·Nelson's· COMFORT PRINT™ BIBLE CONCORDANCE

·Nelson's· COMFORT PRINT™

BIBLE

CONCORDANCE

Ronald F. Youngblood

THOMAS NELSON PUBLISHERS
Nashville • Atlanta • London • Vancouver

Library of Congress Cataloging-in-Publication Data

Youngblood, Ronald F.
    Nelson's Comfort print Bible concordance / Ronald F. Youngblood.
      p. cm.
    Large print ed. of Nelson's quick reference Bible concordance without the supplements.
    Includes index.
    ISBN 0-8407-1156-5
    1. Bible—Concordances, English—New King James. 2. Large type books. I. Youngblood, Ronald F. Nelson's quick reference Bible concordance. II. Title.
    [BS425.Y748   1995]
    220.5'208—dc20   94-34196
                                                CIP

Printed in the United States of America
1 2 3 4 5 6 7 8 — 00 99 98 97 96 95

PREFACE

A biblical concordance is an alphabetical index of the words found in one or more versions of the Bible, a text-finder that enables the reader to locate a particular verse by looking up a key word contained in it. An *exhaustive* concordance lists every occurrence of every word in every verse, including "and," "the," and the like; a *complete* concordance lists every occurrence of every significant word in every verse, excluding what the compiler considers to be nonessential words; a *compact* concordance restricts itself to the most important occurrences of every significant word in the most commonly read verses where each appears.

Nelson's Quick Reference™ *Bible Concordance* is a compact concordance with the following features:

• Based on the *New King James Version,* it will also prove helpful to users of other versions in the Authorized Version tradition (for example *King James Version, American Standard Version, Revised Standard Version*). Synonyms in the subject headings will often assist the reader in comparing two or more versions.

• Accompanying each word are the most important Scripture references where it is found, as well as the surrounding context in the verse where the word is used.

• The verses under each entry are listed in canonical order (from Genesis to Revelation).

• Care has been taken to include most New Testament quotations of Old Testament verses by repeating the identical surrounding context in each reference.

• Choice of references to be included has focused on key doctrines, familiar verses, and passages that the average Bible reader is most likely to want to look up.

• A dagger (†) following an entry heading means that every occurrence of that entry is listed.

Nelson's Quick-Reference™ *Bible Concordance* goes forth to its readers with the sincere prayers of the compiler and publisher that it will prove to be an effective tool for individual Bible study, group discussion, and lesson and sermon preparation.

RONALD YOUNGBLOOD

A

AARON (see AARON'S)

Ex	4:14	Is not A the Levite your
Ex	4:27	And the LORD said to A, "Go
Ex	5: 1	A went in and told Pharaoh,
Ex	6:13	the LORD spoke to Moses and A
Ex	7: 1	A your brother shall be your
Ex	7: 7	A eighty-three years old when
Ex	7:10	A cast down his rod before
Ex	8: 5	Say to A, 'Stretch out your
Ex	15:20	prophetess, the sister of A
Ex	17:12	And A and Hur supported His
Ex	29: 9	So you shall consecrate A
Ex	30:10	A shall make atonement upon
Ex	32:35	with the calf which A made
Lev	8:14	Then A and his sons laid their
Lev	10: 1	Nadab and Abihu, the sons of A
Lev	16: 6	A shall offer the bull as a
Lev	16: 9	A shall bring the goat on
Lev	16:11	A shall bring the bull of the
Num	1: 3	A shall number them by their
Num	3:32	And Eleazar the son of A the
Num	12: 1	A spoke against Moses because
Num	12:10	Then A turned toward Miriam,
Num	14: 2	against Moses and A
Num	17: 6	the rod of A was among their
Num	20:23	A in Mount Hor by the border
Num	20:28	A died there on the top of
Num	26:59	and to Amram she bore A and
Num	33:39	A was one hundred and
Deut	9:20	LORD was very angry with A
Josh	24:33	And Eleazar the son of A died
1Sa	12: 6	who raised up Moses and A
Ps	77:20	By the hand of Moses and A
Ps	133: 2	on the beard, The beard of A
Mic	6: 4	and I sent before you Moses, A
Luke	1: 5	was of the daughters of A
Acts	7:40	saying to A, 'Make us gods to
Heb	5: 4	called by God, just as A was
Heb	7:11	according to the order of A

AARON'S (see AARON)

Ex	7:12	But A rod swallowed up their
Ex	28:30	they shall be over A heart
Ex	28:38	So it shall be on A forehead
Heb	9: 4	A rod that budded, and the

ABADDON†

Rev	9:11	whose name in Hebrew is A

ABASE (see ABASED, HUMBLE)

ABASED† (see HUMBLE, HUMBLED)

Phil	4:12	I know how to be a, and I know

ABASING (see ABASED)

ABATED (see DIMINISHED, RECEDED, SUBSIDED)

ABBA†

Mark	14:36	A, Father, all things are
Rom	8:15	whom we cry out, "A, Father"
Gal	4: 6	crying out, "A, Father

ABED-NEGO

Dan	1: 7	and to Azariah, A
Dan	3:12	Shadrach, Meshach, and A

ABEL

Gen	4: 2	this time his brother A
Gen	4: 9	Where is A your brother
Luke	11:51	from the blood of A to the
Heb	11: 4	By faith A offered to God a
Heb	12:24	better things than that of A

ABHOR

Lev	20:23	things, and therefore I a them
Lev	26:11	and My soul shall not a you
Job	9:31	and my own clothes will a me
Job	19:19	All my close friends a me
Job	42: 6	Therefore I a myself, and
Ps	36: 4	He does not a evil
Mic	3: 9	who a justice and pervert all
Rom	2:22	You who a idols, do you rob
Rom	12: 9	A what is evil

ABIATHAR

1Sa	30: 7	David said to A the priest
2Sa	20:25	Zadok and A were the priests
Mark	2:26	the days of A the high priest

ABIB (see NISAN)

Ex	13: 4	are going out, in the month A
Deut	16: 1	Observe the month of A, and

ABIDE (see ABIDES, ABIDING)

Deut	12:11	chooses to make His name a
Job	24:13	its ways nor a in its paths
Ps	15: 1	who may a in Your tabernacle
Ps	91: 1	of the Most High Shall
Luke	24:29	A with us, for it is toward
John	8:31	If you a in My word, you are
John	12:46	Me should not a in darkness
John	14:16	that He may a with you
John	15: 4	A in Me, and I in you
1Co	13:13	And now a faith, hope, love,
1Jn	2:24	Therefore let that a in you
1Jn	3:17	does the love of God a in him
1Jn	4:13	this we know that we a in Him

ABIDES (see ABIDE)

Ps	119:90	the earth, and it a
John	3:36	but the wrath of God a on him
John	6:56	and drinks My blood a in Me
1Pe	1:23	God which lives and a forever,
1Jn	2: 6	He who says he a in Him ought
1Jn	3: 6	Whoever a in Him does not sin
1Jn	4:12	God a in us, and His love has
2Jn	2	of the truth which a in us

ABIDING (see ABIDE)

John	5:38	do not have His word a in you

ABIGAIL
1Sa	25:39	David sent and proposed to A

ABIHU
Ex	24: 1	you and Aaron, Nadab and A

ABIJAH (*see* ABIJAM)
2Ch	13: 1	A became king over Judah
Matt	1: 7	Rehoboam, Rehoboam begot A
Luke	1: 5	of the division of A

ABIJAM (*see* ABIJAH)
1Ki	15: 1	A became king over Judah

ABILITY (*see* ABLE)
Neh	5: 8	According to our a we have
Dan	1: 4	who had a to serve in the
Matt	25:15	each according to his own a
Acts	11:29	each according to his a,
2Co	8: 3	that according to their a
2Co	8: 3	yes, and beyond their a, they
1Pe	4:11	with the a which God supplies

ABIMELECH (*see* AHIMELECH)
Gen	20: 3	But God came to A in a dream
Gen	26: 1	Isaac went to A king of the
Judg	9: 1	A the son of Jerubbaal went
Judg	9: 6	and made A king beside the

ABINADAB
1Sa	7: 1	the house of A on the hill
2Sa	6: 3	it out of the house of A,

ABIRAM
Num	16:24	tents of Korah, Dathan, and A

ABISHAG
1Ki	1: 3	found A the Shunammite, and

ABISHAI
2Sa	2:18	Joab and A and Asahel
2Sa	16: 9	Then A the son of Zeruiah
2Sa	20: 6	And David said to A, "Now

ABLE (*see* ABILITY)
Gen	13: 6	was not a to support them
Gen	15: 5	if you are a to number them
Num	11:14	I am not a to bear all these
Num	13:30	we are well a to overcome it
Num	13:31	We are not a to go up against
1Sa	17: 9	If he is a to fight with me
1Ki	3: 9	For who is a to judge this
2Ki	3:21	all who were a to bear arms
2Ch	2: 6	But who is a to build Him a
Neh	4:10	are not a to build the wall
Job	41:10	Who then is a to stand
Ps	40:12	so that I am not a to look up
Prov	27: 4	but who is a to stand before
Eccl	8:17	he will not be a to find it
Dan	3:17	is a to deliver us from the
Dan	4:18	not a to make known to me the
Amos	7:10	The land is not a to bear all
Matt	3: 9	is a to raise up children to

Matt	10:28	who is a to destroy both soul
Matt	18:25	But as he was not a to pay
Matt	20:22	Are you a to drink the cup
Matt	22:46	no one was a to answer Him a
Luke	14:29	is not a to finish it, all
John	10:29	no one is a to snatch them
Acts	20:32	which is a to build you up and
Rom	8:39	shall be a to separate us
Rom	11:23	for God is a to graft them in
Rom	14: 4	for God is a to make him
Rom	16:25	Now to Him who is a to
1Co	3: 2	you were not a to receive it
1Co	10:13	tempted beyond what you are a
2Co	1: 4	that we may be a to comfort
2Co	9: 8	God is a to make all grace
Eph	3:18	may be a to comprehend with
Eph	3:20	who is a to do exceedingly
Eph	6:11	that you may be a to stand
1Ti	3: 2	hospitable, a to teach
2Ti	1:12	He is a to keep what I have
2Ti	2: 2	be a to teach others also
2Ti	3: 7	and never a to come to the
2Ti	3:15	which are a to make you wise
Tit	1: 9	been taught, that he may be a
Heb	2:18	He is a to aid those who are
Heb	5: 7	tears to Him who was a to
Heb	7:25	Therefore He is also a to
Heb	11:19	God was a to raise him up
Jas	1:21	which is a to save your souls
Jas	3: 2	a also to bridle the whole
Jas	4:12	who is a to save and to
Jude	24	Now to Him who is a to keep
Rev	5: 3	was a to open the scroll, or

ABNER
1Sa	14:50	his army was A the son of Ner

ABOLISHED†
Is	51: 6	righteousness will not be a
Ezek	6: 6	down, and your works may be a
Eph	2:15	having a in His flesh the
2Ti	1:10	Jesus Christ, who has a death

ABOMINABLE
Lev	7:21	or any a unclean thing, and
Ps	14: 1	They have done a works,
Jer	16:18	their detestable and a idols
1Pe	4: 3	parties, and a idolatries
Rev	21: 8	the cowardly, unbelieving, a

ABOMINATION (*see* ABOMINATIONS)
Gen	43:32	is an a to the Egyptians
Lev	7:18	it shall be an a
1Ki	11: 5	Milcom the a of the Ammonites
Prov	3:32	person is an a to the LORD
Prov	6:16	yes, seven are an a to Him
Prov	11: 1	scales are an a to the LORD
Prov	11:20	heart are an a to the LORD
Prov	12:22	lips are an a to the LORD
Prov	28: 9	Even his prayer is an a
Is	1:13	incense is an a to Me
Is	66:17	eating swine's flesh and the a
Jer	2: 7	and made My heritage an a
Jer	6:15	when they had committed a

Dan	11:31	there the **a** of desolation
Dan	12:11	the **a** of desolation is set up
Mal	2:11	an **a** has been committed in
Matt	24:15	the **a** of desolation
Luke	16:15	is an **a** in the sight of God
Rev	21:27	or causes an **a** or a lie, but

ABOMINATIONS (*see* ABOMINATION)

Deut	18: 9	follow the **a** of those nations
Ezra	9: 1	to the **a** of the Canaanites
Prov	26:25	are seven **a** in his heart
Jer	4: 1	away your **a** out of My sight
Jer	13:27	your **a** on the hills in the
Ezek	5: 9	again, because of all your **a**
Ezek	18:24	**a** that the wicked man does
Ezek	20: 4	them the **a** of their fathers
Dan	9:27	on the wing of **a** shall be one
Rev	17: 5	THE **A** OF THE EARTH

ABOUND (*see* ABOUNDED, ABOUNDING)

Gen	1:20	Let the waters **a** with an
Gen	8:17	that they may **a** on the earth
Matt	24:12	And because lawlessness will **a**
Rom	5:20	that the offense might **a**
Rom	6: 1	in sin that grace may **a**
Rom	15:13	that you may **a** in hope by the
2Co	1: 5	sufferings of Christ **a** in us
2Co	4:15	to **a** to the glory of God
2Co	9: 8	make all grace **a** toward you
Eph	1: 8	which He made to **a** toward us
Phil	1: 9	your love may **a** still more
Phil	4:12	be abased, and I know how to **a**
1Th	3:12	**a** in love to one another and
1Th	4: 1	Jesus that you should **a** more

ABOUNDED† (*see* ABOUND)

Gen	1:21	with which the waters **a**,
Ps	105:30	Their land **a** with frogs, Even
Rom	5:15	Man, Jesus Christ, **a** to many
Rom	5:20	But where sin **a**, grace
2Co	8: 2	their deep poverty **a** in the

ABOUNDING (*see* ABOUND)

Ex	34: 6	and **a** in goodness and truth,
Ps	103: 8	Slow to anger, and **a** in mercy
1Co	15:58	always **a** in the work of the
2Co	9:12	but also is **a** through many

ABRAHAM (*see* ABRAHAM'S, ABRAM)

Gen	17: 5	but your name shall be **A**
Gen	17:23	So **A** took Ishmael his son,
Gen	17:24	**A** was ninety-nine years old
Gen	18:17	I hide from **A** what I am doing
Gen	18:22	but **A** still stood before the
Gen	19:29	plain, that God remembered **A**
Gen	20:17	So **A** prayed to God
Gen	21: 2	bore **A** a son in his old age,
Gen	22: 1	things that God tested **A**, and
Gen	22: 8	**A** said, "My son, God will
Gen	22:11	from heaven and said, "**A**, **A**!"
Gen	22:13	So **A** went and took the ram, and
Gen	23:19	**A** buried Sarah his wife in
Gen	24: 1	Now **A** was old, well-advanced
Gen	25: 6	of the concubines which **A** had

Gen	25: 8	Then **A** breathed his last and
Gen	25:10	the field which **A** purchased
Gen	26:24	I am the God of your father **A**
Ex	2:24	His covenant with **A**, with
Ex	3: 6	the God of **A**, the God of
Ex	6: 3	I appeared to **A**, to Isaac, and
Ex	32:13	Remember **A**, Isaac, and Israel,
Deut	1: 8	to **A**, Isaac, and Jacob
Josh	24: 2	Terah, the father of **A** and the
1Ki	18:36	LORD God of **A**, Isaac, and
2Ch	20: 7	of **A** Your friend forever
Is	41: 8	descendants of **A** My friend
Is	51: 2	Look to **A** your father, and to
Matt	1: 1	Son of David, the Son of **A**
Matt	3: 9	We have **A** as our father
Matt	3: 9	to **A** from these stones
Matt	8:11	and west, and sit down with **A**
Matt	22:32	I am the God of **A**, the God
Luke	3:34	son of Isaac, the son of **A**
Luke	16:23	saw **A** afar off, and Lazarus in
John	8:39	to Him, "**A** is our father
John	8:56	Your father **A** rejoiced to see
John	8:58	I say to you, before **A** was
Acts	7: 2	appeared to our father **A** when
Acts	13:26	sons of the family of **A**, and
Rom	4: 1	that **A** our father has found
Rom	4: 3	**A** believed God, and it was
Rom	4:16	who are of the faith of **A**
Rom	9: 7	they are the seed of **A**
Rom	11: 1	Israelite, of the seed of **A**
Gal	3: 6	just as **A** believed God, and
Gal	3: 7	are of faith are sons of **A**
Gal	3: 8	the gospel to **A** beforehand
Gal	3: 9	are blessed with believing **A**
Gal	3:16	Now to **A** and his Seed were the
Gal	3:18	God gave it to **A** by promise
Gal	4:22	written that **A** had two sons
Heb	2:16	give aid to the seed of **A**
Heb	6:13	when God made a promise to **A**
Heb	7: 2	to whom also **A** gave a tenth
Heb	11: 8	By faith **A** obeyed when he was
Jas	2:21	Was not **A** our father
Jas	2:23	**A** believed God, and it was
1Pc	3: 6	as Sarah obeyed **A**, calling

ABRAHAM'S (*see* ABRAHAM)

Gen	20:18	because of Sarah, **A** wife
Luke	16:22	by the angels to **A** bosom
John	8:33	We are **A** descendants, and have
Gal	3:29	Christ's, then you are **A** seed

ABRAM (*see* ABRAHAM)

Gen	11:27	Terah begot **A**, Nahor, and
Gen	12: 1	Now the LORD had said to **A**
Gen	12: 4	**A** was seventy-five years old
Gen	12: 5	Then **A** took Sarai his wife and
Gen	12: 7	Then the LORD appeared to **A**
Gen	12:10	and **A** went down to Egypt to
Gen	13: 2	**A** was very rich in livestock,
Gen	14:13	told **A** the Hebrew, for he
Gen	14:19	Blessed be **A** of God Most High
Gen	15:12	a deep sleep fell upon **A**
Gen	15:18	LORD made a covenant with **A**
Gen	16: 2	**A** heeded the voice of Sarai

Gen	16:16	A was eighty-six years old
Gen	16:16	when Hagar bore Ishmael to A
Gen	17: 1	old, the LORD appeared to A
Gen	17: 5	shall your name be called A
Neh	9: 7	are the LORD God, Who chose A

ABROAD

Gen	11: 8	the LORD scattered them a
Matt	12:30	not gather with Me scatters a
John	11:52	of God who were scattered a
Jas	1: 1	tribes which are scattered a

ABSALOM (see ABSALOM'S)

2Sa	13: 1	this A the son of David had a
2Sa	13:22	A spoke to his brother Amnon
2Sa	14:25	much as A for his good looks
2Sa	14:27	To A were born three sons, and
2Sa	15: 6	So A stole the hearts of the
2Sa	18:10	I just saw A hanging in a
2Sa	18:29	Is the young man A safe
2Sa	18:33	O my son A—my son
2Sa	19: 1	is weeping and mourning for A
2Sa	19: 4	O my son A!

ABSALOM'S (see ABSALOM)

2Sa	18:14	thrust them through A heart
2Sa	18:18	day it is called A Monument

ABSENCE† (see ABSENT)

Luke	22: 6	in the a of the multitude
Phil	2:12	but now much more in my a

ABSENT (see ABSENCE)

Gen	31:49	me when we are a one from
1Co	5: 3	as a in body but present in
2Co	5: 6	body we are a from the Lord
Col	2: 5	though I am a in the flesh

ABSTAIN

Josh	6:18	a from the accursed things
Acts	15:20	to a from things polluted by
1Th	4: 3	that you should a from sexual
1Th	5:22	A from every form of evil
1Ti	4: 3	commanding to a from foods
1Pe	2:11	a from fleshly lusts which

ABUNDANCE (see ABUNDANT)

Gen	1:20	with an a of living creatures
1Sa	1:16	woman, for out of the a of my
1Ki	18:41	is the sound of a of rain
Ps	52: 7	in the a of his riches, And
Ps	72:16	There will be an a of grain
Eccl	5:10	nor he who loves a, with
Is	55: 2	your soul delight itself in a
Matt	12:34	For out of the a of the heart
Matt	13:12	given, and he will have a
Mark	12:44	all put in out of their a
Luke	12:15	does not consist in the a of
Rom	5:17	those who receive a of grace
2Co	8: 2	affliction the a of their joy
2Co	8:14	your a may supply their lack
2Co	9: 8	have an a for every good work

ABUNDANT (see ABUNDANCE, ABUNDANTLY)

Num	14:18	and a in mercy, forgiving
1Ki	10:27	he made cedars as a as the
Neh	9:27	according to Your a mercies
Ps	86: 5	a in mercy to all those who
Ps	130: 7	And with Him is a redemption
Jon	4: 2	a in lovingkindness, One who
2Co	11:23	in labors more a, in stripes
Phil	1:26	for me may be more a in Jesus
1Ti	1:14	of our Lord was exceedingly a
1Pe	1: 3	who according to His a mercy

ABUNDANTLY (see ABUNDANT)

Gen	9: 7	brings forth a in the earth and
Ex	1: 7	were fruitful and increased a
Is	55: 7	our God, for He will a pardon
John	10:10	that they may have it more a
1Co	15:10	labored more a than they all
2Co	1:12	of God, and more a toward you
2Co	12:15	though the more a I love you
Eph	3:20	a above all that we ask or
Tit	3: 6	us a through Jesus Christ our
Heb	6:17	determining to show more a to
2Pe	1:11	to you a into the everlasting

ABUSE

1Sa	31: 4	and thrust me through and a me
Jer	38:19	into their hand, and they a me
Acts	14: 5	Jews, with their rulers, to a
1Co	9:18	that I may not a my authority

ABYSS†

Luke	8:31	them to go out into the a
Rom	10: 7	Who will descend into the a

ACACIA

Ex	27: 1	shall make an altar of a wood

ACCEPT (see ACCEPTABLE, ACCEPTANCE, ACCEPTED, ACCEPTING)

Gen	32:20	perhaps he will a me
Job	2:10	we indeed a good from God
Job	2:10	and shall we not a adversity
Jer	14:12	offering, I will not a them
Mal	1: 8	Would he a you favorably
Matt	19:11	All cannot a this saying, but
Matt	19:12	He who is able to a it, let
Mark	4:20	the word, a it, and bear fruit
1Co	6: 7	Why do you not rather a wrong

ACCEPTABLE (see ACCEPT, ACCEPTABLY)

Ps	19:14	my heart Be a in Your sight
Ps	69:13	to You, O LORD, in the a time
Eccl	12:10	sought to find a words
Is	49: 8	In an a time I have heard You
Is	61: 2	to proclaim the a year of the
Jer	6:20	burnt offerings are not a
Luke	4:19	to proclaim the a year of the
Rom	12: 1	holy, a to God, which is your
Rom	12: 2	prove what is that good and a
2Co	6: 2	In an a time I have heard you
Phil	4:18	an a sacrifice, well pleasing
1Ti	2: 3	a in the sight of God our

1Pe	2: 5	up spiritual sacrifices **a** to

ACCEPTABLY † (see ACCEPTABLE)

Heb	12:28	serve God **a** with reverence

ACCEPTANCE (see ACCEPT)

Rom	11:15	what will their **a** be but life
1Ti	1:15	saying and worthy of all **a**
1Ti	4: 9	saying and worthy of all **a**

ACCEPTED (see ACCEPT)

Gen	4: 7	do well, will you not be **a**
1Sa	18: 5	he was **a** in the sight of all
Job	42: 9	for the LORD had **a** Job
Eccl	9: 7	God has already **a** your works
Is	56: 7	will be **a** on My altar
Luke	4:24	no prophet is **a** in his own
2Co	6: 2	Behold, now is the **a** time
2Co	8:12	it is **a** according to what one
Eph	1: 6	has made us **a** in the Beloved

ACCEPTING † (see ACCEPT)

Heb	11:35	not **a** deliverance, that they

ACCESS †

Esth	1:14	who had **a** to the king's
Rom	5: 2	through whom also we have **a**
Eph	2:18	through Him we both have **a** by
Eph	3:12	**a** with confidence through

ACCOMPANIED (see ACCOMPANY)

Acts	10:23	brethren from Joppa **a** him
1Pe	3: 2	your chaste conduct **a** by fear

ACCOMPANY † (see ACCOMPANIED)

Heb	6: 9	yes, things that **a** salvation

ACCOMPLISH (see ACCOMPLISHED)

Eccl	2: 2	What does it **a**
Is	55:11	but it shall **a** what I please,
Dan	9: 2	that He would **a** seventy years
Luke	9:31	was about to **a** at Jerusalem

ACCOMPLISHED (see ACCOMPLISH)

Dan	11:36	till the wrath has been **a**
Luke	12:50	distressed I am till it is **a**
Luke	18:31	the Son of Man will be **a**
Luke	22:37	written must still be **a** in Me
John	19:28	that all things were now **a**
Rom	15:18	Christ has not **a** through me
Eph	3:11	He **a** in Christ Jesus our Lord

ACCORD

Lev	25: 5	What grows of its own **a** of
Luke	14:18	one **a** began to make excuses
Acts	1:14	with one **a** in prayer and
Acts	2: 1	all with one **a** in one place
Acts	12:10	opened to them of its own **a**
2Co	6:15	what **a** has Christ with Belial
2Co	8:17	he went to you of his own **a**
Phil	2: 2	the same love, being of one **a**

ACCOUNT (see ACCOUNTED, ACCOUNTS)

Gen	20:11	will kill me on **a** of my wife

Gen	26: 9	said, Lest I die on **a** of her
Dan	7:28	This is the end of the **a**
Matt	12:36	they will give **a** of it in the
Luke	1: 3	to write to you an orderly **a**
Luke	16: 2	Give an **a** of your stewardship
Acts	1: 1	The former **a** I made, O
Rom	14:12	give **a** of himself to God
Phil	4:17	fruit that abounds to your **a**
Phm	18	anything, put that on my **a**
Heb	4:13	of Him to whom we must give **a**
Heb	13:17	as those who must give **a**
1Pe	4: 5	They will give an **a** to Him

ACCOUNTED (see ACCOUNT)

Gen	15: 6	LORD, and He **a** it to him for
Ps	44:22	We are **a** as sheep for the
Rom	4: 3	God, and it was **a** to him for
Rom	8:36	we are **a** as sheep for the
Gal	3: 6	God, and it was **a** to him for
Jas	2:23	God, and it was **a** to him for

ACCOUNTS (see ACCOUNT)

Matt	18:23	to settle **a** with his servants

ACCURATE † (see ACCURATELY)

Acts	24:22	having more **a** knowledge of

ACCURATELY (see ACCURATE)

Acts	18:25	taught **a** the things of the

ACCURSED

Deut	21:23	he who is hanged is **a** of God
Rom	9: 3	wish that I myself were **a**
1Co	12: 3	Spirit of God calls Jesus **a**
1Co	16:22	Jesus Christ, let him be **a**
Gal	1: 8	preached to you, let him be **a**
2Pe	2:14	practices, and are **a** children

ACCUSATION (see ACCUSE)

Mark	15:26	of His **a** was written above
Luke	6: 7	might find an **a** against Him
Luke	16: 1	an **a** was brought to him that
Luke	19: 8	from anyone by false **a**, I
John	18:29	What **a** do you bring against

ACCUSE (see ACCUSATION, ACCUSED, ACCUSER, ACCUSES, ACCUSING)

Matt	12:10	that they might **a** Him
Luke	23: 2	And they began to **a** Him,
John	5:45	I shall **a** you to the Father
Acts	25: 5	**a** this man, to see if there

ACCUSED (see ACCUSE)

Dan	6:24	those men who had **a** Daniel
Matt	27:12	while He was being **a** by the
Mark	15: 3	the chief priests **a** Him of
Acts	22:30	why he was **a** by the Jews, he
Rev	12:10	who **a** them before our God day

ACCUSER † (see ACCUSE, ACCUSERS)

Ps	109: 6	let an **a** stand at his right
Rev	12:10	for the **a** of our brethren,

ACCUSERS (*see* ACCUSER)
| John | 8:10 | where are those **a** of yours |
| Acts | 25:16 | meets the **a** face to face, and |

ACCUSES† (*see* ACCUSE)
| John | 5:45 | there is one who **a** you |

ACCUSING† (*see* ACCUSE)
| Rom | 2:15 | **a** or else excusing them) |

ACCUSTOMED
Jer	13:23	do good who are **a** to do evil
Mark	10: 1	to Him again, and as He was **a**
Luke	22:39	Mount of Olives, as He was **a**

ACHAIA
Acts	18:12	Gallio was proconsul of **A**
Acts	19:21	through Macedonia and **A**
2Co	11:10	boasting in the regions of **A**

ACHAN
| Josh | 7: 1 | for **A** the son of Carmi, the |

ACHISH
| 1Sa | 27: 3 | So David dwelt with **A** at Gath |

ACHOR
| Josh | 7:24 | them to the Valley of **A** |
| Hos | 2:15 | the Valley of **A** as a door of |

ACHSAH
| Judg | 1:12 | give my daughter **A** as wife |

ACKNOWLEDGE (*see* ACKNOWLEDGES)
Deut	33: 9	nor did he **a** his brothers, or
Ps	51: 3	For I **a** my transgressions, And
Prov	3: 6	in all your ways **a** Him, and He
1Co	16:18	therefore **a** such men

ACKNOWLEDGES (*see* ACKNOWLEDGE)
| Ps | 142: 4 | For there is no one who **a** me |
| 1Jn | 2:23 | he who **a** the Son has the |

ACQUAINTANCES (*see* ACQUAINTED)
Job	42:11	who had been his **a** before
Luke	2:44	among their relatives and **a**
Luke	23:49	But all His **a**, and the women

ACQUAINTED† (*see* ACQUAINTANCES)
| Ps | 139: 3 | And are **a** with all my ways |
| Is | 53: 3 | of sorrows and **a** with grief |

ACT (*see* ACTED, ACTS)
Deut	4: 5	that you should **a** according
Deut	17:13	no longer **a** presumptuously
Judg	19:23	beg you, do not **a** so wickedly
1Ki	8:32	then hear in heaven, and **a**
2Ch	19: 9	Thus you shall **a** in the fear
Neh	6:13	**a** that way and sin, so that
Ps	119:126	It is time for You to **a**, O
Is	28:16	believes will not **a** hastily
Dan	11:23	him he shall **a** deceitfully

ACT (*see* ACT)
| John | 8: 4 | in adultery, in the very **a** |
| Rom | 5:18 | **a** the free gift came to all |

ACTED (*see* ACT)
Gen	42: 7	but he **a** as a stranger to
Deut	9:12	out of Egypt have **a** corruptly
Judg	9:16	you have **a** in truth
2Ki	10:19	But Jehu **a** deceptively,
2Ki	21:11	**a** more wickedly than all the
Job	36: 9	that they have **a** defiantly
Ezek	20: 9	But I **a** for My name's sake,

ACTS (*see* ACT)
Deut	17:12	the man who **a** presumptuously
Judg	5:11	the righteous **a** of the LORD
1Ki	11:41	the rest of the **a** of Solomon
Job	15:25	and **a** defiantly against the
Ps	103: 7	His **a** to the children of
Ps	145: 6	the might of Your awesome **a**
Ps	150: 2	Praise Him for His mighty **a**
Prov	13:16	prudent man **a** with knowledge
Prov	21:24	he **a** with arrogant pride
Is	64: 4	Who **a** for the one who waits
Ezek	16:20	Were your **a** of harlotry **a**
Rev	19: 8	the righteous **a** of the saints

ADAM
Gen	2:20	So **A** gave names to all cattle
Gen	3: 9	Then the LORD God called to **A**
Gen	3:20	**A** called his wife's name Eve,
Gen	5: 1	book of the genealogy of **A**
Deut	32: 8	He separated the sons of **A**
Job	31:33	my transgressions as **A**, by
Luke	3:38	the son of Seth, the son of **A**
Rom	5:14	death reigned from **A** to Moses
Rom	5:14	of the transgression of **A**
1Co	15:22	For as in **A** all die, even so
1Co	15:45	The last **A** became a
1Ti	2:13	For **A** was formed first, then
1Ti	2:14	**A** was not deceived, but the
Jude	14	Now Enoch, the seventh from **A**

ADAR
| Esth | 9: 1 | that is, the month of **A**, on |

ADD (*see* ADDED, ADDS)
Gen	30:24	The LORD shall **a** to me
Lev	5:16	shall **a** one-fifth to it and
Deut	4: 2	You shall not **a** to the word
2Ki	20: 6	I will **a** to your days fifteen
Ps	69:27	**A** iniquity to their iniquity,
Prov	30: 6	Do not **a** to His words, lest
Is	5: 8	who **a** field to field, till
Is	29: 1	**A** year to year
Is	30: 1	that they may **a** sin to sin
Luke	12:25	of you by worrying can **a** one
Phil	1:16	supposing to **a** affliction to
2Pe	1: 5	**a** to your faith virtue, to
Rev	22:18	God will **a** to him the plagues

ADDED (*see* ADD)
Num	36: 4	**a** to the inheritance of the
Deut	5:22	and He **a** no more
1Sa	12:19	for we have **a** to all our sins

Prov	9:11	of life will be **a** to you
Eccl	3:14	Nothing can be **a** to it, and
Dan	4:36	excellent majesty was **a** to me
Matt	6:33	things shall be **a** to you
Acts	2:41	thousand souls were **a** to them
Acts	2:47	And the Lord **a** to the church

ADDS (see ADD)

Prov	10:22	and He **a** no sorrow with it
Gal	3:15	no one annuls or **a** to it
Heb	10:17	then He **a**, "Their sins and
Rev	22:18	If anyone **a** to these things,

ADJURE (see OATH)

ADMINISTERED (see ADMINISTRATION)

2Co	8:19	which is **a** by us to the glory

ADMINISTRATION† (see ADMINISTERED, ADMINISTRATIONS)

2Co	9:12	For the **a** of this service not

ADMINISTRATIONS† (see ADMINISTRATION)

1Co	12:28	gifts of healings, helps, **a**

ADMIRED†

2Th	1:10	to be **a** among all those who

ADMONISH† (see ADMONISHING, ADMONITION)

Ps	81: 8	O My people, and I will **a** you
Rom	15:14	able also to **a** one another
1Th	5:12	you in the Lord and **a** you,
2Th	3:15	enemy, but **a** him as a brother
Tit	2: 4	that they **a** the young women

ADMONISHING† (see ADMONISH)

Col	3:16	**a** one another in psalms and

ADMONITION† (see ADMONISH)

1Co	10:11	they were written for our **a**
Eph	6: 4	the training and **a** of the Lord
Tit	3:10	after the first and second **a**

ADOPTION†

Rom	8:15	of **a** by whom we cry out
Rom	8:23	eagerly waiting for the **a**
Rom	9: 4	to whom pertain the **a**, the
Gal	4: 5	might receive the **a** as sons
Eph	1: 5	having predestined us to **a** as

ADORN (see ADORNED, ADORNS)

Job	40:10	Then **a** yourself with majesty
Matt	23:29	and **a** the monuments of the
1Ti	2: 9	that the women **a** themselves
Tit	2:10	that they may **a** the doctrine

ADORNED (see ADORN)

Ezek	16:11	I **a** you with ornaments, put
1Pe	3: 5	in God also **a** themselves,
Rev	17: 4	and **a** with gold and precious
Rev	21: 2	as a bride **a** for her husband
Rev	21:19	the wall of the city were **a**

ADORNMENT (see ADORN)

1Pe	3: 3	Do not let your **a** be merely

ADORNS† (see ADORN)

Ps	93: 5	Holiness **a** Your house, O LORD
Is	61:10	as a bride **a** herself with her

ADULLAM

2Sa	23:13	to David at the cave of **A**

ADULTERER† (see ADULTERERS, ADULTERY)

Lev	20:10	his neighbor's wife, the **a**
Job	24:15	The eye of the **a** waits for
Is	57: 3	you offspring of the **a** and

ADULTERERS (see ADULTERER)

Ps	50:18	have been a partaker with **a**
Hos	7: 4	They are all **a**
Mal	3: 5	against sorcerers, against **a**
Luke	18:11	extortioners, unjust, **a**, or
1Co	6: 9	nor idolaters, nor **a**, nor
Heb	13: 4	and **a** God will judge
Jas	4: 4	**A** and adulteresses

ADULTERESS (see ADULTERY)

Lev	20:10	wife, the adulterer and the **a**
Rom	7: 3	man, she will be called an **a**

ADULTERIES (see ADULTERY)

Jer	13:27	I have seen your **a** and your
Hos	2: 2	and her **a** from between her
Matt	15:19	evil thoughts, murders, **a**

ADULTEROUS (see ADULTERY)

Prov	30:20	This is the way of an **a** woman
Ezek	6: 9	I was crushed by their **a**
Ezek	16:32	You are an **a** wife, who takes
Matt	12:39	**a** generation seeks after a
Mark	8:38	of Me and My words in this **a**

ADULTERY (see ADULTERER, ADULTERESS, ADULTERIES, ADULTEROUS)

Ex	20:14	You shall not commit **a**
Jer	3: 8	Israel had committed **a**, I had
Jer	7: 9	you steal, murder, commit **a**
Ezek	23:37	committed **a** with their idols
Hos	3: 1	by a lover and is committing **a**
Hos	4:13	and your brides commit **a**
Matt	5:28	**a** with her in his heart
Matt	5:32	who is divorced commits **a**
Matt	19: 9	and marries another, commits **a**
John	8: 3	to Him a woman caught in **a**
Gal	5:19	**a**, fornication, uncleanness,
2Pe	2:14	having eyes full of **a** and that
Rev	2:22	those who commit **a** with her

ADVANCE (see ADVANCED)

Prov	30:27	king, yet they all **a** in ranks

ADVANCED (see ADVANCE)

Josh	13: 1	Joshua was old, **a** in years
Gal	1:14	I **a** in Judaism beyond many of

ADVANTAGE (see PROFIT)

Eccl	3:19	man has no **a** over animals, for
John	16: 7	It is to your **a** that I go
Rom	3: 1	What **a** then has the Jew, or
2Co	2:11	Satan should take **a** of us
2Co	8:10	It is to your **a** not only to

ADVERSARIES (see ADVERSARY)

Deut	32:43	and render vengeance to His **a**
Ps	27:12	me to the will of my **a**
Ps	71:13	consumed Who are **a** of my life
Is	59:18	He will repay, fury to His **a**
1Co	16: 9	to me, and there are many **a**
Heb	10:27	which will devour the **a**

ADVERSARY (see ADVERSARIES)

Job	16: 9	my **a** sharpens His gaze on me
Is	50: 8	stand together. Who is My **a**
Matt	5:25	Agree with your **a** quickly
1Pe	5: 8	because your **a** the devil

ADVERSITIES (see ADVERSITY)

Ps	31: 7	You have known my soul in **a**

ADVERSITY (see ADVERSITIES)

2Sa	12:11	I will raise up **a** against you
Job	2:10	God, and shall we not accept **a**
Ps	35:15	But in my **a** they rejoiced And
Prov	17:17	and a brother is born for **a**
Is	30:20	Lord gives you the bread of **a**
Jer	15:11	with you in the time of **a**

ADVICE (see ADVISE, COUNSEL)

2Sa	17:14	the good **a** of Ahithophel, to
1Ki	12: 8	But he rejected the **a** which
1Ki	12:14	to the **a** of the young men
2Co	8:10	And in this I give my **a**

ADVISE (see ADVICE, ADVISED, COUNSEL)

1Ki	12: 6	How do you **a** me to answer

ADVISED (see ADVISE)

2Sa	17:15	and so Ahithophel **a**
Acts	27: 9	was already over, Paul **a** them

ADVOCATE†

1Jn	2: 1	we have an **A** with the Father,

AFFAIRS

2Ti	2: 4	with the **a** of this life, that

AFFECTION† (see AFFECTIONATE, AFFECTIONS)

1Ch	29: 3	because I have set my **a** on
1Co	7: 3	to his wife the **a** due her
Phil	1: 8	with the **a** of Jesus Christ
Phil	2: 1	of the Spirit, if any **a** and

AFFECTIONATE† (see AFFECTION, AFFECTIONATELY)

Rom	12:10	Be kindly **a** to one another

AFFECTIONATELY† (see AFFECTIONATE)

1Th	2: 8	a longing for you, we were

AFFECTIONS† (see AFFECTION)

2Co	6:12	are restricted by your own **a**
2Co	7:15	his **a** are greater for you as

AFFIRM

Rom	3: 8	and as some **a** that we say
1Ti	1: 7	nor the things which they **a**

AFFLICT (see AFFLICTED, AFFLICTION)

Gen	15:13	they will **a** them four hundred
Ex	1:11	to **a** them with their burdens
Ps	55:19	**a** them, Even He who abides
Ps	94: 5	O LORD, And **a** Your heritage

AFFLICTED (see AFFLICT)

Ex	1:12	But the more they **a** them, the
Ruth	1:21	me, and the Almighty has **a** me
Ps	22:24	the affliction of the **a**
Ps	82: 3	Do justice to the **a** and needy
Ps	140:12	maintain The cause of the **a**
Is	53: 4	smitten by God, and **a**
Is	53: 7	He was oppressed and He was **a**
Is	63: 9	all their affliction He was **a**
Matt	4:24	were **a** with various diseases
Heb	11:37	goatskins, being destitute, **a**

AFFLICTION (see AFFLICT, AFFLICTIONS)

Gen	16:11	the LORD has heard your **a**
Deut	16: 3	the bread of **a** for you came
Job	30:16	the days of **a** take hold of me
Job	36: 8	held in the cords of **a**,
Ps	22:24	the **a** of the afflicted
Ps	25:18	Look on my **a** and my pain, And
Ps	66:11	You laid **a** on our backs
Ps	88: 9	eye wastes away because of **a**
Ps	106:44	He regarded their **a**, When He
Ps	119:153	Consider my **a** and deliver me,
Is	63: 9	In all their **a** He was
Jer	30:12	Your **a** is incurable, your
Lam	3: 1	**a** by the rod of His wrath
Amos	6: 6	grieved for the **a** of Joseph
Mark	5:29	that she was healed of the **a**
2Co	2: 4	For out of much **a** and anguish
2Co	4:17	For our light **a**, which is but
2Co	8: 2	that in a great trial of **a**
Phil	1:16	to add **a** to my chains
1Th	1: 6	received the word in much **a**
1Th	3: 7	brethren, in all our **a** and
Heb	11:25	choosing rather to suffer **a**

AFFLICTIONS (see AFFLICTION)

Mark	3:10	so that as many as had **a**
Luke	7:21	of their infirmities, **a**, and
Col	1:24	is lacking in the **a** of Christ
2Ti	4: 5	in all things, endure **a**, do

AFRAID

Gen	3:10	I was **a** because I was naked
Gen	15: 1	Do not be **a**, Abram
Gen	18:15	not laugh," for she was **a**

Ex	3: 6	for he was a to look upon God
Deut	20: 3	your heart faint, do not be a
Josh	1: 9	do not be a, nor be dismayed,
Job	9:28	I am a of all my sufferings
Job	15:24	and anguish make him a
Job	23:15	consider this, I am a of Him
Ps	3: 6	I will not be a of ten
Ps	27: 1	Of whom shall I be a
Ps	56: 3	Whenever I am a, I will trust
Ps	56:11	I will not be a
Ps	77:16	waters saw You, they were a
Ps	119:120	And I am a of Your judgments
Prov	3:24	lie down, you will not be a
Prov	31:21	She is not a of snow for her
Eccl	12: 5	when they are a of height
Is	12: 2	I will trust and not be a
Is	17: 2	and no one will make them a
Is	51:12	be a of a man who will die
Jer	30:10	and no one shall make him a
Dan	4: 5	I saw a dream which made me a
Matt	1:20	do not be a to take to you
Matt	2:22	Herod, he was a to go there
Matt	25:25	And I was a, and went and hid
Matt	28:10	Do not be a. Go and tell my
Mark	5:36	Do not be a; only believe.
Mark	9:32	saying, and were a to ask Him
Mark	10: 8	to anyone, for they were a
Luke	1:13	Do not be a, Zacharias, for
Luke	1:30	Do not be a, Mary, for you
Luke	8:25	And they were a, and marveled
Luke	12: 4	do not be a of those who kill
John	6:20	"It is I; do not be a
John	14:27	troubled, neither let it be a
Acts	24:25	judgment to come, Felix was a
Acts	27:24	saying, "Do not be a, Paul
Rom	13: 4	But if you do evil, be a
Gal	4:11	I am a for you, lest I have
Heb	11:23	they were not a of the king's
Heb	12:21	I am exceedingly a and
1Pe	3:14	do not be a of their threats,
2Pe	2:10	they are not a to speak evil
Rev	1:17	Do not be a; I am the First

AGE (see AGED, AGES)

Gen	15:15	be buried at a good old a
Gen	18:11	passed the a of childbearing
Gen	21: 7	borne him a son in his old a
Gen	48:10	of Israel were dim with a
Ruth	4:15	and a nourisher of your old a
Ps	92:14	still bear fruit in old a
Is	46: 4	even to your old a, I am He,
Matt	12:32	this a or in the a to come
Matt	13:39	harvest is the end of the a
Mark	10:30	in the a to come, eternal
Luke	1:36	conceived a son in her old a
Luke	3:23	at about thirty years of a
Luke	8:42	about twelve years of a, and
Luke	20:34	The sons of this a marry and
John	9:21	He is of a; ask him.
1Co	1:20	is the disputer of this a
1Co	2: 6	yet not the wisdom of this a
1Co	2: 8	of the rulers of this a knew
1Co	3:18	seems to be wise in this a
2Co	4: 4	the god of this a has blinded

Gal	1: 4	us from this present evil a
Eph	1:21	not only in this a but also
Eph	6:12	of the darkness of this a
1Ti	6:17	present a not to be haughty
Heb	6: 5	the powers of the a to come

AGED (see AGE)

2Sa	19:32	Barzillai was a very a man
Phm	9	such a one as Paul, the a

AGES† (see AGE)

1Co	2: 7	before the a for our glory
1Co	10:11	the ends of the a have come
Eph	2: 7	that in the a to come He
Eph	3: 5	which in other a was not made
Eph	3: 9	from the beginning of the a
Col	1:26	which has been hidden from a
Heb	9:26	now, once at the end of the a

AGONY†

Is	23: 5	they also will be in a at the
Luke	22:44	And being in a, He prayed more

AGREE (see AGREED, AGREEMENT)

Matt	5:25	A with your adversary quickly
Matt	18:19	of you a on earth concerning
Matt	20.13	Did you not a with me for a
Mark	14:56	their testimonies did not a
Acts	15:15	the words of the prophets a
Rom	7:16	I a with the law that it is
1Jn	5: 8	and these three a as one

AGREED (see AGREE)

Dan	2: 9	For you have a to speak lying
Amos	3: 3	together, unless they are a
Matt	20: 2	Now when he had a with the
Luke	22: 5	glad, and a to give him money
John	9:22	for the Jews had a already

AGREEMENT (see AGREE)

Num	30: 2	to bind himself by some a
Num	30:10	herself by an a with an oath
Dan	11: 6	of the North to make an a
2Co	6:16	what a has the temple of God

AGRIPPA

Acts	25:13	And after some days King A
Acts	26: 1	Then A said to Paul, "You

AHAB

1Ki	16:29	A the son of Omri became king
1Ki	18:16	and A went to meet Elijah
1Ki	19: 1	And A told Jezebel all that
1Ki	21: 2	So A spoke to Naboth, saying,

AHASUERUS

Ezra	4: 6	Now in the reign of A, in the
Esth	1: 1	A (this was the A who
Dan	9: 1	year of Darius the son of A

AHAZ

2Ki	15:38	Then A his son reigned in his
2Ki	16: 1	A the son of Jotham, king of
2Ki	16:10	Now King A went to Damascus

2Ki	18: 1	that Hezekiah the son of A
Matt	1: 9	begot Jotham, Jotham begot A

AHAZIAH (see JEHOAHAZ)

1Ki	22:40	Then A his son reigned in his
1Ki	22:51	A the son of Ahab became king
2Ki	8:25	A the son of Jehoram, king of

AHIJAH (see AHIMELECH)

1Ki	11:29	that the prophet A the
1Ki	15:27	Then Baasha the son of A, of
1Ki	15:29	His servant A the Shilonite

AHIMELECH (see ABIMELECH, AHIJAH)

1Sa	21: 2	So David said to A the priest
1Sa	22:16	You shall surely die, A, you
2Sa	8:17	A the son of Abiathar were
1Ch	24:31	of King David, Zadok, A, and

AHITHOPHEL

2Sa	15:31	counsel of A into foolishness

AI

Gen	12: 8	on the west and A on the east
Gen	13: 3	between Bethel and A,
Josh	7: 2	sent men from Jericho to A
Josh	8:28	So Joshua burned A and made it
Jer	49: 3	O Heshbon, for A is plundered

AID

2Sa	21:17	son of Zeruiah came to his a
Phil	4:16	Thessalonica you sent a once
Heb	2:16	He does not give a to angels

AIJALON

Josh	10:12	and Moon, in the Valley of A
Judg	12:12	and was buried at A in the

AILS

Gen	21:17	What a you, Hagar
Ps	114: 5	What a you, O sea, that you

AIM† (see AIMLESS)

Rom	15:20	it my a to preach the gospel
2Co	5: 9	Therefore we make it our a

AIMLESS† (see AIM)

1Pe	1:18	from your a conduct received

AIR

Gen	1:26	sea, over the birds of the a
Ps	8: 8	The birds of the a, And the
Prov	30:19	the way of an eagle in the a
Matt	6:26	Look at the birds of the a
Matt	8:20	and birds of the a have nests
Mark	4: 4	and the birds of the a came
Mark	4:32	a may nest under its shade
Acts	22:23	and threw dust into the a,
1Co	9:26	not as one who beats the a
1Co	14: 9	will be speaking into the a
Eph	2: 2	prince of the power of the a
1Th	4:17	to meet the Lord in the a
Rev	16:17	out his bowl into the a, and a

AKEL DAMA

Acts	1:19	in their own language, A,

ALABASTER†

Esth	1: 6	on a mosaic pavement of a
Matt	26: 7	an a flask of very costly
Mark	14: 3	a woman came having an a
Luke	7:37	house, brought an a flask of

ALARM (see ALARMED)

Num	10: 9	sound an a with the trumpets
Jer	4:19	of the trumpet, the a of war

ALARMED (see ALARM)

Mark	16: 5	and they were a

ALEXANDER

Mark	15:21	a Cyrenian, the father of A
Acts	4: 6	priest, Caiaphas, John, and A
Acts	19:33	And they drew A out of the
1Ti	1:20	of whom are Hymenaeus and A
2Ti	4:14	A the coppersmith did me much

ALIEN (see ALIENS)

2Sa	1:13	I am the son of an a, an
Ps	69: 8	an a to my mother's children
Mal	3: 5	those who turn away an a

ALIENATE† (see ALIENATED)

Ezek	48:14	they may not a this best part

ALIENATED (see ALIENATE)

Ezek	23:17	them, and a herself from them
Eph	4:18	being a from the life of God,
Col	1:21	And you, who once were a and

ALIENS (see ALIEN)

Deut	24:14	a who is in your land within
1Ch	29:15	For we are a and pilgrims
Hos	7: 9	A have devoured his strength,
Eph	2:12	being a from the commonwealth
Heb	11:34	to flight the armies of the a

ALIVE

Gen	6:19	ark, to keep them a with you
Gen	45:28	Joseph my son is still a
Gen	50:20	day, to save many people a
Ex	1:17	but saved the male children a
Deut	5: 3	today, all of us who are a
Deut	32:39	I kill and I make a
2Sa	12:18	while the child was a
Ps	22:29	he who cannot keep himself a
Ps	30: 3	You have kept me a, that I
Ps	124: 3	would have swallowed us a
Prov	1:12	us swallow them a like Sheol
Matt	27:63	while He was still a, how
Luke	15:24	my son was dead and is a again
Luke	15:32	your brother was dead and is a
Luke	24:23	of angels who said He was a
Acts	1: 3	He also presented Himself a
Acts	20:12	brought the young man in a
Acts	25:19	whom Paul affirmed to be a
Rom	6:11	but a to God in Christ Jesus

Rom	6:13	God as being a from the dead
Rom	7: 9	I was a once without the law,
1Co	15:22	in Christ all shall be made a
Eph	2: 1	And you He made a, who were
1Th	4:17	Then we who are a and remain
1Pe	3:18	but made a by the Spirit,
Rev	1:18	and behold, I am a forevermore
Rev	3: 1	I have a name that you are a
Rev	19:20	These two were cast a into

ALLELUIA

Rev	19: 1	A! Salvation and glory and

ALLOW (see ALLOWED)

Gen	31: 7	God did not a him to hurt me
Ex	12:23	not a the destroyer to come
Ps	16:10	Nor will You a Your Holy One
Ps	66: 9	does not a our feet to be
Ps	121: 3	He will not a your foot to be
Matt	23:13	nor do you a those who are
Mark	1:34	He did not a the demons to
Mark	11:16	And He would not a anyone to
Luke	4:41	did not a them to speak, for
Acts	2:27	nor will You a Your Holy One
1Co	10:13	who will not a you to be
Rev	2:20	you, because you a that woman
Rev	11: 9	not a their dead bodies to be

ALLOWED (see ALLOW)

Deut	8: 3	a you to hunger, and fed you
Job	31:30	(Indeed I have not a my mouth
Matt	3:15	Then he a Him
Matt	24:43	not a his house to be broken
Acts	14:16	a all nations to walk in

ALMIGHTY

Gen	17: 1	I am A God; walk before Me
Gen	35:11	said to him: I am God A
Ex	6: 3	Isaac, and to Jacob, as God A
Ruth	1:21	me, and the A has afflicted me
Job	6: 4	arrows of the A are within me
Job	11: 7	find out the limits of the A
Job	23:16	weak, and the A terrifies me
Job	24: 1	are not hidden from the A
Job	31:35	that the A would answer me,
Job	33: 4	breath of the A gives me life
Ps	91: 1	under the shadow of the A
Is	13: 6	as destruction from the A
Ezek	1:24	like the voice of the A, a
Ezek	10: 5	like the voice of A God when
2Co	6:18	and daughters, says the LORD A
Rev	1: 8	was and who is to come, the A
Rev	4: 8	Holy, holy, holy, Lord God A
Rev	16:14	of that great day of God A
Rev	19:15	fierceness and wrath of A God

ALMOND

Eccl	12: 5	when the a tree blossoms, the
Jer	1:11	I see a branch of an a tree

ALMS

Luke	12:33	Sell what you have and give a
Acts	3: 3	into the temple, asked for a

Acts	10: 2	who gave a generously to the
Acts	10: 4	your a have come up for a

ALOES

Prov	7:17	perfumed my bed with myrrh, a
Song	4:14	of frankincense, myrrh and a
John	19:39	a mixture of myrrh and a,

ALOUD

Gen	45: 2	And he wept a, and the
1Ki	18:27	Cry a, for he is a god
Ps	51:14	my tongue shall sing a of
Prov	1:20	Wisdom calls a outside
Is	58: 1	Cry a, spare not
Mark	15: 8	Then the multitude, crying a

ALPHA†

Rev	1: 8	I am the A and the Omega
Rev	1:11	I am the A and the Omega
Rev	21: 6	I am the A and the Omega
Rev	22:13	I am the A and the Omega

ALTAR (see ALTARS, CENSER)

Gen	8:20	Noah built an a to the LORD
Gen	22: 9	And Abraham built an a there
Gen	22: 9	his son and laid him on the a
Gen	35: 1	make an a there to God, who
Ex	17:15	And Moses built an a and called
Ex	27: 1	make an a of acacia wood,
Ex	29:37	make atonement for the a and
Lev	4: 7	blood on the horns of the a
Num	4:13	away the ashes from the a
Josh	8:30	Now Joshua built an a to the
Josh	22:10	a great, impressive a
Judg	6:25	tear down the a of Baal that
Judg	13:20	in the flame of the a
1Sa	14:35	Saul built an a to the LORD
1Ki	1:50	hold of the horns of the a
1Ki	8:22	Solomon stood before the a of
1Ki	18:35	water ran all around the a
2Ki	16:10	saw an a that was at Damascus
2Ki	23:16	tombs and burned them on the a
Ps	26: 6	So I will go about Your a
Ps	43: 4	I will go to the a of God
Ps	51:19	shall offer bulls on Your a
Ps	118:27	cords to the horns of the a
Is	6: 6	with the tongs from the a
Ezek	8: 5	and there, north of the a gate
Ezek	40:46	who have charge of the a
Mal	1: 7	offer defiled food on My a
Matt	5:23	you bring your gift to the a
Matt	23:18	And, 'Whoever swears by the a
Luke	1:11	side of the a of incense
Luke	11:51	who perished between the a
Acts	17:23	I even found an a with this
1Co	10:18	sacrifices partakers of the a
Heb	13:10	We have an a from which those
Jas	2:21	Isaac his son on the a
Rev	6: 9	I saw under the a the souls
Rev	8: 3	the saints upon the golden a
Rev	8: 5	it with fire from the a, and
Rev	14:18	angel came out from the a

ALTARS (see ALTAR)

Ex	34:13	But you shall destroy their **a**
Lev	26:30	cut down your incense **a**, and
Num	3:31	table, the lampstand, the **a**
Num	23: 1	Build seven **a** for me here
1Ki	19:10	covenant, torn down Your **a**
2Ki	11:18	priest of Baal before the **a**
Ps	84: 3	Even your **a**, O LORD of hosts,
Is	17: 8	He will not look to the **a**
Is	65: 3	and burn incense on **a** of brick
Jer	11:13	up **a** to that shameful thing
Jer	11:13	**a** to burn incense to Baal
Rom	11: 3	prophets and torn down Your **a**

ALWAYS (see EVER, FOREVER)

Ex	25:30	on the table before Me **a**
Ex	28:38	it shall **a** be on his forehead
Deut	5:29	**a** keep all My commandments,
Deut	14:23	to fear the LORD your God **a**
2Sa	9:10	shall eat bread at my table **a**
1Ki	11:36	**a** have a lamp before Me in
Ps	9:18	shall not **a** be forgotten
Ps	10: 5	His ways are **a** prospering
Ps	16: 8	have set the LORD **a** before me
Ps	73:12	ungodly, Who are **a** at ease
Ps	103: 9	He will not **a** strive with us,
Prov	5:19	**a** be enraptured with her love
Prov	8:30	rejoicing **a** before Him,
Prov	28:14	is the man who is **a** reverent
Eccl	9: 8	Let your garments **a** be white
Is	57:16	nor will I **a** be angry
Jer	20:17	her womb **a** enlarged with me
Matt	26:11	you have the poor with you **a**
Matt	28:20	and lo, I am with you **a**, even
Luke	15:31	him, 'Son, you are **a** with me
Luke	18: 1	that men **a** ought to pray and
John	6:34	Lord, give us this bread **a**
John	18:20	I **a** taught in synagogues and
John	18:20	temple, where the Jews **a** meet
Acts	2:25	the LORD **a** before my face
Rom	1: 9	of you **a** in my prayers,
1Co	1: 4	I thank my God **a** concerning
1Co	15:58	**a** abounding in the work of
2Co	2:14	who **a** leads us in triumph in
2Co	4:10	**a** carrying about in the body
2Co	6:10	as sorrowful, yet **a** rejoicing
2Co	9: 8	**a** having all sufficiency in
Eph	5:20	giving thanks **a** for all
Eph	6:18	praying **a** with all prayer and
Phil	1: 4	**a** in every prayer of mine
Phil	4: 4	Rejoice in the Lord **a**
Col	4: 6	your speech **a** be with grace
1Th	5:16	Rejoice **a**,
2Th	1: 3	bound to thank God **a** for you
2Ti	3: 7	**a** learning and never able to
1Pe	3:15	**a** be ready to give a defense

AM

Gen	4: 9	**A** I my brother's keeper
Gen	15: 1	I **a** your shield, your
Gen	15: 7	I **a** the LORD, who brought you
Gen	17: 1	to him, "I **a** Almighty God
Gen	18:17	from Abraham what I **a** doing
Gen	18:27	I who **a** but dust and ashes
Gen	22: 1	And he said, "Here I **a**."
Gen	26:24	I **a** the God of your father
Gen	26:24	do not fear, for I **a** with you
Gen	28:13	I **a** the LORD God of Abraham
Gen	28:15	I **a** with you and will keep you
Gen	45: 3	to his brothers, "I **a** Joseph
Gen	46: 3	I **a** God, the God of your
Ex	3: 4	And he said, "Here I **a**."
Ex	3: 6	I **a** the God of your father
Ex	3:11	Who **a** I that I should go to
Ex	3:14	said to Moses, "I **A** WHO I **A**
Ex	3:14	I **A** has sent me to you
Ex	6: 2	I **a** the LORD
Ex	6:12	for I **a** of uncircumcised lips
Ex	7: 5	shall know that I **a** the LORD
Ex	15:26	For I **a** the LORD who heals
Ex	20: 5	**a** a jealous God, visiting the
Lev	11:45	be holy, for I **a** holy
Num	18:20	I **a** your portion and your
Deut	5: 9	**a** a jealous God, visiting the
Deut	32:39	I, **a** He, and there is no God
Ruth	3: 9	I **a** Ruth, your maidservant
Ruth	3:12	that I **a** a close relative;
1Sa	3: 5	Here I **a**, for you called me
2Sa	7:18	Who **a** I, O Lord GOD
2Sa	11: 5	and said, "I **a** with child
1Ki	18:22	I alone **a** left a prophet of
2Ki	5: 7	**A** I God, to kill and make
Neh	6: 3	I **a** doing a great work, so
Job	10:15	I **a** full of disgrace
Job	12: 3	I **a** not inferior to you
Job	40: 4	Behold, I **a** vile
Ps	6: 6	I **a** weary with my groaning
Ps	22: 6	But I **a** a worm, and no man
Ps	22:14	I **a** poured out like water, And
Ps	31: 9	O LORD, for I **a** in trouble
Ps	37:25	have been young, and now **a** old
Ps	40:17	But I **a** poor and needy
Ps	46:10	still, and know that I **a** God
Ps	116:16	I **a** Your servant, the son of
Ps	120: 7	I **a** for peace
Ps	139:14	You, for I **a** fearfully and
Song	2:16	beloved is mine, and I **a** his
Song	6: 3	I **a** my beloved's, and my
Is	6: 5	Because I **a** a man of unclean
Is	6: 8	Here **a** I! Send me.
Is	8:18	Here **a** I and the children whom
Is	41: 4	I, the LORD, **a** the first
Is	41:10	Fear not, for I **a** with you
Is	41:10	dismayed, for I **a** your God
Is	42: 8	I **a** the LORD, that is My name
Is	43:11	**a** the LORD, and besides Me
Is	44: 6	**a** the First and I am the Last
Is	45: 5	I **a** the LORD, and there is no
Is	48:12	I **a** He, I am the First, I am
Jer	1: 6	cannot speak, for I **a** a youth
Jer	1: 8	for I **a** with you to deliver
Jer	15:16	for I **a** called by Your name,
Jer	15:20	for I **a** with you to save you
Ezek	6: 7	shall know that I **a** the LORD
Ezek	26: 3	I **a** against you, O Tyre, and
Ezek	28: 2	I **a** a god, I sit in the seat
Ezek	28:22	I **a** against you, O Sidon

Ezek	38: 3	I a against you, O Gog,
Hos	11: 9	For I a God, and not man, the
Matt	3:11	whose sandals I a not worthy
Matt	3:17	Son, in whom I a well pleased
Matt	8: 8	Lord, I a not worthy that You
Matt	8: 9	For I also a a man under
Matt	16:15	But who do you say that I a
Matt	20:22	that I a baptized with
Matt	22:32	I a the God of Abraham, the
Matt	24: 5	I a the Christ,' and will
Matt	27:43	He said, "I a the Son of God
Matt	28:20	I a with you always, even to
Luke	15:19	a no longer worthy to be
Luke	18:11	that I a not like other men
John	1:20	I a not the Christ
John	4:26	I who speak to you a He
John	6:35	them, "I a the bread of life
John	6:51	I a the living bread which
John	7:34	where I a you cannot come
John	8:12	I a the light of the world
John	8:14	came from and where I a going
John	8:23	I a from above
John	8:23	I a not of this world
John	8:24	do not believe that I a He
John	8:58	you, before Abraham was, I A
John	9: 5	As long as I a in the world
John	10: 7	I a the door of the sheep
John	10:11	I a the good shepherd
John	10:36	I said, 'I a the Son of God'
John	11:25	I a the resurrection and the
John	12:26	and where I a, there My
John	12:32	if I a lifted up from the
John	14: 3	that where I a, there you may
John	14: 6	I a the way, the truth, and
John	14:10	that I a in the Father, and
John	14:28	I a going to the Father,'
John	15: 1	I a the true vine, and My
John	17:14	just as I a not of the world
John	18: 5	Jesus said to them, "I a He
John	19:21	I a the King of the Jews
John	20:17	I a ascending to My Father
Acts	9: 5	I a Jesus, whom you are
Acts	10:26	I myself a also a man
Acts	22: 8	I a Jesus of Nazareth, whom
Acts	26:15	I a Jesus, whom you are
Rom	1:15	me, I a ready to preach the
Rom	1:16	For I a not ashamed of the
Rom	7:14	but I a carnal, sold under
Rom	7:24	O wretched man that I a
Rom	8:38	For I a persuaded that
Rom	9: 1	I a not lying, my conscience
1Co	1:12	you says, "I of Paul," or
1Co	9: 1	A I not an apostle
1Co	9: 1	A I not free? Have I not
1Co	13: 2	have not love, I a nothing
1Co	13:12	know just as I also a known
1Co	15: 9	For I a the least of the
1Co	15: 9	who a not worthy to be called
Eph	3: 8	who a less than the least of
Eph	6:20	for which I a an ambassador
Phil	4:11	learned in whatever state I a
Col	2: 5	For though I a absent in the
Col	2: 5	yet I a with you in spirit,
1Ti	1:15	sinners, of whom I a chief

Rev	1: 8	I a the Alpha and the Omega,
Rev	1:17	I a the First and the Last
Rev	1:18	I a He who lives, and was dead
Rev	1:18	behold, I a alive forevermore
Rev	2:23	I a He who searches the minds
Rev	3:17	say, 'I a rich, have become
Rev	16:15	Behold, I a coming as a thief
Rev	22: 7	I a coming quickly
Rev	22:16	I a the Root and the Offspring

AMALEK (see AMALEKITE)

Gen	36:12	son, and she bore A to Eliphaz
Ex	17:13	So Joshua defeated A and his

AMALEKITE (see AMALEK)

1Sa	30:13	from Egypt, servant of an A
2Sa	1: 8	So I answered him, I am an A

AMAZED (see AMAZEMENT, ASTONISHED)

Is	13: 8	they will be a at one another
Matt	12:23	And all the multitudes were a
Mark	6:51	And they were greatly a in
Luke	2:48	they saw Him, they were a
Acts	9:21	Then all who heard were a

AMAZEMENT† (see AMAZED)

Mark	5:42	were overcome with great a
Acts	3:10	a at what had happened to him
Rev	17: 6	her, I marveled with great a

AMAZIAH

2Ki	13:12	against A king of Judah, are
2Ki	14: 1	A the son of Joash, king of
Amos	7:12	Then A said to Amos

AMBASSADOR (see AMBASSADORS)

Eph	6:20	for which I am an a in chains

AMBASSADORS (see AMBASSADOR)

Is	18: 2	which sends a by sea, even in
2Co	5:20	Therefore we are a for Christ

AMBITION† (see AMBITIONS)

Phil	1:16	preach Christ from selfish a
Phil	2: 3	through selfish a or conceit

AMBITIONS† (see AMBITION)

2Co	12:20	wrath, selfish a
Gal	5:20	wrath, selfish a

AMEN

Num	5:22	woman shall say, "A, so be it
Deut	27:16	all the people shall say, 'A
Ps	41:13	everlasting! A and Amen.
Ps	72:19	His glory. A and Amen.
Ps	89:52	forevermore! A and Amen.
Ps	106:48	let all the people say, "A!"
Matt	6:13	and the glory forever. A.
Matt	28:20	to the end of the age." A.
Mark	16:20	the accompanying signs. A.
Luke	24:53	praising and blessing God. A.
John	21:25	that would be written. A.
Rom	15:33	peace be with you all. A.
Rom	16:20	Jesus Christ be with you. A.

1Co	14:16	A" at your giving of thanks,
1Co	16:24	you all in Christ Jesus. A.
2Co	1:20	in Him are Yes, and in Him A
2Co	13:14	Spirit be with you all. A.
Gal	6:18	Christ be with your spirit. A
Eph	3:21	world without end. A.
Col	4:18	Grace be with you. A.
Heb	13:21	be glory forever and ever. A
1Pe	4:11	dominion forever and ever. A.
Rev	1: 7	of Him. Even so, A.
Rev	1:18	I am alive forevermore. A.
Rev	3:14	These things says the A
Rev	5:14	living creatures said, "A!"
Rev	19: 4	saying, "A! Alleluia!"
Rev	22:20	I am coming quickly." A.
Rev	22:21	Christ be with you all. A.

AMISS
Jas	4: 3	receive, because you aska

AMITTAI†
2Ki	14:25	Jonah the son of A
Jon	1: 1	Jonah the son of A

AMMINADAB
Num	1: 7	Judah, Nahshon the son of A
Ruth	4:19	begot Ram, and Ram begot A
Luke	3:33	the son of A, the son of Ram,

AMMON (see AMMONITE)
Gen	19:38	the people of A to this day
Deut	3:11	in Rabbah of the people of A

AMMONITE (see AMMON)
Deut	23: 3	An A or Moabite shall not

AMNON
2Sa	13: 1	A the son of David loved her

AMON
2Ki	21:24	had conspired against King A
Jer	1: 2	days of Josiah the son of A
Matt	1:10	and A begot Josiah

AMORITE (see AMORITES)
Gen	10:16	the Jebusite, the A, and the
Deut	2:24	into your hand Sihon the A
Ezek	16: 3	your father was an A and your
Ezek	16:45	a Hittite and your father an A

AMORITES (see AMORITE)
Gen	14: 7	and also the A who dwelt in
Gen	15:16	of the A is not yet complete
Gen	15:21	the A, the Canaanites, the
Ex	3: 8	and the Hittites and the A and
Num	21:21	to Sihon king of the A,
Deut	31: 4	and Og, the kings of the A
Ps	135:11	Sihon king of the A, Og king

AMOS
Amos	1: 1	The words of A, who was among
Amos	7: 8	A, what do you see

AMOZ
Is	1: 1	vision of Isaiah the son of A

AMPHIPOLIS†
Acts	17: 1	they had passed through A

AMRAM
Num	26:59	to A she bore Aaron and Moses

ANAK (see ANAKIM)
Num	13:33	of A came from the giants)

ANAKIM (see ANAK)
Deut	2:11	as giants, like the A, but

ANANIAS
Acts	5: 3	A, why has Satan filled your
Acts	9:10	disciple at Damascus named A

ANATHOTH
Jer	1: 1	in A in the land of Benjamin
Jer	29:27	not reproved Jeremiah of A
Jer	32: 7	Buy my field which is in A

ANCHOR† (see ANCHORS)
Heb	6:19	we have as an a of the soul

ANCHORS (see ANCHOR)
Acts	27:29	dropped four a from the stern

ANCIENT
Deut	33:15	things of the a mountains
Ps	77: 5	of old, The years of a times
Prov	22:28	Do not remove the a landmark
Eccl	1:10	been in a times before us
Is	19:11	the wise, the son of a kings
Is	23: 7	antiquity is from a days,
Jer	5:15	nation, it is an a nation
Dan	7: 9	and the A of Days was seated
2Pe	2: 5	and did not spare the a world

ANDREW
Matt	10: 2	Peter, and A his brother
Mark	1:29	the house of Simon and A, with
John	12:22	Philip came and told A
Acts	1:13	Peter, James, John, and A

ANGEL (see ANGELS)
Gen	16: 7	Now the A of the LORD found
Gen	16:11	the A of the LORD said to her
Gen	21:17	Then the a of God called to
Gen	24: 7	He will send His a before you
Gen	48:16	the A who has redeemed me
Ex	3: 2	the A of the LORD appeared to
Num	22:23	Now the donkey saw the A of
Judg	13: 6	countenance of the A of God
1Sa	29: 9	in my sight as an a of God
2Sa	14:17	for as the a of God, so is my
2Sa	14:20	to the wisdom of the a of God
2Sa	24:16	when the a stretched out His
2Sa	24:17	a who was striking the people
Ps	34: 7	The a of the LORD encamps all
Ps	35: 5	let the a of the LORD chase

A

Is	63: 9	the A of His Presence saved
Dan	3:28	and Abed-Nego, who sent His A
Dan	6:22	My God sent His a and shut the
Hos	12: 4	Yes, he struggled with the A
Zech	1: 9	So the a who talked with me
Zech	1:11	answered the A of the LORD
Matt	1:20	an a of the Lord appeared to
Luke	1:26	a Gabriel was sent by God to
Luke	2:13	a a multitude of the heavenly
Acts	12: 7	an a of the Lord stood by him
2Co	11:14	himself into an a of light
Gal	1: 8	or an a from heaven, preach
Rev	1: 1	by His a to His servant John
Rev	2: 1	To the a of the church of
Rev	8: 5	Then the a took the censer,
Rev	9:11	the a of the bottomless pit
Rev	21:17	of a man, that is, of an a

ANGELS (see ANGEL)

Gen	19: 1	Now the two a came to Sodom
Gen	28:12	and there the a of God were
Ps	8: 5	him a little lower than the a
Ps	91:11	give His a charge over you
Ps	103:20	Bless the LORD, you His a
Ps	104: 4	Who makes His a spirits, His
Ps	148: 2	Praise Him, all His a
Matt	4: 6	He shall give His a charge
Matt	13:39	age, and the reapers are the a
Matt	16:27	of His Father with His a, and
Matt	24:31	He will send His a with a
Matt	25:31	and all the holy a with Him
Matt	26:53	more than twelve legions of a
Luke	2:15	when the a had gone away from
Luke	15:10	a of God over one sinner who
John	1:51	the a of God ascending and
John	20:12	And she saw two a in white
Rom	8:38	nor a nor principalities nor
1Co	6: 3	know that we shall judge a
1Co	11:10	on her head, because of the a
1Co	13: 1	the tongues of men and of a
1Ti	3:16	in the Spirit, seen by a,
Heb	1: 4	so much better than the a
Heb	2: 7	a little lower than the a
Heb	12:22	an innumerable company of a
Heb	13: 2	unwittingly entertained a
1Pe	1:12	things which a desire to look
2Pe	2: 4	not spare the a who sinned
Jude	6	the a who did not keep their
Rev	1:20	the a of the seven churches
Rev	5:11	of many a around the throne
Rev	8: 2	I saw the seven a who stand
Rev	12: 7	the dragon and his a fought,
Rev	21:12	twelve a at the gates, and

ANGER (see ANGRY)

Gen	27:45	a turns away from you, and he
Ex	4:14	So the a of the LORD was
Ex	32:19	So Moses' a became hot, and he
Num	22:22	Then God's a was aroused
Num	22:27	so Balaam's a was aroused
Num	24:10	Then Balak's a was aroused
Deut	4:25	your God to provoke Him to a
Deut	13:17	from the fierceness of His a
Deut	32:22	For a fire is kindled in My a

1Sa	20:34	from the table in fierce a
Neh	9:17	and merciful, slow to a,
Job	21:17	God distributes in His a
Job	35:15	He has not punished in His a
Ps	6: 1	do not rebuke me in Your a
Ps	7: 6	Arise, O LORD, in Your a
Ps	30: 5	For His a is but for a moment
Ps	69:24	wrathful a take hold of them
Ps	78:50	He made a path for His a
Ps	85: 5	Your a to all generations
Ps	90:11	Who knows the power of Your a
Ps	103: 8	and gracious, Slow to a, and
Ps	103: 9	will He keep His a forever
Prov	15: 1	but a harsh word stirs up a
Eccl	5:17	much sorrow and sickness and a
Is	10: 5	to Assyria, the rod of My a
Is	48: 9	name's sake I will defer My a
Is	63: 3	I have trodden them in My a
Jer	17: 4	My a which shall burn forever
Hos	13:11	I gave you a king in My a
Hos	14: 4	for My a has turned away from
Joel	2:13	and merciful, slow to a, and of
Amos	1:11	his a tore perpetually, and he
Jon	4: 2	and merciful God, slow to a
Mic	7:18	does not retain His a forever
Nah	1: 3	the LORD is slow to a and
Zeph	2: 3	in the day of the LORD's a
Eph	4:31	Let all bitterness, wrath, a
Col	3: 8	a, wrath, malice, blasphemy,

ANGRY (see ANGER)

Gen	4: 5	And Cain was very a, and his
Gen	18:30	Let not the Lord be a, and I
Gen	31:36	Then Jacob was a and rebuked
Gen	34: 7	men were grieved and very a
Ps	2:12	Kiss the Son, lest He be a
Ps	4: 4	Be a, and do not sin
Ps	7:11	And God is a with the wicked
Ps	79: 5	Will You be a forever
Prov	21:19	with a contentious and a woman
Prov	22:24	no friendship with an a man
Prov	25:23	tongue an a countenance
Prov	29:22	An a man stirs up strife, and
Eccl	7: 9	hasten in your spirit to be a
Jer	3: 5	Will He remain a forever
Dan	2:12	this reason the king was a
Jon	4: 1	exceedingly, and he became a
Jon	4: 4	Is it right for you to be a
Matt	2:16	wise men, was exceedingly a
Matt	5:22	a with his brother without a
Matt	18:34	And his master was a, and
Eph	4:26	Be a, and do not sin"
Heb	3:10	Therefore I was a with that
Heb	3:17	whom was He a forty years
Rev	11:18	The nations were a, and Your

ANGUISH

Gen	42:21	for we saw the a of his soul
Ex	6: 9	Moses, because of a of spirit
Ps	77:10	This is my a; but I will
Ps	119:143	a have overtaken me, Yet Your
Prov	1:27	distress and a come upon you
Jer	15: 8	I will cause a and terror to
Jer	49:24	A and sorrows have taken her

John	16:21	she no longer remembers the **a**
Rom	2: 9	tribulation and **a**, on every
2Co	2: 4	**a** of heart I wrote to you,

ANIMAL (*see* ANIMALS, BEAST)

Gen	7: 2	seven each of every clean **a**
Gen	8:19	Every **a**, every creeping thing
Lev	18:23	Nor shall you mate with any **a**
Deut	4:17	the likeness of any **a** that is
Deut	14: 6	And you may eat every **a** with
Eccl	3:21	and the spirit of the **a**

ANIMALS (*see* ANIMAL, BEASTS)

Gen	7: 2	two each of **a** that are
Gen	7: 8	Of clean **a**, of animals that
Gen	7: 8	of **a** that are unclean, of
Ex	11: 5	and all the firstborn of the **a**
Lev	20:25	distinguish between clean **a**
Num	18:15	of unclean **a** you shall redeem
Deut	14: 6	chews the cud, among the **a**
Eccl	3:19	man has no advantage over **a**
Acts	10:12	four-footed **a** of the earth
1Cor	15:39	of men, another flesh of **a**

ANNA†

Luke	2:36	Now there was one, **A**, **a**

ANNAS

Luke	3: 2	**A** and Caiaphas being high

ANNUL† (*see* ANNULLING, ANNULS)

Job	40: 8	you indeed **a** My judgment
Is	14:27	purposed, and who will **a** it
Gal	3:17	cannot **a** the covenant that

ANNULLING† (*see* ANNUL)

Heb	7:18	**a** of the former commandment

ANNULS† (*see* ANNUL)

Gal	3:15	no one **a** or adds to it

ANOINT (*see* ANOINTED, ANOINTING)

Ex	28:41	You shall **a** them, consecrate
Ex	29: 7	pour it on his head, and **a** him
Ex	30:30	And you shall **a** Aaron and his
Ex	40: 9	**a** the tabernacle and all that
Judg	9: 8	forth to **a** **a** king over them
1Sa	15: 1	The LORD sent me to **a** you
1Sa	15:17	did not the LORD **a** you king
1Sa	16:12	the LORD said, Arise, **a** him
1Ki	1:34	Nathan the prophet **a** him king
Ps	23: 5	You **a** my head with oil
Dan	9:24	and to **a** the Most Holy
Mark	14: 8	to **a** My body for burial
Rev	3:18	**a** your eyes with eye salve,

ANOINTED (*see* ANOINT)

Gen	31:13	where you **a** the pillar and
Lev	16:32	And the priest, who is **a** and
1Sa	2:10	and exalt the horn of His **a**
1Sa	2:35	walk before My **a** forever
1Sa	12: 3	the LORD and before His **a**
1Sa	16:13	**a** him in the midst of his
2Sa	2: 4	there they **a** David king over

2Sa	22:51	king, and shows mercy to His **a**
1Ki	1:39	the tabernacle and **a** Solomon
1Ch	16:22	Do not touch My **a** ones, and do
Ps	2: 2	the LORD and against His **A**
Ps	18:50	king, And shows mercy to His **a**
Ps	45: 7	has **a** You With the oil of
Ps	105:15	Do not touch My **a** ones, And do
Is	61: 1	because the LORD has **a** Me to
Ezek	28:14	You were the **a** cherub who
Zech	4:14	These are the two **a** ones, who
Mark	6:13	**a** with oil many who were sick
Luke	4:18	because He has **a** Me to preach
Luke	7:38	**a** them with the fragrant oil
Luke	7:46	but this woman has **a** My feet
John	9: 6	He **a** the eyes of the blind
John	11: 2	It was that Mary who **a** the
John	12: 3	**a** the feet of Jesus, and wiped
Heb	1: 9	has **a** You with the oil of

ANOINTING (*see* ANOINT)

Ex	25: 6	and spices for the **a** oil and
Jas	5:14	**a** him with oil in the name of
1Jn	2:20	But you have an **a** from the

ANT† (*see* ANTS)

Prov	6: 6	Go to the **a**, you sluggard

ANTICHRIST† (*see* ANTICHRISTS)

1Jn	2:18	heard that the **A** is coming
1Jn	2:22	He is **a** who denies the Father
1Jn	4: 3	this is the spirit of the **A**
2Jn	7	This is a deceiver and an **a**

ANTICHRISTS† (*see* ANTICHRIST)

1Jn	2:18	even now many **a** have come

ANTIOCH

Acts	11:26	first called Christians in **A**
Acts	13: 1	in the church that was at **A**

ANTITYPE† (see TYPE)

1Pe	3:21	There is also an **a** which now

ANTS† (*see* ANT)

Prov	30:25	the **a** are a people not strong

ANXIETY (*see* ANXIOUS)

Prov	12:25	**A** in the heart of man causes
Ezek	4:16	eat bread by weight and with **a**
Ezek	12:18	water with trembling and **a**

ANXIOUS (*see* ANXIETY, ANXIOUSLY)

1Sa	9:20	do not be **a** about them, for
Luke	12:26	why are you **a** for the rest
Phil	4: 6	Be **a** for nothing, but in

ANXIOUSLY† (*see* ANXIOUS)

Luke	2:48	father and I have sought You **a**

APOLLONIA†

Acts	17: 1	through Amphipolis and **A**, they

APOLLOS

Acts	18:24	Now **a** certain Jew named **A**

1Co	1:12	I am of **A**," or "I am of
1Co	3: 6	**A** watered, but God gave the

APOLLYON†

Rev	9:11	in Greek he has the name **A**

APOSTLE (see APOSTLES, APOSTLESHIP)

Rom	1: 1	Christ, called to be an **a**
Rom	11:13	as I am an **a** to the Gentiles
1Co	9: 1	Am I not an **a**?
1Co	15: 9	not worthy to be called an **a**
Gal	1: 1	Paul, an **a** (not from men nor
1Ti	2: 7	appointed a preacher and an **a**
Heb	3: 1	calling, consider the **A** and

APOSTLES (see APOSTLE, APOSTLES')

Matt	10: 2	of the twelve **a** are these
Luke	6:13	twelve whom He also named **a**
Luke	11:49	will send them prophets and **a**
Acts	1:26	numbered with the eleven **a**
Acts	5:18	and laid their hands on the **a**
1Co	9: 5	wife, as do also the other **a**
1Co	12:28	first **a**, second prophets,
1Co	12:29	Are all **a**? Are all prophets?
1Co	15: 7	by James, then by all the **a**
1Co	15: 9	For I am the least of the **a**
2Co	11:13	For such are false **a**,
Eph	2:20	on the foundation of the **a**
Eph	3: 5	by the Spirit to His holy **a**
Eph	4:11	He Himself gave some to be **a**
Rev	2: 2	those who say they are **a** and
Rev	21:14	of the twelve **a** of the Lamb

APOSTLES' (see APOSTLES)

Acts	2:42	steadfastly in the **a** doctrine
Acts	4:35	and laid them at the **a** feet
Acts	8:18	the laying on of the **a** hands

APOSTLESHIP (see APOSTLE)

Acts	1:25	and **a** from which Judas by
1Co	9: 2	the seal of my **a** in the Lord

APPALLED (see CONFOUNDED)

APPAREL

2Sa	13:18	virgin daughters wore such **a**
Is	63: 1	One who is glorious in His **a**
Is	63: 2	Why is Your **a** red, and Your
Acts	1:10	men stood by them in white **a**
1Ti	2: 9	adorn themselves in modest **a**
Jas	2: 2	with gold rings, in fine **a**

APPEAL (see APPEALED)

Acts	25:11	I **a** to Caesar
Phm	9	love's sake I rather **a** to you
Phm	10	I **a** to you for my son
Heb	13:22	I **a** to you, brethren, bear

APPEALED (see APPEAL)

Acts	25:12	You have **a** to Caesar

APPEAR (see APPEARANCE, APPEARED, APPEARING, APPEARS)

Gen	1: 9	and let the dry land **a**"
Ex	23:17	shall **a** before the Lord GOD
Ps	90:16	Let Your work **a** to Your
Ps	102:16	He shall **a** in His glory
Song	2:12	The flowers **a** on the earth
Matt	6:16	may **a** to men to be fasting
Matt	24:30	Son of Man will **a** in heaven
Luke	19:11	of God would **a** immediately
Rom	7:13	But sin, that it might **a** sin
2Co	5:10	For we must all **a** before the
Col	3: 4	also will **a** with Him in glory
Heb	9:24	now to **a** in the presence of
Heb	9:28	Him He will **a** a second time
1Pe	4:18	the ungodly and the sinner **a**

APPEARANCE (see APPEAR)

Gen	29:17	was beautiful of form and **a**
1Sa	16: 7	man looks at the outward **a**
Ezek	1:26	the **a** of a man high above it
Dan	8:15	me one having the **a** of a man
Dan	10: 6	face like the **a** of lightning
Luke	9:29	the **a** of His face was altered
John	7:24	Do not judge according to **a**
2Co	10: 7	according to the outward **a**
Phil	2: 8	And being found in **a** as a man

APPEARED (see APPEAR)

Gen	12: 7	Then the LORD **a** to Abram and
Ex	3: 2	the Angel of the LORD **a** to
Dan	5: 5	the fingers of a man's hand **a**
Matt	1:20	the Lord **a** to him in a dream
Matt	2: 7	them what time the star **a**
Matt	17: 3	Elijah **a** to them, talking
Matt	27:53	the holy city and **a** to many
Mark	16: 9	He **a** first to Mary Magdalene,
Mark	16:12	He **a** in another form to two
Mark	16:14	Later He **a** to the eleven
Luke	9: 8	and by some that Elijah had **a**
Luke	24:34	indeed, and has **a** to Simon
Acts	2: 3	Then there **a** to them divided
Acts	7:35	who **a** to him in the bush
Acts	9:17	who **a** to you on the road as
Acts	16: 9	a vision **a** to Paul in the
Tit	2:11	salvation has **a** to all men
Tit	3: 4	God our Savior toward man **a**

APPEARING† (see APPEAR)

1Ti	6:14	our Lord Jesus Christ's **a**
2Ti	1:10	now been revealed by the **a** of
2Ti	4: 1	living and the dead at His **a**
2Ti	4: 8	to all who have loved His **a**
Tit	2:13	glorious **a** of our great God

APPEARS (see APPEAR)

Ps	84: 7	Each one of them **a** before
Mal	3: 2	And who can stand when He **a**
Col	3: 4	When Christ who is our life **a**
Jas	4:14	that **a** for a little time and
1Pe	5: 4	and when the Chief Shepherd **a**
1Jn	2:28	abide in Him, that when He **a**

APPLE (see APPLES)

Deut	32:10	kept him as the **a** of His eye
Song	2: 3	Like an **a** tree among the

APPLES (*see* APPLE)

| Prov | 25:11 | like **a** of gold in settings of |

APPLY

Prov	2: 2	**a** your heart to understanding
Prov	22:17	**a** your heart to my knowledge
Prov	23:12	A your heart to instruction,

APPOINT (*see* APPOINTED, APPOINTS)

2Sa	6:21	to **a** me ruler over the people
Job	9:19	who will **a** my day in court
Matt	24:51	**a** him his portion with the
1Th	5: 9	For God did not **a** us to wrath

APPOINTED (*see* APPOINT)

Gen	4:25	For God has **a** another seed
Gen	18:14	At the **a** time I will return
Num	10:10	gladness, in your **a** feasts
1Sa	25:30	has **a** you ruler over Israel,
2Ch	8:13	the three **a** yearly feasts
Job	34:13	Or who **a** Him over the whole
Ps	78: 5	**a** a law in Israel, Which He
Ps	79:11	those who are **a** to die
Ps	104:19	He **a** the moon for seasons
Is	1:14	your **a** feasts my soul hates
Jer	43:11	to death those **a** for death
Ezek	45:17	at all the **a** seasons of the
Dan	8:19	for at the **a** time the end
Hos	9: 5	What will you do in the **a** day
Hab	1:12	You have **a** them for judgment
Zeph	3:18	sorrow over the **a** assembly
Matt	28:16	which Jesus had **a** for them
Mark	3:14	Then He **a** twelve, that they
Luke	3:13	more than what is **a** for you
Luke	10: 1	Lord **a** seventy others also
John	15:16	**a** you that you should go and
Acts	13:48	And as many as had been **a** to
Acts	14:23	So when they had **a** elders in
Acts	17:31	because He has **a** a day on
Rom	13: 1	that exist are **a** by God
1Co	12:28	God has **a** these in the church
2Co	10:13	of the sphere which God **a** us
Gal	3:19	it was **a** through angels by
Gal	4: 2	the time **a** by the father
Phil	1:17	knowing that I am **a** for the
1Ti	2: 7	for which I was **a** a preacher
Heb	1: 2	whom He has **a** heir of all
Heb	3: 2	was faithful to Him who **a** Him
Heb	9:27	as it is **a** for men to die
1Pe	2: 8	to which they also were **a**

APPOINTS† (*see* APPOINT)

Dan	5:21	**a** over it whomever He chooses
Heb	7:28	For the law **a** as high priests
Heb	7:28	law, **a** the Son who has been

APPREHENDED† (*see* ARRESTED)

| Phil | 3:13 | do not count myself to have **a** |

APPROACH (*see* APPROACHES, APPROACHING)

Lev	18:14	You shall not **a** his wife
Lev	18:19	Also you shall not **a** a woman
Deut	31:14	the days **a** when you must die

Job	31:37	like a prince I would **a** Him
Job	41:13	Who can **a** him with a double
Ps	65: 4	You choose, And cause to **a** You
Ezek	43:19	who **a** Me to minister to Me,'
Luke	8:19	could not **a** Him because of
Heb	10: 1	make those who **a** perfect

APPROACHES† (*see* APPROACH)

| Lev | 20:16 | If a woman **a** any beast and |
| Luke | 12:33 | where no thief **a** nor moth |

APPROACHING† (*see* APPROACH)

| Is | 58: 2 | they take delight in **a** God |
| Heb | 10:25 | the more as you see the Day **a** |

APPROVE (*see* APPROVED, APPROVES)

Ps	49:13	posterity who **a** their sayings
Lam	3:36	the Lord does not **a**
Luke	11:48	**a** the deeds of your fathers
Rom	2:18	and **a** the things that are

APPROVED (*see* APPROVE)

Rom	14:18	acceptable to God and **a** by men
Rom	16:10	Greet Apelles, **a** in Christ
1Co	11:19	that those who are **a** may be
2Co	10:18	he who commends himself is **a**
2Co	13: 7	not that we should appear **a**
1Th	2: 4	But as we have been **a** by God
2Ti	2:15	to present yourself **a** to God

APPROVES† (*see* APPROVE)

| Rom | 14:22 | condemn himself in what he **a** |

AQUILA

Acts	18: 2	found a certain Jew named A
Acts	18:18	Priscilla and A were with him
Acts	18:26	When A and Priscilla heard him

ARABAH

| Deut | 3:17 | Sea of the A (the Salt Sea) |

ARABIA (*see* ARABS)

1Ki	10:15	from all the kings of A, and
Gal	1:17	but I went to A, and returned
Gal	4:25	Hagar is Mount Sinai in A

ARABS† (*see* ARABIA)

| Neh | 4: 7 | when Sanballat, Tobiah, the A |
| Acts | 2:11 | Cretans and A—we hear them |

ARAM (*see* ARAMAIC, MESOPOTAMIA, SYRIA)

| Num | 23: 7 | of Moab has brought me from A |

ARAMAIC (*see* ARAM)

2Ki	18:26	speak to your servants in A
Ezra	4: 7	was written in A script, and
Dan	2: 4	spoke to the king in A, "O

ARARAT

| Gen | 8: 4 | month, on the mountains of A |
| 2Ki | 19:37 | escaped into the land of A |

ARAUNAH

| 2Sa | 24:16 | floor of A the Jebusite |

ARCHANGEL†

| 1Th | 4:16 | shout, with the voice of an **a** |
| Jude | 9 | Yet Michael the **a**, in |

ARCHELAUS†

| Matt | 2:22 | But when he heard that **A** was |

AREOPAGITE† (*see* AREOPAGUS)

| Acts | 17:34 | among them Dionysius the **A** |

AREOPAGUS† (*see* AREOPAGITE)

| Acts | 17:19 | him and brought him to the **A** |
| Acts | 17:22 | stood in the midst of the **A** |

ARGUMENTS†

Job	23: 4	Him, and fill my mouth with **a**
2Co	10: 5	casting down **a** and every high
1Ti	6: 4	**a** over words, from which come

ARIMATHEA

Matt	27:57	there came a rich man from **A**
Mark	15:43	Joseph of **A**, a prominent
Luke	23:51	He was from **A**, a city of the

ARISE (*see* ARISEN, AROSE)

Gen	13:17	**A**, walk in the land through
Gen	19:15	**A**, take your wife and your two
Gen	21:18	**A**, lift up the lad and hold
Gen	27:19	please **a**, sit and eat of my
Josh	1: 2	Now therefore, **a**, go over
1Sa	16:12	**A**, anoint him; for this
2Ki	23:25	after him did any **a** like him
Ps	3: 7	**A**, O LORD; Save me
Ps	88:10	Shall the dead **a** and praise
Is	26:19	my dead body they shall **a**
Is	52: 2	yourself from the dust, **a**
Is	60: 1	**A**, shine; For your light
Jon	1: 2	**A**, go to Nineveh, that great
Jon	3: 2	**A**, go to Nineveh, that great
Mal	4: 2	**a** with healing in His wings
Matt	2:13	**A**, take the young Child and
Matt	9: 5	forgiven you,' or to say, '**A**
Matt	9: 6	**A**, take up your bed, and go to
Luke	15:18	I will **a** and go to my father,
John	14:31	**A**, let us go from here
Acts	9:34	**A** and make your bed
Acts	9:40	body he said, "Tabitha, **a**.
Acts	22:10	And the Lord said to me, '**A**
Acts	22:16	**A** and be baptized, and wash
Eph	5:14	**a** from the dead, and Christ

ARISEN† (*see* ARISE)

Deut	34:10	**a** in Israel a prophet like
Dan	11: 4	And when he has **a**, his kingdom
John	7:52	prophet has **a** out of Galilee

ARK

Gen	6:14	yourself an **a** of gopherwood
Gen	7: 1	Come into the **a**, you and all
Gen	8:16	Go out of the **a**, you and your
Ex	2: 3	she took an **a** of bulrushes
Ex	25:10	make an **a** of acacia wood
Ex	25:21	mercy seat on top of the **a**

Ex	25:22	are on the **a** of the Testimony
Num	10:33	the **a** of the covenant of the
Deut	10: 8	tribe of Levi to bear the **a**
1Sa	4:19	the **a** of God was captured
1Sa	5: 1	Philistines took the **a** of God
2Sa	6: 7	he died there by the **a** of God
1Ki	8: 7	cherubim overshadowed the **a**
Matt	24:38	day that Noah entered the **a**
Heb	9: 4	and the **a** of the covenant
Heb	11: 7	prepared an **a** for the saving
1Pe	3:20	Noah, while the **a** was being
Rev	11:19	the **a** of His covenant was

ARM (*see* ARMED, ARMPITS, ARMS)

Ex	6: 6	you with an outstretched **a**
Ex	15:16	by the greatness of Your **a**
Num	11:23	the LORD's **a** been shortened
Deut	4:34	hand and an outstretched **a**
Job	35: 9	of the **a** of the mighty
Ps	44: 3	Nor did their own **a** save them
Ps	44: 3	was Your right hand, Your **a**
Ps	77:15	You have with Your **a** redeemed
Ps	89:21	Also My **a** shall strengthen
Ps	98: 1	His holy **a** have gained Him
Song	8: 6	heart, as a seal upon your **a**
Is	40:10	and His **a** shall rule for Him
Is	40:11	gather the lambs with His **a**
Is	51: 5	and on My **a** they will trust
Is	51: 9	on strength, O **a** of the LORD
Is	52:10	holy **a** in the eyes of all the
Is	53: 1	to whom has the **a** of the LORD
Is	63:12	of Moses, with His glorious **a**
Jer	48:25	his **a** is broken," says the
Zech	11:17	his **a** shall completely wither
John	12:38	to whom has the **a** of the LORD
Acts	13:17	with an uplifted **a** He brought
1Pe	4: 1	**a** yourselves also with the

ARMAGEDDON†

| Rev | 16:16 | the place called in Hebrew, **A** |

ARMED (*see* ARM)

Gen	14:14	he **a** his three hundred and
Judg	18:11	**a** with weapons of war
1Sa	17: 5	he was **a** with a coat of mail,
1Ch	20: 1	Joab led out the **a** forces
Prov	6:11	and your need like an **a** man
Luke	11:21	When a strong man, fully **a**

ARMIES (*see* ARMY)

Ex	6:26	of Egypt according to their **a**
Ex	7: 4	hand on Egypt and bring My **a**
Ex	12:17	**a** out of the land of Egypt
Ex	12:41	**a** of the LORD went out from
1Sa	17:10	I defy the **a** of Israel this
1Sa	17:23	from the **a** of the Philistines
1Sa	17:26	the **a** of the living God
Matt	22: 7	And he sent out his **a**,
Luke	21:20	see Jerusalem surrounded by **a**
Heb	11:34	to flight the **a** of the aliens
Rev	19:14	the **a** in heaven, clothed in

ARMOR (*see* ARMORBEARER)

| 1Sa | 14: 1 | the young man who bore his **a** |

1Sa	17:38	Saul clothed David with his **a**
Luke	11:22	all his **a** in which he trusted
Rom	13:12	let us put on the **a** of light
2Co	6: 7	by the **a** of righteousness on
Eph	6:11	the whole **a** of God
Eph	6:13	the whole **a** of God

ARMORBEARER (see ARMOR)

Judg	9:54	to the young man, his **a**, and
1Sa	14:12	called to Jonathan and his **a**
1Sa	31: 4	Then Saul said to his **a**

ARMPITS† (see ARM)

Jer	38:12	clothes and rags under your **a**

ARMS (see ARM, HANDS)

Gen	49:24	the **a** of his hands were made
Deut	33:27	are the everlasting **a**
Judg	15:14	**a** became like flax that is
Judg	16:12	them off his **a** like a thread
Ps	18:32	It is God who **a** me with
Ps	18:34	So that my **a** can bend a bow
Ps	37:17	For the **a** of the wicked shall
Prov	5:20	in the **a** of a seductress
Prov	31:17	and strengthens her **a**
Is	51: 5	My **a** will judge the peoples
Ezek	13:20	I will tear them from your **a**
Dan	2:32	**a** of silver, its belly and
Dan	10: 6	like torches of fire, his **a**
Hos	7:15	and strengthened their **a**, yet
Hos	11: 3	walk, taking them by their **a**
Mark	9:36	He had taken him in His **a**

ARMY (see ARMIES)

Gen	21:22	the commander of his **a**,
Ex	14: 4	Pharaoh and over all his **a**
Ex	15: 4	his **a** He has cast into the
Num	31:14	with the officers of the **a**
Josh	5:14	but as Commander of the **a** of
Judg	4:15	all his **a** with the edge of
Judg	8: 6	should give bread to your **a**
1Sa	4: 2	men of the **a** in the field
1Sa	14:48	And he gathered an **a** and
1Sa	17:21	battle array, **a** against **a**
2Sa	8:16	son of Zeruiah was over the **a**
1Ki	11:15	the **a** had gone up to bury the
1Ki	20:25	you shall muster an **a** like
1Ki	22:36	a shout went throughout the **a**
2Ki	3: 9	there was no water for the **a**
2Ki	6:14	chariots and a great **a** there
2Ki	7: 6	the noise of a great **a**
2Ki	25: 5	All his **a** was scattered from
1Ch	7:40	among the **a** fit for battle
1Ch	12:22	a great **a**, like the **a** of God
1Ch	27:34	of the king's **a** was Joab
2Ch	13: 3	with an **a** of valiant warriors
2Ch	14:13	before the LORD and His **a**
2Ch	16: 8	the Lubim not a huge **a** with
2Ch	24:24	very great **a** into their hand
2Ch	26:14	for them, for the entire **a**
Job	29:25	so I dwelt as a king in the **a**
Ps	27: 3	Though an **a** may encamp
Ps	33:16	by the multitude of an **a**
Ps	136:15	his **a** in the Red Sea, For His

Song	6: 4	awesome as an **a** with banners
Is	43:17	the chariot and horse, the **a**
Jer	32: 2	**a** besieged Jerusalem, and
Jer	34: 7	**a** fought against Jerusalem
Jer	39: 5	the Chaldean **a** pursued them
Ezek	1:24	tumult like the noise of an **a**
Ezek	26: 7	and an **a** with many people
Ezek	27:10	were in your **a** as men of war
Ezek	27:11	your **a** were on your walls all
Ezek	29:18	his **a** to labor strenuously
Ezek	29:19	will be the wages for his **a**
Ezek	37:10	feet, an exceedingly great **a**
Ezek	38:13	gathered your **a** to take booty
Ezek	38:15	a great company and a mighty **a**
Dan	4:35	His will in the **a** of heaven
Dan	11:25	with a very great and mighty **a**
Dan	11:26	his **a** shall be swept away, and
Joel	2:11	LORD gives voice before His **a**
Joel	2:20	far from you the northern **a**
Rev	9:16	Now the number of the **a** of
Rev	19:19	on the horse and against His **a**

ARNON

Num	21:13	on the other side of the **A**
Deut	2:24	and cross over the River **A**

AROMA

Gen	8:21	the LORD smelled a soothing **a**
Ex	29:18	it is a sweet **a**, an offering
Ex	29:25	as a sweet **a** before the LORD
Lev	1: 9	fire, a sweet **a** to the LORD
2Co	2:16	the **a** of death leading to death
Phil	4:18	from you, a sweet-smelling **a**

AROSE (see ARISE)

Gen	19:33	she lay down or when she **a**
Gen	22: 3	for the burnt offering, and **a**
Gen	37: 7	Then behold, my sheaf **a** and
Ex	1: 8	Now there **a** a new king over
Judg	4: 9	Then Deborah **a** and went with
Judg	5: 7	**a** a mother in Israel
Ruth	3:14	and she **a** before one could
1Sa	3: 6	So Samuel **a** and went to Eli,
2Ch	36:16	the LORD **a** against His people
Ezra	1: 5	**a** to go up and build the house
Ezra	3: 9	**a** as one to oversee those
Ezra	9: 5	sacrifice I **a** from my fasting
Esth	7: 7	Then the king **a** in his wrath
Esth	8: 4	So Esther **a** and stood before
Job	1:20	Then Job **a**, tore his robe
Job	29: 8	saw me and hid, and the aged **a**
Ps	76: 9	When God **a** to judgment, To
Song	5: 5	I **a** to open for my beloved,
Dan	6:19	Then the king **a** very early in
Dan	8:27	afterward I **a** and went about
Jon	1: 3	But Jonah **a** to flee to
Jon	3: 3	So Jonah **a** and went to Nineveh
Jon	3: 6	he **a** from his throne and laid
Jon	4: 8	it happened, when the sun **a**
Matt	8:15	And she **a** and served them
Matt	8:24	a great tempest **a** on the sea
Matt	8:26	Then He **a** and rebuked the
Matt	9:25	by the hand, and the girl **a**
Matt	25: 7	Then all those virgins **a** and

Matt	26:62	And the high priest **a** and said
Luke	1:39	Now Mary **a** in those days and
Luke	4:38	Now He **a** from the synagogue
Luke	6:48	And when the flood **a**, the
Luke	9:46	Then a dispute **a** among them
Luke	15:14	there a severe famine in
Luke	15:20	And he **a** and came to his father
Luke	24:12	But Peter **a** and ran to the
John	3:25	Then there a **a** dispute
Acts	5: 6	young men **a** and wrapped
Acts	6: 1	there **a** a complaint against
Acts	8: 1	**a** against the church which
Acts	9: 8	Then Saul **a** from the ground,
Acts	10:41	Him after He **a** from the dead
Acts	23: 7	a dissension **a** between the
Acts	23: 9	Then there **a** a loud outcry
Acts	23: 9	of the Pharisees' party **a**
Acts	23:10	Now when there a **a** great
Acts	27:14	a tempestuous head wind **a**
Heb	7:14	that our Lord **a** from Judah
Rev	9: 2	smoke **a** out of the pit like

AROUSED

Gen	30: 2	anger was **a** against Rachel
Num	11: 1	heard it, and His anger was **a**
Deut	6:15	your God be **a** against you
Job	13: 7	My wrath is **a** against you
Matt	1:24	being **a** from sleep, did as

ARRAYED

Matt	6:29	was not **a** like one of these
Luke	23:11	**a** Him in a gorgeous robe, and
Acts	12:21	**a** in royal apparel, sat on
Rev	7:13	Who are these **a** in white
Rev	17: 4	The woman was **a** in purple

ARREST (see ARRESTED)

Judg	15:10	We have come up to **a** Samson
1Ki	13: 4	the altar, saying, "**A** him
Mark	13:11	But when they **a** you and
2Co	11:32	garrison, desiring to **a** me;

ARRESTED† (see ARREST)

2Sa	4:10	I **a** him and had him executed
Luke	22:54	Then, having **a** Him, they led
John	18:12	officers of the Jews **a** Jesus
Acts	1:16	a guide to those who **a** Jesus
Acts	12: 4	when he had **a** him

ARROGANCE (see ARROGANT)

1Sa	2: 3	let no **a** come from your mouth
Prov	8:13	pride and **a** and the evil way and
Is	13:11	will halt the **a** of the proud
Jas	4:16	But now you boast in your **a**

ARROGANT (see ARROGANCE)

Prov	21:24	he acts with **a** pride
Is	10:12	of the **a** heart of the king of
Ezek	24:21	your **a** boast, the desire of
Ezek	30:18	her **a** strength shall cease in
Zeph	2: 8	made **a** threats against their

ARROW (see ARROWS)

| Ex | 19:13 | be stoned or shot with an **a** |

1Sa	20:36	ran, he shot an **a** beyond him
Job	41:28	The **a** cannot make him flee
Ps	11: 2	ready their **a** on the string
Ps	91: 5	Nor of the **a** that flies by
Prov	7:23	till an **a** struck his liver
Prov	25:18	a club, a sword, and a sharp **a**
Is	34:15	There the **a** snake shall make
Jer	9: 8	Their tongue is an **a** shot out
Lam	3:12	me up as a target for the **a**
Zech	9:14	and His **a** will go forth like
Heb	12:20	or shot with an **a**

ARROWS (see ARROW)

Num	24: 8	and pierce them with his **a**
Deut	32:23	I will spend My **a** upon them
Deut	32:42	I will make My **a** drunk with
1Sa	20:20	three **a** to the side of it
2Sa	22:15	He sent out **a** and scattered
Job	6: 4	For the **a** of the Almighty are
Ps	7:13	He makes His **a** into fiery
Ps	18:14	He sent out His **a** and
Ps	21:12	You will make ready Your **a** on
Ps	38: 2	For Your **a** pierce me deeply,
Ps	45: 5	Your **a** are sharp in the heart
Ps	57: 4	Whose teeth are spears and **a**
Ps	58: 7	Let his **a** be as if cut in
Ps	77:17	Your **a** also flashed about
Ps	120: 4	Sharp **a** of the warrior, With
Ps	127: 4	Like **a** in the hand of a
Ps	144: 6	Shoot out Your **a** and destroy
Ezek	21:21	he shakes the **a**, he consults
Ezek	39: 3	cause the **a** to fall out of
Hab	3: 9	oaths were sworn over Your **a**
Hab	3:11	the light of Your **a** they went
Hab	3:14	**a** the head of his villages

ARTAXERXES

| Ezra | 4: 7 | wrote to **A** king of Persia |
| Neh | 13: 6 | of **A** king of Babylon I had |

ARTICLES

Ex	3:22	**a** of silver, **a** of gold
Ex	12:35	**a** of gold, and clothing
Ex	22: 7	neighbor money or **a** to keep
Num	18: 3	near the **a** of the sanctuary
Num	31: 6	the priest, with the holy **a**
2Sa	8:10	**a** of gold, and **a** of bronze
1Ki	7:45	All these **a** which Hiram made
2Ki	14:14	all the **a** that were found in
2Ki	23: 4	the **a** that were made for Baal
2Ki	24:13	he cut in pieces all the **a** of
2Ki	25:16	these **a** was beyond measure
2Ch	36:10	with the costly **a** from the
Ezra	1: 7	**a** of the house of the LORD

ARTISAN

| Ex | 36: 1 | every gifted **a** in whom the |

ASA

1Ki	15: 8	Then **A** his son reigned in his
1Ki	15: 9	**A** became king over Judah
1Ki	15:11	**A** did what was right in the
Matt	1: 7	Abijah, and Abijah begot **A**

ASAHEL

2Sa	2:18	A was as fleet of foot as a
2Sa	23:24	A the brother of Joab was one

ASAPH

1Ch	15:19	the singers, Heman, A, and
1Ch	25: 6	A, Jeduthun, and Heman were
2Ch	29:30	of David and of A the seer
Ezra	3:10	and the Levites, the sons of A

ASCEND (see ASCENDED, ASCENDING)

Deut	30:12	Who will a into heaven for
Ps	24: 3	Who may a into the hill of
Ps	139: 8	If I a into heaven, You are
Is	14:13	I will a into heaven, I will
Is	34:10	its smoke shall a forever
John	6:62	of Man a where He was before
Acts	2:34	did not a into the heavens
Rom	10: 6	Who will a into heaven
Rev	17: 8	will a out of the bottomless

ASCENDED (see ASCEND)

Josh	8:20	smoke of the city a
Ps	68:18	You have a on high, You have
Prov	30: 4	Who has a into heaven, or
John	3:13	No one has a to heaven but He
John	20:17	I have not yet a to My Father
Eph	4: 8	When He a on high, He led
Rev	8: 4	a before God from the angel's
Rev	11:12	they a to heaven in a cloud,

ASCENDING (see ASCEND)

Gen	28:12	the angels of God were a and
John	1:51	open, and the angels of God a
John	20:17	I am a to My Father and your

ASHAMED

Gen	2:25	and his wife, and were not a
Ps	6:10	Let all my enemies be a and
Ps	22: 5	trusted in You, and were not a
Ps	25: 3	no one who waits on You be a
Ps	31:17	Do not let me be a, O LORD,
Ps	34: 5	And their faces were not a
Ps	37:19	not be a in the evil time
Ps	69: 6	of hosts, be a because of me
Ps	70: 2	Let them be a and confounded
Is	41:11	against you shall be a and
Is	49:23	not be a who wait for Me
Mark	8:38	For whoever is a of Me and My
Mark	8:38	a when He comes in the glory
Rom	1:16	for I am not a of the gospel
Phil	1:20	that in nothing I shall be a
2Th	3:14	with him, that he may be a
2Ti	1: 8	Therefore do not be a of the
2Ti	1:12	nevertheless I am not a, for
2Ti	1:16	me, and was not a of my chain
Heb	2:11	not a to call them brethren
Heb	11:16	Therefore God is not a to be
1Pe	4:16	a Christian, let him not be a
1Jn	2:28	not be a before Him at His

ASHDOD

Josh	11:22	in Gaza, in Gath, and in A
Is	20: 1	him, and he fought against A

ASHER

Ex	1: 4	Dan, Naphtali, Gad, and A
Luke	2:36	of Phanuel, of the tribe of A
Rev	7: 6	of the tribe of A twelve

ASHERAH (see ASHERAHS)

1Ki	15:13	made an obscene image of A
1Ki	18:19	four hundred prophets of A
2Ki	23: 4	were made for Baal, for A

ASHERAHS† (see ASHERAH)

Judg	3: 7	God, and served the Baals and A

ASHES

Lev	6:11	carry the a outside the camp
Num	19: 9	gather up the a of the heifer
Esth	4: 1	and put on sackcloth and a, and
Job	2: 8	he sat in the midst of the a
Job	42: 6	and repent in dust and a
Is	61: 3	to give them beauty for a
Dan	9: 3	with fasting, sackcloth, and a
Heb	9:13	the a of a heifer, sprinkling

ASHKELON

1Sa	6:17	one for Gaza, one for A, one
2Sa	1:20	it is not in the streets of A

ASHTORETH (see ASHTORETHS)

1Ki	11:33	worshiped A the goddess of

ASHTORETHS (see ASHTORETH)

Judg	2:13	LORD and served Baal and the A

ASIA

Acts	2: 9	and Cappadocia, Pontus and A
Acts	16: 6	to preach the word in A
Rev	1: 4	seven churches which are in A

ASLEEP

Jon	1: 5	had lain down, and was fast a
Matt	8:24	the waves. But He was a
Matt	26:40	the disciples and found them a
Matt	27:52	who had fallen a were raised
Acts	7:60	he had said this, he fell a
1Co	15: 6	but some have fallen a
1Co	15:18	a in Christ have perished
1Th	4:15	means precede those who are a

ASPS†

Ps	140: 3	The poison of a is under
Rom	3:13	The poison of a is under

ASSEMBLE (see ASSEMBLED, ASSEMBLING, ASSEMBLY)

2Sa	20: 4	A the men of Judah for me
Dan	11:10	a a multitude of great forces

ASSEMBLED (see ASSEMBLE, GATHERED)

Ex	38: 8	who a at the door of the
Num	1:18	they a all the congregation
Josh	18: 1	Israel a together at Shiloh
1Ki	8: 1	Now Solomon a the elders of
John	20:19	where the disciples were a

Acts	1: 4	being **a** together with them,
Acts	4:31	were **a** together was shaken
Acts	15:25	being **a** with one accord, to

ASSEMBLIES† (see ASSEMBLY)

Is	1:13	Sabbaths, and the calling of **a**
Is	4: 5	of Mount Zion, and above her **a**
Amos	5:21	I do not savor your sacred **a**

ASSEMBLING† (see ASSEMBLE)

Heb	10:25	not forsaking the **a** of

ASSEMBLY (see ASSEMBLE, ASSEMBLIES, COMPANY, CONGREGATION)

Gen	28: 3	you may be an **a** of peoples
Ex	12: 6	Then the whole **a** of the
Ex	16: 3	kill this whole **a** with hunger
Lev	4:21	is a sin offering for the **a**
Lev	23:36	It is a sacred **a**, and you
Num	14: 5	**a** of the congregation of the
2Ki	10:20	Proclaim a solemn **a** for Baal
Ezra	10:14	leaders of our entire **a** stand
Neh	5:13	And all the **a** said, "Amen
Neh	8:18	day there was a sacred **a**,
Ps	22:22	of the **a** I will praise You.
Ps	35:18	You thanks in the great **a**
Ps	89: 5	also in the **a** of the saints.
Ps	89: 7	feared in the **a** of the saints
Ps	107:32	also in the **a** of the people
Ps	111: 1	In the **a** of the upright and in
Prov	21:16	rest in the **a** of the dead
Jer	15:17	sit in the **a** of the mockers
Lam	1:10	commanded Not to enter Your **a**
Joel	1:14	a fast, call a sacred **a**
Acts	19:39	be determined in the lawful **a**
Heb	2:12	in the midst of the **a** I will
Heb	12:23	to the general **a** and church of
Jas	2: 2	your **a** a man with gold rings

ASSURANCE† (see ASSURE)

Deut	28:66	night, and have no **a** of life
Is	32:17	quietness and **a** forever
Acts	17:31	He has given **a** of this to all
Col	2: 2	the full **a** of understanding
1Th	1: 5	the Holy Spirit and in much **a**
Heb	6:11	full **a** of hope until the end
Heb	10:22	true heart in full **a** of faith

ASSURE† (see ASSURANCE, ASSURED, ASSUREDLY)

1Jn	3:19	shall **a** our hearts before Him

ASSURED† (see ASSURE)

Jer	14:13	you **a** peace in this place
Dan	4:26	kingdom shall be **a** to you
2Ti	3:14	you have learned and been **a** of
Heb	11:13	them afar off were **a** of them

ASSUREDLY (see ASSURE)

Matt	5:18	For **a**, I say to you, till
Matt	5:26	**A**, I say to you, you will by
Matt	6: 2	**A**, I say to you, they have
John	1:51	Most **a**, I say to you,

John	3: 3	Most **a**, I say to you, unless
Acts	2:36	know **a** that God has made this

ASSYRIA

Gen	2:14	goes toward the east of **A**
Gen	10:11	From that land he went to **A**
2Ki	16: 7	to Tiglath-Pileser king of **A**
2Ki	18: 9	of **A** came up against Samaria
2Ki	18:19	the great king, the king of **A**
Is	10: 5	Woe to **A**, the rod of My anger
Is	19:23	be a highway from Egypt to **A**

ASTONISHED (see AMAZED, ASTONISHMENT)

Lev	26:32	dwell in it shall be **a** at it
1Ki	9: 8	who passes by it will be **a**
Is	52:14	Just as many were **a** at you
Matt	7:28	people were **a** at His teaching
Luke	5: 9	**a** at the catch of fish which
Luke	24:22	at the tomb early, **a** us
Acts	10:45	who believed were **a**, as many

ASTONISHMENT (see ASTONISHED, DESOLATION)

Deut	28:37	And you shall become an **a**, a
Jer	8:21	**a** has taken hold of me

ASTRAY

Ex	23: 4	ox or his donkey going **a**, you
Ps	58: 3	They go **a** as soon as they are
Ps	95:10	who go **a** in their hearts, And
Ps	119:176	I have gone **a** like a lost
Prov	5:23	of his folly he shall go **a**
Prov	10:17	he who refuses correction goes **a**
Is	53: 6	All we like sheep have gone **a**
Matt	18:13	ninety-nine that did not go **a**
Heb	3:10	always go **a** in their heart
Heb	5: 2	who are ignorant and going **a**
1Pe	2:25	you were like sheep going **a**

ASTROLOGER† (see ASTROLOGERS)

Dan	2:10	things of any magician, **a**

ASTROLOGERS (see ASTROLOGER)

Is	47:13	let now the **a**, the stargazers
Dan	1:20	**a** who were in all his realm

ATE (see EAT)

Gen	3: 6	she took of its fruit and **a**
Gen	3:13	serpent deceived me, and I **a**
Ex	16:35	of Israel **a** manna forty years
2Sa	9:13	for he **a** continually at the
Ps	41: 9	Who **a** my bread, Has lifted up
Ps	78:25	Men **a** angels' food
Ps	78:29	So they **a** and were well filled
Ps	106:28	**a** sacrifices made to the dead
Jer	15:16	I **a** them, and Your word was to
Ezek	3: 3	So I **a** it, and it was in my
Dan	1:15	**a** the portion of the king's
Dan	4:33	from men and **a** grass like oxen
Matt	12: 4	**a** the showbread which was not
Matt	14:20	So they all **a** and were filled,
Mark	1: 6	he **a** locusts and wild honey
Mark	14:18	Now as they sat and **a**, Jesus
Luke	6: 1	**a** them, rubbing them in their

Luke	15:16	the pods that the swine **a**
Luke	24:43	it and **a** in their presence
John	6:31	Our fathers **a** the manna in
Acts	9: 9	sight, and neither **a** nor drank
1Co	10: 3	all **a** the same spiritual food
Rev	10:10	**a** it, and it was as sweet as

ATHALIAH

2Ki	11: 1	When **A** the mother of Ahaziah
2Ch	22:11	hid him from **A** so that she

ATHENIANS† (see ATHENS)

Acts	17:21	For all the **A** and the

ATHENS† (see ATHENIANS)

Acts	17:15	Paul brought him to **A**
Acts	17:16	Paul waited for them at **A**
Acts	17:22	Men of **A**, I perceive that in
Acts	18: 1	things Paul departed from **A**
1Th	3: 1	it good to be left in **A** alone

ATHLETICS†

2Ti	2: 5	also if anyone competes in **a**

ATONED (see ATONEMENT, ATONING)

1Sa	3:14	not be **a** for by sacrifice or

ATONEMENT (see ATONED)

Ex	29:33	with which the **a** was made
Ex	29:36	day as a sin offering for **a**
Ex	29:37	shall make **a** for the altar
Ex	30:10	Aaron shall make **a** upon its
Ex	30:15	to make **a** for yourselves
Ex	30:16	you shall take the **a** money of
Ex	32:30	I can make **a** for your sin
Lev	1: 4	his behalf to make **a** for him
Lev	4:20	priest shall make **a** for them
Lev	6: 7	**a** for him before the LORD
Lev	6:30	to make **a** in the holy place,
Lev	14:21	be waved, to make **a** for him
Lev	14:53	make **a** for the house, and it
Lev	16:17	to make **a** in the Holy Place
Lev	17:11	that makes **a** for the soul
Lev	23:27	a month shall be the Day of **A**
Num	8:12	to make **a** for the Levites
Deut	21: 8	Provide **a**, O LORD, for Your
Is	22:14	there will be no **a** for you
Ezek	43:20	cleanse it and make **a** for it
Ezek	43:26	shall make **a** for the altar
Ezek	45:15	to make **a** for them," says
Ezek	45:17	**a** for the house of Israel
Ezek	45:20	shall make **a** for the temple

ATONING† (see ATONED)

Lev	16:20	end of **a** for the Holy Place

ATTACK (see ATTACKED)

Gen	32:11	**a** me and the mother with the
Num	25:17	the Midianites, and **a** them
Josh	7: 3	thousand men go up and **a** Ai
Ps	62: 3	How long will you **a** a man
Jer	18:18	let us **a** him with the tongue,
Dan	11:40	king of the South shall **a** him
Acts	18:10	no one will **a** you to hurt you

ATTACKED (see ATTACK)

Gen	14:15	and he and his servants **a** them
Gen	36:35	who **a** Midian in the field of
Judg	15: 8	So he **a** them hip and thigh

ATTAIN (see ATTAINED, ATTAINING)

2Sa	23:19	he did not **a** to the first
Ps	139: 6	It is high, I cannot **a** it
Prov	1: 5	will **a** a wise counsel,
Hos	8: 5	be until they **a** to innocence
Luke	20:35	counted worthy to **a** that age
Phil	3:11	I may **a** to the resurrection

ATTAINED (see ATTAIN)

Rom	9:30	have **a** to righteousness, even
Rom	9:31	has not **a** to the law of
Phil	3:12	Not that I have already **a**

ATTAINING† (see ATTAIN)

Col	2: 2	**a** to all riches of the full

ATTENTION (see ATTENTIVE)

1Ki	18:29	one answered, no one paid **a**
Prov	4: 1	I give **a** to know understanding
Prov	4:20	My son, give **a** to my words
Prov	5: 1	My son, pay **a** to my wisdom
Acts	26:26	of these things escapes his **a**
1Ti	4:13	I come, give **a** to reading, to
Jas	2: 3	you pay **a** to the one wearing

ATTENTIVE (see ATTENTION)

2Ki	20:13	And Hezekiah was **a** to them
2Ch	6:40	let Your ears be **a** to the
Neh	1:11	be **a** to the prayer of Your
Neh	8: 3	were **a** to the Book of the Law
Luke	19:48	were very **a** to hear Him

ATTRIBUTES†

Rom	1:20	invisible **a** are clearly seen

AUGUSTUS† (see CAESAR)

Luke	2: 1	**A** that all the world should
Acts	25:21	for the decision of **A**, I
Acts	25:25	he himself had appealed to **A**

AUSTERE

Luke	19:21	you, because you are an **a** man

AUTHOR† (see CAPTAIN)

1Co	14:33	For God is not the **a** of
Heb	5: 9	He became the **a** of eternal
Heb	12: 2	looking unto Jesus, the **a**

AUTHORITIES† (see AUTHORITY)

Luke	12:11	and magistrates and **a**, do not
Acts	16:19	into the marketplace to the **a**
Rom	13: 1	be subject to the governing **a**
Rom	13: 1	God, and the **a** that exist are
Tit	3: 1	to be subject to rulers and **a**
1Pe	3:22	hand of God, angels and **a** and

AUTHORITY (see AUTHORITIES)

Gen	41:35	grain under the **a** of Pharaoh

Num	5:19	while under your husband's **a**
Matt	7:29	taught them as one having **a**
Matt	8: 9	For I also am a man under **a**
Matt	20:25	great exercise **a** over them
Matt	21:23	By what **a** are You doing these
Matt	28:18	All **a** has been given to Me in
Luke	4:32	for His word was with **a**
Luke	4:36	For with **a** and power He
Luke	9: 1	**a** over all demons, and to cure
Luke	10:19	I give you the **a** to trample
Luke	19:17	have **a** over ten cities
John	5:27	has given Him **a** to execute
John	7:17	whether I speak on My own **a**
John	12:49	I have not spoken on My own **a**
John	17: 2	given Him **a** over all flesh
Acts	1: 7	Father has put in His own **a**
Acts	8:27	**a** eunuch of great **a** under
Acts	26:12	journeyed to Damascus with **a**
Rom	13: 1	there is no **a** except from God
Rom	13: 2	whoever resists the **a** resists
1Co	7: 4	not have **a** over her own body
1Co	9:18	not abuse my **a** in the gospel
1Co	11:10	**a** symbol of **a** on her head
1Co	15:24	an end to all rule and all **a**
2Co	13:10	according to the **a** which the
2Th	3: 9	not because we do not have **a**
1Ti	2: 2	for kings and all who are in **a**
1Ti	2:12	teach or to have **a** over a man
Tit	2:15	exhort, and rebuke with all **a**
2Pe	2:10	of uncleanness and despise **a**
Jude	8	defile the flesh, reject **a**
Rev	9: 5	were not given **a** to kill them
Rev	13: 4	who gave **a** to the beast
Rev	18: 1	from heaven, having great **a**

AVAILS

Esth	5:13	Yet all this **a** me nothing
Gal	5: 6	nor uncircumcision **a** anything
Jas	5:16	of a righteous man **a** much

AVENGE (see AVENGED, AVENGER)

Deut	32:43	for He will **a** the blood of
Hos	1: 4	in a little while I will **a**
Luke	18: 7	shall God not **a** His own elect
Luke	18: 8	that He will **a** them speedily
Rom	12:19	do not **a** yourselves, but
Rev	6:10	and **a** our blood on those who

AVENGED (see AVENGE)

Gen	4:24	If Cain shall be **a** sevenfold
Rev	19: 2	He has **a** on her the blood of

AVENGER (see AVENGE)

Num	35:12	of refuge for you from the **a**
Num	35:19	The **a** of blood himself shall
Ps	8: 2	silence the enemy and the **a**
Rom	13: 4	an **a** to execute wrath on him
1Th	4: 6	the Lord is the **a** of all such

AWAKE (see AWAKEN, AWOKE, RISE)

Judg	5:12	A, awake, Deborah!
Ps	57: 8	A, lute and harp
Ps	59: 4	A to help me, and behold
Ps	127: 1	The watchman stays **a** in vain

Ps	139:18	When I **a**, I am still with You
Prov	6:22	and when you **a**, they will
Song	5: 2	I sleep, but my heart is **a**
Is	51: 9	A, awake, put on strength, O
Is	51:17	A, awake! Stand up, O
Dan	12: 2	the dust of the earth shall **a**
Hab	2:19	to him who says to wood, 'A
Mal	2:12	man who does this, being **a**
Luke	9:32	and when they were fully **a**
Rom	13:11	high time to **a** out of sleep
1Co	15:34	A to righteousness, and do not
Eph	5:14	A, you who sleep, arise from

AWAKEN (see AWAKE)

Ps	57: 8	I will **a** the dawn
Song	2: 7	do not stir up nor **a** love

AWARE

Matt	24:50	an hour that he is not **a** of
Matt	26:10	But when Jesus was **a** of it
Luke	11:44	over them are not **a** of them
Acts	5: 2	his wife also being **a** of it

AWESOME

Gen	28:17	said, "How **a** is this place
Deut	7:21	great and **a** God, is among you
Deut	28:58	**a** name, THE LORD YOUR
Job	37:22	with God is **a** majesty
Ps	45: 4	hand shall teach You **a** things
Ps	47: 2	For the LORD Most High is **a**
Ps	65: 5	By **a** deeds in righteousness
Ps	66: 3	God, "How **a** are Your works
Ps	111: 9	Holy and **a** is His name
Ezek	1:18	they were so high they were **a**
Ezek	1:22	the color of an **a** crystal
Dan	2:31	and its form was **a**
Dan	9: 4	**a** God, who keeps His covenant

AWL†

Ex	21: 6	pierce his ear with an **a**
Deut	15:17	then you shall take an **a** and

AWOKE (see AWAKE)

Gen	9:24	So Noah **a** from his wine, and
Ps	3: 5	I **a**, for the LORD sustained
Ps	78:65	Then the Lord **a** as one out of
Matt	8:25	came to Him and **a** Him, saying,

AX (see AXES)

1Sa	13:20	plowshare, his mattock, his **a**
2Ki	6: 5	the iron **a** head fell into the
Matt	3:10	even now the **a** is laid to the

AXES (see AX)

1Sa	13:21	mattocks, the forks, and the **a**

AZARIAH (see AHAZIAH, EZRA, UZZIAH)

2Ki	14:21	the people of Judah took A
2Ki	15: 1	A the son of Amaziah, king of
2Ki	15: 6	Now the rest of the acts of A
2Ki	15: 7	So A rested with his fathers
2Ki	15: 8	year of A king of Judah,
2Ch	22: 6	A the son of Jehoram, king of
2Ch	31:10	A the chief priest, from the

| Dan | 1: 6 | Hananiah, Mishael, and **A** |
| Dan | 1: 7 | and to **A**, Abed-Nego |

B

BAAL (see BAALS)

Num	22:41	up to the high places of **B**
Num	25: 3	was joined to **B** of Peor, and
Judg	2:13	forsook the LORD and served **B**
Judg	6:28	there was the altar of **B**
1Ki	18:19	and fifty prophets of **B**, and
1Ki	18:21	but if **B**, then follow him
1Ki	19:18	knees have not bowed to **B**
Rom	11: 4	have not bowed the knee to **B**

BAALS (see BAAL)

Judg	2:11	of the LORD, and served the **B**
Judg	8:33	played the harlot with the **B**
Hos	11: 2	They sacrificed to the **B**

BAAL-ZEBUB (see BEELZEBUB)

| 2Ki | 1: 2 | Go, inquire of **B**, the god of |

BAASHA

| 1Ki | 15:16 | **B** king of Israel all their |

BABBLER (see BABBLINGS)

| Acts | 17:18 | What does this **b** want to say |

BABBLINGS† (see BABBLER)

| 1Ti | 6:20 | the profane and vain **b** and |
| 2Ti | 2:16 | But shun profane and vain **b** |

BABE (see BABES)

Luke	1:41	that the **b** leaped in her womb
Luke	2:12	You will find a **B** wrapped in
Luke	2:16	and the **B** lying in a manger

BABEL† (see BABYLON)

| Gen | 10:10 | of his kingdom was **B**, Erech, |
| Gen | 11: 9 | its name is called **B**, because |

BABES (see BABE)

Ps	8: 2	Out of the mouth of **b** and
Matt	11:25	and have revealed them to **b**
Matt	21:16	read, 'Out of the mouth of **b**
Rom	2:20	the foolish, a teacher of **b**
1Co	3: 1	to carnal, as to **b** in Christ
1Pe	2: 2	as newborn **b**, desire the pure

BABYLON (see BABEL, CHALDEA)

2Ki	17:24	Assyria brought people from **B**
2Ki	20:14	from a far country, from **B**
2Ki	20:17	day, shall be carried to **B**
2Ki	25: 1	that Nebuchadnezzar king of **B**
Ps	137: 1	By the rivers of **B**, There we
Ps	137: 8	O daughter of **B**, who are to
Is	13: 1	The burden against **B** which
Is	13:19	And **B**, the glory of kingdoms,
Is	14: 4	proverb against the king of **B**
Is	21: 9	**B** is fallen, is fallen
Is	47: 1	dust, O virgin daughter of **B**

Is	48:20	Go forth from **B**
Jer	25:11	the king of **B** seventy years
Jer	51:41	How **B** has become desolate
Dan	1: 1	king of **B** came to Jerusalem
Dan	2:12	destroy all the wise men of **B**
Dan	2:48	over the whole province of **B**
Dan	2:48	over all the wise men of **B**
Dan	3: 1	of Dura, in the province of **B**
Dan	4:30	Is not this great **B**, that I
Dan	7: 1	year of Belshazzar king of **B**
Mic	4:10	and you shall go even to **B**
Zech	2: 7	dwell with the daughter of **B**
Matt	1:11	they were carried away to **B**
Matt	1:17	until the captivity in **B** are
Acts	7:43	will carry you away beyond **B**
1Pe	5:13	She who is in **B**, elect
Rev	14: 8	**B** is fallen, is fallen, that
Rev	16:19	great **B** was remembered before
Rev	17: 5	**B** THE GREAT, THE
Rev	18: 2	**B** the great is fallen, is

BACKBITERS†

| Rom | 1:30 | **b**, haters of God, violent, |

BACKS

| Neh | 9:26 | cast Your law behind their **b** |
| Prov | 19:29 | beatings for the **b** of fools |

BACKSLIDING

Is	57:17	he went on **b** in the way of
Jer	3: 6	seen what **b** Israel has done
Hos	11: 7	people are bent on **b** from Me

BAD

Gen	24:50	speak to you either **b** or good
Gen	37: 2	Joseph brought a **b** report of
Num	13:32	a **b** report of the land which
2Ki	2:19	but the water is **b**, and the
Prov	25:19	of trouble is like a **b** tooth
Jer	24: 2	**b** figs which could not be
Jer	49:23	for they have heard **b** news
Amos	8: 6	even sell the **b** wheat
Matt	6:23	But if your eye is **b**, your
Matt	7:17	but a **b** tree bears **b** fruit
Matt	13:48	vessels, but threw the **b** away
Matt	22:10	all whom they found, both **b**
2Co	5:10	has done, whether good or **b**

BAG

Deut	25:13	in your **b** differing weights
1Sa	17:40	and put them in a shepherd's **b**
Prov	7:20	He has taken a **b** of money
Hag	1: 6	to put into a **b** with holes
Matt	10:10	nor **b** for your journey, nor
Mark	6: 8	no **b**, no bread, no copper in
Luke	9: 3	neither staffs nor **b** nor
Luke	10: 4	Carry neither money **b**, sack,

BAKE† (see BAKED, BAKER)

Gen	11: 3	bricks and **b** them thoroughly
Ex	16:23	**B** what you will **b** today,
Lev	24: 5	and **b** twelve cakes with it
Lev	26:26	ten women shall **b** your bread

Ezek	4:12	and **b** it using fuel of human
Ezek	46:20	where they shall **b** the grain

BAKED (*see* BAKE)

Gen	19: 3	**b** unleavened bread, and they
Gen	40:17	kinds of **b** goods for Pharaoh
Ex	12:39	they **b** unleavened cakes of
Lev	2: 4	grain offering **b** in the oven
Lev	6:17	It shall not be **b** with leaven
Is	44:19	I have also **b** bread on its

BAKER (*see* BAKE)

Gen	40: 1	the **b** of the king of Egypt
Gen	40: 2	chief butler and the chief **b**
Hos	7: 4	like an oven heated by a **b**
Hos	7: 6	their **b** sleeps all night

BALAAM

Num	22: 5	**B** the son of Beor at Pethor
Num	22:30	So the donkey said to **B**, "Am
Josh	24:10	But I would not listen to **B**
Neh	13: 2	but hired **B** against them to
2Pe	2:15	the way of **B** the son of Beor
Jude	11	in the error of **B** for profit
Rev	2:14	who hold the doctrine of **B**

BALAK (*see* BALAK'S)

Num	22: 2	Now **B** the son of Zippor saw
Josh	24: 9	Then **B** the son of Zippor,
Mic	6: 5	remember now what **B** king of
Rev	2:14	Balaam, who taught **B** to put a

BALANCE (*see* BALANCES)

Is	40:12	in scales and the hills in a **b**

BALANCES (*see* BALANCE)

Dan	5:27	have been weighed in the **b**

BALDHEAD†

2Ki	2:23	said to him, "Go up, you **b**

BALM

Gen	37:25	camels, bearing spices, **b**
Jer	8:22	Is there no **b** in Gilead, is

BAND (*see* BANDS)

Gen	49:15	and became a **b** of slaves
Ex	28: 8	woven **b** of the ephod, which
Job	38: 9	darkness its swaddling **b**
Dan	4:15	earth, bound with a **b** of iron
Rev	1:13	the chest with a golden **b**

BANDS (*see* BAND)

Hos	11: 4	with **b** of love, and I was to

BANK (*see* BANKERS)

Gen	41: 3	cows on the **b** of the river
Ex	2: 3	in the reeds by the river's **b**
Luke	19:23	you not put my money in the **b**

BANKERS† (*see* BANK)

Matt	25:27	deposited my money with the **b**

BANNER

Ps	60: 4	You have given a **b** to those
Song	2: 4	and his **b** over me was love
Is	5:26	He will lift up a **b** to the
Is	11:10	stand as a **b** to the people
Zech	9:16	lifted like a **b** over His land

BAPTISM (*see* BAPTISMS, BAPTIZE)

Matt	3: 7	and Sadducees coming to his **b**
Matt	20:22	be baptized with the **b** that I
Matt	21:25	The **b** of John, where was it
Mark	1: 4	preaching a **b** of repentance
Luke	3: 3	preaching a **b** of repentance
Acts	10:37	the **b** which John preached
Rom	6: 4	with Him through **b** into death
Eph	4: 5	one Lord, one faith, one **b**
Col	2:12	buried with Him in **b**, in
1Pe	3:21	which now saves us—**b**

BAPTISMS† (*see* BAPTISM)

Heb	6: 2	of the doctrine of **b**, of

BAPTIST (*see* BAPTIZE, JOHN)

Matt	3: 1	the **B** came preaching in the
Matt	11:11	one greater than John the **B**
Mark	6:24	The head of John the **B**
Mark	6:25	of John the **B** on a platter
Luke	7:33	For John the **B** came neither

BAPTIZE (*see* BAPTISM, BAPTIST, BAPTIZED, BAPTIZES, BAPTIZING)

Matt	3:11	I indeed **b** you with water
Matt	3:11	He will **b** you with the Holy
John	4: 2	Jesus Himself did not **b**, but
1Co	1:17	Christ did not send me to **b**

BAPTIZED (*see* BAPTIZE)

Matt	3: 6	were **b** by him in the Jordan,
Matt	3:14	I have need to be **b** by You
Matt	3:16	Jesus, when He had been **b**
Matt	20:22	be **b** with the baptism that I
Mark	1: 8	I indeed **b** you with water,
Mark	1: 9	was **b** by John in the Jordan
Luke	3: 7	that came out to be **b** by him
Luke	12:50	I have a baptism to be **b** with
John	3:23	And they came and were **b**
John	4: 1	**b** more disciples than John
Acts	1: 5	for John truly **b** with water
Acts	1: 5	but you shall be **b** with the
Acts	2:38	let every one of you be **b** in
Acts	2:41	received his word were **b**
Acts	8:12	both men and women were **b**
Acts	8:36	What hinders me from being **b**
Acts	8:38	into the water, and he **b** him
Acts	16:15	she and her household were **b**
Acts	16:33	he and all his family were **b**
Acts	18: 8	hearing, believed and were **b**
Acts	22:16	Arise and be **b**, and wash away
Rom	6: 3	were **b** into Christ Jesus were
Rom	6: 3	Jesus were **b** into His death
1Co	1:14	I thank God that I **b** none of
1Co	1:15	that I had **b** in my own name
1Co	10: 2	all were **b** into Moses in the

B

1Co   12:13   we were all **b** into one body
1Co   15:29   do who are **b** for the dead
Gal   3:27   **b** into Christ have put on

BAPTIZES† (*see* BAPTIZE)
John   1:33   this is He who **b** with the

BAPTIZING (*see* BAPTIZE)
Matt   28:19   **b** them in the name of the
Mark   1: 4   John came **b** in the wilderness
John   1:28   the Jordan, where John was **b**
John   1:31   therefore I came **b** with water
John   3:23   Now John also was **b** in Aenon

BARABBAS
Matt   27:16   a notorious prisoner called **B**
Matt   27:17   **B**, or Jesus who is called

BARAK
Judg   4:12   reported to Sisera that **B** the
Judg   4:14   Then Deborah said to **B**, "Up
Heb   11:32   me to tell of Gideon and **B**

BARBARIAN† (*see* BARBARIANS)
Col   3:11   nor uncircumcised, **b**,

BARBARIANS† (*see* BARBARIAN)
Rom   1:14   debtor both to Greeks and to **b**

BARE (*see* BAREFOOT)
Ps   29: 9   And strips the forests **b**
Is   52:10   The LORD has made **b** His holy

BAREFOOT (*see* BARE)
2Sa   15:30   his head covered and went **b**
Is   20: 2   he did so, walking naked and **b**

BAR-JONAH† (*see* SIMON)
Matt   16:17   Blessed are you, Simon **B**, for

BARLEY
Ruth   1:22   at the beginning of **b** harvest
Ruth   3: 2   he is winnowing **b** tonight at
John   6: 9   here who has five **b** loaves

BARN (*see* BARNS)
Matt   3:12   gather His wheat into the **b**

BARNABAS
Acts   4:36   who was also named **B** by the
Acts   13: 2   Now separate to Me **B** and Saul

BARNS (*see* BARN)
Matt   6:26   nor reap nor gather into **b**
Luke   12:18   ·I will pull down my **b** and

BARREN
Gen   11:30   But Sarai was **b**
Gen   25:21   his wife, because she was **b**
Gen   29:31   but Rachel was **b**
Ex   23:26   or be **b** in your land
Judg   13: 2   and his wife was **b** and had no
1Sa   2: 5   Even the **b** has borne seven,
2Ki   2:19   water is bad, and the ground **b**

Job   3: 7   Oh, may that night be **b**
Ps   113: 9   He grants the **b** woman a home
Prov   30:16   the **b** womb, the earth that is
Is   54: 1   Sing, O **b**, you who have not
Luke   1: 7   because Elizabeth was **b**, and
Luke   1:36   for her who was called **b**
Luke   23:29   will say, 'Blessed are the **b**
Gal   4:27   Rejoice, O **b**, you who do not
2Pe   1: 8   you will be neither **b** nor

BARS
Ex   26:26   shall make **b** of acacia wood
Ex   35:11   it clasps, it boards, its **b**
Num   3:36   of the tabernacle, its **b**, its
Deut   3: 5   with high walls, gates, and **b**
1Sa   23: 7   a town that has gates and **b**
Neh   3: 3   its doors with its bolts and **b**
Job   38:10   My limit for it, and set **b**
Job   40:18   his ribs like **b** of iron
Ps   107:16   And cut the **b** of iron in two
Prov   18:19   are like the **b** of a castle
Lam   2: 9   has destroyed and broken her **b**
Jon   2: 6   the earth with its **b** closed

BARTHOLOMEW (*see* NATHANAEL)
Mark   3:18   Andrew, Philip, **B**, Matthew,

BARTIMAEUS†
Mark   10:46   and a great multitude, blind **B**

BARUCH
Jer   32:12   deed to **B** the son of Neriah
Jer   36: 4   **B** wrote on a scroll of a book

BASE
Ex   19:12   the mountain or touch its **b**
Ex   29:12   beside the **b** of the altar
2Sa   6:20   as one of the **b** fellows
Is   3: 5   the **b** toward the honorable
Mal   2: 9   and **b** before all the people,
1Co   1:28   and **b** things of the world and

BASHAN
Num   32:33   the kingdom of Og king of **B**
Josh   21: 6   half-tribe of Manasseh in **B**
Ps   22:12   Strong bulls of **B** have
Is   2:13   up, and upon all the oaks of **B**
Amos   4: 1   Hear this word, you cows of **B**

BASIN (*see* BASINS)
Ex   12:22   in the blood that is in the **b**
John   13: 5   He poured water into a **b**

BASINS (*see* BASIN)
Ex   24: 6   half the blood and put it in **b**

BASKET (*see* BASKETS)
Gen   40:17   them out of the **b** on my head
Jer   24: 2   One **b** had very good figs,
Amos   8: 1   Behold, a **b** of summer fruit
Matt   5:15   a lamp and put it under a **b**
Mark   4:21   put under a **b** or under a bed
Luke   11:33   a secret place or under a **b**

B

Acts	9:25	through the wall in a large **b**
2Co	11:33	a **b** through a window in the

BASKETS (*see* BASKET)

Gen	40:16	had three white **b** on my head
Matt	14:20	they took up twelve **b** full of
Matt	15:37	they took up seven large **b**
Mark	8: 8	large **b** of leftover fragments

BATHE (*see* BATHED, BATHING)

Lev	15: 5	**b** in water, and be unclean
Lev	15:13	**b** his body in running water
Lev	15:18	they both shall **b** in water

BATHED† (*see* BATHE)

1Ki	22:38	his blood while the harlots **b**
Job	29: 6	my steps were **b** with cream
Is	34: 5	My sword shall be **b** in heaven
John	13:10	He who is **b** needs only to

BATHING† (*see* BATHE)

2Sa	11: 2	the roof he saw a woman **b**

BATHSHEBA

2Sa	11: 3	Is this not **B**, the daughter
2Sa	12:24	David comforted **B** his wife
1Ki	2:13	to **B** the mother of Solomon

BATTLE (*see* BATTLES)

Gen	14: 8	joined together in **b** in the
Num	31:28	men of war who went out to **b**
Judg	20:20	**b** array to fight against them
Judg	20:34	Gibeah, and the **b** was fierce
1Sa	17:47	for the **b** is the LORD's, and
2Sa	11: 1	time when kings go out to **b**
Ps	18:39	me with strength for the **b**
Ps	24: 8	mighty, The LORD mighty in **b**
Ps	78: 9	Turned back in the day of **b**
Ps	144: 1	for war, And my fingers for **b**
Prov	21:31	is prepared for the day of **b**
Eccl	9:11	nor the **b** to the strong, nor
Is	9: 5	sandal from the noisy **b**, and
Is	13: 4	hosts musters the army for **b**
Is	16: 9	for **b** cries have fallen over
Is	28: 6	turn back the **b** at the gate
Is	42:25	anger and the strength of **b**
Jer	8: 6	the horse rushes into the **b**
Jer	18:21	be slain by the sword in **b**
Jer	50:22	A sound of **b** is in the land,
Ezek	13: 5	in **b** on the day of the LORD
Hos	1: 7	by bow, nor by sword or **b**
Zech	9:10	the **b** bow shall be cut off
Zech	14: 3	as He fights in the day of **b**
1Co	14: 8	will prepare himself for **b**
Heb	11:34	strong, became valiant in **b**
Rev	9: 7	like horses prepared for **b**
Rev	16:14	to gather them to the **b** of
Rev	20: 8	to gather them together to **b**

BATTLES (*see* BATTLE)

1Sa	8:20	out before us and fight our **b**
1Sa	18:17	for me, and fight the LORD's **b**

BEAM

Num	4:10	and put it on a carrying **b**
1Sa	17: 7	spear was like a weaver's **b**
2Ki	6: 2	every man take a **b** from there
Hab	2:11	the **b** from the timbers will

BEAR (*see* BEARING, BEARS, BORE, BORNE)

Gen	4:13	is greater than I can **b**
Gen	16:11	child, and you shall **b** a son
Gen	17:17	ninety years old, **b** a child
Gen	17:21	whom Sarah shall **b** to you at
Gen	43: 9	you, then let me **b** the blame
Gen	49:15	his shoulder to **b** a burden
Ex	20:16	You shall not **b** false witness
Ex	25:27	for the poles to **b** the table
Ex	27: 7	sides of the altar to **b** it
Ex	28:12	So Aaron shall **b** their names
Ex	28:30	So Aaron shall **b** the judgment
Ex	28:38	that Aaron may **b** the iniquity
Lev	16:22	The goat shall **b** on itself
Lev	19:17	and not **b** sin because of him
Lev	19:18	nor **b** any grudge against the
Lev	24:15	his God shall **b** his sin
Num	11:14	I am not able to **b** all these
Num	11:17	they shall **b** the burden of
Deut	10: 8	the tribe of Levi to the
Deut	29:23	it is not sown, nor does it **b**
Josh	3: 8	who **b** the ark of the covenant
Judg	5:14	who **b** the recruiter's staff
Judg	13: 3	you shall conceive and **b** a son
Ruth	1:12	tonight and should also **b** sons
1Sa	17:36	has killed both lion and **b**
2Sa	17: 8	like a **b** robbed of her cubs
2Ki	19:30	downward, and **b** fruit upward
Job	9: 9	He made the **B**, Orion, and the
Job	38:32	the Great **B** with its cubs
Ps	28: 9	also, And **b** them up forever
Ps	55:12	Then I could **b** it
Ps	89:50	How I **b** in my bosom the
Ps	91:12	They shall **b** you up in their
Ps	92:14	still **b** fruit in old age
Prov	18:14	but who can **b** a broken spirit
Prov	28:15	and a charging **b** is a wicked
Is	7:14	**b** a Son, and shall call His
Is	11: 7	The cow and the **b** shall graze
Is	53:11	many, for He shall **b** their
Jer	17:21	**b** no burden on the Sabbath
Lam	3:10	to me like a **b** lying in wait
Lam	3:27	to **b** the yoke in his youth
Ezek	16:52	**b** your own shame also,
Ezek	18:19	not **b** the guilt of the father
Dan	7: 5	beast, a second, like a **b**
Amos	5:19	from a lion, and a **b** met him
Amos	7:10	not able to **b** all his words
Mic	7: 9	I will **b** the indignation of
Zech	6:13	He shall **b** the glory, and
Matt	1:23	**b** a Son, and they shall call
Matt	3: 8	Therefore **b** fruits worthy of
Matt	3:10	not **b** good fruit is cut down
Matt	4: 6	hands they shall **b** you up
Matt	7:18	good tree cannot **b** bad fruit
Matt	17:17	How long shall I **b** with you
Matt	19:18	You shall not **b** false witness

Matt	23: 4	bind heavy burdens, hard to **b**
Matt	27:32	they compelled to **b** His cross
Luke	14:27	whoever does not **b** his cross
John	1: 7	to **b** witness of the Light,
John	10:25	name, they **b** witness of Me
John	15: 2	not **b** fruit He takes away
John	15: 2	that it may **b** more fruit
John	15: 8	that you **b** much fruit
John	16:12	but you cannot **b** them now
Rom	7: 4	that we should **b** fruit to God
Rom	10: 2	For I **b** them witness that
Rom	13: 4	for he does not **b** the sword
Rom.	15: 1	who are strong ought to **b**
1Co	10:13	that you may be able to **b** it
1Co	15:49	we shall also **b** the image of
Gal	6: 2	**B** one another's burdens, and
Gal	6: 5	each one shall **b** his own load
Gal	6:17	for I **b** in my body the marks
Heb	9:28	once to **b** the sins of many
1Jn	5: 7	three who **b** witness in heaven
1Jn	5: 8	three that **b** witness on earth
Rev	13: 2	were like the feet of a **b**

BEARD (see BEARDS)

Lev	13:29	a sore on the head or the **b**
1Sa	17:35	me, I caught it by its **b**, and
1Sa	21:13	his saliva fall down on his **b**
Ps	133: 2	head, Running down on the **b**

BEARDS (see BEARD)

2Sa	10: 4	shaved off half of their **b**

BEARING (see BEAR)

Gen	16: 2	restrained me from **b** children
Gen	29:35	Then she stopped **b**
Gen	37:25	**b** spices, balm, and myrrh, on
Ps	126: 6	**B** seed for sowing, Shall
Is	1:14	to Me, I am weary of **b** them
Matt	21:43	a nation **b** the fruits of it
John	19:17	**b** His cross, went out to a
Acts	14: 3	who was **b** witness to the word
Rom	2:15	conscience also **b** witness
Eph	4: 2	**b** with one another in love,
Heb	13:13	the camp, **b** His reproach

BEARS (see BEAR)

Lev	5: 1	does not tell it, he **b** guilt
Lev	12: 5	But if she **b** a female child,
2Ki	2:24	two female **b** came out of the
Prov	25:18	A man who **b** false witness
Matt	7:17	every good tree **b** good fruit
Luke	18: 7	though He **b** long with them
John	5:32	another who **b** witness of Me
John	8:18	I am One who **b** witness of
John	8:18	who sent Me **b** witness of Me
John	15: 2	branch that **b** fruit He prunes
John	15: 5	Me, and I in him, **b** much fruit
Acts	22: 5	the high priest **b** me witness
Rom	8:16	The Spirit Himself **b** witness
1Co	13: 7	**b** all things, believes all
Heb	6: 8	but if it **b** thorns and briars,

BEAST (see ANIMAL, BEASTS)

Gen	1:25	God made the **b** of the earth
Gen	3: 1	was more cunning than any **b**
Gen	6: 7	of the earth, both man and **b**
Gen	7:14	every **b** after its kind, all
Gen	9: 5	of every **b** I will require it
Dan	4:16	Let him be given the heart of a **b**
Dan	7: 5	And suddenly another **b**, a
Dan	7: 6	The **b** also had four heads, and
Rev	11: 7	the **b** that ascends out of the
Rev	13: 3	marveled and followed the **b**
Rev	13: 4	who gave authority to the **b**
Rev	13: 4	and they worshiped the **b**,
Rev	13:17	the mark or the name of the **b**
Rev	13:18	calculate the number of the **b**
Rev	16: 2	men who had the mark of the **b**
Rev	20:10	fire and brimstone where the **b**

BEASTS (see ANIMALS, BEAST)

Gen	7:21	birds and cattle and **b** and every
Ps	49:12	He is like the **b** that perish
Dan	4:15	let him graze with the **b** on
Dan	7: 3	four great **b** came up from the
1Co	15:32	have fought with **b** at Ephesus
Tit	1:12	are always liars, evil **b**,
Jude	10	know naturally, like brute **b**

BEAT (see BEATEN, BEATING, BEATINGS, BEATS)

Ex	39: 3	they **b** the gold into thin
Ruth	2:17	**b** out what she had gleaned,
Ps	78:66	And He **b** back His enemies
Ps	89:23	I will **b** down his foes before
Prov	23:13	for if you **b** him with a rod,
Is	2: 4	they shall **b** their swords
Joel	3:10	**B** your plowshares into swords
Jon	4: 8	the sun **b** on Jonah's head, so
Mic	4: 3	they shall **b** their swords
Matt	7:25	winds blew and **b** on that house
Matt	26:67	spat in His face and **b** Him

BEATEN (see BEAT)

Ex	37: 7	made two cherubim of **b** gold
Luke	12:47	shall be **b** with many stripes
Acts	16:22	them to be **b** with rods
2Co	11:25	Three times I was **b** with rods
1Pe	2:20	if, when you are **b** for your

BEATING† (see BEAT)

Ex	2:11	he saw an Egyptian **b** a Hebrew
Nah	2: 7	of doves, **b** their breasts
Mark	12: 5	**b** some and killing some
Acts	21:32	soldiers, they stopped **b** Paul

BEATINGS† (see BEAT)

Prov	19:29	and **b** for the backs of fools

BEATS† (see BEAT)

Ex	21:20	if a man **b** his male or female
1Co	9:26	not as one who **b** the air

BEAUTIES

Ps	110: 3	In the **b** of holiness, from

BEAUTIFUL (see BEAUTY)

Gen	6: 2	of men, that they were **b**
Gen	12:11	are a woman of **b** countenance

Gen	24:16	woman was very **b** to behold
Gen	29:17	but Rachel was **b** of form
Ex	2: 2	she saw that he was a **b** child
Ps	48: 2	**B** in elevation, The joy of
Eccl	3:11	made everything **b** in its time
Song	7: 1	How **b** are your feet in
Is	4: 2	Branch of the LORD shall be **b**
Is	52: 7	How **b** upon the mountains are
Matt	23:27	indeed appear **b** outwardly
Luke	21: 5	it was adorned with **b** stones
Acts	3: 2	the temple which is called **B**
Acts	3:10	at the **B** Gate of the temple
Rom	10:15	How **b** are the feet of those
Heb	11:23	they saw he was a **b** child

BEAUTY (see BEAUTIFUL)

1Ch	16:29	the LORD in the **b** of holiness
Esth	1:11	to show her **b** to the people
Ps	27: 4	To behold the **b** of the LORD
Ps	29: 2	the LORD in the **b** of holiness
Ps	50: 2	of Zion, the perfection of **b**
Ps	96: 6	and **b** are in His sanctuary
Prov	31:30	**b** is passing, but a woman who
Is	33:17	will see the King in His **b**
Is	53: 2	there is no **b** that we should
Is	61: 3	to give them **b** for ashes

BED (see BEDRIDDEN, BEDS, BEDSTEAD)

Gen	47:31	himself on the head of the **b**
Gen	48: 2	himself and sat up on the **b**
Gen	49: 4	went up to your father's **b**
Gen	49:33	drew his feet up into the **b**
2Ki	4:32	child, lying dead on his **b**
Ps	4: 4	within your heart on your **b**
Ps	6: 6	All night I make my **b** swim
Ps	36: 4	devises wickedness on his **b**
Ps	139: 8	If I make my **b** in hell,
Matt	9: 2	Him a paralytic lying on a **b**
Matt	9: 6	Arise, take up your **b**, and go
Mark	2: 4	they let down the **b** on which
Mark	4:21	under a basket or under a **b**
Mark	7:30	her daughter lying on the **b**
Luke	11: 7	my children are with me in **b**
Luke	17:34	will be two men in one **b**
Heb	13: 4	among all, and the **b** undefiled

BEDRIDDEN† (see BED)

Acts	9:33	who had been **b** eight years

BEDS (see BED)

Ps	149: 5	them sing aloud on their **b**
Song	6: 2	to the **b** of spices, to feed
Hos	7:14	when they wailed upon their **b**
Amos	6: 4	who lie on **b** of ivory,
Mic	2: 1	And work out evil on their **b**
Mark	6:55	on **b** those who were sick to
Acts	5:15	the streets and laid them on **b**

BEDSTEAD† (see BED)

Deut	3:11	his **b** was an iron **b**

BEELZEBUB (see BAAL-ZEBUB)

Matt	10:25	the master of the house **B**
Matt	12:24	cast out demons except by **B**

BEER LAHAI ROI

Gen	16:14	the well was called **B**
Gen	25:11	And Isaac dwelt at **B**

BEERSHEBA

Gen	22:19	and Abraham dwelt at **B**
1Sa	3:20	all Israel from Dan to **B** knew

BEG (see BEGGAR, BEGGED, BEGGING)

Job	9:15	I would **b** mercy of my Judge
Luke	8:28	I **b** You, do not torment me
Luke	16: 3	I am ashamed to **b**

BEGET (see BEGOT, BEGOTTEN)

Deut	28:41	You shall **b** sons and daughters

BEGGAR (see BEG)

1Sa	2: 8	lifts the **b** from the ash heap
Luke	16:20	was a certain **b** named Lazarus

BEGGARLY†

Gal	4: 9	and **b** elements, to which you

BEGGED (see BEG)

Matt	8:31	So the demons **b** Him, saying,
John	9: 8	Is not this he who sat and **b**

BEGGING (see BEG)

Ps	37:25	Nor his descendants **b** bread
Mark	10:46	of Timaeus, sat by the road **b**
Acts	3:10	**b** alms at the Beautiful Gate

BEGINNING (see BEGINNINGS)

Gen	1: 1	In the **b** God created the
Ex	12: 2	shall be your **b** of months
Ruth	1:22	at the **b** of barley harvest
Job	42:12	days of Job more than his **b**
Ps	111:10	the LORD is the **b** of wisdom
Prov	1: 7	LORD is the **b** of knowledge
Prov	8:22	me at the **b** of His way,
Prov	9:10	the LORD is the **b** of wisdom
Is	46:10	Declaring the end from the **b**
Is	48: 3	the former things from the **b**
Is	64: 4	For since the **b** of the world
Matt	14:30	and **b** to sink he cried out,
Matt	19: 4	them at the **b** 'made them male
Matt	19: 8	but from the **b** it was not so
Matt	24: 8	these are the **b** of sorrows
Matt	24:21	the **b** of the world until this
Mark	1: 1	The **b** of the gospel of Jesus
Luke	1: 2	from the **b** were eyewitnesses
Luke	24:27	And **b** at Moses and all the
Luke	24:47	all nations, **b** at Jerusalem
John	1: 1	In the **b** was the Word, and the
John	1: 2	He was in the **b** with God
John	2:11	This **b** of signs Jesus did in
John	8:44	He was a murderer from the **b**
John	15:27	have been with Me from the **b**
Eph	3: 9	which from the **b** of the ages
Phil	4:15	that in the **b** of the gospel
Col	1:18	the church, who is the **b**
2Th	2:13	because God from the **b** chose
Heb	1:10	in the **b** laid the foundation

Heb	7: 3	having neither **b** of days nor
2Pe	2:20	is worse for them than the **b**
2Pe	3: 4	were from the **b** of creation
1Jn	1: 1	That which was from the **b**
1Jn	2:13	known Him who is from the **b**
1Jn	3: 8	devil has sinned from the **b**
Rev	1: 8	the Alpha and the Omega, the **B**
Rev	3:14	the **B** of the creation of God

BEGINNINGS (see BEGINNING)

Mark	13: 8	These are the **b** of sorrows

BEGOT (see BEGET)

Gen	6:10	And Noah **b** three sons
Gen	25:19	Abraham **b** Isaac
Deut	32:18	Of the Rock who **b** you, you
Ruth	4:22	and Jesse **b** David
1Ch	1:10	Cush **b** Nimrod
Prov	23:22	to your father who **b** you, and
Matt	1: 2	Abraham **b** Isaac
Matt	1: 6	and Jesse **b** David the king
Matt	1:16	Jacob **b** Joseph the husband of
Acts	7: 8	and so Abraham **b** Isaac
Acts	7: 8	Jacob **b** the twelve patriarchs
1Jn	5: 1	who **b** also loves him who is

BEGOTTEN (see BEGET)

Lev	18:11	daughter, **b** by your father
Job	38:28	or who has **b** the drops of dew
Ps	2: 7	My Son, Today I have **b** You
John	1:14	of the only **b** of the Father
John	1:18	The only **b** Son, who is in the
John	3:16	that He gave His only **b** Son
John	3:18	name of the only **b** Son of God
Acts	13:33	My Son, today I have **b** You
1Co	4:15	have **b** you through the gospel
Phm	10	whom I have **b** while in my
Heb	1: 5	My Son, today I have **b** You"
Heb	11:17	offered up his only **b** son
1Pe	1: 3	**b** us again to a living hope
1Jn	4: 9	His only **b** Son into the world
1Jn	5: 1	loves him who is **b** of Him

BEHALF

Is	8:19	the dead on **b** of the living
2Co	5:20	we implore you on Christ's **b**
Phil	1:29	been granted on **b** of Christ
Col	1: 7	minister of Christ on your **b**

BEHAVE (see BEHAVED, BEHAVING, BEHAVIOR)

Deut	25:16	all who **b** unrighteously, are
Ps	101: 2	I will **b** wisely in a perfect
1Co	13: 5	does not **b** rudely, does not

BEHAVED (see BEHAVE)

Ex	18:11	thing in which they **b** proudly
Num	5:27	**b** unfaithfully toward her
Judg	2:19	**b** more corruptly than their
1Sa	18: 5	Saul sent him, and **b** wisely
1Ki	21:26	And he **b** very abominably in
1Th	2:10	blamelessly we **b** ourselves

BEHAVING (see BEHAVE)

1Co	3: 3	not carnal and **b** like mere men
1Co	7:36	he is **b** improperly toward his

BEHAVIOR (see BEHAVE)

1Sa	8: 9	show them the **b** of the king
Ezek	16:27	were ashamed of your lewd **b**
1Ti	3: 2	sober-minded, of good **b**,
Tit	2: 3	that they be reverent in **b**

BEHEADED

2Sa	4: 7	**b** him and took his head, and
Matt	14:10	sent and had John **b** in prison
Rev	20: 4	**b** for their witness to Jesus

BEHELD (see BEHOLD)

Jer	4:23	I **b** the earth, and indeed it
John	1:14	we **b** His glory, the glory as

BEHOLD (see BEHELD, BEHOLDING)

Gen	3:22	**B**, the man has become like
Gen	28:13	And **b**, the LORD stood above it
Gen	37: 7	Then **b**, my sheaf arose and
Deut	11:26	**B**, I set before you today a
1Sa	15:22	**B**, to obey is better than
1Ki	19:11	And **b**, the LORD passed by,
Job	19:27	myself, and my eyes shall **b**
Ps	27: 4	To **b** the beauty of the LORD,
Ps	40: 7	Then I said, "**B**, I come
Ps	133: 1	**B**, how good and how pleasant
Is	5: 7	He looked for justice, but **b**
Is	5: 7	for righteousness, but **b**,
Is	6: 7	**B**, this has touched your lips
Is	7:14	**B**, the virgin shall conceive
Is	40: 9	cities of Judah, "**B** your God
Is	42: 1	**B**! My Servant whom I uphold
Is	52:13	**B**, My Servant shall deal
Is	65: 6	**B**, it is written before Me
Zech	6:12	**B**, the Man whose name is the
Zech	9: 9	**B**, your King is coming to you
Mal	3: 1	**B**, I send My messenger, and he
Mal	3: 1	**B**, He is coming," says the
Matt	1:23	**B**, a virgin shall be with
Matt	2: 1	the days of Herod the king, **b**
Matt	2: 9	and **b**, the star which they had
Matt	3:16	and **b**, the heavens were opened
Matt	11:10	**B**, I send My messenger
Matt	12:18	**B**, My Servant whom I have
Luke	1:38	**B** the maidservant of the Lord
Luke	2:10	Do not be afraid, for **b**, I
Luke	24:39	**B** My hands and My feet, that
John	1:29	**B**! The Lamb of God
John	1:36	he said, "**B** the Lamb of God
John	17:24	am, that they may **b** My glory
John	19: 5	said to them, "**B** the Man
John	19:14	to the Jews, "**B** your King
John	19:26	mother, "Woman, **b** your son
John	19:27	the disciple, **B** your mother
1Co	15:51	**B**, I tell you a mystery
2Co	5:17	**b**, all things have become new
2Co	6: 2	**B**, now is the accepted time
2Co	6: 2	**b**, now is the day of
1Jn	3: 1	**B** what manner of love the

Rev	3:11	**B**, I come quickly
Rev	3:20	**B**, I stand at the door and
Rev	22: 7	**B**, I am coming quickly

BEHOLDING† (*see* BEHOLD)

2Co	3:18	**b** as in a mirror the glory of

BELIAL†

2Co	6:15	what accord has Christ with **B**

BELIEF† (*see* BELIEVE, UNBELIEF)

2Th	2:13	the Spirit and **b** in the truth,

BELIEVE (*see* BELIEF, BELIEVED, BELIEVER, BELIEVES, BELIEVING)

Ex	4: 8	will be, if they do not **b** you
Matt	27:42	the cross, and we will **b** Him
Mark	1:15	Repent, and **b** in the gospel
Mark	5:36	Do not be afraid; only **b**
Mark	9:23	If you can **b**, all things are
Mark	9:24	Lord, I **b**; help my unbelief
Mark	9:42	ones who **b** in Me to stumble
Luke	24:25	slow of heart to **b** in all
Luke	24:41	they still did not **b** for joy
John	1: 7	that all through him might **b**
John	1:12	to those who **b** in His name
John	1:50	under the fig tree,' do you **b**
John	3:12	things and you do not **b**, how
John	3:12	how will you **b** if I tell you
John	3:36	he who does not **b** the Son
John	4:21	**b** Me, the hour is coming when
John	5:46	Moses, you would **b** Me
John	5:47	if you do not **b** his writings
John	5:47	how will you **b** My words
John	6:29	that you **b** in Him whom He
John	6:30	that we may see it and **b** You
John	6:36	have seen Me and yet do not **b**
John	7: 5	His brothers did not **b** in Him
John	8:24	if you do not **b** that I am He
John	8:45	the truth, you do not **b** Me
John	9:35	Do you **b** in the Son of God
John	9:38	Then he said, "Lord, I **b**!"
John	10:38	**b** the works, that you may
John	10:38	**b** that the Father is in Me,
John	11:26	never die. Do you **b** this
John	11:27	I **b** that You are the Christ,
John	11:48	this, everyone will **b** in Him
John	12:36	**b** in the light, that you may
John	12:47	hears My words and does not **b**
John	14: 1	you **b** in God, **b** also in Me
John	14:11	or else **b** Me for the sake of
John	17:21	world may **b** that You sent Me
John	19:35	the truth, so that you may **b**
John	20:25	into His side, I will not **b**
John	20:31	**b** that Jesus is the Christ
Acts	8:37	If you **b** with all your heart,
Acts	16:31	**B** on the Lord Jesus Christ,
Rom	4:11	the father of all those who **b**
Rom	4:24	**b** in Him who raised up Jesus
Rom	10: 9	**b** in your heart that God has
Rom	10:14	how shall they **b** in Him of
Eph	1:19	of His power toward us who **b**
Phil	1:29	Christ, not only to **b** in Him
1Th	2:13	works in you who **b**

1Th	4:14	For if we **b** that Jesus died
2Th	2:11	that they should **b** the lie
1Ti	4:10	especially of those who **b**
Heb	11: 6	to God must **b** that He is, and
Jas	2:19	You **b** that there is one God
Jas	2:19	Even the demons **b**
1Jn	5:10	he who does not **b** God has
1Jn	5:13	**b** in the name of the Son of

BELIEVED (*see* BELIEVE, FULFILLED)

Gen	15: 6	And he **b** in the LORD, and He
Ex	14:31	**b** the LORD and His servant
Ps	116:10	I **b**, therefore I spoke, 'I
Is	53: 1	Who has **b** our report
Jon	3: 5	the people of Nineveh **b** God
Matt	8:13	and as you have **b**, so let it
Luke	1:45	Blessed is she who **b**, for
John	2:11	and His disciples **b** in Him
John	2:22	they **b** the Scripture and the
John	2:23	many **b** in His name when they
John	4:39	**b** in Him because of the word
John	5:46	For if you **b** Moses, you would
John	7:48	or the Pharisees **b** in Him
John	12:38	Lord, who has **b** our report
John	16:27	have **b** that I came forth from
John	17: 8	they have **b** that You sent Me
John	20: 8	and he saw and **b**
John	20:29	you have seen Me, you have **b**
Acts	11:17	we **b** on the Lord Jesus Christ
Acts	11:21	them, and a great number **b**
Acts	13:48	appointed to enternal life **b**
Acts	16:34	having **b** in God with all his
Acts	17:34	some men joined him and **b**
Acts	19: 2	the Holy Spirit when you **b**
Rom	4: 3	Abraham **b** God, and it was
Rom	10:14	Him in whom they have not **b**
Rom	10:16	Lord, who has **b** our report
Rom	13:11	nearer than when we first **b**
1Co	15:11	so we preach and so you **b**
Gal	3: 6	**b** God, and it was accounted to
Eph	1:13	in whom also, having **b**, you
2Th	1:10	our testimony among you was **b**
1Ti	3:16	**b** on in the world, received
2Ti	1:12	for I know whom I have **b**
Jas	2:23	Abraham **b** God, and it was
1Jn	5:10	because he has not **b** the

BELIEVER† (*see* BELIEVE, BELIEVERS, UNBELIEVER)

2Co	6:15	has a **b** with an unbeliever

BELIEVERS (*see* BELIEVER)

Acts	5:14	**b** were increasingly added to
1Ti	4:12	an example to the **b** in word

BELIEVES (*see* BELIEVE)

Mark	9:23	are possible to him who **b**
John	3:15	that whoever **b** in Him should
John	3:36	He who **b** in the Son has
John	5:24	and **b** in Him who sent Me has
John	6:40	**b** in Him may have everlasting
John	11:26	and **b** in Me shall never die
Rom	1:16	salvation for everyone who **b**
Rom	4: 5	**b** on Him who justifies the

Rom	9:33	whoever **b** on Him will not be
Rom	10: 4	to everyone who **b**
Rom	10:10	heart one **b** unto righteousness
1Co	13: 7	**b** all things, hopes all
1Pe	2: 6	he who **b** on Him will by no
1Jn	5: 1	Whoever **b** that Jesus is the
1Jn	5:10	He who **b** in the Son of God

BELIEVING (*see* BELIEVE)

Matt	21:22	whatever you ask in prayer, **b**
John	20:27	Do not be unbelieving, but **b**
John	20:31	that **b** you may have life in
1Co	9: 5	right to take along a **b** wife
Gal	3: 9	are blessed with **b** Abraham
1Ti	5:16	If any **b** man or woman has
1Ti	6: 2	And those who have **b** masters
1Pe	1: 8	now you do not see Him, yet **b**

BELLY

Gen	3:14	on your **b** you shall go, and
Dan	2:32	and arms of silver, its **b** and
Jon	1:17	Jonah was in the **b** of the
Jon	2: 1	his God from the fish's **b**
Matt	12:40	in the **b** of the great fish
Rom	16:18	Jesus Christ, but their own **b**
Phil	3:19	whose god is their **b**, and

BELONG (*see* BELONGS)

Gen	40: 8	not interpretations **b** to God
Deut	29:29	The secret things **b** to the
1Pe	4:11	to whom **b** the glory and the

BELONGS (*see* BELONG)

Lev	7:20	offering that **b** to the LORD
Ps	3: 8	Salvation **b** to the LORD
Rev	7:10	Salvation **b** to our God who

BELOVED (*see* BELOVED'S)

Song	1:16	you are handsome, my **b**
Song	7:11	Come, my **b**, let us go forth
Is	5: 1	my **B** regarding His vineyard
Jer	12: 7	I have given the dearly **b** of
Dan	10:11	O Daniel, man greatly **b**,
Matt	3:17	This is My **b** Son, in whom I
Mark	12: 6	still having one son, his **b**
Acts	15:25	to you with our **b** Barnabas
Rom	1: 7	**b** of God, called to be saints
Rom	9:25	were not My people, and her **b**
Rom	11:28	the election they are **b** for
Rom	12:19	**B**, do not avenge yourselves,
1Co	4:14	but as my **b** children I warn
1Co	4:17	Timothy to you, who is my **b**
1Co	10:14	Therefore, my **b**, flee from
1Co	15:58	my **b** brethren, be steadfast,
Eph	1: 6	has made us accepted in the **B**
Eph	6:21	a **b** brother and faithful
Phil	4: 1	Therefore, my **b** and longed-for
Phil	4: 1	so stand fast in the Lord, **b**
Col	3:12	the elect of God, holy and **b**
Col	4:14	Luke the **b** physician and Demas
1Th	1: 4	**b** brethren, your election by
2Th	2:13	you, brethren **b** by the Lord,
1Ti	6: 2	benefited are believers and **b**
2Ti	1: 2	To Timothy, a **b** son

Phm	1	To Philemon our **b** friend
Phm	16	as a **b** brother, especially to
2Pe	1:17	This is My **b** Son, in whom I
2Pe	3:15	as also our **b** brother Paul,
1Jn	3: 2	**B**, now we are children of God
1Jn	4: 7	**B**, let us love one another,
1Jn	4:11	**B**, if God so loved us, we
Rev	20: 9	of the saints and the **b** city

BELOVED'S (*see* BELOVED)

| Song | 6: 3 | I am my **b**, and my beloved is |

BELSHAZZAR

| Dan | 5: 1 | **B** the king made a great feast |

BELT

| Matt | 3: 4 | with a leather **b** around his |

BELTESHAZZAR (*see* DANIEL)

| Dan | 1: 7 | he gave Daniel the name **B** |
| Dan | 4: 9 | **B**, chief of the magicians, |

BEN-HADAD

| 1Ki | 20: 1 | Now **B** the king of Syria |

BENEFITS

| Ps | 103: 2 | soul, And forget not all His **b** |

BENJAMIN

Gen	35:18	but his father called him **B**
Gen	35:24	of Rachel were Joseph and **B**
Num	1:37	numbered of the tribe of **B**
Phil	3: 5	of Israel, of the tribe of **B**

BENT

| Ps | 37:14 | have **b** their bow, To cast |
| Dan | 11:27 | hearts shall be **b** on evil |

BEOR

| Num | 22: 5 | Balaam the son of **B** at Pethor |
| 2Pe | 2:15 | way of Balaam the son of **B** |

BEREA

| Acts | 17:13 | God was preached by Paul at **B** |

BEREAVE (*see* BEREAVED)

Jer	15: 7	I will **b** them of children
Ezek	36:13	**b** your nation of children,'
Hos	9:12	yet I will **b** them to the last

BEREAVED (*see* BEREAVE)

| Gen | 27:45 | Why should I be **b** also of you |
| Gen | 42:36 | You have **b** me of my children |

BERITH†

| Judg | 9:46 | of the temple of the god **B** |

BESEECH

| Rom | 12: 1 | I **b** you therefore, brethren, |
| Eph | 4: 1 | **b** you to have a walk worthy |

BESIEGE (*see* BESIEGED)

| Deut | 20:19 | When you **b** a city for a long |

BESIEGED (see BESIEGE)

2Sa	11:16	while Joab **b** the city, that
Dan	1: 1	came to Jerusalem and **b** it

BEST

Gen	43:11	Take some of the **b** fruits of
Judg	14:20	who had been his **b** man
Matt	23: 6	the **b** seats in the synagogues
Mark	12:39	and the **b** places at feasts,
Luke	15:22	Bring out the **b** robe and put
1Co	12:31	earnestly desire the **b** gifts
Heb	12:10	us as seemed **b** to them, but

BESTOW (see BESTOWED)

Luke	22:29	I **b** upon you a kingdom, just
1Co	12:23	on these we **b** greater honor
1Co	13: 3	though I **b** all my goods to

BESTOWED (see BESTOW)

Luke	22:29	as My Father **b** one upon Me
2Co	8: 1	of God **b** on the churches of
1Jn	3: 1	love the Father has **b** on us

BETHANY

Matt	21:17	and went out of the city to **B**
Matt	26: 6	when Jesus was in **B** at the
John	11: 1	man was sick, Lazarus of **B**
John	11:18	Now **B** was near Jerusalem,

BETHEL

Gen	12: 8	to the mountain east of **B**
Gen	13: 3	at the beginning, between **B**
Gen	28:19	the name of that place **B**
Gen	31:13	I am the God of **B**, where you
Gen	35: 8	she was buried below **B** under
Josh	12: 9	king of Ai, which is beside **B**
Josh	18:13	of Luz (which is **B**) southward
Judg	21:19	Shiloh, which is north of **B**
1Sa	7:16	to year on a circuit to **B**
1Ki	12:29	And he set up one in **B**, and the
1Ki	13: 1	to **B** by the word of the LORD
1Ki	13:11	Now an old prophet dwelt in **B**
1Ki	16:34	days Hiel of **B** built Jericho
2Ki	10:29	golden calves that were at **B**
Jer	48:13	of Israel was ashamed of **B**
Hos	10:15	it shall be done to you, O **B**
Hos	12: 4	He found Him in **B**, and there
Amos	4: 4	Come to **B** and transgress, at
Amos	5: 5	and **B** shall come to nothing
Amos	7:10	of **B** sent to Jeroboam king of
Amos	7:13	But never again prophesy at **B**

BETHESDA†

John	5: 2	which is called in Hebrew, **B**

BETHLEHEM

Gen	35:19	way to Ephrath (that is, **B**)
Judg	17: 7	a young man from **B** in Judah
Ruth	1: 1	And a certain man of **B**, Judah,
Ruth	2: 4	Now behold, Boaz came from **B**
Ruth	4:11	Ephrathah and be famous in **B**
1Sa	16: 4	the LORD said, and went to **B**
1Sa	17:15	feed his father's sheep at **B**

2Sa	23:15	the water from the well of **B**
Mic	5: 2	**B** Ephrathah, though you are
Matt	2: 1	in **B** of Judea in the days of
Matt	2: 6	But you, **B**, in the land of
Matt	2: 8	And he sent them to **B** and said,
Matt	2:16	male children who were in **B**
Luke	2: 4	of David, which is called **B**
Luke	2:15	Let us now go to **B** and see
John	7:42	David and from the town of **B**

BETHSAIDA

Matt	11:21	Woe to you, **B**! For if the
John	1:44	Now Philip was from **B**, the
John	12:21	who was from **B** of Galilee

BETRAY (see BETRAYED, BETRAYER, BETRAYING, BETRAYS)

Matt	24:10	will **b** one another, and will
Matt	26:16	sought opportunity to **b** Him
Matt	26:21	to you, one of you will **b** Me
Matt	26:23	with Me in the dish will **b** Me

BETRAYED (see BETRAY, DELIVERED)

Matt	10: 4	Iscariot, who also **b** Him
Luke	22:22	to that man by whom He is **b**
John	18: 2	And Judas, who **b** Him, also
1Co	11:23	in which He was **b** took bread

BETRAYER (see BETRAY)

Matt	26:46	See, My **b** is at hand
Matt	27: 3	Then Judas, His **b**, seeing

BETRAYING† (see BETRAY)

Matt	26:25	Then Judas, who was **b** Him
Matt	27: 4	sinned by **b** innocent blood
Luke	22:48	are you **b** the Son of Man with

BETRAYS† (see BETRAY)

Matt	26:73	because your speech **b** you
John	21:20	who is the one who **b** You

BETROTH (see BETROTHED)

Deut	28:30	You shall **b** a wife, but
Hos	2:19	I will **b** you to Me forever

BETROTHED (see BETROTH)

Ex	22:16	entices a virgin who is not **b**
Matt	1:18	mother Mary was **b** to Joseph
Luke	1:27	to a virgin **b** to a man whose
Luke	2: 5	his **b** wife, who was with

BEWARE

Gen	24: 6	**B** that you do not take my son
Matt	7:15	**B** of false prophets, who come
Matt	10:17	But **b** of men, for they will
Matt	16: 6	and **b** of the leaven of the
Mark	12:38	**B** of the scribes, who desire
Luke	12:15	**b** of covetousness, for one's
Phil	3: 2	**B** of dogs, **b** of evil workers
Phil	3: 2	**b** of the mutilation
Col	2: 8	**B** lest anyone cheat you
2Ti	4:15	You also must **b** of him, for
2Pe	3:17	**b** lest you also fall from

BEWITCHED†
Gal 3: 1 Who has **b** you that you should

BILDAD
Job 2:11 **B** the Shuhite, and Zophar the

BILLOWS†
Ps 42: 7 waves and **b** have gone over me
Jon 2: 3 all Your **b** and Your waves

BIND (see BINDING, BINDS, BOUND)
Ex 28:28 They shall **b** the breastplate
Deut 6: 8 You shall **b** them as a sign on
Josh 2:18 you **b** this line of scarlet
Judg 16: 7 If they **b** me with seven fresh
Ps 118:27 **B** the sacrifice with cords to
Ps 149: 8 To **b** their kings with chains,
Prov 3: 3 **b** them around your neck,
Is 8:16 **B** up the testimony, Seal the
Is 49:18 **b** them on you as a bride does
Ezek 34:16 **b** up the broken and strengthen
Hos 6: 1 stricken, but He will **b** us up
Matt 13:30 **b** them in bundles to burn
Matt 16:19 whatever you **b** on earth will
Matt 22:13 **B** him hand and foot, take him
Matt 23: 4 For they **b** heavy burdens,
Mark 5: 3 and no one could **b** him, not
Acts 9:14 **b** all who call on Your name

BINDING (see BIND)
Gen 37: 7 were, **b** sheaves in the field
Gen 49:11 **B** his donkey to the vine, and
Num 30:12 the agreement **b** her, it shall
Num 30:13 every **b** oath to afflict her
Ps 56:12 made to You are **b** upon me

BINDS (see BIND)
Num 30: 3 **b** herself by some agreement
Job 5:18 For He bruises, but He **b** up
Job 12:18 **b** their waist with a belt
Job 26: 8 He **b** up the water in His
Job 36:13 cry for help when He **b** them
Ps 129: 7 hand, Nor he who **b** sheaves
Ps 147: 3 And **b** up their wounds
Prov 26: 8 Like one who **b** a stone in a
Matt 12:29 he first **b** the strong man

BIRD (see BIRDS)
Gen 1:21 every winged **b** according to
Gen 7:14 every **b** after its kind, every
Gen 8:20 animal and of every clean **b**
Job 28: 7 That path no **b** knows, nor has
Job 41: 5 you play with him as with a **b**
Ps 11: 1 Flee as a **b** to your mountain
Ps 124: 7 as a **b** from the snare of the
Eccl 12: 4 rises up at the sound of a **b**
Dan 7: 6 on its back four wings of a **b**
Hos 9:11 glory shall fly away like a **b**
Rev 18: 2 for every unclean and hated **b**

BIRDS (see BIRD)
Gen 1:20 let **b** fly above the earth
Gen 1:26 over the **b** of the air, and

Gen 15:10 he did not cut the **b** in two
Deut 14:11 All clean **b** you may eat
1Ki 4:33 spoke also of animals, of **b**
Job 35:11 us wiser than the **b** of heaven
Ps 50:11 I know all the **b** of the
Ps 104:17 Where the **b** make their nests
Is 18: 6 for the mountain **b** of prey
Is 31: 5 Like **b** flying about, so will
Jer 5:27 As a cage is full of **b**, so
Dan 4:12 the **b** of the heavens dwelt in
Matt 6:26 Look at the **b** of the air, for
Matt 8:20 **b** of the air have nests, but
Matt 13: 4 the **b** came and devoured them
Luke 12:24 more value are you than the **b**
Luke 13:19 the **b** of the air nested in
Acts 10:12 things, and **b** of the air
Rom 1:23 and **b** and four-footed beasts
1Co 15:39 of fish, and another of **b**

BIRTH (see BIRTHDAY, BIRTHRIGHT, BORN)
Gen 25:24 fulfilled for her to give **b**
Ex 1:19 give **b** before the midwives
Ruth 2:11 mother and the land of your **b**
1Sa 4:19 she bowed herself and gave **b**
1Ki 3:17 I gave **b** while she was in the
Job 3: 1 and cursed the day of his **b**
Job 3:11 Why did I not die at **b**
Ps 22:10 I was cast upon You from **b**
Ps 29: 9 LORD makes the deer give **b**
Ps 71: 6 I have been upheld from my **b**
Eccl 7: 1 death than the day of one's **b**
Is 66: 7 she travailed, she gave **b**
Is 66: 8 be made to give **b** in one day
Jer 2:27 to a stone, 'You gave **b** to me
Jer 48:41 heart of a woman in **b** pangs
Ezek 16: 3 Your **b** and your nativity are
Hos 9:11 no **b**, no pregnancy, and no
Matt 1:18 Now the **b** of Jesus Christ was
Luke 1:14 and many will rejoice at his **b**
John 9: 1 a man who was blind from **b**
Rom 8:22 labors with **b** pangs together
Gal 4:19 for whom I labor in **b** again
Gal 4:24 which gives **b** to bondage,
Jas 1:15 conceived, it gives **b** to sin
Rev 12: 2 in labor and in pain to give **b**
Rev 12:13 who gave **b** to the male Child

BIRTHDAY (see BIRTH)
Gen 40:20 day, which was Pharaoh's **b**
Matt 14: 6 when Herod's **b** was celebrated

BIRTHRIGHT (see BIRTH)
Gen 25:33 him, and sold his **b** to Jacob
Gen 25:34 Thus Esau despised his **b**
Heb 12:16 one morsel of food sold his **b**

BISHOP
1Ti 3: 2 A **b** then must be blameless,

BITE
Eccl 10:11 A serpent may **b** when it is
Gal 5:15 But if you **b** and devour one

BITS

Jas	3: 3	we put **b** in horses' mouths

BITTER (see BITTERLY, BITTERNESS)

Ex	1:14	lives **b** with hard bondage
Ex	12: 8	with **b** herbs they shall eat
Ex	15:23	of Marah, for they were **b**
Num	5:18	**b** water that brings a curse
Prov	5: 4	the end she is **b** as wormwood
Jer	31:15	**b** weeping, Rachel weeping for
Col	3:19	and do not be **b** toward them
Rev	8:11	water, because it was made **b**

BITTERLY (see BITTER)

Ruth	1:20	has dealt very **b** with me
Hos	12:14	provoked Him to anger most **b**
Luke	22:62	Then Peter went out and wept **b**

BITTERNESS (see BITTER)

1Sa	1:10	And she was in **b** of soul, and
Acts	8:23	that you are poisoned by **b**
Rom	3:14	mouth is full of cursing and **b**
Eph	4:31	Let all **b**, wrath, anger,
Heb	12:15	lest any root of **b** springing

BLACK

1Ki	18:45	the sky became **b** with clouds
Job	30:30	My skin grows **b** and falls from
Song	5:11	are wavy, and **b** as a raven
Matt	5:36	make one hair white or **b**

BLADE

Judg	3:22	the hilt went in after the **b**
Mark	4:28	first the **b**, then the head,

BLAME (see BLAMELESS)

Gen	43: 9	let me bear the **b** forever
2Co	8:20	that anyone should **b** us in
Eph	1: 4	without **b** before Him in love,

BLAMELESS (see BLAME, BLAMELESSLY)

Gen	17: 1	walk before Me and be **b**
Gen	44:10	my slave, and you shall be **b**
Num	32:22	and be **b** before the LORD and
Josh	2:17	We will be **b** of this oath of
Job	1: 1	and that man was **b** and upright,
Job	9:21	I am **b**, yet I do not know
Job	9:22	I say, 'He destroys the **b**
Ps	19:13	Then I shall be **b**, And I shall
Ps	51: 4	speak, And **b** when You judge
Prov	13: 6	keeps him whose way is **b**, but
Matt	12: 5	profane the Sabbath, and are **b**
1Co	1: 8	that you may be **b** in the day
Phil	3: 6	which is in the law, **b**
Col	1:22	to present you holy, and **b**
1Th	5:23	body be preserved **b** at the
1Ti	3: 2	A bishop then must be **b**, the
1Ti	3:10	as deacons, being found **b**
1Ti	6:14	spot, **b** until our Lord Jesus
Tit	1: 6	if a man is **b**, the husband of
2Pe	3:14	in peace, without spot and **b**

BLAMELESSLY † (see BLAMELESS)

Prov	28:18	Whoever walks **b** will be saved
1Th	2:10	**b** we behaved ourselves among

BLASPHEME (see BLASPHEMED, BLASPHEMER, BLASPHEMES, BLASPHEMING, BLASPHEMOUS, BLASPHEMY)

1Ti	1:20	that they may learn not to **b**
Jas	2: 7	Do they not **b** that noble name
Rev	13: 6	to **b** His name, His tabernacle

BLASPHEMED (see BLASPHEME)

1Ki	21:13	Naboth has **b** God and the king
Is	52: 5	And My name is **b** continually
Matt	27:39	And those who passed by **b** Him
Luke	23:39	who were hanged **b** Him, saying
Acts	18: 6	when they opposed him and **b**
Rom	2:24	The name of God is **b** among
1Ti	6: 1	and His doctrine may not be **b**
Tit	2: 5	the word of God may not be **b**
2Pe	2: 2	the way of truth will be **b**
Rev	16:11	And they **b** the God of heaven

BLASPHEMER † (see BLASPHEME, BLASPHEMERS)

1Ti	1:13	although I was formerly a **b**

BLASPHEMERS † (see BLASPHEMER)

Acts	19:37	temples nor **b** of your goddess
2Ti	3: 2	of money, boasters, proud, **b**

BLASPHEMES (see BLASPHEME)

Lev	24:16	whoever **b** the name of the
Matt	9: 3	themselves, "This Man **b**!"
Mark	3:29	but he who **b** against the Holy

BLASPHEMIES (see BLASPHEMY)

Dan	11:36	shall speak **b** against the God
Matt	15:19	thefts, false witness, **b**
Mark	2: 7	this Man speaks **b** like this
Rev	13: 5	speaking great things and **b**

BLASPHEMING † (see BLASPHEME)

John	10:36	into the world, 'You are **b**
Acts	13:45	and contradicting and **b**, they

BLASPHEMOUS † (see BLASPHEME, BLASPHEMOUSLY)

Acts	6:11	speak **b** words against Moses
Acts	6:13	**b** words against this holy
Rev	13: 1	and on his heads a **b** name

BLASPHEMOUSLY † (see BLASPHEMOUS)

Luke	22:65	they **b** spoke against Him

BLASPHEMY (see BLASPHEME, BLASPHEMIES)

Matt	12:31	**b** will be forgiven men, but
Matt	12:31	but the **b** against the Spirit
Matt	26:65	He has spoken **b**
Mark	7:22	an evil eye, **b**, pride,
John	10:33	do not stone You, but for **b**
Col	3: 8	anger, wrath, malice, **b**,

Rev 17: 3 which was full of names of **b**

BLEATING†

1Sa 15:14 What then is this **b** of the

BLEMISH

Ex 12: 5 Your lamb shall be without **b**
Num 19: 2 you a red heifer without **b**
Eph 5:27 should be holy and without **b**
1Pe 1:19 as of a lamb without **b** and

BLESS (see BLESSED, BLESSEDNESS, BLESSING)

Gen 12: 2 I will **b** you and make your
Gen 12: 3 I will **b** those who **b** you,
Gen 17:16 And I will **b** her and also give
Gen 27:34 **B** me, even me also, O my
Gen 32:26 let You go unless You **b** me
Ex 12:32 and **b** me also
Num 6:24 The LORD **b** you and keep you
Deut 27:12 Mount Gerizim to **b** the people
Judg 5: 9 with the people. **B** the LORD!
Ruth 2: 4 The LORD **b** you
Ps 16: 7 I will **b** the LORD who has
Ps 34: 1 I will **b** the LORD at all
Ps 62: 4 They **b** with their mouth, But
Ps 67: 1 **b** us, And cause His face to
Ps 67: 6 God, our own God, shall **b** us
Ps 96: 2 Sing to the LORD, **b** His name
Ps 100: 4 to Him, and **b** His name
Ps 103: 1 **B** the LORD, O my soul
Ps 103: 1 is within me, **b** His holy name
Matt 5:44 **b** those who curse you, do
Acts 3:26 Jesus, sent Him to **b** you, in
Rom 12:14 **B** those who persecute you
Rom 12:14 **b** and do not curse
1Co 4:12 Being reviled, we **b**
1Co 10:16 cup of blessing which we **b**
1Co 14:16 if you **b** with the spirit, how
Heb 6:14 Surely blessing I will **b** you
Jas 3: 9 With it we **b** our God and

BLESSED (see BLESS, HAPPY)

Gen 1:22 And God **b** them, saying,
Gen 2: 3 Then God **b** the seventh day and
Gen 12: 3 of the earth shall be **b**
Gen 14:19 **B** be Abram of God Most High,
Gen 14:20 **b** be God Most High, Who has
Gen 17:20 Behold, I have **b** him, and will
Gen 27:33 and indeed he shall be **b**
Ex 20:11 the LORD **b** the Sabbath day
Num 23:20 He has **b**, and I cannot reverse
Deut 28: 4 **B** shall be the fruit of your
Judg 5:24 Most **b** among women is Jael,
Ruth 2:19 **B** be the one who took notice
Ruth 4:14 **B** be the LORD, who has not
2Sa 22:47 **B** be my Rock! Let God be
Job 1:10 You have **b** the work of his
Job 1:21 **b** be the name of the LORD
Job 42:12 Now the LORD **b** the latter
Ps 1: 1 **B** is the man Who walks not in
Ps 32: 1 **B** is he whose transgression
Ps 32: 2 **B** is the man to whom the LORD
Ps 33:12 **B** is the nation whose God is

Ps 34: 8 **B** is the man who trusts in
Ps 118:26 **B** is he who comes in the name
Prov 31:28 rise up and call her **b**
Jer 20:14 Let the day not be **b** in which
Dan 2:19 So Daniel **b** the God of heaven
Dan 4:34 I **b** the Most High and praised
Dan 12:12 **B** is he who waits, and comes
Mal 3:12 all nations will call you **b**
Matt 5: 3 **B** are the poor in spirit, for
Matt 11: 6 **b** is he who is not offended
Matt 16:17 **B** are you, Simon Bar-Jonah,
Matt 21: 9 **B** is He who comes in the
Matt 25:34 you **b** of My Father, inherit
Matt 26:26 **b** it and broke it, and gave it
Mark 14:61 the Christ, the Son of the **B**
Luke 1:42 **B** are you among women, and
Luke 1:42 **b** is the fruit of your womb
Luke 1:48 generations will call me **b**
Luke 6:20 **B** are you poor, for yours is
Luke 11:27 **B** is the womb that bore You,
Luke 13:35 **B** is He who comes in the
Luke 24:30 them, that He took bread, **b**
Acts 20:35 It is more **b** to give than to
Rom 1:25 the Creator, who is **b** forever
Rom 4: 8 **b** is the man to whom the LORD
Rom 9: 5 over all, the eternally **b** God
2Co 1: 3 **B** be the God and Father of our
Gal 3: 8 all the nations shall be **b**
Gal 3: 9 are **b** with believing Abraham
Eph 1: 3 who has **b** us with every
Tit 2:13 looking for the **b** hope and
Heb 7: 6 **b** him who had the promises
Heb 7: 7 the lesser is **b** by the better
Heb 11:21 **b** each of the sons of Joseph,
Jas 1:12 **B** is the man who endures
Rev 1: 3 **B** is he who reads and those
Rev 14:13 **B** are the dead who die in
Rev 22: 7 **B** is he who keeps the words

BLESSEDNESS (see BLESS)

Rom 4: 6 the **b** of the man to whom God

BLESSING (see BLESS, BLESSINGS)

Gen 12: 2 and you shall be a **b**
Gen 27:35 and has taken away your **b**
Gen 27:38 Have you only one **b**, my
Gen 28: 4 and give you the **b** of Abraham
Deut 11:26 I set before you today a **b**
Deut 11:29 put the **b** on Mount Gerizim
Deut 30:19 before you life and death, **b**
Ps 24: 5 shall receive **b** from the LORD
Ezek 34:26 there shall be showers of **b**
Mal 3:10 pour out for you such **b** That
Luke 24:53 the temple praising and **b** God
1Co 10:16 The cup of **b** which we bless,
Gal 3:14 that the **b** of Abraham might
Eph 1: 3 us with every spiritual **b** in
Heb 6: 7 receives **b** from God
Heb 12:17 he wanted to inherit the **b**
Jas 3:10 of the same mouth proceed **b**
Rev 5:12 and honor and glory and **b**
Rev 7:12 **B** and glory and wisdom,

B

BLESSINGS (see BLESSING)

Gen	49:25	you with **b** of heaven above
Deut	28: 2	all these **b** shall come upon

BLEW (see BLOW)

Ex	10:19	and **b** them into the Red Sea
Judg	7:19	they **b** the trumpets and broke
Matt	7:25	floods came, and the winds **b**

BLIND (see BLINDED, BLINDFOLD, BLINDNESS)

Ex	4:11	deaf, the seeing, or the **b**
2Sa	5: 8	Jebusites (the lame and the **b**
Ps	146: 8	LORD opens the eyes of the **b**
Is	29:18	the eyes of the **b** shall see
Is	42: 7	To open **b** eyes, to bring out
Is	42:19	Who is **b** but My servant, or
Matt	9:27	two **b** men followed Him,
Matt	11: 5	The **b** see and the lame
Matt	15:14	are **b** leaders of the **b**
Matt	15:14	And if the **b** leads the **b**
Matt	23:16	**b** guides, who say, "Whoever
Matt	23:17	Fools and **b**! For which is
Matt	23:24	**B** guides, who strain out a
Matt	23:26	**B** Pharisee, first cleanse the
Mark	10:46	**b** Bartimaeus, the son of
Luke	4:18	and recovery of sight to the **b**
John	9: 1	a man who was **b** from birth
John	9: 6	of the **b** man with the clay
John	9:25	that though I was **b**, now I
John	9:39	those who see may be made **b**
Rom	2:19	yourself are a guide to the **b**
Rev	3:17	wretched, miserable, poor, **b**

BLINDED (see BLIND)

John	12:40	He has **b** their eyes and
2Co	4: 4	the god of this age has **b**
1Jn	2:11	the darkness has **b** his eyes

BLINDFOLD† (see BLIND)

Mark	14:65	to **b** Him, and to beat Him, and

BLINDNESS (see BLIND)

Gen	19:11	doorway of the house with **b**

BLOCK

Is	44:19	fall down before a **b** of wood
Ezek	3:20	lay a stumbling **b** before him
Rom	11: 9	and a trap, a stumbling **b** and a
1Co	1:23	to the Jews a stumbling **b**

BLOOD (see BLOODSHED, BLOODTHIRSTY)

Gen	4:10	**b** cries out to Me from the
Gen	4:11	brother's **b** from your hand
Gen	9: 4	with its life, that is, its **b**
Gen	9: 6	Whoever sheds man's **b**, by man
Gen	37:26	our brother and conceal his **b**
Gen	42:22	his **b** is now required of us
Ex	4: 9	will become **b** on the dry land
Ex	7:19	water, that they may become **b**
Ex	12: 7	they shall take some of the **b**
Ex	12:13	Now the **b** shall be a sign
Ex	12:13	And when I see the **b**, I will
Ex	12:22	dip it in the **b** that is in
Ex	12:23	He sees the **b** on the lintel
Ex	24: 6	half the **b** he sprinkled on
Ex	24: 8	the **b** of the covenant which
Lev	12: 4	in the **b** of her purification
Lev	16:15	bring its **b** inside the veil,
Lev	17:11	life of the flesh is in the **b**
Lev	17:11	the **b** that makes atonement
Lev	19:26	not eat anything with the **b**
Lev	20: 9	His **b** shall be upon him
Num	35:27	the avenger of **b** kills the
Josh	2:19	his **b** shall be on our head if
Josh	20: 3	refuge from the avenger of **b**
1Ch	28: 3	a man of war and have shed **b**
Job	16:18	O earth, do not cover my **b**
Ps	50:13	Or drink the **b** of goats
Ps	72:14	shall be their **b** in His sight
Ps	106:38	the land was polluted with **b**
Prov	6:17	hands that shed innocent **b**
Is	1:15	Your hands are full of **b**
Is	9: 5	And garments rolled in **b**,
Ezek	3:18	but his **b** I will require at
Joel	2:30	**b** and fire and pillars of smoke
Joel	2:31	darkness, and the moon into **b**
Matt	9:20	a woman who had a flow of **b**
Matt	23:35	from the **b** of righteous Abel
Matt	23:35	Abel to the **b** of Zechariah
Matt	26:28	For this is My **b** of the new
Matt	27:24	of the **b** of this just Person
Matt	27:25	His **b** be on us and on our
Luke	13: 1	**b** Pilate had mingled with
Luke	22:20	is the new covenant in My **b**
John	1:13	who were born, not of **b**, nor
John	6:54	drinks My **b** has eternal life,
John	19:34	a spear, and immediately **b**
Acts	1:19	Dama, that is, Field of B
Acts	2:19	**b** and fire and vapor of smoke
Acts	2:20	darkness, and the moon into **b**
Acts	15:20	things strangled, and from **b**
Acts	17:26	He has made from one **b** every
Acts	20:28	He purchased with His own **b**
Acts	22:20	when the **b** of Your martyr
Rom	3:15	feet are swift to shed **b**
Rom	3:25	to be a propitiation of His **b**
Rom	5: 9	now been justified by His **b**
1Co	10:16	communion of the **b** of Christ
1Co	11:25	is the new covenant in My **b**
1Co	11:27	of the body and **b** of the Lord
1Co	15:50	**b** cannot inherit the kingdom
Gal	1:16	confer with flesh and **b**,
Eph	1: 7	have redemption through His **b**
Eph	2:13	brought near by the **b** of Christ
Eph	6:12	wrestle against flesh and **b**
Col	1:20	through the **b** of His cross
Heb	9: 7	once a year, not without **b**
Heb	9:12	Not with the **b** of goats and
Heb	9:12	but with His own **b** He entered
Heb	9:13	For if the **b** of bulls and
Heb	9:14	more shall the **b** of Christ
Heb	9:22	all things are purified with **b**
Heb	9:22	without shedding of **b** there
Heb	10: 4	possible that the **b** of bulls
Heb	10:29	counted the **b** of the covenant
Heb	13:12	the people with His own **b**
Heb	13:20	sheep, through the **b** of the

1Pe	1:19	with the precious **b** of Christ
1Jn	1: 7	the **b** of Jesus Christ His Son
1Jn	5: 6	is He who came by water and **b**
1Jn	5: 8	Spirit, the water, and the **b**
Rev	1: 5	us from our sins in His own **b**
Rev	5: 9	by Your **b** out of every tribe
Rev	6:12	and the moon became like **b**
Rev	7:14	white in the **b** of the Lamb
Rev	8: 8	a third of the sea became **b**
Rev	17: 6	with the **b** of the saints and
Rev	17: 6	with the **b** of the martyrs of
Rev	18:24	was found the **b** of prophets
Rev	19:13	with a robe dipped in **b**, and

BLOODSHED (*see* BLOOD)

Ex	22: 3	shall be guilt for his **b**
Lev	17: 4	**b** shall be imputed to that
Heb	12: 4	have not yet resisted to **b**

BLOODTHIRSTY (*see* BLOOD)

Ps	59: 2	And save me from **b** men

BLOSSOM (*see* BLOSSOMS)

Hab	3:17	Though the fig tree may not **b**

BLOSSOMS (*see* BLOSSOM)

Eccl	12: 5	when the almond tree **b**, the

BLOT (*see* BLOTTED)

Ex	17:14	that I will utterly **b** out the
Ex	32:32	**b** me out of Your book which
Deut	9:14	**b** out their name from under
Ps	51: 1	**B** out my transgressions
Ps	51: 9	And **b** out all my iniquities
Rev	3: 5	I will not **b** out his name

BLOTTED (*see* BLOT)

Deut	25: 6	may not be **b** out of Israel
Ps	69:28	Let them be **b** out of the book
Is	44:22	I have **b** out, like a thick
Acts	3:19	that your sins may be **b** out

BLOW (*see* BLEW, BLOWS)

Num	10: 8	priests, shall **b** the trumpets
Judg	7:18	When I **b** the trumpet, I and
Ps	39:10	by the **b** of Your hand
Ps	78:26	east wind to **b** in the heavens
Jer	6: 1	**B** the trumpet in Tekoa, and
Jer	6:29	the bellows **b** fiercely, the
Ezek	22:21	**b** on you with the fire of My
Joel	2: 1	**B** the trumpet in Zion,
Joel	2:15	**B** the trumpet in Zion,
Luke	12:55	when you see the south wind **b**
Rev	7: 1	should not **b** on the earth

BLOWS (*see* BLOW)

Deut	25: 3	Forty **b** he may give him and no
Prov	17:10	than a hundred **b** on a fool
Is	40: 7	breath of the LORD **b** upon it
John	3: 8	The wind **b** where it wishes,

BOANERGES†

Mark	3:17	to whom He gave the name **B**

BOAST (*see* BOASTED, BOASTERS, BOASTING, BOASTS)

Ps	34: 2	shall make its **b** in the LORD
Ps	49: 6	**b** in the multitude of their
Prov	27: 1	Do not **b** about tomorrow, for
Rom	2:17	law, and make your **b** in God
Rom	2:23	who make your **b** in the law
1Co	9:16	I have nothing to **b** of, for
2Co	12: 6	though I might desire to **b**
2Co	12: 9	rather **b** in my infirmities
Eph	2: 9	works, lest anyone should **b**

BOASTED (*see* BOAST)

2Co	7:14	I have **b** to him about you

BOASTERS† (*see* BOAST)

Rom	1:30	of God, violent, proud, **b**
2Ti	3: 2	lovers of money, **b**, proud,

BOASTING (*see* BOAST)

Rom	3:27	Where is **b** then
1Co	9:15	anyone should make my **b** void
2Co	1:12	For our **b** is this
2Co	7: 4	great is my **b** on your behalf
2Co	9: 4	ashamed of this confident **b**
2Co	10:15	not **b** of things beyond
2Co	12:11	I have become a fool in **b**
Jas	4:16	All such **b** is evil

BOASTS (*see* BOAST)

Ps	10: 3	For the wicked **b** of his
Prov	25:14	Whoever falsely **b** of giving
Jas	3: 5	member and **b** great things

BOAT (*see* BOATS)

Matt	4:21	in the **b** with Zebedee their
Matt	9: 1	So He got into a **b**, crossed
John	21: 6	on the right side of the **b**

BOATS (*see* BOAT)

Mark	4:36	other little **b** were also with
Luke	5: 2	saw two **b** standing by the

BOAZ

Ruth	2: 3	of the field belonging to **B**
Ruth	2: 4	**B** came from Bethlehem, and
Ruth	4:13	So **B** took Ruth and she became
Ruth	4:21	and **B** begot Obed
Matt	1: 5	**B** begot Obed by Ruth, Obed
Luke	3:32	the son of Obed, the son of **B**

BODIES (*see* BODY)

Dan	3:27	whose **b** the fire had no power
Matt	27:52	many **b** of the saints who had
John	19:31	that the **b** should not remain
Rom	8:11	**b** through His Spirit who
Rom	12: 1	your **b** a living sacrifice
1Co	6:15	your **b** are members of Christ
1Co	15:40	celestial **b** and terrestrial
Eph	5:28	own wives as their own **b**
Heb	10:22	our **b** washed with pure water
Rev	11: 9	not allow their dead **b** to be

BODILY (*see* BODY)

Luke	3:22	Holy Spirit descended in **b**
Col	2: 9	the fullness of the Godhead **b**
1Ti	4: 8	For **b** exercise profits a

BODY (*see* BODIES, BODILY)

Gen	15: 4	your own **b** shall be your heir
Lev	21:11	shall he go near any dead **b**
Prov	18: 8	go down into the inmost **b**
Is	26:19	my dead **b** they shall arise
Dan	4:33	his **b** was wet with the dew of
Mic	6: 7	the fruit of my **b** for the sin
Matt	5:29	than for your whole **b** to be
Matt	6:22	The lamp of the **b** is the eye
Matt	6:25	nor about your **b**, what you
Matt	6:25	and the **b** more than clothing
Matt	10:28	both soul and **b** in hell
Matt	26:26	Take, eat; this is My **b**
Matt	27:58	and asked for the **b** of Jesus
Matt	27:59	when Joseph had taken the **b**
Mark	14: 8	to anoint My **b** for burial
Luke	24:23	When they did not find His **b**
John	2:21	of the temple of His **b**
John	19:40	Then they took the **b** of Jesus
Rom	6:6	that the **b** of sin might be
Rom	6:12	sin reign in your mortal **b**
Rom	7:24	me from this **b** of death
Rom	8:10	the **b** is dead because of sin,
Rom	8:13	to death the deeds of the **b**
Rom	8:23	the redemption of our **b**
Rom	12: 4	we have many members in one **b**
Rom	12: 5	many, are one **b** in Christ, and
1Co	5: 3	as absent in **b** but present in
1Co	6:13	Lord, and the Lord for the **b**
1Co	6:16	to a harlot is one **b** with her
1Co	6:18	sins against his own **b**
1Co	6:19	**b** is the temple of the Holy
1Co	6:20	glorify God in your **b** and in
1Co	7: 4	have authority over her own **b**
1Co	9:27	But I discipline my **b** and
1Co	10:16	communion of the **b** of Christ
1Co	10:17	many, are one bread and one **b**
1Co	11:24	this is My **b** which is broken
1Co	11:27	will be guilty of the **b** and
1Co	11:29	not discerning the Lord's **b**
1Co	12:12	For as the **b** is one and has
1Co	12:13	were all baptized into one **b**
1Co	12:27	Now you are the **b** of Christ
1Co	13: 3	I give my **b** to be burned, but
1Co	15:42	The **b** is sown in corruption,
1Co	15:44	It is sown a natural **b**, it is
1Co	15:44	it is raised a spiritual **b**
2Co	4:10	carrying about in the **b** the
2Co	5: 8	to be absent from the **b** and to
2Co	5:10	the things done in the **b**,
2Co	12: 2	out of the **b** I do not know
Gal	6:17	for I bear in my **b** the marks
Eph	2:16	in one **b** through the cross
Eph	4: 4	There is one **b** and one Spirit,
Eph	4:12	edifying of the **b** of Christ
Eph	4:16	from whom the whole **b**, joined
Eph	5:23	and He is the Savior of the **b**
Phil	1:20	will be magnified in my **b**

Phil	3:21	will transform our lowly **b**
Phil	3:21	conformed to His glorious **b**
Col	1:18	And He is the head of the **b**
Col	3:15	also you were called in one **b**
1Th	5:23	**b** be preserved blameless at
Heb	10: 5	but a **b** You have prepared for
Jas	3: 2	also to bridle the whole **b**
1Pe	2:24	sins in His own **b** on the tree
Jude	9	disputed about the **b** of Moses

BOIL (*see* BOILS)

Ex	23:19	You shall not **b** a young goat
Lev	13:18	body develops a **b** in the skin

BOILS (*see* BOIL)

Ex	9:10	they caused **b** that break out
Deut	28:27	you with the **b** of Egypt, with
Job	2: 7	struck Job with painful **b**

BOLD (*see* BOLDLY, BOLDNESS)

Prov	28: 1	the righteous are **b** as a lion
Acts	13:46	Then Paul and Barnabas grew **b**
Rom	10:20	But Isaiah is very **b** and says
1Th	2: 2	we were **b** in our God to speak

BOLDLY (*see* BOLD)

Acts	9:27	and how he had preached **b** at
Acts	18:26	to speak **b** in the synagogue
Heb	4:16	Let us therefore come **b** to

BOLDNESS (*see* BOLD)

Acts	4:13	when they saw the **b** of Peter
Acts	4:31	spoke the word of God with **b**
Heb	10:19	having **b** to enter the Holiest

BOND (*see* BONDAGE, BONDS, BONDWOMAN)

Deut	32:36	no one remaining, **b** or free
Eph	4: 3	the Spirit in the **b** of peace
Col	3:14	which is the **b** of perfection

BONDAGE (*see* BOND)

Ex	1:14	lives bitter with hard **b**
Ex	13: 3	Egypt, out of the house of **b**
Rom	8:15	the spirit of **b** again to fear
Rom	8:21	the **b** of corruption into the
1Co	7:15	is not under **b** in such cases
Gal	5: 1	again with a yoke of **b**

BONDS (*see* BOND)

Judg	15:14	his **b** broke loose from his
Ps	2: 3	us break Their **b** in pieces
Is	58: 6	to loose the **b** of wickedness,

BONDWOMAN (*see* BOND)

Gen	21:10	Cast out this **b** and her son
Gal	4:22	the one by a **b**, the other by

BONE (*see* BONES)

Gen	2:23	This is now **b** of my bones
Judg	9: 2	that I am your own flesh and **b**
Job	19:20	My **b** clings to my skin and to
Ezek	37: 7	came together, **b** to **b**

BONES (see BONE)

Gen	2:23	This is now bone of my **b** and
Gen	50:25	shall carry up my **b** from here
Ex	12:46	shall you break one of its **b**
Ex	13:19	Moses took the **b** of Joseph
2Ki	13:21	and touched the **b** of Elisha
Ps	22:14	all My **b** are out of joint
Ps	22:17	I can count all My **b**
Ps	32: 3	my **b** grew old Through my
Ps	51: 8	That the **b** which You have
Prov	12: 4	is like rottenness in his **b**
Prov	16:24	the soul and health to the **b**
Eccl	11: 5	or how the **b** grow in the womb
Jer	20: 9	burning fire shut up in my **b**
Ezek	37: 3	Son of man, can these **b** live
Ezek	37: 4	and say to them, 'O dry **b**
Dan	6:24	broke all their **b** in pieces
Matt	23:27	are full of dead men's **b** and
Luke	24:39	flesh and **b** as you see I have
John	19:36	Not one of His **b** shall be
Eph	5:30	of His flesh and of His **b**
Heb	11:22	instructions concerning his **b**

BOOK (see BOOKS)

Ex	24: 7	he took the **B** of the Covenant
Ex	32:32	blot me out of Your **b** which
Num	21:14	the **B** of the Wars of the LORD
Deut	17:18	a copy of this law in a **b**
Deut	28:61	written in this **B** of the law
Josh	8:31	in the **B** of the Law of Moses
Josh	10:13	written in the **B** of Jasher
Josh	24:26	in the **B** of the Law of God
1Ki	11:41	the **b** of the acts of Solomon
1Ki	14:29	**b** of the chronicles of the
2Ki	23:21	in this **B** of the Covenant
2Ch	24:27	annals of the **b** of the kings
2Ch	35:12	is written in the **B** of Moses
Neh	8: 3	attentive to the **B** of the Law
Neh	8: 5	And Ezra opened the **b** in the
Ps	40: 7	of the **B** it is written of me
Jer	36: 2	Take a scroll of a **b** and write
Jer	36:10	**b** the words of Jeremiah in
Jer	36:18	wrote them with ink in the **b**
Dan	12: 1	who is found written in the **b**
Dan	12: 4	seal the **b** until the time of
Mal	3:16	so a **b** of remembrance was
Matt	1: 1	The **b** of the genealogy of
Luke	4:17	He was handed the **b** of the
Luke	20:42	said in the **B** of Psalms, 'The
John	20:30	are not written in this **b**
Acts	7:42	in the **b** of the Prophets
Gal	3:10	written in the **b** of the law
Phil	4: 3	names are in the **B** of Life
Heb	9:19	sprinkled both the **b** itself
Heb	10: 7	of the **b** it is written of Me
Rev	3: 5	his name from the **B** of Life
Rev	10: 2	he had a little **b** open in his
Rev	20:12	another **b** was opened, which
Rev	22: 9	who keep the words of this **b**

BOOKS (see BOOK)

Eccl	12:12	Of making many **b** there is no
Dan	7:10	seated, and the **b** were opened
Dan	9: 2	understood by the **b** the
John	21:25	the **b** that would be written
2Ti	4:13	and the **b**, especially the
Rev	20:12	before God, and **b** were opened

BOOTHS

Lev	23:42	dwell in **b** for seven days

BORDER (see HEM)

Gen	10:19	the **b** of the Canaanites was
Josh	15: 5	The east **b** was the Salt Sea
1Ki	4:21	as far as the **b** of Egypt
Mal	1: 5	beyond the **b** of Israel

BORE (see BEAR)

Gen	4: 1	conceived and **b** Cain, and said,
Gen	21: 2	**b** Abraham a son in his old
Ex	19: 4	how I **b** you on eagles' wings
Is	53:12	He **b** the sin of many, and made
Hos	1: 3	she conceived and **b** him a son
Hos	1: 6	again and **b** a daughter
Matt	8:17	and **b** our sicknesses
Mark	14:57	**b** false witness against Him,
Luke	11:27	is the womb that **b** You, and
John	1:15	John **b** witness of Him and
1Pe	2:24	who Himself **b** our sins in His
Rev	12: 5	she **b** a male Child who was to

BORN (see BIRTH, BORNE)

Gen	6: 1	and daughters were **b** to them
Gen	15: 3	indeed one **b** in my house is
Gen	17:27	**b** in the house or bought with
Ex	1:22	Every son who is **b** you shall
Job	3: 3	day perish on which I was **b**
Job	5: 7	yet man is **b** to trouble, as
Job	14: 1	Man who is **b** of woman is of
Prov	17:17	a brother is **b** for adversity
Eccl	3: 2	A time to be **b**, and a time to
Is	9: 6	For unto us a Child is **b**,
Jer	1: 5	before you were **b** I
Jer	20:14	be the day in which I was **b**
Matt	1:16	of whom was **b** Jesus who is
Matt	2: 2	has been **b** King of the Jews
Matt	11:11	among those **b** of women there
Matt	26:24	that man if he had never been **b**
Luke	1:35	**b** will be called the Son of
Luke	2:11	For there is **b** to you this
John	1:13	who were **b**, not of blood, nor
John	3: 3	to you, unless one is **b** again
John	3: 4	his mother's womb and be **b**
John	3: 5	you, unless one is **b** of water
John	3: 6	That which is **b** of the flesh
John	3: 6	that which is **b** of the Spirit
John	9: 2	parents, that he was **b** blind
1Co	15: 8	as by one **b** out of due time
Gal	4: 4	**b** of a woman, **b** under the law
Gal	4:23	was **b** according to the flesh
Gal	4:29	was **b** according to the Spirit
1Pe	1:23	having been **b** again, not of
1Jn	3: 9	Whoever has been **b** of God

BORNE (see BEAR, BORN)

Gen	16: 1	wife, had **b** him no children
Ruth	4:15	than seven sons, has **b** him

1Sa	2: 5	Even the barren has **b** seven
Ps	69: 7	Your sake I have **b** reproach
Is	53: 4	Surely He has **b** our griefs
Jer	15:10	my mother, that you have **b** me
1Co	15:49	as we have **b** the image of the

BORROW

Matt	5:42	from him who wants to **b** from

BOSOM

Ex	4: 6	Now put your hand in your **b**
Num	11:12	to me, 'Carry them in your **b**
Ruth	4:16	child and laid him on her **b**
2Sa	12: 3	his own cup and lay in his **b**
1Ki	3:20	laid her dead child in my **b**
Ps	89:50	How I bear in my **b** the
Prov	6:27	can a man take fire to his **b**
Is	40:11	arm, and carry them in His **b**
Luke	16:22	by the angels to Abraham's **b**
John	1:18	who is in the **b** of the Father
John	13:23	Jesus' **b** one of His disciples

BOTTLE

Ps	56: 8	Put my tears into Your **b**

BOTTOM (see BOTTOMLESS)

Ex	15: 5	sank to the **b** like a stone
Dan	6:24	ever came to the **b** of the den
Matt	27:51	was torn in two from top to **b**

BOTTOMLESS (see BOTTOM)

Rev	9: 1	given the key to the **b** pit

BOUGHT (see BUY)

Gen	17:27	born in the house or **b** with
Josh	24:32	of ground which Jacob had **b**
Jer	32: 9	So I **b** the field from
Hos	3: 2	So I **b** her for myself for
Matt	13:46	sold all that he had and **b** it
Matt	21:12	and drove out all those who **b**
Matt	27: 7	and **b** with them the potter's
1Co	6:20	For you were **b** at a price
2Pe	2: 1	denying the Lord who **b** them

BOUND (see BIND)

Gen	22: 9	he **b** Isaac his son and laid
Gen	44:30	since his life is **b** up in the
Josh	2:21	she **b** the scarlet cord in the
Judg	15:13	they **b** him with two new ropes
Ps	119:61	cords of the wicked have **b** me
Prov	22:15	Foolishness is **b** up in the
Prov	30: 4	Who has **b** the waters in a
Is	1: 6	have not been closed or **b** up
Is	61: 1	the prison to those who are **b**
Ezek	34: 4	nor **b** up the broken, nor
Dan	3:24	Did we not cast three men **b**
Matt	14: 3	**b** him, and put him in prison
Matt	16:19	on earth will be **b** in heaven
Matt	27: 2	And when they had **b** Him, they
Mark	6:17	**b** him in prison for the sake
Mark	15: 1	they **b** Jesus, led Him away,
Luke	13:16	of Abraham, whom Satan has **b**
John	11:44	who had died came out **b** hand
John	18:12	Jews arrested Jesus and **b** Him

John	19:40	**b** it in strips of linen with
Acts	9: 2	bring them **b** to Jerusalem
Acts	10:11	sheet **b** at the four corners
Acts	12: 6	**b** with two chains between two
Acts	20:22	now I go **b** in the spirit to
Acts	23:12	**b** themselves under an oath,
Rom	7: 2	**b** by the law to her husband
1Co	7:27	Are you **b** to a wife
1Co	7:39	A wife is **b** by law as long as
2Th	1: 3	We are **b** to thank God always
Rev	20: 2	**b** him for a thousand years

BOUNTIFULLY

Ps	13: 6	He has dealt **b** with me
2Co	9: 6	who sows **b** will also reap **b**

BOW (see BOWED, BOWING)

Gen	37:10	brothers indeed come to **b**
Gen	41:43	out before him, "**B** the knee
Ex	20: 5	you shall not **b** down to them
2Sa	1:18	of Judah the Song of the **B**
1Ki	22:34	man drew a **b** at random, and
Ps	7:12	He bends His **b** and makes it
Ps	11: 2	The wicked bend their **b**, They
Ps	86: 1	**B** down Your ear, O LORD, hear
Ps	95: 6	let us worship and **b** down
Ps	144: 5	**B** down Your heavens, O LORD,
Eccl	12: 3	and the strong men **b** down
Is	45:23	that to Me every knee shall **b**
Is	46: 2	stoop, they **b** down together
Lam	3:12	He has bent His **b** and set me
Ezek	39: 3	the **b** out of your left hand
Hos	1: 5	day that I will break the **b**
Hos	7:16	they are like a treacherous **b**
Mic	6: 6	**b** myself before the High God
Zech	9:10	the battle **b** shall be cut off
Zech	9:13	For I have bent Judah, My **b**
Rom	11:10	and **b** down their back always
Rom	14:11	every knee shall **b** to Me
Eph	3:14	For this reason I **b** my knees
Phil	2:10	of Jesus every knee should **b**

BOWED (see BOW)

Gen	33: 3	**b** himself to the ground seven
Gen	37: 7	around and **b** down to my sheaf
Gen	37: 9	the eleven stars **b** down to me
1Ki	19:18	knees have not **b** to Baal, and
Matt	27:29	they **b** the knee before Him and
Luke	24: 5	**b** their faces to the earth,
Rom	11: 4	have not **b** the knee to Baal

BOWING (see BOW)

Mark	15:19	**b** the knee, they worshiped
John	19:30	**b** His head, He gave up His

BOWL (see BOWLS)

Eccl	12: 6	or the golden **b** is broken
Rev	16: 2	out his **b** upon the earth, and
Rev	16: 3	poured out his **b** on the sea

BOWLS (see BOWL)

Ex	8: 3	and into your kneading **b**
Ex	25:31	shaft, its branches, its **b**
Num	4: 7	the dishes, the pans, the **b**

Amos	6: 6	who drink wine from **b**, and
Rev	15: 7	**b** full of the wrath of God
Rev	17: 1	who had the seven **b** came and

BOX
Is	41:19	pine and the **b** tree together,
John	13:29	because Judas had the money **b**

BOY
Gen	21:15	she placed the **b** under one of
1Sa	3: 1	Then the **b** Samuel ministered
Luke	2:43	The **B** Jesus lingered behind

BRACELETS
Gen	24:47	nose and the **b** on her wrists

BRAIDED
1Ti	2: 9	not with **b** hair or gold or

BRAMBLE
Judg	9:14	all the trees said to the **b**
Luke	6:44	gather grapes from a **b** bush

BRANCH (see BRANCHES)
Ex	25:33	like almond blossoms on one **b**
Job	15:32	and his **b** will not be green
Job	18:16	below, and his **b** withers above
Is	4: 2	In that day the **B** of the LORD
Is	11: 1	a **B** shall grow out of his
Jer	1:11	I see a **b** of an almond tree
Jer	23: 5	to David a **B** of righteousness
Ezek	8:17	they put the **b** to their nose
Dan	11: 7	But from a **b** of her roots one
Zech	3: 8	forth My Servant the **B**
Zech	6:12	the Man whose name is the **B**
Zech	6:12	From His place He shall **b** out
Mal	4: 1	leave them neither root nor **b**
Matt	24:32	When its **b** has already become
John	15: 2	every **b** that bears fruit He

BRANCHES (see BRANCH)
Gen	40:10	and in the vine were three **b**
Gen	40:12	The three **b** are three days
Ex	25:31	Its shaft, its **b**, its bowls,
Lev	23:40	**b** of palm trees, the boughs
Neh	8:15	mountain, and bring olive **b**
Ps	80:11	Sea, And her **b** to the River
Jer	11:16	on it, and its **b** are broken
Ezek	17:22	highest **b** of the high cedar
Ezek	36: 8	you shall shoot forth your **b**
Dan	4:12	of the heavens dwelt in its **b**
Hos	14: 6	His **b** shall spread
Zech	4:12	olive **b** that drip into the
Matt	13:32	the air come and nest in its **b**
Mark	4:32	herbs, and shoots out large **b**
John	12:13	took **b** of palm trees and went
John	15: 5	I am the vine, you are the **b**
Rom	11:16	root is holy, so are the **b**
Rom	11:21	did not spare the natural **b**
Rev	7: 9	with palm **b** in their hands,

BRAND†
Zech	3: 2	Is this not a **b** plucked from

BRASS
1Co	13: 1	**b** or a clanging cymbal
Rev	1:15	His feet were like fine **b**

BRAVE†
1Co	16:13	stand fast in the faith, be **b**

BRAWLER
Prov	20: 1	Strong drink is a brawler

BREACH
Ps	106:23	one stood before Him in the **b**

BREAD
Gen	3:19	eat **b** till you return to the
Gen	14:18	king of Salem brought out **b**
Gen	19: 3	feast, and baked unleavened **b**
Gen	41:55	people cried to Pharaoh for **b**
Gen	47:13	was no **b** in all the land
Ex	12:15	you shall eat unleavened **b**
Ex	12:17	the Feast of Unleavened **B**
Ex	16: 4	I will rain **b** from heaven for
Deut	8: 3	man shall not live by **b** alone
Deut	16: 3	the **b** of affliction (for you
Ruth	1: 6	His people in giving them **b**
1Sa	21: 6	So the priest gave him holy **b**
1Ki	17: 6	The ravens brought him **b** and
Neh	9:15	You gave them **b** from heaven
Ps	37:25	Nor his descendants begging **b**
Ps	41: 9	whom I trusted, Who ate my **b**
Ps	78:24	given them of the **b** of heaven
Ps	80: 5	fed them with the **b** of tears
Ps	127: 2	late, To eat the **b** of sorrows
Ps	132:15	will satisfy her poor with **b**
Prov	4:17	they eat the **b** of wickedness
Prov	6:26	is reduced to a crust of **b**
Prov	9:17	**b** eaten in secret is pleasant
Prov	20:17	**B** gained by deceit is sweet
Prov	22: 9	he gives of his **b** to the poor
Prov	25:21	is hungry, give him **b** to eat
Prov	31:27	not eat the **b** of idleness
Eccl	9: 7	Go, eat your **b** with joy, and
Eccl	11: 1	Cast your **b** upon the waters,
Is	55: 2	spend money for what is not **b**
Is	55:10	the sower and **b** to the eater,
Is	58: 7	share your **b** with the hungry
Amos	7:12	There eat **b**, and there
Amos	8:11	the land, not a famine of **b**
Matt	4: 3	that these stones become **b**
Matt	4: 4	Man shall not live by **b** alone
Matt	6:11	Give us this day our daily **b**
Matt	7: 9	who, if his son asks for **b**
Matt	26:26	were eating, Jesus took **b**
Mark	7: 2	disciples eat **b** with defiled
Mark	7: 5	but eat **b** with unwashed hands
Mark	14: 1	and the Feast of Unleavened **B**
Mark	14:12	the first day of Unleavened **B**
Luke	7:33	eating **b** nor drinking wine
Luke	11: 3	us day by day our daily **b**
Luke	14: 1	to eat **b** on the Sabbath, that
Luke	14:15	eat **b** in the kingdom of God
Luke	15:17	hired servants have **b** enough
Luke	22: 7	came the Day of Unleavened **B**

Luke	22:19	And He took **b**, gave thanks and
Luke	24:35	to them in the breaking of **b**
John	6:31	He gave them **b** from heaven
John	6:32	you the true **b** from heaven
John	6:33	For the **b** of God is He who
John	6:34	Lord, give us this **b** always
John	6:35	I am the **b** of life
John	6:41	I am the **b** which came down
John	6:51	I am the living **b** which came
John	6:51	the **b** that I shall give is My
John	6:58	He who eats this **b** will live
John	13:26	of **b** when I have dipped it
John	21: 9	and fish laid on it, and **b**
Acts	2:42	in the breaking of **b**, and in
Acts	2:46	and breaking **b** from house to
Acts	27:35	said these things, he took **b**
1Co	5: 8	the unleavened **b** of sincerity
1Co	10:16	The **b** which we break, is it
1Co	10:17	For we, though many, are one **b**
1Co	10:17	we all partake of that one **b**
1Co	11:23	which He was betrayed took **b**
1Co	11:26	as often as you eat this **b**
1Co	11:27	**b** or drinks this cup of the

BREADTH

Judg	20:16	sling a stone at a hair's **b**
Rev	21:16	Its length, **b**, and height are

BREAK (see BREAKING, BREAKS, BROKE, BROKEN)

Gen	19: 9	came near to **b** down the door
Ex	9: 9	that **b** out in sores on man
Ex	12:46	nor shall you **b** one of its
Ex	13:13	it, then you shall **b** its neck
Lev	26:15	but **b** My covenant,
Num	9:12	nor **b** one of its bones
Deut	21: 4	they shall **b** the heifer's
Ps	2: 3	Let us **b** Their bonds in
Ps	2: 9	You shall **b** them with a rod
Ps	58: 6	**B** their teeth in their mouth,
Ps	89:31	If they **b** My statutes And do
Ps	98: 4	**B** forth in song, rejoice, and
Eccl	3: 3	a time to **b** down, and a time
Is	42: 3	A bruised reed He will not **b**
Jer	4: 3	**B** up your fallow ground, and
Jer	19:10	Then you shall **b** the flask in
Jer	28: 4	for I will **b** the yoke of the
Hos	10:12	**b** up your fallow ground, for
Matt	6:19	destroy and where thieves **b** in
Matt	9:17	or else the wineskins **b**, the
Matt	12:20	A bruised reed He will not **b**
John	19:33	dead, they did not **b** His legs
Acts	20: 7	came together to **b** bread,
1Co	10:16	The bread which we **b**, is it

BREAKING (see BREAK)

Ex	22: 2	If the thief is found **b** in
Luke	24:35	to them in the **b** of bread
Rom	2:23	God through **b** the law

BREAKS (see BREAK)

Gen	32:26	Let Me go, for the day **b**
Lev	13:12	if leprosy **b** out all over the
Ps	29: 5	of the LORD **b** the cedars, Yes

Prov	25:15	and a gentle tongue **b** a bone
Jer	19:11	as one **b** a potter's vessel,
Dan	2:40	inasmuch as iron **b** in pieces

BREAST (see BREASTPLATE, BREASTS)

Ex	29:26	the **b** of the ram of Aaron's
Luke	18:13	to heaven, but beat his **b**
John	13:25	leaning back on Jesus' **b**
John	21:20	leaned on His **b** at the supper

BREASTPLATE (see BREAST)

Ex	28: 4	a **b**, an ephod, a robe, a
Is	59:17	put on righteousness as a **b**
Eph	6:14	put on the **b** of righteousness
1Th	5: 8	putting on the **b** of faith

BREASTS (see BREAST)

Ps	22: 9	while on My mother's **b**
Song	1:13	lies all night between my **b**
Song	4: 5	Your two **b** are like two fawns
Hos	2: 2	adulteries from between her **b**
Luke	11:27	and the **b** which nursed You

BREATH (see BREATHE)

Gen	2: 7	his nostrils the **b** of life
Gen	7:22	the **b** of the spirit of life
2Sa	22:16	of the **b** of His nostrils
Job	4: 9	by the **b** of His anger they
Job	7: 7	remember that my life is a **b**
Job	9:18	not allow me to catch my **b**
Job	15:30	by the **b** of His mouth he will
Job	19:17	My **b** is offensive to my wife,
Job	32: 8	the **b** of the Almighty gives
Job	34:14	Himself His Spirit and His **b**
Ps	104:29	You take away their **b**, they
Ps	144: 4	Man is like a **b**
Ps	150: 6	that has **b** praise the LORD
Ezek	37: 6	you with skin and put **b** in you
Acts	17:25	since He gives to all life, **b**
2Th	2: 8	with the **b** of His mouth and
Rev	13:15	**b** to the image of the beast

BREATHE† (see BREATH, BREATHED, BREATHING)

Ps	27:12	me, And such as **b** out violence
Ezek	37: 9	**b** on these slain, that they

BREATHED (see BREATHE)

Gen	2: 7	and **b** into his nostrils the
Gen	25: 8	Then Abraham **b** his last and
Mark	15:37	a loud voice, and **b** His last
John	20:22	He **b** on them, and said to them

BREATHING (see BREATHE)

Acts	9: 1	still **b** threats and murder

BRETHREN (see BROTHER)

Gen	13: 8	your herdsmen; for we are **b**
Deut	17:15	one from among your **b** you
Deut	18:18	like you from among their **b**
Ruth	4:10	be cut off from among his **b**
Ps	133: 1	how pleasant it is For **b** to
Prov	6:19	one who sows discord among **b**
Matt	23: 8	the Christ, and you are all **b**

Matt	25:40	of the least of these My **b**
Matt	28:10	tell My **b** to go to Galilee,
Luke	22:32	to Me, strengthen your **b**
John	20:17	but go to My **b** and say to them
Acts	1:16	Men and **b**, this Scripture had
Acts	3:22	a Prophet like me from your **b**
Rom	1:13	not want you to be unaware, **b**
Rom	8:29	be the firstborn among many **b**
Rom	9: 3	accursed from Christ for my **b**
Rom	10: 1	**B**, my heart's desire and
Rom	12: 1	I beseech you therefore, **b**
1Co	1:26	For you see your calling, **b**
1Co	8:12	you thus sin against the **b**
1Co	15: 6	over five hundred **b** at once
2Co	1: 8	want you to be ignorant, **b**
2Co	11:26	sea, in perils among false **b**
Eph	6:10	Finally, my **b**, be strong in
Eph	6:23	Peace to the **b**, and love with
Phil	1:12	But I want you to know, **b**
Phil	3: 1	Finally, my **b**, rejoice in the
Phil	4: 8	Finally, **b**, whatever things
Col	1: 2	faithful **b** in Christ who are
1Th	1: 4	knowing, beloved **b**, your
1Th	4:13	want you to be ignorant, **b**
1Th	5:25	**B**, pray for us
1Th	5:26	Greet all the **b** with a holy
2Th	2: 1	Now, **b**, concerning the coming
2Th	2:13	you, **b** beloved by the Lord,
2Th	2:15	Therefore, **b**, stand fast and
2Th	3: 1	Finally, **b**, pray for us, that
Heb	2:11	is not ashamed to call them **b**
Heb	2:12	declare Your name to My **b**
Heb	2:17	He had to be made like His **b**
Heb	3: 1	Therefore, holy **b**, partakers
Heb	10:19	Therefore, **b**, having boldness
Heb	13:22	And I appeal to you, **b**, bear
Jas	1: 2	My **b**, count it all joy when
Jas	1:16	not be deceived, my beloved **b**
1Pe	1:22	in sincere love of the **b**,
1Jn	2: 7	**B**, I write no new commandment
1Jn	3:13	Do not marvel, my **b**, if the
1Jn	3:14	life, because we love the **b**
1Jn	3:16	lay down our lives for the **b**
Rev	12:10	for the accuser of our **b**
Rev	22: 9	of your **b** the prophets, and of

BRIBE

Ex	23: 8	And you shall take no **b**, for a
Ex	23: 8	for a **b** blinds the discerning
Deut	10:17	no partiality nor takes a **b**

BRICK (see BRICKS)

Gen	11: 3	They had **b** for stone, and
Ex	1:14	in mortar, in **b**, and in all
Ex	5: 7	straw to make **b** as before

BRICKS (see BRICK)

Gen	11: 3	Come, let us make **b** and bake

BRIDE (see BRIDEGROOM)

Is	49:18	bind them on you as a **b** does
Is	61:10	as a **b** adorns herself with
Is	62: 5	rejoices over the **b**, so shall
Jer	7:34	and the voice of the **b**

Rev	21: 2	prepared as a **b** adorned for
Rev	22:17	And the Spirit and the **b** say

BRIDEGROOM (see BRIDE)

Ps	19: 5	Which is like a **b** coming out
Is	62: 5	as the **b** rejoices over the
Jer	7:34	gladness, the voice of the **b**
Matt	9:15	Can the friends of the **b** mourn
Matt	9:15	as long as the **b** is with them
Matt	25: 1	and went out to meet the **b**
Matt	25: 6	Behold, the **b** is coming
Mark	2:19	Can the friends of the **b** fast
John	2: 9	of the feast called the **b**
Rev	18:23	And the voice of the **b** and bride

BRIDLE

Prov	26: 3	a **b** for the donkey, and a rod
Jas	1:26	does not **b** his tongue but
Jas	3: 2	able also to **b** the whole body

BRIGHT (see BRIGHTER, BRIGHTNESS)

Rev	19: 8	in fine linen, clean and **b**
Rev	22:16	the Offspring of David, the **B**

BRIGHTER (see BRIGHT)

Prov	4:18	that shines ever **b** unto the
Acts	26:13	**b** than the sun, shining

BRIGHTNESS (see BRIGHT)

Ezek	1: 4	and **b** was all around it and
Ezek	10: 4	of the **b** of the LORD's glory
Dan	12: 3	like the **b** of the firmament
2Th	2: 8	with the **b** of His coming
Heb	1: 3	who being the **b** of His glory

BRIM

John	2: 7	they filled them up to the **b**

BRIMSTONE

Gen	19:24	Then the LORD rained **b** and
Luke	17:29	**b** from heaven and destroyed
Rev	9:17	mouths came fire, smoke, and **b**
Rev	19:20	lake of fire burning with **b**

BROAD (see WIDE)

Ps	119:96	commandment is exceedingly **b**
Amos	8: 9	the earth in **b** daylight
Matt	7:13	**b** is the way that leads to
Matt	23: 5	make their phylacteries **b**

BROKE (see BREAK)

Ex	34: 1	the first tablets which you **b**
Num	2:34	standards and so they **b** camp
Deut	10: 2	first tablets, which you **b**
Judg	7:20	trumpets and **b** the pitchers
Judg	15:14	his bonds **b** loose from his
Judg	16: 9	But he **b** the bowstrings as
Judg	16:12	But he **b** them off his arms
1Sa	5: 9	and tumors **b** out on them
1Ki	19:11	**b** the rocks in pieces before
2Ki	10:27	Then they **b** down the sacred
2Ki	14:13	**b** down the wall of Jerusalem
1Ch	15:13	LORD our God **b** out against us
1Ch	20: 4	war **b** out at Gezer with the

2Ch	26:19	leprosy **b** out on his forehead
Job	29:17	I **b** the fangs of the wicked,
Ps	74:13	You **b** the heads of the sea
Ps	74:14	You **b** the heads of Leviathan
Ps	74:15	You **b** open the fountain and
Ps	76: 3	There He **b** the arrows of the
Ps	106:29	the plague **b** out among them
Jer	28:10	Jeremiah's neck and **b** it
Jer	31:32	My covenant which they **b**
Ezek	17:16	and whose covenant he **b**
Dan	2:34	and clay, and **b** them in pieces
Dan	2:45	that it **b** in pieces the iron,
Dan	7:19	**b** in pieces, and trampled the
Dan	8: 7	the ram, and **b** his two horns
Matt	14:19	up to heaven, He blessed and **b**
Matt	15:36	**b** them and gave them to His
Matt	26:26	and **b** it, and gave it to the
Mark	8:19	When I **b** the five loaves for
Mark	8:20	when I **b** the seven for the
Mark	14: 3	she **b** the flask and poured it
John	5:18	He not only **b** the Sabbath
John	19:32	**b** the legs of the first and of
1Co	11:24	He had given thanks, He **b** it
Rev	12: 7	And war **b** out in heaven

BROKEN (see BREAK, BROKE,
  BROKENHEARTED, DASHED)

Gen	7:11	of the great deep were **b** up
Gen	17:14	he has **b** My covenant
Lev	13:20	which has **b** out of the boil
Num	15:31	has **b** His commandment, that
Ps	34:20	Not one of them is **b**
Ps	51: 8	You have **b** may rejoice
Ps	51:17	a **b** spirit, A **b** and a
Ps	55:20	He has **b** his covenant
Prov	6:15	he shall be **b** without remedy
Eccl	4:12	cord is not quickly **b**
Eccl	12: 6	or the golden bowl is **b**, or
Eccl	12: 6	or the wheel **b** at the well
Is	24: 5	**B** the everlasting covenant
Is	36: 6	in the staff of this **b** reed
Jer	2:13	**b** cisterns that can hold no
Jer	23: 9	My heart within me is **b**
Jer	28: 2	I have **b** the yoke of the
Lam	3:16	He has also **b** my teeth with
Dan	11: 4	his kingdom shall be **b** up
Jon	1: 4	the ship was about to be **b** up
Matt	21:44	falls on this stone will be **b**
Matt	24:43	his house to be **b** into
Mark	2: 4	And when they had **b** through
Mark	5: 4	and the shackles **b** in pieces
Luke	20:18	falls on that stone will be **b**
John	7:23	law of Moses should not be **b**
John	10:35	and the Scripture cannot be **b**)
John	19:31	that their legs might be **b**
John	19:36	one of His bones shall be **b**
John	21:11	so many, the net was not **b**
Rom	11:17	of the branches were **b** off
Rom	11:19	Branches were **b** off that I
1Co	11:24	is My body which is **b** for you
Eph	2:14	has **b** down the middle wall of

BROKENHEARTED† (see BROKEN, HEART)

Ps	147: 3	He heals the **b** And binds up

Is	61: 1	He has sent Me to heal the **b**
Luke	4:18	He has sent Me to heal the **b**

BRONZE

Gen	4:22	of every craftsman in **b** and
Ex	25: 3	gold, silver, and **b**
Num	21: 9	he looked at the **b** serpent
Judg	16:21	They bound him with **b** fetters
1Sa	17: 5	He had a **b** helmet on his head
2Sa	22:35	my arms can bend a bow of **b**
1Ki	14:27	made **b** shields in their place
2Ki	18: 4	broke in pieces the **b** serpent
Ps	18:34	my arms can bend a bow of **b**
Jer	1:18	**b** walls against the whole
Jer	15:20	people a fortified **b** wall
Jer	39: 7	bound him with **b** fetters to
Ezek	1: 7	like the color of burnished **b**
Dan	2:32	its belly and thighs of **b**
Dan	2:39	another, a third kingdom of **b**
Dan	10: 6	like burnished **b** in color
Zech	6: 1	mountains were mountains of **b**
Rev	18:12	of most precious wood, **b**,

BROOD

Is	1: 4	a **b** of evildoers, children
Matt	3: 7	said to them, "**B** of vipers
Luke	13:34	gathers her **b** under her wings

BROOK (see BROOKS)

Gen	32:23	them, sent them over the **b**
Lev	23:40	trees, and willows of the **b**
Josh	15:47	as far as the **B** of Egypt and
1Sa	17:40	five smooth stones from the **b**
2Sa	15:23	crossed over the **B** Kidron
1Ki	8:65	of Hamath to the **B** of Egypt
1Ki	17: 5	and stayed by the **B** Cherith
1Ki	17: 7	a while that the **b** dried up
1Ki	18:40	them down to the **B** Kishon
2Ki	23: 6	burned it at the **B** Kidron
2Ki	24: 7	the **B** of Egypt to the River
Job	6:15	dealt deceitfully like a **b**
Job	40:22	willows by the **b** surround him
Ps	110: 7	drink of the **b** by the wayside
Prov	18: 4	of wisdom is a flowing **b**
Is	15: 7	away to the **B** of the Willows
John	18: 1	disciples over the **B** Kidron

BROOKS (see BROOK)

Deut	8: 7	land, a land of **b** of water
Job	6:15	of the **b** that pass away,
Job	22:24	among the stones of the **b**
Ps	42: 1	deer pants for the water **b**

BROOM

1Ki	19: 4	and sat down under a **b** tree

BROTHER (see BRETHREN, BROTHERHOOD,
  BROTHERLY, BROTHER'S, BROTHERS)

Gen	4: 8	Cain rose against Abel his **b**
Gen	9: 5	the hand of every man's **b** I
Gen	27:40	and you shall serve your **b**
Gen	42:15	your youngest **b** comes here
Gen	43: 3	unless your **b** is with you
Gen	45: 4	I am Joseph your **b**, whom you

Lev	19:17	not hate your **b** in your heart
Deut	15:12	If your **b**, a Hebrew man, or a
Deut	17:15	over you, who is not your **b**
Deut	23: 7	an Edomite, for he is your **b**
Deut	23:19	not charge interest to your **b**
Deut	25: 5	duty of a husband's **b** to her
Deut	25: 6	to the name of his dead **b**
2Sa	1:26	for you, my **b** Jonathan
2Sa	13:12	No, my **b**, do not force me,
Neh	5: 7	is exacting usury from his **b**
Ps	35:14	though he were my friend or **b**
Ps	49: 7	can by any means redeem his **b**
Ps	50:20	sit and speak against your **b**
Prov	17:17	a **b** is born for adversity
Prov	18:24	who sticks closer than a **b**
Prov	27:10	nearby than a **b** far away
Jer	31:34	neighbor, and every man his **b**
Jer	34: 9	keep a Jewish **b** in bondage
Jer	34:14	man set free his Hebrew **b**
Hos	12: 3	He took his **b** by the heel in
Mal	1: 2	Was not Esau Jacob's **b**
Matt	5:22	whoever is angry with his **b**
Matt	5:24	First be reconciled to your **b**
Matt	7: 4	Or how can you say to your **b**
Matt	10:21	Now **b** will deliver up **b**
Matt	17: 1	Peter, James, and John his **b**
Matt	18:15	if your **b** sins against you
Matt	22:24	his **b** shall marry his wife and
Matt	22:24	raise up offspring for his **b**
Mark	3:35	does the will of God is My **b**
Mark	12:19	to us that if a man's **b** dies
Mark	12:19	his **b** should take his wife and
Mark	12:19	raise up offspring for his **b**
Luke	3: 1	his **b** Philip tetrarch of
Luke	12:13	tell my **b** to divide the
Luke	15:32	be glad, for your **b** was dead
Luke	17: 3	If your **b** sins against you,
John	1:41	first found his own **b** Simon
John	11: 2	whose **b** Lazarus was sick
John	11:21	my **b** would not have died
John	11:23	her, "Your **b** will rise again
Acts	9:17	**B** Saul, the Lord Jesus, who
Acts	12: 2	the **b** of John with the sword
Rom	14:10	But why do you judge your **b**
Rom	14:10	you show contempt for your **b**
1Co	6: 6	**b** goes to law against **b**
1Co	7:12	If any **b** has a wife who does
1Co	8:11	shall the weak **b** perish, for
1Co	8:13	if food makes my **b** stumble
1Co	16:12	Now concerning our **b** Apollos
2Co	1: 1	will of God, and Timothy our **b**
2Co	2:13	I did not find Titus my **b**
Gal	1:19	except James, the Lord's **b**
Eph	6:21	doing, Tychicus, a beloved **b**
Col	1: 1	will of God, and Timothy our **b**
Col	4: 9	a faithful and beloved **b**, who
1Th	4: 6	defraud his **b** in this matter,
2Th	3: 6	every **b** who walks disorderly
2Th	3:15	but admonish him as a **b**
Phm	16	than a slave, as a beloved **b**
Heb	8:11	his neighbor, and none his **b**
Jas	1: 9	Let the lowly **b** glory in his
Jas	2:15	If a **b** or sister is naked and
Jas	4:11	He who speaks evil of a **b**
1Pe	5:12	our faithful **b** as I consider
2Pe	3:15	as also our beloved **b** Paul
1Jn	2: 9	in the light, and hates his **b**
1Jn	2:10	He who loves his **b** abides in
1Jn	3:17	goods, and sees his **b** in need
1Jn	5:16	If anyone sees his **b** sinning
Jude	1	**b** of James, To those who are
Rev	1: 9	I, John, both your **b** and

BROTHERHOOD (*see* BROTHER)

Amos	1: 9	remember the covenant of **b**
1Pe	2:17	Love the **b**. Fear God

BROTHERLY (*see* BROTHER)

Rom	12:10	to one another with **b** love
Heb	13: 1	Let **b** love continue
2Pe	1: 7	to godliness **b** kindness, and

BROTHER'S (*see* BROTHER)

Gen	4: 9	Am I my **b** keeper
Gen	4:10	The voice of your **b** blood
Gen	38: 8	Go in to your **b** wife and marry
Mark	6:18	for you to have your **b** wife

BROTHERS (*see* BROTHER)

Gen	9:22	and told his two **b** outside
Gen	37: 5	dream, and he told it to his **b**
Gen	37:11	his **b** envied him, but his
Gen	37:28	so the **b** pulled Joseph up and
Gen	42: 3	So Joseph's ten **b** went down
Gen	42: 4	brother Benjamin with his **b**
Gen	42: 6	And Joseph's **b** came and bowed
Gen	42:13	Your servants are twelve **b**
Gen	45: 1	made himself known to his **b**
Gen	45:15	Moreover he kissed all his **b**
Gen	49:26	who was separate from his **b**
Gen	50:15	When Joseph's **b** saw that
Lev	25:48	One of his **b** may redeem him
Deut	25: 5	If **b** dwell together, and one
Josh	2:13	my father, my mother, my **b**
Judg	9:56	by killing his seventy **b**
Judg	11: 3	Then Jephthah fled from his **b**
Judg	21:22	**b** come to us to complain,
1Sa	16:13	him in the midst of his **b**
1Ch	4: 9	was more honorable than his **b**
1Ch	5: 2	Judah prevailed over his **b**
Job	6:15	My **b** have dealt deceitfully
Job	19:13	has removed my **b** far from me
Job	42:15	an inheritance among their **b**
Ps	69: 8	become a stranger to my **b**
Prov	19: 7	All the **b** of the poor hate
Jer	12: 6	For even your **b**, the house of
Matt	1: 2	Jacob begot Judah and his **b**
Matt	12:46	**b** stood outside, seeking to
Matt	12:48	is My mother and who are My **b**
Matt	20:24	displeased with the two **b**
Matt	22:25	there were with us seven **b**
Mark	3:31	His **b** and His mother came
Mark	3:33	Who is My mother, or My **b**
Mark	3:34	Here are My mother and My **b**
Luke	14:26	mother, wife and children, **b**
Acts	7:13	was made known to his **b**, and
Acts	28:11	figurehead was the Twin **B**

1Co	9: 5	the **b** of the Lord, and Cephas
1Pe	3: 8	love as **b**, be tenderhearted,

BRUISE (*see* BRUISED, BRUISES)

Gen	3:15	He shall **b** your head, and you
Is	53:10	it pleased the LORD to **b** Him

BRUISED (*see* BRUISE)

Is	42: 3	A **b** reed He will not break,
Is	53: 5	He was **b** for our iniquities
Matt	12:20	A **b** reed He will not break,

BRUISES† (*see* BRUISE)

Job	5:18	For He **b**, but He binds up
Is	1: 6	in it, but wounds and **b** and

BUCKET†

Is	40:15	nations are as a drop in a **b**

BUCKLER

Ps	35: 2	Take hold of shield and **b**, And

BUDDED (*see* BUDDING, BUDS)

Heb	9: 4	the manna, Aaron's rod that **b**

BUDDING (*see* BUDDED, BUDS)

Luke	21:30	When they are already **b**, you

BUDS (*see* BUDDDED, BUDDING)

Num	17: 8	had sprouted and put forth **b**

BUILD (*see* BUILDER, BUILDING, BUILDS, BUILT)

Gen	11: 4	let us **b** ourselves a city, and
Josh	24:13	and cities which you did not **b**
2Sa	7: 5	Would you **b** a house for Me to
2Sa	7:13	He shall **b** a house for My
2Sa	7:27	saying, 'I will **b** you a house
1Ki	5: 5	I propose to **b** a house for
1Ch	28: 6	Solomon who shall **b** My house
2Ch	36:23	He has commanded me to **b**
Ezra	1: 2	He has commanded me to **b**
Neh	2:17	Come and let us **b** the wall of
Neh	2:18	Let us rise up and **b**
Neh	4:10	we are not able to **b** the wall
Ps	51:18	**B** the walls of Jerusalem
Ps	127: 1	They labor in vain who **b** it
Prov	24:27	and afterward **b** your house
Eccl	3: 3	break down, and a time to **b** up
Jer	1:10	and to throw down, to **b** and to
Jer	18: 9	and concerning a kingdom, to **b**
Jer	29: 5	**B** houses and dwell in them
Dan	9:25	**b** Jerusalem until Messiah the
Matt	16:18	this rock I will **b** My church
Matt	26:61	God and to **b** it in three days
John	2:20	years to **b** this temple, and
Acts	7:49	What house will you **b** for Me
Acts	20:32	which is able to **b** you up
Rom	15:20	lest I should **b** on another
Gal	2:18	For if I **b** again those things

BUILDER† (*see* BUILD, BUILDERS)

1Co	3:10	as a wise master **b** I have
Heb	11:10	has foundations, whose **b** and

BUILDERS (*see* BUILDER)

1Ki	5:18	Solomon's **b**, Hiram's **b**
2Ki	12:11	**b** who worked on the house of
Ps	118:22	The stone which the **b**
Matt	21:42	The stone which the **b**
Acts	4:11	which was rejected by you **b**
1Pe	2: 7	The stone which the **b**

BUILDING (*see* BUILD)

Gen	11: 8	and they ceased **b** the city
1Ki	6:38	So he was seven years in **b** it
Ezra	4: 4	They troubled them in **b**,
Luke	6:48	He is like a man **b** a house
1Co	3: 9	God's field, you are God's **b**
2Co	5: 1	we have a **b** from God, a
Eph	2:21	in whom the whole **b**, being
Jude	20	**b** yourselves up on your most

BUILDS (*see* BUILD)

Ps	127: 1	Unless the LORD **b** the house
Ps	147: 2	The LORD **b** up Jerusalem
1Co	3:10	one take heed how he **b** on it
1Co	3:12	Now if anyone **b** on this

BUILT (*see* BUILD)

Gen	4:17	he **b** a city, and called the
Gen	8:20	Then Noah **b** an altar to the
Gen	11: 5	which the sons of men had **b**
Gen	12: 7	there he **b** an altar to the
Ex	1:11	they **b** for Pharaoh supply
Ex	17:15	Moses **b** an altar and called
Ex	24: 4	**b** an altar at the foot of the
Ezra	6:14	And they **b** and finished it,
Neh	4: 6	so we **b** the wall, and the
Ps	122: 3	Jerusalem is **b** As a city that
Prov	9: 1	Wisdom has **b** her house, she
Prov	24: 3	Through wisdom a house is **b**
Eccl	2: 4	I **b** myself houses, and planted
Is	5: 2	He **b** a tower in its midst, and
Jer	7:31	they have **b** the high places
Jer	30:18	the city shall be **b** upon its
Jer	45: 4	what I have **b** I will break
Jer	52: 4	they **b** a siege wall against
Dan	4:30	that I have **b** for a royal
Dan	9:25	the street shall be **b** again
Amos	5:11	though you have **b** houses of
Hag	1: 2	the LORD's house should be **b**
Zech	1:16	my house shall be **b** in it
Zech	8: 9	that the temple might be **b**
Matt	7:24	who **b** his house on the rock
Matt	7:26	who **b** his house on the sand
Matt	21:33	winepress in it and **b** a tower
Mark	12: 1	for the wine vat and **b** a tower
Luke	4:29	on which their city was **b**
Luke	7: 5	and has **b** us a synagogue
Luke	17:28	sold, they planted, they **b**
Acts	7:47	But Solomon **b** Him a house
Eph	2:22	**b** together for a habitation
Col	2: 7	**b** up in Him and established in
1Pe	2: 5	are being **b** up a spiritual

BULL (*see* BULLS)

Ex	29: 1	Take one young **b** and two rams

Ex	29:10	hands on the head of the **b**
Ex	29:11	kill the **b** before the LORD
Ex	29:12	some of the blood of the **b**
Lev	4: 3	**b** without blemish as a sin
Lev	4:21	carry the **b** outside the camp
1Ki	18:23	choose one **b** for themselves
1Ki	18:23	and I will prepare the other **b**
1Ki	18:33	cut the **b** in pieces, and laid

BULLS (*see* BULL)

Ps	22:12	Many **b** have surrounded Me
Ps	22:12	Strong **b** of Bashan have
Ps	51:19	shall offer **b** on Your altar
Is	1:11	not delight in the blood of **b**
Heb	9:13	For if the blood of **b** and
Heb	10: 4	possible that the blood of **b**

BULRUSHES†

Ex	2: 3	she took an ark of **b** for him

BURDEN (*see* BURDENED, BURDENS, BURDENSOME)

Gen	49:15	his shoulder to bear a **b**, and
Ex	18:22	they shall bear the **b** with you
Ps	55:22	Cast your **b** on the LORD, And
Ps	81: 6	his shoulder from the **b**
Eccl	12: 5	the grasshopper is a **b**, and
Is	9: 4	have broken the yoke of his **b**
Is	30:27	His anger, and His **b** is heavy
Is	46: 1	a **b** to the weary beast
Is	46: 2	they could not deliver the **b**
Jer	17:21	bear no **b** on the Sabbath day,
Ezek	12:10	This **b** concerns the prince in
Hos	8:10	because of the **b** of the king
Nah	1: 1	The **b** against Nineveh
Zeph	3:18	to whom its reproach is a **b**
Zech	9: 1	The **b** of the word of the LORD
Zech	12: 1	The **b** of the word of the LORD
Mal	1: 1	The **b** of the word of the LORD
Matt	11:30	yoke is easy and My **b** is light
Matt	20:12	to us who have borne the **b**
Acts	15:28	to lay upon you no greater **b**
2Co	11: 9	I was a **b** to no one, for what
2Co	12:16	as it may, I did not **b** you
Rev	2:24	I will put on you no other **b**

BURDENED (*see* BURDEN)

2Co	1: 8	that we were **b** beyond measure
2Co	5: 4	in this tent groan, being **b**
2Co	8:13	should be eased and you **b**
1Ti	5:16	and do not let the church be **b**

BURDENS (*see* BURDEN)

Gen	49:14	lying down between two **b**
Ex	1:11	to afflict them with their **b**
Ex	6: 6	under the **b** of the Egyptians
Deut	1:12	bear your problems and your **b**
Is	58: 6	to undo the heavy **b**, to let
Matt	23: 4	For they bind heavy **b**, hard
Luke	11:46	load men with **b** hard to bear
Luke	11:46	**b** with one of your fingers
Gal	6: 2	Bear one another's **b**, and so

BURDENSOME (*see* BURDEN)

1Ki	12: 4	lighten the **b** service of your
Is	15: 4	his life will be **b** to him
2Co	11: 9	myself from being **b** to you
1Jn	5: 3	His commandments are not **b**

BURIAL (*see* BURY)

Gen	23: 4	for a **b** place among you, that
Gen	23: 6	the choicest of our **b** places
Gen	47:30	and bury me in their **b** place
Gen	50:13	as property for a **b** place
Eccl	6: 3	or indeed he has no **b**, I say
Jer	22:19	buried with the **b** of a donkey
Ezek	39:11	Gog a **b** place there in Israel
Matt	26:12	My body, she did it for My **b**
Mark	14: 8	to anoint My body for **b**
John	12: 7	kept this for the day of My **b**
Acts	8: 2	men carried Stephen to his **b**

BURIED (*see* BURY)

Gen	15:15	you shall be **b** at a good old
Gen	23:19	Abraham **b** Sarah his wife in
Gen	25:10	Abraham was **b**, and Sarah
Gen	50:13	and **b** him in the cave of the
Judg	12:10	died and was **b** at Bethlehem
Ruth	1:17	die, and there will I be **b**
1Ki	2:10	was **b** in the City of David
1Ki	14:31	was **b** with his fathers in the
Matt	14:12	**b** it, and went and told Jesus
Luke	16:22	rich man also died and was **b**
Acts	2:29	that he is both dead and **b**
Acts	5: 6	up, carried him out, and **b** him
Acts	5: 9	**b** your husband are at the
Acts	5:10	her out, **b** her by her husband
Acts	13:36	was **b** with his fathers, and
Rom	6: 4	Therefore we were **b** with Him
1Co	15: 4	and that He was **b**, and that He
Col	2:12	**b** with Him in baptism, in

BURN (*see* BURNED, BURNING, BURNS, BURNT)

Ex	3: 3	why the bush does not **b**
Ex	12:10	morning you shall **b** with fire
Ex	21:25	**b** for **b**, wound for wound,
Ex	27:20	the lamp to **b** continually
Ex	29:13	them, and **b** them on the altar
Ex	32:10	wrath may **b** hot against them
Deut	12:31	for they **b** even their sons and
Deut	32:22	shall **b** to the lowest hell
Josh	11: 6	**b** their chariots with fire
Is	1:31	both will **b** together, and no
Jer	4: 4	**b** so that no one can quench
Jer	7: 9	**b** incense to Baal, and walk
Jer	7:31	to **b** their sons and their
Jer	36:25	the king not to **b** the scroll
Jer	44:17	to **b** incense to the queen of
Mal	4: 1	is coming shall **b** them up
Matt	3:12	but He will **b** up the chaff
Matt	13:30	them in bundles to **b** them
Luke	1: 9	his lot fell to **b** incense
Luke	3:17	but the chaff He will **b** with
Luke	24:32	Did not our heart **b** within us
1Co	7: 9	marry than to **b** with passion

| 2Co | 11:29 | I do not **b** with indignation |
| Rev | 17:16 | her flesh and **b** her with fire |

BURNED (see BURN)

Gen	38:24	Bring her out and let her be **b**
Ex	32:20	**b** it in the fire, and ground
Deut	4:11	the mountain **b** with fire to
Josh	6:24	But they **b** the city and all
Josh	11: 9	**b** their chariots with fire
Josh	11:11	Then he **b** Hazor with fire
Josh	11:13	Israel **b** none of them, except
Judg	15:14	like flax that is **b** with fire
1Ki	3: 3	**b** incense at the high places
1Ki	9:16	**b** it with fire, had killed
1Ki	13: 2	men's bones shall be **b** on you
1Ki	15:13	and **b** it by the Brook Kidron
1Ki	16:18	**b** the king's house down upon
2Ki	1:14	**b** up the first two captains
2Ki	10:26	the temple of Baal and **b** them
2Ki	23: 6	**b** it at the Brook Kidron and
2Ki	23:11	he **b** the chariots of the sun
2Ki	23:15	and **b** the wooden image
2Ki	23:20	and **b** men's bones on them
2Ki	25: 9	He **b** the house of the LORD and
2Ki	25: 9	the great men, he **b** with fire
2Ch	36:19	**b** all its palaces with fire,
Neh	1: 3	and its gates are **b** with fire
Neh	4: 2	stones that are **b**
Esth	1:12	and his anger **b** within him
Job	1:16	and **b** up the sheep and the
Ps	39: 3	I was musing, the fire **b**
Ps	74: 8	They have **b** up all the
Ps	80:16	It is **b** with fire, it is cut
Ps	102: 3	my bones are **b** like a hearth
Ps	106:18	The flame **b** up the wicked
Prov	6:27	and his clothes not be **b**
Is	5: 5	its hedge, and it shall be **b**
Is	9:19	of hosts the land is **b** up
Is	24: 6	of the earth are **b**, and few
Is	44:19	I have **b** half of it in the
Jer	19:13	on whose roofs they have **b**
Jer	36:29	You have **b** this scroll,
Jer	39: 8	the Chaldeans **b** the king's
Jer	49: 2	villages shall be **b** with fire
Jer	51:30	they have **b** her dwelling
Jer	51:32	reeds they have **b** with fire
Hos	11: 2	**b** incense to carved images
Joel	1:19	a flame has **b** all the trees
Amos	2: 1	because he **b** the bones of the
Matt	13:40	**b** in the fire, so it will be
Matt	22: 7	murderers, and **b** up their city
John	15: 6	into the fire, and they are **b**
Rom	1:27	**b** in their lust for one
1Co	3:15	If anyone's work is **b**, he
1Co	13: 3	though I give my body to be **b**
Heb	6: 8	cursed, whose end is to be **b**
Heb	12:18	and that **b** with fire, and to
Heb	13:11	sin, are **b** outside the camp
2Pe	3:10	that are in it will be **b** up
Rev	8: 7	third of the trees were **b** up
Rev	8: 7	and all green grass was **b** up
Rev	18: 8	will be utterly **b** with fire

BURNING (see BURN)

Gen	15:17	a **b** torch that passed between
Ex	3: 2	the bush was **b** with fire, but the
Deut	5:23	the mountain was **b** with fire
Ps	58: 9	As in His living and **b** wrath
Ps	140:10	Let **b** coals fall upon them
Prov	16:27	is on his lips like a **b** fire
Is	4: 4	and by the spirit of **b**,
Jer	20: 9	a **b** fire shut up in my bones
Dan	3: 6	midst of a **b** fiery furnace
Amos	4:11	firebrand plucked from the **b**
Mal	4: 1	**b** like an oven, and all the
Mark	12:26	in the **b** bush passage, how
Luke	12:35	be girded and your lamps **b**
John	5:35	He was the **b** and shining lamp,
Rev	4: 5	of fire were **b** before the throne
Rev	8: 8	like a great mountain **b** with
Rev	8:10	**b** like a torch, and it fell on
Rev	18: 9	they see the smoke of her **b**
Rev	19:20	lake of fire **b** with brimstone

BURNS (see BURN)

Ps	97: 3	**b** up His enemies round about
Is	44:16	He **b** half of it in the fire
Rev	21: 8	in the lake which **b** with fire

BURNT (see BURN)

Gen	8:20	offered **b** offerings on the
Gen	22: 2	and offer him there as a **b**
Gen	22: 3	the wood for the **b** offering
Gen	22: 7	is the lamb for a **b** offering
Gen	22:13	ram, and offered it up for a **b**
Ex	30:28	the altar of **b** offering with
1Sa	15:22	great delight in **b** offerings
1Ki	18:33	and pour it on the **b** sacrifice
1Ki	18:38	and consumed the **b** sacrifice
2Ki	3:27	offered him as a **b** offering
Ps	51:16	do not delight in **b** offering
Ps	66:13	Your house with **b** offerings
Ps	66:15	I will offer You **b** sacrifices
Is	1:11	enough of **b** offerings of rams
Is	40:16	sufficient for a **b** offering
Is	61: 8	I hate robbery for **b** offering
Jer	19: 5	fire for **b** offerings to Baal
Jer	51:25	and make you a **b** mountain
Ezek	40:38	they washed the **b** offering
Ezek	46:12	prince makes a voluntary **b**
Hos	6: 6	of God more than **b** offerings
Mic	6: 6	before Him with **b** offerings
Mark	12:33	all the whole **b** offerings
Heb	10: 6	In **b** offerings and sacrifices

BURST (see BURSTS)

Judg	20:33	**b** forth from their position
Job	32:19	it is ready to **b** like new
Job	38: 8	with doors, when it **b** forth
Is	35: 6	For waters shall **b** forth in
Jer	2:20	your yoke and **b** your bonds
Luke	5:37	new wine will **b** the wineskins
Acts	1:18	he **b** open in the middle and

BURSTS† (see BURST)

| Mark | 2:22 | the new wine **b** the wineskins |

BURY (see BURIAL, BURIED)

Gen	23: 4	that I may **b** my dead out of
Gen	47:29	Please do not **b** me in Egypt
Jer	7:32	for they will **b** in Tophet
Jer	19:11	till there is no place to **b**
Ezek	39:11	because there they will **b** Gog
Ezek	39:14	**b** those bodies remaining on
Matt	8:21	me first go and **b** my father
Matt	8:22	let the dead **b** their own dead
Matt	27: 7	field, to **b** strangers in

BUSH

Ex	3: 2	the **b** was burning with fire, but
Deut	33:16	of Him who dwelt in the **b**
Mark	12:26	in the burning **b** passage
Acts	7:30	him in a flame of fire in a **b**
Acts	7:35	who appeared to him in the **b**

BUSINESS

Dan	8:27	and went about the king's **b**
Luke	2:49	I must be about My Father's **b**
1Th	4:11	life, to mind your own **b**, and

BUSY

1Ki	18:27	he is meditating, or he is **b**

BUSYBODIES† (see BUSYBODY)

2Th	3:11	not working at all, but are **b**
1Ti	5:13	idle but also gossips and **b**

BUSYBODY† (see BUSYBODIES)

1Pe	4:15	or as a **b** in other people's

BUTLER

Gen	40: 1	after these things that the **b**

BUY (see BOUGHT, BUYS)

Gen	41:57	to Joseph in Egypt to **b** grain
Ex	21: 2	If you **b** a Hebrew servant, he
Ruth	4: 5	On the day you **b** the field
Ruth	4: 5	you must also **b** it from Ruth
Prov	23:23	**B** the truth, and do not sell
Is	55: 1	who have no money, come, **b**
Is	55: 1	**b** wine and milk without money
Jer	32: 7	**B** my field which is in
Amos	8: 6	that we may **b** the poor for
Matt	14:15	villages and **b** themselves food
Matt	25:10	And while they went to **b**, the
Mark	6:36	and **b** themselves bread
Mark	6:37	**b** two hundred denarii worth
Luke	9:13	**b** food for all these people
Luke	22:36	him sell his garment and **b** one
John	4: 8	away into the city to **b** food
John	6: 5	Where shall we **b** bread, that
John	13:29	**B** those things we need for
1Co	7:30	those who **b** as though they
Jas	4:13	a city, spend a year there, **b**
Rev	3:18	I counsel you to **b** from Me
Rev	13:17	that no one may **b** or sell

BUYS† (see BUY)

Lev	22:11	But if the priest **b** a person
Prov	31:16	She considers a field and **b** it

Matt	13:44	that he has and **b** that field
Rev	18:11	over her, for no one **b** their

BYWORD

Deut	28:37	a **b** among all nations where
1Ki	9: 7	and a **b** among all peoples
Job	30: 9	yes, I am their **b**
Ps	69:11	I became a **b** to them
Jer	24: 9	harm, to be a reproach and a **b**
Ezek	16:56	a **b** in your mouth in the days
Ezek	23:10	She became a **b** among women

C

CAESAR (see AUGUSTUS, CAESAR'S, CLAUDIUS, TIBERIUS)

Matt	22:17	it lawful to pay taxes to **C**
Mark	12:17	Render to **C** the things that
Luke	2: 1	**C** Augustus that all the world
Luke	3: 1	of the reign of Tiberius **C**
John	19:12	a king speaks against **C**
John	19:15	We have no king but **C**
Acts	11:28	in the days of Claudius **C**
Acts	17: 7	contrary to the decrees of **C**
Acts	25: 8	nor against **C** have I offended
Acts	25:11	me to them. I appeal to **C**

CAESAREA

Acts	8:40	the cities till he came to **C**
Acts	10: 1	man in **C** called Cornelius
Acts	25:13	came to **C** to greet Festus

CAESAREA PHILIPPI

Matt	16:13	came into the region of **C**

CAESAR'S (see CAESAR)

John	19:12	Man go, you are not **C** friend
Acts	25:10	I stand at **C** judgment seat,
Phil	4:22	those who are of **C** household

CAIAPHAS

Matt	26:57	Him away to **C** the high priest
Luke	3: 2	**C** were high priests, the
Acts	4: 6	as Annas the high priest, **C**

CAIN

Gen	4: 1	and she conceived and bore **C**
Gen	4: 8	that **C** rose against Abel his
Gen	4:15	And the Lord set a mark on **C**
Heb	11: 4	excellent sacrifice than **C**
1Jn	3:12	not as **C** who was of the
Jude	11	have gone in the way of **C**

CAKE (see CAKES)

Hos	7: 8	Ephraim is a **c** unturned

CAKES (see CAKE)

Gen	18: 6	knead it and make **c**
Ex	12:39	they baked unleavened **c** of
Lev	7:12	or **c** of blended flour
Jer	7:18	to make **c** for the queen of

Ezek	4:12	you shall eat it as barley c
Hos	3: 1	the raisin c of the pagans

CALAMITY

Gen	42:38	If any c should befall him
Deut	32:35	the day of their c is at hand
1Ki	9: 9	brought all this c on them
2Ki	21:12	such c upon Jerusalem and
Job	30:13	up my path, they promote my c
Ps	18:18	me in the day of my c, But
Prov	1:26	I also will laugh at your c
Is	45: 7	I make peace and create c
Jer	1:14	Out of the north c shall
Jer	48:16	The c of Moab is near at hand
Jer	49: 8	bring the c of Esau upon him
Amos	3: 6	If there is c in a city, will

CALEB

Num	13: 6	Judah, C the son of Jephunneh
Num	14:24	But My servant C, because he

CALF (see CALVES)

Gen	18: 7	herd, took a tender and good c
Ex	32: 4	
Prov	15:17	than a fatted c with hatred
Jer	34:18	when they cut the c in two
Jer	34:19	between the parts of the c
Luke	15:30	killed the fatted c for him

CALL (see CALLED, CALLING, CALLS)

Gen	2:19	to see what he would c them
Gen	4:26	Then men began to c on the
Gen	16:11	You shall c his name Ishmael,
Gen	30:13	daughters will c me blessed
Ex	2: 7	c a nurse for you from the
Deut	4: 7	reason we may c upon Him
Deut	4:26	I c heaven and earth to
Deut	30: 1	you c them to mind among all
Judg	18:12	(Therefore they c that place
Ruth	1:20	to them, "Do not c me Naomi
Ruth	1:20	c me Mara, for the Almighty
1Sa	3: 6	I did not c, my son
1Sa	3: 8	Here I am, for you did c me
1Sa	12:17	I will c to the LORD, and He
1Sa	14:17	Now c the roll and see who has
2Sa	22: 4	I will c upon the LORD, who
1Ki	18:25	c on the name of your god,
Job	14:15	You shall c, and I will answer
Job	19:16	I c my servant, but he gives
Ps	4: 1	Hear me when I c, O God of my
Ps	4: 3	will hear when I c to Him
Ps	50: 4	He shall c to the heavens
Ps	50:15	C upon Me in the day of
Ps	72:17	nations shall c Him blessed
Ps	77: 6	I c to remembrance my song in
Ps	91:15	He shall c upon Me, and I will
Ps	116: 2	Therefore I will c upon Him
Ps	145:18	is near to all who c upon Him
Prov	31:28	rise up and c her blessed
Is	5:20	Woe to those who c evil good
Is	7:14	shall c His name Immanuel
Is	31: 2	will not c back His words,
Is	55: 6	c upon Him while He is near
Is	58: 5	Would you c this a fast, and

Is	58:13	c the Sabbath a delight, the
Is	61: 6	men shall c you the Servants
Jer	3:19	You shall c Me, 'My Father,
Jer	9:17	c for the mourning women,
Jer	33: 3	C to Me, and I will answer
Hos	1: 4	C his name Jezreel, for in a
Hos	1: 6	C her name Lo-Ruhamah, for I
Hos	1: 9	C his name Lo-Ammi, for you
Jon	1: 6	Arise, c on your God
Mal	3:12	nations will c you blessed
Matt	1:21	you shall c His name JESUS,
Matt	9:13	not come to c the righteous
Matt	19:17	Why do you c Me good
Matt	20: 8	C the laborers and give them
Matt	22:43	in the Spirit c Him Lord
Mark	15:12	you c the King of the Jews
Luke	1:13	you shall c his name John
Luke	1:48	generations will c me blessed
Luke	6:46	But why do you c Me 'Lord
John	4:16	c your husband, and come here
John	13:13	You c me Teacher and Lord,
John	15:15	No longer do I c you servants
Acts	2:39	as the Lord our God will c
Acts	10:28	c any man common or unclean
Acts	24:14	the Way which they c a sect
Rom	9:25	I will c them My people, who
Rom	10:12	is rich to all who c upon Him
Rom	10:14	How then shall they c on Him
1Co	1: 2	c on the name of Jesus Christ
2Co	1:23	Moreover I c God as witness
1Th	4: 7	For God did not c us to
2Ti	1: 5	when I c to remembrance the
Heb	2:11	ashamed to c them brethren
Jas	5:14	Let him c for the elders of
3Jn	10	I will c to mind his deeds

CALLED (see CALL)

Gen	1: 5	God c the light Day, and the
Gen	12: 8	c on the name of the LORD
Gen	21:12	in Isaac your seed shall be c
Gen	32:28	shall no longer be c Jacob
Gen	35:10	So He c his name Israel
1Sa	3: 4	that the LORD c Samuel
1Sa	9: 9	for he who is now c a prophet
1Sa	9: 9	prophet was formerly c a seer
2Sa	12:24	son, and he c his name Solomon
2Sa	12:25	so he c his name Jedidiah,
2Ch	7:14	if My people who are c by My
Ps	18: 6	my distress I c upon the LORD
Is	9: 6	His name will be c Wonderful
Is	56: 7	for My house shall be c a
Jer	7:10	house which is c by My name
Jer	25:29	city which is c by My name
Hos	11: 1	and out of Egypt I c My son
Matt	1:16	born Jesus who is c Christ
Matt	1:25	And he c His name JESUS
Matt	2:15	Out of Egypt I c My Son
Matt	2:23	He shall be c a Nazarene
Matt	5: 9	they shall be c sons of God
Matt	5:19	so, shall be c least in the
Matt	5:19	he shall be c great in the
Matt	10: 1	And when He had c His twelve
Matt	20:16	For many are c, but few
Matt	21:13	shall be c a house of prayer

C

Matt	27:22	do with Jesus who is c Christ
Matt	27:33	come to a place c Golgotha
Luke	1:35	born will be c the Son of God
Luke	1:36	for her who was c barren
Luke	15:19	worthy to be c your son
Luke	19:29	at the mountain c Olivet
Luke	23:33	come to the place c Calvary
Luke	24:13	day to a village c Emmaus
John	1:42	You shall be c Cephas"
John	1:48	Before Philip c you, when you
John	4:25	is coming" (who is c Christ)
John	9:11	A Man c Jesus made clay and
John	12:17	He c Lazarus out of his tomb
John	15:15	but I have c you friends, for
John	19:13	place that is c The Pavement
John	19:17	Skull, which is c in Hebrew,
Acts	3: 2	temple which is c Beautiful
Acts	3:11	porch which is c Solomon's
Acts	9:11	go to the street c Straight
Acts	11:26	first c Christians in Antioch
Acts	13: 2	work to which I have c them
Rom	1: 1	c to be an apostle, separated
Rom	1: 6	are the c of Jesus Christ
Rom	1: 7	of God, c to be saints
Rom	8:28	God, to those who are the c
Rom	8:30	predestined, these He also c
Rom	9: 7	In Isaac your seed shall be c
1Co	1:24	but to those who are c, both
1Co	1:26	mighty, not many noble, are c
1Co	7:15	But God has c us to peace
1Co	7:20	calling in which he was c
1Co	15: 9	not worthy to be c an apostle
Gal	1:15	and c me through His grace,
Gal	5:13	have been c to liberty
Eph	2:11	who are c Uncircumcision by
Col	3:15	also you were c in one body
2Th	2: 4	is c God or that is worshiped
1Ti	6:20	what is falsely c knowledge
2Ti	1: 9	c us with a holy calling, not
Heb	9: 3	which is c the Holiest of All
Heb	9:15	that those who are c may
Heb	11: 8	was c to go out to the place
Heb	11:16	not ashamed to be c their God
Heb	11:18	In Isaac your seed shall be c
Heb	11:24	refused to be c the son of
Jas	2: 7	noble name by which you are c
Jas	2:23	he was c the friend of God
1Pe	1:15	but as He who c you is holy
1Pe	2: 9	the praises of Him who c you
1Pe	2:21	For to this you were c,
1Pe	5:10	who c us to His eternal glory
1Jn	3: 1	should be c children of God
Rev	1: 9	was on the island that is c
Rev	11: 8	which spiritually is c Sodom
Rev	12: 9	c the Devil and Satan, who
Rev	16:16	to the place c in Hebrew,
Rev	19: 9	c to the marriage supper of
Rev	19:11	who sat on him was c Faithful
Rev	19:13	His name is c The Word of God

CALLING (see CALL)

Num	10: 2	use them for c the assembly
Matt	27:47	This Man is c for Elijah
John	11:28	has come and is c for you

Acts	22:16	c on the name of the Lord
Rom	11:29	the c of God are irrevocable
1Co	1:26	For you see your c, brethren,
1Co	7:20	same c in which he was called
Eph	1:18	what is the hope of His c
Eph	4: 1	you to walk worthy of the c
2Ti	1: 9	us and called us with a holy c
Heb	3: 1	partakers of the heavenly c

CALLS (see CALL)

1Sa	3: 9	and it shall be, if He c you
Ps	42: 7	Deep c unto deep at the noise
Ps	147: 4	He c them all by name
Prov	1:20	Wisdom c aloud outside
Is	64: 7	is no one who c on Your name
Joel	2:32	c on the name of the LORD
John	10: 3	he c his own sheep by name and
Acts	2:21	c on the name of the LORD
Rom	9:11	of works but of Him who c)
Rom	10:13	whoever c upon the name of
1Co	12: 3	of God c Jesus accursed, and
1Th	2:12	c you into His own kingdom
1Th	5:24	He who c you is faithful, who

CALM

Prov	17:27	is of a c spirit
Jon	1:11	that the sea may be c for us
Mark	4:39	ceased and there was a great c

CALVARY † (see GOLGOTHA)

Luke	23:33	come to the place called C

CALVES (see CALF)

1Sa	14:32	and took sheep, oxen, and c
1Ki	12:28	counsel and made two c of gold
Hos	13: 2	men who sacrifice kiss the c
Mic	6: 6	offerings, with c a year old
Heb	9:12	with the blood of goats and c

CAMEL (see CAMEL'S, CAMELS)

Matt	19:24	it is easier for a c to go
Matt	23:24	out a gnat and swallow a c

CAMEL'S (see CAMEL)

Gen	31:34	put them in the c saddle
Matt	3: 4	himself was clothed in c hair

CAMELS (see CAMEL)

Gen	24:11	And he made his c kneel down

CAMP

Ex	14: 2	you shall c before it by the
Ex	16:13	at evening and covered the c
Ex	16:13	the dew lay all around the c
Ex	19:17	out of the c to meet with God
Ex	29:14	burn with fire outside the c
Ex	32:17	is a noise of war in the c
Ex	32:26	in the entrance of the c, and
Ex	36: 6	proclaimed throughout the c
Lev	4:12	the c to a clean place, where
Lev	4:21	carry the bull outside the c
Lev	14: 3	priest shall go out of the c
Lev	17: 3	or who kills it outside the c
Lev	24:10	fought each other in the c

C

CANA (continued)

Num	1:50	it and c around the tabernacle
Num	2: 2	shall c by his own standard
Num	2: 3	c according to their armies
Num	4:15	when the c is set to go, then
Num	5: 2	put out of the c every leper
Num	11: 1	in the outskirts of the c
Num	11: 9	fell on the c in the night
Num	11:31	other side, all around the c
Num	12:14	shut out of the c seven days
Num	15:35	him with stones outside the c
Deut	23:14	walks in the midst of your c
Deut	23:14	your c shall be holy, that He
Deut	29:11	the stranger who is in your c
Josh	5: 8	the c till they were healed
Josh	6:18	make the c of Israel a curse,
Josh	10: 6	to Joshua at the c at Gilgal
Judg	7: 8	Now the c of Midian was below
Ps	106: 16	they envied Moses in the c
Nah	3:17	which c in the hedges on a
Zech	9: 8	I will c around My house
Heb	13:11	sin, are burned outside the c
Rev	20: 9	the c of the saints and the

CANA

John	2: 1	was a wedding in C of Galilee
John	21: 2	Nathanael of C in Galilee

CANAAN (see CANAANITE)

Gen	9:18	And Ham was the father of C
Gen	9:25	Cursed be C; A servant
Gen	28: 1	wife from the daughters of C
Gen	42: 5	famine was in the land of C
Lev	25:38	to give you the land of C
Num	13: 2	men to spy out the land of C
Deut	32:49	view the land of C, which I
Is	19:18	will speak the language of C

CANAANITE (see CANAAN, CANAANITES)

Ex	33: 2	and I will drive out the C
Matt	10: 4	Simon the C, and Judas

CANAANITES (see CANAANITE)

Gen	10:19	the border of the C was from
Gen	12: 6	the C were then in the land
Gen	13: 7	The C and the Perizzites then
Gen	15:21	the Amorites, the C, the
Gen	24: 3	from the daughters of the C
Ex	3:17	of Egypt to the land of the C
Num	21: 3	Israel and delivered up the C
Josh	3:10	out from before you the C
Josh	12: 8	Hittites, the Amorites, the C
Josh	16:10	out the C who dwelt in Gezer
Josh	17:12	but the C were determined to
Josh	17:13	put the C to forced labor
Josh	17:18	for you shall drive out the C
Judg	1: 3	we may fight against the C
Judg	1: 4	and the LORD delivered the C
Judg	1: 5	and they defeated the C and the
Judg	1:10	the C who dwelt in Hebron
Judg	1:17	and they attacked the C who
Judg	1:28	they put the C under tribute
Judg	1:32	Asherites dwelt among the C
Ezra	9: 1	to the abominations of the C
Obad	20	of the C as far as Zarephath

CAPERNAUM

Matt	4:13	He came and dwelt in C, which
Matt	8: 5	Now when Jesus had entered C
Matt	11:23	And you, C, who are exalted to
Luke	4:23	we have heard done in C, do
Luke	10:15	And you, C, who are exalted to
John	2:12	After this He went down to C
John	4:46	whose son was sick at C
John	6:17	and went over the sea toward C
John	6:24	got into boats and came to C
John	6:59	synagogue as He taught in C

CAPTAIN (see AUTHOR, CAPTAINS)

Gen	39: 1	c of the guard, an Egyptian,
Prov	6: 7	which, having no c, overseer
Jon	1: 6	So the c came to him, and said
Heb	2:10	glory, to make the c of their

CAPTAINS (see CAPTAIN)

Ex	14: 7	with c over every one of them

CAPTIVE (see CAPTIVES, CAPTIVITY, CAPTURED)

Gen	14:14	that his brother was taken c
2Ki	25:21	away c from its own land
1Ch	9: 1	But Judah was carried away c
Ezra	4:10	and noble Osnapper took c and
Ps	68:18	You have led captivity c
Ps	137: 3	away c required of us a song
Song	7: 5	king is held c by its tresses
Is	52: 2	neck, O c daughter of Zion
Jer	40: 1	carried away c from Jerusalem
Jer	48:46	your sons have been taken c
Jer	48:46	c, and your daughters c
Jer	52:28	Nebuchadnezzar carried away c
Ezek	39:28	none of them c any longer
Dan	11: 8	carry their gods c to Egypt
Amos	4:10	along with your c horses
Luke	21:24	and be led away c into all
Eph	4: 8	on high, He led captivity c
2Ti	2:26	having been taken c by him to

CAPTIVES (see CAPTIVE)

Gen	31:26	like c taken with the sword
Num	31:12	Then they brought the c, the
Deut	21:11	among the c a beautiful woman
Deut	32:42	blood of the slain and the c
Judg	5:12	Barak, and lead your c away
2Ki	24:14	men of valor, ten thousand c
2Ch	28:11	therefore, and return the c
2Ch	28:13	shall not bring the c here
Ezra	1:11	the c who were brought from
Esth	2: 6	from Jerusalem with the c who
Is	20: 4	and the Ethiopians as c, young
Is	49:24	or the c of the righteous be
Is	49:25	"Even the c of the mighty
Is	61: 1	to proclaim liberty to the c
Jer	32:44	will cause their c to return
Jer	48:47	Yet I will bring back the c
Ezek	1: 1	as I was among the c by the
Ezek	3:11	And go, get to the c, to the
Ezek	3:15	I came to the c at Tel Abib
Ezek	16:53	the c of your captivity among

Ezek	29:14	bring back the c of Egypt
Ezek	39:25	bring back the c of Jacob
Dan	2:25	found a man of the c of Judah
Hos	6:11	I return the c of My people
Joel	3: 1	I bring back the c of Judah
Obad	20	The c of Jerusalem who are in
Hab	1: 9	They gather c like sand
Zech	6:10	Receive the gift from the c
Luke	4:18	preach deliverance to the c
2Ti	3: 6	and make c of gullible women

CAPTIVITY (see CAPTIVE)

Num	21:29	and his daughters into c, to
Deut	21:13	put off the clothes of her c
Deut	28:41	for they shall go into c
Deut	30: 3	will bring you back from c
Judg	18:30	the day of the c of the land
2Ki	24:14	carried into c all Jerusalem
2Ki	24:15	c from Jerusalem to Babylon
2Ki	25:27	thirty-seventh year of the c
1Ch	5: 6	of Assyria carried into c
2Ch	6:37	to You in the land of their c
2Ch	29: 9	and our wives are in c
Ezra	2: 1	who came back from the c, of
Ezra	3: 8	out of the c to Jerusalem
Ezra	6:16	of the descendants of the c
Ezra	9: 7	the lands, to the sword, to c
Ezra	10: 6	the guilt of those from the c
Neh	1: 2	who had survived the c, and
Neh	1: 3	who are left from the c in
Neh	4: 4	as plunder to a land of c
Neh	8:17	from the c made booths and sat
Ps	14: 7	back the c of his people
Ps	53: 6	back the c of His people, Let
Ps	68:18	high, You have led c captive
Ps	78:61	delivered His strength into c
Ps	85: 1	brought back the c of Jacob
Ps	126: 1	brought back the c of Zion
Ps	126: 4	Bring back our c, O LORD, As
Is	5:13	my people have gone into c
Jer	22:22	your lovers shall go into c
Jer	29:28	saying, 'This c is long
Jer	29:31	Send to all those in c,
Jer	30: 3	back from c My people Israel
Jer	30:10	seed from the land of their c
Jer	30:18	back the c of Jacob's tents
Jer	31:23	when I bring back their c
Jer	43:11	those appointed for c, and to
Jer	46:19	prepare yourself to go into c
Jer	48: 7	Chemosh shall go forth into c
Jer	49: 3	go into c with his priests
Jer	52:31	thirty-seventh year of the c
Lam	1: 3	Judah has gone into c, under
Lam	1:18	my young men have gone into c
Lam	4:22	no longer send you into c
Ezek	1: 2	year of King Jehoiachin's c
Ezek	11:25	So I spoke to those in c of
Dan	11:33	fall by sword and flame, by c
Amos	5:27	you into c beyond Damascus
Obad	12	brother in the day of his c
Matt	1:17	from the c in Babylon until
Rom	7:23	bringing me into c to the law
2Co	10: 5	c to the obedience of Christ
Eph	4: 8	He led c captive, and gave

CAPTURED (see CAPTIVE)

Josh	11:17	He c all their kings, and
1Sa	4:11	Also the ark of God was c
Rev	19:20	Then the beast was c, and with

CARCHEMISH

Jer	46: 2	by the River Euphrates in C

CARE (see CAREFUL, CARES)

Deut	15: 5	to observe with c all these
2Sa	18: 3	they will not c about us
1Ki	1: 2	king, and let her c for him
2Ki	4:13	for us with all this c
2Ch	19: 7	take c and do it, for there is
Esth	2: 8	into the c of Hegai the
Job	10:12	and Your c has preserved my
Ps	27:10	the LORD will take c of me
Is	21: 7	diligently with great c
Luke	10:34	to an inn, and took c of him
Luke	10:40	do You not c that my sister
John	10:13	does not c about the sheep
Acts	27: 3	to his friends and receive c
1Co	7:32	I want you to be without c
1Co	12:25	the same c for one another
Phil	2:20	sincerely c for your state
Phil	4:10	though you surely did c, but
1Ti	3: 5	how will he take c of the
Heb	2: 6	of man that You take c of him
1Pe	5: 7	casting all your c upon Him

CAREFUL (see CARE, CAREFULLY, DILIGENT)

Deut	4: 6	Therefore be c to observe
Tit	3: 8	be c to maintain good works

CAREFULLY (see CAREFUL, DILIGENTLY)

Prov	12:26	should choose his friends c

CARES (see CARE)

Ps	142: 4	No one c for my soul
Matt	13:22	the c of this world and the
Luke	8:14	go out and are choked with c
Luke	21:34	c of this life, and that Day
1Co	7:32	He who is unmarried c for the
1Co	7:34	The unmarried woman c about
1Pe	5: 7	upon Him, for He c for you

CARMEL

1Ki	18:20	prophets together on Mount C
Jer	46:18	as C by the sea, so he shall

CARNAL (see CARNALLY)

Rom	7:14	law is spiritual, but I am c
Rom	8: 7	Because the c mind is enmity
1Co	3: 1	spiritual people but as to c
1Co	3: 3	for you are still c
2Co	10: 4	not c but mighty in God for

CARNALLY (see CARNAL)

Gen	19: 5	to us that we may know them c
Lev	18:20	c with your neighbor's wife
Lev	19:20	'Whoever lies c with a woman
Judg	19:22	house, that we may know him c
Rom	8: 6	For to be c minded is death,

CARPENTER† (*see* CARPENTER'S)

Mark	6: 3	Is this not the c, the Son of

CARPENTER'S† (*see* CARPENTER)

Matt	13:55	Is this not the c son

CARRIED (*see* CARRY)

Ex	25:14	that the ark may be c by them
Num	13:23	they c it between two of them
Deut	1:31	how the LORD your God c you
Judg	11:39	he c out his vow with her
2Ki	15:29	he c them captive to Assyria
Ps	46: 2	though the mountains be c
Ps	137: 3	For there those who c us away
Is	53: 4	our griefs and c our sorrows
Jer	52:28	Nebuchadnezzar c away captive
Matt	1:11	they were c away to Babylon
Mark	2: 3	who was c by four men
Luke	7:12	a dead man being c out
Luke	16:22	and was c by the angels to
Luke	24:51	from them and c up into heaven
John	20:15	Sir, if You have c Him away
Acts	5: 6	up, c him out, and buried him
Acts	8: 2	devout men c Stephen to his
1Co	12: 2	c away to these dumb idols,
Gal	2:13	c away with their hypocrisy
Eph	4:14	c about with every wind of
Heb	13: 9	Do not be c about with
2Pe	2:17	clouds c by a tempest, to
Jude	12	water, c about by the winds
Rev	12:15	her to be c away by the flood
Rev	17: 3	he c me away in the Spirit
Rev	21:10	he c me away in the Spirit

CARRIES (*see* CARRY)

Lev	11:28	'Whoever c any such carcass
Lev	15:10	He who c any of those things
Num	11:12	as a guardian c a nursing
Num	24:22	Asshur c you away captive
Deut	1:31	you, as a man c his son, in
Job	21:18	chaff that a storm c away
Job	27:21	The east wind c him away, and
Rev	17: 7	and of the beast that c her

CARRY (*see* CARRIED, CARRIES, CARRYING)

Gen	37:25	on their way to c them down
Gen	47:30	you shall c me out of Egypt
Gen	50:25	you shall c up my bones from
Lev	6:11	c the ashes outside the camp
Num	1:50	they shall c the tabernacle
Num	11:12	'C them in your bosom, as a
Deut	14:24	are not able to c the tithe
2Ch	36: 6	to c him off to Babylon
Ezra	5:15	c them to the temple site
Job	5:12	cannot c out their plans
Ps	49:17	dies he shall c nothing away
Ps	90: 5	You c them away like a flood
Eccl	5:15	he may c away in his hand
Eccl	10:20	of the air may c your voice
Is	30: 6	they will c their riches on
Is	40:11	and c them in His bosom, and
Is	41:16	the wind shall c them away
Is	46: 4	to gray hairs I will c you

Ezek	29:19	c off her spoil, and remove
Dan	11: 8	he shall also c their gods
Dan	11:32	and c out great exploits
Matt	3:11	sandals I am not worthy to c
Mark	6:55	and began to c about on beds
Mark	11:16	to c wares through the temple
Luke	10: 4	C neither money bag, sack,
John	5:10	lawful for you to c your bed
John	21:18	c you where you do not wish
Acts	5: 9	door, and they will c you out
1Ti	6: 7	certain we can c nothing out

CARRYING (*see* CARRY)

Num	4:12	and put them on a c beam
Num	4:24	Gershonites, in serving and c
Num	10:17	set out, c the tabernacle
Num	10:21	set out, c the holy things
Deut	32:11	them up, c them on its wings,
Jer	1: 3	until the c away of Jerusalem
Jer	17:27	such as not c a burden when
Zech	5:10	Where are they c the basket
Mark	14:13	meet you c a pitcher of water
Acts	5.10	c her out, buried her by her
2Co	4:10	always c about in the body

CARVED

Ex	20: 4	make for yourself any c image

CASE (*see* CASES)

Ex	18:26	every small c themselves
Deut	1:17	The c that is too hard for
1Sa	24:15	and me, and see and plead my c
Job	23: 4	would present my c before Him
Acts	19:38	have a c against anyone, the

CASES (*see* CASE)

Ex	18:26	the hard c they brought to
1Co	7:15	not under bondage in such c

CAST (*see* CASTING, CASTS, REJECTED)

Gen	21:10	C out this bondwoman and her
Gen	37:24	took him and c him into a pit
Gen	39: 7	wife c longing eyes on Joseph
Ex	1:22	you shall c into the river
Ex	4: 3	He said, "C it on the ground
Ex	4:25	c it at Moses' feet, and said,
Ex	7: 9	c it before Pharaoh, and let
Ex	7:10	Aaron c down his rod before
Ex	15: 4	army He has c into the sea
Ex	32:19	he c the tablets out of his
Ex	32:24	I c it into the fire, and this
Lev	16: 8	Then Aaron shall c lots for
Deut	9: 4	God has c them out before you
Josh	10:11	that the LORD c down large
Josh	10:27	c them into the cave where
1Sa	18:11	Saul c the spear, for he said
1Ki	7:15	he c two pillars of bronze,
1Ki	9: 7	name I will c out of My sight
1Ki	14: 9	have c Me behind your back
1Ch	28: 9	He will c you off forever
2Ch	25:12	c them down from the top of
2Ch	26:14	bows, and slings to c stones
2Ch	29:19	c aside in his transgression
Neh	9:26	c Your law behind their backs

C

Esth	3: 7	they c Pur (that is, the lot)
Job	8:20	God will not c away the
Job	15: 4	you c off fear, and restrain
Job	18: 8	For he is c into a net by his
Job	30:11	they have c off restraint
Ps	2: 3	c away Their cords from us
Ps	17:13	Confront him, c him down
Ps	22:10	I was c upon You from birth
Ps	22:18	for My clothing they c lots
Ps	37:24	shall not be utterly c down
Ps	42: 5	Why are you c down, O my soul
Ps	44:23	Do not c us off forever
Ps	50:17	And c My words behind you
Ps	51:11	Do not c me away from Your
Ps	55:22	C your burden on the LORD,
Ps	60: 8	Over Edom I will c My shoe
Ps	71: 9	Do not c me off in the time
Ps	78:49	He c on them the fierceness
Ps	89:44	And c his throne down to the
Ps	102:10	lifted me up and c me away
Ps	140:10	Let them be c into the fire,
Prov	1:14	c in your lot among us, let
Prov	16:33	The lot is c into the lap,
Prov	29:18	the people c off restraint
Eccl	3: 5	a time to c away stones, and a
Eccl	11: 1	C your bread upon the waters,
Is	25: 7	covering c over all people
Is	26:19	earth shall c out the dead
Is	38:17	for You have c all my sins
Is	57:20	rest, whose waters c up mire
Jer	7:15	I will c you out of My sight,
Jer	38: 6	c him into the dungeon of
Ezek	23:35	Me and c Me behind your back,
Ezek	27:30	and c dust on their heads
Ezek	31:16	when I c it down to hell
Ezek	32:18	c them down to the depths of
Dan	3:20	c them into the burning fiery
Dan	3:21	were c into the midst of the
Dan	3:24	Did we not c three men bound
Dan	6:16	c him into the den of lions
Dan	8:12	he c truth down to the ground
Hos	9:17	My God will c them away,
Amos	1:11	the sword, and c off all pity
Obad	11	gates and c lots for Jerusalem
Jon	1: 7	So they c lots, and the lot
Jon	2: 3	For You c me into the deep,
Mic	7:19	You will c all our sins into
Matt	5:29	pluck it out and c it from you
Matt	5:29	whole body to be c into hell
Matt	7: 6	nor c your pearls before
Matt	7:22	c out demons in Your name, and
Matt	8:12	be c out into outer darkness
Matt	8:16	He c out the spirits with a
Matt	13:42	will c them into the furnace
Matt	17:27	c in a hook, and take the fish
Matt	18: 8	cut if off and c it from you
Matt	18: 8	to be c into the everlasting
Matt	18: 9	eyes, to be c into hell fire
Matt	21:21	be c into the sea,' it will
Matt	22:13	c him into outer darkness
Matt	25:30	c the unprofitable servant
Matt	27:35	for My clothing they c lots
Mark	3:23	How can Satan c out Satan
Mark	16: 9	of whom He had c seven demons

John	6:37	Me I will by no means c out
John	9:35	heard that they had c him out
John	12:31	of this world will be c out
John	15: 6	he is c out as a branch and is
John	21: 6	C the net on the right side
Acts	1:26	they c their lots, and the lot
Rom	11: 2	God has not c away His people
Rom	11:15	For if their being c away is
Rom	13:12	Therefore let us c off the
Gal	4:30	C out the bondwoman and her
2Pe	2: 4	but c them down to hell and
Rev	12: 9	So the great dragon was c out
Rev	12: 9	angels were c out with him
Rev	20: 3	he c him into the bottomless
Rev	20:10	was c into the lake of fire

CASTING (see CAST)

Prov	18:18	C lots causes contentions to
Matt	4:18	brother, c a net into the sea
Matt	27:35	c lots, that it might be
Mark	1:39	all Galilee, and c out demons
2Co	10: 5	c down arguments and every
1Pe	5: 7	c all your care upon Him, for

CASTS (see CAST)

Ps	147: 6	He c the wicked down to the
Matt	9:34	He c out demons by the ruler
Matt	12:26	if Satan c out Satan, he is
Mark	3:22	of the demons He c out demons
Luke	11:15	He c out demons by Beelzebub,
1Jn	4:18	but perfect love c out fear

CATCH (see CATCHES, CAUGHT)

Job	9:18	not allow me to c my breath
Ps	10: 9	He lies in wait to c the poor
Mark	12:13	to c Him in His words
Luke	5: 4	and let down your nets for a c
Luke	5: 9	the c of fish which they had
Luke	5:10	From now on you will c men

CATCHES (see CATCH)

Job	5:13	He c the wise in their own
1Co	3:19	He c the wise in their own

CATTLE

Gen	1:24	c and creeping thing and beast
Gen	2:20	So Adam gave names to all c
Ps	50:10	the c on a thousand hills
Matt	22: 4	fatted c are killed, and all

CAUGHT (see CATCH, TOOK)

Gen	22:13	c in a thicket by its horns
Gen	39:12	that she c him by his garment
Eccl	9:12	net, like birds c in a snare
Ezek	12:13	and he shall be c in My snare
Luke	5: 5	toiled all night and c nothing
Luke	5: 6	they c a great number of fish
John	8: 3	to Him a woman c in adultery
Acts	8:39	of the Lord c Philip away
Acts	27:15	So when the ship was c, and
2Co	12: 4	how he was c up into Paradise
1Th	4:17	remain shall be c up together
Rev	12: 5	And her Child was c up to God

CAUSE (see CAUSED, CAUSES)

Ex	22: 9	the c of both parties shall
1Sa	19: 5	to kill David without a c
1Ki	8:59	maintain the c of His servant
Job	2: 3	him, to destroy him without c
Job	5: 8	and to God I would commit my c
Ps	17: 1	Hear a just c, O LORD, Attend
Ps	35: 1	Plead my c, O LORD, with
Ps	35:27	Who favor my righteous c
Ps	67: 1	c His face to shine upon us
Ps	74:22	O God, plead Your own c
Ps	80: 3	C Your face to shine, And we
Ps	119:154	Plead my c and redeem me
Ps	140:12	The c of the afflicted, And
Prov	22:23	the LORD will plead their c
Prov	29: 7	considers the c of the poor
Is	1:23	nor does the c of the widow
Is	34: 8	recompense for the c of Zion
Is	42: 2	nor c His voice to be heard
Jer	11:20	to You I have revealed my c
Lam	3:36	or subvert a man in his c
Jon	1: 8	For whose c is this trouble
John	15:25	They hated Me without a c
John	18:37	For this c I was born, and for
Acts	13:28	found no c for death in Him

CAUSED (see CAUSE)

1Sa	20:17	Jonathan again c David to vow
2Sa	7:11	have c you to rest from all
Job	29:13	I c the widow's heart to sing
Job	38:12	c the dawn to know its place,
Ps	78:13	sea and c them to pass through
Ps	78:26	He c an east wind to blow in
Ps	119:49	which You have c me to hope
Jer	29: 7	have c you to be carried away
Jer	48:33	I have c wine to fail from
Jer	51:49	As Babylon has c the slain of
Ezek	3: 2	He c me to eat that scroll
Dan	9:21	being c to fly swiftly,
Hos	4:12	harlotry has c them to stray
Jon	3: 7	he c it to be proclaimed and
Mal	2: 8	you have c many to stumble at
Acts	15: 3	they c great joy to all the
2Co	2: 5	But if anyone has c grief

CAUSES (see CAUSE)

Ps	37: 8	it only c harm
Ps	104:14	He c the grass to grow for
Ps	107:40	And c them to wander in the
Ps	135: 7	He c the vapors to ascend
Ps	147:18	He c His wind to blow, and the
Prov	10: 5	harvest is a son who c shame
Prov	10:10	winks with the eye c trouble
Prov	17: 2	rule over a son who c shame
Is	64: 2	as fire c water to boil
Lam	3:32	Though He c grief, yet He
Ezek	14: 3	which c them to stumble into
Ezek	26: 3	as the sea c its waves to
Matt	5:29	your right eye c you to sin
Matt	5:32	c her to commit adultery
Matt	18: 9	And if your eye c you to sin
Mark	9:42	whoever c one of these little
Mark	9:43	your hand c you to sin

Mark	9:45	your foot c you to sin
Mark	9:47	And if your eye c you to sin,
2Co	9:11	which c thanksgiving through
Eph	4:16	c growth of the body for the
Rev	21:27	or c an abomination or a lie,

CAVE (see CAVES)

Gen	19:30	two daughters dwelt in a c
Gen	23: 9	that he may give me the c of
Gen	23:11	field and the c that is in it
Gen	23:19	Sarah his wife in the c of
Gen	25: 9	him in the c of Machpelah
Josh	10:18	against the mouth of the c
Josh	10:27	cast them into the c where
1Sa	24: 7	And Saul got up from the c
2Sa	23:13	to David at the c of Adullam
John	11:38	It was a c, and a stone lay

CAVES (see CAVE)

Judg	6: 2	themselves the dens, the c
1Sa	13: 6	then the people hid in c
Heb	11:38	in dens and c of the earth
Rev	6:15	man, hid themselves in the c

CEASE (see CEASED, CEASING)

Gen	8:22	and day and night shall not c
Ex	9:29	the thunder will c, and there
Num	8:25	must c performing this work
Deut	15:11	will never c from the land
Josh	22:25	c fearing the LORD
Judg	2:19	They did not c from their own
Judg	9: 9	Should I c giving my oil,
Neh	4:11	them and cause the work to c
Job	3:17	the wicked c from troubling
Ps	46: 9	He makes wars c to the end of
Eccl	12: 3	when the grinders c because
Is	1:16	My eyes. C to do evil,
Hos	2:11	also cause all her mirth to c
Acts	5:42	they did not c teaching and
Acts	6:13	This man does not c to speak
Acts	13:10	will you not c perverting the
Acts	20:31	not c to warn everyone night
1Co	13: 8	are tongues, they will c
Eph	1:16	do not c to give thanks for
Col	1: 9	do not c to pray for you, and
2Pe	2:14	and that cannot c from sin

CEASED (see CEASE)

Gen	11: 8	and they c building the city
Ex	9:33	the thunder and the hail c
Josh	5:12	Now the manna c on the day
Judg	5: 7	life c, it c in Israel
1Sa	2: 5	were hungry have c to hunger
2Ki	4: 6	vessel." So the oil c
Job	32: 1	three men c answering Job
Ps	77: 8	Has His mercy c forever
Is	14: 4	How the oppressor has c, the
Jer	51:30	of Babylon have c fighting
Lam	5:14	The elders have c gathering
Lam	5:15	The joy of our heart has c
Hos	4:10	they have c obeying the LORD
Jon	1:15	the sea c from its raging
Matt	14:32	got into the boat, the wind c
Luke	7:45	but this woman has not c to

C

Luke	9:36	And when the voice had c,
Acts	20: 1	After the uproar had c, Paul
Gal	5:11	offense of the cross has c
Heb	10: 2	they not have c to be offered
1Pe	4: 1	in the flesh has c from sin

CEASING (see CEASE)

1Sa	12:23	the LORD in c to pray for you
Rom	1: 9	that without c I make mention
1Th	1: 3	without c your work of faith
1Th	2:13	we also thank God without c
1Th	5:17	pray without c,
2Ti	1: 3	as without c I remember you

CEDAR (see CEDARS)

Lev	14: 4	c wood, scarlet, and hyssop
2Sa	7: 2	now, I dwell in a house of c
1Ki	4:33	from the c tree of Lebanon
Ezek	17:22	branches of the high c and set
Ezek	17:23	fruit, and be a majestic c

CEDARS (see CEDAR)

Judg	9:15	and devour the c of Lebanon
2Ki	19:23	I will cut down its tall c
Ps	29: 5	of the LORD breaks the c, Yes

CELESTIAL

1Co	15:40	There are also c bodies and

CENSER (see ALTAR)

Lev	10: 1	of Aaron, each took his c
Heb	9: 4	which had the golden c
Rev	8: 3	angel, having a golden c,

CENSUS

Num	1: 2	Take a c of all the
Num	26: 4	Take a c of the people from
Luke	2: 2	This c first took place while
Acts	5:37	rose up in the days of the c

CENTER

Judg	9:37	down from the c of the land
Ezek	48:15	and the city shall be in the c
John	19:18	side, and Jesus in the c

CENTURION

Matt	8: 5	a c came to Him, pleading
Luke	7: 6	the c sent friends to Him,
Acts	10:22	Cornelius the c, a just man,
Acts	24:23	commanded the c to keep Paul
Acts	27: 1	a c of the Augustan Regiment
Acts	28:16	the c delivered the prisoners

CEPHAS (see PETER, SIMON)

John	1:42	You shall be called C"
1Co	3:22	whether Paul or Apollos or C
1Co	15: 5	and that He was seen by C,
Gal	2: 9	and when James, C, and John,

CERTAIN (see CERTAINLY, CERTAINTY, UNCERTAIN)

Josh	23:13	know for c that the LORD your
Dan	2:45	The cream is c, and its
Acts	25:26	I have nothing c to write to

1Ti	6: 7	it is c we can carry nothing
Heb	10:27	but a c fearful expectation

CERTAINLY (see CERTAIN)

2Ki	8:10	to him, "You shall c recover
Luke	23:47	C this was a righteous Man
Rom	3: 6	C not! For then how will God
Rom	3:31	law through faith? C not!
Rom	6: 2	C not! How shall we who
Rom	6:15	law but under grace? C not!
Rom	7: 7	Is the law sin? C not!
Rom	11: 1	cast away His people? C not!
1Co	6:15	members of a harlot? C not!
Gal	2:17	a minister of sin? C not!
Gal	3:21	the promises of God? C not!

CERTAINTY (see CERTAIN)

Luke	1: 4	that you may know the c of

CERTIFICATE (see CERTIFIED)

Deut	24: 1	he writes her a c of divorce
Matt	5:31	him give her a c of divorce

CHAFF

Job	21:18	like c that a storm carries
Ps	1: 4	But are like the c which the
Ps	35: 5	be like c before the wind
Is	5:24	and the flame consumes the c
Is	29: 5	be as c that passes away
Is	33:11	You shall conceive c, you
Jer	23:28	What is the c to the wheat
Hos	13: 3	away, like c blown off from a
Matt	3:12	the c with unquenchable fire

CHAIN (see CHAINED, CHAINS)

Gen	41:42	put a gold c around his neck
Lam	3: 7	He has made my c heavy
Dan	5:29	put a c of gold around his
Acts	28:20	Israel I am bound with this c
2Ti	1:16	and was not ashamed of my c
Rev	20: 1	pit and a great c in his hand

CHAINED† (see CHAIN)

Mark	15: 7	who was c with his fellow
2Ti	2: 9	but the word of God is not c
Heb	13: 3	prisoners as if c with them

CHAINS (see CHAIN)

Ex	28:14	you shall make two c of pure
Ps	107:14	And broke their c in pieces
Ps	149: 8	To bind their kings with c
Prov	1: 9	head, and c about your neck
Song	1:10	your neck with c of gold
Is	40:19	silversmith casts silver c
Jer	40: 1	he had taken him bound in c
Ezek	19: 9	They put him in a cage with c
Mark	5: 3	bind him, not even with c
Mark	5: 4	the c had been pulled apart
Acts	12: 6	bound with two c between two
Acts	12: 7	And his c fell off his hands
Acts	16:26	and everyone's c were loosed
Acts	22: 5	to Damascus to bring in c
Acts	23:29	him worthy of death or c
Acts	26:29	as I am, except for these c

Eph	6:20	which I am an ambassador in c
Phil	1: 7	inasmuch as both in my c
Phil	1:13	rest, that my c are in Christ
Phil	1:16	to add affliction to my c
Col	4: 3	for which I am also in c
Col	4:18	Remember my c. Grace be with
Phm	10	I have begotten while in my c
Phm	13	to me in my c for the gospel
Heb	10:34	had compassion on me in my c
Heb	11:36	and scourgings, yes, and of c
2Pe	2: 4	them into c of darkness, to
Jude	6	c under darkness for the

CHALDEA (*see* BABYLON, CHALDEAN, CHALDEANS)

Jer	51:24	all the inhabitants of C for
Ezek	23:15	of the Babylonians of C, the

CHALDEAN† (*see* CHALDEA, CHALDEANS)

Ezra	5:12	king of Babylon, the C, who
Jer	39: 5	But the C army pursued them
Dan	2:10	magician, astrologer, or C

CHALDEANS (*see* CHALDEA, CHALDEAN)

Gen	11:28	native land, in Ur of the C
Neh	9: 7	him out of Ur of the C, and
Jer	39: 8	the C burned the king's house
Dan	1: 4	and literature of the C
Dan	5:11	the magicians, astrologers, C
Dan	5:30	Belshazzar, king of the C
Acts	7: 4	came out of the land of the C

CHAMBER (*see* CHAMBERS)

Gen	43:30	And he went into his c and wept
Judg	3:24	to his needs in the cool c
2Ki	23:12	the roof, the upper c of Ahaz
Ps	19: 5	coming out of his c, And
Joel	2:16	bridegroom go out from his c

CHAMBERS (*see* CHAMBER)

Prov	7:27	descending to the c of death
Song	1: 4	has brought me into his c

CHANCE

1Sa	6: 9	it was by c that it happened
Eccl	9:11	time and c happen to them all
Luke	10:31	Now by c a certain priest

CHANGE (*see* CHANGED, CHANGERS', CHANGES, UNCHANGEABLE)

Gen	35: 2	and c your garments
Jer	13:23	Can the Ethiopian c his skin
Dan	5:10	nor let your countenance c
Dan	7:25	and shall intend to c times
Mal	3: 6	For I am the LORD, I do not c
Acts	6:14	c the customs which Moses
Heb	7:12	there is also a c of the law

CHANGED (*see* CHANGE)

Gen	31: 7	c my wages ten times, but God
Gen	41:14	c his clothing, and came to
1Sa	21:13	So he c his behavior before
2Ki	23:34	and c his name to Jehoiakim
2Ki	24:17	and c his name to Zedekiah

Ps	106:20	Thus they c their glory Into
Jer	34:11	afterward they c their minds
Jer	48:11	him, and his scent has not c
Dan	2: 9	before me till the time has c
Dan	3:19	on his face c toward Shadrach
Dan	4:16	Let his heart be c from that
Dan	5: 6	Then the king's countenance c
Mic	2: 4	He has c the heritage of my
Acts	28: 6	they c their minds and said
Rom	1:23	and c the glory of the
1Co	15:51	sleep, but we shall all be c
Heb	1:12	them up, and they will be c
Heb	7:12	For the priesthood being c

CHANGERS'† (*see* CHANGE)

John	2:15	and poured out the c money

CHANGES (*see* CHANGE)

Gen	45:22	to each man, c of garments
Lev	13:16	Or if the raw flesh c and
Job	10:17	c and war are ever with me
Dan	2:21	He c the times and the seasons
Hab	1:11	Then his mind c, and he

CHARACTER

Rom	5: 4	and perseverance, c
Phil	2:22	But you know his proven c

CHARGE (*see* CHARGED, CHARGES)

Gen	26: 5	obeyed My voice and kept My c
Gen	28: 6	blessed him he gave him a c
Ex	22:25	you shall not c him interest
Deut	23:19	You shall not c interest to
Deut	23:20	foreigner you may c interest
2Sa	3: 8	you c me today with a fault
Job	1:22	not sin nor c God with wrong
Job	34:13	Who gave Him c over the earth
Ps	91:11	give His angels c over you
Song	2: 7	I c you, O daughters of
Is	10: 6	of My wrath I will give him c
Jer	39:11	king of Babylon gave c
Dan	6: 4	c against Daniel concerning
Dan	6: 4	they could find no c or fault
Jon	1:14	do not c us without innocent
Nah	3: 3	Horsemen c with bright sword
Luke	4:10	give His angels c over You
Acts	7:60	do not c them with this sin
Acts	25:16	concerning the c against him
Rom	8:33	Who shall bring a c against
1Co	9:18	gospel of Christ without c
2Co	11: 7	of God to you free of c
2Th	3: 8	eat anyone's bread free of c
1Ti	1: 3	may c some that they teach no
1Ti	1:18	This c I commit to you, son

CHARGED (*see* CHARGE)

2Ti	4:16	May it not be c against them

CHARGES (*see* CHARGE)

Job	4:18	if He c His angels with error

CHARIOT (*see* CHARIOTEERS, CHARIOTS)

Gen	41:43	in the second c which he had
Gen	46:29	So Joseph made ready his c

2Sa	8: 4	hamstrung all the c horses
1Ki	10:26	he stationed in the c cities
2Ki	2:11	that suddenly a c of fire
2Ki	2:12	the c of Israel and its
Ps	104: 3	Who makes the clouds His c
Acts	8:28	And sitting in his c, he was
Acts	8:29	Go near and overtake this c

CHARIOTEERS† (see CHARIOT)

2Sa	10:18	David killed seven hundred c
1Ch	19:18	David killed seven thousand c

CHARIOTS (see CHARIOT)

Ex	14: 7	and all the c of Egypt with
Ex	14: 9	c of Pharaoh, his horsemen and
Josh	11: 6	and burn their c with fire
Josh	17:16	of the valley have c of iron
1Ki	4:26	stalls of horses for his c
2Ki	6:17	c of fire all around Elisha
2Ki	13:14	the c of Israel and their
2Ki	23:11	he burned the c of the sun
Ps	20: 7	Some trust in c, and some in
Dan	11:40	him like a whirlwind, with c
Nah	2: 4	The c rage in the streets,
Nah	3: 2	horses, of clattering c

CHARITABLE

Matt	6: 1	do your c deeds before men
Acts	9:36	and c deeds which she did

CHARM†

Prov	31:30	C is deceitful and beauty is

CHASE (see CHASED)

Lev	26: 7	You will c your enemies, and
Lev	26: 8	Five of you shall c a hundred
Ps	35: 5	the angel of the LORD c them
Hos	2: 7	She will c her lovers, but

CHASED (see CHASE)

Deut	1:44	c you as bees do, and drove
Josh	10:10	c them along the road that
Judg	20:43	c them, and easily trampled
Job	18:18	and c out of the world
Job	20: 8	Yes, he will be c away like a
Is	17:13	be c like the chaff of the

CHASTE†

2Co	11: 2	you as a c virgin to Christ
Tit	2: 5	to be discreet, c, homemakers
1Pe	3: 2	when they observe your c

CHASTEN (see CHASTENED, CHASTENING, CHASTENS)

2Sa	7:14	I will c him with the rod of
Ps	6: 1	anger, Nor c me in Your hot
Prov	19:18	C your son while there is
Heb	12: 7	whom a father does not c
Rev	3:19	many as I love, I rebuke and c

CHASTENED (see CHASTEN)

Job	33:19	Man is also c with pain on
Ps	69:10	c my soul with fasting, That
Ps	73:14	plagued, And c every morning

Ps	118:18	The LORD has c me severely
Heb	12:10	c us as seemed best to them

CHASTENING (see CHASTEN)

Deut	11: 2	the c of the LORD your God
Job	5:17	despise the c of the Almighty
Prov	3:11	not despise the c of the LORD
Heb	12: 5	not despise the c of the LORD
Heb	12: 7	If you endure c, God deals
Heb	12:11	Now no c seems to be joyful

CHASTENS† (see CHASTEN)

Deut	8: 5	heart that as a man c his son
Deut	8: 5	so the LORD your God c you
Heb	12: 6	For whom the LORD loves He c

CHASTISE (see CHASTISED, CHASTISEMENT)

1Ki	12:11	whips, but I will c you with
Luke	23:16	I will therefore c Him
Luke	23:22	I will therefore c Him and

CHASTISED (see CHASTISE)

1Ki	12:11	my father c you with whips,

CHASTISEMENT† (see CHASTISE)

Is	53: 5	the c for our peace was upon
Jer	30:14	with the c of a cruel one,

CHEAT† (see CHEATED)

Lev	19:13	You shall not c your neighbor
1Co	6: 8	you yourselves do wrong and c
Col	2:18	Let no one c you of your
Col	2: 8	Beware lest anyone c you

CHEATED (see CHEAT)

1Sa	12: 3	I taken, or whom have I c
2Co	7: 2	no one, we have c no one

CHEEK (see CHEEKS)

Matt	5:39	slaps you on your right c
Luke	6:29	who strikes you on the one c

CHEEKS (see CHEEK)

Deut	18: 3	priest the shoulder, the c
Song	1:10	Your c are lovely with
Lam	1: 2	night, her tears are on her c

CHEER (see CHEERFUL)

Eccl	11: 9	let your heart c you in the
Matt	9: 2	Son, be of good c
Matt	9:22	Be of good c, daughter
Matt	14:27	Be of good c! It is I
John	16:33	but be of good c, I have
Acts	23:11	Be of good c, Paul

CHEERFUL† (see CHEER, CHEERFULNESS)

Ruth	3: 7	and drunk, and his heart was c
1Ki	21: 7	food, and let your heart be c
Prov	15:13	heart makes a c countenance
Zech	8:19	c feasts for the house of
2Co	9: 7	for God loves a c giver
Jas	5:13	Is anyone c? Let him sing

CHEERFULNESS† (*see* CHEERFUL)

Rom 12: 8 he who shows mercy, with **c**

CHEMOSH

1Ki 11: 7 built a high place for **C** the
1Ki 11:33 **C** the god of the Moabites, and

CHERISHES†

Eph 5:29 **c** it, just as the Lord does
1Th 2: 7 mother **c** her own children

CHERITH

1Ki 17: 3 and hide by the Brook **C**,

CHERUB (*see* CHERUBIM)

Ex 25:19 Make one **c** at one end, and tho
2Sa 22:11 He rode upon a **c**, and flew
Ezek 10: 2 among the wheels, under the **c**

CHERUBIM (*see* CHERUB)

Gen 3:24 He placed **c** at the east of
Ex 25:18 you shall make two **c** of gold
1Sa 4: 4 who dwells between the **c**
Heb 9: 5 above it were the **c** of glory

CHEST

Dan 2:32 head was of fine gold, its **c**
Rev 1:13 girded about the **c** with a

CHEW

Lev 11: 7 yet does not **c** the cud, is

CHICKS†

Matt 23:37 gathers her **c** under her wings

CHIEF

Gen 36:15 were **C** Teman, Chief
Gen 40: 2 **c** butler and the **c** baker
2Ki 25:18 took Seraiah the **c** priest
Ezra 7: 5 the son of Aaron the **c** priest
Ps 118:22 Has become the **c** cornerstone
Ps 137: 6 Jerusalem Above my **c** joy
Song 5.10 ruddy, **c** among ten thousand
Dan 10:13 Michael, one of the **c** princes
Hab 3:19 To the **C** Musician
Matt 16:21 **c** priests and scribes, and be
Matt 21:42 has become the **c** cornerstone
Luke 19: 2 who was a **c** tax collector
Acts 14:12 because he was the **c** speaker
Acts 19:14 of Sceva, a Jewish **c** priest
Eph 2:20 being the **c** cornerstone,
1Ti 1:15 save sinners, of whom I am **c**
1Pe 2: 6 I lay in Zion a **c** cornerstone
1Pe 5: 4 when the **C** Shepherd appears,

CHILD (*see* CHILDHOOD, CHILDISH, CHILDLESS, CHILDREN, CHILD'S)

Gen 11:30 was barren; she had no **c**
Gen 16:11 Behold, you are with **c**, and
Gen 17:10 Every male **c** among you shall
Gen 44:20 a **c** of his old age, who is
Ex 2: 2 saw that he was a beautiful **c**
Ex 21:22 fight, and hurt a woman with **c**

Num 11:12 guardian carries a nursing **c**
Judg 11:34 and she was his only **c**
Judg 13: 8 do for the **c** who will be born
1Sa 1:27 For this **c** I prayed, and the
1Sa 2:11 But the **c** ministered to the
1Sa 2:26 the **c** Samuel grew in stature,
1Sa 15: 3 woman, infant and nursing **c**
2Sa 12:15 the LORD struck the **c** that
2Sa 12:18 came to pass that the **c** died
1Ki 3:20 laid her dead **c** in my bosom
1Ki 3:25 Divide the living **c** in two
2Ki 4:31 The **c** has not awakened
2Ki 4:34 And he went up and lay on the **c**
2Ki 4:34 flesh of the **c** became warm
2Ki 5:14 like the flesh of a little **c**
2Ki 8:12 rip open their women with **c**
Job 3:16 not hidden like a stillborn **o**
Prov 20:11 Even a **c** is known by his
Prov 22: 6 Train up a **c** in the way he
Prov 22:15 bound up in the heart of a **c**
Prov 23:13 withhold correction from a **c**
Prov 23:24 a wise **c** will delight in him
Prov 29:15 but a **c** left to himself
Eccl 10:16 O land, when your king is a **c**
Is 3: 5 the **c** will be insolent toward
Is 7:16 For before the **C** shall know
Is 9: 6 For unto us a **C** is born, unto
Is 10:19 that a **c** may write them
Is 11: 6 a little **c** shall lead them
Is 11: 8 The nursing **c** shall play by
Is 26:17 As a woman with **c** is in pain
Is 49:15 a woman forget her nursing **c**
Is 54: 1 who have not travailed with **c**
Jer 30: 6 a man is ever in labor with **c**
Jer 31:20 Is he a pleasant **c**
Hos 11: 1 When Israel was a **c**, I loved
Matt 1:18 with **c** of the Holy Spirit
Matt 1:23 a virgin shall be with **c**
Matt 2: 8 diligently for the young **C**
Matt 2: 9 over where the young **C** was
Matt 2:13 Arise, take the young **C** and
Matt 2:13 the young **C** to destroy Him
Matt 17:18 the **c** was cured from that
Matt 18: 2 called a little **c** to Him, set
Matt 18: 4 **c** is the greatest in the
Mark 5:39 The **c** is not dead, but
Mark 5:40 entered where the **c** was lying
Mark 5:41 He took the **c** by the hand
Mark 9:24 the father of the **c** cried out
Mark 10:15 **c** will by no means enter it
Luke 1:59 they came to circumcise the **c**
Luke 1:66 What kind of **c** will this be
Luke 1:76 and you, **c**, will be called the
Luke 1:80 So the **c** grew and became
Luke 2:21 for the circumcision of the **C**
Luke 2:27 brought in the **C** Jesus, to do
Luke 2:34 this **C** is destined for the
Luke 2:40 the **C** grew and became strong
Luke 9:42 unclean spirit, healed the **c**
Luke — 9:48 receives this little **c** in My
Acts 7: 5 even when Abraham had no **c**
1Co 13:11 I was a **c**, I spoke as a **c**
Gal 4: 1 heir, as long as he is a **c**
Heb 11:11 she bore a **c** when she was

Heb	11:23	they saw he was a beautiful **c**
Rev	12: 2	Then being with **c**, she cried
Rev	12: 5	her **C** was caught up to God and

CHILDBEARING†

Gen	18:11	Sarah had passed the age of **c**
1Ti	2:15	she will be saved in **c** if

CHILDHOOD (see CHILD)

2Ti	3:15	that from **c** you have known

CHILDISH† (see CHILD)

1Co	13:11	a man, I put away **c** things

CHILDLESS (see CHILD)

Gen	15: 2	You give me, seeing I go **c**
Jer	22:30	Write this man down as **c**
Luke	20:30	her as wife, and he died **c**

CHILDREN (see CHILD, CHILDREN'S, GRANDCHILDREN)

Gen	3:16	pain you shall bring forth **c**
Gen	16: 1	wife, had borne him no **c**
Gen	25:22	But the **c** struggled together
Gen	30: 1	Give me **c**, or else I die
Gen	36:31	reigned over the **c** of Israel
Gen	45:10	your children's **c**
Ex	2: 6	This is one of the Hebrews' **c**
Ex	12:26	when your **c** say to you, "What
Ex	12:37	men on foot, besides **c**
Ex	17: 3	of Egypt, to kill us and our **c**
Ex	20: 5	fathers on the **c** to the third
Ex	21: 4	her **c** shall be her master's,
Ex	34: 7	of the fathers upon the **c**
Lev	6:18	the **c** of Aaron may eat it
Lev	25:45	the **c** of the strangers who
Lev	25:46	for your **c** after you, to
Lev	26:22	which shall rob you of your **c**
Num	1: 2	of the **c** of Israel, by their
Num	1:20	Now the **c** of Reuben, Israel's
Num	1:22	From the **c** of Simeon, their
Num	1:24	From the **c** of Gad, their
Num	1:26	From the **c** of Judah, their
Num	1:28	From the **c** of Issachar, their
Num	1:30	From the **c** of Zebulun, their
Num	1:32	the **c** of Ephraim, their
Num	1:34	From the **c** of Manasseh, their
Num	1:36	From the **c** of Benjamin, their
Num	1:38	From the **c** of Dan, their
Num	1:40	From the **c** of Asher, their
Num	1:42	From the **c** of Naphtali, their
Num	5:28	be free and may conceive **c**
Num	14: 3	and **c** should become victims
Deut	1:39	your little ones and your **c**
Deut	4: 9	And teach them to your **c** and
Deut	4:25	When you beget **c** and
Deut	4:40	you and with your **c** after you
Deut	5: 9	upon the **c** to the third and
Deut	5:29	them and with their **c** forever
Deut	11:19	shall teach them to your **c**
Deut	11:21	the days of your **c** may be
Deut	14: 1	You are the **c** of the LORD
Deut	17:20	his **c** in the midst of Israel
Deut	21:15	and they have borne him **c**

Deut	23: 8	The **c** of the third generation
Deut	24:16	be put to death for their **c**
Deut	32: 5	they are not His **c**, because
Deut	32: 8	the number of the **c** of Israel
Deut	32:20	**c** in whom is no faith
Deut	34: 8	And the **c** of Israel wept for
Deut	34: 9	so the **c** of Israel heeded him
Josh	4:12	armed before the **c** of Israel
Josh	4:21	When your **c** ask their fathers
Josh	4:22	you shall let your **c** know
Josh	5:10	So the **c** of Israel camped in
Josh	11:14	the **c** of Israel took as booty
Josh	11:19	peace with the **c** of Israel
Josh	11:22	the land of the **c** of Israel
Josh	12: 1	whom the **c** of Israel defeated
Josh	12: 6	the **c** of Israel had conquered
Josh	14: 1	are the areas which the **c** of
Josh	14: 4	For the **c** of Joseph were two
Josh	15:13	portion among the **c** of Judah
Josh	16: 5	border of the **c** of Ephraim
Josh	19: 1	inheritance of the **c** of Judah
Josh	22:12	whole congregation of the **c**
Josh	22:33	thing pleased the **c** of Israel
Josh	22:33	the **c** of Israel blessed God
Josh	24: 4	and his **c** went down to Egypt
Judg	1:21	Jebusites dwell with the **c** of
Judg	1:34	the Amorites forced the **c** of
Judg	2:11	Then the **c** of Israel did evil
Judg	13: 2	wife was barren and had no **c**
Judg	21:10	including the women and **c**
1Sa	1: 2	Peninnah had **c**
1Sa	1: 2	but Hannah had no **c**
1Sa	2: 5	she who has many **c** has become
2Sa	6:23	no **c** to the day of her death
2Sa	12: 3	with him and with his **c**
1Ki	20: 3	loveliest wives and **c** are mine
1Ki	20: 5	gold, your wives and your **c**"
2Ki	8:12	and you will dash their **c**, and
2Ki	14: 6	But the **c** of the murderers he
2Ki	14: 6	not be put to death for the **c**
2Ki	14: 6	nor shall the **c** be put to
2Ki	17:31	**c** in fire to Adrammelech and
2Ki	19: 3	for the **c** have come to birth,
1Ch	14: 4	**c** whom he had in Jerusalem
1Ch	16:13	you **c** of Jacob, His chosen
2Ch	25: 4	he did not execute their **c**
2Ch	28: 3	burned his **c** in the fire,
Ezra	10:44	had wives by whom they had **c**
Neh	5: 5	our **c** as their **c**
Neh	9:23	**c** as the stars of heaven, and
Job	17: 5	the eyes of his **c** will fail
Job	19:17	to the **c** of my own body
Job	19:18	Even young **c** despise me
Job	24: 5	food for them and for their **c**
Job	27:14	If his **c** are multiplied, it
Job	29: 5	me, when my **c** were around me
Job	41:34	king over all the **c** of pride
Job	42:16	and forty years, and saw his **c**
Ps	14: 2	from heaven upon the **c** of men
Ps	17:14	They are satisfied with **c**
Ps	34:11	Come, you **c**, listen to me
Ps	53: 2	from heaven upon the **c** of men
Ps	69: 8	And an alien to my mother's **c**
Ps	72: 4	will save the **c** of the needy

Ps	73:15	to the generation of Your **c**
Ps	78: 4	not hide them from their **c**
Ps	78: 5	make them known to their **c**
Ps	78: 6	and declare them to their **c**
Ps	82: 6	all of you are **c** of the Most
Ps	83: 8	They have helped the **c** of Lot
Ps	89:47	You created all the **c** of men
Ps	90: 3	And say, "Return, O **c** of men
Ps	90:16	And Your glory to their **c**
Ps	102:28	The **c** of Your servants will
Ps	103:13	As a father pities his **c**, So
Ps	103:17	righteousness to children's **c**
Ps	107: 8	works to the **c** of men
Ps	109: 9	Let his **c** be fatherless, And
Ps	113: 9	Like a joyful mother of **c**
Ps	127: 3	**c** are a heritage from the
Ps	127: 4	So are the **c** of one's youth
Ps	128: 3	Your **c** like olive plants All
Ps	128: 6	may you see your children's **c**
Ps	147:13	has blessed your **c** within you
Ps	148:12	Old men and **c**
Prov	4: 1	Hear, my **c**, the instruction
Prov	13:22	to his children's **c**, but the
Prov	17: 6	Children's **c** are the crown of
Prov	17: 6	and the glory of **c** is their
Prov	31:28	Her **c** rise up and call her
Is	1: 2	nourished and brought up **c**
Is	1: 4	**c** who are corrupters
Is	8:18	the **c** whom the LORD has given
Is	23: 4	not labor, nor bring forth **c**
Is	30: 1	Woe to the rebellious **c**,"
Is	54: 1	For more are the **c** of the
Is	54: 1	the **c** of the married woman
Jer	3:14	Return, O backsliding **c**,"
Jer	4:22	They are silly **c**, and they
Jer	18:21	widows and bereaved of their **c**
Jer	31:15	Rachel weeping for her **c**
Jer	31:15	to be comforted for her **c**
Jer	32:39	of them and their **c** after them
Jer	38:23	wives and **c** to the Chaldeans
Jer	40: 7	to him men, women, **c**, and the
Jer	49:11	Leave your fatherless **c**, I
Lam	1:16	My **c** are desolate because the
Lam	2:19	for the life of your young **c**
Lam	4:10	women have cooked their own **c**
Ezek	2: 4	are impudent and stubborn **c**
Ezek	20:21	the **c** rebelled against Me
Ezek	33: 2	speak to the **c** of your people
Dan	2:38	wherever the **c** of men dwell
Hos	1: 2	**c** of harlotry, for the land
Hos	2: 4	will not have mercy on her **c**
Mal	4: 6	of the fathers to the **c**, and
Mal	4: 6	of the **c** to their fathers
Matt	2:16	male **c** who were in Bethlehem
Matt	2:18	Rachel weeping for her **c**
Matt	3: 9	up **c** to Abraham from these
Matt	7:11	to give good gifts to your **c**
Matt	11:19	wisdom is justified by her **c**
Matt	14:21	men, besides women and **c**
Matt	18: 3	and become as little **c**, you
Matt	19:14	Let the little **c** come to Me
Matt	19:29	mother or wife or **c** or lands
Matt	27:25	blood be on us and on our **c**
Luke	1:16	he will turn many of the **c** of

John	1:12	the right to become **c** of God
John	8:39	If you were Abraham's **c**, you
John	13:33	Little **c**, I shall be with you
John	21: 5	**C**, have you any food
Acts	2:39	is to you and to your **c**, and to
Rom	8:16	spirit that we are **c** of God
Rom	8:17	and if **c**, then heirs
Rom	8:21	liberty of the **c** of God
Rom	9: 8	who are the **c** of the flesh
Rom	9: 8	but the **c** of the promise are
Rom	9:27	Though the number of the **c** of
1Co	14:20	do not be **c** in understanding
2Co	6:13	the same (I speak as to **c**)
2Co	12:14	For the **c** ought not to lay up
2Co	12:14	but the parents for the **c**
Gal	4:25	and is in bondage with her **c**
Gal	4:20	Isaac was, are **c** of promise
Gal	4:31	we are not **c** of the bondwoman
Eph	2: 3	and were by nature **c** of wrath
Eph	4:14	that we should no longer be **c**
Eph	5: 1	be followers of God as dear **c**
Eph	5: 8	Walk as **c** of light
Eph	6: 1	**C**, obey your parents in the
Eph	6: 4	not provoke your **c** to wrath
Phil	2:15	**c** of God without fault in the
Col	3:20	**C**, obey your parents in all
Col	3:21	do not provoke your **c**, lest
1Th	2: 7	mother cherishes her own **c**
1Th	2:11	as a father does his own **c**
1Ti	3: 4	having his **c** in submission
1Ti	3:12	of one wife, ruling their **c**
1Ti	5: 4	widow has **c** or grandchildren
1Ti	5:10	if she has brought up **c**, if
1Ti	5:14	younger widows marry, bear **c**
Tit	1: 6	having faithful **c** not accused
Tit	2: 4	husbands, to love their **c**
Heb	2:13	the **c** whom God has given Me
Heb	11:22	departure of the **c** of Israel
1Pe	1:14	as obedient **c**, not conforming
2Pe	2:14	practices, and are accursed **c**
1Jn	2: 1	My little **c**, these things I
1Jn	2:18	Little **c**, it is the last hour
1Jn	2:28	And now, little **c**, abide in
1Jn	3: 1	we should be called **c** of God
1Jn	3: 2	Beloved, now we are **c** of God
1Jn	3: 7	Little **c**, let no one deceive
1Jn	3:10	In this the **c** of God and the
1Jn	3:10	God and the **c** of the devil are
1Jn	3:18	My little **c**, let us not love
1Jn	5: 2	that we love the **c** of God
1Jn	5:21	Little **c**, keep yourselves
2Jn	1	To the elect lady and her **c**
3Jn	4	hear that my **c** walk in truth
Rev	2:14	block before the **c** of Israel
Rev	2:23	I will kill her **c** with death
Rev	7: 4	the **c** of Israel were sealed

CHILDREN'S (see CHILDREN)

Ex	34: 7	the **c** children to the third
Prov	17: 6	**C** children are the crown of
Jer	31:29	the **c** teeth are set on edge
Matt	15:26	not good to take the **c** bread
Mark	7:28	table eat from the **c** crumbs

CHILD'S (*see* CHILD)

Ex	2: 8	went and called the **c** mother
Job	33:25	flesh shall be young like a **c**
Matt	2:20	the young **C** life are dead

CHOICE (*see* CHOICEST, CHOOSE)

Gen	27: 9	there two **c** kids of the goats
Prov	8:10	knowledge rather than **c** gold

CHOICEST (*see* CHOICE)

Is	5: 2	and planted it with the **c** vine

CHOKE† (*see* CHOKED)

Matt	13:22	of riches **c** the word and he
Mark	4:19	things entering in **c** the word

CHOKED (*see* CHOKE)

Matt	13: 7	thorns sprang up and **c** them
Mark	4: 7	**c** it, and it yielded no crop
Luke	8:14	are **c** with cares, riches, and

CHOOSE (*see* CHOICE, CHOOSES, CHOOSING, CHOSE, CHOSEN)

Ex	17: 9	**C** us some men and go out,
Deut	7: 7	**c** you because you were more
Deut	30:19	therefore **c** life, that both
Josh	24:15	**c** for yourselves this day
1Ki	18:25	**C** one bull for yourselves and
Ps	65: 4	Blessed is the man whom You **c**
Is	7:15	refuse the evil and **c** the good
Is	14: 1	Jacob, and will still **c** Israel
Zech	1:17	and will again **c** Jerusalem
John	6:70	Did I not **c** you, the twelve,
John	15:16	You did not **c** Me, but I chose

CHOOSES (*see* CHOOSE)

Deut	12: 5	where the LORD your God **c**
Dan	4:25	and gives it to whomever He **c**

CHOOSING† (*see* CHOOSE)

Heb	11:25	**c** rather to suffer affliction

CHOSE (*see* CHOOSE)

Gen	6: 2	themselves of all whom they **c**
Gen	13:11	Then Lot **c** for himself all
Ex	18:25	Moses **c** able men out of all
Judg	5: 8	They **c** new gods
1Sa	17:40	he **c** for himself five smooth
Ps	78:70	He also **c** David His servant,
Mark	13:20	the elect's sake, whom He **c**
Luke	6:13	from them He **c** twelve whom
John	15:16	not choose Me, but I **c** you
John	15:19	but I **c** you out of the world,
Eph	1: 4	just as He **c** us in Him before
2Th	2:13	God from the beginning **c** you

CHOSEN (*see* CHOOSE)

Deut	7: 6	the LORD your God has **c** you
Judg	10:14	to the gods which you have **c**
1Sa	10:20	the tribe of Benjamin was **c**
1Sa	10:21	And Saul the son of Kish was **c**
1Sa	16: 8	has the Lord **c** this one
1Sa	16:10	The LORD has not **c** these

1Sa	20:30	**c** the son of Jesse to your
1Ki	3: 8	Your people whom You have **c**
2Ch	6: 6	I have **c** David to be over My
Neh	1: 9	**c** as a dwelling for My name
Ps	33:12	has **c** as His own inheritance
Ps	89: 3	made a covenant with My **c**
Ps	89:19	exalted one **c** from the people
Ps	105: 6	children of Jacob, His **c** ones
Ps	106:23	Had not Moses His **c** one stood
Ps	119:30	I have **c** the way of truth
Ps	119:173	For I have **c** Your precepts
Ps	132:13	For the LORD has **c** Zion
Ps	135: 4	For the LORD has **c** Jacob for
Prov	16:16	is to be **c** rather than silver
Prov	22: 1	A good name is to be **c** rather
Is	41: 8	servant, Jacob, whom I have **c**
Is	41: 9	are My servant, I have **c** you
Is	43:10	And My servant whom I have **c**
Is	44: 1	and Israel whom I have **c**
Is	44: 2	you, Jeshurun, whom I have **c**
Is	58: 5	Is it a fast that I have **c**
Is	66: 3	as they have **c** their own ways
Jer	8: 3	Then death shall be **c** rather
Jer	33:24	families which the LORD has **c**
Jer	49:19	who is a **c** man that I may
Matt	12:18	My Servant whom I have **c**
Matt	20:16	many are called, but few **c**
Luke	10:42	Mary has **c** that good part,
Luke	23:35	is the Christ, the **c** of God
John	13:18	I know whom I have **c**
Acts	1: 2	to the apostles whom He had **c**
Acts	1:24	which of these two You have **c**
Acts	9:15	for he is a **c** vessel of Mine
Acts	15:22	to send **c** men of their own
1Co	1:27	But God has **c** the foolish
Jas	2: 5	Has God not **c** the poor of
1Pe	2: 4	but **c** by God and precious,
1Pe	2: 9	But you are a **c** generation
Rev	17:14	are with Him are called, **c**

CHRIST (*see* CHRIST'S, CHRISTS, JESUS)

Matt	1: 1	of the genealogy of Jesus **C**
Matt	1:16	born Jesus who is called **C**
Matt	2: 4	where the **C** was to be born
Matt	16:16	You are the **C**, the Son of the
Matt	23: 8	One is your Teacher, the **C**
Matt	27:22	do with Jesus who is called **C**
Mark	1: 1	of the gospel of Jesus **C**, the
Luke	2:11	a Savior, who is **C** the Lord
Luke	2:26	he had seen the Lord's **C**
Luke	20:41	say that the **C** is David's Son
Luke	23:35	save Himself if He is the **C**
Luke	24:26	Ought not the **C** to have
Luke	24:46	necessary for the **C** to suffer
John	1:17	and truth came through Jesus **C**
John	1:20	I am not the **C**
John	1:25	baptize if you are not the **C**
John	7:27	but when the **C** comes, no one
John	11:27	I believe that You are the **C**
John	12:34	that the **C** remains forever
John	17: 3	Jesus **C** whom You have sent
John	20:31	believe that Jesus is the **C**
Acts	2:31	the resurrection of the **C**
Acts	2:36	you crucified, both Lord and **C**

Acts	2:38	in the name of Jesus C for	1Co	11: 3	the head of every man is C
Acts	3: 6	name of Jesus C of Nazareth	1Co	11: 3	man, and the head of C is God
Acts	4:26	the LORD and against His C	1Co	12:12	are one body, so also is C
Acts	8: 5	and preached C to them	1Co	15: 3	that C died for our sins
Acts	8:37	Jesus C is the Son of God	1Co	15:13	the dead, then C is not risen
Acts	9:20	the C in the synagogues, that	1Co	15:17	if C is not risen, your faith
Acts	10:36	peace through Jesus C	1Co	15:18	asleep in C have perished
Acts	11:17	believed on the Lord Jesus C	1Co	15:19	life only we have hope in C
Acts	16:31	Believe on the Lord Jesus C	1Co	15:20	But now C is risen from the
Acts	17: 3	that the C had to suffer and	1Co	15:23	C the firstfruits, afterward
Acts	17: 3	whom I preach to you is the C	2Co	2:14	leads us in triumph in C, and
Acts	18: 5	the Jews that Jesus is the C	2Co	3:14	the veil is taken away in C
Acts	26:23	that the C would suffer, that	2Co	4: 6	of God in the face of Jesus C
Rom	1: 1	Paul, a servant of Jesus C	2Co	5:10	before the judgment seat of C
Rom	1: 3	His Son Jesus C our Lord, who	2Co	5:14	the love of C constrains us
Rom	1: 6	are the called of Jesus C	2Co	5:17	Therefore, if anyone is in C
Rom	1:16	ashamed of the gospel of C	2Co	5:19	that God was in C reconciling
Rom	2:16	the secrets of men by Jesus C	2Co	5:20	we are ambassadors for C, as
Rom	3:24	redemption that is in C Jesus	2Co	6:15	what accord has C with Belial
Rom	5: 6	in due time C died for the	2Co	12: 2	I know a man in C who
Rom	5: 8	still sinners, C died for us	2Co	12: 9	power of C may rest upon me
Rom	5:17	life through the One, Jesus C	Gal	1:12	the revelation of Jesus C
Rom	5:21	life through Jesus C our Lord	Gal	2:16	be justified by faith in C
Rom	6: 3	C Jesus were baptized into	Gal	2:20	I have been crucified with C
Rom	6: 4	that just as C was raised	Gal	2:20	I who live, but C lives in me
Rom	6: 8	Now if we died with C, we	Gal	3:13	C has redeemed us from the
Rom	6:23	life in C Jesus our Lord	Gal	3:16	And to your Seed," who is C
Rom	8: 2	of the Spirit of life in C	Gal	3:24	our tutor to bring us to C
Rom	8:10	If C is in you, the body is	Gal	3:27	into C have put on C
Rom	8:11	He who raised C from the dead	Gal	3:28	you are all one in C Jesus
Rom	8:17	of God and joint heirs with C	Gal	4: 7	then an heir of God through C
Rom	8:34	It is C who died, and	Gal	4:19	until C is formed in you,
Rom	8:35	us from the love of C	Gal	5: 1	by which C has made us free
Rom	8:39	which is in C Jesus our Lord	Gal	6: 2	and so fulfill the law of C
Rom	9: 1	I tell the truth in C, I am	Eph	1: 3	in the heavenly places in C
Rom	9: 3	from C for my brethren, my	Eph	1:12	we who first trusted in C
Rom	10: 4	For C is the end of the law	Eph	2: 6	heavenly places in C Jesus
Rom	10: 6	to bring C down from above)	Eph	2:13	made near by the blood of C
Rom	12: 5	being many, are one body in C	Eph	3:17	that C may dwell in your
Rom	13:14	But put on the Lord Jesus C	Eph	3:19	to know the love of C which
Rom	14: 9	For to this end C died and	Eph	5: 2	as C also has loved us and
Rom	14:10	before the judgment seat of C	Eph	5:23	as also C is head of the
Rom	16:16	The churches of C greet you	Phil	1:15	preach C even from envy and
1Co	1: 1	C through the will of God	Phil	1:21	For to me, to live is C, and
1Co	1: 2	who are sanctified in C Jesus	Phil	2:11	confess that Jesus C is Lord
1Co	1: 8	the day of our Lord Jesus C	Phil	3: 8	knowledge of C Jesus my Lord
1Co	1:12	of Cephas," or "I am of C."	Phil	3:18	the enemies of the cross of C
1Co	1:13	Is C divided?	Phil	4:13	through C who strengthens me
1Co	1:17	For C did not send me to	Phil	4:19	riches in glory by C Jesus
1Co	1:17	lest the cross of C should be	Col	1:27	which is C in you, the hope
1Co	1:23	but we preach C crucified	Col	3: 1	which are above, where C is
1Co	1:24	C the power of God and the	1Th	2:19	Lord Jesus C at His coming
1Co	1:30	But of Him you are in C Jesus	1Th	4:16	the dead in C will rise first
1Co	2:16	But we have the mind of C	1Ti	1:15	that C Jesus came into the
1Co	3: 1	to carnal, as to babes in C	1Ti	2: 5	God and men, the Man C Jesus
1Co	3:11	is laid, which is Jesus C	2Ti	2: 3	as a good soldier of Jesus C
1Co	3:23	are Christ's, and C is God's	2Ti	3:12	godly in C Jesus will suffer
1Co	5: 7	For indeed C, our Passover,	Tit	2:13	great God and Savior Jesus C
1Co	6:15	your bodies are members of C	Phm	1	Paul, a prisoner of C Jesus
1Co	8: 6	and one Lord Jesus C, through	Heb	9:11	But C came as High Priest of
1Co	8:11	perish, for whom C died	Heb	9:14	more shall the blood of C
1Co	10: 4	them, and that Rock was C	Heb	9:24	For C has not entered the
1Co	10:16	communion of the blood of C	Heb	9:28	so C was offered once to bear
1Co	11: 1	me, just as I also imitate C	Heb	10:10	body of Jesus C once for all

Heb	11:26	of C greater riches than the
Heb	13: 8	Jesus C is the same yesterday
Heb	13:21	in His sight, through Jesus C
Jas	2: 1	the faith of our Lord Jesus C
1Pe	1: 1	Peter, an apostle of Jesus C
1Pe	1: 2	of the blood of Jesus C
1Pe	1: 3	and Father of our Lord Jesus C
1Pe	1: 3	of Jesus C from the dead,
1Pe	1: 7	at the revelation of Jesus C
1Pe	1:11	the sufferings of C and the
1Pe	1:13	at the revelation of Jesus C
1Pe	1:19	with the precious blood of C
1Pe	3:18	For C also suffered once for
1Pe	4:14	reproached for the name of C
1Pe	5: 1	of the sufferings of C, and
1Pe	5:10	His eternal glory by C Jesus
2Pe	1: 1	of our God and Savior Jesus C
2Pe	1: 8	knowledge of our Lord Jesus C
1Jn	1: 3	and with His Son Jesus C
1Jn	1: 7	the blood of Jesus C His Son
1Jn	2: 1	Father, Jesus C the righteous
1Jn	2:22	denies that Jesus is the C
1Jn	3:23	the name of His Son Jesus C
1Jn	4: 3	C has come in the flesh is
1Jn	5: 1	Jesus is the C is born of God
1Jn	5: 6	by water and blood—Jesus C
2Jn	7	C as coming in the flesh
2Jn	9	of C has both the Father and
Jude	1	Jude, a servant of Jesus C
Jude	4	Lord God and our Lord Jesus C
Rev	1: 1	The Revelation of Jesus C
Rev	1: 2	to the testimony of Jesus C
Rev	1: 5	and from Jesus C, the faithful
Rev	1: 9	and patience of Jesus C, was
Rev	1: 9	for the testimony of Jesus C
Rev	11:15	of our Lord and of His C, and
Rev	12:17	have the testimony of Jesus C
Rev	20: 4	reigned with C for a thousand
Rev	20: 6	be priests of God and of C
Rev	22:21	Lord Jesus C be with you all

CHRISTIAN† (*see* CHRISTIANS)

Acts	26:28	persuade me to become a C
1Pe	4:16	Yet if anyone suffers as a C

CHRISTIANS† (*see* CHRISTIAN)

Acts	11:26	first called C in Antioch

CHRIST'S (*see* CHRIST)

1Co	3:23	And you are C, and Christ is
1Co	4:10	We are fools for C sake, but
1Co	15:23	those who are C at His coming
2Co	5:20	we implore you on C behalf
Eph	4: 7	to the measure of C gift
1Ti	6:14	our Lord Jesus C appearing
1Pe	4:13	you partake of C sufferings

CHRISTS (*see* CHRIST)

Matt	24:24	For false c and false prophets

CHURCH (*see* CHURCHES)

Matt	16:18	this rock I will build My c
Matt	18:17	hear them, tell it to the c
Acts	2:47	the Lord added to the c daily

Acts	8: 1	arose against the c which was
Acts	8: 3	Saul, he made havoc of the c
Acts	14:23	appointed elders in every c
Acts	20:28	to shepherd the c of God
1Co	4:17	I teach everywhere in every c
1Co	11:18	when you come together as a c
1Co	11:22	do you despise the c of God
1Co	14: 4	who prophesies edifies the c
1Co	14:28	let him keep silent in c
1Co	14:35	for women to speak in c
1Co	15: 9	I persecuted the c of God
1Co	16:19	with the c that is in their
Eph	1:22	head over all things to the c
Eph	3:21	to Him be glory in the c by
Eph	5:23	also Christ is head of the c
Eph	5:24	just as the c is subject to
Eph	5:25	as Christ also loved the c
Eph	5:27	it to Himself a glorious c
Eph	5:32	concerning Christ and the c
Phil	3: 6	zeal, persecuting the c
Col	1:18	the head of the body, the c
1Ti	3: 5	he take care of the c of God
1Ti	3:15	which is the c of the living
Heb	12:23	c of the firstborn who are
Jas	5:14	call for the elders of the c
Rev	2: 1	of the c of Ephesus write

CHURCHES (*see* CHURCH)

Acts	9:31	Then the c throughout all
1Co	14:34	women keep silent in the c
Rev	1:11	the seven c which are in Asia
Rev	2: 7	what the Spirit says to the c

CIRCLE

Job	22:14	walks above the c of heaven
Prov	8:27	when He drew a c on the face
Is	40:22	sits above the c of the earth

CIRCUIT

Ps	19: 6	And its c to the other end

CIRCUMCISE (*see* CIRCUMCISED, CIRCUMCISION, UNCIRCUMCISED)

Deut	10:16	Therefore c the foreskin of
Deut	30: 6	your God will c your heart
Jer	4: 4	C yourselves to the LORD, and
Luke	1:59	that they came to c the child
John	7:22	you c a man on the Sabbath
Acts	15: 5	It is necessary to c them
Acts	21:21	that they ought not to c

CIRCUMCISED (*see* CIRCUMCISE)

Gen	17:10	child among you shall be c
Gen	17:11	you shall be c in the flesh
Gen	17:26	very same day Abraham was c
Gen	21: 4	Then Abraham c his son Isaac
Jer	9:25	are c with the uncircumcised
Acts	7: 8	and c him on the eighth day
Acts	15: 1	Unless you are c according to
Acts	15:24	souls, saying, "You must be c
Acts	16: 3	c him because of the Jews who
Rom	3:30	will justify the c by faith
Gal	2: 3	Greek, was compelled to be c
Gal	2: 7	gospel for the c was to Peter

Gal	2: 9	the Gentiles and they to the **c**
Gal	5: 3	to every man who becomes **c**
Gal	6:12	try to compel you to be **c** ⚹
Gal	6:13	those who are **c** keep the law
Gal	6:13	**c** that they may glory in your
Phil	3: 5	**c** the eighth day, of the
Col	2:11	In Him you were also **c** with
Col	3:11	nor Jew, **c** nor uncircumcised,

CIRCUMCISION (see CIRCUMCISE)

Ex	4:26	because of the **c**
Luke	2:21	for the **c** of the Child, His
John	7:22	Moses therefore gave you **c**
John	7:23	man receives **c** on the Sabbath
Acts	7: 8	He gave him the covenant of **c**
Acts	10:45	those of the **c** who believed
Rom	2:25	For **c** is indeed profitable if
Rom	2:27	with your written code and **c**
Rom	2:29	**c** is that of the heart, in
Rom	3: 1	or what is the profit of **c**
Rom	4:11	And he received the sign of **c**
Rom	4:12	the father of **c** to those who
Rom	15: 8	to the **c** for the truth of God
1Co	7:19	**C** is nothing and
Gal	5: 6	**c** nor uncircumcision avails
Gal	5:11	brethren, if I still preach **c**
Eph	2:11	by what is called the **C** made
Phil	3: 3	For we are the **c**, who worship
Col	2:11	with the **c** made without hands
Col	2:11	flesh, by the **c** of Christ,
Tit	1:10	especially those of the **c**

CIRCUMSPECTLY†

Eph	5:15	See then that you walk **c**, not

CISTERN (see CISTERNS)

2Ki	18:31	drink the waters of his own **c**
Prov	5:15	Drink water from your own **c**

CISTERNS (see CISTERN)

Jer	2:13	waters, and hewn themselves **c**
Jer	2:13	broken **c** that can hold no

CITIES (see CITY)

Gen	13:12	dwelt in the **c** of the plain
Gen	19:25	So He overthrew those **c**, all
Ex	1:11	built for Pharaoh supply **c**
Lev	25:32	the **c** of the Levites, and the
Num	13:28	the **c** are fortified and very
Num	35: 6	shall appoint six **c** of refuge
Josh	10: 2	city, like one of the royal **c**
Josh	16: 9	all the **c** with their villages
2Sa	10:12	and for the **c** of our God
1Ki	9:19	all the storage **c** that
1Ki	10:26	he stationed in the chariot **c**
2Ch	28:18	invaded the **c** of the lowland
Is	64:10	Your holy **c** are a wilderness,
Jer	2:28	of your **c** are your gods, O
Matt	9:35	And Jesus went about all the **c**
Matt	11: 1	teach and to preach in their **c**
Matt	11:20	He began to upbraid the **c** in
Luke	19:17	have authority over ten **c**
2Pe	2: 6	and turning the **c** of Sodom

CITIZEN (see CITIZENS)

Acts	22:28	But I was born a **c**

CITIZENS (see CITIZEN)

Eph	2:19	but fellow **c** with the saints

CITIZENSHIP

Phil	3:20	For our **c** is in heaven, from

CITY (see CITIES)

Gen	4:17	And he built a **c**, and called
Gen	11: 5	LORD came down to see the **c**
Gen	11: 8	and they ceased building the **c**
Gen	18:24	fifty righteous within the **c**
Gen	19:14	the LORD will destroy this **c**
Lev	14:40	unclean place outside the **c**
Num	35:26	the **c** of refuge where he fled
Deut	28: 3	Blessed shall you be in the **c**
Deut	28:16	Cursed shall you be in the **c**
Deut	34: 3	the **c** of palm trees, as far
Josh	2:15	her house was on the **c** wall
Josh	6: 4	around the **c** seven times, and
Josh	10: 2	because Gibeon was a great **c**
Josh	15:62	the **C** of Salt, and En Gedi
Judg	9:31	fortifying the **c** against you
Judg	9:33	rise early and rush upon the **c**
Judg	9:51	was a strong tower in the **c**
Judg	16: 3	doors of the gate of the **c**
Judg	17: 8	**c** of Bethlehem in Judah to
Judg	19:15	in the open square of the **c**
Judg	19:17	in the open square of the **c**
Judg	20:32	from the **c** to the highways
Judg	20:48	from every **c**, men and beasts,
Ruth	1:19	that all the **c** was excited
1Sa	1: 3	from his **c** yearly to worship
1Sa	5:12	the cry of the **c** went up to
1Sa	8:22	Every man go to his **c**
1Sa	9: 6	is in this **c** a man of God
1Sa	9:11	went up the hill to the **c**
1Sa	9:25	the high place into the **c**
1Sa	9:27	to the outskirts of the **c**
1Sa	20:29	has a sacrifice in the **c**, and
1Sa	22:19	Nob, the **c** of the priests, he
1Sa	27: 5	dwell in the royal **c** with you
1Sa	30: 3	and his men came to the **c**
2Sa	5: 9	and called it the **C** of David
2Sa	15:14	strike the **c** with the edge of
2Sa	15:24	crossing over from the **c**
2Sa	15:25	ark of God back into the **c**
2Sa	15:27	Return to the **c** in peace, and
2Sa	17:23	home to his house, to his **c**
2Sa	19:37	that I may die in my own **c**
2Sa	20:15	a siege mound against the **c**
1Ki	1:41	Why is the **c** in such a noisy
1Ki	1:45	so that the **c** is in an uproar
1Ki	8:44	the **c** which You have chosen
1Ki	8:48	the **c** which You have chosen
1Ki	9:16	Canaanites who dwelt in the **c**
1Ki	14:12	When your feet enter the **c**
1Ki	22:36	Every man to his **c**, and every
2Ki	2:23	some youths came from the **c**
2Ki	7: 4	**c**,' the famine is in the **c**
2Ki	7:10	to the gatekeepers of the **c**

C

2Ki	10: 5	he who was in charge of the **c**
2Ki	10: 6	with the great men of the **c**
2Ki	11:20	the **c** was quiet, for they had
2Ki	17: 9	watchtower to fortified **c**
2Ki	18: 8	watchtower to fortified **c**
2Ki	19:33	he shall not come into this **c**
2Ki	19:34	For I will defend this **c**
2Ki	20: 6	defend this **c** for My own sake
2Ki	20:20	and brought water into the **c**
2Ki	23:27	and will cast off this **c**
2Ki	24:11	of Babylon came against the **c**
2Ki	25: 4	Then the **c** wall was broken
2Ki	25:11	people who remained in the **c**
2Ch	28:15	Jericho, the **c** of palm trees
2Ch	32: 5	the Millo in the **C** of David
2Ch	32: 6	the open square of the **c** gate
Ezra	4:12	the rebellious and evil **c**, and
Neh	11: 1	in Jerusalem, the holy **c**, and
Job	24:12	The dying groan in the **c**, and
Ps	46: 4	shall make glad the **c** of God
Ps	48: 1	praised In the **c** of our God
Ps	48: 2	The **c** of the great King
Ps	87: 3	are spoken of you, O **c** of God
Ps	107: 4	They found no **c** to dwell in
Ps	127: 1	Unless the LORD guards the **c**
Prov	9: 3	the highest places of the **c**,
Prov	10:15	man's wealth is his strong **c**
Is	1:21	How the faithful **c** has become
Is	1:26	called the **c** of righteousness
Is	19:18	called the **C** of Destruction
Is	22: 9	the damage to the **c** of David
Is	52: 1	O Jerusalem, the holy **c**
Jer	29: 7	seek the peace of the **c** where
Lam	1: 1	How lonely sits the **c** that
Ezek	48:15	be for general use by the **c**
Ezek	48:15	the **c** shall be in the center
Ezek	48:18	food for the workers of the **c**
Ezek	48:30	These are the exits of the **c**
Hos	6: 8	Gilead is a **c** of evildoers,
Joel	2: 9	They run to and fro in the **c**
Amos	3: 6	If a trumpet is blown in a **c**
Amos	3: 6	If there is calamity in a **c**
Amos	4: 7	I made it rain on one **c**, I
Jon	1: 2	go to Nineveh, that great **c**
Jon	3: 2	go to Nineveh, that great **c**
Jon	3: 3	was an exceedingly great **c**
Nah	3: 1	Woe to the bloody **c**
Zeph	2:15	**c** that dwelt securely, that
Zech	8: 3	be called the **C** of Truth, the
Matt	2:23	dwelt in a **c** called Nazareth,
Matt	4: 5	took Him up into the holy **c**
Matt	5:14	A **c** that is set on a hill
Matt	8:34	the whole **c** came out to meet
Matt	9: 1	over, and came to His own **c**
Matt	10:11	Now whatever **c** or town you
Matt	10:14	depart from that house or **c**
Matt	12:25	and every **c** or house divided
Matt	21:17	went out of the **c** to Bethany
Matt	23:34	and persecute from **c** to **c**
Luke	1:26	was sent by God to a **c** of
Luke	2: 3	everyone to his own **c**
Luke	2:11	in the **c** of David a Savior
Luke	7:11	He went into a **c** called Nain
Luke	9:10	to the **c** called Bethsaida
Luke	10:11	The very dust of your **c**
Luke	10:12	Day for Sodom than for that **c**
Luke	23:19	insurrection made in the **c**
Luke	23:51	a **c** of the Jews, who himself
John	1:44	the **c** of Andrew and Peter
John	4: 5	So He came to a **c** of Samaria
John	4: 8	away into the **c** to buy food
John	4:30	Then they went out of the **c**
John	4:39	of the Samaritans of that **c**
John	19:20	was crucified was near the **c**
Acts	8: 8	there was great joy in that **c**
Acts	8: 9	practiced sorcery in the **c**
Acts	11: 5	I was in the **c** of Joppa
Acts	12:10	iron gate that leads to the **c**
Acts	14:19	and dragged him out of the **c**
Acts	14:21	preached the gospel to that **c**
Acts	16:13	out of the **c** to the riverside
Acts	16:14	purple from the **c** of Thyatira
Acts	16:39	them to depart from the **c**
Acts	17: 5	set all the **c** in an uproar and
Acts	17:16	the **c** was given over to idols
Acts	18:10	I have many people in this **c**
Acts	19:35	when the **c** clerk had quieted
Acts	19:35	**c** of the Ephesians is temple
Acts	20:23	Spirit testifies in every **c**
Acts	21:39	a citizen of no mean **c**
Acts	24:12	in the synagogues or in the **c**
Acts	25:23	and the prominent men of the **c**
Rom	16:23	the treasurer of the **c**,
2Co	11:26	Gentiles, in perils in the **c**
Tit	1: 5	in every **c** as I commanded you
Heb	11:10	the **c** which has foundations
Heb	11:16	He has prepared a **c** for them
Heb	12:22	to the **c** of the living God,
Heb	13:14	here we have no continuing **c**
Rev	3:12	the name of the **c** of My God
Rev	11: 8	in the street of the great **c**
Rev	11:13	and a tenth of the **c** fell
Rev	14: 8	is fallen, that great **c**,
Rev	14:20	was trampled outside the **c**
Rev	16:19	Now the great **c** was divided
Rev	18:10	**c** Babylon, that mighty **c**
Rev	20: 9	the saints and the beloved **c**
Rev	21: 2	Then I, John, saw the holy **c**
Rev	21:15	a gold reed to measure the **c**
Rev	21:16	the **c** is laid out as a square
Rev	21:18	the **c** was pure gold, like
Rev	21:21	street of the **c** was pure gold
Rev	21:23	the **c** had no need of the sun
Rev	22:19	Book of Life, from the holy **c**

CLAIMING†

Acts	5:36	rose up, **c** to be somebody
Acts	8: 9	**c** that he was someone great,

CLANGING†

1Co	13: 1	sounding brass or a **c** cymbal

CLAP†

Job	27:23	Men shall **c** their hands at
Ps	47: 1	**c** your hands, all you peoples
Ps	98: 8	Let the rivers **c** their hands
Is	55:12	the field shall **c** their hands

Lam	2:15	All who pass by c their hands
Nah	3:19	will c their hands over you

CLAUDIUS (see CAESAR)

Acts	11:28	in the days of C Caesar

CLAY

Job	4:19	who dwell in houses of c,
Job	10: 9	that You have made me like c
Job	33: 6	have been formed out of c
Job	38:14	on form like c under a seal
Ps	40: 2	pit, Out of the miry c, And
Is	41:25	as the potter treads c
Is	45: 9	Shall the c say to him who
Jer	18: 4	c was marred in the hand of
Ezek	4: 1	son of man, takes a c tablet
Dan	2:33	partly of iron and partly of c
John	9: 6	and made c with the saliva
John	9: 6	of the blind man with the c
John	9:11	A Man called Jesus made c
John	9:15	He put c on my eyes, and I
Rom	9:21	potter have power over the c
2Ti	2:20	silver, but also of wood and c

CLEAN (see CLEANNESS, CLEANSE, UNCLEAN)

Gen	7: 2	seven each of every c animal
Gen	7: 8	Of c beasts, of beasts that
Gen	8:20	animal and of every c bird
Lev	7:19	And as for the c flesh, all
Lev	10:10	and between unclean and c,
Lev	12: 7	she shall be c from the flow
Lev	13:40	head, he is bald, but he is c
Lev	14: 4	c birds, cedar wood, scarlet,
Lev	22: 7	sun goes down he shall be c
Num	5:28	not defiled herself, and is c
Num	19:19	The c person shall sprinkle
Num	19:19	and at evening he shall be c
Num	31:23	the fire, and it shall be c
Deut	12:15	the c may eat of it, of the
Deut	14:11	All c birds you may eat
2Ki	5:14	a little child, and he was c
Ezra	6:20	all of them were ritually c
Job	11: 4	pure, And I am c in your eyes
Ps	19: 9	The fear of the LORD is c
Ps	24: 4	He who has c hands and a pure
Ps	51: 7	with hyssop, and I shall be c
Ps	51:10	Create in me a c heart, O God
Prov	14: 4	no oxen are, the trough is c
Prov	20: 9	I have made my heart c, I am
Eccl	9: 2	to the good, the c, and the
Is	1:16	yourselves, make yourselves c
Is	66:20	bring an offering in a c
Zech	3: 5	Let them put a c turban on
Matt	3:12	thoroughly c out his threshing
Matt	8: 2	willing, You can make me c
Matt	23:26	outside of them may be c also
Luke	3:17	thoroughly c out his thresing
Matt	27:59	wrapped it in a c linen cloth
Luke	11:39	outside of the cup and dish c
Luke	11:41	all things are c to you
John	13:10	his feet, but is completely c
John	13:10	and you are c, but not all of
John	15: 3	You are already c because of
Rev	19:14	in fine linen, white and c

CLEANNESS (see CLEAN)

2Sa	22:25	according to my c in His eyes
Amos	4: 6	Also I gave you c of teeth in

CLEANSE (see CLEAN, CLEANSED, CLEANSES, CLEANSING)

Ex	29:36	You shall c the altar when
Lev	14:49	to c the house, two birds,
Num	8: 6	Israel and c them ceremonially
Num	8:21	atonement for them to c them
Neh	13: 9	commanded them to c the rooms
Job	9:30	and c my hands with soap,
Ps	19:12	C me from secret faults
Ps	51: 2	iniquity, And c me from my sin
Ps	119: 9	How can a young man c his way
Prov	20:30	Blows that hurt c away evil
Ezek	39:12	them, in order to c the land
Ezek	45:18	blemish and c the sanctuary
Matt	10: 8	c the lepers, raise the dead,
Matt	23:25	For you c the outside of the
Matt	23:26	first c the inside of the cup
2Co	7: 1	let us c ourselves from all
Eph	5:26	and c it with the washing of
Heb	9:14	c your conscience from
Jas	4: 8	C your hands, you sinners
1Jn	1: 9	our sins and to c us from all

CLEANSED (see CLEANSE)

Lev	14: 7	is to be c from the leprosy
Lev	14:19	to be c from his uncleanness
Lev	14:31	is to be c before the LORD
Dan	8:14	then the sanctuary shall be c
Matt	8: 3	I am willing; be c."
Matt	8: 3	immediately his leprosy was c
Matt	11: 5	the lepers are c and the deaf
Luke	4:27	none of them was c except
Luke	17:17	Were there not ten c
Acts	10:15	What God has c you must not
2Pe	1:19	he was c from his old sins

CLEANSES† (see CLEANSE)

1Ti	2:21	Therefore if anyone c himself
1Jn	1: 7	His Son c us from all sin

CLEANSING (see CLEANSE)

Lev	13: 7	seen by the priest for his c

CLEAR (see CLEARED, CLEARING, CLEARLY)

Gen	24:41	You will be c from this oath
Rev	21:11	a jasper stone, c as crystal
Rev	21:18	was pure gold, like c glass

CLEARED (see CLEAR)

Is	5: 2	c out its stones, and planted

CLEARING (see CLEAR)

Ex	34: 7	sin, by no means c the guilty

CLEARLY (see CLEAR)

Matt	7: 5	then you will see c to remove
Rom	1:20	attributes are c seen, being
Gal	3: 1	was c portrayed among you as
1Ti	5:24	Some men's sins are c evident

CLEFT
Ex	33:22	put you in the c of the rock

CLIFF
Luke	4:29	throw Him down over the c

CLING (see CLINGS, CLUNG)
Ps	102: 5	My bones c to my skin
Ps	137: 6	Let my tongue c to the roof
Rom	12: 9	C to what is good

CLINGS (see CLING)
Job	19:20	My bone c to my skin and to my
Ps	22:15	And My tongue c to My jaws
Lam	4: 4	c to the roof of its mouth
Lam	4: 8	their skin c to their bones,

CLOAK
Matt	5:40	let him have your c also
1Th	2: 5	nor a c for covetousness
2Ti	4:13	Bring the c that I left with
1Pe	2:16	your liberty as a c for vice

CLOSE (see CLOSED, CLOSER)
Ruth	2: 8	but stay c by my young women
Job	19:14	my c friends have forgotten
Luke	19:43	and c you in on every side,
Phil	2:30	of Christ he came c to death

CLOSED (see CLOSE)
Gen	2:21	c up the flesh in its place
Num	16:33	the earth c over them, and
Judg	3:22	the fat c over the blade, for
1Sa	1: 5	the LORD had c her womb
Dan	12: 9	for the words are c up and
Jon	2: 5	the deep c around me
Luke	4:20	Then he c the book, and gave

CLOSER (see CLOSE)
Prov	18:24	who sticks c than a brother

CLOTH (see CLOTHS)
Num	4: 8	spread over them a scarlet c
Matt	9:16	unshrunk c on an old garment
Matt	27:59	wrapped it in a clean linen c
John	11:44	his face was wrapped with a c

CLOTHE (see CLOTHED, CLOTHES)
Job	10:11	c me with skin and flesh, and
Ps	132:18	enemies I will c with shame
Is	15: 3	c themselves with sackcloth
Matt	6:30	will He not much more c you
Matt	25:38	You in, or naked and c You

CLOTHED (see CLOTHE)
Gen	3:21	tunics of skin, and c them
Gen	41:42	he c him in garments of fine
1Sa	17:38	So Saul c David with his
2Sa	1:24	who c you in scarlet, with
1Ch	21:16	c in sackcloth, fell on their
2Ch	6:41	be c with salvation, and let
Job	8:22	hate you will be c with shame
Job	29:14	on righteousness, and it c me

Ps	61:10	for He has c me with the
Ps	65: 6	strength, Being c with power
Ps	93: 1	reigns, He is c with majesty
Ps	104: 1	You are c with honor and
Prov	31:21	household is c with scarlet
Is	30:11	and c me with gladness,
Zech	3: 3	Now Joshua was c with filthy
Matt	3: 4	himself was c in camel's hair
Matt	11: 8	A man c in soft garments
Matt	25:36	I was naked and you c Me
Mark	5:15	had the legion, sitting and c
Mark	15:17	And they c Him with purple
Mark	16: 5	man c in a long white robe
1Co	4:11	and thirst, and we are poorly c
2Co	5: 2	earnestly desiring to be c
1Pe	5: 5	and be c with humility, for
Rev	1:13	c with a garment down to the
Rev	3: 5	shall be c in white garments
Rev	19:13	He was c with a robe dipped

CLOTHES (see CLOTHE, CLOTHING)
Gen	27:15	c of her elder son Esau,
Gen	37:34	Then Jacob tore his c, put
Ex	19:10	and let them wash their c
Lev	10: 6	your heads nor tear your c
Lev	13: 6	scab, and he shall wash his c
Deut	21:13	off the c of her captivity
Deut	29: 5	Your c have not worn out on
Judg	17:10	silver per year, a suit of c
Job	9:31	and my own c will abhor me
Jer	38:12	Please put these old c and
Amos	2: 8	altar on c taken in pledge
Matt	6:30	Now if God so c the grass of
Matt	17: 2	His c became as white as the
Matt	21: 7	colt, laid their c on them
Matt	21: 8	spread their c on the road;
Matt	26:65	the high priest tore his c
Matt	27:31	off Him, put His own c on Him
Mark	5:28	If only I may touch His c
Mark	13:16	not go back to get his c
Luke	19:36	spread their c on the road
Jas	2: 2	in a poor man in filthy c
Jas	2: 3	to the one wearing the fine c

CLOTHING (see CLOTHES)
Gen	27:27	he smelled the smell of his c
Gen	41:14	and he shaved, changed his c
Judg	14:12	and thirty changes of c
Ps	22:18	And for My c they cast lots
Ps	35:13	were sick, My c was sackcloth
Prov	31:22	her c is fine linen and purple
Prov	31:25	Strength and honor are her c
Matt	6:25	food and the body more than c
Matt	6:28	So why do you worry about c
Matt	7:15	who come to you in sheep's c
Matt	11: 8	those who wear soft c are in
Matt	27:35	and for My c they cast lots
Matt	28: 3	and his c as white as snow
Luke	10:30	who stripped him of his c
Acts	10:30	stood before me in bright c
1Ti	2: 9	or gold or pearls or costly c

CLOTHS (see CLOTH)
Ezek	16: 4	nor swathed in swaddling c

Luke	2:12	a Babe wrapped in swaddling **c**
Luke	24:12	he saw the linen **c** lying by
John	20: 7	not lying with the linen **c**

CLOUD (see CLOUDS)

Gen	9:13	I set My rainbow in the **c**
Ex	13:21	a pillar of **c** to lead the way
Ex	13:22	of **c** by day or the pillar of
Ex	14:24	the pillar of fire and **c**, and
Ex	16:10	of the LORD appeared in the **c**
Ex	19:16	a thick **c** on the mountain
Ex	34: 5	the LORD descended in the **c**
Lev	16: 2	in the **c** above the mercy seat
Lev	16:13	that the **c** of incense may
Num	9:15	the **c** covered the tabernacle,
1Ki	18:44	There is a **c**, as small as a
Is	19: 1	the LORD rides on a swift **c**
Is	44:22	blotted out, like a thick **c**
Hos	6: 4	is like a morning **c**, and like
Matt	17: 5	a bright **c** overshadowed them
Matt	17: 5	a voice came out of the **c**
Luke	12:54	When you see a **c** rising out
Luke	21:27	Man coming in a **c** with power
Acts	1: 9	a **c** received Him out of their
1Co	10: 1	our fathers were under the **c**
1Co	10: 2	baptized into Moses in the **c**
Heb	12: 1	by so great a **c** of witnesses
Rev	10: 1	from heaven, clothed with a **c**
Rev	11:12	ascended to heaven in a **c**
Rev	14:14	looked, and behold, a white **c**
Rev	14:14	on the **c** sat One like the Son

CLOUDS (see CLOUD)

Ps	36: 5	faithfulness reaches to the **c**
Ps	68: 4	Extol Him who rides on the **c**
Ps	104: 3	Who makes the **c** His chariot
Dan	7:13	coming with the **c** of heaven
Matt	24:30	on the **c** of heaven with power
Matt	26:64	and coming on the **c** of heaven
1Th	4:17	together with them in the **c**
2Pe	2:17	**c** carried by a tempest, to
Jude	12	they are **c** without water,
Rev	1: 7	Behold, He is coming with **c**

CLOVEN

Deut	14: 7	chew the cud or have **c** hooves

CLUNG (see CLING)

Ruth	1:14	but Ruth **c** to her

CLUSTER

Num	13:23	a branch with one **c** of grapes

COAL (see COALS)

Is	6: 6	having in his hand a live **c**

COALS (see COAL)

Lev	16:12	**c** of fire from the altar
Ps	140:10	Let burning **c** fall upon them
Prov	25:22	heap **c** of fire on his head
John	18:18	made a fire of **c** stood there
Rom	12:20	heap **c** of fire on his head

CODE†

Rom	2:27	who, even with your written **c**

COFFIN†

Gen	50:26	and he was put in a **c** in Egypt
2Sa	3:31	And King David followed the **c**
Luke	7:14	He came and touched the open **c**

COIN† (see COINS)

Matt	10:29	sparrows sold for a copper **c**
Luke	15: 8	coins, if she loses one **c**

COINS (see COIN)

Ps	119:72	thousands of **c** of gold
Luke	12: 6	sold for two copper **c**
Luke	15: 8	woman, having ten silver **c**

COLD

Gen	8:22	seedtime and harvest, and **c**
Ps	147:17	Who can stand before His **c**
Prov	25:13	Like the **c** of snow in time of
Prov	25:20	away a garment in **c** weather
Prov	25:25	As **c** water to a weary soul,
Matt	10:42	of **c** water in the name of a
Matt	24:12	the love of many will grow **c**
John	18:18	stood there, for it was **c**
2Co	11:27	in fastings often, in **c** and
Rev	3:15	you are neither **c** nor hot

COLLECT (see COLLECTED, COLLECTING, COLLECTION, COLLECTOR)

Gen	41:34	to **c** one-fifth of the produce
Luke	19:21	You **c** what you did not

COLLECTED† (see COLLECT)

Luke	19:23	might have **c** it with interest

COLLECTING† (see COLLECT)

Eccl	2:26	the work of gathering and **c**
Luke	19:22	**c** what I did not deposit and

COLLECTION (see COLLECT, COLLECTIONS)

2Ch	24: 9	to bring to the LORD the **c**
Is	57:13	let your **c** of idols deliver
1Co	16: 1	the **c** for the saints, as I

COLLECTIONS (see COLLECTION)

1Co	16: 2	there be no **c** when I come

COLLECTOR (see COLLECT, COLLECTORS)

Matt	10: 3	Thomas and Matthew the tax **c**
Luke	5:27	and saw a tax **c** named Levi,
Luke	18:10	Pharisee and the other a tax **c**
Luke	19: 2	who was a chief tax **c**, and he

COLLECTORS (see COLLECTOR)

Matt	5:46	even the tax **c** do the same
Matt	9:10	that behold, many tax **c** and
Matt	9:11	your Teacher eat with tax **c**
Matt	11:19	winebibber, a friend of tax **c**
Luke	7:29	even the tax **c** justified God,

COLORS

Gen	37: 3	he made him a tunic of many **c**
2Sa	13:18	she had on a robe of many **c**
Ps	45:14	the King in robes of many **c**

COLOSSE†

Col	1: 2	in Christ who are in **C**

COLT

Gen	49:11	his donkey's **c** to the choice
Zech	9: 9	and riding on a donkey, a **c**
Matt	21: 2	donkey tied, and a **c** with her
Luke	19:35	their own garments on the **c**
John	12:15	sitting on a donkey's **c**

COLUMN† (see COLUMNS)

Judg	20:40	from the city in a **c** of smoke
Joel	2: 8	one marches in his own **c**

COLUMNS† (see COLUMN)

Jer	36:23	had read three or four **c**,

COMELINESS†

Is	53: 2	He has no form or **c**

COMFORT (see COMFORTED, COMFORTERS, COMFORTS)

Gen	5:29	This one will **c** us concerning
Gen	37:35	his daughters arose to **c** him
Job	2:11	mourn with him, and to **c** him
Job	6:10	Then I would still have **c**
Job	7:13	When I say, "My bed will **c** me
Job	10:20	that I may take a little **c**
Ps	23: 4	rod and Your staff, they **c** me
Ps	71:21	And **c** me on every side
Ps	119:50	This is my **c** in my affliction
Is	40: 1	**C**, yes, **c** My people
Is	40: 2	Speak **c** to Jerusalem, and cry
Is	51: 3	For the LORD will **c** Zion, He
Is	61: 2	to **c** all who mourn,
Zech	1:17	the LORD will again **c** Zion
Acts	9:31	in the **c** of the Holy Spirit,
Rom	15: 4	**c** of the Scriptures might
Rom	15: 5	**c** grant you to be like-minded
2Co	1: 3	of mercies and God of all **c**
2Co	1: 4	to **c** those who are in any
2Co	7: 4	I am filled with **c**
2Co	13:11	Be of good **c**, be of one mind,
Eph	6:22	and that he may **c** your hearts
Phil	2: 1	if any **c** of love, if any
Col	4:11	have proved to be a **c** to me
1Th	4:18	Therefore **c** one another with
1Th	5:14	**c** the fainthearted, uphold

COMFORTED (see COMFORT)

Gen	24:67	So Isaac was **c** after his
Gen	37:35	but he refused to be **c**, and he
Gen	50:21	he **c** them and spoke kindly to
Ruth	2:13	for you have **c** me, and have
Job	42:11	**c** him for all the adversity
Ps	77: 2	My soul refused to be **c**
Is	49:13	For the LORD has **c** His people
Jer	31:15	refusing to be **c** for her

Matt	2:18	children, refusing to be **c**
Matt	5: 4	mourn, for they shall be **c**
Acts	20:12	and they were not a little **c**
2Co	1: 4	we ourselves are **c** by God
2Co	7:13	have been **c** in your comfort
1Th	3: 7	distress we were **c** concerning

COMFORTERS (see COMFORT)

Job	16: 2	miserable **c** are you all

COMFORTS (see COMFORT)

Is	51:12	I, even I, am He who **c** you
2Co	1: 4	who **c** us in all our
2Co	7: 6	who **c** the downcast, comforted

COMMAND (see COMMANDED, COMMANDER, COMMANDING, COMMANDMENT, COMMANDS)

Gen	18:19	that he may **c** his children
Ex	7: 2	shall speak all that I **c** you
Josh	1:16	All that you **c** us we will do,
Ps	147:15	sends out His **c** to the earth
Prov	6:20	My son, keep your father's **c**
Jer	1: 7	send you, and whatever I **c** you
Jer	23:32	I did not send them or **c** them
Dan	9:25	forth of the **c** to restore
Matt	4: 3	**c** that these stones become
Matt	19: 7	Why then did Moses **c** to give
Matt	27:64	Therefore **c** that the tomb be
Mark	9:25	I **c** you, come out of him, and
Luke	9:54	do You want us to **c** fire to
John	10:18	This **c** I have received from
John	11:57	the Pharisees had given a **c**
John	12:49	who sent Me gave Me a **c**, what
John	15:14	if you do whatever I **c** you
Acts	15: 5	to **c** them to keep the law of
Acts	16:18	I **c** you in the name of Jesus
1Co	7:10	Now to the married I **c**, yet
2Th	3: 6	But we **c** you, brethren, in
1Ti	4:11	These things **c** and teach
Heb	11:23	not afraid of the king's **c**
Rev	3:10	have kept My **c** to persevere

COMMANDED (see COMMAND)

Gen	2:16	And the LORD God **c** the man
Gen	3:11	from the tree of which I **c**
Gen	6:22	to all that God **c** him, so he
Gen	7: 9	and female, as God had **c** Noah
Gen	7:16	went in as God had **c** him
Gen	12:20	So Pharaoh **c** his men
Ex	1:22	So Pharaoh **c** all his people,
Ex	4:28	the signs which He had **c** him
Ex	5: 6	**c** the taskmasters of the
Ex	7: 6	just as the LORD **c** them, so
Ex	12:50	as the LORD **c** Moses and Aaron,
Ex	16:24	up till morning, as Moses **c**
Ex	34:18	unleavened bread, as I **c** you
Ex	39: 1	as the LORD had **c** Moses
Num	36:13	judgments which the LORD **c**
Deut	1:16	Then I **c** your judges at that
Deut	5:15	**c** you to keep the Sabbath day
Deut	6: 1	your God has **c** to teach you
Deut	6:17	statutes which He has **c** you
Deut	6:24	the LORD **c** us to observe all

Deut	9:12	from the way which I c them
Deut	13: 5	LORD your God c you to walk
Deut	31:25	that Moses c the Levites, who
Deut	33: 4	Moses c a law for us, a
Josh	1: 7	which Moses My servant c you
Josh	1: 9	Have I not c you
Josh	7:11	My covenant which I c them
Ruth	2: 9	Have I not c the young men
Ruth	2:15	Boaz c his young men, saying,
2Sa	7: 7	whom I c to shepherd My
1Ki	17: 4	I have c the ravens to feed
Job	42: 9	and did as the LORD c them
Ps	33: 9	He c, and it stood fast
Ps	105: 8	forever, The word which He c
Ps	133: 3	there the LORD c the blessing
Lam	2:17	which He c in days of old
Lam	3:37	when the Lord has not c it
Ezek	12: 7	So I did as I was c
Ezek	37: 7	So I prophesied as I was c
Matt	1:24	the angel of the Lord c him
Matt	8: 4	offer the gift that Moses c
Matt	16:20	Then He c His disciples that
Matt	27:58	Then Pilate c the body to be
Matt	28:20	all things that I have c you
Mark	1:44	those things which Moses c
Luke	8:29	For He had c the unclean
Luke	14:22	Master, it is done as you c
Acts	1: 4	He c them not to depart from
Acts	4:18	c them not to speak at all
Acts	10:42	And He c us to preach to the
Acts	10:48	he c them to be baptized in
Acts	16:22	c them to be beaten with rods
Acts	23: 2	the high priest Ananias c
Acts	23:30	also c his accusers to state
Acts	24:23	So he c the centurion to keep
1Co	9:14	Even so the Lord has c that
2Co	4: 6	who c light to shine out of
1Th	4:11	your own hands, as we c you
Tit	1: 5	in every city as I c you
Heb	9:20	covenant which God has c you
Heb	12:20	could not endure what was c
Rev	9: 4	They were c not to harm the

COMMANDER (see COMMAND)

Josh	5:15	Then the C of the LORD's army
Is	55: 4	a leader and c for the people

COMMANDING† (see COMMAND)

Gen	49:33	Jacob had finished c his sons
Matt	11: 1	when Jesus finished c His
Acts	16:23	c the jailer to keep them

COMMANDMENT (see COMMAND, COMMANDMENTS)

Ex	36: 6	So Moses gave a c, and they
Deut	8: 1	Every c which I command you
Josh	22: 5	diligent heed to do the c
Ps	19: 8	The c of the LORD is pure,
Prov	6:23	For the c is a lamp, and the
Prov	13:18	fears the c will be rewarded
Prov	19:16	keeps the c keeps his soul
Matt	22:36	is the great c in the law
Matt	22:38	This is the first and great c
Mark	7: 8	For laying aside the c of God

Luke	23:56	Sabbath according to the c
John	13:34	A new c I give to you, that
John	14:31	and as the Father gave Me c
John	15:12	This is My c, that you love
Rom	7: 8	taking opportunity by the c
Rom	7: 9	the law, but when the c came
Rom	7:12	the c holy and just and good
Rom	7:13	so that sin through the c
1Co	7: 6	as a concession, not as a c
1Co	7:25	I have no c from the Lord
2Co	8: 8	I speak not by c, but I am
Eph	6: 2	is the first c with promise
1Ti	1: 1	by the c of God our Savior and
1Ti	1: 5	Now the purpose of the c is
1Ti	6:14	you keep this c without spot
Heb	7: 5	have a c to receive tithes
Heb	7:16	to the law of a fleshly c
Heb	7:18	c because of its weakness
2Pe	2:21	the holy c delivered to them
2Pe	3: 2	of the c of us the apostles
1Jn	2: 7	I write no new c to you, but
1Jn	3:23	And this is His c
1Jn	4:21	And this c we have from Him
2Jn	5	though I wrote a new c to you

COMMANDMENTS (see COMMANDMENT)

Ex	20: 6	who love Me and keep My c
Ex	24:12	c which I have written, that
Ex	34:28	of the covenant, the Ten C
Deut	4:13	perform, that is, the Ten C
Deut	10: 4	the first writing, the Ten C
Deut	11:13	c which I command you today
1Ki	14: 8	servant David, who kept My c
Ezra	9:10	For we have forsaken Your c
Ezra	9:14	should we again break Your c
Ps	119:10	let me not wander from Your c
Ps	119:19	Do not hide Your c from me
Ps	119:21	cursed, Who stray from Your c
Ps	119:35	me walk in the path of Your c
Ps	119:47	will delight myself in Your c
Ps	119:66	For I believe Your c
Ps	119:86	All Your c are faithful
Ps	119:127	I love Your c More than gold
Ps	119:143	Yet Your c are my delights
Ps	119:151	LORD, And all Your c are truth
Ps	119:176	For I do not forget Your c
Eccl	12:13	Fear God and Keep His c, for
Dan	9: 4	and with those who keep His c
Matt	5:19	one of the least of these c
Matt	15: 9	as doctrines the c of men
Matt	19:17	enter into life, keep the c
Matt	22:40	On these two c hang all the
Mark	12:29	The first of all the c is
John	14:15	If you love Me, keep My c
John	15:10	as I have kept My Father's c
Rom	13: 9	For the c, "You shall not
Eph	2:15	the law of c contained in
1Jn	2: 3	we know Him, if we keep His c
1Jn	3:24	who keeps His c abides in Him
1Jn	5: 2	we love God and keep His c
1Jn	5: 3	And His c are not burdensome

COMMANDS (see COMMAND)

Prov	2: 1	and treasure my c within you

Prov	7: 2	Keep my c and live, and my law
Luke	8:25	For He c even the winds and
Acts	17:30	but now c all men everywhere

COMMEND (see COMMENDATION)

Acts	20:32	I c you to God and to the word
1Co	8: 8	But food does not c us to God
2Co	3: 1	we begin again to c ourselves

COMMENDATION (see COMMEND)

2Co	3: 1	you or letters of c from you

COMMIT (see COMMITS, COMMITTED, COMMITTING)

Ex	20:14	You shall not c adultery
Lev	20: 5	him to c harlotry with Molech
Job	5: 8	and to God I would c my cause
Ps	31: 5	Into Your hand I c my spirit
Ps	37: 5	C your way to the LORD, Trust
Prov	16: 3	C your works to the LORD, and
Matt	5:27	You shall not c adultery
Luke	16:11	who will c to your trust the
Luke	23:46	into Your hands I c My spirit
1Co	10: 8	Nor let us c sexual
2Co	11: 7	Did I c sin in abasing myself
1Ti	1:18	This charge I c to you, son
2Ti	2: 2	c these to faithful men who
Jas	2: 9	show partiality, you c sin
1Jn	5:16	c sin not leading to death
Rev	2:14	and to c sexual immorality

COMMITS (see COMMIT)

Lev	20:10	The man who c adultery with
Num	5: 6	When a man or woman c any
Matt	5:32	who is divorced c adultery
John	8:34	whoever c sin is a slave of
1Co	6:18	the body, but he who c sexual
1Jn	3: 4	sin also c lawlessness, and

COMMITTED (see COMMIT)

Ex	32:31	have c a great sin
Num	15:24	if it is unintentionally c
Jer	2:13	My people have c two evils
Luke	12:48	and to whom much has been c
John	5:22	but has c all judgment to the
Acts	25:25	had c nothing worthy of death
Rom	3: 2	were c the oracles of God
Rom	11:32	For God has c them all to
2Co	5:19	and has c to us the word of
2Ti	1:12	have c to Him until that Day
2Ti	1:14	good thing which was c to you
Heb	9: 7	people's sins c in ignorance
Jas	5:15	And if he has c sins, he will
1Pe	2:22	Who c no sin, nor was guile
1Pe	2:23	but c Himself to Him who
Jude	15	they have c in an ungodly way
Rev	20: 4	and judgment was c to them

COMMITTING (see COMMIT)

Rom	1:27	men with men c what is

COMMON

Lev	4:27	If anyone of the c people
Num	16:29	by the c fate of all men,

1Sa	21: 4	There is no c bread on hand
1Ki	10:27	as c in Jerusalem as stones
Prov	22: 2	and the poor have this in c
Prov	29:13	the oppressor have this in c
Eccl	6: 1	the sun, and it is c among men
Ezek	42:20	the holy areas from the c
Mark	12:37	the c people heard Him gladly
Acts	2:44	and had all things in c,
Acts	5:18	and put them in the c prison
Acts	10:14	eaten anything c or unclean
1Co	10:13	except such as is c to man
Tit	1: 4	my true son in our c faith
Heb	10:29	he was sanctified a c thing
Jude	3	concerning our c salvation

COMMONWEALTH†

Eph	2:12	aliens from the c of Israel

COMMUNION

1Co	10:16	is it not the c of the blood
2Co	6:14	And what c has light with
2Co	13:14	the c of the Holy Spirit be

COMPANION (see COMPANIONS)

Ex	2:13	Why are you striking your c
Ex	32:27	his brother, every man his c
Job	30:29	jackals, and a c of ostriches
Ps	55:13	was you, a man my equal, My c
Ps	119:63	I am a c of all those who
Prov	2:17	forsakes the c of her youth
Prov	13:20	but the c of fools will be
Prov	28: 7	but a c of gluttons shames
Prov	29: 3	but a c of harlots wastes his
Eccl	4:10	fall, one will lift up his c
Zech	13: 7	against the Man who is My C
Mal	2:14	yet she is your c and your
Phil	4: 3	And I urge you also, true c
Rev	1: 9	c in tribulation, and in the

COMPANIONS (see COMPANION)

Num	16:40	become like Korah and his c
Ps	45: 7	of gladness more than Your c
Dan	2:13	they sought Daniel and his c
Acts	19:29	Macedonians, Paul's travel c
Heb	1: 9	of gladness more than Your c

COMPANY (see ASSEMBLY)

Ps	68:11	Great was the c of those who
Ps	107:32	Him in the c of the elders
Luke	2:44	Him to have been in the c
Luke	24:22	and certain women of our c
Rom	15:24	may enjoy your c for a while
1Co	5: 9	keep c with sexually immoral
1Co	15:33	Evil c corrupts good habits
Heb	12:22	to an innumerable c of angels

COMPARABLE (see COMPARE)

Gen	2:18	make him a helper c to him

COMPARE (see COMPARABLE, COMPARED, COMPARING)

Is	40:18	likeness will you c to Him
Is	46: 5	c Me, that we should be alike
Luke	13:18	And to what shall I c it

COMPARED (*see* COMPARE)

| Ps | 89: 6 | heavens can be c to the LORD |
| Rom | 8:18 | time are not worthy to be c |

COMPARING† (*see* COMPARE)

| 1Co | 2:13 | c spiritual things with |
| 2Co | 10:12 | c themselves among themselves |

COMPASSION (*see* COMPASSIONS)

Ex	2: 6	So she had c on him, and said,
Ex	33:19	I will have c on whom I will
Deut	32:36	have c on His servants, when
1Sa	23:21	LORD, for you have c on me
1Ki	3:26	yearned with c for her son
1Ki	8:50	grant them c before those who
2Ch	30: 9	will be treated with c by
Ps	78:38	But He, being full of c,
Ps	86:15	O Lord, are a God full of c
Ps	111: 4	LORD is gracious and full of c
Is	49:15	not have c on the son of her
Lam	3:32	yet He will show c according
Matt	9:36	He was moved with c for them
Matt	15:32	I have c on the multitude,
Matt	20:34	So Jesus had c and touched
Mark	9:22	have c on us and help us
Luke	15:20	his father saw him and had c
Rom	9:15	I will have c on whomever I
1Pe	3: 8	having c for one another

COMPASSIONS† (*see* COMPASSION)

| Lam | 3:22 | because His c fail not |

COMPEL (*see* COMPELLED, COMPELS)

| Luke | 14:23 | c them to come in, that my |
| Gal | 2:14 | why do you c Gentiles to live |

COMPELLED (*see* COMPEL)

| Matt | 27:32 | Him they c to bear His cross |
| Gal | 2: 3 | was c to be circumcised |

COMPELS† (*see* COMPEL)

Job	32:18	the spirit within me c me
Matt	5:41	whoever c you to go one mile,
2Co	5:14	For the love of Christ c us

COMPETES†

1Co	9:25	everyone who c for the prize
2Ti	2: 5	also if anyone c in athletics
2Ti	2: 5	he c according to the rules

COMPLAIN (*see* COMPLAINED, COMPLAINERS, COMPLAINING, COMPLAINT)

| Num | 14:27 | who c against me |

COMPLAINED (*see* COMPLAIN)

| Ex | 15:24 | the people c against Moses |
| Num | 14:29 | you who have c against Me |

COMPLAINERS† (*see* COMPLAIN)

| Jude | 16 | These are murmurers, c, |

COMPLAINING (*see* COMPLAIN)

| Phil | 2:14 | Do all things without c |

COMPLAINT (*see* COMPLAIN)

Ps	142: 2	I pour out my c before Him
Mic	6: 2	has a c against his people
Col	3:13	has a c against another

COMPLETE (*see* COMPLETED, COMPLETELY)

Gen	15:16	of the Amorites is not yet c
2Co	13: 9	pray, that you may be made c
2Co	13:11	Become c. Be of good comfort
Phil	1: 6	a good work in you will c it
Col	2:10	and you are c in Him, who is
Col	4:12	and c in all the will of God
2Ti	3:17	that the man of God may be c
Heb	13:21	make you c in every good work
Jas	1: 4	that you may be perfect and c

COMPLETED (*see* COMPLETE)

Lev	23:15	seven Sabbaths shall be c
Jer	25:12	when seventy years are c
Jer	29:10	years are c at Babylon, I
Luke	2:21	when eight days were c for

COMPLETELY (*see* COMPLETE)

Judg	1:28	but did not c drive them out
1Ki	9:21	not been able to destroy c
John	9:34	You were c born in sins, and
John	13:10	wash his feet, but is c clean
1Th	5:23	peace Himself sanctify you c

COMPREHEND†

Job	37: 5	things which we cannot c
Ps	139: 3	You c my path and my lying
Luke	24:45	they might c the Scriptures
John	1: 5	and the darkness did not c it
Eph	3:18	may be able to c with all the

COMPULSION†

| Phm | 14 | good deed might not be by c |
| 1Pe | 5: 2 | not by c but willingly, not |

CONCEAL

| Gen | 37:26 | our brother and c his blood |
| Prov | 25: 2 | glory of God to c a matter |

CONCEIT† (*see* CONCEITED)

| Phil | 2: 3 | through selfish ambition or c |

CONCEITED† (*see* CONCEIT)

| Gal | 5:26 | Let us not become c, |

CONCEIVE (*see* CONCEIVED, CONCEIVES)

Job	15:35	They c trouble and bring forth
Is	7:14	Behold, the virgin shall c
Is	59: 4	they c evil and bring forth
Luke	1:31	you will c in your womb and

CONCEIVED (*see* CONCEIVE)

Gen	4: 1	knew Eve his wife, and she c
Ps	51: 5	And in sin my mother c me
Matt	1:20	for that which is c in her is
Luke	1:24	days his wife Elizabeth c
Luke	1:36	also c a son in her old age
Luke	2:21	before He was c in the womb

Acts	5: 4	Why have you c this thing in
Jas	1:15	Then, when desire has c, it

CONCEIVES† (see CONCEIVE)

Ps	7:14	C trouble and brings forth

CONCESSION†

1Co	7: 6	But I say this as a c, not as

CONCLUDING (see CONCLUSION)

Heb	11:19	c that God was able to raise

CONCLUSION (see CONCLUDING)

Eccl	12:13	Let us hear the c of the

CONCUBINE (see CONCUBINES)

Gen	35:22	with Bilhah his father's c
Judg	19: 2	But his c played the harlot
1Ch	1:32	born to Keturah, Abraham's c

CONCUBINES (see CONCUBINE)

Gen	25: 6	of the c which Abraham had
2Sa	5:13	And David took more c and
1Ki	11: 3	and three hundred c
Song	6: 8	are sixty queens and eighty c

CONDEMN (see CONDEMNATION, CONDEMNED, CONDEMNS)

Deut	25: 1	righteous and c the wicked,
Job	9:20	my own mouth would c me
Ps	94:21	And c innocent blood
Ps	109:31	save him from those who c him
Prov	12: 2	of wicked devices He will c
Is	50: 9	who is he who will c Me
Matt	12:41	c it, because they repented
Matt	20:18	they will c Him to death,
Luke	6:37	C not, and you shall not be
John	3:17	into the world to c the world
John	8:11	Neither do I c you
Rom	2: 1	judge another you c yourself
Rom	14:22	Happy is he who does not c
2Co	7: 3	I do not say this to c
1Jn	3:21	if our heart does not c us

CONDEMNATION (see CONDEMN)

Matt	23:14	you will receive greater c
Matt	23:33	can you escape the c of hell
Mark	3:29	but is subject to eternal c"
Luke	23:40	you are under the same c
John	3:19	And this is the c, that the
John	5:29	to the resurrection of c
Rom	3: 8	Their c is just
Rom	5:16	one offense resulted in c
Rom	8: 1	There is therefore now no c
2Co	3: 9	the ministry of c had glory
1Ti	3: 6	into the same c as the devil
Jude	4	were marked out for this c

CONDEMNED (see CONDEMN)

Job	9:29	If I am c, why then do I
Job	32: 3	no answer, and yet had c Job
Ps	34:21	hate the righteous shall be c
Ps	34:22	who trust in Him shall be c
Matt	12: 7	not have c the guiltless

Matt	12:37	by your words you will be c
Matt	27: 3	seeing that He had been c
Luke	24:20	Him to be c to death, and
John	3:18	who believes in Him is not c
John	3:18	does not believe is c already
Rom	8: 3	He c sin in the flesh,
Rom	14:23	he who doubts is c if he eats
1Co	4: 9	last, as men c to death
1Co	11:32	may not be c with the world
Tit	2: 8	sound speech that cannot be c
Heb	11: 7	by which he c the world and
2Pe	2: 6	c them to destruction, making

CONDEMNS (see CONDEMN)

Job	15: 6	Your own mouth c you, and not
Rom	8:34	Who is he who c
1Jn	3:20	For if our heart c us, God is

CONDITION

John	5: 6	been in that c a long time

CONDUCT

Ps	37:14	those who are of upright c
Phil	1:27	Only let your c be worthy of
1Ti	3:15	to c yourself in the house of
1Ti	4:12	the believers in word, in c
Jas	3:13	Let him show by good c that

CONFER (see COUNSEL)

Gal	1:16	not immediately c with flesh

CONFESS (see CONFESSED, CONFESSES, CONFESSING, CONFESSION)

Lev	5: 5	that he shall c that he has
Lev	16:21	c over it all the iniquities
Num	5: 7	then he shall c the sin
1Ki	8:33	c Your name, and pray and
Ps	32: 5	I will c my transgressions to
Matt	10:32	him I will also c before My
Luke	12: 8	c before the angels of God
John	12:42	Pharisees they did not c Him
Rom	10: 9	that if you c with your mouth
Rom	14:11	every tongue shall c to God
Phil	2:11	that every tongue should c
Jas	5:16	C your trespasses to one
1Jn	1: 9	If we c our sins, He is
1Jn	4: 3	c that Jesus Christ has come
2Jn	7	c Jesus Christ as coming in
Rev	3: 5	but I will c his name before

CONFESSED (see CONFESS)

John	1:20	He c, and did not deny, but
John	9:22	anyone c that He was Christ
1Ti	6:12	have c the good confession in
Heb	11:13	c that they were strangers and

CONFESSES (see CONFESS)

Matt	10:32	whoever c Me before men, him
1Jn	4: 2	Every spirit that c that

CONFESSING (see CONFESS)

Ezra	10: 1	praying, and while he was c
Dan	9:20	c my sin and the sin of my

Matt	3: 6	in the Jordan, c their sins
Acts	19:18	many who had believed came c

CONFESSION (see CONFESS)

Rom	10:10	with the mouth c is made to
2Co	9:13	c to the gospel of Christ
1Ti	6:13	good c before Pontius Pilate
Heb	3: 1	and High Priest of our c,
Heb	4:14	God, let us hold fast our c
Heb	10:23	the c of our hope without

CONFIDENCE (see CONFIDENT)

Ps	65: 5	You who are the c of all the
Ps	118: 8	the LORD Than to put c in man
Prov	3:26	for the LORD will be your c
Is	30:15	and c shall be your strength
2Co	2: 3	having c in you all that my
Eph	3:12	access with c through faith
Phil	3: 3	and have no c in the flesh,
2Th	3: 4	And we have c in the Lord
Phm	21	Having c in your obedience, I
Heb	3: 6	we are if we hold fast the c
Heb	3:14	of our c steadfast to the end
Heb	10:35	do not cast away your c,
1Jn	5:14	Now this is the c that we

CONFIDENT (see CONFIDENCE)

Ps	27: 3	me, In this I will be c
Phil	1: 6	being c of this very thing,
Phil	1:14	having become c by my chains
Heb	6: 9	we are c of better things
Heb	13:18	for we are c that we have a

CONFIRM (see CONFIRMED, CONFIRMING)

Rom	15: 8	to c the promises made to the

CONFIRMED (see CONFIRM, ESTABLISHED)

1Co	1: 6	of Christ was c in you,
Heb	6:17	His counsel, c it by an oath,

CONFIRMING† (see CONFIRM)

Mark	16:20	and c the word through the

CONFORMED (see CONFORMING)

Rom	8:29	be c to the image of His Son
Rom	12: 2	do not be c to this world,
Phil	3:10	being c to His death,

CONFORMING† (see CONFORMED)

1Pe	1:14	not c yourselves to the

CONFOUNDED (see APPALLED)

Ps	70: 2	and c Who seek my life

CONFUSE† (see CONFUSED, CONFUSION)

Gen	11: 7	there c their language, that

CONFUSED (see CONFUSE)

1Sa	7:10	and so c them that they were
Job	6:20	they come there and are c
Ps	70: 2	back and c Who desire my hurt
Acts	19:32	for the assembly was c, and

CONFUSION (see CONFUSE)

1Co	14:33	the author of c but of peace

CONGEALED†

Ex	15: 8	the depths c in the heart of

CONGREGATION (see ASSEMBLY)

Ex	12: 3	Speak to all the c of Israel
Ex	16:22	all the rulers of the c came
Lev	4:15	the elders of the c shall lay
Num	1: 2	Take a census of all the c of
Num	8: 9	c of the chidren of Israel.
Num	10: 2	use them for calling the c
Num	16: 3	for all the c is holy, every
Num	20: 2	there was no water for the c
Deut	33: 4	a heritage of the c of Jacob
Josh	9:21	water carriers for all the c
Ps	1: 5	in the c of the righteous
Ps	22:16	The c of the wicked has
Ps	82: 1	stands in the c of the mighty
Is	14:13	sit on the mount of the c on
Acts	13:43	Now when the c had broken up,

CONQUER (see CONQUERED, CONQUERORS)

Rev	6: 2	went out conquering and to c

CONQUERED (see CONQUER)

Josh	10:40	So Joshua c all the land

CONQUERORS† (see CONQUER)

Rom	8:37	things we are more than c

CONSCIENCE (see CONSCIENCE')

John	8: 9	being convicted by their c
Acts	23: 1	I have lived in all good c
Rom	2:15	their c also bearing witness,
1Co	8: 7	and their c, being weak, is
1Co	10:29	C, I say, not your own, but
1Co	10:29	judged by another man's c
2Co	1:12	the testimony of our c that
2Co	4: 2	man's c in the sight of God
1Ti	1: 5	a pure heart, from a good c
1Ti	1:19	having faith and a good c,
1Ti	3: 9	of the faith with a pure c
1Ti	4: 2	having their own c seared
Tit	1:15	their mind and c are defiled
Heb	9:14	purge your c from dead works
Heb	10:22	sprinkled from an evil c and
1Pe	2:19	if because of c toward God

CONSCIENCE' (see CONSCIENCE)

Rom	13: 5	of wrath but also for c sake
1Co	10:25	no questions for c sake

CONSECRATE (see CONSECRATED)

Ex	28:41	c them, and sanctify them,
Ex	29:33	the atonement was made, to c
Lev	25:10	you shall c the fiftieth year
Joel	1:14	C a fast, call a sacred
Mic	4:13	I will c their gain to the

CONSECRATED (see CONSECRATE)

Ex	29:29	in them and to be c in them

Lev	7:35	This is the c portion for
Lev	8:15	the alter, and c it, to make
Lev	8:30	he c Aaron, his garments,
Lev	16:32	c to minister as priest in
Lev	21:10	who is c to wear the garments
Num	6: 9	him, and he defiles his c head
Num	6:19	he has shaved his c hair,
Judg	17:12	So Micah c the Levite, and the
1Sa	16: 5	Then he c Jesse and his sons
1Ki	8:64	c the middle of the court
2Ch	29:33	The c things were six hundred
Heb	10:20	living way which He c for us

CONSENT (see CONSENTING)

Gen	34:22	the men c to dwell with us
Prov	1:10	sinners entice you, do not c
Acts	18:20	time with them, he did not c

CONSENTING (see CONSENT)

Acts	8: 1	Now Saul was c to his death

CONSIDER (see CONSIDERED, CONSIDERING, CONSIDERS)

Deut	4:39	c it in your heart, that the
Judg	19:30	C it, take counsel, and speak
1Sa	12:24	for c what great things He
Job	23:15	when I c this, I am afraid of
Job	37:14	c the wondrous works of God
Ps	5: 1	O LORD, C my meditation
Ps	8: 3	When I c Your heavens, the
Ps	13: 3	C and hear me, O LORD my God
Ps	25:19	C my enemies, for they are
Ps	64: 9	they shall wisely c His doing
Ps	119:95	But I will c Your testimonies
Ps	119:128	all things I c to be right
Ps	119:153	C my affliction and deliver me
Prov	6: 6	C her ways and be wise,
Prov	23: 1	C carefully what is before
Prov	24:12	He who weighs the hearts c it
Prov	28:22	does not c that poverty will
Eccl	2:12	I turned myself to c wisdom
Is	1: 3	not know, My people do not c
Is	43:18	nor c the things of old
Jer	2:10	c diligently, and see if there
Jer	30:24	the latter days you will c it
Lam	1: 9	she did not c her destiny
Lam	1:11	See, O LORD, and c, for I am
Ezek	12: 3	It may be that they will c
Dan	9:23	therefore c the matter, and
Hos	7: 2	They do not c in their hearts
Hag	1: 5	LORD of hosts: "C your ways
Hag	2:15	carefully c from this day
Matt	6:28	C the lilies of the field,
Matt	7: 3	but do not c the plank in
Luke	12:24	C the ravens, for they
Luke	14:31	c whether he is able with ten
John	11:50	nor do you c that it is
Acts	15: 6	together to c this matter
Rom	4:19	he did not c his own body,
Rom	8:18	For I c that the sufferings
Rom	11:22	Therefore c the goodness and
Phil	2: 6	did not c it robbery to be
2Ti	2: 7	C what I say, and may the Lord
Heb	3: 1	c the Apostle and High Priest

Heb	7: 4	Now c how great this man was,
Heb	10:24	let us c one another in order
Heb	12: 3	For c Him who endured such
1Pe	5:12	faithful brother as I c him

CONSIDERED (see CONSIDER)

Neh	13:13	for they were c faithful, and
Job	1: 8	Have you c My servant Job,
Job	2: 3	Have you c My servant Job,
Ps	31: 7	For You have c my trouble
Ps	77: 5	I have c the days of old, The
Prov	17:28	his lips, he is c perceptive
Mark	10:42	c rulers over the Gentiles
Luke	1:29	c what manner of greeting
Luke	22:24	them should be c the greatest
Phil	2:25	Yet I c it necessary to send

CONSIDERING (see CONSIDER)

Dan	7: 8	I was c the horns, and there
Acts	17:23	c the objects of your worship
Heb	13: 7	c the outcome of their

CONSIDERS (see CONSIDER)

Prov	31:16	She c a field and buys it
Is	44:19	no one c in his heart, nor is

CONSIST†

Luke	12:15	not c in the abundance of the
Col	1:17	and in Him all things c

CONSOLATION

Job	21: 2	speech, and let this be your c
Jer	16: 7	men give them the cup of c to
Luke	2:25	waiting for the C of Israel
Phil	2: 1	if there is any c in Christ
2Th	2:16	us and given us everlasting c

CONSPIRED

Gen	37:18	they c against him to kill
Amos	7:10	Amos has c against you in the

CONSTRAINED

Luke	24:29	But they c Him, saying
Acts	18: 5	Paul was c by the Spirit, and

CONSUME (see CONSUMED, CONSUMING)

Ex	32:10	against them and I may c them
Num	16:21	that I may c them in a moment
Deut	5:25	For this great fire will c us
Deut	28:38	in, for the locust shall c it
Job	24:19	heat c the snow waters, so
Ps	59:13	C them in wrath
Ezek	13:13	hailstones in fury to c it
Dan	7:26	take away his dominion, to c
Luke	9:54	c them, just as Elijah did
2Th	2: 8	whom the Lord will c with the

CONSUMED (see CONSUME)

Gen	19:15	here, lest you be c in the
Gen	31:15	also completely c our money
Ex	3: 2	fire, but the bush was not c
Ex	15: 7	which c them like stubble
Ps	73:19	are utterly c with terrors
Ps	104:35	sinners be c from the earth

Ps	119:139	My zeal has **c** me, Because my
Prov	5:11	your flesh and your body are **c**
Is	1:28	forsake the LORD shall be **c**
Jer	20:18	days should be **c** with shame
Jer	36:23	until all the scroll was **c** in
Lam	3:22	LORD's mercies we are not **c**
Amos	7: 4	and it **c** the great deep and
Mal	3: 6	therefore you are not **c**, O
Gal	5:15	lest you be **c** by one another

CONSUMING (see CONSUME)

Ex	24:17	a **c** fire on the top of the
Deut	4:24	the LORD your God is a **c** fire
Ezek	21:28	polished for slaughter, for **c**
Joel	1: 4	left, the **c** locust has eaten
Heb	12:29	For our God is a **c** fire

CONTAIN

1Ki	8:27	of heavens cannot **c** You
John	21:25	not **c** the books that would be

CONTEMPT (see CONTEMPTIBLE)

Deut	27:16	father or his mother with **c**
Esth	1:18	there will be excessive **c**
Job	12:21	He pours **c** on princes, and
Ps	119:22	from me reproach and **c**
Ps	123: 3	are exceedingly filled with **c**
Ps	123: 4	ease, With the **c** of the proud
Is	23: 9	and to bring into **c** all the
Dan	12: 2	to shame and everlasting **c**
Luke	23:11	of war, treated Him with **c**
Rom	14:10	you show **c** for your brother

CONTEMPTIBLE (see CONTEMPT)

Mal	1: 7	The table of the LORD is **c**
Mal	2: 9	I also have made you **c** and
2Co	10:10	is weak, and his speech **c**

CONTEND (see CONTENDED, CONTENDING)

Ex	17: 2	Why do you **c** with me
Ex	21:18	If men **c** with each other, and
Job	9: 3	If one wished to **c** with Him
Job	10: 2	show me why You **c** with me
Job	13: 8	Will you **c** for God
Prov	28: 4	as keep the law **c** with them
Is	43:26	let us **c** together
Is	57:16	For I will not **c** forever, nor
Jer	12: 5	how can you **c** with horses
Jude	3	to **c** earnestly for the faith

CONTENDED (see CONTEND)

Ex	17: 2	the people **c** with Moses, and
Num	20:13	of Israel **c** with the LORD
Deut	33: 8	with whom You **c** at the waters
Acts	11: 2	the circumcision **c** with him

CONTENDING† (see CONTEND)

Jude	9	in **c** with the devil, when he

CONTENT (see CONTENTMENT)

Ex	2:21	Then Moses was **c** to live with
Luke	3:14	and be **c** with your wages
Phil	4:11	whatever state I am, to be **c**

1Ti	6: 8	with these we shall be **c**
Heb	13: 5	be **c** with such things as you

CONTENTION (see CONTENTIONS, CONTENTIOUS)

Jer	15:10	a man of **c** to the whole earth

CONTENTIONS (see CONTENTION)

Prov	23:29	Who has sorrow? who has **c**?
1Co	1:11	that there are **c** among you

CONTENTIOUS (see CONTENTION)

Prov	21: 9	a house shared with a **c** woman
1Co	11:16	But if anyone seems to be **c**

CONTENTMENT† (see CONTENT)

1Ti	6: 6	with **c** is great gain

CONTINUAL (see CONTINUALLY, CONTINUE)

Ex	29:42	This shall be a **c** burnt
2Ch	2: 4	for the **c** showbread, for the
Prov	15:15	a merry heart has a **c** feast
Prov	19:13	of a wife are a **c** dripping
Is	14: 6	in wrath with a **c** stroke, he
Jer	48: 5	they ascend with **c** weeping
Luke	18: 5	her, lest by her **c** coming she
Rom	9: 2	sorrow and **c** grief in my heart

CONTINUALLY (see CONTINUAL)

Gen	6: 5	of his heart was only evil **c**
Gen	8: 3	receded **c** from the earth
Ex	27:20	to cause the lamp to burn **c**
2Sa	9: 7	shall eat bread at my table **c**
Ps	34: 1	praise shall **c** be in my mouth
Ps	42: 3	night, While they **c** say to me
Ps	52: 1	The goodness of God endures **c**
Ps	126: 6	He who **c** goes forth weeping,
Prov	6:21	Bind them **c** upon your heart
Is	49:16	your walls are **c** before Me
Luke	24:53	were **c** in the temple praising
Acts	6: 4	give ourselves **c** to prayer
Heb	7: 3	of God, remains a priest **c**
Heb	10: 1	they offer **c** year by year

CONTINUE (see CONTINUAL, CONTINUED, CONTINUES, CONTINUING)

1Sa	13:14	now your kingdom shall not **c**
2Sa	7:29	that it may **c** forever before
Acts	14:22	them to **c** in the faith, and
Rom	6: 1	Shall we **c** in sin that grace
Rom	11:22	if you **c** in His goodness
Rom	11:23	if they do not **c** in unbelief
1Ti	2:15	if they **c** in faith, love, and
Heb	8: 9	they did not **c** in My covenant
Heb	13: 1	Let brotherly love **c**
2Pe	3: 4	all things **c** as they were

CONTINUED (see CONTINUE)

Acts	1:14	These all **c** with one accord
Acts	2:42	they **c** steadfastly in the
1Jn	2:19	us, they would have **c** with us

CONTINUES (see CONTINUE)

Heb	7:24	But He, because He **c** forever

CONTINUING (*see* CONTINUE)

Acts	2:46	So c daily with one accord in
Rom	12:12	c steadfastly in prayer
Heb	13:14	For here we have no c city

CONTRADICTION† (*see* CONTRARY)

Heb	7: 7	Now beyond all c the lesser

CONTRARY (*see* CONTRADICTION)

Lev	26:21	Then, if you walk c to Me
Lev	26:24	I also will walk c to you
Matt	14:24	the waves, for the wind was c
Luke	22:26	on the c, he who is greatest
Acts	17: 7	these are all acting c to the
Acts	18:13	to worship God c to the law
Rom	4:18	c to hope, in hope believed,
Rom	10:21	to a disobedient and c people
Rom	11:24	were grafted c to nature into
Rom	16:17	c to the doctrine which you
1Ti	1:10	that is c to sound doctrine

CONTRIBUTION

Rom	15:26	c for the poor among the

CONTRITE

Ps	34:18	saves such as have a c spirit
Ps	51:17	spirit, A broken and a c heart
Is	57:15	place, with him who has a c

CONTROVERSY

Jer	25:31	LORD has a c with the nations
1Ti	3:16	And without c great is the

CONVENIENT

Acts	24:25	when I have a c time I will
1Co	16:12	come when he has a c time

CONVERSATION†

Jer	38:27	for the c had not been heard
Luke	24:17	What kind of c is this that

CONVERTED† (*see* CONVERTING)

Ps	51:13	And sinners shall be c to You
Matt	18: 3	say to you, unless you are c
Acts	3:19	Repent therefore and be c,

CONVERTING† (*see* CONVERTED)

Ps	19: 7	LORD is perfect, c the soul

CONVICT† (*see* CONVICTS)

John	16: 8	He will c the world of sin,
Tit	1: 9	and c those who contradict
Jude	15	all, to c all who are ungodly

CONVICTS† (*see* CONVICT)

John	8:46	Which of you c Me of sin

CONVINCED

Acts	26:26	for I am c that none of these
Rom	4:21	being fully c that what He
Rom	14: 5	be fully c in his own mind
Rom	14:14	am c by the Lord Jesus that
1Co	14:24	he is c by all, he is judged

CONVOCATION

Ex	12:16	day there shall be a holy c

CONVULSES†

Luke	9:39	it c him so that he foams at

COOL

Gen	3: 8	garden in the c of the day
Luke	16:24	in water and c my tongue

COPIED† (*see* COPY)

Prov	25: 1	of Hezekiah king of Judah c

COPIES (*see* COPY)

Heb	9:23	the c of the things in the

COPY (*see* COPIED, COPIES)

Deut	17:18	are c of this law in a book
Josh	8:32	a c of the law of Moses,
Heb	8: 5	who serve the c and shadow of

CORBAN†

Mark	7:11	from me is C (that is,

CORD (*see* CORDS)

Gen	38:18	Your signet and c, and your
Josh	2:21	the scarlet c in the window
Eccl	4:12	a threefold c is not quickly
Eccl	12: 6	before the silver c is loosed

CORDS (*see* CORD)

Ps	2: 3	And cast away Their c from us
Ps	119:61	The c of the wicked have
Is	54: 2	lengthen your c, and
Hos	11: 4	I drew them with gentle c

CORIANDER†

Ex	16:31	And it was like white c seed
Num	11: 7	Now the manna was like c seed

CORINTH (*see* CORINTHIANS)

Acts	18: 1	from Athens and went to C
1Co	1: 2	church of God which is at C

CORINTHIANS† (*see* CORINTH)

Acts	18: 8	And many of the C, hearing,
2Co	6:11	O C! We have spoken openly

CORNELIUS

Acts	10: 1	man in Caesarea called C, a

CORNER (*see* CORNERS, CORNERSTONE)

1Sa	24: 4	cut off a c of Saul's robe
Prov	7: 8	along the street near her c
Prov	7:12	square, lurking at every c
Prov	21: 9	to dwell in a c of a housetop
Acts	26:26	thing was not done in a c

CORNERS (*see* CORNER)

Ex	27: 2	make its horns on its four c
Lev	19: 9	reap the c of your field, nor
Deut	22:12	make tassels on the four c of
Is	11:12	from the four c of the earth

Acts   10:11 sheet bound at the four c
Rev   7: 1 at the four c of the earth

CORNERSTONE (see CORNER)

Ps   118:22 Has become the chief c
Is   28:16 a tried stone, a precious c
Zech   10: 4 From him comes the c, from
Matt   21:42 has become the chief c
1Pe   2: 6 I lay in Zion a chief c,

CORPSE (see CORPSES, DEAD)

Lev   22: 4 anything made unclean by a c

CORPSES (see CORPSE)

2Ki   19:35 the morning, there were the c

CORRECT (see CORRECTED, CORRECTION)

Job   40: 2 with the Almighty c Him
Ps   39:11 You c man for iniquity, You
Ps   94:10 the nations, shall He not c
Prov   29:17 C your son, and he will give
Jer   2:19 own wickedness will c you
Jer   10:24 LORD, c me, but with justice

CORRECTED† (see CORRECT)

Prov   29:19 will not be c by mere words
Hab   2: 1 answer when I am c
Heb   12: 9 had human fathers who c us

CORRECTION (see CORRECT)

Prov   3:11 of the LORD, nor detest His c
Prov   22:15 but the rod of c will drive
Prov   23:13 not withhold c from a child
2Ti   3:16 doctrine, for reproof, for c

CORRESPONDING (see CORRESPONDS)

Ex   38:18 c to the hangings of the

CORRESPONDS† (see CORRESPONDING)

Gal   4:25 c to Jerusalem which now is,

CORRODED†

Jas   5: 3 Your gold and silver are c

CORRUPT (see CORRUPTED, CORRUPTIBLE, CORRUPTION, CORRUPTS)

Gen   6:11 earth also was c before God
1Sa   2:12 Now the sons of Eli were c
Ps   14: 1 They are c, They have done
Dan   2: 9 c words before me till the
Dan   11:32 he shall c with flattery
Eph   4:22 the old man which grows c
Eph   4:29 Let no c communication
1Ti   6: 5 wranglings of men of c minds
Jude   10 things they c themselves

CORRUPTED (see CORRUPT)

Gen   6:12 for all flesh had c their way
Ex   8:24 The land was c because of the
Mal   2: 8 You have c the covenant of
2Co   11: 3 so your minds may be c from
Jas   5: 2 Your riches are c, and your
Rev   19: 2 who c the earth with her

CORRUPTIBLE (see CORRUPT)

Rom   1:23 into an image made like c man
1Co   15:53 For this c must put on
1Pe   1:18 not redeemed with c things
1Pe   1:23 born again, not of c seed but

CORRUPTION (see CORRUPT)

2Ki   23:13 the south of the Mount of C
Ps   16:10 allow Your Holy One to see c
Is   38:17 my soul from the pit of c
Acts   2:27 allow Your Holy One to see c
Acts   2:31 nor did His flesh see c
Rom   8:21 from the bondage of c into
1Co   15:42 The body is sown in c, it is
1Co   15:50 nor does c inherit
Gal   6: 8 will of the flesh reap c, but
2Pe   1: 4 having escaped the c that is
2Pe   2:19 themselves are slaves of c

CORRUPTS† (see CORRUPT)

1Co   15:33 Evil company c good habits

COST (see COSTS)

Prov   7:23 it would c his life.
Luke   14:28 sit down first and count the c

COSTS (see COST)

2Sa   24:24 with that which c me nothing

COUNCIL (see COUNCILS)

Matt   5:22 shall be in danger of the c
Luke   22:66 and led Him into their c,
Acts   22: 5 all the c of the elders, from
Acts   23: 6 he cried out in the c, "Men

COUNCILS (see COUNCIL)

Matt   10:17 they will deliver you up to c

COUNSEL (see ADVICE, ADVISE, CONFER, COUNSELOR, DECISION, INQUIRE, INSTRUCTION, PLOT, PURPOSE, WILL)

Num   31:16 through the c of Balaam, to
2Sa   15:31 turn the c of Ahithophel into
Job   38: 2 Who is this who darkens c by
Ps   1: 1 not in the c of the ungodly
Ps   2: 2 And the rulers take c together
Ps   55:14 We took sweet c together, And
Ps   73:24 You will guide me with Your c
Ps   107:11 despised the c of the Most
Prov   1: 5 will attain wise c,
Prov   12:15 but he who heeds c is wise
Is   5:19 let the c of the Holy One of
Is   11: 2 the Spirit of c and might,
Is   28:29 hosts, Who is wonderful in c
Is   30: 1 Who take c, but not of Me, and
Jer   18:18 nor c from the wise, nor the
Acts   20:27 to you the whole c of God
Eph   1:11 to the c of His will,
Heb   6:17 the immutability of His c

COUNSELOR (see COUNSEL, COUNSELORS)

Is   9: 6 will be called wonderful, C

Is	40:13	or as His c has taught Him
Rom	11:34	Or who has become His c

COUNSELORS (see COUNSELOR)

Prov	11:14	of c there is safety
Is	1:26	your c as at the beginning
Dan	3: 2	the governors, the c, the

COUNT (see COUNTED)

Gen	15: 5	c the stars if you are able
Lev	23:16	C fifty days to the day
Lev	25: 8	you shall c seven sabbaths of
Num	23:10	Who can c the dust of Jacob,
Deut	16: 9	begin to c the seven weeks
Ps	22:17	I can c all My bones
Luke	14:28	c the cost, whether he has
Phil	3: 8	But indeed I also c all
Phil	3: 8	c them as rubbish, that I may
Phil	3:13	I do not c myself to have
2Th	1:11	c you worthy of this calling
Phm	17	If then you c me as a partner
Jas	1: 2	c it all joy when you fall
2Pe	3: 9	as some c slackness, but is

COUNTED (see COUNT)

Gen	16:10	shall not be c for multitude
Matt	14: 5	because they c him as a
Matt	26:15	And they c out to him thirty
Mark	11:32	for all c John to have been a
Luke	20:35	But those who are c worthy to
Acts	5:41	rejoicing that they were c
Rom	2:26	be c as circumcision
Rom	4: 4	the wages are not c as grace
Rom	9: 8	the promise are c as the seed
Phil	3: 7	me, these I have c loss for
2Th	1: 5	that you may be c worthy of
1Ti	1:12	because He c me faithful,
1Ti	5:17	be c worthy of double honor
Heb	3: 3	For this One has been c
Heb	10:29	c the blood of the covenant

COUNTENANCE (see FACE)

Gen	4: 5	was very angry, and his c fell
Gen	12:11	are a woman of beautiful c
Gen	31: 2	And Jacob saw the c of Laban
Gen	31: 5	I see your father's c, that
Num	6:26	LORD lift up His c upon you
Deut	28:50	a nation of fierce c, which
Judg	13: 6	the c of the Angel of God
1Sa	14:27	and his c brightened
2Ki	8:11	Then he set his c in a stare
Job	14:20	You change his c and send him
Ps	4: 6	the light of Your c upon us
Ps	10: 4	his proud c does not seek God
Ps	42: 5	Him For the help of His c
Ps	44: 3	arm, and the light of Your c
Ps	80:16	at the rebuke of Your c
Prov	15:13	heart makes a cheerful c, but
Prov	25:23	backbiting tongue an angry c
Prov	27:17	sharpens the c of his friend
Eccl	7: 3	for by a sad c the heart is
Dan	5: 6	Then the king's c changed
Matt	28: 3	His c was like lightning, and

2Co	3: 7	because of the glory of his c
Rev	1:16	and His c was like the sun

COUNTRIES (see COUNTRY)

Gen	41:57	So all c came to Joseph in
Ps	110: 6	execute the heads of many c
Is	8: 9	Give ear, all you from far c
Jer	23: 3	of My flock out of all c
Ezek	35:10	these two c shall be mine, and
Dan	11:41	many c shall be overthrown
Zech	10: 9	shall remember Me in a far c

COUNTRY (see COUNTRIES)

Gen	12: 1	Get out of your c, from your
Deut	28: 3	blessed shall you be in the c
Deut	28:16	cursed shall you be in the c
Josh	6:22	men who had spied out the c
Josh	9: 6	We have come from a far c
Josh	11:16	the mountain c, all the South
Prov	25:25	so is good news from a far c
Is	1: 7	Your c is desolate, your
Jer	2: 7	you into a bountiful c, to
Jer	6:22	people comes from the north c
Matt	2:12	for their own c another way
Matt	13:57	honor except in his own c
Matt	21:33	and went into a far c
Mark	5:14	it in the city and in the c
Luke	1:39	into the hill c with haste
Luke	1:65	all the hill c of Judea
Luke	2: 8	Now there were in the same c
Luke	4:24	is accepted in his own c
John	4:44	has no honor in his own c
Acts	7: 3	to him, 'Get out of your c
Heb	11:16	better, that is, a heavenly c

COUPLE (see COUPLED)

Ex	26: 9	you shall c five curtains by
1Ki	17:12	I am gathering a c of sticks

COUPLED (see COUPLE)

Ex	26: 3	shall be c to one another
Ex	26:24	They shall be c together at
Ex	36:10	he c five curtains to one
Ex	36:29	they were c at the bottom and
Ex	36:29	c together at the top by one

COURAGE (see COURAGEOUS)

Num	13:20	Be of good c
Deut	31: 6	Be strong and of good c, do
2Ch	15: 8	Oded the prophet, he took c
Acts	28:15	he thanked God and took c

COURAGEOUS (see COURAGE)

Josh	1: 7	Only be strong and very c,

COURSE (see COURSES)

Eph	2: 2	to the c of this world,
Jas	3: 6	set on fire the c of nature

COURSES† (see COURSE)

Judg	5:20	the stars from their c fought

COURT (see COURTS, COURTYARD)

Ex	27: 9	make the c of the tabernacle

2Ch	4: 9	he made the c of the priests
2Ch	29:16	c of the house of the LORD
Neh	3:25	was by the c of the prison
Esth	1: 5	in the c of the garden of the
Esth	6: 4	c of the king's palace to
Job	9:19	who will appoint my day in c
Job	9:32	we should go to c together
Job	11:19	yes, many would c your favor
Prov	25: 8	Do not go hastily to c
Jer	32: 2	up in the c of the prison
Jer	36:10	in the upper c at the entry
Ezek	10: 3	the cloud filled the inner c
Ezek	46:22	of the c were enclosed courts
Dan	7:10	The c was seated, and the
1Co	4: 3	judged by you or by a human c
Gal	4:17	They zealously c you, but for
Rev	11: 2	But leave out the c which is

COURTEOUS† (see COURTESY)

| 1Pe | 3: 8 | be tenderhearted, be c |

COURTESY† (see COURTEOUS)

| Acts | 24: 4 | I beg you to hear, by your c |

COURTS (see COURT)

2Ki	23:12	had made in the two c of the
Ps	65: 4	That he may dwell in Your c
Ps	84: 2	faints For the c of the LORD
Ps	84:10	For a day in Your c is better
Ps	92:13	flourish in the c of our God
Ps	100: 4	And into His c with praise
Is	1:12	your hand, to trample My c
Jas	2: 6	you and drag you into the c

COURTYARD (see COURT)

| Matt | 26:69 | Peter sat outside in the c |

COVENANT (see COVENANTS, TESTAMENT)

Gen	6:18	will establish My c with you
Gen	9: 9	I establish My c with you
Gen	9:13	the sign of the c between Me
Gen	9:16	the everlasting c between God
Gen	15:18	the LORD made a c with Abram
Gen	17: 9	for you, you shall keep My c
Gen	17:11	be a sign of the c between Me
Ex	19: 5	obey My voice and keep My c
Ex	23:32	You shall make no c with them
Ex	24: 7	he took the Book of the C
Ex	24: 8	the blood of the c which the
Ex	31:16	generations as a perpetual c
Ex	34:28	tablets the words of the c
Num	10:33	the ark of the c of the LORD
Num	18:19	it is a c of salt forever
Num	25:12	I give to him My c of peace
Deut	9:11	stone, the tablets of the c
Deut	29:14	I make this c and this oath,
Josh	3: 8	who bear the ark of the c
1Sa	4: 3	c of the LORD from Shiloh to
1Sa	4: 4	of the c of the LORD of hosts
1Sa	4: 4	with the ark of the c of God
1Sa	18: 3	Jonathan and David made a c
1Ki	19:10	Israel have forsaken Your c
2Ki	13:23	because of His c with Abraham
2Ki	23: 2	words of the Book of the C

2Ch	13: 5	and his sons, by a c of salt
Neh	9:32	and awesome God, Who keeps c
Neh	13:29	the c of the priesthood and
Job	31: 1	I have made a c with my eyes
Ps	44:17	we dealt falsely with Your c
Ps	50: 5	made a c with Me by sacrifice
Ps	50:16	Or take My c in your mouth,
Ps	89:34	My c I will not break, Nor
Ps	103:18	To such as keep His c, And to
Ps	105: 8	has remembered His c forever
Ps	111: 5	will ever be mindful of His c
Ps	132:12	If your sons will keep My c
Prov	2:17	and forgets the c of her God
Is	24: 5	Broken the everlasting c
Is	28:15	We have made a c with death
Is	42: 6	give You as a c to the people
Is	54:10	nor shall My c of peace be
Jer	31:31	when I will make a new c with
Jer	31:32	My c which they broke, though
Jer	33:20	can break My c with the day
Ezek	34:25	I will make a c of peace with
Dan	9:27	a c with many for one week
Dan	11:22	and also the prince of the c
Dan	11:28	be moved against the holy c
Hos	2:18	In that day I will make a c
Amos	1: 9	remember the c of brotherhood
Zech	9:11	of the blood of your c, I
Mal	2: 4	you, that My c with Levi may
Mal	2:14	companion and your wife by c
Mal	3: 1	even the Messenger of the c
Matt	26:28	this is My blood of the new c
Luke	1:72	and to remember His holy c
Luke	22:20	cup is the new c in My blood
Acts	3:25	of the c which God made with
Acts	7: 8	him the c of circumcision
Rom	11:27	For this is My c with them
2Co	3: 6	as ministers of the new c
Gal	3:17	cannot annul the c that was
Heb	7:22	become a surety of a better c
Heb	8: 6	also Mediator of a better c
Heb	8: 7	For if that first c had been
Heb	8: 8	when I will make a new c with
Heb	9: 4	the ark of the c overlaid on
Heb	9: 4	and the tablets of the c
Heb	9:15	is the Mediator of the new c
Heb	13:20	blood of the everlasting c
Rev	11:19	the ark of His c was seen in

COVENANTS† (see COVENANT)

Rom	9: 4	adoption, the glory, the c
Gal	4:24	For these are the two c
Eph	2:12	from the c of promise, having

COVER (see COVERED, COVERING, COVERINGS, COVERS)

Gen	6:14	c it inside and outside with
Ex	33:22	will c you with My hand while
Deut	23:13	it and turn and c your refuse
1Sa	19:13	put a c of goats' hair for
1Sa	25:20	went down under c of the hill
1Ki	7:18	c the capitals that were on
2Ch	4:13	to c the two bowl-shaped
Neh	4: 5	Do not c their iniquity, and
Job	16:18	do not c my blood, and let my

Job	21:26	in the dust, and worms c them
Job	22:14	Thick clouds c Him, so that
Job	38:34	abundance of water may c you
Ps	91: 4	He shall c you with His
Ps	104: 2	Who c Yourself with light as
Is	11: 9	LORD as the waters c the sea
Is	26:21	and will no more c her slain
Is	58: 7	see the naked, that you c him
Is	60: 2	darkness shall c the earth
Ezek	7:18	horror will c them
Ezek	24:17	do not c your lips, and do not
Ezek	32: 7	I will c the sun with a cloud
Ezek	37: 6	c you with skin and put breath
Hos	2: 9	given to c her nakedness
Hos	10: 8	say to the mountains, "C us
Hab	2:14	LORD, as the waters c the sea
Zech	5: 8	the lead c over its mouth
Luke	23:30	and to the hills, 'C us
1Co	11: 7	ought not to c his head,
Jas	5:20	and c a multitude of sins
1Pe	4: 8	love will c a multitude of

COVERED (see COVER)

Gen	7:20	and the mountains were c
Gen	9:23	and c the nakedness of their
Gen	24:65	she took a veil and c herself
Ex	14:28	c the chariots, the horsemen,
Ex	15: 5	The depths have c them
Ex	24:15	and a cloud c the mountain
Ex	37: 9	c the mercy seat with their
Num	9:15	the cloud c the tabernacle,
Ps	32: 1	is forgiven, Whose sin is c
Ps	65:13	valleys also are c with grain
Ps	68:13	wings of a dove c with silver
Ps	80:10	The hills were c with its
Ps	85: 2	You have c all their sin
Is	6: 2	with two he c his face, with
Is	61:10	He has c me with the robe of
Matt	10:26	For there is nothing c that
Rom	4: 7	forgiven, and whose sins are c
1Co	11: 4	having his head c, dishonors
1Co	11: 6	For if a woman is not c, let

COVERING (see COVER, COVERINGS)

Gen	8:13	Noah removed the c of the ark
Ex	22:27	For that is his only c, it is
Ex	25:20	c the mercy seat with their
Ps	105:39	He spread a cloud for a c
Is	25: 7	of the c cast over all people
1Co	11:15	hair is given to her for a c

COVERINGS (see COVER, COVERING)

Gen	3: 7	together and made themselves c

COVERS (see COVER)

Prov	10:12	strife, but love c all sins
Luke	8:16	c it with a vessel or puts it

COVET (see COVETED, COVETOUS)

Ex	20:17	You shall not c your
Rom	7: 7	You shall not c
Jas	4: 2	You murder and c and cannot

COVETOUS (see COVET, COVETOUSNESS)

1Co	5:10	of this world, or with the c
1Co	6:10	nor thieves, nor c, nor
Eph	5: 5	unclean person, nor c man
1Ti	3: 3	not quarrelsome, not c

COVETOUSNESS (see COVETOUS)

Luke	12:15	Take heed and beware of c, for
Rom	1:29	immorality, wickedness, c
Rom	7: 7	c unless the law had said
1Th	2: 5	you know, nor a cloak for c
Heb	13: 5	Let your conduct be without c

COW (see COWS)

Is	11: 7	The c and the bear shall graze

COWS (see COW)

Gen	41: 2	up out of the river seven c
1Sa	6: 7	and hitch the c to the cart
Amos	4: 1	you c of Bashan, who are on

CRAFTINESS (see CRAFTY)

Job	5:13	the wise in their own c, and
1Co	3:19	the wise in their own c"
2Co	11: 3	serpent deceived Eve by his c

CRAFTSMAN

Gen	4:22	of every c in bronze and iron
Prov	8:30	was beside Him, as a master c

CRAFTY (see CRAFTINESS)

1Sa	23:22	I am told that he is very c
Job	5:12	the devices of the c, so that
Job	15: 5	choose the tongue of the c
Ps	83: 3	They have taken c counsel
Prov	7:10	of a harlot, and a c heart

CREATE (see CREATED, CREATION, CREATOR, CREATURE)

Neh	4: 8	Jerusalem and c confusion
Ps	51:10	C in me a clean heart, O God,
Is	4: 5	then the LORD will c above
Is	45: 7	c darkness, I make peace and
Is	45: 7	I make peace and c calamity
Is	45:18	it, Who did not c it in vain
Is	65:17	I c new heavens and a new
Is	65:18	rejoice forever in what I c
Is	65:18	I c Jerusalem as a rejoicing,
Eph	2:15	so as to c in Himself one new

CREATED (see CREATE)

Gen	1: 1	beginning God c the heavens
Gen	1:21	So God c great sea creatures
Gen	1:27	So God c man in His own image
Gen	1:27	male and female He c them
Gen	6: 7	destroy man whom I have c
Ps	104:30	forth Your Spirit, they are c
Ps	148: 5	He commanded and they were c
Is	41:20	Holy One of Israel has c it
Is	43: 7	whom I have c for My glory
Is	45: 8	I, the LORD, have c it
Mal	2:10	Has not one God c us
Mark	13:19	which God c until this time

Rom	8:39	depth, nor any other c thing
1Co	11: 9	Nor was man c for the woman,
Eph	2:10	c in Christ Jesus for good
Eph	3: 9	c all things through Jesus
Col	1:16	All things were c through Him
Col	3:10	to the image of Him who c him
Rev	4:11	for You c all things, and by

CREATION (see CREATE)

Mark	10: 6	from the beginning of the c
Mark	13:19	of c which God created until
Rom	1:20	For since the c of the world
Rom	8:19	the c eagerly waits for the
Rom	8:20	For the c was subjected to
Rom	8:22	know that the whole c groans
2Co	5:17	is in Christ, he is a new c
Gal	6:15	avails anything, but a new c
Col	1:15	God, the firstborn over all c
Heb	9:11	hands, that is, not of this c
2Pe	3: 4	were from the beginning of c
Rev	3:14	the Beginning of the c of God

CREATOR (see CREATE)

Eccl	12: 1	Remember now your C in the
Is	40:28	the C of the ends of the
Is	43:15	the C of Israel, your King
Rom	1:25	creature rather than the C
1Pe	4:19	good, as to a faithful C

CREATURE (see CREATE, CREATURES)

Gen	1:24	c according to its kind
Gen	2:19	Adam called each living c
Ezek	1:15	living c with its four faces
Mark	16:15	preach the gospel to every c
Acts	28: 5	shook off the c into the fire
Rom	1:25	served the c rather than the
Col	1:23	to every c under heaven, of
1Ti	4: 4	For every c of God is good,
Jas	3: 7	c of the sea, is tamed and has
Rev	4: 7	living c was like a lion, the
Rev	5:13	every c of which is in heaven and
Rev	16: 3	every living c in the sea

CREATURES (see CREATURE)

Gen	1:21	So God created great sea c
Ezek	1: 5	the likeness of four living c
Rev	4: 6	were four living c full of

CREEP (see CREEPING)

Lev	11:20	c on all fours shall be an
2Ti	3: 6	those who c into households

CREEPING (see CREEP)

Gen	1:24	c thing and beast of the earth
Gen	6: 7	c thing and birds of the air,
Acts	10:12	c things, and birds of the air
Rom	1:23	beasts and c things

CRETANS† (see CRETE)

Acts	2:11	C and Arabs—we hear them
Tit	1:12	C are always liars, evil

CRETE (see CRETANS)

Acts	27: 7	the shelter of C off Salmone

Acts	27:12	a harbor of C opening toward
Tit	1: 5	this reason I left you in C

CRIED (see CRY)

Gen	41:55	the people c to Pharaoh for
Ex	14:10	of Israel c out to the LORD
Deut	22:27	betrothed young woman c out
Job	29:12	delivered the poor who c out
Ps	34: 6	This poor man c out, and the
Ps	66:17	I c to Him with my mouth, And
Ps	88: 1	I have c out day and night
Ps	107: 6	Then they c out to the LORD
Ps	130: 1	of the depths I have c to You
Is	6: 3	And one c to another and said
Dan	3: 4	Then a herald c aloud
Dan	5: 7	The king c aloud to bring in
Dan	6:20	he c out with a lamenting
Jon	1: 5	every man c out to his god,
Jon	2: 2	out of the belly of Sheol I c
Matt	14:30	and beginning to sink he c out
Matt	20:30	passing by, c out, saying,
Matt	20:31	but they c out all the more,
Matt	27:46	Jesus c out with a loud voice
Mark	6:49	it was a ghost, and c out
Mark	9:24	the father of the child c out
Mark	9:26	Then the spirit c out,
Mark	15:39	saw that He c out like this
Luke	16:24	Then he c and said, 'Father
John	19: 6	officers saw Him, they c out
John	19:12	Him, but the Jews c out,
John	19:15	But they c out, "Away with
Acts	23: 6	he c out in the council,
Rev	18: 2	he c mightily with a loud
Rev	18:19	c out, weeping and wailing, and

CRIES (see CRY)

Gen	4:10	of your brother's blood c out
Ps	72:12	deliver the needy when he c
Prov	1:21	She c out in the chief
Prov	20:14	for nothing," c the buyer
Is	26:17	c out in her pangs, when she
Mic	6: 9	LORD's voice c to the city
Heb	5: 7	with vehement c and tears to
Jas	5: 4	the c of the reapers have

CRIMINALS

Luke	23:32	There were also two others, c

CRIMSON

Is	1:18	though they are red like c

CROOKED

Deut	32: 5	a perverse and c generation
Eccl	1:15	What is c cannot be made
Eccl	7:13	straight what He has made c
Is	42:16	them, and c places straight

CROSS (see CROSSED)

Num	35:10	When you c the Jordan into
Josh	4: 5	C over before the ark of the
Is	11:15	and make men c over dryshod
Is	51:10	for the redeemed to c over
Ezek	47: 5	a river that I could not c
Matt	16:24	himself, and take up his c

Matt	27:32	they compelled to bear His **c**
Matt	27:40	of God, come down from the **c**
Mark	4:35	Let us **c** over to the other
Luke	9:23	and take up his **c** daily, and
Luke	23:26	on him they laid the **c** that
John	19:17	And He, bearing His **c**, went
John	19:19	a title and put it on the **c**
John	19:25	by the **c** of Jesus His mother
1Co	1:17	lest the **c** of Christ should
1Co	1:18	For the message of the **c** is
Gal	5:11	offense of the **c** has ceased
Gal	6:14	**c** of our Lord Jesus Christ
Eph	2:16	God in one body through the **c**
Phil	2: 8	even the death of the **c**
Phil	3:18	enemies of the **c** of Christ
Col	1:20	through the blood of His **c**
Col	2:14	having nailed it to the **c**
Heb	12: 2	set before Him endured the **c**

CROSSED (see CROSS)

Josh	3:17	and all Israel **c** over on dry

CROW (see CROWED, CROWING, CROWS)

Luke	22:34	the rooster will not **c** this

CROWD

Mark	2: 4	near Him because of the **c**
Mark	5:27	she came behind Him in the **c**
Mark	15:11	priests stirred up the **c**, so
Luke	4:42	the **c** sought Him and came to

CROWED (see CROW)

Matt	26:74	Immediately a rooster **c**.

CROWING† (see CROW)

Mark	13:35	at the **c** of the rooster, or

CROWN (see CROWNED, CROWNS)

Ex	29: 6	put the holy **c** on the head of
Job	2: 7	his foot to the **c** of his head
Ps	65:11	You **c** the year with Your
Prov	12: 4	wife is the **c** of her husband
Prov	14:24	The **c** of the wise is their
Prov	16:31	head is a **c** of glory, if it
Prov	17: 6	children are the **c** of old men
Zech	9:16	be like the jewels of a **c**
Matt	27:29	had twisted a **c** of thorns
1Co	9:25	it to obtain a perishable **c**
Phil	4: 1	brethren, my joy and **c**, so
1Th	2:19	or joy, or **c** of rejoicing
2Ti	4: 8	for me the **c** of righteousness
Jas	1:12	he will receive the **c** of life
Rev	6: 2	a **c** was given to him, and he
Rev	14:14	having on His head a golden **c**

CROWNED (see CROWN)

Ps	8: 5	You have **c** him with glory and
Heb	2: 7	You **c** him with glory and honor

CROWNS (see CROWN)

Ps	103: 4	Who **c** you with lovingkindness
Rev	4:10	and cast their **c** before the
Rev	19:12	and on His head were many **c**

CROWS (see CROW)

Matt	26:34	night, before the rooster **c**

CRUCIFIED (see CRUCIFY)

Matt	26: 2	will be delivered up to be **c**
Matt	27:31	Him, and led Him away to be **c**
Matt	27:38	two robbers were **c** with Him
Matt	28: 5	that you seek Jesus who was **c**
Luke	23:33	Calvary, there they **c** Him
Luke	24: 7	hands of sinful men, and be **c**
Luke	24:20	condemned to death, and **c** Him
John	19:20	Jesus was **c** was near the city
John	19:41	He was **c** there was a garden
Acts	4:10	of Nazareth, whom you **c**, whom
Rom	6: 6	our old man was **c** with Him
1Co	1:13	Was Paul **c** for you
1Co	1:23	but we preach Christ **c**, to
1Co	2: 2	except Jesus Christ and Him **c**
1Co	2: 8	not have **c** the Lord of glory
Gal	2:20	I have been **c** with Christ
Gal	5:24	**c** the flesh with its passions
Gal	6:14	the world has been **c** to me
Rev	11: 8	where also our Lord was **c**

CRUCIFY (see CRUCIFIED)

Matt	20:19	to mock and to scourge and to **c**
John	19: 6	saying, "**C** Him, **c** Him
John	19:10	that I have power to **c** You
John	19:15	them, "Shall I **c** your King
Heb	6: 6	since they **c** again for

CRUEL

Ex	6: 9	of spirit and **c** bondage

CRUMBS

Matt	15:27	the **c** which fall from their

CRUSH (see CRUSHED)

Amos	4: 1	who **c** the needy, who say to
Rom	16:20	will **c** Satan under your feet

CRUSHED (see CRUSH)

Lev	22:24	the LORD what is bruised or **c**
Judg	9:53	head and **c** his skull
2Co	4: 8	on every side, yet not **c**

CRY (see CRIED, CRIES, CRYING)

Ex	2:23	and their **c** came up to God
Ex	12:30	there was a great **c** in Egypt
Ps	5: 2	heed to the voice of my **c**
Ps	17: 1	cause, O LORD, Attend to my **c**
Ps	18: 6	my **c** came before Him, even to
Ps	22: 2	I **c** in the daytime, but You
Ps	28: 1	To You I will **c**, O LORD my
Ps	28: 2	supplications When I **c** to You
Ps	34:15	His ears are open to their **c**
Ps	34:17	The righteous **c** out, and the
Ps	39:12	O LORD, And give ear to my **c**
Ps	40: 1	inclined to me, And heard my **c**
Ps	61: 1	Hear my **c**, O God
Ps	84: 2	my flesh **c** out for the living
Ps	86: 3	For I **c** to You all day long
Ps	142: 6	Attend to my **c**, For I am

Ps	147: 9	And to the young ravens that c
Prov	8: 1	Does not wisdom c out, and
Prov	21:13	shuts his ears to the c of
Is	5: 7	but behold, a c for help.
Is	24:14	shall c aloud from the sea
Is	40: 6	The voice said, "C out
Is	40: 6	What shall I c
Is	42: 2	He will not c out, nor raise
Is	42:14	Now I will c like a woman in
Is	58: 1	C aloud, spare not
Jer	2: 2	c in the hearing of Jerusalem
Jer	14: 2	the c of Jerusalem has gone
Jer	25:34	Wail, shepherds, and c
Jer	46:12	your c has filled the land
Jer	48: 5	have heard a c of destruction
Jer	48:20	Wail and c! Tell it in
Jer	51:54	The sound of a c comes from
Lam	2:19	c out in the night, at the
Lam	3:56	sighing, from my c for help
Ezek	9: 4	c over all the abominations
Ezek	21:12	C and wail, son of man
Hos	8: 2	Israel will c to Me, 'My God,
Joel	1:19	O LORD, to You I c out
Joel	1:20	the field also c out to You
Amos	3: 4	a young lion c out of his den
Jon	1: 2	city, and c out against it
Hab	1: 2	O LORD, how long shall I c
Zeph	1:10	mournful c from the Fish Gate
Matt	12:19	He will not quarrel nor c out
Matt	25: 6	And at midnight a c was heard
Mark	10:47	Nazareth, he began to c out
Luke	18: 7	His own elect who c out day
Luke	19:40	would immediately c out
Rom	8:15	adoption by whom we c out

CRYING (see CRY)

2Sa	13:19	head and went away c bitterly
Ps	69: 3	I am weary with my c
Is	40: 3	The voice of one c in the
Mal	2:13	with tears, with weeping and c
Matt	3: 3	The voice of one c in the
Matt	21:15	the children c out in the
Mark	5: 5	c out and cutting himself with
John	1:23	of one c in the wilderness
Acts	8: 7	c with a loud voice, came out
Gal	4: 6	Son into your hearts, c out,
Rev	14:15	c with a loud voice to Him
Rev	21: 4	more death, nor sorrow, nor c

CRYSTAL

Rev	21:11	a jasper stone, clear as c
Rev	22: 1	of water of life, clear as c

CUBIT (see CUBITS)

Gen	6:16	finish it to a c from above
Matt	6:27	can add one c to his stature

CUBITS (see CUBIT)

Gen	6:15	ark shall be three hundred c
Gen	7:20	prevailed fifteen c upward
Dan	3: 1	whose height was sixty c
Rev	21:17	one hundred and forty-four c

CUD

Lev	11: 3	hooves and chewing the c

CUMI†

Mark	5:41	Talitha, c," which is

CUMMIN

Matt	23:23	tithe of mint and anise and c

CUNNING (see CUNNINGLY)

Gen	3: 1	Now the serpent was more c
Eph	4:14	in the c craftiness by which

CUNNINGLY† (see CUNNING)

2Pe	1:16	For we did not follow c

CUP (see CUPBEARER)

Gen	40:11	Pharaoh's c was in my hand
Gen	44: 2	Also put my c, the silver c
Gen	44:12	the c was found in Benjamin's
Ps	23: 5	My c runs over
Ps	116:13	take up the c of salvation
Prov	23:31	when it sparkles in the c
Is	51:17	of the LORD the c of His fury
Jer	16: 7	c of consolation to drink for
Matt	10:42	a c of cold water in the name
Matt	20:22	c that I am about to drink
Matt	23:25	cleanse the outside of the c
Matt	26:27	Then He took the c, and gave
Matt	26:39	let this c pass from Me
Luke	22:20	also took the c after supper
Luke	22:20	This c is the new covenant in
Luke	22:42	will, remove this c from Me
1Co	10:16	The c of blessing which we
1Co	10:21	drink the c of the Lord and
1Co	10:21	the Lord and the c of demons
1Co	11:26	this bread and drink this c
Rev	14:10	into the c of His indignation
Rev	16:19	to give her the c of the wine
Rev	17: 4	golden c full of abominations
Rev	18: 6	in the c which she has mixed,

CUPBEARER† (see CUP)

Neh	1:11	For I was the king's c

CURDS

Is	7:15	C and honey He shall eat, that

CURSE (see CURSED, CURSES, CURSING)

Gen	8:21	I will never again c the
Gen	12: 3	I will c him who curses you
Num	5:18	bitter water that brings a c
Num	23: 8	How shall I c whom God has
Deut	11:26	you today a blessing and a c
Neh	13: 2	Balaam against them to c them
Job	1:11	he will surely c You to Your
Job	2: 9	C God and die
Job	3: 8	May those c it who c the day
Ps	62: 4	mouth, But they c inwardly
Ps	109:28	Let them c, but You bless
Eccl	10:20	Do not c the king, even in
Eccl	10:20	do not c the rich, even in
Is	8:21	c their king and their God, and

Jer	24: 9	and a byword, a taunt and a c
Mal	2: 2	and I will c your blessings
Mal	4: 6	and strike the earth with a c
Matt	5:44	bless those who c you, do
Matt	26:74	Then he began to c and swear,
Gal	3:10	of the law are under the c
Gal	3:13	us from the c of the law,
Gal	3:13	having become a c for us (for
Jas	3: 9	Father, and with it we c men
Rev	22: 3	And there shall be no more c

CURSED (see CURSE)

Gen	3:14	this, you are c more than all
Gen	3:17	C is the ground for your sake
Gen	4:11	now you are c from the earth
Gen	9:25	C be Canaan
Deut	27:20	C is the one who lies with
Deut	28:16	C shall you be in the city,
Deut	28:16	c shall you be in the country
Deut	28:17	C shall be your basket and
1Sa	17:43	the Philistine c David by his
2Sa	16: 7	Shimei said thus when he c
Job	1: 5	and c God in their hearts
Job	3: 1	and c the day of his birth
Ps	37:22	But those who are c by Him
Ps	119:21	the c, Who stray from Your
Eccl	7:22	that even you have c others
Jer	17: 5	C is the man who trusts in
Jer	20:14	C be the day in which I was
Jer	20:15	Let the man c who brought
Mal	3: 9	You are c with a curse, for
Matt	25:41	hand, 'Depart from Me, you c
Mark	11:21	which You c has withered away
Gal	3:10	C is everyone who does not
Gal	3:13	C is everyone who hangs on a
Heb	6: 8	rejected and near to being c

CURSES (see CURSE)

Gen	12: 3	and I will curse him who c you
Ex	21:17	he who c his father or his
Lev	24:15	Whoever c his God shall bear
Num	5:23	shall write these c in a book
Jer	15:10	every one of them c me
Matt	15: 4	He who c father or mother,
Mark	7:10	He who c father or mother,

CURSING (see CURSE, CURSINGS)

Deut	30:19	life and death, blessing and c
Ps	10: 7	His mouth is full of c and
Ps	59:12	in their pride, And for the c
Ps	109:17	As he loved c, so let it come
Ps	109:18	with c as with his garment
Rom	3:14	Whose mouth is full of c and
Jas	3:10	mouth proceed blessings and c

CURSINGS† (see CURSING)

Josh	8:34	law, the blessings and the c
Hos	7:16	for the c of their tongue

CURTAIN (see CURTAINS)

Ex	26: 2	The length of each c shall be

CURTAINS (see CURTAIN)

Ex	26: 1	the tabernacle with ten c

CUSH (see ETHIOPIA)

Gen	2:13	the whole land of C
Gen	10: 8	C begot Nimrod

CUSTOM (see CUSTOMS)

Gen	19:31	as is the c of all the earth
2Ki	11:14	by a pillar according to c
Ezra	4:13	not pay tax, tribute, or c
Ps	119:132	As Your c is toward those who
Dan	6:10	as was his c since early days
Luke	2:27	according to the c of the law
Luke	2:42	to the c of the feast
Luke	4:16	And as His c was, He went into
John	19:40	as the c of the Jews is to
Acts	15: 1	according to the c of Moses
Acts	17: 2	Then Paul, as his c was, went
Acts	25:16	It is not the c of the

CUSTOMS (see CUSTOM)

Lev	18:30	any of these abominable c
Acts	6:14	and change the c which Moses
Rom	13: 7	c to whom c, fear to

CUT

Gen	9:11	be c off by the waters of the
Gen	15:10	and c them in two, down the
Gen	17:14	be c off from his people
Ex	4:25	c off the foreskin of her son
Ex	34: 1	C two tablets of stone like
Ex	34:13	c down their wooden images
Lev	22:24	or crushed, or torn or c
Deut	19: 5	the ax to c down the tree
Judg	20: 6	c her in pieces, and sent her
1Sa	24: 5	because he had c Saul's robe
1Ki	18:28	c themselves, as was their
1Ki	18:33	c the bull in pieces, and laid
Job	14: 7	for a tree, if it is c down
Ps	34:16	To c off the remembrance of
Ps	37: 2	soon be c down like the grass
Ps	37: 9	For evildoers shall be c off
Ps	90:10	For it is soon c off, and we
Ps	109:13	Let his posterity be c off
Ps	109:15	That He may c off the memory
Ps	143:12	In Your mercy c off my
Prov	2:22	will be c off from the earth
Prov	10:31	perverse tongue will be c out
Prov	23:18	your hope will not be c off
Prov	24:14	your hope will not be c off
Is	6:13	remains when it is c down
Is	10:34	He will c down the thickets
Is	14:22	c off from Babylon the name
Is	15: 2	and every beard c off
Is	53: 8	For He was c off from the
Is	55:13	sign that shall not be c off
Is	56: 5	name that shall not be c off
Jer	16: 6	them, c themselves, nor make
Jer	34:18	when they c the calf in two
Jer	44: 7	to c off from you man and
Jer	48:25	The horn of Moab is c off
Jer	50:16	C off the sower from Babylon,
Jer	50:23	whole earth has been c apart
Ezek	5:16	c off your supply of bread
Ezek	6: 6	incense altars may be c down

Ezek	14:13	c off man and beast from it
Ezek	16: 4	your navel cord was not c
Ezek	17: 9	c off its fruit, and leave it
Dan	2: 5	you shall be c in pieces
Dan	2:34	stone was c out without hands
Dan	9:26	weeks Messiah shall be c off
Hos	10: 7	her king is c off like a twig
Hos	10:15	Israel shall be c off utterly
Obad	9	may be c off by slaughter
Mic	1:16	c off your hair, because of
Mic	5:10	That I will c off your horses
Mic	5:12	I will c off sorceries from
Nah	2:13	I will c off your prey from
Hab	3:17	flock be c off from the fold
Zech	9:10	I will c off the chariot from
Zech	9:10	the battle bow shall be c off
Matt	3:10	not bear good fruit is c down
Matt	5:30	c it off and cast it from you
Matt	26:51	high priest, and c off his ear
Mark	9:43	hand makes you sin, c it off
Mark	11: 8	others c down leafy branches
John	18:26	of him whose ear Peter c off
Acts	2:37	they were c to the heart, and
Acts	7:54	they were c to the heart, and
Acts	18:18	his hair c off at Cenchrea
Acts	27:32	Then the soldiers c away the
Rom	9:28	c it short in righteousness,
Rom	11:22	you also will be c off

CYMBAL† (see CYMBALS)

1Co	13: 1	brass or a clanging c

CYMBALS (see CYMBAL)

Ps	150: 5	Praise Him with loud c

CYPRUS

Dan	11:30	For ships from C shall come
Acts	15:39	took Mark and sailed to C

CYRENIAN

Mark	15:21	a certain man, Simon a C, the

CYRUS

2Ch	36:22	year of C king of Persia,
Ezra	5:13	year of C king of Babylon
Ezra	5:17	C to build this house of God
Is	44:28	who says of C, 'He is My
Is	45: 1	LORD to His anointed, to C
Dan	6:28	in the reign of C the Persian

D

DAGON

Judg	16:23	sacrifice to D their god, and
1Sa	5: 2	it into the temple of D

DAILY

Ex	5:19	any bricks from your d quota
Ex	16: 5	as much as they gather d
Lev	6:20	flour as a d grain offering
Judg	16:16	pestered him d with her words
Prov	8:30	and I was d His delight,

Dan	1: 5	a d provision of the king's
Dan	11:31	take away the d sacrifices
Matt	6:11	Give us this day our d bread
Matt	26:55	I sat d with you, teaching in
Luke	9:23	and take up his cross d, and
Acts	2:47	Lord added to the church d
Acts	6: 1	in the d distribution
Acts	16: 5	and increased in number d
Acts	17:11	searched the Scriptures d to
1Co	15:31	Jesus our Lord, I die d
Heb	10:11	priest stands ministering d
Jas	2:15	naked and destitute of d food

DAMASCUS

Gen	15: 2	of my house is Eliezer of D
2Sa	8: 5	When the Syrians of D came to
2Ki	5:12	the Pharpar, the rivers of D
2Ki	16:10	and saw an altar that was at D
Is	7: 8	For the head of Syria is D
Amos	1: 3	For three transgressions of D
Acts	9:10	disciple at D named Ananias

DAN (see LAISH)

Gen	14:14	went in pursuit as far as D
Gen	49:16	D shall judge his people as
Num	1:38	From the children of D, their
Num	26:42	These are the sons of D
Deut	33:22	D is a lion's whelp
Deut	34: 1	land of Gilead as far as D
Josh	19:47	They called Leshem, D, after
Josh	21:23	and from the tribe of D,
Judg	5:17	why did D remain on ships
Judg	18:29	called the name of the city D
Judg	20: 1	from D to Beersheba, as well
1Sa	3:20	And all Israel from D to
2Sa	3:10	Judah, from D to Beersheba
2Ki	10:29	that were at Bethel and D
Amos	8:14	say, As your god lives, O D

DANCE (see DANCED, DANCES, DANCING)

Ps	150: 4	Him with the timbrel and d
Eccl	3: 4	time to mourn, and a time to d
Matt	11:17	for you, and you did not d

DANCED (see DANCE)

2Sa	6:14	Then David d before the LORD
Matt	14: 6	of Herodias d before them

DANCES (see DANCE)

Ex	15:20	her with timbrels and with d

DANCING (see DANCE)

Ex	32:19	that he saw the calf and the d
Judg	11:34	meet him with timbrels and d
1Sa	18: 6	of Israel, singing and d, to

DANGER

Matt	5:21	will be in d of the judgment
Matt	5:22	shall be in d of hell fire

DANIEL (see BELTESHAZZAR)

Ezek	14:20	even though Noah, D, and Job
Ezek	28: 3	(Behold, you are wiser than D
Dan	1: 7	he gave D the name

D

Dan	1:17	**D** had understanding in all
Dan	1:19	all none was found like **D**
Dan	2:19	So **D** blessed the God of
Dan	2:48	Then the king promoted **D** and
Dan	5:29	and they clothed **D** with purple
Dan	6: 2	governors, of whom **D** was one
Dan	6:10	Now when **D** knew that the
Dan	6:11	found **D** praying and making
Dan	6:20	**D**, servant of the living God,
Dan	6:23	take **D** up out of the den
Dan	6:27	Who has delivered **D** from the
Dan	6:28	So this **D** prospered in the
Dan	7: 1	**D** had a dream and visions of
Dan	8:27	And I, **D**, fainted and was sick
Dan	10: 7	And I, **D**, alone saw the vision
Dan	10:11	O **D**, man greatly beloved,
Dan	12: 4	But you, **D**, shut up the words
Matt	24:15	spoken of by **D** the prophet
Mark	13:14	spoken of by **D** the prophet

DARE (see DARED)

Esth	7: 5	who would **d** presume in his
Job	41:10	that he would **d** stir him up
Amos	6:10	For we **d** not mention the name
Matt	22:46	anyone **d** question Him
Rom	5: 7	someone would even **d** to die
Rom	15:18	For I will not **d** to speak of

DARED (see DARE)

2Sa	17:17	for they **d** not be seen coming
Job	32: 6	**d** not declare my opinion to
Mark	12:34	that no one **d** question Him
John	21:12	of the disciples **d** ask Him
Acts	5:13	none of the rest **d** join them
Acts	7:32	Moses trembled and **d** not look

DARIUS

Ezra	4: 5	the reign of **D** king of Persia
Dan	5:31	And **D** the Mede received the
Dan	6: 6	King **D**, live forever
Dan	6: 9	Therefore King **D** signed the
Hag	1: 1	In the second year of King **D**
Zech	1: 1	month of the second year of **D**

DARK (see DARKENED, DARKNESS)

Gen	15:17	the sun went down and it was **d**
Num	12: 8	plainly, and not in **d** sayings
1Ki	8:12	He would dwell in the **d** cloud
Ps	74:20	For the **d** places of the earth
Song	1: 5	I am **d**, but lovely, O
Is	45:19	in a **d** place of the earth
Ezek	34:12	on a cloudy and **d** day
Joel	2:10	the sun and moon grow **d**, and
Amos	5: 8	and makes the day **d** as night
John	6:17	And it was now **d**, and Jesus had
John	20: 1	early, while it was still **d**
2Pe	1:19	that shines in a **d** place,

DARKENED (see DARK, DARKENS)

Ex	10:15	earth, so that the land was **d**
Eccl	12: 2	moon and the stars, are not **d**
Matt	24:29	those days the sun will be **d**
Luke	23:45	Then the sun was **d**, and the
Rom	1:21	their foolish hearts were **d**

Rom	11:10	let their eyes be **d**, that
Eph	4:18	having their understanding **d**
Rev	8:12	that a third of them were **d**

DARKENS (see DARKENED)

Job	38: 2	Who is this who **d** counsel by

DARKNESS (see DARK)

Gen	1: 2	**d** was on the face of the deep
Gen	1: 4	divided the light from the **d**
Gen	1: 5	Day, and the **d** He called Night
Gen	1:18	divide the light from the **d**
Gen	15:12	and great **d** fell upon him
Ex	10:21	**d** which may even be felt
Ex	20:21	the thick **d** where God was
Job	10:21	not return, to the land of **d**
Job	26:10	at the boundary of light and **d**
Job	28: 3	Man puts an end to **d**, and
Ps	91: 6	pestilence that walks in **d**
Ps	139:12	the **d** shall not hide from You
Ps	139:12	The **d** and the light are both
Is	9: 2	in **d** have seen a great light
Is	45: 3	give you the treasures of **d**
Is	45: 7	I form the light and create **d**
Joel	2: 2	a day of clouds and thick **d**
Joel	2:31	sun shall be turned into **d**
Amos	5:18	It will be **d**, and not light
Amos	5:20	Is not the day of the LORD **d**
Zeph	1:15	a day of clouds and thick **d**
Matt	4:16	sat in **d** saw a great light
Matt	6:23	whole body will be full of **d**
Matt	6:23	how great is that **d**
Matt	8:12	will be cast out into outer **d**
Matt	27:45	there was **d** over all the land
Luke	22:53	your hour, and the power of **d**
John	1: 5	And the light shines in the **d**
John	1: 5	the **d** did not comprehend it
John	3:19	men loved **d** rather than light
John	8:12	Me shall not walk in **d**, but
Acts	2:20	sun shall be turned into **d**
Rom	13:12	us cast off the works of **d**
2Co	4: 6	light to shine out of **d** who
2Co	6:14	communion has light with **d**
Eph	5:11	the unfruitful works of **d**
Eph	6:12	rulers of the **d** of this age
Col	1:13	us from the power of **d** and
1Pe	2: 9	of **d** into His marvelous light
1Jn	1: 5	and in Him is no **d** at all
1Jn	1: 6	with Him, and walk in **d**, we
1Jn	2:11	who hates his brother is in **d**
Rev	16:10	his kingdom became full of **d**

DARTS

Eph	6:16	the fiery **d** of the wicked one

DASH (see DASHED, DASHES)

Ps	2: 9	You shall **d** them in pieces
Ps	91:12	Lest you **d** your foot against
Matt	4: 6	lest you **d** your foot against

DASHED (see BROKEN, DASH)

Ex	15: 6	has **d** the enemy in pieces
Rev	2:27	they shall be **d** to pieces

DASHES† (see DASH)

Ps	137: 9	**d** Your little ones against

DATHAN

Num	16:24	from the tents of Korah, **D**

DAUGHTER (see DAUGHTERS, GRANDDAUGHTER)

Gen	20:12	She is the **d** of my father,
Gen	29: 6	his **d** Rachel is coming with
Gen	34: 5	he had defiled Dinah his **d**
Ex	1:22	every **d** you shall save alive
Ex	2: 5	Then the **d** of Pharaoh came
Ex	2:21	gave Zipporah his **d** to Moses
Ex	20:10	you, nor your son, nor your **d**
Judg	11:35	"Alas, my **d**! You have brought
Judg	19:24	Look, here is my virgin **d**
2Sa	12: 3	and it was like a **d** to him
1Ki	3: 1	Egypt, and married Pharaoh's **d**
2Ki	19:21	the **d** of Zion, has despised
Ps	45:13	The royal **d** is all glorious
Ps	137: 8	O **d** of Babylon, who are to be
Is	10:32	the mount of the **d** of Zion,
Is	47: 1	dust, O virgin **d** of Babylon
Lam	2:13	you, O virgin **d** of Zion
Ezek	16:44	Like mother, like **d**
Hos	1: 6	conceived again and bore a **d**
Zech	9: 9	Rejoice greatly, O **d** of Zion
Zech	9: 9	Shout, O **d** of Jerusalem
Mal	2:11	the **d** of a foreign god
Matt	9:18	My **d** has just died, but come
Matt	10:35	a **d** against her mother, and a
Matt	10:37	he who loves son or **d** more
Matt	14: 6	the **d** of Herodias danced
Matt	15:28	her **d** was healed from that
Matt	21: 5	Tell the **d** of Zion, 'Behold,
Luke	8:42	for he had an only **d** about
Luke	12:53	father, mother against **d** and
Luke	13:16	being a **d** of Abraham, whom
John	12:15	Fear not, **d** of Zion
Heb	11:24	called the son of Pharaoh's **d**

DAUGHTERS (see DAUGHTER)

Gen	5: 4	and he begot sons and **d**
Gen	6: 1	and **d** were born to them,
Gen	6: 2	sons of God saw the **d** of men
Gen	19: 8	I have two **d** who have not
Gen	19:36	Thus both the **d** of Lot were
Gen	31:41	fourteen years for your two **d**
Num	27: 1	Then came the **d** of Zelophehad
Deut	12:31	**d** in the fire to their gods
Ezra	9:12	do not give your **d** as wives
Neh	10:30	nor take their **d** for our sons
Job	1: 2	and three **d** were born to him
Job	42:13	had seven sons and three **d**
Prov	30:15	The leech has two **d**, crying,
Prov	31:29	Many **d** have done well, but
Eccl	12: 4	and all the **d** of music are
Song	1: 5	O **d** of Jerusalem, like the
Jer	16: 2	have sons or **d** in this place
Lam	3:51	of all the **d** of my city
Ezek	13:17	against the **d** of your people
Ezek	14:16	deliver neither sons nor **d**
Ezek	14:18	deliver neither sons nor **d**
Ezek	16:46	of you, is Sodom and her **d**
Ezek	23: 2	women, the **d** of one mother
Ezek	30:18	her **d** shall go into captivity
Ezek	32:16	the **d** of the nations shall
Hos	4:13	Therefore your **d** commit
Joel	2:28	your **d** shall prophesy, your
Luke	1: 5	wife was of the **d** of Aaron
Luke	23:28	**D** of Jerusalem, do not weep
Acts	2:17	your **d** shall prophesy, your
Acts	21: 9	four virgin **d** who prophesied
2Co	6:18	and you shall be My sons and **d**
1Pe	3: 6	whose **d** you are if you do

DAVID

Ruth	4:17	of Jesse, the father of **D**
1Sa	16:13	upon **D** from that day forward
1Sa	16:23	that **D** would take a harp and
1Sa	17:14	**D** was the youngest
1Sa	17:43	So the Philistine said to **D**
1Sa	17:54	And **D** took the head of the
1Sa	18: 1	was knit to the soul of **D**
1Sa	18: 3	**D** made a covenant, because he
1Sa	18: 7	and **D** his ten thousands
1Sa	18: 9	So Saul eyed **D** from that day
1Sa	18:10	So **D** played music with his
1Sa	18:11	I will pin **D** to the wall with
1Sa	18:11	But **D** escaped his presence
1Sa	18:12	Now Saul was afraid of **D**,
1Sa	18:16	all Israel and Judah loved **D**
1Sa	18:20	Saul's daughter, loved **D**
1Sa	18:28	knew that the LORD was with **D**
1Sa	19: 2	So Jonathan told **D**, saying
1Sa	25:23	Now when Abigail saw **D**, she
1Sa	27:12	So Achish believed **D**, saying,
2Sa	2: 4	there they anointed **D** king
2Sa	5: 3	they anointed **D** king over
2Sa	5: 7	Zion (that is, the City of **D**)
2Sa	5:17	anointed **D** king over Israel
2Sa	6:14	Then **D** danced before the LORD
2Sa	7: 5	Go and tell My servant **D**
2Sa	11: 6	And Joab sent Uriah to **D**
2Sa	12: 1	the LORD sent Nathan to **D**
2Sa	12:24	Then **D** comforted Bathsheba
2Sa	20: 1	We have no part in **D**, nor do
2Sa	22:51	mercy to His anointed, to **D**
2Sa	23: 1	these are the last words of **D**
2Sa	24:24	So **D** bought the threshing
2Sa	24:25	**D** built there an altar to the
1Ki	1: 1	Now King **D** was old, advanced
1Ki	1:31	my lord King **D** live forever
1Ki	1:37	the throne of my lord King **D**
1Ki	2: 1	Then the days of **D** drew near
1Ki	2:10	So **D** rested with his fathers,
1Ki	2:10	was buried in the City of **D**
1Ki	2:33	But upon **D** and his descendants
1Ki	2:45	and the throne of **D** shall be
1Ki	3: 3	the statutes of his father **D**
1Ki	3: 6	to your servant **D** my father
1Ki	3: 7	king instead of my father **D**
1Ki	3:14	as your father **D** walked,
1Ki	5: 1	for Hiram had always loved **D**
1Ki	5: 7	for He has given **D** a wise son
1Ki	8:16	but I chose **D** to be over My

1Ki	8:24	Your servant **D** my father
1Ki	11:21	**D** rested with his fathers
1Ki	12:16	What portion have we in **D**
1Ki	12:16	see to your own house, O **D**
1Ki	14: 8	have not been as My servant **D**
1Ki	15: 5	because **D** did what was right
1Ch	9:22	**D** and Samuel the seer had
1Ch	11:10	of the mighty men whom **D** had
1Ch	13:12	**D** was afraid of God that day,
1Ch	18: 3	**D** defeated Hadadezer king of
1Ch	19:19	they made peace with **D** and
1Ch	21: 1	and moved **D** to number Israel
1Ch	22: 5	Now **D** said, "Solomon my son
1Ch	27:24	of the chronicles of King **D**
1Ch	29:29	Now the acts of King **D**, first
2Ch	6:42	the mercies of Your servant **D**
2Ch	8:14	for so **D** the man of God had
2Ch	29:26	with the instruments of **D**
2Ch	32:33	upper tombs of the sons of **D**
Neh	3:16	in front of the tombs of **D**
Neh	12:24	of **D** the man of God
Neh	12:37	the stairs of the City of **D**
Neh	12:37	wall, beyond the house of **D**
Neh	12:46	For in the days of **D** and Asaph
Ps	18:50	mercy to His anointed, To **D**
Ps	72:20	The prayers of **D** the son of
Ps	89:49	You swore to **D** in Your truth
Ps	132: 1	Lord, remember **D** And all his
Ps	132:17	will make the horn of **D** grow
Prov	1: 1	of Solomon the son of **D**, king
Eccl	1: 1	of the Preacher, the son of **D**
Song	4: 4	neck is like the tower of **D**
Is	7:13	Hear now, O house of **D**
Is	9: 7	no end, upon the throne of **D**
Is	16: 5	truth, in the tabernacle of **D**
Is	22:22	The key of the house of **D** I
Is	29: 1	Ariel, the city where **D** dwelt
Is	55: 3	the sure mercies of **D**
Jer	21:12	O house of **D**!
Jer	22: 2	who sit on the throne of **D**
Jer	23: 5	That I will raise to **D** a
Jer	33:15	**D** a Branch of righteousness
Jer	33:17	**D** shall never lack a man to
Ezek	34:23	shall feed them—My servant **D**
Hos	3: 5	**D** their king, and fear the
Amos	6: 5	musical instruments like **D**
Amos	9:11	raise up The tabernacle of **D**
Zech	12:10	I will pour on the house of **D**
Matt	1: 1	of Jesus Christ, the Son of **D**
Matt	1: 6	and Jesse begot **D** the king
Matt	1: 6	**D** the king begot Solomon by
Matt	1:17	to **D** are fourteen generations
Matt	1:20	Joseph, son of **D**, do not be
Matt	9:27	Son of **D**, have mercy on us
Matt	12: 3	what **D** did when he was hungry
Matt	20:30	mercy on us, O Lord, Son of **D**
Matt	21: 9	Hosanna to the Son of **D**
Matt	22:43	How then does **D** in the Spirit
Matt	22:45	If **D** then calls Him 'Lord,'
Mark	12:35	the Christ is the Son of **D**
Luke	1:27	was Joseph, of the house of **D**
Luke	1:32	the throne of His father **D**
Luke	2: 4	into Judea, to the city of **D**
Luke	2: 4	of the house and lineage of **D**

Luke	2:11	day in the city of **D** a Savior
Luke	20:41	the Christ is the Son of D?
John	7:42	comes from the seed of **D** and
John	7:42	of Bethlehem, where **D** was
Acts	1:16	mouth of **D** concerning Judas
Acts	2:29	to you of the patriarch **D**
Acts	13:34	you the sure mercies of **D**
Acts	15:16	of **D** which has fallen down
Rom	1: 3	of **D** according to the flesh
Rom	11: 9	And **D** says: "Let their table
2Ti	2: 8	Christ, of the seed of **D**, was
Heb	4: 7	a certain day, saying in **D**
Heb	11:32	Samson and Jephthah, also of **D**
Rev	3: 7	He who has the key of **D**, He
Rev	5: 5	tribe of Judah, the Root of **D**
Rev	22:16	Root and the Offspring of **D**

DAWN (*see* DAWNED, DAWNS)

Ps	46: 5	her, just at the break of **d**
Ps	57: 8	I will awaken the **d**
Is	58:10	light shall **d** in the darkness
Matt	28: 1	day of the week began to **d**

DAWNED (*see* DAWN)

Matt	4:16	shadow of death light has **d**

DAWNS† (*see* DAWN)

2Pe	1:19	a dark place, until the day **d**

DAY (*see* DAY'S, DAYS, DAYSPRING)

Gen	1: 5	God called the light **D**, and
Gen	1: 5	the morning were the first **d**
Gen	1:16	greater light to rule the **d**
Gen	2: 2	He rested on the seventh **d**
Gen	2: 3	God blessed the seventh **d**
Gen	2:17	for in the **d** that you eat of
Gen	3: 8	garden in the cool of the **d**
Gen	8:22	and winter and summer, and **d**
Gen	18: 1	door in the heat of the **d**
Gen	27: 2	do not know the **d** of my death
Ex	12:15	first **d** until the seventh **d**
Ex	12:17	you shall observe this **d**
Ex	20: 8	Remember the Sabbath **d**, to
Ex	20:11	them, and rested the seventh **d**
Ex	20:11	LORD blessed the Sabbath **d**
Ex	31:15	any work on the Sabbath **d**
Lev	23:27	shall be the **D** of Atonement
Num	15:32	sticks on the Sabbath **d**
Deut	6:24	us alive, as it is this **d**
Deut	34: 6	one knows his grave to this **d**
Josh	1: 8	you shall meditate in it **d**
Josh	10:13	go down for about a whole **d**
Josh	10:14	there has been no **d** like that
Josh	24:15	this **d** whom you will serve
Ruth	4: 9	You are witnesses this **d**
2Ki	17:23	Assyria, as it is to this **d**
Neh	4: 2	Will they complete it in a **d**
Neh	10:31	to sell on the Sabbath **d**, we
Neh	13:17	you profane the Sabbath **d**
Neh	13:22	to sanctify the Sabbath **d**
Job	3: 1	cursed the **d** of his birth
Job	3: 3	May the **d** perish on which I
Job	9:19	will appoint my **d** in court
Job	21:30	reserved for the **d** of doom

D

Ps	1: 2	And in His law he meditates **d**
Ps	18:18	me in the **d** of my calamity
Ps	19: 2	**D** unto day utters speech
Ps	20: 1	I you in the **d** of trouble
Ps	25: 5	On You I wait all the **d**
Ps	32: 3	my groaning all the **d** long
Ps	32: 4	For **d** and night Your hand was
Ps	44:22	sake we are killed all **d** long
Ps	74:16	The **d** is Yours, the night
Ps	81: 3	moon, on our solemn feast **d**
Ps	84:10	For a **d** in Your courts is
Ps	91: 5	of the arrow that flies by **d**
Ps	118:24	This is the **d** which the LORD
Ps	121: 6	sun shall not strike you by **d**
Ps	136: 8	The sun to rule by **d**, For His
Prov	4:18	brighter unto the perfect **d**
Prov	6:34	spare in the **d** of vengeance
Prov	27: 1	know what a **d** may bring forth
Prov	27:15	dripping on a very rainy **d**
Eccl	7: 1	than the **d** of one's birth
Eccl	12: 3	in the **d** when the keepers of
Song	2:17	Until the **d** breaks and the
Song	8: 8	the **d** when she is spoken for
Is	2:11	shall be exalted in that **d**
Is	2:12	For the **d** of the LORD of
Is	9: 4	as in the **d** of Midian
Is	13:13	in the **d** of His fierce anger
Is	19:16	In that **d** Egypt will be like
Is	19:24	In that **d** Israel will be one
Is	49: 8	in the **d** of salvation I have
Is	60:19	no longer be your light by **d**
Is	61: 2	the **d** of vengeance of our God
Jer	9: 1	of tears, that I might weep **d**
Jer	17:22	but hallow the Sabbath **d**
Jer	20:14	Cursed be the **d** in which I
Jer	31:35	the sun for a light by **d**, and
Jer	33:20	break My covenant with the **d**
Jer	51: 2	For in the **d** of doom they
Jer	52:34	a portion for each **d**
Lam	1:12	in the **d** of His fierce anger
Lam	1:13	desolate and faint all the **d**
Lam	2: 7	as on the **d** of a set feast
Lam	2:16	is the **d** we have waited for
Lam	2:18	tears run down like a river **d**
Ezek	1:28	in a cloud on a rainy **d**, so
Ezek	4: 6	laid on you a **d** for each year
Ezek	7:19	**d** of the wrath of the LORD
Ezek	22:24	on in the **d** of indignation
Ezek	24:27	on that **d** your mouth will be
Ezek	30: 3	even the **d** of the LORD is
Ezek	30: 3	it will be a **d** of clouds, the
Ezek	34:12	on a cloudy and dark **d**
Dan	6:10	his knees three times that **d**
Dan	6:13	his petition three times a **d**
Hos	1: 5	**d** that I will break the bow
Hos	2: 3	as in the **d** she was born, and
Hos	2:21	in that **d** that I will answer
Hos	6: 2	on the third **d** He will raise
Joel	1:15	Alas for the **d**
Joel	1:15	For the **d** of the LORD is at
Joel	2: 2	a **d** of darkness and gloominess
Joel	2: 2	a **d** of clouds and thick
Joel	2:31	and terrible **d** of the LORD
Amos	1:14	in the **d** of the whirlwind
Amos	2:16	shall flee naked in that **d**
Amos	5:18	who desire the **d** of the LORD
Amos	6: 3	who put far off the **d** of doom
Jon	4: 7	next **d** God prepared a worm
Mic	2: 4	In that **d** one shall take up a
Nah	2: 3	in the **d** of his preparation
Nah	3:17	in the hedges on a cold **d**
Zeph	1:14	The great **d** of the LORD is
Zeph	1:15	That **d** is a day of wrath,
Zeph	1:15	a **d** of trouble and distress
Zeph	1:15	a **d** of darkness and gloominess
Hag	2:15	consider from this **d** forward
Zech	3: 9	of that land in one **d**
Zech	4:10	the **d** of small things
Zech	13: 1	In that **d** a fountain shall be
Zech	14: 1	the **d** of the LORD is coming.
Zech	14: 4	in that **d** His feet will stand
Zech	14: 7	neither **d** nor night
Zech	14:20	In that **d** "HOLINESS TO THE
Mal	3: 2	endure the **d** of His coming
Mal	4: 1	the **d** is coming, burning like
Mal	4: 5	and dreadful **d** of the LORD
Matt	6:11	Give us this **d** our daily
Matt	7:22	Many will say to Me in that **d**
Matt	11:24	**d** of judgment than for you
Matt	16:21	be raised again the third **d**
Matt	20: 2	laborers for a denarius a **d**
Matt	24:36	But of that **d** and hour no one
Matt	24:38	until the **d** that Noah entered
Matt	25:13	for you know neither the **d**
Matt	26:29	**d** when I drink it new with
Matt	27:62	followed the **D** of Preparation
Matt	27:64	made secure until the third **d**
Luke	1:59	so it was, on the eighth **d**
Luke	2:11	this **d** in the city of David a
Luke	4:16	synagogue on the Sabbath **d**
Luke	10:12	**D** for Sodom than for that
Luke	11: 3	Give us **d** by day our daily
Luke	24:46	from the dead the third **d**
John	6:39	raise it up at the last **d**
John	6:40	raise him up at the last **d**
John	8:56	Abraham rejoiced to see My **d**
John	9: 4	Him who sent Me while it is **d**
John	11:24	resurrection at the last **d**
John	12: 7	this for the **d** of My burial
John	20: 1	On the first **d** of the week
John	20:19	the same **d** at evening
John	20:19	being the first **d** of the week
Acts	1: 2	until the **d** in which He was
Acts	2: 1	Now when the **D** of Pentecost
Acts	2:20	and notable **d** of the LORD
Acts	10:40	God raised up on the third **d**
Acts	13:14	synagogue on the Sabbath **d**
Acts	17:31	**d** on which He will judge the
Rom	2: 5	wrath in the **d** of wrath and
Rom	8:36	sake we are killed all **d** long
Rom	10:21	All **d** long I have stretched
Rom	13:12	far spent, the **d** is at hand
Rom	13:13	us walk properly, as in the **d**
Rom	14: 5	another esteems every **d** alike
1Co	1: 8	**d** of our Lord Jesus Christ
1Co	3:13	for the **D** will declare it,
1Co	16: 2	On the first **d** of the week
2Co	1:14	in the **d** of the Lord Jesus

2Co	6: 2	now is the **d** of salvation
Eph	4:30	for the **d** of redemption
Eph	6:13	to withstand in the evil **d**
Phil	3: 5	circumcised the eighth **d**, of
1Th	2: 9	for laboring night and **d**, that
1Th	5: 5	of light and sons of the **d**
1Th	5: 8	us who are of the **d** be sober
2Th	1:10	when He comes, in that **D**, to
2Ti	1:12	committed to Him until that **D**
Heb	10:25	as you see the **D** approaching
1Pe	2:12	God in the **d** of visitation
2Pe	1:19	dark place, until the **d** dawns
2Pe	3: 7	fire until the **d** of judgment
2Pe	3: 8	one **d** is as a thousand years
Rev	16:14	that great **d** of God Almighty
Rev	21:25	by **d** (there shall be no night)

DAY'S (see DAY)

Num	11:31	about a **d** journey on this
Jon	3: 4	the city on the first **d** walk
Acts	1:12	a Sabbath **d** journey

DAYS (see DAY, DAYS')

Gen	1:14	signs and seasons, and for **d**
Gen	3:14	dust all the **d** of your life
Gen	6: 4	on the earth in those **d**, and
Gen	7: 4	For after seven more **d** I will
Gen	7: 4	to rain on the earth forty **d**
Gen	8:10	he waited yet another seven **d**
Gen	17:12	He who is eight **d** old among
Gen	29:20	they seemed but a few **d** to
Gen	35:29	being old and full of **d**
Gen	49: 1	befall you in the last **d**
Ex	12:19	For seven **d** no leaven shall
Ex	20: 9	Six **d** you shall labor and do
Ex	20:11	For in six **d** the LORD made
Ex	20:12	that your **d** may be long upon
Ex	23:15	eat unleavened bread seven **d**
Ex	24:18	was on the mountain forty **d**
Lev	12: 4	the **d** of her purification are
Lev	23:16	Count fifty **d** to the day
Num	6: 4	All the **d** of his separation
Num	6: 5	All the **d** of the vow of his
Num	14:34	spied out the land, forty **d**
Deut	4: 9	heart all the **d** of your life
Deut	9:25	forty **d** and forty nights I
Deut	33:25	as your **d**, so shall your
Judg	17: 6	In those **d** there was no king
Ruth	1: 1	in the **d** when the judges
1Sa	3: 1	the LORD was rare in those **d**
2Ki	20: 6	add to your **d** fifteen years
Neh	1: 4	wept, and mourned for many **d**
Esth	9:26	So they called these **d** Purim
Job	2:13	him on the ground seven **d**
Job	7:16	for my **d** are but a breath
Job	14: 1	is born of woman is of few **d**
Job	29: 4	as I was in the **d** of my prime
Job	30:16	the **d** of affliction take hold
Job	42:12	latter **d** of Job more than his
Job	42:17	So Job died, old and full of **d**
Ps	21: 4	Length of **d** forever and ever
Ps	23: 6	me All the **d** of my life
Ps	27: 4	the LORD All the **d** of my life
Ps	37:18	knows the **d** of the upright

Ps	44: 1	in their days, In **d** of old
Ps	49: 5	I fear in the **d** of evil, When
Ps	55:23	not live out half their **d**
Ps	90:10	The **d** of our lives are
Ps	90:12	So teach us to number our **d**
Ps	90:14	rejoice and be glad all our **d**
Ps	102: 3	For my **d** are consumed like
Ps	102:11	My **d** are like a shadow that
Ps	103:15	for man, his **d** are like grass
Prov	3: 2	for length of **d** and long life
Prov	10:27	fear of the LORD prolongs **d**
Prov	31:12	evil all the **d** of her life
Eccl	2: 3	all the **d** of their lives
Eccl	6:12	all the **d** of his vain life
Eccl	7:15	all things in my **d** of vanity
Eccl	12: 1	in the **d** of your youth,
Eccl	12: 1	before the difficult **d** come
Is	39: 8	be peace and truth in my **d**
Is	53:10	seed, He shall prolong His **d**
Jer	7:32	the **d** are coming," says the
Jer	23: 6	In His **d** Judah will be saved,
Jer	31:31	the **d** are coming," says the
Jer	52:33	king all the **d** of his life
Lam	5:21	renew our **d** as of old,
Ezek	3:15	astonished among them seven **d**
Ezek	16:22	remember the **d** of your youth
Ezek	16:56	mouth in the **d** of your pride
Ezek	36:38	at Jerusalem on its feast **d**
Dan	1:12	test your servants for ten **d**
Dan	2:28	what will be in the latter **d**
Dan	7: 9	the Ancient of **D** was seated
Dan	8:14	two thousand three hundred **d**
Dan	10:14	your people in the latter **d**
Dan	10:14	refers to many **d** yet to come
Dan	12:13	at the end of the **d**
Hos	2:15	as in the **d** of her youth, as
Hos	3: 3	You shall stay with me many **d**
Hos	3: 4	many **d** without king or prince
Hos	3: 5	His goodness in the latter **d**
Hos	6: 2	After two **d** He will revive us
Joel	2:29	pour out My Spirit in those **d**
Amos	5:21	hate, I despise your feast **d**
Amos	9:11	rebuild it as in the **d** of old
Jon	1:17	the belly of the fish three **d**
Jon	3: 4	Yet forty **d**, and Nineveh shall
Hab	1: 5	I will work a work in your **d**
Matt	2: 1	in the **d** of Herod the king
Matt	3: 1	In those **d** John the Baptist
Matt	4: 2	And when He had fasted forty **d**
Matt	12:40	For as Jonah was three **d** and
Matt	12:40	the Son of Man be three **d**
Matt	24:19	nursing babies in those **d**
Matt	24:22	unless those **d** were shortened
Matt	24:29	**d** the sun will be darkened
Matt	24:37	But as the **d** of Noah were, so
Matt	26: 2	after two **d** is the Passover
Matt	27:40	temple and build it in three **d**
Matt	27:63	After three **d** I will rise
Mark	2:20	they will fast in those **d**
Luke	1: 5	There was in the **d** of Herod
Luke	1:39	Now Mary arose in those **d**
Luke	2:21	when eight **d** were completed
Luke	2:46	three **d** they found Him in the
Luke	4: 2	in those **d** He ate nothing, and

Luke	4:25	in Israel in the **d** of Elijah
Luke	17:22	of the **d** of the Son of Man
Luke	17:28	it was also in the **d** of Lot
John	2:12	did not stay there many **d**
John	11:17	been in the tomb four **d**
John	11:39	for he has been dead four **d**
Acts	1: 3	seen by them during forty **d**
Acts	1: 5	Spirit not many **d** from now
Acts	1:15	in those **d** Peter stood up in
Acts	2:17	come to pass in the last **d**
Acts	2:18	pour out My Spirit in those **d**
Acts	3:24	have also foretold these **d**
Acts	12: 3	the **D** of Unleavened Bread
Acts	13:31	He was seen for many **d** by
Acts	13:41	for I work a work in your **d**
Acts	21:26	of the **d** of purification, at
Gal	1:18	remained with him fifteen **d**
Eph	5:16	time, because the **d** are evil
2Ti	3: 1	that in the last **d** perilous
Heb	1: 2	has in these last **d** spoken to
Heb	5: 7	in the **d** of His flesh, when
Heb	7: 3	of **d** nor end of life, but
Jas	5: 3	up treasure in the last **d**
1Pe	3:10	would love life and see good **d**
1Pe	3:20	God waited in the **d** of Noah
2Pe	3: 3	will come in the last **d**,
Rev	11: 3	two hundred and sixty **d**,
Rev	11: 9	dead bodies three and a half **d**

DAYS' *(see* DAYS*)*

Gen	30:36	Then he put three **d** journey
Ex	3:18	let us go three **d** journey

DAYSPRING† *(see* DAY*)*

Luke	1:78	with which the **D** from on high

DEACONS

Phil	1: 1	with the bishops and **d**
1Ti	3: 8	Likewise **d** must be reverent,
1Ti	3:12	Let **d** be the husbands of one

DEAD *(see* CORPSE, DEADLY, DIE*)*

Gen	20: 3	him, "Indeed you are a **d** man
Gen	23: 4	may bury my **d** out of my sight
Ex	12:33	We shall all be **d**
Ex	14:30	Egyptians **d** on the seashore
Num	6: 6	he shall not go near a **d** body
Deut	18:11	or one who calls up the **d**
Deut	25: 5	the widow of the **d** man shall
Deut	25: 6	to the name of his **d** brother
Josh	1: 2	Moses My servant is **d**
Ruth	2:20	to the living and the **d**
Ruth	4: 5	of the **d** on his inheritance
Ruth	4:10	that the name of the **d** may
1Sa	24:14	Whom do you pursue? A **d** dog?
2Sa	11:21	Uriah the Hittite is **d** also
2Sa	12:18	tell him that the child was **d**
1Ki	3:20	laid her **d** child in my bosom
1Ki	3:22	son, and the **d** one is your son
2Ki	4:32	the child, lying **d** on his bed
2Ki	8: 5	he had restored the **d** to life
Ps	88:10	Shall the **d** arise and praise
Ps	106:28	ate sacrifices made to the **d**
Ps	115:17	The **d** do not praise the LORD,

Prov	2:18	death, and her paths to the **d**
Eccl	9: 4	dog is better than a **d** lion
Is	26:19	Your **d** shall live
Jer	22:10	Weep not for the **d**, nor
Jer	31:40	whole valley of the **d** bodies
Matt	8:22	let the **d** bury their own
Matt	10: 8	the lepers, raise the **d**, cast
Matt	14: 2	he is risen from the **d**, and
Matt	22:31	the resurrection of the **d**
Matt	22:32	God is not the God of the **d**
Matt	23:27	are full of **d** men's bones
Matt	28: 7	that He is risen from the **d**
Luke	7:22	the **d** are raised, the poor
Luke	8:52	she is not **d**, but sleeping
Luke	15:24	for this my son was **d** and is
Luke	15:32	glad, for your brother was **d**
Luke	16:31	though one rise from the **d**
Luke	24:46	rise from the **d** the third day
John	5:21	as the Father raises the **d**
John	5:25	is, when the **d** will hear the
John	11:14	them plainly, "Lazarus is **d**
John	11:39	for he has been **d** four days
John	20: 9	He must rise again from the **d**
Acts	2:29	David, that he is both **d** and
Acts	3:15	whom God raised from the **d**
Acts	10:42	Judge of the living and the **d**
Acts	14:19	city, supposing him to be **d**
Acts	17:32	of the resurrection of the **d**
Acts	20: 9	third story and was taken up **d**
Acts	23: 6	of the **d** I am being judged
Rom	4:17	God, who gives life to the **d**
Rom	4:24	up Jesus our Lord from the **d**
Rom	6: 4	**d** by the glory of the Father
Rom	6:11	to be **d** indeed to sin, but
Rom	6:13	God as being alive from the **d**
Rom	7: 4	you also have become **d** to the
Rom	8:10	the body is **d** because of sin,
Rom	8:11	from the **d** dwells in you, He
Rom	10: 9	God has raised Him from the **d**
1Co	15:16	For if the **d** do not rise,
1Co	15:20	Christ is risen from the **d**
1Co	15:29	do who are baptized for the **d**
1Co	15:52	and the **d** will be raised
Eph	2: 5	when we were **d** in trespasses
Eph	5:14	who sleep, arise from the **d**
Col	1:18	the firstborn from the **d**
1Th	4:16	the **d** in Christ will rise
1Ti	5: 6	pleasure is **d** while she lives
2Ti	4: 1	the **d** at His appearing and His
Heb	6: 1	of repentance from **d** works
Heb	9:14	**d** works to serve the living
Heb	9:17	is in force after men are **d**
Heb	11: 4	it he being **d** still speaks
Heb	11:12	one man, and him as good as **d**
Heb	11:19	raise him up, even from the **d**
Heb	11:35	their **d** raised to life again
Heb	13:20	up our Lord Jesus from the **d**
Jas	2:20	that faith without works is **d**
Jas	2:26	body without the spirit is **d**
Rev	1: 5	the firstborn from the **d**
Rev	1:17	Him, I fell at His feet as **d**
Rev	1:18	I am He who lives, and was **d**
Rev	2: 8	First and the Last, who was **d**
Rev	3: 1	you are alive, but you are **d**

Rev	14:13	Blessed are the **d** who die in
Rev	20:12	And I saw the **d**, small and
Rev	20:12	the **d** were judged according
Rev	20:13	gave up the **d** who were in it

DEADLY (see DEAD)

Jas	3: 8	unruly evil, full of **d** poison

DEAF

Ex	4:11	Or who makes the mute, the **d**
Is	29:18	In that day the **d** shall hear
Is	42:19	or **d** as My messenger whom I
Mark	7:32	brought to Him one who was **d**
Mark	9:25	You **d** and dumb spirit, I
Luke	7:22	the **d** hear, the dead are

DEAL (see DEALINGS, DEALT)

Gen	19: 9	now we will **d** worse with you
Gen	24:49	Now if you will **d** kindly and
Ex	1:10	let us **d** wisely with them,
Ps	119:17	**D** bountifully with Your
Is	52:13	My Servant shall **d** prudently

DEALINGS (see DEAL)

John	4: 9	have no **d** with Samaritans

DEALT (see DEAL)

Gen	16: 6	when Sarai **d** harshly with her
Gen	33:11	because God has **d** graciously
Ex	1:20	Therefore God **d** well with the
Ruth	1:20	for the Almighty has **d** very
Ps	103:10	He has not **d** with us
Rom	12: 3	as God has **d** to each one a

DEATH (see DIE)

Gen	25:11	after the **d** of Abraham, that
Gen	27: 2	I do not know the day of my **d**
Ex	19:12	shall surely be put to **d**
Num	35:25	remain there until the **d** of
Num	35:28	the **d** of the high priest
Num	35:30	a person for the **d** penalty
Deut	24:16	be put to **d** for their fathers
Deut	24:16	be put to **d** for his own sin
Deut	30:19	have set before you life and **d**
Josh	1: 1	After the **d** of Moses the
Judg	1: 1	Now after the **d** of Joshua it
Judg	16:30	his **d** were more than he had
Ruth	1:17	if anything but **d** parts you
2Sa	22: 5	the waves of **d** encompassed me
2Ki	15: 5	leper until the day of his **d**
2Ki	20: 1	Hezekiah was sick and near **d**
Job	18:13	the firstborn of **d** devours
Job	28:22	and **D** say, We have heard a
Job	38:17	Have the gates of **d** been
Ps	13: 3	Lest I sleep the sleep of **d**
Ps	18: 5	The snares of **d** confronted me
Ps	23: 4	the valley of the shadow of **d**
Ps	49:14	**D** shall feed on them
Ps	102:20	To loose those apointed to **d**
Ps	116: 8	have delivered my soul from **d**
Ps	116:15	LORD Is the **d** of His saints
Prov	2:18	for her house leads down to **d**
Prov	7:27	to the chambers of **d**
Prov	10: 2	righteousness delivers from **d**

Prov	14:12	but its end is the way of **d**
Song	8: 6	for love is as strong as **d**
Is	9: 2	the land of the shadow of **d**
Is	25: 8	He will swallow up **d** forever
Is	28:15	have made a covenant with **d**
Is	53: 9	but with the rich at His **d**
Is	53:12	He poured out His soul unto **d**
Jer	21: 8	way of life and the way of **d**
Ezek	33:11	in the **d** of the wicked, but
Hos	13:14	I will redeem them from **d**
Hos	13:14	O **D**, I will be your plagues
Matt	2:16	and put to **d** all the male
Matt	4:16	shadow of **d** light has dawned
Matt	26:38	sorrowful, even to **d**
Matt	26:66	He is deserving of **d**
Mark	9: 1	here who will not taste **d**
Luke	1:79	darkness and the shadow of **d**
Luke	2:26	that he would not see **d**
John	5:24	has passed from **d** into life
John	11: 4	This sickness is not unto **d**
John	12:33	by what **d** He would die
Rom	1:32	such things are worthy of **d**
Rom	5:10	God through the **d** of His Son
Rom	5:12	and **d** through sin
Rom	5:14	Nevertheless **d** reigned from
Rom	6: 3	were baptized into His **d**
Rom	6: 9	**D** no longer has dominion over
Rom	6:23	For the wages of sin is **d**
Rom	7:24	me from this body of **d**
Rom	8: 2	free from the law of sin and **d**
Rom	8: 6	to be carnally minded is **d**
Rom	8:38	that neither **d** nor life, nor
1Co	11:26	the Lord's **d** till He comes
1Co	15:26	that will be destroyed is **d**
1Co	15:54	**D** is swallowed up in victory
1Co	15:55	O **D**, where is your sting
2Co	2:16	are the aroma of **d** to **d**
2Co	3: 7	But if the ministry of **d**,
Phil	1:20	body, whether by life or by **d**
Phil	2: 8	obedient to the point of **d**
Phil	2: 8	even the **d** of the cross
Phil	3:10	being conformed to His **d**
2Ti	1:10	Christ, who has abolished **d**
Heb	2: 9	might taste **d** for everyone
Heb	11: 5	so that he did not see **d**
Jas	1:15	is full-grown, brings forth **d**
Jas	5:20	way will save a soul from **d**
1Jn	3:14	we have passed from **d** to life
1Jn	5:16	sin which does not lead to **d**
Rev	1:18	the keys of Hades and of **D**
Rev	2:10	Be faithful until **d**, and I
Rev	2:11	not be hurt by the second **d**
Rev	20:14	Then **D** and Hades were cast
Rev	21: 4	there shall be no more **d**, nor

DEBORAH

Gen	35: 8	Now **D**, Rebekah's nurse, died,
Judg	4: 4	Now **D**, a prophetess, the wife

DEBT (see DEBTOR, DEBTS)

Matt	18:27	him, and forgave him the **d**
Rom	4: 4	not counted as grace but as **d**

DEBTOR (see DEBT, DEBTORS)
Rom   1:14 I am a **d** both to Greeks and to

DEBTORS (see DEBTOR)
Matt   6:12 debts, As we forgive our **d**
Rom   8:12 Therefore, brethren, we are **d**

DEBTS (see DEBT)
Matt   6:12 And forgive us our **d**, As we

DECAPOLIS
Matt   4:25 from Galilee, and from **D**,

DECEIT (see DECEITFUL, DECEIVE)
Ps   32: 2 in whose spirit there is no **d**
Ps   34:13 your lips from speaking **d**
Prov   20:17 Bread gained by **d** is sweet to
Is   53: 9 nor was any **d** in His mouth
Amos   8: 5 falsifying the balances by **d**
John   1:47 indeed, in whom is no **d**!"
Rom   1:29 of envy, murder, strife, **d**
Rom   3:13 they have practiced **d**"
1Pe   2:22 Nor was **d** found in His
1Pe   3:10 And his lips from speaking **d**.
Rev   14: 5 in their mouth was found no **d**,

DECEITFUL (see DECEIT, DECEITFULLY, DECEITFULNESS)
Prov   14:25 but a **d** witness speaks lies
Prov   31:30 Charm is **d** and beauty is vain,
Jer   17: 9 The heart is **d** above all
Hos   7:16 they are like a **d** bow.
Hos   12: 7 **d** scales are in his hand
Mic   6:11 and with the bag of **d** weights
Eph   4:14 craftiness of **d** plotting,
Eph   4:22 according to the **d** lusts,

DECEITFULLY (see DECEITFUL)
Ps   24: 4 soul to an idol, Nor sworn **d**
Jer   48:10 does the work of the LORD **d**
2Co   4: 2 handling the word of God **d**

DECEITFULNESS (see DECEITFUL)
Matt   13:22 the **d** of riches choke the
Heb   3:13 hardened through the **d** of sin

DECEIVE (see DECEIT, DECEIVED, DECEIVERS, DECEIVES, DECEIVING)
2Ki   18:29 Do not let Hezekiah **d** you
2Ki   19:10 God in whom you trust **d** you
Matt   24: 5 the Christ,' and will **d** many
Matt   24:24 signs and wonders, so as to **d**
Rom   16:18 and flattering speech **d** the
1Co   3:18 Let no one **d** himself
1Jn   1: 8 we **d** ourselves, and the truth
Rev   20: 8 will go out to **d** the nations

DECEIVED (see DECEIVE)
Gen   3:13 The serpent **d** me, and I ate
Deut   11:16 lest your heart be **d**, and you
Josh   7:11 and have both stolen and **d**
Jer   4:10 have greatly **d** this people
Obad   3 pride of your heart has **d** you

Matt   2:16 that he was **d** by the wise men
Luke   21: 8 Take heed that you not be **d**
John   7:47 Are you also **d**
Rom   7:11 **d** me, and by it killed me
1Co   6: 9 Do not be **d**
1Co   15:33 Do not be **d**
2Co   11: 3 as the serpent **d** Eve by his
Gal   6: 7 Do not be **d**, God is not
1Ti   2:14 And Adam was not **d**, but the
Rev   18:23 all the nations were **d**
Rev   20:10 who **d** them, was cast into the

DECEIVERS (see DECEIVE)
2Jn   7 For many **d** have gone out into

DECEIVES (see DECEIVE)
Prov   26:19 is the man who **d** his neighbor
Matt   24: 4 Take heed that no one **d** you
John   7:12 the contrary, He **d** the people
Gal   6: 3 he is nothing, he **d** himself
Jas   1:26 tongue but **d** his own heart
Rev   12: 9 Satan, who **d** the whole world

DECEIVING (see DECEIVE)
1Ti   4: 1 giving heed to **d** spirits
2Ti   3:13 will grow worse and worse, **d**
Jas   1:22 hearers only, **d** yourselves

DECENTLY †
1Co   14:40 Let all things be done **d** and

DECISION (see COUNSEL)
Prov   16:33 but its every **d** is from the
Joel   3:14 multitudes in the valley of **d**

DECLARE (see DECLARED)
Deut   5: 5 to **d** to you the word of the
1Ch   16:24 **D** His glory among the nations
Ps   2: 7 I will **d** the decree
Ps   9:11 **D** His deeds among the people
Ps   19: 1 The heavens **d** the glory of
Is   53: 8 who will **d** His generation
Is   66:19 they shall **d** My glory among
Acts   8:33 who will **d** His generation
1Co   3:13 for the Day will **d** it,
1Jn   1: 3 seen and heard we **d** to you
1Jn   1: 5 **d** to you, that God is light

DECLARED (see DECLARE)
John   1:18 of the Father, He has **d** Him
Rom   1: 4 **d** to be the Son of God with

DECREASE
John   3:30 must increase, but I must **d**

DECREE
Ezra   5:13 King Cyrus issued a **d** to
Ps   2: 7 I will declare the **d**
Dan   2:13 So the **d** went out, and they
Dan   4:17 is by the **d** of the watchers
Dan   4:24 this is the **d** of the Most
Luke   2: 1 that a **d** went out from Caesar

DEDICATED (see DEDICATION)

Heb	9:18	covenant was **d** without blood

DEDICATION (see DEDICATED)

Ezra	6:17	at the **d** of this house of God
Neh	12:27	Now at the **d** of the wall of
John	10:22	the Feast of **D** in Jerusalem

DEED (see DEEDS)

Gen	44:15	What **d** is this you have done
Judg	20: 3	how did this wicked **d** happen
Jer	32:10	And I signed the **d** and sealed
Matt	6: 2	when you do a charitable **d**
Luke	23:51	to their counsel and **d**
Luke	24:19	who was a Prophet mighty in **d**
Rom	15:18	through me, in word and **d**, to
Tit	2:14	us from every lawless **d** and
Phm	14	that your good **d** might not be
1Jn	3:18	word or in tongue, but in **d**

DEEDS (see DEED)

Gen	20: 9	You have done **d** to me that
Deut	3:24	Your works and Your mighty **d**
1Ch	16: 8	make known His **d** among the
1Ch	17:21	a name by great and awesome **d**
Neh	13:14	do not wipe out my good **d**
Ps	9:11	Declare His **d** among the
Ps	28: 4	to them according to their **d**
Ps	44: 1	What **d** You did in their days,
Ps	105: 1	Make known His **d** among the
Prov	20:11	a child is known by his **d**
Prov	24:12	each man according to his **d**
Is	12: 4	declare His **d** among the
Jer	11:15	having done lewd **d** with many
Jer	32:44	buy fields for money, sign **d**
Ezek	9:10	their **d** on their own head
Dan	9:18	because of our righteous **d**
Hos	4: 9	and reward them for their **d**
Hos	12: 2	according to his **d** He will
Matt	6: 1	your charitable **d** before men
Luke	23:41	the due reward of our **d**
John	3:19	because their **d** were evil
John	3:20	lest his **d** should be exposed
John	8:41	You do the **d** of your father
Acts	7:22	and was mighty in words and **d**
Acts	19:18	confessing and telling their **d**
Rom	2: 6	each one according to his **d**"
Rom	3:28	apart from the **d** of the law
Rom	4: 7	whose lawless **d** are forgiven
Rom	8:13	to death the **d** of the body
2Co	12:12	signs and wonders and mighty **d**
Col	3: 9	off the old man with his **d**
Rev	2: 6	that you hate the **d** of the
Rev	2:22	unless they repent of their **d**

DEEP (see DEEPLY)

Gen	1: 2	was on the face of the **d**
Gen	2:21	a **d** sleep to fall on Adam
Gen	7:11	of the great **d** were broken up
Job	4:13	when **d** sleep falls on men,
Job	11: 7	out the **d** things of God
Ps	2: 5	them in His **d** displeasure
Ps	42: 7	**D** calls unto **d** at the

Ps	69:14	me, And out of the **d** waters
Prov	8:27	a circle on the face of the **d**
Dan	2:22	He reveals **d** and secret things
Dan	8:18	I was in a **d** sleep
Jon	2: 3	For You cast me into the **d**
Jon	2: 5	the **d** closed around me
Luke	5: 4	Launch out into the **d** and let
John	4:11	draw with, and the well is **d**
1Co	2:10	yes, the **d** things of God

DEEPLY (see DEEP)

Matt	26:37	be sorrowful and **d** distressed
Mark	8:12	But He sighed **d** in His spirit

DEER

2Sa	22:34	my feet like the feet of **d**
Ps	42: 1	As the **d** pants for the water
Prov	5:19	As a loving **d** and a graceful
Is	35: 6	the lame shall leap like a **d**

DEFEAT (see DEFEATED)

Ex	32:18	of those who cry out in **d**
Deut	7:23	and will inflict **d** upon them
2Sa	17:14	to **d** the good counsel of

DEFEATED (see DEFEAT)

Josh	12: 1	whom the children of Israel **d**
Judg	1: 5	they **d** the Canaanites and the
1Sa	4: 3	Why has the LORD **d** us today
Esth	9: 5	Thus the Jews **d** all their
Ps	135:10	He **d** many nations And slew

DEFEND (see DEFENDER, DEFENSE)

Job	13:15	I will **d** my own ways before
Ps	5:11	for joy, because You **d** them
Ps	20: 1	of the God of Jacob **d** you
Is	1:17	**d** the fatherless, plead for
Is	31: 5	the LORD of hosts **d** Jerusalem
Is	37:35	For I will **d** this city, to

DEFENDER† (see DEFEND)

Ps	68: 5	a **d** of widows, Is God in His

DEFENSE (see DEFEND)

2Ch	11: 5	built cities for **d** in Judah
Ps	59: 9	For God is my **d**
Acts	19:33	to make his **d** to the people
1Pe	3:15	always be ready to give a **d**

DEFERRED†

Prov	13:12	Hope **d** makes the heart sick,

DEFILE (see DEFILED, DEFILES, DEFILING, UNDEFILED)

Lev	18:20	wife, to **d** yourself with her
Lev	18:23	beast, to **d** yourself with it
Dan	1: 8	**d** himself with the portion of
Dan	11:31	they shall **d** the sanctuary
Amos	2: 7	same girl, to **d** My holy name
Matt	15:18	the heart, and they **d** a man
Mark	7:18	man from outside cannot **d** him
Jude	8	these dreamers **d** the flesh

DEFILED (*see* DEFILE)

Gen	34: 5	he had **d** Dinah his daughter
Num	5: 2	becomes **d** by a dead body
2Ki	23: 8	**d** the high places where the
2Ki	23:10	he **d** Topheth, which is in the
2Ch	36:14	**d** the house of the LORD which
Ezra	2:62	from the priesthood as **d**
Ps	74: 7	They have **d** the dwelling
Is	24: 5	The earth is also **d** under its
Mal	1: 7	You offer **d** food on My altar
Mal	1: 7	In what way have we **d** You
Mal	1:12	The table of the LORD is **d**
Mark	7: 2	disciples eat bread with **d**
1Co	8: 7	conscience, being weak, is **d**
Tit	1:15	pure, but to those who are **d**
Heb	12:15	and by this many become **d**
Jude	23	the garment **d** by the flesh
Rev	3: 4	who have not **d** their garments
Rev	14: 4	who were not **d** with women

DEFILES (*see* DEFILE)

Num	19:13	**d** the tabernacle of the LORD
Num	35:33	for blood **d** the land, and no
Matt	15:11	goes into the mouth **d** a man
Jas	3: 6	that it **d** the whole body, and
Rev	21:27	enter it anything that **d**, or

DEFILING (*see* DEFILE)

Is	56: 2	who keeps from **d** the Sabbath

DEGENERATE†

Jer	2:21	the **d** plant of an alien vine
Ezek	16:30	How **d** is your heart

DEGREES

2Ki	20: 9	the shadow go forward ten **d**

DELAY (*see* DELAYED, DELAYING)

1Sa	20:38	Make haste, hurry, do not **d**
Ps	40:17	Do not **d**, O my God

DELAYED (*see* DELAY)

Ex	32: 1	Moses **d** coming down from the

DELAYING (*see* DELAY)

Matt	24:48	My master is **d** his coming

DELIGHT (*see* DELIGHTS)

Deut	21:14	be, if you have no **d** in her
1Sa	15:22	as great **d** in burnt offerings
Ps	1: 2	But his **d** is in the law of
Ps	16: 3	ones, in whom is all my **d**
Ps	37: 4	**D** yourself also in the LORD,
Ps	40: 8	I **d** to do Your will, O my God
Ps	119:77	For Your law is my **d**
Prov	8:30	and I was daily His **d**,
Prov	11: 1	but a just weight is His **d**
Prov	29:17	he will give **d** to your soul
Is	1:11	I do not **d** in the blood of
Is	11: 3	His **d** is in the fear of the
Is	58:13	day, and call the Sabbath a **d**
Jer	9:24	For in these I **d**," says the
Ezek	24:21	your eyes, the **d** of your soul

Mal	3: 1	the covenant, in whom you **d**
Rom	7:22	For I **d** in the law of God

DELIGHTS (*see* DELIGHT)

Num	14: 8	If the LORD **d** in us, then He
Esth	6: 6	man whom the king **d** to honor
Ps	22: 8	Him, since He **d** in Him
Ps	37:23	the LORD, And He **d** in his way
Ps	119:143	Your commandments are my **d**
Prov	3:12	a father the son in whom he **d**
Is	42: 1	Elect One in whom My soul **d**

DELILAH

Judg	16: 6	So **D** said to Samson, "Please

DELIVER (*see* DELIVERANCE, DELIVERED, DELIVERER, DELIVERS, GRANT)

Gen	37:22	that he might **d** him out of
Ex	3: 8	So I have come down to **d** them
Deut	32:39	any who can **d** from My hand
Ps	6: 4	Return, O LORD, **d** me
Ps	7: 2	while there is none to **d**
Ps	17:13	**D** my life from the wicked
Ps	22: 8	Let Him **d** Him, since He
Ps	22:20	**D** Me from the sword, My
Ps	72:12	For He will **d** the needy when
Ps	119:170	**D** me according to Your word
Ps	144: 7	**d** me out of great waters,
Prov	2:16	to **d** you from the immoral
Prov	23:14	rod, and **d** his soul from hell
Is	44:17	**D** me, for you are my god
Jer	1: 8	for I am with you to **d** you
Jer	18:21	Therefore **d** up their children
Jer	24: 9	I will **d** them to trouble
Jer	43:11	**d** to death those appointed
Ezek	14:14	they would **d** only themselves
Ezek	34:10	for I will **d** My flock from
Dan	3:17	whom we serve is able to **d** us
Matt	6:13	but **d** us from the evil one
Matt	10:17	for they will **d** you up to
Matt	10:21	Now brother will **d** up brother
Matt	20:19	**d** Him to the Gentiles to mock
Matt	24: 9	Then they will **d** you up to
Matt	27:43	let Him **d** Him now if He will
Mark	10:33	and **d** Him to the Gentiles
Luke	12:58	judge, the judge **d** you to the
Acts	26:17	I will **d** you from the Jewish
Rom	7:24	Who will **d** me from this body
1Co	5: 5	**d** such a one to Satan for the
Gal	1: 4	that He might **d** us from this
2Ti	4:18	the Lord will **d** me from every
2Pe	2: 9	how to **d** the godly out of

DELIVERANCE (*see* DELIVER, LIBERTY)

Ps	32: 7	surround me with songs of **d**
Prov	21:31	battle, but **d** is of the LORD

DELIVERED (*see* BETRAYED, DELIVER)

Ex	2:19	An Egyptian **d** us from the
Ex	12:27	Egyptians and **d** our households
Judg	12: 3	the LORD **d** them into my hand
2Sa	12: 7	I **d** you from the hand of Saul
2Sa	22:20	He **d** me, because He delighted
Job	16:11	God has **d** me to the ungodly,

D

Ps	22: 4	They trusted, and You **d** them
Ps	22: 5	They cried to You, and were **d**
Ps	34: 4	me, And **d** me from all my fears
Ps	81: 7	called in trouble, and I **d** you
Ps	86:13	You have **d** my soul from the
Ps	106:43	Many times He **d** them
Prov	11: 8	righteous is **d** from trouble
Prov	11: 9	the righteous will be **d**
Ezek	3:21	you will have **d** your soul
Ezek	31:14	they have all been **d** to death
Dan	6:27	Who has **d** Daniel from the
Matt	11:27	been **d** to Me by My Father
Matt	18:34	**d** him to the torturers until
Matt	25:14	and **d** his goods to them
Matt	25:20	you **d** to me five talents
Matt	26: 2	will be **d** up to be crucified
Matt	27: 2	**d** Him to Pontius Pilate the
Luke	1: 2	of the word **d** them to us,
Luke	1:57	time came for her to be **d**
Luke	2: 6	completed for her to be **d**
Luke	10:22	been **d** to Me by My Father
Luke	19:13	**d** to them ten minas, and said
Luke	24: 7	The Son of Man must be **d**
Luke	24:20	and our rulers **d** Him to be
John	18:35	priests have **d** You to me
John	18:36	I should not be **d** to the Jews
Acts	2:23	being **d** by the determined
Acts	3:13	Servant Jesus, whom you **d** up
Acts	6:14	customs which Moses **d** to us
Acts	7:10	**d** him out of all his troubles
Rom	7: 6	we have been **d** from the law
Rom	8:21	will be **d** from the bondage of
Rom	8:32	but **d** Him up for us all, how
1Co	11:23	that which I also **d** to you
1Co	15: 3	For I **d** to you first of all
2Co	1:10	who **d** us from so great a
Col	1:13	He has **d** us from the power of
1Ti	1:20	whom I **d** to Satan that they
2Ti	4:17	I was **d** out of the mouth of
Jude	3	once for all **d** to the saints
Rev	20:13	Hades **d** up the dead who were

DELIVERER (see DELIVER, DELIVERERS)

Judg	3: 9	the LORD raised up a **d** for
2Sa	22: 2	my rock, my fortress and my **d**
Ps	40:17	You are my help and my **d**
Acts	7:35	a **d** by the hand of the Angel
Rom	11:26	The **D** will come out of Zion,

DELIVERS (see DELIVER)

Ex	22: 7	If a man **d** to his neighbor
Ps	34: 7	who fear Him, And **d** them
Ps	34:17	And **d** them out of all their
Prov	10: 2	righteousness **d** from death
Prov	14:25	A true witness **d** souls, but a
Dan	6:27	He **d** and rescues, and He works
1Co	15:24	when He **d** the kingdom to God
1Th	1:10	even Jesus who **d** us from the

DEMON (see DEMON-POSSESSED, DEMONS)

Matt	9:33	when the **d** was cast out, the
Matt	11:18	and they say, 'He has a **d**
Matt	17:18	And Jesus rebuked the **d**, and he

Luke	4:33	had a spirit of an unclean **d**
John	8:48	are a Samaritan and have a **d**

DEMON-POSSESSED (see DEMON)

Matt	4:24	torments, and those who were **d**
Matt	8:28	there met Him two **d** men,
Matt	15:22	My daughter is severely **d**
Mark	1:32	were sick and those who were **d**

DEMONS (see DEMON)

Deut	32:17	They sacrificed to **d**, not to
2Ch	11:15	the high places, for the **d**
Ps	106:37	sons And their daughters to **d**
Matt	7:22	cast out **d** in Your name, and
Matt	8:31	So the **d** begged Him, saying,
Matt	9:34	by the ruler of the **d**
Matt	10: 8	raise the dead, cast out **d**
Matt	12:24	Beelzebub, the ruler of the **d**
Luke	8:2	out of whom had come seven **d**
Luke	9: 1	power and authority over all **d**
1Co	10:20	sacrifice they sacrifice to **d**
1Co	10:21	of the Lord and the cup of **d**
1Ti	4: 1	spirits and doctrines of **d**
Jas	2:19	Even the **d** believe
Rev	9:20	they should not worship **d**

DEMONSTRATION†

1Co	2: 4	but in **d** of the Spirit and of

DEN

Ps	10: 9	secretly, as a lion in his **d**
Is	11: 8	put his hand in the viper's **d**
Jer	7:11	become a **d** of thieves in your
Dan	6: 7	be cast into the **d** of lions
Matt	21:13	have made it a '**d** of thieves

DENIED (see DENY)

Gen	18:15	But Sarah **d** it, saying, "I
Job	31:28	would have **d** God who is above
Matt	26:70	But he **d** it before them all,
Luke	8:45	When all **d** it, Peter and
Luke	12: 9	Me before men will be **d**
John	13:38	you have **d** Me three times
Acts	3:13	**d** in the presence of Pilate,
Acts	3:14	But you **d** the Holy One and the
Acts	19:36	these things cannot be **d**, you
1Ti	5: 8	he has **d** the faith and is
Rev	3: 8	word, and have not **d** My name

DENIES (see DENY)

Matt	10:33	But whoever **d** Me before men,
1Jn	2:22	**d** that Jesus is the Christ
1Jn	2:22	antichrist who **d** the Father
1Jn	2:23	Whoever **d** the Son does not

DENY (see DENIED, DENIES, DENYING)

Matt	10:33	him I will also **d** before My
Matt	16:24	after Me, let him **d** himself
Matt	26:34	you will **d** Me three times
Luke	20:27	who **d** that there is a
John	1:20	He confessed, and did not **d**
Acts	4:16	Jerusalem, and we cannot **d** it
2Ti	2:12	If we **d** Him, He also will **d** us
2Ti	2:13	He cannot **d** Himself

Rev	2:13	did not **d** My faith even in

DENYING† (*see* DENY)

2Ti	3: 5	of godliness but **d** its power
Tit	2:12	**d** ungodliness and worldly
2Pe	2: 1	even **d** the Lord who bought

DEPART (*see* DEPARTED, DEPARTS, DEPARTURE)

Gen	49:10	shall not **d** from Judah, nor a
Deut	4: 9	lest they **d** from your heart
Josh	1: 8	shall not **d** from your mouth
2Ki	15: 9	he did not **d** from the sins of
Ps	6: 8	**D** from me, all you workers of
Ps	34:14	**D** from evil, and do good
Prov	3: 7	fear the LORD and **d** from evil
Prov	22: 6	is old he will not **d** from it
Is	59:21	shall not **d** from your mouth,
Matt	7:23	**d** from Me, you who practice
Matt	8:18	to **d** to the other side
Matt	8:34	Him to **d** from their region
Matt	10:14	when you **d** from that house or
Mark	6:11	when you **d** from there, shake
Luke	2:29	Your servant **d** in peace,
John	7: 3	**D** from here and go into Judea,
John	13: 1	**d** from this world to the
John	16: 7	but if I **d**, I will send Him
Acts	1: 4	them not to **d** from Jerusalem
1Co	7:10	is not to **d** from her husband
1Co	7:11	But even if she does **d**, let
1Co	7:15	unbeliever departs, let him **d**
2Co	12: 8	times that it might **d** from me
Phil	1:23	the two, having a desire to **d**
1Ti	4: 1	some will **d** from the faith
2Ti	2:19	of Christ **d** from iniquity
Jas	2:16	**D** in peace, be warmed and

DEPARTED (*see* DEPART)

Gen	12: 4	So Abram **d** as the LORD had
Gen	31:40	and my sleep **d** from my eyes
Num	12:10	when the cloud **d** from above
Judg	16:20	that the LORD had **d** from him
1Sa	4:21	The glory has **d** from Israel
1Sa	16:14	of the LORD **d** from Saul, and a
Matt	27:60	the door of the tomb, and **d**
Mark	1:35	out and **d** to a solitary place
Luke	8:35	from whom the demons had **d**
Acts	18:23	spent some time there, he ˙**d**
Acts	20: 1	them, and **d** to go to Macedonia
Acts	28:29	said these words, the Jews **d**
Phm	15	For perhaps he **d** for a while

DEPARTS (*see* DEPART)

1Co	7:15	But if the unbeliever **d**, let

DEPARTURE (*see* DEPART)

2Ti	4: 6	the time of my **d** is at hand
Heb	11:22	made mention of the **d** of the

DEPTH (*see* DEPTHS)

Prov	25: 3	for height and the earth for **d**
Matt	13: 5	they had no **d** of earth
Matt	18: 6	drowned in the **d** of the sea
Rom	8:39	nor height nor **d**, nor any

Rom	11:33	the **d** of the riches both of
Eph	3:18	is the width and length and **d**

DEPTHS (*see* DEPTH)

Ex	15: 5	The **d** have covered them
Job	36:30	and covers the **d** of the sea
Ps	71:20	again from the **d** of the earth
Ps	86:13	my soul from the **d** of Sheol
Ps	130: 1	Out of the **d** I have cried to
Prov	8:24	When there were no **d** I was
Prov	9:18	guests are in the **d** of hell
Prov	20:27	all the inner **d** of his heart
Is	14:15	to the lowest **d** of the Pit
Rev	2:24	have not known the **d** of Satan

DERISION

Ps	2: 4	The LORD shall hold them in **d**
Ps	44:13	a **d** to those all around us
Ps	59: 8	have all the nations in **d**
Ps	119:51	The proud have me in great **d**
Jer	20: 8	to me a reproach and a **d** daily
Ezek	23:32	laughed to scorn and held in **d**
Hos	7:16	This shall be their **d** in the

DESCEND (*see* DESCENDANTS, DESCENDED, DESCENDING)

2Ki	20:18	your sons who will **d** from you
Ezek	26:20	with those who **d** into the Pit
Mark	15:32	**d** now from the cross, that we
Rom	10: 7	Who will **d** into the abyss
1Th	4:16	**d** from heaven with a shout
Jas	3:15	wisdom does not **d** from above

DESCENDANTS (*see* DESCEND)

Gen	9: 9	you and with your **d** after you
Gen	12: 7	To your **d** I will give this
Gen	16:10	multiply your **d** exceedingly
Gen	22:17	your **d** shall possess the gate
Gen	32:12	make your **d** as the sand of
Num	13:22	the **d** of Anak, were there
Deut	23: 2	none of his **d** shall enter the
Josh	24: 3	Canaan, and multiplied his **d**
Ps	18:50	To David and his **d** forevermore
Ps	37:25	Nor his **d** begging bread
Is	41: 8	the **d** of Abraham My friend
Is	44: 3	will pour My Spirit on your **d**
John	8:33	We are Abraham's **d**, and have
Acts	7: 5	and to his **d** after him
Rom	4:18	So shall your **d** be

DESCENDED (*see* DESCEND)

Ex	19:18	the LORD **d** upon it in fire
Ex	33: 9	that the pillar of cloud **d**
Ex	34: 5	Then the LORD **d** in the cloud
Prov	30: 4	ascended into heaven, or **d**
Is	57: 9	and even **d** to Sheol
Matt	7:25	and the rain **d**, the floods
Matt	28: 2	of the Lord **d** from heaven
Luke	3:22	the Holy Spirit **d** in bodily
Eph	4: 9	**d** into the lower parts of the

DESCENDING (*see* DESCEND)

Gen	28:12	God were ascending and **d** on it
Ps	133: 3	**D** upon the mountains of Zion

Prov	7:27	**d** to the chambers of death
Matt	3:16	Spirit of God **d** like a dove
John	1:51	and **d** upon the Son of Man
Acts	10:11	**d** to him and let down to the
Acts	11: 5	an object **d** like a great
Rev	21:10	**d** out of heaven from God,

DESERT (see WILDERNESS)

Ex	3: 1	flock to the back of the **d**
Ps	73:27	those who **d** You for harlotry
Ps	106:14	And tested God in the **d**
Is	23:13	it for wild beasts of the **d**
Is	35: 1	and the **d** shall rejoice and
Is	35: 6	and streams in the **d**
Is	40: 3	make straight in the **d** a
Is	43:19	wilderness and rivers in the **d**
Matt	24:26	to you, 'Look, He is in the **d**
John	6:31	ate the manna in the **d**

DESERVE (see DESERVING)

Ezra	9:13	us less than our iniquities **d**
Ps	28: 4	Render to them what they **d**
Jer	26:16	This man does not **d** to die

DESERVING (see DESERVE)

Deut	17: 6	Whoever is **d** of death
Matt	26:66	and said, 'He is **d** of death

DESIRABLE (see DESIRE)

Gen	3: 6	a tree **d** to make one wise,
Prov	21:20	There is **d** treasure, and oil
Hos	13:15	the treasury of every **d** prize
Acts	6: 2	It is not **d** that we should

DESIRE (see DESIRABLE, DESIRED, DESIRES, DESIRING)

Gen	3:16	Your **d** shall be for your
Gen	4: 7	its **d** is for you, but you
1Sa	9:20	whom is all the **d** of Israel
Ps	10: 3	boasts of his heart's **d**
Ps	45:11	will greatly **d** your beauty
Ps	51: 6	You **d** truth in the inward
Ps	51:16	For You do not **d** sacrifice
Ps	59:10	let me see my **d** on my enemies
Ps	73:25	earth that I **d** besides You
Ps	145:16	satisfy the **d** of every living
Ps	145:19	He will fulfill the **d** of
Prov	13:19	A **d** accomplished is sweet to
Eccl	12: 5	is a burden, and **d** fails
Is	53: 2	beauty that we should **d** Him
Ezek	24:16	the **d** of your eyes with one
Hos	6: 6	For I **d** mercy and not
Amos	5:18	Woe to you who **d** the day of
Hag	2: 7	come to the **D** of All Nations
Matt	9:13	I **d** mercy and not sacrifice
Matt	15:28	Let it be to you as you **d**
Rom	7: 8	in me all manner of evil **d**
Rom	10: 1	Brethren, my heart's **d** and
1Co	12:31	But earnestly **d** the best
1Co	14: 1	and **d** spiritual gifts, but
2Co	7: 7	he told us of your earnest **d**
Phil	1:23	having a **d** to depart and be
Col	3: 5	uncleanness, passion, evil **d**

2Ti	3:12	all who **d** to live godly in
Heb	10: 5	and offering You did not **d**
Heb	10: 8	for sin You did not **d**, nor
Heb	11:16	But now they **d** a better, that
Jas	1:15	when **d** has conceived, it
1Pe	1:12	which angels **d** to look into
1Pe	2: 2	**d** the pure milk of the word,

DESIRED (see DESIRE)

Ps	19:10	More to be **d** are they than
Ps	27: 4	thing I have **d** of the LORD
Ps	107:30	guides them to their **d** haven
Eccl	2:10	Whatever my eyes **d** I did not
Luke	22:15	**d** to eat this Passover with

DESIRES (see DESIRE)

Deut	12:20	as much meat as your heart **d**
Job	7: 2	who earnestly **d** the shade
Job	23:13	And whatever His soul **d**, that
Ps	34:12	Who is the man who **d** life
Ps	37: 4	give you the **d** of your heart
Prov	21:10	The soul of the wicked **d** evil
Matt	16:24	If anyone **d** to come after Me,
Matt	16:25	For whoever **d** to save his
Gal	5:24	flesh with its passions and **d**
Eph	2: 3	fulfilling the **d** of the flesh
1Ti	2: 4	who **d** all men to be saved and
1Ti	3: 1	If a man **d** the position of a
1Ti	3: 1	of a bishop, he **d** a good work
Jas	1:14	he is drawn away by his own **d**

DESIRING (see DESIRE)

Luke	8:20	outside, **d** to see You
2Co	5: 2	earnestly **d** to be clothed

DESOLATE (see DESOLATION)

Ex	23:29	year, lest the land become **d**
Lev	26:34	sabbaths as long as it lies **d**
2Sa	13:20	So Tamar remained **d** in her
Ps	25:16	have mercy on me, For I am **d**
Is	62: 4	land any more be termed **D**
Jer	9:11	make the cities of Judah **d**
Dan	9:17	on Your sanctuary, which is **d**
Dan	9:27	shall be one who makes **d**,
Dan	9:27	is poured out on the **d**
Matt	23:38	Your house is left to you **d**

DESOLATION (see ASTONISHMENT, DESOLATE)

Is	51:19	**D** and destruction, famine and
Is	64:10	a wilderness, Jerusalem a **d**
Jer	22: 5	this house shall become a **d**
Jer	25:12	I will make it a perpetual **d**
Dan	8:13	and the transgression of **d**
Dan	11:31	there the abomination of **d**
Dan	12:11	abomination of **d** is set up
Matt	24:15	you see the 'abomination of **d**
Luke	21:20	then know that its **d** is near

DESPAIR (see DESPAIRED, DESPERATELY)

2Co	4: 8	are perplexed, but not in **d**

DESPAIRED (see DESPAIR)

2Co	1: 8	so that we **d** even of life

DESPERATELY (see DESPAIR)

| Jer | 17: 9 | above all things, and **d** wicked |

DESPISE (see DESPISED, DESPISES, DESPISING)

Ps	51:17	These, O God, You will not **d**
Prov	1: 7	knowledge, but fools **d** wisdom
Prov	3:11	do not **d** the chastening of
Amos	5:21	I **d** your feast days, and I do
Mal	1: 6	to you priests who **d** My name
Matt	6:24	to the one and **d** the other
Matt	18:10	**d** one of these little ones
Rom	2: 4	Or do you **d** the riches of His
Rom	14: 3	eats **d** him who does not eat
1Co	11:22	Or do you **d** the church of God
1Ti	4:12	Let no one **d** your youth, but

DESPISED (see DESPISE)

Gen	16: 4	mistress became **d** in her eyes
Gen	25:34	Thus Esau **d** his birthright
Num	11:20	because you have **d** the LORD
2Sa	6:16	and she **d** him in her heart
Ps	22: 6	of men, and **d** of the people
Ps	107:11	**d** the counsel of the Most
Is	5:24	**d** the word of the Holy One of
Is	53: 3	He is **d** and rejected by men, a
Is	53: 3	He was **d**, and we did not
Mal	1: 6	what way have we **d** Your name
1Co	1:28	which are **d** God has chosen

DESPISES (see DESPISE)

Prov	11:12	of wisdom **d** his neighbor, but
Prov	13:13	He who **d** the word will be
Prov	14: 2	is perverse in his ways **d** Him
Prov	14:21	He who **d** his neighbor sins
Prov	15: 5	A fool **d** his father's
Prov	15:20	a foolish man **d** his mother
Prov	15:32	instruction **d** his own soul

DESPISING† (see DESPISE)

| Heb | 12: 2 | **d** the shame, and has sat down |

DESTINED

| Luke | 2:34 | this Child is **d** for the fall |

DESTITUTE

Ps	102:17	regard the prayer of the **d**
Ps	141: 8	Do not leave my soul **d**
Prov	15:21	him who is **d** of discernment
1Ti	6: 5	**d** of the truth, who suppose
Heb	11:37	and goatskins, being **d**,
Jas	2:15	is naked and **d** of daily food,

DESTROY (see DESTROYED, DESTROYER, DESTROYS, DESTRUCTION)

Gen	6: 7	I will **d** man whom I have
Gen	9:11	be a flood to **d** the earth
Gen	18:28	forty-five, I will not **d** it
Gen	19:14	for the LORD will **d** this city
Deut	20:19	you shall not **d** its trees by
Judg	21:11	shall utterly **d** every male
Job	14:19	so You **d** the hope of man
Ps	21:10	You shall **d** from the earth
Ps	40:14	Who seek to **d** my life

Ps	106:23	He said that He would **d** them
Eccl	5: 6	and **d** the work of your hands
Eccl	7:16	why should you **d** yourself
Is	11: 9	nor **d** in all My holy mountain
Jer	1:10	out and to pull down, to **d**
Matt	2:13	seek the young Child to **d** Him
Matt	5:17	to **d** the Law or the Prophets
Matt	5:17	not come to **d** but to fulfill
Matt	6:19	earth, where moth and rust **d**
Matt	10:28	who is able to **d** both soul
Matt	12:14	Him, how they might **d** Him
Matt	27:40	You who **d** the temple and build
Luke	6: 9	evil, to save life or to **d** it
John	2:19	**D** this temple, and in three
John	10:10	to steal, and to kill, and to **d**
Rom	14:15	Do not **d** with your food the
Rom	14:20	Do not **d** the work of God for
1Co	1:19	I will **d** the wisdom of the
1Co	3:17	temple of God, God will **d** him
1Co	6:13	foods, but God will **d** both it
Heb	2:14	**d** him who had the power of
1Jn	3: 8	that He might **d** the works of

DESTROYED (see DESTROY)

Gen	7:23	So He **d** all living things
Gen	13:10	(before the LORD **d** Sodom and
Gen	19:17	the mountains, lest you be **d**
Josh	6:21	they utterly **d** all that was
Ezra	5:12	who **d** this temple and carried
Job	19:26	and after my skin is **d**, this I
Ps	11: 3	If the foundations are **d**,
Ps	78:51	**d** all the firstborn in Egypt,
Ps	137: 8	of Babylon, who are to be **d**
Prov	13:13	despises the word will be **d**
Prov	13:20	companion of fools will be **d**
Prov	29: 1	his neck, will suddenly be **d**
Jer	22:20	for all your lovers are **d**
Lam	2: 5	He has **d** her strongholds, and
Ezek	28:16	I **d** you, O covering cherub,
Dan	2:44	which shall never be **d**
Dan	7:11	was slain, and its body **d** and
Hos	4: 6	My people are **d** for lack of
Matt	22: 7	**d** those murderers, and burned
Luke	9:25	and is himself **d** or lost
Luke	17:27	the flood came and **d** them all
Acts	13:19	when He had **d** seven nations
1Co	10: 9	and were **d** by serpents
1Co	10:10	and were **d** by the destroyer
1Co	15:26	enemy that will be **d** is death
2Co	4: 9	struck down, but not **d**
2Co	5: 1	house, this tent, is **d**, we
Heb	11:28	lest he who **d** the firstborn
Rev	8: 9	a third of the ships were **d**

DESTROYER (see DESTROY)

| Ex | 12:23 | not allow the **d** to come into |
| 1Co | 10:10 | and were destroyed by the **d** |

DESTROYS (see DESTROY)

| Matt | 6:20 | where neither moth nor rust **d** |

DESTRUCTION (see DESTROY)

| Lev | 27:29 | become doomed to **d** among |
| Deut | 32:24 | by pestilence and bitter **d** |

Josh	6:17	be doomed by the LORD to **d**
1Sa	5: 9	the city with a very great **d**
2Sa	24:16	the LORD relented from the **d**
Esth	4: 8	written decree for their **d**
Esth	9: 5	sword, with slaughter and **d**
Job	5:21	be afraid of **d** when it comes
Job	5:22	You shall laugh at **d** and
Job	26: 6	Him, and **D** has no covering
Job	28:22	**D** and Death say, 'We have
Job	31: 3	Is it not **d** for the wicked,
Job	31:12	be a fire that consumes to **d**
Job	31:23	For **d** from God is a terror to
Ps	5: 9	Their inward part is **d**
Ps	35: 8	Let **d** come upon him
Ps	52: 2	Your tongue devises **d**, Like a
Ps	55:23	them down to the pit of **d**
Ps	78:49	angels of **d** among them
Ps	88:11	in the place of **d**
Ps	91: 6	Nor of the **d** that lays waste
Ps	103: 4	Who redeems your life from **d**
Prov	1:27	your **d** comes like a whirlwind
Prov	10:15	the **d** of the poor is their
Prov	15:11	Hell and **D** are before the LORD
Prov	16:18	Pride goes before **d**, and a
Prov	18: 7	A fool's mouth is his **d**, and
Prov	18:12	Before **d** the heart of a man
Prov	27:20	Hell and **D** are never full
Is	14:23	sweep it with the broom of **d**
Is	19:18	will be called the City of **D**
Is	28:22	a **d** determined even upon the
Is	59: 7	and **d** are in their paths
Jer	4: 6	from the north, and great **d**
Jer	4:20	**D** upon destruction is cried
Jer	17:18	and destroy them with double **d**
Lam	2:11	the **d** of the daughter of my
Dan	11:16	Land with **d** in his power
Hos	13:14	O Grave, I will be your **d**
Amos	3:14	I will also visit **d** on the
Matt	7:13	is the way that leads to **d**
Rom	3:16	**d** and misery are in their ways
Rom	9:22	of wrath prepared for **d**,
1Co	5: 5	Satan for the **d** of the flesh
2Co	10: 8	edification and not for your **d**
Phil	3:19	whose end is **d**, whose god is
1Th	5: 3	then sudden **d** comes upon
2Th	1: 9	**d** from the presence of the
1Ti	6: 9	lusts which drown men in **d**
2Pe	2: 1	bring on themselves swift **d**
2Pe	2: 6	ashes, condemned them to **d**
2Pe	3:16	unstable twist to their own **d**

DETAIL

Heb	9: 5	we cannot now speak in **d**

DETERMINED

Josh	17:12	were **d** to dwell in that land
Ruth	1:18	that she was **d** to go with her
Job	14: 5	Since his days are **d**, the
Job	38: 5	Who **d** its measurements
Dan	9:24	weeks are **d** for your people
Dan	9:26	of the war desolations are **d**
Dan	11:36	what has been **d** shall be done
Matt	2: 7	**d** from them what time the
Luke	22:22	of Man goes as it has been **d**

Acts	2:23	delivered by the **d** counsel
Acts	3:13	when he was **d** to let Him go
Acts	11:29	**d** to send relief to the
Acts	15: 2	they **d** that Paul and Barnabas
Acts	17:26	and has **d** their preappointed
1Co	2: 2	For I **d** not to know anything

DEVICES

Job	5:12	the **d** of the crafty, so that
2Co	2:11	we are not ignorant of his **d**

DEVIL

Matt	4: 1	to be tempted by the **d**
Matt	4: 5	Then the **d** took Him up into
Matt	13:39	enemy who sowed them is the **d**
Matt	25:41	fire prepared for the **d** and
Luke	4: 2	for forty days by the **d**
Luke	8:12	then the **d** comes and takes
John	6:70	twelve, and one of you is a **d**
John	8:44	You are of your father the **d**
John	13: 2	the **d** having already put it
Acts	10:38	who were oppressed by the **d**
Acts	13:10	all fraud, you son of the **d**
Eph	4:27	nor give place to the **d**
Eph	6:11	against the wiles of the **d**
1Ti	3: 6	same condemnation as the **d**
1Ti	3: 7	and the snare of the **d**
Heb	2:14	of death, that is, the **d**,
Jas	4: 7	Resist the **d** and he will flee
1Pe	5: 8	**d** walks about like a roaring
1Jn	3: 8	He who sins is of the **d**, for
1Jn	3: 8	destroy the works of the **d**
Jude	9	in contending with the **d**
Rev	12: 9	serpent of old, called the **D**
Rev	20:10	And the **d**, who deceived them,

DEVISE

Mic	2: 1	Woe to those who **d** iniquity

DEVOTED (*see* DEVOUT)

Lev	27:28	every **d** offering is most holy
Ps	119:38	Who is **d** to fearing You
1Co	16:15	that they have **d** themselves

DEVOUR (*see* DEVOURED, DEVOURS)

2Sa	2:26	Shall the sword **d** forever
Ps	21: 9	And the fire shall **d** them
Prov	30:14	to **d** the poor from off the
Jer	17:27	it shall **d** the palaces of
Ezek	7:15	and pestilence will **d** him
Ezek	20:47	it shall **d** every green tree
Dan	7: 5	Arise, **d** much flesh
Dan	7:23	and shall **d** the whole earth,
Amos	1: 7	which shall **d** its palaces
Matt	23:14	For you **d** widows' houses, and
Gal	5:15	**d** one another, beware lest
Heb	10:27	which will **d** the adversaries
1Pe	5: 8	lion, seeking whom he may **d**

DEVOURED (*see* DEVOUR)

Gen	37:33	A wild beast has **d** him
Gen	41: 7	thin heads **d** the seven plump
Hos	7: 9	Aliens have **d** his strength

DEVOURS (see DEVOUR)

Num	13:32	a land that **d** its inhabitants
2Sa	11:25	for the sword **d** one as well
Hab	1:13	**d** one more righteous than he

DEVOUT (see DEVOTED)

Luke	2:25	and this man was just and **d**
Acts	2: 5	**d** men, from every nation
Acts	10: 2	a **d** man and one who feared

DEW

Gen	27:28	give you of the **d** of heaven
Ex	16:13	in the morning the **d** lay all
Deut	32: 2	my speech distill as the **d**
Deut	33:28	His Heavens shall also drop **d**
Judg	6:37	if there is **d** on the fleece
Ps	110: 3	You have the **d** of Your youth
Prov	3:20	up, and clouds drop down the **d**
Dan	4:33	his body was wet with the **d**
Hos	6: 4	like the early **d** it goes away

DIAL†

Is	38: 8	**d** by which it had gone down

DIANA

Acts	19:28	Great is **D** of the Ephesians

DIE (see DEAD, DEATH, DIED, DIES, DYING)

Gen	2:17	eat of it you shall surely **d**
Gen	3: 3	you touch it, lest you **d**
Gen	3: 4	You will not surely **d**
Gen	27: 4	soul may bless you before I **d**
Gen	30: 1	Give me children, or else I **d**
Ex	14:12	we should **d** in the wilderness
Deut	5:25	therefore, why should we **d**
Deut	18:20	gods, that prophet shall **d**
Ruth	1:17	Where you **d**, I will **d**, and
1Ki	21:10	and stone him, that he may **d**
2Ki	13:14	illness of which he would **d**
2Ch	25: 4	shall **d** for his own sin
Job	2: 9	Curse God and **d**
Job	3:11	Why did I not **d** at birth
Job	12: 2	and wisdom will **d** with you
Ps	79:11	those who are appointed to **d**
Ps	82: 7	But you shall **d** like men, And
Prov	23:13	him with a rod, he will not **d**
Eccl	3: 2	to be born, and a time to **d**
Eccl	7:17	why should you **d** before your
Is	22:13	and drink, for tomorrow we **d**
Is	66:24	For their worm does not **d**
Jer	11:22	men shall **d** by the sword,
Jer	20: 6	Babylon, and there you shall **d**
Jer	26:11	This man deserves to **d**
Jer	31:30	But every one shall **d** for his
Ezek	3:18	wicked, 'You shall surely **d**
Ezek	3:18	man shall **d** in his iniquity
Ezek	18: 4	the soul who sins shall **d**
Ezek	18:31	For why should you **d**, O house
Amos	6: 9	in one house, they shall **d**
Amos	7:11	Jeroboam shall **d** by the sword
Jon	4: 3	for me to **d** than to live
Hab	1:12	We shall not **d**
Matt	26:35	Even if I have to **d** with You

Mark	9:44	where 'their worm does not **d**
John	8:21	Me, and will **d** in your sin
John	11:25	in Me, though he may **d**, he
John	11:26	believes in Me shall never **d**
John	11:50	man should **d** for the people
John	11:51	Jesus would **d** for the nation
John	12:33	by what death He would **d**
John	21:23	this disciple would not **d**
Rom	5: 7	a righteous man will one **d**
Rom	5: 7	someone would even dare to **d**
Rom	8:13	to the flesh you will **d**
Rom	14: 8	if we **d**, we **d** to the Lord
Rom	14: 8	whether we live or **d**, we are
1Co	15:22	For as in Adam all **d**, even so
1Co	15:31	Jesus our Lord, I **d** daily
1Co	15:32	and drink, for tomorrow we **d**
Phil	1:21	is Christ, and to **d** is gain
Heb	9:27	appointed for men to **d** once
Rev	14:13	who **d** in the Lord from now on

DIED (see DIE)

Gen	25: 8	**d** in a good old age, an old
Num	15:36	him with stones, and he **d**
1Sa	25:37	that his heart **d** within him
1Sa	25:38	LORD struck Nabal, and he **d**
2Sa	11:17	and Uriah the Hittite **d** also
2Sa	12:18	came to pass that the child **d**
2Sa	18:33	if only I had **d** in your place
Job	42:17	So Job **d**, old and full of days
Is	6: 1	the year that King Uzziah **d**
Is	14:28	in the year that King Ahaz **d**
Ezek	24:18	and at evening my wife **d**
Hos	13: 1	he offended in Baal, he **d**
Matt	9:18	My daughter has just **d**, but
Matt	22:27	last of all the woman **d** also
Luke	16:22	So it was that the beggar **d**
Luke	16:22	The rich man also **d** and was
Luke	20:29	a wife, and **d** without children
John	11:21	my brother would not have **d**
John	11:44	he who had **d** came out bound
Acts	7:15	and he **d**, he and our fathers
Acts	12:23	he was eaten by worms and **d**
Rom	5: 6	time Christ **d** for the ungodly
Rom	5: 8	sinners, Christ **d** for us
Rom	5:15	the one man's offense many **d**
Rom	6: 2	How shall we who **d** to sin
Rom	6: 8	Now if we **d** with Christ, we
Rom	6:10	For the death that He **d**, He
Rom	6:10	He **d** to sin once for all
Rom	7: 9	came, sin revived and I **d**
1Co	15: 3	that Christ **d** for our sins
2Co	5:14	One **d** for all, then all **d**
Gal	2:19	For I through the law **d** to
Gal	2:21	law, then Christ **d** in vain
Col	3: 3	For you **d**, and your life is
1Th	4:14	if we believe that Jesus **d**
Heb	11:13	These all **d** in faith, not
1Pe	2:24	having **d** to sins, might live
Rev	8: 9	living creatures in the sea **d**

DIES (see DIE)

Lev	7:24	of a beast that **d** naturally
Num	27: 8	If a man **d** and has no son,

Deut 13:10 him with stones until he **d**
Deut 14:21 eat anything that **d** of itself
Deut 24: 3 or if the latter husband **d**
2Sa   3:33 Should Abner die as a fool **d**
Job   14:10 But man **d** and is laid away
Job   14:14 If a man **d**, shall he live
Job   21:23 One **d** in his full strength,
Prov 11: 7 When a wicked man **d**, his
Eccl   3:19 as one **d**, so **d** the other
Matt 22:24 Moses said that if a man **d**
Mark 12:19 us that if a man's brother **d**
Luke 20:28 he **d** without children, his
John   4:49 come down before my child **d**
John 12:24 falls into the ground and **d**
John 12:24 but if it **d**, it produces much
Rom   6: 9 from the dead, **d** no more
Rom   7: 2 But if the husband **d**, she is
Rom 14: 7 and no one **d** to himself
1Co 15:36 is not made alive unless it **d**
Heb 10:28 law **d** without mercy on the

DIFFER (see DIFFERENCE, DIFFERENT, DIFFERING)
1Co   4: 7 who makes you **d** from another

DIFFERENCE (see DIFFER)
Ex   8:23 I will make a **d** between My
Ex   11: 7 a **d** between the Egyptians
Ezek 22:26 the **d** between the unclean
Rom   3:22 For there is no **d**

DIFFERENT (see DIFFER, VARIOUS)
Num 14:24 he has a **d** spirit in him and
1Co 12:10 to another **d** kinds of tongues
2Co 11: 4 or if you receive a **d** spirit
Gal   1: 6 of Christ, to a **d** gospel,

DIFFERING† (see DIFFER)
Deut 25:13 have in your bag **d** weights
Deut 25:14 have in your house **d** measures
Rom 12: 6 Having then gifts **d** according

DIG (see DUG)
Deut   6:11 wells which you did not **d**
Deut   8: 9 whose hills you can **d** copper

DILIGENCE (see DILIGENT)
Prov   4:23 Keep your heart with all **d**
Rom 12: 8 he who leads, with **d**
Rom 12:11 not lagging in **d**, fervent in
2Co   8: 7 in knowledge, in all **d**, and

DILIGENT (see CAREFUL, DILIGENCE, DILIGENTLY)
2Co   8:22 often proved **d** in many things
2Ti   4: 9 Be **d** to come to me quickly
Heb   4:11 be **d** to enter that rest, lest
2Pe   3:14 be **d** to be found by Him in

DILIGENTLY (see CAREFULLY, DILIGENT, EARNESTLY)
Deut   6: 7 teach them **d** to your children
Prov   8:17 who seek me **d** will find me

Heb 11: 6 of those who **d** seek Him
Heb 12:17 he sought it **d** with tears

DIM (see DIMLY)
Gen 27: 1 his eyes were so **d** that he
Deut 34: 7 His eyes were not **d** nor his
Eccl 12: 3 through the windows grows **d**

DIMINISH (see DIMINISHED)
Jer 26: 2 Do not **d** a word

DIMINISHED (see DIMINISH)
Deut 34: 7 dim nor his natural vigor **d**

DIMLY† (see DIM)
1Co 13:12 For now we see in a mirror, **d**

DINAH
Gen 34: 3 to **D** the daughter of Jacob

DINNER
Prov 15:17 Better is a **d** of herbs where
Luke 11:38 had not first washed before **d**
1Co 10:27 not believe invites you to **d**

DIP (see DIPPED, DIPS)
Ex 12:22 **d** it in the blood that is in
Num 19:18 **d** it in the water, sprinkle
Luke 16:24 **d** the tip of his finger in

DIPPED (see DIP)
Gen 37:31 and **d** the tunic in the blood
Lev   9: 9 he **d** his finger in the blood,
2Ki   5:14 **d** seven times in the Jordan,
Matt 26:23 He who **d** his hand with Me in
John 13:26 of bread when I have **d** it
Rev 19:13 with a robe **d** in blood, and

DIPS† (see DIP)
Mark 14:20 who **d** with Me in the dish

DIRE
Lam   1: 3 overtake her in **d** straits

DIRECT (see DIRECTED, DIRECTS)
Ps 119:133 **D** my steps by Your word, And
Prov   3: 6 Him, and He shall **d** your paths
Is   45:13 and I will **d** all his ways
2Th   3: 5 Now may the Lord **d** your

DIRECTED (see DIRECT)
Ps 119: 5 that my ways were **d** To keep
Is   40:13 Who has **d** the Spirit of the
Matt 27:10 field, as the LORD **d** me

DIRECTS† (see DIRECT)
Prov 16: 9 way, but the LORD **d** his steps

DIRT
1Sa   4:12 clothes torn and **d** on his head
Is 57:20 waters cast up mire and **d**

DISAPPOINT†
Rom   5: 5 Now hope does not **d**, because

DISARMED

Col	2:15	Having **d** principalities and

DISASTER

Neh	13:18	God bring all this **d** on us
Job	31: 3	**d** for the workers of iniquity
Jer	4: 6	I will bring **d** from the north
Jer	18: 8	I will relent of the **d** that I
Ezek	7:26	**D** will come upon **d**
Jon	3:10	God relented from the **d** that
Acts	27:10	this voyage will end with **d**

DISCERN (see DISCERNED, DISCERNER, DISCERNING)

Jon	4:11	**d** between their right hand
Matt	16: 3	but you cannot **d** the signs of

DISCERNED† (see DISCERN)

1Co	2:14	they are spiritually **d**

DISCERNER† (see DISCERN)

Heb	4:12	is a **d** of the thoughts and

DISCERNING (see DISCERN)

1Co	11:29	not **d** the Lord's body
1Co	12:10	to another **d** of spirits, to

DISCIPLE (see DISCIPLES, DISCIPLINE)

Matt	10:24	A **d** is not above his teacher,
Matt	10:42	cold water in the name of a **d**
Matt	27:57	had also become a **d** of Jesus
Luke	14:27	come after Me cannot be My **d**
John	19:26	the **d** whom He loved standing
John	20: 4	the other **d** outran Peter and
John	21:20	saw the **d** whom Jesus loved
John	21:23	that this **d** would not die
Acts	9:36	was a certain **d** named Tabitha

DISCIPLES (see DISCIPLE, DISCIPLES')

Is	8:16	Seal the law among my **d**
Matt	5: 1	was seated His **d** came to Him
Matt	8:23	a boat, His **d** followed Him
Matt	9:14	Then the **d** of John came to
Matt	9:14	often, but Your **d** do not fast
Matt	10: 1	called His twelve **d** to Him
Matt	24: 3	the **d** came to Him privately,
Matt	26:26	broke it, and gave it to the **d**
Matt	26:36	Gethsemane, and said to the **d**
Matt	26:56	Then all the **d** forsook Him
Matt	28: 7	tell His **d** that He is risen
Matt	28:16	Then the eleven **d** went away
Matt	28:19	make **d** of all the nations,
Mark	10:10	in the house His **d** asked Him
Mark	10:24	the **d** were astonished at His
Mark	14:14	eat the Passover with My **d**
Luke	6: 1	His **d** plucked the heads of
Luke	9:40	Your **d** to cast it out, but
Luke	9:54	And when His **d** James and John
Luke	22:45	prayer, and had come to His **d**
John	1:35	John stood with two of his **d**
John	2:12	His brothers, and His **d**
John	2:17	Then His **d** remembered that it
John	4: 1	and baptized more **d** than John

John	6: 8	One of His **d**, Andrew, Simon
John	6:61	His **d** murmured about this
John	8:31	My word, you are My **d** indeed
John	9:27	you also want to become His **d**
John	9:28	disciple, but we are Moses' **d**
John	11: 8	The **d** said to Him, "Rabbi,
John	11:16	Didymus, said to his fellow **d**
John	12: 4	Then one of His **d**, Judas
John	13:23	on Jesus' bosom one of His **d**
John	13:35	will know that you are My **d**
John	18:17	not also one of this Man's **d**
John	20:19	where the **d** were assembled
John	20:20	Then the **d** were glad when
John	21: 1	the **d** at the Sea of Tiberias
John	21:14	**d** after He was raised from
Acts	1:15	up in the midst of the **d**
Acts	6: 1	of the **d** was multiplying,
Acts	6: 7	and the number of the **d**
Acts	9:19	days with the **d** at Damascus
Acts	9:25	Then the **d** took him by night
Acts	11:26	And the **d** were first called
Acts	14:21	to that city and made many **d**
Acts	20: 1	Paul called the **d** to him
Acts	20: 7	when the **d** came together to

DISCIPLES'† (see DISCIPLES)

John	13: 5	and began to wash the **d** feet

DISCIPLINE (see DISCIPLE, DISCIPLINES)

1Co	9:27	But I **d** my body and bring it

DISCIPLINES† (see DISCIPLINE)

Prov	13:24	who loves him **d** him promptly

DISCORD

Prov	6:19	one who sows **d** among brethren

DISCOURAGED

Deut	1:21	do not fear or be **d**
Is	42: 4	He will not fail nor be **d**
Heb	12: 5	nor be **d** when you are rebuked

DISCREET† (see DISCRETION)

Tit	2: 5	to be **d**, chaste, homemakers,

DISCRETION (see DISCREET)

Prov	1: 4	the young man knowledge and **d**

DISEASE (see DISEASES)

2Ki	8: 8	Shall I recover from this **d**
Matt	4:23	and all kinds of **d** among the
John	5: 4	well of whatever **d** he had

DISEASES (see DISEASE)

Deut	28:60	on you all the **d** of Egypt
Ps	103: 3	Who heals all your **d**,
Matt	4:24	were afflicted with various **d**
Luke	6:17	Him and be healed of their **d**
Luke	9: 1	over all demons, and to cure **d**
Acts	19:12	the **d** left them and the evil

DISGRACEFUL

Deut	22:21	has done a **d** thing in Israel
2Sa	13:12	Do not do this **d** thing

DISGUISED
| 1Sa | 28: 8 | So Saul **d** himself and put on |

DISH
2Ki	21:13	Jerusalem as one wipes a **d**
Matt	23:25	the outside of the cup and **d**
Matt	26:23	Me in the **d** will betray Me
Luke	11:39	**d** clean, but your inward part

DISHONEST
1Sa	8: 3	turned aside after **d** gain
Tit	1:11	not, for the sake of **d** gain
1Pe	5: 2	not for **d** gain but eagerly

DISHONOR (see DISHONORED, DISHONORS)
Ps	35:26	and **d** Who magnify themselves
Ps	44:15	My **d** is continually before me
Ps	69:19	reproach, my shame, and my **d**
John	8:49	honor My Father, and you **d** Me
Rom	1:24	to **d** their bodies among
Rom	2:23	do you **d** God through breaking
Rom	9:21	for honor and another for **d**
1Co	11:14	long hair, it is a **d** to him
1Co	15:43	It is sown in **d**, it is raised
2Ti	2:20	some for honor and some for **d**

DISHONORED† (see DISHONOR)
| 1Co | 4:10 | distinguished, but we are **d** |
| Jas | 2: 6 | But you have **d** the poor man |

DISHONORS† (see DISHONOR)
Mic	7: 6	For son **d** father, daughter
1Co	11: 4	his head covered, **d** his head
1Co	11: 5	her head uncovered **d** her head

DISMAYED
Deut	31: 8	do not fear nor be **d**
Josh	1: 9	do not be afraid, nor be **d**
Ps	83:17	be confounded and **d** forever
Is	41:10	be not **d**, for I am your God
Jer	1:17	Do not be **d** before their

DISOBEDIENCE (see DISOBEDIENT)
Rom	5:19	For as by one man's **d** many
Rom	11:30	mercy through their **d**,
Eph	2: 2	now works in the sons of **d**
Heb	2: 2	**d** received a just reward,
Heb	4: 6	did not enter because of **d**

DISOBEDIENT (see DISOBEDIENCE)
Neh	9:26	Nevertheless they were **d** and
Acts	26:19	I was not **d** to the heavenly
Rom	1:30	of evil things, **d** to parents,
Rom	10:21	stretched out My hands to a **d**
Rom	11:30	For as you were once **d** to God
1Pe	2: 8	being **d** to the word, to which
1Pe	3:20	who formerly were **d**, when

DISPENSATION†
| Eph | 1:10 | that in the **d** of the fullness |
| Eph | 3: 2 | you have heard of the **d** of |

DISPERSED (see DISPERSION)
| Is | 11:12 | and gather together the **d** of |

DISPERSION† (see DISPERSED)
| John | 7:35 | go to the **D** among the Greeks |
| 1Pe | 1: 1 | pilgrims of the **D** in Pontus |

DISPLEASED (see DISPLEASURE)
| Jon | 4: 1 | But it **d** Jonah exceedingly, |

DISPLEASURE (see DISPLEASED)
| Ps | 2: 5 | distress them in His deep **d** |
| Ps | 6: 1 | Nor chasten me in Your hot **d** |

DISPOSSESS
| Deut | 9: 1 | go in to **d** nations greater and |

DISPUTE (see DISPUTED, DISPUTER, DISPUTES, DISPUTING)
Deut	25: 1	If there is a **d** between men
Mark	8:11	out and began to **d** with Him
Luke	9:46	Then a **d** arose among them as

DISPUTED (see DISPUTE)
| Jude | 9 | when he **d** about the body of |

DISPUTER† (see DISPUTE)
| 1Co | 1:20 | Where is the **d** of this age |

DISPUTES (see DISPUTE)
Rom	14: 1	but not to **d** over doubtful
1Ti	1: 4	which cause **d** rather than
2Ti	2:23	avoid foolish and ignorant **d**

DISPUTING (see DISPUTE)
| Acts | 24:12 | found me in the temple **d** with |
| Phil | 2:14 | without murmuring and **d** |

DISQUALIFIED
| 1Co | 9:27 | I myself should become **d** |

DISQUIETED
| Ps | 42: 5 | And why are you **d** within me |

DISSENSION
| Acts | 15: 2 | and Barnabas had no small **d** |

DISSOLVED
| Is | 34: 4 | the host of heaven shall be **d** |
| 2Pe | 3:12 | will be **d** being on fire, and |

DISTINCTION (see DISTINGUISH)
| Acts | 15: 9 | made no **d** between us and them, |
| Rom | 10:12 | For there is no **d** between Jew |

DISTINGUISH (see DISTINCTION)
| Lev | 10:10 | that you may **d** between holy |
| Lev | 11:47 | To **d** between the unclean and |

DISTRACTED† (see DISTRACTION)
| Luke | 10:40 | But Martha was **d** with much |

DISTRACTION† (see DISTRACTED)
1Co	7:35	may serve the Lord without **d**

DISTRESS (see DISTRESSED, DISTRESSING)
Gen	35: 3	me in the day of my **d** and has
Ps	2: 5	wrath, And **d** them in His deep
Ps	4: 1	relieved me when I was in **d**
Ps	18: 6	In my **d** I called upon the
Rom	8:35	Shall tribulation, or **d**, or
1Co	7:26	good because of the present **d**
Phil	4:14	well that you shared in my **d**

DISTRESSED (see DISTRESS)
1Sa	28:15	I am deeply **d**
2Sa	1:26	I am **d** for you, my brother
Matt	26:37	to be sorrowful and deeply **d**
Luke	12:50	and how **d** I am till it is

DISTRESSING (see DISTRESS)
1Sa	16:14	and a **d** spirit from the LORD
Is	21: 2	a **d** vision is declared to me

DISTRIBUTE (see DISTRIBUTED, DISTRIBUTING, DISTRIBUTION)
Neh	13:13	was to **d** to their brethren
Luke	18:22	**d** to the poor, and you will

DISTRIBUTED (see DISTRIBUTE)
Josh	13:32	**d** as an inheritance in the
John	6:11	He **d** them to the disciples
Acts	4:35	they **d** to each as anyone had
1Co	7:17	But as God has **d** to each one

DISTRIBUTING† (see DISTRIBUTE)
Rom	12:13	**d** to the needs of the saints,
1Co	12:11	**d** to each one individually as

DISTRIBUTION† (see DISTRIBUTE)
Acts	6: 1	were neglected in the daily **d**

DISTURBED
1Sa	28:15	Why have you **d** me by bringing
Neh	2:10	they were deeply **d** that a man
Acts	21:30	And all the city was **d**

DITCH
Ps	7:15	into the **d** which he made
Matt	15:14	both will fall into a **d**

DIVERSE (see DIVERSITIES)
Prov	20:23	**D** weights are an abomination

DIVERSITIES (see DIVERSE)
1Co	12: 4	Now there are **d** of gifts, but

DIVIDE (see DIVIDED, DIVIDING, DIVISION)
Gen	1: 6	let it **d** the waters from the
Gen	1:14	to **d** the day from the night
Ex	14:16	hand over the sea and **d** it
Josh	13: 7	**d** this land as an inheritance
1Ki	3:25	**D** the living child in two, and
Ps	22:18	**d** My garments among them

Is	9: 3	rejoice when they **d** the spoil
Is	53:12	Therefore I will **d** Him a
Is	53:12	He shall **d** the spoil with the
Luke	12:13	tell my brother to **d** the

DIVIDED (see DIVIDE, SEPARATED)
Gen	1: 4	and God **d** the light from the
Gen	1: 7	**d** the waters which were under
Gen	10:25	in his days the earth was **d**
Ex	14:21	land, and the waters were **d**
1Ki	16:21	Israel were **d** into two parts
Ps	136:13	To Him who **d** the Red Sea in
Dan	2:41	iron, the kingdom shall be **d**
Dan	5:28	Your kingdom has been **d**, and
Matt	12:25	Every kingdom **d** against
Matt	27:35	**d** His garments, casting lots,
Mark	6:41	two fish He **d** among them all
Luke	12:53	Father will be **d** against son
Acts	2: 3	appeared to them **d** tongues
Acts	2:45	**d** them among all, as anyone
1Co	1:13	Is Christ **d**? Was Paul

DIVIDING
2Ti	2:15	rightly **d** the word of truth

DIVINATION (see DIVINE)
Lev	19:26	you practice **d** or soothsaying
Acts	16:16	with a spirit of **d** met us

DIVINE (see DIVINATION, DIVINELY)
Mic	3:11	and her prophets **d** for money
Acts	17:29	the **D** Nature is like gold or

DIVINELY (see DIVINE)
Matt	2:12	being **d** warned in a dream
Heb	11: 7	being **d** warned of things not

DIVISION (see DIVIDE, DIVISIONS)
1Ch	28:13	also for the **d** of the priests
Luke	1: 5	Zacharias, of the **d** of Abijah
John	7:43	there was a **d** among them
Heb	4:12	even to the **d** of soul and

DIVISIONS (see DIVISION)
1Ch	28:21	Here are the **d** of the priests
Rom	16:17	note those who cause **d** and
1Co	1:10	that there be no **d** among you

DIVORCE (see DIVORCED, DIVORCES)
Deut	22:19	he cannot **d** her all his days
Deut	24: 1	writes her a certificate of **d**
Mal	2:16	Israel says that He hates **d**
Matt	5:31	give her a certificate of **d**
Matt	19: 3	to **d** his wife for just any
1Co	7:11	husband is not to **d** his wife

DIVORCED (see DIVORCE)
Deut	24: 4	**d** her must not take her back
Matt	5:32	who is **d** commits adultery

DIVORCES (see DIVORCE)
Jer	3: 1	say, 'If a man **d** his wife
Matt	5:32	**d** his wife for any reason
Matt	19: 9	whoever **d** his wife, except

DOCTRINE (see DOCTRINES)

Matt	16:12	but of the **d** of the Pharisees
Mark	1:27	What new **d** is this
John	7:16	My **d** is not Mine, but His who
Acts	2:42	in the apostles' **d** and
Rom	16:17	contrary to the **d** which you
Eph	4:14	about with every wind of **d**
1Ti	1: 3	that they teach no other **d**
1Ti	1:10	that is contrary to sound **d**
1Ti	4:16	heed to yourself and to the **d**
1Ti	6: 1	His **d** may not be blasphemed
2Ti	3:16	God, and is profitable for **d**
2Ti	4: 3	they will not endure sound **d**
Tit	2:10	that they may adorn the **d** of
Heb	6: 2	of the **d** of baptisms, of
2Jn	9	does not abide in the **d** of
Rev	2:14	who hold the **d** of Balaam, who
Rev	2:15	hold the **d** of the Nicolaitans

DOCTRINES (see DOCTRINE)

Matt	15: 9	worship Me, teaching as **d** the
Col	2:22	commandments and **d** of men
1Ti	4: 1	spirits and **d** of demons,
Heb	13: 9	with various and strange **d**

DOER (see DOERS, DOINGS)

| Jas | 1:23 | hearer of the word and not a **d** |
| Jas | 4:11 | you are not a **d** of the law |

DOERS† (see DOER, EVILDOERS)

| Rom | 2:13 | but the **d** of the law will be |
| Jas | 1:22 | But be **d** of the word, and not |

DOG (see DOGS)

Ex	11: 7	shall a **d** move its tongue
Deut	23:18	a **d** to the house of the LORD
Judg	7: 5	with his tongue, as a **d** laps
1Sa	17:43	Am I a **d**, that you come to me
Ps	22:20	life from the power of the **d**
Prov	26:11	As a **d** returns to his own
Prov	26:17	one who takes a **d** by the ears
Eccl	9: 4	for a living **d** is better than
2Pe	2:22	A **d** returns to his own vomit,

DOGS (see DOG)

Ex	22:31	you shall throw it to the **d**
1Ki	21:19	**d** shall lick your blood, even
1Ki	21:23	The **d** shall eat Jezebel by
Ps	22:16	For **d** have surrounded Me
Matt	7: 6	give what is holy to the **d**
Matt	15:26	and throw it to the little **d**
Luke	16:21	Moreover the **d** came and licked
Phil	3: 2	Beware of **d**, beware of evil
Rev	22:15	But outside are **d** and

DOINGS (see DOER)

| Deut | 28:20 | of the wickedness of your **d** |
| Jer | 7: 3 | Amend your ways and your **d** |

DOMINION (see DOMINIONS)

Gen	1:26	let them have **d** over the fish
Num	24:19	Out of Jacob One shall have **d**
Ps	8: 6	have **d** over the works of Your
Ps	19:13	Let them not have **d** over me
Ps	49:14	The upright shall have **d** over
Ps	72: 8	He shall have **d** also from sea
Ps	103:22	works, In all places of His **d**
Ps	114: 2	sanctuary, And Israel His **d**
Ps	145:13	Your **d** endures throughout all
Dan	4: 3	His **d** is from generation to
Dan	4:34	His **d** is an everlasting **d**
Dan	7:14	Then to Him was given **d** and
Dan	7:14	**d** is an everlasting **d**
Zech	9:10	His **d** shall be 'from sea to
Rom	6: 9	no longer has **d** over Him
Rom	7: 1	that the law has **d** over a man
Rev	1: 6	be glory and **d** forever and ever

DOMINIONS† (see DOMINION)

| Dan | 7:27 | all **d** shall serve and obey Him |
| Col | 1:16 | whether thrones or **d** or |

DONKEY (see DONKEYS)

Gen	22: 3	the morning and saddled his **d**
Ex	13:13	a **d** you shall redeem with a
Ex	20:17	nor his ox, nor his **d**, nor
Ex	21:33	an ox or a **d** falls in it,
Num	22:30	So the **d** said to Balaam, "Am
Judg	15:15	found a fresh jawbone of a **d**
Jer	22:19	buried with the burial of a **d**
Zech	9: 9	lowly and riding on a **d**, a
Matt	21: 5	you, lowly, and sitting on a **d**
2Pe	2:16	a dumb **d** speaking with a

DONKEYS (see DONKEY)

| Gen | 12:16 | He had sheep, oxen, male **d** |

DOOM

| Job | 21:30 | are reserved for the day of **d** |
| Amos | 6: 3 | who put far off the day of **d** |

DOOR (see DOORKEEPER, DOORPOST, DOORS)

Gen	4: 7	do well, sin lies at the **d**
Gen	6:16	set the **d** of the ark in its
Gen	19: 9	came near to break down the **d**
Ex	12:23	the LORD will pass over the **d**
Ex	29: 4	to the **d** of the tabernacle of
Deut	15:17	it through his ear to the **d**
Ps	141: 3	watch over the **d** of my lips
Prov	26:14	As a **d** turns on its hinges,
Song	5: 4	hand by the latch of the **d**
Is	6: 4	And the posts of the **d** were
Hos	2:15	of Achor as a **d** of hope
Matt	6: 6	and when you have shut your **d**
Matt	27:60	against the **d** of the tomb
Matt	28: 2	back the stone from the **d**
Mark	2: 2	them, not even near the **d**
John	10: 2	the **d** is the shepherd of the
John	10: 7	you, I am the **d** of the sheep
John	10: 9	I am the **d**. If anyone
1Co	16: 9	effective **d** has opened to me,
2Co	2:12	a **d** was opened to me by the
Col	4: 3	open to us a **d** for the word
Jas	5: 9	Judge is standing at the **d**
Rev	3: 8	have set before you an open **d**
Rev	3:20	Behold, I stand at the **d** and
Rev	3:20	hears My voice and opens the **d**

DOORKEEPER (*see* DOOR)

Ps	84:10	I would rather be a **d** in the
John	10: 3	To him the **d** opens, and the

DOORPOST (*see* DOOR, DOORPOSTS)

Ex	21: 6	him to the door, or to the **d**
1Sa	1: 9	**d** of the tabernacle of the

DOORPOSTS (*see* DOORPOST)

Ex	12: 7	blood and put it on the two **d**
Deut	6: 9	them on the **d** of your house

DOORS (*see* DOOR)

Job	3:10	up the **d** of my mother's womb
Ps	24: 7	lifted up, you everlasting **d**
Eccl	12: 4	when the **d** are shut in the
Mic	7: 5	Guard the **d** of your mouth
Matt	24:33	it is near, at the very **d**
John	20:19	when the **d** were shut where

DORCAS (*see* TABITHA)

Acts	9:36	which is translated **D**

DOTHAN

Gen	37:17	brothers and found them in **D**

DOUBLE

Gen	43:12	Take **d** money in your hand, and
Ex	22: 4	or sheep, he shall restore **d**
Deut	21:17	firstborn by giving him a **d**
1Sa	1: 5	he would give a **d** portion
2Ki	2: 9	Please let a **d** portion of
Is	40: 2	hand **d** for all her sins
Jer	17:18	them with **d** destruction
1Ti	5:17	be counted worthy of **d** honor

DOUBLE-MINDED†

Ps	119:113	I hate the **d**, But I love Your
Jas	1: 8	he is a **d** man, unstable in
Jas	4: 8	and purify your hearts, you **d**

DOUBT (*see* DOUBTED, DOUBTFUL, DOUBTING, DOUBTLESS, DOUBTS)

Job	12: 2	No **d** you are the people, and
Matt	14:31	little faith, why did you **d**
Mark	11:23	does not **d** in his heart, but
Acts	28: 4	No **d** this man is a murderer,

DOUBTED† (*see* DOUBT)

Matt	28:17	worshipped Him: but some **d**

DOUBTFUL† (*see* DOUBT)

Rom	14: 1	not to disputes over **d** things

DOUBTING (*see* DOUBT)

Acts	10:20	and go with them, **d** nothing
1Ti	2: 8	hands, without wrath and **d**
Jas	1: 6	him ask in faith, with no **d**

DOUBTLESS (*see* DOUBT)

Ps	126: 6	Shall **d** come again with
Is	63:16	**D** You are our Father, though
2Co	12: 1	It is **d** not profitable for me

DOUBTS† (*see* DOUBT)

Luke	24:38	why do **d** arise in your hearts
Rom	14:23	But he who **d** is condemned if
Gal	4:20	for I have **d** about you
Jas	1: 6	for he who **d** is like a wave

DOVE (*see* DOVES)

Gen	8:10	sent the **d** out from the ark
Ps	55: 6	Oh, that I had wings like a **d**
Song	5: 2	me, my sister, my love, my **d**
Hos	7:11	also is like a silly **d**,
Luke	3:22	bodily form like a **d** upon Him

DOVES (*see* DOVE)

Song	5:12	His eyes are like **d** by the
Is	59:11	bears, and moan sadly like **d**
Matt	10:16	as serpents and harmless as **d**
Matt	21:12	the seats of those who sold **d**

DRAG (*see* DRAGGED)

Luke	12:58	lest he **d** you to the judge,
Jas	2: 6	you and **d** you into the courts

DRAGGED (*see* DRAG)

Jer	22:19	the burial of a donkey, **d**
John	21:11	**d** the net to land, full of
Acts	14:19	and **d** him out of the city,
Acts	16:19	**d** them into the marketplace

DRAGON

Rev	12: 3	fiery red **d** having seven

DRANK (*see* DRINK)

Gen	9:21	Then he **d** of the wine and was
Ex	24:11	saw God, and they ate and **d**
1Ki	17: 6	and he **d** from the brook
Dan	1: 8	nor with the wine which he **d**
Mark	14:23	them, and they all **d** from it
Luke	13:26	**d** in Your presence, and You
John	4:12	**d** from it himself, as well as
Acts	9: 9	sight, and neither ate nor **d**
Acts	10:41	**d** with Him after He arose
1Co	10: 4	and all **d** the same spiritual

DRAW (*see* DRAWN, DRAWS, DREW)

Gen	24:11	when women go out to **d** water
Ex	15: 9	I will **d** my sword, my hand
Judg	3:22	for he did not **d** the dagger
1Sa	14:36	Let us **d** near to God here
Ps	69:18	**D** near to my soul, and redeem
Ps	73:28	good for me to **d** near to God
Eccl	12: 1	the years **d** near when you say
Is	29:13	**d** near to Me with their
Matt	15: 8	These people **d** near to Me
John	4: 7	of Samaria came to **d** water
John	12:32	will **d** all peoples to Myself
Heb	7:19	which we **d** near to God
Heb	10:22	let us **d** near with a true
Jas	4: 8	**D** near to God
Jas	4: 8	and He will **d** near to you

DRAWN (*see* DRAW)

Num	22:23	with His **d** sword in His hand

Jer	31: 3	lovingkindness I have **d** you
Luke	21: 8	He,' and, 'The time has **d** near
Jas	1:14	is **d** away by his own desires

DRAWS (see DRAW)

Luke	21:28	your redemption **d** near
John	6:44	the Father who sent Me **d** him

DREAD (see DREADFUL)

Gen	9: 2	and the **d** of you shall be on
Is	7:16	the land that you **d** will be

DREADFUL (see DREAD)

Dan	7: 7	and behold, a fourth beast, **d**
Dan	7:19	all the others, exceedingly **d**
Mal	4: 5	great and **d** day of the LORD

DREAM (see DREAMER, DREAMS)

Gen	20: 3	to Abimelech in a **d** by night
Gen	31:10	lifted my eyes and saw in a **d**
Gen	37: 5	Now Joseph had a **d**, and
Gen	40: 5	in the prison, had a **d**
Gen	40: 9	butler told his **d** to Joseph
Gen	41: 1	years, that Pharaoh had a **d**
Gen	41:11	interpretation of his own **d**
Num	12: 6	and I speak to him in a **d**
1Ki	3: 5	to Solomon in a **d** by night
Job	20: 8	He will fly away like a **d**
Job	33:15	In a **d**, in a vision of the
Ps	73:20	As a **d** when one awakes, So,
Ps	126: 1	We were like those who **d**
Jer	23:28	has a **d**, let him tell a dream
Dan	2: 3	I have had a **d**, and my spirit
Dan	2: 5	do not make known the **d** to me
Dan	4: 5	I saw a **d** which made me
Dan	7: 1	of Babylon, Daniel had a **d**
Joel	2:28	your old men shall **d** dreams
Matt	1:20	Lord appeared to him in a **d**
Matt	2:12	being divinely warned in a **d**
Acts	2:17	your old men shall **d** dreams

DREAMER (see DREAM)

Gen	37:19	Look, this **d** is coming
Deut	13: 1	a prophet or a **d** of dreams

DREAMS (see DREAM)

Gen	37: 8	hated him even more for his **d**
Gen	37:20	see what will become of his **d**
Gen	41:12	he interpreted our **d** for us
Gen	41:25	The **d** of Pharaoh are one
Deut	13: 1	a prophet or a dreamer of **d**
1Sa	28: 6	either by **d** or by Urim or by
Dan	2: 1	reign, Nebuchadnezzar had **d**
Joel	2:28	your old men shall dream **d**
Acts	2:17	your old men shall dream **d**

DREW (see DRAW)

Gen	8: 9	**d** her into the ark to himself
Gen	24:45	down to the well and **d** water
Ex	2:10	Because I **d** him out of the
Hos	11: 4	I **d** them with gentle cords,
John	18:10	**d** it and struck the high

DRIED (see DRY)

Gen	8: 7	had **d** up from the earth
Judg	16: 7	fresh bowstrings, not yet **d**
Ps	106: 9	the Red Sea also, and it **d** up
Is	51:10	not the One who **d** up the sea
Mark	5:29	of her blood was **d** up, and she
Mark	11:20	fig tree **d** up from the roots

DRINK (see DRANK, DRINKING, DRINKS, DRUNK)

Gen	19:32	let us make our father **d** wine
Gen	21:19	water, and gave the lad a **d**
Gen	24:14	also give your camels a **d**'
Gen	35:14	he poured a **d** offering on it,
Ex	32: 6	people sat down to eat and **d**
Lev	10: 9	Do not **d** wine
Num	6:20	that the Nazirite may **d** wine
Judg	7: 6	on their knees to **d** water
Judg	13: 7	**d** no wine or similar **d**
2Sa	23:16	he would not **d** it, but poured
Neh	8:10	**d** the sweet, and send portions
Job	21:20	let him **d** of the wrath of the
Job	22: 7	given the weary water to **d**
Ps	50:13	Or **d** the blood of goats
Ps	69:21	they gave me vinegar to **d**
Ps	102: 9	mingled my **d** with weeping,
Ps	110: 7	He shall **d** of the brook by
Prov	4:17	and **d** the wine of violence
Prov	5:15	**D** water from your own cistern
Prov	23:35	that I may seek another **d**
Prov	25:21	thirsty, give him water to **d**
Prov	31: 4	it is not for kings to **d** wine
Prov	31: 6	Give strong **d** to him who is
Prov	31: 7	Let him **d** and forget his
Eccl	2:24	than that he should eat and **d**
Eccl	9: 7	and **d** your wine with an merry
Song	5: 1	**D**, yes, **d** deeply, O beloved
Is	22:13	Let us eat and **d**, for tomorrow
Is	24: 9	strong **d** is bitter to those
Is	28: 7	erred through intoxicating **d**
Is	62: 8	shall not **d** your new wine
Is	65:13	behold, My servants shall **d**
Jer	2:18	to **d** the waters of the River
Jer	8:14	given us water of gall to **d**
Jer	25:27	**D**, be drunk, and vomit
Jer	35: 6	We will **d** no wine, for
Jer	44:17	pour out **d** offerings to her,
Lam	3:15	He has made me **d** wormwood
Lam	5: 4	We pay for the water we **d**
Ezek	12:18	**d** your water with trembling
Ezek	25: 4	and they shall **d** your milk
Ezek	34:19	they **d** what you have fouled
Ezek	39:17	you may eat flesh and **d** blood
Ezek	44:21	No priest shall **d** wine when
Dan	1:10	has appointed your food and **d**
Dan	5: 2	concubines might **d** from them
Hos	2: 5	and my linen, my oil and my **d**
Hos	4:18	Their **d** is rebellion, they
Amos	2: 8	the wine of the condemned
Amos	2:12	gave the Nazirites wine to **d**
Amos	6: 6	who **d** wine from bowls, and
Matt	6:25	will eat or what you will **d**
Matt	20:22	Are you able to **d** the cup

Matt	25:35	was thirsty and you gave Me **d**
Matt	26:27	**D** from it, all of you
Matt	26:29	I will not **d** of this fruit of
Matt	26:29	I **d** it new with you in My
Matt	27:34	wine mingled with gall to **d**
Mark	9:41	cup of water to **d** in My name
Mark	16:18	if they **d** anything deadly, it
Luke	1:15	and shall **d** neither wine nor
Luke	12:19	eat, **d**, and be merry
Luke	12:29	eat or what you should **d**, nor
John	4: 7	said to her, "Give Me a **d**."
John	4: 9	ask a **d** from me, a Samaritan
John	6:53	**d** His blood, you have no life
John	6:55	and My blood is **d** indeed
John	7:37	let him come to Me and **d**
Rom	12:20	if he thirsts, give him a **d**
1Co	9: 7	does not **d** of the milk of the
1Co	10: 4	drank the same spiritual **d**
1Co	10: 7	people sat down to eat and **d**
1Co	10:21	You cannot **d** the cup of the
1Co	10:31	whether you eat or **d**, or
1Co	11:25	This do, as often as you **d** it
1Co	12:13	made to **d** into one Spirit
1Co	15:32	Let us eat and **d**, for tomorrow
Col	2:16	one judge you in food or in **d**
1Ti	5:23	No longer **d** only water, but
2Ti	4: 6	poured out as a **d** offering
Rev	14: 8	she has made all nations **d** of
Rev	16: 6	have given them blood to **d**

DRINKING (see DRINK)

Ruth	3: 3	he has finished eating and **d**
Is	5:22	Woe to men mighty at **d** wine
Matt	11:19	Son of Man came eating and **d**
Matt	24:38	flood, they were eating and **d**
Rom	14:17	of God is not eating and **d**,

DRINKS (see DRINK)

Gen	44: 5	the one from which my lord **d**
Num	23:24	and **d** the blood of the slain
Job	6: 4	my spirit **d** in their poison
Job	15:16	Who **d** iniquity like water
Job	34: 7	Job, who **d** scorn like water,
Ezek	31:14	that no tree which **d** water
Mark	2:16	and **d** with tax collectors and
John	4:13	Whoever **d** of this water will
John	6:54	**d** My blood has eternal life,
John	6:56	**d** My blood abides in Me, and I
1Co	11:27	**d** this cup of the Lord in an
1Co	11:29	**d** in an unworthy manner eats
1Co	11:29	**d** judgment to himself, not
Heb	9:10	only with foods and **d**, various

DRIVE (see DRIVEN, DRIVES, DRIVING, DROVE)

Ex	33: 2	I will **d** out the Canaanite and
Judg	1:28	did not completely **d** them out
Prov	22:15	will **d** it far from him

DRIVEN (see DRIVE)

Gen	4:14	Surely You have **d** me out this
Ex	12:39	they were **d** out of Egypt and
Dan	4:33	he was **d** from men and ate
Luke	8:29	was **d** by the demon into the

Jas	1: 6	is like a wave of the sea **d**
Jas	3: 4	are **d** by fierce winds, they

DRIVES (see DRIVE)

Deut	18:12	the LORD your God **d** them out
2Ki	9:20	of Nimshi, for he **d** furiously
Ps	1: 4	chaff which the wind **d** away

DRIVING (see DRIVE)

Acts	26:24	Much learning is **d** you mad

DROP (see DROPS)

Deut	33:28	His Heavens shall also **d** dew
Is	40:15	are as a **d** in a bucket, and

DROPS (see DROP)

Luke	22:44	**d** of blood falling down to

DROUGHT

Ps	32: 4	turned into the **d** of summer
Is	58:11	and satisfy your soul in **d**

DROVE (see DRIVE)

Gen	3:24	So He **d** out the man
Gen	15:11	carcasses, Abram **d** them away
Josh	24:18	the LORD **d** out from before us
Judg	4:21	**d** the peg into his temple, and
Neh	13:28	therefore I **d** him from me
Matt	21:12	**d** out all those who bought and
Mark	1:12	immediately the Spirit **d** Him
John	2:15	He **d** them all out of the

DROWN† (see DROWNED)

Song	8: 7	love, nor can the floods **d** it
1Ti	6: 9	which **d** men in destruction

DROWNED (see DROWN)

Ex	15: 4	also are **d** in the Red Sea
Matt	18: 6	he were **d** in the depth of the
Heb	11:29	attempting to do so, were **d**

DRUNK (see DRINK)

Gen	9:21	he drank of the wine and was **d**
1Sa	1:13	Eli thought she was **d**
Is	63: 6	made them **d** in My fury, and
Dan	5:23	have **d** wine from them
Luke	5:39	And no one, having **d** old wine,
John	2:10	when the guests have well **d**
Acts	2:15	For these are not **d**, as you
1Co	11:21	one is hungry and another is **d**
Eph	5:18	And do not be **d** with wine, in
Rev	17: 6	**d** with the blood of the

DRUNKENNESS (see DRUNK)

Rom	13:13	the day, not in revelry and **d**
Gal	5:21	envy, murders, **d**, revelries,
1Pe	4: 3	in licentiousness, lusts, **d**

DRY (see DRIED)

Gen	1: 9	and let the **d** land appear"
Ex	14:21	and made the sea into **d** land
Josh	3:17	crossed over on **d** ground,
Judg	6:40	It was **d** on the fleece only,
1Ki	17:16	nor did the jar of oil run **d**

Ps	63: 1	My flesh longs for You In a **d**
Is	53: 2	and as a root out of **d** ground
Ezek	37: 4	O **d** bones, hear the word of
Jon	2:10	it vomited Jonah onto **d** land
Luke	23:31	what will be done in the **d**
Heb	11:29	the Red Sea as by **d** land,

DUE

Deut	18: 3	priest's **d** from the people
Deut	32:35	foot shall slip in **d** time
Ps	29: 2	LORD the glory **d** to His name
Ps	104:27	them their food in **d** season
Matt	24:45	to give them food in **d** season
Rom	5: 6	in **d** time Christ died for the
Rom	13: 7	taxes to whom taxes are **d**
1Co	7: 3	his wife the affection **d** her
1Co	15: 8	as by one born out of **d** time
Gal	6: 9	for in **d** season we shall reap
1Pe	5: 6	He may exalt you in **d** time

DUG (see DIG)

Gen	21:30	that I have **d** this well
Gen	26:18	Isaac **d** again the wells of
Ex	7:24	So all the Egyptians **d** all
Ps	57: 6	They have **d** a pit before me
Ps	94:13	the pit is **d** for the wicked
Is	5: 2	He **d** it up and cleared out its
Is	5: 6	it shall not be pruned or **d**
Is	51: 1	the pit from which you were **d**
Jer	13: 7	I went to the Euphrates and **d**
Ezek	8: 8	when I **d** into the wall, there
Matt	21:33	**d** a winepress in it and built
Matt	25:18	**d** in the ground, and hid his
Luke	6:48	house, who **d** deep and laid the

DULL

Is	6:10	the heart of this people **d**
Matt	13:15	of this people has grown **d**
Acts	28:27	of this people has grown **d**
Heb	5:11	you have become **d** of hearing

DUMB†

Is	35: 6	and the tongue of the **d** sing
Is	56:10	they are all **d** dogs, they
Mark	9:25	**d** spirit, I command you, come
1Co	12: 2	carried away to these **d** idols
2Pe	2:16	a **d** donkey speaking with a

DUST

Gen	2: 7	man of the **d** of the ground
Gen	3:14	you shall eat **d** all the days
Gen	3:19	for **d** you are, and to **d** you
Gen	3:19	and to **d** you shall return
Gen	13:16	as the **d** of the earth
Gen	18:27	Indeed now, I who am but **d**
2Sa	1: 2	clothes torn and **d** on his head
Job	34:15	and man would return to **d**
Job	42: 6	abhor myself, and repent in **d**
Ps	22:15	brought Me to the **d** of death
Ps	30: 9	Will the **d** praise You
Ps	72: 9	His enemies will lick the **d**
Ps	103:14	He remembers that we are **d**
Eccl	12: 7	Then the **d** will return to the
Is	26:19	and sing, you who dwell in **d**

Is	65:25	**d** shall be the serpent's food
Dan	12: 2	**d** of the earth shall awake
Matt	10:14	shake off the **d** from your
1Co	15:47	was of the earth, made of **d**
1Co	15:48	As was the man of **d**, so also
Rev	18:19	they threw **d** on their heads

DWELL (see DWELLING, DWELLS, DWELT)

Gen	4:20	of those who **d** in tents and
Gen	9:27	may he **d** in the tents of Shem
Gen	13: 6	they could not **d** together
Ex	25: 8	that I may **d** among them
Num	35:34	for I the LORD **d** among the
Deut	8:12	beautiful houses and **d** in them
Deut	25: 5	If brothers **d** together, and
2Sa	7: 2	I **d** in a house of cedar, but
2Sa	7: 5	build a house for Me to **d** in
1Ki	8:12	He would **d** in the dark cloud
1Ki	8:27	God indeed **d** on the earth
Ps	15: 1	Who may **d** in Your holy hill
Ps	23: 6	I will **d** in the house of the
Ps	24: 1	world and those who **d** therein
Ps	27: 4	That I may **d** in the house of
Ps	98: 7	world and those who **d** in it
Ps	107: 4	They found no city to **d** in
Ps	123: 1	O You who **d** in the heavens
Ps	133: 1	to **d** together in unity
Ps	139: 9	**d** in the uttermost parts of
Ps	143: 3	He has made me **d** in darkness
Prov	1:33	listens to me will **d** safely
Prov	2:21	upright will **d** in the land
Prov	21: 9	It is better to **d** in a corner
Song	8:13	You who **d** in the gardens, the
Is	6: 5	I **d** in the midst of a people
Is	10:24	who **d** in Zion, do not be
Is	11: 6	also shall **d** with the lamb
Is	26: 5	down those who **d** on high, the
Is	26:19	and sing, you who **d** in dust
Is	47: 8	who **d** securely, who say in
Is	57:15	I **d** in the high and holy place
Is	58:12	Restorer of Streets to **D** In
Jer	7: 3	cause you to **d** in this place
Jer	27:11	they shall till it and **d** in it
Jer	29: 5	Build houses and **d** in them
Jer	33:16	and Jerusalem will **d** safely
Jer	44: 1	who **d** in the land of Egypt
Jer	49: 8	turn back, **d** in the depths, O
Jer	50:39	**d** there with the jackals, and
Ezek	37:25	Then they shall **d** in the land
Ezek	43: 9	and I will **d** in their midst
Hos	14: 7	Those who **d** under his shadow
Hag	1: 4	to **d** in your paneled houses
Zech	2:11	And I will **d** in your midst
Acts	7:48	the Most High does not **d** in
Acts	17:24	does not **d** in temples made
Acts	17:26	to **d** on all the face of the
Acts	28:16	but Paul was permitted to **d**
Eph	3:17	that Christ may **d** in your
Col	1:19	Him all the fullness should **d**
Col	3:16	Let the word of Christ **d** in
1Pe	3: 7	husbands, **d** with them with
Rev	2:13	your works, and where you **d**
Rev	3:10	test those who **d** on the earth
Rev	7:15	the throne will **d** among them

Rev	13: 6	and those who **d** in heaven
Rev	21: 3	He will **d** with them, and they

DWELLING (*see* DWELL, DWELLINGS)

Gen	25:27	was a mild man, **d** in tents
Ex	15:17	You have made for Your own **d**
1Ki	8:30	hear in heaven Your **d** place
2Ch	30:27	came up to His holy **d** place
Neh	1: 9	chosen as a **d** for My name
Job	38:19	is the way to the **d** of light
Ps	76: 2	And His **d** place in Zion
Ps	90: 1	You have been our **d** place in
Ps	91: 9	the Most High, your **d** place,
Ps	107: 7	to a city for a **d** place.
Ps	132: 5	A **d** place for the Mighty God
Ps	132:13	desired it for His **d** place:
Dan	2:11	whose **d** is not with flesh
Dan	4:30	a royal **d** by my mighty power
Dan	5:21	and his **d** was with the wild
Mark	5: 3	who had his **d** among the tombs
Acts	1:19	to all those **d** in Jerusalem
Acts	7:46	asked to find a **d** for the God
Eph	2:22	for a **d** place of God
1Ti	6:16	**d** in unapproachable light,
Heb	11: 9	**d** in tents with Isaac and
2Pe	2: 8	**d** among them, tormented his
Rev	18: 2	become a **d** place of demons,

DWELLINGS (*see* DWELLING)

Ex	10:23	Israel had light in their **d**
Lev	7:26	any blood in any of your **d**
Lev	23:21	**d** throughout your generations
Num	24: 5	your **d**, O Israel
Ps	55:15	For wickedness is in their **d**
Ps	87: 2	More than all the **d** of Jacob
Is	32:18	habitation, in secure **d**, and
Jer	9:19	have been cast out of our **d**
Acts	17:26	the boundaries of their **d**,

DWELLS (*see* DWELL)

1Sa	4: 4	who **d** between the cherubim
2Sa	6: 2	who **d** between the cherubim
Ps	9:11	to the LORD, who **d** in Zion
Ps	26: 8	the place where Your glory **d**
Ps	91: 1	He who **d** in the secret place
Ps	113: 5	LORD our God, Who **d** on high,
Jer	49:31	nation that **d** securely,"
Dan	2:22	darkness, and light **d** with Him
John	14:10	but the Father who **d** in Me
John	14:17	for He **d** with you and will be
Rom	7:17	do it, but sin that **d** in me
Rom	7:18	in my flesh) nothing good **d**
Rom	7:20	do it, but sin that **d** in me
Rom	8: 9	the Spirit of God **d** in you
Rom	8:11	Jesus from the dead **d** in you
Col	2: 9	For in Him **d** all the fullness
Jas	4: 5	The Spirit who **d** in us yearns
2Pe	3:13	in which righteousness **d**
Rev	2:13	among you, where Satan **d**

DWELT (*see* DWELL)

Gen	4:16	**d** in the land of Nod on the
Gen	13:12	Abram **d** in the land of Canaan
Gen	13:12	Lot **d** in the cities of the

2Sa	5: 9	So David **d** in the stronghold,
2Sa	7: 6	For I have not **d** in a house
Ps	74: 2	Mount Zion where You have **d**
Matt	2:23	**d** in a city called Nazareth,
John	1:14	**d** among us, and we beheld His
Acts	7: 2	before he **d** in Haran,
2Ti	1: 5	in you, which **d** first in your

DYING (*see* DIE)

Luke	8:42	years of age, and she was **d**
John	11:37	have kept this man from **d**
2Co	4:10	body the **d** of the Lord Jesus
2Co	6: 9	as **d**, and behold we live

E

EAGERLY

Rom	8:19	**e** waits for the revealing of
Rom	8:23	**e** waiting for the adoption,
Heb	9:28	To those who **e** wait for Him

EAGLE (*see* EAGLE'S, EAGLES)

Prov	30:19	the way of an **e** in the air
Ezek	1:10	the four had the face of an **e**
Mic	1:16	your baldness like an **e**, for

EAGLE'S† (*see* EAGLE)

Ps	103: 5	youth is renewed like the **e**
Dan	7: 4	like a lion, and had **e** wings

EAGLES (*see* EAGLE, EAGLES')

2Sa	1:23	they were swifter than **e**,
Is	40:31	mount up with wings like **e**
Matt	24:28	there the **e** will be gathered

EAGLES'† (*see* EAGLES)

Ex	19: 4	and how I bore you on **e** wings
Dan	4:33	had grown like **e** feathers

EAR (*see* EARS)

Ex	15:26	give **e** to His commandments
Ex	21: 6	pierce his **e** with an awl
Ex	29:20	tip of the right **e** of Aaron
2Ki	19:16	Incline Your **e**, O LORD, and
Job	42: 5	You by the hearing of the **e**
Ps	5: 1	Give **e** to my words, O LORD,
Ps	17: 6	Incline Your **e** to me, and hear
Ps	94: 9	He who planted the **e**, shall
Prov	2: 2	you incline your **e** to wisdom
Prov	20:12	The hearing **e** and the seeing
Is	50: 5	The Lord GOD has opened My **e**
Amos	3:12	two legs or a piece of an **e**
Luke	22:51	And He touched his **e** and
John	18:26	of him whose **e** Peter cut off
1Co	2: 9	nor **e** heard, nor have entered
Rev	2: 7	He who has an **e**, let him hear

EARLY

Gen	19:27	Abraham went **e** in the morning
Gen	21:14	Abraham rose **e** in the morning
Gen	22: 3	Abraham rose **e** in the morning
Deut	11:14	the **e** rain and the latter rain

Ps	63: 1	E will I seek You; My soul
Ps	90:14	satisfy us e with Your
Dan	6:10	as was his custom since e
Dan	6:19	Then the king arose very e in
Hos	6: 4	And like the e dew it goes
Hos	13: 3	cloud And like the e dew
Mark	16: 9	Now when He rose e on the
Luke	21:38	Then e in the morning all the
Luke	24: 1	very e in the morning, they,
Luke	24:22	who arrived at the tomb e,
John	8: 2	Now e in the morning He came
John	18:28	and it was e morning. But
John	20: 1	Magdalene went to the tomb e,
Acts	5:21	they entered the temple e in
Acts	21:16	an e disciple, with whom we
Jas	5: 7	it until it receives the e

EARNEST (see EARNESTLY)

Rom	8:19	For the e expectation of the
2Co	7: 7	when he told us of your e
Phil	1:20	according to my e expectation
Heb	2: 1	must give the more e heed

EARNESTLY (see DILIGENTLY, EARNEST)

1Sa	20: 6	David e asked permission of
1Co	12:31	But e desire the best gifts.
1Co	14:39	desire e to prophesy, and do
2Co	5: 2	e desiring to be clothed
Col	4: 2	Continue e in prayer, being
Jas	5:17	and he prayed e that it
Jude	3	exhorting you to contend e

EARS (see EAR)

Ex	32: 2	which are in the e of your
Lev	8:24	on the tips of their right e,
Deut	29: 4	and eyes to see and e to
Judg	17: 2	even saying it in my e—
1Sa	3:11	in Israel at which both e
1Sa	15:14	of the sheep in my e,
2Sa	7:22	we have heard with our e.
2Sa	22: 7	And my cry entered His e.
2Ki	21:12	both his e will tingle.
2Ch	7:15	eyes will be open and My e
Neh	8: 3	and the e of all the people
Job	15:21	sounds are in his e;
Job	33:16	Then He opens the e of men,
Ps	34:15	And His e are open to
Ps	40: 6	My e You have opened.
Ps	44: 1	We have heard with our e,
Ps	78: 1	Incline your e to the words
Ps	115: 6	They have e, but they do not
Prov	21:13	Whoever shuts his e to the
Prov	23:12	And your e to words of
Prov	26:17	one who takes a dog by the e.
Is	6:10	And their e heavy, And
Is	6:10	eyes, And hear with their e,
Is	11: 3	by the hearing of His e;
Is	42:20	not observe; Opening the e,
Is	43: 8	And the deaf who have e.
Ezek	40: 4	eyes and hear with your e,
Matt	11:15	He who has e to hear, let him
Matt	13:15	Their e are hard of
Acts	17:20	some strange things to our e.
Acts	28:27	Their e are hard of

Rom	11: 8	e that they should not
2Ti	4: 3	because they have itching e,
1Pe	3:12	And His e are open to

EARTH (see EARTHEN, EARTHLY, EARTHQUAKE)

Gen	1: 1	the heavens and the e.
Gen	1: 2	The e was without form, and
Gen	1:10	God called the dry land E,
Gen	1:24	thing and beast of the e,
Gen	1:28	fill the e and subdue it;
Gen	2: 5	caused it to rain on the e,
Gen	2: 6	a mist went up from the e
Gen	4:11	you are cursed from the e,
Gen	4:14	and a vagabond on the e,
Gen	6: 4	There were giants on the e in
Gen	6: 5	of man was great in the e,
Gen	6:11	The e also was corrupt
Gen	7:17	and it rose high above the e.
Gen	8:11	had receded from the e.
Gen	8:22	While the e remains,
Gen	9: 1	and multiply, and fill the e.
Gen	11: 1	Now the whole e had one
Gen	11: 9	the language of all the e;
Gen	12: 3	all the families of the e
Gen	13:16	number the dust of the e,
Gen	14:19	Possessor of heaven and e;
Gen	18:25	not the Judge of all the e
Ex	15:12	The e swallowed them.
Ex	19: 5	for all the e is Mine.
Ex	20: 4	is in the water under the e;
Num	14:21	all the e shall be filled
Num	16:32	and the e opened its mouth
Deut	4:26	I call heaven and e to
Deut	13: 7	from one end of the e to
Deut	28: 1	above all nations of the e.
Deut	32: 1	I will speak; And hear, O e,
Deut	32:13	ride in the heights of the e,
Deut	33:17	To the ends of the e;
Josh	23:14	going the way of all the e.
Judg	5: 4	The e trembled and the
1Sa	4: 5	so loudly that the e shook.
1Sa	28:13	ascending out of the e.
2Sa	18: 9	hanging between heaven and e.
1Ki	1:40	that the e seemed to split
1Ki	8:23	God in heaven above or on e
2Ki	5:17	be given two mule-loads of e;
Ezra	5:11	of the God of heaven and e,
Job	1: 7	going to and fro on the e,
Job	1: 8	is none like him on the e,
Job	3:14	and counselors of the e,
Job	19:25	shall stand at last on the e;
Job	20: 4	Since man was placed on e,
Job	26: 7	He hangs the e on nothing.
Ps	2: 2	The kings of the e set
Ps	2: 8	And the ends of the e for
Ps	2:10	you judges of the e.
Ps	7: 5	him trample my life to the e,
Ps	8: 1	is Your name in all the e,
Ps	19: 4	gone out through all the e,
Ps	24: 1	The e is the LORD's, and
Ps	33: 5	The e is full of the
Ps	33: 8	Let all the e fear the
Ps	37:11	the meek shall inherit the e,

Ps	46: 2	Even though the e be
Ps	46: 6	His voice, the e melted.
Ps	46:10	I will be exalted in the e
Ps	47: 2	a great King over all the e.
Ps	48: 2	The joy of the whole e,
Ps	57: 5	glory be above all the e.
Ps	63: 9	the lower parts of the e.
Ps	67: 7	And all the ends of the e
Ps	72: 6	showers that water the e.
Ps	72: 8	River to the ends of the e.
Ps	72:16	flourish like grass of the e.
Ps	74:20	the dark places of the e
Ps	82: 8	Arise, O God, judge the e;
Ps	83:10	became as refuse on the e.
Ps	83:18	the Most High over all the e.
Ps	89:11	the e also is Yours; The
Ps	90: 2	ever You had formed the e
Ps	96:13	He is coming to judge the e.
Ps	97: 1	Let the e rejoice; Let the
Ps	98: 3	All the ends of the e have
Ps	103:11	heavens are high above the e,
Ps	104: 9	not return to cover the e.
Ps	104:14	bring forth food from the e,
Ps	104:30	You renew the face of the e.
Ps	115:16	But the e He has given to
Ps	121: 2	Who made heaven and e.
Ps	135: 6	He does, In heaven and in e,
Prov	3:19	by wisdom founded the e;
Prov	8:23	before there was ever an e.
Eccl	1: 4	But the e abides forever.
Eccl	5: 2	is in heaven, and you on e;
Eccl	12: 7	dust will return to the e
Song	2:12	The flowers appear on the e;
Is	1: 2	O e For the LORD has
Is	6: 3	The whole e is full of His
Is	11: 9	For the e shall be full of
Is	40:22	above the circle of the e,
Is	40:28	Creator of the ends of the e,
Is	45:18	Who formed the e and made
Is	45:22	All you ends of the e For
Is	55: 9	are higher than the e,
Is	55:10	there, But water the e,
Is	65:17	new heavens and a new e;
Is	66: 1	And e is My footstool
Jer	15:10	contention to the whole e
Jer	22:29	O e, earth, earth, Hear
Dan	2:35	and filled the whole e.
Dan	4:22	dominion to the end of the e.
Dan	12: 2	sleep in the dust of the e
Amos	3: 2	of all the families of the e;
Mic	1: 2	you peoples! Listen, O e,
Hab	2:14	For the e will be filled
Hab	2:20	Let all the e keep silence
Hag	2: 6	I will shake heaven and e,
Zech	1:10	to and fro throughout the e.
Zech	4:14	the Lord of the whole e.
Zech	9:10	River to the ends of the e.
Zech	14: 9	shall be King over all the e.
Mal	4: 6	I come and strike the e
Matt	5: 5	they shall inherit the e.
Matt	5:13	"You are the salt of the e;
Matt	5:18	till heaven and e pass away,
Matt	6:10	Your will be done On e as
Matt	6:19	yourselves treasures on e,

Matt	9: 6	Son of Man has power on e
Matt	10:34	I came to bring peace on e.
Matt	16:19	and whatever you bind on e
Matt	24:35	Heaven and e will pass away,
Matt	28:18	to Me in heaven and on e.
Luke	2:14	And on e peace, goodwill
Luke	10:21	Father, Lord of heaven and e,
Luke	18: 8	really find faith on the e?
John	3:31	he who is of the e is
John	12:32	if I am lifted up from the e,
John	17: 4	have glorified You on the e.
Acts	1: 8	and to the end of the e.
Acts	7:49	And e is My footstool.
Acts	10:11	to him and let down to the e.
Rom	9:17	declared in all the e.
Rom	10:18	gone out to all the e,
1Co	10:26	the e is the LORD's,
1Co	15:47	The first man was of the e,
Eph	6: 3	may live long on the e.
Phil	2:10	in heaven, and of those on e,
Col	3: 2	not on things on the e.
Col	3: 5	members which are on the e:
Heb	11:13	and pilgrims on the e
Heb	11:38	in dens and caves of the e.
Heb	12:25	refused Him who spoke on e,
Heb	12:26	whose voice then shook the e;
Heb	12:26	I shake not only the e,
2Pe	3: 5	and the e standing out of
2Pe	3:13	for new heavens and a new e
1Jn	5: 8	three that bear witness on e:
Rev	1: 5	over the kings of the e.
Rev	1: 7	And all the tribes of the e
Rev	3:10	those who dwell on the e.
Rev	5:10	And we shall reign on the e.
Rev	5:13	on the earth and under the e
Rev	6:13	of heaven fell to the e,
Rev	7: 1	at the four corners of the e,
Rev	7: 1	the four winds of the e,
Rev	7: 3	saying, "Do not harm the e,
Rev	12: 9	world; he was cast to the e,
Rev	12:16	and the e opened its mouth
Rev	13:11	beast coming up out of the e,
Rev	17: 5	ABOMINATIONS OF THE E.
Rev	21: 1	saw a new heaven and a new e,
Rev	21: 1	heaven and the first e had

EARTHEN (see EARTH)

Lev	6:28	But the e vessel in which it
Num	5:17	take holy water in an e
Jer	19: 1	Go and get a potter's e
Jer	32:14	and put them in an e vessel,
Hab	1:10	For they heap up e mounds
2Co	4: 7	we have this treasure in e

EARTHLY (see EARTH)

John	3:12	If I have told you e things
John	3:31	he who is of the earth is
2Co	5: 1	For we know that if our e
Phil	3:19	who set their mind on e

EARTHQUAKE (see EARTH, EARTHQUAKES)

1Ki	19:11	and after the wind an e,
1Ki	19:11	the LORD was not in the e;

E

Amos	1: 1	two years before the e.
Matt	27:54	saw the e and the things

EARTHQUAKES (see EARTHQUAKE)

Matt	24: 7	and e in various places.

EASE

Amos	6: 1	Woe to you who are at e in
Luke	12:19	for many years; take your e;

EASIER (see EASY)

Matt	9: 5	"For which is e,
Matt	19:24	it is e for a camel to go
Luke	16:17	And it is e for heaven and

EASILY (see EASY)

Heb	12: 1	and the sin which so e

EAST

Gen	3:24	He placed cherubim at the e
Gen	4:16	in the land of Nod on the e
Gen	13:11	Jordan, and Lot journeyed e.
Ex	14:21	to go back by a strong e
Ps	103:12	As far as the e is from the
Jon	4: 8	God prepared a vehement e
Matt	2: 1	wise men from the E came to
Matt	2: 2	have seen His star in the E
Matt	8:11	that many will come from e

EASY (see EASIER, EASILY)

Matt	11:30	For My yoke is e and My

EAT (see ATE, EATEN, EATER, EATING, EATS)

Gen	2:16	the garden you may freely e;
Gen	2:17	and evil you shall not e,
Gen	3:14	And you shall e dust All
Gen	9: 4	But you shall not e flesh
Gen	40:19	and the birds will e your
Ex	12:11	So you shall e it in haste.
Lev	3:17	you shall e neither fat nor
Lev	11: 4	these you shall not e among
Lev	11:39	any animal which you may e
Lev	17:14	You shall not e the blood of
Lev	19:25	in the fifth year you may e
Lev	22: 4	shall not e the holy
Lev	22: 6	and shall not e the holy
Lev	22: 7	and afterward he may e the
Lev	22: 8	by beasts he shall not e,
Lev	22:13	she may e her father's food;
Lev	22:16	of trespass when they e
Lev	25:19	and you will e your fill,
Lev	26:38	of your enemies shall e you
Num	6: 3	nor e fresh grapes or
Num	6: 4	of his separation he shall e
Num	11:13	'Give us meat, that we may e.
Deut	2: 6	with money, that you may e;
Deut	4:28	neither see nor hear nor e
Deut	8: 9	a land in which you will e
Deut	12:15	you may slaughter and e meat
Deut	12:16	Only you shall not e the
Deut	12:23	you may not e the life with
Deut	14: 7	hooves, you shall not e,
Deut	14: 9	you may e all that have fins
Deut	14:10	and scales you shall not e;
Deut	14:11	"All clean birds you may e.
Deut	16: 3	seven days you shall e
Deut	18: 8	have equal portions to e,
Deut	28:55	his children whom he will e,
Neh	8:10	e the fat, drink the sweet,
Job	31: 8	let me sow, and another e;
Ps	14: 4	Who e up my people as they
Ps	22:26	The poor shall e and be
Ps	78:24	down manna on them to e,
Ps	127: 2	To e the bread of sorrows;
Prov	25:16	E only as much as you need,
Prov	25:21	hungry, give him bread to e;
Eccl	2:24	a man than that he should e
Eccl	8:15	under the sun than to e,
Eccl	9: 7	e your bread with joy, And
Is	1:19	You shall e the good of the
Is	7:15	"Curds and honey He shall e,
Is	11: 7	And the lion shall e straw
Is	22:13	Let us e and drink, for
Is	55: 1	no money, Come, buy and e.
Is	65:25	The lion shall e straw like
Ezek	3: 1	e this scroll, and go, speak
Dan	1:12	give us vegetables to e and
Dan	4:32	They shall make you e grass
Amos	7:12	There e bread, And there
Matt	6:25	what you will e or what you
Matt	6:31	saying, 'What shall we e?
Matt	9:11	Why does your Teacher e with
Matt	12: 1	heads of grain and to e.
Matt	12: 4	was not lawful for him to e,
Matt	15:20	but to e with unwashed hands
Matt	15:27	yet even the little dogs e
Matt	26:17	us to prepare for You to e
Matt	26:26	and said, "Take, e;
Mark	7:28	dogs under the table e from
Luke	5:30	Why do You e and drink with
Luke	5:33	but Yours e and drink?"
Luke	12:19	years; take your ease; e,
Luke	15:23	and let us e and be merry;
Luke	22:16	I will no longer e of it
Luke	22:30	that you may e and drink at
John	4:31	Him, saying, "Rabbi, e.
John	4:32	I have food to e of which you
John	6: 5	buy bread, that these may e?
John	6:31	bread from heaven to e
John	6:52	Man give us His flesh to e?
Acts	10:13	"Rise, Peter; kill and e.
Acts	23:12	that they would neither e
Rom	14: 2	For one believes he may e all
Rom	14: 3	let not him who does not e
Rom	14:21	It is good neither to e
Rom	14:23	because he does not e
1Co	5:11	not even to e with such a
1Co	8:10	is weak be emboldened to e
1Co	8:13	I will never again e meat,
1Co	9:13	minister the holy things e
1Co	10: 7	people sat down to e
1Co	10:27	e whatever is set before
1Co	10:31	whether you e or drink, or
1Co	11:20	it is not to e the Lord's
1Co	11:24	it and said, "Take, e;
1Co	11:26	For as often as you e this
1Co	11:28	and so let him e of the
1Co	11:33	when you come together to e,

1Co	11:34	let him e at home, lest you
Gal	2:12	he would e with the
2Th	3:10	not work, neither shall he e.
Heb	13:10	have no right to e.
Jas	5: 3	against you and will e your
Rev	2: 7	overcomes I will give to e
Rev	2:14	to e things sacrificed to
Rev	2:17	of the hidden manna to e.
Rev	10: 9	Take and e it; and it will
Rev	17:16	e her flesh and burn her
Rev	19:18	that you may e the flesh of

EATEN (see EAT)

Gen	3:11	Have you e from the tree of
Ps	69: 9	zeal for Your house has e
Prov	9:17	And bread e in secret is
Jer	24: 2	figs which could not be e,
Jer	31:29	The fathers have e sour
Ezek	18: 2	The fathers have e sour
John	2:17	for Your house has e
John	6:13	left over by those who had e.
Acts	12:23	And he was e by worms and

EATER (see EAT)

Judg	14:14	Out of the e came something
Is	55:10	sower And bread to the e,

EATING (see EAT)

Matt	11:18	For John came neither e nor
Matt	11:19	The Son of Man came e and
Matt	24:38	they were e and drinking,
1Co	8: 4	Therefore concerning the e of
1Co	8:10	you who have knowledge e in
1Co	11:21	For in e, each one takes

EATS (see EAT)

Ex	12:15	For whoever e leavened bread
Lev	7:18	and the person who e of it
Lev	7:21	and who e the flesh of the
Lev	7:25	For whoever e the fat of the
Lev	7:27	Whoever e any blood, that
Lev	11:40	He who e of its carcass shall
Lev	22:14	And if a man e the holy
1Sa	14:24	Cursed is the man who e any
Job	40:15	He e grass like an ox.
Prov	30:20	She e and wipes her mouth,
Eccl	5:12	Whether he e little or
Eccl	5:17	All his days he also e in
Is	44:16	With this half he e meat;
Mark	2:16	How is it that He e and
Mark	14:18	one of you who e with Me
Luke	15: 2	Man receives sinners and e
John	6:51	If anyone e of this bread,
John	6:54	Whoever e My flesh and drinks
John	6:58	He who e this bread will
Rom	14: 2	but he who is weak e only
Rom	14: 3	Let not him who e despise him
Rom	14: 6	He who e, eats to the Lord,
Rom	14:23	doubts is condemned if he e,
1Co	11:27	Therefore whoever e this
1Co	11:29	in an unworthy manner e and

EBAL

Deut	11:29	and the curse on Mount E.

EBENEZER

1Sa	4: 1	and encamped beside E;

EDEN

Gen	2: 8	a garden eastward in E,
Gen	2:10	Now a river went out of E to
Ezek	28:13	You were in E,
Ezek	31: 9	So that all the trees of E

EDGE

Jer	31:29	teeth are set on e.
Ezek	18: 2	teeth are set on e'?
Luke	21:24	they will fall by the e
Heb	11:34	escaped the e of the sword,

EDIFICATION (see EDIFY)

Rom	15: 2	for his good, leading to e.
1Co	14: 3	he who prophesies speaks e
1Co	14:26	Let all things be done for e.
1Ti	1: 4	rather than godly e which

EDIFIED (see EDIFY)

1Co	14:17	well, but the other is not e.

EDIFIES (see EDIFY)

1Co	8: 1	puffs up, but love e.
1Co	14: 4	He who speaks in a tongue e

EDIFY (see EDIFICATION, EDIFIED, EDIFIES, EDIFYING)

1Co	10:23	for me, but not all things e.

EDIFYING (see EDIFY)

Eph	4:12	for the e of the body of

EDOM (see ESAU, IDUMEA)

Gen	25:30	his name was called E.
Gen	32: 3	of Seir, the country of E.
Gen	36: 1	genealogy of Esau, who is E.
Is	63: 1	is this who comes from E,
Amos	1:11	three transgressions of E,

EFFECT (see EFFECTIVE)

Matt	15: 6	commandment of God of no e
Mark	7:13	the word of God of no e
Rom	4:14	and the promise made of no e,
Gal	3:17	make the promise of no e.

EFFECTIVE (see EFFECT, EFFECTIVELY)

1Co	16: 9	For a great and e door has
Jas	5:16	The e, fervent prayer

EFFECTIVELY (see EFFECTIVE)

1Th	2:13	which also e works in you

EGG

Luke	11:12	"Or if he asks for an e,

EGLON

Josh	10: 3	Lachish, and Debir king of E,
Judg	3:14	children of Israel served E

E

EGYPT (see EGYPTIAN, GOSHEN)

Gen	12:10	and Abram went down to E to
Gen	15:18	from the river of E to the
Gen	37:28	And they took Joseph to E.
Gen	41: 8	for all the magicians of E
Gen	41:33	set him over the land of E.
Gen	41:46	before Pharaoh king of E.
Gen	50:26	he was put in a coffin in E.
Ex	1: 5	persons (for Joseph was in E
Ex	1: 8	arose a new king over E,
Ex	3:12	brought the people out of E,
Ex	12:12	against all the gods of E I
Ex	13: 9	has brought you out of E.
Ex	20: 2	you out of the land of E,
Num	13:22	seven years before Zoan in E.
Num	14: 3	better for us to return to E?
Deut	4:20	the iron furnace, out of E,
Deut	6:21	were slaves of Pharaoh in E,
Deut	6:21	LORD brought us out of E
Deut	28:27	you with the boils of E,
Deut	28:60	on you all the diseases of E,
2Sa	7:23	redeemed for Yourself from E,
1Ki	3: 1	with Pharaoh king of E,
1Ki	4:30	East and all the wisdom of E.
1Ki	10:28	had horses imported from E
1Ki	11:40	Jeroboam arose and fled to E,
1Ki	11:40	Egypt, to Shishak king of E,
2Ki	17: 4	messengers to So, king of E,
2Ki	18:21	staff of this broken reed, E,
2Ki	18:24	and put your trust in E for
2Ki	23:29	days Pharaoh Necho king of E
2Ch	1:17	and imported from E a
2Ch	26: 8	as far as the entrance of E,
Ps	68:31	Envoys will come out of E;
Ps	78:43	He worked His signs in E,
Ps	80: 8	have brought a vine out of E;
Ps	105:38	E was glad when they
Ps	106:21	had done great things in E,
Ps	114: 1	When Israel went out of E,
Ps	135: 8	destroyed the firstborn of E,
Ps	136:10	To Him who struck E in their
Is	7:18	part of the rivers of E,
Is	11:15	the tongue of the Sea of E;
Is	19: 1	The burden against E.
Is	19: 1	The idols of E will totter
Is	19:18	five cities in the land of E
Is	19:23	will be a highway from E to
Is	19:24	will be one of three with E
Is	19:25	Blessed is E My people, and
Is	20: 4	uncovered, to the shame of E.
Is	27:12	the River to the Brook of E;
Is	30: 2	to trust in the shadow of E!
Is	43: 3	I gave E for your ransom,
Jer	43:12	the houses of the gods of E,
Jer	46:11	O virgin, the daughter of E;
Jer	46:14	"Declare in E,
Ezek	17:15	sending his ambassadors to E,
Ezek	20: 7	with the idols of E.
Ezek	23: 3	committed harlotry in E,
Ezek	30: 4	The sword shall come upon E,
Ezek	30: 8	I have set a fire in E And
Ezek	30:19	will execute judgments on E,
Ezek	32:12	shall plunder the pomp of E,

Ezek	32:16	shall lament for her, for E,
Hos	7:11	sense—They call to E,
Hos	11: 1	And out of E I called My
Hos	11:11	trembling like a bird from E,
Hos	12: 1	And oil is carried to E.
Amos	4:10	plague after the manner of E;
Amos	8: 8	subside Like the River of E.
Nah	3: 9	Ethiopia and E were her
Zech	10:11	And the scepter of E shall
Matt	2:13	and His mother, flee to E,
Matt	2:15	Out of E I called My
Matt	2:19	in a dream to Joseph in E,
Acts	7: 9	envious, sold Joseph into E.
Acts	7:10	he made him governor over E
Acts	7:15	"So Jacob went down to E;
Heb	11:26	than the treasures in E;
Heb	11:27	By faith he forsook E,
Jude	5	people out of the land of E,
Rev	11: 8	is called Sodom and E,

EGYPTIAN (see EGYPT, EGYPTIANS)

Gen	16: 1	And she had an E maidservant
Gen	21: 9	saw the son of Hagar the E,
Gen	39: 1	captain of the guard, an E,
Ex	2:12	he killed the E and hid him
Acts	7:24	and struck down the E.

EGYPTIANS (see EGYPTIAN)

Gen	12:14	that the E saw the woman,
Gen	41:55	Pharaoh said to all the E,
Gen	41:56	and sold to the E.
Gen	43:32	because the E could not eat
Gen	43:32	is an abomination to the E.
Gen	47:15	all the E came to Joseph and
Gen	50: 3	and the E mourned for him
Ex	1:13	So the E made the children of
Ex	3: 8	out of the hand of the E,
Ex	3: 9	oppression with which the E
Ex	3:21	favor in the sight of the E;
Ex	3:22	So you shall plunder the E.
Ex	7: 5	And the E shall know that I
Ex	7:18	and the E will loathe to
Ex	9:11	magicians and on all the E.
Ex	11: 3	favor in the sight of the E.
Ex	11: 7	a difference between the E
Ex	12:23	pass through to strike the E;
Ex	14:17	harden the hearts of the E,
Ex	14:30	and Israel saw the E dead on
Acts	7:22	in all the wisdom of the E,

EHUD

Judg	3:16	Now E made himself a dagger

EIGHT (see EIGHTH)

Gen	17:12	He who is e days old among
Gen	21: 4	his son Isaac when he was e
Luke	2:21	And when e days were
1Pe	3:20	e souls, were saved through
2Pe	2: 5	one of e people, a

EIGHTH (see EIGHT)

Luke	1:59	on the e day, that they came
Acts	7: 8	and circumcised him on the e
Phil	3: 5	circumcised the e day, of the

EIGHTY

Ex	7: 7	And Moses was e years old
Ps	90:10	of strength they are e

EKRON

Jer	25:20	(namely, Ashkelon, Gaza, E,

ELAM (see ELAMITES, PERSIA)

Gen	14: 1	Chedorlaomer king of E,
Dan	8: 2	is in the province of E;

ELAMITES (see ELAM, PERSIAN)

Acts	2: 9	"Parthians and Medes and E,

ELDER (see ELDERS)

Gen	10:21	the brother of Japheth the e.
Gen	27:15	the choice clothes of her e
Gen	29:16	the name of the e was Leah,
Is	3: 2	And the diviner and the e;
Ezek	16:46	Your e sister is Samaria,
Ezek	23: 4	Oholah the e and Oholibah
1Ti	5:19	an accusation against an e
1Pe	5: 1	I who am a fellow e and a
2Jn	1	The E, To the elect lady
3Jn	1	The E, To the beloved

ELDERS (see ELDER)

Gen	50: 7	the e of his house, and all
Ex	3:16	Go and gather the e of Israel
Ex	24: 1	and seventy of the e of
Lev	4:15	And the e of the congregation
Num	11:25	same upon the seventy e;
Deut	21: 2	then your e and your judges
Josh	24:31	and all the days of the e
Judg	11: 5	that the e of Gilead went to
Ruth	4: 2	he took ten men of the e of
Ruth	4:11	were at the gate, and the e,
Ps	105:22	And teach his e wisdom.
Ezek	8: 1	I sat in my house with the e
Ezek	8:11	them seventy men of the e
Matt	15: 2	the tradition of the e?
Matt	16:21	many things from the e and
Matt	26:47	the chief priests and e of
Matt	27:41	with the scribes and e,
Acts	14:23	appointed e in every church,
Acts	15: 2	to the apostles and e,
Acts	15: 6	Now the apostles and e came
Acts	20:17	and called for the e of the
Acts	22: 5	and all the council of the e,
Acts	23:14	to the chief priests and e,
1Ti	5:17	Let the e who rule well be
Tit	1: 5	and appoint e in every city
Heb	11: 2	For by it the e obtained a
Jas	5:14	Let him call for the e of
1Pe	5: 1	The e who are among you I
1Pe	5: 5	submit yourselves to your e.
Rev	4: 4	thrones I saw twenty-four e

ELEAZAR

Ex	6:23	she bore him Nadab, Abihu, E,
Ex	6:25	E, Aaron's son, took for

ELECT (see ELECT'S, ELECTION)

Is	42: 1	My E One in whom My soul
Is	45: 4	sake, And Israel My e,
Matt	24:24	if possible, even the e.
Matt	24:31	will gather together His e
Rom	8:33	a charge against God's e?
Rom	11: 7	but the e have obtained it,
Col	3:12	as the e of God, holy and
1Ti	5:21	Lord Jesus Christ and the e
2Ti	2:10	things for the sake of the e,
Tit	1: 1	to the faith of God's e and
1Pe	1: 2	e according to the
1Pe	2: 6	A chief cornerstone, e,
2Jn	1	To the e lady and her
2Jn	13	The children of your e sister

ELECT'S (see ELECT)

Matt	24:22	but for the e sake those

ELECTION† (see ELECT)

Rom	9:11	of God according to e might
Rom	11: 5	a remnant according to the e
Rom	11:28	but concerning the e they
1Th	1: 4	your e by God.
2Pe	1:10	to make your call and e

ELEMENTS

Gal	4: 9	to the weak and beggarly e,
2Pe	3:10	and the e will melt with

ELEVATION

Ps	48: 2	Beautiful in e,

ELEVEN (see ELEVENTH)

Gen	32:22	and his e sons, and crossed
Gen	37: 9	and the e stars bowed down
Matt	28:16	Then the e disciples went

ELEVENTH (see ELEVEN)

Matt	20: 6	And about the e hour he went

ELI (see ELOI)

1Sa	1: 3	Also the two sons of E,
1Sa	1: 9	Now E the priest was sitting
Matt	27:46	"E, Eli, lama sabachthani?"

ELIEZER

Gen	15: 2	the heir of my house is E
1Ch	23:15	of Moses were Gershon and E.

ELIHU

Job	32: 4	E had waited to speak to

ELIJAH

1Ki	17: 1	And E the Tishbite, of the
1Ki	17:23	And E said, "See, your son
1Ki	18:16	him; and Ahab went to meet E.
1Ki	18:25	Now E said to the prophets
1Ki	18:31	And E took twelve stones,
1Ki	18:46	of the LORD came upon E;
1Ki	19:20	the oxen and ran after E,
2Ki	1:13	fell on his knees before E,
2Ki	1:15	angel of the LORD said to E,

2Ki	2: 1	that E went with Elisha from
2Ki	2: 2	Then E said to Elisha, "Stay
2Ki	2: 8	Now E took his mantle, rolled
2Ki	2:11	and E went up by a whirlwind
2Ki	2:13	also took up the mantle of E
2Ki	2:14	Then he took the mantle of E
2Ki	2:14	is the LORD God of E?
2Ki	2:15	The spirit of E rests on
2Ki	9:36	He spoke by His servant E
Mal	4: 5	I will send you E the
Matt	11:14	he is E who is to come.
Matt	16:14	John the Baptist, some E,
Matt	17: 3	Moses and E appeared to
Matt	17: 4	one for Moses, and one for E.
Matt	17:10	do the scribes say that E
Matt	17:12	But I say to you that E has
Matt	27:47	This Man is calling for E!"
Mark	6:15	Others said, "It is E.
Luke	1:17	in the spirit and power of E,
Luke	4:25	in Israel in the days of E,
Luke	9:54	just as E did?"
John	1:21	him, "What then? Are you E?
John	1:25	are not the Christ, nor E,
Rom	11: 2	what the Scripture says of E,
Jas	5:17	E was a man with a nature

ELIM

Ex	15:27	Then they came to E,
Num	33: 9	from Marah and came to E.

ELIPHAZ

Job	4: 1	Then E the Temanite answered

ELISHA

1Ki	19:16	And E the son of Shaphat of
2Ki	2: 2	Then Elijah said to E,
2Ki	2:15	spirit of Elijah rests on E.
2Ki	5: 8	when E the man of God heard
Luke	4:27	in Israel in the time of E

ELIZABETH

Luke	1: 7	because E was barren, and

ELOI (see ELI)

Mark	15:34	"E, Eloi, lama sabachthani?"

ELOQUENT†

Ex	4:10	"O my Lord, I am not e,
Acts	18:24	an e man and mighty in the

EMBRACE (see EMBRACED, EMBRACES, EMBRACING)

Gen	16: 5	I gave my maid into your e;
Eccl	3: 5	gather stones; A time to e,

EMBRACED (see EMBRACE)

Gen	29:13	and e him and kissed him,
1Ki	9: 9	and have e other gods, and
Acts	20: 1	e them, and departed to go
Heb	11:13	e them and confessed that

EMBRACES† (see EMBRACE)

Song	2: 6	And his right hand e me.
Song	8: 3	And his right hand e me.

EMBRACING† (see EMBRACE)

Eccl	3: 5	a time to refrain from e;
Acts	20:10	and e him said, "Do not

EMMAUS†

Luke	24:13	day to a village called E,

EMPTY (see EMPTY-HANDED, VAIN)

Gen	37:24	a pit. And the pit was e;
Gen	41:27	and the seven e heads
Ex	23:15	shall appear before Me e);
Judg	7:16	with e pitchers, and torches
Ruth	1:21	has brought me home again e.
Job	11: 3	Should your e talk make men
Job	21:34	can you comfort me with e
Job	22: 9	You have sent widows away e,
Job	26: 7	out the north over e space;
Is	24: 1	the LORD makes the earth e
Is	29: 8	and his soul is still e;
Matt	12:44	he comes, he finds it e,
Luke	1:53	the rich He has sent away e.
1Co	15:14	then our preaching is e and
1Co	15:14	and your faith is also e.
Eph	5: 6	no one deceive you with e
Col	2: 8	you through philosophy and e

EMPTY-HANDED (see EMPTY)

Ex	3:21	go, that you shall not go e.
Ex	34:20	shall appear before Me e.
Ruth	3:17	Do not go e to your
Mark	12: 3	him and sent him away e.

EN DOR

1Sa	28: 7	a woman who is a medium a E

EN GEDI

1Sa	23:29	and dwelt in strongholds at E

ENABLED†

1Ti	1:12	Jesus our Lord who has e me,

ENCOURAGE (see ENCOURAGED, ENCOURAGEMENT)

Deut	3:28	and e him and strengthen
2Sa	11:25	So e him."
1Th	3: 2	to establish you and e you

ENCOURAGED (see ENCOURAGE)

Acts	16:40	they e them and departed.
Acts	20: 2	gone over that region and e
Acts	27:36	Then they were all e,
Rom	1:12	that I may be e together
1Co	14:31	may learn and all may be e.
Phil	2:19	that I also may be e when I
Col	2: 2	that their hearts may be e,

ENCOURAGEMENT (see ENCOURAGE)

2Ch	30:22	And Hezekiah gave e to all
Acts	4:36	is translated Son of E),
Acts	15:31	it, they rejoiced over its e.

END (see ENDED, ENDLESS, ENDS)

Gen	6:13	The e of all flesh has come

Gen	8: 6	at the e of forty days, that
Gen	41: 1	at the e of two full years,
Ex	23:16	of Ingathering at the e of
Ex	25:19	other cherub at the other e;
Deut	8:16	you, to do you good in the e—
Job	8: 7	Yet your latter e would
Job	16: 3	words of wind have an e?
Job	22: 5	And your iniquity without e?
Job	28: 3	Man puts an e to darkness,
Ps	7: 9	of the wicked come to an e,
Ps	19: 4	And their words to the e of
Ps	19: 6	its circuit to the other e;
Ps	39: 4	make me to know my e,
Ps	73:17	Then I understood their e.
Ps	102:27	Your years will have no e.
Ps	107:27	And are at their wits' e.
Ps	119:112	Forever, to the very e.
Prov	5: 4	But in the e she is bitter
Prov	14:12	But its e is the way of
Prov	14:13	And the e of mirth may be
Prov	16:25	But its e is the way of
Prov	25: 8	what will you do in the e,
Eccl	3:11	God does from beginning to e.
Eccl	4: 8	Yet there is no e to all
Eccl	12:12	many books there is no e,
Is	7: 3	at the e of the aqueduct
Is	9: 7	peace There will be no e,
Is	46:10	Declaring the e from the
Is	48:20	Utter it to the e of the
Jer	3: 5	Will He keep it to the e?
Jer	4:27	I will not make a full e.
Jer	5:31	what will you do in the e?
Jer	51:13	Your e has come, The
Ezek	22: 4	and have come to the e of
Dan	1:15	And at the e of ten days
Dan	6:26	shall endure to the e.
Dan	7:28	This is the e of the
Dan	8:17	refers to the time of the e.
Dan	8:19	at the appointed time the e
Dan	9:24	To make an e of sins, To
Dan	9:26	And till the e of the war
Dan	9:27	week He shall bring an e
Dan	11:35	until the time of the e;
Dan	11:40	At the time of the e the
Dan	12: 4	book until the time of the e;
Dan	12: 8	what shall be the e of
Dan	12: 9	till the time of the e.
Dan	12:13	go your way till the e;
Dan	12:13	to your inheritance at the e
Hos	1: 4	And bring an e to the
Matt	10:22	But he who endures to the e
Matt	13:39	the harvest is the e of the
Matt	24: 6	but the e is not yet.
Matt	24:14	and then the e will come.
Matt	24:31	from one e of heaven to the
Matt	28:20	even to the e of the age."
Mark	3:26	cannot stand, but has an e.
Luke	1:33	kingdom there will be no e.
Luke	21: 9	but the e will not come
John	13: 1	He loved them to the e.
Acts	1: 8	and to the e of the earth."
Rom	6:21	For the e of those things
Rom	10: 4	For Christ is the e of the
Heb	7: 3	beginning of days nor e of

1Pe	4: 7	But the e of all things is
1Pe	4:17	what will be the e of those
2Pe	2:20	the latter e is worse for
Rev	1: 8	the Beginning and the E,
Rev	21: 6	the Beginning and the E.
Rev	22:13	the Beginning and the E,

ENDEAVORING†

Eph	4: 3	e to keep the unity of the

ENDED (see END)

Gen	2: 2	And on the seventh day God e
Is	40: 2	her, That her warfare is e,
Jer	8:20	is past, The summer is e,

ENDLESS† (see END)

1Ti	1: 4	give heed to fables and e
Heb	7:16	to the power of an e life.

ENDS (see END)

Ps	2: 8	And the e of the earth for
Ps	22:27	All the e of the world
Matt	12:42	for she came from the e of
1Co	10:11	upon whom the e of the ages

ENDUED†

Luke	24:49	of Jerusalem until you are e

ENDURANCE (see ENDURE)

Heb	12: 1	and let us run with e the

ENDURE (see ENDURANCE, ENDURED, ENDURES, ENDURING)

Ps	9: 7	But the LORD shall e
Ps	30: 5	Weeping may e for a night,
Ps	72: 5	long as the sun and moon e,
Ps	72:17	His name shall e forever;
Ps	102:26	will perish, but You will e;
Is	1:13	I cannot e iniquity and the
Dan	6:26	And His dominion shall e
Mal	3: 2	But who can e the day of His
1Co	9:12	but e all things lest we
1Th	3: 1	when we could no longer e it,
2Th	1: 4	and tribulations that you e,
2Ti	2: 3	You therefore must e hardship
2Ti	2:12	we e, We shall also reign
2Ti	4: 3	come when they will not e
2Ti	4: 5	e afflictions, do the work
Heb	12: 7	If you e chastening, God
Jas	5:11	we count them blessed who e.

ENDURED (see ENDURE)

2Ti	3:11	Lystra—what persecutions I e.
Heb	6:15	so, after he had patiently e,
Heb	10:32	you e a great struggle with
Heb	11:27	for he e as seeing Him who
Heb	12: 2	that was set before Him e
Heb	12: 3	For consider Him who e such

ENDURES (see ENDURE)

1Ch	16:34	is good! For His mercy e
Ps	52: 1	The goodness of God e
Ps	100: 5	And His truth e to all
Ps	106: 1	is good! For His mercy e

E

Ps	111: 3	And His righteousness e
Ps	111:10	His praise e forever.
Ps	117: 2	the truth of the LORD e
Ps	119:90	Your faithfulness e to all
Ps	119:160	Your righteous judgments e
Ps	136: 1	is good! For His mercy e
Ps	145:13	And Your dominion e
Matt	10:22	But he who e to the end will
John	6:27	but for the food which e to
1Co	13: 7	all things, e all things.
Jas	1:12	Blessed is the man who e
1Pe	1:25	word of the LORD e
1Pe	2:19	conscience toward God one e

ENDURING (*see* ENDURE)

1Sa	25:28	make for my lord an e house,
Ps	19: 9	e forever; The judgments of
Prov	8:18	E riches and righteousness.
Heb	10:34	you have a better and an e

ENEMIES (*see* ENEMY)

Gen	14:20	Who has delivered your e
Gen	22:17	possess the gate of their e.
Num	10: 9	will be saved from your e.
Judg	5:31	Thus let all Your e perish, O
2Sa	7:11	you to rest from all your e.
2Sa	19: 6	in that you love your e and
Job	19:11	counts me as one of His e.
Ps	18: 3	shall I be saved from my e.
Ps	23: 5	me in the presence of my e;
Ps	25: 2	Let not my e triumph over
Ps	27: 2	My e and foes, They
Ps	31:11	am a reproach among all my e,
Ps	35:19	me who are wrongfully my e;
Ps	37:20	And the e of the LORD,
Ps	38:19	But my e are vigorous, and
Ps	41: 5	My e speak evil of me:
Ps	42:10	My e reproach me, While
Ps	54: 5	He will repay my e for their
Ps	54: 7	seen its desire upon my e.
Ps	56: 2	My e would hound me all
Ps	59:10	me see my desire on my e.
Ps	60:12	who shall tread down our e.
Ps	71:10	For my e speak against me;
Ps	72: 9	And His e will lick the
Ps	78:53	the sea overwhelmed their e.
Ps	78:66	And He beat back His e;
Ps	80: 6	And our e laugh among
Ps	89:10	You have scattered Your e
Ps	89:42	You have made all his e
Ps	92: 9	For behold, Your e,
Ps	92: 9	Your e shall perish; All
Ps	106:11	The waters covered their e;
Ps	110: 1	Till I make Your e Your
Ps	110: 2	in the midst of Your e!
Ps	139:20	Your e take Your name in
Ps	139:22	hatred; I count them my e.
Prov	16: 7	He makes even his e to be
Is	1:24	And take vengeance on My e.
Is	59:18	Recompense to His e;
Matt	5:44	I say to you, love your e,
Mark	12:36	Till I make Your e
Luke	1:71	should be saved from our e
Luke	6:27	to you who hear: Love your e,

Rom	5:10	For if when we were e we were
Rom	11:28	the gospel they are e for
1Co	15:25	reign till He has put all e
Heb	1:13	Till I make Your e
Rev	11: 5	mouth and devours their e.

ENEMY (*see* ENEMIES)

Ex	15: 6	has dashed the e in pieces.
1Sa	18:29	So Saul became David's e
1Sa	24: 4	I will deliver your e into
2Sa	22:18	me from my strong e,
1Ki	8:33	are defeated before an e
1Ki	8:37	when their e besieges them
1Ki	21:20	"Have you found me, O my e?
2Ch	26:13	help the king against the e.
Esth	7: 6	The adversary and e is this
Esth	8: 1	the e of the Jews. And
Job	13:24	And regard me as Your e?
Job	33:10	me, He counts me as His e;
Ps	8: 2	That You may silence the e
Ps	13: 2	How long will my e be
Ps	18:17	me from my strong e,
Ps	41:11	Because my e does not
Ps	42: 9	of the oppression of the e?
Ps	61: 3	A strong tower from the e.
Ps	64: 1	my life from fear of the e.
Ps	74:10	Will the e blaspheme Your
Ps	78:42	He redeemed them from the e,
Ps	89:22	The e shall not outwit him,
Prov	24:17	Do not rejoice when your e
Prov	25:21	If your e is hungry, give
Prov	27: 6	But the kisses of an e are
Lam	1: 5	into captivity before the e.
Lam	2: 5	The Lord was like an e.
Mic	7:10	Then she who is my e will
Matt	5:43	neighbor and hate your e.
Matt	13:25	his e came and sowed tares
Luke	10:19	over all the power of the e,
Acts	13:10	you e of all righteousness,
Rom	12:20	If your e is hungry,
1Co	15:26	The last e that will be
2Th	3:15	do not count him as an e,
Jas	4: 4	world makes himself an e of

ENJOY

2Ti	6:17	us richly all things to e.

ENLARGE

Gen	9:27	May God e Japheth, And may
Is	54: 2	E the place of your tent,

ENLIGHTENED (*see* ENLIGHTENING)

Eph	1:18	your understanding being e;
Heb	6: 4	for those who were once e,

ENLIGHTENING† (*see* ENLIGHTENED)

Ps	19: 8	LORD is pure, e the eyes;

ENLISTED†

2Ti	2: 4	he may please him who e him

ENMITY

Gen	3:15	And I will put e Between
Rom	8: 7	the carnal mind is e

Eph	2:15	abolished in His flesh the **e**,
Eph	2:16	putting to death the **e**.
Jas	4: 4	with the world is **e** with

ENOCH

Gen	5:24	And **E** walked with God; and he
1Ch	1: 3	**E**, Methuselah, Lamech,
Heb	11: 5	By faith **E** was taken away so
Jude	14	**E**, the seventh from Adam,

ENTER (see ENTERED, ENTERING, ENTERS)

Deut	29:12	that you may **e** into covenant
Ps	95:11	They shall not **e** My rest.'"
Ps	100: 4	**E** into His gates with
Dan	11:41	He shall also **e** the Glorious
Joel	2: 9	They **e** at the windows like
Jon	3: 4	And Jonah began to **e** the city
Matt	5:20	you will by no means **e** the
Matt	7:13	**E** by the narrow gate; for
Matt	7:21	shall **e** the kingdom of
Matt	10: 5	and do not **e** a city of the
Matt	12:45	and they **e** and dwell there;
Matt	18: 9	It is better for you to **e**
Matt	19:23	is hard for a rich man to **e**
Matt	19:24	than for a rich man to **e**
Matt	25:21	**E** into the joy of your
Matt	26:41	lest you **e** into temptation.
Mark	1:45	could no longer openly **e**
Mark	3:27	No one can **e** a strong man's
Mark	5:12	that we may **e** them."
Mark	9:43	It is better for you to **e**
Mark	10:15	child will by no means **e** it.
Mark	13:15	nor **e** to take anything out
Luke	7: 6	not worthy that You should **e**
Luke	11:52	You did not **e** in yourselves,
Luke	24:26	these things and to **e** into
John	3: 4	Can he **e** a second time into
John	3: 5	he cannot **e** the kingdom of
John	10: 1	he who does not **e** the
Heb	3:11	They shall not **e** My
Heb	3:19	we see that they could not **e**
Heb	4: 6	was first preached did not **e**
Heb	10:19	having boldness to **e** the
Rev	21:27	there shall by no means **e**
Rev	22:14	and may **e** through the gates

ENTERED (see ENTER)

Gen	7:13	sons with them, **e** the ark—
Gen	7:16	So those that **e**,
Ex	33: 9	when Moses **e** the tabernacle,
2Ch	15:12	Then they **e** into a covenant
Jer	34:10	who had **e** into the covenant,
Mark	1:21	on the Sabbath He **e** the
Mark	5:13	spirits went out and **e** the
Mark	5:40	and **e** where the child was
Mark	6:56	Wherever He **e** into villages,
Luke	1:40	and **e** the house of Zacharias
Luke	4:38	from the synagogue and **e**
Luke	8:30	because many demons had **e**
Luke	9:34	they were fearful as they **e**
Luke	22: 3	Then Satan **e** Judas, surnamed
John	4:38	and you have **e** into their
John	6:22	and that Jesus had not **e** the
John	18:33	Then Pilate **e** the Praetorium

Acts	3: 2	to ask alms from those who **e**
Acts	11: 8	or unclean has at any time **e**
Acts	16:40	went out of the prison and **e**
Acts	18:19	but he himself **e** the
Acts	23:16	he went and **e** the barracks
Rom	5:12	as through one man sin **e**
Rom	5:20	Moreover the law **e** that the
1Co	2: 9	Nor have **e** into the
Heb	4:10	For he who has **e** His rest has
Heb	6:20	where the forerunner has **e**
Heb	9:12	but with His own blood He **e**
Heb	9:24	For Christ has not **e** the holy

ENTERING (see ENTER)

Deut	23:20	in the land which you are **e**
Mark	4:19	desires for other things **e**
Mark	16: 5	And **e** the tomb, they saw a
Acts	8: 3	**e** every house, and dragging
Heb	4: 1	a promise remains of **e** His

ENTERS (see ENTER)

Num	4:30	everyone who **e** the service
Job	22: 4	And **e** into judgment with
Prov	2:10	When wisdom **e** your heart,
Matt	15:17	understand that whatever **e**
Mark	7:18	perceive that whatever **e** a
John	10: 2	But he who **e** by the door is
John	10: 9	If anyone **e** by Me, he will
Heb	6:19	and which **e** the Presence
Heb	9:25	as the high priest **e** the

ENTERTAIN† (see ENTERTAINED)

Heb	13: 2	Do not forget to **e** strangers,

ENTERTAINED (see ENTERTAIN)

Heb	13: 2	some have unwittingly **e**

ENTICE (see ENTICED)

Prov	1:10	if sinners **e** you, Do not

ENTICED (see ENTICE)

Jas	1:14	by his own desires and **e**.

ENTRANCE

Ps	119:130	The **e** of Your words gives

ENTREAT (see ENTREATED)

Ex	8: 8	**E** the LORD that He may take
Ruth	1:16	**E** me not to leave you, Or
1Ki	13: 6	Please **e** the favor of the
1Co	4:13	being defamed, we **e**.

ENTREATED (see ENTREAT)

Ex	8:30	went out from Pharaoh and **e**
Ezra	8:23	So we fasted and **e** our God
Ps	119:58	I **e** Your favor with my

ENTRUSTED†

1Co	9:17	I have been **e** with a
1Th	2: 4	been approved by God to be **e**
1Pe	5: 3	as being lords over those **e**

ENVIED (see ENVY)

Gen	30: 1	Rachel **e** her sister, and

E

Gen	37:11	And his brothers e him, but
Ps	106:16	When they e Moses in the
Eccl	4: 4	skillful work a man is e by

ENVIOUS (*see* ENVY)

Ps	37: 1	Nor be e of the workers of
Ps	73: 3	For I was e of the
Prov	24: 1	Do not be e of evil men,
Prov	24:19	Nor be e of the wicked;
Acts	7: 9	the patriarchs, becoming e,

ENVY (*see* ENVIED, ENVIOUS, ENVYING)

Ps	68:16	Why do you fume with e,
Prov	3:31	Do not e the oppressor,
Prov	14:30	But e is rottenness to the
Prov	23:17	Do not let your heart e
Matt	27:18	handed Him over because of e.
Acts	13:45	they were filled with e;
Rom	1:29	maliciousness; full of e,
Rom	13:13	lust, not in strife and e.
1Co	13: 4	is kind; love does not e;
Gal	5:21	e, murders, drunkenness,
Phil	1:15	preach Christ even from e
Tit	3: 3	living in malice and e,
Jas	3:14	But if you have bitter e and
1Pe	2: 1	all deceit, hypocrisy, e,

ENVYING† (*see* ENVY)

Gal	5:26	e one another.

EPAPHRAS

Col	4:12	E, who is one of you,
Phm	1:23	E, my fellow prisoner in

EPAPHRODITUS†

Phil	2:25	necessary to send to you E,
Phil	4:18	having received from E the

EPHESIANS (*see* EPHESUS)

Acts	19:28	Great is Diana of the E!"

EPHESUS (*see* EPHESIANS)

Acts	19:17	and Greeks dwelling in E;
Eph	1: 1	To the saints who are in E,
1Ti	1: 3	remain in E that you may
2Ti	1:18	he ministered to me at E.
Rev	1:11	which are in Asia: to E,
Rev	2: 1	the angel of the church of E

EPHOD

Ex	25: 7	stones to be set in the e
Ex	28: 4	make: a breastplate, an e,
Lev	8: 7	and with it tied the e on
Judg	8:27	Gideon made it into an e
1Sa	2:18	a child, wearing a linen e.
2Sa	6:14	David was wearing a linen e.
Hos	3: 4	without e or teraphim.

EPHPHATHA†

Mark	7:34	sighed, and said to him, "E,

EPHRAIM

Gen	41:52	of the second he called E:
Gen	46:20	were born Manasseh and E,

Num	1:32	of Joseph, the children of E,
Deut	34: 2	Naphtali and the land of E
Josh	17:15	since the mountains of E are
2Sa	18: 6	battle was in the woods of E.
2Ki	14:13	from the Gate of E to the
2Ch	31: 1	all Judah, Benjamin, E,
Is	7: 5	'Because Syria, E,
Is	7: 8	Within sixty-five years E
Is	7: 9	The head of E is Samaria,
Jer	31: 9	And E is My firstborn.
Jer	31:20	Is E My dear son? Is he
Ezek	37:16	'For Joseph, the stick of E,
Hos	4:17	E is joined to idols, Let
Hos	7: 8	E is a cake unturned.
Hos	7:11	E also is like a silly dove,
Hos	11: 8	"How can I give you up, E?
Hos	11: 9	I will not again destroy E.
Hos	12: 1	E feeds on the wind, And

EPHRATHAH

Mic	5: 2	"But you, Bethlehem E,

EPICUREAN†

Acts	17:18	Then certain E and Stoic

EPISTLE (*see* EPISTLES)

Rom	16:22	Tertius, who wrote this e,
1Co	5: 9	I wrote to you in my e not
2Co	3: 2	You are our e written in our
2Co	3: 3	clearly you are an e of
Col	4:16	Now when this e is read
Col	4:16	that you likewise read the e
1Th	5:27	you by the Lord that this e
2Th	2:15	whether by word or our e.
2Pe	3: 1	write to you this second e

EPISTLES† (*see* EPISTLE)

2Co	3: 1	e of commendation to you or
2Pe	3:16	as also in all his e,

EQUAL (*see* EQUITY, UNEQUALLY)

Deut	18: 8	They shall have e portions to
Job	28:17	gold nor crystal can e it,
Ps	55:13	it was you, a man my e,
Is	40:25	Or to whom shall I be e?
Is	46: 5	and make Me e And compare
Luke	20:36	for they are e to the angels
John	5:18	making Himself e with God.
Phil	2: 6	consider it robbery to be e
Rev	21:16	breadth, and height are e.

EQUIPPED† (*see* EQUIPPING)

1Ch	12:23	the divisions that were e
2Ti	3:17	thoroughly e for every good

EQUIPPING† (*see* EQUIPPED)

Eph	4:12	for the e of the saints for

EQUITY (*see* EQUAL)

Ps	98: 9	And the peoples with e.
Ps	99: 4	You have established e;
Prov	1: 3	Justice, judgment, and e;
Is	11: 4	And decide with e for the
Mal	2: 6	with Me in peace and e,

ERROR (*see* ERRORS)

Job	4:18	He charges His angels with **e**,
Jas	5:20	turns a sinner from the **e**
1Jn	4: 6	of truth and the spirit of **e**.

ERRORS (*see* ERROR)

Ps	19:12	Who can understand his **e**?

ESAU (*see* EDOM)

Gen	25:25	so they called his name **E**.
Gen	25:27	And **E** was a skillful hunter,
Gen	25:28	And Isaac loved **E** because he
Gen	25:34	Thus **E** despised his
Gen	27:11	**E** my brother is a hairy
Gen	27:22	hands are the hands of **E**.
Mal	1: 3	But **E** I have hated, And
Rom	9:13	but **E** I have hated."
Heb	12:16	or profane person like **E**,

ESCAPE (*see* ESCAPED)

Gen	19:17	'**E** for your life! Do not look
Matt	23:33	of vipers! How can you **e**
Luke	21:36	may be counted worthy to **e**
Rom	2: 3	that you will **e** the judgment
1Co	10:13	will also make the way of **e**,
Heb	2: 3	how shall we **e** if we neglect
Heb	12:25	more shall we not **e** if

ESCAPED (*see* ESCAPE)

Job	1:15	and I alone have **e** to tell
Job	19:20	And I have **e** by the skin of
John	10:39	but He **e** out of their hand.
Acts	28: 4	though he has **e** the sea, yet
2Co	11:33	and **e** from his hands.
Heb	11:34	**e** the edge of the sword, out
2Pe	1: 4	having **e** the corruption
2Pe	2:20	after they have **e** the

ESHCOL

Num	13:24	was called the Valley of **E**,

ESPECIALLY

1Ti	4:10	**e** of those who believe.
2Ti	4:13	**e** the parchments.

ESTABLISH (*see* ESTABLISHED, ESTABLISHES)

Gen	6:18	But I will **e** My covenant with
Gen	9: 9	I **e** My covenant with you and
Gen	17: 7	And I will **e** My covenant
2Sa	7:12	and I will **e** his kingdom.
2Sa	7:13	and I will **e** the throne of
2Sa	7:25	**e** it forever and do as You
Ps	48: 8	God will **e** it forever.
Ps	87: 5	Most High Himself shall **e**
Ps	89: 4	Your seed I will **e** forever,
Ps	90:17	**e** the work of our hands.
Is	9: 7	To order it and **e** it with
Is	26:12	You will **e** peace for us,
Jer	33: 2	LORD who formed it to **e** it
Ezek	34:23	I will **e** one shepherd over
Dan	6: 8	**e** the decree and sign the
Amos	5:15	**E** justice in the gate. It
Rom	3:31	the contrary, we **e** the law.

Rom	10: 3	and seeking to **e** their own
Rom	16:25	to Him who is able to **e** you
1Th	3: 2	to **e** you and encourage you
1Th	3:13	so that He may **e** your hearts
2Th	2:17	comfort your hearts and **e** you
2Th	3: 3	who will **e** you and guard
Heb	10: 9	the first that He may **e** the
1Pe	5:10	suffered a while, perfect, **e**,

ESTABLISHED (*see* CONFIRMED, ESTABLISH, MADE)

Gen	9:17	the covenant which I have **e**
Gen	41:32	because the thing is **e** by
Ex	6: 4	I have also **e** My covenant
Ex	15:17	which Your hands have **e**.
Deut	19:15	the matter shall be **e**.
Deut	32: 6	Has He not made you and **e**
1Sa	3:20	that Samuel had been **e** as
1Sa	13:13	now the LORD would have **e**
2Sa	7:16	Your throne shall be **e**
2Sa	7:26	of Your servant David be **e**
1Ki	2:12	and his kingdom was firmly **e**.
1Ki	2:24	and who has **e** a house for
1Ch	16:30	The world also is firmly **e**,
1Ch	17:14	and his throne shall be **e**
1Ch	17:24	of Your servant David be **e**
2Ch	12: 1	when Rehoboam had **e** the
2Ch	23:18	as it was **e** by David.
Ps	24: 2	And **e** it upon the waters.
Ps	40: 2	And **e** my steps.
Ps	78: 5	For He **e** a testimony in
Ps	81: 5	This He **e** in Joseph as a
Ps	93: 2	Your throne is **e** from of
Ps	96:10	The world also is firmly **e**,
Ps	103:19	The LORD has **e** His throne
Ps	119:90	You **e** the earth, and it
Prov	8:23	I have been **e** from
Is	2: 2	LORD's house Shall be **e**
Is	7: 9	Surely you shall not be **e**.
Is	42: 4	Till He has **e** justice in
Is	45:18	Who has **e** it, Who did not
Mic	4: 1	LORD's house Shall be **e**
Matt	18:16	every word may be **e**.
Col	2: 7	and built up in Him and **e**

ESTABLISHES (*see* ESTABLISH)

Prov	29: 4	The king **e** the land by
Hab	2:12	Who **e** a city by iniquity!

ESTEEM (*see* ESTEEMED, ESTEEMING, ESTEEMS)

Is	53: 3	and we did not **e** Him.
Phil	2: 3	of mind let each **e** others

ESTEEMED (*see* ESTEEM)

Is	53: 4	Yet we **e** Him stricken,

ESTEEMING† (*see* ESTEEM)

Heb	11:26	**e** the reproach of Christ

ESTEEMS† (*see* ESTEEM)

Rom	14: 5	One person **e** one day above
Rom	14: 5	another **e** every day alike.

ESTHER

Esth	2: 7	up Hadassah, that is, E,
Esth	5: 3	"What do you wish, Queen E?

ESTRANGED

Job	19:13	are completely e from me.
Ps	58: 3	The wicked are e from the
Gal	5: 4	You have become e from

ETERNAL (see ETERNITY, EVERLASTING)

Deut	33:27	The e God is your refuge,
Eccl	12: 5	For man goes to his e home,
Matt	19:16	I do that I may have e life?
Mark	10:30	in the age to come, e life.
Luke	10:25	what shall I do to inherit e
John	3:15	not perish but have e life.
John	6:54	and drinks My blood has e
John	10:28	And I give them e life, and
John	17: 2	that He should give e life
John	17: 3	And this is e life, that they
Acts	13:48	as had been appointed to e
Rom	1:20	even His e power and
Rom	6:23	but the gift of God is e
2Co	4:17	a far more exceeding and e
2Co	5: 1	e in the heavens.
Eph	3:11	according to the e purpose
1Ti	1:17	Now to the King e,
Tit	1: 2	in hope of e life which God,
Heb	5: 9	He became the author of e
Heb	6: 2	and of e judgment.
Heb	9:14	who through the e Spirit
1Pe	5:10	who called us to His e glory
1Jn	1: 2	and declare to you that e
1Jn	5:13	you may know that you have e
1Jn	5:20	This is the true God and e
Jude	7	the vengeance of e fire.
Jude	21	our Lord Jesus Christ unto e

ETERNITY† (see ETERNAL)

Eccl	3:11	Also He has put e in their
Is	57:15	Lofty One Who inhabits e,
Acts	15:18	Known to God from e are all

ETHIOPIA (see CUSH, ETHIOPIAN)

Esth	1: 1	provinces, from India to E),
Ps	68:31	E will quickly stretch out
Is	18: 1	is beyond the rivers of E,
Acts	8:27	went. And behold, a man of E,

ETHIOPIAN (see ETHIOPIA, ETHIOPIANS)

Num	12: 1	for he had married an E
Jer	13:23	Can the E change his skin or

ETHIOPIANS (see ETHIOPIAN)

Acts	8:27	Candace the queen of the E,

EUNICE†

2Ti	1: 5	Lois and your mother E,

EUNUCH (see EUNUCHS)

Acts	8:34	So the e answered Philip and

EUNUCHS (see EUNUCH)

Dan	1: 7	To them the chief of the e
Matt	19:12	For there are e who were born

EUPHRATES

Gen	2:14	The fourth river is the E.
Gen	15:18	the great river, the River E—
2Ki	24: 7	of Egypt to the River E.
2Ch	35:20	against Carchemish by the E;
Rev	9:14	bound at the great river E.

EUTYCHUS†

Acts	20: 9	a certain young man named E,

EVANGELIST† (see EVANGELISTS)

Acts	21: 8	the house of Philip the e,
2Ti	4: 5	do the work of an e,

EVANGELISTS† (see EVANGELIST)

Eph	4:11	some prophets, some e,

EVE†

Gen	3:20	called his wife's name E,
Gen	4: 1	Now Adam knew E his wife, and
2Co	11: 3	as the serpent deceived E by
1Ti	2:13	was formed first, then E.

EVENING

Gen	1: 5	So the e and the morning
Ps	104:23	to his labor until the e.

EVER (see ALWAYS)

Ex	15:18	shall reign forever and e.
Ps	10:16	LORD is King forever and e;
Ps	45: 6	O God, is forever and e;
Ps	90: 2	Or e You had formed the
Ps	145: 1	Your name forever and e.
Prov	4:18	That shines e brighter unto
Dan	7:18	forever, even forever and e.
Dan	12: 3	the stars forever and e.
John	4:39	He told me all that I e
John	7:46	No man e spoke like this
Gal	1: 5	whom be glory forever and e.
Heb	1: 8	God, is forever and e;
Rev	4: 9	who lives forever and e,
Rev	11:15	He shall reign forever and e!

EVERLASTING (see ETERNAL)

Gen	9:16	look on it to remember the e
Gen	17: 7	for an e covenant, to be God
Gen	21:33	of the LORD, the E God.
Num	25:13	after him a covenant of an e
Deut	33:27	And underneath are the e
Ps	24: 7	you e doors! And the King
Ps	90: 2	Even from e to everlasting,
Ps	93: 2	of old; You are from e.
Ps	100: 5	is good; His mercy is e,
Ps	103:17	of the LORD is from e to
Ps	139:24	And lead me in the way e.
Ps	145:13	Your kingdom is an e
Is	9: 6	E Father, Prince of Peace.
Is	24: 5	Broken the e covenant.
Is	35:10	With e joy on their heads.

Is	40:28	The **e** God, the LORD, The
Is	54: 8	But with **e** kindness I will
Is	55:13	For an **e** sign that shall
Is	56: 5	I will give them an **e** name
Is	61: 7	**E** joy shall be theirs.
Is	63:16	Our Redeemer from **E** is
Jer	31: 3	I have loved you with an **e**
Dan	4: 3	His kingdom is an **e**
Dan	9:24	To bring in **e**
Dan	12: 2	Some to **e** life, Some to
Dan	12: 2	Some to shame and **e**
Mic	5: 2	are from of old, From **e**.
Matt	18: 8	to be cast into the **e** fire.
Matt	25:41	into the **e** fire prepared for
Matt	25:46	these will go away into **e**
John	3:16	not perish but have **e** life.
John	3:36	believes in the Son has **e**
John	4:14	of water springing up into **e**
Rom	6:22	and the end, **e** life.
Rom	16:26	to the commandment of the **e**
2Th	1: 9	shall be punished with **e**
1Ti	6:16	to whom be honor and **e**
Heb	13:20	through the blood of the **e**
2Pe	1:11	to you abundantly into the **e**
Jude	6	He has reserved in **e** chains
Rev	14: 6	having the **e** gospel to

EVIDENCE (see EVIDENT)

Heb	11: 1	the **e** of things not seen.

EVIDENT (see EVIDENCE)

Gal	5:19	the works of the flesh are **e**,
1Ti	5:24	men's sins are clearly **e**,
Heb	7:14	For it is **e** that our Lord

EVIL (see EVILDOER, EVILDOERS, EVILS, WICKED)

Gen	2: 9	the knowledge of good and **e**.
Gen	6: 5	of his heart was only **e**
Gen	8:21	of man's heart is **e** from
Gen	48:16	has redeemed me from all **e**,
Gen	50:20	you meant **e** against me; but
Deut	1:39	no knowledge of good and **e**,
Deut	30:15	life and good, death and **e**,
2Sa	14:17	in discerning good and **e**.
1Ki	11: 6	Solomon did **e** in the sight of
Job	1: 1	who feared God and shunned **e**.
Job	28:28	And to depart from **e** is
Ps	23: 4	of death, I will fear no **e**;
Ps	34:13	Keep your tongue from **e**,
Ps	34:14	Depart from **e** and do good;
Ps	38:20	Those also who render **e** for
Ps	51: 4	And done this **e** in Your
Ps	91:10	No **e** shall befall you, Nor
Ps	121: 7	preserve you from all **e**;
Prov	6:24	To keep you from the **e**
Prov	16:17	upright is to depart from **e**;
Prov	24: 1	Do not be envious of **e** men,
Prov	28:22	A man with an **e** eye hastens
Prov	31:12	She does him good and not **e**
Eccl	2:21	is vanity and a great **e**.
Eccl	12:14	thing, Whether good or **e**.
Is	1:16	My eyes. Cease to do **e**,
Is	5:20	call evil good, and good **e**;

Is	7:15	He may know to refuse the **e**
Jer	13:23	who are accustomed to do **e**.
Jer	18:20	Shall **e** be repaid for good?
Amos	5:13	For it is an **e** time.
Amos	5:14	Seek good and not **e**,
Amos	5:15	Hate **e**, love good;
Hab	1:13	purer eyes than to behold **e**,
Matt	5:11	and say all kinds of **e**
Matt	5:45	makes His sun rise on the **e**
Matt	6:13	But deliver us from the **e**
Matt	7:11	"If you then, being **e**,
Matt	9: 4	Why do you think **e** in your
Matt	12:35	evil treasure brings forth **e**
Matt	12:39	An **e** and adulterous
Matt	15:19	out of the heart proceed **e**
Matt	27:23	what **e** has He done?" But
Mark	3: 4	to do good or to do **e**,
Mark	7:21	proceed **e** thoughts,
Mark	7:22	an **e** eye, blasphemy, pride,
John	3:19	because their deeds were **e**.
Acts	23: 9	We find no **e** in this man; but
Rom	3: 8	Let us do **e** that good may
Rom	7: 8	in me all manner of **e**.
Rom	12: 9	hypocrisy. Abhor what is **e**.
Rom	12:17	Repay no one evil for **e**.
Rom	12:21	but overcome **e** with good.
1Co	13: 5	is not provoked, thinks no **e**;
1Co	15:33	**E** company corrupts good
Gal	1: 4	us from this present **e** age,
Eph	4:31	and **e** speaking be put away
Eph	5:16	time, because the days are **e**.
Eph	6:13	able to withstand in the **e**
1Th	5:15	no one renders evil for **e**
1Th	5:22	Abstain from every form of **e**.
1Ti	6:10	a root of all kinds of **e**,
2Ti	3:13	But **e** men and impostors will
Heb	3:12	there be in any of you an **e**
Heb	5:14	to discern both good and **e**.
Heb	10:22	hearts sprinkled from an **e**
Jas	1:13	God cannot be tempted by **e**,
Jas	3: 8	tongue. It is an unruly **e**,
Jas	4:11	speaks **e** of the law and
Jas	4:16	All such boasting is **e**.
1Pe	3: 9	not returning evil for **e** or
1Jn	3:12	Because his works were **e** and
3Jn	11	but he who does **e** has not
Rev	2: 2	cannot bear those who are **e**.

EVILDOER (see EVIL, EVILDOERS)

John	18:30	him, "If He were not an **e**,
2Ti	2: 9	I suffer trouble as an **e**,

EVILDOERS (see DOERS, EVILDOER)

Ps	37: 1	Do not fret because of **e**,
Prov	24:19	Do not fret because of **e**,
1Pe	2:12	they speak against you as **e**,

EVILS (see EVIL)

Jer	2:13	people have committed two **e**:

EWE

2Sa	12: 3	except one little **e** lamb

EXALT (see EXALTED, EXALTS, MAGNIFY)

Ps	34: 3	And let us e His name
Ps	137: 6	If I do not e Jerusalem
Is	14:13	I will e my throne above
Dan	8:25	And he shall e himself in
Dan	11:36	he shall e and magnify
1Pe	5: 6	that He may e you in due

EXALTED (see EXALT, MAGNIFIED)

Num	24: 7	And his kingdom shall be e.
1Sa	2: 1	My horn is e in the LORD.
2Sa	22:47	be my Rock! Let God be e,
Job	10:16	If my head is e,
Ps	18:46	God of my salvation be e.
Ps	46:10	I will be e in the earth!
Ps	57: 5	Be e, O God, above the
Ps	118:16	right hand of the LORD is e;
Ps	148:13	For His name alone is e;
Is	2: 2	And shall be e above the
Is	2:11	the LORD alone shall be e
Is	40: 4	Every valley shall be e And
Dan	8:11	He even e himself as high as
Matt	23:12	humbles himself will be e.
Acts	5:31	Him God has e to His right
2Co	12: 7	lest I be e above measure.
Phil	2: 9	God also has highly e Him

EXALTS (see EXALT)

Prov	14:34	Righteousness e a nation,
Matt	23:12	And whoever e himself will be

EXAMINE (see LOOK)

1Co	11:28	But let a man e himself,
Gal	6: 4	But let each one e his own

EXAMPLE (see EXAMPLES)

Matt	1:19	to make her a public e,
John	13:15	"For I have given you an e,
Phil	3:17	join in following my e,
1Ti	4:12	but be an e to the believers
Jas	5:10	as an e of suffering and
1Pe	2:21	for us, leaving us an e,

EXAMPLES (see EXAMPLE)

1Co	10:11	things happened to them as e,
1Th	1: 7	so that you became e to all
1Pe	5: 3	but being e to the flock;

EXCEEDING (see EXCEEDINGLY, EXCEEDS)

Ps	43: 4	To God my e joy; And on
Eph	1:19	and what is the e greatness
Jude	24	of His glory with e joy,

EXCEEDINGLY (see EXCEEDING)

Gen	15: 1	your e great reward."
Ps	21: 6	You have made him e glad
Prov	30:24	But they are e wise:
Jon	3: 3	Now Nineveh was an e great
Matt	2:10	they rejoiced with e great
Matt	5:12	Rejoice and be e glad, for
Matt	26:38	My soul is e sorrowful, even
Eph	3:20	to Him who is able to do e

EXCEEDS (see EXCEEDING)

Matt	5:20	unless your righteousness e

EXCEL

Prov	31:29	But you e them all."
1Co	14:12	church that you seek to e.

EXCELLENCE (see EXCELLENT)

Ex	15: 7	in the greatness of Your e
Ps	47: 4	The e of Jacob whom He
1Co	2: 1	did not come with e of
2Co	4: 7	that the e of the power may
Phil	3: 8	all things loss for the e

EXCELLENT (see EXCELLENCE)

Job	37:23	He is e in power, In
Ps	8: 1	How e is Your name in all
Ps	150: 2	Him according to His e
Prov	12: 4	An e wife is the crown of
Is	12: 5	For He has done e things;
Luke	1: 3	most e Theophilus,
Acts	23:26	to the most e governor
Rom	2:18	the things that are e,
1Co	12:31	And yet I show you a more e
Phil	1:10	the things that are e,
Heb	1: 4	obtained a more e name than
Heb	11: 4	Abel offered to God a more e
2Pe	1:17	voice came to Him from the E

EXCHANGE (see EXCHANGED)

Matt	16:26	Or what will a man give in e

EXCHANGED (see EXCHANGE)

Rom	1:25	who e the truth of God for
Rom	1:26	For even their women e the

EXCUSE (see EXCUSING)

John	15:22	but now they have no e for
Rom	1:20	so that they are without e,
2Co	12:19	do you think that we e

EXCUSING† (see EXCUSE)

Rom	2:15	thoughts accusing or else e

EXECUTE (see EXECUTED, EXECUTES)

Ex	12:12	the gods of Egypt I will e
Ezek	45: 9	e justice and righteousness,
Zech	7: 9	E true justice, Show mercy
John	5:27	has given Him authority to e
Rom	13: 4	an avenger to e wrath on
Jude	15	to e judgment on all, to

EXECUTED (see EXECUTE)

1Ki	18:40	to the Brook Kishon and e
Ps	99: 4	You have e justice and
Dan	5:19	Whomever he wished, he e;

EXECUTES (see EXECUTE)

Ps	103: 6	The LORD e righteousness
Ps	146: 7	Who e justice for the

EXERCISE

1Ki	21: 7	You now e authority over

Luke	22:25	and those who e authority
1Co	7: 9	but if they cannot e
1Ti	4: 7	and e yourself toward
1Ti	4: 8	For bodily e profits a

EXHORT (see EXHORTATION, EXHORTS)

1Th	4: 1	we urge and e in the Lord
1Ti	5: 1	but e him as a father,
1Ti	6: 2	Teach and e these things.
2Ti	4: 2	season. Convince, rebuke, e,
Tit	2: 6	Likewise e the young men to
Tit	2: 9	E bondservants to be
Heb	3:13	but e one another daily,
1Pe	5: 1	elders who are among you I e,

EXHORTATION (see EXHORT)

Acts	13:15	if you have any word of e
Rom	12: 8	he who exhorts, in e;
1Ti	4:13	attention to reading, to e,
Heb	13:22	bear with the word of e,

EXHORTS† (see EXHORT)

Rom	12: 8	he who e, in exhortation;

EXIST (see EXISTED)

Rom	4:17	those things which do not e
Rev	4:11	And by Your will they e and

EXISTED† (see EXIST)

Eccl	4: 3	both is he who has never e,
2Pe	3: 6	which the world that then e

EXPECT (see EXPECTATION, UNEXPECTEDLY)

Matt	24:44	at an hour you do not e.

EXPECTATION (see EXPECT)

Ps	62: 5	For my e is from Him.
Luke	3:15	Now as the people were in e,
Acts	12:11	of Herod and from all the e
Rom	8:19	For the earnest e of the
Phil	1:20	according to my earnest e and
Heb	10:27	but a certain fearful e of

EXPEDIENT†

John	11:50	do you consider that it is e
John	18:14	the Jews that it was e that

EXPLAIN (see EXPLAINED)

Gen	41:24	was no one who could e it
Deut	1: 5	Moses began to e this law,
Dan	4: 9	e to me the visions of my
Dan	5:16	give interpretations and e
Matt	13:36	E to us the parable of the
Heb	5:11	much to say, and hard to e,

EXPLAINED (see EXPLAIN)

Acts	18:26	they took him aside and e to

EXPOSED

John	3:20	lest his deeds should be e.

EXPOUNDED†

Luke	24:27	He e to them in all the

EXPRESS (see EXPRESSLY)

Heb	1: 3	of His glory and the e

EXPRESSLY (see EXPRESS)

1Ti	4: 1	Now the Spirit e says that in

EXTOL† (see EXTOLLED)

Ps	30: 1	I will e You, O LORD, for
Ps	68: 4	E Him who rides on the
Ps	145: 1	I will e You, my God, O
Dan	4:37	praise and e and honor the

EXTOLLED (see EXTOL)

Is	52:13	He shall be exalted and e

EYE (see EYELIDS, EYES, EYESERVICE)

Ex	21:24	e for eye, tooth for tooth,
Deut	7:16	your e shall have no pity on
Deut	15: 9	and your e be evil against
Deut	19:21	e for eye, tooth for tooth,
Deut	32:10	him as the apple of His e.
Job	7: 8	The e of him who sees me
Job	17: 7	My e has also grown dim
Job	20: 9	The e that saw him will
Job	24:15	No e will see me'; And he
Job	42: 5	But now my e sees You.
Ps	6: 7	My e wastes away because of
Ps	32: 8	I will guide you with My e.
Ps	33:18	the e of the LORD is on
Ps	54: 7	And my e has seen its
Ps	94: 9	hear? He who formed the e,
Prov	20:12	hearing ear and the seeing e,
Prov	28:22	A man with an evil e hastens
Eccl	1: 8	The e is not satisfied with
Is	52: 8	For they shall see e to eye
Lam	1:16	my e overflows with water;
Ezek	5:11	My e will not spare, nor
Matt	5:29	If your right e causes you to
Matt	6:22	lamp of the body is the e.
Matt	6:22	If therefore your e is good,
Matt	7: 3	speck in your brother's e,
Matt	7: 3	the plank in your own e?
Matt	18: 9	And if your e causes you to
Matt	18: 9	enter into life with one e,
Matt	19:24	a camel to go through the e
1Co	2: 9	E has not seen, nor ear
1Co	12:16	say, "Because I am not an e,
1Co	12:17	If the whole body were an e,
1Co	15:52	in the twinkling of an e,
Rev	1: 7	and every e will see Him,
Rev	3:18	and anoint your eyes with e

EYELIDS (see EYE)

Ps	132: 4	my eyes Or slumber to my e,
Prov	6:25	her allure you with her e.

EYES (see EYE)

Gen	3: 5	the day you eat of it your e
Gen	3: 6	it was pleasant to the e,
Gen	6: 8	Noah found grace in the e
Gen	13:14	Lift your e now and look from
Gen	27: 1	when Isaac was old and his e
Gen	29:17	Leah's e were delicate, but

E

Gen	39: 7	wife cast longing e on
Gen	46: 4	will put his hand on your e.
Ex	13: 9	as a memorial between your e,
Ex	13:16	as frontlets between your e,
Num	5:13	and it is hidden from the e
Num	22:31	the LORD opened Balaam's e,
Deut	3:27	east; behold it with your e,
Deut	6:22	and wonders before our e,
Deut	12: 8	is right in his own e—
Deut	28:65	a trembling heart, failing e,
Deut	34: 7	His e were not dim nor his
Josh	23:13	sides and thorns in your e,
Judg	16:21	took him and put out his e,
Judg	17: 6	was right in his own e.
Ruth	2:10	have I found favor in your e,
1Ki	16:25	Omri did evil in the e of the
2Ki	4:35	and the child opened his e.
2Ki	9:30	and she put paint on her e
2Ki	25: 7	put out the e of Zedekiah,
2Ch	16: 9	For the e of the LORD run to
Job	19:27	And my e shall behold, and
Job	31: 1	made a covenant with my e;
Job	32: 1	was righteous in his own e.
Ps	19: 8	is pure, enlightening the e;
Ps	25:15	My e are ever toward the
Ps	34:15	The e of the LORD are on
Ps	36: 1	no fear of God before his e.
Ps	36: 2	himself in his own e,
Ps	115: 5	E they have, but they do
Ps	116: 8	My e from tears, And my
Ps	118:23	It is marvelous in our e.
Ps	119:18	Open my e, that I may see
Ps	121: 1	I will lift up my e to the
Ps	139:16	Your e saw my substance,
Prov	3: 7	not be wise in your own e;
Prov	6:13	He winks with his e,
Prov	12:15	fool is right in his own e,
Prov	23:29	cause? Who has redness of e?
Is	5:21	are wise in their own e,
Is	6: 5	For my e have seen the
Is	6:10	Lest they see with their e,
Is	11: 3	judge by the sight of His e,
Is	33:17	Your e will see the King in
Is	42: 7	To open blind e,
Jer	7:11	a den of thieves in your e?
Jer	9: 1	And my e a fountain of
Lam	2:11	My e fail with tears, My
Ezek	24:21	boast, the desire of your e,
Ezek	24:25	glory, the desire of their e,
Dan	7:20	that horn which had e and a
Dan	8: 5	a notable horn between his e.
Hab	1:13	You are of purer e than to
Zech	8: 6	it also be marvelous in My e?
Matt	9:29	Then He touched their e,
Matt	9:30	And their e were opened. And
Matt	13:15	see with their e and
Matt	20:34	and touched their e.
Matt	20:34	And immediately their e
Matt	21:42	is marvelous in our e'?
Matt	26:43	for their e were heavy.
Mark	8:23	when He had spit on his e
Luke	2:30	For my e have seen Your
Luke	10:23	Blessed are the e which see
Luke	24:16	But their e were restrained,

Luke	24:31	Then their e were opened and
John	4:35	lift up your e and look at
John	9: 6	and He anointed the e of the
John	9:10	How were your e opened?"
John	9:11	made clay and anointed my e
John	9:32	of that anyone opened the e
John	12:40	He has blinded their e
John	12:40	should see with their e,
Acts	9: 8	and when his e were opened
Acts	9:18	there fell from his e
Rom	3:18	of God before their e.
Rom	11:10	Let their e be darkened,
Eph	1:18	the e of your understanding
Heb	4:13	naked and open to the e of
1Pe	3:12	For the e of the LORD
2Pe	2:14	having e full of adultery and
1Jn	1: 1	we have seen with our e,
1Jn	2:11	darkness has blinded his e.
1Jn	2:16	the flesh, the lust of the e,
Rev	1:14	and His e like a flame of
Rev	3:18	and anoint your e with eye
Rev	4: 6	living creatures full of e
Rev	5: 6	seven horns and seven e,
Rev	21: 4	away every tear from their e;

EYESERVICE † (see EYE)

Eph	6: 6	not with e,
Col	3:22	to the flesh, not with e,

EYEWITNESSES † (see WITNESS)

Luke	1: 2	from the beginning were e
2Pe	1:16	but were e of His majesty.

EZEKIEL †

Ezek	1: 3	LORD came expressly to E
Ezek	24:24	Thus E is a sign to you;

EZRA (see AZARIAH)

Ezra	7: 6	this E came up from Babylon;
Ezra	7:12	To E the priest, a scribe of

F

FABLES

1Ti	1: 4	nor give heed to f and
1Ti	4: 7	profane and old wives' f,
Tit	1:14	not giving heed to Jewish f
2Pe	1:16	follow cunningly devised f

FACE (see COUNTENANCE, FACES)

Gen	1: 2	God was hovering over the f
Gen	3:19	In the sweat of your f you
Gen	11: 4	scattered abroad over the f
Gen	17: 3	Then Abram fell on his f,
Gen	32:30	I have seen God face to f,
Ex	33:11	spoke to Moses face to f,
Ex	34:30	the skin of his f shone, and
Ex	34:33	them, he put a veil on his f.
Num	6:25	The LORD make His f shine
Num	12: 8	I speak with him f to face,
Deut	34:10	whom the LORD knew f to
2Ch	7:14	and pray and seek My f,

Neh	2: 2	Why is your f sad, since you
Job	1:11	surely curse You to Your f!
Job	4:15	a spirit passed before my f;
Ps	24: 6	seek Him, Who seek Your f.
Ps	27: 8	heart said to You, "Your f,
Ps	27: 9	Do not hide Your f from me;
Ps	67: 1	And cause His f to shine
Ps	104:30	And You renew the f of the
Ps	105: 4	Seek His f evermore!
Prov	7:13	With an impudent f she said
Is	6: 2	with two he covered his f,
Jer	32: 4	speak with him face to f,
Jer	33: 5	I have hidden My f from
Lam	3:35	due a man Before the f of
Lam	4:16	The f of the LORD scattered
Ezek	7:18	Shame will be on every f,
Ezek	9: 8	and I fell on my f and cried
Ezek	10:14	the first f was the face of
Ezek	10:14	the second f the face of a
Ezek	10:14	the third the f of a lion,
Ezek	10:14	and the fourth the f of an
Ezek	38:18	My fury will show in My f.
Dan	3:19	and the expression on his f
Dan	10: 9	with my f to the ground.
Hos	5:15	Then they will seek My f;
Nah	3: 5	lift your skirts over your f,
Matt	6:17	your head and wash your f,
Matt	11:10	messenger before Your f,
Matt	16: 3	know how to discern the f
Matt	17: 2	His f shone like the sun,
Matt	18:10	angels always see the f of
Matt	26:39	farther and fell on His f,
Matt	26:67	Then they spat in His f and
Luke	9:29	the appearance of His f was
Luke	17:16	and fell down on his f at
Luke	22:64	they struck Him on the f and
John	11:44	and his f was wrapped with a
Acts	6:15	saw his f as the face of an
Acts	7:45	God drove out before the f
Acts	17:26	of men to dwell on all the f
Acts	20:25	will see my f no more.
Acts	25:16	meets the accusers face to f,
1Co	13:12	but then f to face. Now I
1Co	14:25	so, falling down on his f,
2Co	3: 7	not look steadily at the f
2Co	3:18	But we all, with unveiled f,
2Co	4: 6	of the glory of God in the f
2Co	11:20	if one strikes you on the f.
Gal	2:11	I withstood him to his f,
Col	2: 1	many as have not seen my f
1Th	2:17	more eagerly to see your f
Jas	1:23	man observing his natural f
1Pe	3:12	But the f of the
2Jn	12	to come to you and speak f
Rev	4: 7	living creature had a f
Rev	6:16	on us and hide us from the f
Rev	10: 1	his f was like the sun, and
Rev	22: 4	They shall see His f,

FACES (see FACE)

Is	25: 8	wipe away tears from all f;
Is	53: 3	our f from Him; He was

FADE (see FADES)

1Pe	1: 4	and that does not f away,
1Pe	5: 4	of glory that does not f

FADES (see FADE)

Is	40: 7	grass withers, the flower f,

FAIL (see FAILING, FAILS)

1Sa	17:32	Let no man's heart f because
Ps	69: 3	My eyes f while I wait for
Ps	73:26	My flesh and my heart f;
Is	42: 4	He will not f nor be
Jer	15:18	stream, As waters that f?
Lam	3:22	Because His compassions f
Luke	16:17	one tittle of the law to f.
1Co	13: 8	are prophecies, they will f;
Heb	1:12	Your years will not f.
Heb	11:32	For the time would f me to

FAILING (see FAIL)

Luke	21:26	men's hearts f them from fear

FAILS (see FAIL)

Ps	38:10	my strength f me; As for
Ps	40:12	Therefore my heart f me.
Eccl	12: 5	is a burden, And desire f.
Is	15: 6	withered away; The grass f,
1Co	13: 8	Love never f.

FAINT (see FAINTED, FAINTS)

Is	40:30	Even the youths shall f and
Is	40:31	They shall walk and not f.
Jer	8:18	My heart is f in me.
Jon	4: 8	head, so that he grew f.
Matt	15:32	lest they f on the way."

FAINTED (see FAINT)

Jon	2: 7	When my soul f within me, I

FAINTS† (see FAINT)

Ps	84: 2	even f For the courts of
Ps	119:81	My soul f for Your
Is	1: 5	sick, And the whole heart f.
Is	40:28	Neither f nor is weary.

FAIR (see FAIRER, FAIREST)

Song	1:15	Behold, you are f,
Matt	16: 2	It will be f weather, for
Acts	27: 8	we came to a place called F
Col	4: 1	what is just and f,

FAIRER† (see FAIR)

Ps	45: 2	You are f than the sons of

FAIREST (see FAIR)

Song	1: 8	O f among women, Follow in

FAITH (see FAITHFUL, FAITHLESS)

Deut	32:20	Children in whom is no f.
Hab	2: 4	the just shall live by his f.
Matt	6:30	you, O you of little f?
Matt	8:10	have not found such great f,
Matt	9: 2	bed. When Jesus saw their f,

Matt	9:22	your f has made you well."
Matt	15:28	great is your f! Let it be
Matt	17:20	if you have f as a mustard
Matt	23:23	law: justice and mercy and f.
Mark	11:22	Have f in God.
Luke	7: 9	have not found such great f,
Luke	7:50	Your f has saved you. Go in
Luke	17: 5	the Lord, "Increase our f.
Luke	17:19	Your f has made you well."
Luke	22:32	that your f should not fail;
Acts	3:16	the f which comes through
Acts	6: 5	a man full of f and the Holy
Acts	6: 7	were obedient to the f.
Acts	11:24	of the Holy Spirit and of f.
Acts	14: 9	and seeing that he had f to
Acts	14:22	them to continue in the f,
Acts	14:27	He had opened the door of f
Acts	15: 9	purifying their hearts by f.
Acts	16: 5	were strengthened in the f,
Acts	26:18	who are sanctified by f in
Rom	1: 8	that your f is spoken of
Rom	1:12	with you by the mutual f
Rom	1:17	is revealed from faith to f;
Rom	1:17	just shall live by f.
Rom	3:25	by His blood, through f,
Rom	3:28	that a man is justified by f
Rom	4:13	the righteousness of f.
Rom	4:19	And not being weak in f,
Rom	10: 6	But the righteousness of f
Rom	10: 8	the word of f which we
Rom	10:17	So then f comes by hearing,
Rom	12: 3	to each one a measure of f.
Rom	12: 6	in proportion to our f;
Rom	14:23	for whatever is not from f
1Co	13: 2	and though I have all f,
1Co	13:13	And now abide f,
1Co	15:17	your f is futile; you are
1Co	16:13	Watch, stand fast in the f,
2Co	5: 7	For we walk by f,
Gal	2:16	we might be justified by f
Gal	2:20	in the flesh I live by f in
Gal	3: 2	law, or by the hearing of f?
Gal	3:11	just shall live by f.
Gal	5: 6	but f working through love.
Gal	6:10	are of the household of f.
Eph	2: 8	have been saved through f,
Eph	4: 5	one Lord, one f,
Eph	4:13	come to the unity of the f
Eph	6:16	taking the shield of f with
Col	1: 4	since we heard of your f in
Col	1:23	indeed you continue in the f,
1Th	3:10	what is lacking in your f?
1Th	5: 8	on the breastplate of f and
1Ti	1: 2	Timothy, a true son in the f:
1Ti	1: 5	and from sincere f,
1Ti	4: 1	some will depart from the f,
1Ti	6:12	Fight the good fight of f,
2Ti	4: 7	the race, I have kept the f.
Heb	10:22	heart in full assurance of f,
Heb	10:38	just shall live by f;
Heb	11: 1	Now f is the substance of
Heb	11: 3	By f we understand that the
Heb	11: 6	But without f it is
Heb	12: 2	and finisher of our f,

Jas	1: 3	that the testing of your f
Jas	2:14	if someone says he has f but
Jas	2:20	that f without works is
Jas	5:15	And the prayer of f will save
1Pe	1: 5	the power of God through f
1Pe	1: 9	receiving the end of your f—
1Pe	5: 9	him, steadfast in the f,
2Pe	1: 1	obtained like precious f
2Pe	1: 5	add to your f virtue, to
1Jn	5: 4	has overcome the world—our f.
Jude	20	up on your most holy f,

FAITHFUL (see FAITH, FAITHFULLY, FAITHFULNESS)

Num	12: 7	He is f in all My house.
Deut	7: 9	the f God who keeps covenant
1Sa	2:35	will raise up for Myself a f
Ps	89:37	Even like the f witness in
Ps	119:86	Your commandments are f;
Prov	27: 6	F are the wounds of a
Is	1:21	How the f city has become a
Is	49: 7	of the LORD who is f,
Matt	24:45	Who then is a f and wise
Matt	25:21	good and f servant; you were
Matt	25:21	you were f over a few
Luke	16:10	in what is least is f
1Co	1: 9	God is f, by whom you were
1Co	4: 2	stewards that one be found f.
1Co	10:13	common to man; but God is f,
1Th	5:24	He who calls you is f,
1Ti	1:15	This is a f saying and
2Ti	2: 2	commit these to f men who
2Ti	2:13	are faithless, He remains f;
Heb	10:23	for He who promised is f.
1Pe	4:19	as to a f Creator.
1Jn	1: 9	He is f and just to forgive
Rev	1: 5	the f witness, the firstborn
Rev	2:10	Be f until death, and I will
Rev	3:14	the F and True Witness, the

FAITHFULLY (see FAITHFUL)

Jer	23:28	let him speak My word f.

FAITHFULNESS (see FAITHFUL)

Ps	36: 5	Your f reaches to the
Lam	3:23	morning; Great is Your f.
Hos	2:20	will betroth you to Me in f,
Gal	5:22	kindness, goodness, f,

FAITHLESS (see FAITH)

Matt	17:17	O f and perverse generation,
2Ti	2:13	If we are f, He remains

FALL (see FALLEN, FALLING, FALLS, FELL)

Gen	2:21	caused a deep sleep to f on
Ps	91: 7	A thousand may f at your
Ps	140:10	Let burning coals f upon
Prov	16:18	a haughty spirit before a f.
Eccl	10: 8	He who digs a pit will f
Is	40:30	young men shall utterly f,
Is	47:11	And trouble shall f upon
Jer	46: 6	They will stumble and f
Hos	10: 8	to the hills, "F on us!"
Matt	7:25	that house; and it did not f,

Matt	7:27	it fell. And great was its **f**.
Matt	15:14	both will **f** into a ditch."
Matt	15:27	dogs eat the crumbs which **f**
Luke	2:34	is destined for the **f** and
Luke	10:18	I saw Satan **f** like lightning
Luke	23:30	F on us!" and to the
Rom	3:23	for all have sinned and **f**
1Co	10:12	stands take heed lest he **f**.
Heb	6: 6	if they **f** away, to renew them
Heb	10:31	It is a fearful thing to **f**
Jas	1: 2	count it all joy when you **f**
Jas	5:12	lest you **f** into judgment.

FALLEN (see FALL)

Gen	4: 6	why has your countenance **f**?
2Sa	1:19	How the mighty have **f**!
2Sa	3:38	and a great man has **f** this
Ps	7:15	And has **f** into the ditch
Ps	16: 6	The lines have **f** to me in
Is	14:12	How you are **f** from heaven,
Gal	5: 4	you have **f** from grace.
Rev	2: 5	from where you have **f**;
Rev	14: 8	saying, "Babylon is **f**,
Rev	17:10	seven kings. Five have **f**,

FALLING (see FALL)

Ps	116: 8	tears, And my feet from **f**.
Is	34: 4	And as fruit **f** from a fig
Luke	8:47	and **f** down before Him, she
Luke	22:44	like great drops of blood **f**
Acts	1:18	and **f** headlong, he burst
1Co	14:25	**f** down on his face, he will
2Th	2: 3	not come unless the **f**

FALLOW

Ex	23:11	shall let it rest and lie **f**,
Jer	4: 3	Break up your **f** ground, And

FALLS (see FALL)

Ex	21:33	and an ox or a donkey **f** in
Num	24: 4	Who **f** down, with eyes wide
Num	33:54	shall be whatever **f** to him
Deut	22: 8	your household if anyone **f**
2Sa	3:29	who leans on a staff or **f** by
2Sa	17:12	fall on him as the dew **f** on
Job	4:13	When deep sleep **f** on men,
Job	30:30	My skin grows black and **f**
Prov	13:17	A wicked messenger **f** into
Prov	17:20	who has a perverse tongue **f**
Prov	24:17	rejoice when your enemy **f**,
Eccl	9:12	When it **f** suddenly upon
Matt	12:11	and if it **f** into a pit on
Matt	17:15	for he often **f** into the fire
Matt	21:44	And whoever **f** on this stone
Matt	21:44	broken; but on whomever it **f**,
Luke	11:17	divided against a house **f**.
Luke	15:12	the portion of goods that **f**
John	12:24	unless a grain of wheat **f**
Rom	14: 4	own master he stands or **f**.
Jas	1:11	the grass; its flower **f**,
1Pe	1:24	And its flower **f** away,
Rev	11: 6	so that no rain **f** in the

FALSE (see FALSEHOOD, FALSELY, FALSIFYING)

Ex	20:16	You shall not bear **f** witness
Ps	119:104	Therefore I hate every **f**
Ps	119:128	I hate every **f** way.
Prov	6:19	A **f** witness who speaks
Jer	8: 8	the **f** pen of the scribe
Jer	23:32	those who prophesy **f** dreams,
Zech	8:17	And do not love a **f** oath.
Matt	7:15	Beware of **f** prophets, who
Matt	19:18	You shall not bear **f**
Matt	24:11	Then many **f** prophets will
Matt	24:24	For false christs and **f**
Matt	26:60	But at last two **f** witnesses
Luke	19: 8	anything from anyone by **f**
Rom	13: 9	You shall not bear **f**
2Co	11:13	For such are **f** apostles,
2Co	11:26	in perils among **f** brethren;
Col	2:18	taking delight in **f**
2Pe	2: 1	But there were also **f**
2Pe	2: 1	even as there will be **f**
Rev	20:10	where the beast and the **f**

FALSEHOOD (see FALSE)

Job	31: 5	"If I have walked with **f**,
Ps	5: 6	destroy those who speak **f**;
Ps	7:14	trouble and brings forth **f**.
Ps	119:78	treated me wrongfully with **f**;
Prov	30: 8	Remove **f** and lies far from
Is	57: 4	Offspring of **f**,
Jer	8: 8	the scribe certainly works **f**.
Jer	10:14	For his molded image is **f**,

FALSELY (see FALSE)

Gen	21:23	God that you will not deal **f**
Lev	6: 3	concerning it, and swears **f**—
Lev	19:11	shall not steal, nor deal **f**,
Lev	19:12	shall not swear by My name **f**,
Deut	19:18	who has testified **f** against
Jer	5:31	The prophets prophesy **f**,
Jer	6:13	priest, Everyone deals **f**.
Jer	43: 2	You speak **f**! The LORD our
Matt	5:11	kinds of evil against you **f**
Matt	5:33	old, 'You shall not swear **f**,
1Ti	6:20	contradictions of what is **f**

FALSIFYING† (see FALSE)

Amos	8: 5	F the scales by deceit,

FAME

Matt	4:24	Then His **f** went throughout

FAMILIES (see FAMILY)

Gen	12: 3	And in you all the **f** of the
Ps	68: 6	God sets the solitary in **f**;
Amos	3: 2	have I known of all the **f**
Acts	3:25	in your seed all the **f**

FAMILY (see FAMILIES)

Gen	12: 1	From your **f** And from your
Esth	2:10	not revealed her people or **f**,
Jer	3:14	from a city and two from a **f**,
Jer	8: 3	who remain of this evil **f**,
Amos	3: 1	against the whole **f** which I

F

Zech	12:12	the f of the house of David
Acts	4: 6	as many as were of the f of
Acts	7:13	and Joseph's f became known
Acts	13:26	sons of the f of Abraham,
Acts	16:33	he and all his f were
Eph	3:15	from whom the whole f in

FAMINE (see FAMINES)

Gen	12:10	for the f was severe in the
Gen	26: 1	besides the first f that was
Gen	41:27	wind are seven years of f.
Ruth	1: 1	that there was a f in the
Jer	5:12	Nor shall we see sword or f.
Amos	8:11	Not a f of bread, Nor a
Luke	4:25	and there was a great f
Rom	8:35	or persecution, or f,

FAMINES (see FAMINE)

| Matt | 24: 7 | kingdom. And there will be f, |

FAN

| Jer | 15: 7 | them with a winnowing f in |
| Matt | 3:12 | His winnowing f is in His |

FANGS

| Job | 29:17 | I broke the f of the wicked, |

FAREWELL

| Luke | 9:61 | me first go and bid them f |
| 2Co | 13:11 | Finally, brethren, f. |

FARMER

Gen	9:20	And Noah began to be a f,
2Ti	2: 6	The hard-working f must be
Jas	5: 7	See how the f waits for the

FAST (see FASTED, FASTING)

Deut	4: 4	But you who held f to the
Judg	4:21	for he was f asleep and
1Ki	21: 9	saying, Proclaim a f,
Esth	4:16	My maids and I will f
Job	2: 3	And still he holds f to his
Job	27: 6	My righteousness I hold f,
Ps	33: 9	commanded, and it stood f.
Ps	111: 8	They stand f forever and
Is	56: 4	And hold f My covenant,
Is	58: 4	You will not f as you do
Is	58: 5	Would you call this a f,
Joel	1:14	Consecrate a f,
Jon	1: 5	and was f asleep.
Jon	3: 5	believed God, proclaimed a f,
Zech	8:19	And the f of the tenth,
Matt	6:16	"Moreover, when you f,
Matt	9:14	do we and the Pharisees f
Matt	9:14	but Your disciples do not f?
Luke	18:12	I f twice a week; I give
Acts	27: 9	now dangerous because the F
Acts	27:41	and the prow stuck f and
1Co	15: 2	if you hold f that word
1Co	16:13	stand in the faith, be
Gal	5: 1	Stand f therefore in the
Phil	1:27	that you stand f in one
Phil	2:16	holding f the word of life,
Phil	4: 1	so stand f in the Lord,

Col	2:19	and not holding f to the
1Th	5:21	hold f what is good.
2Ti	1:13	Hold f the pattern of sound
Tit	1: 9	holding f the faithful word
Heb	3: 6	house we are if we hold f
Heb	4:14	let us hold f our
Rev	2:13	And you hold f to My name,
Rev	3:11	I am coming quickly! Hold f

FASTED (see FAST)

Judg	20:26	before the LORD and f that
1Sa	31:13	and f seven days.
2Sa	12:16	and David f and went in and
Ezra	8:23	So we f and entreated our God
Is	58: 3	'Why have we f,
Matt	4: 2	And when He had f forty days
Acts	13: 3	having f and prayed, and

FASTING (see FAST, FASTINGS)

Ezra	9: 5	sacrifice I arose from my f;
Neh	1: 4	I was f and praying before
Neh	9: 1	Israel were assembled with f,
Ps	35:13	I humbled myself with f;
Ps	69:10	chastened my soul with f,
Ps	109:24	My knees are weak through f,
Jer	36: 6	house on the day of f.
Dan	6:18	palace and spent the night f;
Dan	9: 3	and supplications, with f,
Matt	6:16	may appear to men to be f.
Matt	17:21	out except by prayer and f.
Mark	2:18	and of the Pharisees were f.
Acts	14:23	church, and prayed with f,
1Co	7: 5	you may give yourselves to f

FASTINGS† (see FASTING)

Luke	2:37	but served God with f and
2Co	6: 5	in sleeplessness, in f;
2Co	11:27	in f often, in cold and

FAT (see FATNESS, FATTED)

Gen	4: 4	of his flock and of their f.
Gen	41: 2	cows, fine looking and f;
1Sa	15:22	And to heed than the f of
Neh	8:10	"Go your way, eat the f,
Ezek	34:16	but I will destroy the f and
Ezek	34:20	will judge between the f

FATHER (see FATHER-IN-LAW, FATHER'S, FATHERLESS, FATHERS)

Gen	2:24	a man shall leave his f and
Gen	9:22	saw the nakedness of his f,
Gen	11:28	And Haran died before his f
Gen	17: 5	for I have made you a f of
Gen	19:31	Our f is old, and there is
Gen	19:32	the lineage of our f.
Gen	19:33	went in and lay with her f,
Gen	19:36	were with child by their f.
Gen	20:12	She is the daughter of my f,
Gen	22: 7	My f!" And he said, "Here I
Gen	26: 3	I swore to Abraham your f.
Gen	26:24	I am the God of your f
Gen	27:38	O my f!" And Esau lifted up
Gen	31: 5	but the God of my f has been
Gen	31:53	swore by the Fear of his f

Gen	37:11	but his f kept the matter
Gen	43: 7	Is your f still alive? Have
Gen	46: 1	to the God of his f Isaac.
Gen	50: 5	let me go up and bury my f,
Gen	50:10	days of mourning for his f.
Ex	3: 6	"I am the God of your f—
Ex	20:12	Honor your f and your
Ex	21:15	And he who strikes his f or
Ex	21:17	And he who curses his f or
Lev	18: 7	The nakedness of your f or
Josh	24: 2	father of Abraham and the f
Josh	24: 3	Then I took your f Abraham
2Sa	7:14	"I will be his F,
1Ki	12:11	my f chastised you with
1Ki	15:26	walked in the way of his f,
2Ki	14: 3	he did everything as his f
2Ki	21:21	served the idols that his f
1Ch	22:10	son, and I will be his F;
1Ch	28: 4	and among the sons of my f,
1Ch	29:10	LORD God of Israel, our F,
2Ch	7:18	covenanted with David your f,
Esth	2: 7	for she had neither f nor
Job	17:14	corruption, 'You are my f,
Job	29:16	I was a f to the poor, And
Job	38:28	Has the rain a f?
Job	42:15	and their f gave them an
Ps	68: 5	A f of the fatherless, a
Ps	89:26	cry to Me, 'You are my F,
Ps	103:13	As a f pities his children,
Prov	1: 8	the instruction of your f,
Prov	3:12	Just as a f the son in
Prov	10: 1	A wise son makes a glad f,
Prov	17:21	And the f of a fool has no
Prov	17:25	son is a grief to his f,
Prov	20:20	Whoever curses his f or his
Prov	20:24	Whoever robs his f or his
Prov	29: 3	loves wisdom makes his f
Prov	30:17	The eye that mocks his f,
Is	8: 4	My f' and 'My mother,' the
Is	9: 6	Mighty God, Everlasting F,
Is	22:21	He shall be a f to the
Is	43:27	Your first f sinned, And
Is	45:10	to him who says to his f,
Is	51: 2	Look to Abraham your f,
Is	58:14	the heritage of Jacob your f.
Is	63:16	Doubtless You are our F,
Is	63:16	You, O LORD, are our F;
Jer	2:27	to a tree, 'You are my f,
Jer	3:19	'You shall call Me, "My F,
Jer	12: 6	the house of your f,
Jer	20:15	Who brought news to my f,
Jer	22:15	Did not your f eat and
Jer	31: 9	For I am a F to Israel,
Ezek	16: 3	your f was an Amorite and
Ezek	16:45	was a Hittite and your f
Ezek	18: 4	The soul of the f As well
Ezek	18:14	all the sins which his f
Ezek	18:17	for the iniquity of his f;
Ezek	18:18	"As for his f,
Ezek	18:19	not bear the guilt of the f?
Ezek	18:20	nor the f bear the guilt of
Dan	5:11	King Nebuchadnezzar your f—
Amos	2: 7	A man and his f go in to
Mic	7: 6	For son dishonors f,

Mal	1: 6	"A son honors his f,
Mal	1: 6	master. If then I am the F,
Mal	2:10	Have we not all one F?
Matt	2:22	over Judea instead of his f
Matt	3: 9	'We have Abraham as our f.
Matt	4:21	boat with Zebedee their f
Matt	5:16	works and glorify your F in
Matt	6: 4	and your F who sees in
Matt	6: 9	Our F in heaven, Hallowed
Matt	6:26	yet your heavenly F feeds
Matt	7:21	he who does the will of My F
Matt	8:21	me first go and bury my f.
Matt	10:35	a man against his f,
Matt	10:37	He who loves f or mother more
Matt	11:25	and said, "I thank You, F,
Matt	11:26	"Even so, F, for so it
Matt	11:27	knows the Son except the F.
Matt	13:43	in the kingdom of their F.
Matt	15: 4	Honor your f and your
Matt	15: 4	He who curses f or
Matt	16:17	but My F who is in heaven.
Matt	16:27	come in the glory of His F
Matt	19: 5	man shall leave his f
Matt	19:29	or brothers or sisters or f
Matt	23: 9	call anyone on earth your f;
Matt	23: 9	father; for One is your F,
Matt	25:34	'Come, you blessed of My F,
Matt	28:19	them in the name of the F
Mark	13:32	nor the Son, but only the F.
Mark	14:36	And He said, "Abba, F,
Luke	1:32	give Him the throne of His f
Luke	2:48	Your f and I have sought You
Luke	3: 8	'We have Abraham as our f.
Luke	9:59	me first go and bury my f.
Luke	15:18	'I will arise and go to my f,
Luke	15:27	your f has killed the fatted
Luke	16:24	F Abraham, have mercy on me,
Luke	18:20	Honor your f and your
Luke	23:34	Then Jesus said, "F,
Luke	24:49	I send the Promise of My F
John	1:14	the only begotten of the F,
John	1:18	who is in the bosom of the F,
John	3:35	The F loves the Son, and has
John	4:23	will worship the F in
John	5:17	My F has been working until
John	5:30	will but the will of the F
John	5:36	that the F has sent Me.
John	5:45	I shall accuse you to the F;
John	6:44	can come to Me unless the F
John	8:39	to Him, "Abraham is our f.
John	8:44	You are of your f the devil,
John	8:44	for he is a liar and the f
John	8:56	Your f Abraham rejoiced to
John	10:15	Me, even so I know the F;
John	10:30	I and My F are one."
John	11:41	up His eyes and said, "F,
John	13: 1	from this world to the F,
John	14: 6	No one comes to the F except
John	14: 8	Him, "Lord, show us the F,
John	14: 9	has seen Me has seen the F;
John	14:12	do, because I go to My F.
John	14:16	"And I will pray the F,
John	14:28	for My F is greater than I.
John	15: 1	and My F is the vinedresser.

F

John	15: 8	By this My **F** is glorified,
John	15:16	that whatever you ask the **F**
John	15:23	He who hates Me hates My **F**
John	15:26	who proceeds from the **F**,
John	16:23	whatever you ask the **F** in My
John	16:28	I came forth from the **F** and
John	17: 1	to heaven, and said: "**F**,
John	17:21	all may be one, as You, **F**,
John	18:11	not drink the cup which My **F**
John	20:17	to My Father and your **F**,
John	20:21	Peace to you! As the **F** has
Acts	1: 4	for the Promise of the **F**,
Rom	1: 7	you and peace from God our **F**
Rom	6: 4	dead by the glory of the **F**,
Rom	8:15	whom we cry out, "Abba, **F**.
Rom	15: 6	mouth glorify the God and **F**
1Co	8: 6	us there is one God, the **F**,
2Co	1: 3	the **F** of mercies and God of
Eph	1:17	the **F** of glory, may give to
Eph	2:18	by one Spirit to the **F**.
Eph	4: 6	one God and **F** of all, who is
Phil	2:11	to the glory of God the **F**.
Col	3:17	giving thanks to God the **F**
Heb	1: 5	will be to Him a **F**,
Heb	7: 3	without **f**, without mother,
Heb	12: 9	be in subjection to the **F**
Jas	1:17	and comes down from the **F** of
Jas	1:27	before God and the **F** is
1Pe	1: 2	foreknowledge of God the **F**,
1Jn	1: 2	life which was with the **F**
1Jn	1: 3	fellowship is with the **F**
1Jn	2: 1	have an Advocate with the **F**,
1Jn	2:15	the love of the **F** is not in
1Jn	3: 1	what manner of love the **F**
1Jn	5: 7	witness in heaven: the **F**,

FATHER-IN-LAW (see FATHER)

Ex	3: 1	the flock of Jethro his **f**,
Ex	18: 1	priest of Midian, Moses' **f**,
John	18:13	for he was the **f** of Caiaphas

FATHER'S (see FATHER)

Gen	12: 1	your family And from your **f**
1Ki	12:10	shall be thicker than my **f**
Prov	4: 3	When I was my **f** son, Tender
Prov	13: 1	A wise son heeds his **f**
Luke	2:49	that I must be about My **F**
John	10:29	to snatch them out of My **F**
John	14: 2	In My **F** house are many
John	15:10	just as I have kept My **F**
1Co	5: 1	that a man has his **f** wife!
Rev	14: 1	having His **F** name written on

FATHERLESS (see FATHER)

Ex	22:22	not afflict any widow or **f**
Ex	22:24	widows, and your children **f**.
Deut	10:18	justice for the **f** and the
Deut	14:29	and the stranger and the **f**
Ps	10:14	You are the helper of the **f**.
Ps	68: 5	A father of the **f**; Defend the **f**,
Is	1:17	oppressor; Defend the **f**,
Hos	14: 3	For in You the **f** finds
Zech	7:10	oppress the widow or the **f**,

FATHERS (see FATHER)

Gen	15:15	you shall go to your **f** in
Gen	49:29	bury me with my **f** in the
Ex	3:13	The God of your **f** has sent me
Ex	20: 5	the iniquity of the **f** on
Num	20:15	how our **f** went down to Egypt,
Deut	4: 1	the LORD God of your **f** is
Deut	24:16	**F** shall not be put to death
Deut	31:16	you will rest with your **f**;
Josh	4:21	your children ask their **f**
Judg	2:10	had been gathered to their **f**,
2Sa	7:12	and you rest with your **f**,
1Ki	2:10	So David rested with his **f**,
2Ch	25: 4	be put to death for their **f**;
2Ch	26:23	they buried him with his **f**
Neh	9: 9	saw the affliction of our **f**
Ps	22: 4	Our **f** trusted in You; They
Ps	78: 3	And our **f** have told us.
Jer	31:29	The **f** have eaten sour grapes,
Jer	34:14	But your **f** did not obey Me
Jer	44: 3	they nor you nor your **f**.
Jer	44: 9	the wickedness of your **f**,
Jer	50: 7	LORD, the hope of their **f**.
Lam	5: 7	Our **f** sinned and are no
Ezek	5:10	and sons shall eat their **f**;
Ezek	18: 2	The **f** have eaten sour grapes,
Ezek	20: 4	the abominations of their **f**.
Dan	2:23	praise You, O God of my **f**;
Dan	11:38	and a god which his **f** did
Amos	2: 4	Lies which their **f**
Mic	7:20	You have sworn to our **f**
Zech	1: 2	been very angry with your **f**.
Zech	8:14	to punish you When your **f**
Mal	2:10	the covenant of the **f**?
Mal	4: 6	turn The hearts of the **f**
Matt	23:30	lived in the days of our **f**,
Luke	1:17	the hearts of the **f**
Luke	1:55	As He spoke to our **f**,
Luke	1:72	the mercy promised to our **f**
John	4:20	Our **f** worshiped on this
John	6:31	Our **f** ate the manna in the
Acts	5:30	The God of our **f** raised up
Acts	7: 2	he said, "Brethren and **f**,
Acts	7:32	am the God of your **f**—
Acts	7:44	Our **f** had the tabernacle of
Acts	15:10	which neither our **f** nor we
Acts	22: 1	"Brethren and **f**,
Acts	26: 6	promise made by God to our **f**.
Acts	28:17	or the customs of our **f**,
Rom	9: 5	of whom are the **f** and from
Rom	11:28	for the sake of the **f**.
Rom	15: 8	the promises made to the **f**,
1Co	4:15	you do not have many **f**;
1Co	10: 1	to be unaware that all our **f**
Gal	1:14	for the traditions of my **f**.
Eph	6: 4	And you, **f**, do not provoke
1Ti	1: 9	for murderers of **f** and
Heb	1: 1	spoke in time past to the **f**
Heb	3: 9	Where your **f** tested Me,
Heb	12: 9	we have had human **f** who
2Pe	3: 4	For since the **f** fell asleep,
1Jn	2:13	I write to you, **f**,

FATLING†
Is   11: 6   and the young lion and the **f**

FATNESS (see FAT)
Gen   27:28   Of the **f** of the earth, And

FATTED (see FAT)
Luke   15:27   your father has killed the **f**

FAULT (see FAULTLESS, FAULTS)
1Sa   29: 3   this day I have found no **f**
Mark   7: 2   unwashed hands, they found **f**.
Luke   23: 4   I find no **f** in this Man."
Rom   9:19   "Why does He still find **f**?
Phil   2:15   children of God without **f** in
Rev   14: 5   for they are without **f**

FAULTLESS (see FAULT)
Jude   24   And to present you **f**

FAULTS (see FAULT)
Gen   41: 9   I remember my **f** this day.
Ps   19:12   Cleanse me from secret **f**.

FAVOR (see FAVORED, FAVORITISM)
Gen   18: 3   if I have now found **f** in
Gen   39: 4   So Joseph found **f** in his
Deut   28:50   the elderly nor show **f** to
Ruth   2: 2   in whose sight I may find **f**.
1Sa   2:26   and in **f** both with the LORD
Esth   2:15   And Esther obtained **f** in the
Prov   3: 4   And so find **f** and high
Prov   8:35   And obtains **f** from the
Prov   11:27   earnestly seeks good finds **f**,
Prov   12: 2   A good man obtains **f** from
Luke   1:30   for you have found **f** with
Luke   2:52   and in **f** with God and men.
Acts   2:47   praising God and having **f**

FAVORED (see FAVOR)
Luke   1:28   highly **f** one, the Lord is

FAVORITISM† (see FAVOR)
Luke   20:21   You do not show personal **f**,
Gal   2: 6   God shows personal **f** to no

FEAR (see FEARED, FEARFUL, FEARING,
   FEARS)
Gen   9: 2   And the **f** of you and the
Gen   20:11   surely the **f** of God is not
Gen   21:17   **F** not, for God has heard the
Gen   22:12   for now I know that you **f**
Gen   31:42   God of Abraham and the **F** of
Lev   19:14   but shall **f** your God: I am
Deut   2:25   to put the dread and **f** of
Deut   4:10   that they may learn to **f** Me
Deut   6:13   You shall **f** the LORD your
Deut   28:66   you shall **f** day and night,
Deut   31: 8   do not **f** nor be dismayed."
Josh   24:14   **f** the LORD, serve Him in
1Sa   11: 7   And the **f** of the LORD
1Sa   12:24   Only **f** the LORD, and serve
2Ch   17:10   And the **f** of the LORD fell

Esth   8:17   because **f** of the Jews fell
Job   1: 9   Does Job **f** God for nothing?
Job   4:14   **F** came upon me, and
Job   6:14   though he forsakes the **f** of
Job   15: 4   Yes, you cast off **f**,
Job   21: 9   houses are safe from **f**,
Job   25: 2   Dominion and **f** belong to
Job   28:28   the **f** of the Lord, that is
Job   39:22   He mocks at **f**,
Ps   2:11   Serve the LORD with **f**,
Ps   15: 4   But he honors those who **f**
Ps   19: 9   The **f** of the LORD is
Ps   22:23   And **f** Him, all you
Ps   22:25   My vows before those who **f**
Ps   23: 4   I will **f** no evil; For You
Ps   25:14   LORD is with those who **f**
Ps   27: 1   salvation; Whom shall I **f**?
Ps   27: 3   me, My heart shall not **f**;
Ps   31:13   **F** is on every side; While
Ps   33: 8   Let all the earth **f** the
Ps   34: 7   all around those who **f** Him,
Ps   34: 9   is no want to those who **f**
Ps   34:11   I will teach you the **f** of
Ps   36: 1   There is no **f** of God
Ps   40: 3   Many will see it and **f**,
Ps   46: 2   Therefore we will not **f**,
Ps   52: 6   also shall see and **f**,
Ps   53: 5   in great fear Where no **f**
Ps   55:19   Therefore they do not **f**
Ps   60: 4   a banner to those who **f** You,
Ps   64: 1   Preserve my life from **f** of
Ps   67: 7   ends of the earth shall **f**
Ps   85: 9   is near to those who **f** Him,
Ps   86:11   Unite my heart to **f** Your
Ps   103:11   His mercy toward those who **f**
Ps   111:10   The **f** of the LORD is the
Ps   118: 4   Let those who **f** the LORD
Prov   1: 7   The **f** of the LORD is the
Prov   2: 5   you will understand the **f**
Prov   9:10   The **f** of the LORD is the
Prov   24:21   **f** the LORD and the king;
Is   7: 4   do not **f** or be fainthearted
Is   24:17   **F** and the pit and the snare
Is   41:10   **F** not, for I am with you
Is   43: 1   **F** not, for I have redeemed
Is   44: 2   **F** not, O Jacob My servant;
Is   44: 8   Do not **f**, nor be afraid;
Jer   2:19   And the **f** of Me is not in
Jer   6:25   **F** is on every side.
Jer   48:43   **F** and the pit and the snare
Dan   10:12   he said to me, "Do not **f**,
Dan   10:19   **f** not! Peace be to you; be
Amos   3: 8   has roared! Who will not **f**?
Matt   10:28   But rather **f** Him who is able
Luke   1:12   and **f** fell upon him.
Luke   1:50   His mercy is on those who **f**
Luke   1:74   Might serve Him without **f**,
Luke   12:32   "Do not **f**, little flock,
Luke   21:26   hearts failing them from **f**
Luke   23:40   Do you not even **f** God, seeing
John   12:15   **F** not, daughter of Zion;
John   20:19   for **f** of the Jews, Jesus
Acts   5: 5   So great **f** came upon all
Rom   3:18   There is no **f** of God

F

Rom	8:15	spirit of bondage again to f,
Rom	13: 7	whom customs, fear to whom f,
2Co	7: 1	holiness in the f of God.
Phil	1:14	to speak the word without f.
Phil	2:12	your own salvation with f
2Ti	1: 7	not given us a spirit of f,
Heb	5: 7	heard because of His godly f,
Heb	11: 7	yet seen, moved with godly f,
Heb	13: 6	helper; I will not f.
1Pe	2:17	F God. Honor the king.
1Pe	2:18	to your masters with all f,
1Jn	4:18	but perfect love casts out f,
Rev	11:11	and great f fell on those
Rev	11:18	And those who f Your name,
Rev	14: 7	F God and give glory to Him,

FEARED (see FEAR)

Ex	1:17	But the midwives f God, and
Ex	14:31	so the people f the LORD,
2Ki	17:33	They f the LORD, yet served
Job	1: 1	and one who f God and
Ps	96: 4	He is to be f above all
Mark	6:20	for Herod f John, knowing
Luke	19:21	For I f you, because you are
Acts	10: 2	a devout man and one who f

FEARFUL (see FEAR, FEARFULLY)

Heb	10:27	but a certain f expectation
Heb	10:31	It is a f thing to fall into

FEARFULLY (see FEARFUL)

Ps	139:14	for I am f and wonderfully

FEARING (see FEAR)

Col	3:22	sincerity of heart, f God.

FEARS (see FEAR)

Job	1: 8	one who f God and shuns
Ps	34: 4	delivered me from all my f.
Ps	128: 1	is every one who f the
Prov	31:30	But a woman who f the
Acts	10:22	one who f God and has a good
Acts	10:35	in every nation whoever f

FEAST (see FEASTING, FEASTS)

Gen	19: 3	house. Then he made them a f,
Ex	5: 1	that they may hold a f to Me
Ex	12:17	you shall observe the F
Ex	23:16	and the F of Harvest, the
Ex	23:16	and the F of Ingathering at
Deut	16:16	and at the F of Tabernacles;
Job	1: 4	his sons would go and f in
Dan	5: 1	the king made a great f for
Hos	2:11	Her f days, Her New Moons,
Amos	5:21	I despise your f days, And
Mark	6:21	on his birthday gave a f
Mark	14: 1	the Passover and the F of
Luke	2:41	every year at the F of the
Luke	14: 8	by anyone to a wedding f,
Luke	23:17	one to them at the f).
John	2: 8	it to the master of the f.
John	4:45	they also had gone to the f.
John	5: 1	After this there was a f of
John	7: 8	not yet going up to this f,

John	7:37	that great day of the f,
John	13: 1	Now before the f of the
Acts	18:21	means keep this coming f in
1Co	5: 8	Therefore let us keep the f,
2Pe	2:13	own deceptions while they f

FEASTING (see FEAST)

Esth	9:19	of Adar with gladness and f,
Job	1: 5	when the days of f had run
Prov	17: 1	Than a house full of f
Jer	16: 8	not go into the house of f
Hab	3:14	Their rejoicing was like f

FEASTS (see FEAST)

2Ch	8:13	the three appointed yearly f—
Mal	2: 3	The refuse of your solemn f;
Matt	23: 6	love the best places at f,
Jude	12	are spots in your love f,

FEATHERS

Ps	91: 4	shall cover you with His f,
Dan	4:33	had grown like eagles' f

FED (see FEED)

Deut	8: 3	and f you with manna which
Ezek	34: 8	but the shepherds f
Dan	5:21	They f him with grass like
Mark	5:14	So those who f the swine
1Co	3: 2	I f you with milk and not

FEEBLE

Is	35: 3	And make firm the f knees.
Heb	12:12	and the f knees,

FEED (see FED, FEEDING, FEEDS)

1Ki	17: 4	commanded the ravens to f
Song	4: 5	Which f among the lilies.
Is	40:11	He will f His flock like a
Is	65:25	wolf and the lamb shall f
Ezek	34:16	and f them in judgment."
Matt	25:37	did we see You hungry and f
John	21:15	F My lambs."
John	21:17	F My sheep.
Rom	12:20	f him; If he is
1Co	13: 3	I bestow all my goods to f

FEEDING (see FEED)

Gen	37: 2	was f the flock with his
Matt	8:30	was a herd of many swine f.

FEEDS (see FEED)

Hos	12: 1	Ephraim f on the wind, And
Matt	6:26	yet your heavenly Father f

FEEL

Gen	27:12	Perhaps my father will f me,
Judg	16:26	Let me f the pillars which

FEET (see FOOT)

Gen	18: 4	be brought, and wash your f,
Gen	49:10	lawgiver from between his f,
Gen	49:33	he drew his f up into the
Ex	3: 5	Take your sandals off your f,
Ex	4:25	and cast it at Moses' f,

Josh	3:13	soon as the soles of the f
Josh	9: 5	patched sandals on their f,
Ruth	3: 8	a woman was lying at his f.
2Sa	4: 4	son who was lame in his f.
2Sa	4:12	cut off their hands and f,
1Ki	15:23	age he was diseased in his f.
Neh	9:21	not wear out And their f
Job	13:27	You put my f in the stocks,
Job	29:15	And I was f to the lame.
Ps	8: 6	put all things under his f,
Ps	22:16	pierced My hands and My f;
Ps	40: 2	And set my f upon a rock,
Ps	56:13	Have You not kept my f
Ps	66: 9	And does not allow our f to
Ps	73: 2	my f had almost stumbled;
Ps	115: 7	F they have, but they do
Ps	116: 8	And my f from falling.
Ps	119:101	I have restrained my f from
Ps	119:105	word is a lamp to my f
Prov	1:16	For their f run to evil,
Prov	5: 5	Her f go down to death, Her
Is	6: 2	with two he covered his f,
Is	52: 7	the mountains Are the f of
Dan	2:33	its f partly of iron and
Dan	7: 4	and made to stand on two f
Nah	1:15	on the mountains The f of
Zech	14: 4	And in that day His f will
Matt	10:14	off the dust from your f.
Matt	15:30	laid them down at Jesus' f,
Matt	18: 8	having two hands or two f,
Matt	18:29	servant fell down at his f
Matt	28: 9	came and held Him by the f
Mark	7:25	she came and fell at His f.
Mark	9:45	rather than having two f,
Luke	1:79	To guide our f in the way
Luke	7:38	and she began to wash His f
Luke	7:38	and she kissed His f and
Luke	8:35	sitting at the f of Jesus,
Luke	24:39	"Behold My hands and My f,
John	13: 5	to wash the disciples' f,
John	13: 9	not my f only, but also my
John	13:14	to wash one another's f.
John	20:12	head and the other at the f,
Acts	4:35	them at the apostles' f;
Acts	7:58	down their clothes at the f
Acts	13:25	the sandals of whose f I am
Acts	22: 3	up in this city at the f of
Rom	3:15	Their f are swift to
Rom	10:15	beautiful are the f
Rom	16:20	crush Satan under your f
1Co	12:21	nor again the head to the f,
1Co	15:27	all things under His f.
Eph	6:15	and having shod your f with
1Ti	5:10	she has washed the saints' f,
Heb	2: 8	subjection under his f.
Heb	12:13	straight paths for your f,
Rev	1:15	His f were like fine brass,
Rev	1:17	I fell at His f as dead. But
Rev	10: 1	and his f like pillars of
Rev	12: 1	with the moon under her f,
Rev	13: 2	his feet were like the f

FEIGNED†

| 1Sa | 21:13 | f madness in their hands, |

FELIX

| Acts | 23:26 | most excellent governor F: |

FELL (see FALL)

Gen	4: 5	angry, and his countenance f.
Gen	17: 3	Then Abram f on his face, and
Gen	33: 4	and f on his neck and kissed
1Ki	18:38	the fire of the LORD f and
Ps	27: 2	foes, They stumbled and f.
Matt	2:11	and f down and worshiped
Matt	7:27	beat on that house; and it f.
Matt	13: 4	some seed f by the wayside;
Matt	13: 5	Some f on stony places, where
Luke	10:30	and f among thieves, who
Acts	10:44	the Holy Spirit f upon all
Acts	12: 7	quickly!" And his chains f
Acts	19:17	and fear f on them all, and
1Ti	2:14	f into transgression.
Rev	1:17	I f at His feet as dead. But
Rev	6:13	And the stars of heaven f to
Rev	16:21	And great hail from heaven f

FELLOW (see FELLOWSHIP)

1Sa	21:15	Shall this f come into my
Matt	26:71	This f also was with Jesus
John	9:29	to Moses; as for this f,
John	11:16	said to his f disciples,
Rom	16: 3	my f workers in Christ
1Co	3: 9	For we are God's f workers;
Eph	2:19	but f citizens with the
Phil	2:25	f worker, and fellow
Phil	2:25	and f soldier, but your
1Th	3: 2	and our f laborer in the
Phm	1: 1	our beloved friend and f
1Pe	5: 1	I who am a f elder and a

FELLOWSHIP (see FELLOW)

Acts	2:42	the apostles' doctrine and f,
1Co	1: 9	you were called into the f
1Co	10:20	I do not want you to have f
2Co	6:14	For what f has righteousness
Gal	2: 9	Barnabas the right hand of f,
Eph	3: 9	make all see what is the f
Eph	5:11	And have no f with the
Phil	1: 5	for your f in the gospel from
Phil	2: 1	if any f of the Spirit, if
Phil	3:10	and the f of His sufferings,
1Jn	1: 3	and truly our f is with the
1Jn	1: 6	If we say that we have f with
1Jn	1: 7	we have f with one another,

FEMALE (see MAIDSERVANT, MAIDSERVANTS)

Gen	1:27	male and f He created them.
Gen	7: 2	unclean, a male and his f;
Ex	20:10	nor your f servant, nor your
Matt	19: 4	'made them male and f,
Gal	3:28	there is neither male nor f;

FERVENT (see FERVENTLY)

Prov	26:23	F lips with a wicked heart
Luke	22:15	With f desire I have desired
Rom	12:11	f in spirit, serving the
Jas	5:16	f prayer of a righteous man

F

1Pe	4: 8	And above all things have **f**
2Pe	3:10	elements will melt with **f**

FERVENTLY † (see FERVENT)

Col	4:12	always laboring **f** for you in
1Pe	1:22	love one another **f** with a

FESTUS

Acts	24:27	after two years Porcius **F**

FEVER

Matt	8:14	mother lying sick with a **f**.
John	4:52	at the seventh hour the **f**

FIELD (see FIELDS)

Gen	2: 5	and before any herb of the **f**
Gen	2:19	formed every beast of the **f**
Gen	4: 8	when they were in the **f**,
Gen	25:27	hunter, a man of the **f**;
Ruth	2: 3	went and gleaned in the **f**
Ruth	2: 3	to come to the part of the **f**
Ruth	4: 5	On the day you buy the **f** from
1Sa	4: 2	men of the army in the **f**.
1Sa	20:24	Then David hid in the **f**.
2Sa	2:16	that place was called the **F**
2Sa	14:30	servants set the **f** on fire.
2Ki	18:17	highway to the Fuller's **F**.
Job	5:23	And the beasts of the **f**
Ps	78:12	in the **f** of Zoan.
Ps	96:12	Let the **f** be joyful, and all
Ps	103:15	grass; As a flower of the **f**,
Prov	31:16	She considers a **f** and buys
Song	7:11	Let us go forth to the **f**;
Is	5: 8	They add **f** to field, Till
Is	29:17	And the fruitful **f** be
Is	37:27	were as the grass of the **f**
Is	40: 6	is like the flower of the **f**.
Is	55:12	And all the trees of the **f**
Jer	26:18	shall be plowed like a **f**,
Jer	32: 7	Buy my **f** which is in
Ezek	17: 5	planted it in a fertile **f**;
Ezek	34:27	Then the trees of the **f** shall
Dan	4:25	be with the beasts of the **f**,
Hos	10: 4	in the furrows of the **f**.
Mic	3:12	shall be plowed like a **f**,
Matt	6:28	Consider the lilies of the **f**,
Matt	6:30	clothes the grass of the **f**,
Matt	13:24	who sowed good seed in his **f**;
Matt	13:36	of the tares of the **f**.
Matt	13:38	The **f** is the world, the good
Matt	13:44	that he has and buys that **f**.
Matt	24:40	two men will be in the **f**:
Matt	27: 7	with them the potter's **f**,
Matt	27: 8	field has been called the **F**
Luke	15:25	his older son was in the **f**.
Acts	1:19	that is, **F** of Blood.)
1Co	3: 9	workers; you are God's **f**,
Jas	1:10	as a flower of the **f** he

FIELDS (see FIELD)

Jer	32:43	And **f** will be bought in this
Luke	2: 8	living out in the **f**,
John	4:35	your eyes and look at the **f**,

FIERCE

Gen	49: 7	their anger, for it is **f**;
Ex	32:12	Turn from Your **f** wrath, and
Judg	20:34	Gibeah, and the battle was **f**.
Is	13:13	And in the day of His **f**

FIERY (see FIRE)

Num	21: 6	So the LORD sent **f** serpents
Ps	7:13	He makes His arrows into **f**
Eph	6:16	be able to quench all the **f**
Heb	10:27	and **f** indignation which will
1Pe	4:12	it strange concerning the **f**
Rev	12: 3	**f** red dragon having seven

FIFTEEN (see FIFTEENTH)

Gen	7:20	The waters prevailed **f** cubits
2Ki	20: 6	I will add to your days **f**

FIFTEENTH (see FIFTEEN)

Ex	16: 1	on the **f** day of the second
Luke	3: 1	Now in the **f** year of the

FIFTH (see FIVE)

Gen	1:23	and the morning were the **f**
Lev	19:25	And in the **f** year you may eat

FIFTIES (see FIFTY)

Ex	18:21	of hundreds, rulers of **f**,

FIFTY (see FIFTIES)

Gen	6:15	its width **f** cubits, and its
Gen	18:24	Suppose there were **f**
Lev	23:16	Count **f** days to the day after
Num	4: 3	even to **f** years old, all who
John	8:57	You are not yet **f** years old,

FIG (see FIGS)

Gen	3: 7	and they sewed **f** leaves
Deut	8: 8	of vines and **f** trees and
Judg	9:10	the trees said to the **f**
Mic	4: 4	his vine and under his **f**
Hab	3:17	Though the **f** tree may not
Matt	21:20	How did the **f** tree wither
Matt	24:32	this parable from the **f**
John	1:50	I saw you under the **f** tree,'

FIGHT (see FIGHTING, FIGHTS, FOUGHT)

Ex	1:10	also join our enemies and **f**
Ex	14:14	The LORD will **f** for you, and
Deut	25:11	If two men **f** together, and
1Sa	18:17	and the LORD's battles."
2Ch	13:12	do not **f** against the LORD
Neh	4:20	Our God will **f** for us."
Jer	1:19	They will **f** against you,
Jer	15:20	And they will **f** against
John	18:36	world, My servants would **f**,
Acts	5:39	you even be found to **f**
1Co	9:26	with uncertainty. Thus I **f**:
1Ti	6:12	**F** the good fight of faith,
2Ti	4: 7	I have fought the good **f**,
Jas	4: 2	You **f** and war. Yet you do
Rev	2:16	to you quickly and will **f**

FIGHTING (*see* FIGHT)

Ex	2:13	two Hebrew men were f,
Acts	7:26	two of them as they were f,

FIGHTS (*see* FIGHT)

Ex	14:25	for the LORD f for them
Josh	23:10	LORD your God is He who f
Jas	4: 1	Where do wars and f come

FIGS (*see* FIG)

2Ki	20: 7	said, "Take a lump of f.
Song	2:13	tree puts forth her green f,
Jer	24: 2	One basket had very good f,
Jer	24: 5	Israel: 'Like these good f,
Jer	29:17	will make them like rotten f
Mark	11:13	it was not the season for f.
Luke	6:44	For men do not gather f
Jas	3:12	or a grapevine bear f?
Rev	6:13	a fig tree drops its late f

FIGURATIVE (*see* FIGURE)

John	16:25	I have spoken to you in f
Heb	11:19	he also received him in a f

FIGURE† (*see* FIGURATIVE)

Deut	4:16	image in the form of any f:
Is	44:13	And makes it like the f of
John	16:29	and using no f of speech!

FILL (*see* FILLED, FILLS, FULL)

Gen	1:22	and f the waters in the
Gen	1:28	f the earth and subdue it;
Gen	9: 1	and f the earth.
1Ki	18:33	F four waterpots with water,
Prov	7:18	let us take our f of love
Jer	23:24	Do I not f heaven and
John	2: 7	F the waterpots with water."
Rom	15:13	Now may the God of hope f you
Eph	4:10	that He might f all things.)
Col	1:24	and f up in my flesh what is

FILLED (*see* FILL)

Gen	6:11	and the earth was f with
Gen	24:16	f her pitcher, and came up.
Ex	1: 7	and the land was f with
Num	14:21	all the earth shall be f
Deut	11:15	that you may eat and be f.
1Ki	18:35	and he also f the trench
Neh	9:25	So they ate and were f and
Ps	72:19	let the whole earth be f
Ps	78:29	So they ate and were well f,
Ps	126: 2	Then our mouth was f with
Prov	3:10	So your barns will be f with
Eccl	1: 8	Nor the ear f with hearing.
Is	6: 1	and the train of His robe f
Is	6: 4	and the house was f with
Jer	15:17	For You have f me with
Ezek	43: 5	the glory of the LORD f the
Dan	2:35	a great mountain and f the
Hab	2:14	For the earth will be f
Matt	5: 6	For they shall be f.
Matt	14:20	So they all ate and were f,
Luke	1:15	He will also be f with the

Luke	1:41	and Elizabeth was f with the
Luke	1:53	He has f the hungry with
Luke	1:67	his father Zacharias was f
Luke	2:40	f with wisdom; and the grace
Luke	6:21	now, For you shall be f.
John	2: 7	And they f them up to the
John	6:13	and f twelve baskets from
John	6:26	ate of the loaves and were f.
John	16: 6	sorrow has f your heart.
Acts	2: 2	and it f the whole house
Acts	2: 4	And they were all f with the
Acts	3:10	and they were f with wonder
Acts	5: 3	why has Satan f your heart
Acts	5:17	and they were f with
Acts	5:28	you have f Jerusalem with
Acts	13: 9	f with the Holy Spirit,
Acts	13:45	they were f with envy; and
Acts	13:52	And the disciples were f with
Rom	1:29	being f with all
Rom	15:14	f with all knowledge, able
Eph	3:19	that you may be f with all
Phil	1:11	being f with the fruits of
Jas	2:16	in peace, be warmed and f,
Rev	15: 8	The temple was f with smoke

FILLS (*see* FILL)

Ps	107: 9	And f the hungry soul with
Eph	1:23	the fullness of Him who f

FILTHY

Is	64: 6	righteousnesses are like f
Col	3. 8	f language out of your
Rev	22:11	be unjust still; he who is f,

FINALLY

2Co	13.11	F, brethren, farewell.
Eph	6:10	F, my brethren, be strong
Phil	4: 8	F, brethren, whatever
2Th	3: 1	F, brethren, pray for us,
2Ti	4: 8	F, there is laid up for me

FIND (*see* FINDING, FINDS, FOUND)

Gen	18:26	If I f in Sodom fifty
Gen	33:15	Let me f favor in the sight
Gen	34:11	Let me f favor in your eyes,
Num	32:23	and be sure your sin will f
Deut	4:29	and you will f Him if you
Ps	132: 5	Until I f a place for the
Prov	2: 5	And f the knowledge of God.
Prov	8: 9	And right to those who f
Prov	8:17	seek me diligently will f
Prov	14: 6	wisdom and does not f it,
Prov	19: 8	keeps understanding will f
Prov	20: 6	But who can f a faithful
Prov	31:10	Who can f a virtuous wife?
Eccl	3:11	except that no one can f out
Song	3: 1	but I did not f him.
Song	5: 8	If you f my beloved, That
Is	41:12	shall seek them and not f
Jer	29:13	And you will seek Me and f
Matt	7: 7	to you; seek, and you will f;
Matt	7:14	and there are few who f it.
Matt	10:39	his life for My sake will f
Matt	11:29	and you will f rest for your

F

Mark	13:36	he f you sleeping.
Luke	2:12	You will f a Babe wrapped in
Luke	2:45	So when they did not f Him,
Luke	12:43	whom his master will f so
Luke	13: 7	on this fig tree and f none.
Luke	18: 8	will He really f faith on
Luke	23: 4	I f no fault in this Man."
Luke	24:23	When they did not f His body,
John	7:34	You will seek Me and not f
John	10: 9	and will go in and out and f
John	21: 6	and you will f some." So
Acts	5:22	officers came and did not f
Acts	7:46	before God and asked to f a
Acts	17: 6	But when they did not f them,
Acts	17:11	the Scriptures daily to f
Acts	17:27	might grope for Him and f
Acts	23: 9	We f no evil in this man; but
Rom	7:18	what is good I do not f.
Rom	9:19	Why does He still f fault?
2Co	9: 4	come with me and f you
Heb	4:16	we may obtain mercy and f
Rev	9: 6	seek death and will not f

FINDING (see FIND)

Gen	4:15	lest anyone f him should
Rom	11:33	and His ways past f out!

FINDS (see FIND)

Gen	4:14	happen that anyone who f
Num	35:27	and the avenger of blood f
Prov	3:13	Happy is the man who f
Prov	8:35	For whoever f me finds life,
Prov	18:22	He who finds a wife f a
Eccl	9:10	Whatever your hand f to do,
Hos	14: 3	For in You the fatherless f
Matt	7: 8	receives, and he who seeks f,
Matt	10:39	He who f his life will lose
Matt	12:44	he f it empty, swept, and
Luke	15: 4	which is lost until he f it?

FINE

Gen	41:42	him in garments of f linen
Num	6:15	cakes of f flour mixed with
Ps	19:10	than much f gold; Sweeter
Prov	31:22	Her clothing is f linen
Jas	2: 2	in f apparel, and there
Rev	1:15	His feet were like f brass,
Rev	19:14	clothed in f linen, white

FINGER (see FINGERS)

Ex	8:19	This is the f of God." But
Ex	31:18	written with the f of God.
Lev	4: 6	The priest shall dip his f in
Lev	16:14	some of the blood with his f
1Ki	12:10	My little f shall be thicker
Luke	11:20	I cast out demons with the f
Luke	16:24	he may dip the tip of his f
John	8: 6	on the ground with His f,
John	20:25	and put my f into the print

FINGERS (see FINGER)

2Sa	21:20	who had six f on each hand
Ps	8: 3	heavens, the work of Your f,
Prov	7: 3	Bind them on your f;

Dan	5: 5	In the same hour the f of a
Dan	5:24	Then the f of the hand were
Matt	23: 4	them with one of their f.
Mark	7:33	and put His f in his ears,

FINISH (see FINISHED, FINISHER)

Ps	90: 9	We f our years like a sigh.
Dan	9:24	To f the transgression, To
Zech	4: 9	His hands shall also f it.
Luke	14:30	build and was not able to f.
John	4:34	and to f His work.
Acts	20:24	so that I may f my race with

FINISHED (see FINISH)

Gen	2: 1	all the host of them, were f.
Ex	40:33	So Moses f the work.
Dan	5:26	your kingdom, and f it;
Dan	12: 7	all these things shall be f.
Matt	11: 1	when Jesus f commanding His
Matt	13:53	when Jesus had f these
John	17: 4	I have f the work which You
John	19:30	It is f!" And bowing His
2Ti	4: 7	I have f the race, I have

FINISHER† (see FINISH)

Heb	12: 2	the author and f of our

FIRE (see FIERY)

Gen	19:24	rained brimstone and f on
Gen	22: 6	and he took the f in his
Gen	22: 7	the f and the wood, but
Ex	3: 2	to him in a flame of f from
Ex	3: 2	the bush was burning with f,
Ex	13:22	by day or the pillar of f
Ex	19:18	LORD descended upon it in f.
Ex	24:17	was like a consuming f on
Ex	32:24	me, and I cast it into the f,
Lev	10: 1	and offered profane f before
Deut	4:24	your God is a consuming f,
Deut	18:10	daughter pass through the f,
Deut	32:22	For a f is kindled by my
Josh	8: 8	you shall set the city on f.
Josh	11:11	Then he burned Hazor with f.
1Ki	18:24	and the God who answers by f,
1Ki	18:25	but put no f under it."
1Ki	18:38	Then the f of the LORD fell
1Ki	19:12	and after the earthquake a f,
1Ki	19:12	the LORD was not in the f;
1Ki	19:12	and after the f a still
2Ki	1:10	And f came down from
2Ki	1:12	And the f of God came down
2Ki	2:11	appeared with horses of f,
2Ki	6:17	of horses and chariots of f
2Ki	16: 3	his son pass through the f,
2Ki	19:18	cast their gods into the f;
2Ki	21: 6	his son pass through the f,
2Ki	23:10	daughter pass through the f
Neh	1: 3	gates are burned with f.
Neh	2: 3	its gates are burned with f?
Job	1:16	The f of God fell from heaven
Job	20:26	An unfanned f will consume
Job	41:19	Sparks of f shoot out.
Ps	18: 8	And devouring f from His
Ps	18:12	hailstones and coals of f.

Ps	50: 3	A f shall devour before
Ps	66:12	We went through f and
Ps	68: 2	As wax melts before the f,
Ps	74: 7	They have set f to Your
Ps	79: 5	Your jealousy burn like f?
Ps	83:14	sets the mountains on f,
Ps	89:46	Will Your wrath burn like f?
Ps	104: 4	His ministers a flame of f.
Ps	148: 8	F and hail, snow and clouds
Prov	6:27	Can a man take f to his
Prov	16:27	on his lips like a burning f.
Prov	25:22	you will heap coals of f on
Prov	26:20	the f goes out; And where
Prov	30:16	And the f never says,
Song	8: 6	Its flames are flames of f,
Is	1: 7	cities are burned with f;
Is	43: 2	When you walk through the f,
Is	44:16	burns half of it in the f;
Is	66:24	And their f is not
Jer	15:14	For a f is kindled in My
Jer	20: 9	in my heart like a burning f
Jer	23:29	"Is not My word like a f?
Dan	3:24	into the midst of the f?
Dan	3:27	and the smell of f was not
Joel	2:30	Blood and f and pillars of
Amos	1: 4	But I will send a f into the
Mic	1: 4	split Like wax before the f,
Zeph	1:18	shall be devoured By the f
Zech	2: 5	will be a wall of f all
Zech	3: 2	a brand plucked from the f?
Mal	1:10	that you would not kindle f
Mal	3: 2	He is like a refiner's f
Matt	3:10	down and thrown into the f.
Matt	3:11	with the Holy Spirit and f.
Matt	3:12	chaff with unquenchable f.
Matt	5:22	shall be in danger of hell f.
Matt	13:42	them into the furnace of f.
Matt	13:50	them into the furnace of f.
Matt	17:15	he often falls into the f
Matt	18: 8	cast into the everlasting f.
Mark	9:44	And the f is not
Mark	9:49	will be seasoned with f,
Mark	14:54	and warmed himself at the f.
Luke	9:54	do You want us to command f
Luke	12:49	I came to send f on the
Luke	17:29	out of Sodom it rained f
John	21: 9	they saw a f of coals there,
Acts	2: 3	divided tongues, as of f,
Acts	2:19	Blood and f and vapor
Acts	7:30	to him in a flame of f in a
Acts	28: 5	off the creature into the f
Rom	12:20	will heap coals of f
1Co	3:13	it will be revealed by f;
1Co	3:13	and the f will test each
1Co	3:15	saved, yet so as through f.
2Th	1: 8	in flaming f taking vengeance
Heb	1: 7	ministers a flame of f.
Heb	12:29	our God is a consuming f.
Jas	3: 5	great a forest a little f
Jas	3: 6	and sets on f the course of
Jas	3: 6	and it is set on f by hell.
1Pe	1: 7	though it is tested by f,
2Pe	3: 7	are reserved for f until the
2Pe	3:12	be dissolved, being on f,

Jude	7	the vengeance of eternal f.
Rev	1:14	His eyes like a flame of f;
Rev	3:18	Me gold refined in the f,
Rev	8: 5	filled it with f from the
Rev	10: 1	his feet like pillars of f.
Rev	11: 5	f proceeds from their mouth
Rev	14:10	He shall be tormented with f
Rev	19:20	alive into the lake of f
Rev	20: 9	And f came down from God out
Rev	20:10	was cast into the lake of f

FIRM

Is	35: 3	And make f the feeble

FIRMAMENT

Gen	1: 6	Let there be a f in the midst
Gen	1: 8	And God called the f Heaven.
Ps	19: 1	And the f shows His
Ps	150: 1	Praise Him in His mighty f!
Ezek	1:26	And above the f over their
Dan	12: 3	the brightness of the f,

FIRST (see FIRSTBORN, FIRSTFRUIT)

Gen	1: 5	and the morning were the f
Gen	26: 1	besides the f famine that
Ex	12: 5	a male of the f year. You
Judg	1: 1	Who shall be f to go up for
1Ki	3:27	Give the f woman the living
2Ch	36:22	Now in the f year of Cyrus
Ezra	1: 1	Now in the f year of Cyrus
Job	40:19	He is the f of the ways of
Ps	105:36	The f of all their
Is	41: 4	'I, the LORD, am the f;
Is	43:27	Your f father sinned, And
Is	44: 6	I am the F and I am the
Hos	2: 7	will go and return to my f
Matt	5:24	F be reconciled to your
Matt	6:33	But seek f the kingdom of God
Matt	7: 5	Hypocrite! F remove the plank
Matt	8:21	let me f go and bury my
Matt	12:45	that man is worse than the f.
Matt	17:10	say that Elijah must come f?
Matt	19:30	But many who are f will be
Matt	20:27	whoever desires to be f
Matt	22:38	This is the f and great
Mark	4:28	f the blade, then the head,
Mark	9:35	"If anyone desires to be f,
Mark	12:28	Which is the f commandment of
Mark	13:10	And the gospel must f be
Mark	16: 9	He appeared f to Mary
Luke	2: 2	This census f took place
John	1:41	He f found his own brother
Acts	11:26	And the disciples were f
Acts	13:24	after John had f preached,
Rom	1: 8	F, I thank my God
Rom	1:16	for the Jew f and also for
Rom	13:11	is nearer than when we f
1Co	12:28	f apostles, second prophets,
1Co	14:30	let the f keep silent.
1Co	15:45	The f man Adam became a
1Co	16: 2	On the f day of the week let
2Co	8: 5	but they f gave themselves
2Co	8:12	For if there is f a willing
Gal	4:13	the gospel to you at the f.

F

Eph	1:12	that we who f trusted in
Eph	4: 9	it mean but that He also f
Eph	6: 2	which is the f commandment
1Th	4:16	dead in Christ will rise f.
2Th	2: 3	the falling away comes f,
1Ti	2:13	For Adam was formed f,
2Ti	1: 5	which dwelt f in your
2Ti	2: 6	farmer must be f to partake
2Ti	4:16	At my f defense no one stood
Heb	2: 3	which at the f began to be
Heb	5:12	to teach you again the f
Heb	7:27	f for His own sins and then
Heb	8: 7	For if that f covenant had
Heb	8:13	He has made the f
Heb	9: 8	made manifest while the f
Heb	10: 9	He takes away the f that
Jas	3:17	that is from above is f
1Pe	4:17	and if it begins with us f,
2Pe	1:20	knowing this f,
1Jn	4:19	We love Him because He f
Rev	1:11	the F and the Last," and,
Rev	1:17	I am the F and the Last.
Rev	2: 4	that you have left your f
Rev	2: 5	repent and do the f works,
Rev	20: 5	This is the f resurrection.
Rev	21: 1	for the f heaven and the
Rev	21: 1	the first heaven and the f
Rev	22:13	the F and the Last."

FIRSTBORN (see FIRST)

Gen	4: 4	Abel also brought of the f of
Gen	19:33	And the f went in and lay
Gen	27:19	father, "I am Esau your f;
Ex	4:22	"Israel is My son, My f.
Ex	4:23	I will kill your son, your f.
Ex	11: 5	from the f of Pharaoh who
Ex	13: 2	"Consecrate to Me all the f,
Deut	21:17	the right of the f is his.
Mic	6: 7	Shall I give my f for my
Matt	1:25	she had brought forth her f
Rom	8:29	that He might be the f among
Col	1:15	the f over all creation.
Col	1:18	the f from the dead, that in
Heb	12:23	and church of the f who

FIRSTFRUIT† (see FIRST, FIRSTFRUITS)

Rom	11:16	For if the f is holy, the

FIRSTFRUITS (see FIRSTFRUIT)

Ex	23:16	the f of your labors which
Lev	2:12	for the offering of the f,
Jer	2: 3	The f of His increase. All
Rom	8:23	but we also who have the f
Rom	16: 5	who is the f of Achaia to
1Co	15:20	and has become the f of
1Co	15:23	his own order: Christ the f,
Jas	1:18	we might be a kind of f of

FISH

Gen	1:26	have dominion over the f of
Num	11: 5	We remember the f which we
Deut	4:18	or the likeness of any f
Ps	8: 8	And the f of the sea That
Jon	1:17	was in the belly of the f

Matt	7:10	"Or if he asks for a f,
Matt	12:40	in the belly of the great f,
Matt	14:17	only five loaves and two f.
Matt	15:34	"Seven, and a few little f.
Luke	11:11	him a serpent instead of a f?
Luke	24:42	Him a piece of a broiled f
1Co	15:39	of animals, another of f,

FISHERS

Matt	4:19	and I will make you f of

FIT (see FITLY, FITTING)

Luke	9:62	is f for the kingdom of
Acts	22:22	for he is not f to live!"

FITLY (see FIT)

Prov	25:11	A word f spoken is like

FITTING (see FIT)

Prov	26: 1	So honor is not f for a
Matt	3:15	for thus it is f for us to
Rom	1:28	those things which are not f;
Col	3:18	as is f in the Lord.

FIVE (see FIFTH)

Gen	18:28	Suppose there were f less
Josh	13: 3	the f lords of the
1Sa	6: 4	F golden tumors and five
Matt	14:17	We have here only f loaves
Matt	14:21	who had eaten were about f
Matt	25: 2	and f were foolish.
Matt	25:15	And to one he gave f talents,
John	4:18	for you have had f husbands,
1Co	15: 6	that He was seen by over f

FLAME (see FLAMING)

Ex	3: 2	appeared to him in a f of
Ps	104: 4	His ministers a f of fire.
Acts	7:30	Lord appeared to him in a f
Heb	1: 7	And His ministers a f
Rev	1:14	and His eyes like a f of

FLAMING (see FLAME)

Gen	3:24	and a f sword which turned
2Th	1: 8	in f fire taking vengeance on

FLASK

1Sa	10: 1	Then Samuel took a f of oil
Jer	19: 1	and get a potter's earthen f,
Mark	14: 3	Then she broke the f and
Luke	7:37	brought an alabaster f of

FLAVOR

Matt	5:13	but if the salt loses its f,

FLAX

Judg	15:14	on his arms became like f
Prov	31:13	She seeks wool and f,
Is	42: 3	And smoking f He will not
Matt	12:20	And smoking f He will

FLED (see FLEE)

Gen	31:22	third day that Jacob had f.
Ex	4: 3	and Moses f from it.

Ex	14: 5	Egypt that the people had **f**,
Num	35:25	of refuge where he had **f**,
1Sa	4:10	and every man **f** to his tent.
1Sa	17:51	champion was dead, they **f**.
1Sa	21:10	Then David arose and **f** that
2Sa	4: 4	his nurse took him up and **f**.
1Ki	2:28	So Joab **f** to the tabernacle
2Ki	7: 7	and they **f** for their lives.
Ps	104: 7	At Your rebuke they **f**;
Ps	114: 5	ails you, O sea, that you **f**?
Is	21:15	For they **f** from the swords,
Jer	4:25	birds of the heavens had **f**.
Jer	26:21	it, he was afraid and **f**,
Dan	10: 7	so that they **f** to hide
Amos	5:19	will be as though a man **f**
Jon	1:10	For the men knew that he **f**
Jon	4: 2	Therefore I **f** previously to
Matt	26:56	disciples forsook Him and **f**.
Mark	5:14	So those who fed the swine **f**,
Mark	14:52	left the linen cloth and **f**
Mark	16: 8	they went out quickly and **f**
Acts	16:27	the prisoners had **f**,
Rev	20:11	the earth and the heaven **f**

FLEE (see FLED)

Gen	19:20	city is near enough to **f**
Gen	31:27	Why did you **f** away secretly,
Lev	26:17	and you shall **f** when no one
Num	35: 6	to which a manslayer may **f**.
Num	35:11	person accidentally may **f**
Num	35:15	a person accidentally may **f**
Deut	28: 7	against you one way and **f**
Deut	28:25	one way against them and **f**
Josh	8:20	So they had no power to **f**
2Sa	15:14	"Arise, and let us **f**;
2Sa	19: 3	steal away when they **f** in
Job	41:28	The arrow cannot make him **f**;
Ps	31:11	Those who see me outside **f**
Ps	64: 8	All who see them shall **f**
Ps	68: 1	those also who hate Him **f**
Ps	68:12	"Kings of armies **f**,
Ps	68:12	of armies flee, they **f**,
Ps	139: 7	Or where can I **f** from Your
Prov	28: 1	The wicked **f** when no one
Song	2:17	breaks And the shadows **f**
Song	4: 6	breaks And the shadows **f**
Is	30:17	One thousand shall **f** at
Is	35:10	sorrow and sighing shall **f**
Matt	24:16	those who are in Judea **f** to
1Co	6:18	**F** sexual immorality. Every
1Co	10:14	**f** from idolatry.
2Ti	2:22	**F** also youthful lusts; but
Jas	4: 7	the devil and he will **f**

FLEECE

Judg	6:37	if there is dew on the **f**

FLESH (see FLESHLY)

Gen	2:21	and closed up the **f** in its
Gen	2:23	my bones And flesh of my **f**;
Gen	2:24	and they shall become one **f**.
Gen	6: 3	forever, for he is indeed **f**;
Gen	6:12	for all **f** had corrupted
Gen	6:13	The end of all **f** has come

Gen	9: 4	But you shall not eat **f** with
Gen	17:11	be circumcised in the **f** of
Gen	17:13	covenant shall be in your **f**
Gen	37:27	is our brother and our **f**.
Ex	4: 7	restored like his other **f**.
Lev	17:11	For the life of the **f** is in
Lev	21: 5	make any cuttings in their **f**.
Num	16:22	God of the spirits of all **f**,
2Ki	5:14	and his **f** was restored like
Job	7: 5	My **f** is caked with worms and
Job	19:26	That in my **f** I shall see
Job	34:15	All **f** would perish together,
Ps	16: 9	My **f** also will rest in
Ps	27: 2	against me To eat up my **f**,
Ps	38: 7	is no soundness in my **f**.
Ps	56: 4	What can **f** do to me?
Ps	63: 1	My **f** longs for You In a
Ps	65: 2	To You all **f** will come.
Ps	73:26	My **f** and my heart fail;
Ps	78:39	that they were but **f**,
Ps	84: 2	My heart and my **f** cry out
Ps	119:120	My **f** trembles for fear of
Ps	136:25	Who gives food to all **f**,
Ps	145:21	And all **f** shall bless His
Prov	3: 8	It will be health to your **f**,
Eccl	12:12	study is wearisome to the **f**.
Is	31: 3	God; And their horses are **f**,
Is	40: 5	And all **f** shall see it
Is	40: 6	All **f** is grass, And all its
Is	49:26	All **f** shall know That I,
Is	65: 4	tombs; Who eat swine's **f**,
Is	66:24	be an abhorrence to all **f**.
Jer	17: 5	trusts in man And makes **f**
Jer	32:27	the LORD, the God of all **f**.
Ezek	11:19	stony heart out of their **f**,
Ezek	11:19	and give them a heart of **f**,
Ezek	37: 6	sinews on you and bring **f**
Ezek	44: 7	heart and uncircumcised in **f**,
Dan	1:15	better and fatter in **f** than
Joel	2:28	pour out My Spirit on all **f**;
Matt	16:17	for **f** and blood has not
Matt	19: 5	two shall become one **f**'
Matt	24:22	no **f** would be saved; but for
Matt	26:41	but the **f** is weak."
Luke	24:39	for a spirit does not have **f**
John	1:13	nor of the will of the **f**,
John	1:14	And the Word became **f** and
John	3: 6	which is born of the **f**
John	6:52	this Man give us His **f** to
John	6:53	unless you eat the **f** of the
John	6:55	For My **f** is food indeed, and
John	6:63	the **f** profits nothing. The
John	17: 2	Him authority over all **f**,
Acts	2:17	of My Spirit on all **f**;
Rom	1: 3	of David according to the **f**,
Rom	3:20	by the deeds of the law no **f**
Rom	7:18	in my **f**) nothing good
Rom	8: 1	not walk according to the **f**,
Rom	8: 3	it was weak through the **f**,
Rom	8: 3	in the likeness of sinful **f**,
Rom	8: 3	He condemned sin in the **f**,
Rom	8: 5	minds on the things of the **f**,
Rom	8: 9	But you are not in the **f** but
Rom	8:12	to live according to the **f**.

F

Rom	13:14	make no provision for the f,
1Co	1:26	many wise according to the f,
1Co	1:29	that no f should glory in His
1Co	5: 5	for the destruction of the f,
1Co	6:16	"shall become one f.
1Co	15:39	another f of animals,
2Co	3: 3	of stone but on tablets of f,
2Co	4:11	manifested in our mortal f.
2Co	10: 3	For though we walk in the f,
2Co	12: 7	a thorn in the f was given
Gal	1:16	immediately confer with f
Gal	2:16	by the works of the law no f
Gal	2:20	which I now live in the f I
Gal	5:13	as an opportunity for the f,
Gal	5:16	fulfill the lust of the f.
Gal	5:17	and the Spirit against the f;
Gal	5:24	have crucified the f with
Gal	6: 8	For he who sows to his f will
Eph	2:15	having abolished in His f the
Eph	5:29	no one ever hated his own f,
Eph	5:30	of His f and of His bones.
Eph	5:31	two shall become one f.
Eph	6:12	we do not wrestle against f
Phil	3: 3	have no confidence in the f,
Col	1:22	in the body of His f through
Col	1:24	and fill up in my f what is
Col	2: 5	though I am absent in the f,
Col	2:23	the indulgence of the f.
1Ti	3:16	was manifested in the f,
Heb	5: 7	who, in the days of His f,
Heb	10:20	the veil, that is, His f,
1Pe	1:24	All f is as grass, And
1Pe	4: 1	he who has suffered in the f
2Pe	2:10	who walk according to the f
1Jn	2:16	the world—the lust of the f,
1Jn	4: 2	Christ has come in the f is
Jude	7	and gone after strange f,

FLESHLY (see FLESH)

2Co	1:12	not with f wisdom but by the
1Pe	2:11	abstain from f lusts which

FLEW (see FLY)

2Sa	22:11	rode upon a cherub, and f;
Ps	18:10	He f upon the wings of the
Is	6: 2	his feet, and with two he f.
Is	6: 6	Then one of the seraphim f

FLIES (see FLY)

Ex	8:21	I will send swarms of f on
Ps	91: 5	Nor of the arrow that f
Eccl	10: 1	Dead f putrefy the

FLIGHT (see FLY)

Lev	26: 8	shall put ten thousand to f;
Heb	11:34	turned to f the armies of

FLINT (see FLINTY)

Josh	5: 2	Make f knives for yourself,
Is	50: 7	I have set My face like a f,
Zech	7:12	made their hearts like f,

FLINTY (see FLINT)

Deut	32:13	And oil from the f rock;

FLOCK (see FLOCKS)

Gen	4: 4	of the firstborn of his f
Gen	30:40	not put them with Laban's f.
Ex	2:16	to water their father's f.
Ex	3: 1	Now Moses was tending the f
Lev	5:18	without blemish from the f,
Song	4: 1	Your hair is like a f of
Is	40:11	He will feed His f like a
Jer	23: 2	"You have scattered My f,
Ezek	34: 3	but you do not feed the f.
Ezek	34:15	"I will feed My f,
Amos	7:15	took me as I followed the f,
Luke	2: 8	keeping watch over their f
Luke	12:32	"Do not fear, little f,
John	10:16	and there will be one f and
1Pe	5: 2	Shepherd the f of God which
1Pe	5: 3	but being examples to the f;

FLOCKS (see FLOCK)

Gen	24:35	and He has given him f and
Gen	30:36	fed the rest of Laban's f.
Ezek	34: 2	not the shepherds feed the f?

FLOOD (see FLOODS, FLOODWATERS)

Gen	7: 7	of the waters of the f.
Gen	9:11	again shall there be a f to
Ps	29:10	sat enthroned at the F,
Is	59:19	the enemy comes in like a f,
Matt	24:38	as in the days before the f,

FLOODS (see FLOOD)

Song	8: 7	Nor can the f drown it. If
Jon	2: 3	And the f surrounded me;
Matt	7:25	the f came, and the winds

FLOODWATERS (see FLOOD, WATERS)

Gen	6:17	I Myself am bringing f on

FLOOR

Num	5:17	of the dust that is on the f
Num	18:27	the grain of the threshing f
Ruth	3:14	came to the threshing f.

FLOURISH (see FLOURISHES)

Job	8:11	Can the reeds f without
Ps	72: 7	days the righteous shall f,
Ps	72:16	those of the city shall f
Ps	92: 7	the workers of iniquity f,
Ps	92:12	The righteous shall f like a
Ps	92:13	house of the LORD Shall f
Prov	11:28	But the righteous will f
Prov	14:11	tent of the upright will f.
Is	66:14	And your bones shall f like
Ezek	17:24	tree and made the dry tree f;

FLOURISHES (see FLOURISH)

Ps	90: 6	In the morning it f and

FLOW (see FLOWING)

Lev	12: 7	shall be clean from the f
Ps	147:18	to blow, and the waters f.
Is	2: 2	And all nations shall f to
Is	8: 6	waters of Shiloah that f

Is	48:21	He caused the waters to **f**
Jer	14:17	Let my eyes **f** with tears
Lam	3:49	My eyes **f** and do not cease,
Joel	3:18	A fountain shall **f** from the
Amos	9:13	And all the hills shall **f**
Mic	4: 1	And peoples shall **f** to it.
Zech	14: 8	living waters shall **f** from
Mark	5:25	Now a certain woman had a **f**
John	7:38	out of his heart will **f**

FLOWER (see FLOWERS)

1Sa	2:33	house shall die in the **f** of
Job	14: 2	.He comes forth like a **f** and
Ps	103:15	As a **f** of the field, so he
Is	18: 5	grape is ripening in the **f**,
Is	40: 8	the **f** fades, But the word
1Co	7:36	if she is past the **f** of
Jas	1:10	because as a **f** of the field
1Pe	1:24	And its **f** falls away,

FLOWERS (see FLOWER)

Song	2:12	The **f** appear on the earth;

FLOWING (see FLOW)

Ex	13: 5	a land **f** with milk and
Ezek	47: 1	the water was **f** from under

FLUTE

Gen	4:21	who play the harp and **f**.
Matt	9:23	and saw the **f** players and

FLY (see FLEW, FLIES, FLIGHT)

Gen	1:20	and let birds **f** above the
Job	5: 7	As the sparks **f** upward.
Ps	90:10	and we **f** away.
Is	7:18	LORD will whistle for the **f**

FOAL†

Zech	9: 9	the **f** of a donkey.' ”
Matt	21: 5	the **f** of a donkey.' ”

FOAMING† (see FOAMS)

Mark	9:20	**f** at the mouth.
Jude	13	**f** up their own shame;

FOAMS (see FOAMING)

Mark	9:18	he **f** at the mouth, gnashes

FOLD (see FOLDED, FOLDING, FOLDS)

Neh	5:13	Then I shook out the **f** of my
Ezek	34:14	shall lie down in a good **f**
John	10:16	have which are not of this **f**;
Heb	1:12	a cloak You will **f**

FOLDED† (see FOLD)

John	20: 7	but **f** together in a place by

FOLDING (see FOLD)

Prov	6:10	A little **f** of the hands to

FOLDS (see FOLD)

Num	32:36	and **f** for sheep.
Job	41:23	The **f** of his flesh are
Eccl	4: 5	The fool **f** his hands And

FOLLOW (see FOLLOWED, FOLLOWERS, FOLLOWING, FOLLOWS)

Deut	8:19	and **f** other gods, and serve
1Ki	11: 6	and did not fully **f** the
1Ki	18:21	**f** Him; but if Baal, follow
Ps	23: 6	goodness and mercy shall **f**
Ps	94:15	the upright in heart will **f**
Jer	13:10	who **f** the dictates of their
Matt	4:19	**F** Me, and I will make you
Matt	8:19	I will **f** You wherever You
Matt	8:22	**F** Me, and let the dead bury
Matt	10:38	not take his cross and **f**
Matt	16:24	up his cross and **f** Me.
Matt	19:21	and come, **f** Me.”
Mark	1:17	**F** Me, and I will make you
Mark	5:37	And He permitted no one to **f**
Mark	16:17	And these signs will **f** those
Luke	9:57	I will **f** You wherever You
John	1:43	said to him, **F** Me.”
John	10: 4	and the sheep **f** him, for
John	10:27	and they **f** Me.
John	13:36	I am going you cannot **f** Me
John	13:36	but you shall **f** Me
Acts	3:24	from Samuel and those who **f**,
1Ti	5:24	but those of some men **f**
1Pe	1:11	and the glories that would **f**.
1Pe	2:21	that you should **f** His steps:
2Pe	1:16	For we did not **f** cunningly
Rev	14:13	and their works **f** them.”

FOLLOWED (see FOLLOW, WALKED)

Num	14:24	spirit in him and has **f** Me
Num	32:11	they have not wholly **f** Me,
Judg	2:12	and they **f** other gods from
Amos	7:15	the LORD took me as I **f**
Matt	4:20	left their nets and **f** Him.
Matt	4:22	their father, and **f** Him.
Matt	4:25	Great multitudes **f** Him—from
Matt	8:23	His disciples **f** Him.
Matt	9:27	two blind men **f** Him, crying
Matt	19:27	we have left all and **f** You.
Matt	26:58	But Peter **f** Him at a distance
Matt	27:55	And many women who **f** Jesus
Matt	27:62	which **f** the Day of
Mark	14:51	Now a certain young man **f**
Luke	5:11	they forsook all and **f** Him.
Luke	18:43	and **f** Him, glorifying God.
John	1:40	and **f** Him, was Andrew, Simon
John	18:15	And Simon Peter **f** Jesus, and
Acts	13:43	Jews and devout proselytes **f**
1Co	10: 4	that spiritual Rock that **f**
1Ti	5:10	if she has diligently **f**
2Ti	3:10	But you have carefully **f** my
Rev	6: 8	and Hades **f** with him. And
Rev	8: 7	sounded: And hail and fire **f**,
Rev	13: 3	all the world marveled and **f**

FOLLOWERS (see FOLLOW)

1Th	1: 6	And you became **f** of us and of

FOLLOWING (see FOLLOW)

Judg	2:19	by **f** other gods, to serve
Ruth	1:16	Or to turn back from **f**

F

FOLLOWS (see FOLLOW)

Ps	63: 8	My soul f close behind You;
John	8:12	He who f Me shall not walk

FOLLY (see FOOL)

1Sa	25:25	and f is with him. But I,
Job	42: 8	you according to your f;
Prov	26: 4	a fool according to his f,
Eccl	1:17	and to know madness and f.
Eccl	7:25	To know the wickedness of f,
2Ti	3: 9	for their f will be manifest

FOOD (see FOODS)

Gen	1:29	to you it shall be for f.
Gen	1:30	every green herb for f";
Gen	2: 9	to the sight and good for f.
Job	23:12	More than my necessary f.
Ps	42: 3	My tears have been my f day
Ps	69:21	also gave me gall for my f,
Ps	78:25	Men ate angels' f;
Ps	78:25	He sent them f to the full.
Ps	104:14	That he may bring forth f
Ps	104:21	And seek their f from God.
Ps	104:27	You may give them their f
Ps	136:25	Who gives f to all flesh,
Ps	146: 7	Who gives f to the hungry.
Prov	6: 8	And gathers her f in the
Prov	23: 3	For they are deceptive f.
Prov	31:14	She brings her f from afar.
Prov	31:15	And provides f for her
Is	65:25	shall be the serpent's f.
Mal	3:10	That there may be f in My
Matt	3: 4	and his f was locusts and
Matt	6:25	Is not life more than f and
Matt	10:10	a worker is worthy of his f.
Matt	24:45	to give them f in due
Matt	25:35	was hungry and you gave Me f;
Luke	9:13	unless we go and buy f for
Luke	12:23	"Life is more than f,
Luke	24:41	Have you any f here?"
John	4: 8	away into the city to buy f.
John	4:32	I have f to eat of which you
John	4:34	My f is to do the will of Him
John	6:27	Do not labor for the f which
John	6:27	but for the f which endures
John	6:55	For My flesh is f indeed, and
John	21: 5	"Children, have you any f?
Acts	27:21	after long abstinence from f,
Rom	14:15	Do not destroy with your f
1Co	3: 2	milk and not with solid f;
1Co	8: 8	But f does not commend us to
1Co	8:13	if f makes my brother
1Co	10: 3	all ate the same spiritual f,
1Co	10:30	I evil spoken of for the f
2Co	9:10	the sower, and bread for f,
Col	2:16	So let no one judge you in f
Heb	12:16	who for one morsel of f sold
Jas	2:15	and destitute of daily f,

FOODS (see FOOD)

1Co	6:13	and the stomach for f,

FOOL (see FOLLY, FOOL'S, FOOLISH, FOOLS)

Ps	14: 1	The f has said in his heart,
Prov	11:29	And the f will be servant
Prov	12:15	The way of a f is right in
Prov	15: 5	A f despises his father's
Prov	17:10	Than a hundred blows on a f.
Prov	26: 4	Do not answer a f according
Prov	26: 5	Answer a f according to his
Prov	26:12	is more hope for a f than
Matt	5:22	You f!' shall be in danger of
Luke	12:20	F! This night your soul will
2Co	11:23	of Christ?—I speak as a f—

FOOL'S (see FOOL)

Prov	12:16	A f wrath is known at once,
Prov	18: 7	A f mouth is his
Prov	26: 3	And a rod for the f back.
Eccl	5: 3	And a f voice is known by

FOOLISH (see FOOL, FOOLISHNESS)

Job	2:10	You speak as one of the f
Prov	10: 1	But a f son is the grief
Ezek	13: 3	Woe to the f prophets, who
Matt	25: 2	were wise, and five were f.
Luke	24:25	O f ones, and slow of heart
Rom	1:21	and their f hearts were
1Co	1:20	Has not God made f the
1Co	1:27	But God has chosen the f
Gal	3: 1	O f Galatians! Who has
2Ti	2:23	But avoid f and ignorant
Tit	3: 9	But avoid f disputes,

FOOLISHNESS (see FOOLISH)

Prov	15: 2	mouth of fools pours forth f.
Prov	22:15	F is bound up in the heart
1Co	1:18	message of the cross is f
1Co	1:21	it pleased God through the f
1Co	1:23	block and to the Greeks f,
1Co	1:25	Because the f of God is wiser
1Co	2:14	for they are f to him; nor
1Co	3:19	wisdom of this world is f

FOOLS (see FOOL)

Prov	1: 7	But f despise wisdom and
Prov	19:29	beatings for the backs of f.
Prov	26: 7	a proverb in the mouth of f.
Eccl	5: 4	He has no pleasure in f.
Eccl	10:15	The labor of f wearies them,
Matt	23:17	F and blind! For which is
Rom	1:22	to be wise, they became f,
1Co	4:10	We are f for Christ's sake,
Eph	5:15	not as f but as wise,

FOOT (see FEET, FOOTSTOOL, FOUR-FOOTED)

Gen	8: 9	place for the sole of her f,
Ex	21:24	hand for hand, foot for f,
Ex	29:20	the big toe of their right f,
Lev	11:26	animal which divides the f,
Lev	13:12	sore, from his head to his f,
Job	2: 7	from the sole of his f to
Ps	38:16	when my f slips, they exalt
Ps	66: 6	went through the river on f.
Ps	91:12	Lest you dash your f

Ps	121: 3	He will not allow your **f** to
Prov	1:15	Keep your **f** from their
Is	1: 6	From the sole of the **f** even
Matt	4: 6	Lest you dash your **f**
Matt	18: 8	If your hand or **f** causes you
Matt	22:13	'Bind him hand and **f**,
John	11:44	came out bound hand and **f**
1Co	12:15	If the **f** should say,

FOOTSTOOL (see FOOT)

2Ch	9:18	with a **f** of gold, which
Ps	99: 5	God, And worship at His **f**—
Ps	110: 1	I make Your enemies Your **f**.
Is	66: 1	throne, And earth is My **f**.
Matt	5:35	the earth, for it is His **f**;
Matt	22:44	Your enemies Your **f**'"?
Acts	7:49	And earth is My **f**.
Heb	1:13	Your enemies Your **f**"?
Jas	2: 3	or, "Sit here at my **f**,

FORBEARANCE

Rom	2: 4	riches of His goodness, **f**,
Rom	3:25	because in His **f** God had

FORBID

1Sa	24: 6	The LORD **f** that I should do
Matt	19:14	and do not **f** them; for of
Acts	10:47	Can anyone **f** water, that
Gal	6:14	But God **f** that I should boast

FORCE

Matt	11:12	and the violent take it by **f**.
John	6:15	to come and take Him by **f**

FOREHEAD (see FOREHEADS)

Ex	28:38	it shall always be on his **f**,
1Sa	17:49	the Philistine in his **f**,
Rev	14: 9	receives his mark on his **f**
Rev	17: 5	And on her **f** a name was

FOREHEADS (see FOREHEAD)

Ezek	9: 4	and put a mark on the **f** of
Rev	9: 4	the seal of God on their **f**.
Rev	13:16	right hand or on their **f**,
Rev	14: 1	name written on their **f**.

FOREIGN (see FOREIGNER)

Gen	35: 2	Put away the **f** gods that are
Ex	2:22	have been a stranger in a **f**
Ex	21: 8	no right to sell her to a **f**
Josh	24:23	put away the **f** gods which
1Ki	11: 1	King Solomon loved many **f**
1Ki	11: 8	did likewise for all his **f**
Ps	81: 9	shall you worship any **f** god.
Ps	137: 4	the LORD's song In a **f**
Jer	5:19	forsaken Me and served **f**
Mal	2:11	married the daughter of a **f**
Heb	11: 9	land of promise as in a **f**

FOREIGNER (see FOREIGN, FOREIGNERS, STRANGER)

Gen	17:12	with money from any **f** who
Ex	12:43	No **f** shall eat it.
Deut	17:15	you may not set a **f** over

Ruth	2:10	of me, since I am a **f**?
Ezek	44: 9	says the Lord GOD: "No **f**,
Luke	17:18	glory to God except this **f**?
1Co	14:11	I shall be a **f** to him who

FOREIGNERS (see FOREIGNER)

Deut	31:16	with the gods of the **f** of
Is	25: 2	A palace of **f** to be a city
Jer	30: 8	**F** shall no more enslave
Lam	5: 2	aliens, And our houses to **f**.
Acts	17:21	all the Athenians and the **f**
Eph	2:19	no longer strangers and **f**,

FOREKNEW (see FOREKNOWLEDGE)

Rom	11: 2	away His people whom He **f**.

FOREKNOWLEDGE† (see FOREKNEW)

Acts	2:23	determined purpose and **f** of
1Pe	1: 2	elect according to the **f** of

FOREORDAINED†

1Pe	1:20	He indeed was **f** before the

FORERUNNER†

Heb	6:20	where the **f** has entered for

FORESEEING

Gal	3: 8	**f** that God would justify the

FORESKIN (see FORESKINS)

Gen	17:14	in the flesh of his **f**,
Ex	4:25	stone and cut off the **f** of

FORESKINS (see FORESKIN)

1Sa	18:25	any dowry but one hundred **f**

FOREST (see FORESTS)

Jas	3: 5	See how great a **f** a little

FORESTS (see FOREST)

Ps	29: 9	And strips the **f** bare; And

FORETOLD

Acts	3:18	those things which God **f** by
Acts	3:24	have also **f** these days.

FOREVER (see ALWAYS, FOREVERMORE, WORLD)

Gen	3:22	and eat, and live **f**"—
Gen	6: 3	shall not strive with man **f**,
Gen	13:15	you and your descendants **f**.
Ex	3:15	to you. This is My name **f**,
Ex	12:24	for you and your sons **f**.
Ex	15:18	The LORD shall reign **f** and
2Sa	7:13	the throne of his kingdom **f**.
2Sa	7:16	shall be established **f**
2Sa	7:24	Your very own people **f**;
2Sa	7:25	establish it **f** and do as
2Sa	7:26	let Your name be magnified **f**,
2Sa	7:29	that it may continue **f**
2Sa	7:29	of Your servant be blessed **f**.
2Ki	8:19	lamp to him and his sons **f**.
1Ch	16:15	Remember His covenant **f**,
1Ch	16:34	For His mercy endures **f**.

F

Neh	2: 3	May the king live f! Why
Ps	10:16	The LORD is King f and
Ps	19: 9	LORD is clean, enduring f;
Ps	21: 4	Length of days f and ever.
Ps	23: 6	in the house of the LORD F.
Ps	29:10	the LORD sits as King f.
Ps	30:12	I will give thanks to You f.
Ps	44:23	Do not cast us off f.
Ps	73:26	of my heart and my portion f.
Ps	74: 1	why have You cast us off f?
Ps	89: 1	the mercies of the LORD f;
Ps	106: 1	For His mercy endures f.
Ps	110: 4	You are a priest f
Ps	111: 3	His righteousness endures f.
Ps	117: 2	of the LORD endures f.
Ps	119:44	continually, F and ever.
Ps	119:89	F, O LORD, Your word
Ps	125: 1	be moved, but abides f.
Ps	125: 2	From this time forth and f.
Ps	135:13	name, O LORD, endures f,
Ps	136: 1	For His mercy endures f.
Ps	145: 1	I will bless Your name f
Ps	145: 2	I will praise Your name f
Ps	146:10	The LORD shall reign f—
Eccl	1: 4	But the earth abides f.
Is	9: 7	that time forward, even f.
Is	25: 8	He will swallow up death f,
Is	26: 4	Trust in the LORD f,
Is	40: 8	the word of our God stands f.
Lam	3:31	the Lord will not cast off f.
Lam	5:20	Why do You forget us f,
Ezek	37:25	their children's children, f;
Ezek	43: 9	shall be their prince f.
Dan	2: 4	live f! Tell your servants
Dan	2:44	and it shall stand f.
Dan	4:34	and honored Him who lives f:
Dan	6: 6	"King Darius, live f!
Dan	12: 3	Like the stars f and ever.
Dan	12: 7	and swore by Him who lives f,
Hos	2:19	will betroth you to Me f;
Matt	6:13	the power and the glory f.
Luke	1:55	Abraham and to his seed f.
John	6:58	eats this bread will live f.
John	8:35	forever, but a son abides f.
John	14:16	that He may abide with you f—
Rom	1:25	Creator, who is blessed f.
Rom	11:36	things, to whom be glory f.
Rom	16:27	glory through Jesus Christ f.
2Co	9: 9	righteousness endures f.
2Co	11:31	Christ, who is blessed f,
Gal	1: 5	to whom be glory f and ever.
Heb	1: 8	is f and ever; A
Heb	5: 6	You are a priest f
Heb	7:24	He, because He continues f,
Heb	10:12	one sacrifice for sins f,
Heb	10:14	offering He has perfected f
Heb	13: 8	same yesterday, today, and f.
Heb	13:21	to whom be glory f and
1Pe	1:25	of the LORD endures f.
2Pe	2:17	the blackness of darkness f.
1Jn	2:17	the will of God abides f.
2Jn	2	in us and will be with us f:
Rev	11:15	and He shall reign f and

Rev	14:11	of their torment ascends f
Rev	22: 5	And they shall reign f and

FOREVERMORE (see FOREVER)

Ps	16:11	right hand are pleasures f.
Ps	113: 2	From this time forth and f!
Ps	133: 3	the blessing—Life f.
Rev	1:18	and behold, I am alive f.

FORGAVE (see FORGIVE)

Ps	32: 5	And You f the iniquity of
Eph	4:32	just as God in Christ f you.
Col	3:13	even as Christ f you, so you

FORGET (see FORGETFULNESS, FORGETS, FORGETTING, FORGOT, FORGOTTEN)

Deut	4:23	lest you f the covenant of
Deut	6:12	lest you f the LORD who
Ps	13: 1	Will You f me forever? How
Ps	50:22	you who f God, Lest I tear
Ps	103: 2	And f not all His benefits:
Ps	119:16	I will not f Your word.
Ps	137: 5	If I f you, O Jerusalem,
Ps	137: 5	Let my right hand f its
Is	49:15	her womb? Surely they may f,
Is	49:15	Yet I will not f you.
Heb	13: 2	Do not f to entertain
Heb	13:16	But do not f to do good and

FORGETFULNESS† (see FORGET)

Ps	88:12	in the land of f?

FORGETS (see FORGET)

Prov	2:17	And f the covenant of her
Jas	1:24	and immediately f what kind

FORGETTING† (see FORGET)

Phil	3:13	f those things which are

FORGIVE (see FORGAVE, FORGIVEN, FORGIVES, FORGIVING, UNFORGIVING)

Ex	32:32	if You will f their sin—but
2Ch	7:14	and will f their sin and
Dan	9:19	f! O Lord, listen and act!
Matt	6:12	And f us our debts, As we
Matt	6:14	For if you f men their
Matt	6:14	heavenly Father will also f
Matt	9: 6	Man has power on earth to f
Matt	18:35	does not f his brother his
Mark	2: 7	Who can f sins but God
Luke	11: 4	And f us our sins, For we
Luke	23:34	f them, for they do not know
1Jn	1: 9	He is faithful and just to f

FORGIVEN (see FORGIVE, FORGIVENESS)

Ps	32: 1	whose transgression is f,
Matt	9: 2	your sins are f you."
Matt	12:31	the Spirit will not be f
Luke	6:37	Forgive, and you will be f.
1Jn	2:12	Because your sins are f you

FORGIVENESS (see FORGIVEN)

Ps	130: 4	But there is f with You,
Dan	9: 9	our God belong mercy and f,

Acts 5:31 repentance to Israel and **f**
Eph   1: 7 the **f** of sins, according to

FORGIVES (see FORGIVE)
Ps   103: 3 Who **f** all your iniquities,
Luke 7:49   Who is this who even **f**

FORGIVING (see FORGIVE)
Ex   34: 7 **f** iniquity and transgression
Eph   4:32   **f** one another, just as God

FORGOT (see FORGET)
Gen   40:23 Joseph, but **f** him.
Judg 3: 7   They **f** the LORD their God,
Hos   2:13   her lovers; But Me she **f**,

FORGOTTEN (see FORGET)
Deut 32:18 And have **f** the God who
Job   19:14 my close friends have **f** me.
Hos   8:14   For Israel has **f** his Maker,

FORM (see FORMED, FORMS, UNFORMED)
Gen   1: 2   The earth was without **f**,
Gen   29:17 Rachel was beautiful of **f**
Gen   39: 6 Now Joseph was handsome in **f**
Deut 4:12   of the words, but saw no **f**;
Job   4:16   A **f** was before my eyes;
Is   45: 7 I **f** the light and create
Is   52:14 And His **f** more than the
Is   53: 2 He has no **f** or comeliness;
Luke 3:22   descended in bodily **f** like
John 5:37   at any time, nor seen His **f**.
Phil 2: 6   being in the **f** of God, did
Phil 2: 7   taking the **f** of a
1Th   5:22   Abstain from every **f** of evil.
2Ti   3: 5   having a **f** of godliness but

FORMED (see FORM)
Gen   2: 7   And the LORD God **f** man of
Ps   90: 2   Or ever You had **f** the earth
Ps   95: 5   And His hands **f** the dry
Ps   139:13 For You **f** my inward parts;
Is   29:16   Or shall the thing **f** say of
Is   43: 1   And He who **f** you, O Israel:
Is   45:18   Who **f** it to be inhabited:
Jer   1: 5   Before I **f** you in the womb I
Rom   9:20   Will the thing **f** say to him
Gal   4:19   again until Christ is **f** in

FORMER
Is   42: 9   the **f** things have come to
Is   46: 9   Remember the **f** things of
Hos   6: 3   Like the latter and **f** rain
Rev   21: 4   for the **f** things have passed

FORMS (see FORM)
Is   45: 9   the clay say to him who **f**

FORNICATION (see FORNICATOR)
Gal   5:19   which are: adultery, **f**,

FORNICATOR (see FORNICATION, FORNICATORS)
Eph   5: 5   For this you know, that no **f**,

FORNICATORS (see FORNICATOR)
1Co   6: 9   not be deceived. Neither **f**,

FORSAKE (see FORSAKEN, FORSAKES, FORSAKING, FORSOOK)
Deut 31: 6   He will not leave you nor **f**
Josh 1: 5   I will not leave you nor **f**
Ps   138: 8 Do not the works of Your
Is   55: 7   Let the wicked **f** his way,
Heb   13: 5   never leave you nor **f**

FORSAKEN (see FORSAKE)
Judg 6:13   But now the LORD has **f** us
Judg 10:13   Yet you have **f** Me and served
Ps   37:25   not seen the righteous **f**,
Jer   2:13   They have **f** Me, the
Matt 27:46   why have You **f** Me?"
2Co   4: 9   persecuted, but not **f**;
2Ti   4:10   for Demas has **f** me, having

FORSAKES (see FORSAKE)
Prov 28:13   But whoever confesses and **f**

FORSAKING† (see FORSAKE)
Heb   10:25   not **f** the assembling of

FORSOOK (see FORSAKE)
Matt 26:56   Then all the disciples **f**
2Ti   4:16   but all **f** me. May it not be

FORTIETH (see FORTY)
Num   33:38   and died there in the **f** year

FORTIFIED (see FORTRESS)
Num   13:28   the cities are **f** and very
Jer   1:18   have made you this day A **f**
Jer   15:20   make you to this people a **f**

FORTRESS (see FORTIFIED)
Ps   18: 2   LORD is my rock and my **f**
Ps   91: 2   "He is my refuge and my **f**;
Jer   16:19   LORD, my strength and my **f**,

FORTUNE-TELLING†
Acts 16:16   her masters much profit by **f**.

FORTY (see FORTIETH)
Gen   7: 4   the earth forty days and **f**
Gen   7:12   the rain was on the earth **f**
Gen   18:29   not do it for the sake of **f**."
Ex   16:35   of Israel ate manna **f** years,
Ex   24:18   Moses was on the mountain **f**
Ex   24:18   mountain forty days and **f**
Num   13:25   spying out the land after **f**
Num   14:33   in the wilderness **f** years,
Num   14:34   namely **f** years, and you
Deut 8: 4   did your foot swell these **f**
Deut 25: 3   **F** blows he may give him and
Judg 3:11   So the land had rest for **f**
1Sa   4:18   And he had judged Israel **f**
1Ki   11:42   over all Israel was **f**
1Ki   19: 8   the strength of that food **f**
Neh   9:21   **F** years You sustained them

F

Ps	95:10	For f years I was grieved
Jon	3: 4	Yet f days, and Nineveh shall
Matt	4: 2	had fasted forty days and f
Mark	1:13	there in the wilderness f
Luke	4: 2	being tempted for f days by
Acts	1: 3	being seen by them during f
2Co	11:24	Jews five times I received f
Heb	3:17	Now with whom was He angry f

FORTY-FOUR

Rev	14: 1	with Him one hundred and f

FOUGHT (see FIGHT)

Josh	10:14	for the LORD f for Israel.
Judg	5:20	stars from their courses f
1Co	15:32	I have f with beasts at
2Ti	4: 7	I have f the good fight, I

FOUND (see FIND, FOUNDED)

Gen	2:20	for Adam there was not f a
Gen	6: 8	But Noah f grace in the eyes
Gen	18: 3	if I have now f favor in
Deut	21: 1	If anyone is f slain, lying
Deut	22:14	and when I came to her I f
Deut	22:22	If a man is f lying with a
Deut	22:28	and they are f out,
Deut	24: 1	in his eyes because he has f
Deut	24: 7	If a man is f kidnapping any
Judg	15:15	He f a fresh jawbone of a
Ruth	2:10	Why have I f favor in your
1Sa	13:19	was no blacksmith to be f
1Sa	29: 3	And to this day I have f no
1Sa	29: 6	For to this day I have not f
2Sa	7:27	Your servant has f it in
1Ki	13:14	and f him sitting under an
1Ki	13:28	Then he went and f his corpse
1Ki	20:36	a lion f him and killed him.
1Ki	21:20	I have f you, because you
2Ki	12:18	and all the gold f in the
2Ki	14:14	the articles that were f in
2Ki	22: 8	I have f the Book of the Law
1Ch	26:31	and there were f among them
1Ch	28: 9	He will be f by you; but if
2Ch	29:16	all the debris that they f
2Ch	34:14	Hilkiah the priest f the
Neh	8:14	And they f written in the
Neh	9: 8	You f his heart faithful
Job	19:28	the root of the matter is f
Job	28:12	where can wisdom be f?
Job	32:13	We have f wisdom'; God will
Ps	17: 3	have tried me and have f
Ps	32: 6	In a time when You may be f;
Ps	69:20	comforters, but I f none.
Ps	84: 3	Even the sparrow has f a
Ps	89:20	I have f My servant David;
Ps	107: 4	They f no city to dwell in.
Ps	109: 7	let him be f guilty, And
Ps	116: 3	I f trouble and sorrow.
Ps	132: 6	We f it in the fields of
Prov	10:13	Wisdom is f on the lips of
Prov	30: 6	and you be f a liar.
Prov	30:10	and you be f guilty.
Song	3: 4	When I f the one I love. I
Is	51: 3	Joy and gladness will be f

Is	55: 6	the LORD while He may be f,
Jer	15:16	Your words were f,
Jer	29:14	I will be f by you, says the
Dan	5:27	and f wanting;
Dan	12: 1	Every one who is f written
Matt	1:18	she was f with child of the
Matt	2: 8	and when you have f Him,
Matt	8:10	I have not f such great
Matt	13:44	which a man f and hid; and
Matt	13:46	when he had f one pearl of
Luke	1:30	for you have f favor with
Luke	2:16	they came with haste and f
Luke	2:46	after three days they f Him
Luke	15: 6	for I have f my sheep which
Luke	15: 9	for I have f the piece which
Luke	15:32	again, and was lost and is f.
Luke	23:14	I have f no fault in this
Luke	23:22	I have f no reason for death
John	1:41	He first f his own brother
John	1:41	We have f the Messiah"
John	1:45	We have f Him of whom Moses
John	12:14	when He had f a young
Acts	5:10	the young men came in and f
Acts	5:23	we f no one inside!"
Acts	5:39	lest you even be f to fight
Acts	9:30	When the brethren f out, they
Acts	17:23	I even f an altar with this
Acts	22:29	was also afraid after he f
Acts	23:29	I f out that he was accused
Rom	7:10	I f to bring death.
1Co	4: 2	in stewards that one be f
2Co	5: 3	we shall not be f naked.
2Co	12:20	and that I shall be f by
Phil	3: 9	and be f in Him, not having
Heb	11: 5	death, "and was not f,
Heb	12:17	for he f no place for
Rev	20:15	And anyone not f written in

FOUNDATION (see FOUNDATIONS)

1Ki	5:17	to lay the f of the temple.
Ps	102:25	Of old You laid the f of the
Ps	137: 7	To its very f!"
Is	28:16	lay in Zion a stone for a f,
Is	28:16	cornerstone, a sure f;
Matt	13:35	kept secret from the f
Rom	15:20	build on another man's f,
1Co	3:11	For no other f can anyone lay
1Co	3:12	if anyone builds on this f
Eph	1: 4	us in Him before the f of
Eph	2:20	having been built on the f of
2Ti	2:19	Nevertheless the solid f of
Rev	13: 8	of the Lamb slain from the f
Rev	17: 8	the Book of Life from the f
Rev	21:19	the first f was jasper, the

FOUNDATIONS (see FOUNDATION)

Job	38: 4	were you when I laid the f
Heb	11:10	for the city which has f,
Rev	21:14	of the city had twelve f,

FOUNDED (see FOUND)

Ps	24: 2	For He has f it upon the
Prov	3:19	The LORD by wisdom f the
Matt	7:25	for it was f on the rock.

FOUNTAIN (see FOUNTAINS)

Prov	14:27	fear of the LORD is a f
Eccl	12: 6	pitcher shattered at the f,
Jer	2:13	the f of living waters,
Jer	9: 1	And my eyes a f of tears,
Jer	17:13	The f of living waters."
Joel	3:18	A f shall flow from the
John	4:14	him will become in him a f
Rev	21: 6	I will give of the f of the

FOUNTAINS (see FOUNTAIN)

Gen	8: 2	The f of the deep and the

FOUR (see FOUR-FOOTED, FOURTH)

Gen	2:10	there it parted and became f
Gen	14. 9	f kings against five.
Gen	23:16	f hundred shekels of silver,
Prov	30:18	f which I do not
Prov	30:29	f which are stately in
Jer	49:36	the four winds From the f
Ezek	1: 6	Each one had f faces, and
Ezek	1: 6	and each one had f wings.
Dan	7: 3	And f great beasts came up
Dan	7: 6	The beast also had f heads,
Dan	7:17	are f kings which arise
Amos	1: 3	of Damascus, and for f,
Matt	24:31	His elect from the f winds,
Mark	2: 3	who was carried by f men.
John	4:35	There are still f months and
John	11:39	for he has been dead f
Acts	10:11	a great sheet bound at the f

FOUR-FOOTED (see FOOT, FOUR)

Acts	10:12	In it were all kinds of f
Rom	1:23	and birds and f animals and

FOURTEEN

Gen	31:41	I served you f years for
Matt	1:17	from Abraham to David are f

FOURTH (see FOUR)

Gen	1:19	and the morning were the f
Gen	2:14	The f river is the
Gen	15:16	But in the f generation they
Num	14:18	children to the third and f
Dan	2:40	And the f kingdom shall be as
Dan	7: 7	a f beast, dreadful and

FOWLER†

Ps	91: 3	you from the snare of the f
Prov	6: 5	bird from the hand of the f.

FOX (see FOXES)

Luke	13:32	to them, "Go, tell that f,

FOXES (see FOX)

Judg	15: 4	turned the f tail to tail,
Song	2:15	The little f that spoil the
Matt	8:20	F have holes and birds of the

FRAGMENTS

Matt	14:20	baskets full of the f that

FRAGRANCE (see FRAGRANT)

Song	1:12	spikenard sends forth its f.
Song	7: 8	The f of your breath like
John	12: 3	house was filled with the f
2Co	2:14	through us diffuses the f
2Co	2:15	For we are to God the f of

FRAGRANT (see FRAGRANCE)

Song	4:13	F henna with spikenard,
Matt	26: 7	flask of very costly f oil,
Matt	26:12	For in pouring this f oil on
Luke	7:46	has anointed My feet with f
Luke	23:56	and prepared spices and f

FRAME (see FRAMED)

Ps	103:14	For He knows our f;
Ps	139:15	My f was not hidden from

FRAMED† (see FRAME)

Heb	11: 3	that the worlds were f by

FRANKINCENSE

Ex	30:34	and pure f with these sweet
Song	3: 6	Perfumed with myrrh and f,
Matt	2:11	gifts to Him: gold, f,
Rev	18:13	incense, fragrant oil and f,

FREE (see FREELY, FREEWILL, FREEWOMAN)

Ex	21: 2	seventh he shall go out f
Lev	19: 5	offer it of your own f will.
Deut	32:36	no one remaining, bond or f.
Judg	16:20	and shake myself f!" But he
Is	45:13	city And let My exiles go f,
Jer	34: 9	that every man should set f
John	8:32	the truth shall make you f.
John	8:36	you shall be f indeed.
Rom	5:15	But the f gift is not like
Rom	6:18	And having been set f from
Rom	6:20	you were f in regard to
Rom	8: 2	Christ Jesus has made me f
1Co	7:22	he who is called while f
1Co	9: 1	I not an apostle? Am I not f?
2Co	11: 7	the gospel of God to you f ·
Gal	3:28	there is neither slave nor f,
Gal	4:26	but the Jerusalem above is f,
Gal	4:31	the bondwoman but of the f.
Gal	5: 1	which Christ has made us f,
2Th	3: 8	did we eat anyone's bread f
1Pe	2:16	as f, yet not using

FREELY (see FREE)

Gen	2:16	of the garden you may f eat;
Hos	14: 4	I will love them f,
Matt	10: 8	F you have received, freely
Rom	3:24	being justified f by His
Rom	8:32	He not with Him also f give
Rev	21: 6	of the water of life f to
Rev	22:17	him take the water of life f.

FREEWILL (see FREE)

Ex	36: 3	continued bringing to him f
Ps	119:108	the f offerings of my mouth,

FREEWOMAN (see FREE)
Gal   4:30   with the son of the **f**.

FRESH
Judg   15:15   He found a **f** jawbone of a
Judg   16: 7   they bind me with seven **f**

FRET
Ps   37: 1   Do not **f** because of

FRIEND (see FRIENDS, FRIENDSHIP)
Ex   33:11   as a man speaks to his **f**.
1Ki   4: 5   a priest and the king's **f**;
2Ch   20: 7   of Abraham Your **f** forever?
Ps   41: 9   Even my own familiar **f** in
Prov   17:17   A **f** loves at all times, And
Prov   18:24   But there is a **f** who
Prov   27: 6   are the wounds of a **f**,
Is   41: 8   descendants of Abraham My **f**.
Matt   11:19   a **f** of tax collectors and
John   3:29   but the **f** of the bridegroom,
John   19:12   go, you are not Caesar's **f**.
Phm   1: 1   To Philemon our beloved **f**
Jas   2:23   And he was called the **f** of

FRIENDS (see FRIEND)
Job   2:11   Now when Job's three **f** heard
Job   19:19   All my close **f** abhor me,
Job   42:10   when he prayed for his **f**.
Zech   13: 6   wounded in the house of my **f**.
Matt   9:15   Can the **f** of the bridegroom
Luke   15: 6   he calls together his **f** and
Luke   15: 9   she calls her **f** and
Luke   23:12   Pilate and Herod became **f**
John   15:13   down one's life for his **f**.
John   15:14   You are My **f** if you do
John   15:15   but I have called you **f**,

FRIENDSHIP (see FRIEND)
Jas   4: 4   Do you not know that **f** with

FROGS
Ex   8: 2   all your territory with **f**.

FRONTLETS
Ex   13:16   a sign on your hand and as **f**
Deut   6: 8   and they shall be as **f**

FRUIT (see FRUITFUL, FRUITS)
Amos   2: 9   Yet I destroyed his **f** above
Amos   7:14   And a tender of sycamore **f**.
Amos   8: 1   Behold, a basket of summer **f**.
Mic   6: 7   The **f** of my body for the
Matt   7:17   every good tree bears good **f**,
Matt   12:33   a tree is known by its **f**.
Matt   21:19   Let no **f** grow on you ever
Matt   26:29   I will not drink of this **f**
Luke   1:42   and blessed is the **f** of
John   4:36   and gathers **f** for eternal
John   15: 2   in Me that does not bear **f**
John   15: 2   every branch that bears **f**
John   15:16   and that your **f** should
Rom   1:13   that I might have some **f**

Rom   7: 4   that we should bear **f** to
1Co   9: 7   and does not eat of its **f**?
Gal   5:22   But the **f** of the Spirit is
Heb   12:11   it yields the peaceable **f**
Heb   13:15   the **f** of our lips, giving
Jas   3:18   Now the **f** of righteousness is
Rev   22: 2   each tree yielding its **f**

FRUITFUL (see FRUIT, UNFRUITFUL)
Gen   .1:22   Be **f** and multiply, and fill
Gen   9: 1   Be **f** and multiply, and fill
Gen   17: 6   will make you exceedingly **f**;
Is   5: 1   has a vineyard On a very **f**
Col   1:10   being **f** in every good work

FRUITS (see FRUIT)
Gen   43:11   Take some of the best **f** of
Matt   3: 8   Therefore bear **f** worthy of
Matt   7:16   will know them by their **f**.
Matt   21:43   to a nation bearing the **f**
Phil   1:11   being filled with the **f** of
Rev   22: 2   of life, which bore twelve **f**,

FULFILL (see FULFILLED, FULFILLMENT)
Gen   29:27   **F** her week, and we will give
Lev   22:21   to **f** his vow, or a freewill
Deut   9: 5   and that He may **f** the word
1Ki   5: 9   And you shall **f** my desire by
Matt   3:15   it is fitting for us to **f**
Matt   5:17   not come to destroy but to **f**.
Rom   13:14   to **f** its lusts.
Gal   5:16   and you shall not **f** the lust
Gal   6: 2   and so **f** the law of Christ.
Phil   2: 2   **f** my joy by being
2Ti   4: 5   **f** your ministry.

FULFILLED (see BELIEVED, FULFILL)
Gen   25:24   So when her days were **f** for
Num   6:13   days of his separation are **f**,
1Ki   8:20   So the LORD has **f** His word
2Ch   36:22   mouth of Jeremiah might be **f**,
Ezra   1: 1   mouth of Jeremiah might be **f**,
Dan   4:33   very hour the word was **f**
Dan   10: 3   three whole weeks were **f**.
Matt   1:22   was done that it might be **f**
Matt   5:18   from the law till all is **f**.
Mark   1:15   and saying, "The time is **f**,
Luke   1: 1   which have been **f** among us,
Luke   4:21   Today this Scripture is **f** in
Luke   21:24   times of the Gentiles are **f**.
Luke   22:16   eat of it until it is **f** in
John   17:13   that they may have My joy **f**
John   18:32   saying of Jesus might be **f**
Rom   8: 4   of the law might be **f** in us
Rev   17:17   until the words of God are **f**.

FULFILLMENT (see FULFILL)
Rom   13:10   therefore love is the **f** of

FULL (see FILL, FULL-GROWN, FULLNESS, FULLY, VALUE)
Gen   25: 8   an old man and **f** of years,
Gen   35:29   being old and **f** of days.
Gen   41: 7   the seven plump and **f** heads.

Deut	6:11	you have eaten and are f—
Ruth	1:21	"I went out f,
Job	14: 1	woman Is of few days and f
Job	42:17	old and f of days.
Ps	29: 4	voice of the LORD is f of
Ps	33: 5	The earth is f of the
Ps	78:38	being f of compassion,
Ps	81: 3	At the f moon, on our
Ps	104:24	The earth is f of Your
Ps	119:64	is f of Your mercy; Teach
Ps	127: 5	man who has his quiver f of
Ps	144:13	That our barns may be f,
Eccl	1: 7	sea, Yet the sea is not f;
Is	1:15	Your hands are f of blood.
Is	6: 3	The whole earth is f of
Is	11: 9	For the earth shall be f of
Jer	20. 0	Within two f years I will
Lam	1: 1	sits the city That was f
Ezek	37: 1	and it was f of bones.
Ezek	39:19	shall eat fat till you are f,
Mic	3: 8	But truly I am f of power
Mic	6:12	For her rich men are f of
Hab	3: 3	And the earth was f of His
Matt	6:22	your whole body will be f of
Matt	13:48	"which, when it was f,
Matt	14:20	took up twelve baskets f of
Matt	23:27	but inside are f of dead
Matt	23:28	but inside you are f of
Mark	6:43	took up twelve baskets f of
Mark	15:36	ran and filled a sponge f
Luke	1:57	Now Elizabeth's f time came
Luke	5:12	a man who was f of leprosy
Luke	6:25	Woe to you who are f,
Luke	11:34	your whole body also is f of
Luke	16:20	f of sores, who was laid at
John	1:14	f of grace and truth.
John	15:11	and that your joy may be f.
John	16:24	that your joy may be f.
John	21:11	f of large fish, one hundred
Acts	2:13	They are f of new wine."
Acts	2:28	You will make me f of
Acts	6: 3	f of the Holy Spirit and
Acts	6: 5	a man f of faith and the
Acts	6: 8	f of faith and power, did
1Co	4: 8	You are already f! You are
Phil	4:12	I have learned both to be f
Jas	3: 8	f of deadly poison.
1Pe	1: 8	joy inexpressible and f of
2Pe	2:14	having eyes f of adultery and
1Jn	1: 4	you that your joy may be f.

FULL-GROWN† (see FULL, GROW)

Jas	1:15	sin; and sin, when it is f,

FULLNESS (see FULL)

Ps	16:11	In Your presence is f of
Ps	24: 1	the LORD's, and all its f,
John	1:16	And of His f we have all
Rom	11:25	to Israel until the f of
Rom	15:29	I shall come in the f of the
1Co	10:26	LORD's, and all its f.
Gal	4: 4	But when the f of the time
Eph	1:10	in the dispensation of the f
Eph	1:23	the f of Him who fills all

Eph	3:19	be filled with all the f of
Eph	4:13	of the stature of the f of
Col	1:19	that in Him all the f
Col	2: 9	For in Him dwells all the f

FULLY (see FULL)

Num	14:24	in him and has followed Me f,
John	7: 8	for My time has not yet f
Col	1:10	f pleasing Him, being
1Pe	1:13	and rest your hope f upon

FURNACE

Gen	19:28	up like the smoke of a f.
Ex	19:18	like the smoke of a f,
Deut	4:20	you out of the iron f,
1Ki	8:51	of Egypt, out of the iron f),
Is	48:10	I have tested you in the f
Jer	11: 4	of Egypt, from the iron f,
Dan	3: 6	midst of a burning fiery f.
Matt	13:42	will cast them into the f

FURTHERANCE†

Phil	1:12	turned out for the f of the

FURY

Gen	27:44	until your brother's f turns
Prov	6:34	jealousy is a husband's f;
Is	51:17	the LORD The cup of His f;
Is	59:18	F to His adversaries,
Is	63: 3	And trampled them in My f;
Is	63: 6	Made them drunk in My f,
Jer	25:15	Take this wine cup of f from
Jer	33: 5	slay in My anger and My f,
Ezek	9: 8	in pouring out Your f on
Dan	9:16	let Your anger and Your f be
Amos	5: 9	So that f comes upon the
Mic	5:15	vengeance in anger and f
Nah	1: 6	His f is poured out like

FUTILE (see FUTILITY)

Rom	1:21	but became f in their
1Co	15:17	not risen, your faith is f;

FUTILITY (see FUTILE)

Rom	8:20	creation was subjected to f,
Eph	4:17	in the f of their mind,

FUTURE

Jer	29:11	to give you a f and a hope.
Jer	31:17	There is hope in your f,
Dan	8:26	to many days in the f.

G

GABBATHA†

John	19:13	Pavement, but in Hebrew, G.

GABRIEL

Dan	9:21	in prayer, the man G,
Luke	1:19	and said to him, "I am G,

GAD

Gen	30:11	So she called his name G.
Num	2:14	"Then comes the tribe of G,
1Sa	13: 7	the Jordan to the land of G
1Sa	22: 5	Now the prophet G said to

GAIN (see GAINED, GAINS)

1Sa	8: 3	aside after dishonest g,
Job	18: 2	G understanding, and
Ps	90:12	That we may g a heart of
Prov	1:19	everyone who is greedy for g;
Eccl	3: 6	A time to g, And a time
Dan	2: 8	for certain that you would g
Phil	1:21	is Christ, and to die is g.
Phil	3: 7	But what things were g to me,
Phil	3: 8	that I may g Christ
1Ti	6: 5	godliness is a means of g.
1Ti	6: 6	with contentment is great g.
Tit	1:11	for the sake of dishonest g.
Jude	16	flattering people to g

GAINED (see GAIN)

Ps	98: 1	and His holy arm have g Him
Prov	20:17	Bread g by deceit is sweet
Eccl	1:16	and have g more wisdom than
Ezek	28: 4	understanding You have g
Matt	18:15	you have g your brother.
Matt	25:17	he who had received two g

GAINS (see GAIN)

Prov	3:13	And the man who g
Mark	8:36	it profit a man if he g the
Luke	9:25	is it to a man if he g the

GALATIA (see GALATIANS)

Gal	1: 2	me, To the churches of G:
1Pe	1: 1	the Dispersion in Pontus, G,

GALATIANS† (see GALATIA)

Gal	3: 1	O foolish G! Who has

GALILEAN (see GALILEE)

Mark	14:70	of them; for you are a G,

GALILEE (see GALILEAN)

Josh	20: 7	they appointed Kedesh in G,
1Ki	9:11	cities in the land of G.
Is	9: 1	In G of the Gentiles.
Matt	4:15	G of the Gentiles:
Matt	4:23	And Jesus went about all G,
Matt	4:25	followed Him—from G,
Matt	21:11	prophet from Nazareth of G.
Luke	4:31	to Capernaum, a city of G,
John	2: 1	was a wedding in Cana of G,
Acts	1:11	who also said, "Men of G,

GALL

Ps	69:21	They also gave me g for my
Lam	3:19	The wormwood and the g.
Matt	27:34	sour wine mingled with g to

GALLOWS

Esth	7: 9	to the king, "Look! The g,

GAMALIEL

Acts	5:34	stood up, a Pharisee named G,
Acts	22: 3	this city at the feet of G,

GAME

Gen	25:28	because he ate of his g,
Gen	27:31	arise and eat of his son's g,

GAP

Ezek	22:30	and stand in the g before Me

GARDEN (see GARDENER)

Gen	2: 8	The LORD God planted a g
Gen	3: 8	LORD God walking in the g
Is	1: 8	As a hut in a g of
Ezek	28:13	the g of God; Every
John	18: 1	Kidron, where there was a g,
John	19:41	was crucified there was a g,
John	19:41	and in the g a new tomb in

GARDENER† (see GARDEN)

John	20:15	supposing Him to be the g,

GARLIC†

Num	11: 5	leeks, the onions, and the g;

GARMENT (see GARMENTS)

Gen	9:23	Shem and Japheth took a g,
Gen	25:25	He was like a hairy g all
Gen	39:12	But he left his g in her
Ex	22:26	ever take your neighbor's g
Lev	19:19	Nor shall a g of mixed linen
Deut	22: 5	a man put on a woman's g,
Ruth	3: 3	put on your best g and go
Ps	69:11	I also made sackcloth my g;
Ps	102:26	will all grow old like a g;
Dan	7: 9	His g was white as snow,
Matt	9:16	unshrunk cloth on an old g;
Matt	9:16	patch pulls away from the g,
Matt	9:20	and touched the hem of His g.
Matt	22:11	did not have on a wedding g.
Mark	10:50	And throwing aside his g,
Luke	22:36	let him sell his g and buy
John	21: 7	he put on his outer g (for
Heb	1:11	all grow old like a g;
Jude	23	hating even the g defiled by

GARMENTS (see GARMENT)

Gen	38:14	she took off her widow's g,
Gen	45:22	silver and five changes of g.
Ex	28: 3	that they may make Aaron's g,
Deut	8: 4	Your g did not wear out on
Josh	9: 5	and old g on themselves; and
2Sa	10: 4	cut off their g in the
2Sa	13:31	king arose and tore his g
Ezra	2:69	and one hundred priestly g.
Ps	22:18	They divide My g among them,
Ps	45: 8	All Your g are scented with
Ps	133: 2	down on the edge of his g.
Prov	31:24	She makes linen g and sells
Eccl	9: 8	Let your g always be white,
Song	4:11	And the fragrance of your g
Is	3:22	the mantles; The outer g,

Is	9: 5	And **g** rolled in blood,
Is	61:10	He has clothed me with the **g**
Is	63: 1	With dyed **g** from Bozrah,
Is	63: 3	blood is sprinkled upon My **g**,
Dan	3:27	not singed nor were their **g**
Joel	2:13	your heart, and not your **g**;
Zech	3: 3	was clothed with filthy **g**,
Matt	11: 8	see? A man clothed in soft **g**?
Matt	27:35	They divided My **g** among
Luke	24: 4	stood by them in shining **g**.
John	13: 4	supper and laid aside His **g**,
Acts	18: 6	he shook his **g** and said to
Jas	5: 2	and your **g** are moth-eaten.
Rev	3: 4	who have not defiled their **g**;
Rev	3: 5	shall be clothed in white **g**,

GATE (see GATES)

Gen	19: 1	Lot was sitting in the **g** of
Gen	22:17	shall possess the **g** of
Deut	22:15	elders of the city at the **g**.
Ruth	4: 1	Now Boaz went up to the **g** and
Neh	3:26	in front of the Water **G**
Esth	5: 9	saw Mordecai in the king's **g**,
Esth	5:13	Jew sitting at the king's **g**.
Job	5: 4	They are crushed in the **g**,
Prov	22:22	the afflicted at the **g**;
Is	28: 6	back the battle at the **g**.
Is	29:21	him who reproves in the **g**,
Jer	19: 2	the entry of the Potsherd **G**;
Jer	36:10	at the entry of the New **G**
Jer	38: 7	king was sitting at the **G**
Jer	51:30	The bars of her **g** are
Jer	52: 7	at night by way of the **g**
Ezek	8: 3	to the door of the north **g**
Ezek	40: 7	between the **g** chambers was
Ezek	44: 2	This **g** shall be shut; it
Amos	1: 5	I will also break the **g** bar
Amos	5:10	the one who rebukes in the **g**,
Matt	7:13	"Enter by the narrow **g**;
Matt	7:13	for wide is the **g** and broad
Luke	16:20	sores, who was laid at his **g**,
John	5: 2	Jerusalem by the Sheep **G** a
Acts	3:10	alms at the Beautiful **G** of
Acts	12:10	they came to the iron **g** that
Acts	12:13	knocked at the door of the **g**,
Heb	13:12	suffered outside the **g**.
Rev	21:21	each individual **g** was of one

GATES (see GATE)

Ex	20:10	who is within your **g**.
Deut	3: 5	fortified with high walls, **g**,
Deut	6: 9	of your house and on your **g**.
Deut	12:12	Levite who is within your **g**,
Deut	14:21	alien who is within your **g**,
Ps	24: 7	O you **g**! And be lifted up,
Ps	100: 4	Enter into His **g** with
Ps	122: 2	been standing Within your **g**,
Prov	31:23	husband is known in the **g**,
Prov	31:31	works praise her in the **g**.
Matt	16:18	and the **g** of Hades shall not
Rev	21:12	and high wall with twelve **g**,

GATH

Josh	11:22	remained only in Gaza, in **G**,

1Sa	6:17	one for Ashkelon, one for **G**,
1Sa	17: 4	named Goliath, from **G**,
2Sa	1:20	Tell it not in **G**,
Mic	1:10	Tell it not in **G**,

GATHER (see GATHERED, GATHERING, GATHERS)

Ex	5: 7	Let them go and **g** straw for
Ruth	2: 7	Please let me glean and **g**
Eccl	3: 5	And a time to **g** stones; A
Song	6: 2	And to **g** lilies.
Is	11:12	And **g** together the
Is	34:15	and **g** them under her
Is	40:11	He will **g** the lambs with
Is	43: 5	And **g** you from the west;
Matt	3:12	and **g** His wheat into the
Matt	13:30	First **g** together the tares
Matt	23:37	her! How often I wanted to **g**
Matt	25:26	and **g** where I have not
Mark	13:27	and **g** together His elect
Luke	6:44	For men do not **g** figs from
Luke	6:44	nor do they **g** grapes from a
John	6:12	**G** up the fragments that
John	11:52	but also that He would **g**
John	15: 6	and they **g** them and throw
Rev	19:17	Come and **g** together for the

GATHERED (see ASSEMBLED, GATHER)

Gen	1: 9	under the heavens be **g**
Gen	12: 5	possessions that they had **g**,
Gen	25:17	and was **g** to his people.
Ex	15: 8	nostrils The waters were **g**
Ex	16:18	he who **g** much had nothing
Ex	16:18	and he who **g** little had no
Ex	16:21	So they **g** it every morning,
Num	11:32	and **g** the quail (he who
Josh	24: 1	Then Joshua **g** all the tribes
1Sa	13: 5	Then the Philistines **g**
2Sa	14:14	which cannot be **g** up again.
2Sa	21:13	and they **g** the bones of
2Ki	22:20	and you shall be **g** to your
2Ch	13: 7	Then worthless rogues **g** to
Ezra	3: 1	the people **g** together as one
Neh	8:13	were **g** to Ezra the scribe
Neh	12:28	the sons of the singers **g**
Esth	2:19	When virgins were **g** together
Ps	35:15	Attackers **g** against me,
Ps	107: 3	And **g** out of the lands,
Prov	30: 4	Who has **g** the wind in His
Eccl	2: 8	I also **g** for myself silver
Is	22: 9	And you **g** together the
Is	27:12	And you will be **g** one by
Is	34:16	and His Spirit has **g** them.
Is	49: 5	So that Israel is **g** to Him
Jer	8: 2	They shall not be **g** nor
Ezek	29: 5	shall not be picked up or **g**.
Matt	2: 4	And when he had **g** all the
Matt	13:40	as the tares are **g** and
Matt	18:20	where two or three are **g**
Matt	22:41	While the Pharisees were **g**
Mark	1:33	And the whole city was **g**
Mark	4: 1	And a great multitude was **g**
Mark	6:30	Then the apostles **g** to Jesus
Luke	15:13	the younger son **g** all

John	6:13	Therefore they **g** them up,
Acts	4: 6	were **g** together at
Acts	14:20	when the disciples **g** around
Acts	14:27	Now when they had come and **g**
2Co	8:15	He who **g** much had
Rev	19:19	**g** together to make war

GATHERING (see GATHER)

Gen	1:10	and the **g** together of the
Num	15:32	they found a man **g** sticks on
Matt	25:24	and **g** where you have not
2Th	2: 1	Lord Jesus Christ and our **g**

GATHERS (see GATHER)

Matt	23:37	as a hen **g** her chicks under
John	4:36	and **g** fruit for eternal

GAVE (see GIVE)

Gen	2:20	So Adam **g** names to all
Gen	35:12	The land which I **g** Abraham
Gen	39:21	and He **g** him favor in the
2Sa	12: 8	I **g** you your master's house
1Ki	4:29	And God **g** Solomon wisdom and
Neh	8: 8	and they **g** the sense, and
Neh	9:15	You **g** them bread from heaven
Neh	9:20	You also **g** Your good Spirit
Neh	9:20	And **g** them water for their
Job	1:21	I return there. The LORD **g**,
Job	42:10	Indeed the LORD **g** Job twice
Ps	68:11	The Lord **g** the word; Great
Ps	69:21	They also **g** me gall for my
Eccl	12: 7	will return to God who **g** it.
Is	43: 3	I **g** Egypt for your ransom,
Is	50: 6	I **g** My back to those who
Dan	1:17	God **g** them knowledge and
Dan	6:10	and prayed and **g** thanks
Hos	2: 8	she did not know That I **g**
Hos	13:11	I **g** you a king in My anger,
Amos	4: 6	Also I **g** you cleanness of
Matt	10: 1	He **g** them power over
Matt	25:35	for I was hungry and you **g** Me
Mark	3:16	to whom He **g** the name Peter;
Mark	6:28	and **g** it to the girl; and
Luke	2:38	coming in that instant she **g**
Luke	5:29	Then Levi **g** Him a great feast
Luke	7:21	and to many blind He **g**
Luke	7:44	you **g** Me no water for My
Luke	9: 1	disciples together and **g**
Luke	9:42	and **g** him back to his
Luke	10:35	**g** them to the innkeeper,
Luke	18:43	**g** praise to God.
Luke	22:17	and **g** thanks, and said,
Luke	22:19	**g** thanks and broke it, and
Luke	23:24	So Pilate **g** sentence that it
Luke	24:42	So they **g** Him a piece of a
John	1:12	to them He **g** the right to
John	3:16	so loved the world that He **g**
John	4:12	who **g** us the well, and drank
John	6:31	He **g** them bread from
John	13:26	He **g** it to Judas Iscariot,
John	14:31	and as the Father **g** Me
John	17:12	Those whom You **g** Me I have
John	17:22	And the glory which You **g** Me
John	19: 9	But Jesus **g** him no answer.

John	19:30	He **g** up His spirit.
Acts	2: 4	as the Spirit **g** them
Acts	7:42	Then God turned and **g** them up
Acts	8:10	to whom they all **g** heed, from
Acts	14:17	**g** us rain from heaven and
Rom	1:24	Therefore God also **g** them up
1Co	3: 5	as the Lord **g** to each one?
1Co	3: 6	but God **g** the increase.
2Co	8: 5	but they first **g** themselves
Gal	1: 4	who **g** Himself for our sins,
Gal	2:20	who loved me and **g** Himself
Eph	1:22	and **g** Him to be head over
Eph	4: 8	And **g** gifts to men."
Eph	4:11	And He Himself **g** some to be
Eph	5:25	also loved the church and **g**
1Ti	2: 6	who **g** Himself a ransom for
Heb	7: 2	to whom also Abraham **g** a
Heb	11:22	and **g** instructions
Jas	5:18	and the heaven **g** rain, and
1Jn	3:23	as He **g** us commandment.
Rev	1: 1	which God **g** Him to show His
Rev	11:13	the rest were afraid and **g**
Rev	12:13	persecuted the woman who **g**
Rev	13: 2	The dragon **g** him his power,
Rev	13: 4	worshiped the dragon who **g**
Rev	15: 7	the four living creatures **g**
Rev	20:13	The sea **g** up the dead who

GAZA

Judg	16: 1	Now Samson went to **G** and saw
Amos	1: 6	three transgressions of **G**,
Acts	8:26	down from Jerusalem to **G**.

GAZELLE (see GAZELLES)

2Sa	2:18	fleet of foot as a wild **g**.
Song	2: 9	My beloved is like a **g** or a
Song	4: 5	two fawns, Twins of a **g**,

GAZELLES (see GAZELLE)

Song	2: 7	By the **g** or by the does of

GAZING

Acts	1:11	why do you stand **g** up into

GENEALOGIES (see GENEALOGY)

1Ti	1: 4	heed to fables and endless **g**,
Tit	3: 9	avoid foolish disputes, **g**,

GENEALOGY (see GENEALOGIES)

Gen	5: 1	This is the book of the **g** of
Gen	6: 9	This is the **g** of Noah. Noah
Matt	1: 1	The book of the **g** of Jesus
Heb	7: 3	without mother, without **g**,

GENERATION (see GENERATIONS)

Gen	7: 1	before Me in this **g**.
Gen	15:16	But in the fourth **g** they
Gen	50:23	children to the third **g**.
Deut	1:35	of these men of this evil **g**
Deut	23: 2	even to the tenth **g** none of
Deut	32: 5	A perverse and crooked **g**.
Ps	22:30	of the Lord to the next **g**,
Ps	24: 6	the **g** of those who seek Him,
Ps	78: 8	A stubborn and rebellious **g**,

Ps	112: 2	The **g** of the upright will
Ps	145: 4	One **g** shall praise Your
Eccl	1: 4	One **g** passes away, and
Is	53: 8	And who will declare His **g**?
Dan	4: 3	His dominion is from **g** to
Dan	4:34	And His kingdom is from **g**
Matt	11:16	to what shall I liken this **g**?
Matt	12:39	An evil and adulterous **g**
Matt	12:41	in the judgment with this **g**
Matt	12:45	also be with this wicked **g**.
Matt	17:17	"O faithless and perverse **g**,
Matt	24:34	this **g** will by no means pass
Mark	8:12	Why does this **g** seek a sign?
Mark	8:38	this adulterous and sinful **g**,
Luke	11:29	to say, "This is an evil **g**.
Luke	11:30	Son of Man will be to this **g**.
Luke	11:31	with the men of this **g** and
Luke	11:50	may be required of this **g**,
Luke	16: 8	are more shrewd in their **g**
Acts	8:33	who will declare His **g**?
Phil	2:15	of a crooked and perverse **g**,
Heb	3:10	was angry with that **g**,
1Pe	2: 9	But you are a chosen **g**,

GENERATIONS (see GENERATION)

Gen	6: 9	a just man, perfect in his **g**.
Gen	9:12	with you, for perpetual **g**:
Ex	3:15	is My memorial to all **g**.
Ex	20: 5	to the third and fourth **g**
Ex	31:16	Sabbath throughout their **g**
Deut	7: 9	and mercy for a thousand **g**
Job	42:16	grandchildren for four **g**.
Ps	49:11	dwelling places to all **g**;
Ps	61: 6	life, His years as many **g**.
Ps	72: 5	endure, Throughout all **g**.
Ps	79:13	forth Your praise to all **g**.
Ps	89: 1	Your faithfulness to all **g**.
Ps	90: 1	our dwelling place in all **g**.
Ps	100: 5	His truth endures to all **g**.
Ps	102:24	years are throughout all **g**.
Ps	106:31	for righteousness To all **g**
Ps	119:90	endures to all **g**;
Is	51: 9	In the **g** of old. Are You
Is	60:15	excellence, A joy of many **g**.
Is	61: 4	The desolations of many **g**.
Joel	2: 2	Even for many successive **g**.
Matt	1:17	So all the **g** from Abraham to
Eph	3:21	by Christ Jesus to all **g**,

GENEROUS

Ps	51:12	And uphold me by Your **g**

GENTILES

Gen	10: 5	coastland peoples of the **G**
Is	9: 1	Jordan, In Galilee of the **G**.
Is	11:10	For the **G** shall seek Him,
Is	42: 1	bring forth justice to the **G**.
Is	49: 6	give You as a light to the **G**,
Is	66:19	declare My glory among the **G**.
Jer	10: 2	not learn the way of the **G**;
Ezek	30: 3	of clouds, the time of the **G**.
Matt	4:15	Galilee of the **G**:
Matt	6:32	all these things the **G** seek.
Matt	12:18	justice to the **G**.

Matt	12:21	And in His name **G** will
Matt	20:19	and deliver Him to the **G** to
Luke	2:32	bring revelation to the **G**,
Luke	18:32	will be delivered to the **G**
Luke	21:24	will be trampled by **G** until
Luke	21:24	until the times of the **G**
Acts	9:15	to bear My name before **G**,
Acts	10:45	had been poured out on the **G**
Acts	13:46	behold, we turn to the **G**.
Acts	13:47	as a light to the **G**,
Acts	14: 2	Jews stirred up the **G** and
Acts	14:27	the door of faith to the **G**.
Acts	15: 3	the conversion of the **G**;
Acts	18: 6	now on I will go to the **G**.
Acts	26:23	Jewish people and to the **G**.
Acts	28:28	God has been sent to the **G**,
Rom	1:13	just as among the other **G**.
Rom	2:24	blasphemed among the **G**
Rom	3:29	not also the God of the **G**?
Rom	11:11	has come to the **G**.
Rom	11:13	as I am an apostle to the **G**,
Rom	11:25	until the fullness of the **G**
Rom	15:11	all you **G**! Laud Him,
Rom	15:12	In Him the **G** shall
Rom	16: 4	all the churches of the **G**.
1Co	5: 1	not even named among the **G**—
Gal	1:16	might preach Him among the **G**,
Gal	2:12	he would eat with the **G**;
Gal	2:14	why do you compel **G** to live
Eph	2:11	once **G** in the flesh—who are
Col	1:27	of this mystery among the **G**:
1Ti	2: 7	a teacher of the **G** in faith
1Ti	3:16	Preached among the **G**,
Rev	11: 2	it has been given to the **G**.

GENTLE (see GENTLENESS, GENTLY)

Prov	25:15	And a **g** tongue breaks a
Hos	11: 4	I drew them with **g** cords,
Matt	11:29	for I am **g** and lowly in
1Th	2: 7	But we were **g** among you, just
1Ti	3: 3	not greedy for money, but **g**,
2Ti	2:24	must not quarrel but be **g**
Tit	3: 2	no one, to be peaceable, **g**,
Jas	3:17	pure, then peaceable, **g**,

GENTLENESS (see GENTLE)

1Co	4:21	or in love and a spirit of **g**?
2Co	10: 1	you by the meekness and **g**
Gal	5:23	**g**, self-control. Against
Gal	6: 1	such a one in a spirit of **g**,
Phil	4: 5	Let your **g** be known to all
1 Ti	6:11	faith, love, patience, **g**.

GENTLY (see GENTLE)

Is	40:11	And **g** lead those who are

GENUINENESS

1Pe	1: 7	that the **g** of your faith,

GERIZIM

Deut	11:29	put the blessing on Mount **G**

GET

Gen	12: 1	**G** out of your country, From

G

Prov	4: 5	G wisdom! Get understanding!
Matt	16:23	G behind Me, Satan! You are
Matt	24:18	the field not go back to **g**

GETHSEMANE

Matt	26:36	them to a place called **G**,

GHOST

Mark	6:49	they supposed it was a **g**,

GIANTS

Gen	6: 4	There were **g** on the earth in
Num	13:33	There we saw the **g** (the
Deut	3:13	was called the land of the **g**.

GIBEON

Josh	10:12	"Sun, stand still over **G**;
2Sa	2:13	met them by the pool of **G**.

GIDEON

Judg	6:11	while his son **G** threshed
Judg	6:24	So **G** built an altar there to
Judg	6:34	of the LORD came upon **G**;
Judg	7:20	sword of the LORD and of **G**!
Judg	8:27	Then **G** made it into an ephod
Heb	11:32	would fail me to tell of **G**

GIFT (see GIFTS, GIVE)

Num	8:19	given the Levites as a **g** to
2Sa	11: 8	and a **g** of food from the
Prov	21:14	A **g** in secret pacifies
Eccl	3:13	it is the **g** of God.
Matt	5:23	if you bring your **g** to the
Matt	8: 4	and offer the **g** that Moses
John	4:10	If you knew the **g** of God, and
Acts	2:38	and you shall receive the **g**
Rom	1:11	to you some spiritual **g**,
Rom	5:15	But the free **g** is not like
Rom	5:17	of grace and of the **g** of
Rom	6:23	but the **g** of God is eternal
1Co	7: 7	But each one has his own **g**
1Co	13: 2	And though I have the **g** of
1Co	16: 3	I will send to bear your **g**
2Co	1:11	on our behalf for the **g**
2Co	8: 4	that we would receive the **g**
2Co	9: 5	and prepare your generous **g**
2Co	9:15	God for His indescribable **g**!
Eph	2: 8	it is the **g** of God,
Eph	3: 7	minister according to the **g**
Eph	4: 7	to the measure of Christ's **g**.
Phil	4:17	Not that I seek the **g**,
2Ti	4:14	Do not neglect the **g** that is
Heb	6: 4	have tasted the heavenly **g**,
Jas	1:17	Every good **g** and every
1Pe	4:10	As each one has received a **g**,

GIFTS (see GIFT)

Ps	68:18	You have received **g** among
Dan	2: 6	you shall receive from me **g**,
Dan	2:48	and gave him many great **g**;
Dan	5:17	Let your **g** be for yourself,
Matt	2:11	they presented **g** to Him;
Matt	7:11	know how to give good **g** to
Rom	11:29	For the **g** and the calling of

Rom	12: 6	Having then **g** differing
1Co	12: 1	Now concerning spiritual **g**,
1Co	12: 4	There are diversities of **g**,
1Co	12: 9	to another **g** of healings by
1Co	12:31	earnestly desire the best **g**.
Eph	4: 8	And gave **g** to men."
Heb	2: 4	and **g** of the Holy Spirit,
Heb	8: 4	are priests who offer the **g**
Heb	11: 4	God testifying of his **g**;
Rev	11:10	and send **g** to one another,

GILEAD

Num	26:29	and Machir begot **G**;
Num	32:29	give them the land of **G** as
Josh	17: 1	of Manasseh, the father of **G**,
Josh	22:13	Manasseh, into the land of **G**,
Judg	11: 1	and **G** begot Jephthah.
1Sa	13: 7	to the land of Gad and **G**.
2Ki	10:33	including **G** and Bashan.
Ps	60: 7	**G** is Mine, and Manasseh is
Song	6: 5	of goats Going down from **G**.
Jer	8:22	Is there no balm in **G**,
Hos	12:11	Though **G** has idols—Surely
Amos	1: 3	they have threshed **G** with
Amos	1:13	the women with child in **G**,
Obad	19	Benjamin shall possess **G**.

GILGAL

Josh	4:19	and they camped in **G** on the
Josh	4:20	Jordan, Joshua set up in **G**.
Hos	12:11	they sacrifice bulls in **G**,

GIRD (see GIRDED)

1Sa	25:13	Every man **g** on his sword."
2Sa	3:31	**g** yourselves with sackcloth,
John	21:18	and another will **g** you and
1Pe	1:13	Therefore **g** up the loins of

GIRDED (see GIRD)

1Ki	18:46	and he **g** up his loins and
Ps	93: 1	He has **g** Himself with
John	13: 4	took a towel and **g** Himself.
Eph	6:14	having **g** your waist with

GIRL

Judg	5:30	To every man a **g** or two;
Amos	2: 7	father go in to the same **g**,
Matt	9:24	for the **g** is not dead, but
Matt	9:25	and the **g** arose.
Matt	14:11	a platter and given to the **g**,
Matt	26:69	And a servant **g** came to him,
Mark	5:41	is translated, "Little **g**,
Acts	12:13	a **g** named Rhoda came to
Acts	16:16	that a certain slave **g**
Acts	16:17	This **g** followed Paul and us,

GIVE (see GAVE, GIFT, GIVEN, GIVER, GIVES, GIVING)

Gen	1:15	of the heavens to **g** light
Gen	12: 7	your descendants I will **g**
Gen	13:15	the land which you see I **g**
Gen	28:13	on which you lie I will **g**
Gen	30: 1	**G** me children, or else I
Ex	6: 8	the land which I swore to **g**

Ex	33:14	and I will **g** you rest."
Deut	18: 3	they shall **g** to the priest
Judg	21:18	we cannot **g** them wives from
Ruth	4:12	which the LORD will **g** you
1Sa	2:10	He will **g** strength to His
1Sa	6: 5	and you shall **g** glory to the
1Sa	8: 6	**G** us a king to judge us." So
2Sa	3:14	**G** me my wife Michal, whom I
2Sa	22:50	Therefore I will **g** thanks to
1Ki	3: 5	Ask! What shall I **g** you?"
1Ki	3: 9	Therefore **g** to Your servant
1Ki	3:25	and **g** half to one, and half
1Ki	3:26	**g** her the living child, and
1Ki	11:13	I will **g** one tribe to your
1Ki	17:19	**G** me your son." So he took
1Ki	21: 6	**G** me your vineyard for money;
1Ki	21: 6	I will not **g** you my
2Ki	6:28	**G** your son, that we may eat
2Ki	8:19	as He promised him to **g** a
1Ch	16: 8	**g** thanks to the LORD! Call
1Ch	16:29	**G** to the LORD the glory
1Ch	22: 9	for I will **g** peace and
1Ch	22:12	Only may the LORD **g** you
2Ch	1:10	Now **g** me wisdom and
2Ch	25:18	**G** your daughter to my son as
2Ch	30:12	of God was on Judah to **g**
2Ch	31: 2	to **g** thanks, and to praise
Ezra	9: 8	enlighten our eyes and **g** us
Ezra	9: 9	and to **g** us a wall in Judah
Ezra	9:12	do not **g** your daughters as
Neh	9:12	To **g** them light on the road
Neh	9:15	Which You had sworn to **g**
Job	2: 4	all that a man has he will **g**
Job	10: 1	I will **g** free course to my
Job	33:31	**G** ear, Job, listen to me;
Ps	2: 8	and I will **g** You The
Ps	5: 1	**G** ear to my words, O LORD,
Ps	5: 2	**G** heed to the voice of my
Ps	6: 5	In the grave who will **g** You
Ps	18:49	Therefore I will **g** thanks to
Ps	28: 4	**G** them according to the
Ps	29: 1	**G** unto the LORD glory and
Ps	29:11	The LORD will **g** strength to
Ps	30:12	I will **g** thanks to You
Ps	37: 4	And He shall **g** you the
Ps	49: 7	Nor **g** to God a ransom for
Ps	51:16	or else I would **g** it; You
Ps	84:11	The LORD will **g** grace and
Ps	91:11	For He shall **g** His angels
Ps	92: 1	It is good to **g** thanks to
Ps	96: 7	**G** to the LORD, O families
Ps	97:12	And **g** thanks at the
Ps	105: 1	**g** thanks to the LORD! Call
Ps	106:47	To **g** thanks to Your holy
Ps	108:12	**G** us help from trouble, For
Ps	109: 4	But I **g** myself to
Ps	118: 1	**g** thanks to the LORD, for
Ps	118:29	**g** thanks to the LORD, for
Ps	119:62	midnight I will rise to **g**
Ps	132: 4	I will not **g** sleep to my
Ps	136: 1	**g** thanks to the LORD, for
Ps	136: 2	**g** thanks to the God of gods!
Ps	136: 3	**g** thanks to the Lord of
Ps	143: 1	**G** ear to my supplications!
Ps	145:15	And You **g** them their food
Prov	1: 4	To **g** prudence to the simple,
Prov	4: 2	For I **g** you good doctrine:
Prov	4:20	**g** attention to my words;
Prov	5: 9	Lest you **g** your honor to
Prov	6: 4	**G** no sleep to your eyes,
Prov	9: 9	**G** instruction to a wise
Prov	23:26	**g** me your heart, And let
Prov	25:21	**g** him bread to eat; And if
Prov	29:17	he will **g** delight to your
Prov	30:15	Give and **G**! There are
Prov	31: 3	Do not **g** your strength to
Prov	31: 6	**G** strong drink to him who is
Prov	31:31	**G** her of the fruit of her
Eccl	5: 1	to hear rather than to **g**
Song	7:12	There I will **g** you my love.
Song	8: 7	If a man would **g** for love
Is	1: 2	and **g** ear, O earth! For the
Is	7:14	the Lord Himself will **g** you
Is	42: 8	And My glory I will not **g**
Jer	32:39	then I will **g** them one heart
Ezek	11:19	Then I will **g** them one heart,
Ezek	11:19	and **g** them a heart of flesh,
Ezek	36:26	I will **g** you a new heart and
Hos	11: 8	How can I **g** you up, Ephraim?
Mic	6: 7	Shall I **g** my firstborn for
Matt	4: 6	He shall **g** His angels
Matt	5:42	**G** to him who asks you, and
Matt	6:11	**G** us this day our daily
Matt	7: 6	Do not **g** what is holy to the
Matt	7: 9	will **g** him a stone?
Matt	7:11	know how to **g** good gifts to
Matt	10: 8	you have received, freely **g**.
Matt	11:28	and I will **g** you rest.
Matt	16:26	Or what will a man **g** in
Matt	20:28	and to **g** His life a ransom
Matt	24:45	to **g** them food in due
Mark	10:21	whatever you have and **g** to
Luke	1:79	To **g** light to those who sit
Luke	4: 6	and I **g** it to whomever I
Luke	4:10	He shall **g** His angels
Luke	6:30	**G** to everyone who asks of
Luke	6:38	"**G**, and it will be given
Luke	11: 3	**G** us day by day our daily
Luke	11.11	will he **g** him a serpent
Luke	11:13	know how to **g** good gifts to
Luke	11:13	your heavenly Father **g** the
Luke	12:32	Father's good pleasure to **g**
Luke	12:33	Sell what you have and **g**
Luke	15:12	**g** me the portion of goods
Luke	18:12	I **g** tithes of all that I
Luke	19: 8	I **g** half of my goods to the
John	1:22	that we may **g** an answer to
John	4: 7	**G** Me a drink."
John	4:14	of the water that I shall **g**
John	4:15	**g** me this water, that I may
John	6:34	**g** us this bread always."
John	6:51	the bread that I shall **g** is
John	6:51	which I shall **g** for the life
John	9:24	**G** God the glory! We know that
John	10:28	And I **g** them eternal life,
John	13:26	It is he to whom I shall **g** a
John	13:34	A new commandment I **g** to you,
John	14:16	and He will **g** you another

John	14:27	My peace I **g** to you; not as
John	15:16	Father in My name He may **g**
John	17: 2	that He should **g** eternal
Acts	3: 6	but what I do have I **g** you:
Acts	12:23	because he did not **g** glory
Acts	20:35	It is more blessed to **g** than
Rom	8:32	not with Him also freely **g**
Rom	12:20	**g** him a drink; For in
Rom	14:12	So then each of us shall **g**
Rom	16: 4	to whom not only I **g** thanks,
1Co	7: 5	that you may **g** yourselves to
1Co	10:32	**G** no offense, either to the
1Co	13: 3	and though I **g** my body to be
1Co	14:17	For you indeed **g** thanks well,
2Co	8:10	And in this I **g** advice: It is
2Co	9: 7	So let each one **g** as he
Eph	1:16	do not cease to **g** thanks for
Eph	4:27	nor **g** place to the devil.
Eph	4:28	he may have something to **g**
Eph	5:14	And Christ will **g** you
Col	1: 3	We **g** thanks to the God and
1Th	5:18	in everything **g** thanks; for
1Ti	1: 4	nor **g** heed to fables and
1Ti	4:13	**g** attention to reading, to
1Ti	5:14	**g** no opportunity to the
2Ti	4: 8	will **g** to me on that Day,
Heb	2: 1	Therefore we must **g** the more
1Pe	3:15	and always be ready to **g**
1Jn	5:16	and He will **g** him life for
Rev	2: 7	him who overcomes I will **g**
Rev	2:10	and I will **g** you the crown
Rev	2:17	And I will **g** him a white
Rev	2:28	and I will **g** him the morning
Rev	4: 9	the living creatures **g**
Rev	14: 7	Fear God and **g** glory to Him,
Rev	16: 9	they did not repent and **g**
Rev	22:12	to **g** to every one according

GIVEN (*see* GIVE)

Gen	1:30	I have **g** every green herb
Gen	9: 3	I have **g** you all things,
Gen	15:18	your descendants I have **g**
Esth	7: 3	let my life be **g** me at my
Ps	16: 7	bless the LORD who has **g**
Ps	115:16	But the earth He has **g** to
Eccl	9: 9	vain life which He has **g**
Is	8:18	whom the LORD has **g** me!
Is	9: 6	is born, Unto us a Son is **g**;
Dan	5:28	and **g** to the Medes and
Matt	7: 7	and it will be **g** to you;
Matt	9: 8	who had **g** such power to men.
Matt	12:39	and no sign will be **g** to it
Matt	13:12	has, to him more will be **g**,
Matt	21:43	be taken from you and **g** to
Matt	22:30	neither marry nor are **g** in
Matt	28:18	All authority has been **g** to
Mark	14:23	and when He had **g** thanks He
Luke	6:38	and it will be **g** to you:
Luke	11: 9	and it will be **g** to you;
Luke	11:29	and no sign will be **g** to it
Luke	22:19	This is My body which is **g**
John	1:17	For the law was **g** through
John	3:27	unless it has been **g** to him
John	3:35	and has **g** all things into

John	4:10	and He would have **g** you
John	5:27	and has **g** Him authority to
John	5:36	which the Father has **g** Me
John	6:11	and when He had **g** thanks He
John	7:39	Holy Spirit was not yet **g**,
John	10:29	who has **g** them to Me, is
John	13: 3	that the Father had **g** all
John	13:15	For I have **g** you an example,
John	16:21	but as soon as she has **g**
John	17: 2	as You have **g** Him authority
John	17: 4	the work which You have **g**
John	17: 6	to the men whom You have **g**
John	17: 8	For I have **g** to them the
John	17: 8	the words which You have **g**
John	17: 9	for those whom You have **g**
John	17:14	I have **g** them Your word; and
John	17:22	which You gave Me I have **g**
John	17:24	My glory which You have **g**
John	18:11	cup which My Father has **g**
Acts	4:12	no other name under heaven **g**
Acts	5:32	Holy Spirit whom God has **g**
Acts	8:18	hands the Holy Spirit was **g**,
Acts	17:31	He has **g** assurance of this
Rom	5: 5	by the Holy Spirit who was **g**
Rom	11: 8	God has **g** them a spirit
Rom	12: 3	through the grace **g** to me,
Rom	12:13	**g** to hospitality.
1Co	11:15	for her hair is **g** to her
1Co	11:24	and when He had **g** thanks, He
1Co	12: 7	of the Spirit is **g** to each
1Co	12: 8	for to one is **g** the word of
1Co	12:24	having **g** greater honor to
2Co	5:18	and has **g** us the ministry of
2Co	9: 9	He has **g** to the poor;
Gal	3:22	in Jesus Christ might be **g**
Gal	4:15	out your own eyes and **g**
Eph	3: 8	the saints, this grace was **g**,
Eph	4: 7	each one of us grace was **g**
Eph	4:19	have **g** themselves over to
Eph	5: 2	also has loved us and **g**
Eph	6:19	that utterance may be **g** to
Phil	2: 9	has highly exalted Him and **g**
2Th	2:16	who has loved us and **g** us
1Ti	3: 3	not **g** to wine, not violent,
2Ti	1: 7	For God has not **g** us a spirit
2Ti	3:16	All Scripture is **g** by
Heb	2:13	whom God has **g** Me.
Heb	4: 8	For if Joshua had **g** them
Jas	1: 5	and it will be **g** to him.
2Pe	3:15	according to the wisdom **g** to
1Jn	4:13	because He has **g** us of His
1Jn	5:10	testimony that God has **g** of
1Jn	5:11	that God has **g** us eternal
Rev	6: 2	and a crown was **g** to him,
Rev	8: 2	and to them were **g** seven
Rev	9: 1	To him was **g** the key to the
Rev	9: 3	And to them was **g** power, as
Rev	11: 1	Then I was **g** a reed like a
Rev	16: 8	and power was **g** to him to

GIVER† (*see* GIVE)

2Co	9: 7	for God loves a cheerful **g**.

GIVES (see GIVE)

Job	32: 8	the breath of the Almighty **g**
Job	35:10	Who **g** songs in the night,
Ps	119:130	entrance of Your words **g**
Ps	119:130	It **g** understanding to the
Ps	127: 2	For so He **g** His beloved
Ps	136:25	Who **g** food to all flesh,
Ps	146: 7	Who **g** food to the hungry.
Prov	3:34	But **g** grace to the humble.
Matt	5:15	and it **g** light to all who
Matt	10:42	And whoever **g** one of these
Mark	9:41	For whoever **g** you a cup of
John	1: 9	was the true Light which **g**
John	5:21	even so the Son **g** life to
John	6:63	It is the Spirit who **g** life;
John	10:11	The good shepherd **g** His life
John	14:27	not as the world **g** do I give
Acts	17:25	since He **g** to all life,
Rom	4:17	who **g** life to the dead and
Rom	12: 8	in exhortation; he who **g**,
1Co	3: 7	but God who **g** the increase.
1Co	15:57	who **g** us the victory through
2Co	3: 6	but the Spirit **g** life.
1Ti	6:17	who **g** us richly all things
Jas	1: 5	who **g** to all liberally and
Jas	1:15	it **g** birth to sin; and sin,
Jas	4: 6	But **g** grace to the
Rev	22: 5	for the Lord God **g** them

GIVING (see GIVE)

Ruth	1: 6	had visited His people by **g**
Matt	24:38	marrying and **g** in marriage,
Luke	17:16	**g** Him thanks. And he was a
Acts	15: 8	acknowledged them by **g** them
Rom	4:20	**g** glory to God,
Rom	9: 4	the **g** of the law, the
Rom	12:10	in honor **g** preference to one
Col	1:12	**g** thanks to the Father who
1Ti	4: 1	**g** heed to deceiving spirits
Tit	1:14	not **g** heed to Jewish fables
Heb	13:15	**g** thanks to His name.
1Pe	3: 7	**g** honor to the wife, as to
2Pe	1: 5	**g** all diligence, add to your

GLAD (see GLADLY, GLADNESS)

Ps	9: 2	I will be **g** and rejoice in
Ps	14: 7	rejoice and Israel be **g**.
Ps	16: 9	Therefore my heart is **g**,
Ps	34: 2	shall hear of it and be **g**.
Ps	45: 8	which they have made You **g**.
Ps	46: 4	whose streams shall make **g**
Ps	104:15	And wine that makes **g** the
Ps	118:24	We will rejoice and be **g** in
Ps	122: 1	I was **g** when they said to
Ps	126: 3	for us, And we are **g**.
Prov	10: 1	A wise son makes a **g**
Is	52: 7	Who brings **g** tidings of
Matt	5:12	and be exceedingly **g**,
John	8:56	and he saw it and was **g**.
John	20:20	Then the disciples were **g**
Rom	10:15	Who bring **g** tidings of
Phil	2:17	I am **g** and rejoice with you
Rev	19: 7	Let us be **g** and rejoice and

GLADLY (see GLAD)

Mark	12:37	common people heard Him **g**.
2Co	12: 9	Therefore most **g** I will

GLADNESS (see GLAD)

Deut	28:47	your God with joy and **g** of
Esth	8:16	The Jews had light and **g**,
Esth	9:17	it a day of feasting and **g**.
Ps	4: 7	You have put **g** in my heart,
Ps	30:11	and clothed me with **g**,
Ps	45: 7	You With the oil of **g** more
Ps	51: 8	Make me hear joy and **g**,
Ps	100: 2	Serve the LORD with **g**;
Is	35:10	They shall obtain joy and **g**,
Jer	7:34	of mirth and the voice of **g**,
Heb	1: 9	You With the oil of **g**

GLEAN (see GLEANED)

Lev	19:10	And you shall not **g** your
Ruth	2: 7	Please let me **g** and gather

GLEANED (see GLEAN)

Ruth	2:17	So she **g** in the field until

GLORIES† (see GLORY)

Jer	9:24	But let him who **g** glory in
1Co	1:31	it is written, "He who **g**,
2Co	10:17	But "he who **g**,
1Pe	1:11	of Christ and the **g** that

GLORIFIED (see GLORIFY)

Is	49: 3	Israel, In whom I will be **g**.
Dan	5:23	your ways, you have not **g**.
Matt	9: 8	they marveled and **g** God, who
John	7:39	because Jesus was not yet **g**.
John	11: 4	that the Son of God may be **g**
John	12:28	I have both **g** it and will
John	13:31	and God is **g** in Him.
John	14:13	that the Father may be **g** in
John	17: 4	I have **g** You on the earth. I
Rom	8:30	justified, these He also **g**.
2Th	1:12	Lord Jesus Christ may be **g**
1Pe	4:14	but on your part He is **g**.

GLORIFY (see GLORIFIED, GLORIFYING, GLORY)

Matt	5:16	see your good works and **g**
John	12:28	**g** Your name." Then a voice
John	12:28	glorified it and will **g**
John	17: 1	**G** Your Son, that Your Son
John	21:19	by what death he would **g**
Rom	1:21	they did not **g** Him as God,
1Co	6:20	therefore **g** God in your body
Heb	5: 5	So also Christ did not **g**

GLORIFYING (see GLORIFY)

Luke	2:20	**g** and praising God for all

GLORIOUS (see GLORY)

Ex	15: 6	has become **g** in power; Your
Ps	72:19	And blessed be His **g** name
Ps	87: 3	**G** things are spoken of you,
Dan	8: 9	and toward the **G** Land.
Eph	5:27	present her to Himself a **g**

Phil	3:21	it may be conformed to His **g**	Ezek	43: 5	the **g** of the LORD filled
Col	1:11	according to His **g** power,	Dan	7:14	Him was given dominion and **g**
1Ti	1:11	according to the **g** gospel of	Hag	2: 3	this temple in its former **g**?
Tit	2:13	for the blessed hope and **g**	Hag	2: 9	The **g** of this latter temple
			Matt	6:13	and the power and the **g**

GLORY (see GLORIES, GLORIFY, GLORIOUS, GLORYING)

			Matt	6:29	even Solomon in all his **g**
Ex	24:16	Now the **g** of the LORD rested	Matt	16:27	of Man will come in the **g**
Ex	29:43	shall be sanctified by My **g**.	Matt	19:28	sits on the throne of His **g**,
Ex	33:18	"Please, show me Your **g**.	Matt	24:30	with power and great **g**.
Ex	33:22	while My **g** passes by, that I	Luke	2: 9	and the **g** of the Lord shone
Ex	40:34	and the **g** of the LORD	Luke	2:14	**G** to God in the highest, And
Num	14:21	shall be filled with the **g**	Luke	2:32	And the **g** of Your people
Num	14:22	men who have seen My **g** and	Luke	19:38	Peace in heaven and **g** in
Josh	7:19	give **g** to the LORD God of	Luke	24:26	and to enter into His **g**?
1Sa	4:21	The **g** has departed from	John	1:14	us, and we beheld His **g**,
1Ch	16:24	Declare His **g** among the	John	2:11	and manifested His **g**;
1Ch	16:29	Give to the LORD the **g** due	John	17: 5	with the **g** which I had with
1Ch	29:11	The power and the **g**,	John	17:22	And the **g** which You gave Me I
Ps	4: 2	Will you turn my **g** to	Acts	7: 2	The God of **g** appeared to our
Ps	8: 1	Who have set Your **g** above	Rom	1:23	and changed the **g** of the
Ps	8: 5	You have crowned him with **g**	Rom	3:23	and fall short of the **g** of
Ps	19: 1	The heavens declare the **g** of	Rom	5: 2	rejoice in hope of the **g** of
Ps	24: 7	doors! And the King of **g**	Rom	6: 4	from the dead by the **g** of
Ps	29: 1	Give unto the LORD **g** and	Rom	8:18	to be compared with the **g**
Ps	29: 3	The God of **g** thunders; The	Rom	9: 4	pertain the adoption, the **g**,
Ps	29: 9	everyone says, "**G**!"	Rom	9:23	known the riches of His **g**
Ps	62: 7	is my salvation and my **g**;	Rom	9:23	prepared beforehand for **g**,
Ps	64:10	the upright in heart shall **g**.	Rom	11:36	to whom be **g** forever. Amen.
Ps	72:19	earth be filled with His **g**.	Rom	16:27	be **g** through Jesus Christ
Ps	73:24	afterward receive me to **g**.	1Co	1:29	that no flesh should **g** in His
Ps	79: 9	For the **g** of Your name;	1Co	2: 7	before the ages for our **g**,
Ps	84:11	LORD will give grace and **g**;	1Co	2: 8	have crucified the Lord of **g**.
Ps	85: 9	That **g** may dwell in our	1Co	10:31	do all to the **g** of God.
Ps	90:16	And Your **g** to their	1Co	11: 7	since he is the image and **g**
Ps	96: 3	Declare His **g** among the	1Co	11: 7	but woman is the **g** of man.
Ps	97: 6	all the peoples see His **g**.	1Co	15:43	dishonor, it is raised in **g**.
Ps	102:16	He shall appear in His **g**.	2Co	3: 7	of Moses because of the **g**
Ps	104:31	May the **g** of the LORD	2Co	3: 7	which **g** was passing away,
Ps	105: 3	**G** in His holy name	2Co	3:18	same image from glory to **g**,
Ps	106:20	Thus they changed their **g**	2Co	4:17	and eternal weight of **g**,
Ps	108: 5	And Your **g** above all the	Gal	1: 5	to whom be **g** forever and
Ps	113: 4	His **g** above the heavens.	Eph	1: 6	to the praise of the **g** of His
Ps	138: 5	For great is the **g** of the	Eph	1:17	Christ, the Father of **g**,
Ps	145:11	They shall speak of the **g** of	Eph	1:18	are the riches of the **g** of
Ps	148:13	His **g** is above the earth	Eph	3:21	to Him be **g** in the church by
Ps	149: 5	the saints be joyful in **g**;	Phil	2:11	to the **g** of God the Father.
Prov	17: 6	And the **g** of children is	Phil	4:19	to His riches in **g** by
Prov	25: 2	It is the **g** of God to	Col	1:27	are the riches of the **g** of
Prov	25: 2	But the **g** of kings is to	Col	1:27	Christ in you, the hope of **g**.
Is	6: 3	earth is full of His **g**!"	Col	3: 4	will appear with Him in **g**.
Is	28: 5	will be For a crown of **g**	1Th	2:20	For you are our **g** and joy.
Is	40: 5	The **g** of the LORD shall be	1Ti	3:16	the world, Received up in **g**.
Is	41:16	And **g** in the Holy One of	2Ti	2:10	Christ Jesus with eternal **g**.
Is	42: 8	And My **g** I will not give to	Heb	1: 3	the brightness of His **g**
Is	43: 7	I have created for My **g**;	Heb	2: 7	crowned him with **g** and
Is	46:13	in Zion, For Israel My **g**.	Heb	2:10	in bringing many sons to **g**,
Is	60: 1	light has come! And the **g**	Heb	13:21	to whom be **g** forever and
Is	60:19	light, And your God your **g**.	Jas	2: 1	Christ, the Lord of **g**,
Jer	9:23	Let not the wise man **g** in	1Pe	1: 8	inexpressible and full of **g**,
Ezek	1:28	of the likeness of the **g** of	1Pe	4:13	that when His **g** is revealed,
Ezek	3:23	the **g** of the LORD stood	1Pe	4:14	for the Spirit of **g** and of
Ezek	8: 4	the **g** of the God of Israel	1Pe	5: 1	and also a partaker of the **g**
Ezek	10: 4	brightness of the LORD's **g**.	1Pe	5: 4	will receive the crown of **g**
			1Pe	5:10	called us to His eternal **g**

1Pe	5:11	To Him be the **g** and the
Jude	24	the presence of His **g** with
Rev	4:11	To receive **g** and honor and

GLORYING† (see GLORY)

1Co	5: 6	Your **g** is not good. Do you

GLUTTON

Deut	21:20	he is a **g** and a drunkard.'
Matt	11:19	a **g** and a winebibber, a

GNASHING

Matt	8:12	There will be weeping and **g**
Matt	13:42	There will be wailing and **g**

GNAT†

Matt	23:24	who strain out a **g** and

GOAD† (see GOADS)

Judg	3:31	the Philistines with an ox **g**;

GOADS (see GOAD)

Eccl	12:11	words of the wise are like **g**,
Acts	9: 5	you to kick against the **g**.

GOAL†

Phil	3:14	I press toward the **g** for the

GOAT (see GOATS)

Gen	15: 9	a three-year-old female **g**,
Ex	23:19	shall not boil a young **g** in
Lev	16:20	he shall bring the live **g**.
Lev	16:26	And he who released the **g** as
Is	11: 6	lie down with the young **g**,
Dan	8: 5	suddenly a male **g** came from

GOATS (see GOAT)

Gen	27:16	skins of the kids of the **g**
Matt	25:32	his sheep from the **g**.
Matt	25:33	but the **g** on the left.
Heb	9:12	Not with the blood of **g** and
Heb	9:13	if the blood of bulls and **g**
Heb	10: 4	the blood of bulls and **g**

GOD (see GOD'S, GODHEAD, GODLY, ONE, YOU-ARE-THE-GOD-WHO-SEES)

Gen	1: 1	In the beginning **G** created
Gen	1: 3	Then **G** said, "Let there be
Gen	1:10	And **G** saw that it was
Gen	1:26	Then **G** said, "Let Us make
Gen	1:27	So **G** created man in His own
Gen	2: 7	And the LORD **G** formed man
Gen	5:22	Enoch walked with **G** three
Gen	6: 4	when the sons of **G** came in
Gen	6: 9	Noah walked with **G**.
Gen	7: 9	as **G** had commanded Noah.
Gen	8: 1	Then **G** remembered Noah, and
Gen	9:16	covenant between **G** and
Gen	14:18	he was the priest of **G** Most
Gen	17: 1	to him, "I am Almighty **G**;
Gen	20:11	surely the fear of **G** is not
Gen	21:17	Then the angel of **G** called
Gen	21:33	the LORD, the Everlasting **G**.
Gen	22: 8	**G** will provide for Himself

Gen	28: 3	May **G** Almighty bless you,
Gen	31:11	Then the Angel of **G** spoke to
Gen	32:30	For I have seen **G** face to
Gen	41:38	in whom is the Spirit of **G**?
Gen	50:20	but **G** meant it for good, in
Ex	2:24	So **G** heard their groaning,
Ex	3: 1	to Horeb, the mountain of **G**.
Ex	3: 4	**G** called to him from the
Ex	3:15	the **G** of Abraham, the God of
Ex	3:18	The LORD **G** of the Hebrews
Ex	3:18	sacrifice to the LORD our **G**.
Ex	6: 7	people, and I will be your **G**.
Ex	8:19	"This is the finger of **G**.
Ex	18:12	sacrifices to offer to **G**.
Ex	18:15	come to me to inquire of **G**.
Ex	20: 2	"I am the LORD your **G**,
Ex	20: 5	your God, am a jealous **G**,
Ex	20: 7	name of the LORD your **G** in
Ex	24:11	lay His hand. So they saw **G**,
Ex	31: 3	him with the Spirit of **G**,
Ex	31:18	written with the finger of **G**.
Ex	34: 6	"The LORD, the LORD **G**,
Lev	18:21	profane the name of your **G**:
Lev	21:17	to offer the bread of his **G**.
Num	16:22	the **G** of the spirits of all
Num	22: 9	Then **G** came to Balaam and
Num	23: 8	How shall I curse whom **G** has
Num	23:19	**G** is not a man, that He
Num	27:16	the **G** of the spirits of all
Deut	4:24	consuming fire, a jealous **G**.
Deut	4:25	sight of the LORD your **G**
Deut	4:29	will seek the LORD your **G**,
Deut	5:14	Sabbath of the LORD your **G**.
Deut	5:26	the voice of the living **G**
Deut	6: 4	O Israel: The LORD our **G**,
Deut	6: 5	shall love the LORD your **G**
Deut	6:16	not tempt the LORD your **G**
Deut	7: 9	the LORD your God, He is **G**,
Deut	7: 9	the faithful **G** who keeps
Deut	7:21	God, the great and awesome **G**,
Deut	21:23	is hanged is accursed of **G**.
Deut	28:58	name, THE LORD YOUR **G**,
Deut	32: 3	Ascribe greatness to our **G**.
Deut	32:17	to demons, not to **G**,
Deut	32:39	And there is no **G** besides
Deut	33:27	The eternal **G** is your
Josh	1:11	land which the LORD your **G**
Josh	3:10	know that the living **G** is
Josh	24:26	in the Book of the Law of **G**.
Josh	24:27	to you, lest you deny your **G**.
Judg	13: 5	shall be a Nazirite to **G**
Judg	13: 6	A Man of **G** came to me, and
Judg	13: 6	of the Angel of **G**,
Judg	13:22	because we have seen **G**!"
Judg	18:31	the time that the house of **G**
Ruth	1:16	people, And your God, my **G**.
1Sa	2: 2	there any rock like our **G**.
1Sa	10:10	then the Spirit of **G** came
1Sa	16:23	whenever the spirit from **G**
1Sa	17:26	the armies of the living **G**?
1Sa	18:10	distressing spirit from **G**
1Sa	19:20	the Spirit of **G** came upon
2Sa	5:10	and the LORD **G** of hosts
2Sa	6: 7	died there by the ark of **G**.

G

2Sa	7:22	You are great, O Lord G.
2Sa	7:22	nor is there any G
2Sa	7:28	now, O Lord GOD, You are G,
2Sa	14:17	for as the angel of G,
1Ki	4:29	And G gave Solomon wisdom
1Ki	8:27	But will G indeed dwell on
1Ki	13: 1	a man of G went from Judah
1Ki	18:21	opinions? If the LORD is G,
1Ki	18:24	who answers by fire, He is G.
1Ki	18:36	LORD G of Abraham, Isaac,
1Ki	18:39	He is G! The LORD, He is
1Ki	19: 8	as Horeb, the mountain of G.
1Ki	20:28	The LORD is G of the hills,
1Ki	21:10	You have blasphemed G and the
2Ki	18:22	'We trust in the LORD our G,
2Ki	19: 4	to reproach the living G,
2Ki	19:10	Do not let your G in whom you
2Ki	19:15	the cherubim, You are G,
1Ch	9:11	officer over the house of G;
2Ch	15: 1	Now the Spirit of G came upon
Ezra	1: 3	God of Israel (He is G),
Ezra	7: 9	to the good hand of his G
Neh	1: 5	O great and awesome G,
Neh	8:18	the Book of the Law of G.
Neh	13:31	times. Remember me, O my G,
Job	1: 1	and one who feared G and
Job	1: 5	have sinned and cursed G in
Job	1: 9	Does Job fear G for nothing?
Job	1:16	The fire of G fell from
Job	1:22	Job did not sin nor charge G
Job	2: 9	Curse G and die!"
Job	2:10	we indeed accept good from G,
Job	3:23	And whom G has hedged in?
Job	11: 7	out the deep things of G?
Job	13: 3	I desire to reason with G.
Job	19:26	in my flesh I shall see G,
Job	33: 4	The Spirit of G has made me,
Job	33:12	For G is greater than man.
Job	38: 7	And all the sons of G
Job	40:19	the first of the ways of G;
Ps	5: 2	of my cry, My King and my G,
Ps	14: 1	heart, "There is no G.
Ps	14: 2	who understand, who seek G.
Ps	16: 1	Preserve me, O G,
Ps	18: 2	and my deliverer; My G,
Ps	18:29	By my G I can leap over a
Ps	18:46	be my Rock! Let the G of
Ps	19: 1	declare the glory of G;
Ps	22: 1	My God, My G, why have
Ps	29: 3	The G of glory thunders;
Ps	31: 5	O LORD G of truth.
Ps	33:12	is the nation whose G is
Ps	36: 1	There is no fear of G
Ps	40: 8	to do Your will, O my G,
Ps	42: 1	pants my soul for You, O G.
Ps	42: 2	My soul thirsts for G,
Ps	42: 3	to me, "Where is your G?
Ps	42: 5	within me? Hope in G,
Ps	45: 6	Your throne, O G,
Ps	45: 7	Therefore God, Your G,
Ps	46: 1	G is our refuge and
Ps	46: 4	make glad the city of G,
Ps	46: 5	G is in the midst of her,
Ps	46: 5	G shall help her, just at
Ps	46: 7	The G of Jacob is our
Ps	46:10	still, and know that I am G;
Ps	48: 1	In the city of our G,
Ps	51: 1	Have mercy upon me, O G,
Ps	51:10	in me a clean heart, O G,
Ps	65: 9	The river of G is full of
Ps	66: 1	Make a joyful shout to G,
Ps	66: 5	Come and see the works of G;
Ps	66: 8	Oh, bless our G,
Ps	66:19	But certainly G has heard
Ps	67: 3	the peoples praise You, O G;
Ps	68: 5	Is G in His holy
Ps	68: 6	G sets the solitary in
Ps	68:15	A mountain of G is the
Ps	68:17	The chariots of G are
Ps	68:19	The G of our salvation!
Ps	68:26	Bless G in the
Ps	68:31	stretch out her hands to G.
Ps	68:34	Ascribe strength to G;
Ps	69: 1	O G! For the waters have
Ps	69:35	For G will save Zion And
Ps	70: 1	Make haste, O G,
Ps	70: 4	Let G be magnified!"
Ps	71: 5	You are my hope, O Lord G;
Ps	71:19	have done great things; O G,
Ps	71:22	O my G! To You I will sing
Ps	73: 1	Truly G is good to Israel,
Ps	74:12	For G is my King from of
Ps	75: 1	We give thanks to You, O G,
Ps	76:11	vows to the LORD your G,
Ps	77: 1	I cried out to G with my
Ps	77:13	is so great a God as our G?
Ps	78:56	and provoked the Most High G,
Ps	79: 9	O G of our salvation, For
Ps	79:10	say, "Where is their G?
Ps	82: 8	Arise, O G, judge
Ps	83: 1	O G! Do not hold Your
Ps	84: 2	cry out for the living G.
Ps	84: 3	of hosts, My King and my G.
Ps	84:11	For the LORD G is a sun
Ps	86:15	are a G full of compassion,
Ps	87: 3	O city of G! Selah
Ps	89:26	'You are my Father, My G,
Ps	90: 2	to everlasting, You are G.
Ps	98: 3	seen the salvation of our G.
Ps	100: 3	that the LORD, He is G;
Ps	115: 3	But our G is in heaven; He
Ps	119:115	the commandments of my G!
Ps	136: 2	give thanks to the G of
Ps	139:23	Search me, O G,
Ps	144:15	are the people whose G is
Prov	2: 5	And find the knowledge of G.
Prov	2:17	the covenant of her G.
Prov	30: 5	Every word of G is pure;
Prov	30: 9	profane the name of my G.
Eccl	2:24	saw, was from the hand of G.
Eccl	3:13	labor—it is the gift of G.
Eccl	5: 2	For G is in heaven, and
Eccl	5: 4	When you make a vow to G,
Eccl	12: 7	the spirit will return to G
Eccl	12:13	Fear G and keep His
Eccl	12:14	For G will bring every work
Is	7:13	but will you weary my G
Is	8:10	For G is with us."

Is	8:21	curse their king and their **G**,	Matt	22:32	the **G** of Isaac, and
Is	9: 6	Counselor, Mighty **G**,	Matt	27:40	If You are the Son of **G**,
Is	10:21	of Jacob, To the Mighty **G**.	Matt	27:43	"He trusted in **G**;
Is	14:13	throne above the stars of **G**;	Matt	27:46	that is, "My God, My **G**,
Is	25: 8	And the Lord **G** will wipe	Matt	27:54	this was the Son of **G**!
Is	31: 3	are men, and not **G**;	Mark	1: 1	Jesus Christ, the Son of **G**.
Is	40: 1	My people!" Says your **G**.	Mark	1:14	gospel of the kingdom of **G**,
Is	40: 3	desert A highway for our **G**.	Mark	4:11	mystery of the kingdom of **G**;
Is	40: 8	But the word of our **G**	Mark	10:14	of such is the kingdom of **G**.
Is	40: 9	Behold your **G**!"	Luke	1:35	will be called the Son of **G**.
Is	40:18	whom then will you liken **G**?	Luke	1:37	For with **G** nothing will be
Is	40:28	heard? The everlasting **G**,	Luke	1:47	my spirit has rejoiced in **G**
Is	41:10	dismayed, for I am your **G**.	Luke	2:13	the heavenly host praising **G**
Is	44: 6	Besides Me there is no **G**.	Luke	2:14	Glory to **G** in the highest,
Is	45: 5	There is no **G** besides Me.	Luke	2:52	and in favor with **G** and men.
Is	45:14	There is no other **G**.	Luke	3: 2	the word of **G** came to John
Is	45:21	A just **G** and a Savior;	Luke	3:38	son of Adam, the son of **G**.
Is	52:10	see The salvation of our **G**.	Luke	4: 4	but by every word of **G**.
Is	53: 4	Him stricken, Smitten by **G**,	Luke	9:20	and said, "The Christ of **G**.
Is	55: 7	mercy on him; And to our **G**,	Luke	11:20	demons with the finger of **G**,
Is	57:21	is no peace," Says my **G**,	Luke	23:35	the Christ, the chosen of **G**.
Is	61: 1	The Spirit of the Lord **G** is	John	1: 1	and the Word was with **G**,
Is	61: 2	day of vengeance of our **G**;	John	1: 1	with God, and the Word was **G**.
Jer	1: 6	Lord **G**! Behold, I cannot	John	1: 2	was in the beginning with **G**.
Jer	24: 7	and I will be their **G**,	John	1: 6	There was a man sent from **G**,
Jer	32:18	them—the Great, the Mighty **G**,	John	1:12	to become children of **G**,
Ezek	1: 1	and I saw visions of **G**.	John	1:13	of the will of man, but of **G**.
Ezek	11:24	a vision by the Spirit of **G**	John	1:18	No one has seen **G** at any
Ezek	13: 9	know that I am the Lord **G**.	John	1:29	Behold! The Lamb of **G** who
Dan	1:17	**G** gave them knowledge and	John	1:49	You are the Son of **G**! You
Dan	2:19	So Daniel blessed the **G** of	John	3: 2	are a teacher come from **G**;
Dan	2:28	But there is a **G** in heaven	John	3: 3	cannot see the kingdom of **G**.
Dan	3:25	fourth is like the Son of **G**.	John	3:16	For **G** so loved the world that
Dan	3:26	servants of the Most High **G**,	John	3:17	For **G** did not send His Son
Dan	4: 8	the Spirit of the Holy **G**),	John	3:36	but the wrath of **G** abides on
Dan	5:14	that the Spirit of **G** is in	John	4:10	"If you knew the gift of **G**,
Dan	5:26	**G** has numbered your kingdom,	John	4:24	**G** is Spirit, and those who
Dan	9: 4	Lord, great and awesome **G**,	John	5:18	making Himself equal with **G**.
Hos	1: 9	And I will not be your **G**.	John	6:28	we may work the works of **G**?
Hos	1:10	are sons of the living **G**.	John	6:29	"This is the work of **G**,
Hos	4: 1	or mercy Or knowledge of **G**	John	6:33	For the bread of **G** is He who
Hos	6: 6	And the knowledge of **G** more	John	6:69	the Son of the living **G**.
Amos	4:12	you, Prepare to meet your **G**,	John	8:41	we have one Father—**G**.
Jon	3:10	and **G** relented from the	John	9:16	"This Man is not from **G**,
Jon	4: 2	a gracious and merciful **G**,	John	9:24	Give **G** the glory! We know
Mic	6: 6	bow myself before the High **G**?	John	10:33	being a Man, make Yourself **G**.
Mic	6: 8	to walk humbly with your **G**?	John	11:22	that whatever You ask of **G**,
Mal	2:10	Has not one **G** created us?	John	11:27	are the Christ, the Son of **G**,
Mal	2:17	Where is the **G** of justice?"	John	13: 3	and that He had come from **G**
Mal	3: 8	"Will a man rob **G**?	John	13:31	and **G** is glorified in Him.
Mal	3:15	They even tempt **G** and go	John	14: 1	troubled; you believe in **G**,
Matt	1:23	translated, "**G** with us."	John	17: 3	know You, the only true **G**,
Matt	3:16	and He saw the Spirit of **G**	John	19: 7	He made Himself the Son of **G**.
Matt	4: 3	"If You are the Son of **G**,	John	20:17	and to My **G** and your God.'
Matt	4: 4	from the mouth of **G**.	John	20:28	My Lord and my **G**!"
Matt	4: 7	tempt the LORD your **G**.	John	21:19	death he would glorify **G**.
Matt	5: 8	heart, For they shall see **G**.	Acts	2:11	the wonderful works of **G**.
Matt	5: 9	shall be called sons of **G**.	Acts	2:23	and foreknowledge of **G**,
Matt	6:24	You cannot serve **G** and	Acts	2:32	This Jesus **G** has raised up,
Matt	6:33	seek first the kingdom of **G**	Acts	2:33	to the right hand of **G**,
Matt	12:28	demons by the Spirit of **G**,	Acts	3: 8	leaping, and praising **G**.
Matt	14:33	"Truly You are the Son of **G**.	Acts	3:15	whom **G** raised from the dead,
Matt	16:16	the Son of the living **G**.	Acts	5: 4	not lied to men but to **G**.
Matt	19:17	good but One, that is, **G**.	Acts	5:29	We ought to obey **G** rather

G

Acts	5:39	be found to fight against G.	Rom	16:20	And the G of peace will crush
Acts	7: 2	The G of glory appeared to	1Co	1: 4	I thank my G always
Acts	8:37	Jesus Christ is the Son of G.	1Co	1: 9	G is faithful, by whom you
Acts	10: 2	man and one who feared G	1Co	1:14	I thank G that I baptized
Acts	10:15	What G has cleansed you must	1Co	1:20	Has not G made foolish the
Acts	15:18	Known to G from eternity are	1Co	1:21	since, in the wisdom of G,
Acts	16:17	servants of the Most High G,	1Co	1:24	Christ the power of G and
Acts	17:23	TO THE UNKNOWN G.	1Co	1:25	and the weakness of G is
Acts	20:24	the gospel of the grace of G.	1Co	2:10	yes, the deep things of G.
Acts	20:27	you the whole counsel of G.	1Co	2:14	things of the Spirit of G,
Acts	26:18	the power of Satan to G,	1Co	3: 6	but G gave the increase.
Acts	26:20	should repent, turn to G,	1Co	3:16	you are the temple of G and
Rom	1: 1	to the gospel of G	1Co	4: 1	of the mysteries of G.
Rom	1: 7	to you and peace from G our	1Co	4:20	For the kingdom of G is not
Rom	1: 9	For G is my witness, whom I	1Co	6:20	therefore glorify G in your
Rom	1:16	for it is the power of G to	1Co	7:40	I also have the Spirit of G.
Rom	1:17	in it the righteousness of G	1Co	8: 6	yet for us there is one G,
Rom	1:18	For the wrath of G is	1Co	10:13	but G is faithful, who will
Rom	1:21	although they knew G,	1Co	10:20	to demons and not to G,
Rom	1:21	did not glorify Him as G,	1Co	10:31	do, do all to the glory of G.
Rom	1:23	of the incorruptible G into	1Co	11: 3	and the head of Christ is G.
Rom	1:24	Therefore G also gave them up	1Co	11: 7	is the image and glory of G;
Rom	1:25	who exchanged the truth of G	1Co	14:33	For G is not the author of
Rom	2:11	is no partiality with G.	1Co	15: 9	I persecuted the church of G.
Rom	3: 2	committed the oracles of G.	1Co	15:28	that G may be all in all.
Rom	3: 4	let G be true but every man	1Co	15:57	But thanks be to G,
Rom	3:11	none who seeks after G.	2Co	2:15	For we are to G the fragrance
Rom	3:23	fall short of the glory of G,	2Co	2:17	many, peddling the word of G;
Rom	3:29	Or is He the G of the Jews	2Co	4: 4	who is the image of G,
Rom	4: 3	say? "Abraham believed G,	2Co	5: 1	we have a building from G,
Rom	4:20	waver at the promise of G	2Co	5:19	that G was in Christ
Rom	5: 1	we have peace with G through	2Co	5:20	behalf, be reconciled to G.
Rom	5: 8	But G demonstrates His own	2Co	6:16	the temple of the living G.
Rom	5:10	we were reconciled to G	2Co	6:16	I will be their G,
Rom	5:15	much more the grace of G and	2Co	10: 4	not carnal but mighty in G
Rom	6:10	that He lives, He lives to G.	2Co	13:11	and the G of love and peace
Rom	6:22	having become slaves of G,	Gal	2:20	by faith in the Son of G,
Rom	6:23	but the gift of G is	Gal	3: 6	as Abraham "believed G,
Rom	8: 7	mind is enmity against G;	Gal	4: 4	G sent forth His Son, born
Rom	8: 7	not subject to the law of G,	Gal	6: 7	G is not mocked; for
Rom	8: 8	in the flesh cannot please G.	Gal	6:16	and upon the Israel of G.
Rom	8:14	are led by the Spirit of G,	Eph	2: 8	it is the gift of G,
Rom	8:14	of God, these are sons of G.	Eph	2:10	which G prepared beforehand
Rom	8:16	that we are children of G,	Eph	2:12	no hope and without G in
Rom	8:17	heirs of G and joint heirs	Eph	2:19	of the household of G,
Rom	8:21	liberty of the children of G.	Eph	3:19	with all the fullness of G.
Rom	8:28	for good to those who love G,	Eph	4: 6	one G and Father of all, who
Rom	8:31	If G is for us, who can	Eph	4:30	grieve the Holy Spirit of G,
Rom	8:33	It is G who justifies.	Eph	4:32	just as G in Christ forgave
Rom	8:39	us from the love of G which	Eph	5: 1	Therefore be imitators of G
Rom	9: 5	the eternally blessed G.	Eph	6:11	Put on the whole armor of G,
Rom	10: 1	desire and prayer to G for	Phil	2: 6	who, being in the form of G,
Rom	10: 2	that they have a zeal for G,	Phil	2: 6	robbery to be equal with G,
Rom	10:17	and hearing by the word of G.	Phil	2: 9	Therefore G also has highly
Rom	11: 1	has G cast away His people?	Phil	2:13	for it is G who works in you
Rom	11:23	for G is able to graft them	Phil	3:14	of the upward call of G in
Rom	11:29	gifts and the calling of G	Phil	4: 6	requests be made known to G;
Rom	11:33	wisdom and knowledge of G!	Phil	4: 7	and the peace of G,
Rom	12: 1	by the mercies of G,	Phil	4: 9	and the G of peace will be
Rom	12: 1	holy, acceptable to G,	Phil	4:19	And my G shall supply all
Rom	12: 2	and perfect will of G.	Col	1:15	the image of the invisible G,
Rom	13: 1	no authority except from G,	Col	3:12	as the elect of G,
Rom	15: 5	Now may the G of patience and	Col	3:15	And let the peace of G rule
Rom	15:13	Now may the G of hope fill	1Th	1: 8	Your faith toward G has gone

1Th	1: 9	and how you turned to **G** from
1Th	1: 9	serve the living and true **G**,
1Th	2: 4	but **G** who tests our hearts.
1Th	2:13	is in truth, the word of **G**,
1Th	4: 5	Gentiles who do not know **G**;
1Th	4:16	and with the trumpet of **G**.
1Th	5: 9	For **G** did not appoint us to
1Th	5:18	for this is the will of **G** in
1Ti	1:17	to **G** who alone is wise, be
1Ti	2: 5	For there is one **G** and one
1Ti	2: 5	and one Mediator between **G**
1Ti	3:15	the church of the living **G**,
1Ti	3:16	**G** was manifested in the
1Ti	6:11	But you, O man of **G**,
2Ti	1: 6	you to stir up the gift of **G**
2Ti	2:15	yourself approved to **G**,
2Ti	3: 4	rather than lovers of **G**,
2Ti	3:16	given by inspiration of **G**,
Tit	2:13	appearing of our great **G**
Heb	1: 8	"Your throne, O **G**,
Heb	1: 9	Therefore God, Your **G**,
Heb	4: 9	a rest for the people of **G**.
Heb	4:12	For the word of **G** is living
Heb	5:10	called by **G** as High Priest
Heb	5:12	of the oracles of **G**;
Heb	6: 5	tasted the good word of **G**
Heb	6:18	it is impossible for **G** to
Heb	7: 1	priest of the Most High **G**,
Heb	7: 3	but made like the Son of **G**,
Heb	9:14	works to serve the living **G**?
Heb	10: 7	do Your will, O **G**.
Heb	10:12	down at the right hand of **G**,
Heb	10:29	has trampled the Son of **G**
Heb	10:31	the hands of the living **G**.
Heb	11: 3	were framed by the word of **G**,
Heb	11: 4	By faith Abel offered to **G**
Heb	11:10	builder and maker is **G**.
Heb	12:29	For our **G** is a consuming
Heb	13:20	Now may the **G** of peace who
Jas	1: 5	wisdom, let him ask of **G**,
Jas	1:13	for **G** cannot be tempted by
Jas	1:27	undefiled religion before **G**
Jas	2:23	"Abraham believed **G**,
Jas	2:23	was called the friend of **G**.
Jas	4: 4	the world is enmity with **G**?
Jas	4: 6	**G** resists the proud, But
Jas	4: 8	Draw near to **G** and He will
1Pe	1: 2	to the foreknowledge of **G**
1Pe	1: 5	are kept by the power of **G**
1Pe	2:10	but are now the people of **G**,
1Pe	3: 4	precious in the sight of **G**.
1Pe	4:10	of the manifold grace of **G**.
1Pe	4:11	speak as the oracles of **G**.
1Pe	4:17	to begin at the house of **G**;
1Pe	5: 2	Shepherd the flock of **G** which
1Pe	5: 5	**G** resists the proud, But
1Pe	5:10	But may the **G** of all grace,
2Pe	1:21	but holy men of **G** spoke as
1Jn	1: 5	that **G** is light and in Him
1Jn	2:14	and the word of **G** abides in
1Jn	2:17	he who does the will of **G**
1Jn	3: 2	now we are children of **G**;
1Jn	3: 9	Whoever has been born of **G**
1Jn	4: 2	come in the flesh is of **G**,

1Jn	4: 7	who loves is born of **G** and
1Jn	4: 8	for **G** is love.
1Jn	4:10	is love, not that we loved **G**,
1Jn	4:12	No one has seen **G** at any
1Jn	4:16	**G** is love, and he who abides
1Jn	5: 1	is the Christ is born of **G**,
1Jn	5: 5	that Jesus is the Son of **G**?
1Jn	5:12	does not have the Son of **G**
1Jn	5:13	in the name of the Son of **G**,
1Jn	5:20	This is the true **G** and
Jude	25	To **G** our Savior, Who alone
Rev	1: 2	witness to the word of **G**,
Rev	1: 6	kings and priests to His **G**
Rev	2: 7	midst of the Paradise of **G**.
Rev	3: 1	has the seven Spirits of **G**
Rev	7:17	And **G** will wipe away every
Rev	14:10	the wine of the wrath of **G**,
Rev	16:11	They blasphemed the **G** of
Rev	19: 6	Alleluia! For the Lord **G**
Rev	19:13	name is called The Word of **G**.
Rev	19:17	the supper of the great **G**,
Rev	21: 4	And **G** will wipe away every
Rev	22:18	**G** will add to him the
Rev	22:19	**G** shall take away his part

GOD'S (see GOD)

Matt	22:21	to God the things that are **G**.
1Co	3:23	Christ's, and Christ is **G**.
1Co	6:20	in your spirit, which are **G**.

GODDESS

1Ki	11: 5	went after Ashtoreth the **g**

GODHEAD† (see GOD)

Rom	1:20	His eternal power and **G**,
Col	2: 9	all the fullness of the **G**

GODLINESS (see GODLY)

1Ti	2: 2	and peaceable life in all **g**
1Ti	3:16	great is the mystery of **g**:
1Ti	4: 8	but **g** is profitable for all
1Ti	6: 6	Now **g** with contentment is
2Ti	3: 5	having a form of **g** but
2Pe	1: 3	that pertain to life and **g**,
2Pe	1: 7	to **g** brotherly kindness, and

GODLY (see GOD, GODLINESS, UNGODLY)

2Co	7:10	For **g** sorrow produces
2Ti	3:12	all who desire to live **g** in
Heb	11: 7	moved with **g** fear, prepared
Heb	12:28	with reverence and **g** fear.

GODS (see GOD)

Gen	31:30	but why did you steal my **g**?
Gen	35: 2	Put away the foreign **g** that
Ex	12:12	and against all the **g** of
Ex	18:11	is greater than all the **g**;
Ex	20: 3	You shall have no other **g**
Ex	20:23	**g** of silver or gods of gold
Deut	10:17	LORD your God is God of **g**
Ruth	1:15	to her people and to her **g**;
Ps	82: 6	I said, "You are **g**,
Ps	95: 3	the great King above all **g**.
Ps	96: 4	is to be feared above all **g**.

G

Ps	97: 7	Worship Him, all you **g**.
Ps	97: 9	are exalted far above all **g**.
Ps	136: 2	give thanks to the God of **g**!
Is	42:17	images, 'You are our **g**.
Jer	10:11	The **g** that have not made the
Jer	11:13	of your cities were your **g**,
Ezek	28: 2	I sit in the seat of **g**,
Dan	2:47	your God is the God of **g**,
Dan	5: 4	and praised the **g** of gold
Dan	5:11	like the wisdom of the **g**,
Dan	5:23	And you have praised the **g**
John	10:34	You are **g**"?
John	10:35	"If He called them **g**,
Acts	7:40	Make us **g** to go before
1Co	8: 5	if there are so-called **g**,
Gal	4: 8	which by nature are not **g**.

GOG (see MAGOG)

Ezek	38: 2	man, set your face against **G**,
Rev	20: 8	**G** and Magog, to gather them

GOLD (see GOLDEN)

Gen	2:12	And the **g** of that land is
Gen	13: 2	in silver, and in **g**.
Ex	20:23	of silver or gods of **g**
Ex	25:11	shall overlay it with pure **g**,
Ex	32:31	for themselves a god of **g**!
Deut	17:17	multiply silver and **g** for
1Ki	10:11	which brought **g** from Ophir,
1Ki	22:48	ships to go to Ophir for **g**;
Job	23:10	me, I shall come forth as **g**.
Job	28: 1	And a place where **g** is
Job	28:15	cannot be purchased for **g**,
Job	31:24	If I have made **g** my hope, Or
Ps	19:10	be desired are they than **g**,
Ps	21: 3	You set a crown of pure **g**
Ps	72:15	And the **g** of Sheba will be
Ps	115: 4	idols are silver and **g**,
Prov	11:22	As a ring of **g** in a swine's
Prov	16:16	better to get wisdom than **g**!
Prov	17: 3	silver and the furnace for **g**,
Song	5:11	head is like the finest **g**;
Jer	10: 9	And **g** from Uphaz, The work
Dan	2:32	image's head was of fine **g**,
Dan	2:35	and the **g** were crushed
Dan	2:38	all—you are this head of **g**.
Dan	2:45	clay, the silver, and the **g**—
Dan	3: 5	fall down and worship the **g**
Dan	3:18	nor will we worship the **g**
Dan	5: 3	Then they brought the **g**
Dan	5: 4	and praised the gods of **g**
Dan	5: 7	and have a chain of **g**
Dan	10: 5	waist was girded with **g** of
Hos	8: 4	From their silver and **g**
Nah	2: 9	of silver! Take spoil of **g**!
Hag	2: 8	and the **g** is Mine,' says
Zech	4: 2	is a lampstand of solid **g**
Zech	4:12	the receptacles of the two **g**
Zech	13: 9	And test them as **g** is
Matt	2:11	presented gifts to Him: **g**,
Acts	3: 6	Silver and **g** I do not have,
Acts	17:29	the Divine Nature is like **g**
1Co	3:12	on this foundation with **g**,
1Ti	2: 9	not with braided hair or **g**

2Ti	2:20	are not only vessels of **g**
Heb	9: 4	overlaid on all sides with **g**,
Jas	2: 2	your assembly a man with **g**
1Pe	1: 7	much more precious than **g**
1Pe	1:18	things, like silver or **g**,
Rev	3:18	counsel you to buy from Me **g**
Rev	4: 4	and they had crowns of **g** on
Rev	21:15	who talked with me had a **g**
Rev	21:18	and the city was pure **g**,

GOLDEN (see GOLD)

Ex	28:34	a **g** bell and a pomegranate, a
1Sa	6: 4	Five **g** tumors and five golden
2Ki	10:29	from the **g** calves that were
Eccl	12: 6	Or the **g** bowl is broken,
Jer	51: 7	Babylon was a **g** cup in the

GOLGOTHA† (see CALVARY)

Matt	27:33	had come to a place called **G**,
Mark	15:22	brought Him to the place **G**,
John	19:17	which is called in Hebrew, **G**,

GOLIATH

1Sa	17: 4	of the Philistines, named **G**,
2Sa	21:19	killed the brother of **G**
1Ch	20: 5	Lahmi the brother of **G** the

GOMER

Ezek	38: 6	**G** and all its troops; the
Hos	1: 3	So he went and took **G** the

GOMORRAH

Gen	19:24	and fire on Sodom and **G**,
Is	1: 9	would have been made like **G**.
Jer	50:40	God overthrew Sodom and **G**
Matt	10:15	for the land of Sodom and **G**
Mark	6:11	tolerable for Sodom and **G**
Rom	9:29	have been made like **G**.

GOOD (see GOODNESS)

Gen	1: 4	the light, that it was **g**;
Gen	1:31	and indeed it was very **g**.
Gen	2: 9	pleasant to the sight and **g**
Gen	2: 9	tree of the knowledge of **g**
Gen	2:18	It is not **g** that man should
Gen	3: 5	knowing **g** and evil."
Gen	44: 4	have you repaid evil for **g**?
Gen	50:20	me; but God meant it for **g**,
Ex	18:17	thing that you do is not **g**.
Lev	27:10	**g** for bad or bad for good;
Lev	27:12	whether it is **g** or bad; as
Num	13:20	Be of **g** courage. And bring
Deut	6:18	do what is right and **g** in
Deut	8:16	to do you **g** in the end—
Deut	10:13	command you today for your **g**?
Deut	30:15	before you today life and **g**,
Deut	31:23	Be strong and of **g** courage;
Josh	1: 9	Be strong and of **g** courage;
1Ki	8:56	failed one word of all His **g**
2Ki	3:19	and ruin every **g** piece of
2Ki	7: 9	This day is a day of **g**
1Ch	16:34	for He is **g**! For His
2Ch	14: 2	Asa did what was **g** and
2Ch	30:18	May the **g** LORD provide

Ezra	8:18	by the **g** hand of our God
Neh	5: 9	you are doing is not **g**.
Neh	5:19	Remember me, my God, for **g**,
Esth	10: 3	seeking the **g** of his people
Job	2:10	Shall we indeed accept **g**
Ps	14: 1	There is none who does **g**.
Ps	16: 6	I have a **g** inheritance.
Ps	25: 8	G and upright is the LORD
Ps	34: 8	and see that the LORD is **g**;
Ps	34:10	LORD shall not lack any **g**
Ps	34:14	Depart from evil and do **g**;
Ps	35:12	They reward me evil for **g**,
Ps	37: 3	in the LORD, and do **g**;
Ps	37:23	The steps of a **g** man are
Ps	38:20	also who render evil for **g**,
Ps	40: 9	I have proclaimed the **g** news
Ps	45: 1	is overflowing with a **g**
Ps	51:18	Do **g** in Your good pleasure
Ps	52: 3	You love evil more than **g**,
Ps	69:16	Your lovingkindness is **g**;
Ps	73: 1	Truly God is **g** to Israel,
Ps	84:11	No **g** thing will He
Ps	100: 5	For the LORD is **g**;
Ps	103: 5	satisfies your mouth with **g**
Ps	106: 1	for He is **g**! For His
Ps	109: 5	have rewarded me evil for **g**,
Ps	133: 1	how **g** and how pleasant it
Ps	143:10	my God; Your Spirit is **g**.
Ps	145: 9	The LORD is **g** to all, And
Prov	3:27	Do not withhold **g** from
Prov	4: 2	For I give you **g** doctrine:
Prov	12: 2	A **g** man obtains favor from
Prov	15: 3	watch on the evil and the **g**.
Prov	15:30	And a **g** report makes the
Prov	17:13	Whoever rewards evil for **g**,
Prov	17:22	A merry heart does **g**,
Prov	18:22	who finds a wife finds a **g**
Prov	20:14	It is **g** for nothing,"
Prov	20:23	dishonest scales are not **g**.
Prov	22: 1	A **g** name is to be chosen
Prov	25:25	So is **g** news from a far
Prov	28:21	show partiality is not **g**,
Prov	31:12	She does him **g** and not evil
Eccl	4: 8	toil and deprive myself of **g**?
Eccl	7: 1	A **g** name is better than
Is	1:17	Learn to do **g**;
Is	1:19	You shall eat the **g** of the
Is	7:15	the evil and choose the **g**.
Is	52: 7	the feet of him who brings **g**
Is	52: 7	brings glad tidings of **g**
Is	61: 1	has anointed Me To preach **g**
Jer	8:15	but no **g** came; And for a
Jer	13:23	Then may you also do **g** who
Jer	18:10	will relent concerning the **g**
Jer	18:20	Shall evil be repaid for **g**?
Lam	3:25	The LORD is **g** to those who
Amos	5:14	Seek **g** and not evil, That
Amos	5:15	Hate evil, love **g**;
Mic	6: 8	shown you, O man, what is **g**;
Matt	5:13	It is then **g** for nothing but
Matt	5:16	that they may see your **g**
Matt	5:44	do **g** to those who hate you,
Matt	5:45	on the evil and on the **g**,
Matt	6:22	If therefore your eye is **g**,

Matt	7:11	know how to give **g** gifts to
Matt	7:17	every **g** tree bears good
Matt	9: 2	be of **g** cheer; your sins are
Matt	11:26	for so it seemed **g** in Your
Matt	12:12	it is lawful to do **g** on the
Matt	12:35	A **g** man out of the good
Matt	13: 8	But others fell on **g** ground
Matt	19:16	G Teacher, what good thing
Matt	19:17	No one is **g** but One, that
Matt	25:21	**g** and faithful servant; you
Matt	26:10	For she has done a **g** work
Matt	26:24	It would have been **g** for
Mark	3: 4	on the Sabbath to do **g** or
Luke	2:10	I bring you **g** tidings of
Luke	6: 9	on the Sabbath to do **g** or
Luke	6:27	do **g** to those who hate you,
Luke	6:38	**g** measure, pressed down,
Luke	10:21	for so it seemed **g** in Your
John	1:46	Can anything **g** come out of
John	2:10	You have kept the **g** wine
John	10:11	I am the **g** shepherd. The good
Acts	10:38	who went about doing **g** and
Acts	15:28	For it seemed **g** to the Holy
Rom	3: 8	Let us do evil that **g** may
Rom	3:12	is none who does **g**,
Rom	5: 7	yet perhaps for a **g** man
Rom	7:12	holy and just and **g**.
Rom	7:18	in my flesh) nothing **g**
Rom	7:19	For the **g** that I will to
Rom	8:28	things work together for **g**
Rom	10:15	bring glad tidings of **g**
Rom	12: 2	may prove what is that **g**
Rom	12: 9	is evil. Cling to what is **g**.
Rom	12:21	but overcome evil with **g**.
1Co	5: 6	Your glorying is not **g**.
1Co	7: 1	It is **g** for a man not to
2Co	13:11	Be of **g** comfort, be of one
Gal	6: 9	not grow weary while doing **g**,
Eph	2:10	in Christ Jesus for **g** works,
Phil	1: 6	that He who has begun a **g**
Phil	2:13	to will and to do for His **g**
Phil	4: 8	whatever things are of **g**
Col	1:10	being fruitful in every **g**
1Th	5:21	things; hold fast what is **g**.
2Th	2:17	and establish you in every **g**
2Th	3:13	not grow weary in doing **g**.
1Ti	1: 5	from a **g** conscience, and
1Ti	2: 3	For this is **g** and acceptable
1Ti	6:12	Fight the **g** fight of faith,
2Ti	1:14	That **g** thing which was
2Ti	2: 3	must endure hardship as a **g**
2Ti	2:21	prepared for every **g** work.
2Ti	3:17	equipped for every **g** work.
2Ti	4: 7	I have fought the **g** fight, I
Tit	2:14	zealous for **g** works.
Heb	6: 5	and have tasted the **g** word of
Heb	10: 1	having a shadow of the **g**
Heb	11: 2	it the elders obtained a **g**
Heb	11:12	and him as **g** as dead, were
Heb	13:21	make you complete in every **g**
Jas	1:17	Every **g** gift and every
1Pe	3:16	having a **g** conscience, that
1Pe	4:10	as **g** stewards of the

G

GOODNESS (see GOOD)

Ex	33:19	I will make all My **g** pass
Ps	23: 6	Surely **g** and mercy shall
Ps	27:13	That I would see the **g** of
Ps	33: 5	The earth is full of the **g**
Ps	65:11	crown the year with Your **g**,
Eccl	6: 3	soul is not satisfied with **g**,
Hos	3: 5	fear the LORD and His **g** in
Rom	2: 4	despise the riches of His **g**,
Rom	2: 4	not knowing that the **g** of
Gal	5:22	longsuffering, kindness, **g**,

GOODS

Luke	12:19	you have many **g** laid up for
Luke	15:12	give me the portion of **g**
Luke	19: 8	I give half of my **g** to the
1Co	13: 3	though I bestow all my **g** to
1Jn	3:17	whoever has this world's **g**,

GOODWILL

Luke	2:14	**g** toward men!"

GOSHEN (see EGYPT)

Gen	45:10	shall dwell in the land of **G**,

GOSPEL

Matt	11: 5	up and the poor have the **g**
Matt	24:14	And this **g** of the kingdom
Matt	26:13	wherever this **g** is preached
Mark	1: 1	The beginning of the **g** of
Mark	1:15	Repent, and believe in the **g**.
Mark	13:10	And the **g** must first be
Mark	16:15	the world and preach the **g**
Luke	4:18	Me To preach the **g**
Rom	1: 1	separated to the **g** of God
Rom	1:15	I am ready to preach the **g**
Rom	1:16	I am not ashamed of the **g**
Rom	10:15	those who preach the **g**
Rom	10:16	have not all obeyed the **g**.
Rom	15:16	ministering the **g** of God,
1Co	1:17	baptize, but to preach the **g**,
1Co	9:12	things lest we hinder the **g**
1Co	9:14	that those who preach the **g**
1Co	9:16	me if I do not preach the **g**!
1Co	9:18	abuse my authority in the **g**.
2Co	4: 3	But even if our **g** is veiled,
2Co	4: 4	lest the light of the **g** of
2Co	11: 4	or a different **g** which you
Gal	1: 6	of Christ, to a different **g**,
Gal	1: 7	and want to pervert the **g**
Gal	1: 8	preach any other **g** to you
Gal	2: 5	that the truth of the **g**
Gal	3: 8	preached the **g** to Abraham
Eph	6:15	the preparation of the **g** of
Eph	6:19	known the mystery of the **g**,
Phil	1: 5	for your fellowship in the **g**
Phil	1: 7	and confirmation of the **g**,
Phil	1:12	for the furtherance of the **g**,
Phil	1:17	for the defense of the **g**.
Phil	1:27	conduct be worthy of the **g**
Phil	1:27	for the faith of the **g**,
Phil	2:22	he served with me in the **g**.
Phil	4:15	in the beginning of the **g**,

Col	1:23	away from the hope of the **g**
1Th	1: 5	For our **g** did not come to you
1Th	2: 4	to be entrusted with the **g**,
1Ti	1:11	according to the glorious **g**
2Ti	1:10	to light through the **g**,
Phm	1:13	to me in my chains for the **g**.
Heb	4: 2	For indeed the **g** was preached
1Pe	4:17	those who do not obey the **g**
Rev	14: 6	having the everlasting **g** to

GOVERNMENT

Is	9: 6	And the **g** will be upon His
Is	9: 7	Of the increase of His **g**

GRACE (see GRACIOUS)

Gen	6: 8	But Noah found **g** in the eyes
Ps	45: 2	**G** is poured upon Your lips;
Prov	3:34	But gives **g** to the humble.
Zech	4: 7	capstone With shouts of "**G**,
Luke	2:40	and the **g** of God was upon
John	1:14	full of **g** and truth.
John	1:16	received, and grace for **g**.
John	1:17	but **g** and truth came
Acts	4:33	And great **g** was upon them
Acts	14: 3	witness to the word of His **g**,
Acts	20:24	to the gospel of the **g** of
Rom	1: 5	Him we have received **g** and
Rom	1: 7	**G** to you and peace from God
Rom	3:24	justified freely by His **g**
Rom	4: 4	wages are not counted as **g**
Rom	5: 2	access by faith into this **g**
Rom	5:15	of God and the gift by the **g**
Rom	5:20	**g** abounded much more,
Rom	5:21	even so **g** might reign
Rom	6: 1	we continue in sin that **g**
Rom	6:14	not under law but under **g**.
Rom	12: 3	through the **g** given to me,
Rom	16:20	The **g** of our Lord Jesus
1Co	15:10	But by the **g** of God I am what
2Co	4:15	are for your sakes, that **g**,
2Co	6: 1	you not to receive the **g**
2Co	8: 1	we make known to you the **g**
2Co	8: 9	For you know the **g** of our
2Co	9:14	because of the exceeding **g**
2Co	12: 9	My **g** is sufficient for you,
Gal	1:15	and called me through His **g**,
Gal	5: 4	law; you have fallen from **g**.
Eph	1: 6	praise of the glory of His **g**,
Eph	1: 7	to the riches of His **g**
Eph	2: 5	together with Christ (by **g**
Eph	2: 7	exceeding riches of His **g**
Eph	2: 8	For by **g** you have been saved
Eph	4: 7	But to each one of us **g** was
Phil	1: 7	are partakers with me of **g**.
Col	3:16	singing with **g** in your
Col	4: 6	speech always be with **g**,
1Ti	1: 2	a true son in the faith: **G**,
Tit	3: 7	been justified by His **g** we
Heb	2: 9	by the **g** of God, might taste
Heb	4:16	boldly to the throne of **g**,
Heb	4:16	may obtain mercy and find **g**
Heb	10:29	and insulted the Spirit of **g**?
Heb	12:15	anyone fall short of the **g**
Jas	4: 6	But He gives more **g**.

GRACIOUS (see GRACE)

Jas	4: 6	But gives **g** to the
1Pe	1:10	who prophesied of the **g**
1Pe	1:13	your hope fully upon the **g**
1Pe	3: 7	heirs together of the **g** of
1Pe	4:10	stewards of the manifold **g**
1Pe	5: 5	But gives **g** to the
1Pe	5:10	But may the God of all **g**,
Rev	1: 4	**G** to you and peace from Him
Rev	22:21	The **g** of our Lord Jesus

GRACIOUS (see GRACE)

Ex	33:19	I will be **g** to whom I will
Ex	34: 6	LORD God, merciful and **g**,
Num	6:25	And be **g** to you;
Neh	9:17	**G** and merciful, Slow to
Ps	86:15	full of compassion, and **g**,
Ps	103: 8	LORD is merciful and **g**,
Ps	111: 4	The LORD is **g** and full of
Jon	4: 2	for I know that You are a **g**
1Pe	2: 3	tasted that the Lord is **g**.

GRAFTED

Rom	11:17	were **g** in among them, and
Rom	11:24	be **g** into their own olive

GRAIN (see MEAL)

Gen	41: 5	suddenly seven heads of **g**
Gen	41:57	to Joseph in Egypt to buy **g**,
Gen	42:25	to fill their sacks with **g**,
Ex	30: 9	or a **g** offering; nor shall
Deut	7:13	your **g** and your new wine and
Deut	25: 4	while it treads out the **g**.
Hos	2: 8	not know That I gave her **g**,
Hos	2:22	earth shall answer With **g**,
Amos	8: 5	be past, That we may sell **g**?
Amos	9: 9	As **g** is sifted in a sieve;
Matt	12: 1	began to pluck heads of **g**
John	12:24	unless a **g** of wheat falls
John	12:24	it dies, it produces much **g**.
1Co	9: 9	it treads out the **g**.
1Ti	5:18	it treads out the **g**,

GRANDCHILDREN (see CHILDREN)

Deut	4: 9	to your children and your **g**,
Job	42:16	and saw his children and **g**

GRANDDAUGHTER (see DAUGHTER)

2Ki	8:26	name was Athaliah the **g** of

GRANDMOTHER (see MOTHER)

2Ti	1: 5	which dwelt first in your **g**

GRANDSON (see SON)

Deut	6: 2	you and your son and your **g**,

GRANT (see DELIVER, GRANTED)

Ps	85: 7	And **g** us Your salvation.
Mark	10:37	**G** us that we may sit, one on
2Ti	1:16	The Lord **g** mercy to the

GRANTED (see GRANT)

Esth	5: 6	It shall be **g** you. What is
John	6:65	to Me unless it has been **g**
Phil	1:29	For to you it has been **g** on

GRAPE (see GRAPES, GRAPEVINE)

Num	6: 3	shall he drink any **g** juice,

GRAPES (see GRAPE)

Gen	49:11	clothes in the blood of **g**.
Num	6: 3	nor eat fresh **g** or raisins.
Num	13:23	branch with one cluster of **g**;
Is	5: 2	But it brought forth wild **g**.
Jer	31:29	fathers have eaten sour **g**,
Ezek	18: 2	fathers have eaten sour **g**,
Amos	9:13	And the treader of **g** him

GRAPEVINE† (see GRAPE, VINE)

Num	6: 4	that is produced by the **g**,
Jas	3:12	or a **g** bear figs? Thus no

GRASS (see GRASSHOPPERS)

Gen	1:11	the earth bring forth **g**,
Job	40:15	He eats **g** like an ox.
Ps	72:16	city shall flourish like **g**
Ps	90: 5	the morning they are like **g**
Ps	92: 7	the wicked spring up like **g**,
Ps	103:15	man, his days are like **g**;
Prov	19:12	favor is like dew on the **g**.
Is	40: 6	I cry?" "All flesh is **g**,
Is	40: 7	The **g** withers, the flower
Is	40: 7	Surely the people are **g**.
Dan	4:25	they shall make you eat **g**
Matt	6:30	if God so clothes the **g**
Mark	6:39	in groups on the green **g**.
1Pe	1:24	"All flesh is as **g**,

GRASSHOPPERS (see GRASS)

Num	13:33	and we were like **g** in our
Is	40:22	its inhabitants are like **g**,

GRAVE (see GRAVECLOTHES, GRAVES)

Gen	18:20	because their sin is very **g**,
Gen	37:35	I shall go down into the **g**
Gen	42:38	hair with sorrow to the **g**.
Deut	34: 6	but no one knows his **g** to
Job	10:19	from the womb to the **g**.
Job	21:13	in a moment go down to the **g**.
Ps	30: 3	my soul up from the **g**;
Ps	31:17	Let them be silent in the **g**.
Ps	88: 5	the slain who lie in the **g**,
Ps	141: 7	at the mouth of the **g**,
Eccl	9:10	or wisdom in the **g** where
Song	8: 6	Jealousy as cruel as the **g**;
Is	14:19	you are cast out of your **g**
Is	53: 9	And they made His **g** with the
Jer	20:17	mother might have been my **g**,
Hos	13:14	I will be your plagues! O **G**,

GRAVECLOTHES† (see GRAVE)

John	11:44	bound hand and foot with **g**,

GRAVES (see GRAVE)

2Ki	23: 6	threw its ashes on the **g** of
Jer	8: 1	of Jerusalem, out of their **g**.
Ezek	37:12	I will open your **g** and cause
Ezek	37:12	you to come up from your **g**,
Matt	27:52	and the **g** were opened; and

G

Matt	27:53	and coming out of the g after
John	5:28	which all who are in the g

GRAZE

Is	11: 7	cow and the bear shall g;
Dan	4:15	And let him g with the

GREAT (see GREATER, GREATEST, GREATLY, GREATNESS)

Gen	1:16	Then God made two g lights:
Gen	1:21	So God created g sea
Gen	6: 5	wickedness of man was g in
Gen	7:11	all the fountains of the g
Gen	12: 2	I will make you a g nation;
Gen	12: 2	you And make your name g;
Gen	15: 1	your exceedingly g reward."
Gen	21: 8	And Abraham made a g feast
Ex	3: 3	turn aside and see this g
Ex	6: 6	outstretched arm and with g
Ex	14:31	Thus Israel saw the g work
Ex	32:11	of the land of Egypt with g
Ex	32:30	You have committed a g sin.
Num	34: 6	you shall have the G Sea for
Deut	1:17	the small as well as the g;
Deut	1:28	the cities are g and
Deut	4: 7	For what g nation is there
Deut	9: 2	a people g and tall, the
Deut	10:17	the g God, mighty and
1Sa	12:22	for His g name's sake,
1Sa	12:24	for consider what g things
1Sa	15:22	Has the LORD as g delight
2Sa	3:38	know that a prince and a g
2Sa	7: 9	and have made you a g name,
2Sa	7:22	"Therefore You are g,
2Sa	7:23	and to do for Youself g and
Neh	6: 3	I am doing a g work, so that
Job	38:32	Or can you guide the G Bear
Ps	19:11	in keeping them there is g
Ps	19:13	I shall be innocent of g
Ps	25:11	my iniquity, for it is g.
Ps	31:19	how g is Your goodness,
Ps	47: 2	He is a g King over all
Ps	48: 1	G is the LORD, and greatly
Ps	48: 2	The city of the g King.
Ps	68:11	G was the company of those
Ps	71:19	You who have done g things;
Ps	77:13	Who is so g a God as our
Ps	86:13	For g is Your mercy toward
Ps	92: 5	how g are Your works! Your
Ps	95: 3	For the LORD is the g God,
Ps	95: 3	And the g King above all
Ps	104: 1	LORD my God, You are very g:
Ps	108: 4	For Your mercy is g above
Ps	119:156	G are Your tender mercies,
Ps	119:165	G peace have those who love
Ps	126: 3	The LORD has done g things
Ps	136: 4	To Him who alone does g
Ps	139:17	O God! How g is the sum of
Ps	145: 3	G is the LORD, and greatly
Ps	145: 8	Slow to anger and g in
Is	9: 2	in darkness Have seen a g
Is	32: 2	As the shadow of a g rock
Is	53:12	Him a portion with the g,
Jer	33: 3	and show you g and mighty

Jer	45: 5	And do you seek g things for
Lam	3:23	G is Your faithfulness.
Dan	4:30	Is not this g Babylon, that I
Dan	5: 1	the king made a g feast for
Dan	7: 3	And four g beasts came up
Dan	9: 4	g and awesome God, who keeps
Dan	9:18	but because of Your g
Hos	1: 2	the land has committed g
Hos	13: 5	In the land of g drought.
Joel	2:11	the day of the LORD is g
Joel	2:13	and of g kindness; And He
Jon	1: 2	that g city, and cry out
Jon	1: 4	But the LORD sent out a g
Jon	1:17	the LORD had prepared a g
Nah	3: 3	A g number of bodies,
Zeph	1:14	The g day of the LORD is
Zech	4: 7	O g mountain? Before
Zech	7:12	Thus g wrath came from the
Mal	1:11	For My name shall be g
Mal	1:14	For I am a g King," Says
Mal	4: 5	Before the coming of the g
Matt	2:10	rejoiced with exceedingly g
Matt	2:18	and g mourning, Rachel
Matt	4:16	darkness have seen a g
Matt	4:25	G multitudes followed
Matt	5:12	for g is your reward in
Matt	5:19	he shall be called g in the
Matt	5:35	for it is the city of the g
Matt	6:23	how g is that darkness!
Matt	7:27	And g was its fall."
Matt	8:10	I have not found such g
Matt	8:24	And suddenly a g tempest
Matt	8:26	and there was a g calm.
Matt	12:40	in the belly of the g fish,
Matt	13:46	he had found one pearl of g
Matt	15:28	g is your faith! Let it be
Matt	19:22	for he had g possessions.
Matt	20:26	whoever desires to become g
Matt	22:38	This is the first and g
Matt	24:21	For then there will be g
Matt	24:24	will rise and show g signs
Matt	24:30	of heaven with power and g
Matt	24:31	send His angels with a g
Matt	28: 2	there was a g earthquake;
Mark	5:19	and tell them what g things
Mark	13: 2	Do you see these g buildings?
Luke	1:32	"He will be g,
Luke	1:49	He who is mighty has done g
Luke	2:10	bring you good tidings of g
Luke	8:39	and tell what g things God
Luke	9:48	among you all will be g.
Luke	10: 2	"The harvest truly is g,
John	7:37	that g day of the feast,
Acts	4:33	And with g power the apostles
Acts	4:33	And g grace was upon them
Acts	5: 5	So g fear came upon all
Acts	19:28	G is Diana of the
Rom	9: 2	that I have g sorrow and
1Co	16: 9	For a g and effective door
2Co	1:10	who delivered us from so g a
2Co	3:12	we use g boldness of speech—
Eph	2: 4	because of His g love with
Eph	5:32	This is a g mystery, but I
1Th	2:17	to see your face with g

1Ti	3:13	a good standing and **g**
1Ti	3:16	And without controversy **g** is
1Ti	6: 6	with contentment is **g** gain.
Tit	2:13	glorious appearing of our **g**
Heb	2: 3	escape if we neglect so **g** a
Heb	4:14	then that we have a **g** High
Heb	7: 4	Now consider how **g** this man
Heb	12: 1	we are surrounded by so **g** a
Heb	13:20	that **g** Shepherd of the
Jas	3: 5	a little member and boasts **g**
Jas	3: 5	See how **g** a forest a little
2Pe	3:10	will pass away with a **g**
Rev	6:12	there was a **g** earthquake;
Rev	6:17	For the **g** day of His wrath
Rev	7: 9	a **g** multitude which no one
Rev	8:10	And a **g** star fell from
Rev	9:14	who are bound at the **g**
Rev	12: 1	Now a **g** sign appeared in
Rev	12: 9	So the **g** dragon was cast out,
Rev	12:12	having **g** wrath, because he
Rev	13: 2	and **g** authority.
Rev	13: 5	was given a mouth speaking **g**
Rev	14: 8	that **g** city, because she has
Rev	16:14	to the battle of that **g** day
Rev	17: 5	MYSTERY, BABYLON THE **G**,
Rev	18:10	that **g** city Babylon, that
Rev	19:17	for the supper of the **g** God,
Rev	20:11	Then I saw a **g** white throne
Rev	20:12	I saw the dead, small and **g**,
Rev	21:10	and showed me the **g** city,

GREATER (see GREAT)

Gen	1:16	the **g** light to rule the day,
Gen	4:13	My punishment is **g** than I
Job	33:12	For God is **g** than man.
Matt	11:11	there has not risen one **g**
Matt	12:41	and indeed a **g** than Jonah
Matt	12:42	and indeed a **g** than Solomon
John	1:50	You will see **g** things than
John	4:12	Are You **g** than our father
John	5:20	and He will show Him **g** works
John	8:53	Are You **g** than our father
John	10:29	is **g** than all; and no one is
John	13:16	a servant is not **g** than his
John	14:12	and **g** works than these he
John	14:28	for My Father is **g** than I.
John	15:13	**G** love has no one than this,
1Co	12:23	on these we bestow **g** honor;
Heb	6:13	He could swear by no one **g**,
Heb	11:26	the reproach of Christ **g**
1Jn	4: 4	He who is in you is **g** than

GREATEST (see GREAT)

Jon	3: 5	from the **g** to the least of
Matt	18: 4	this little child is the **g**
Matt	23:11	But he who is **g** among you
Mark	9:34	who would be the **g**.
1Co	13:13	but the **g** of these is love.

GREATLY (see GREAT)

Gen	3:16	I will **g** multiply your sorrow
1Ch	16:25	the LORD is great and **g**
Ps	48: 1	and **g** to be praised In the
Ps	62: 2	I shall not be **g** moved.

Ps	96: 4	the LORD is great and **g**
1Pe	1: 6	In this you **g** rejoice, though

GREATNESS (see GREAT)

1Ch	29:11	Yours, O LORD, is the **g**,
Ps	145: 3	And His **g** is unsearchable.
Ps	145: 6	And I will declare Your **g**.
Ps	150: 2	to His excellent **g**!
Prov	5:23	And in the **g** of his folly
Ezek	31: 2	are you like in your **g**?
Eph	1:19	what is the exceeding **g** of

GREECE (see GREEK)

Dan	8:21	goat is the kingdom of **G**.

GREEDY

1Ti	3: 3	not **g** for money, but gentle,

GREEK (see GREECE, GREEKS)

Luke	23:38	over Him in letters of **G**,
Acts	16: 1	but his father was **G**.
Rom	1:16	Jew first and also for the **G**.
Rom	10:12	between Jew and **G**,
Gal	3:28	There is neither Jew nor **G**,

GREEKS (see GREEK)

Rom	1:14	I am a debtor both to **G** and
1Co	1:22	and **G** seek after wisdom;
1Co	1:24	are called, both Jews and **G**,

GREEN

Gen	1:30	I have given every **g** herb
Gen	9: 3	even as the **g** herbs.
Ps	23: 2	makes me to lie down in **g**
Ps	37: 2	And wither as the **g** herb.
Luke	23:31	do these things in the **g**

GREET

Rom	16:16	**G** one another with a holy
Phil	4:21	**G** every saint in Christ
Heb	13:24	**G** all those who rule over
1Pe	5:14	**G** one another with a kiss of

GREW (see GROW)

Gen	21: 8	So the child **g** and was
Ex	1: 7	multiplied and **g** exceedingly
Ex	2:10	And the child **g**,
Ex	7:13	And Pharaoh's heart **g** hard,
Luke	1:80	So the child **g** and became
Luke	2:40	And the Child **g** and became

GRIEF (see GRIEFS, GRIEVE)

Job	2:13	for they saw that his **g** was
Ps	6: 7	eye wastes away because of **g**;
Ps	10:14	You observe trouble and **g**,
Ps	31:10	For my life is spent with **g**,
Prov	10: 1	a foolish son is the **g** of
Eccl	1:18	in much wisdom is much **g**,
Is	53: 3	and acquainted with **g**.
Is	53:10	Him; He has put Him to **g**.
Rom	9: 2	sorrow and continual **g** in
Heb	13:17	so with joy and not with **g**,
1Pe	2:19	toward God one endures **g**,

G

GRIEFS† (see GRIEF)
Is   53: 4 Surely He has borne our g

GRIEVE (see GRIEF, GRIEVED)
Zech   12:10 and g for Him as one grieves
Eph   4:30 And do not g the Holy Spirit

GRIEVED (see GRIEVE)
Gen   6: 6 and He was g in His heart.

GRIND (see GRINDER, GRINDING)
Matt   21:44 it will g him to powder."

GRINDER† (see GRIND, GRINDERS)
Judg   16:21 and he became a g in the

GRINDERS† (see GRINDER)
Eccl   12: 3 When the g cease because

GRINDING (see GRIND)
Eccl   12: 4 And the sound of g is low;
Matt   24:41 Two women will be g at the

GROAN (see GROANING, GROANS)
Rom   8:23 even we ourselves g within

GROANING (see GROAN, GROANINGS)
Ex   2:24 So God heard their g,
Ps   6: 6 I am weary with my g;
Ps   22: 1 from the words of My g?
Ps   32: 3 grew old Through my g all

GROANINGS (see GROANING)
Rom   8:26 intercession for us with g

GROANS† (see GROAN)
Rom   8:22 that the whole creation g

GROUND (see GROUNDED)
Gen   2: 5 was no man to till the g;
Gen   2: 7 man of the dust of the g,
Gen   3:17 Cursed is the g for your
Gen   3:19 Till you return to the g,
Gen   3:23 of Eden to till the g from
Gen   4: 2 Cain was a tiller of the g.
Gen   4:10 cries out to Me from the g.
Gen   8:21 never again curse the g for
Ex   3: 5 where you stand is holy g.
Ex   14:22 of the sea on the dry g,
Ex   32:20 and g it to powder; and he
Num   16:31 that the g split apart under
Josh   24:32 in the plot of g which Jacob
Judg   6:40 there was dew on all the g.
2Sa   8: 2 Forcing them down to the g,
2Sa   17:12 as the dew falls on the g.
2Ki   2: 8 them crossed over on dry g.
Job   1:20 and he fell to the g and
Job   2:13 sat down with him on the g
Job   5: 6 trouble spring from the g;
Job   14: 8 its stump may die in the g,
Job   39:14 she leaves her eggs on the g,
Is   14:12 you are cut down to the g,
Is   29: 4 a medium's, out of the g;

Is   35: 7 The parched g shall become a
Is   44: 3 And floods on the dry g;
Is   53: 2 And as a root out of dry g.
Jer   4: 3 "Break up your fallow g,
Lam   5:13 Young men g at the
Dan   8: 5 without touching the g;
Dan   8: 7 he cast him down to the g
Hos   10:12 Break up your fallow g,
Amos   9: 9 grain shall fall to the g.
Hag   1:11 on whatever the g brings
Matt   13: 8 But others fell on good g and
Matt   15:35 to sit down on the g.
Matt   25:25 and hid your talent in the g.
Mark   4: 8 other seed fell on good g
Luke   12:16 The g of a certain rich man
Luke   14:18 'I have bought a piece of g,
Luke   22:44 blood falling down to the g.
John   4: 5 near the plot of g that
John   8: 6 down and wrote on the g
John   9: 6 He spat on the g and made
John 12:24 of wheat falls into the g
Acts   7:33 you stand is holy g.
Acts   9: 8 Then Saul arose from the g,
Acts 22: 7 And I fell to the g and heard
Acts 26:14 we all had fallen to the g,
1Ti   3:15 the pillar and g of the

GROUNDED (see GROUND)
Eph   3:17 being rooted and g in love,

GROW (see FULL-GROWN, GREW, GROWN, GROWS)
Gen   2: 9 LORD God made every tree g
Num   6: 5 of the hair of his head g.
Judg 16:22 hair of his head began to g
Ps 102:26 they will all g old like a
Eccl 11: 5 Or how the bones g in the
Is   11: 1 And a Branch shall g out of
Is   51: 6 The earth will g old like a
Is   53: 2 For He shall g up before Him
Joel   3:15 The sun and moon will g
Jon   4:10 not labored, nor made it g,
Matt   6:28 of the field, how they g:
Matt   13:30 Let both g together until the
Matt   21:19 Let no fruit g on you ever
Matt   24:12 the love of many will g
Luke   12:33 money bags which do not g
Gal   6: 9 And let us not g weary while
Eph   4:15 may g up in all things into
2Th   3:13 do not g weary in doing
2Ti   3:13 men and impostors will g
Heb   1:11 And they will all g
1Pe   2: 2 that you may g thereby,
2Pe   3:18 but g in the grace and

GROWN (see GROW)
Gen   2: 5 any herb of the field had g.
Gen 18:12 After I have g old, shall I
Ruth   1:13 for them till they were g?
Dan   4:33 heaven till his hair had g

GROWS (see GROW)
Ps   90: 5 are like grass which g up:
Ps   90: 6 morning it flourishes and g

Eph	2:21	**g** into a holy temple in the
2Th	1: 3	because your faith **g**

GRUDGINGLY†

2Co	9: 7	not **g** or of necessity; for

GUARANTEE†

2Co	1:22	Spirit in our hearts as a **g**.
2Co	5: 5	given us the Spirit as a **g**.
Eph	1:14	who is the **g** of our

GUARD (see GUARDIANS, GUARDS)

Gen	3:24	to **g** the way to the tree of
Gen	37:36	and captain of the **g**.
Num	10:25	children of Dan (the rear **g**
Job	7:12	That You set a **g** over me?
Ps	39: 1	I will **g** my ways, Lest I sin
Ps	141: 3	Set a **g**, O LORD, over
Mic	7: 5	**G** the doors of your mouth
Matt	27:66	the stone and setting the **g**.
Phil	1:13	to the whole palace **g**,
Phil	4: 7	will **g** your hearts and minds
2Th	3: 3	who will establish you and **g**
1Ti	6:20	O Timothy! **G** what was

GUARDIANS (see GUARD)

Gal	4: 2	but is under **g** and stewards

GUARDS (see GUARD)

Ps	34:20	He **g** all his bones; Not one
Ps	127: 1	Unless the LORD **g** the

GUESTS

John	2:10	and when the **g** have well

GUIDE (see GUIDES)

Ps	31: 3	Lead me and **g** me.
Ps	32: 8	I will **g** you with My eye.
Ps	48:14	He will be our **g** Even to
Prov	23:19	And **g** your heart in the
Luke	1:79	To **g** our feet into the way
John	16:13	He will **g** you into all
Rom	2:19	that you yourself are a **g**

GUIDES (see GUIDE)

Matt	23:16	"Woe to you, blind **g**,
Acts	8:31	unless someone **g** me?" And

GUILT (see GUILTLESS, GUILTY)

Lev	5: 1	not tell it, he bears **g**.
Deut	19:13	you shall put away the **g**
2Ch	28:13	for our **g** is great, and
Ezra	9:13	deeds and for our great **g**,
Ezek	18:19	the son not bear the **g** of
Ezek	18:20	nor the father bear the **g** of
Matt	23:32	measure of your fathers' **g**.

GUILTLESS (see GUILT)

Ex	20: 7	LORD will not hold him **g**
Matt	12: 7	not have condemned the **g**.

GUILTY (see GUILT)

Ex	34: 7	by no means clearing the **g**,
Lev	6: 4	he has sinned and is **g**,

Num	14:18	by no means clears the **g**,
Num	35:27	he shall not be **g** of blood,
Ps	5:10	Pronounce them **g**,
Ps	109: 7	judged, let him be found **g**,
Prov	21: 8	The way of a **g** man is
Rom	3:19	all the world may become **g**
1Co	11:27	an unworthy manner will be **g**
Jas	2:10	he is **g** of all.

GULF†

Luke	16:26	and you there is a great **g**

H

HABAKKUK†

Hab	1: 1	burden which the prophet H
Hab	3: 1	A prayer of H the prophet, on

HABITATION (see HOME)

Ex	15:13	strength To Your holy **h**.
Ps	68: 5	Is God in His holy **h**.
Is	32:18	will dwell in a peaceful **h**,
Is	34:13	It shall be a **h** of jackals,
Is	63:15	heaven, And see from Your **h**,
Hab	3:11	moon stood still in their **h**;
2Co	5: 2	to be clothed with our **h**

HABITS†

1Co	15:33	company corrupts good **h**.

HADES

Matt	11:23	will be brought down to H;
Matt	16:18	and the gates of H shall not
Acts	2:27	not leave my soul in H,
1Co	15:55	is your sting? O H,
Rev	1:18	And I have the keys of H and
Rev	20:14	Then Death and H were cast

HAGAR

Gen	16: 3	took H her maid, the
Gen	16:15	So H bore Abram a son; and
Gal	4:25	for this H is Mount Sinai in

HAGGAI

Ezra	5: 1	Then the prophet H and
Ezra	6:14	the prophesying of H the

HAIL (see HAILSTONES)

Ex	9:23	the LORD sent thunder and **h**,
Matt	27:29	and mocked Him, saying, "H,
Rev	16:21	And great **h** from heaven fell

HAILSTONES (see HAIL)

Josh	10:11	the LORD cast down large **h**
Ps	18:13	H and coals of fire.

HAIR (see HAIRS, HAIRY)

Gen	42:38	would bring down my gray **h**
Ex	25: 4	fine linen, and goats' **h**;
Lev	14: 9	day he shall shave all the **h**
Num	6: 5	let the locks of the **h** of
Num	6:19	shaved his consecrated **h**,

Judg	16:22	the **h** of his head began to
2Sa	14:26	he weighed the **h** of his head
Neh	13:25	them and pulled out their **h**,
Job	4:15	The **h** on my body stood up.
Song	4: 1	Your **h** is like a flock of
Is	7:20	The head and the **h** of the
Ezek	8: 3	took me by a lock of my **h**;
Dan	3:27	the **h** of their head was not
Dan	4:33	the dew of heaven till his **h**
Dan	7: 9	And the **h** of His head was
Zech	13: 4	not wear a robe of coarse **h**
Matt	3: 4	was clothed in camel's **h**,
Matt	5:36	you cannot make one **h** white
Luke	7:38	and wiped them with the **h**
Luke	21:18	But not a **h** of your head
John	11: 2	wiped His feet with her **h**,
Acts	18:18	He had his **h** cut off at
Acts	27:34	since not a **h** will fall from
1Co	11:14	you that if a man has long **h**,
1Co	11:15	But if a woman has long **h**,
1Co	11:15	for her **h** is given to her
1Ti	2: 9	not with braided **h** or gold
1Pe	3: 3	outward—arranging the **h**,
Rev	1:14	His head and **h** were white

HAIRS (see HAIR)

Ps	40:12	They are more than the **h** of
Matt	10:30	But the very **h** of your head

HAIRY (see HAIR)

Gen	25:25	He was like a **h** garment
Gen	27:11	Esau my brother is a **h** man,

HALF

Ex	24: 6	and **h** the blood he sprinkled
1Ki	3:25	and give **h** to one, and half
Esth	5: 6	up to **h** the kingdom? It
Is	44:16	He burns **h** of it in the
Dan	7:25	For a time and times and **h**
Dan	12: 7	and **h** a time; and when the
Mark	6:23	up to **h** of my kingdom."
Luke	10:30	leaving him **h** dead.
Luke	19: 8	I give **h** of my goods to the

HALF-TRIBE

Num	34:14	and the **h** of Manasseh has

HALLOW (see HALLOWED)

Is	29:23	They will **h** My name, And
Jer	17:22	but **h** the Sabbath day, as I

HALLOWED (see HALLOW)

Ex	20:11	the Sabbath day and **h** it.
Ex	29:21	and his garments shall be **h**,
Matt	6: 9	**H** be Your name.
Luke	11: 2	**H** be Your name. Your

HAM

Gen	5:32	old, and Noah begot Shem, **H**,
Ps	105:27	wonders in the land of **H**.

HAMAN

Esth	7: 6	this wicked Haman!" So **H**

HAMMER

Judg	4:21	a tent peg and took a **h** in
Jer	23:29	And like a **h** that breaks the

HANANIAH (see SHADRACH)

Jer	28: 5	spoke to the prophet **H** in
Dan	1: 6	sons of Judah were Daniel, **H**,

HAND (see HANDIWORK, HANDS)

Gen	4:11	brother's blood from your **h**.
Gen	9: 2	They are given into your **h**.
Gen	9: 5	and from the **h** of man. From
Gen	14:22	I have raised my **h** to the
Gen	22:12	Do not lay your **h** on the lad,
Gen	24: 2	put your **h** under my thigh,
Gen	24:49	I may turn to the right **h**
Gen	38:30	the scarlet thread on his **h**.
Gen	39: 3	he did to prosper in his **h**.
Gen	39:12	he left his garment in her **h**,
Gen	46: 4	and Joseph will put his **h** on
Gen	48:13	Ephraim with his right **h**
Ex	3: 8	to deliver them out of the **h**
Ex	3:19	no, not even by a mighty **h**.
Ex	3:20	So I will stretch out My **h**
Ex	4: 2	"What is that in your **h**?
Ex	4: 4	Reach out your **h** and take it
Ex	4: 4	it became a rod in his **h**),
Ex	4: 6	Now put your **h** in your
Ex	4: 6	his **h** was leprous, like
Ex	6: 1	and with a strong **h** he will
Ex	7: 5	when I stretch out My **h** on
Ex	8: 6	So Aaron stretched out his **h**
Ex	9: 3	the **h** of the LORD will be
Ex	13: 9	as a sign to you on your **h**
Ex	14:22	to them on their right **h**
Ex	15: 6	"Your right **h**,
Ex	15: 6	in power; Your right **h**,
Ex	16: 3	that we had died by the **h** of
Ex	17:11	when Moses held up his **h**,
Ex	18: 9	had delivered out of the **h**
Ex	19:13	Not a **h** shall touch him, but
Ex	21:24	tooth for tooth, hand for **h**,
Ex	29:20	the thumb of their right **h**
Ex	32:11	power and with a mighty **h**?
Ex	33:22	and will cover you with My **h**
Lev	4: 4	lay his **h** on the bull's
Lev	21:19	a broken foot or broken **h**,
Num	5:25	jealousy from the woman's **h**,
Num	27:18	and lay your **h** on him;
Num	35:21	he strikes him with his **h**
Deut	2: 7	in all the work of your **h**.
Deut	2:15	For indeed the **h** of the LORD
Deut	3:24	greatness and Your mighty **h**,
Deut	5:15	out from there by a mighty **h**
Deut	6: 8	them as a sign on your **h**,
Deut	10: 3	the two tablets in my **h**.
Deut	11:18	them as a sign on your **h**,
Deut	14:25	take the money in your **h**,
Deut	15: 9	the year of release, is at **h**,
Deut	15:10	all to which you put your **h**.
Deut	19:21	**h** for hand, foot for foot.
Deut	19:21	tooth for tooth, hand for **h**,
Deut	25:12	you shall cut off her **h**;

Deut	28:12	bless all the work of your **h**.
Deut	32:35	of their calamity is at **h**,
Deut	32:39	who can deliver from My **h**.
Deut	32:40	For I raise My **h** to heaven,
Deut	33: 3	His saints are in Your **h**;
Josh	5:13	His sword drawn in His **h**.
Josh	6: 2	given Jericho into your **h**,
Josh	10:32	Lachish into the **h** of
Josh	14: 2	had commanded by the **h** of
Josh	20: 5	the slayer into his **h**,
Judg	2:15	the **h** of the LORD was
Judg	2:16	delivered them out of the **h**
Judg	2:23	He deliver them into the **h**
Judg	3: 8	and He sold them into the **h**
Judg	3:21	Ehud reached with his left **h**,
Judg	4: 9	will sell Sisera into the **h**
Judg	4:21	and took a hammer in her **h**,
Judg	5:26	She stretched her **h** to the
Judg	7: 2	My own **h** has saved me.'
Judg	7:16	a trumpet into every man's **h**,
Judg	9:48	took an ax in his **h** and cut
1Sa	5:11	the **h** of God was very heavy
2Sa	4:11	require his blood at your **h**
2Sa	6: 6	Uzzah put out his **h** to the
2Sa	21:20	had six fingers on each **h**
1Ki	18:44	cloud, as small as a man's **h**,
Ezra	7: 9	according to the good **h** of
Neh	2: 8	me according to the good **h**
Job	1:11	stretch out Your **h** and touch
Job	1:12	only do not lay a **h** on his
Job	26:13	His **h** pierced the fleeing
Ps	16: 8	He is at my right **h** I
Ps	16:11	At Your right **h** are
Ps	31: 5	Into Your **h** I commit my
Ps	31: 8	not shut me up into the **h**
Ps	31:15	My times are in Your **h**;
Ps	32: 4	For day and night Your **h** was
Ps	37:24	upholds him with His **h**.
Ps	45: 4	And Your right **h** shall
Ps	63: 8	Your right **h** upholds me.
Ps	71: 4	out of the **h** of the wicked,
Ps	77:10	the years of the right **h** of
Ps	78:54	mountain which His right **h**
Ps	80:17	upon the man of Your right **h**,
Ps	80:25	Also I will set his **h** over
Ps	89:42	have exalted the right **h** of
Ps	91: 7	ten thousand at your right **h**;
Ps	95: 7	And the sheep of His **h**.
Ps	98: 1	His right **h** and His holy
Ps	108: 6	Save with Your right **h**,
Ps	110: 1	Lord, "Sit at My right **h**,
Ps	110: 5	Lord is at Your right **h**;
Ps	121: 5	your shade at your right **h**.
Ps	127: 4	Like arrows in the **h** of a
Ps	136:12	With a strong **h**,
Ps	137: 5	Let my right **h** forget its
Ps	138: 7	And Your right **h** will save
Ps	139: 5	And laid Your **h** upon me.
Ps	139:10	Even there Your **h** shall lead
Ps	139:10	And Your right **h** shall hold
Prov	3:16	of days is in her right **h**,
Prov	3:27	it is in the power of your **h**
Prov	12:24	The **h** of the diligent will
Prov	19:24	A lazy man buries his **h** in
Prov	21: 1	king's heart is in the **h**
Prov	26:15	The lazy man buries his **h**
Prov	31:19	And her **h** holds the
Prov	31:20	She extends her **h** to the
Eccl	2:24	was from the **h** of God.
Eccl	9: 1	their works are in the **h**
Eccl	9:10	Whatever your **h** finds to do,
Eccl	11: 6	do not withhold your **h**;
Song	2: 6	And his right **h** embraces
Is	1:12	required this from your **h**,
Is	6: 6	having in his **h** a live coal
Is	9:12	But His **h** is stretched out
Is	11: 8	child shall put his **h** in
Is	13: 6	day of the LORD is at **h**!
Is	40: 2	received from the LORD's **h**
Is	40:12	in the hollow of His **h**,
Is	41:10	with My righteous right **h**.
Is	41:13	God, will hold your right **h**,
Is	45: 1	whose right **h** I have
Is	49:22	I will lift My **h** in an oath
Is	50: 2	Is My **h** shortened at all
Is	51:16	you with the shadow of My **h**,
Is	53:10	LORD shall prosper in His **h**.
Is	59: 1	the LORD's **h** is not
Is	62: 8	has sworn by His right **h**
Is	64: 8	we are the work of Your **h**.
Jer	1: 9	the LORD put forth His **h**
Jer	15:17	sat alone because of Your **h**,
Jer	18: 4	of clay was marred in the **h**
Jer	18: 6	clay is in the potter's **h**,
Jer	18: 6	hand, so are you in My **h**,
Jer	22:24	the signet on My right **h**,
Jer	25:15	wine cup of fury from My **h**,
Jer	36:14	Take in your **h** the scroll
Jer	40: 4	chains that were on your **h**.
Jer	43: 9	large stones in your **h**,
Jer	44:30	his enemies and into the **h**
Lam	1: 7	her people fell into the **h**
Lam	4: 6	With no **h** to help her!
Ezek	1: 3	and the **h** of the LORD was
Ezek	3:18	I will require at your **h**.
Ezek	10: 8	have the form of a man's **h**
Ezek	20: 5	Israel and raised My **h** in
Ezek	33: 8	I will require at your **h**.
Dan	4:35	No one can restrain His **h**
Dan	5: 5	the fingers of a man's **h**
Hos	11: 8	How can I **h** you over,
Joel	1:15	day of the LORD is at **h**;
Amos	5:19	Leaned his **h** on the wall,
Jon	4:11	between their right **h** and
Matt	3: 2	kingdom of heaven is at **h**!
Matt	5:30	And if your right **h** causes
Matt	6: 3	do not let your left **h** know
Matt	8:15	So He touched her **h**,
Matt	12:10	a man who had a withered **h**.
Matt	20:21	one on Your right **h** and the
Matt	22:44	"Sit at My right **h**,
Matt	25:33	set the sheep on His right **h**,
Matt	26:18	says, "My time is at **h**;
Matt	26:23	He who dipped his **h** with Me
Matt	26:45	Behold, the hour is at **h**,
Mark	1:15	the kingdom of God is at **h**.
Mark	5:41	He took the child by the **h**,
Mark	8:23	took the blind man by the **h**

Mark	16:19	and sat down at the right **h**
Luke	1: 1	as many have taken in **h** to
Luke	23:33	one on the right **h** and the
John	3:35	given all things into His **h**.
John	7:30	but no one laid a **h** on Him,
John	10:28	snatch them out of My **h**.
John	10:29	them out of My Father's **h**.
John	20:25	and put my **h** into His side,
Acts	2:33	exalted to the right **h** of
Acts	7:50	Has My **h** not made all
Acts	9:12	in and putting his **h** on
Acts	26: 1	So Paul stretched out his **h**
Acts	28: 3	heat, and fastened on his **h**.
Rom	13:12	far spent, the day is at **h**.
1Co	12:15	say, "Because I am not a **h**,
1Co	16:21	The salutation with my own **h—**
Gal	2: 9	me and Barnabas the right **h**
Gal	3:19	through angels by the **h** of
Gal	6:11	to you with my own **h**!
Phil	4: 5	all men. The Lord is at **h**.
2Ti	4: 6	time of my departure is at **h**.
Phm	1:19	am writing with my own **h**.
Heb	1: 3	sat down at the right **h** of
Heb	1:13	"Sit at My right **h**,
Jas	5: 8	coming of the Lord is at **h**.
1Pe	4: 7	end of all things is at **h**;
1Pe	5: 6	under the mighty **h** of God,
Rev	1:16	He had in His right **h** seven
Rev	1:17	But He laid His right **h** on
Rev	6: 5	a pair of scales in his **h**.
Rev	10: 2	a little book open in his **h**.
Rev	10: 5	on the land raised up his **h**
Rev	13:16	a mark on their right **h** or

HANDIWORK (see HAND)

Ps	19: 1	the firmament shows His **h**.

HANDKERCHIEF (see HANDKERCHIEFS)

Luke	19:20	I have kept put away in a **h**.

HANDKERCHIEFS† (see HANDKERCHIEF)

Acts	19:12	so that even **h** or aprons were

HANDLE (see HANDLED)

Ps	115: 7	hands, but they do not **h**;
Luke	24:39	**H** Me and see, for a spirit

HANDLED (see HANDLE)

1Jn	1: 1	upon, and our hands have **h**,

HANDS (see ARMS, HAND)

Gen	5:29	work and the toil of our **h**,
Gen	27:22	but the hands are the **h** of
Gen	27:23	because his **h** were hairy
Ex	17:12	But Moses' **h** became heavy;
Lev	16:21	Aaron shall lay both his **h** on
Deut	4:28	gods, the work of men's **h**,
Deut	34: 9	for Moses had laid his **h** on
Judg	2:14	He delivered them into the **h**
Judg	2:14	and He sold them into the **h**
Judg	12: 3	I took my life in my **h** and
Judg	15:14	bonds broke loose from his **h**.
2Sa	4:12	cut off their **h** and feet,
2Ki	11:12	and they clapped their **h** and

Neh	2:18	Then they set their **h** to
Neh	6: 9	O God, strengthen my **h**.
Job	1:10	blessed the work of his **h**,
Job	10: 3	despise the work of Your **h**,
Ps	8: 6	over the works of Your **h**;
Ps	22:16	They pierced My **h** and My
Ps	24: 4	He who has clean **h** and a
Ps	47: 1	Oh, clap your **h**,
Ps	90:17	establish the work of our **h**.
Ps	91:12	In their **h** they shall bear
Ps	115: 4	gold, The work of men's **h**.
Ps	138: 8	forsake the works of Your **h**.
Prov	6:10	A little folding of the **h**
Prov	6:17	**H** that shed innocent blood,
Prov	31:13	willingly works with her **h**.
Prov	31:31	her of the fruit of her **h**,
Song	5: 5	And my **h** dripped with
Is	1:15	Your **h** are full of blood.
Is	19:25	and Assyria the work of My **h**,
Is	35: 3	Strengthen the weak **h**,
Is	45: 9	say, 'He has no **h**'?
Ezek	23:37	and blood is on their **h**.
Dan	2:34	stone was cut out without **h**,
Zech	4: 9	The **h** of Zerubbabel Have
Matt	4: 6	In their **h** they shall
Matt	15:20	but to eat with unwashed **h**
Matt	18:28	and he laid **h** on him and
Matt	26:50	Then they came and laid **h**
Matt	27:24	took water and washed his **h**
Mark	14:58	this temple made with **h**,
Mark	16:18	they will lay **h** on the sick,
Luke	6: 1	rubbing them in their **h**.
Luke	23:46	into Your **h** I commit My
Luke	24:39	Behold My **h** and My feet, that
John	7:44	but no one laid **h** on Him.
John	13: 3	given all things into His **h**,
John	20:20	He showed them His **h** and
John	20:25	Unless I see in His **h** the
Acts	2:23	you have taken by lawless **h**,
Acts	5:18	and laid their **h** on the
Acts	7:48	dwell in temples made with **h**,
Acts	17:25	is He worshiped with men's **h**,
Acts	19:26	gods which are made with **h**.
Rom	10:21	stretched out My **h** To
1Co	4:12	working with our own **h**.
2Co	5: 1	God, a house not made with **h**,
Col	2:11	circumcision made without **h**,
1Th	4:11	and to work with your own **h**,
1Ti	2: 8	lifting up holy **h**,
Heb	1:10	are the work of Your **h**.
Heb	6: 2	baptisms, of laying on of **h**,
Heb	9:11	tabernacle not made with **h**,
Heb	10:31	thing to fall into the **h** of
Heb	12:12	Therefore strengthen the **h**
Jas	4: 8	near to you. Cleanse your **h**,
1Jn	1: 1	and our **h** have handled,
Rev	7: 9	palm branches in their **h**,
Rev	20: 4	foreheads or on their **h**.

HANDSOME

Gen	39: 6	Now Joseph was **h** in form and
1Sa	16:18	and a **h** person; and the
Song	1:16	Behold, you are **h**,

HANDWRITING†

| Col | 2:14 | having wiped out the **h** of |

HANG (see HANGED, HANGS, HUNG)

Gen	40:19	off your head from you and **h**
Matt	22:40	these two commandments **h**
Heb	12:12	the hands which **h** down,

HANGED (see HANG)

| Deut | 21:23 | for he who is **h** is accursed |
| Matt | 27: 5 | and went and **h** himself. |

HANGS† (see HANG)

| Job | 26: 7 | He **h** the earth on nothing. |
| Gal | 3:13 | is everyone who **h** on |

HANNAH

| 1Sa | 1: 2 | but H had no children. |

HAPPY (see BLESSED)

1Ki	10: 8	H are your men and happy
Ps	127: 5	H is the man who has his
Ps	137: 8	H the one who repays you as
Ps	144:15	H are the people whose God

HARAN

Gen	11:26	begot Abram, Nahor, and **H.**
Gen	11:27	H begot Lot.
Gen	11:32	years, and Terah died in **H.**
Acts	7: 2	before he dwelt in **H,**

HARD (see HARDEN, HARDNESS)

Gen	18:14	Is anything too **h** for the
Ex	1:14	their lives bitter with **h**
Ex	7:13	And Pharaoh's heart grew **h,**
Ex	18:26	the **h** cases they brought to
1Ki	10: 1	she came to test him with **h**
2Ki	2:10	You have asked a **h** thing.
Jer	32:17	There is nothing too **h** for
Matt	13:15	Their ears are **h** of
Matt	25:24	I knew you to be a **h** man,
Acts	9: 5	It is **h** for you to kick
2Co	4: 8	We are **h** pressed on every
Heb	5:11	and **h** to explain, since you
2Pe	3:16	in which are some things **h**

HARDEN (see HARD, HARDENED, HARDENS)

Ex	7: 3	And I will **h** Pharaoh's heart,
Ps	95: 8	Do not **h** your hearts, as in
Heb	3: 8	Do not **h** your hearts

HARDENED (see HARDEN)

Ex	10:20	But the LORD **h** Pharaoh's
Neh	9:16	H their necks, And did not
Dan	5:20	and his spirit was **h** in
Mark	6:52	because their heart was **h.**

HARDENS (see HARDEN)

Prov	28:14	But he who **h** his heart will
Prov	29: 1	and **h** his neck, Will
Rom	9:18	and whom He wills He **h.**

HARDNESS (see HARD)

| Matt | 19: 8 | because of the **h** of your |

HARLOT (see HARLOTRY, HARLOTS)

Gen	34:31	he treat our sister like a **h?**
Gen	38:15	her, he thought she was a **h,**
Ex	34:16	and his daughters play the **h**
Deut	23:17	shall be no ritual **h** of
Josh	2: 1	and came to the house of a **h**
Judg	11: 1	but he was the son of a **h;**
Judg	16: 1	went to Gaza and saw a **h**
Prov	7:10	With the attire of a **h,**
Prov	23:27	For a **h** is a deep pit, And
Is	1:21	city has become a **h!** It
Ezek	16:30	the deeds of a brazen **h.**
Ezek	16:34	one solicited you to be a **h.**
Hos	2: 5	mother has played the **h;**
Amos	7:17	Your wife shall be a **h** in the
1Co	6:15	make them members of a **h?**
1Co	6:16	he who is joined to a **h** is
Heb	11:31	By faith the **h** Rahab did not
Jas	2:25	was not Rahab the **h** also
Rev	17: 1	the judgment of the great **h**

HARLOTRY (see HARLOT)

Gen	38:24	she is with child by **h.**
Num	25: 1	the people began to commit **h**
Ezek	16:25	multiplied your acts of **h.**
Hos	1: 2	take yourself a wife of **h**
Hos	1: 2	land has committed great **h**
Hos	5: 4	For the spirit of **h** is in

HARLOTS (see HARLOT)

1Ki	3:16	Now two women who were **h**
1Ki	22:38	up his blood while the **h**
Matt	21:31	that tax collectors and **h**
Luke	15:30	your livelihood with **h,**
Rev	17: 5	THE MOTHER OF H

HARM (see HARMLESS)

Gen	26:29	'that you will do us no **h,**
Gen	31:29	is in my power to do you **h,**
Ex	21:23	But if any **h** follows, then
Lev	5:16	make restitution for the **h**
1Ch	16:22	And do My prophets no **h.**
Rom	13:10	Love does no **h** to a neighbor;

HARMLESS† (see HARM)

| Matt | 10:16 | be wise as serpents and **h** |
| Phil | 2:15 | may become blameless and **h,** |

HARP (see HARPS)

Gen	4:21	of all those who play the **h**
1Sa	16:23	that David would take a **h**
Ps	33: 2	Praise the LORD with the **h;**
Ps	57: 8	lute and **h!** I will awaken
Rev	5: 8	the Lamb, each having a **h,**

HARPS (see HARP)

| Ps | 137: 2 | We hung our **h** Upon the |

HARVEST

| Gen | 8:22 | remains, Seedtime and **h,** |

Gen	30:14	went in the days of wheat **h**
Ex	23:16	"and the Feast of H,
Lev	19: 9	the gleanings of your **h.**
Ruth	1:22	at the beginning of barley **h.**
Ruth	2:23	barley harvest and wheat **h;**
Jer	8:20	The **h** is past, The summer is
Amos	4: 7	still three months to the **h.**
Matt	9:37	The **h** truly is plentiful,
Matt	9:38	pray the Lord of the **h** to
Matt	9:38	send out laborers into His **h.**
Matt	13:39	the **h** is the end of the age,
Luke	10: 2	The **h** truly is great, but
Luke	10: 2	send out laborers into His **h.**
John	4:35	are already white for **h!**

HASTE (see HASTEN, HASTILY)

Ex	12:11	So you shall eat it in **h.**
Ps	38:22	Make **h** to help me, O Lord,
Prov	1:16	And they make **h** to shed
Song	8:14	Make **h,** my beloved,
Is	59: 7	And they make **h** to shed

HASTEN (see HASTE, HASTENING, HASTENS)

Ps	22:19	**h** to help Me!

HASTENING (see HASTEN)

2Pe	3:12	looking for and **h** the coming

HASTENS (see HASTEN)

Zeph	1:14	It is near and **h** quickly.

HASTILY (see HASTE, QUICKLY)

1Ti	5:22	Do not lay hands on anyone **h,**

HATE (see HATED, HATERS, HATES, HATRED)

Gen	50:15	Perhaps Joseph will **h** us, and
Ex	20: 5	generations of those who **h**
Lev	19:17	You shall not **h** your brother
Deut	32:41	And repay those who **h** Me.
Judg	14:16	You only **h** me! You do not
Ps	25:19	And they **h** me with cruel
Ps	45: 7	love righteousness and **h**
Ps	119:104	Therefore I **h** every false
Ps	139:22	I **h** them with perfect
Prov	1:22	And fools **h** knowledge.
Prov	8:13	fear of the LORD is to **h**
Eccl	3: 8	to love, And a time to **h;**
Amos	5:15	**H** evil, love good
Mic	3: 2	You who **h** good and love
Matt	5:43	love your neighbor and **h**
Matt	5:44	do good to those who **h** you,
Matt	6:24	for either he will **h** the one
Luke	6:22	Blessed are you when men **h**
John	7: 7	The world cannot **h** you, but
Rom	7:15	not practice; but what I **h,**

HATED (see HATE)

Gen	27:41	So Esau **h** Jacob because of
Gen	37: 4	they **h** him and could not
2Sa	13:15	the hatred with which he **h**
Esth	9: 1	overpowered those who **h**
Ps	44: 7	put to shame those who **h** us.
Prov	1:29	Because they **h** knowledge
Prov	5:12	How I have **h** instruction,

Prov	14:20	The poor man is **h** even by
Eccl	2:17	Therefore I **h** life because
Mal	1: 3	But Esau I have **h,**
Matt	10:22	And you will be **h** by all for
John	15:18	it hated Me before it **h**
John	15:24	they have seen and also **h**
John	15:25	They **h** Me without a
John	17:14	and the world has **h** them
Rom	9:13	but Esau I have **h.**
Eph	5:29	For no one ever **h** his own
Heb	1: 9	righteousness and **h**

HATERS (see HATE)

Rom	1:30	**h** of God, violent, proud,

HATES (see HATE)

Deut	19:11	But if anyone **h** his
Job	16: 9	and **h** me; He gnashes at me
Prov	6:16	six things the LORD **h,**
Prov	12: 1	But he who **h** correction is
Prov	13: 5	A righteous man **h** lying,
Prov	13:24	He who spares his rod **h** his
Prov	15:27	But he who **h** bribes will
Is	1:14	appointed feasts My soul **h;**
John	7: 7	but it **h** Me because I
John	12:25	and he who **h** his life in
John	15:18	If the world **h** you, you know
John	15:23	He who **h** Me hates My Father
1Jn	2: 9	and **h** his brother, is in
1Jn	3:13	if the world **h** you.

HATRED (see HATE)

Ps	25:19	they hate me with cruel **h.**
Ps	109: 5	And **h** for my love.
Ps	139:22	I hate them with perfect **h;**
Prov	10:12	**H** stirs up strife, But love
Prov	15:17	Than a fatted calf with **h.**

HAUGHTY

Prov	16:18	And a **h** spirit before a
Prov	21: 4	A **h** look, a proud heart,

HAY

1Co	3:12	precious stones, wood, **h,**

HAZOR

Josh	11:11	Then he burned **H** with fire.

HEAD (see HEADS)

Gen	3:15	He shall bruise your **h,**
Gen	40:13	Pharaoh will lift up your **h**
Gen	40:19	will lift off your **h** from
Ex	29: 7	oil, pour it on his **h,**
Ex	29:10	put their hands on the **h** of
Lev	13:12	from his **h** to his foot,
Lev	16:21	lay both his hands on the **h**
Num	6: 5	razor shall come upon his **h;**
Num	6: 5	locks of the hair of his **h**
Judg	13: 5	razor shall come upon his **h,**
Judg	16:19	off the seven locks of his **h.**
1Sa	1:11	razor shall come upon his **h.**
1Sa	5: 4	The **h** of Dagon and both the
2Sa	1: 2	torn and dust on his **h.**
2Sa	3: 8	Am I a dog's **h** that belongs

2Sa	18: 9	and his **h** caught in the
2Ki	4:19	said to his father, "My **h**,
2Ki	6: 5	the iron ax **h** fell into
2Ki	9:30	her eyes and adorned her **h**,
Esth	2:17	the royal crown upon her **h**
Esth	6:12	mourning and with his **h**
Esth	9:25	should return on his own **h**,
Job	1:20	his robe, and shaved his **h**;
Job	2: 7	foot to the crown of his **h**.
Job	2:12	and sprinkled dust on his **h**
Job	10:15	I cannot lift up my **h**.
Job	20: 6	And his **h** reaches to the
Job	29: 3	His lamp shone upon my **h**,
Ps	3: 3	the One who lifts up my **h**.
Ps	7:16	shall return upon his own **h**,
Ps	21: 3	of pure gold upon his **h**.
Ps	22: 7	tho lip, they shake the **h**,
Ps	23: 5	You anoint my **h** with oil;
Ps	38: 4	have gone over my **h**;
Ps	40:12	more than the hairs of my **h**;
Ps	110: 7	He shall lift up the **h**.
Ps	133: 2	the precious oil upon the **h**,
Prov	1: 9	graceful ornament on your **h**,
Prov	16:31	The silver-haired **h** is a
Prov	20:29	of old men is their gray **h**.
Prov	25:22	heap coals of fire on his **h**,
Eccl	9: 8	And let your **h** lack no
Song	2: 6	left hand is under my **h**,
Is	1: 5	The whole **h** is sick, And
Is	3:17	a scab The crown of the **h**
Is	7: 8	For the **h** of Syria is
Is	9:14	the LORD will cut off **h**
Is	19:15	Which the **h** or tail, Palm
Is	59:17	helmet of salvation on His **h**;
Jer	9: 1	that my **h** were waters, And
Jer	18:16	astonished And shake his **h**.
Jer	23:19	fall violently on the **h** of
Jer	48:37	For every **h** shall be bald,
Jer	52:31	lifted up the **h** of
Ezek	5: 1	and pass it over your **h** and
Ezek	10: 1	that was above the **h** of the
Ezek	17:19	will recompense on his own **h**.
Ezek	24:17	bind your turban on your **h**,
Ezek	33: 4	blood shall be on his own **h**.
Dan	2:28	and the visions of your **h**
Dan	2:38	you are this **h** of gold.
Dan	4: 5	bed and the visions of my **h**
Dan	7: 9	And the hair of His **h** was
Matt	5:36	shall you swear by your **h**,
Matt	8:20	has nowhere to lay His **h**.
Matt	10:30	the very hairs of your **h**
Matt	14: 8	me John the Baptist's **h**
Matt	26: 7	and she poured it on His **h**
Matt	27:30	reed and struck Him on the **h**.
Matt	27:37	And they put up over His **h**
Mark	4:28	first the blade, then the **h**,
Luke	7:38	them with the hair of her **h**;
John	13: 9	also my hands and my **h**!"
Rom	12:20	coals of fire on his **h**.
1Co	11: 3	the **h** of woman is man, and
1Co	11: 3	and the **h** of Christ is God.
1Co	11:10	of authority on her **h**,
Eph	1:22	and gave Him to be **h** over
Eph	4:15	things into Him who is the **h—**

Eph	5:23	For the husband is **h** of the
Eph	5:23	as also Christ is **h** of the
Col	1:18	And He is the **h** of the body,
Col	2:19	not holding fast to the **H**,

HEADLONG

Acts	1:18	of iniquity; and falling **h**,

HEADS (see HEAD)

Gen	41: 5	and suddenly seven **h** of
Gen	43:28	And they bowed their **h**
Ex	18:25	and made them **h** over the
Josh	7: 6	and they put dust on their **h**.
Ps	24: 7	Lift up your **h**,
Is	35:10	everlasting joy on their **h**.
Dan	7: 6	The beast also had four **h**,
Acts	18: 6	blood be upon your own **h**;
Rev	12: 3	red dragon having seven **h**

HEAL (see HEALED, HEALING, HEALS)

2Ch	7:14	will forgive their sin and **h**
Ps	41: 4	**H** my soul, for I have
Eccl	3: 3	to kill, And a time to **h**;
Is	61: 1	He has sent Me to **h** the
Jer	17:14	**H** me, O LORD, and I shall
Matt	8: 7	I will come and **h** him."
Matt	10: 8	**H** the sick, cleanse the
Matt	12:10	Is it lawful to **h** on the
Luke	4:18	He has sent Me to **h**
Luke	4:23	**h** yourself! Whatever we have

HEALED (see HEAL)

Is	6:10	heart, And return and be **h**.
Is	53: 5	And by His stripes we are **h**.
Hos	11: 3	they did not know that I **h**
Matt	8:13	And his servant was **h** that
Matt	15:28	And her daughter was **h**
Luke	8: 2	women who had been **h** of
Luke	8:36	been demon-possessed was **h**.
Luke	8:43	and could not be **h** by any,
Luke	22:51	And He touched his ear and **h**
John	5:13	But the one who was **h** did not
Acts	3:11	as the lame man who was **h**
Acts	5:16	spirits, and they were all **h**.
Acts	14: 9	that he had faith to be **h**,
Acts	28: 8	laid His hands on him and **h**
Heb	12:13	dislocated, but rather be **h**.
1Pe	2:24	whose stripes you were **h**.
Rev	13: 3	and his deadly wound was **h**.

HEALING (see HEAL, HEALINGS)

Is	58: 8	Your **h** shall spring forth
Jer	14:19	us so that there is no **h**
Jer	14:19	good; And for the time of **h**,
Mal	4: 2	shall arise With **h** in His
Matt	4:23	and **h** all kinds of sickness
Luke	9: 6	preaching the gospel and **h**
Luke	9:11	those who had need of **h**.
Acts	10:38	went about doing good and **h**
Rev	22: 2	of the tree were for the **h**

HEALINGS (see HEALING)

1Co	12: 9	to another gifts of **h** by the

H

HEALS (*see* HEAL)

Ex	15:26	For I am the LORD who **h**
Ps	103: 3	Who **h** all your diseases,
Ps	147: 3	He **h** the brokenhearted And
Acts	9:34	Jesus the Christ **h** you.

HEALTH

Prov	16:24	to the soul and **h** to the

HEAP (*see* HEAPED)

Gen	31:46	took stones and made a **h**,
Gen	31:48	This **h** is a witness between
Ex	15: 8	stood upright like a **h**;
Prov	25:22	For so you will **h** coals of
Rom	12:20	in so doing you will **h**

HEAPED (*see* HEAP)

Jas	5: 3	You have **h** up treasure in

HEAR (*see* HEARD, HEARERS, HEARING, HEARS)

Ex	22:27	he cries to Me, I will **h**,
Deut	1:16	H the cases between your
Deut	4:33	Did any people ever **h** the
Deut	5: 1	and said to them: "**H**,
Deut	6: 4	"**H**, O Israel: The LORD
1Sa	15:14	lowing of the oxen which I **h**?
1Ki	4:34	came to **h** the wisdom of
1Ki	8:30	H in heaven Your dwelling
Job	26:14	how small a whisper we **h** of
Job	31:35	that I had one to **h** me!
Ps	4: 1	H me when I call, O God of
Ps	4: 1	and **h** my prayer.
Ps	10:17	will cause Your ear to **h**,
Ps	13: 3	Consider and **h** me, O LORD
Ps	17: 1	H a just cause, O LORD,
Ps	28: 2	H the voice of my
Ps	34: 2	The humble shall **h** of it
Ps	39:12	H my prayer, O LORD, And
Ps	51: 8	Make me **h** joy and gladness,
Ps	61: 1	H my cry, O God
Ps	94: 9	the ear, shall He not **h**?
Ps	115: 6	have ears, but they do not **h**;
Eccl	12:13	Let us **h** the conclusion of
Is	1:10	H the word of the LORD,
Is	1:15	many prayers, I will not **h**.
Is	6:10	And **h** with their ears, And
Is	29:18	that day the deaf shall **h**
Is	55: 3	your ear, and come to Me. **H**,
Is	59: 1	ear heavy, That it cannot **h**.
Jer	5:21	And who have ears and **h**
Jer	11: 2	H the words of this covenant,
Jer	11:10	who refused to **h** My words,
Jer	13:15	H and give ear: Do not be
Jer	14:12	I will not **h** their cry; and
Jer	22:29	H the word of the LORD!
Jer	49:20	Therefore **h** the counsel of
Lam	1:18	H now, all peoples, And
Ezek	2: 5	whether they **h** or whether
Ezek	2: 7	whether they **h** or whether
Ezek	2: 8	**h** what I say to you. Do not
Ezek	3:27	He who hears, let him **h**;
Ezek	8:18	I will not **h** them."

Ezek	12: 2	and ears to **h** but does not
Ezek	24:26	come to you to let you **h**
Ezek	37: 4	**h** the word of the LORD!
Dan	3:15	are ready at the time you **h**
Dan	5:23	which do not see or **h** or
Dan	9:17	**h** the prayer of Your
Hos	5: 1	H this, O priests! Take
Joel	1: 2	H this, you elders, And
Amos	4: 1	H this word, you cows of
Amos	7:16	**h** the word of the LORD:
Mic	3: 9	Now **h** this, You heads of
Mic	6: 1	And let the hills **h** your
Zech	7:12	refusing to **h** the law and
Mal	2: 2	If you will not **h**,
Matt	10:14	will not receive you nor **h**
Matt	10:27	and what you **h** in the ear,
Matt	11: 4	John the things which you **h**
Matt	11: 5	are cleansed and the deaf **h**;
Matt	11:15	"He who has ears to **h**,
Matt	12:19	Nor will anyone **h** His
Matt	12:42	the ends of the earth to **h**
Matt	13:13	and hearing they do not **h**,
Matt	13:15	with their eyes and **h**
Matt	13:18	Therefore **h** the parable of
Matt	17: 5	well pleased. "**H** Him!"
Matt	18:17	But if he refuses even to **h**
Matt	24: 6	And you will **h** of wars and
Mark	4:15	word is sown. When they **h**,
Mark	4:24	them, "Take heed what you **h**.
Mark	4:24	to you; and to you who **h**,
Mark	7:37	He makes both the deaf to **h**
Mark	12:29	the commandments is: '**H**,
Luke	5:15	came together to **h**,
Luke	6:17	who came to **h** Him and be
Luke	7:22	are cleansed, the deaf **h**,
Luke	8:12	wayside are the ones who **h**;
Luke	8:18	take heed how you **h**.
Luke	15: 1	drew near to Him to **h** Him.
Luke	16: 2	What is this I **h** about you?
Luke	16:31	If they do not **h** Moses and
Luke	18: 6	H what the unjust judge said.
John	3: 8	and you **h** the sound of it,
John	5:25	when the dead will **h** the
John	5:25	and those who **h** will live.
John	5:28	who are in the graves will **h**
John	9:31	we know that God does not **h**
John	10: 3	and the sheep **h** his voice;
Acts	2:11	we **h** them speaking in our own
Acts	2:22	**h** these words: Jesus of
Acts	7:37	Him you shall **h**.
Acts	13: 7	and Saul and sought to **h**
Acts	15: 7	mouth the Gentiles should **h**
Acts	17:21	but either to tell or to **h**
Acts	17:32	We will **h** you again on this
Acts	22: 1	**h** my defense before you
Acts	26: 3	Therefore I beg you to **h** me
Acts	26:29	but also all who **h** me today,
Acts	28:26	"Hearing you will **h**,
Acts	28:27	with their eyes and **h**
Rom	10:14	And how shall they **h** without
Rom	11: 8	that they should not **h**,
1Co	11:18	I **h** that there are divisions
Gal	4:21	do you not **h** the law?
Phil	1:30	you saw in me and now **h** is

Heb	3: 7	if you will **h** His
1Jn	4: 6	is not of God does not **h** us.
Rev	1: 3	he who reads and those who **h**
Rev	2: 7	let him **h** what the Spirit
Rev	9:20	which can neither see nor **h**
Rev	13: 9	anyone has an ear, let him **h**.

HEARD (see HEAR)

Gen	3:10	I **h** Your voice in the garden,
Deut	4:12	you only **h** a voice.
1Ki	10: 1	when the queen of Sheba **h**
Neh	9:27	You **h** from heaven; And
Job	42: 5	I have **h** of You by the
Ps	3: 4	And He **h** me from His holy
Ps	6: 8	For the LORD has **h** the
Ps	10:17	You have **h** the desire of the
Ps	18: 6	He **h** my voice from His
Ps	19: 3	Where their voice is not **h**.
Ps	22:24	when He cried to Him, He **h**.
Ps	34: 4	and He **h** me, And delivered
Ps	34: 6	and the LORD **h** him, And
Ps	40: 1	And **h** my cry.
Ps	44: 1	We have **h** with our ears, O
Ps	48: 8	As we have **h**,
Ps	81: 5	Where I **h** a language I did
Ps	106:44	When He **h** their cry;
Ps	120: 1	And He **h** me.
Ps	132: 6	we **h** of it in Ephrathah; We
Song	2:12	of the turtledove Is **h** in
Is	6: 8	Also I **h** the voice of the
Is	40:21	not known? Have you not **h**?
Is	49: 8	an acceptable time I have **h**
Is	52:15	And what they had not **h**
Jer	31:15	A voice was **h** in Ramah,
Matt	2:18	A voice was **h** in Ramah,
Matt	5:21	You have **h** that it was said
Matt	6: 7	think that they will be **h**
Mark	12:37	And the common people **h**
Luke	1:13	for your prayer is **h**;
Luke	1:41	when Elizabeth **h** the
Luke	1:58	neighbors and relatives **h**
Luke	2:18	And all those who **h** it
Luke	2:20	the things that they had **h**
Luke	2:47	And all who **h** Him were
Luke	7:22	things you have seen and **h**:
Luke	12: 3	in the dark will be **h** in
Luke	15:25	he **h** music and dancing.
Luke	22:71	For we have **h** it ourselves
John	3:32	"And what He has seen and **h**,
John	4:42	for we ourselves have **h** Him
John	8:26	those things which I **h** from
John	8:40	told you the truth which I **h**
John	11: 6	when He **h** that he was sick,
John	11:41	I thank You that You have **h**
John	12:34	We have **h** from the law that
Acts	1: 4	you have **h** from Me;
Acts	4:20	which we have seen and **h**.
Acts	8:30	and **h** him reading the
Acts	19: 2	We have not so much as **h**
Acts	22:15	of what you have seen and **h**.
Rom	10:14	Him of whom they have not **h**?
1Co	2: 9	not seen, nor ear **h**,
Eph	1:13	after you **h** the word of
Eph	1:15	after I **h** of your faith in

Phil	4: 9	learned and received and **h**
Col	1: 4	since we **h** of your faith in
Col	1: 9	since the day we **h** it, do
2Ti	1:13	words which you have **h** from
2Ti	2: 2	the things that you have **h**
Jas	5:11	You have **h** of the
2Pe	1:18	And we **h** this voice which
1Jn	1: 1	beginning, which we have **h**,
1Jn	1: 3	which we have seen and **h** we
1Jn	1: 5	the message which we have **h**
Rev	1:10	and I **h** behind me a loud
Rev	3: 3	how you have received and **h**;
Rev	5:11	and I **h** the voice of many
Rev	6: 1	and I **h** one of the four
Rev	10: 4	but I **h** a voice from heaven
Rev	12:10	Then I **h** a loud voice saying
Rev	18:22	trumpeters shall not be **h**
Rev	18:23	and bride shall not be **h** in
Rev	22: 8	saw and **h** these things. And

HEARERS (see HEAR)

Rom	2:13	(for not the **h** of the law
Eph	4:29	it may impart grace to the **h**.
Jas	1:22	and not **h** only, deceiving

HEARING (see HEAR)

Ex	24: 7	Covenant and read in the **h**
Job	42: 5	have heard of You by the **h**
Prov	20:12	The **h** ear and the seeing
Eccl	1: 8	Nor the ear filled with **h**.
Is	6: 9	this people: 'Keep on **h**,
Amos	8:11	But of **h** the words of the
Matt	13:13	and **h** they do not hear, nor
Matt	13:14	**H** you will hear and
Matt	13:15	ears are hard of **h**,
Mark	6: 2	And many **h** Him were
Luke	4:21	is fulfilled in your **h**.
Luke	7: 1	all His sayings in the **h** of
Acts	5: 5	**h** these words, fell down and
Acts	9: 7	**h** a voice but seeing no one.
Acts	28:26	**H** you will hear, and
Acts	28:27	ears are hard of **h**,
Rom	10:17	So then faith comes by **h**,
Rom	10:17	and **h** by the word of God.
1Co	12:17	eye, where would be the **h**?
Gal	3: 2	or by the **h** of faith?
Phm	1: 5	**h** of your love and faith
Heb	5:11	you have become dull of **h**.
2Pe	2: 8	day to day by seeing and **h**

HEARS (see HEAR)

1Sa	3:10	"Speak, for Your servant **h**.
Matt	7:24	Therefore whoever **h** these
Matt	13:19	When anyone **h** the word of the
Matt	13:23	the good ground is he who **h**
Luke	10:16	He who **h** you hears Me, he who
John	5:24	he who **h** My word and
John	8:47	He who is of God **h** God's
John	12:47	And if anyone **h** My words and
John	18:37	who is of the truth **h** My
1Jn	4: 5	and the world **h** them.
1Jn	4: 6	He who knows God **h** us; he
Rev	3:20	If anyone **h** My voice and
Rev	22:17	Come!" And let him who **h**

H

HEART (*see* BROKENHEARTED, HEART'S, HEARTS)

Gen	6: 5	of the thoughts of his **h**
Gen	6: 6	and He was grieved in His **h**.
Gen	8:21	the imagination of man's **h**
Gen	17:17	laughed, and said in his **h**,
Ex	7: 3	I will harden Pharaoh's **h**,
Ex	7:13	And Pharaoh's **h** grew hard,
Ex	10:20	LORD hardened Pharaoh's **h**,
Ex	35: 5	Whoever is of a willing **h**,
Lev	26:16	eyes and cause sorrow of **h**.
Deut	4:29	you seek Him with all your **h**
Deut	6: 5	your God with all your **h**,
Deut	6: 6	you today shall be in your **h**.
Deut	8: 2	to know what was in your **h**,
Deut	8:14	when your **h** is lifted up, and
Deut	10:12	your God with all your **h**
Deut	10:16	the foreskin of your **h**,
Deut	11:13	serve Him with all your **h**
Deut	12:15	whatever your **h** desires,
Deut	26:16	them with all your **h** and
Deut	30:14	in your mouth and in your **h**,
Josh	5: 1	that their **h** melted; and
Judg	5:16	have great searchings of **h**.
Judg	16:17	that he told her all his **h**,
Judg	19: 6	and let your **h** be merry."
1Sa	2: 1	My **h** rejoices in the LORD;
1Sa	13:14	a man after His own **h**,
1Sa	16: 7	but the LORD looks at the **h**.
1Ki	11: 3	his wives turned away his **h**.
1Ki	14: 8	followed Me with all his **h**,
2Ch	36:13	his neck and hardened his **h**
Job	19:27	How my **h** yearns within me!
Job	41:24	His **h** is as hard as stone,
Ps	4: 7	have put gladness in my **h**,
Ps	7:10	Who saves the upright in **h**.
Ps	9: 1	O LORD, with my whole **h**;
Ps	12: 2	lips and a double **h** they
Ps	14: 1	The fool has said in his **h**,
Ps	15: 2	speaks the truth in his **h**;
Ps	16: 9	Therefore my **h** is glad, and
Ps	17: 3	You have tested my **h**;
Ps	19: 8	are right, rejoicing the **h**;
Ps	19:14	and the meditation of my **h**
Ps	22:14	My **h** is like wax; It has
Ps	24: 4	has clean hands and a pure **h**,
Ps	27: 3	My **h** shall not fear;
Ps	38:10	My **h** pants, my strength
Ps	40: 8	Your law is within my **h**.
Ps	44:21	knows the secrets of the **h**.
Ps	45: 1	My **h** is overflowing with a
Ps	51:10	Create in me a clean **h**,
Ps	51:17	A broken and a contrite **h**—
Ps	66:18	I regard iniquity in my **h**,
Ps	73: 1	To such as are pure in **h**.
Ps	86:11	Unite my **h** to fear Your
Ps	90:12	That we may gain a **h** of
Ps	101: 2	my house with a perfect **h**.
Ps	101: 4	A perverse **h** shall depart
Ps	101: 5	a haughty look and a proud **h**,
Ps	109:22	And my **h** is wounded within
Ps	119:11	word I have hidden in my **h**,
Ps	119:70	Their **h** is as fat as grease,
Ps	119:80	Let my **h** be blameless
Ps	139:23	me, O God, and know my **h**;
Prov	2: 2	And apply your **h** to
Prov	2:10	When wisdom enters your **h**,
Prov	3: 3	them on the tablet of your **h**,
Prov	3: 5	in the LORD with all your **h**,
Prov	4:23	Keep your **h** with all
Prov	13:12	Hope deferred makes the **h**
Prov	14:10	The **h** knows its own
Prov	14:14	The backslider in **h** will be
Prov	14:30	A sound **h** is life to the
Prov	14:33	But what is in the **h** of
Prov	15:15	But he who is of a merry **h**
Prov	16: 9	A man's **h** plans his way,
Prov	17:16	Since he has no **h** for
Prov	17:20	He who has a deceitful **h**
Prov	20: 5	Counsel in the **h** of man is
Prov	20: 9	I have made my **h** clean, I am
Prov	20:27	the inner depths of his **h**.
Prov	21: 1	The king's **h** is in the hand
Prov	21: 4	A haughty look, a proud **h**,
Prov	22:15	is bound up in the **h** of a
Prov	22:17	And apply your **h** to my
Prov	23: 7	For as he thinks in his **h**,
Prov	23:17	Do not let your **h** envy
Prov	23:19	And guide your **h** in the
Prov	23:26	My son, give me your **h**,
Prov	25:20	who sings songs to a heavy **h**.
Prov	26:25	seven abominations in his **h**;
Prov	27:19	So a man's **h** reveals the
Prov	28:14	But he who hardens his **h**
Prov	28:25	He who is of a proud **h** stirs
Prov	28:26	He who trusts in his own **h**
Eccl	1:16	I communed with my **h**,
Eccl	1:17	And I set my **h** to know wisdom
Eccl	5:20	busy with the joy of his **h**.
Eccl	8: 9	and applied my **h** to every
Eccl	8:16	When I applied my **h** to know
Song	4: 9	You have ravished my **h**,
Song	8: 6	me as a seal upon your **h**,
Is	1: 5	And the whole **h** faints.
Is	6:10	Make the **h** of this people
Is	6:10	And understand with their **h**,
Is	57:15	And to revive the **h** of the
Jer	8:18	My **h** is faint in me.
Jer	9:26	are uncircumcised in the **h**.
Jer	15:16	joy and rejoicing of my **h**;
Jer	17: 9	The **h** is deceitful above
Jer	17:10	I, the LORD, search the **h**,
Jer	29:13	for Me with all your **h**.
Ezek	11:19	I will give them one **h**,
Ezek	11:19	and take the stony **h** out of
Ezek	11:19	and give them a **h** of flesh,
Ezek	36:26	I will give you a new **h** and
Ezek	36:26	I will take the **h** of stone
Ezek	36:26	your flesh and give you a **h**
Hos	11: 8	My **h** churns within Me; My
Joel	2:13	So rend your **h**,
Matt	5: 8	Blessed are the pure in **h**,
Matt	5:28	adultery with her in his **h**.
Matt	6:21	there your **h** will be also.
Matt	11:29	I am gentle and lowly in **h**,
Matt	12:34	of the abundance of the **h**
Matt	12:35	the good treasure of his **h**

Matt	15:19	For out of the **h** proceed evil
Matt	22:37	God with all your **h**,
Luke	2:19	and pondered them in her **h**.
Luke	2:51	all these things in her **h**.
Luke	6:45	the good treasure of his **h**
Luke	24:25	and slow of **h** to believe in
Luke	24:32	Did not our **h** burn within us
John	7:38	out of his **h** will flow
John	14: 1	Let not your **h** be troubled;
Acts	4:32	who believed were of one **h**
Acts	5: 3	why has Satan filled your **h**
Acts	7:51	and uncircumcised in **h** and
Acts	8:37	you believe with all your **h**,
Acts	13:22	a man after My own **h**,
Acts	15: 8	"So God, who knows the **h**,
Rom	2:29	is that of the **h**,
Rom	6:17	yet you obeyed from the **h**
Rom	10: 6	"Do not say in your **h**,
Rom	10: 9	Jesus and believe in your **h**
Rom	10:10	For with the **h** one believes
1Co	2: 9	entered into the **h** of
1Co	14:25	thus the secrets of his **h**
2Co	2: 4	affliction and anguish of **h**
2Co	3: 3	flesh, that is, of the **h**.
2Co	3:15	read, a veil lies on their **h**.
2Co	6:11	our **h** is wide open.
2Co	9: 7	as he purposes in his **h**,
Gal	6: 9	reap if we do not lose **h**.
Eph	5:19	and making melody in your **h**
Eph	6: 5	trembling, in sincerity of **h**,
Eph	6: 6	the will of God from the **h**,
Phil	1: 7	because I have you in my **h**,
1Ti	1: 5	is love from a pure **h**,
Phm	1:12	him, that is, my own **h**,
Phm	1:20	refresh my **h** in the Lord.
Heb	3:12	be in any of you an evil **h**
Heb	4:12	and intents of the **h**.
Heb	10:22	us draw near with a true **h**
Jas	1:26	but deceives his own **h**,
1Pe	1:22	fervently with a pure **h**,
1Pe	3: 4	the hidden person of the **h**,
1Jn	3:17	and shuts up his **h** from him,
1Jn	3:20	For if our **h** condemns us, God
1Jn	3:20	God is greater than our **h**,

HEART'S (see HEART)

Rom	10: 1	my **h** desire and prayer to

HEARTILY

Col	3:23	And whatever you do, do it **h**,

HEARTS (see HEART)

Ex	14:17	I indeed will harden the **h**
1Sa	10:26	whose **h** God had touched.
1Ki	8:58	that He may incline our **h** to
1Ch	28: 9	for the LORD searches all **h**
Job	1: 5	and cursed God in their **h**.
Ps	95: 8	"Do not harden your **h**,
Prov	17: 3	But the LORD tests the **h**.
Prov	21: 2	But the LORD weighs the **h**.
Eccl	3:11	has put eternity in their **h**,
Jer	31:33	and write it on their **h**;
Mal	4: 6	And he will turn The **h** of
Matt	13:15	understand with their **h**

Matt	19: 8	of the hardness of your **h**,
Luke	1:17	to turn the **h** of the
Luke	1:51	the imagination of their **h**.
Luke	2:35	that the thoughts of many **h**
Luke	16:15	men, but God knows your **h**.
Luke	21:26	men's **h** failing them from
Luke	24:38	do doubts arise in your **h**?
Acts	15: 9	purifying their **h** by faith.
Rom	1:21	and their foolish **h** were
Rom	1:24	in the lusts of their **h**,
Rom	2:15	the law written in their **h**,
Rom	8:27	Now He who searches the **h**
1Co	4: 5	reveal the counsels of the **h**.
2Co	1:22	us the Spirit in our **h** as a
2Co	3: 2	our epistle written in our **h**,
2Co	4: 6	who has shone in our **h** to
2Co	7: 2	Open your **h** to us. We have
Gal	4: 6	of His Son into your **h**,
Eph	3:17	Christ may dwell in your **h**
Eph	6:22	that he may comfort your **h**.
Phil	4: 7	will guard your **h** and minds
Col	3:15	peace of God rule in your **h**,
Col	3:16	with grace in your **h** to the
Col	4: 8	and comfort your **h**,
1Th	2: 4	men, but God who tests our **h**.
1Th	3:13	that He may establish your **h**
Heb	3: 8	Do not harden your **h**
Heb	8:10	write them on their **h**;
Heb	10:16	My laws into their **h**,
Heb	10:22	having our **h** sprinkled from
Jas	3:14	and self-seeking in your **h**,
Jas	4: 8	sinners; and purify your **h**,
2Pe	1:19	morning star rises in your **h**;
1Jn	3:19	and shall assure our **h**
Rev	2:23	who searches the minds and **h**.
Rev	17:17	God has put it into their **h**

HEAT (see HEATED)

Gen	8:22	and harvest, Cold and **h**,
Ps	19: 6	is nothing hidden from its **h**.
2Pe	3:10	will melt with fervent **h**;

HEATED (see HEAT)

Dan	3:19	more than it was usually **h**.

HEATHEN

Matt	6: 7	vain repetitions as the **h**

HEAVE

Ex	29:28	their **h** offering to the

HEAVEN (see HEAVENLY, HEAVENS)

Gen	1: 8	God called the firmament **H**.
Gen	7:11	and the windows of **h** were
Gen	14:19	Possessor of **h** and earth;
Gen	22:17	as the stars of the **h** and
Gen	28:12	and its top reached to **h**;
Gen	28:17	and this is the gate of **h**!
Ex	16: 4	I will rain bread from **h** for
Ex	20: 4	of anything that is in **h**
Deut	1:28	great and fortified up to **h**;
Deut	2:25	nations under the whole **h**,
Deut	4:26	I call **h** and earth to witness
Deut	10:14	Indeed **h** and the highest

Deut	30:12	Who will ascend into **h** for us
2Sa	18: 9	was left hanging between **h**
1Ki	8:27	**h** and the heaven of heavens
1Ki	8:30	Hear in **h** Your dwelling
2Ki	1:10	let fire come down from **h**
2Ki	2: 1	to take up Elijah into **h** by
2Ch	7:14	then I will hear from **h**,
Job	1:16	fire of God fell from **h**
Job	2:12	dust on his head toward **h**.
Job	16:19	even now my witness is in **h**,
Job	22:14	walks above the circle of **h**.
Ps	11: 4	The LORD's throne is in **h**;
Ps	19: 6	rising is from one end of **h**,
Ps	73:25	Whom have I in **h** but You?
Ps	78:24	given them of the bread of **h**.
Ps	115: 3	But our God is in **h**,
Ps	119:89	Your word is settled in **h**.
Ps	136:26	give thanks to the God of **h**!
Ps	139: 8	If I ascend into **h**,
Eccl	1:13	all that is done under **h**;
Is	14:12	you are fallen from **h**,
Is	14:13	'I will ascend into **h**,
Is	66: 1	**H** is My throne, And earth
Jer	7:18	cakes for the queen of **h**;
Jer	23:24	Do I not fill **h** and earth?"
Jer	49:36	From the four quarters of **h**,
Dan	2:19	Daniel blessed the God of **h**.
Dan	2:28	But there is a God in **h** who
Dan	4:15	it be wet with the dew of **h**,
Dan	4:26	you come to know that **H**
Dan	7:13	with the clouds of **h**! He
Hag	2:21	I will shake **h** and earth.
Mal	3:10	for you the windows of **h**
Matt	3: 2	for the kingdom of **h** is at
Matt	5: 3	theirs is the kingdom of **h**.
Matt	5:12	great is your reward in **h**,
Matt	5:16	and glorify your Father in **h**.
Matt	5:18	till **h** and earth pass away,
Matt	5:19	least in the kingdom of **h**;
Matt	5:34	swear at all: neither by **h**,
Matt	5:45	be sons of your Father in **h**;
Matt	6: 9	pray: Our Father in **h**,
Matt	6:10	On earth as it is in **h**.
Matt	6:20	yourselves treasures in **h**,
Matt	7:21	the will of My Father in **h**.
Matt	11:11	is least in the kingdom of **h**
Matt	11:25	Lord of **h** and earth, that
Matt	12:50	the will of My Father in **h**
Matt	16:19	the keys of the kingdom of **h**,
Matt	16:19	on earth will be bound in **h**,
Matt	18: 1	greatest in the kingdom of **h**?
Matt	18:10	of My Father who is in **h**.
Matt	18:14	of your Father who is in **h**
Matt	19:14	of such is the kingdom of **h**.
Matt	19:21	you will have treasure in **h**;
Matt	24:30	Son of Man will appear in **h**,
Matt	24:30	coming on the clouds of **h**
Matt	24:35	**H** and earth will pass away,
Matt	28:18	has been given to Me in **h**
Mark	10:21	you will have treasure in **h**;
Mark	16:19	He was received up into **h**,
Luke	2:15	gone away from them into **h**,
Luke	10:18	fall like lightning from **h**.
Luke	10:20	your names are written in **h**.

Luke	15: 7	there will be more joy in **h**
Luke	15:18	I have sinned against **h** and
Luke	17:29	fire and brimstone from **h**
Luke	19:38	the LORD!' Peace in **h**
Luke	24:51	them and carried up into **h**.
John	1:32	the Spirit descending from **h**
John	1:51	hereafter you shall see **h**
John	3:13	No one has ascended to **h** but
John	3:13	the Son of Man who is in **h**.
John	3:31	He who comes from **h** is above
John	6:31	gave them bread from **h**
John	17: 1	lifted up His eyes to **h**,
Acts	1:11	you stand gazing up into **h**?
Acts	1:11	was taken up from you into **h**,
Acts	2: 2	there came a sound from **h**,
Acts	2: 5	from every nation under **h**.
Acts	2:19	will show wonders in **h**
Acts	3:21	whom **h** must receive until the
Acts	4:12	is no other name under **h**
Acts	17:24	since He is Lord of **h** and
Rom	1:18	of God is revealed from **h**
Rom	10: 6	'Who will ascend into **h**?
1Co	8: 5	whether in **h** or on earth (as
2Co	12: 2	was caught up to the third **h**.
Eph	3:15	whom the whole family in **h**
Phil	2:10	should bow, of those in **h**,
Phil	3:20	For our citizenship is in **h**,
Col	1: 5	is laid up for you in **h**,
Col	1:16	were created that are in **h**
Col	1:20	on earth or things in **h**,
1Th	1:10	to wait for His Son from **h**,
1Th	4:16	Himself will descend from **h**
2Th	1: 7	Jesus is revealed from **h**
Heb	12:23	who are registered in **h**,
1Pe	1: 4	reserved in **h** for you,
1Pe	1:12	the Holy Spirit sent from **h**—
1Jn	5: 7	three that bear witness in **h**:
Rev	3:12	which comes down out of **h**
Rev	9: 1	I saw a star fallen from **h**
Rev	18: 5	her sins have reached to **h**,
Rev	19:11	Now I saw **h** opened, and
Rev	20: 9	came down from God out of **h**
Rev	21: 1	Now I saw a new **h** and a new
Rev	21: 1	for the first **h** and the

HEAVENLY (*see* HEAVEN)

Matt	6:14	your **h** Father will also
Matt	18:35	So My **h** Father also will do
Luke	2:13	angel a multitude of the **h**
John	3:12	you believe if I tell you **h**
Acts	26:19	was not disobedient to the **h**
1Co	15:48	and as is the **h** Man, so
Eph	1: 3	spiritual blessing in the **h**
Heb	3: 1	partakers of the **h** calling,
Heb	6: 4	and have tasted the **h** gift,
Heb	8: 5	the copy and shadow of the **h**
Heb	11:16	a **h** country. Therefore God
Heb	12:22	the **h** Jerusalem, to an

HEAVENS (*see* HEAVEN)

Gen	1: 1	beginning God created the **h**
Gen	11: 4	tower whose top is in the **h**;
Ex	20:11	days the LORD made the **h**
Deut	10:14	heaven and the highest **h**

Deut	32: 1	"Give ear, O **h**,
1Ki	8:27	heaven and the heaven of **h**
Ps	2: 4	He who sits in the **h** shall
Ps	8: 1	set Your glory above the **h**!
Ps	8: 3	When I consider Your **h**,
Ps	19: 1	The **h** declare the glory of
Ps	33: 6	the word of the LORD the **h**
Ps	68:33	who rides on the heaven of **h**,
Ps	96:11	Let the **h** rejoice, and let
Ps	103:11	For as the **h** are high above
Ps	104: 2	Who stretch out the **h** like
Ps	136: 5	Him who by wisdom made the **h**,
Prov	8:27	When He prepared the **h**,
Is	34: 4	And the **h** shall be rolled
Is	40:22	Who stretches out the **h**
Is	51: 6	For the **h** will vanish away
Is	55: 9	For as the **h** are higher than
Is	64: 1	that You would rend the **h**!
Is	65:17	I create new **h** and a new
Jer	4:23	form, and void; And the **h**,
Ezek	1: 1	that the **h** were opened and
Dan	4:11	Its height reached to the **h**,
Joel	2:30	I will show wonders in the **h**
Zech	8:12	And the **h** shall give their
Matt	3:16	the **h** were opened to Him,
Matt	24:29	and the powers of the **h** will
Mark	1:10	He saw the **h** parting and the
Luke	12:33	a treasure in the **h** that
Acts	2:34	did not ascend into the **h**,
Acts	7:56	Look! I see the **h** opened and
2Co	5: 1	with hands, eternal in the **h**.
Eph	4:10	ascended far above all the **h**,
Heb	1:10	And the **h** are the
Heb	4:14	who has passed through the **h**,
Heb	7:26	has become higher than the **h**;
Heb	8: 1	of the Majesty in the **h**,
2Pe	3:10	in which the **h** will pass
2Pe	3:13	look for new **h** and a new
Rev	12:12	"Therefore rejoice, O **h**,

HEAVY

Ex	17:12	But Moses' hands became **h**;
Num	11:14	the burden is too **h** for me.
1Ki	12:10	'Your father made our yoke **h**,
Is	6:10	dull, And their ears **h**,
Matt	11:28	all you who labor and are **h**
Matt	23: 4	For they bind **h** burdens, hard
Matt	26:43	again, for their eyes were **h**.

HEBREW (see HEBREWS)

Gen	14:13	came and told Abram the **H**,
Gen	39:17	The **H** servant whom you
Ex	1:15	king of Egypt spoke to the **H**
Ex	21: 2	If you buy a **H** servant, he
2Ki	18:26	and do not speak to us in **H**
Luke	23:38	of Greek, Latin, and **H**:
Phil	3: 5	a **H** of the Hebrews;

HEBREWS (see HEBREW)

Ex	3:18	The LORD God of the **H** has

HEBRON

Gen	23: 2	**H**) in the land of Canaan,
Josh	14:13	and gave **H** to Caleb the son

2Sa	2:11	that David was king in **H**
2Sa	15:10	Absalom reigns in **H**!'"

HEDGE (see HEDGED, HEDGES)

Job	1:10	Have You not made a **h** around
Is	5: 5	I will take away its **h**,
Hos	2: 6	I will **h** up your way with

HEDGED (see HEDGE)

Ps	139: 5	You have **h** me behind and

HEDGES (see HEDGE)

Luke	14:23	out into the highways and **h**,

HEED (see HEEDED, HEEDS)

Deut	4:23	Take **h** to yourselves, lest
1Sa	15:22	And to **h** than the fat of
Ps	119: 9	By taking **h** according to
Matt	24: 4	Take **h** that no one deceives
Mark	13: 5	Take **h** that no one deceives
Luke	8:18	Therefore take **h** how you
1Co	10:12	who thinks he stands take **h**
Col	4:17	Take **h** to the ministry which
1Ti	1: 4	nor give **h** to fables and
1Ti	4: 1	giving **h** to deceiving
1Ti	4:16	Take **h** to yourself and to the
Tit	1:14	not giving **h** to Jewish fables
Heb	2: 1	give the more earnest **h** to
2Pe	1:19	which you do well to **h** as a

HEEDED (see HEED)

Gen	3:17	Because you have **h** the voice
Gen	16: 2	And Abram **h** the voice of
Ex	6:12	of Israel have not **h** me.
Ex	18:24	So Moses **h** the voice of his
Josh	10:14	that the LORD **h** the voice
Judg	2:20	and has not **h** My voice,
2Ch	25:16	done this and have not **h** my
Neh	9:34	Nor **h** Your commandments and
Is	48:18	that you had **h** My
Dan	9: 6	Neither have we **h** Your
Acts	8: 6	with one accord **h** the

HEEDS (see HEED)

Prov	13: 1	A wise son **h** his father's

HEEL

Gen	3:15	And you shall bruise His **h**.
Gen	25:26	hand took hold of Esau's **h**;
Ps	41: 9	Has lifted up his **h**
Hos	12: 3	took his brother by the **h**
John	13:18	Me has lifted up his **h**

HEIFER

Gen	15: 9	Me a three-year-old **h**,
Num	19: 2	that they bring you a red **h**
Num	19: 9	gather up the ashes of the **h**
Heb	9:13	goats and the ashes of a **h**,

HEIGHT (see HEIGHTS)

1Sa	16: 7	his appearance or at the **h**
Prov	25: 3	As the heavens for **h** and
Eccl	12: 5	Also they are afraid of **h**,
Is	7:11	in the depth or in the **h**

H

Rom	8:39	nor **h** nor depth, nor any
Eph	3:18	and length and depth and **h**—
Rev	21:16	and **h** are equal.

HEIGHTS (*see* HEIGHT)

Ps	148: 1	Praise Him in the **h**!
Is	14:14	I will ascend above the **h** of

HEIR (*see* HEIRS)

Gen	15: 2	and the **h** of my house is
Gen	15: 3	born in my house is my **h**!"
Gen	15: 4	one shall not be your **h**,
Gen	21:10	bondwoman shall not be **h**
2Sa	14: 7	and we will destroy the **h**
Matt	21:38	themselves, 'This is the **h**.
Rom	4:13	that he would be the **h** of
Gal	4: 1	Now I say that the **h**,
Gal	4: 7	then an **h** of God through
Gal	4:30	shall not be **h** with
Heb	1: 2	whom He has appointed **h** of
Heb	11: 7	the world and became **h** of

HEIRS (*see* HEIR)

2Ki	11: 1	destroyed all the royal **h**.
Rom	4:14	who are of the law are **h**,
Rom	8:17	and if children, then **h**—
Rom	8:17	**h** of God and joint
Rom	8:17	and joint **h** with Christ,
Gal	3:29	and **h** according to the
Heb	11: 9	the **h** with him of the same
1Pe	3: 7	and as being **h** together of

HELD (*see* HOLD)

Ps	18:35	Your right hand has **h** me
Song	3: 4	I **h** him and would not let
Is	45: 1	whose right hand I have **h**—
Acts	5:34	a teacher of the law **h** in

HELL

Deut	32:22	shall burn to the lowest **h**;
Ps	139: 8	If I make my bed in **h**,
Prov	7:27	Her house is the way to **h**,
Is	14: 9	**H** from beneath is excited
Matt	5:22	shall be in danger of **h**
Matt	5:29	whole body to be cast into **h**.
Matt	10:28	both soul and body in **h**.
Matt	23:15	twice as much a son of **h** as
Jas	3: 6	and it is set on fire by **h**.
2Pe	2: 4	but cast them down to **h** and

HELMET

1Sa	17: 5	He had a bronze **h** on his
Is	59:17	And a **h** of salvation on His
Eph	6:17	And take the **h** of salvation,
1Th	5: 8	and as a **h** the hope of

HELP (*see* HELPED, HELPER, HELPFUL, HELPING, HELPS)

2Ch	25: 8	for God has power to **h** and
Job	6:13	Is my **h** not within me? And
Ps	3: 2	There is no **h** for him in
Ps	20: 2	May He send you **h** from the
Ps	22:11	For there is none to **h**.
Ps	22:19	hasten to **h** Me!

Ps	33:20	He is our **h** and our
Ps	38:22	Make haste to **h** me, O Lord,
Ps	40:17	You are my **h** and my
Ps	42: 5	yet praise Him For the **h**
Ps	42:11	The **h** of my countenance and
Ps	46: 1	A very present **h** in
Ps	46: 5	God shall **h** her, just at
Ps	60:11	For the **h** of man is
Ps	70: 5	O God! You are my **h** and my
Ps	94:17	the LORD had been my **h**,
Ps	115: 9	He is their **h** and their
Ps	121: 1	whence comes my **h**?
Ps	121: 2	My **h** comes from the LORD,
Ps	124: 8	Our **h** is in the name of the
Ps	146: 5	the God of Jacob for his **h**,
Eccl	4:10	For he has no one to **h**
Is	30: 7	For the Egyptians shall **h** in
Is	31: 1	who go down to Egypt for **h**,
Is	41:13	you, 'Fear not, I will **h** you
Is	50: 7	For the Lord God will **h** Me
Is	63: 5	but there was no one to **h**,
Jer	37: 7	army which has come up to **h**
Lam	1: 7	With no one to **h** her, The
Lam	4:17	Watching vainly for our **h**;
Dan	11:34	be aided with a little **h**;
Mark	9:24	**h** my unbelief!"
Luke	5: 7	the other boat to come and **h**
Acts	16: 9	over to Macedonia and **h** us.
Acts	26:22	having obtained **h** from God,
Phil	4: 3	**h** these women who labored
Heb	4:16	mercy and find grace to **h**

HELPED (*see* HELP)

1Sa	7:12	Thus far the LORD has **h**
Neh	8: 7	**h** the people to understand
Is	49: 8	day of salvation I have **h**
Luke	1:54	He has **h** His servant Israel,

HELPER (*see* HELP)

Gen	2:18	I will make him a **h**
John	14:16	He will give you another **H**,
John	16: 7	the **H** will not come to you;
Heb	13: 6	"The LORD is my **h**;

HELPFUL (*see* HELP)

1Co	6:12	me, but all things are not **h**.
1Co	10:23	me, but not all things are **h**;

HELPING (*see* HELP)

Ps	22: 1	are You so far from **h** Me,

HELPS (*see* HELP)

Rom	8:26	Likewise the Spirit also **h** in

HEM (*see* BORDER)

Matt	9:20	behind and touched the **h** of
Matt	14:36	they might only touch the **h**

HEN

Matt	23:37	as a **h** gathers her chicks

HENCEFORTH†

Luke	1:48	**h** all generations will call

HERB *(see* HERBS*)*

Gen	1:11	the **h** that yields seed,
Gen	1:30	have given every green **h**
Gen	2: 5	the earth and before any **h**
Gen	3:18	And you shall eat the **h** of
Ex	9:25	and the hail struck every **h**
Ps	37: 2	And wither as the green **h**.

HERBS *(see* HERB*)*

Gen	9: 3	things, even as the green **h**.
Num	9:11	bread and bitter **h**.
Prov	15:17	Better is a dinner of **h**
Matt	13:32	it is greater than the **h**
Mark	4:32	becomes greater than all **h**,

HERD *(see* HERDS, HERDSMEN*)*

Gen	18: 7	And Abraham ran to the **h**,
2Sa	17:29	sheep and cheese of the **h**,
Hab	3:17	And there be no **h** in the
Matt	8:31	us to go away into the **h** of
Mark	5:13	and the **h** ran violently down

HERDS *(see* HERD*)*

Gen	13: 5	had flocks and **h** and tents.
Ex	12:32	take your flocks and your **h**,
Deut	12: 6	and the firstborn of your **h**
Joel	1:18	the animals groan! The **h**

HERDSMEN

Gen	13: 7	was strife between the **h** of
Gen	13: 7	Abram's livestock and the **h**
Gen	26:20	quarreled with Isaac's **h**,

HERESIES†

Gal	5:20	ambitions, dissensions, **h**,
2Pe	2: 1	bring in destructive **h**,

HERITAGE

Ex	6: 8	will give it to you as a **h**:
Job	27:13	And the **h** of oppressors,
Ps	94: 5	O LORD, And afflict Your **h**.
Ps	111: 6	In giving them the **h** of the
Ps	119:111	I have taken as a **h** forever,
Ps	127: 3	children are a **h** from the
Eccl	2:21	yet he must leave his **h** to a
Jer	2: 7	My land And made My **h** an
Jer	50:11	You destroyers of My **h**,
Joel	3: 2	My **h** Israel, Whom they have

HERMON

Deut	3: 8	the River Arnon to Mount **H**
Ps	133: 3	It is like the dew of **H**,

HEROD *(see* HERODIANS*)*

Matt	2: 1	of Judea in the days of **H**
Matt	2:12	they should not return to **H**,
Matt	2:13	for **H** will seek the young
Matt	2:15	there until the death of **H**,
Matt	14: 3	For **H** had laid hold of John
Luke	3: 1	**H** being tetrarch of Galilee,

HERODIANS *(see* HEROD*)*

Mark	12:13	of the Pharisees and the **H**,

HERODIAS

Matt	14: 6	the daughter of **H** danced

HEWN

2Ki	22: 6	and to buy timber and **h** stone
Prov	9: 1	She has **h** out her seven
Is	51: 1	rock from which you were **h**,
Matt	27:60	his new tomb which he had **h**

HEZEKIAH

2Ki	18: 1	that **H** the son of Ahaz,
2Ki	19:15	Then **H** prayed before the
2Ki	20: 1	In those days **H** was sick and
2Ki	20:20	the rest of the acts of **H**—
2Ki	20:21	So **H** rested with his fathers.
2Ki	21: 3	the high places which **H** his
1Ch	3:13	**H** his son, Manasseh his son,
2Ch	30:22	And **H** gave encouragement to
2Ch	31: 9	Then **H** questioned the priests
2Ch	32: 2	And when **H** saw that
2Ch	32:26	Then **H** humbled himself for
2Ch	32:27	**H** had very great riches and
Prov	25: 1	Solomon which the men of **H**
Is	1: 1	Uzziah, Jotham, Ahaz, and **H**,
Hos	1: 1	Uzziah, Jotham, Ahaz, and **H**,
Mic	1: 1	days of Jotham, Ahaz, and **H**,
Zeph	1: 1	son of Amariah, the son of **H**,
Matt	1: 9	begot Ahaz, and Ahaz begot **H**.

HID *(see* HIDE*)*

Gen	3: 8	and Adam and his wife **h**
Ex	2: 2	she **h** him three months.
Ex	3: 6	And Moses **h** his face, for
1Sa	3:18	and **h** nothing from him. And
2Ch	22:11	**h** him from Athaliah so that
Is	53: 3	with grief. And we **h**,
Jer	13: 5	So I went and **h** it by the
Matt	13:33	which a woman took and **h** in
Matt	13:44	which a man found and **h**;
Matt	25:25	and went and **h** your talent

HIDDEN *(see* HIDE*)*

Gen	4:14	I shall be **h** from Your face;
2Sa	18:13	For there is nothing **h** from
Job	3:21	search for it more than **h**
Ps	19: 6	And there is nothing **h** from
Ps	22:24	Nor has He **h** His face from
Ps	32: 5	my iniquity I have not **h**.
Ps	51: 6	And in the **h** part You will
Ps	69: 5	And my sins are not **h** from
Ps	119:11	Your word I have **h** in my
Ps	139:15	My frame was not **h** from You,
Prov	2: 4	search for her as for **h**
Matt	5:14	is set on a hill cannot be **h**.
Matt	10:26	and **h** that will not be
Matt	11:25	that You have **h** these things
Matt	13:44	of heaven is like treasure **h**
Mark	7:24	it, but He could not be **h**.
Luke	19:42	peace! But now they are **h**
1Co	2: 7	the **h** wisdom which God
1Co	4: 5	both bring to light the **h**
Eph	3: 9	of the ages has been **h** in
Col	1:26	the mystery which has been **h**

Col	2: 3	in whom are **h** all the
Col	3: 3	and your life is **h** with
Heb	4:13	And there is no creature **h**
Heb	11:23	was **h** three months by his
1Pe	3: 4	rather let it be the the **h**
Rev	2:17	I will give some of the **h**

HIDE (*see* HID, HIDDEN, HIDES, HIDING)

Gen	18:17	Shall I **h** from Abraham what I
Ex	2: 3	when she could no longer **h**
Lev	4:11	But the bull's **h** and all its
Deut	31:17	I will **h** My face from them,
Ps	17: 8	**H** me under the shadow of
Ps	27: 5	time of trouble He shall **h**
Ps	27: 5	His tabernacle He shall **h**
Ps	139:12	the darkness shall not **h**

HIDES (*see* HIDE)

Job	42: 3	Who is this who **h** counsel

HIDING (*see* HIDE)

Ps	119:114	You are my **h** place and my

HIGH (*see* HIGHER, HIGHEST, HIGHLY, LOUD)

Gen	7:17	and it rose **h** above the
Gen	7:19	and all the **h** hills under
Gen	14:18	the priest of God Most **H.**
Lev	21:10	He who is the **h** priest
Lev	26:30	I will destroy your **h** places,
Num	35:28	until the death of the **h**
Deut	32: 8	When the Most **H** divided
2Sa	22:14	And the Most **H** uttered His
1Ki	11: 7	Then Solomon built a **h** place
2Ki	23:15	and the **h** place which
1Ch	17:17	to the rank of a man of **h**
2Ch	31: 1	and threw down the **h** places
2Ch	33: 3	For he rebuilt the **h** places
2Ch	33:17	still sacrificed on the **h**
Esth	7: 9	The gallows, fifty cubits **h,**
Job	16:19	And my evidence is on **h.**
Ps	7:17	the name of the LORD Most **H.**
Ps	9: 2	to Your name, O Most **H.**
Ps	18:13	And the Most **H** uttered His
Ps	18:33	And sets me on my **h** places.
Ps	21: 7	the mercy of the Most **H** he
Ps	27: 5	He shall set me **h** upon a
Ps	46: 4	the tabernacle of the Most **H.**
Ps	47: 2	For the LORD Most **H** is
Ps	49: 2	Both low and **h,**
Ps	57: 2	will cry out to God Most **H,**
Ps	62: 9	Men of **h** degree are a lie;
Ps	68:18	You have ascended on **h,**
Ps	75: 5	not lift up your horn on **h;**
Ps	77:10	the right hand of the Most **H.**
Ps	82: 6	are children of the Most **H.**
Ps	91: 1	secret place of the Most **H**
Ps	92: 1	to Your name, O Most **H;**
Ps	103:11	For as the heavens are **h**
Ps	107:11	the counsel of the Most **H,**
Ps	107:41	Yet He sets the poor on **h,**
Ps	139: 6	wonderful for me; It is **h,**
Is	6: 1	**h** and lifted up. and the
Is	14:14	I will be like the Most **H.**
Is	52:13	and extolled and be very **h.**

Is	57:15	For thus says the **H** and
Is	57:15	I dwell in the **h** and holy
Dan	3:26	servants of the Most **H** God,
Dan	4:24	is the decree of the Most **H,**
Dan	4:25	you know that the Most **H**
Dan	4:34	and I blessed the Most **H** and
Dan	7:22	of the saints of the Most **H,**
Dan	8: 3	and the two horns were **h;**
Mic	6: 6	bow myself before the **H** God?
Matt	4: 8	Him up on an exceedingly **h**
Matt	17: 1	led them up on a **h** mountain
Mark	5: 7	Son of the Most **H** God? I
Luke	1:78	the Dayspring from on **h** has
Luke	3: 2	Annas and Caiaphas were **h**
Luke	6:35	will be sons of the Most **H.**
Luke	8:28	Son of the Most **H** God? I beg
Luke	24:49	endued with power from on **h.**
Acts	7:48	the Most **H** does not dwell in
Acts	16:17	the servants of the Most **H**
Eph	4: 8	He ascended on **h,**
Heb	1: 3	hand of the Majesty on **h,**
Heb	2:17	be a merciful and faithful **H**
Heb	3: 1	consider the Apostle and **H**
Heb	4:14	then that we have a great **H**
Heb	6:20	having become **H** Priest
Heb	7: 1	priest of the Most **H** God,
Heb	9:11	But Christ came as **H** Priest

HIGHER (*see* HIGH)

Ps	61: 2	me to the rock that is **h**
Is	55: 9	For as the heavens are **h**
Is	55: 9	So are My ways **h** than your
Luke	14:10	say to you, 'Friend, go up **h.**
Heb	7:26	and has become **h** than the

HIGHEST (*see* HIGH)

Matt	21: 9	LORD!' Hosanna in the **h**!
Luke	1:32	be called the Son of the **H;**
Luke	1:35	and the power of the **H** will
Luke	2:14	"Glory to God in the **h,**
Luke	19:38	in heaven and glory in the **h**!

HIGHLY† (*see* HIGH)

1Sa	18:30	so that his name became **h**
1Ch	14: 2	for his kingdom was **h**
Luke	1:28	**h** favored one, the Lord is
Luke	16:15	For what is **h** esteemed among
Acts	5:13	the people esteemed them **h.**
Rom	12: 3	to think of himself more **h**
Phil	2: 9	Therefore God also has **h**
1Th	5:13	and to esteem them very **h** in

HIGHWAY (*see* HIGHWAYS)

Is	19:23	that day there will be a **h**
Is	40: 3	straight in the desert A **h**

HIGHWAYS (*see* HIGHWAY)

Matt	22: 9	Therefore go into the **h,** and

HILL (*see* HILLS)

1Ki	14:23	images on every high **h** and
Ps	2: 6	set My King On My holy **h**
Ps	15: 1	may dwell in Your holy **h**?
Ps	24: 3	Who may ascend into the **h** of

Is	5: 1	On a very fruitful **h**.
Matt	5:14	A city that is set on a **h**

HILLS (see HILL)

Gen	7:19	and all the high **h** under the
Ps	50:10	the cattle on a thousand **h**.
Ps	114: 4	The little **h** like lambs.
Ps	121: 1	lift up my eyes to the **h**—
Prov	8:25	were settled, Before the **h**,
Is	2: 2	shall be exalted above the **h**;
Is	55:12	The mountains and the **h**
Jer	4:24	And all the **h** moved back
Jer	17: 2	green trees on the high **h**.
Jer	26:18	the temple Like the bare **h**
Hos	10: 8	"Cover us!" And to the **h**,
Mic	4: 1	shall be exalted above the **h**;
Nah	1: 5	The **h** melt, And the earth
Zeph	1:10	a loud crashing from the **h**.
Luke	23:30	on us!" and to the **h**,

HINDER (see HINDERED, HINDERS)

Gen	24:56	Do not **h** me, since the LORD
Job	9:12	who can **h** Him? Who can say

HINDERED (see HINDER)

Rom	1:13	to come to you (but was **h**
Gal	5: 7	Who **h** you from obeying the
1Th	2:18	but Satan **h** us.
1Pe	3: 7	your prayers may not be **h**.

HINDERS (see HINDER)

Acts	8:36	What **h** me from being

HINNOM

Josh	15: 8	the Valley of the Son of H
Neh	11:30	Beersheba to the Valley of H.

HIP

Gen	32:25	and the socket of Jacob's **h**
Judg	15: 8	So he attacked them **h** and

HIRED (see HIRELING)

Gen	30:16	for I have surely **h** you with
Ex	12:45	A sojourner and a **h** servant
Deut	15.10	he has been worth a double **h**
1Sa	2: 5	who were full have **h**
2Ch	24:12	and they **h** masons and
Neh	13: 2	but **h** Balaam against them to
Job	7: 1	also like the days of a **h**
Is	7:20	the Lord will shave with a **h**
Hos	8: 9	Ephraim has **h** lovers.
Matt	20: 7	Because no one **h** us.' He said
Matt	20: 9	when those came who were **h**
Mark	1:20	in the boat with the **h**
Luke	15:19	Make me like one of your **h**

HIRELING (see HIRED)

John	10:13	The **h** flees because he is a

HISTORY

Gen	2: 4	This is the **h** of the

HITTITE (see HITTITES)

Gen	49:29	in the field of Ephron the **H**,

2Sa	11: 3	the wife of Uriah the **H**?
Ezek	16: 3	Amorite and your mother a **H**.

HITTITES (see HITTITE)

Ex	3: 8	of the Canaanites and the **H**

HIVITES

Josh	3:10	and the Hittites and the **H**

HOLD (see HELD, HOLDING, HOLDS)

Gen	19:16	the men took **h** of his hand,
Ex	5: 1	that they may **h** a feast to
Ex	20: 7	for the LORD will not **h**
Deut	5:11	for the LORD will not **h**
Deut	10:20	and to Him you shall **h** fast,
Judg	16: 3	took **h** of the doors of the
Judg	16:29	And Samson took **h** of the two
1Ki	2: 9	do not **h** him guiltless, for
1Ch	13: 9	Uzza put out his hand to **h**
Job	2: 9	Do you still **h** fast to your
Job	6:24	and I will **h** my tongue;
Job	9:28	I know that You will not **h**
Job	21: 6	And trembling takes **h** of my
Job	27: 6	My righteousness I **h** fast,
Ps	2: 4	The LORD shall **h** them in
Ps	73:23	You **h** me by my right hand.
Ps	94:18	O LORD, will **h** me up.
Ps	116: 3	the pangs of Sheol laid **h**
Ps	119:53	Indignation has taken **h** of
Ps	139:10	Your right hand shall **h** me.
Prov	3:18	of life to those who take **h**
Prov	4:13	Take firm **h** of instruction,
Prov	5: 5	Her steps lay **h** of hell.
Prov	24:11	And **h** back those stumbling
Is	4: 1	seven women shall take **h** of
Jer	2:13	broken cisterns that can **h** no
1Co	15: 2	if you **h** fast that word
Phil	3:12	that I may lay **h** of that for
Phil	3:12	Jesus has also laid **h** of me.
1Th	5:21	**h** fast what is good.
2Th	2:15	stand fast and **h** the
1Ti	6:12	lay **h** on eternal life, to
2Ti	1:13	**H** fast the pattern of sound
Heb	4:14	let us **h** fast our

HOLDING (see HOLD)

Jer	6:11	I am weary of **h** it in.
Phil	2:16	**h** fast the word of life, so
Col	2:19	and not **h** fast to the Head,
1Ti	3: 9	**h** the mystery of the faith
Tit	1: 9	**h** fast the faithful word as

HOLDS (see HOLD)

Job	2: 3	And still he **h** fast to his

HOLES

Matt	8:20	Foxes have **h** and birds of the

HOLIEST (see HOLY)

Heb	9: 3	which is called the **H** of
Heb	10:19	boldness to enter the **H** by

HOLINESS (see HOLY)

Ex	28:36	**H** TO THE LORD.

H

1Ch	16:29	LORD in the beauty of **h**!
Ps	89:35	Once I have sworn by My **h**;
Ps	93: 5	**H** adorns Your house, O
Is	35: 8	be called the Highway of **H**.
Zech	14:20	**H** TO THE LORD" shall be
Luke	1:75	In **h** and righteousness
Rom	1: 4	according to the Spirit of **h**,
2Co	7: 1	perfecting **h** in the fear of
Eph	4:24	in true righteousness and **h**.
1Ti	2:15	in faith, love, and **h**,
Heb	12:10	may be partakers of His **h**.

HOLLOW

Is	40:12	the waters in the **h** of His

HOLY (*see* HOLIEST, HOLINESS, SPIRIT, UNHOLY)

Ex	3: 5	place where you stand is **h**
Ex	16:23	a **h** Sabbath to the LORD.
Ex	19: 6	a kingdom of priests and a **h**
Ex	20: 8	Sabbath day, to keep it **h**.
Ex	22:31	And you shall be **h** men to
Ex	29:37	the altar shall be most **h**.
Ex	31:15	**h** to the LORD. Whoever does
Ex	35: 2	the seventh day shall be a **h**
Lev	10:10	may distinguish between **h**
Lev	11:44	shall be holy; for I am **h**.
Lev	16: 2	at just any time into the **H**
Lev	16: 3	Aaron shall come into the **H**
Lev	16:17	to make atonement in the **H**
Lev	21: 8	who sanctify you, am **h**.
Lev	22:15	shall not profane the **h**
Lev	27:14	his house to be **h** to the
Num	4:15	they shall not touch any **h**
Num	4:19	they approach the most **h**
Num	16: 5	who is His and who is **h**,
Num	31: 6	with the **h** articles and the
Num	35:25	who was anointed with the **h**
Deut	5:12	Sabbath day, to keep it **h**,
Deut	7: 6	For you are a **h** people to
Deut	26:13	I have removed the **h** tithe
Deut	26:15	Look down from Your **h**
Josh	5:15	place where you stand is **h**.
Josh	24:19	for He is a **h** God. He is a
1Sa	2: 2	No one is **h** like the LORD,
1Sa	21: 6	So the priest gave him **h**
1Ki	7:50	the inner room (the Most **H**
1Ki	8: 4	and all the **h** furnishings
2Ki	4: 9	I know that this is a **h** man
2Ki	19:22	Against the **H** One of
1Ch	16:10	Glory in His **h** name; Let
1Ch	29: 3	I have prepared for the **H**
2Ch	23: 6	may go in, for they are **h**;
2Ch	30:27	prayer came up to His **h**
2Ch	35: 3	Put the **h** ark in the house
Ezra	9: 2	sons, so that the **h** seed is
Neh	8: 9	This day is **h** to the LORD
Neh	9:14	made known to them Your **h**
Neh	10:31	or on a **h** day; and we would
Neh	11: 1	the **h** city, and nine-tenths
Ps	2: 6	My King On My **h** hill of Zion
Ps	3: 4	He heard me from His **h** hill.
Ps	11: 4	The LORD is in His **h**
Ps	15: 1	Who may dwell in Your **h**

Ps	16:10	Nor will You allow Your **H**
Ps	24: 3	Or who may stand in His **h**
Ps	51:11	And do not take Your **H**
Ps	68: 5	Is God in His **h**
Ps	103: 1	bless His **h** name!
Ps	111: 9	**H** and awesome is His name.
Prov	9:10	And the knowledge of the **H**
Prov	30: 3	have knowledge of the **H** One.
Is	1: 4	provoked to anger The **H**
Is	6: 3	and said: "Holy, **h**,
Is	6:13	So the **h** seed shall be
Is	10:17	And his **H** One for a flame;
Is	11: 9	hurt nor destroy in all My **h**
Is	12: 6	For great is the **H** One of
Is	52:10	LORD has made bare His **h**
Is	57:15	eternity, whose name is **H**:
Is	57:15	I dwell in the high and **h**
Is	63:10	rebelled and grieved His **H**
Is	63:11	Where is He who put His **H**
Dan	4:18	for the Spirit of the **H** God
Dan	9:24	be moved against the **h**
Hos	11: 9	my **H** One? We shall not die.
Hab	2:20	as His inheritance in the **H**
Matt	1:18	found with child of the **H**
Matt	3:11	will baptize you with the **H**
Matt	4: 5	took Him up into the **h** city,
Matt	12:32	speaks against the **H** Spirit,
Matt	28:19	and of the Son and of the **H**
Mark	1:24	the **H** One of God!"
Mark	13:11	but the **H** Spirit.
Luke	1:15	also be filled with the **H**
Luke	1:35	The **H** Spirit will come upon
Luke	1:35	that **H** One who is to be born
Luke	3:16	will baptize you with the **H**
Luke	3:22	And the **H** Spirit descended in
Luke	4: 1	being filled with the **H**
John	1:33	He who baptizes with the **H**
John	7:39	for the **H** Spirit was not yet
John	14:26	the **H** Spirit, whom the
John	17:11	**H** Father, keep through Your
John	20:22	Receive the **H** Spirit.
Acts	1: 2	after He through the **H**
Acts	1: 5	shall be baptized with the **H**
Acts	1: 8	receive power when the **H**
Acts	2: 4	were all filled with the **H**
Acts	2:33	Father the promise of the **H**
Acts	2:38	receive the gift of the **H**
Acts	3:14	But you denied the **H** One and
Acts	5: 3	your heart to lie to the **H**
Acts	6: 3	full of the **H** Spirit and
Acts	7:33	where you stand is **h**
Acts	7:51	You always resist the **H**
Acts	8:15	they might receive the **H**
Acts	9:17	and be filled with the **H**
Acts	11:16	shall be baptized with the **H**
Acts	13:35	will not allow Your **H**
Acts	13:52	with joy and with the **H**
Acts	15:28	For it seemed good to the **H**
Acts	19: 2	heard whether there is a **H**
Rom	5: 5	out in our hearts by the **H**
Rom	7:12	Therefore the law is **h**,
Rom	7:12	and the commandment **h** and
Rom	9: 1	bearing me witness in the **H**
Rom	12: 1	bodies a living sacrifice, **h**,

Rom	14:17	and peace and joy in the **H**
Rom	15:13	hope by the power of the **H**
Rom	15:16	sanctified by the **H** Spirit.
Rom	16:16	Greet one another with a **h**
1Co	3:17	For the temple of God is **h**,
1Co	6:19	body is the temple of the **H**
1Co	7:14	unclean, but now they are **h**.
1Co	12: 3	is Lord except by the **H**
2Co	13:14	and the communion of the **H**
Eph	1:13	you were sealed with the **H**
Eph	2:21	grows into a **h** temple in the
Eph	4:30	And do not grieve the **H**
1Th	4: 8	who has also given us His **H**
1Ti	2: 8	lifting up **h** hands, without
2Ti	1:14	keep by the **H** Spirit who
Heb	6: 4	become partakers of the **H**
Heb	9:12	blood He entered the Most **H**
Heb	9:25	priest enters the Most **H**
1Pe	1:15	as He who called you is **h**,
1Pe	1:16	"Be holy, for I am **h**.
1Pe	2: 5	a **h** priesthood, to offer up
1Pe	2: 9	a **h** nation, His own special
2Pe	1:21	but **h** men of God spoke as
2Pe	1:21	they were moved by the **H**
1Jn	2:20	an anointing from the **H** One,
1Jn	5: 7	and the **H** Spirit; and these
Jude	20	up on your most **h** faith,
Jude	20	praying in the **H** Spirit,
Rev	3: 7	things says He who is **h**,
Rev	4: 8	saying: "Holy, holy, **h**,
Rev	6:10	**h** and true, until You judge
Rev	11: 2	And they will tread the **h**
Rev	14:10	in the presence of the **h**
Rev	15: 4	name? For You alone are **h**.
Rev	18:20	and you **h** apostles and
Rev	20: 6	Blessed and **h** is he who has
Rev	21:10	the **h** Jerusalem, descending
Rev	22:11	righteous still; he who is **h**,
Rev	22:11	let him be **h** still."

HOME (*see* HABITATION, HOMELESS, HOMEMAKERS)

Prov	7:19	For my husband is not at **h**;
Eccl	12: 5	man goes to his eternal **h**,
Matt	8: 6	my servant is lying at **h**
John	14:23	come to him and make Our **h**
John	19:27	took her to his own **h**.
1Co	14:35	ask their own husbands at **h**;

HOMELESS† (*see* HOME)

1Co	4:11	clothed, and beaten, and **h**.

HOMEMAKERS† (*see* HOME)

Tit	2: 5	to be discreet, chaste, **h**,

HOMOSEXUALS†

1Co	6: 9	nor adulterers, nor **h**,

HONEST (*see* JUST)

Gen	42:11	we are **h** men; your
Lev	19:36	You shall have **h** scales,

HONEY (*see* HONEYCOMB)

Ex	3: 8	land flowing with milk and **h**,

Ex	16:31	like wafers made with **h**.
Judg	14:18	"What is sweeter than **h**?
Ps	19:10	Sweeter also than **h** and the
Ps	81:16	And with **h** from the rock I
Is	7:15	Curds and **h** He shall eat,
Ezek	3: 3	it was in my mouth like **h**
Matt	3: 4	food was locusts and wild **h**.

HONEYCOMB (*see* HONEY)

Ps	19:10	also than honey and the **h**.
Luke	24:42	of a broiled fish and some **h**.

HONOR (*see* HONORABLE, HONORED, HONORS)

Ex	20:12	**H** your father and your
1Ki	3:13	not asked: both riches and **h**,
1Ch	16:27	**H** and majesty are before
Ps	8: 5	crowned him with glory and **h**.
Ps	21: 5	**H** and majesty You have
Ps	104: 1	You are clothed with **h** and
Prov	3: 9	**H** the LORD with your
Prov	31:25	Strength and **h** are her
Is	29:13	with their mouths And **h** Me
Is	61: 7	you shall have double **h**,
Matt	13:57	A prophet is not without **h**
Matt	15: 4	**H** your father and your
Matt	15: 8	And **h** Me with their
John	4:44	that a prophet has no **h** in
John	8:49	but I **h** My Father, and you
John	8:54	If I **h** Myself, My honor is
John	12:26	Me, him My Father will **h**.
Rom	9:21	to make one vessel for **h**
Rom	12:10	in **h** giving preference to
Rom	13: 7	whom fear, honor to whom **h**.
1Co	12:23	on these we bestow greater **h**;
1Ti	1:17	be **h** and glory forever and
1Ti	5:17	counted worthy of double **h**,
2Ti	2:21	he will be a vessel for **h**,
Heb	2: 7	him with glory and **h**,
1Pe	1: 7	may be found to praise, **h**,
1Pe	2:17	**H** all people. Love the
1Pe	2:17	Fear God. **H** the king.
1Pe	3: 7	giving **h** to the wife, as to
Rev	19: 1	Salvation and glory and **h**

HONORABLE (*see* HONOR)

Heb	13: 4	Marriage is **h** among all, and

HONORED (*see* HONOR)

Dan	4:34	Most High and praised and **h**
1Co	12:26	it; or if one member is **h**,

HONORS (*see* HONOR)

Mal	1: 6	A son **h** his father, And a
Mark	7: 6	This people **h** Me with
John	8:54	It is My Father who **h** Me, of

HOOKS

Is	2: 4	their spears into pruning **h**;
Joel	3:10	swords And your pruning **h**

HOPE (*see* HOPED, HOPES)

Ruth	1:12	If I should say I have **h**,
Job	14: 7	For there is **h** for a tree,
Job	17:15	Where then is my **h**?

Ps	16: 9	flesh also will rest in **h**.
Ps	31:24	All you who **h** in the LORD.
Ps	42: 5	**H** in God, for I shall yet
Ps	71: 5	For You are my **h**,
Ps	119:81	But I **h** in Your word.
Ps	119:166	I **h** for Your salvation, And
Ps	130: 7	**h** in the LORD; For with
Prov	13:12	**H** deferred makes the heart
Prov	19:18	your son while there is **h**,
Prov	26:12	There is more **h** for a
Jer	14: 8	O the **H** of Israel, his
Jer	29:11	to give you a future and a **h**.
Lam	3:21	my mind, Therefore I have **h**.
Hos	2:15	of Achor as a door of **h**;
Acts	16:19	masters saw that their **h** of
Acts	17:27	in the **h** that they might
Rom	4:18	who, contrary to **h**,
Rom	5: 2	and rejoice in **h** of the
Rom	5: 4	character; and character, **h**.
Rom	5: 5	Now **h** does not disappoint,
Rom	8:20	Him who subjected it in **h**;
Rom	8:24	but **h** that is seen is not
Rom	12:12	rejoicing in **h**,
Rom	15: 4	the Scriptures might have **h**.
Rom	15:12	the Gentiles shall **h**.
Rom	15:13	Now may the God of **h** fill you
1Co	9:10	who plows should plow in **h**,
1Co	13:13	And now abide faith, **h**,
1Co	15:19	in this life only we have **h**
1Co	16: 7	but I **h** to stay a while with
Gal	5: 5	eagerly wait for the **h** of
Eph	1:18	you may know what is the **h**
Eph	2:12	having no **h** and without God
Eph	4: 4	as you were called in one **h**
Col	1:23	not moved away from the **h**
Col	1:27	the **h** of glory.
1Th	2:19	For what is our **h**,
1Th	4:13	as others who have no **h**.
1Th	5: 8	and as a helmet the **h** of
1Ti	1: 1	the Lord Jesus Christ, our **h**,
Tit	1: 2	in **h** of eternal life which
Tit	2:13	looking for the blessed **h** and
Heb	3: 6	and the rejoicing of the **h**
Heb	6:19	This **h** we have as an anchor
Heb	7:19	bringing in of a better **h**,
Heb	10:23	the confession of our **h**
1Pe	1: 3	us again to a living **h**
1Pe	1:21	so that your faith and **h** are
1Pe	3:15	asks you a reason for the **h**
1Jn	3: 3	And everyone who has this **h**

HOPED (see HOPE)

| Heb | 11: 1 | is the substance of things **h** |

HOPES† (see HOPE)

| 1Co | 13: 7 | **h** all things, endures all |

HOREB (see SINAI)

| Ex | 33: 6 | their ornaments by Mount **H**. |
| Deut | 5: 2 | made a covenant with us in **H**. |

HORN (see HORNS)

| Josh | 6: 5 | long blast with the ram's **h**, |
| 1Sa | 2: 1 | My **h** is exalted in the |

1Sa	16: 1	Fill your **h** with oil, and
Ps	89:17	And in Your favor our **h** is
Ps	132:17	There I will make the **h** of
Dan	3: 5	you hear the sound of the **h**,
Dan	7: 8	and there was another **h**,
Dan	7:20	and the other **h** which came
Dan	8: 5	the goat had a notable **h**
Dan	8: 8	the large **h** was broken, and
Dan	8: 9	one of them came a little **h**
Luke	1:69	And has raised up a **h** of

HORNS (see HORN)

Gen	22:13	caught in a thicket by its **h**.
Ex	29:12	bull and put it on the **h**
Ex	30:10	make atonement upon its **h**
Josh	6: 4	seven trumpets of rams' **h**
1Ki	1:51	he has taken hold of the **h**
Ps	22:21	mouth And from the **h** of
Ezek	43:15	with four **h** extending upward
Dan	7: 7	before it, and it had ten **h**.
Dan	7:24	The ten **h** are ten kings
Dan	8: 3	was a ram which had two **h**,
Zech	1:18	and there were four **h**.
Rev	5: 6	having seven **h** and seven
Rev	9:13	a voice from the four **h** of
Rev	12: 3	having seven heads and ten **h**,
Rev	13: 1	and on his **h** ten crowns, and

HORSE (see HORSEMEN, HORSES)

Ex	15: 1	gloriously! The **h** and its
Zech	1: 8	a man riding on a red **h**,
Rev	6: 2	and behold, a white **h**.
Rev	19:19	Him who sat on the **h** and

HORSEMEN (see HORSE)

| Ex | 15:19 | with his chariots and his **h** |
| 2Ki | 2:12 | chariot of Israel and its **h**! |

HORSES (see HORSE)

Ex	14: 9	all the **h** and chariots of
Ex	14:23	of the sea, all Pharaoh's **h**,
Deut	17:16	he shall not multiply **h**
1Ki	10:28	Also Solomon had **h** imported
Is	31: 1	for help, And rely on **h**,
Is	31: 3	And their **h** are flesh, and
Jer	12: 5	how can you contend with **h**?
Amos	6:12	Do **h** run on rocks? Does
Hab	1: 8	Their **h** also are swifter
Zech	6: 2	first chariot were red **h**,
Rev	19:14	followed Him on white **h**.

HOSANNA

Matt	21: 9	**H** to the Son of David!
Matt	21: 9	name of the LORD!' **H**
Mark	11: 9	**H**! 'Blessed is He who

HOSEA

| Hos | 1: 1 | of the LORD that came to **H** |
| Rom | 9:25 | As He says also in **H**: |

HOSPITALITY

| Rom | 12:13 | of the saints, given to **h**. |

HOST (*see* HOSTS)

Gen	2: 1	and all the **h** of them, were
Deut	4:19	all the **h** of heaven, you
2Ki	17:16	and worshiped all the **h** of
2Ki	21: 5	built altars for all the **h**
Neh	9: 6	The **h** of heaven worships
Ps	33: 6	And all the **h** of them by
Is	40:26	Who brings out their **h** by
Dan	8:10	it cast down some of the **h**
Luke	2:13	multitude of the heavenly **h**

HOSTILITY†

Heb	12: 3	Him who endured such **h** from

HOSTS (*see* HOST)

1Sa	1: 3	sacrifice to the LORD of **h**
1Sa	4: 4	covenant of the LORD of **h**,
1Sa	15: 2	"Thus says the LORD of **h**:
1Sa	17:45	the name of the LORD of **h**,
2Sa	6: 2	by the Name, the LORD of H,
1Ki	19:10	for the LORD God of **h**,
Ps	24:10	of glory? The LORD of **h**,
Ps	46: 7	The LORD of **h** is with us;
Ps	48: 8	the city of the LORD of **h**,
Ps	80: 4	O LORD God of **h**,
Ps	80: 7	Restore us, O God of **h**;
Ps	84: 3	Your altars, O LORD of **h**,
Ps	103:21	the LORD, all you His **h**,
Ps	148: 2	Praise Him, all His **h**!
Is	1: 9	Unless the LORD of **h** Had
Is	5:24	the law of the LORD of **h**,
Is	6: 3	holy is the LORD of **h**;
Is	6: 5	the King, The LORD of **h**.
Is	13:13	the wrath of the LORD of **h**
Is	14:24	The LORD of **h** has sworn,
Zech	8: 3	Mountain of the LORD of **h**,
Zech	8:21	And seek the LORD of **h**.
Mal	2: 7	messenger of the LORD of **h**.
Eph	6:12	against spiritual **h** of

HOT

Ps	6: 1	Nor chasten me in Your **h**
Prov	6:28	Can one walk on **h** coals,
Dan	3:22	the furnace exceedingly **h**,
Luke	12:55	There will be **h** weather'; and
1Ti	4: 2	conscience seared with a **h**
Rev	3:15	you are neither cold nor **h**.

HOUR

Matt	8:13	was healed that same **h**.
Matt	20:12	men have worked only one **h**,
Matt	24:36	But of that day and **h** no one
Matt	24:42	for you do not know what **h**
Matt	25:13	neither the day nor the **h**
Matt	26:40	you not watch with Me one **h**?
Matt	26:45	the **h** is at hand, and the
Matt	27:45	sixth hour until the ninth **h**
Mark	13:11	is given you in that **h**,
Mark	14:35	the **h** might pass from Him.
Luke	1:10	praying outside at the **h** of
Luke	20:19	and the scribes that very **h**
Luke	24:33	So they rose up that very **h**
John	1:39	it was about the tenth **h**).

John	2: 4	My **h** has not yet come."
John	4:21	the **h** is coming when you
John	4:52	Yesterday at the seventh **h**
John	5:25	the **h** is coming, and now is,
John	12:27	save Me from this **h**'?
John	12:27	purpose I came to this **h**.
John	13: 1	when Jesus knew that His **h**
John	16:32	Indeed the **h** is coming, yes,
John	17: 1	the **h** has come. Glorify Your
John	19:27	mother!" And from that **h**
Acts	2:15	it is only the third **h** of
Acts	3: 1	to the temple at the **h** of
Acts	3: 1	hour of prayer, the ninth **h**.
Acts	10: 9	to pray, about the sixth **h**
Acts	23:23	to Caesarea at the third **h**
1Co	4:11	To the present **h** we both
1Co	15:30	we stand in jeopardy every **h**?
1Jn	2:18	children, it is the last **h**;
Rev	3: 3	you will not know what **h** I
Rev	3:10	will keep you from the **h** of
Rev	14: 7	for the **h** of His judgment
Rev	18:10	mighty city! For in one **h**

HOUSE (*see* HOUSEHOLD, HOUSES, HOUSETOP)

Gen	12: 1	And from your father's **h**,
Gen	14:14	who were born in his own **h**,
Gen	15: 2	and the heir of my **h** is
Gen	15: 3	indeed one born in my **h** is
Gen	17:12	he who is born in your **h** or
Gen	24: 7	took me from my father's **h**
Gen	28:22	as a pillar shall be God's **h**,
Ex	12:46	of the flesh outside the **h**,
Ex	13: 3	out of the **h** of bondage; for
Ex	16:31	And the **h** of Israel called
Ex	19: 3	you shall say to the **h**
Ex	20: 2	out of the **h** of bondage.
Ex	20:17	not covet your neighbor's **h**;
Ex	23:19	you shall bring into the **h**
Lev	14:35	is some plague in the **h**,
Lev	14:36	that they empty the **h**,
Lev	14:39	spread on the walls of the **h**,
Lev	14:47	he who lies down in the **h**
Lev	14:47	and he who eats in the **h**
Lev	14:48	shall pronounce the **h** clean,
Lev	14:53	and make atonement for the **h**,
Lev	22:13	returned to her father's **h**
Num	1: 4	the head of his father's **h**.
Num	1:20	by their fathers' **h**,
Num	3:30	leader of the fathers' **h** of
Num	12: 7	He is faithful in all My **h**.
Num	30: 3	while in her father's **h** in
Num	30:10	she vowed in her husband's **h**,
Deut	5: 6	out of the **h** of bondage.
Deut	5:21	not desire your neighbor's **h**,
Deut	6: 7	them when you sit in your **h**,
Deut	6: 9	on the doorposts of your **h**
Deut	20: 5	who has built a new **h** and
Josh	2:15	for her **h** was on the city
Josh	24:15	But as for me and my **h**,
Judg	6:15	the least in my father's **h**.
Ruth	1: 8	each to her mother's **h**.
Ruth	1: 9	each in the **h** of her
2Sa	7: 2	I dwell in a **h** of cedar, but
2Sa	7: 5	Would you build a **h** for Me to

H

2Sa	7: 7	have you not built Me a **h**
2Sa	7:13	He shall build a **h** for My
2Sa	7:16	And your **h** and your kingdom
2Sa	7:27	'I will build you a **h**.
2Sa	7:29	it please You to bless the **h**
2Sa	11: 2	on the roof of the king's **h**.
1Ki	3: 1	finished building his own **h**,
1Ki	3:17	and I dwell in the same **h**;
1Ki	3:17	while she was in the **h**.
1Ki	3:18	the two of us in the **h**.
1Ki	5: 3	David could not build a **h**
1Ki	5: 5	he shall build the **h** for My
1Ki	6:37	the foundation of the **h** of
1Ki	6:38	the **h** was finished in all
1Ki	7: 1	years to build his own **h**;
1Ki	14:17	to the threshold of the **h**,
1Ki	14:26	treasures of the king's **h**;
1Ki	15:29	that he killed all the **h** of
1Ki	16:18	the citadel of the king's **h**
1Ki	16:18	and burned the king's **h**
1Ki	18: 3	who was in charge of his **h**.
1Ki	21: 2	it is near, next to my **h**;
1Ki	21: 4	So Ahab went into his **h**
1Ki	22:39	the ivory **h** which he built
2Ki	4: 2	what do you have in the **h**?
2Ki	4: 2	has nothing in the **h** but a
2Ki	10: 5	who was in charge of the **h**,
2Ki	10:11	all who remained of the **h**
2Ki	11: 5	watch over the king's **h**,
2Ki	11:15	let her be killed in the **h**
2Ki	12:10	that was found in the **h** of
2Ki	12:11	who worked on the **h** of the
2Ki	12:12	repair the damage of the **h**
2Ki	12:14	and they repaired the **h** of
2Ki	12:20	and killed Joash in the **h** of
2Ki	15: 5	so he dwelt in an isolated **h**.
2Ki	20: 1	Set your **h** in order, for you
2Ki	20:15	have they seen in your **h**?
2Ki	20:15	seen all that is in my **h**;
2Ki	21:13	and the plummet of the **h** of
2Ki	21:18	in the garden of his own **h**,
2Ki	21:23	killed the king in his own **h**.
2Ki	22: 5	to those who are in the **h**
2Ki	22: 5	repair the damages of the **h**—
2Ki	22: 8	Book of the Law in the **h** of
2Ki	22: 9	that was found in the **h**,
2Ki	22: 9	who oversee the **h** of the
2Ki	23: 6	the wooden image from the **h**
2Ki	25: 9	He burned the **h** of the LORD
1Ch	6:48	of the tabernacle of the **h**
1Ch	7:23	tragedy had come upon his **h**.
1Ch	14: 1	carpenters, to build him a **h**.
1Ch	25: 6	for the music in the **h** of
1Ch	25: 6	for the service of the **h** of
1Ch	29: 3	have prepared for the holy **h**,
2Ch	3: 1	began to build the **h** of the
2Ch	5:14	of the LORD filled the **h**
2Ch	7: 5	the people dedicated the **h**
2Ch	7:11	Thus Solomon finished the **h**
2Ch	10:19	in rebellion against the **h**
2Ch	21:13	like the harlotry of the **h**
2Ch	22:12	hidden with them in the **h**
2Ch	23:14	Do not kill her in the **h** of
2Ch	24: 7	dedicated things of the **h**
2Ch	29:15	to cleanse the **h** of the
2Ch	31:10	from the **h** of Zadok,
2Ch	33:15	and the idol from the **h** of
2Ch	33:15	built in the mount of the **h**
2Ch	35: 3	Put the holy ark in the **h**
2Ch	36:14	and defiled the **h** of the
2Ch	36:23	me to build Him a **h** at
Ezra	1: 2	me to build Him a **h** at
Ezra	1: 3	and build the **h** of the LORD
Ezra	3: 8	to oversee the work of the **h**
Ezra	5:13	a decree to build this **h** of
Ezra	5:15	and let the **h** of God be
Ezra	6: 7	of the Jews build this **h** of
Ezra	6:17	at the dedication of this **h**
Ezra	7:27	to beautify the **h** of the
Ezra	9: 9	to repair the **h** of our God,
Ps	23: 6	And I will dwell in the **h**
Ps	27: 4	That I may dwell in the **h**
Ps	69: 9	Because zeal for Your **h** has
Ps	84: 4	those who dwell in Your **h**;
Ps	84:10	be a doorkeeper in the **h** of
Ps	93: 5	Holiness adorns Your **h**,
Ps	112: 3	riches will be in his **h**,
Ps	114: 1	The **h** of Jacob from a
Ps	115:10	O **h** of Aaron, trust in the
Ps	115:12	He will bless the **h** of
Ps	116:19	the courts of the LORD's **h**,
Ps	118: 3	Let the **h** of Aaron now say,
Ps	119:54	been my songs In the **h** of
Ps	122: 1	Let us go into the **h** of the
Ps	127: 1	the LORD builds the **h**,
Ps	132: 3	go into the chamber of my **h**,
Ps	134: 1	by night stand in the **h** of
Ps	135: 2	You who stand in the **h** of
Ps	135:19	O **h** of Israel! Bless the
Prov	2:18	For her **h** leads down to
Prov	5: 8	go near the door of her **h**,
Prov	6:31	all the substance of his **h**.
Prov	7: 6	For at the window of my **h**
Prov	7:27	Her **h** is the way to hell,
Prov	9: 1	Wisdom has built her **h**,
Prov	9:14	sits at the door of her **h**,
Prov	11:29	He who troubles his own **h**
Prov	12: 7	But the **h** of the righteous
Prov	14: 1	The wise woman builds her **h**,
Prov	14:11	The **h** of the wicked will be
Prov	17: 1	Than a **h** full of feasting
Prov	21: 9	Than in a **h** shared with a
Prov	24: 3	Through wisdom a **h** is built,
Prov	25:17	foot in your neighbor's **h**,
Prov	25:24	Than in a **h** shared with a
Prov	27:10	Nor go to your brother's **h**
Eccl	5: 1	when you go to the **h** of God;
Eccl	12: 3	when the keepers of the **h**
Song	3: 4	I had brought him to the **h**
Is	2: 2	mountain of the LORD's **h**
Is	2: 3	To the **h** of the God of
Is	5: 7	LORD of hosts is the **h** of
Is	5: 8	to those who join house to **h**;
Is	6: 4	and the **h** was filled with
Is	7: 2	And it was told to the **h** of
Is	7:17	people and your father's **h**—
Is	22:15	Shebna, who is over the **h**,
Is	22:22	The key of the **h** of David I

Is	38: 1	Set your **h** in order, for you
Is	42: 7	darkness from the prison **h**.
Is	46: 3	all the remnant of the **h** of
Is	48: 1	O **h** of Jacob, Who are
Is	56: 7	My house shall be called a **h**
Is	60: 7	And I will glorify the **h** of
Jer	7:10	stand before Me in this **h**
Jer	18: 2	go down to the potter's **h**,
Jer	31:31	a new covenant with the **h**
Jer	36:22	was sitting in the winter **h**
Ezek	2: 5	they are a rebellious **h**—
Ezek	18:31	O **h** of Israel?
Dan	1: 2	of the articles of the **h** of
Dan	1: 2	into the treasure **h** of his
Dan	2:17	Then Daniel went to his **h**,
Dan	5: 3	from the temple of the **h** of
Dan	5:23	the vessels of His **h** before
Amos	2: 8	of the condemned in the **h**
Amos	3:15	I will destroy the winter **h**
Amos	3:15	along with the summer **h**;
Amos	5: 3	have ten left to the **h** of
Amos	6: 1	To whom the **h** of Israel
Amos	7: 9	the sword against the **h** of
Amos	7:10	you in the midst of the **h**
Obad	18	But the **h** of Esau shall
Mic	4: 1	mountain of the LORD's **h**
Mic	4: 2	To the **h** of the God of
Hag	1: 2	the time that the LORD's **h**
Hag	1:14	came and worked on the **h** of
Zech	1:16	My **h** shall be built in
Zech	13: 6	I was wounded in the **h** of
Zech	14:20	The pots in the LORD's **h**
Mal	3:10	there may be food in My **h**,
Matt	2:11	they had come into the **h**,
Matt	5:15	to all who are in the **h**.
Matt	7:24	a wise man who built his **h**
Matt	7:25	blew and beat on that **h**;
Matt	7:26	foolish man who built his **h**
Matt	10: 6	to the lost sheep of the **h**
Matt	10:25	called the master of the **h**
Matt	12:29	one enter a strong man's **h**
Matt	12:29	then he will plunder his **h**.
Matt	21:13	My **h** shall be called a
Mark	3:25	And if a **h** is divided against
Mark	3:25	that **h** cannot stand.
Luke	2: 4	because he was of the **h** and
Luke	13:35	See! Your **h** is left to you
Luke	15: 8	light a lamp, sweep the **h**,
Luke	18:29	is no one who has left **h** or
Luke	19: 9	salvation has come to this **h**,
John	2:16	make My Father's house a **h**
John	2:17	Zeal for Your **h** has
John	8:35	does not abide in the **h**
John	11:20	Mary was sitting in the **h**.
John	12: 3	And the **h** was filled with
John	14: 2	In My Father's **h** are many
Acts	2: 2	and it filled the whole **h**
Acts	2:46	bread from house to **h**,
Acts	5:42	the temple, and in every **h**,
Acts	8: 3	the church, entering every **h**,
Acts	10: 6	whose **h** is by the sea. He
Acts	10:30	ninth hour I prayed in my **h**,
Acts	16:32	and to all who were in his **h**.
Acts	19:16	that they fled out of that **h**

Acts	20:20	publicly and from house to **h**,
Acts	28:30	years in his own rented **h**,
Rom	16: 5	church that is in their **h**.
1Co	16:19	church that is in their **h**.
2Co	5: 1	know that if our earthly **h**,
2Co	5: 1	a **h** not made with hands,
1Ti	3: 4	one who rules his own **h** well,
1Ti	3:15	to conduct yourself in the **h**
Heb	3: 2	was faithful in all His **h**.
Heb	3: 6	as a Son over His own **h**,
Heb	3: 6	whose **h** we are if we hold
Heb	8: 8	covenant with the **h** of
Heb	8: 8	Israel and with the **h**
Heb	10:21	a High Priest over the **h** of
1Pe	2: 5	being built up a spiritual **h**,
1Pe	4:17	judgment to begin at the **h**

HOUSEHOLD (*see* HOUSE, HOUSEHOLDER, HOUSEHOLDS)

Gen	7: 1	the ark, you and all your **h**,
Judg	18:14	**h** idols, a carved image, and
2Sa	17:23	Then he put his **h** in order,
Prov	31:15	And provides food for her **h**,
Prov	31:21	not afraid of snow for her **h**,
Matt	10:36	be those of his own **h**.
John	4:53	believed, and his whole **h**.
Acts	10: 2	feared God with all his **h**,
Acts	16:31	be saved, you and your **h**.
Gal	6:10	to those who are of the **h**
Eph	2:19	saints and members of the **h**
Phil	4:22	those who are of Caesar's **h**.
Heb	11: 7	ark for the saving of his **h**,

HOUSEHOLDER† (*see* HOUSEHOLD)

Matt	13:52	of heaven is like a **h** who

HOUSEHOLDS (*see* HOUSEHOLD)

Ex	1:21	that He provided **h** for them.
Tit	1:11	stopped, who subvert whole **h**,

HOUSES (*see* HOUSE)

Ex	6:14	heads of their fathers' **h**:
Ex	12: 7	and on the lintel of the **h**
Amos	3:15	The **h** of ivory shall
Hag	1: 4	to dwell in your paneled **h**,
Matt	11: 8	clothing are in kings' **h**.
Matt	23:14	For you devour widows' **h**,

HOUSETOP (*see* HOUSE, HOUSETOPS)

Prov	21: 9	to dwell in a corner of a **h**,
Matt	24:17	Let him who is on the **h** not
Acts	10: 9	Peter went up on the **h** to

HOUSETOPS (*see* HOUSETOP)

Luke	12: 3	will be proclaimed on the **h**.

HOVERING† (*see* HOVERS)

Gen	1: 2	And the Spirit of God was **h**

HOVERS† (*see* HOVERING)

Deut	32:11	**H** over its young,

HUMAN

Rom	6:19	I speak in **h** terms because
Heb	12: 9	we have had **h** fathers who

HUMBLE (see ABASE, HUMBLED, HUMBLES, HUMBLY)

Ex	10: 3	long will you refuse to **h**
Num	12: 3	the man Moses was very **h**,
Deut	8: 2	to **h** you and test you, to
2Ch	7:14	are called by My name will **h**
Job	22:29	Then He will save the **h**
Ps	9:12	not forget the cry of the **h**.
Ps	10:12	hand! Do not forget the **h**.
Ps	10:17	heard the desire of the **h**;
Ps	25: 9	And the **h** He teaches His
Ps	34: 2	The **h** shall hear of it
Ps	147: 6	The LORD lifts up the **h**;
Prov	3:34	But gives grace to the **h**.
Prov	16:19	Better to be of a **h** spirit
Is	57:15	revive the spirit of the **h**,
Ezek	21:26	humble, and **h** the exalted
Dan	10:12	and to **h** yourself before
Jas	4: 6	gives grace to the **h**.
Jas	4:10	**H** yourselves in the sight of
1Pe	5: 5	gives grace to the **h**.
1Pe	5: 6	Therefore **h** yourselves under

HUMBLED (see ABASED, HUMBLE)

Deut	8: 3	So He **h** you, allowed you to
Deut	21:14	because you have **h** her.
Deut	22:29	be his wife because he has **h**
2Ch	33:23	as his father Manasseh had **h**
Ps	35:13	I **h** myself with fasting;
Is	2:11	looks of man shall be **h**,
Dan	5:22	have not **h** your heart,
Matt	23:12	exalts himself will be **h**
Phil	2: 8	He **h** Himself and became

HUMBLES (see HUMBLE)

Matt	23:12	and he who **h** himself will be

HUMBLY (see HUMBLE)

Mic	6: 8	And to walk **h** with your

HUMILITY

Prov	15:33	And before honor is **h**.
Prov	22: 4	By **h** and the fear of the
Zeph	2: 3	Seek righteousness, seek **h**.
Acts	20:19	the Lord with all **h**,
Col	2:18	taking delight in false **h**
Col	3:12	tender mercies, kindness, **h**,
Tit	3: 2	showing all **h** to all men.
1Pe	5: 5	and be clothed with **h**,

HUNDRED (see HUNDREDFOLD)

Gen	5: 3	And Adam lived one **h** and
Gen	5:22	walked with God three **h**
Deut	34: 7	Moses was one **h** and twenty
1Ki	11: 3	And he had seven **h** wives,
1Ki	11: 3	and three **h** concubines; and
Matt	18:12	If a man has a **h** sheep, and
Matt	18:28	servants who owed him a **h**
Mark	4: 8	some sixty, and some a **h**.

Mark	4:20	some sixty, and some a **h**.
Luke	16: 6	A **h** measures of oil.' So he
John	19:39	about a **h** pounds.
Acts	7: 6	and oppress them four **h**
Acts	13:20	judges for about four **h** and
1Co	15: 6	He was seen by over five **h**
Rev	7: 4	One **h** and forty-four
Rev	11: 3	prophesy one thousand two **h**
Rev	21:17	one **h** and forty-four

HUNDREDFOLD (see HUNDRED)

Gen	26:12	reaped in the same year a **h**;
Matt	13: 8	and yielded a crop: some a **h**,
Matt	13:23	fruit and produces: some a **h**,
Mark	10:30	who shall not receive a **h** now

HUNG (see HANG)

Ex	40:21	**h** up the veil of the
Ex	40:33	and **h** up the screen of the
2Sa	21:12	where the Philistines had **h**
Neh	3: 1	they consecrated it and **h**
Ps	137: 2	We **h** our harps Upon the
Lam	5:12	Princes were **h** up by their
Matt	18: 6	him if a millstone were **h**

HUNGER (see HUNGRY)

Deut	8: 3	you, allowed you to **h**,
Deut	32:24	shall be wasted with **h**,
1Sa	2: 5	hungry have ceased to **h**.
Neh	9:15	from heaven for their **h**,
Ps	34:10	lions lack and suffer **h**;
Prov	19:15	an idle person will suffer **h**.
Is	49:10	They shall neither **h** nor
Lam	4: 9	Than those who die of **h**;
Mic	6:14	**H** shall be in your midst.
Matt	5: 6	Blessed are those who **h** and
John	6:35	comes to Me shall never **h**,
1Co	4:11	the present hour we both **h**
2Co	11:27	in **h** and thirst, in fastings
Rev	6: 8	to kill with sword, with **h**,

HUNGRY (see HUNGER)

1Sa	2: 5	And the **h** have ceased to
Job	22: 7	withheld bread from the **h**.
Ps	107: 5	**H** and thirsty, Their soul
Ps	107: 9	And fills the **h** soul with
Ps	146: 7	Who gives food to the **h**.
Prov	25:21	If your enemy is **h**,
Prov	27: 7	But to a **h** soul every
Is	29: 8	shall even be as when a **h**
Is	32: 6	To keep the **h** unsatisfied,
Is	58: 7	share your bread with the **h**,
Is	65:13	eat, But you shall be **h**;
Ezek	18: 7	has given his bread to the **h**
Matt	4: 2	nights, afterward He was **h**.
Matt	12: 1	And His disciples were **h**,
Matt	12: 3	what David did when he was **h**,
Matt	15:32	not want to send them away **h**,
Matt	25:35	for I was **h** and you gave Me
Mark	11:12	out from Bethany, He was **h**.
Acts	10:10	Then he became very **h** and
Rom	12:20	"If your enemy is **h**,
1Co	11:34	But if anyone is **h**,
Phil	4:12	both to be full and to be **h**,

HUNTER

Gen	10: 9	He was a mighty **h** before the

HURT

Ex	21:22	and **h** a woman with child, so
Ps	15: 4	He who swears to his own **h**
Ps	35: 4	to confusion Who plot my **h.**
Ps	38:12	Those who seek my **h** speak
Ps	105:18	They **h** his feet with
Prov	23:35	struck me, but I was not **h**;
Eccl	10: 9	quarries stones may be **h** by
Is	11: 9	They shall not **h** nor destroy
Jer	8:11	For they have healed the **h**
Dan	3:25	the fire; and they are not **h,**
Dan	6:22	so that they have not **h** me,
Rev	2:11	overcomes shall not be **h** by

HUSBAND (see HUSBANDS)

Gen	3:16	desire shall be for your **h,**
Ex	4:25	Surely you are a **h** of blood
Prov	12: 4	wife is the crown of her **h,**
Prov	31:23	Her **h** is known in the gates,
Is	54: 5	For your Maker is your **h,**
Jer	31:32	though I was a **h** to them,
Hos	2: 2	nor am I her **H!** Let her
Hos	2: 7	go and return to my first **h,**
Hos	2:16	you will call Me 'My **H,**
Rom	7: 2	But if the **h** dies, she is
1Co	7: 2	each woman have her own **h.**
1Co	7: 3	Let the **h** render to his wife
1Co	7: 4	but the **h** does. And
1Co	7:10	is not to depart from her **h.**
1Co	7:11	or be reconciled to her **h.**
1Co	7:11	And a **h** is not to divorce
1Co	7:14	wife is sanctified by the **h**;
1Co	7:16	you will save your **h?**
1Co	7:34	she may please her **h.**
Eph	5:23	For the **h** is head of the
Eph	5:33	that she respects her **h.**
1Ti	3: 2	the **h** of one wife,
Rev	21: 2	as a bride adorned for her **h.**

HUSBANDS (see HUSBAND)

John	4:18	"for you have had five **h,**
1Co	14:35	let them ask their own **h** at
Eph	5:22	Wives, submit to your own **h,**
1Ti	3:12	Let deacons be the **h** of one
Tit	2: 4	young women to love their **h,**
Tit	2: 5	obedient to their own **h,**
1Pe	3: 1	be submissive to your own **h,**

HYMN† (see HYMNS)

Matt	26:30	And when they had sung a **h,**
Mark	14:26	And when they had sung a **h,**

HYMNS† (see HYMN)

Acts	16:25	were praying and singing **h**
Eph	5:19	one another in psalms and **h**
Col	3:16	one another in psalms and **h**

HYPOCRISY (see HYPOCRITE)

Matt	23:28	but inside you are full of **h**
Luke	12: 1	of the Pharisees, which is **h.**
Rom	12: 9	Let love be without **h.**

HYPOCRITE (see HYPOCRISY, HYPOCRITES)

Job	8:13	And the hope of the **h** shall
Job	20: 5	And the joy of the **h** is
Matt	7: 5	**H!** First remove the plank

HYPOCRITES (see HYPOCRITE)

Matt	6: 5	you shall not be like the **h.**
Matt	16: 3	**H!** You know how to discern
Matt	23:13	**h!** For you shut up the

HYSSOP

Ex	12:22	you shall take a bunch of **h,**
Ps	51: 7	Purge me with **h,**
John	19:29	with sour wine, put it on **h,**
Heb	9:19	water, scarlet wool, and **h,**

I

ICHABOD†

1Sa	4:21	Then she named the child **I,**

IDLE (see IDLENESS)

Prov	14:23	But **i** chatter leads only
Prov	19:15	And an **i** person will suffer
Matt	12:36	say to you that for every **i**
Matt	20: 3	and saw others standing **i**
1Ti	6:20	the profane and **i** babblings
Tit	1:10	both **i** talkers and

IDLENESS (see IDLE)

Prov	31:27	does not eat the bread of **i.**

IDOL (see IDOLATER, IDOLATRY, IDOLS)

Ps	24: 4	lifted up his soul to an **i,**
1Co	8: 4	we know that an **i** is
1Co	8: 7	as a thing offered to an **i**;
1Co	10:19	That an **i** is anything, or

IDOLATER† (see IDOL, IDOLATERS)

1Co	5:11	or covetous, or an **i,**
Eph	5: 5	covetous man, who is an **i,**

IDOLATERS (see IDOLATER)

1Co	5:10	or extortioners, or **i,**
1Co	6: 9	Neither fornicators, nor **i,**
1Co	10: 7	And do not become **i** as were
Rev	21: 8	immoral, sorcerers, **i,**

IDOLATRY (see IDOL)

1Sa	15:23	is as iniquity and **i.**
1Co	10:14	my beloved, flee from **i.**
Col	3: 5	and covetousness, which is **i.**

IDOLS (see IDOL)

Gen	31:19	had stolen the household **i**
Lev	26:30	the lifeless forms of your **i**;
Judg	17: 5	an ephod and household **i**;
1Ch	16:26	gods of the peoples are **i,**
2Ch	11:15	and the calf **i** which he had
Ps	31: 6	those who regard useless **i**;
Ps	115: 4	Their **i** are silver and
Zech	10: 2	For the **i** speak delusion;
Acts	15:20	from things polluted by **i,**

Acts	15:29	from things offered to i,
Acts	17:16	the city was given over to i.
Rom	2:22	adultery? You who abhor i,
1Co	8: 4	of things offered to i,
1Co	12: 2	carried away to these dumb i,
2Co	6:16	has the temple of God with i?
1Th	1: 9	you turned to God from i to
1Jn	5:21	keep yourselves from i.
Rev	2:14	eat things sacrificed to i,
Rev	9:20	and i of gold, silver,

IDUMEA† (*see* EDOM)

Mark	3: 8	and Jerusalem and I and

IGNORANCE (*see* IGNORANT)

Ezek	45:20	unintentionally or in i.
Acts	3:17	I know that you did it in i,
Acts	17:30	these times of i God
Heb	9: 7	sins committed in i;
1Pe	1:14	former lusts, as in your i;
1Pe	2:15	may put to silence the i of

IGNORANT (*see* IGNORANCE, IGNORANTLY)

Ps	73:22	I was so foolish and i;
Is	63:16	Though Abraham was i of us,
Rom	10: 3	For they being i of God's
Rom	11:25	that you should be i of this
1Co	12: 1	I do not want you to be i:
2Co	2:11	for we are not i of his
2Ti	2:23	But avoid foolish and i
Heb	5: 2	on those who are i and

IGNORANTLY† (*see* IGNORANT)

1Ti	1:13	mercy because I did it i

ILLEGITIMATE

Heb	12: 8	then you are i and not sons.

IMAGE (*see* IMAGES)

Gen	1:26	"Let Us make man in Our i,
Gen	1:27	created man in His own i;
Gen	5: 3	own likeness, after his i,
Gen	9: 6	For in the i of God He
Ex	20: 4	make for yourself a carved i,
Deut	9:12	made themselves a molded i.
Ps	106:20	their glory Into the i of
Is	40:19	The workman molds an i,
Is	44:17	into a god, His carved i.
Jer	10:14	For his molded i is
Ezek	8: 3	where the seat of the i of
Dan	2:31	a great i! This great image,
Dan	3: 1	the king made an i of gold,
Dan	3: 3	for the dedication of the i
Dan	3: 5	down and worship the gold i
Hab	2:18	"What profit is the i,
Matt	22:20	Whose i and inscription is
Rom	1:23	incorruptible God into an i
Rom	8:29	to be conformed to the i
1Co	11: 7	since he is the i and glory
1Co	15:49	And as we have borne the i of
1Co	15:49	we shall also bear the i of
2Co	3:18	transformed into the same i
2Co	4: 4	who is the i of God, should
Col	1:15	He is the i of the invisible

Col	3:10	according to the i of Him
Heb	1: 3	glory and the express i of
Heb	10: 1	and not the very i of the
Rev	13:14	on the earth to make an i
Rev	13:15	as would not worship the i
Rev	14:11	worship the beast and his i,

IMAGES (*see* IMAGE)

Ex	34:13	cut down their wooden i
Num	33:52	destroy all their molded i,
Deut	7: 5	and burn their carved i with
Judg	3:19	back from the stone i that
1Sa	6: 5	images of your tumors and i
2Ch	34: 7	had beaten the carved i into
Ezek	21:21	arrows, he consults the i,
Acts	7:43	I which you made to

IMAGINATION

Gen	8:21	although the i of man's
Luke	1:51	the proud in the i of

IMITATE† (*see* IMITATORS)

1Co	4:16	i me.
1Co	11: 1	just as I also i Christ.
Heb	6:12	but i those who through
3Jn	11	do not i what is evil, but

IMITATORS (*see* IMITATE)

1Th	2:14	became i of the churches of

IMMANUEL†

Is	7:14	and shall call His name I.
Is	8: 8	breadth of Your land, O I.
Matt	1:23	shall call His name I,

IMMEDIATELY

Matt	3:16	Jesus came up i from the
Matt	8: 3	I his leprosy was
Mark	1:12	I the Spirit drove Him into
Mark	1:31	and i the fever left her.
Mark	4: 5	and i it sprang up because
Luke	19:11	of God would appear i.
Luke	19:40	the stones would i cry
John	5: 9	And i the man was made well,
John	6:21	and i the boat was at the
John	19:34	and i blood and water came
John	21: 3	They went out and i got
Acts	3: 7	and i his feet and ankle
Acts	9:20	I he preached the Christ in
Acts	9:34	your bed." Then he arose i.
Acts	16:26	and i all the doors were
Gal	1:16	I did not i confer with
Jas	1:24	and i forgets what kind of
Rev	4: 2	I I I was in the Spirit; and

IMMORAL (*see* IMMORALITY)

Prov	2:16	To deliver you from the i
Prov	5: 3	For the lips of an i woman
Prov	7: 5	they may keep you from the i
Prov	22:14	The mouth of an i woman is

IMMORALITY (*see* IMMORAL)

Matt	5:32	any reason except sexual i
Acts	15:29	strangled, and from sexual i.

Rom	1:29	unrighteousness, sexual i,
1Co	5: 1	and such sexual i as is not
1Co	6:13	body is not for sexual i
1Co	6:18	Flee sexual i
1Th	4: 3	should abstain from sexual i;

IMMORTAL† (*see* IMMORTALITY)

1Ti	1:17	Now to the King eternal, i,

IMMORTALITY (*see* IMMORTAL)

1Co	15:53	this mortal must put on i.
1Ti	6:16	who alone has i,
2Ti	1:10	and brought life and i to

IMMOVABLE†

Acts	27:41	stuck fast and remained i,
1Co	15:58	brethren, be steadfast, i,

IMMUTABLE†

Heb	6:18	that by two i things, in

IMPENITENT†

Rom	2: 5	your hardness and your i

IMPERISHABLE†

1Co	9:25	but we for an i crown.

IMPLANTED†

Jas	1:21	receive with meekness the i

IMPLORE

Mark	5: 7	I i You by God that You do
2Co	5:20	we i you on Christ's

IMPOSSIBLE

Matt	17:20	and nothing will be i for
Matt	19:26	them, "With men this is i,
Luke	1:37	with God nothing will be i.
Heb	6: 4	For it is i for those who
Heb	6:18	in which it is i for God to
Heb	11: 6	But without faith it is i

IMPOSTORS†

2Ti	3:13	But evil men and i will grow

IMPUDENT

Prov	7:13	With an i face she said to

IMPUTE† (*see* IMPUTED, IMPUTES, IMPUTING)

1Sa	22:15	from me! Let not the king i
2Sa	19:19	Do not let my lord i iniquity
Ps	32: 2	to whom the LORD does not i
Rom	4: 8	the LORD shall not i

IMPUTED (*see* IMPUTE)

Lev	17: 4	of bloodshed shall be i to
Rom	4:23	sake alone that it was i to
Rom	4:24	It shall be i to us who
Rom	5:13	but sin is not i when there

IMPUTES† (*see* IMPUTE)

Rom	4: 6	of the man to whom God i

IMPUTING (*see* IMPUTE)

2Co	5:19	not i their trespasses to

INCENSE

Ex	30: 1	make an altar to burn i on;
Ex	30: 7	shall burn on it sweet i
Ex	30: 8	a perpetual i before the
Ex	30: 9	shall not offer strange i
Ex	30:27	utensils, and the altar of i;
Is	1:13	I is an abomination to Me.
Luke	1: 9	his lot fell to burn i when

INCITED

Job	2: 3	although you i Me against

INCLINE (*see* INCLINED)

Josh	24:23	and i your heart to the
1Ki	8:58	that He may i our hearts to
2Ki	19:16	I Your ear, O LORD, and
Ps	17: 6	I Your ear to me, and hear
Ps	119:36	I my heart to Your

INCLINED (*see* INCLINE)

Ps	116: 2	Because He has i His ear to

INCLUDING

Eccl	12:14	I every secret thing,

INCORRUPTIBLE (*see* INCORRUPTION)

Rom	1:23	changed the glory of the i
1Co	15:52	the dead will be raised i,
1Pe	1: 4	to an inheritance i and
1Pe	1:23	of corruptible seed but i,

INCORRUPTION (*see* INCORRUPTIBLE)

1Co	15:42	it is raised in i.
1Co	15:53	corruptible must put on i,

INCREASE (*see* INCREASED, INCREASES, INCREASING)

Lev	19:25	it may yield to you its i:
Job	10:17	And i Your indignation
Ps	67: 6	the earth shall yield her i;
Is	9: 7	Of the i of His government
Dan	12: 4	fro, and knowledge shall i.
Luke	17: 5	I our faith."
John	3:30	"He must i,
1Co	3: 6	watered, but God gave the i.
1Th	3:12	And may the Lord make you i
1Th	4:10	that you i more and more;

INCREASED (*see* INCREASE)

Gen	7:17	The waters i and lifted up
Gen	19:19	and you have i your mercy
Ex	1: 7	Israel were fruitful and i
Job	1:10	and his possessions have i
Ps	105:24	He i His people greatly,
Is	9: 3	the nation And i its joy;
Is	26:15	You have i the nation; You
Jer	5: 6	Their backslidings have i
Jer	30:14	Because your sins have i.
Ezek	23:14	But she i her harlotry; She
Ezek	28: 5	wisdom in trade you have i

Hos 4: 7 "The more they i,
Mark 4: 8 i and produced: some
Luke 2:52 And Jesus i in wisdom and
Acts 9:22 But Saul i all the more in
Acts 16: 5 and i in number daily.
2Co 10:15 that as your faith is i,

INCREASES (see INCREASE)
Prov 16:21 And sweetness of the lips i
Prov 23:28 And i the unfaithful among
Prov 29:16 multiplied, transgression i;
Eccl 1:18 he who increases knowledge i
Eccl 8: 6 Though the misery of man i
Is 40:29 who have no might He i
Hab 2: 6 Woe to him who i What is

INCREASING† (see INCREASE)
Col 1:10 in every good work and i in

INCURABLE
Job 34: 6 my right? My wound is i,
Jer 15:18 perpetual And my wound i,
Jer 30:15 Your sorrow is i.

INDESCRIBABLE†
2Co 9:15 Thanks be to God for His i

INDIGNATION
Deut 29:28 in wrath, and in great i,
2Ki 3:27 and there was great i
Job 10:17 And increase Your i toward
Ps 69:24 Pour out Your i upon them,
Ps 78:49 of His anger, Wrath, i,
Is 13: 5 LORD and His weapons of i,
Is 30:27 His lips are full of i,
Is 66:14 And His i to His enemies.
Jer 10:10 not be able to endure His i.
Jer 15:17 You have filled me with i.
Dan 8:19 in the latter time of the i;
Nah 1: 6 Who can stand before His i?
Acts 5:17 and they were filled with i,
Rom 2: 8 i and wrath,
Heb 10:27 and fiery i which will
Rev 14:10 into the cup of His i.

INDIVIDUALLY
Rom 12: 5 and i members of one
1Co 12:11 distributing to each one i
1Co 12:27 of Christ, and members i.

INEXPRESSIBLE†
2Co 12: 4 up into Paradise and heard i
1Pe 1: 8 you rejoice with joy i and

INFALLIBLE†
Acts 1: 3 His suffering by many i

INFANTS
Ps 8: 2 of babes and nursing i You
Matt 21:16 of babes and nursing i
Luke 18:15 Then they also brought i to

INFERIOR
Job 12: 3 I am not i to you.

Dan 2:39 arise another kingdom i to
John 2:10 have well drunk, then the i.

INFINITE†
Ps 147: 5 His understanding is i.

INFIRMITIES (see INFIRMITY)
Matt 8:17 He Himself took our i
2Co 12: 5 not boast, except in my i.
1Ti 5:23 sake and your frequent i.

INFIRMITY (see INFIRMITIES)
Luke 13:11 woman who had a spirit of i

INGATHERING
Ex 34:22 and the Feast of I at the

INHABIT (see INHABITANT, INHABITED, INHABITS)
Num 15: 2 into the land you are to i,
Prov 10:30 But the wicked will not i
Is 65:21 shall build houses and i

INHABITANT (see INHABIT, INHABITANTS)
Is 6:11 are laid waste and without i,
Is 12: 6 O i of Zion, For great is

INHABITANTS (see INHABITANT)
Ps 75: 3 The earth and all its i are
Is 24: 1 And scatters abroad its i.
Jer 23:14 And her i like Gomorrah.
Ezek 27:35 All the i of the isles will
Rev 8:13 woe to the i of the earth,

INHABITED (see INHABIT)
Ex 16:35 until they came to an i
Is 45:18 vain, Who formed it to be i:

INHABITS (see INHABIT)
Is 57:15 High and Lofty One Who i

INHERIT (see INHERITANCE)
Gen 15: 7 to give you this land to i
Gen 15: 8 shall I know that I will i
Num 32:19 For we will not i with them
Ps 25:13 his descendants shall i the
Ps 37:11 But the meek shall i the
Ps 37:29 The righteous shall i the
Ps 82: 8 For You shall i all
Prov 8:21 cause those who love me to i
Prov 11:29 his own house will i the
Prov 14:18 The simple i folly, But the
Prov 28:10 But the blameless will i
Is 57:13 And shall i My holy
Is 65: 9 My elect shall i it, And
Matt 5: 5 For they shall i the earth.
Matt 19:29 and i eternal life.
Matt 25:34 i the kingdom prepared for
Mark 10:17 what shall I do that I may i
1Co 6: 9 the unrighteous will not i
1Co 6:10 nor extortioners will i the
1Co 15:50 flesh and blood cannot i
1Co 15:50 nor does corruption i
Heb 1:14 for those who will i

Heb	6:12	faith and patience i the
Heb	12:17	when he wanted to i the
Rev	21: 7	He who overcomes shall i all

INHERITANCE (see INHERIT)

Gen	31:14	still any portion or i for
Ex	15:17	In the mountain of Your i,
Josh	13:14	of Levi he had given no i;
Josh	13:33	God of Israel was their i,
Ruth	4: 5	of the dead through his i.
Ps	16: 6	Yes, I have a good i.
Ps	78:71	people, And Israel His i.
Is	19:25	of My hands, and Israel My i.
Is	47: 6	I have profaned My i,
Matt	21:38	us kill him and seize his i.
Luke	12:13	my brother to divide the i
Gal	3:18	For if the i is of the law,
Eph	1:11	also we have obtained an i,
Eph	1:14	is the guarantee of our i
Eph	1:18	of the glory of His i in
Eph	5: 5	has any i in the kingdom of
Col	1:12	us to be partakers of the i
Col	3:24	receive the reward of the i;
Heb	1: 4	as He has by i obtained a
Heb	9:15	the promise of the eternal i.
Heb	11: 8	he would receive as an i.
1Pe	1: 4	to an i incorruptible and

INIQUITIES (see INIQUITY)

Lev	16:21	confess over it all the i of
Ps	51: 9	sins, And blot out all my i.
Ps	90: 8	You have set our i before
Ps	103: 3	Who forgives all your i,
Ps	103:10	us according to our i.
Ps	130: 3	You, LORD, should mark i,
Is	53: 5	He was bruised for our i;
Is	53:11	For He shall bear their i.
Is	64: 6	fade as a leaf, And our i,
Amos	3: 2	punish you for all your i.

INIQUITY (see INIQUITIES)

Gen	15:16	for the i of the Amorites
Ex	20: 5	visiting the i of the
Ex	34: 7	forgiving i and
Ex	04. 9	and pardon our i and our
Josh	22:20	not perish alone in his i.
1Sa	15:23	And stubbornness is as i
1Sa	25:24	on me let this i be! And
2Sa	7:14	be My son. If he commits i,
2Sa	14: 9	let the i be on me and on
2Sa	14:32	but if there is i in me, let
2Sa	19:19	not let my lord impute i
Neh	4: 5	Do not cover their i,
Job	4: 8	Those who plow i And sow
Job	7:21	And take away my i?
Job	10:14	will not acquit me of my i.
Job	11: 6	from you Less than your i
Job	15:16	Who drinks i like water!
Job	22:23	You will remove i far from
Job	31: 3	for the workers of i?
Job	31:11	it would be i deserving
Job	31:33	By hiding my i in my bosom,
Job	33: 9	and there is no i in me.
Job	34:10	the Almighty to commit i.

Ps	7: 3	If there is i in my hands,
Ps	7:14	the wicked brings forth i;
Ps	10: 7	his tongue is trouble and i.
Ps	18:23	And I kept myself from my i.
Ps	25:11	sake, O LORD, Pardon my i,
Ps	32: 2	the LORD does not impute i,
Ps	32: 5	And You forgave the i of
Ps	38:18	For I will declare my i;
Ps	51: 2	me thoroughly from my i,
Ps	51: 5	I was brought forth in i,
Ps	53: 1	and have done abominable i;
Ps	66:18	If I regard i in my heart,
Ps	69:27	Add i to their iniquity,
Ps	85: 2	You have forgiven the i of
Ps	92: 7	when all the workers of i
Ps	109:14	Let the i of his fathers be
Ps	119:133	And let no i have dominion
Ps	125: 3	reach out their hands to i.
Prov	16: 6	Atonement is provided for i;
Prov	19:28	of the wicked devours i.
Prov	22: 8	He who sows i will reap
Is	1: 4	A people laden with i,
Is	1:13	I cannot endure i and the
Is	6: 7	Your i is taken away, And
Is	40: 2	That her i is pardoned;
Is	53: 6	LORD has laid on Him the i
Is	59: 7	thoughts are thoughts of i;
Is	64: 9	Nor remember i forever;
Jer	9: 5	weary themselves to commit i.
Jer	16:17	nor is their i hidden from
Jer	16:18	repay double for their i
Jer	31:30	one shall die for his own i;
Jer	31:34	For I will forgive their i,
Jer	36: 3	that I may forgive their i
Ezek	3:18	man shall die in his i;
Ezek	4: 4	it, you shall bear their i.
Ezek	14: 3	them to stumble into i.
Ezek	18:17	shall not die for the i
Ezek	18:18	he shall die for his i.
Ezek	28:18	By the i of your trading;
Ezek	33: 8	man shall die in his i;
Dan	9: 5	have sinned and committed i,
Dan	9:24	make reconciliation for i,
Hos	4: 8	set their heart on their i.
Hos	8:13	He will remember their i
Hos	10:13	You have reaped i.
Hos	13:12	The i of Ephraim is bound
Mic	2: 1	Woe to those who devise i,
Mic	7:18	Pardoning i And passing
Hab	2:12	establishes a city by i!
Mal	2: 6	And turned many away from i.
Luke	13:27	Me, all you workers of i.
Acts	1:18	a field with the wages of i;
Acts	8:23	by bitterness and bound by i.
1Co	13: 6	does not rejoice in i,
2Ti	2:19	name of Christ depart from i.
Jas	3: 6	is a fire, a world of i.
2Pe	2:16	but he was rebuked for his i:

INN (see INNKEEPER)

| Luke | 2: 7 | was no room for them in the i |
| Luke | 10:34 | animal, brought him to an i |

INNER

Eph	3:16	through His Spirit in the i

INNKEEPER† (see INN)

Luke	10:35	denarii, gave them to the i,

INNOCENCE (see INNOCENT)

Gen	20: 5	integrity of my heart and i
Ps	26: 6	I will wash my hands in i;

INNOCENT (see INNOCENCE)

Ex	23: 7	do not kill the i and
Deut	19:10	lest i blood be shed in the
Deut	27:25	takes a bribe to slay an i
Job	4: 7	who ever perished being i?
Job	9:23	at the plight of the i.
Job	9:28	that You will not hold me i.
Job	22:30	deliver one who is not i;
Job	33: 9	transgression; I am i,
Ps	15: 5	take a bribe against the i.
Ps	19:13	And I shall be i of great
Ps	94:21	And condemn i blood.
Ps	106:38	And shed i blood, The blood
Prov	1:11	us lurk secretly for the i
Prov	6:17	Hands that shed i blood,
Prov	6:29	touches her shall not be i.
Is	59: 7	they make haste to shed i
Jer	2:35	you say, 'Because I am i,
Dan	6:22	because I was found i before
Jon	1:14	and do not charge us with i
Matt	27: 4	have sinned by betraying i
Matt	27:24	I am i of the blood of this
Acts	20:26	to you this day that I am i

INNUMERABLE

Heb	12:22	to an i company of angels,

INQUIRE (see COUNSEL, INQUIRED)

Deut	17: 4	then you shall i diligently.
1Sa	9: 9	when a man went to i of God,
Ps	27: 4	And to i in His temple.

INQUIRED (see INQUIRE)

1Sa	28: 6	And when Saul i of the LORD,
Matt	2: 4	he i of them where the
John	4:52	Then he i of them the hour
1Pe	1:10	the prophets have i and

INSANE

1Sa	21:14	"Look, you see the man is i.

INSCRIBED (see INSCRIPTION)

Job	19:23	that they were i in a book!
Is	49:16	I have i you on the palms

INSCRIPTION (see INSCRIBED)

Ex	39:30	and wrote on it an i like
Dan	5:25	And this is the i that was
Matt	22:20	Whose image and i is this?"
Mark	15:26	And the i of His accusation
Acts	17:23	found an altar with this i:

INSPIRATION†

2Ti	3:16	Scripture is given by i of

INSTRUCT (see INSTRUCTED, INSTRUCTION)

Deut	17:11	of the law in which they i
Neh	9:20	gave Your good Spirit to i
Ps	32: 8	I will i you and teach you
1Co	2:16	LORD that he may i

INSTRUCTED (see INSTRUCT)

Ps	2:10	be wise, O kings; Be i,
Is	40:14	and who i Him, And taught
Luke	1: 4	things in which you were i.
Acts	18:25	This man had been i in the
Rom	2:18	being i out of the law,

INSTRUCTION (see COUNSEL, INSTRUCT, INSTRUCTIONS)

Prov	1: 2	To know wisdom and i,
Prov	1: 7	fools despise wisdom and i.
Prov	1: 8	hear the i of your father,
Prov	13: 1	son heeds his father's i,
Prov	15: 5	fool despises his father's i,
Prov	15:33	fear of the LORD is the i
Jer	36:27	Baruch had written at the i
2Ti	3:16	for i in righteousness,

INSTRUCTIONS (see INSTRUCTION)

Heb	11:22	and gave i concerning his

INSTRUMENTS

Ps	150: 4	Praise Him with stringed i
Amos	6: 5	to the sound of stringed i,
Rom	6:13	present your members as i

INTEGRITY

Gen	20: 5	In the i of my heart and
Job	2: 3	still he holds fast to his i,
Job	31: 6	That God may know my i.
Ps	7: 8	And according to my i
Ps	26: 1	For I have walked in my i.
Prov	10: 9	He who walks with i walks
Prov	11: 3	The i of the upright will
Tit	2: 7	in doctrine showing i,

INTENT (see INTENTS)

Gen	6: 5	and that every i of the
Prov	21:27	he brings it with wicked i!
Eph	3:10	to the i that now the

INTENTS (see INTENT)

Heb	4:12	of the thoughts and i of

INTERCESSION

Is	53:12	And made i for the
Jer	7:16	nor make i to Me; for I will
Rom	8:26	the Spirit Himself makes i
Heb	7:25	He always lives to make i

INTEREST (see INTERESTS)

Lev	25:36	Take no usury or i from him;
Deut	23:19	You shall not charge i to

Deut   23:20   a foreigner you may charge i,
Matt   25:27   received back my own with i.

INTERESTS (see INTEREST)

Phil   2: 4   but also for the i of

INTERPRET (see INTERPRETATION,
INTERPRETED, INTERPRETER,
INTERPRETING, INTERPRETS)

Gen   41:15   there is no one who can i
1Co   12:30   speak with tongues? Do all i?
1Co   14:13   a tongue pray that he may i.

INTERPRETATION (see INTERPRET,
INTERPRETATIONS)

Dan   2: 6   you tell the dream and its i,
Dan   4: 6   make known to me the i of
Dan   5: 7   writing, and tells me its i,
Dan   5:26   This is the i of each word.
1Co   12:10   to another the i of tongues.
1Co   14:26   has a revelation, has an i.
2Pe   1:20   is of any private i,

INTERPRETATIONS† (see INTERPRETATION)

Gen   40: 8   Do not i belong to God? Tell
Dan   5:16   that you can give i and

INTERPRETED (see INTERPRET)

Gen   40:22   as Joseph had i to them.
Gen   41:12   and he i our dreams for us;

INTERPRETER (see INTERPRET)

Gen   42:23   spoke to them through an i.
1Co   14:28   But if there is no i,

INTERPRETING† (see INTERPRET)

Dan   5:12   i dreams, solving riddles,

INTERPRETS† (see INTERPRET)

Deut   18:10   or one who i omens, or a
1Co   14: 5   tongues, unless indeed he i,

INVISIBLE†

Rom   1:20   creation of the world His i
Col   1:15   He is the image of the i God,
Col   1:16   are on earth, visible and i,
1Ti   1:17   King eternal, immortal, i,
Heb   11:27   as seeing Him who is i.

INVITE (see INVITED)

1Sa   16: 3   Then i Jesse to the
Job   1: 4   and would send and i their
Matt   22: 9   i to the wedding.'
Luke   14:13   i the poor, the maimed,

INVITED (see INVITE)

1Sa   16: 5   and i them to the sacrifice.
Esth   5:12   Queen Esther i no one but me
Matt   22: 3   to call those who were i to
Luke   14: 8   When you are i by anyone to a
Luke   14:10   "But when you are i,
John   2: 2   and His disciples were i to

INWARD (see INWARDLY)

Ps   51: 6   You desire truth in the i
Ps   64: 6   Both the i thought and
Ps   139:13   For You formed my i parts;
Rom   7:22   of God according to the i
2Co   4:16   yet the i man is being

INWARDLY† (see INWARD)

Ps   62: 4   mouth, But they curse i.
Matt   7:15   but i they are ravenous
Rom   2:29   he is a Jew who is one i;

IRON

Gen   4:22   craftsman in bronze and i.
Deut   3:11   his bedstead was an i
2Ki   6: 6   and he made the i float.
Job   19:24   on a rock With an i pen
Job   28: 2   I is taken from the earth,
Ps   2: 9   break them with a rod of i;
Prov   27:17   As i sharpens iron, So a
Jer   1:18   A fortified city and an i
Dan   2:33   "its legs of i,
Dan   2:33   its feet partly of i and
Dan   7: 7   It had huge i teeth; it was
1Ti   4: 2   seared with a hot i,
Rev   2:27   them with a rod of i;
Rev   19:15   rule them with a rod of i.

IRREVOCABLE†

Rom   11:29   the calling of God are i

ISAAC

Gen   17:19   you shall call his name I;
Gen   21: 3   whom Sarah bore to him—I.
Gen   21: 4   circumcised his son I when
Gen   21:12   for in I your seed shall be
Gen   22: 2   your son, your only son I,
Gen   24: 4   and take a wife for my son I.
Gen   24:67   So I was comforted after his
Gen   27: 1   when I was old and his eyes
Gen   31:42   of Abraham and the Fear of I,
2Ki   13:23   His covenant with Abraham, I,
Matt   8:11   and sit down with Abraham, I,
Rom   9: 7   In I your seed shall be
Heb   11:17   he was tested, offered up I,
Heb   11:20   By faith I blessed Jacob and
Jas   2:21   by works when he offered I

ISAIAH

2Ki   19: 2   to I the prophet, the son of
Is   1: 1   The vision of I the son of
Is   20: 3   Just as My servant I has
Matt   4:14   which was spoken by I the
Matt   13:14   in them the prophecy of I
Luke   4:17   the book of the prophet I.
Acts   8:28   he was reading I the
Rom   10:16   For I says, "Lord, who
Rom   10:20   But I is very bold and says:

ISCARIOT (see JUDAS)

Matt   26:14   the twelve, called Judas I,
John   14:22   Judas (not I) said to Him,

ISHMAEL (see ISHMAELITES)

Gen	16:16	years old when Hagar bore I
Gen	17:26	circumcised, and his son I;
Gen	25: 9	And his sons Isaac and I
Jer	40:15	and I will kill I the son of

ISHMAELITES (see ISHMAEL)

Gen	37:28	and sold him to the I for
Judg	8:24	because they were I.

ISLAND

Rev	1: 9	was on the i that is called

ISRAEL (see ISRAELITE, JACOB)

Gen	32:28	be called Jacob, but I;
Gen	32:32	this day the children of I
Gen	35:10	but I shall be your name."
Gen	36:31	over the children of I:
Gen	37: 3	Now I loved Joseph more than
Gen	42: 5	And the sons of I went to buy
Gen	43: 8	Then Judah said to I his
Gen	46: 8	names of the children of I,
Gen	46:29	Goshen to meet his father I;
Gen	46:30	And I said to Joseph, "Now
Gen	47:29	the time drew near that I
Gen	48: 8	Then I saw Joseph's sons,
Gen	48:10	Now the eyes of I were dim
Gen	49: 2	And listen to I your
Gen	49: 7	Jacob And scatter them in I.
Gen	49:24	Shepherd, the Stone of I),
Gen	49:28	are the twelve tribes of I,
Gen	50: 2	So the physicians embalmed I.
Ex	1: 1	names of the children of I
Ex	1: 7	But the children of I were
Ex	3:10	My people, the children of I,
Ex	3:11	bring the children of I out
Ex	3:16	and gather the elders of I
Ex	4:22	I is My son, My firstborn.
Ex	5: 1	says the LORD God of I:
Ex	5: 2	obey His voice to let I go?
Ex	6:14	Reuben, the firstborn of I,
Ex	10:23	But all the children of I
Ex	11: 7	between the Egyptians and I.
Ex	12: 3	to all the congregation of I,
Ex	12:15	shall be cut off from I.
Ex	14: 8	he pursued the children of I;
Ex	14:10	and the children of I cried
Ex	14:19	went before the camp of I,
Ex	14:30	So the LORD saved I that
Ex	15: 1	Moses and the children of I
Ex	15:22	So Moses brought I from the
Ex	16: 2	of the children of I
Ex	16:31	And the house of I called its
Ex	16:35	And the children of I ate
Ex	17:11	that I prevailed; and when
Ex	19: 2	So I camped there before the
Ex	24: 1	seventy of the elders of I,
Ex	24: 9	seventy of the elders of I,
Ex	24:10	and they saw the God of I.
Ex	28: 9	the names of the sons of I:
Ex	32: 4	"This is your god, O I,
Ex	32:13	Abraham, Isaac, and I,
Ex	34:27	covenant with you and with I.

Ex	39: 7	stones for the sons of I,
Lev	4:13	the whole congregation of I
Lev	10: 6	the whole house of I,
Lev	20: 2	the strangers who dwell in I,
Lev	24:10	woman's son and a man of I
Lev	27:34	Moses for the children of I
Num	1: 3	able to go to war in I.
Num	1:16	heads of the divisions in I.
Num	1:44	with the leaders of I,
Num	1:45	of the children of I,
Num	24:17	Scepter shall rise out of I,
Deut	5: 1	said to them: "Hear, O I,
Deut	6: 4	"Hear, O I: The LORD
Deut	9: 1	"Hear, O I: You are to
Deut	10:12	"And now, I, what does
Deut	13:11	So all I shall hear and fear,
Deut	18: 1	part nor inheritance with I;
Deut	21: 8	O LORD, for Your people I,
Deut	21:21	and all I shall hear and
Deut	23:17	harlot of the daughters of I,
Deut	23:17	one of the sons of I.
Deut	25: 6	may not be blotted out of I.
Deut	25: 7	a name to his brother in I;
Deut	31:11	when all I comes to appear
Deut	34:10	there has not arisen in I a
Deut	34:12	in the sight of all I.
Josh	10:14	for the LORD fought for I.
Josh	24:31	I served the LORD all the
Judg	3:31	and he also delivered I.
Judg	5: 7	arose, Arose a mother in I.
Judg	17: 6	there was no king in I;
Ruth	4:14	may his name be famous in I!
1Sa	4:21	glory has departed from I!
1Sa	7:10	they were overcome before I.
1Sa	7:15	And Samuel judged I all the
1Sa	8: 1	made his sons judges over I.
1Sa	8:22	Samuel said to the men of I,
1Sa	9: 9	(Formerly in I, when a man
1Sa	9:21	smallest of the tribes of I,
1Sa	13:13	your kingdom over I forever.
1Sa	14:23	So the LORD saved I that
1Sa	15:17	LORD anoint you king over I?
1Sa	15:26	you from being king over I.
1Sa	15:29	And also the Strength of I
1Sa	17: 8	cried out to the armies of I,
1Sa	17:10	I defy the armies of I this
1Sa	17:45	the God of the armies of I,
1Sa	17:46	that there is a God in I.
1Sa	23:17	You shall be king over I,
1Sa	24: 2	chosen men from all I,
1Sa	25:30	appointed you ruler over I,
1Sa	25:32	is the LORD God of I,
1Sa	31: 1	Philistines fought against I;
1Sa	31: 1	and the men of I fled from
2Sa	1:19	The beauty of I is slain on
2Sa	1:24	"O daughters of I,
2Sa	3:10	the throne of David over I
2Sa	3:38	man has fallen this day in I?
2Sa	5: 2	shall shepherd My people I,
2Sa	5: 3	anointed David king over I.
2Sa	7: 6	I brought the children of I
2Sa	7: 7	to shepherd My people I,
2Sa	7: 8	ruler over My people, over I.
2Sa	7:11	to be over My people I,

2Sa	7:24	You have made Your people I	Neh	13:26	God made him king over all I.
2Sa	7:27	O LORD of hosts, God of I,	Ps	14: 7	Let Jacob rejoice and I be
2Sa	10:18	the Syrians fled before I;	Ps	22: 3	in the praises of I.
2Sa	10:19	they made peace with I and	Ps	22:23	all you offspring of I!
2Sa	11:11	The ark and I and Judah are	Ps	25:22	Redeem I, O God
2Sa	12: 7	'I anointed you king over I,	Ps	41:13	be the LORD God of I
2Sa	12: 8	and gave you the house of I	Ps	59: 5	God of hosts, the God of I,
2Sa	13:13	like one of the fools in I.	Ps	68:26	Lord, from the fountain of I.
2Sa	14:25	Now in all I there was no	Ps	68:34	His excellence is over I,
2Sa	15: 6	the hearts of the men of I.	Ps	71:22	the harp, O Holy One of I.
2Sa	17:15	Absalom and the elders of I,	Ps	73: 1	Truly God is good to I,
2Sa	19:22	be put to death today in I?	Ps	76: 1	His name is great in I.
2Sa	19:22	that today I am king over I?	Ps	78: 5	And appointed a law in I,
2Sa	20:19	a city and a mother in I.	Ps	78:41	limited the Holy One of I.
2Sa	21: 5	any of the territories of I,	Ps	78:71	And I His inheritance.
2Sa	21:17	you quench the lamp of I.	Ps	80: 1	Give ear, O Shepherd of I,
2Sa	23: 1	And the sweet psalmist of I:	Ps	81: 4	this is a statute for I,
2Sa	23: 3	The God of I said, The Rock	Ps	81:11	And I would have none of
2Sa	23: 3	The Rock of I spoke to me:	Ps	81:13	That I would walk in My
2Sa	24: 1	LORD was aroused against I,	Ps	103: 7	acts to the children of I.
2Sa	24: 1	number I and Judah."	Ps	105:10	To I as an everlasting
2Sa	24:25	plague was withdrawn from I.	Ps	106:48	be the LORD God of I
1Ki	1:20	the eyes of all I are on	Ps	114: 1	When I went out of Egypt,
1Ki	2: 4	a man on the throne of I.	Ps	114: 2	And I His dominion.
1Ki	2:11	that David reigned over I	Ps	115: 9	O I, trust in the LORD;
1Ki	4: 1	Solomon was king over all I.	Ps	118: 2	Let I now say, "His mercy
1Ki	4: 7	twelve governors over all I,	Ps	121: 4	He who keeps I Shall
1Ki	4:25	And Judah and I dwelt safely,	Ps	122: 4	To the Testimony of I,
1Ki	6:13	will not forsake My people I.	Ps	124: 1	Let I now say—
1Ki	8:16	no city from any tribe of I	Ps	125: 5	Peace be upon I!
1Ki	8:16	David to be over My people I.	Ps	128: 6	Peace be upon I!
1Ki	8:20	and sit on the throne of I,	Ps	130: 8	And He shall redeem I From
1Ki	8:23	he said: "LORD God of I,	Ps	135: 4	I for His special treasure.
1Ki	8:34	the sin of Your people I,	Ps	136:22	A heritage to I His servant,
1Ki	8:52	of Your people I,	Ps	149: 2	Let I rejoice in their
1Ki	9: 5	of your kingdom over I	Prov	1: 1	the son of David, king of I:
1Ki	9: 7	I will be a proverb and a	Eccl	1:12	was king over I in
1Ki	11:25	He was an adversary of I all	Is	1: 3	But I does not know, My
1Ki	11:42	in Jerusalem over all I	Is	1: 4	to anger The Holy One of I,
1Ki	12: 1	for all I had gone to	Is	1:24	hosts, the Mighty One of I,
1Ki	12:16	O I! Now, see to your own	Is	5: 7	of hosts is the house of I,
1Ki	12:19	So I has been in rebellion	Is	9:14	cut off head and tail from I,
1Ki	12:28	Here are your gods, O I,	Is	10:17	So the Light of I will be
1Ki	14: 7	you ruler over My people I,	Is	10:20	day That the remnant of I,
1Ki	14:15	He will uproot I from this	Is	12: 6	great is the Holy One of I
1Ki	14:16	who sinned and who made I	Is	19:25	and I My inheritance."
1Ki	18:17	that you, O troubler of I?	Is	27: 6	I shall blossom and bud,
1Ki	18:36	God of Abraham, Isaac, and I,	Is	29:23	And fear the God of I.
1Ki	19:18	reserved seven thousand in I,	Is	40:27	O Jacob, And speak, O I:
2Ki	2:12	the chariot of I and its	Is	41:14	You men of I! I will help
2Ki	13:14	the chariots of I and their	Is	41:14	Redeemer, the Holy One of I.
2Ki	17:34	of Jacob, whom He named I,	Is	43: 1	And He who formed you, O I:
1Ch	21: 1	Now Satan stood up against I,	Is	43:15	Holy One, The Creator of I,
1Ch	21:14	LORD sent a plague upon I,	Is	43:22	have been weary of Me, O I.
Ezra	3: 2	the altar of the God of I,	Is	44: 1	And I whom I have chosen.
Ezra	3:10	ordinance of David king of I.	Is	44:23	And glorified Himself in I.
Ezra	4: 1	temple of the LORD God of I,	Is	45: 4	And I My elect, I have
Ezra	6:22	house of God, the God of I.	Is	46: 3	remnant of the house of I,
Ezra	7:10	statutes and ordinances in I.	Is	46:13	For I My glory.
Ezra	10: 5	and all I swear an oath that	Is	48: 2	And lean on the God of I;
Ezra	10:10	adding to the guilt of I.	Is	49: 3	'You are My servant, O I,
Neh	1: 6	sins of the children of I	Jer	2: 3	I was holiness to the
Neh	10:33	to make atonement for I,	Jer	2:14	Is I a servant? Is he a
Neh	13: 3	the mixed multitude from I.	Jer	3: 6	you seen what backsliding I

Jer	3:23	God Is the salvation of I.
Jer	14: 8	O the Hope of I,
Ezek	3:17	watchman for the house of I;
Ezek	11:22	the glory of the God of I
Ezek	18:31	should you die, O house of I?
Ezek	33:11	should you die, O house of I?
Ezek	34: 2	against the shepherds of I,
Hos	1: 5	I will break the bow of I
Hos	1: 6	have mercy on the house of I,
Hos	3: 5	Afterward the children of I
Hos	5: 5	The pride of I testifies to
Hos	5: 5	Therefore I and Ephraim
Hos	7: 1	I would have healed I,
Hos	8: 8	I is swallowed up
Hos	8:14	For I has forgotten his
Hos	9:10	I found I Like grapes in
Hos	10:15	At dawn the king of I
Hos	11: 1	When I was a child, I loved
Hos	11: 8	How can I hand you over, I?
Hos	13: 1	He exalted himself in I;
Hos	13: 9	"O I, you are destroyed,
Hos	14: 5	I will be like the dew to I;
Joel	3: 2	of My people, My heritage I,
Amos	2: 6	three transgressions of I,
Amos	5: 2	The virgin of I has fallen;
Amos	5: 3	ten left to the house of I.
Amos	6: 1	To whom the house of I
Amos	7: 9	And the sanctuaries of I
Amos	7:10	sent to Jeroboam king of I,
Amos	7:11	And I shall surely be led
Amos	7:15	prophesy to My people I.
Amos	7:16	'Do not prophesy against I,
Amos	7:17	And I shall surely be led
Amos	8: 2	has come upon My people I;
Amos	9:14	the captives of My people I;
Mic	2:12	gather the remnant of I;
Mic	3: 8	his transgression And to I
Mic	5: 2	Me The One to be Ruler in I,
Nah	2: 2	Like the excellence of I,
Zeph	3:15	your enemy. The King of I,
Matt	2: 6	shepherd My people I.
Matt	8:10	not even in I!
Matt	10: 6	lost sheep of the house of I.
Matt	10:23	gone through the cities of I
Matt	15:24	lost sheep of the house of I.
Matt	19:28	the twelve tribes of I.
Matt	27:42	save. If He is the King of I,
Mark	12:29	is: 'Hear, O I,
Mark	15:32	the Christ, the King of I,
Luke	1:54	He has helped His servant I,
Luke	1:68	is the Lord God of I,
Luke	1:80	of his manifestation to I.
Luke	2:25	for the Consolation of I,
Luke	2:32	the glory of Your people I.
Luke	2:34	fall and rising of many in I,
Luke	24:21	He who was going to redeem I.
John	1:31	He should be revealed to I,
John	1:49	God! You are the King of I!
John	3:10	"Are you the teacher of I,
John	12:13	LORD!' The King of I!"
Acts	1: 6	restore the kingdom to I?
Acts	2:22	"Men of I, hear these
Acts	3:12	to the people: "Men of I,
Acts	4:27	Gentiles and the people of I,

Acts	5:31	to give repentance to I and
Acts	13:16	his hand said, "Men of I,
Acts	13:23	God raised up for I a
Rom	9: 6	For they are not all I who
Rom	9:27	of the children of I
Rom	10: 1	and prayer to God for I is
Rom	10:21	But to I he says: "All
Rom	11: 7	I has not obtained what it
Rom	11:25	in part has happened to I
Rom	11:26	And so all I will be saved,
1Co	10:18	Observe I after the flesh:
Gal	6:16	and upon the I of God.
Eph	2:12	from the commonwealth of I
Phil	3: 5	day, of the stock of I,
Heb	8: 8	with the house of I
Rev	21:12	tribes of the children of I:

ISRAELITE (*see* ISRAEL, ISRAELITES)

John	1:47	an I indeed, in whom is no
Rom	11: 1	not! For I also am an I,

ISRAELITES (*see* ISRAELITE)

Rom	9: 4	who are I, to whom pertain
2Co	11:22	So am I. Are they I?

ISSACHAR

Gen	35:23	and Simeon, Levi, Judah, I,

ISSUES†

Prov	4:23	out of it spring the i of

ITCHING†

2Ti	4: 3	because they have i ears,

IVORY

1Ki	10:18	made a great throne of i,
1Ki	22:39	the i house which he built
Ps	45: 8	Out of the i palaces, by
Song	7: 4	Your neck is like an i
Amos	3:15	The houses of i shall
Amos	6: 4	Who lie on beds of i,

J

JABBOK

Gen	32:22	crossed over the ford of J.

JACOB (*see* ISRAEL, JACOB'S, JAMES)

Gen	25:27	but J was a mild man,
Gen	25:28	game, but Rebekah loved J.
Gen	25:29	Now J cooked a stew; and
Gen	25:33	and sold his birthright to J.
Gen	25:34	And J gave Esau bread and
Gen	27:30	and J had scarcely gone out
Gen	27:36	"Is he not rightly named J?
Gen	27:41	So Esau hated J because of
Gen	27:41	I will kill my brother J.
Gen	28:16	Then J awoke from his sleep
Gen	28:20	Then J made a vow, saying,
Gen	29:11	Then J kissed Rachel, and
Gen	29:15	Then Laban said to J,
Gen	29:18	Now J loved Rachel; so he

Gen	29:20	So J served seven years for
Gen	30:40	Then J separated the lambs,
Gen	30:41	that J placed the rods
Gen	31: 1	J has taken away all that was
Gen	31:25	So Laban overtook J.
Gen	31:45	So J took a stone and set it
Gen	31:47	but J called it Galeed.
Gen	31:53	And J swore by the Fear of
Gen	32: 7	So J was greatly afraid and
Gen	32:24	Then J was left alone; and a
Gen	32:28	shall no longer be called J,
Gen	34: 3	to Dinah the daughter of J,
Gen	35: 4	and J hid them under the
Gen	35:10	name shall not be called J
Gen	35:14	So J set up a pillar in the
Gen	35:20	And J set a pillar on her
Gen	35:22	Now the sons of J were
Gen	37: 2	This is the history of J.
Gen	37:34	Then J tore his clothes, put
Gen	46: 5	Then J arose from Beersheba;
Gen	46:26	the persons who went with J
Gen	47: 7	and J blessed Pharaoh.
Gen	47: 8	Pharaoh said to J,
Gen	49: 2	and hear, you sons of J,
Gen	50:24	Abraham, to Isaac, and to J.
Ex	3: 6	of Isaac, and the God of J.
Ex	3:16	Abraham, of Isaac, and of J,
Lev	26:42	remember My covenant with J,
Num	23: 7	curse J for me, And come,
Num	24: 5	O J! Your dwellings, O
Num	24:17	A Star shall come out of J;
Deut	33: 4	of the congregation of J.
Deut	33:28	The fountain of J alone,
Josh	24: 4	To Isaac I gave J and Esau.
2Sa	23: 1	anointed of the God of J,
1Ki	18:31	the tribes of the sons of J,
Ps	14: 7	Let J rejoice and Israel
Ps	20: 1	the name of the God of J
Ps	24: 6	This is J, the generation
Ps	44: 4	Command victories for J.
Ps	46: 7	The God of J is our
Ps	46:11	The God of J is our
Ps	47: 4	The excellence of J whom He
Ps	75: 9	sing praises to the God of J.
Ps	76: 6	At Your rebuke, O God of J,
Ps	77:15	The sons of J and Joseph.
Ps	78: 5	established a testimony in J,
Ps	78:21	a fire was kindled against J,
Ps	78:71	To shepherd J His people,
Ps	81: 1	joyful shout to the God of J.
Ps	84: 8	O God of J! Selah
Ps	85: 1	back the captivity of J.
Ps	94: 7	Nor does the God of J
Ps	105:10	And confirmed it to J for a
Ps	105:23	And J dwelt in the land of
Ps	114: 7	the presence of the God of J,
Ps	132: 2	vowed to the Mighty One of J:
Ps	135: 4	For the LORD has chosen J
Ps	147:19	He declares His word to J,
Is	2: 3	the house of the God of J;
Is	10:21	return, the remnant of J,
Is	17: 4	pass That the glory of J
Is	29:23	hallow the Holy One of J,
Is	41: 8	J whom I have chosen, The
Is	41:14	"Fear not, you worm J,
Is	41:21	says the King of J.
Is	43: 1	LORD, who created you, O J,
Is	44: 1	O J My servant, And Israel
Is	45:19	did not say to the seed of J,
Is	46: 3	to Me, O house of J,
Is	49: 5	To bring J back to Him, So
Is	49:26	the Mighty One of J.
Is	58: 1	And the house of J their
Is	58:14	you with the heritage of J
Jer	10:16	The Portion of J is not
Jer	10:25	For they have eaten up J,
Jer	31: 7	"Sing with gladness for J,
Jer	31:11	the LORD has redeemed J,
Lam	2: 3	He has blazed against J
Ezek	39:25	bring back the captives of J,
Hos	12: 2	And will punish J according
Amos	6: 8	"I abhor the pride of J,
Amos	7: 2	that J may stand, For he
Amos	8: 7	has sworn by the pride of J:
Obad	10	against your brother J,
Mic	1: 5	for the transgression of J
Mic	3: 1	"Hear now, O heads of J,
Mic	3: 8	To declare to J his
Mal	1: 2	Yet J I have loved;
Mal	3: 6	not consumed, O sons of J.
Matt	8:11	and J in the kingdom of
Matt	22:32	and the God of J'?
Luke	1:33	reign over the house of J
Luke	13:28	see Abraham and Isaac and J
Luke	20:37	and the God of J.
John	4:12	greater than our father J,
Acts	3:13	God of Abraham, Isaac, and J,
Acts	7: 8	and J begot the twelve
Rom	9:13	J I have loved, but Esau
Rom	11:26	away ungodliness from J;
Heb	11: 9	in tents with Isaac and J,
Heb	11:20	By faith Isaac blessed J and

JACOB'S (see JACOB)

Gen	27:22	The voice is J voice, but
Gen	32:25	and the socket of J hip was
Jer	30: 7	And it is the time of J
Mal	1: 2	Was not Esau J brother?"
John	4: 6	Now J well was there. Jesus

JAILER†

Acts	16:23	commanding the j to keep

JAIRUS

Mark	5:22	J by name. And when he saw

JAMES (see JACOB)

Matt	4:21	J the son of Zebedee, and
Matt	10: 3	J the son of Alphaeus, and
Matt	17: 1	six days Jesus took Peter, J,
1Co	15: 7	After that He was seen by J,
Jude	1	Christ, and brother of J,

JAPHETH

Gen	7:13	sons, Shem, Ham, and J,
Gen	9:27	May God enlarge J,

J

JAWBONE (*see* JAWS)
Judg 15:15 He found a fresh j of a

JAWS (*see* JAWBONE)
Ps 22:15 My tongue clings to My j;

JEALOUS (*see* JEALOUSY)
Ex 20: 5 am a j God, visiting the
Ex 34:14 the LORD, whose name is J,
Num 5:14 upon him and he becomes j
Deut 5: 9 am a j God, visiting the
Ezek 39:25 and I will be j for My holy
2Co 11: 2 For I am j for you with godly

JEALOUSY (*see* JEALOUS)
Num 5:14 if the spirit of j comes upon
Num 5:15 it is a grain offering of j,
Deut 29:20 anger of the LORD and His j
Deut 32:16 They provoked Him to j with
Ps 78:58 And moved Him to j with
Ps 79: 5 Will Your j burn like fire?
Prov 6:34 For j is a husband's fury;
Song 8: 6 J as cruel as the grave;
Ezek 8: 3 the seat of the image of j
Ezek 23:25 I will set My j against you,
Zeph 1:18 By the fire of His j,
Rom 10:19 will provoke you to j
1Co 10:22 do we provoke the Lord to j?
2Co 11: 2 jealous for you with godly j.

JEHOAHAZ (*see* AHAZIAH)
2Ki 13: 1 J the son of Jehu became
2Ki 14: 1 year of Joash the son of J,

JEHOASH (*see* JOASH)
2Ki 12:18 And J king of Judah took all
2Ki 14: 9 And J king of Israel sent to

JEHOIACHIN
2Ki 24: 8 J was eighteen years old
2Ki 24:15 And he carried J captive to
2Ki 25:27 released J king of Judah
2Ch 36: 9 J was eight years old when

JEHOIAKIM
2Ki 23:34 and changed his name to J.
2Ki 24: 5 the rest of the acts of J,
Jer 36:32 words of the book which J
Dan 1: 1 year of the reign of J king

JEHORAM (*see* JORAM)
1Ki 22:50 Then J his son reigned in
2Ki 3: 1 Now J the son of Ahab became
2Ki 3: 6 So King J went out of
2Ki 8:16 J the son of Jehoshaphat,
2Ki 8:25 Israel, Ahaziah the son of J,
2Ki 9:24 full strength and shot J
2Ch 22: 6 And Azariah the son of J,

JEHOSHAPHAT
2Sa 8:16 J the son of Ahilud was
1Ki 15:24 Then J his son reigned in
1Ki 22: 2 that J the king of Judah

1Ki 22:41 J the son of Asa had become
1Ki 22:45 the rest of the acts of J,
1Ki 22:50 And J rested with his
2Ki 9: 2 there for Jehu the son of J,
2Ch 18: 1 J had riches and honor in
2Ch 18: 7 the king of Israel said to J,
2Ch 19: 4 So J dwelt at Jerusalem; and
2Ch 20: 1 came to battle against J.
2Ch 20: 3 And J feared, and set himself
2Ch 20:18 And J bowed his head with
2Ch 20:30 Then the realm of J was
2Ch 20:34 the rest of the acts of J,
2Ch 20:37 prophesied against J,
2Ch 21:12 not walked in the ways of J
Joel 3: 2 them down to the Valley of J;
Matt 1: 8 J begot Joram, and Joram

JEHU
1Ki 16: 1 word of the LORD came to J
1Ki 16: 7 LORD came by the prophet J
1Ki 19:17 J will kill; and whoever
2Ki 9:14 So J the son of Jehoshaphat,
2Ki 9:16 So J rode in a chariot and
2Ki 9:20 is like the driving of J
2Ki 9:22 happened, when Joram saw J,
2Ki 9:22 he said, "Is it peace, J?
2Ki 9:27 So J pursued him, and said,
2Ki 9:30 Now when J had come to
2Ki 10: 1 And J wrote and sent letters
2Ki 10:11 So J killed all who remained
2Ki 10:19 But J acted deceptively,
2Ki 10:28 Thus J destroyed Baal from
2Ki 10:31 But J took no heed to walk in
2Ki 10:34 the rest of the acts of J,
2Ki 10:35 So J rested with his fathers,
2Ki 13: 1 Jehoahaz the son of J became

JEOPARDY
1Co 15:30 And why do we stand in j

JEPHTHAH
Judg 11: 1 Now J the Gileadite was a
Judg 11:30 And J made a vow to the
Judg 11:40 to lament the daughter of J
1Sa 12:11 sent Jerubbaal, Bedan, J,
Heb 11:32 and Barak and Samson and J,

JEREMIAH
2Ch 35:25 J also lamented for Josiah.
2Ch 36:12 not humble himself before J
2Ch 36:22 the LORD by the mouth of J
Ezra 1: 1 the LORD by the mouth of J
Jer 1: 1 The words of J the son of
Jer 1:11 came to me, saying, "J,
Jer 7: 1 The word that came to J from
Jer 18:18 us devise plans against J;
Jer 20: 2 Then Pashhur struck J the
Jer 20: 3 day that Pashhur brought J
Jer 26: 9 were gathered against J in
Jer 36: 4 Then J called Baruch the son
Jer 36: 5 And J commanded Baruch,
Jer 36:19 "Go and hide, you and J;
Jer 36:27 at the instruction of J,
Jer 36:32 Then J took another scroll

Jer	36:32	it at the instruction of J
Jer	37:12	that J went out of Jerusalem
Jer	37:13	and he seized J the prophet,
Jer	37:15	princes were angry with J,
Jer	37:16	When J entered the dungeon
Jer	37:21	Thus J remained in the court
Jer	38: 6	and they let J down with
Jer	38: 6	So J sank in the mire.
Jer	38:10	and lift J the prophet out
Jer	38:11	ropes into the dungeon to J.
Jer	38:12	the Ethiopian said to J,
Jer	38:15	J said to Zedekiah, "If I
Jer	38:16	the king swore secretly to J,
Jer	38:19	Zedekiah the king said to J,
Jer	39:14	they sent someone to take J
Jer	40: 2	captain of the guard took J
Jer	40: 6	Then J went to Gedaliah the
Jer	45: 1	book at the instruction of J,
Jer	51:60	So J wrote in a book all the
Jer	51:64	Thus far are the words of J.
Dan	9: 2	word of the LORD through J
Matt	2:17	what was spoken by J the
Matt	16:14	and others J or one of the
Matt	27: 9	what was spoken by J the

JERICHO

Num	22: 1	the Jordan across from J.
Deut	34: 3	the plain of the Valley of J,
Josh	2: 1	view the land, especially J.
Josh	4:13	battle, to the plains of J.
Josh	6: 1	Now J was securely shut up
Matt	20:29	Now as they went out of J,
Luke	10:30	down from Jerusalem to J,
Heb	11:30	By faith the walls of J fell

JEROBOAM

1Ki	11:26	J the son of Nebat, an
1Ki	13: 4	it came to pass when King J
1Ki	13:34	the sin of the house of J,
2Ki	14:28	the rest of the acts of J,
Hos	1: 1	and in the days of J the son
Amos	1: 1	and in the days of J the son
Amos	7: 9	sword against the house of J.

JERUSALEM (*see* SALEM)

Josh	10: 1	when Adoni-Zedek king of J
Josh	15: 8	Jebusite city (which is J)
Josh	18:28	Eleph, Jebus (which is J),
2Sa	9:13	So Mephibosheth dwelt in J,
2Sa	11: 1	But David remained at J.
2Sa	14:23	and brought Absalom to J.
2Sa	15:29	the ark of God back to J.
2Sa	20: 3	David came to his house at J.
2Sa	24:16	out His hand over J to
1Ki	2:36	yourself a house in J
1Ki	8: 1	Israel, to King Solomon in J,
1Ki	9:15	the Millo, the wall of J,
2Ki	23: 6	the Brook Kidron outside J,
2Ki	24:10	of Babylon came up against J,
2Ki	24:15	into captivity from J to
2Ch	24:18	wrath came upon Judah and J
2Ch	36:23	me to build Him a house at J
Ezra	1: 2	me to build Him a house at J
Ezra	1: 3	and let him go up to J which

Ezra	1:11	brought from Babylon to J.
Ezra	3: 8	out of the captivity to J,
Neh	2:12	put in my heart to do at J;
Neh	2:13	and viewed the walls of J
Neh	2:17	how J lies waste, and its
Neh	2:17	let us build the wall of J,
Neh	11: 1	one out of ten to dwell in J,
Neh	12:27	dedication of the wall of J
Neh	12:43	so that the joy of J was
Ps	51:18	Zion; Build the walls of J.
Ps	79: 1	They have laid J in heaps.
Ps	79: 3	shed like water all around J,
Ps	102:21	Zion, And His praise in J,
Ps	116:19	In the midst of you, O J.
Ps	122: 2	Within your gates, O J!
Ps	122: 3	J is built As a city that
Ps	122: 6	Pray for the peace of J:
Ps	125: 2	As the mountains surround J,
Ps	128: 5	may you see the good of J
Ps	135:21	Who dwells in J! Praise
Ps	137: 5	If I forget you, O J,
Ps	137: 6	If I do not exalt J Above
Ps	147: 2	The LORD builds up J;
Ps	147:12	O J! Praise your God, O
Eccl	1: 1	the son of David, king in J.
Eccl	1:12	was king over Israel in J.
Eccl	1:16	all who were before me in J.
Song	5: 8	charge you, O daughters of J,
Song	6: 4	as Tirzah, Lovely as J,
Is	1: 1	saw concerning Judah and J
Is	3: 8	For J stumbled, And Judah
Is	4: 4	and purged the blood of J
Is	10:12	work on Mount Zion and on J,
Is	10:32	of Zion, The hill of J.
Is	27:13	LORD in the holy mount at J.
Is	40: 2	"Speak comfort to J,
Is	44:26	messengers; Who says to J,
Is	51:17	awake! Stand up, O J,
Is	52: 1	beautiful garments, O J,
Is	52: 9	You waste places of J! For
Is	52: 9	people, He has redeemed J.
Is	62: 6	watchmen on your walls, O J;
Is	62: 7	And till He makes J a
Is	64:10	J a desolation.
Is	65:18	I create J as a rejoicing,
Jer	1: 3	until the carrying away of J
Jer	1:15	entrance of the gates of J,
Jer	2: 2	and cry in the hearing of J,
Jer	4: 4	Judah and inhabitants of J,
Jer	4:16	Yes, proclaim against J,
Jer	5: 1	fro through the streets of J;
Jer	6: 1	to flee from the midst of J!
Jer	6: 6	And build a mound against J.
Jer	7:34	and from the streets of J
Jer	8: 1	of the inhabitants of J,
Jer	9:11	I will make J a heap of
Jer	11: 6	and in the streets of J,
Jer	13: 9	and the great pride of J.
Jer	14:16	cast out in the streets of J
Jer	15: 5	will have pity on you, O J?
Jer	17:27	entering the gates of J on
Jer	17:27	devour the palaces of J,
Jer	19: 7	the counsel of Judah and J
Jer	23:14	thing in the prophets of J:

J

Jer	24: 8	the residue of J who remain
Jer	27:20	the nobles of Judah and J—
Jer	29: 1	carried away captive from J
Jer	32: 2	of Babylon's army besieged J,
Jer	33:16	And J will dwell safely.
Jer	35:17	on all the inhabitants of J
Jer	37:11	left the siege of J for
Jer	38:28	prison until the day that J
Jer	39: 8	broke down the walls of J.
Jer	40: 1	carried away captive from J
Jer	44: 6	and in the streets of J;
Jer	44: 9	and in the streets of J?
Jer	44:13	Egypt, as I have punished J,
Jer	52:29	carried away captive from J
Lam	1: 8	J has sinned gravely,
Lam	1:17	J has become an unclean
Lam	2:10	The virgins of J Bow their
Lam	2:13	liken you, O daughter of J?
Lam	4:12	Could enter the gates of J—
Dan	1: 1	king of Babylon came to J
Dan	6:10	his windows open toward J,
Dan	9:25	To restore and build J
Zech	14: 4	Which faces J on the east.
Zech	14: 8	waters shall flow from J,
Matt	23:37	"O Jerusalem, J,
Luke	9:51	set His face to go to J,
Luke	24:47	all nations, beginning at J.
Luke	24:49	but tarry in the city of J
John	4:20	and you Jews say that in J
John	4:21	on this mountain, nor in J,
Acts	1: 8	be witnesses to Me in J,
Acts	8: 1	the church which was at J;
Acts	8:26	road which goes down from J
Acts	8:27	and had come to J to
Acts	9: 2	might bring them bound to J.
Acts	9:13	has done to Your saints in J.
Acts	9:21	who called on this name in J,
Acts	11:27	days prophets came from J
Acts	16: 4	the apostles and elders at J.
Acts	20:16	he was hurrying to be at J,
Acts	20:22	go bound in the spirit to J,
Acts	21: 4	the Spirit not to go up to J.
Acts	21:13	but also to die at J for the
Acts	21:31	of the garrison that all J
Acts	24:11	days since I went up to J
Acts	25: 1	went up from Caesarea to J.
Acts	26:20	those in Damascus and in J,
Acts	28:17	as a prisoner from J into
Rom	15:25	But now I am going to J to
Rom	15:26	the saints who are in J.
Gal	1:17	nor did I go up to J to those
Gal	1:18	three years I went up to J
Gal	2: 1	years I went up again to J
Gal	4:25	and corresponds to J which
Gal	4:26	but the J above is free,
Heb	12:22	living God, the heavenly J,
Rev	3:12	city of My God, the New J,
Rev	21: 2	saw the holy city, New J,
Rev	21:10	the great city, the holy J,

JESHUA (see JOSHUA)

Ezra	2: 2	came with Zerubbabel were J,

JESSE

Ruth	4:22	Obed begot J,
Ruth	4:22	and J begot David.
1Sa	16: 1	I am sending you to J the
1Sa	16:10	Thus J made seven of his sons
1Sa	17:17	Then J said to his son David,
1Sa	22: 8	a covenant with the son of J;
2Sa	20: 1	inheritance in the son of J;
Ps	72:20	of David the son of J are
Is	11: 1	a Rod from the stem of J,
Is	11:10	there shall be a Root of J,
Matt	1: 6	and J begot David the king.
Acts	13:22	found David the son of J,
Rom	15:12	shall be a root of J;

JESUS (see CHRIST, JESUS')

Matt	1: 1	book of the genealogy of J
Matt	1:16	of whom was born J who is
Matt	1:18	Now the birth of J Christ
Matt	1:21	you shall call His name J,
Matt	2: 1	Now after J was born in
Matt	3:13	Then J came from Galilee to
Matt	4: 1	Then J was led up by the
Matt	4:12	Now when J heard that John
Matt	7:28	when J had ended these
Matt	8: 3	Then J put out His hand and
Matt	8:13	Then J said to the centurion,
Matt	8:20	And J said to him, "Foxes
Matt	8:22	But J said to him, "Follow
Matt	8:29	have we to do with You, J,
Matt	8:34	city came out to meet J.
Matt	9: 2	When J saw their faith, He
Matt	9:35	Then J went about all the
Matt	10: 5	These twelve J sent out and
Matt	11: 1	when J finished commanding
Matt	12:25	But J knew their thoughts,
Matt	15:32	Now J called His disciples
Matt	16:20	tell no one that He was J
Matt	16:21	From that time J began to
Matt	27:17	or J who is called Christ?"
Matt	27:37	THIS IS J THE KING OF THE
Matt	27:58	and asked for the body of J.
Mark	1: 1	of the gospel of J Christ,
Mark	1:24	J of Nazareth? Did You come
Mark	14:62	J said, "I am. And you will
Mark	16: 6	You seek J of Nazareth, who
Luke	1:31	and shall call His name J.
Luke	2:21	His name was called J,
Luke	2:43	the Boy J lingered behind in
Luke	2:52	And J increased in wisdom and
Luke	4:14	Then J returned in the power
Luke	4:34	J of Nazareth? Did You come
Luke	5:10	And J said to Simon, "Do
Luke	5:12	was full of leprosy saw J;
Luke	8:35	sitting at the feet of J,
Luke	8:45	And J said, "Who touched
Luke	9:42	Then J rebuked the unclean
Luke	9:58	And J said to him, "Foxes
Luke	9:60	J said to him, "Let the dead
Luke	10:21	In that hour J rejoiced in
Luke	13:14	because J had healed on the
Luke	17:13	their voices and said, "J,
Luke	18:38	he cried out, saying, "J,

Luke	19: 9	And J said to him, "Today	John	12:11	went away and believed in J.
Luke	19:35	and they set J on him.	John	12:16	but when J was glorified,
Luke	22:47	them and drew near to J to	John	12:21	"Sir, we wish to see J.
Luke	22:52	Then J said to the chief	John	13:23	whom J loved.
Luke	22:63	Now the men who held J	John	19:19	J OF NAZARETH, THE KING
Luke	23: 8	Now when Herod saw J,	John	20:19	J came and stood in the
Luke	23:20	wishing to release J,	John	20:26	J came, the doors being
Luke	23:25	but he delivered J to their	John	20:30	And truly J did many other
Luke	23:26	he might bear it after J.	John	20:31	that you may believe that J
Luke	23:34	Then J said, "Father,	John	21: 7	that disciple whom J loved
Luke	23:46	And when J had cried out with	Acts	1:11	up into heaven? This same J,
Luke	23:52	and asked for the body of J.	Acts	1:14	and Mary the mother of J,
Luke	24:19	The things concerning J of	Acts	3:13	glorified His Servant J,
Luke	24:36	J Himself stood in the midst	Acts	3:26	raised up His Servant J,
John	1:17	and truth came through J	Acts	4:10	that by the name of J Christ
John	1:37	speak, and they followed J.	Acts	16:18	you in the name of J Christ
John	1:45	J of Nazareth, the son of	Acts	16:31	Believe on the Lord J Christ,
John	1:47	J saw Nathanael coming toward	Acts	17: 7	there is another king—J.
John	2: 2	Now both J and His disciples	Acts	19:13	call the name of the Lord J
John	2: 4	J said to her, "Woman, what	Acts	19:15	J I know, and Paul I know;
John	2: 7	J said to them, "Fill the	Acts	20:24	I received from the Lord J,
John	2:11	This beginning of signs J did	Acts	22: 8	I am J of Nazareth, whom you
John	2:13	and J went up to Jerusalem.	Acts	26:15	Lord?' And He said, 'I am J,
John	3: 2	This man came to J by night	Acts	28:23	them concerning J from both
John	4:26	J said to her, "I who speak	Rom	1: 1	a bondservant of J Christ,
John	4:34	J said to them, "My food is	Rom	1: 3	concerning His Son J Christ
John	4:46	So J came again to Cana of	Rom	1: 6	you also are the called of J
John	4:50	J said to him, "Go your way;	Rom	1: 7	our Father and the Lord J
John	4:54	again is the second sign J	Rom	2:16	the secrets of men by J
John	5: 6	When J saw him lying there,	Rom	3:22	through faith in J Christ,
John	5:16	reason the Jews persecuted J,	Rom	3:26	the one who has faith in J.
John	6: 3	And J went up on the	Rom	4:24	in Him who raised up J our
John	6: 5	Then J lifted up His eyes,	Rom	6: 3	were baptized into Christ J
John	6:11	And J took the loaves, and	Rom	6:23	is eternal life in Christ J
John	6:14	had seen the sign that J	Rom	8: 1	to those who are in Christ J,
John	6:24	came to Capernaum, seeking J.	Rom	8: 2	Spirit of life in Christ J
John	6:42	they said, "Is not this J,	Rom	8:11	Spirit of Him who raised J
John	6:67	Then J said to the twelve,	Rom	8:39	of God which is in Christ J
John	7: 1	After these things J walked	Rom	10: 9	with your mouth the Lord J
John	7:14	the middle of the feast J	Rom	13:14	But put on the Lord J Christ,
John	7:39	because J was not yet	Rom	15:16	I might be a minister of J
John	7:50	Nicodemus (he who came to J	Rom	15:17	reason to glory in Christ J
John	8: 1	But J went to the Mount of	Rom	16: 3	fellow workers in Christ J,
John	8: 6	But J stooped down and wrote	1Co	1: 1	to be an apostle of J
John	8:59	but J hid Himself and went	1Co	1: 2	are sanctified in Christ J,
John	9:11	A Man called J made clay and	1Co	1: 8	in the day of our Lord J
John	9:14	Now it was a Sabbath when J	1Co	2: 2	anything among you except J
John	9:35	J heard that they had cast	1Co	5: 4	with the power of our Lord J
John	9:39	And J said, "For judgment I	1Co	8: 6	and one Lord J Christ,
John	10: 6	J used this illustration, but	1Co	9: 1	Have I not seen J Christ our
John	10:23	And J walked in the temple,	1Co	11:23	that the Lord J on the same
John	11: 5	Now J loved Martha and her	1Co	12: 3	by the Spirit of God calls J
John	11:13	J spoke of his death, but	1Co	12: 3	and no one can say that J is
John	11:21	Then Martha said to J,	1Co	15:57	victory through our Lord J
John	11:23	J said to her, "Your brother	2Co	1: 2	our Father and the Lord J
John	11:25	J said to her, "I am the	2Co	4: 5	but Christ J the Lord, and
John	11:33	when J saw her weeping, and	2Co	4: 6	of God in the face of J
John	11:35	J wept.	2Co	4:10	body the dying of the Lord J,
John	11:39	J said, "Take away the	2Co	4:10	that the life of J also may
John	11:44	J said to them, "Loose him,	2Co	4:14	will also raise us up with J,
John	11:51	year he prophesied that J	Gal	1:12	through the revelation of J
John	12: 1	J came to Bethany, where	Gal	2:16	of the law but by faith in J
John	12: 3	anointed the feet of J,	Gal	3:14	the Gentiles in Christ J,
John	12: 7	But J said, "Let her alone;	Gal	3:28	you are all one in Christ J.

J

Gal	5: 6	For in Christ J neither
Gal	6:14	in the cross of our Lord J
Gal	6:17	body the marks of the Lord J.
Eph	1: 1	and faithful in Christ J:
Eph	2: 6	heavenly places in Christ J,
Eph	2:10	created in Christ J for good
Eph	2:20	J Christ Himself being the
Eph	3: 1	the prisoner of Christ J for
Eph	4:21	by Him, as the truth is in J:
Eph	6:24	those who love our Lord J
Phil	1: 1	bondservants of J Christ,
Phil	1: 8	all with the affection of J
Phil	1:19	supply of the Spirit of J
Phil	2: 5	which was also in Christ J,
Phil	2:10	that at the name of J every
Phil	2:11	tongue should confess that J
Phil	2:19	But I trust in the Lord J to
Phil	3: 8	of the knowledge of Christ J
Phil	3:14	call of God in Christ J.
Phil	4: 7	and minds through Christ J.
Phil	4:19	riches in glory by Christ J.
Phil	4:21	every saint in Christ J.
Col	1:28	man perfect in Christ J.
Col	4:11	and J who is called Justus.
1Th	1:10	even J who delivers us from
1Th	3:13	at the coming of our Lord J
1Th	4:14	For if we believe that J died
1Th	4:14	Him those who sleep in J.
1Th	5:23	at the coming of our Lord J
2Th	1: 8	the gospel of our Lord J
2Th	2: 1	the coming of our Lord J
2Th	2:14	of the glory of our Lord J
1Ti	1:15	that Christ J came into the
1Ti	2: 5	and men, the Man Christ J,
1Ti	4: 6	will be a good minister of J
1Ti	6:14	blameless until our Lord J
2Ti	1: 1	of life which is in Christ J,
2Ti	2: 3	as a good soldier of J
2Ti	3:12	to live godly in Christ J
Tit	1: 4	the Father and the Lord J
Tit	2:13	our great God and Savior J
Phm	1: 1	a prisoner of Christ J,
Phm	1:23	fellow prisoner in Christ J,
Heb	2: 9	But we see J,who was made
Heb	3: 1	of our confession, Christ J,
Heb	4:14	J the Son of God, let us
Heb	7:22	by so much more J has become
Heb	10:10	offering of the body of J
Heb	10:19	Holiest by the blood of J,
Heb	12: 2	looking unto J,
Heb	12:24	to J the Mediator of the new
Heb	13: 8	J Christ is the same
Heb	13:20	who brought up our Lord J
Heb	13:21	through J Christ, to whom
1Pe	1: 1	an apostle of J Christ, To
1Pe	1: 7	glory at the revelation of J
1Pe	5:10	eternal glory by Christ J,
2Pe	1: 1	and apostle of J Christ,
1Jn	1: 7	and the blood of J Christ
1Jn	2: 1	J Christ the righteous.
1Jn	2:22	but he who denies that J is
1Jn	4: 2	spirit that confesses that J
1Jn	4:15	Whoever confesses that J is
1Jn	5: 5	but he who believes that J

1Jn	5: 6	J Christ; not only by water,
Jude	1	and preserved in J Christ
Rev	1: 1	The Revelation of J Christ,
Rev	1: 2	and to the testimony of J
Rev	1: 9	kingdom and patience of J
Rev	17: 6	blood of the martyrs of J.
Rev	22:21	The grace of our Lord J

JESUS' (*see* JESUS)

Matt	15:30	and they laid them down at J
Luke	10:39	who also sat at J feet and
John	12: 9	not for J sake only, but
John	13:25	leaning back on J breast, he

JETHRO (*see* REUEL)

Ex	3: 1	was tending the flock of J
Ex	18: 6	"I, your father-in-law J,

JEW (*see* JEWISH, JEWS, JUDAISM)

Esth	8: 7	Esther and Mordecai the J,
John	4: 9	is it that You, being a J,
Acts	21:39	I am a J from Tarsus, in
Acts	22: 3	"I am indeed a J,
Rom	1:16	for the J first and also for
Rom	2:28	For he is not a J who is
Rom	3: 1	advantage then has the J,
Rom	10:12	is no distinction between J
1Co	9:20	to the Jews I became as a J,
Gal	2:14	all, "If you, being a J,
Gal	3:28	There is neither J nor Greek,

JEWELS

Mal	3:17	day that I make them My j.

JEWISH (*see* JEW)

Zech	8:23	grasp the sleeve of a J man,
Acts	24:24	his wife Drusilla, who was J,
Tit	1:14	not giving heed to J fables

JEWS (*see* JEW)

Esth	4: 3	great mourning among the J,
Esth	4:14	will arise for the J from
Esth	8:16	The J had light and gladness,
Matt	2: 2	has been born King of the J?
Matt	27:37	JESUS THE KING OF THE J.
John	2:13	Now the Passover of the J
John	3: 1	Nicodemus, a ruler of the J.
John	4: 9	For J have no dealings
John	4:20	and you J say that in
John	4:22	for salvation is of the J.
John	7: 1	because the J sought to kill
John	7:13	of Him for fear of the J.
John	18:12	and the officers of the J
John	18:33	"Are You the King of the J?
John	18:36	not be delivered to the J;
John	19:19	THE KING OF THE J.
John	19:20	Then many of the J read this
John	19:21	write, 'The King of the J,
John	19:38	secretly, for fear of the J,
John	19:40	as the custom of the J is to
John	20:19	assembled, for fear of the J,
Acts	2: 5	were dwelling in Jerusalem J,
Acts	2:10	both J and proselytes,
Acts	9:23	the J plotted to kill him.

Acts	13: 5	in the synagogues of the J.
Acts	14: 2	But the unbelieving J stirred
Acts	14: 5	by both the Gentiles and J,
Acts	18: 4	and persuaded both J and
Acts	18: 5	and testified to the J that
Acts	18:14	mouth, Gallio said to the J,
Acts	18:19	and reasoned with the J.
Acts	18:28	he vigorously refuted the J
Acts	20: 3	And when the J plotted
Acts	20:19	me by the plotting of the J;
Acts	20:21	"testifying to J,
Acts	21:20	how many myriads of J there
Acts	21:21	you that you teach all the J
Acts	24: 5	dissension among all the J
Acts	24: 9	And the J also assented,
Acts	24:27	wanting to do the J a favor,
Acts	25: 2	and the chief men of the J
Acts	25: 8	against the law of the J,
Acts	26: 2	which I am accused by the J,
Rom	3: 9	previously charged both J
Rom	3:29	Or is He the God of the J
Rom	9:24	not of the J only, but also
1Co	1:22	For J request a sign, and
1Co	1:23	to the J a stumbling block
1Co	1:24	both J and Greeks, Christ
1Co	9:20	and to the J I became as a
1Co	10:32	either to the J or to the
2Co	11:24	From the J five times I
Gal	2:14	compel Gentiles to live as J?
Gal	2:15	We who are J by nature, and
Rev	2: 9	of those who say they are J
Rev	3: 9	who say they are J and are

JEZEBEL

1Ki	19: 1	And Ahab told J all that
1Ki	21:23	The dogs shall eat J by the
Rev	2:20	you allow that woman J,

JEZREEL (see JEZREELITE)

Josh	17:16	who are of the Valley of J.
Hos	1: 4	to him: "Call his name J,
Hos	1: 5	of Israel in the Valley of J.
Hos	2:22	oil; They shall answer J.

JEZREELITE (see JEZREEL)

1Ki	21: 7	the vineyard of Naboth the J
2Ki	9:21	the property of Naboth the J
2Ki	9:25	of the field of Naboth the J

JOAB

2Sa	2:14	Then Abner said to J,
2Sa	3:22	the servants of David and J
2Sa	11: 6	And J sent Uriah to David.

JOASH (see JEHOASH)

Judg	7:14	sword of Gideon the son of J,
2Ki	13:14	Then J the king of Israel
Hos	1: 1	of Jeroboam the son of J,
Amos	1: 1	of Jeroboam the son of J,

JOB (see JOB'S)

Job	1: 1	of Uz, whose name was J;
Job	1: 8	you considered My servant J,
Job	1:22	In all this J did not sin

Job	2: 7	and struck J with painful
Job	3: 1	After this J opened his mouth
Job	31:40	The words of J are ended.
Ezek	14:14	men, Noah, Daniel, and J,
Ezek	14:20	and J were in it, as I
Jas	5:11	of the perseverance of J

JOB'S† (see JOB)

Job	2:11	Now when J three friends
Job	42:10	And the LORD restored J

JOEL

Joel	1: 1	of the LORD that came to J
Acts	2:16	was spoken by the prophet J:

JOHN (see BAPTIST, MARK*)

Matt	3: 1	In those days J the Baptist
Matt	9:14	Then the disciples of J came
Matt	11:11	not risen one greater than J
Matt	11:12	And from the days of J the
Matt	11:13	the law prophesied until J.
Matt	11:18	For J came neither eating nor
Matt	14: 3	For Herod had laid hold of J
Matt	14: 8	Give me J the Baptist's head
Matt	14:10	So he sent and had J beheaded
Matt	16:14	Some say J the Baptist, some
Matt	21:25	"The baptism of J—
Mark	1: 9	and was baptized by J in the
Mark	1:19	and J his brother, who also
Mark	1:29	and Andrew, with James and J.
Mark	3:17	the son of Zebedee and J
Mark	6:14	J the Baptist is risen from
Mark	6:25	me at once the head of J
Mark	9: 2	took Peter, James, and J,
Luke	1:13	you shall call his name J.
Luke	5:33	Why do the disciples of J
Luke	7:24	When the messengers of J had
Luke	16:16	the prophets were until J.
Luke	20: 6	they are persuaded that J
Luke	22: 8	And He sent Peter and J,
John	1: 6	from God, whose name was J.
John	1:15	J bore witness of Him and
John	1:19	this is the testimony of J,
John	1:32	And J bore witness, saying,
John	3:24	For J had not yet been thrown
John	4: 1	more disciples than J
John	5:33	"You have sent to J,
John	10:41	J performed no sign, but all
Acts	1: 5	for J truly baptized with
Acts	1:13	staying: Peter, James, J,
Acts	3:11	held on to Peter and J,
Acts	4:13	the boldness of Peter and J,
Acts	12:12	the mother of J whose
Acts	12:25	they also took with them J
Acts	15:37	to take with them J called
Acts	18:25	knew only the baptism of J.
Gal	2: 9	when James, Cephas, and J,
Rev	1: 1	His angel to His servant J,

JOIN (see JOINED)

Ex	1:10	that they also j our enemies
Is	5: 8	Woe to those who j house to

J

JOINED (see JOIN)

Gen	2:24	father and mother and be j
Matt	19: 5	and mother and be j
Matt	19: 6	Therefore what God has j
Acts	17:34	some men j him and believed,
1Co	1:10	but that you be perfectly j
1Co	6:16	not know that he who is j
1Co	6:17	But he who is j to the Lord
Eph	2:21	being j together, grows into
Eph	4:16	j and knit together by what
Eph	5:31	and mother and be j

JOINT (see JOINTS)

Gen	32:25	of Jacob's hip was out of j
Ps	22:14	all My bones are out of j;
Rom	8:17	heirs of God and j heirs with
Eph	4:16	together by what every j

JOINTS (see JOINT)

Col	2:19	and knit together by j and
Heb	4:12	and of j and marrow, and is

JOKING†

Gen	19:14	he seemed to be j.
Prov	26:19	I was only j!"

JONAH

2Ki	14:25	through His servant J the
Jon	1: 1	word of the LORD came to J
Jon	3: 1	word of the LORD came to J
Matt	12:39	the sign of the prophet J.
Matt	12:40	For as J was three days and
Matt	12:41	and indeed a greater than J
John	1:42	"You are Simon the son of J.
John	21:16	time, "Simon, son of J,

JONATHAN

1Sa	13:22	who were with Saul and J.
1Sa	18: 3	Then J and David made a
2Sa	1:26	for you, my brother J;

JOPPA

2Ch	2:16	to you in rafts by sea to J,
Jon	1: 3	the LORD. He went down to J,
Acts	11:13	said to him, 'Send men to J,

JORAM (see JEHORAM)

2Ki	9:21	Then J king of Israel and
Matt	1: 8	Jehoshaphat begot J,

JORDAN

Gen	13:11	himself all the plain of J,
Num	13:29	and along the banks of the J.
Num	26: 3	the plains of Moab by the J,
Deut	1: 1	on this side of the J in
Deut	3:25	the good land beyond the J,
Josh	1: 2	arise, go over this J,
1Ki	17: 3	which flows into the J.
2Ki	5:10	Go and wash in the J seven
Is	9: 1	way of the sea, beyond the J,
Matt	3: 6	baptized by him in the J,
Matt	3:13	Galilee to John at the J to
Matt	4:15	the sea, beyond the J,

JOSEPH

Gen	30:25	when Rachel had borne J,
Gen	37: 3	Now Israel loved J more than
Gen	37: 5	Now J had a dream, and he
Gen	37:33	Without doubt J is torn to
Gen	39: 2	The LORD was with J,
Gen	39: 4	So J found favor in his
Gen	39: 6	Now J was handsome in form
Gen	39: 7	wife cast longing eyes on J,
Gen	39:10	as she spoke to J day by
Gen	40: 3	the place where J was
Gen	40: 4	of the guard charged J with
Gen	40: 9	butler told his dream to J,
Gen	40:22	as J had interpreted to
Gen	40:23	butler did not remember J,
Gen	41:14	Pharaoh sent and called J,
Gen	41:46	J was thirty years old when
Gen	41:50	And to J were born two sons
Gen	42: 6	Now J was governor over the
Gen	42: 8	So J recognized his brothers,
Gen	42: 9	Then J remembered the dreams
Gen	43:16	When J saw Benjamin with
Gen	45: 1	Then J could not restrain
Gen	45: 3	Then J said to his brothers,
Gen	45: 3	to his brothers, "I am J;
Gen	45: 4	I am J your brother, whom
Gen	45:26	J is still alive, and he is
Gen	45:28	J my son is still alive. I
Gen	47: 7	Then J brought in his father
Gen	47:17	and J gave them bread in
Gen	47:20	Then J bought all the land
Gen	47:26	And J made it a law over the
Gen	48:13	And J took them both, Ephraim
Gen	48:15	And he blessed J,
Gen	49:22	J is a fruitful bough, A
Gen	49:26	shall be on the head of J,
Gen	50: 7	So J went up to bury his
Gen	50:15	Perhaps J will hate us, and
Gen	50:17	And J wept when they spoke
Gen	50:22	And J lived one hundred and
Gen	50:23	J saw Ephraim's children to
Ex	1: 8	Egypt, who did not know J.
Ex	13:19	Moses took the bones of J
Num	13:11	from the tribe of J,
Num	27: 1	of Manasseh the son of J;
Josh	14: 4	For the children of J were
Josh	24:32	The bones of J,
Judg	1:22	And the house of J also went
Ps	77:15	The sons of Jacob and J.
Ps	78:67	He rejected the tent of J,
Ps	80: 1	You who lead J like a
Ps	81: 5	This He established in J as
Ps	105:17	sent a man before them—J—
Ezek	37:16	and write on it, 'For J,
Amos	5: 6	like fire in the house of J,
Amos	5:15	gracious to the remnant of J.
Amos	6: 6	for the affliction of J.
Obad	18	And the house of J a flame;
Matt	1:18	Mary was betrothed to J,
Matt	1:19	Then J her husband, being a
Matt	1:20	him in a dream, saying, "J,
Matt	2:13	of the Lord appeared to J
Matt	2:19	appeared in a dream to J in

Matt	27:59	When J had taken the body, he
Mark	15:43	J of Arimathea, a prominent
Mark	15:45	he granted the body to J.
Luke	1:27	to a man whose name was J,
Luke	2: 4	J also went up from Galilee,
Luke	2:16	haste and found Mary and J,
Luke	2:33	And J and His mother marveled
Luke	3:23	was supposed) the son of J,
John	1:45	of Nazareth, the son of J.
Acts	1:23	J called Barsabas, who was
Acts	7: 9	sold J into Egypt. But God
Heb	11:21	each of the sons of J,
Heb	11:22	By faith J, when he was
Rev	7: 8	of the tribe of J twelve

JOSHUA (see JESHUA)

Ex	17:10	So J did as Moses said to
Ex	17:13	So J defeated Amalek and his
Ex	24:13	arose with his assistant J,
Ex	33:11	but his servant J the son of
Num	11:28	So J the son of Nun, Moses'
Num	13:16	Hoshea the son of Nun, J.
Deut	31:23	Then He inaugurated J the son
Josh	4: 4	Then J called the twelve men
Josh	8:30	Now J built an altar to the
Josh	9: 3	of Gibeon heard what J had
Josh	9:15	So J made peace with them,
Josh	10: 6	the men of Gibeon sent to J
Josh	10:18	So J said, "Roll large
Josh	10:24	brought out those kings to J,
Josh	10:27	down of the sun that J
Josh	10:40	So J conquered all the landJ
Josh	11:13	which J burned.
Josh	11:18	J made war a long time with
Josh	11:21	J utterly destroyed them
Josh	12: 7	which J gave to the tribes
Josh	13: 1	Now J was old, advanced in
Josh	14:13	And J blessed him, and gave
Josh	18:10	and there J divided the land
Josh	23: 1	that J was old, advanced in
Josh	24:25	So J made a covenant with the
Josh	24:26	Then J wrote these words in
Josh	24:31	of the elders who outlived J,
Judg	1: 1	Now after the death of J it
Judg	2.21	any of the nations which J
Hag	1: 1	and to J the son of
Zech	3: 1	Then he showed me J the high
Zech	3: 3	Now J was clothed with filthy
Zech	3: 8	'Hear, O J, the high priest
Acts	7:45	also brought with J into the
Heb	4: 8	For if J had given them rest,

JOSIAH

1Ki	13: 2	J by name, shall be born to
2Ki	22: 1	J was eight years old when
2Ki	22: 3	eighteenth year of King J,
2Ch	35:25	Jeremiah also lamented for J.
Jer	1: 2	LORD came in the days of J
Zeph	1: 1	in the days of J the son of
Matt	1:10	begot Amon, and Amon begot J.

JOT†

Matt	5:18	one j or one tittle will by

JOTHAM

Judg	9: 5	But J the youngest son of
Judg	9:21	And J ran away and fled; and
Judg	9:57	on them came the curse of J
2Ki	15:36	the rest of the acts of J,
2Ki	15:38	So J rested with his fathers,
2Ki	16: 1	Remaliah, Ahaz the son of J,
Is	1: 1	in the days of Uzziah, J,
Is	7: 1	days of Ahaz the son of J,
Hos	1: 1	in the days of Uzziah, J,
Mic	1: 1	Moresheth in the days of J,
Matt	1: 9	Uzziah begot J,

JOURNEY (see JOURNEYED, JOURNEYS)

Gen	30:36	Then he put three days' j
Gen	31:23	him for seven days' j,
Ex	5: 3	let us go three days' j into
Deut	1: 2	It is eleven days' j from
Jon	3: 3	a three-day j in extent.
Matt	10:10	"nor bag for your j,
Mark	6: 8	to take nothing for the j
John	4: 6	being wearied from His j,
Acts	1:12	Jerusalem, a Sabbath day's j.

JOURNEYED (see JOURNEY)

Gen	11: 2	as they j from the east,
Luke	15:13	j to a far country, and

JOURNEYS (see JOURNEY)

Ex	40:38	throughout all their j.
2Co	11:26	in j often, in perils of

JOY (see JOYFUL)

Neh	8:10	for the j of the LORD is
Esth	8.17	the Jews had j and gladness,
Job	20: 5	And the j of the hypocrite
Job	38: 7	sons of God shouted for j?
Ps	16:11	presence is fullness of j;
Ps	21: 1	The king shall have j in
Ps	27: 6	I will offer sacrifices of j
Ps	30: 5	But j comes in the
Ps	32:11	righteous; And shout for j,
Ps	43: 4	God, To God my exceeding j;
Ps	48: 2	The j of the whole earth,
Ps	51: 8	Make me hear j and gladness,
Ps	51:12	Restore to me the j of Your
Ps	67: 4	be glad and sing for j!
Ps	126: 5	in tears Shall reap in j.
Ps	137: 6	Jerusalem Above my chief j.
Eccl	9: 7	Go, eat your bread with j,
Is	12: 3	Therefore with j you will
Is	22:13	j and gladness, Slaying
Is	35:10	With everlasting j on their
Is	55:12	you shall go out with j,
Is	61: 3	The oil of j for mourning,
Jer	15:16	Your word was to me the j
Jer	31:13	turn their mourning to j,
Matt	2:10	with exceedingly great j.
Matt	13:20	receives it with j;
Matt	25:21	Enter into the j of your
Matt	28: 8	tomb with fear and great j,
Luke	1:14	And you will have j and
Luke	1:44	babe leaped in my womb for j.

Luke	2:10	you good tidings of great j
Luke	15: 7	there will be more j in
John	15:11	that My j may remain in you,
John	15:11	and that your j may be
John	16:20	sorrow will be turned into j.
John	16:24	that your j may be full.
Acts	20:24	I may finish my race with j,
Rom	14:17	and peace and j in the Holy
Rom	15:13	of hope fill you with all j
2Co	2: 3	in you all that my j is
2Co	8: 2	the abundance of their j
Gal	5:22	of the Spirit is love, j,
Phil	2: 2	fulfill my j by being
Phil	4: 1	my j and crown, so stand
1Th	1: 6	with j of the Holy Spirit,
1Th	2:20	For you are our glory and j.
Heb	12: 2	who for the j that was set
Jas	1: 2	count it all j when you fall
1Pe	1: 8	you rejoice with j
1Pe	4:13	be glad with exceeding j.
1Jn	1: 4	we write to you that your j
3Jn	4	I have no greater j than to
Jude	24	His glory with exceeding j,

JOYFUL (see JOY, JOYFULLY)

Ps	63: 5	shall praise You with j
Ps	66: 1	Make a j shout to God, all
Ps	98: 8	Let the hills be j together
Ps	100: 1	Make a j shout to the LORD,
2Co	7: 4	I am exceedingly j in all
Heb	12:11	no chastening seems to be j

JOYFULLY (see JOYFUL)

Ps	98: 4	Shout j to the LORD, all
Eccl	9: 9	Live j with the wife whom
Luke	19: 6	down, and received Him j.

JUBILEE

Lev	25:11	fiftieth year shall be a J
Lev	25:28	it until the Year of J;

JUDAH (see JUDEA)

Gen	35:23	and Simeon, Levi, J,
Gen	37:26	So J said to his brothers,
Gen	49:10	shall not depart from J,
Ex	1: 2	Reuben, Simeon, Levi, and J;
Judg	17: 7	man from Bethlehem in J,
Ruth	4:12	Perez, whom Tamar bore to J,
2Sa	3:10	David over Israel and over J,
2Ki	14:12	And J was defeated by Israel,
2Ki	25:21	He sent them against J to
2Ch	16:11	the book of the kings of J
2Ch	36:23	at Jerusalem which is in J.
Ezra	1: 2	at Jerusalem which is in J.
Ezra	1: 8	Sheshbazzar the prince of J.
Ezra	2: 1	returned to Jerusalem and J,
Ezra	4: 1	when the adversaries of J
Ezra	9: 9	and to give us a wall in J
Neh	2: 5	I ask that you send me to J,
Neh	5:14	governor in the land of J,
Neh	13:12	Then all J brought the tithe
Neh	13:24	not speak the language of J,
Ps	48:11	Let the daughters of J be
Ps	60: 7	J is My lawgiver.

Ps	69:35	And build the cities of J,
Ps	76: 1	In J God is known; His
Ps	97: 8	And the daughters of J
Ps	114: 2	J became His sanctuary,
Prov	25: 1	men of Hezekiah king of J
Is	1: 1	which he saw concerning J
Is	2: 1	son of Amoz saw concerning J
Is	5: 7	And the men of J are His
Is	7:17	that Ephraim departed from J.
Is	11:13	Ephraim shall not envy J,
Is	26: 1	be sung in the land of J:
Is	36: 1	the fortified cities of J
Is	40: 9	Say to the cities of J,
Is	48: 1	from the wellsprings of J;
Jer	1: 3	the son of Josiah, king of J,
Jer	1:15	against all the cities of J.
Jer	1:18	land—Against the kings of J,
Jer	2:28	cities Are your gods, O J.
Jer	3: 7	And her treacherous sister J
Jer	4: 5	Declare in J and proclaim in
Jer	8: 1	the bones of the kings of J,
Jer	9:11	I will make the cities of J
Jer	10:22	To make the cities of J
Jer	11:13	cities were your gods, O J;
Jer	13: 9	I will ruin the pride of J
Jer	13:19	J shall be carried away
Jer	14: 2	J mourns, And her gates
Jer	14:19	You utterly rejected J?
Jer	17: 1	The sin of J is written with
Jer	19: 7	make void the counsel of J
Jer	19:13	the houses of the kings of J
Jer	23: 6	In His days J will be saved,
Jer	28: 4	with all the captives of J
Jer	29: 2	the princes of J and
Jer	29:22	up by all the captivity of J
Jer	30: 3	My people Israel and J,
Jer	32:35	to cause J to sin.'
Jer	33: 7	cause the captives of J and
Jer	33:16	In those days J will be
Jer	34: 7	and all the cities of J
Jer	36:31	and on the men of J all the
Jer	39: 6	killed all the nobles of J.
Jer	39:10	guard left in the land of J
Jer	40: 5	over the cities of J,
Jer	40:11	had left a remnant of J,
Jer	44: 6	kindled in the cities of J
Jer	44: 9	wickedness of the kings of J,
Jer	44:26	in the mouth of any man of J
Jer	51: 5	is not forsaken, nor J,
Jer	51:59	with Zedekiah the king of J
Lam	1: 3	J has gone into captivity,
Lam	1:15	The virgin daughter of J.
Ezek	8: 1	house with the elders of J
Ezek	37:19	with it, with the stick of J,
Dan	1: 2	gave Jehoiakim king of J
Dan	1: 6	those of the sons of J were
Dan	5:13	one of the captives from J,
Hos	1: 1	and Hezekiah, kings of J,
Hos	1: 7	have mercy on the house of J,
Hos	5: 5	J also stumbles with them.
Hos	5:12	And to the house of J like
Hos	5:13	And J saw his wound, Then
Hos	5:14	young lion to the house of J.
Hos	6: 4	what shall I do to you? O J,

Hos	11:12	But **J** still walks with God,
Hos	12: 2	brings a charge against **J**,
Joel	3: 1	back the captives of **J** and
Joel	3:20	But **J** shall abide forever,
Amos	1: 1	the days of Uzziah king of **J**,
Amos	2: 4	three transgressions of **J**,
Amos	2: 5	I will send a fire upon **J**,
Amos	7:12	seer! Flee to the land of **J**.
Mic	5: 2	among the thousands of **J**,
Matt	1: 2	and Jacob begot **J** and his
Matt	2: 6	in the land of **J**,
Matt	2: 6	among the rulers of **J**;
Rev	5: 5	the Lion of the tribe of **J**,
Rev	7: 5	of the tribe of **J** twelve

JUDAISM (see JEW)

Gal	1:13	of my former conduct in **J**,

JUDAS (see ISCARIOT, JUDE, THADDAEUS)

Matt	10: 4	and **J** Iscariot, who also
Luke	22: 3	Then Satan entered **J**,
John	12: 4	**J** Iscariot, Simon's son,
John	13: 2	put it into the heart of **J**
John	13:29	because **J** had the money box,
John	14:22	**J** (not Iscariot) said to Him,
Acts	1:13	and **J** the son of James.
Acts	5:37	**J** of Galilee rose up in the

JUDE† (see JUDAS)

Jude	1	**J**, a bondservant of Jesus

JUDEA (see JUDAH)

Matt	2: 1	was born in Bethlehem of **J**
Luke	1:65	all the hill country of **J**.
Luke	3: 1	Pilate being governor of **J**,
Acts	1: 8	and in all **J** and Samaria,

JUDGE (see JUDGED, JUDGES, JUDGMENT)

Gen	18:25	it from You! Shall not the **J**
Ex	2:14	made you a prince and a **j**
Ex	18:13	that Moses sat to **j** the
Deut	17: 8	is too hard for you to **j**,
Judg	2:18	the LORD was with the **j** and
Judg	11:27	me. May the LORD, the **J**,
1Sa	8: 6	Give us a king to **j** us." So
1Sa	24:12	Let the LORD **j** between you
1Ki	3: 9	an understanding heart to **j**
1Ch	16:33	For He is coming to **j** the
Ps	7:11	God is a just **j**,
Ps	9: 8	He shall **j** the world in
Ps	50: 6	For God Himself is **J**.
Ps	51: 4	And blameless when You **j**.
Ps	58: 1	Do you **j** uprightly, you
Ps	82: 8	**j** the earth; For You shall
Ps	96:13	for He is coming to **j** the
Ps	96:13	He shall **j** the world with
Is	2: 4	He shall **j** between the
Is	11: 3	And He shall not **j** by the
Is	11: 4	righteousness He shall **j**
Is	33:22	(For the LORD is our **J**,
Ezek	34:17	I shall **j** between sheep and
Ezek	34:20	I Myself will **j** between the
Amos	2: 3	And I will cut off the **j**
Mic	3:11	Her heads **j** for a bribe,

Mic	4: 3	He shall **j** between many
Matt	5:25	deliver you to the **j**,
Matt	7: 1	**J** not, that you be not
Matt	7: 2	with what judgment you **j**,
Luke	12:14	who made Me a **j** or an
Luke	12:58	lest he drag you to the **j**,
Luke	18: 6	Hear what the unjust **j** said.
Luke	19:22	of your own mouth I will **j**
John	7:24	but **j** with righteous
John	7:51	Does our law **j** a man before
John	8:15	You **j** according to the flesh;
John	8:15	I **j** no one.
John	8:16	"And yet if I do **j**,
John	12:47	for I did not come to **j** the
John	12:48	that I have spoken will **j**
John	18:31	You take Him and **j** Him
Acts	7:27	you a ruler and a **j**
Acts	10:42	ordained by God to be **J**
Acts	13:46	and **j** yourselves unworthy of
Acts	17:31	a day on which He will **j**
Acts	18:15	for I do not want to be a **j**
Acts	23: 3	wall! For you sit to **j** me
Rom	2: 1	O man, whoever you are who **j**,
Rom	2: 1	for in whatever you **j**
Rom	2:16	in the day when God will **j**
Rom	3: 6	For then how will God **j** the
Rom	14: 3	not him who does not eat **j**
Rom	14: 4	Who are you to **j** another's
Rom	14:10	But why do you **j** your
Rom	14:13	Therefore let us not **j** one
1Co	6: 2	know that the saints will **j**
1Co	6: 3	you not know that we shall **j**
1Co	10:15	**j** for yourselves what I say.
1Co	11:31	For if we would **j** ourselves,
Col	2:16	So let no one **j** you in food
2Ti	4: 1	who will **j** the living and
2Ti	4: 8	the Lord, the righteous **J**,
Heb	10:30	The LORD will **j** His
Heb	12:23	to God the **J** of all, to the
Heb	13: 4	and adulterers God will **j**.
Jas	4:11	But if you **j** the law, you
Jas	4:12	Who are you to **j** another?
Jas	5: 9	the **J** is standing at the
1Pe	4: 5	to Him who is ready to **j**
Rev	6:10	until You **j** and avenge our

JUDGED (see JUDGE)

Ex	18:26	but they **j** every small case
Judg	3:10	and he **j** Israel. He went out
Ps	37:33	condemn him when he is **j**.
Matt	7: 1	not, that you be not **j**.
John	16:11	the ruler of this world is **j**.
Acts	23: 6	of the dead I am being **j**!"
Rom	2:12	sinned in the law will be **j**
1Co	6: 2	And if the world will be **j**
Heb	11:11	because she **j** Him faithful
Rev	11:18	dead, that they should be **j**,
Rev	19: 2	because He has **j** the great
Rev	20:12	And the dead were **j**

JUDGES (see JUDGE)

Ex	21: 6	shall bring him to the **j**.
Deut	16:18	You shall appoint **j** and
Judg	2:16	the LORD raised up **j** who

J

Judg	2:17	would not listen to their j,
Ruth	1: 1	in the days when the j
1Sa	8: 1	old that he made his sons j
Ps	2:10	you j of the earth.
Ps	58:11	Surely He is God who j in
Ps	82: 1	He j among the gods.
Ps	148:11	Princes and all j of the
Is	1:26	I will restore your j as at
Zeph	3: 3	Her j are evening wolves
John	5:22	For the Father j no one, but
Acts	13:20	After that He gave them j
1Co	2:15	But he who is spiritual j all
1Co	4: 4	but He who j me is the Lord.
Jas	2: 4	and become j with evil
Jas	4:11	evil of the law and j the
1Pe	1:17	who without partiality j
1Pe	2:23	Himself to Him who j

JUDGMENT (see JUDGE, JUDGMENTS)

Ex	12:12	of Egypt I will execute j:
Ex	28:15	make the breastplate of j.
Deut	1:17	not show partiality in j;
Ps	1: 5	shall not stand in the j,
Eccl	11: 9	God will bring you into j.
Eccl	12:14	will bring every work into j,
Is	4: 4	by the spirit of j and by
Is	9: 7	it and establish it with j
Is	53: 8	taken from prison and from j,
Jer	5: 4	The j of their God.
Jer	8: 7	My people do not know the j
Jer	39: 5	where he pronounced j on
Jer	51: 9	For her j reaches to heaven
Jer	51:47	coming That I will bring j
Ezek	23:24	I will delegate j to them,
Ezek	34:16	strong, and feed them in j.
Dan	7:22	and a j was made in favor
Hos	10: 4	Thus j springs up like
Joel	3: 2	And I will enter into j
Hab	1: 4	Therefore perverse j
Hab	1:12	have appointed them for j;
Zech	8:16	Give j in your gates for
Matt	5:21	will be in danger of the j.
Matt	7: 2	For with what j you judge,
Matt	10:15	and Gomorrah in the day of j
Matt	12:41	will rise up in the j with
Matt	12:42	South will rise up in the j
Matt	27:19	he was sitting on the j
Luke	10:14	for Tyre and Sidon at the j
John	5:22	but has committed all j to
John	5:24	and shall not come into j,
John	5:27	Him authority to execute j
John	5:30	and My j is righteous,
John	8:16	My j is true; for I am not
John	9:39	For j I have come into this
John	12:31	Now is the j of this world;
John	16: 8	of righteousness, and of j:
John	19:13	out and sat down in the j
Acts	24:25	and the j to come, Felix was
Acts	25:10	I stand at Caesar's j seat,
Rom	1:32	knowing the righteous j of
Rom	5:18	one man's offense j came
Rom	13: 2	who resist will bring j on
Rom	14:10	all stand before the j seat
1Co	1:10	same mind and in the same j.

1Co	7:25	yet I give j as one whom the
1Co	11:29	manner eats and drinks j to
1Co	11:34	lest you come together for j.
Gal	5:10	you shall bear his j,
2Th	1: 5	evidence of the righteous j
Heb	6: 2	the dead, and of eternal j.
Heb	9:27	once, but after this the j,
Heb	10:27	fearful expectation of j,
Jas	2:13	For j is without mercy to the
Jas	2:13	mercy. Mercy triumphs over j.
Jas	3: 1	shall receive a stricter j.
Jas	5:12	"No," lest you fall into j.
1Pe	4:17	the time has come for j
2Pe	2: 4	to be reserved for j;
2Pe	2: 9	punishment for the day of j,
2Pe	3: 7	for fire until the day of j
1Jn	4:17	boldness in the day of j;
Jude	6	under darkness for the j of
Jude	15	to execute j on all, to
Rev	14: 7	for the hour of His j has
Rev	17: 1	I will show you the j of the
Rev	20: 4	and j was committed to them.

JUDGMENTS (see JUDGMENT)

Ex	6: 6	arm and with great j.
Lev	18: 5	keep My statutes and My j,
Ps	19: 9	The j of the LORD are
Ps	89:30	law And do not walk in My j,
Ps	119:39	For Your j are good.
Ps	119:52	I remembered Your j of old,
Hos	6: 5	And your j are like light
Rom	11:33	How unsearchable are His j
Rev	16: 7	and righteous are Your j.

JUST (see HONEST, JUSTICE, JUSTIFY, JUSTLY, UNJUST)

Gen	6: 9	Noah was a j man, perfect in
Judg	6:39	but let me speak j once
Ps	51: 4	That You may be found j when
Prov	4:18	But the path of the j is
Prov	11: 1	But a j weight is His
Is	45:21	A j God and a Savior;
Is	49: 4	Yet surely my j reward is
Is	52:14	J as many were astonished at
Hab	2: 4	But the j shall live by his
Zech	9: 9	He is j and having
Matt	1:19	being a j man, and not
Matt	5:45	and sends rain on the j and
Matt	27:19	nothing to do with that j
Matt	27:24	of the blood of this j
Luke	2:25	and this man was j and
Luke	6:31	And j as you want men to do
Luke	14:14	at the resurrection of the j.
Luke	15: 7	than over ninety-nine j
Acts	10:22	a j man, one who fears God
Acts	22:14	and see the J One, and hear
Rom	1:17	The j shall live by
Rom	3: 8	say. Their condemnation is j.
Rom	3:26	that He might be j and the
Rom	7:12	the commandment holy and j
1Co	13:12	but then I shall know j as I
Gal	3:11	the j shall live by
Eph	4:32	j as God in Christ forgave
Eph	5:25	j as Christ also loved the

Phil	4: 8	whatever things are j,
Col	4: 1	your bondservants what is j
1Th	5:11	j as you also are doing.
Tit	1: 8	is good, sober-minded, j,
Heb	2: 2	disobedience received a j
Heb	10:38	Now the j shall live
Heb	12:23	to the spirits of j men made
Jas	5: 6	you have murdered the j;
1Pe	3:18	the j for the unjust, that
1Jn	1: 9	He is faithful and j to
1Jn	2: 6	himself also to walk j as
1Jn	3: 3	j as He is pure.
1Jn	3: 7	j as He is righteous.
Rev	15: 3	Lord God Almighty! J and
Rev	16: 6	For it is their j due."

JUSTICE (see JUST)

Gen	18:19	to do righteousness and j,
Ex	23: 2	after many to pervert j.
1Ki	3:11	understanding to discern j,
Job	8: 3	does the Almighty pervert j?
Ps	33: 5	loves righteousness and j;
Ps	37: 6	And your j as the noonday.
Ps	82: 3	Do j to the afflicted and
Ps	89:14	Righteousness and j are the
Ps	101: 1	I will sing of mercy and j;
Is	1:17	Learn to do good; Seek j,
Is	5: 7	plant. He looked for j,
Is	9: 7	it with judgment and j
Is	10: 2	To rob the needy of j,
Is	30:18	the LORD is a God of j;
Is	42: 1	He will bring forth j to
Is	42: 4	Till He has established j
Is	59: 9	Therefore j is far from us,
Amos	5: 7	You who turn j to wormwood,
Amos	5:12	the poor from j at the
Amos	5:15	Establish j in the gate.
Amos	5:24	But let j run down like
Mal	2:17	"Where is the God of j?
Matt	12:18	And He will declare j
Matt	12:20	Till He sends forth j
Matt	23:23	j and mercy and faith. These
Luke	11:42	and pass by j and the love

JUSTIFICATION (see JUSTIFY)

Rom	4:25	was raised because of our j.

JUSTIFIED (see JUSTIFY)

Matt	11:19	sinners!' But wisdom is j
Matt	12:37	by your words you will be j,
Luke	18:14	man went down to his house j
Acts	13:39	everyone who believes is j
Acts	13:39	which you could not be j by
Rom	2:13	doers of the law will be j;
Rom	3: 4	That You may be j in
Rom	3:20	the law no flesh will be j
Rom	3:24	being j freely by His grace
Rom	3:28	we conclude that a man is j
Rom	4: 2	For if Abraham was j by
Rom	5: 1	having been j by faith, we
Rom	8:30	He called, these He also j;
Gal	2:16	that we might be j by faith
Gal	2:16	the law no flesh shall be j.
Gal	3:24	that we might be j by faith.

1Ti	3:16	J in the Spirit, Seen by
Jas	2:21	not Abraham our father j by
Jas	2:24	see then that a man is j by
Jas	2:25	not Rahab the harlot also j

JUSTIFIER† (see JUSTIFY)

Rom	3:26	He might be just and the j

JUSTIFIES (see JUSTIFY)

Prov	17:15	He who j the wicked, and he
Rom	4: 5	but believes on Him who j
Rom	8:33	elect? It is God who j.

JUSTIFY (see JUST, JUSTIFICATION, JUSTIFIED, JUSTIFIER, JUSTIFIES)

Ex	23: 7	For I will not j the wicked.
Is	53:11	My righteous Servant shall j
Gal	3: 8	foreseeing that God would j

JUSTLY (see JUST)

Mic	6: 8	require of you But to do j,
Luke	23:41	"And we indeed j,

JUSTUS

Acts	1:23	Barsabas, who was surnamed J,
Col	4:11	and Jesus who is called J

K

KADESH BARNEA

Num	32: 8	away from K to see the land
Deut	1: 2	by way of Mount Seir to K
Deut	1:19	Then we came to K
Deut	2:14	K until we crossed over
Josh	14: 7	me from K to spy out the land

KEEP (see KEEPER, KEEPING, KEEPS, KEPT)

Gen	2:15	of Eden to tend and k it.
Gen	17: 9	you shall k My covenant, you
Ex	19: 5	indeed obey My voice and k
Ex	20: 6	to those who love Me and k
Ex	20: 8	Sabbath day, to k it holy.
Ex	23:14	Three times you shall k a
Num	6:24	The LORD bless you and k
Deut	8: 2	whether you would k His
2Ki	23:21	K the Passover to the LORD
Ps	19:13	K back Your servant also
Ps	25:10	To such as k His covenant
Ps	34:13	K your tongue from evil,
Ps	91:11	To k you in all your ways.
Ps	140: 4	K me, O LORD, from the
Prov	1:15	K your foot from their
Prov	4: 4	K my commands, and live.
Prov	4:13	K her, for she is your
Prov	4:23	K your heart with all
Prov	6:24	To k you from the evil
Eccl	3: 7	A time to k silence, And a
Eccl	12:13	Fear God and k His
Is	6: 9	K on hearing, but do not
Is	26: 3	You will k him in perfect
Dan	9: 4	and with those who k His
Amos	5:13	Therefore the prudent k

Hab	2:20	Let all the earth k silence
Matt	19:17	k the commandments."
Matt	26:18	I will k the Passover at
Luke	4:10	over you, To k you,'
Luke	11:28	hear the word of God and k
Luke	19:40	you that if these should k
John	8:55	but I do know Him and k His
John	9:16	because He does not k the
John	12:25	life in this world will k
John	14:15	k My commandments.
John	14:23	he will k My word; and My
John	17:11	k through Your name those
Acts	5: 3	lie to the Holy Spirit and k
Acts	10:28	it is for a Jewish man to k
Acts	15: 5	and to command them to k
Acts	15:24	must be circumcised and k
Acts	15:29	If you k yourselves from
Acts	16:23	commanding the jailer to k
Acts	18: 9	and do not k silent;
1Co	5: 8	Therefore let us k the feast,
1Co	11: 2	me in all things and k the
1Co	14:28	let him k silent in church,
1Co	14:34	Let your women k silent in
Gal	5: 3	that he is a debtor to k
Gal	6:13	those who are circumcised k
Eph	4: 3	endeavoring to k the unity of
2Th	3:14	that person and do not k
1Ti	5:22	k yourself pure.
2Ti	1:12	that He is able to k what I
2Ti	1:14	k by the Holy Spirit who
Phm	1:13	whom I wished to k with me,
Jas	1:27	and to k oneself unspotted
Jas	2:10	For whoever shall k the whole
1Jn	2: 3	if we k His commandments.
1Jn	5:21	k yourselves from idols.
Jude	6	And the angels who did not k
Jude	24	to Him who is able to k you
Rev	1: 3	and k those things which are
Rev	3:10	I also will k you from the
Rev	22: 9	and of those who k the words

KEEPER (see KEEP, KEEPERS)

Gen	4: 2	Now Abel was a k of sheep,
Gen	4: 9	know. Am I my brother's k?
Ps	121: 5	The LORD is your k;
Luke	13: 7	Then he said to the k of his
Acts	16:27	And the k of the prison,

KEEPERS (see KEEPER)

Eccl	12: 3	In the day when the k of the

KEEPING (see KEEP)

Ex	34: 7	k mercy for thousands,
Ps	19:11	And in k them there is
Luke	2: 8	k watch over their flock by

KEEPS (see KEEP)

Ps	121: 3	He who k you will not
Ps	121: 4	He who k Israel Shall
Prov	29:18	But happy is he who k the
John	8:51	if anyone k My word he shall
John	14:21	has My commandments and k
1Jn	2: 5	But whoever k His word, truly
1Jn	5:18	who has been born of God k

Rev	2:26	and k My works until the
Rev	22: 7	Blessed is he who k the

KEPT (see KEEP)

Gen	37:11	but his father k the matter
Num	9: 5	And they k the Passover on
Job	31:16	If I have k the poor from
Ps	18:23	And I k myself from my
Ps	30: 3	You have k me alive, that I
Ps	32: 3	When I k silent, my bones
Dan	7:28	but I k the matter in my
Matt	19:20	All these things I have k
Matt	26:63	But Jesus k silent. And the
Matt	27:36	they k watch over Him there.
Mark	10:20	all these things I have k
Luke	1:66	all those who heard them k
Luke	2:19	But Mary k all these things
Luke	2:51	but His mother k all these
Luke	8:29	and he was k under guard,
Luke	18:21	All these things I have k
Luke	20:26	at His answer and k silent.
John	2:10	You have k the good wine
John	11:37	also have k this man from
John	12: 7	she has k this for the day
John	15:10	just as I have k My Father's
John	18:17	Then the servant girl who k
Acts	5: 2	And he k back part of the
Acts	12: 5	Peter was therefore k in
Acts	25: 4	that Paul should be k at
Rom	16:25	revelation of the mystery k
2Co	11: 9	And in everything I k myself
Gal	3:23	we were k under guard by the
Gal	3:23	k for the faith which would
2Ti	4: 7	I have k the faith.
Heb	11:28	By faith he k the Passover
1Pe	1: 5	who are k by the power of God
Rev	3: 8	have k My word, and have not
Rev	3:10	you have k My command

KEY (see KEYS)

Is	22:22	The k of the house of David
Luke	11:52	you have taken away the k
Rev	3: 7	He who has the k of
Rev	9: 1	To him was given the k to
Rev	20: 1	having the k to the

KEYS† (see KEY)

Matt	16:19	And I will give you the k of
Rev	1:18	And I have the k of Hades

KICK

Acts	9: 5	It is hard for you to k

KIDRON

2Sa	15:23	crossed over the Brook K,
John	18: 1	disciples over the Brook K,

KIDS

Gen	27:16	she put the skins of the k

KILL (see KILLED, KILLING, KILLS)

Gen	4:14	anyone who finds me will k
Gen	37:18	conspired against him to k
Ex	2:14	Do you intend to k me as you

Ex	12:21	and **k** the Passover lamb.
Ex	29:11	Then you shall **k** the bull
Deut	32:39	I **k** and I make alive; I
2Ki	5: 7	to **k** and make alive, that
Eccl	3: 3	A time to **k**, And a time
Jer	20:17	Because he did not **k** me from
Jer	40:15	and I will **k** Ishmael the son
Matt	10:28	do not fear those who **k**
Matt	10:28	kill the body but cannot **k**
Matt	17:23	and they will **k** Him, and the
Matt	21:38	let us **k** him and seize his
Matt	24: 9	you up to tribulation and **k**
Mark	3: 4	evil, to save life or to **k**?
Mark	9:31	and they will **k** Him. And
Mark	10:34	and **k** Him. And the third day
Luke	13:31	for Herod wants to **k** You."
Luke	15:23	the fatted calf here and **k**
Luke	22: 2	sought how they might **k** Him,
John	5:16	and sought to **k** Him, because
John	7: 1	the Jews sought to **k** Him.
John	10:10	except to steal, and to **k**,
Acts	5:33	furious and plotted to **k**
Acts	9:23	the Jews plotted to **k** him.
Acts	10:13	"Rise, Peter; **k** and eat."
Acts	27:42	the soldiers' plan was to **k**
Rev	2:23	I will **k** her children with

KILLED (see KILL)

Gen	4: 8	Abel his brother and **k** him.
Ex	2:12	he **k** the Egyptian and hid
Lev	6:25	the burnt offering is **k**,
Judg	9:54	A woman **k** him.'" So his
Judg	16:30	So the dead that he **k** at his
Judg	16:30	were more than he had **k** in
1Sa	17:36	Your servant has **k** both lion
1Sa	17:50	struck the Philistine and **k**
2Sa	12: 9	You have **k** Uriah the Hittite
2Sa	14: 6	one struck the other and **k**
1Ki	18.13	what I did when Jezebel **k**
1Ki	19:10	and **k** Your prophets with the
2Ki	10:11	So Jehu **k** all who remained of
2Ki	10:17	he **k** all who remained to
2Ki	23:29	And Pharaoh Necho **k** him at
2Ki	25:25	ten men and struck and **k**
Job	1:15	indeed they have **k** the
Job	1:17	and **k** the servants with the
Ps	44:22	Yet for Your sake we are **k**
Jer	39: 6	Then the king of Babylon **k**
Dan	3:22	the flame of the fire **k**
Amos	4:10	Your young men I **k** with a
Matt	16:21	and scribes, and be **k**,
Mark	9:31	kill Him. And after He is **k**,
Mark	12: 5	sent another, and him they **k**;
Luke	9:22	and scribes, and be **k**,
Luke	11:48	for they indeed **k** them, and
Luke	12: 5	Fear Him who, after He has **k**,
Luke	15:27	your father has **k** the fatted
Luke	22: 7	when the Passover must be **k**.
Acts	3:15	and **k** the Prince of life,
Acts	10:39	whom they **k** by hanging on a
Acts	12: 2	Then he **k** James the brother
Rom	7:11	and by it **k** me.
Rom	8:36	Your sake we are **k**
Rom	11: 3	they have **k** Your

2Co	6: 9	as chastened, and yet not **k**;
1Th	2:15	who **k** both the Lord Jesus and
Rev	2:13	who was **k** among you, where
Rev	9:18	a third of mankind was **k**—
Rev	13:15	image of the beast to be **k**.
Rev	19:21	And the rest were **k** with the

KILLING (see KILL)

Hos	4: 2	**K** and stealing and

KILLS (see KILL)

Gen	4:15	whoever **k** Cain, vengeance
Lev	17: 3	or who **k** it outside the
Lev	24:17	Whoever **k** any man shall
Deut	19: 4	Whoever **k** his neighbor
1Sa	2: 6	The LORD **k** and makes alive;
1Sa	17:26	be done for the man who **k**
Matt	23:37	the one who **k** the prophets
John	16: 2	is coming that whoever **k**
2Co	3: 6	the Spirit; for the letter **k**,

KIND (see KINDLY, KINDNESS, KINDS)

Gen	1:11	fruit according to its **k**,
Matt	17:21	this **k** does not go out
Luke	1:66	What **k** of child will this
1Co	13: 4	Love suffers long and is **k**;
Eph	4:32	And be **k** to one another,
1Th	1: 5	as you know what **k** of men we
Jas	1:24	immediately forgets what **k**

KINDLED (see KINDLES)

Ex	4:14	the anger of the LORD was **k**
Deut	32:22	For a fire is **k** by my anger,
Ps	2:12	When His wrath is **k** but a

KINDLES (see KINDLED)

Jas	3: 5	a forest a little fire **k**!

KINDLY (see KIND)

Gen	24:49	Now if you will deal **k** and
Ruth	1: 8	The LORD deal **k** with you,
Rom	12:10	Be **k** affectionate to one

KINDNESS (see KIND)

Gen	24:12	and show **k** to my master
Ruth	2:20	who has not forsaken His **k**
Ruth	3:10	For you have shown more **k**
Neh	9:17	to anger, Abundant in **k**,
Ps	117: 2	For His merciful **k** is great
Is	54: 8	But with everlasting **k** I
Is	54:10	But My **k** shall not depart
Joel	2:13	to anger, and of great **k**;
Gal	5:22	joy, peace, longsuffering, **k**,
Eph	2: 7	of His grace in His **k**
Col	3:12	put on tender mercies, **k**,
2Pe	1: 7	to godliness brotherly **k**,

KINDS (see KIND)

Lev	11:27	among all **k** of animals that
Matt	4:23	and healing all **k** of
Matt	5:11	and say all **k** of evil
1Co	12:10	to another different **k** of
1Ti	6:10	of money is a root of all **k**

K

KING (see KING'S, KINGS)

Gen	14:18	Then Melchizedek **k** of Salem
Gen	41:46	he stood before Pharaoh **k**
Ex	1: 8	Now there arose a new **k** over
Deut	17:15	you shall surely set a **k** over
Judg	17: 6	those days there was no **k**
1Sa	2:10	will give strength to His **k**,
1Sa	8: 5	Now make us a **k** to judge us
1Sa	8:10	people who asked him for a **k**.
1Sa	10:24	Long live the **k**!"
1Sa	11:15	and there they made Saul **k**
1Sa	12:12	LORD your God was your **k**.
1Sa	15:23	rejected you from being **k**.
2Sa	2: 4	there they anointed David **k**
2Sa	16:16	Long live the **k**! Long live
2Sa	18:33	Then the **k** was deeply moved,
2Sa	19: 1	the **k** is weeping and
2Sa	19: 2	The **k** is grieved for his
2Sa	19: 4	But the **k** covered his face,
2Sa	19:12	the last to bring back the **k**?
2Sa	19:15	to escort the **k** across the
2Sa	19:16	the men of Judah to meet **K**
2Sa	19:22	not know that today I am **k**
2Sa	19:23	And the **k** swore to him.
2Sa	19:30	Mephibosheth said to the **k**,
2Sa	19:36	And why should the **k** repay
2Sa	19:43	have ten shares in the **k**;
2Sa	20: 2	remained loyal to their **k**.
2Sa	20: 3	And the **k** took the ten
1Ki	1: 1	Now **K** David was old,
1Ki	1: 4	and she cared for the **k**,
1Ki	1: 5	I will be **k**"; and he
1Ki	1:13	then has Adonijah become **k**?
1Ki	1:15	Shunammite was serving the **k**.
1Ki	1:16	and did homage to the **k**.
1Ki	1:18	look! Adonijah has become **k**;
1Ki	1:19	all the sons of the **k**,
1Ki	1:25	Long live **K** Adonijah!'
1Ki	1:29	And the **k** took an oath and
1Ki	1:30	Solomon your son shall be **k**
1Ki	1:31	Let my lord **K** David live
1Ki	1:34	the prophet anoint him **k**
1Ki	1:34	Long live **K** Solomon!'
1Ki	1:37	than the throne of my lord **K**
1Ki	1:43	David has made Solomon **k**.
1Ki	1:45	prophet have anointed him **k**
1Ki	1:51	Adonijah is afraid of **K**
1Ki	1:53	So **K** Solomon sent them to
1Ki	2:26	to Abiathar the priest the **k**
1Ki	3: 4	Now the **k** went to Gibeon to
1Ki	3: 7	You have made Your servant **k**
1Ki	3:16	were harlots came to the **k**,
1Ki	3:24	brought a sword before the **k**.
1Ki	3:25	And the **k** said, "Divide the
1Ki	3:28	of the judgment which the **k**
1Ki	3:28	and they feared the **k**,
1Ki	4: 7	who provided food for the **k**
1Ki	4:27	and for all who came to **K**
1Ki	5: 1	Now Hiram **k** of Tyre sent his
1Ki	7:45	which Huram made for **K**
1Ki	9:15	for the labor force which **K**
1Ki	9:26	**K** Solomon also built a fleet
1Ki	10: 3	so difficult for the **k** that

1Ki	10: 6	Then she said to the **k**:
1Ki	10:10	the queen of Sheba gave to **K**
1Ki	10:22	For the **k** had merchant ships
1Ki	10:23	So **K** Solomon surpassed all
1Ki	10:27	The **k** made silver as common
1Ki	11: 1	But **K** Solomon loved many
1Ki	12: 6	Then **K** Rehoboam consulted
1Ki	12:15	So the **k** did not listen to
1Ki	12:28	Therefore the **k** asked advice,
1Ki	14:25	in the fifth year of **K**
1Ki	14:25	Rehoboam that Shishak **k** of
1Ki	21:10	blasphemed God and the **k**.
2Ki	3: 4	Now Mesha **k** of Moab was a
2Ki	11:12	Long live the **k**!"
2Ki	15:19	Pul **k** of Assyria came against
2Ki	16: 7	to Tiglath-Pileser **k** of
2Ki	18:13	Sennacherib **k** of Assyria
2Ki	23:29	In his days Pharaoh Necho **k**
2Ki	25: 2	until the eleventh year of **K**
2Ki	25: 5	the Chaldeans pursued the **k**,
2Ki	25: 6	So they took the **k** and
2Ki	25: 6	and brought him up to the **k**
2Ki	25:21	Then the **k** of Babylon struck
2Ki	25:22	whom Nebuchadnezzar **k** of
2Ki	25:24	in the land and serve the **k**
2Ki	25:27	captivity of Jehoiachin **k**
2Ki	25:27	that Evil-Merodach **k** of
2Ki	25:27	released Jehoiachin **k** of
2Ki	25:30	ration given him by the **k**,
1Ch	11: 3	Then they anointed David **k**
1Ch	15:29	through a window and saw **K**
1Ch	18: 3	David defeated Hadadezer **k**
1Ch	21:24	Then **K** David said to Ornan,
1Ch	23: 1	he made his son Solomon **k**
1Ch	25: 6	under the authority of the **k**.
1Ch	26:32	whom **K** David made officials
1Ch	27:24	of the chronicles of **K**
1Ch	27:31	were the officials over **K**
1Ch	28: 2	Then **K** David rose to his feet
1Ch	29:24	and also all the sons of **K**
1Ch	29:29	Now the acts of **K** David,
2Ch	1: 8	and have made me **k** in his
2Ch	1:15	Also the **k** made silver and
2Ch	2:12	for He has given **K** David a
2Ch	7: 5	**K** Solomon offered a sacrifice
2Ch	13: 1	Abijah became **k** over Judah.
2Ch	16: 1	Baasha **k** of Israel came up
2Ch	18: 3	So Ahab **k** of Israel said to
2Ch	18: 3	said to Jehoshaphat **k** of
2Ch	18:12	one accord encourage the **k**.
2Ch	21: 2	the sons of Jehoshaphat **k**
2Ch	23:11	Testimony, and made him **k**.
2Ch	23:12	running and praising the **k**,
2Ch	23:20	and set the **k** on the throne
2Ch	24:23	all their spoil to the **k** of
2Ch	25: 3	murdered his father the **k**.
2Ch	25:17	Now Amaziah **k** of Judah asked
2Ch	25:17	**k** of Israel, saying, "Come,
2Ch	25:18	And Joash **k** of Israel sent to
2Ch	26:18	And they withstood **K** Uzziah
2Ch	26:21	**K** Uzziah was a leper until
2Ch	28:19	Judah low because of Ahaz **k**
2Ch	28:20	Also Tiglath-Pileser **k** of
2Ch	28:22	This is that **K** Ahaz.

2Ch	30: 4	And the matter pleased the **k**	Is	32: 1	a **k** will reign in
2Ch	30: 6	with the letters from the **k**	Is	33:17	Your eyes will see the **K** in
2Ch	30: 6	to the command of the **k:**	Is	33:22	The LORD is our **K;**
2Ch	30:24	For Hezekiah **k** of Judah gave	Is	39: 3	Isaiah the prophet went to **K**
2Ch	32: 1	Sennacherib **k** of Assyria	Is	41:21	says the **K** of Jacob.
2Ch	33:25	who had conspired against **K**	Is	43:15	Creator of Israel, your **K.**
2Ch	33:25	land made his son Josiah **k**	Is	44: 6	the **K** of Israel, And his
2Ch	34:16	carried the book to the **k,**	Jer	8:19	Is not her **K** in her?"
2Ch	34:18	the scribe told the **k,**	Jer	10: 7	O **K** of the nations? For
2Ch	34:18	Shaphan read it before the **k.**	Jer	10:10	God and the everlasting **K.**
2Ch	34:19	when the **k** heard the words	Jer	25: 9	and Nebuchadnezzar the **k** of
2Ch	34:31	Then the **k** stood in his place	Jer	25:26	Also the **k** of Sheshach shall
2Ch	35:20	Necho **k** of Egypt came up to	Jer	27: 3	the **k** of Moab, the king of
2Ch	35:23	And the archers shot **K**	Jer	27: 3	the **k** of the Ammonites, the
2Ch	35:23	and the **k** said to his	Jer	27: 3	the **k** of Tyre, and the king
2Ch	36: 3	Now the **k** of Egypt deposed	Jer	27: 3	and the **k** of Sidon, by the
2Ch	36: 4	brother Eliakim **k** over	Jer	27: 8	under the yoke of the **k** of
2Ch	36: 6	Nebuchadnezzar **k** of Babylon	Jer	30: 9	God, And David their **k,**
2Ch	36:17	brought against them the **k**	Jer	34: 7	when the **k** of Babylon's army
2Ch	36:18	and the treasures of the **k**	Jer	36:21	So the **k** sent Jehudi to bring
2Ch	36:22	in the first year of Cyrus **k**	Jer	36:22	Now the **k** was sitting in the
Ezra	1: 2	Thus says Cyrus **k** of Persia:	Jer	36:23	that the **k** cut it with
Ezra	4: 2	the days of Esarhaddon **k** of	Jer	36:27	Now after the **k** had burned
Ezra	4: 5	until the reign of Darius **k**	Jer	37:18	Moreover Jeremiah said to **K**
Ezra	4: 7	wrote to Artaxerxes **k** of	Jer	37:20	hear now, O my lord the **k.**
Ezra	4:12	Let it be known to the **k** that	Jer	39: 6	Then the **k** of Babylon killed
Ezra	4:17	The **k** sent an answer: To	Jer	44:30	I will give Pharaoh Hophra **k**
Ezra	5:13	in the first year of Cyrus **k**	Jer	46:17	**k** of Egypt, is but a
Ezra	5:13	**K** Cyrus issued a decree to	Jer	50:17	First the **k** of Assyria
Neh	2: 3	May the **k** live forever! Why	Jer	50:17	last this Nebuchadnezzar **k**
Ps	2: 6	Yet I have set My **K** On My	Jer	52:10	Then the **k** of Babylon killed
Ps	5: 2	My **K** and my God, For to	Jer	52:27	Then the **k** of Babylon struck
Ps	10:16	The LORD is **K** forever and	Ezek	26: 7	**k** of kings, with horses,
Ps	24: 7	doors! And the **K** of glory	Ezek	28:12	up a lamentation for the **k**
Ps	33:16	No **k** is saved by the	Ezek	29: 2	your face against Pharaoh **k**
Ps	44: 4	You are my **K,** O God;	Ezek	37:22	and one **k** shall be king over
Ps	47: 2	He is a great **K** over all	Dan	1: 1	of the reign of Jehoiakim **k**
Ps	47: 6	Sing praises to our **K,**	Dan	1: 1	Nebuchadnezzar **k** of Babylon
Ps	47: 7	For God is the **K** of all the	Dan	1: 5	And the **k** appointed for them
Ps	48: 2	The city of the great **K.**	Dan	1: 5	might serve before the **k.**
Ps	74:12	For God is my **K** from of	Dan	1:19	Then the **k** interviewed them,
Ps	84: 3	My **K** and my God.	Dan	1:20	about which the **k** examined
Ps	95: 3	And the great **K** above all	Dan	1:21	until the first year of **K**
Ps	98: 6	before the LORD, the **K.**	Dan	2: 2	the Chaldeans to tell the **k**
Ps	145: 1	will extol You, my God, O **K;**	Dan	2: 4	Chaldeans spoke to the **k** in
Ps	149: 2	of Zion be joyful in their **K.**	Dan	2: 4	the king in Aramaic, "O **k,**
Prov	24:21	fear the LORD and the **k;**	Dan	2:12	For this reason the **k** was
Prov	25: 1	which the men of Hezekiah **k**	Dan	2:15	is the decree from the **k** so
Prov	29:14	The **k** who judges the poor	Dan	2:16	went in and asked the **k** to
Prov	30:27	The locusts have no **k,**	Dan	2:16	that he might tell the **k** the
Prov	31: 1	The words of **K** Lemuel, the	Dan	2:25	brought Daniel before the **k,**
Eccl	1: 1	**k** in Jerusalem.	Dan	2:25	who will make known to the **k**
Eccl	1:12	was **k** over Israel in	Dan	2:28	and He has made known to **K**
Eccl	4:13	Than an old and foolish **k**	Dan	2:29	"As for you, O **k,**
Eccl	10:16	when your **k** is a child,	Dan	2:37	are a **k** of kings. For the
Eccl	10:20	Do not curse the **k,**	Dan	3:18	let it be known to you, O **k,**
Song	1: 4	The **k** has brought me into	Dan	3:30	Then the **k** promoted Shadrach,
Song	3: 9	of Lebanon Solomon the **K**	Dan	4:37	and extol and honor the **K**
Song	3:11	And see **K** Solomon with the	Dan	5: 1	Belshazzar the **k** made a great
Is	6: 1	In the year that **K** Uzziah	Dan	5: 8	or make known to the **k** its
Is	6: 5	For my eyes have seen the **K,**	Dan	5: 9	Then **K** Belshazzar was greatly
Is	7: 6	and set a **k** over them, the	Dan	5:11	and **K** Nebuchadnezzar your
Is	7:17	The LORD will bring the **k** of	Dan	5:17	read the writing to the **k,**
Is	20: 1	when Sargon the **k** of Assyria	Dan	5:30	**k** of the Chaldeans, was

Dan	6: 6	K Darius, live forever!
Dan	6: 7	thirty days, except you, O k,
Dan	6: 9	Therefore K Darius signed the
Dan	6:17	and the k sealed it with his
Dan	6:19	Then the k arose very early
Dan	6:20	The k spoke, saying to
Dan	6:21	Then Daniel said to the k,
Dan	8:23	A k shall arise, Having
Dan	11: 3	Then a mighty k shall arise,
Dan	11: 5	Also the k of the South
Dan	11: 6	the South shall go to the k
Hos	1: 1	son of Joash, k of Israel.
Hos	3: 4	abide many days without k
Hos	3: 5	their God and David their k.
Hos	10: 3	they say, "We have no k,
Hos	13:11	I gave you a k in My anger,
Amos	1: 1	in the days of Uzziah k of
Amos	1: 1	k of Israel, two years
Amos	2: 1	he burned the bones of the k
Amos	7:10	of Bethel sent to Jeroboam k
Jon	3: 6	Then word came to the k of
Mic	6: 5	remember now What Balak k
Zeph	3:15	The K of Israel, the LORD,
Hag	1: 1	In the second year of K
Zech	9: 9	your K is coming to you; He
Zech	14: 5	In the days of Uzziah k of
Zech	14: 9	And the LORD shall be K
Zech	14:17	Jerusalem to worship the K,
Mal	1:14	I am a great K,
Matt	2: 1	in the days of Herod the k,
Matt	2: 2	is He who has been born K
Matt	5:35	is the city of the great K.
Matt	21: 5	your K is coming to
Matt	25:34	Then the K will say to those
Matt	27:11	Are You the K of the Jews?"
Matt	27:29	K of the Jews!"
Matt	27:37	THIS IS JESUS THE K OF THE
Matt	27:42	If He is the K of Israel,
Mark	15:32	the K of Israel, descend now
Luke	1: 5	the k of Judea, a certain
Luke	14:31	"Or what k, going to make
Luke	19:38	Blessed is the K who
Luke	23: 2	He Himself is Christ, a K.
John	1:49	Son of God! You are the K
John	6:15	Him by force to make Him k,
John	12:15	your K is coming,
John	18:37	Are You a k then?" Jesus
John	18:37	say rightly that I am a k.
John	19:12	Whoever makes himself a k
John	19:14	Behold your K!"
John	19:15	"Shall I crucify your K?
John	19:15	We have no k but Caesar!"
John	19:19	THE K OF THE JEWS.
John	19:21	The K of the Jews,' but, 'He
Acts	13:22	up for them David as k,
Acts	25:13	And after some days K
Acts	26: 7	K Agrippa, I am accused by
Acts	26:13	"at midday, O k,
Acts	26:19	K Agrippa, I was not
Acts	26:27	K Agrippa, do you believe the
1Ti	1:17	Now to the K eternal,
1Ti	6:15	the K of kings and Lord of
Heb	7: 1	k of Salem, priest of the

Heb	7: 2	k of righteousness," and
Heb	7: 2	meaning "k of peace,"
Heb	11:27	fearing the wrath of the k;
1Pe	2:13	whether to the k as supreme,
1Pe	2:17	Fear God. Honor the k.
Rev	15: 3	O K of the saints!
Rev	17:14	He is Lord of lords and K
Rev	19:16	K OF KINGS AND LORD OF

KING'S (see KING)

Gen	14:17	the K Valley), after his
1Ki	4: 5	a priest and the k friend;
2Ki	25: 4	which was by the k garden,
Neh	1:11	For I was the k cupbearer.
Amos	7:13	For it is the k sanctuary,
Heb	11:23	were not afraid of the k

KINGDOM (see KINGDOMS)

Gen	10:10	And the beginning of his k
Ex	19: 6	And you shall be to Me a k of
Deut	17:18	sits on the throne of his k,
Deut	17:20	prolong his days in his k,
1Sa	18: 8	more can he have but the k?
2Sa	7:12	and I will establish his k.
2Sa	7:13	the throne of his k forever.
1Ki	2:46	Thus the k was established
Esth	4:14	you have come to the k for
Esth	5: 3	up to half the k!"
Ps	22:28	For the k is the LORD's,
Ps	45: 6	is the scepter of Your k.
Ps	103:19	And His k rules over all.
Ps	145:12	glorious majesty of His k.
Ps	145:13	Your k is an everlasting
Is	9: 7	of David and over His k,
Jer	18: 7	a nation and concerning a k,
Dan	2:39	you shall arise another k
Dan	2:39	a third k of bronze, which
Dan	2:40	And the fourth k shall be as
Dan	2:41	the k shall be divided; yet
Dan	4:25	Most High rules in the k of
Dan	5: 7	be the third ruler in the k.
Dan	5:21	High God rules in the k of
Dan	5:26	God has numbered your k,
Dan	5:28	Your k has been divided, and
Dan	7:23	beast shall be A fourth k
Dan	7:27	His k is an everlasting
Matt	3: 2	for the k of heaven is at
Matt	4:23	the gospel of the k,
Matt	5: 3	For theirs is the k of
Matt	5:19	be called least in the k of
Matt	5:19	be called great in the k of
Matt	5:20	by no means enter the k of
Matt	6:10	Your k come. Your will be
Matt	6:13	For Yours is the k and the
Matt	6:33	But seek first the k of God
Matt	8:11	and Jacob in the k of
Matt	8:12	But the sons of the k will be
Matt	10: 7	The k of heaven is at hand.'
Matt	12:28	surely the k of God has come
Matt	13:11	know the mysteries of the k
Matt	13:24	The k of heaven is like a man
Matt	13:38	seeds are the sons of the k,
Matt	13:41	will gather out of His k

Matt	13:43	forth as the sun in the **k**
Matt	16:19	give you the keys of the **k**
Matt	16:28	Son of Man coming in His **k**.
Matt	18: 1	then is greatest in the **k**
Matt	18: 3	by no means enter the **k** of
Matt	19:12	eunuchs for the **k** of
Matt	19:14	for of such is the **k** of
Matt	19:23	a rich man to enter the **k**
Matt	20:21	other on the left, in Your **k**.
Matt	24: 7	and **k** against kingdom. And
Matt	24:14	And this gospel of the **k** will
Matt	25:34	inherit the **k** prepared for
Matt	26:29	with you in My Father's **k**.
Mark	1:14	the gospel of the **k** of God,
Mark	1:15	and the **k** of God is at hand.
Mark	3:24	that **k** cannot stand.
Mark	4:11	to know the mystery of the **k**
Mark	4:26	The **k** of God is as if a man
Mark	4:30	what shall we liken the **k**
Mark	6:23	give you, up to half of my **k**.
Mark	9: 1	death till they see the **k**
Mark	9:47	for you to enter the **k** of
Mark	10:14	for of such is the **k** of God.
Mark	10:23	have riches to enter the **k**
Mark	10:24	in riches to enter the **k** of
Mark	12:34	You are not far from the **k** of
Mark	14:25	I drink it new in the **k** of
Mark	15:43	himself waiting for the **k**
Luke	1:33	and of His **k** there will be
Luke	8: 1	the glad tidings of the **k**
Luke	9:62	is fit for the **k** of God."
Luke	10: 9	The **k** of God has come near to
Luke	12:32	pleasure to give you the **k**.
Luke	13:18	What is the **k** of God like?
Luke	13:29	and sit down in the **k** of
Luke	14:15	shall eat bread in the **k** of
Luke	17:21	the **k** of God is within
Luke	18:24	have riches to enter the **k**
Luke	19:11	because they thought the **k**
Luke	19:12	to receive for himself a **k**
Luke	22:18	of the vine until the **k** of
Luke	22:30	drink at My table in My **k**,
Luke	23:42	me when You come into Your **k**.
Luke	23:51	was also waiting for the **k**
John	3: 3	he cannot see the **k** of
John	3: 5	he cannot enter the **k** of
John	18:36	My **k** is not of this world. If
Acts	1: 6	at this time restore the **k**
Acts	20:25	I have gone preaching the **k**
Acts	28:23	solemnly testified of the **k**
Rom	14:17	for the **k** of God is not
1Co	6: 9	will not inherit the **k** of
1Co	15:24	when He delivers the **k** to
Eph	5: 5	any inheritance in the **k** of
Col	1:13	and conveyed us into the **k**
Col	4:11	fellow workers for the **k** of
1Th	2:12	who calls you into His own **k**
2Th	1: 5	be counted worthy of the **k**
2Ti	4: 1	at His appearing and His **k**:
2Ti	4:18	me for His heavenly **k**.
Heb	1: 8	the scepter of Your **K**.
Heb	12:28	since we are receiving a **k**
Jas	2: 5	in faith and heirs of the **k**

2Pe	1:11	into the everlasting **k** of
Rev	1: 9	in the tribulation and **k**
Rev	17:17	and to give their **k** to the

KINGDOMS (see KINGDOM)

Josh	11:10	the head of all those **k**.
1Ki	4:21	Solomon reigned over all **k**
2Ki	19:15	of all the **k** of the earth.
2Ch	36:23	All the **k** of the earth the
Ezra	1: 2	All the **k** of the earth the
Jer	1:10	the nations and over the **k**,
Jer	51:20	With you I will destroy **k**;
Dan	8:22	four **k** shall arise out of
Luke	4: 5	showed Him all the **k** of the
Heb	11:33	who through faith subdued **k**,
Rev	11:15	The **k** of this world have
Rev	11:15	world have become the **k**

KINGS (see KING)

Gen	14: 9	four **k** against five.
Gen	17:16	**k** of peoples shall be from
2Sa	11: 1	at the time when **k** go out
1Ch	9: 1	in the book of the **k** of
Job	3:14	With **k** and counselors of the
Ps	2: 2	The **k** of the earth set
Ps	2:10	Now therefore, be wise, O **k**;
Ps	135:10	nations And slew mighty **k**—
Ps	138: 4	All the **k** of the earth shall
Prov	8:15	By me **k** reign, And rulers
Prov	31: 4	It is not for **k** to drink
Is	52:15	**K** shall shut their mouths
Dan	2:21	He removes **k** and raises up
Dan	2:37	O king, are a king of **k**.
Dan	2:47	God of gods, the Lord of **k**,
Dan	7:17	are four **k** which arise out
Dan	7:24	The ten horns are ten **k**
Dan	7:24	And shall subdue three **k**.
Dan	8:20	they are the **k** of Media and
Dan	10:13	left alone there with the **k**
Dan	11: 2	three more **k** will arise in
Hos	7: 7	All their **k** have fallen.
Hos	8: 4	"They set up **k**,
Matt	10:18	before governors and **k** for
Luke	10:24	you that many prophets and **k**
Luke	21:12	You will be brought before **k**
Luke	22:25	The **k** of the Gentiles
Acts	4:26	The **k** of the earth
1Ti	2: 2	for **k** and all who are in
1Ti	6:15	the King of **k** and Lord of
Rev	1: 5	and the ruler over the **k** of
Rev	1: 6	and has made us **k** and priests
Rev	10:11	nations, tongues, and **k**.
Rev	16:12	so that the way of the **k**
Rev	17:10	"There are also seven **k**.
Rev	17:12	which you saw are ten **k** who
Rev	17:14	Lord of lords and King of **k**;
Rev	19:16	KING OF **K** AND LORD OF

KIRJATH JEARIM

1Sa	7: 2	ark remained in **K** a long time

KISS (see KISSED, KISSES)

Gen	27:26	Come near now and **k** me, my

K

Ps	2:12	K the Son, lest He be angry,
Song	1: 2	Let him k me with the kisses
Matt	26:48	sign, saying, "Whomever I k,
Luke	22:48	the Son of Man with a k?
Rom	16:16	one another with a holy k.
1Th	5:26	the brethren with a holy k.
1Pe	5:14	Greet one another with a k of

KISSED (see KISS)

Gen	29:11	Then Jacob k Rachel, and
Ps	85:10	and peace have k.
Matt	26:49	Rabbi!" and k Him.

KISSES (see KISS)

Song	1: 2	Let him kiss me with the k

KNEE (see KNEES)

Gen	41:43	Bow the k!" So he set him
Matt	27:29	And they bowed the k before
Rom	11: 4	have not bowed the k
Rom	14:11	Every k shall bow to
Phil	2:10	at the name of Jesus every k

KNEEL (see KNELT)

Gen	24:11	And he made his camels k down

KNEES (see KNEE)

Gen	30: 3	will bear a child on my k,
Job	4: 4	strengthened the feeble k;
Is	35: 3	And make firm the feeble k.
Heb	12:12	hang down, and the feeble k,

KNELT (see KNEEL)

Dan	6:10	he k down on his knees three
Luke	22:41	and He k down and prayed,

KNEW (see KNOW)

Gen	3: 7	and they k that they were
Gen	4: 1	Now Adam k Eve his wife, and
Deut	34:10	whom the LORD k face to
Judg	19:25	And they k her and abused
Job	23: 3	that I k where I might find
Jer	1: 5	I formed you in the womb I k
Dan	5:21	till he k that the Most High
Dan	6:10	Now when Daniel k that the
Hos	13: 5	I k you in the wilderness,
Matt	7:23	I never k you; depart from
Matt	12:25	But Jesus k their thoughts,
Matt	25:24	I k you to be a hard man,
Matt	25:26	you k that I reap where I
Luke	19:22	You k that I was an austere
Luke	24:31	eyes were opened and they k
John	2: 9	who had drawn the water k),
John	2:25	for He k what was in man.
John	4:10	If you k the gift of God, and
John	13: 1	when Jesus k that His hour
John	13:11	For He k who would betray
John	13:28	But no one at the table k for
Acts	3:10	Then they k that it was he
Acts	18:25	though he k only the baptism
Rom	1:21	although they k God, they
1Co	2: 8	of the rulers of this age k;
2Co	5:21	For He made Him who k no sin

KNIFE

Gen	22: 6	fire in his hand, and a k,
Prov	23: 2	And put a k to your throat

KNIT

1Sa	18: 1	the soul of Jonathan was k
Eph	4:16	joined and k together by
Col	2: 2	being k together in love,
Col	2:19	nourished and k together by

KNOCK (see KNOCKED, KNOCKS)

Matt	7: 7	seek, and you will find; k,
Rev	3:20	I stand at the door and k.

KNOCKED (see KNOCK)

Acts	12:13	And as Peter k at the door of

KNOCKS (see KNOCK)

Song	5: 2	voice of my beloved! He k,
Matt	7: 8	and to him who k it will be

KNOW (see KNEW, KNOWING, KNOWLEDGE, KNOWN, KNOWS, UNKNOWN)

Gen	3:22	to k good and evil. And now,
Gen	19: 5	them out to us that we may k
Gen	19:33	and he did not k when she
Ex	1: 8	who did not k Joseph.
Ex	3: 7	for I k their sorrows.
Ex	33:12	I k you by name, and you have
Deut	8: 2	to k what was in your
Deut	8: 3	manna which you did not k
Deut	13: 3	your God is testing you to k
Deut	29:26	gods that they did not k and
1Sa	2:12	they did not k the LORD.
1Sa	3: 7	(Now Samuel did not yet k the
1Ki	17:24	Now by this I k that you are
Job	19:25	For I k that my Redeemer
Job	38: 5	Surely you k! Or who
Job	42: 2	I k that You can do
Ps	4: 3	But k that the LORD has set
Ps	9:10	And those who k Your name
Ps	9:20	That the nations may k
Ps	20: 6	Now I k that the LORD saves
Ps	35:11	me things that I do not k.
Ps	39: 4	make me to k my end, And
Ps	39: 4	That I may k how frail I
Ps	46:10	and k that I am God; I
Ps	51: 6	part You will make me to k
Ps	69: 5	You k my foolishness; And
Ps	69:19	You k my reproach, my shame,
Ps	73:11	they say, "How does God k?
Ps	79: 6	on the nations that do not k
Ps	83:18	That they may k that You,
Ps	89:15	are the people who k the
Ps	92: 6	A senseless man does not k,
Ps	95:10	And they do not k My ways.'
Ps	100: 3	K that the LORD, He is God
Ps	119:79	Those who k Your
Ps	139: 2	You k my sitting down and my
Ps	139: 4	You k it altogether.
Ps	139:23	and k my heart; Try me, and
Ps	139:23	and k my anxieties;

Prov	1: 2	To k wisdom and instruction,
Prov	7:23	He did not k it would
Prov	24:12	Surely we did not k this,"
Prov	27: 1	For you do not k what a day
Prov	30: 4	His Son's name, If you k?
Eccl	1:17	And I set my heart to k
Eccl	1:17	to know wisdom and to k
Eccl	7:25	I applied my heart to k,
Eccl	7:25	To k the wickedness of
Eccl	8: 7	For he does not k what will
Eccl	9: 5	But the dead k nothing,
Eccl	10:15	For they do not even k how
Eccl	11: 9	But k that for all these
Is	1: 3	But Israel does not k,
Is	7:15	that He may k to refuse the
Is	9: 9	All the people will k—
Is	19:21	and the Egyptians will k the
Is	41:20	That they may see and k,
Is	41:22	And k the latter end of
Is	44: 9	They neither see nor k,
Is	48: 8	hear, Surely you did not k;
Is	49:26	All flesh shall k That I,
Is	51: 7	you who k righteousness,
Is	52: 6	My people shall k My name;
Is	55: 5	call a nation you do not k,
Is	58: 2	And delight to k My ways,
Jer	2:19	K therefore and see that
Jer	5:15	whose language you do not k,
Jer	7: 9	other gods whom you do not k,
Jer	9: 3	And they do not k Me,"
Jer	10:23	I k the way of man is not
Jer	10:25	who do not k You, And on
Jer	14:18	in a land they do not k.
Jer	15:15	O LORD, You k;
Jer	15:15	K that for Your sake I have
Jer	17: 9	Who can k it?
Jer	31:34	K the LORD,' for they all
Jer	31:34	for they all shall k Me,
Jer	44: 3	gods whom they did not k,
Jer	48:17	And all you who k his name,
Ezek	2: 5	yet they will k that a
Ezek	6: 7	and you shall k that I am
Ezek	21: 5	that all flesh may k that I,
Ezek	25:14	and they shall k My
Ezek	37: 3	"O Lord GOD, You k.
Ezek	37:28	The nations also will k that
Ezek	38:16	so that the nations may k
Ezek	39:23	The Gentiles shall k that the
Hos	2: 8	For she did not k That I
Hos	2:20	And you shall k the LORD.
Hos	6: 3	Let us k, Let us pursue
Matt	1:25	and did not k her till she
Matt	6: 3	do not let your left hand k
Matt	7:11	k how to give good gifts to
Matt	7:16	You will k them by their
Matt	7:20	by their fruits you will k
Matt	11:27	Nor does anyone k the Father
Matt	24:42	for you do not k what hour
Matt	25:12	I do not k you.'
Matt	25:13	for you k neither the day
Matt	26:72	I do not k the Man!"
Luke	1:18	How shall I k this? For I am
Luke	1:34	since I do not k a man?"
Luke	2:49	Did you not k that I must be
Luke	22:34	deny three times that you k
Luke	22:57	I do not k Him."
Luke	23:34	for they do not k what they
John	1:10	and the world did not k Him.
John	2: 9	and did not k where it came
John	3: 2	we k that You are a teacher
John	3:10	and do not k these things?
John	3:11	We speak what We k and
John	4:22	worship what you do not k;
John	4:22	we k what we worship, for
John	4:25	I k that Messiah is coming"
John	4:32	to eat of which you do not k.
John	7:28	You both k Me, and you know
John	7:29	But I k Him, for I am from
John	8:28	then you will k that I am
John	8:32	And you shall k the truth,
John	8:55	but I k Him. And if I say,
John	8:55	but I do k Him and keep His
John	9:20	We k that this is our son,
John	9:21	he now sees we do not k,
John	9:21	opened his eyes we do not k.
John	9:25	I do not know. One thing I k,
John	10: 4	for they k his voice.
John	10:14	and I k My sheep, and am
John	10:15	even so I k the Father; and
John	11:24	I k that he will rise again
John	13:12	Do you k what I have done to
John	13:17	If you k these things,
John	13:18	I k whom I have chosen; but
John	14: 4	"And where I go you k,
John	14: 4	you know, and the way you k.
John	14: 5	and how can we k the way?"
John	14: 7	and from now on you k Him
John	14:17	but you k Him, for He dwells
John	14:31	But that the world may k that
John	15:18	you k that it hated Me
John	17: 3	that they may k You, the
John	17:23	and that the world may k
John	21:15	You k that I love You." He
John	21:17	You k all things; You know
John	21:24	and we k that his testimony
Acts	1: 7	It is not for you to k times
Acts	7:18	king arose who did not k
Acts	17:19	May we k what this new
Acts	19:15	and said, "Jesus I k,
Rom	6: 3	Or do you not k that as many
Rom	6:16	Do you not k that to whom you
Rom	7:18	For I k that in me (that is,
Rom	8:28	And we k that all things work
1Co	1:21	through wisdom did not k
1Co	2: 2	For I determined not to k
1Co	2:14	nor can he k them, because
1Co	3:16	Do you not k that you are the
1Co	6:15	Do you not k that your bodies
1Co	9:13	Do you not k that those who
1Co	13: 9	For we k in part and we
1Co	13:12	Now I k in part, but then I
2Co	8: 9	For you k the grace of our
2Co	12: 2	I k a man in Christ who
2Co	12: 2	in the body I do not k,
2Co	12: 3	out of the body I do not k,
Gal	4: 8	when you did not k God, you

K

Eph	1:18	that you may **k** what is the
Eph	3:19	to **k** the love of Christ which
Phil	3:10	that I may **k** Him and the
1Th	1: 5	as you **k** what kind of men we
2Ti	1:12	for I **k** whom I have believed
Tit	1:16	They profess to **k** God, but in
Heb	8:11	**K** the LORD,' for all
Heb	8:11	for all shall **k** Me,
1Jn	2: 3	by this we know that we **k**
1Jn	2: 4	I **k** Him," and does not keep
1Jn	2: 5	By this we **k** that we are in
1Jn	3: 1	the world does not **k** us,
1Jn	3: 1	because it did not **k** Him.
1Jn	3: 2	but we **k** that when He is
1Jn	3:14	We **k** that we have passed from
1Jn	3:15	and you **k** that no murderer
1Jn	3:16	By this we **k** love, because
1Jn	3:24	And by this we **k** that He
1Jn	4: 2	By this you **k** the Spirit of
1Jn	4: 8	who does not love does not **k**
1Jn	4:13	By this we **k** that we abide in
1Jn	5: 2	By this we **k** that we love the
1Jn	5:13	that you may **k** that you have
1Jn	5:18	We **k** that whoever is born of
1Jn	5:19	We **k** that we are of God, and
1Jn	5:20	And we **k** that the Son of God
1Jn	5:20	that we may **k** Him who is
Rev	2: 2	I **k** your works, your labor,
Rev	2: 9	I **k** your works, tribulation,
Rev	2: 9	and I **k** the blasphemy of
Rev	2:13	I **k** your works, and where you
Rev	3: 3	and you will not **k** what hour
Rev	3:15	I **k** your works, that you are

KNOWING (*see* KNOW)

Gen	3: 5	**k** good and evil."
1Co	15:58	**k** that your labor is not in
2Ti	3:14	**k** from whom you have learned
Heb	11: 8	not **k** where he was going.
1Pe	1:18	**k** that you were not redeemed

KNOWLEDGE (*see* KNOW)

Gen	2: 9	and the tree of the **k** of
2Ch	1:10	"Now give me wisdom and **k**,
Job	34:35	'Job speaks without **k**,
Job	35:16	multiplies words without **k**.
Job	38: 2	counsel By words without **k**?
Job	42: 3	who hides counsel without **k**?
Ps	19: 2	night unto night reveals **k**.
Ps	73:11	And is there **k** in the Most
Ps	94:10	He who teaches man **k**?
Ps	139: 6	Such **k** is too wonderful
Ps	144: 3	that You take **k** of him? Or
Prov	1: 7	LORD is the beginning of **k**,
Prov	2: 5	And find the **k** of God.
Prov	9:10	And the **k** of the Holy One
Eccl	1:18	And he who increases **k**
Eccl	9:10	is no work or device or **k**
Eccl	12: 9	he still taught the people **k**;
Is	11: 2	The Spirit of **k** and of the
Is	11: 9	shall be full of the **k** of
Is	53:11	By His **k** My righteous
Dan	12: 4	and **k** shall increase."
Hos	4: 1	is no truth or mercy Or **k**

Hos	4: 6	are destroyed for lack of **k**.
Hos	4: 6	Because you have rejected **k**,
Hos	6: 3	Let us pursue the **k** of the
Hos	6: 6	And the **k** of God more than
Hab	2:14	will be filled With the **k**
Luke	11:52	have taken away the key of **k**.
Acts	24:22	having more accurate **k** of
Rom	1:28	to retain God in their **k**,
Rom	2:20	having the form of **k** and
Rom	10: 2	God, but not according to **k**.
Rom	11:33	both of the wisdom and **k** of
Rom	15:14	goodness, filled with all **k**,
1Co	8: 1	**K** puffs up, but love
1Co	12: 8	to another the word of **k**
1Co	13: 2	all mysteries and all **k**,
1Co	13: 8	cease; whether there is **k**,
2Co	2:14	the fragrance of His **k** in
2Co	4: 6	to give the light of the **k**
Eph	3:19	of Christ which passes **k**;
Col	1: 9	may be filled with the **k** of
Col	1:10	and increasing in the **k** of
Col	2: 3	treasures of wisdom and **k**.
Col	3:10	new man who is renewed in **k**
1Ti	2: 4	saved and to come to the **k**
1Ti	6:20	of what is falsely called **k**—
2Ti	3: 7	never able to come to the **k**
2Pe	1: 5	faith virtue, to virtue **k**,
2Pe	1: 6	to **k** self-control, to
2Pe	3:18	but grow in the grace and **k**

KNOWN (*see* KNOW)

Gen	18:19	For I have **k** him, in order
Gen	19: 8	daughters who have not **k** a
Gen	45: 1	while Joseph made himself **k**
Ex	2:14	Surely this thing is **k**!"
Ex	6: 3	My name LORD I was not **k**
Num	12: 6	make Myself **k** to him in a
Ps	76: 1	In Judah God is **k**;
Ps	78: 3	Which we have heard and **k**,
Ps	89: 1	my mouth will I make **k** Your
Ps	91:14	because he has **k** My name.
Ps	105: 1	Make **k** His deeds among the
Ps	139: 1	You have searched me and **k**
Is	40:21	Have you not **k**?
Is	45: 4	though you have not **k** Me.
Is	59: 8	way of peace they have not **k**,
Amos	3: 2	You only have I **k** of all the
Hab	3: 2	of the years make it **k**;
Matt	10:26	hidden that will not be **k**.
Matt	12: 7	But if you had **k** what this
Matt	12:16	them not to make Him **k**,
Matt	12:33	for a tree is **k** by its
Matt	24:43	master of the house had **k**
Luke	2:15	which the Lord has made **k** to
Luke	2:17	they made widely **k** the
Luke	8:17	hidden that will not be **k**
Luke	24:35	and how He was **k** to them in
John	8:19	If you had **k** Me, you would
John	8:19	you would have **k** My Father
John	8:55	Yet you have not **k** Him, but I
John	10:14	and am **k** by My own.
John	14: 7	If you had **k** Me, you would
John	14: 7	you would have **k** My Father
John	17:25	but I have **k** You; and these

John	17:25	and these have **k** that You
Acts	15:18	**K** to God from eternity are
Rom	1:19	because what may be **k** of God
Rom	3:17	peace they have not **k**.
Rom	7: 7	I would not have **k** sin
Rom	9:22	and to make His power **k**,
Rom	9:23	and that He might make **k** the
Rom	11:34	For who has **k** the mind
Rom	16:26	Scriptures has been made **k**
1Co	2: 8	age knew; for had they **k**,
1Co	2:16	who has **k** the mind of
1Co	8: 3	this one is **k** by Him.
1Co	13:12	know just as I also am **k**.
2Co	3: 2	**k** and read by all men;
Eph	3: 3	by revelation He made **k** to
Eph	3:10	of God might be made **k** by
Eph	6:19	my mouth boldly to make **k**
Phil	4: 5	Let your gentleness be **k** to
Phil	4: 6	let your requests be made **k**
2Ti	3:15	from childhood you have **k**
Heb	3:10	And they have not **k**
2Pe	1:16	fables when we made **k** to
2Pe	2:21	than having **k** it, to turn
1Jn	2:13	Because you have **k** Him who
1Jn	2:14	Because you have **k** Him who
1Jn	3: 6	has neither seen Him nor **k**
1Jn	4:16	And we have **k** and believed
Rev	2:24	who have not **k** the depths of

KNOWS (see KNOW, KNOWLEDGE)

Gen	3: 5	For God **k** that in the day you
Deut	34: 6	but no one **k** his grave to
Ps	1: 6	For the LORD **k** the way of
Ps	90:11	Who **k** the power of Your
Ps	94:11	The LORD **k** the thoughts of
Ps	103:14	For He **k** our frame; He
Ps	104:19	The sun **k** its going down.
Ps	139:14	And that my soul **k** very
Eccl	2:19	And who **k** whether he will be
Is	1: 3	The ox **k** its owner And the
Jer	9:24	That he understands and **k**
Matt	6: 8	For your Father **k** the things
Matt	6:32	For your heavenly Father **k**
Matt	11:27	and no one **k** the Son except
Matt	24:36	that day and hour no one **k**,
Luke	16:15	but God **k** your hearts. For
John	7:27	no one **k** where He is from."
John	10:15	As the Father **k** Me, even so I
John	14:17	it neither sees Him nor **k**
Acts	15: 8	who **k** the heart,
Rom	8:27	He who searches the hearts **k**
1Co	2:11	For what man **k** the things of
1Co	3:20	The LORD **k** the thoughts
1Co	8: 2	if anyone thinks that he **k**
1Co	8: 2	he **k** nothing yet as he ought
2Co	12: 2	body I do not know, God **k**—
2Ti	2:19	The Lord **k** those who are
Jas	4:17	to him who **k** to do good and
1Jn	3:20	and **k** all things.
1Jn	4: 6	He who **k** God hears us; he
1Jn	4: 7	loves is born of God and **k**
Rev	2:17	name written which no one **k**

KORAH

Num	16: 6	**K** and all your company;
Jude	11	in the rebellion of **K̇**.

L

LABAN

Gen	29:15	Then **L** said to Jacob,
Gen	29:16	Now **L** had two daughters: the
Gen	46:18	whom **L** gave to Leah his
Gen	46:25	whom **L** gave to Rachel his

LABOR (see LABORED, LABORER, LABORS)

Gen	35:16	and she had hard **l**.
Ex	20: 9	Six days you shall **l** and do
Josh	17:13	the Canaanites to forced **l**,
Josh	24:13	land for which you did not **l**,
Is	21: 3	the pangs of a woman in **l**.
Jer	20:18	from the womb to see **l** and
Matt	11:28	all you who **l** and are heavy
John	6:27	Do not **l** for the food which
1Co	3: 8	according to his own **l**.
1Co	15:58	knowing that your **l** is not
Eph	4:28	longer, but rather let him **l**,
Col	1:29	To this end I also **l**,
1Th	1: 3	**l** of love, and patience of
1Th	2: 9	our **l** and toil; for laboring
1Th	3: 5	and our **l** might be in vain.
Rev	2: 2	"I know your works, your **l**,

LABORED (see LABOR)

Eccl	2:21	to a man who has not **l** for
Is	49: 4	I have **l** in vain, I have
Dan	6:14	and he **l** till the going down
Jon	4:10	for which you have not **l**,
John	4:38	for which you have not **l**;
John	4:38	not labored; others have **l**,
Rom	16:12	who have **l** in the Lord.
1Co	15:10	but I **l** more abundantly than
Gal	4:11	lest I have **l** for you in
Phil	2:16	I have not run in vain or **l**
Phil	4: 3	help these women who **l** with
Rev	2: 3	and have **l** for My name's

LABORER† (see LABOR, LABORERS)

Luke	10: 7	for the **l** is worthy of his
1Th	3: 2	and our fellow **l** in the
1Ti	5:18	The **l** is worthy of his
Phm	1: 1	beloved friend and fellow **l**,

LABORERS (see LABORER)

Matt	9:37	but the **l** are few.
Matt	9:38	of the harvest to send out **l**
Matt	20: 1	in the morning to hire **l**
Phm	1:24	Demas, Luke, my fellow **l**.

LABORS (see LABOR)

Ex	23:16	the firstfruits of your **l**
Eccl	4: 8	is no end to all his **l**,
Jer	31: 8	child And the one who **l**
John	4:38	have entered into their **l**.

L

Rom	8:22	whole creation groans and l
2Co	6: 5	in tumults, in l,
2Co	10:15	that is, in other men's l,
2Co	11:23	in l more abundant, in
Rev	14:13	they may rest from their l,

LACHISH

Is	36: 2	with a great army from L to

LACK (see LACKED, LACKING, LACKS)

Hos	4: 6	people are destroyed for l
Amos	4: 6	And l of bread in all your
Mark	10:21	to him, "One thing you l:
2Co	8:14	may supply their l,
2Co	8:15	little had no l.
1Th	4:12	and that you may l nothing.

LACKED (see LACK)

Acts	4:34	anyone among them who l;
Phil	4:10	but you l opportunity.

LACKING (see LACK)

Eccl	1:15	And what is l cannot be
1Co	16:17	for what was l on your part
Phil	2:30	to supply what was l in your
Col	1:24	up in my flesh what is l in

LACKS (see LACK)

Eccl	10: 3	He l wisdom, And he shows
Jas	1: 5	If any of you l wisdom, let

LAD (see LADS)

Gen	21:17	God heard the voice of the l.
Gen	22: 5	the l and I will go yonder
John	6: 9	There is a l here who has

LADDER†

Gen	28:12	a l was set up on the

LADEN†

Is	1: 4	A people l with iniquity,
Matt	11:28	who labor and are heavy l,

LADS (see LAD)

Gen	48:16	from all evil, Bless the l;

LAID (see LAY)

Gen	9:23	l it on both their
Gen	22: 6	of the burnt offering and l
Gen	22: 9	he bound Isaac his son and l
Ex	2: 3	and l it in the reeds by
Ex	16:24	So they l it up till morning,
Num	27:23	And he l his hands on him and
1Ki	3:20	and l her dead child in my
1Ki	16:34	He l its foundation with
Ps	102:25	Of old You l the foundation
Is	53: 6	And the LORD has l on Him
Zech	4: 9	hands of Zerubbabel Have l
Matt	3:10	And even now the ax is l to
Matt	18:28	and he l hands on him and
Matt	27:60	and l it in his new tomb
Mark	15:47	observed where He was l.
Mark	16: 6	See the place where they l
Luke	2: 7	and l Him in a manger,

Luke	12:19	you have many goods l up for
John	7:30	but no one l a hand on Him,
John	13: 4	rose from supper and l aside
John	20: 2	not know where they have l
Acts	4: 3	And they l hands on them, and
Acts	4:35	and l them at the apostles'
Acts	7:58	And the witnesses l down
Acts	16:23	And when they had l many
Acts	19: 6	And when Paul had l hands on
1Co	3:10	master builder I have l the
1Co	3:11	lay than that which is l,
1Co	9:16	for necessity is l upon me;
Phil	3:12	Christ Jesus has also l
Col	1: 5	of the hope which is l up
2Ti	4: 8	there is l up for me the
Heb	1:10	in the beginning l the
1Jn	3:16	because He l down His life
Rev	1:17	But He l His right hand on
Rev	21:16	The city is l out as a

LAIN (see LIE)

Luke	23:53	where no one had ever l
John	20:12	the body of Jesus had l.

LAISH (see DAN)

Judg	18:29	of the city formerly was L.

LAKE

Luke	8:22	to the other side of the l.
Luke	8:23	windstorm came down on the l,
Rev	20:10	was cast into the l of fire

LAMA†

Matt	27:46	l sabachthani?" that is,
Mark	15:34	l sabachthani?" which is

LAMB (see LAMB'S, LAMBS)

Gen	22: 7	but where is the l for a
Gen	22: 8	provide for Himself the l
Ex	12: 3	a l for a household.
Ex	12:21	and kill the Passover l.
Ex	13:13	you shall redeem with a l;
2Sa	12: 3	except one little ewe l
2Sa	12: 4	but he took the poor man's l
Is	11: 6	also shall dwell with the l,
Is	53: 7	He was led as a l to the
Is	65:25	The wolf and the l shall
Mark	14:12	they killed the Passover l,
John	1:29	Behold! The L of God who
John	1:36	Behold the L of God!"
Acts	8:32	And as a l before its
1Pe	1:19	as of a l without blemish
Rev	5: 8	fell down before the L,
Rev	5:12	Worthy is the L who was slain
Rev	6:16	and from the wrath of the L!
Rev	7:14	white in the blood of the L.
Rev	13: 8	in the Book of Life of the L
Rev	15: 3	God, and the song of the L,
Rev	17:14	will make war with the L,
Rev	19: 9	marriage supper of the L!'
Rev	21:14	the twelve apostles of the L.
Rev	21:23	The L is its light.

LAMB'S (see LAMB)

Rev	21:27	who are written in the L

LAMBS (see LAMB)

Gen	30:40	Then Jacob separated the l,
Lev	14:10	day he shall take two male l
Ezra	6:20	slaughtered the Passover l
Ps	114: 4	The little hills like l.
Is	40:11	He will gather the l with
Luke	10: 3	I send you out as l among
John	21:15	He said to him, "Feed My l.

LAME

Lev	21:18	approach: a man blind or l,
2Sa	4: 4	had a son who was l in
Is	35: 6	Then the l shall leap like a
Matt	11: 5	The blind see and the l
Luke	7:22	the l walk, the lepers are
Acts	3: 2	And a certain man l from his
Acts	8: 7	who were paralyzed and l
Heb	12:13	so that what is l may not be

LAMECH

Gen	4:23	Then L said to his wives:
Gen	5:30	L lived five hundred and

LAMENT (see LAMENTATION, LAMENTED)

Judg	11:40	four days each year to l
2Sa	3:33	And the king sang a l over
Lam	2: 8	the rampart and wall to l;

LAMENTATION (see LAMENT)

Gen	50:10	a great and very solemn l.
2Sa	1:17	David lamented with this l
Jer	31:15	L and bitter weeping,
Mic	2: 4	And lament with a bitter l,
Matt	2:18	was heard in Ramah, L,

LAMENTED (see LAMENT)

2Sa	1:17	Then David l with this
2Ch	35:25	Jeremiah also l for Josiah.

LAMP (see LAMPS, LAMPSTAND)

Ex	27:20	to cause the l to burn
1Sa	3: 3	and before the l of God went
2Sa	22:29	"For You are my l,
1Ki	11:36	David may always have a l
Ps	119:105	Your word is a l to my
Prov	31:18	And her l does not go out
Matt	5:15	Nor do they light a l and put
Matt	6:22	The l of the body is the
Luke	8:16	one, when he has lit a l,
Luke	15: 8	one coin, does not light a l,
John	5:35	the burning and shining l,
Rev	22: 5	They need no l nor light of

LAMPS (see LAMP)

Ex	25:37	You shall make seven l for
Ex	30: 8	when Aaron lights the l
Zeph	1:12	will search Jerusalem with l,
Zech	4: 2	seven pipes to the seven l.
Matt	25: 1	ten virgins who took their l
Rev	4: 5	Seven l of fire were

LAMPSTAND (see LAMP, LAMPSTANDS)

Ex	25:31	You shall also make a l of
Ex	37:19	branches coming out of the l.
Dan	5: 5	and wrote opposite the l on
Matt	5:15	under a basket, but on a l,
Rev	2: 5	quickly and remove your l

LAMPSTANDS (see LAMPSTAND)

1Ki	7:49	the l of pure gold, five on
Rev	1:12	turned I saw seven golden l,
Rev	11: 4	olive trees and the two l

LAND (see LANDMARK, LANDOWNER, LANDS)

Gen	1: 9	and let the dry l appear";
Gen	12: 1	To a l that I will show
Gen	12: 7	I will give this l.
Gen	12:10	there was a famine in the l,
Gen	35:12	The l which I gave Abraham
Gen	37: 1	in the l of Canaan.
Gen	42: 5	for the famine was in the l
Gen	45:18	give you the best of the l
Gen	45:18	will eat the fat of the l.
Ex	3: 8	land to a good and large l,
Ex	3:17	to a l flowing with milk and
Ex	14:21	and made the sea into dry l,
Ex	14:29	Israel had walked on dry l
Ex	18: 3	a stranger in a foreign l'
Ex	20: 2	brought you out of the l of
Ex	20:12	days may be long upon the l
Ex	22:21	you were strangers in the l
Ex	23:30	and you inherit the l.
Ex	32: 1	brought us up out of the l
Ex	32:11	have brought out of the l
Ex	34:15	the inhabitants of the l,
Ex	34:24	will any man covet your l
Lev	18:25	For the l is defiled;
Lev	18:25	and the l vomits out its
Lev	19: 9	reap the harvest of your l,
Lev	19:29	lest the l fall into
Lev	24:16	as him who is born in the l.
Lev	25: 2	When you come into the l
Lev	25: 4	of solemn rest for the l,
Lev	25: 5	is a year of rest for the l.
Lev	25:10	and you will dwell in the l
Lev	25:19	Then the l will yield its
Lev	25:23	The l shall not be sold
Lev	25:23	for the l is Mine; for you
Lev	25:24	grant redemption of the l.
Lev	26: 4	the l shall yield its
Lev	26: 5	and dwell in your l safely.
Lev	26: 6	I will give peace in the l,
Lev	26: 6	I will rid the l of evil
Lev	27:30	'And all the tithe of the l,
Num	9:14	and the native of the l.
Num	13: 2	Send men to spy out the l of
Num	13:20	whether the l is rich or
Num	13:20	some of the fruit of the l.
Num	14: 2	only we had died in the l
Num	14: 3	LORD brought us to this l
Num	14: 7	is an exceedingly good l.
Num	14:36	a bad report of the l,
Num	15:19	eat of the bread of the l,
Num	18:20	no inheritance in their l,

Num	20:18	shall not pass through my l,	2Ch	6:27	and send rain on Your l
Num	20:23	Hor by the border of the l	2Ch	6:36	take them captive to a l
Num	21: 4	to go around the l of Edom;	2Ch	6:38	all their soul in the l of
Num	32: 8	Kadesh Barnea to see the l.	2Ch	6:38	and pray toward their l
Num	32:22	and the l is subdued before	2Ch	7:13	the locusts to devour the l,
Num	33:53	for I have given you the l	2Ch	7:14	their sin and heal their l.
Num	33:54	And you shall divide the l by	2Ch	15: 8	idols from all the l of
Num	35:14	you shall appoint in the l	2Ch	32: 4	brook that ran through the l,
Num	35:33	you shall not pollute the l	2Ch	34: 8	when he had purged the l and
Num	35:33	for blood defiles the l,	2Ch	36: 3	and he imposed on the l a
Deut	1: 8	I have set the l before you;	Ezra	9:11	The l which you are entering
Deut	1: 8	go in and possess the l	Ezra	9:11	to possess is an unclean l,
Deut	1:22	let them search out the l	Ezra	9:12	and eat the good of the l,
Deut	1:25	It is a good l which the	Neh	5:14	be their governor in the l
Deut	2:20	was also regarded as a l of	Neh	9:25	strong cities and a rich l,
Deut	2:27	'Let me pass through your l;	Esth	10: 1	imposed tribute on the l
Deut	3:18	God has given you this l to	Job	1: 1	There was a man in the l of
Deut	3:25	over and see the good l	Job	1:10	have increased in the l.
Deut	4:22	"But I must die in this l,	Job	10:21	To the l of darkness and
Deut	4:40	prolong your days in the l	Job	39: 6	And the barren l his
Deut	5:15	you were a slave in the l	Job	42:15	In all the l were found no
Deut	6:18	go in and possess the good l	Ps	10:16	have perished out of His l.
Deut	6:23	to give us the l of which He	Ps	27:13	of the LORD In the l of
Deut	8: 7	bringing you into a good l,	Ps	37: 3	and do good; Dwell in the l,
Deut	8: 7	a l of brooks of water, of	Ps	37:29	shall inherit the l,
Deut	8: 8	a l of wheat and barley, of	Ps	42: 6	remember You from the l of
Deut	8: 8	a l of olive oil and honey;	Ps	52: 5	And uproot you from the l
Deut	8: 9	a l whose stones are iron	Ps	63: 1	You In a dry and thirsty l
Deut	9:28	able to bring them to the l	Ps	66: 6	turned the sea into dry l;
Deut	10: 7	a l of rivers of water.	Ps	74: 8	places of God in the l.
Deut	10:19	you were strangers in the l	Ps	85: 1	been favorable to Your l;
Deut	11:11	over to possess is a l of	Ps	85: 9	glory may dwell in our l.
Josh	1: 4	all the l of the Hittites,	Ps	85:12	And our l will yield its
Josh	2: 1	saying, "Go, view the l,	Ps	88:12	Your righteousness in the l
Josh	4:18	feet touched the dry l,	Ps	95: 5	His hands formed the dry l.
Josh	10:40	Joshua conquered all the l:	Ps	101: 6	be on the faithful of the l,
Josh	14: 5	did; and they divided the l.	Ps	101: 8	all the wicked of the l,
Josh	14: 7	Barnea to spy out the l,	Ps	105:23	And Jacob dwelt in the l of
Judg	9:37	from the center of the l,	Ps	105:36	all the firstborn in their l,
Ruth	1: 1	there was a famine in the l.	Ps	106:24	they despised the pleasant l;
1Ki	15:20	with all the l of Naphtali.	Ps	106:38	And the l was polluted with
1Ki	17: 7	had been no rain in the l.	Ps	107:34	A fruitful l into
2Ki	4:38	was a famine in the l.	Ps	107:35	And dry l into
2Ki	5: 2	a young girl from the l of	Ps	116: 9	before the LORD In the l
2Ki	8: 1	it will come upon the l for	Ps	135:12	And gave their l as a
2Ki	8: 3	for her house and for her l.	Ps	137: 4	LORD's song In a foreign l?
2Ki	11: 3	Athaliah reigned over the l.	Ps	143: 6	for You like a thirsty l.
2Ki	11:20	So all the people of the l	Ps	143:10	Lead me in the l of
2Ki	13:20	from Moab invaded the l in	Prov	2:21	upright will dwell in the l,
2Ki	15:19	Assyria came against the l;	Prov	29: 4	The king establishes the l
2Ki	17:26	rituals of the God of the l;	Prov	31:23	among the elders of the l.
2Ki	18:32	a l of grain and new wine, a	Song	2:12	Is heard in our l.
2Ki	18:32	a l of bread and vineyards,	Is	1:19	shall eat the good of the l;
2Ki	18:32	a l of olive groves and	Is	6:11	The l is utterly desolate,
2Ki	19: 7	and return to his own l;	Is	7:16	the l that you dread will be
2Ki	23:33	and he imposed on the l a	Is	8: 8	fill the breadth of Your l,
2Ki	23:35	but he taxed the l to give	Is	9: 1	land of Zebulun and the l
2Ki	24:14	the poorest people of the l.	Is	32: 2	of a great rock in a weary l.
2Ki	25: 3	food for the people of the l.	Jer	2: 2	In a l not sown.
2Ki	25:21	away captive from its own l	Jer	24: 5	into the l of the Chaldeans.
2Ki	25:22	who remained in the l of	Jer	51:47	Her whole l shall be
2Ki	25:24	Dwell in the l and serve the	Jer	52:16	some of the poor of the l
1Ch	5:25	gods of the peoples of the l,	Jer	52:25	mustered the people of the l,
1Ch	28: 8	you may possess this good l,	Jer	52:27	away captive from its own l.

Ezek	7: 2	the four corners of the l.
Ezek	8:12	the LORD has forsaken the l.
Ezek	8:17	For they have filled the l
Ezek	9: 9	and the l is full of
Ezek	12:19	so that her l may be emptied
Ezek	14:13	when a l sins against Me by
Ezek	14:17	I bring a sword on that l,
Ezek	14:19	a pestilence into that l
Ezek	17:13	away the mighty of the l,
Ezek	19:13	In a dry and thirsty l.
Ezek	20:46	against the forest l,
Ezek	21:30	In the l of your nativity.
Ezek	23:19	played the harlot in the l
Ezek	23:48	lewdness to cease from the l,
Ezek	26:20	establish glory in the l of
Ezek	29:14	to the l of their origin,
Ezek	32: 8	bring darkness upon your l,
Ezek	32:23	Who caused terror in the l
Ezek	33: 2	I bring the sword upon a l,
Ezek	33:24	the l has been given to us
Ezek	34:27	shall be safe in their l;
Ezek	36:18	blood they had shed on the l,
Ezek	37:14	will place you in your own l.
Ezek	38: 2	of the l of Magog, the
Ezek	38: 9	covering the l like a cloud,
Ezek	38:16	like a cloud, to cover the l.
Ezek	38:19	a great earthquake in the l
Ezek	39:12	in order to cleanse the l.
Ezek	45: 1	when you divide the l by lot
Ezek	48:14	this best part of the l,
Dan	8: 9	and toward the Glorious L.
Dan	11:39	and divide the l for gain.
Dan	11:41	also enter the Glorious L,
Hos	1: 2	For the l has committed
Hos	2: 3	And set her like a dry l,
Hos	4: 1	knowledge of God in the l.
Hos	4: 3	Therefore the l will mourn;
Hos	7:16	be their derision in the l
Hos	9: 3	not dwell in the LORD's l,
Hos	12: 9	Ever since the l of Egypt;
Joel	1:10	The l mourns; For the
Joel	2:18	will be zealous for His l,
Joel	3:19	innocent blood in their l.
Amos	7: 2	eating the grass of the l,
Amos	7:10	The l is not able to bear
Amos	7:11	captive From their own l.
Amos	7:12	you seer! Flee to the l of
Amos	7:17	away captive From his own l.
Amos	8: 4	And make the poor of the l
Jon	1: 9	made the sea and the dry l.
Jon	1:13	rowed hard to return to l,
Jon	2:10	it vomited Jonah onto dry l.
Mic	5: 5	Assyrian comes into our l,
Mic	5: 6	And the l of Nimrod at its
Hab	2: 8	And the violence of the l
Hab	3: 7	The curtains of the l of
Hag	1:11	for a drought on the l and
Hag	2: 6	and earth, the sea and dry l;
Zech	2:12	inheritance in the Holy L,
Zech	3: 9	the iniquity of that l in
Zech	7:14	for they made the pleasant l
Zech	8: 7	save My people from the l
Zech	8: 7	of the east And from the l
Zech	9:16	like a banner over His l—

Zech	11: 6	the inhabitants of the l,
Zech	11:16	up a shepherd in the l who
Zech	12:12	And the l shall mourn, every
Mal	3:12	you will be a delightful l,
Matt	2: 6	in the l of Judah,
Matt	2:20	and go to the l of Israel,
Matt	4:15	The l of Zebulun and the
Matt	10:15	be more tolerable for the l
Matt	23:15	For you travel l and sea to
Matt	27:45	was darkness over all the l.
Mark	1: 5	Then all the l of Judea, and
Luke	4:25	famine throughout all the l;
Luke	5: 3	put out a little from the l.
Luke	5:11	had brought their boats to l,
Luke	15:14	a severe famine in that l,
Luke	21:23	be great distress in the l
John	3:22	disciples came into the l
John	6:21	the boat was at the l where
John	21: 9	soon as they had come to l,
John	21:11	up and dragged the net to l,
Acts	4:37	having l, sold it, and
Acts	5: 8	me whether you sold the l
Acts	7:45	with Joshua into the l
Acts	27:44	they all escaped safely to l.
Heb	11: 9	By faith he dwelt in the l of
Heb	11:29	the Red Sea as by dry l,
Jas	5:17	and it did not rain on the l
Jude	5	the people out of the l of
Rev	10: 2	and his left foot on the l,

L

LANDMARK (see LAND)

Deut	19:14	not remove your neighbor's l,
Prov	22:28	Do not remove the ancient l

LANDOWNER (see LAND)

Matt	20: 1	of heaven is like a l who

LANDS (see LAND)

Gen	10:31	their languages, in their l,
Ps	100: 1	to the LORD, all you l!
Matt	19:29	or wife or children or l,

LANGUAGE (see LANGUAGES)

Gen	10: 5	everyone according to his l,
Gen	11: 1	the whole earth had one l
Gen	11: 7	and there confuse their l,
Ezra	4: 7	into the Aramaic l.
Ps	19: 3	There is no speech nor l
Ps	114: 1	from a people of strange l,
Dan	1: 4	whom they might teach the l
Zeph	3: 9	to the peoples a pure l,
Acts	1:19	is called in their own l,
Acts	2: 6	them speak in his own l.
Acts	21:40	to them in the Hebrew l,
Col	3: 8	filthy l out of your mouth.

LANGUAGES (see LANGUAGE)

Gen	10:20	according to their l,
1Co	14:10	so many kinds of l in the

LAODICEA (see LAODICEANS)

Col	4:15	the brethren who are in L,
Col	4:16	read the epistle from L.
Rev	1:11	to Philadelphia, and to L.

LAODICEANS† (see LAODICEA)

Col	4:16	also in the church of the L,
Rev	3:14	angel of the church of the L

LAP (see LAPS)

Prov	16:33	The lot is cast into the l,

LAPS (see LAP)

Judg	7: 5	with his tongue, as a dog l,

LAST

Gen	25: 8	Then Abraham breathed his l
Job	19:25	And He shall stand at l on
Prov	23:32	At the l it bites like a
Is	41: 4	And with the l I am He.'
Is	44: 6	the First and I am the L;
Matt	5:26	till you have paid the l
Matt	12:45	and the l state of that man
Matt	19:30	who are first will be l,
Mark	15:37	voice, and breathed His l.
Luke	12:59	you have paid the very l
John	6:40	I will raise him up at the l
John	11:24	in the resurrection at the l
John	12:48	will judge him in the l day.
Acts	5: 5	fell down and breathed his l.
Acts	5:10	his feet and breathed her l.
1Co	15: 8	Then l of all He was seen by
1Co	15:26	The l enemy that will be
1Co	15:45	The l Adam became a
1Co	15:52	at the l trumpet. For the
2Ti	3: 1	that in the l days perilous
Heb	1: 2	has in these l days spoken to
Jas	5: 3	heaped up treasure in the l
1Pe	1: 5	to be revealed in the l
1Pe	1:20	but was manifest in these l
2Pe	3: 3	scoffers will come in the l
1Jn	2:18	it is the l hour; and as you
Rev	1:11	Omega, the First and the L,
Rev	1:17	I am the First and the L.
Rev	2: 8	says the First and the L,
Rev	2:19	the l are more than the
Rev	15: 1	angels having the seven l
Rev	21: 9	filled with the seven l
Rev	22:13	End, the First and the L.

LATE (see LATER)

Ps	127: 2	rise up early, To sit up l,
Amos	7: 1	at the beginning of the l
Matt	14:15	and the hour is already l.
Rev	6:13	as a fig tree drops its l

LATER (see LATE)

Mark	14:70	And a little l those who
Acts	5: 7	it was about three hours l
1Ti	5:24	those of some men follow L

LATIN†

Luke	23:38	Him in letters of Greek, L,
John	19:20	in Hebrew, Greek, and L.

LATTER

Deut	4:30	come upon you in the l days,
Deut	11:14	the early rain and the l

Deut	32:29	they would consider their l
Job	42:12	Now the LORD blessed the l
Is	2: 2	shall come to pass in the l
Jer	49:39	shall come to pass in the l
Ezek	38: 8	In the l years you will come
Dan	2:28	what will be in the l days.
Dan	8:19	what shall happen in the l
Dan	10:14	to your people in the l
Dan	11:29	be like the former or the l.
Hos	3: 5	and His goodness in the l
Hos	6: 3	Like the l and former rain
Joel	2:23	And the l rain in the first
Mic	4: 1	shall come to pass in the l
Hag	2: 9	The glory of this l temple
Phil	1:17	but the l out of love,
1Ti	4: 1	expressly says that in l
Jas	5: 7	it receives the early and l
2Pe	2:20	the l end is worse for them

LATTICE

2Ki	1: 2	Ahaziah fell through the l

LAUD†

Ps	117: 1	all you Gentiles! L Him,
Rom	15:11	all you Gentiles! L

LAUGH (see LAUGHED)

Gen	18:13	Abraham, "Why did Sarah l,
Gen	18:15	but you did l!"
Gen	21: 6	said, "God has made me l,
Ps	2: 4	sits in the heavens shall l;
Eccl	3: 4	to weep, And a time to l;
Luke	6:21	weep now, For you shall l.

LAUGHED (see LAUGH)

Gen	17:17	fell on his face and l,
Gen	18:12	Therefore Sarah l within

LAUNCH† (see LAUNCHED)

Luke	5: 4	L out into the deep and let

LAUNCHED† (see LAUNCH)

Luke	8:22	And they l out.

LAVER (see LAVERS)

Ex	30:18	You shall also make a l of

LAVERS (see LAVER)

1Ki	7:38	Then he made ten l of

LAW (see LAWFUL, LAWGIVER, LAWLESS, LAWS, LAWYER)

Num	5:29	This is the l of jealousy,
Deut	17:18	himself a copy of this l in
Deut	29:21	in this Book of the L,
Deut	31: 9	So Moses wrote this l and
Deut	31:11	you shall read this l before
Josh	1: 7	to do according to all the l
Josh	1: 8	This Book of the L shall not
Josh	8:32	the stones a copy of the l
2Ki	22: 8	found the Book of the L in
Ezra	7: 6	a skilled scribe in the L
Neh	8: 7	people to understand the L;
Ps	1: 2	his delight is in the l of

Ps	1: 2	And in His l he meditates
Ps	19: 7	The l of the LORD is
Ps	40: 8	And Your l is within my
Ps	81: 4	A l of the God of Jacob.
Ps	119:18	Wondrous things from Your l.
Ps	119:61	I have not forgotten Your l.
Ps	119:70	But I delight in Your l.
Ps	119:97	how I love Your l! It is
Ps	119:142	And Your l is truth.
Prov	1: 8	And do not forsake the l of
Prov	3: 1	My son, do not forget my l,
Prov	6:23	And the l a light;
Prov	29:18	happy is he who keeps the l.
Prov	31:26	on her tongue is the l of
Is	2: 3	of Zion shall go forth the l,
Is	5:24	they have rejected the l of
Is	8:16	Seal the l among my
Is	8:20	To the l and to the
Is	42: 4	shall wait for His l.
Is	51: 7	in whose heart is My l:
Jer	31:33	I will put My l in their
Mic	4: 2	For out of Zion the l
Mal	2: 9	shown partiality in the l.
Mal	4: 4	Remember the L of Moses, My
Matt	5:17	I came to destroy the L or
Matt	5:18	by no means pass from the l
Matt	7:12	for this is the L and the
Matt	22:36	great commandment in the l?
Matt	22:40	commandments hang all the L
Matt	23:23	weightier matters of the l:
Luke	16:16	The l and the prophets were
Luke	16:17	for one tittle of the l to
John	1:17	For the l was given through
John	7:51	Does our l judge a man before
John	8:17	is also written in your l
Acts	5:34	a teacher of the l held in
Acts	13:39	not be justified by the l
Rom	2:12	as have sinned without l
Rom	2:13	but the doers of the l will
Rom	2:14	are a l to themselves,
Rom	2:15	who show the work of the l
Rom	2:23	who make your boast in the l,
Rom	2:25	you are a breaker of the l,
Rom	2:27	are a transgressor of the l?
Rom	3:19	to those who are under the l,
Rom	3:20	by the deeds of the l no
Rom	3:27	It is excluded. By what l?
Rom	3:27	but by the l of faith.
Rom	3:31	Do we then make void the l
Rom	3:31	contrary, we establish the l.
Rom	5:13	(For until the l sin was in
Rom	5:13	imputed when there is no l.
Rom	6:14	for you are not under l but
Rom	7: 1	that the l has dominion over
Rom	7: 2	a husband is bound by the l
Rom	7: 3	she is free from that l,
Rom	7: 4	have become dead to the l
Rom	7: 7	covetousness unless the l
Rom	7:12	Therefore the l is holy, and
Rom	7:22	For I delight in the l of God
Rom	7:23	But I see another l in my
Rom	7:23	warring against the l of my
Rom	7:23	me into captivity to the l
Rom	8: 2	For the l of the Spirit of

Rom	8: 2	has made me free from the l
Rom	9:32	were, by the works of the l.
Rom	10: 4	Christ is the end of the l
Rom	13:10	is the fulfillment of the l.
1Co	6: 6	But brother goes to l against
1Co	7:39	A wife is bound by l as long
1Co	15:56	strength of sin is the l.
Gal	2:16	not by the works of the l;
Gal	2:19	For I through the l died to
Gal	3:12	Yet the l is not of faith,
Gal	3:13	us from the curse of the l,
Gal	3:18	the inheritance is of the l,
Gal	3:23	kept under guard by the l,
Gal	3:24	Therefore the l was our tutor
Gal	4: 4	of a woman, born under the l,
Gal	5: 3	a debtor to keep the whole l.
Gal	5: 4	to be justified by l;
Gal	5:14	For all the l is fulfilled in
Gal	5:23	Against such there is no l.
Gal	6: 2	and so fulfill the l of
Phil	3: 5	Hebrews; concerning the l,
Heb	7:12	is also a change of the l.
Heb	7:19	for the l made nothing
Heb	7:28	For the l appoints as high
Heb	7:28	oath, which came after the l,
Heb	9:22	And according to the l almost
Heb	10:28	who has rejected Moses' l
Jas	1:25	looks into the perfect l of
Jas	2: 8	really fulfill the royal l
Jas	2:10	shall keep the whole l,
Jas	2:11	a transgressor of the l.
Jas	4:11	law. But if you judge the l,

LAWFUL (see LAW)

Matt	12: 2	are doing what is not l to
Matt	12: 4	showbread which was not l
Matt	12:10	Is it l to heal on the
Matt	12:12	Therefore it is l to do good
Matt	14: 4	It is not l for you to have
Matt	19: 3	Is it l for a man to divorce
Matt	22:17	Is it l to pay taxes to
John	5:10	it is not l for you to carry
John	18:31	It is not l for us to put
Acts	16:21	customs which are not l for
Acts	19:39	shall be determined in the l
Acts	22:25	Is it l for you to scourge a
1Co	6:12	All things are l for me, but
2Co	12: 4	which it is not l for a man

LAWGIVER (see LAW)

| Gen | 49:10 | Nor a l from between his |
| Jas | 4:12 | There is one L, |

LAWLESS (see LAW, LAWLESSNESS)

| 2Th | 2: 9 | The coming of the l one is |

LAWLESSNESS (see LAWLESS)

Matt	23:28	are full of hypocrisy and l.
Matt	24:12	And because l will abound,
2Th	2: 7	For the mystery of l is

LAWS (see LAW)

| Gen | 26: 5 | My statutes, and My l. |
| Neh | 9:13 | just ordinances and true l, |

L

Esth	3: 8	their l are different from
Ps	105:45	His statutes And keep His l.
Is	24: 5	they have transgressed the l,
Dan	9:10	our God, to walk in His l,
Heb	8:10	I will put My l in
Heb	10:16	I will put My l into

LAWYER (see LAW)

Matt	22:35	Then one of them, a l,

LAY (see LAID, LAYING, LAYS, LIE)

Gen	22:12	Do not l your hand on the
Gen	37:22	and do not l a hand on
Lev	3: 2	And he shall l his hand on
Lev	4: 4	l his hand on the bull's
1Ki	5:17	to l the foundation of the
Job	1:12	only do not l a hand on his
Is	54:11	I will l your stones with
Is	54:11	And l your foundations with
Matt	6:19	Do not l up for yourselves
Matt	8:20	Son of Man has nowhere to l
Matt	9:18	but come and l Your hand on
Matt	21:46	But when they sought to l
Matt	23: 4	and l them on men's
Matt	28: 6	the place where the Lord l.
Mark	1:30	But Simon's wife's mother l
Mark	3:21	they went out to l hold of
Mark	12:12	And they sought to l hands on
Mark	16:18	they will l hands on the
John	10:15	and I l down My life for the
John	10:18	I have power to l it down,
John	11:38	and a stone l against it.
John	13:38	Will you l down your life for
John	15:13	than to l down one's life
Acts	8:19	that anyone on whom I l
Rom	9:33	"Behold, I l in Zion a
1Co	3:11	foundation can anyone l
1Co	16: 2	week let each one of you l
Phil	3:12	that I may l hold of that
1Ti	5:22	Do not l hands on anyone
1Ti	6:12	l hold on eternal life, to
Heb	6:18	have fled for refuge to l
Heb	12: 1	let us l aside every weight,
Jas	1:21	Therefore l aside all
1Pe	2: 6	I l in Zion A chief
1Jn	3:16	And we also ought to l down

LAYING (see LAY)

Acts	9:17	and l his hands on him he
1Ti	4:14	you by prophecy with the l
2Ti	1: 6	is in you through the l on
Heb	6: 1	not l again the foundation
Heb	6: 2	of l on of hands, of

LAYS (see LAY)

Luke	12:21	So is he who l up treasure

LAZARUS

Luke	16:20	was a certain beggar named L,
Luke	16:23	and L in his bosom.
John	11: 2	whose brother L was sick.
John	11: 5	Martha and her sister and L.

LAZY (see SLUGGARD)

Prov	19:24	A l man buries his hand in
Matt	25:26	You wicked and l servant, you

LEAD (see LEADER, LEADING, LEADS, LED)

Ex	13:17	that God did not l them by
Ex	13:21	in a pillar of cloud to l
Ex	15:10	They sank like l in the
Job	19:24	rock With an iron pen and l,
Ps	5: 8	L me, O LORD, in Your
Ps	25: 5	L me in Your truth and teach
Ps	27:11	And l me in a smooth path,
Ps	43: 3	and Your truth! Let them l
Ps	61: 2	L me to the rock that is
Ps	80: 1	You who l Joseph like a
Ps	125: 5	The LORD shall l them away
Ps	139:10	there Your hand shall l me,
Ps	139:24	And l me in the way
Ps	143:10	L me in the land of
Is	11: 6	And a little child shall l
Is	40:11	And gently l those who are
Is	42:16	I will l them in paths they
Is	63:14	So You l Your people, To
Jer	32: 5	then he shall l Zedekiah to
Amos	2: 4	Their lies l them astray,
Matt	6:13	And do not l us into
Mark	14:44	seize Him and l Him away
Luke	6:39	Can the blind l the blind?
Luke	11: 4	And do not l us into
Acts	13:11	around seeking someone to l
1Th	4:11	that you also aspire to l a
1Jn	5:16	a sin which does not l
Rev	7:17	will shepherd them and l

LEADER (see LEAD, LEADERS)

Num	14: 4	Let us select a l and return
Is	55: 4	A l and commander for the

LEADERS (see LEADER)

Matt	15:14	They are blind l of the

LEADING (see LEAD)

Acts	15:22	l men among the brethren.

LEADS (see LEAD)

Ps	23: 2	He l me beside the still
Ps	23: 3	He l me in the paths of
Matt	7:13	broad is the way that l to
Matt	7:14	is the way which l to life,
Matt	15:14	And if the blind l the
Rom	2: 4	that the goodness of God l
Rom	12: 8	with liberality; he who l,
2Co	2:14	be to God who always l us

LEAF (see LEAVES)

Gen	8:11	a freshly plucked olive l
Ps	1: 3	Whose l also shall not
Is	64: 6	rags; We all fade as a l,
Jer	17: 8	But its l will be green,

LEAH

Gen	29:16	the name of the elder was L,

| Gen | 29:30 | loved Rachel more than **L**. |
| Ruth | 4:11 | your house like Rachel and **L**, |

LEAN (see LEANED, LEANING, LEANNESS, LEANS)

| Judg | 16:26 | so that I can **l** on them." |
| Prov | 3: 5 | And **l** not on your own |

LEANED (see LEAN)

| Amos | 5:19 | **L** his hand on the wall, |
| John | 21:20 | who also had **l** on His breast |

LEANING (see LEAN)

| John | 13:23 | Now there was **l** on Jesus' |
| Heb | 11:21 | **l** on the top of his staff. |

LEANNESS (see LEAN)

| Ps | 106:15 | But sent **l** into their soul. |

LEANS (see LEAN)

| 2Ki | 18:21 | Egypt, on which if a man **l**, |

LEAPED

| 1Ki | 18:26 | Then they **l** about the altar |
| Luke | 1:41 | that the babe **l** in her womb; |

LEARN (see LEARNED, LEARNING)

Deut	4:10	that they may **l** to fear Me
Prov	22:25	Lest you **l** his ways And set
Is	1:17	**L** to do good; Seek justice
Is	2: 4	Neither shall they **l** war
Is	29:24	those who complained will **l**
Mic	4: 3	Neither shall they **l** war
Matt	9:13	But go and **l** what this
Matt	11:29	My yoke upon you and **l**
Matt	24:32	Now **l** this parable from the
1Co	4: 6	that you may **l** in us not to
1Ti	1:20	to Satan that they may **l**
1Ti	2:11	Let a woman **l** in silence with
1Ti	5:13	And besides they **l** to be
Rev	14: 3	and no one could **l** that song

LEARNED (see LEARN)

John	6:45	who has heard and **l** from
Acts	7:22	And Moses was **l** in all the
Acts	17:13	the Jews from Thessalonica **l**
Acts	23:27	having **l** that he was a
Rom	16:17	to the doctrine which you **l**,
Eph	4:20	But you have not so **l** Christ,
Phil	4: 9	The things which you **l** and
Phil	4:11	for I have **l** in whatever
Phil	4:12	and in all things I have **l**
2Ti	3:14	the things which you have **l**
2Ti	3:14	from whom you have **l** them,
Heb	5: 8	yet He **l** obedience by the

LEARNING (see LEARN)

Prov	1: 5	will hear and increase **l**,
Acts	26:24	are beside yourself! Much **l**
Rom	15: 4	were written for our **l**,
2Ti	3: 7	always **l** and never able to

LEATHER

| 2Ki | 1: 8 | A hairy man wearing a **l** belt |

LEAVEN (see LEAVENED, LEAVENS, UNLEAVENED)

Ex	12:15	day you shall remove **l** from
Ex	12:19	For seven days no **l** shall be
Matt	13:33	kingdom of heaven is like **l**,
Matt	16:11	but to beware of the **l** of
Mark	8:15	of the Pharisees and the **l**
1Co	5: 6	you not know that a little **l**
1Co	5: 7	purge out the old **l**,
1Co	5: 8	nor with the **l** of malice and

LEAVENED (see LEAVEN)

| Hos | 7: 4 | the dough, Until it is **l**. |
| Matt | 13:33 | of meal till it was all **l**. |

LEAVENS† (see LEAVEN)

| 1Co | 5: 6 | know that a little leaven **l** |
| Gal | 5: 9 | A little leaven **l** the whole |

LEAVES (see LEAF)

Gen	3: 7	and they sewed fig **l**
Matt	21:19	found nothing on it but **l**,
Matt	24:32	tender and puts forth **l**,
Mark	11:13	afar a fig tree having **l**,
Rev	22: 2	The **l** of the tree were for

LEBANON

1Ki	5: 6	down cedars for me from **L**;
Song	7: 4	nose is like the tower of **L**
Is	2:13	Upon all the cedars of **L**

LED (see LEAD)

Gen	24:48	who had **l** me in the way of
Ex	3: 1	And he **l** the flock to the
Ex	13:18	So God **l** the people around
Deut	29: 5	And I have **l** you forty years
Judg	2: 1	I **l** you up from Egypt and
2Ch	21:11	and **l** Judah astray.
Is	53: 7	He was **l** as a lamb to the
Matt	4: 1	Then Jesus was **l** up by the
Matt	27:31	and **l** Him away to be
Mark	8:23	blind man by the hand and **l**
Mark	9: 2	and **l** them up on a high
Luke	4:29	and they **l** Him to the brow
Luke	23: 1	of them arose and **l** Him to
Luke	24:50	And He **l** them out as far as
John	18:13	And they **l** Him away to Annas
Acts	8:32	He was **l** as a sheep to
Acts	9: 8	But they **l** him by the hand
Rom	8:14	For as many as are **l** by the
2Co	7: 9	but that your sorrow **l** to
Gal	5:18	But if you are **l** by the
Eph	4: 8	He **l** captivity captive,
2Ti	3: 6	**l** away by various lusts,
2Pe	3:17	being **l** away with the error

LEEKS†

| Num | 11: 5 | cucumbers, the melons, the **l**, |

LEFT (see LEFT-HANDED)

Gen	13: 9	from me. If you take the **l**,
Prov	3:16	In her **l** hand riches and
Prov	4:27	turn to the right or the **l**;

Song	2: 6	His l hand is under my
Matt	6: 3	do not let your l hand know
Matt	20:21	hand and the other on the l,
Matt	20:23	on My right hand and on My l
Matt	25:33	hand, but the goats on the l.
Matt	25:41	also say to those on the l
Matt	27:38	right and another on the l.

LEFT-HANDED† (*see* LEFT)

Judg	3:15	a l man. By him the children
Judg	20:16	select men who were l;

LEGION (*see* LEGIONS)

Mark	5: 9	saying, "My name is L;

LEGIONS† (*see* LEGION)

Matt	26:53	Me with more than twelve l

LEGS

Dan	2:33	its l of iron, its feet
John	19:33	they did not break His l.

LEND

Ex	22:25	If you l money to any of
Lev	25:37	nor l him your food at a
Deut	24:10	When you l your brother
Prov	5: 1	L your ear to my
Luke	6:34	And if you l to those from
Luke	6:34	For even sinners l to
Luke	6:35	your enemies, do good, and l,
Luke	11: 5	l me three loaves;

LENGTH (*see* LENGTHEN)

Prov	3: 2	For l of days and long life
Eph	3:18	what is the width and l

LENGTHEN (*see* LENGTH)

Is	54: 2	L your cords, And

LENTILS

Gen	25:34	Esau bread and stew of l;

LEOPARD

Is	11: 6	The l shall lie down with
Jer	13:23	change his skin or the l
Dan	7: 6	there was another, like a l,
Rev	13: 2	which I saw was like a l,

LEPER (*see* LEPERS, LEPROSY)

Lev	13:45	Now the l on whom the sore
Num	5: 2	put out of the camp every l,
Num	12:10	and there she was, a l.
2Ki	5: 1	man of valor, but a l.
2Ch	26:21	King Uzziah was a l until the
Matt	8: 2	a l came and worshiped Him,
Matt	26: 6	at the house of Simon the l,

LEPERS (*see* LEPER)

Matt	10: 8	the sick, cleanse the l,
Luke	17:12	met Him ten men who were l,

LEPROSY (*see* LEPER, LEPROUS)

Lev	13:12	And if l breaks out all over
2Ki	5:27	Therefore the l of Naaman

2Ch	26:19	l broke out on his forehead,
Matt	8: 3	Immediately his l was

LEPROUS (*see* LEPROSY)

Ex	4: 6	out, behold, his hand was l,
Lev	13: 2	skin of his body like a l
Lev	13:47	if a garment has a l plague
Lev	13:59	This is the law of the l
Num	12:10	suddenly Miriam became l,
2Ki	5:27	went out from his presence l,
2Ki	7: 3	Now there were four l men at
2Ch	26:20	on his forehead, he was l;

LETTER (*see* LETTERS)

2Sa	11:14	that David wrote a l to
Ezra	7:11	This is a copy of the l
Neh	6: 5	with an open l in his hand.
Esth	9:29	to confirm this second l
Jer	29: 1	are the words of the l
Jer	29:29	the priest read this l in
Acts	23:33	and had delivered the l to
Rom	2:29	in the Spirit, not in the l;
Rom	7: 6	not in the oldness of the l.
2Co	3: 6	for the l kills, but the
2Co	7: 8	I made you sorry with my l,
2Th	2: 2	by spirit or by word or by l,

LETTERS (*see* LETTER)

1Ki	21: 8	And she wrote l in Ahab's
Neh	2: 7	let l be given to me for the
Neh	2: 9	and gave them the king's l.
Esth	9:20	these things and sent l to
Luke	23:38	was written over Him in l
John	7:15	"How does this Man know l,
Acts	9: 2	and asked l from him to the
2Co	3: 1	of commendation to you or l
Gal	6:11	See with what large l I have

LEVI (*see* LEVITE, MATTHEW)

Gen	34:25	sons of Jacob, Simeon and L,
Deut	10: 9	Therefore L has no portion
Mal	2: 4	That My covenant with L may
Luke	5:27	saw a tax collector named L,
Heb	7: 5	who are of the sons of L,
Heb	7: 9	Even L, who receives
Rev	7: 7	of the tribe of L twelve

LEVIATHAN

Job	3: 8	who are ready to arouse L.
Job	41: 1	Can you draw out L with a
Ps	74:14	You broke the heads of L in
Is	27: 1	L that twisted serpent;

LEVITE (*see* LEVI, LEVITES)

Ex	4:14	Is not Aaron the L your
Deut	12:12	and the L who is within
Judg	17:12	So Micah consecrated the L,
Luke	10:32	"Likewise a L,
Acts	4:36	a L of the country of

LEVITES (*see* LEVITE)

Ex	6:25	the fathers' houses of the L
Ex	38:21	for the service of the L,
Lev	25:32	the cities of the L,

LEWD (*see* LEWDNESS)

Deut	17: 9	come to the priests, the **L**,
1Ch	15:14	So the priests and the **L**
John	1:19	the Jews sent priests and **L**

LEWD (*see* LEWDNESS)

Ezek	16:27	who were ashamed of your **l**
Ezek	23:44	Oholibah, the **l** women.

LEWDNESS (*see* LEWD)

Judg	20: 6	because they committed **l** and
Ezek	23:21	called to remembrance the **l**
Hos	2:10	Now I will uncover her **l** in
Hos	6: 9	Surely they commit **l**.
Rom	13:13	not in **l** and lust, not in

LIAR (*see* LIARS, LIE)

Job	24:25	so, who will prove me a **l**,
Prov	19:22	poor man is better than a **l**.
Prov	30: 6	you, and you be found a **l**.
John	8:44	for he is a **l** and the father
Rom	3: 4	be true but every man a **l**.
1Jn	1:10	not sinned, we make Him a **l**,
1Jn	2: 4	His commandments, is a **l**,
1Jn	2:22	Who is a **l** but he who denies
1Jn	4:20	hates his brother, he is a **l**;
1Jn	5:10	believe God has made Him a **l**,

LIARS (*see* LIAR)

Ps	116:11	my haste, "All men are **l**.
Tit	1:12	"Cretans are always **l**,
Rev	2: 2	not, and have found them **l**;
Rev	21: 8	and all **l** shall have their

LIBERALITY (*see* LIBERALLY)

Rom	12: 8	he who gives, with **l**;
2Co	8: 2	in the riches of their **l**.

LIBERALLY (*see* LIBERALITY)

Jas	1: 5	who gives to all **l** and

LIBERTY (*see* DELIVERANCE)

Lev	25:10	and proclaim **l** throughout
Ps	119:45	And I will walk at **l**,
Is	61: 1	To proclaim **l** to the
Jer	34:16	slaves, whom he had set at **l**,
Luke	4:18	To proclaim **l** to the
Acts	27: 3	Paul kindly and gave him **l**
Rom	8:21	into the glorious **l** of the
1Co	7:39	she is at **l** to be married to
1Co	8: 9	beware lest somehow this **l**
1Co	10:29	For why is my **l** judged by
2Co	3:17	of the Lord is, there is **l**.
Gal	2: 4	by stealth to spy out our **l**
Gal	5: 1	fast therefore in the **l** by
Gal	5:13	only do not use **l** as an
Jas	1:25	into the perfect law of **l**
Jas	2:12	be judged by the law of **l**.
1Pe	2:16	yet not using **l** as a cloak
2Pe	2:19	While they promise them **l**,

LICK (*see* LICKED)

1Ki	21:19	dogs shall **l** your blood,
Mic	7:17	They shall **l** the dust like a

LICKED (*see* LICK)

1Ki	18:38	and it **l** up the water that
1Ki	21:19	In the place where dogs **l** the
Luke	16:21	the dogs came and **l** his

LIE (*see* LAIN, LAY, LIAR, LIED, LIES, LYING)

Gen	19:32	and we will **l** with him, that
Gen	39: 7	she said, "**L** with me."
Gen	47:30	but let me **l** with my fathers;
Lev	19:11	nor **l** to one another.
Num	23:19	not a man, that He should **l**,
Deut	6: 7	when you **l** down, and when
Ps	23: 2	He makes me to **l** down in
Prov	1:11	Let us **l** in wait to shed
Eccl	4:11	if two **l** down together, they
Is	11: 6	The leopard shall **l** down
Jer	28:15	this people trust in a **l**.
Ezek	4: 4	**L** also on your left side,
Ezek	34:14	There they shall **l** down in a
Amos	2: 8	They **l** down by every altar
Amos	6: 4	Who **l** on beds of ivory,
John	8:44	in him. When he speaks a **l**,
Acts	5: 3	filled your heart to **l** to
Rom	1:25	the truth of God for the **l**,
Gal	1:20	before God, I do not **l**.
Col	3: 9	Do not **l** to one another,
2Th	2:11	they should believe the **l**,
Tit	1: 2	life which God, who cannot **l**,
Heb	6:18	is impossible for God to **l**,
Jas	3:14	do not boast and **l** against
1Jn	1: 6	we **l** and do not practice the
1Jn	2:21	and that no **l** is of the
1Jn	2:27	and is true, and is not a **l**,
Rev	3: 9	are Jews and are not, but **l**—
Rev	22:15	loves and practices a **l**.

LIED (*see* LIE)

Ps	78:36	And they **l** to Him with
Acts	5: 4	You have not **l** to men but to

LIES (*see* LIE)

Gen	4: 7	sin **l** at the door. And its
Ex	22:16	and **l** with her, he shall
Ex	22:19	Whoever **l** with an animal
Judg	16: 5	where his great strength **l**,
Job	14:12	So man **l** down and does not
Prov	30: 8	Remove falsehood and **l** far
2Co	3:15	a veil **l** on their heart.
1Ti	4: 2	speaking **l** in hypocrisy,
1Jn	5:19	and the whole world **l** under

LIFE (*see* LIFE-GIVING, LIVE)

Gen	1:30	earth, in which there is **l**,
Gen	2: 7	his nostrils the breath of **l**;
Gen	2: 9	The tree of **l** was also in
Gen	3:14	dust All the days of your **l**.
Gen	3:24	the way to the tree of **l**.
Gen	7:22	breath of the spirit of **l**,
Gen	9: 4	not eat flesh with its **l**,
Gen	9: 5	I will require the **l** of man.
Gen	44:30	is bound up in the lad's **l**,
Ex	21:23	you shall give life for **l**,
Lev	17:11	For the **l** of the flesh is in

Lev	17:14	Its blood sustains its l.
Num	35:31	take no ransom for the l of
Deut	30:15	have set before you today l
Deut	30:19	cursing; therefore choose l,
1Ki	3:11	and have not asked long l
1Ki	19: 4	Now, LORD, take my l,
1Ki	19:10	and they seek to take my l.
2Ki	8: 5	had restored the dead to l,
Job	2: 4	has he will give for his l.
Job	2: 6	your hand, but spare his l.
Job	7:16	I loathe my l;
Job	33: 4	of the Almighty gives me l.
Job	33:30	with the light of l.
Ps	16:11	will show me the path of l;
Ps	17:13	Deliver my l from the
Ps	22:20	My precious l from the
Ps	23: 6	me All the days of my l;
Ps	27: 1	is the strength of my l;
Ps	27: 4	LORD All the days of my l,
Ps	36: 9	You is the fountain of l;
Ps	91:16	With long l I will satisfy
Ps	119:50	Your word has given me l.
Ps	133: 3	L forevermore.
Prov	2:19	they regain the paths of l—
Prov	3: 2	length of days and long l
Prov	3:18	She is a tree of l to those
Prov	4:23	it spring the issues of l.
Prov	7:23	know it would cost his l.
Prov	8:35	whoever finds me finds l,
Prov	10:11	righteous is a well of l,
Prov	11:30	righteous is a tree of l,
Prov	13:14	the wise is a fountain of l,
Prov	14:27	LORD is a fountain of l,
Prov	16:22	is a wellspring of l to
Prov	21:21	and mercy Finds l,
Prov	22: 4	Are riches and honor and l.
Prov	31:12	evil All the days of her l.
Eccl	6:12	all the days of his vain l
Eccl	9: 9	that is your portion in l,
Is	38:10	In the prime of my l I shall
Is	38:12	My l span is gone, Taken
Is	38:20	All the days of our l,
Jer	18:20	they have dug a pit for my l.
Jer	23:10	Their course of l is evil,
Lam	2:12	As their l is poured out
Lam	3:58	You have redeemed my l.
Ezek	3:18	wicked way, to save his l,
Ezek	33:15	walks in the statutes of l
Dan	12: 2	Some to everlasting l,
Jon	2: 6	You have brought up my l
Jon	4: 3	please take my l from me,
Matt	2:20	sought the young Child's l
Matt	6:25	do not worry about your l,
Matt	6:25	Is not l more than food and
Matt	7:14	is the way which leads to l,
Matt	10:39	He who finds his l will lose
Matt	10:39	and he who loses his l for
Matt	16:25	desires to save his l will
Matt	18: 8	for you to enter into l
Matt	19:16	do that I may have eternal l?
Matt	20:28	and to give His l a ransom
Matt	25:46	the righteous into eternal l.
Mark	3: 4	to save l or to kill?" But
Mark	10:30	the age to come, eternal l.
Mark	10:45	and to give His l a ransom
Luke	1:75	Him all the days of our l.
Luke	6: 9	to save l or to destroy?"
Luke	8:14	riches, and pleasures of l,
Luke	12:15	for one's l does not consist
Luke	12:22	do not worry about your l,
Luke	12:23	L is more than food, and the
Luke	18:30	in the age to come eternal l.
Luke	21:34	and cares of this l,
John	1: 4	In Him was l,
John	1: 4	and the l was the light of
John	3:15	perish but have eternal l.
John	3:16	but have everlasting l.
John	3:36	in the Son has everlasting l;
John	3:36	the Son shall not see l,
John	4:14	up into everlasting l.
John	4:36	gathers fruit for eternal l,
John	5:24	sent Me has everlasting l,
John	5:24	has passed from death into l.
John	5:39	you think you have eternal l;
John	5:40	to Me that you may have l.
John	6:27	endures to everlasting l,
John	6:35	them, "I am the bread of l.
John	6:54	My blood has eternal l,
John	6:63	is the Spirit who gives l;
John	6:63	are spirit, and they are l.
John	6:68	have the words of eternal l.
John	8:12	but have the light of l.
John	10:10	come that they may have l,
John	10:15	and I lay down My l for the
John	10:28	"And I give them eternal l,
John	11:25	the resurrection and the l.
John	11:25	He who loves his l will lose
John	14: 6	way, the truth, and the l.
John	15:13	than to lay down one's l for
John	17: 3	"And this is eternal l,
John	20:31	believing you may have l in
Acts	3:15	"and killed the Prince of l,
Acts	17:25	since He gives to all l,
Rom	5:10	we shall be saved by His l.
Rom	6: 4	should walk in newness of l.
Rom	6:22	and the end, everlasting l.
Rom	6:23	gift of God is eternal l
Rom	8: 2	the law of the Spirit of l
Rom	8: 6	be spiritually minded is l
Rom	8:38	that neither death nor l,
1Co	15:19	If in this l only we have
2Co	2:16	to the other the aroma of l
2Co	3: 6	but the Spirit gives l.
Gal	2:20	and the l which I now live
Gal	6: 8	Spirit reap everlasting l.
Phil	1:20	whether by l or by death.
Phil	2:16	holding fast the word of l,
Phil	4: 3	names are in the Book of L.
Col	3: 3	and your l is hidden with
Col	3: 4	When Christ who is our l
1Ti	6:19	may lay hold on eternal l.
2Ti	1:10	death and brought l and
Heb	7: 3	of days nor end of l,
Heb	7:16	to the power of an endless l.
Jas	1:12	will receive the crown of l
1Pe	3: 7	together of the grace of l,
1Jn	1: 1	concerning the Word of l—
1Jn	1: 2	the l was manifested, and we

1Jn	2:16	the eyes, and the pride of l—
1Jn	3:14	have passed from death to l,
1Jn	5:11	and this l is in His Son.
1Jn	5:12	He who has the Son has l;
1Jn	5:13	know that you have eternal l,
1Jn	5:20	the true God and eternal l.
Rev	2: 7	to eat from the tree of l,
Rev	2:10	will give you the crown of l.
Rev	13: 8	written in the Book of L of
Rev	21: 6	fountain of the water of l
Rev	21:27	in the Lamb's Book of L.
Rev	22: 2	river, was the tree of l,
Rev	22:17	let him take the water of l
Rev	22:19	his part from the Book of L,

LIFE-GIVING† (see LIFE)

1Co	15:45	The last Adam became a l

LIFT (see LIFTED, LIFTING, LIFTS, RAISE)

Gen	13:14	L your eyes now and look from
Num	6:26	The LORD l up His
Ps	24: 7	L up your heads, O you
Ps	25: 1	I l up my soul.
Ps	110: 7	Therefore He shall l up the
Ps	121: 1	I will l up my eyes to the
Is	2: 4	Nation shall not l up sword
Is	49:18	L up your eyes, look around
Is	62:10	L up a banner for the
Lam	3:41	Let us l our hearts and
Mic	4: 3	Nation shall not l up sword
Luke	21:28	look up and l up your heads,
John	8:28	When you l up the Son of Man,
Jas	4:10	and He will l you up

LIFTED (see LIFT, RAISED)

Gen	13:10	And Lot l his eyes and saw
Gen	22:13	Then Abraham l his eyes and
Deut	8:14	when your heart is l up, and
Ps	24: 4	Who has not l up his soul
Ps	24: 7	O you gates! And be l up,
Ps	27: 6	And now my head shall be l
Ps	30: 1	for You have l me up, And
Ps	41: 9	Has l up his heel against
Is	6: 1	high and l up, and the train
Jer	38:13	up with ropes and l him out
Dan	4:34	l my eyes to heaven, and my
Dan	5:20	But when his heart was l up,
Mark	1:31	took her by the hand and l
John	3:14	And as Moses l up the serpent
John	3:14	so must the Son of Man be l
John	12:32	if I am l up from the earth,
John	12:34	The Son of Man must be l up'?

LIFTING (see LIFT)

1Ti	2: 8	l up holy hands, without

LIFTS (see LIFT)

1Sa	2: 7	He brings low and l up.
Ps	3: 3	My glory and the One who l
Ps	147: 6	The LORD l up the humble;
Is	18: 3	When he l up a banner on

LIGAMENTS†

Col	2:19	together by joints and l,

LIGHT (see LIGHTS)

Gen	1: 3	Let there be l"; and there
Gen	1: 4	and God divided the l from
Gen	1: 5	God called the l Day, and the
Gen	1:15	of the heavens to give l on
Gen	1:16	the greater l to rule the
Gen	1:18	and to divide the l from the
Ex	10:23	children of Israel had l in
Ex	13:21	of fire to give them l,
Esth	8:16	The Jews had l and gladness,
Job	3:16	infants who never saw l?
Job	26:10	At the boundary of l and
Job	37:15	And causes the l of His
Ps	4: 6	lift up the l of Your
Ps	18:28	For You will l my lamp; The
Ps	27: 1	The LORD is my l and my
Ps	36: 9	In Your l we see light.
Ps	43: 3	send out Your l and Your
Ps	90: 8	Our secret sins in the l
Ps	119:105	a lamp to my feet And a l
Ps	119:130	of Your words gives l;
Ps	139:11	Even the night shall be l
Ps	139:12	The darkness and the l are
Prov	16:15	In the l of the king's face
Is	2: 5	and let us walk In the l
Is	5:20	Who put darkness for l,
Is	9: 2	Have seen a great l;
Is	9: 2	Upon them a l has shined.
Is	10:17	So the L of Israel will be
Is	42: 6	As a l to the Gentiles,
Is	45: 7	I form the l and create
Is	49: 6	I will also give You as a l
Is	58: 8	Then your l shall break
Is	60: 1	For your l has come! And
Is	60:19	be to you an everlasting l,
Dan	2:22	And l dwells with Him.
Amos	5:18	be darkness, and not l.
Matt	4:16	have seen a great l,
Matt	4:16	and shadow of death L
Matt	5:14	You are the l of the world. A
Matt	5:15	Nor do they l a lamp and put
Matt	5:15	and it gives l to all who
Matt	5:16	Let your l so shine before
Matt	6:22	whole body will be full of l.
Matt	6:23	If therefore the l that is
Matt	11:30	is easy and My burden is l.
Matt	22: 5	But they made l of it and
Matt	24:29	the moon will not give its l;
Luke	1:79	To give l to those who sit
Luke	2:32	A l to bring revelation to
Luke	8:16	who enter may see the l.
Luke	8:17	not be known and come to l.
Luke	12: 3	dark will be heard in the l,
Luke	15: 8	does not l a lamp, sweep the
Luke	16: 8	than the sons of l.
John	1: 4	and the life was the l of
John	1: 5	And the l shines in the
John	1: 7	to bear witness of the L,
John	1: 8	He was not that L,
John	1: 9	That was the true L which
John	3:19	loved darkness rather than l,
John	3:20	practicing evil hates the l
John	3:21	the truth comes to the l,

L

John	8:12	I am the l of the world. He
John	8:12	but have the l of life."
John	9: 5	I am the l of the world."
John	12:35	Walk while you have the l,
John	12:36	the light, believe in the l,
John	12:36	you may become sons of l.
John	12:46	I have come as a l into the
Acts	9: 3	and suddenly a l shone
Acts	12: 7	and a l shone in the prison;
Acts	22: 6	suddenly a great l from
Rom	2:19	a l to those who are in
Rom	13:12	let us put on the armor of l.
1Co	4: 5	who will both bring to l the
2Co	4: 4	lest the l of the gospel of
2Co	4: 6	is the God who commanded l
2Co	4: 6	in our hearts to give the l
2Co	6:14	And what communion has l
2Co	11:14	himself into an angel of l.
Eph	5: 8	but now you are l in the
Eph	5: 8	Walk as children of l
Eph	5:13	are made manifest by the l,
Eph	5:14	And Christ will give you l.
Col	1:12	of the saints in the l.
1Th	5: 5	You are all sons of l and
2Ti	1:10	life and immortality to l
1Pe	2: 9	into His marvelous l;
2Pe	1:19	you do well to heed as a l
1Jn	1: 5	that God is l and in Him is
1Jn	1: 7	But if we walk in the l as He
1Jn	2: 8	and the true l is already
1Jn	2: 9	He who says he is in the l,
1Jn	2:10	his brother abides in the l,
Rev	21:23	it. The Lamb is its l.
Rev	21:24	saved shall walk in its l,
Rev	22: 5	They need no lamp nor l of
Rev	22: 5	the Lord God gives them l.

LIGHTNING (see LIGHTNINGS)

Ex	20:18	the l flashes, the sound of
Ps	135: 7	He makes l for the rain;
Dan	10: 6	like the appearance of l,
Matt	24:27	For as the l comes from the
Matt	28: 3	His countenance was like l,
Luke	10:18	I saw Satan fall like l from

LIGHTNINGS (see LIGHTNING)

Ex	19:16	there were thunderings and l,

LIGHTS (see LIGHT)

Gen	1:14	Let there be l in the
Gen	1:16	Then God made two great l:
Ps	136: 7	To Him who made great l,
Phil	2:15	among whom you shine as l in
Jas	1:17	down from the Father of l,

LIKE-MINDED

Rom	15: 5	comfort grant you to be l
Phil	2: 2	fulfill my joy by being l,

LIKENESS

Gen	1:26	image, according to Our l;
Gen	5: 1	He made him in the l of God.
Gen	5: 3	begot a son in his own l,
Ex	20: 4	or any l of anything that

Deut	4:16	the l of male or female,
Rom	6: 5	we also shall be in the l
Rom	8: 3	His own Son in the l of
Phil	2: 7	and coming in the l of men.
Heb	7:15	in the l of Melchizedek,

LILIES (see LILY)

Song	2:16	his flock among the l.
Matt	6:28	Consider the l of the field,

LILY (see LILIES)

Song	2: 1	And the l of the valleys.

LIMPED

Gen	32:31	and he l on his hip.

LINE (see LINEAGE, LINES)

Ps	19: 4	Their l has gone out through
Is	28:10	L upon line, line upon
Zech	2: 1	a man with a measuring l in

LINEAGE (see LINE)

Luke	2: 4	he was of the house and l

LINEN

Ex	28:42	you shall make for them l
Lev	13:47	is a woolen garment or a l
Deut	22:11	such as wool and l mixed
Jer	13: 1	Go and get yourself a l sash,
Matt	27:59	he wrapped it in a clean l
Luke	24:12	he saw the l cloths lying by
John	19:40	and bound it in strips of l

LINES (see LINE)

Ps	16: 6	The l have fallen to me in

LINTEL

Ex	12: 7	two doorposts and on the l
Ex	12:23	He sees the blood on the l

LION (see LIONS)

Judg	14: 6	and he tore the l apart as
Judg	14:18	what is stronger than a l?
1Sa	17:34	and when a l or a bear came
Ps	22:13	a raging and roaring l.
Ps	91:13	You shall tread upon the l
Prov	28: 1	righteous are bold as a l.
Eccl	9: 4	dog is better than a dead l.
Is	11: 6	The calf and the young l
Is	11: 7	And the l shall eat straw
Ezek	1:10	four had the face of a l on
Dan	7: 4	"The first was like a l,
Amos	3: 8	A l has roared! Who will
Amos	3:12	takes from the mouth of a l
Amos	5:19	though a man fled from a l,
2Ti	4:17	out of the mouth of the l.
1Pe	5: 8	walks about like a roaring l,
Rev	5: 5	the L of the tribe of Judah,

LIONS (see LION)

2Sa	1:23	They were stronger than l.
Ps	35:17	precious life from the l.
Dan	6: 7	be cast into the den of l.
Heb	11:33	stopped the mouths of l,

LIPS

Ex	6:12	for I am of uncircumcised l?
1Sa	1:13	only her l moved, but her
Job	2:10	Job did not sin with his l.
Job	15: 6	your own l testify against
Job	23:12	the commandment of His l;
Job	33: 3	My l utter pure knowledge.
Ps	12: 2	With flattering l and a
Ps	16: 4	take up their names on my l.
Ps	17: 1	is not from deceitful l.
Ps	31:18	Let the lying l be put to
Ps	34:13	And your l from speaking
Ps	40: 9	I do not restrain my l,
Ps	45: 2	Grace is poured upon Your l;
Ps	63: 3	My l shall praise You.
Ps	66:14	Which my l have uttered And
Ps	71:23	My l shall greatly rejoice
Ps	106:33	he spoke rashly with his l.
Ps	141: 3	watch over the door of my l.
Prov	4:24	And put perverse l far from
Prov	5: 3	For the l of an immoral
Prov	7:21	With her flattering l she
Prov	10:18	hides hatred has lying l,
Prov	10:19	But he who restrains his l
Prov	10:32	The l of the righteous know
Prov	12:22	Lying l are an abomination
Prov	14: 3	But the l of the wise will
Prov	14: 7	not perceive in him the l
Prov	16:10	Divination is on the l of
Prov	16:30	He purses his l and brings
Prov	17: 4	gives heed to false l;
Prov	19: 1	who is perverse in his l,
Prov	23:16	will rejoice When your l
Prov	24: 2	And their l talk of
Prov	24:26	a right answer kisses the l.
Prov	26:23	Fervent l with a wicked
Eccl	10:12	But the l of a fool shall
Song	5:13	His l are lilies,
Is	6: 5	l am a man of unclean l,
Is	6: 5	of a people of unclean l;
Is	6: 7	this has touched your l;
Is	11: 4	with the breath of His l He
Is	29:13	And honor Me with their l,
Is	37:29	And My bridle in your l,
Jer	17:16	know what came out of my l;
Ezek	24:17	feet; do not cover your l,
Dan	10:16	the sons of men touched my l;
Hos	14: 2	the sacrifices of our l.
Hab	3:16	My l quivered at the
Mal	2: 7	For the l of a priest should
Matt	15: 8	honor Me with their l,
Rom	3:13	asps is under their l'
1Co	14:21	tongues and other l I
Heb	13:15	that is, the fruit of our l,
1Pe	3:10	And his l from

LISTEN

Gen	4:23	l to my speech! For I have
Ex	4: 1	will not believe me or l to
Deut	1:43	to you; yet you would not l,
Prov	23:22	L to your father who begot
Is	46: 3	L to Me, O house of Jacob,
John	8:43	you are not able to l to My

John	10:20	Why do you l to Him?"
Acts	7: 2	"Brethren and fathers, l:
Acts	13:16	and you who fear God, l:
Jas	2: 5	L, my beloved brethren:

LITTLE

Gen	19:20	and it is a l one; please
Ex	16:18	and he who gathered l had no
Ex	23:30	L by little I will drive them
2Sa	12: 3	except one l ewe lamb which
1Ki	12:10	My l finger shall be thicker
2Ki	5:14	like the flesh of a l child,
Ps	2:12	His wrath is kindled but a l.
Ps	8: 5	For You have made him a l
Ps	37:10	For yet a l while and the
Ps	65:12	And the l hills rejoice on
Ps	114: 4	The l hills like lambs.
Ps	137: 9	who takes and dashes Your l
Prov	6:10	A l sleep, a little slumber,
Prov	24:33	A l folding of the hands to
Prov	30:24	four things which are l
Song	2:15	The l foxes that spoil the
Song	8: 8	We have a l sister, And
Is	11: 6	And a l child shall lead
Is	28:10	Here a little, there a l.
Is	60:22	A l one shall become a
Jer	51:33	Yet a l while And the time
Ezek	34:18	Is it too l for you to have
Dan	7: 8	a l one, coming up among
Dan	8: 9	out of one of them came a l
Dan	11:34	they shall be aided with a l
Hos	1: 4	For in a l while I will
Mic	5: 2	Though you are l among the
Hag	1: 6	sown much, and bring in l;
Matt	6:30	O you of l faith?
Matt	10:42	gives one of these l ones
Matt	14:31	O you of l faith, why did you
Matt	18: 2	Then Jesus called a l child
Matt	18: 3	converted and become as l
Matt	18: 4	humbles himself as this l
Matt	18: 5	Whoever receives one l child
Matt	19:14	Let the l children come to
Matt	26:39	He went a l farther and fell
Mark	4:36	And other l boats were also
Mark	5:23	My l daughter lies at the
Mark	5:41	L girl, I say to you,
Mark	10:15	the kingdom of God as a l
Luke	5: 3	and asked him to put out a l
Luke	7:47	But to whom l is forgiven,
Luke	12:28	O you of l faith?
Luke	12:32	l flock, for it is your
Luke	17: 2	offend one of these l ones.
Luke	19:17	were faithful in a very l,
John	7:33	I shall be with you a l while
John	13:33	L children, I shall be with
John	16:16	A l while, and you will not
1Co	5: 6	Do you not know that a l
2Co	8:15	and he who gathered l
2Co	11:16	that I also may boast a l.
Gal	4:19	My l children, for whom I
Gal	5: 9	A l leaven leavens the whole
1Ti	4: 8	bodily exercise profits a l,
1Ti	5:23	but use a l wine for your
Heb	2: 7	You have made him a l

L

Heb	10:37	For yet a l while, And
Jas	3: 5	Even so the tongue is a l
Jas	3: 5	See how great a forest a l
Jas	4:14	a vapor that appears for a l
1Pe	1: 6	though now for a l while, if
1Jn	2: 1	My l children, these things I
1Jn	5:21	L children, keep yourselves
Rev	3: 8	for you have a l strength,
Rev	10: 2	He had a l book open in his

LIVE (see LIFE, LIVED, LIVES, LIVING)

Gen	3:22	and l forever"—
Gen	45: 3	does my father still l?
Ex	1:16	a daughter, then she shall l.
Ex	33:20	no man shall see Me, and l.
Num	21: 8	when he looks at it, shall l.
Deut	8: 3	know that man shall not l
1Sa	10:24	Long l the king!"
Job	14:14	shall he l again? All the
Ps	63: 4	I will bless You while I l;
Ps	104:33	to the LORD as long as I l;
Is	6: 6	having in his hand a l coal
Is	26:19	Your dead shall l;
Is	38:16	by these things men l;
Is	55: 3	Hear, and your soul shall l;
Ezek	18:23	turn from his ways and l?
Ezek	20:11	he shall l by them.'
Ezek	33:10	in them, how can we then l?
Ezek	37: 3	of man, can these bones l?
Dan	2: 4	l forever! Tell your
Amos	5: 4	of Israel: "Seek Me and l;
Amos	5: 6	Seek the LORD and l,
Amos	5:14	not evil, That you may l;
Hab	2: 4	But the just shall l by his
Matt	4: 4	Man shall not l by bread
Matt	9:18	hand on her and she will l.
Luke	10:28	do this and you will l.
Luke	20:38	for all l to Him."
John	5:25	and those who hear will l.
John	6:51	he will l forever; and the
John	6:57	and I l because of the
John	6:57	so he who feeds on Me will l
John	11:25	he may die, he shall l.
John	14:19	you will l also.
Acts	17:28	for in Him we l and move and
Rom	1:17	The just shall l by
Rom	6: 2	shall we who died to sin l
Rom	6: 8	that we shall also l with
Rom	8:12	to l according to the flesh.
Rom	12:18	l peaceably with all men.
Rom	14: 8	For if we l, we live to
Rom	14: 8	we l to the Lord; and if we
1Co	7:12	and she is willing to l with
1Co	8: 6	and through whom we l.
1Co	9:14	preach the gospel should l
2Co	5:15	that those who l should live
2Co	6: 9	as dying, and behold we l;
2Co	7: 3	to die together and to l
2Co	13: 4	but we shall l with Him by
Gal	2:14	do you compel Gentiles to l
Gal	2:19	to the law that I might l
Gal	2:20	it is no longer I who l,
Gal	2:20	and the life which I now l
Gal	3:11	the just shall l by

Gal	3:12	who does them shall l
Gal	5:25	If we l in the Spirit, let us
Eph	6: 3	with you and you may l
Phil	1:21	to l is Christ, and to die
Phil	1:22	But if I l on in the flesh,
1Th	5:10	we should l together with
2Ti	2:11	We shall also l with Him.
2Ti	3:12	and all who desire to l
Tit	2:12	we should l soberly,
Heb	10:38	Now the just shall l
Heb	13:18	in all things desiring to l
Jas	4:15	we shall l and do this or
1Pe	2:24	might l for righteousness—by
1Pe	4: 2	that he no longer should l
1Pe	4: 6	but l according to God in
2Pe	2: 6	those who afterward would l
2Pe	2:18	escaped from those who l in
1Jn	4: 9	that we might l through Him.
Rev	20: 5	rest of the dead did not l

LIVED (see LIVE)

Num	21: 9	at the bronze serpent, he l.
Deut	5:26	the fire, as we have, and l?
Col	3: 7	once walked when you l in
Rev	20: 4	And they l and reigned with

LIVES (see LIVE)

Gen	9: 3	Every moving thing that l
Deut	8: 3	but man l by every word
Judg	8:19	my mother. As the LORD l,
1Sa	1:26	"O my lord! As your soul l,
2Sa	23:17	in jeopardy of their l?
Job	19:25	I know that my Redeemer l,
Ps	18:46	The LORD l! Blessed be my
Ps	90:10	The days of our l are
Dan	4:34	and honored Him who l
Dan	12: 7	and swore by Him who l
Luke	9:56	not come to destroy men's l
John	4:50	"Go your way; your son l.
John	11:26	And whoever l and believes in
Rom	6:10	He l to God.
Rom	14: 7	For none of us l to himself,
1Co	7:39	law as long as her husband l;
2Co	13: 4	yet He l by the power of
Gal	2:20	but Christ l in me; and the
Heb	7:25	since He always l to make
Heb	9:17	at all while the testator l.
1Pe	1:23	the word of God which l and
1Jn	3:16	ought to lay down our l
Rev	1:18	"I am He who l,
Rev	4: 9	who l forever and ever,

LIVESTOCK

Gen	4:20	dwell in tents and have l.
Gen	13: 2	Abram was very rich in l,
Ex	9: 6	and all the l of Egypt died;
Ex	12:29	and all the firstborn of l.

LIVING (see LIVE)

Gen	1:21	sea creatures and every l
Gen	2: 7	and man became a l being.
Gen	3:20	she was the mother of all l.
Ruth	2:20	His kindness to the l and
1Sa	17:26	defy the armies of the l

1Ki	3:25	Divide the l child in two,
Job	28:13	found in the land of the l.
Ps	27:13	LORD In the land of the l.
Ps	42: 2	for the l God. When shall I
Ps	69:28	out of the book of the l,
Ps	84: 2	my flesh cry out for the l
Ps	104:25	L things both small and
Ps	145:16	the desire of every l thing.
Eccl	9: 4	for a l dog is better than a
Song	4:15	A well of l waters, And
Is	4: 3	who is recorded among the l
Is	8:19	the dead on behalf of the l?
Is	53: 8	off from the land of the l;
Jer	2:13	the fountain of l waters,
Jer	10:10	He is the l God and the
Jer	17:13	The fountain of l waters."
Ezek	1: 5	came the likeness of four l
Dan	6:20	servant of the l God, has
Hos	1:10	You are sons of the l God.'
Matt	16:16	the Son of the l God."
Matt	22:32	of the dead, but of the l.
Luke	2: 8	the same country shepherds l
Luke	24: 5	Why do you seek the l among
John	4:10	He would have given you l
John	6:51	I am the l bread which came
John	7:38	heart will flow rivers of l
Acts	10:42	God to be Judge of the l
Rom	9:26	called sons of the l
Rom	12: 1	you present your bodies a l
1Co	15:45	man Adam became a l
2Co	3: 3	but by the Spirit of the l
2Co	6:16	you are the temple of the l
1Th	1: 9	from idols to serve the l
1Ti	3:15	is the church of the l God,
2Ti	4: 1	who will judge the l and the
Tit	3: 3	l in malice and envy,
Heb	3:12	in departing from the l God;
Heb	4:12	For the word of God is l and
Heb	9:14	dead works to serve the l
Heb	10:20	by a new and l way which He
Heb	10:31	into the hands of the l God.
Heb	12:22	and to the city of the l
1Pe	1: 3	has begotten us again to a l
1Pe	2: 4	Coming to Him as to a l
1Pe	4: 5	who is ready to judge the l
Rev	4: 6	were four l creatures full
Rev	7: 2	having the seal of the l
Rev	7:17	them and lead them to l

LO

Matt	28:20	I have commanded you; and l,

LOAF (*see* LOAVES)

Judg	7:13	a l of barley bread tumbled
Mark	8:14	did not have more than one l

LOATHE

Job	7:16	I l my life; I would not
Ps	139:21	And do I not l those who

LOAVES (*see* LOAF)

Matt	16: 9	or remember the five l of
Matt	16:10	Nor the seven l of the four
Mark	6:41	blessed and broke the l,

LOCUST (*see* LOCUSTS)

Ex	10:19	There remained not one l in
Joel	1: 4	What the chewing l left,
Amos	7: 1	He formed l swarms at the

LOCUSTS (*see* LOCUST)

Prov	30:27	The l have no king, Yet
Mark	1: 6	and he ate l and wild honey.
Rev	9: 3	Then out of the smoke l came

LODGE

Ruth	1:16	wherever you lodge, I will l;

LOFTY

Is	57:15	thus says the High and L

LOINS

1Ki	18:46	and he girded up his l and
Heb	7:10	for he was still in the l of
1Pe	1:13	Therefore gird up the l of

LOIS†

2Ti	1: 5	first in your grandmother L

LONG (*see* LONGER, LONGING, LONGS)

Ex	20:12	that your days may be l upon
Num	9:18	as l as the cloud stayed
Num	14:11	And how l will they not
Num	14:27	How l shall I bear with
Num	20:15	and we dwelt in Egypt a l
Deut	5:16	you, that your days may be l,
Deut	12:20	because you l to eat meat,
Deut	19: 6	him, because the way is l,
Josh	6: 5	when they make a l blast
Josh	11:18	Joshua made war a l time with
1Sa	1:14	How l will you be drunk? Put
1Sa	7: 2	in Kirjath Jearim a l time;
1Sa	10:24	L live the king!"
1Ki	3:11	and have not asked l life
1Ki	18:21	How l will you falter between
Job	3:21	Who l for death, but it does
Job	6: 8	me the thing that I l for!
Job	7:19	How l? Will You not look
Job	18: 2	How l till you put an end to
Job	27: 3	As l as my breath is in me,
Job	27: 6	shall not reproach me as l
Ps	6: 3	But You, O LORD—HOW l?
Ps	13: 1	How l will You hide Your
Ps	32: 3	my groaning all the day l.
Ps	35:28	of Your praise all the day l.
Ps	44:22	sake we are killed all day l;
Ps	62: 3	How l will you attack a man?
Ps	72: 5	They shall fear You As l as
Ps	73:14	For all day l I have been
Ps	80: 4	How l will You be angry
Ps	89:16	name they rejoice all day l,
Ps	90:13	Return, O LORD! How l?
Ps	91:16	With l life I will satisfy
Ps	94: 3	How l will the wicked
Ps	104:33	will sing to the LORD as l
Ps	116: 2	I will call upon Him as l
Ps	119:40	I l for Your precepts;
Ps	129: 3	They made their furrows l.

Ps	143: 3	Like those who have l been
Prov	3: 2	For length of days and l
Prov	6: 9	How l will you slumber, O
Prov	7:19	He has gone on a l journey;
Prov	23:30	Those who linger l at the
Is	6:11	Then I said, "Lord, how l?
Is	22:11	for Him who fashioned it l
Is	65: 2	out My hands all day l to a
Jer	12: 4	How l will the land mourn,
Jer	47: 6	How l until you are quiet?
Ezek	44:20	nor let their hair grow l;
Dan	8:13	How l will the vision be,
Dan	10: 1	the appointed time was l;
Dan	12: 6	How l shall the fulfillment
Mark	12:38	who desire to go around in l
John	9: 5	As l as I am in the world, I
John	14: 9	"Have I been with you so l,
1Co	11:14	you that if a man has l
1Co	11:15	But if a woman has l hair, it
1Co	13: 4	Love suffers l and is kind;
Rev	6:10	loud voice, saying, "How l,

LONGER (see LONG)

Ex	2: 3	But when she could no l hide
Matt	19: 6	they are no l two but one
Mark	14:25	I will no l drink of the
Luke	15:19	and I am no l worthy to be
Luke	22:16	I will no l eat of it until
John	7:33	be with you a little while l,
John	11:54	Therefore Jesus no l walked
John	12:35	A little while l the light is
John	14:19	A little while l and the
John	15:15	No l do I call you servants,
John	16:25	is coming when I will no l
John	17:11	Now I am no l in the world,
Rom	6: 2	who died to sin live any l
Rom	6: 6	that we should no l be
Rom	6: 9	Death no l has dominion over
Rom	7:17	it is no l I who do it,
Rom	11: 6	then it is no l of works;
Rom	11: 6	otherwise grace is no l
Rom	14:15	you are no l walking in
2Co	5:15	who live should live no l
2Co	5:16	now we know Him thus no l.
Gal	2:20	it is no l I who live, but
Gal	3:18	it is no l of promise; but
Gal	3:25	we are no l under a tutor.
Gal	4: 7	Therefore you are no l a
Eph	2:19	you are no l strangers and
Eph	4:14	that we should no l be
Eph	4:17	that you should no l walk as
Eph	4:28	Let him who stole steal no l,
1Th	3: 1	when we could no l endure
1Ti	5:23	No l drink only water, but
Phm	1:16	no l as a slave but more than
Heb	10:18	there is no l an offering
Heb	10:26	there no l remains a
1Pe	4: 2	that he no l should live the
Rev	6:11	should rest a little while l,

LONGING

Ps	107: 9	For He satisfies the l soul,

LONGS (see LONG)

Ps	63: 1	My flesh l for You In a
Ps	84: 2	My soul l, yes, even
Ps	143: 6	My soul l for You like a

LONGSUFFERING

Ex	34: 6	merciful and gracious, l,
Num	14:18	The LORD is l and abundant
Ps	86:15	L and abundant in mercy and
Rom	2: 4	goodness, forbearance, and l,
Rom	9:22	endured with much l the
2Co	6: 6	purity, by knowledge, by l,
Gal	5:22	is love, joy, peace, l,
Eph	4: 2	and gentleness, with l,
Col	1:11	for all patience and l with
Col	3:12	humility, meekness, l;
2Ti	4: 2	with all l and teaching.
1Pe	3:20	when once the Divine l
2Pe	3: 9	but is l toward us, not
2Pe	3:15	and consider that the l of

LOOK (see EXAMINE, LOOKED, LOOKING, LOOKS)

Gen	13:14	Lift your eyes now and l from
Gen	15: 5	L now toward heaven, and
Ex	3: 6	for he was afraid to l upon
Num	15:39	that you may l upon it and
Deut	26:15	L down from Your holy
1Sa	16: 7	Do not l at his appearance or
Job	6:28	be pleased to l at me; For
Job	7:19	Will You not l away from
Job	21: 5	L at me and be astonished
Job	35: 5	L to the heavens and see
Ps	17: 2	Let Your eyes l on the
Ps	22:17	They l and stare at Me.
Ps	25:18	L on my affliction and my
Ps	35:17	how long will You l on?
Ps	80:14	L down from heaven and see,
Ps	84: 9	And l upon the face of Your
Ps	101: 5	one who has a haughty l and
Ps	123: 2	So our eyes l to the LORD
Prov	6:17	A proud l, A lying tongue
Prov	21: 4	A haughty l, a proud heart,
Prov	23:31	Do not l on the wine when it
Is	45:22	L to Me, and be saved, All
Is	51: 1	L to the rock from which
Is	51: 2	L to Abraham your father,
Is	59: 9	We l for light, but there
Is	59:11	We l for justice, but
Is	63:15	L down from heaven, And
Hab	1:13	And cannot l on wickedness.
Hab	1:13	Why do You l on those who
Zech	12:10	then they will l on Me whom
Matt	6:26	L at the birds of the air,
Matt	7: 3	And why do you l at the speck
Matt	11: 3	or do we l for another?"
Matt	24:26	if they say to you, 'L,
Luke	17:23	L here!' or 'Look there!' Do
Luke	21:28	l up and lift up your heads,
Luke	21:29	L at the fig tree, and all
John	4:35	lift up your eyes and l at
John	7:52	from Galilee? Search and l,
John	19:37	They shall l on Him whom

John	20:27	and l at My hands; and reach
Acts	3:12	Or why l so intently at us,
Acts	18:15	l to it yourselves; for I
2Co	10: 7	Do you l at things according
Phil	2: 4	Let each of you l out not
1Pe	1:12	which angels desire to l
2Pe	3:13	l for new heavens and a new
2Jn	8	L to yourselves, that we do
Rev	5: 3	or to l at it.

LOOKED (see LOOK)

Gen	18: 2	So he lifted his eyes and l,
Gen	19:26	But his wife l back behind
Ex	2:12	So he l this way and that
Ex	3: 2	the midst of a bush. So he l,
Job	30:26	But when I l for good, evil
Ps	34: 5	They l to Him and were
Is	5: 7	He l for justice, but
Jer	8:15	We l for peace, but no good
Matt	19:26	But Jesus l at them and said
Mark	6:41	He l up to heaven, blessed
Mark	8:33	He had turned around and l
Mark	14:67	she l at him and said, "You
Luke	1:25	in the days when He l on
Luke	2:38	of Him to all those who l
Luke	21: 1	And He l up and saw the rich
Luke	22:56	l intently at him and said,
Luke	22:61	And the Lord turned and l at
John	1:42	Now when Jesus l at him, He
John	20:11	she stooped down and l
Acts	1:10	And while they l steadfastly
Acts	13: 9	l intently at him
Heb	11:26	for he l to the reward.
1Jn	1: 1	which we have l upon, and
Rev	4: 1	After these things I l,

LOOKING (see LOOK)

Luke	9:62	and l back, is fit for the
Tit	2:13	l for the blessed hope and
Heb	12: 2	l unto Jesus, the author and
2Pe	3:12	l for and hastening the

LOOKS (see LOOK)

1Sa	16: 7	for man l at the outward
1Sa	16: 7	but the LORD l at the
2Sa	14:25	as Absalom for his good l.
Ps	14: 2	The LORD l down from heaven
Matt	5:28	I say to you that whoever l

LOOSE (see LOOSED, RELEASE)

Judg	15:14	and his bonds broke l from
Matt	16:19	and whatever you l on earth
Mark	1: 7	worthy to stoop down and l.

LOOSED (see LOOSE)

Eccl	12: 6	before the silver cord is l,
Matt	18:18	loose on earth will be l in
Acts	2:24	having l the pains of death,

LORD (see LORD'S, LORDS,
    THE-LORD-IS-MY-BANNER,
    THE-LORD-WILL-PROVIDE, YAH)

Gen	2: 4	in the day that the L God
Gen	2: 7	And the L God formed man of

Gen	2: 8	The L God planted a garden
Gen	2: 9	And out of the ground the L
Gen	2:15	Then the L God took the man
Gen	3: 8	heard the sound of the L
Gen	4:26	call on the name of the L.
Gen	6: 8	grace in the eyes of the L.
Gen	7:16	and the L shut him in.
Gen	8:20	built an altar to the L,
Gen	10: 9	mighty hunter before the L;
Gen	11: 5	But the L came down to see
Gen	11: 8	So the L scattered them
Gen	12: 7	Then the L appeared to Abram
Gen	13:10	like the garden of the L,
Gen	15: 2	L GOD, what will You give
Gen	15: 6	And he believed in the L,
Gen	16: 7	Now the Angel of the L
Gen	18:12	my l being old also?"
Gen	18:14	anything too hard for the L?
Gen	18:30	Let not the L be angry, and I
Gen	22:14	In the Mount of The L it
Gen	24: 7	The L God of heaven, who
Gen	28:13	the L stood above it and
Gen	28:13	I am the L God of Abraham
Gen	28:16	Surely the L is in this
Gen	31:49	May the L watch between you
Ex	3: 2	And the Angel of the L
Ex	3:15	The L God of your fathers,
Ex	3:18	The L God of the Hebrews has
Ex	3:18	we may sacrifice to the L
Ex	5: 2	said, "Who is the L,
Ex	5: 2	go? I do not know the L,
Ex	6: 2	said to him: "I am the L.
Ex	6: 3	but by My name L I was not
Ex	6: 6	of Israel: 'I am the L;
Ex	7:16	The L God of the Hebrews has
Ex	8:10	is no one like the L our
Ex	9:12	But the L hardened the heart
Ex	9:30	you will not yet fear the L
Ex	10: 7	that they may serve the L
Ex	10: 9	must hold a feast to the L.
Ex	12:23	For the L will pass through
Ex	12:23	the L will pass over the
Ex	12:27	Passover sacrifice of the L,
Ex	12:29	pass at midnight that the L
Ex	13:12	shall set apart to the L
Ex	13:14	By strength of hand the L
Ex	13:21	And the L went before them
Ex	14:13	see the salvation of the L,
Ex	14:14	The L will fight for you,
Ex	14:21	and the L caused the sea to
Ex	14:27	So the L overthrew the
Ex	14:30	So the L saved Israel that
Ex	14:31	so the people feared the L,
Ex	14:31	and believed the L and His
Ex	15: 1	sang this song to the L,
Ex	15: 1	"I will sing to the L,
Ex	15: 2	The L is my strength and
Ex	15: 3	The L is a man of war;
Ex	15: 3	The L is His name.
Ex	15: 6	"Your right hand, O L,
Ex	15:11	"Who is like You, O L,
Ex	15:16	Your people pass over, O L,
Ex	15:18	The L shall reign forever
Ex	15:19	and the L brought back the

L

Ex	15:26	For I am the L who heals
Ex	16: 7	see the glory of the L;
Ex	16: 7	complaints against the L.
Ex	16:23	a holy Sabbath to the L.
Ex	16:33	and lay it up before the L,
Ex	17: 2	me? Why do you tempt the L?
Ex	17: 4	So Moses cried out to the L,
Ex	18: 9	all the good which the L
Ex	18:10	said, "Blessed be the L,
Ex	19:18	because the L descended
Ex	19:20	Then the L came down upon
Ex	19:21	through to gaze at the L,
Ex	19:22	priests who come near the L
Ex	19:22	lest the L break out
Ex	20: 5	the L your God, am a
Ex	20: 7	not take the name of the L
Ex	20:10	is the Sabbath of the L
Ex	20:11	For in six days the L made
Ex	20:11	Therefore the L blessed the
Ex	22:11	then an oath of the L shall
Ex	22:20	except to the L only, he
Ex	24: 1	Moses, "Come up to the L,
Ex	24: 2	alone shall come near the L,
Ex	24: 5	offerings of oxen to the L.
Ex	24: 7	All that the L has said we
Ex	24: 8	of the covenant which the L
Ex	24:16	Now the glory of the L
Ex	28:36	signet: HOLINESS TO THE L.
Ex	31:13	may know that I am the L
Ex	31:15	of rest, holy to the L.
Ex	31:17	for in six days the L made
Ex	32: 5	is a feast to the L.
Ex	32:14	So the L relented from the
Ex	32:35	So the L plagued the people
Ex	34: 6	And the L passed before him
Ex	34: 6	him and proclaimed, "The L,
Ex	34:14	no other god, for the L,
Ex	35: 2	a Sabbath of rest to the L.
Ex	40:34	and the glory of the L
Ex	40:38	For the cloud of the L was
Lev	1: 2	brings an offering to the L,
Lev	1: 5	kill the bull before the L;
Lev	18: 2	I am the L your God.
Lev	18: 5	live by them: I am the L.
Lev	20: 8	I am the L who sanctifies
Lev	23: 3	it is the Sabbath of the L
Lev	24: 6	gold table before the L.
Lev	25: 1	And the L spoke to Moses on
Lev	25: 2	keep a sabbath to the L.
Lev	26:46	and laws which the L made
Lev	27: 2	certain persons to the L,
Lev	27:28	is most holy to the L.
Num	3: 4	profane fire before the L
Num	4:49	to the commandment of the L
Num	5: 6	against the L,
Num	5: 8	wrong must go to the L
Num	5:16	and set her before the L.
Num	5:21	the L make you a curse and
Num	5:21	when the L makes your thigh
Num	6: 2	separate himself to the L,
Num	6: 6	separates himself to the L
Num	6: 8	he shall be holy to the L.
Num	6:12	shall consecrate to the L
Num	6:24	The L bless you and keep

Num	6:25	The L make His face shine
Num	6:26	The L lift up His
Num	8: 4	to the pattern which the L
Num	8:10	the Levites before the L,
Num	8:11	perform the work of the L.
Num	9: 8	that I may hear what the L
Num	9:13	the offering of the L at
Num	9:18	and at the command of the L
Num	9:19	kept the charge of the L
Num	9:20	to the command of the L
Num	10:29	the place of which the L
Num	10:29	for the L has promised good
Num	10:32	that whatever good the L
Num	10:33	from the mountain of the L
Num	10:33	of the covenant of the L
Num	10:34	And the cloud of the L was
Num	10:35	O L! Let Your enemies be
Num	11: 1	it displeased the L;
Num	11: 1	So the fire of the L burned
Num	11: 2	when Moses prayed to the L,
Num	11:18	in the hearing of the L,
Num	11:28	and said, "Moses my l,
Num	11:31	a wind went out from the L,
Num	11:33	and the L struck the people
Num	12: 2	Has the L indeed spoken only
Num	12: 2	And the L heard it.
Num	12: 6	among you, I, the L,
Num	12: 8	he sees the form of the L.
Num	12: 9	So the anger of the L was
Num	12:11	my l! Please do not lay
Num	14: 3	Why has the L brought us to
Num	14: 8	If the L delights in us,
Num	14: 9	do not rebel against the L,
Num	14:14	these people; that You, L,
Num	14:17	let the power of my L be
Num	14:18	The L is longsuffering and
Num	14:42	for the L is not among
Num	14:43	have turned away from the L,
Num	14:44	of the covenant of the L
Num	15:15	stranger be before the L.
Num	15:30	brings reproach on the L,
Num	15:31	despised the word of the L,
Num	16: 5	Tomorrow morning the L will
Num	16:17	his censer before the L,
Num	16:30	But if the L creates a new
Num	16:30	men have rejected the L.
Num	16:35	a fire came out from the L
Num	21: 6	So the L sent fiery serpents
Num	21:14	Book of the Wars of the L:
Num	22:22	and the Angel of the L took
Num	22:28	Then the L opened the mouth
Num	22:31	Then the L opened Balaam's
Num	23: 5	Then the L put a word in
Num	30: 2	a man makes a vow to the L,
Num	30: 3	woman makes a vow to the L,
Deut	1: 8	the land which the L swore
Deut	1:27	Because the L hates us, He
Deut	1:36	he wholly followed the L.
Deut	2: 7	These forty years the L
Deut	4:12	And the L spoke to you out
Deut	4:15	you saw no form when the L
Deut	4:23	the covenant of the L your
Deut	6: 2	that you may fear the L your
Deut	6: 4	The L our God, the LORD

Deut	6: 5	You shall love the L your
Deut	6:16	shall not tempt the L
Deut	7: 6	are a holy people to the L
Deut	7: 6	the L your God has chosen
Deut	7: 7	The L did not set His love
Deut	7: 8	but because the L loves you,
Deut	7: 9	Therefore know that the L
Deut	7:25	is an abomination to the L
Deut	8: 2	shall remember that the L
Deut	10:17	God is God of gods and L
Deut	10:20	You shall fear the L your
Deut	12: 5	seek the place where the L
Deut	12:21	If the place where the L
Deut	12:29	When the L your God cuts
Deut	13: 3	know whether you love the L
Deut	14: 1	are the children of the L
Deut	14: 2	are a holy people to the L
Deut	14: 2	and the L has chosen you to
Deut	14:23	you may learn to fear the L
Deut	15: 9	and he cry out to the L
Deut	15:15	and the L your God redeemed
Deut	15:19	you shall sanctify to the L
Deut	16: 1	keep the Passover to the L
Deut	16:15	a sacred feast to the L
Deut	16:16	not appear before the L
Deut	17: 1	is an abomination to the L
Deut	18: 2	the L is their inheritance,
Deut	18: 7	stand there before the L.
Deut	18:15	The L your God will raise
Deut	18:21	know the word which the L
Deut	18:22	speaks in the name of the L,
Deut	18:22	is the thing which the L
Deut	20:18	and you sin against the L
Deut	23: 1	enter the assembly of the L.
Deut	23:21	you make a vow to the L
Deut	26: 3	to the country which the L
Deut	26: 4	before the altar of the L
Deut	28: 7	The L will cause your
Deut	28:11	And the L will grant you
Deut	28:21	The L will make the plague
Deut	28:22	The L will strike you with
Deut	28:58	THE L YOUR GOD,
Deut	28:64	Then the L will scatter you
Deut	29:20	and the L would blot out
Deut	29:28	And the L uprooted them from
Deut	30: 6	to love the L your God with
Deut	31:11	to appear before the L
Deut	31:12	may learn to fear the L
Deut	31:27	rebellious against the L,
Deut	31:29	evil in the sight of the L,
Deut	32: 3	proclaim the name of the L:
Deut	33: 2	The L came from Sinai, And
Deut	33:12	The beloved of the L shall
Deut	33:29	a people saved by the L,
Deut	34: 1	And the L showed him all
Deut	34:10	whom the L knew face to
Deut	34:11	and wonders which the L
Josh	1: 1	Moses the servant of the L,
Josh	2:10	we have heard how the L
Josh	2:12	you, swear to me by the L,
Josh	3:11	of the covenant of the L of
Josh	4:23	for the L your God dried up
Josh	5:14	of the army of the L I
Josh	6:11	So he had the ark of the L

Josh	6:19	are consecrated to the L;
Josh	6:19	into the treasury of the L.
Josh	6:27	So the L was with Joshua,
Josh	7: 1	so the anger of the L
Josh	7:19	give glory to the L God of
Josh	14: 8	I wholly followed the L my
Josh	22: 5	to love the L your God, to
Josh	22:16	this day against the L?
Josh	22:22	The L God of gods, the LORD
Josh	22:22	the L God of gods, He
Josh	24:15	house, we will serve the L.
Josh	24:16	we should forsake the L to
Josh	24:18	We also will serve the L,
Josh	24:24	The L our God we will serve,
Josh	24:29	Nun, the servant of the L,
Judg	2: 1	Then the Angel of the L came
Judg	2:16	the L raised up judges who
Judg	2:18	the L was with the judge
Judg	2:18	for the L was moved to pity
Judg	3: 7	They forgot the L their
Judg	3: 9	the L raised up a deliverer
Judg	3:10	The Spirit of the L came
Judg	4: 2	So the L sold them into the
Judg	5:11	the righteous acts of the L,
Judg	6:22	seen the Angel of the L
Judg	6:34	But the Spirit of the L came
Judg	7:20	The sword of the L and of
Judg	8:23	the L shall rule over
Judg	11:30	made a vow to the L,
Judg	13: 3	And the Angel of the L
Judg	13:25	And the Spirit of the L
Judg	16:20	he did not know that the L
Judg	16:28	Samson called to the L,
Ruth	1: 8	The L deal kindly with you,
Ruth	1:17	The L do so to me, and
Ruth	2: 4	The L be with you!" And
Ruth	2: 4	The L bless you!"
Ruth	4:13	the L gave her conception,
Ruth	4:14	Naomi, "Blessed be the L,
1Sa	1:11	I will give him to the L
1Sa	1:28	also have lent him to the L;
1Sa	2: 1	heart rejoices in the L;
1Sa	2: 1	horn is exalted in the L.
1Sa	2: 2	one is holy like the L,
1Sa	2: 6	The L kills and makes alive;
1Sa	2:21	Samuel grew before the L.
1Sa	2:26	in favor both with the L
1Sa	3: 4	that the L called Samuel.
1Sa	3: 7	did not yet know the L,
1Sa	3: 9	you must say, 'Speak, L,
1Sa	7:12	Thus far the L has helped
1Sa	15: 1	The L sent me to anoint you
1Sa	15:19	not obey the voice of the L?
1Sa	15:22	Has the L as great delight
1Sa	15:22	obeying the voice of the L?
1Sa	15:23	rejected the word of the L,
1Sa	15:26	and the L has rejected you
1Sa	15:28	The L has torn the kingdom
1Sa	15:33	in pieces before the L in
1Sa	15:35	and the L regretted that He
1Sa	16: 7	For the L does not see
1Sa	16: 7	but the L looks at the
1Sa	16: 8	Neither has the L chosen
1Sa	16:13	and the Spirit of the L

L

1Sa	16:14	spirit from the L troubled	2Ki	11:17	a covenant between the L,
1Sa	16:18	and the L is with him."	2Ki	13:23	But the L was gracious to
1Sa	20:42	May the L be between you and	2Ki	15: 3	right in the sight of the L,
1Sa	24:12	Let the L judge between you	2Ki	15: 5	Then the L struck the king,
1Sa	25:28	fights the battles of the L,	2Ki	17: 9	secretly did against the L
1Sa	25:38	that the L struck Nabal,	2Ki	17:11	things to provoke the L to
1Sa	26:19	be cursed before the L,	2Ki	17:20	And the L rejected all the
1Sa	26:23	May the L repay every man	2Ki	17:23	until the L removed Israel
1Sa	28: 6	when Saul inquired of the L,	2Ki	17:25	they did not fear the L;
1Sa	28: 6	the L did not answer him,	2Ki	17:25	therefore the L sent lions
1Sa	28:18	not obey the voice of the L	2Ki	17:41	these nations feared the L,
2Sa	2: 6	And now may the L show	2Ki	18: 6	For he held fast to the L;
2Sa	3:39	The L shall repay the	2Ki	18:22	We trust in the L our God,'
2Sa	4: 8	and the L has avenged my	2Ki	19:14	and spread it before the L.
2Sa	6: 2	the L of Hosts, who dwells	2Ki	19:15	prayed before the L,
2Sa	6: 5	played music before the L	2Ki	19:16	"Incline Your ear, O L,
2Sa	6: 9	How can the ark of the L	2Ki	19:16	hear; open Your eyes, O L,
2Sa	6:11	And the L blessed Obed-Edom	2Ki	19:19	O L our God, I pray, save
2Sa	6:14	David danced before the L	2Ki	19:31	The zeal of the L of hosts
2Sa	7:18	O L GOD? And what is my	2Ki	20: 2	wall, and prayed to the L,
2Sa	8: 6	The L preserved David	2Ki	20: 3	"Remember now, O L,
2Sa	12: 1	Then the L sent Nathan to	2Ki	21:22	He forsook the L God of his
2Sa	12:13	have sinned against the L.	2Ki	22: 8	Law in the house of the L.
2Sa	12:14	to the enemies of the L to	2Ki	22: 9	oversee the house of the L.
2Sa	12:15	And the L struck the child	2Ki	22:13	is the wrath of the L
2Sa	14:11	As the L lives, not one	2Ki	23: 3	a covenant before the L,
2Sa	15: 7	vow which I made to the L.	2Ki	23:21	the Passover to the L
2Sa	22: 1	Then David spoke to the L	2Ki	24: 4	which the L would not
2Sa	22:32	who is God, except the L?	2Ki	25: 9	burned the house of the L
2Sa	23: 2	The Spirit of the L spoke by	1Ch	29:11	Yours is the kingdom, O L,
2Sa	24: 1	Again the anger of the L was	2Ch	1: 1	and the L his God was with
1Ki	1:31	Let my l King David live	2Ch	11:16	their heart to seek the L
1Ki	6: 1	to build the house of the L.	2Ch	12: 1	he forsook the law of the L,
1Ki	15: 4	for David's sake the L his	2Ch	16: 9	For the eyes of the L run to
1Ki	18: 7	that you, my l Elijah?"	2Ch	31: 3	written in the Law of the L.
1Ki	18:12	servant have feared the L	2Ch	32: 8	but with us is the L our
1Ki	18:13	the prophets of the L,	2Ch	32:22	Thus the L saved Hezekiah
1Ki	18:21	If the L is God, follow	2Ch	36:22	the L stirred up the spirit
1Ki	18:22	am left a prophet of the L;	Ezra	1: 1	the L stirred up the spirit
1Ki	18:36	L God of Abraham, Isaac, and	Ezra	1: 3	build the house of the L
1Ki	18:38	Then the fire of the L fell	Neh	1: 5	L God of heaven, O great
1Ki	18:39	and they said, "The L,	Neh	8: 9	day is holy to the L
1Ki	19: 4	"It is enough! Now, L,	Neh	8:10	for the joy of the L is
1Ki	19: 7	And the angel of the L came	Neh	9: 3	Book of the Law of the L
1Ki	19:11	the mountain before the L.	Neh	9: 6	You alone are the L;
1Ki	19:11	the L passed by, and a	Job	1: 7	And the L said to Satan,
1Ki	19:11	in pieces before the L,	Job	1:21	The L gave, and the LORD
1Ki	19:11	but the L was not in the	Job	1:21	and the L has taken away;
1Ki	20:28	The L is God of the hills,	Job	1:21	be the name of the L.
1Ki	22: 7	still a prophet of the L	Job	28:28	'Behold, the fear of the L,
1Ki	22:19	I saw the L sitting on His	Job	38: 1	Then the L answered Job out
1Ki	22:28	the L has not spoken by	Job	42: 9	for the L had accepted Job.
2Ki	1:15	And the angel of the L said	Job	42:10	Indeed the L gave Job twice
2Ki	2:14	Where is the L God of	Job	42:12	Now the L blessed the latter
2Ki	2:16	the Spirit of the L has	Ps	1: 2	is in the law of the L,
2Ki	3:15	that the hand of the L came	Ps	1: 6	For the L knows the way of
2Ki	4: 1	your servant feared the L.	Ps	2: 2	Against the L and against
2Ki	5:18	in this thing may the L	Ps	2: 7	The L has said to Me,
2Ki	6:18	him, Elisha prayed to the L,	Ps	2:11	Serve the L with fear, And
2Ki	6:33	calamity is from the L;	Ps	3: 8	belongs to the L.
2Ki	10:16	and see my zeal for the L.	Ps	4: 3	But know that the L has set
2Ki	10:30	And the L said to Jehu,	Ps	4: 3	The L will hear when I
2Ki	10:31	to walk in the law of the L	Ps	5: 6	The L abhors the
2Ki	11:15	in the house of the L.	Ps	5: 8	Lead me, O L,

Ps	6: 2	LORD, for I am weak; O L,
Ps	6: 3	troubled; But You, O L—
Ps	9: 1	I will praise You, O L,
Ps	9:11	Sing praises to the L,
Ps	9:13	O L! Consider my trouble
Ps	10: 1	do You stand afar off, O L?
Ps	10:16	The L is King forever and
Ps	11: 4	The L is in His holy
Ps	11: 5	The L tests the righteous,
Ps	12: 6	The words of the L are
Ps	13: 6	I will sing to the L,
Ps	14: 2	The L looks down from
Ps	14: 7	out of Zion! When the L
Ps	16: 7	I will bless the L who has
Ps	16: 8	I have set the L always
Ps	18: 1	I will love You, O L,
Ps	18: 2	The L is my rock and my
Ps	18:28	The L my God will
Ps	18:46	The L lives! Blessed be
Ps	19: 7	The law of the L is
Ps	19: 7	The testimony of the L is
Ps	19: 8	The statutes of the L are
Ps	19: 8	The commandment of the L
Ps	19: 9	The fear of the L is
Ps	19: 9	The judgments of the L
Ps	19:14	In Your sight, O L,
Ps	21: 7	the king trusts in the L,
Ps	21: 9	The L shall swallow them
Ps	22: 8	"He trusted in the L,
Ps	22:27	remember and turn to the L,
Ps	22:30	will be recounted of the L
Ps	23: 1	The L is my shepherd; I
Ps	23: 6	dwell in the house of the L
Ps	24: 3	into the hill of the L?
Ps	24: 5	receive blessing from the L,
Ps	24: 8	The L strong and mighty,
Ps	24: 8	The L mighty in battle.
Ps	24:10	The L of hosts, He is
Ps	25: 4	Show me Your ways, O L;
Ps	25:12	the man that fears the L?
Ps	26: 1	Vindicate me, O L,
Ps	26: 2	Examine me, O L,
Ps	26: 6	go about Your altar, O L,
Ps	27: 1	The L is my light and my
Ps	27: 1	The L is the strength of
Ps	27: 4	I have desired of the L,
Ps	27: 4	behold the beauty of the L,
Ps	27: 8	said to You, "Your face, L,
Ps	27:11	Teach me Your way, O L,
Ps	27:13	see the goodness of the L
Ps	28: 7	The L is my strength and
Ps	29: 2	Give unto the L the glory
Ps	29: 2	Worship the L in the
Ps	29: 3	The voice of the L is over
Ps	29:10	The L sat enthroned at the
Ps	29:10	And the L sits as King
Ps	29:11	The L will bless His
Ps	30: 1	I will extol You, O L,
Ps	30:10	Hear, O L, and have mercy
Ps	30:10	and have mercy on me; L,
Ps	31:24	All you who hope in the L.
Ps	32: 2	is the man to whom the L
Ps	32: 5	my transgressions to the L,
Ps	33: 2	Praise the L with the harp;
Ps	33: 5	of the goodness of the L.
Ps	33:12	nation whose God is the L,
Ps	33:13	The L looks from heaven;
Ps	33:18	the eye of the L is on
Ps	33:20	Our soul waits for the L;
Ps	34: 1	I will bless the L at all
Ps	34: 2	make its boast in the L;
Ps	34: 3	magnify the L with me, And
Ps	34: 4	I sought the L,
Ps	34: 6	and the L heard him, And
Ps	34: 7	The angel of the L encamps
Ps	34: 8	taste and see that the L
Ps	34:18	The L is near to those who
Ps	37: 3	Trust in the L,
Ps	37: 5	Commit your way to the L,
Ps	37: 7	Rest in the L,
Ps	37:23	man are ordered by the L,
Ps	40: 1	waited patiently for the L;
Ps	46: 7	The L of hosts is with us;
Ps	48: 1	Great is the L,
Ps	50: 1	The Mighty One, God the L,
Ps	55:22	Cast your burden on the L,
Ps	59:11	O L our shield.
Ps	68:11	The L gave the word; Great
Ps	70: 5	help and my deliverer; O L,
Ps	77: 7	Will the L cast off forever?
Ps	84: 2	For the courts of the L;
Ps	84:11	For the L God is a sun and
Ps	84:11	The L will give grace and
Ps	86: 1	Bow down Your ear, O L,
Ps	86:11	Teach me Your way, O L;
Ps	89: 1	of the mercies of the L
Ps	89: 6	can be compared to the L?
Ps	90:17	let the beauty of the L
Ps	93: 1	The L reigns, He is clothed
Ps	94: 1	O L God, to whom vengeance
Ps	94:17	Unless the L had been my
Ps	95: 1	let us sing to the L! Let
Ps	95: 6	Let us kneel before the L
Ps	96: 1	sing to the L a new song!
Ps	96: 7	Give to the L glory and
Ps	96: 9	worship the L in the beauty
Ps	96:10	The L reigns; The world
Ps	100: 1	a joyful shout to the L,
Ps	100: 2	Serve the L with gladness;
Ps	100: 3	Know that the L,
Ps	100: 5	For the L is good; His
Ps	102:19	From heaven the L viewed
Ps	103: 1	Bless the L, O my soul;
Ps	103:13	So the L pities those who
Ps	103:17	But the mercy of the L is
Ps	105: 1	give thanks to the L! Call
Ps	106: 1	Oh, give thanks to the L,
Ps	106: 2	the mighty acts of the L?
Ps	107: 2	Let the redeemed of the L
Ps	107: 6	they cried out to the L in
Ps	110: 1	The L said to my Lord,
Ps	110: 4	The L has sworn And will
Ps	110: 5	The L is at Your right
Ps	111:10	The fear of the L is the
Ps	115:17	dead do not praise the L,
Ps	116: 1	I love the L,
Ps	116:12	shall I render to the L
Ps	116:14	will pay my vows to the L

Ps	118: 8	better to trust in the L
Ps	118:14	The L is my strength and
Ps	118:24	This is the day the L has
Ps	118:26	comes in the name of the L!
Ps	119:89	Forever, O L, Your word is
Ps	119:107	very much; Revive me, O L,
Ps	120: 1	distress I cried to the L,
Ps	121: 2	My help comes from the L,
Ps	121: 5	The L is your keeper; The
Ps	121: 7	The L shall preserve you
Ps	122: 1	go into the house of the L.
Ps	124: 1	If it had not been the L who
Ps	126: 1	When the L brought back the
Ps	126: 2	The L has done great things
Ps	127: 1	Unless the L builds the
Ps	127: 3	are a heritage from the L,
Ps	130: 3	should mark iniquities, O L,
Ps	130: 7	For with the L there is
Ps	135: 1	O you servants of the L!
Ps	135: 6	Whatever the L pleases He
Ps	136: 1	Oh, give thanks to the L,
Ps	139:21	Do I not hate them, O L,
Ps	144: 1	Blessed be the L my Rock,
Ps	144: 5	Bow down Your heavens, O L,
Ps	144:15	people whose God is the L!
Ps	145:10	works shall praise You, O L,
Ps	145:17	The L is righteous in all
Prov	1: 7	The fear of the L is the
Prov	3: 5	Trust in the L with all
Prov	3:12	For whom the L loves He
Prov	3:19	The L by wisdom founded
Prov	6:16	These six things the L
Prov	8:13	The fear of the L is to
Prov	8:22	The L possessed me at the
Prov	8:35	obtains favor from the L;
Prov	9:10	The fear of the L is the
Prov	16: 2	But the L weighs the
Prov	16: 7	a man's ways please the L,
Prov	16: 9	But the L directs his
Prov	16:33	decision is from the L.
Prov	17: 3	But the L tests the
Prov	19:23	The fear of the L leads to
Prov	20:24	man's steps are of the L;
Prov	21: 2	But the L weighs the
Prov	31:30	a woman who fears the L,
Is	1: 2	O earth! For the L has
Is	1: 9	Unless the L of hosts Had
Is	2: 3	up to the mountain of the L,
Is	2: 3	And the word of the L from
Is	5: 7	For the vineyard of the L
Is	6: 1	I saw the L sitting on a
Is	6: 3	holy is the L of hosts;
Is	7:14	Therefore the L Himself will
Is	8:18	and the children whom the L
Is	9: 7	The zeal of the L of hosts
Is	11: 2	The Spirit of the L shall
Is	11: 2	and of the fear of the L.
Is	11: 9	of the knowledge of the L
Is	12: 2	afraid; 'For YAH, the L,
Is	19:19	and a pillar to the L at
Is	25: 8	And the L GOD will wipe
Is	26: 4	For in YAH, the L,
Is	30:33	wood; The breath of the L,
Is	33:22	(For the L is our Judge,
Is	33:22	The L is our King; He
Is	37:36	Then the angel of the L
Is	40: 3	"Prepare the way of the L;
Is	40: 5	The glory of the L shall be
Is	40: 7	the breath of the L blows
Is	40:13	the Spirit of the L,
Is	40:27	way is hidden from the L,
Is	40:28	The everlasting God, the L,
Is	40:31	those who wait on the L
Is	41: 4	the beginning? 'I, the L,
Is	42: 8	I am the L, that is My
Is	42:10	Sing to the L a new song,
Is	43:11	I, even I, am the L,
Is	44:23	for the L has done it!
Is	45: 6	besides Me. I am the L,
Is	48:22	is no peace," says the L,
Is	50: 5	The L GOD has opened My
Is	51: 3	For the L will comfort
Is	51: 3	like the garden of the L;
Is	52: 9	of Jerusalem! For the L
Is	52:10	The L has made bare His
Is	53: 1	whom has the arm of the L
Is	53: 6	And the L has laid on Him
Is	53:10	Yet it pleased the L to
Is	53:10	And the pleasure of the L
Is	55: 6	Seek the L while He may be
Is	55: 7	Let him return to the L,
Is	58: 5	an acceptable day to the L?
Is	58: 9	and the L will answer; You
Is	58:13	The holy day of the L
Is	58:14	delight yourself in the L;
Is	59:19	fear The name of the L
Is	60: 1	And the glory of the L is
Is	60:14	call you The City of the L,
Is	61: 1	The Spirit of the L GOD is
Is	61: 1	Because the L has anointed
Is	61: 2	acceptable year of the L,
Is	61: 3	The planting of the L,
Is	62: 8	The L has sworn by His
Is	62:12	The Redeemed of the L;
Is	63: 7	lovingkindnesses of the L
Is	63:16	acknowledge us. You, O L,
Is	66: 5	Let the L be glorified,
Is	66:15	the L will come with fire
Is	66:16	and by His sword The L
Jer	1: 4	Then the word of the L came
Jer	1: 6	L GOD! Behold, I cannot
Jer	1: 8	deliver you," says the L.
Jer	1:19	am with you," says the L,
Jer	7: 4	LORD, the temple of the L,
Jer	9:24	knows Me, That I am the L,
Jer	9:24	I delight," says the L.
Jer	10:10	But the L is the true God;
Jer	15:20	deliver you," says the L.
Jer	17: 5	heart departs from the L.
Jer	17: 7	the man who trusts in the L,
Jer	17: 7	And whose hope is the L.
Jer	22:16	knowing Me?" says the L.
Jer	23: 6	L OUR RIGHTEOUSNESS.
Jer	23:34	The oracle of the L!' I will
Jer	28: 6	Amen! The L do so; the LORD
Jer	28:15	the L has not sent you, but
Jer	31:31	days are coming, says the L,
Jer	31:32	husband to them, says the L.

Jer	31:33	those days, says the L:
Jer	31:34	saying, 'Know the L,
Jer	33:16	L OUR RIGHTEOUSNESS.'
Jer	47: 6	"O you sword of the L,
Jer	50:25	The L has opened His
Jer	50:28	the vengeance of the L our
Jer	50:35	the Chaldeans," says the L,
Jer	51:39	not awake," says the L.
Jer	51:45	the fierce anger of the L.
Jer	51:48	the north," says the L.
Jer	52:13	burned the house of the L
Jer	52:17	were in the house of the L,
Lam	1: 9	had no comforter. "O L,
Lam	1:15	The L has trampled underfoot
Lam	2: 7	The L has spurned His altar,
Lam	2: 9	find no vision from the L.
Lam	3:18	Have perished from the L.
Lam	3:25	The L is good to those who
Lam	3:31	For the L will not cast off
Lam	3:40	And turn back to the L;
Lam	3:50	Till the L from heaven
Lam	4:11	The L has fulfilled His
Lam	5:21	Turn us back to You, O L,
Ezek	1: 3	and the hand of the L was
Ezek	1:28	of the glory of the L.
Ezek	3:14	but the hand of the L was
Ezek	6: 7	shall know that I am the L.
Ezek	7: 9	know that I am the L who
Ezek	7:19	day of the wrath of the L;
Ezek	8:12	The L does not see us, the
Ezek	8:12	the L has forsaken the
Ezek	8:16	toward the temple of the L
Ezek	9: 9	The L has forsaken the land,
Ezek	10: 4	Then the glory of the L went
Ezek	11: 5	Then the Spirit of the L
Ezek	11:23	And the glory of the L went
Ezek	13: 5	battle on the day of the L.
Ezek	16:23	woe to you!' says the L
Ezek	16:58	abominations," says the L.
Ezek	18:25	The way of the L is not
Ezek	20:12	know that I am the L who
Ezek	20:48	shall see that I, the L,
Ezek	20:49	L GOD! They say of me,
Ezek	25: 5	shall know that I am the L.
Ezek	30: 3	Even the day of the L is
Ezek	33:17	The way of the L is not
Ezek	37: 1	The hand of the L came upon
Ezek	37: 1	out in the Spirit of the L,
Ezek	37: 3	O L GOD, You know."
Ezek	37: 4	hear the word of the L!
Ezek	37:14	performed it," says the L.
Ezek	38:14	Thus says the L GOD: "On
Ezek	39: 6	shall know that I am the L.
Ezek	39: 7	know that I am the L,
Ezek	39:20	says the L GOD.
Ezek	43: 5	the glory of the L filled
Ezek	43:24	a burnt offering to the L.
Ezek	44: 4	the glory of the L filled
Ezek	44:15	says the L GOD.
Ezek	46: 3	this gateway before the L
Ezek	46: 4	the prince offers to the L
Ezek	46: 9	the land come before the L
Ezek	46:14	be made regularly to the L.
Ezek	48:14	for it is holy to the L.
Ezek	48:35	THE L IS THERE."
Dan	2:47	the L of kings, and a
Dan	5:23	yourself up against the L
Dan	9: 2	by the word of the L
Dan	9: 4	And I prayed to the L my
Dan	9: 4	confession, and said, "O L,
Dan	9:19	"O Lord, hear! O L,
Dan	12: 8	Then I said, "My l,
Hos	1: 2	When the L began to speak
Hos	1: 7	Will save them by the L
Hos	2:13	Me she forgot," says the L.
Hos	2:20	And you shall know the L.
Hos	5: 4	And they do not know the L.
Hos	6: 1	and let us return to the L;
Hos	6: 3	the knowledge of the L.
Joel	1:15	day! For the day of the L
Joel	2:31	and awesome day of the L.
Joel	2:32	calls on the name of the L
Joel	3:16	The L also will roar from
Amos	1: 2	The L roars from Zion, And
Amos	5: 6	Seek the L and live, Lest
Amos	5:18	desire the day of the L!
Jon	1:17	Now the L had prepared a
Jon	2: 1	Then Jonah prayed to the L
Jon	2: 9	Salvation is of the L.
Jon	4: 6	And the L God prepared a
Mic	2: 7	Is the Spirit of the L
Mic	3: 8	by the Spirit of the L,
Mic	4: 2	up to the mountain of the L,
Mic	4: 2	And the word of the L from
Mic	6: 6	shall I come before the L,
Mic	6: 7	Will the L be pleased with
Mic	6: 8	And what does the L
Nah	1: 3	The L is slow to anger and
Hab	1:12	O L my God, my Holy One?
Hab	2:20	But the L is in His holy
Zeph	1:12	The L will not do good, Nor
Zeph	1:14	The great day of the L is
Zech	1:12	Then the Angel of the L
Zech	3: 2	And the L said to Satan,
Zech	14: 9	The L is one," And His
Zech	14:20	HOLINESS TO THE L" shall
Mal	2:17	You have wearied the L
Mal	4: 5	and dreadful day of the L.
Matt	1:20	an angel of the L appeared
Matt	1:22	which was spoken by the L
Matt	3: 3	the way of the L;
Matt	4: 7	shall not tempt the L
Matt	4:10	shall worship the L
Matt	7:21	everyone who says to Me, 'L,
Matt	8: 2	worshiped Him, saying, "L,
Matt	8: 8	answered and said, "L,
Matt	8:21	disciples said to Him, "L,
Matt	8:25	and awoke Him, saying, "L,
Matt	11:25	L of heaven and earth, that
Matt	12: 8	For the Son of Man is L even
Matt	14:28	answered Him and said, "L,
Matt	15:27	And she said, "Yes, L,
Matt	16:22	"Far be it from You, L;
Matt	17: 4	and said to Jesus, "L,
Matt	18:21	came to Him and said, "L,
Matt	20:25	rulers of the Gentiles l it
Matt	21: 3	The L has need of them,' and
Matt	21: 9	in the name of the L!

Matt	22:37	You shall love the L	Rom	6:23	life in Christ Jesus our L.
Matt	22:44	The L said to my Lord,	Rom	9:29	Unless the L of Sabaoth
Matt	22:45	David then calls Him 'L,	Rom	10: 9	with your mouth the L Jesus
Matt	24:42	do not know what hour your L	Rom	10:12	for the same L over all is
Matt	25:21	His l said to him, 'Well	Rom	10:13	on the name of the L
Matt	25:21	Enter into the joy of your l.	Rom	10:16	For Isaiah says, "L,
Matt	26:22	began to say to Him, "L,	Rom	11:34	the mind of the L?
Matt	27:10	as the L directed	Rom	12:11	in spirit, serving the L;
Matt	28: 2	for an angel of the L	Rom	12:19	will repay," says the L.
Matt	28: 6	see the place where the L	Rom	13:14	But put on the L Jesus
Mark	12:29	the L is one.	Rom	14: 6	day, observes it to the L;
Mark	12:30	you shall love the L	Rom	14: 6	He who eats, eats to the L,
Luke	1:28	the L is with you; blessed	Rom	14: 8	if we die, we die to the L.
Luke	1:32	and the L God will give Him	Rom	14: 9	that He might be L of both
Luke	1:38	the maidservant of the L!	Rom	16:12	who have labored in the L.
Luke	1:43	that the mother of my L	Rom	16:20	The grace of our L Jesus
Luke	1:46	"My soul magnifies the L,	1Co	1: 9	His Son, Jesus Christ our L.
Luke	2: 9	an angel of the L stood	1Co	1:31	him glory in the L.
Luke	2: 9	and the glory of the L shone	1Co	2: 8	not have crucified the L of
Luke	2:11	Savior, who is Christ the L.	1Co	2:16	the mind of the L
Luke	2:15	which the L has made known	1Co	4: 4	He who judges me is the L.
Luke	2:22	to present Him to the L	1Co	5: 4	In the name of our L Jesus
Luke	4:18	The Spirit of the L is	1Co	5: 4	with the power of our L
Luke	4:19	year of the L.	1Co	6:13	and the L for the body.
Luke	10:27	You shall love the L	1Co	7:10	yet not I but the L.
Luke	24:34	The L is risen indeed, and	1Co	7:12	But to the rest I, not the L,
John	6:23	they ate bread after the L	1Co	7:25	no commandment from the L;
John	12:38	has the arm of the L	1Co	7:32	Lord—how he may please the L.
John	13:13	"You call me Teacher and L,	1Co	7:35	and that you may serve the L
John	13:14	your L and Teacher, have	1Co	8: 6	and one L Jesus Christ,
John	20: 2	They have taken away the L	1Co	9: 1	not seen Jesus Christ our L?
John	20:18	that she had seen the L,	1Co	9: 1	Are you not my work in the L?
John	20:20	glad when they saw the L.	1Co	9: 2	of my apostleship in the L.
John	20:28	My L and my God!"	1Co	10:21	drink the cup of the L and
John	21: 7	It is the L!" Now when Simon	1Co	10:22	Or do we provoke the L to
John	21: 7	heard that it was the L,	1Co	11:23	For I received from the L
Acts	2:20	awesome day of the L.	1Co	11:23	that the L Jesus on the
Acts	2:21	on the name of the L	1Co	11:27	or drinks this cup of the L
Acts	2:36	both L and Christ."	1Co	11:27	the body and blood of the L.
Acts	2:47	And the L added to the	1Co	12: 3	one can say that Jesus is L
Acts	5: 9	to test the Spirit of the L?	1Co	12: 5	ministries, but the same L.
Acts	5:14	increasingly added to the L,	1Co	15:47	the second Man is the L
Acts	5:19	at night an angel of the L	1Co	15:58	in the work of the L,
Acts	7:30	an Angel of the L appeared	1Co	15:58	is not in vain in the L.
Acts	7:59	L Jesus, receive my spirit."	1Co	16:10	he does the work of the L,
Acts	8:26	Now an angel of the L spoke	1Co	16:22	let him be accursed. O L,
Acts	8:39	the Spirit of the L caught	2Co	3:16	when one turns to the L,
Acts	9: 5	he said, "Who are You, L?	2Co	3:17	where the Spirit of the L
Acts	9: 5	Then the L said, "I am	2Co	3:18	a mirror the glory of the L,
Acts	9:42	and many believed on the L.	2Co	4:10	the body the dying of the L
Acts	10:48	in the name of the L.	2Co	5: 6	we are absent from the L.
Acts	11:24	people were added to the L.	2Co	5: 8	and to be present with the L.
Acts	12: 7	an angel of the L stood by	2Co	6:17	be separate, says the L.
Acts	14: 3	speaking boldly in the L,	2Co	10:17	him glory in the L.
Acts	15:35	preaching the word of the L,	2Co	10:18	but whom the L commends.
Acts	16:31	Believe on the L Jesus	2Co	12: 8	thing I pleaded with the L
Acts	17:24	since He is L of heaven and	Gal	6:14	in the cross of our L Jesus
Acts	18: 9	Now the L spoke to Paul in	Gal	6:17	my body the marks of the L
Acts	19:20	So the word of the L grew	Eph	1:15	heard of your faith in the L
Acts	21:14	The will of the L be done."	Eph	2:21	into a holy temple in the L,
Acts	22: 8	I answered, 'Who are You, L?	Eph	4: 1	the prisoner of the L,
Acts	22:10	I said, 'What shall I do, L?	Eph	4: 5	one L, one faith, one
Rom	4: 8	the man to whom the L	Eph	5: 8	now you are light in the L.
Rom	4:24	who raised up Jesus our L	Eph	5:10	what is acceptable to the L.

Eph	5:17	what the will of the L is.
Eph	5:19	in your heart to the L,
Eph	5:22	own husbands, as to the L.
Eph	5:29	just as the L does the
Eph	6: 1	obey your parents in the L,
Eph	6: 7	doing service, as to the L,
Phil	2:11	that Jesus Christ is L,
Phil	4: 1	so stand fast in the L,
Phil	4: 2	be of the same mind in the L.
Phil	4: 4	Rejoice in the L always.
Phil	4: 5	The L is at hand.
Col	1:10	you may walk worthy of the L,
Col	3:16	in your hearts to the L.
Col	3:23	as to the L and not to men,
Col	3:24	for you serve the L Christ.
Col	4: 7	and fellow servant in the L,
1Th	1: 3	patience of hope in our L
1Th	1: 6	followers of us and of the L,
1Th	2:15	who killed both the L Jesus
1Th	2:19	you in the presence of our L
1Th	3: 8	if you stand fast in the L.
1Th	4:17	in the clouds to meet the L
1Th	4:17	shall always be with the L.
2Th	2: 8	whom the L will consume with
2Th	3: 3	But the L is faithful, who
2Th	3:16	Now may the L of peace
1Ti	1: 1	of God our Savior and the L
1Ti	1:12	I thank Christ Jesus our L
1Ti	6:14	blameless until our L Jesus
1Ti	6:15	the King of kings and L of
2Ti	1: 8	of the testimony of our L,
2Ti	2:19	The L knows those who are
2Ti	2:22	those who call on the L out
2Ti	2:24	And a servant of the L must
Phm	1.20	refresh my heart in the L.
Heb	7:14	it is evident that our L
Heb	7:21	The L has sworn And
Heb	8:11	saying, 'Know the L,
Heb	10:30	will repay," says the L.
Heb	10:30	The L will judge His
Heb	12: 5	chastening of the L,
Heb	12: 6	For whom the L loves
Heb	13:20	peace who brought up our L
Jas	1:12	crown of life which the L
Jas	2: 1	the L of glory, with
Jas	5: 4	reached the ears of the L
Jas	5: 8	for the coming of the L is
Jas	5:11	the end intended by the L—
Jas	5:14	oil in the name of the L.
Jas	5:15	and the L will raise him up.
1Pe	2: 3	you have tasted that the L
1Pe	3: 6	Abraham, calling him l,
1Pe	3:15	But sanctify the L God in
2Pe	1:11	kingdom of our L and Savior
2Pe	2: 1	even denying the L who
2Pe	3: 2	the apostles of the L and
2Pe	3: 8	that with the L one day is
2Pe	3: 9	The L is not slack concerning
2Pe	3:10	But the day of the L will
Jude	4	and deny the only L God and
Jude	9	The L rebuke you!"
Jude	14	the L comes with ten
Rev	1: 8	and the End," says the L,
Rev	4: 8	L God Almighty, Who was

Rev	4:11	"You are worthy, O L,
Rev	6:10	saying, "How long, O L,
Rev	11:15	the kingdoms of our L and
Rev	14:13	the dead who die in the L
Rev	17:14	for He is L of lords and
Rev	19: 6	Alleluia! For the L God
Rev	19:16	KING OF KINGS AND L OF
Rev	22:21	The grace of our L Jesus

LORD'S (see LORD)

Ex	9:29	that the earth is the L.
Ex	12:11	It is the L Passover.
1Sa	17:47	for the battle is the L,
Ps	11: 4	The L throne is in
Ps	24: 1	The earth is the L,
Ps	118:23	This was the L doing; It
Ps	137: 4	How shall we sing the L
Is	2: 2	the mountain of the L
Is	40: 2	she has received from the L
Lam	3:22	Through the L mercies we
Mic	4: 1	the mountain of the L
Matt	21:42	This was the L doing,
Luke	2:26	before he had seen the L
Rom	14: 8	we live or die, we are the L.
1Co	10:21	you cannot partake of the L
1Co	10:26	"the earth is the L,
1Co	11:26	you proclaim the L death
1Co	11:29	not discerning the L body.

LORDS (see LORD)

Deut	10.17	God of gods and Lord of l,
Josh	13: 3	the five l of the
Ps	136: 3	thanks to the Lord of l!
1Co	8: 5	are many gods and many l),
1Ti	6:15	King of kings and Lord of l,
Rev	17:14	for He is Lord of l and King
Rev	19:16	OF KINGS AND LORD OF L.

LOSE (see LOSES, LOSS, LOST)

Eccl	3: 6	to gain, And a time to l;
Matt	10:39	who finds his life will l
Gal	6: 9	we shall reap if we do not l

LOSES (see LOSE)

Matt	5:13	but if the salt l its
Matt	10:39	and he who l his life for My
Matt	16:26	and l his own soul? Or what
Luke	15: 4	if he l one of them, does
Luke	15: 8	if she l one coin, does not

LOSS (see LOSE)

| 1Co | 3:15 | is burned, he will suffer l; |
| Phil | 3: 7 | these I have counted l for |

LOST (see LOSE)

Jer	50: 6	My people have been l sheep.
Ezek	34:16	I will seek what was l and
Ezek	37:11	bones are dry, our hope is l,
Matt	10: 6	But go rather to the l sheep
Matt	15:24	was not sent except to the l
Matt	18:11	to save that which was l.
Luke	14:34	but if the salt has l its
Luke	15: 4	go after the one which is l
Luke	15: 6	found my sheep which was l!

L

Luke	15: 9	found the piece which I l!'
Luke	15:24	he was l and is found.' And
Luke	21:18	hair of your head shall be l.
John	17:12	and none of them is l except
John	18: 9	whom You gave Me I have l

LOT (see LOTS)

Num	26:55	land shall be divided by l;
Num	33:54	whatever falls to him by l.
Esth	3: 7	cast Pur (that is, the l),
Ps	16: 5	my cup; You maintain my l.
Prov	16:33	The l is cast into the lap,
Jon	1: 7	and the l fell on Jonah.
Acts	1:26	and the l fell on Matthias.

LOT* (see LOT'S)

Gen	11:27	and Haran. Haran begot L.
Gen	11:31	son Abram and his grandson L,
Gen	19:29	and sent L out of the midst
Gen	19:36	both the daughters of L
Luke	17:28	it was also in the days of L:
2Pe	2: 7	and delivered righteous L,

LOT'S (see LOT*)

Luke	17:32	Remember L wife.

LOTS (see LOT)

Ps	22:18	for My clothing they cast l.
Jon	1: 7	upon us." So they cast l,
Matt	27:35	My clothing they cast l.
Acts	1:26	And they cast their l,

LOUD (see HIGH)

Matt	27:46	Jesus cried out with a l

LOVE (see LOVED, LOVERS, LOVES, LOVESICK, LOVINGKINDNESS, UNLOVED)

Gen	22: 2	only son Isaac, whom you l,
Gen	27: 4	me savory food, such as I l,
Ex	20: 6	to those who l Me and keep
Lev	19:18	but you shall l your
Lev	19:34	and you shall l him as
Deut	6: 5	You shall l the LORD your
Deut	7: 7	LORD did not set His l
Deut	7: 9	with those who l Him and
2Sa	1:26	Surpassing the l of women.
Ps	18: 1	I will l You, O LORD, my
Ps	45: 7	You l righteousness and hate
Ps	52: 3	You l evil more than good,
Ps	116: 1	I l the LORD, because He
Ps	119:47	commandments, Which I l.
Ps	119:97	how I l Your law! It is my
Prov	4: 6	L her, and she will keep
Prov	7:18	let us take our fill of l
Prov	8:17	I l those who love me, And
Prov	10:12	But l covers all sins.
Prov	15:17	a dinner of herbs where l
Eccl	3: 8	A time to l, And a time
Eccl	9: 9	with the wife whom you l
Song	1: 2	For your l is better than
Song	1: 7	Tell me, O you whom I l,
Song	2: 4	his banner over me was l.
Song	2: 7	Do not stir up nor awaken l
Song	3: 3	"Have you seen the one I l?

Song	8: 6	For l is as strong as
Song	8: 7	Many waters cannot quench l,
Jer	31: 3	you with an everlasting l;
Dan	9: 4	and mercy with those who l
Hos	3: 1	l a woman who is loved by
Hos	3: 1	who look to other gods and l
Hos	9:15	I will l them no more. All
Hos	11: 4	cords, With bands of l,
Hos	14: 4	I will l them freely, For
Mic	6: 8	To l mercy, And to walk
Matt	5:43	You shall l your neighbor
Matt	5:44	l your enemies, bless those
Matt	5:46	For if you l those who love
Matt	6: 5	For they l to pray standing
Matt	6:24	he will hate the one and l
Matt	19:19	You shall l your neighbor
Matt	22:37	You shall l the LORD
Matt	24:12	the l of many will grow
Mark	12:33	And to l Him with all the
Luke	16:13	he will hate the one and l
John	11: 3	he whom You l is sick."
John	13:34	that you l one another; as I
John	14:15	If you l Me, keep My
John	14:23	and My Father will l him,
John	14:24	He who does not l Me does not
John	14:31	the world may know that I l
John	15: 9	loved you; abide in My l.
John	15:13	Greater l has no one than
John	21:15	do you l Me more than
John	21:15	You know that I l You." He
Rom	5: 5	because the l of God has
Rom	5: 8	God demonstrates His own l
Rom	8:28	for good to those who l God,
Rom	8:35	separate us from the l of
Rom	12: 9	Let l be without
Rom	12:10	one another with brotherly l,
Rom	13:10	does no harm to a neighbor
1Co	8: 1	but l edifies.
1Co	13: 1	of angels, but have not l,
1Co	13: 8	L never fails. But whether
1Co	13:13	And now abide faith, hope, l,
1Co	13:13	the greatest of these is l.
2Co	13:11	and the God of l and peace
2Co	13:14	and the l of God, and the
Gal	5: 6	but faith working through l.
Gal	5:22	the fruit of the Spirit is l,
Eph	2: 4	because of His great l with
Eph	3:17	rooted and grounded in l,
Eph	3:19	to know the l of Christ which
Eph	4:15	but, speaking the truth in l,
Eph	4:16	the edifying of itself in l.
Eph	5:25	l your wives, just as Christ
Eph	5:28	So husbands ought to l their
Phil	1: 9	that your l may abound still
Phil	2: 1	Christ, if any comfort of l,
Col	1:13	kingdom of the Son of His l,
Col	2: 2	being knit together in l,
Col	3:14	all these things put on l,
1Th	1: 3	work of faith, labor of l,
1Th	3:12	increase and abound in l to
1Ti	6:10	For the l of money is a root
Heb	6:10	your work and labor of l,
Heb	10:24	in order to stir up l and
Heb	13: 1	Let brotherly l continue.

Jas	1:12	has promised to those who l
1Pe	1: 8	whom having not seen you l.
1Pe	2:17	L the brotherhood. Fear God.
1Pe	4: 8	l will cover a multitude
1Pe	5:14	one another with a kiss of l.
1Jn	2:15	Do not l the world or the
1Jn	2:15	the l of the Father is not
1Jn	3: 1	Behold what manner of l the
1Jn	3:17	how does the l of God abide
1Jn	4: 7	for l is of God; and
1Jn	4: 8	not know God, for God is l.
1Jn	4: 9	In this the l of God was
1Jn	4:10	In this is l, not that we
1Jn	4:12	If we l one another, God
1Jn	4:12	and His l has been perfected
1Jn	4:19	We l Him because He first
1Jn	4:20	how can he l God whom he has
1Jn	5: 2	By this we know that we l the
1Jn	5: 2	when we l God and keep His
Rev	2: 4	you have left your first l.

LOVED (see LOVE)

Gen	25:28	And Isaac l Esau because he
Gen	25:28	but Rebekah l Jacob.
Gen	27:14	food, such as his father l.
Gen	29:18	Now Jacob l Rachel; so he
Gen	37: 3	Now Israel l Joseph more than
1Sa	18: 1	and Jonathan l him as his
Jer	31: 3	I have l you with an
Hos	11: 1	I l him, And out of Egypt I
John	3:16	For God so l the world that
John	3:19	and men l darkness rather
John	11: 5	Now Jesus l Martha and her
John	11:36	See how He l him!"
John	13: 1	having l His own who were in
John	13: 1	He l them to the end.
John	13:23	His disciples, whom Jesus l.
John	14:28	If you l Me, you would
John	15: 9	I also have l you; abide in
John	15:12	one another as I have l you.
John	20: 2	other disciple, whom Jesus l,
Rom	8:37	through Him who l us.
Rom	9:13	"Jacob I have l,
Gal	2:20	who l me and gave Himself
Eph	2: 4	great love with which He l
Eph	5: 2	as Christ also has l us and
2Ti	4:10	having l this present world,
1Jn	4:10	not that we l God, but that
1Jn	4:11	if God so l us, we also
1Jn	4:19	love Him because He first l
Rev	1: 5	To Him who l us and washed

LOVELY

Ps	84: 1	How l is Your tabernacle,
Song	1: 5	I am dark, but l,
Song	5:16	Yes, he is altogether l.
Phil	4: 8	pure, whatever things are l,

LOVERS

Hos	2: 5	said, 'I will go after my l,
Luke	16:14	who were l of money, also
2Ti	3: 2	l of money, boasters, proud,
2Ti	3: 4	l of pleasure rather than

LOVES (see LOVE)

Gen	27: 9	your father, such as he l.
Deut	7: 8	but because the LORD l you,
Ps	47: 4	of Jacob whom He l.
Prov	3:12	For whom the LORD l He
Prov	17:17	A friend l at all times,
Matt	10:37	He who l father or mother
Luke	7: 5	for he l our nation, and has
John	12:25	He who l his life will lose
John	14:21	it is he who l Me. And he
2Co	9: 7	for God l a cheerful giver.
Heb	12: 6	For whom the LORD l
1Jn	2:15	If anyone l the world, the
1Jn	4: 7	and everyone who l is born
1Jn	4:21	that he who l God must love

LOVESICK† (see LOVE)

Song	2: 5	me with apples, For I am l.
Song	5: 8	That you tell him I am l!

LOVINGKINDNESS (see LOVE)

Ps	51: 1	O God, According to Your l;
Ps	63: 3	Because Your l is better
Ps	103: 4	Who crowns you with l and
Jer	31: 3	Therefore with l I have
Jer	32:18	You show l to thousands, and
Jon	4: 2	to anger and abundant in l,

LOWING

1Sa	15:14	and the l of the oxen which

LOWLINESS (see LOWLY)

Phil	2: 3	but in l of mind let each

LOWLY (see LOWLINESS)

Ps	136:23	Who remembered us in our l
Zech	9: 9	L and riding on a donkey,
Matt	11:29	for I am gentle and l in
Matt	21: 5	is coming to you, L,

LUCIFER†

Is	14:12	are fallen from heaven, O L,

LUKE

Col	4:14	L the beloved physician and
2Ti	4:11	Only L is with me. Get Mark

LUKEWARM†

Rev	3:16	"So then, because you are l,

LUMP

Rom	9:21	from the same l to make one
Rom	11:16	the l is also holy; and if
1Co	5: 6	leaven leavens the whole l?
1Co	5: 7	that you may be a new l,

LUST (see LUSTS)

Prov	6:25	Do not l after her beauty in
Matt	5:28	looks at a woman to l for
Rom	1:27	burned in their l for one
Gal	5:16	you shall not fulfill the l
2Pe	1: 4	is in the world through l.
1Jn	2:16	the l of the eyes, and the

LUSTS (see LUST)

Rom	13:14	flesh, to fulfill its l.
Gal	5:17	For the flesh l against the
Eph	4:22	according to the deceitful l,
2Ti	2:22	Flee also youthful l;
1Pe	2:11	abstain from fleshly l which

LUTE

Ps	150: 3	Praise Him with the l and

LYDIA

Ezek	27:10	"Those from Persia, L,
Acts	16:14	Now a certain woman named L

LYING (see LIE)

Ps	31:18	Let the l lips be put to
Ps	119:163	I hate and abhor l,
Prov	6:17	A l tongue, Hands that
Prov	12:22	L lips are an abomination
Matt	8: 6	my servant is l at home
Matt	8:14	He saw his wife's mother l
Matt	9: 2	to Him a paralytic l on a
Luke	2:12	l in a manger."
Luke	2:16	and the Babe l in a manger.
Luke	5:25	took up what he had been l
Luke	11:54	l in wait for Him, and
Luke	24:12	he saw the linen cloths l by
John	5: 6	When Jesus saw him l there,
John	11:41	where the dead man was l.
John	20: 5	saw the linen cloths l
John	20: 6	he saw the linen cloths l
Rom	9: 1	truth in Christ, I am not l,
Eph	4:25	Therefore, putting away l,
2Th	2: 9	and l wonders,
1Ti	2: 7	truth in Christ and not l—

M

MACEDONIA

Acts	16: 9	A man of M stood and pleaded
Acts	16: 9	Come over to M and help us."
1Th	1: 8	not only in M and Achaia,

MACHPELAH

Gen	25: 9	buried him in the cave of M,
Gen	50:13	the cave of the field of M,

MAD (see MADMAN, MADNESS)

Acts	26:24	learning is driving you m!

MADE (see ESTABLISHED, MAKE, TOOK)

Gen	1: 7	Thus God m the firmament, and
Gen	1:16	Then God m two great lights:
Gen	1:16	He m the stars also.
Gen	1:31	saw everything that He had m,
Gen	2: 3	which God had created and m.
Gen	3: 7	fig leaves together and m
Gen	5: 1	He m him in the likeness of
Gen	6: 7	for I am sorry that I have m
Gen	9: 6	in the image of God He m
Ex	2:14	Who m you a prince and a

Ex	4:11	has m man's mouth? Or who
Ex	7: 1	I have m you as God to
Ex	20:11	For in six days the LORD m
Ex	29:18	an offering m by fire to the
Josh	9:15	So Joshua m peace with them,
Josh	9:15	and m a covenant with them
Judg	9: 6	and they went and m
Judg	9:27	and m merry. And they went
Judg	11:30	And Jephthah m a vow to the
Judg	17: 4	and he m it into a carved
1Sa	1:11	Then she m a vow and said,
1Sa	3:13	because his sons m
1Sa	8: 1	Samuel was old that he m
1Sa	11:15	and there they m Saul king
1Sa	15:35	regretted that He had m
1Sa	16: 8	and m him pass before
1Sa	16:10	Thus Jesse m seven of his
1Sa	18: 3	Then Jonathan and David m a
1Sa	20:16	So Jonathan m a covenant
2Sa	5: 3	and King David m a covenant
2Sa	7: 9	and have m you a great name,
2Sa	8:13	And David m himself a name
1Ki	1:43	Our lord King David has m
1Ki	1:44	and they have m him ride on
1Ki	3: 1	Now Solomon m a treaty with
1Ki	3: 7	You have m Your servant king
1Ki	4: 7	each one m provision for one
1Ki	5:12	and the two of them m a
1Ki	6: 4	And he m for the house
1Ki	10: 9	therefore He m you king, to
1Ki	12: 4	Your father m our yoke heavy;
1Ki	12:20	and m him king over all
1Ki	12:28	m two calves of gold, and
1Ki	12:31	He m shrines on the high
1Ki	12:31	and m priests from every
1Ki	14: 7	and m you ruler over My
1Ki	14: 9	for you have gone and m for
1Ki	14:16	who sinned and who m Israel
1Ki	14:26	shields which Solomon had m.
1Ki	15:26	in his sin by which he had m
1Ki	15:30	sinned and by which he had m
1Ki	15:34	in his sin by which he had m
1Ki	18:26	the altar which they had m.
1Ki	18:32	and he m a trench around the
1Ki	22:44	Also Jehoshaphat m peace with
1Ki	22:45	and how he m war, are they
1Ki	22:48	Jehoshaphat m merchant ships
1Ki	22:52	who had m Israel sin;
2Ki	6: 6	and he m the iron float.
2Ki	9:21	And his chariot was m
2Ki	11:17	Then Jehoiada m a covenant
2Ki	14:21	and m him king instead of
2Ki	16: 3	indeed he m his son pass
2Ki	17:21	and they m Jeroboam the son
2Ki	17:30	the men of Cuth m Nergal,
2Ki	18: 4	serpent that Moses had m;
2Ki	19:15	You have m heaven and earth.
2Ki	20:20	and how he m a pool and a
2Ki	21: 7	of Asherah that he had m,
2Ki	21:11	and has also m Judah sin
2Ki	21:24	the people of the land m
2Ki	23: 3	stood by a pillar and m a
2Ki	23:34	Then Pharaoh Necho m Eliakim
1Ch	16: 5	but Asaph m music with

1Ch	22: 8	shed much blood and have **m**
1Ch	28: 2	and had **m** preparations to
2Ch	6:29	whatever supplication is **m**
2Ch	6:40	attentive to the prayer **m**
2Ch	12: 9	shields which Solomon had **m.**
2Ch	12:10	Then King Rehoboam **m** bronze
2Ch	25:27	they **m** a conspiracy against
2Ch	26: 5	God **m** him prosper.
2Ch	33:25	the people of the land **m**
2Ch	34:31	stood in his place and **m a**
2Ch	35:25	They **m** it a custom in
2Ch	36:22	so that he **m a** proclamation
Ezra	1: 1	so that he **m a** proclamation
Job	33: 4	The Spirit of God has **m** me,
Ps	8: 5	For You have **m** him a little
Ps	33: 6	The LORD the heavens were **m,**
Ps	100: 3	It is He who has **m** us,
Ps	118:24	is the day the LORD has **m;**
Ps	139:14	fearfully and wonderfully **m;**
Prov	20:12	The LORD has **m** them both.
Eccl	3:11	He has **m** everything beautiful
Is	29:16	For shall the thing **m** say
Is	43: 7	I have **m** him."
Is	52:10	The LORD has **m** bare His
Is	53: 9	And they **m** His grave with
Is	53:12	And **m** intercession for the
Jer	1:18	I have **m** you this day A
Jer	10:11	The gods that have not **m** the
Jer	17:23	but **m** their neck stiff, that
Jer	18: 4	And the vessel that he **m** of
Jer	18: 4	so he **m** it again into
Jer	19:11	which cannot be **m** whole
Jer	25:17	and **m** all the nations drink,
Jer	29:26	The LORD has **m** you priest
Jer	31:32	to the covenant that I **m**
Jer	34:11	changed their minds and **m**
Jer	34:15	and you **m** a covenant before
Jer	46:16	He **m** many fall; Yes, one
Lam	1:13	He has **m** me desolate And
Lam	1:14	He **m** my strength fail; The
Lam	3: 2	He has led me and **m** me walk
Lam	3: 7	He has **m** my chain heavy.
Lam	3:15	He has **m** me drink wormwood.
Ezek	3: 8	I have **m** your face strong
Ezek	3: 9	I have **m** your forehead; do
Ezek	3:17	I have **m** you a watchman for
Ezek	12: 6	for I have **m** you a sign to
Ezek	16:25	and **m** your beauty to be
Ezek	20: 5	and **m** Myself known to them
Ezek	22:12	you have **m** profit from your
Ezek	27:11	They **m** your beauty
Ezek	27:16	the abundance of goods you **m.**
Ezek	29: 9	and I have **m** it.'
Ezek	31: 9	I **m** it beautiful with a
Ezek	33: 7	I have **m** you a watchman for
Dan	2:28	and He has **m** known to King
Dan	2:29	He who reveals secrets has **m**
Dan	3: 1	Nebuchadnezzar the king **m** an
Dan	4: 5	I saw a dream which **m** me
Dan	5: 1	Belshazzar the king **m** a great
Dan	9: 4	and **m** confession, and said,
Dan	10:10	which **m** me tremble on my
Hos	8: 4	silver and gold They **m**
Hos	8: 6	A workman **m** it, and it is

Amos	5: 8	He **m** the Pleiades and Orion;
Jon	1: 9	who **m** the sea and the dry
Jon	4: 5	There he **m** himself a shelter
Jon	4: 6	God prepared a plant and **m**
Jon	4:10	nor **m** it grow, which came up
Zeph	2: 8	And **m** arrogant threats
Mal	2: 9	Therefore I also have **m** you
Matt	9:16	and the tear is **m** worse.
Matt	9:22	your faith has **m** you well."
Matt	15:31	the maimed **m** whole, the
Matt	18:25	had, and that payment be **m.**
Matt	19:12	there are eunuchs who were **m**
Matt	21:13	but you have **m** it a 'den
Matt	24:45	whom his master **m** ruler over
Matt	25:16	and **m** another five talents.
Matt	26:33	Even if all are **m** to stumble
Matt	27:64	command that the tomb be **m**
Matt	27:66	So they went and **m** the tomb
Mark	2:27	The Sabbath was **m** for man,
Mark	10: 6	**m** them male and female.'
Mark	14:58	will destroy this temple **m**
Luke	1:62	So they **m** signs to his
Luke	2:15	which the Lord has **m** known
Luke	2:17	they **m** widely known the
Luke	3: 5	places shall be **m**
Luke	4:38	and they **m** request of Him
Luke	9:15	and **m** them all sit down.
Luke	12:14	who **m** Me a judge or an
Luke	23:19	for a certain rebellion **m**
John	1: 3	All things were **m** through
John	1: 3	nothing was made that was **m.**
John	1:10	and the world was **m** through
John	2: 9	tasted the water that was **m**
John	5: 6	Do you want to be **m** well?"
John	8:33	You will be **m** free'?"
John	19: 7	because He **m** Himself the Son
Acts	17:24	who **m** the world and
Rom	1:20	by the things that are **m,**
Rom	9:29	we would have been **m**
Rom	15:20	And so I have **m** it my aim to
Rom	16:26	Scriptures has been **m** known
1Co	9:19	I have **m** myself a servant to
1Co	12:13	and have all been **m** to drink
1Co	15:22	so in Christ all shall be **m**
1Co	15:28	Now when all things are **m**
2Co	5:21	For He **m** Him who knew no sin
Gal	3:19	to whom the promise was **m;**
Gal	5: 1	by which Christ has **m** us
Eph	1: 6	by which He has **m** us
Eph	1: 8	which He **m** to abound toward
Eph	1: 9	having **m** known to us the
Eph	2: 1	And you He **m** alive, who
Eph	2: 5	**m** us alive together with
Eph	2: 6	and **m** us sit together in
Eph	2:14	who has **m** both one, and has
Phil	2: 7	but **m** Himself of no
Phil	4: 6	let your requests be **m** known
Col	1:20	having **m** peace through the
Col	2:11	with the circumcision **m**
Col	2:13	He has **m** alive together with
Col	2:15	He **m** a public spectacle of
Heb	1: 2	through whom also He **m** the
Heb	2: 7	You have **m** him a
Heb	6:13	For when God **m** a promise to

M

Heb	7: 3	but **m** like the Son of God,
Heb	7:19	for the law **m** nothing
Heb	8: 9	the covenant that I **m**
Heb	8:13	He has **m** the first
Heb	9:11	perfect tabernacle not **m**
Heb	9:24	entered the holy places **m**
Heb	10:13	till His enemies are **m** His
Heb	11: 3	which are seen were not **m**
Heb	11:22	**m** mention of the departure
Heb	11:34	out of weakness were **m**
Heb	12:23	to the spirits of just men **m**
Heb	12:27	as of things that are **m**,
Jas	2:22	and by works faith was **m**
1Pe	3:18	to death in the flesh but **m**
1Pe	3:22	and powers having been **m**
2Pe	1:16	devised fables when we **m**
1Jn	5:10	does not believe God has **m**
Rev	1: 6	and has **m** us kings and

MADMAN (see MAD)

1Sa	21:15	this fellow to play the **m**

MADNESS (see MAD)

1Sa	21:13	feigned **m** in their hands,
Eccl	1:17	to know wisdom and to know **m**

MAGDALENE

Mark	16: 9	He appeared first to Mary **M**,
Luke	8: 2	infirmities—Mary called **M**,
John	20:18	Mary **M** came and told the

MAGGOT†

Job	25: 6	much less man, who is a **m**,

MAGICIANS

Gen	41: 8	and called for all the **m** of
Ex	7:22	Then the **m** of Egypt did so
Dan	2: 2	the command to call the **m**,

MAGNIFIED (see EXALTED, MAGNIFY)

2Sa	7:26	So let Your name be **m**
Ps	138: 2	For You have **m** Your word
Acts	19:17	name of the Lord Jesus was **m**.
Phil	1:20	so now also Christ will be **m**

MAGNIFIES† (see MAGNIFY)

Luke	1:46	My soul **m** the Lord,

MAGNIFY (see EXALT, MAGNIFIED, MAGNIFIES)

Ps	34: 3	**m** the LORD with me, And
Rom	11:13	I **m** my ministry,

MAGOG (see GOG)

Gen	10: 2	of Japheth were Gomer, **M**,
Ezek	38: 2	Gog, of the land of **M**,
Rev	20: 8	of the earth, Gog and **M**,

MAHER-SHALAL-HASH-BAZ

Is	8: 3	to me, "Call his name **M**;

MAID

Gen	16: 2	Please, go in to my **m**;
Gen	16: 8	He said, "Hagar, Sarai's **m**,

MAIDSERVANT (see FEMALE, MAIDSERVANTS, SERVANT)

Gen	16: 1	And she had an Egyptian **m**
Ruth	3: 9	"I am Ruth, your **m**.
1Sa	1:11	on the affliction of Your **m**
Ps	86:16	And save the son of Your **m**.
Luke	1:38	Behold the **m** of the Lord! Let
Luke	1:48	the lowly state of His **m**;

MAIDSERVANTS (see FEMALE, MAIDSERVANT)

Gen	33: 1	Leah, Rachel, and the two **m**.
Ruth	2:13	I am not like one of your **m**.
Prov	31:15	And a portion for her **m**.
Joel	2:29	menservants and on My **m** I
Acts	2:18	and on My **m** I will

MAINTAIN

Ps	16: 5	You **m** my lot.

MAJESTY

Ps	29: 4	of the LORD is full of **m**.
Ps	45: 4	And in Your **m** ride
Ps	93: 1	reigns, He is clothed with **m**;
Ps	96: 6	Honor and **m** are before Him;
Is	2:10	And the glory of His **m**.
Dan	4:30	and for the honor of my **m**?
Heb	1: 3	at the right hand of the **M**
Heb	8: 1	hand of the throne of the **M**
2Pe	1:16	were eyewitnesses of His **m**.
Jude	25	is wise, Be glory and **m**,

MAKE (see MADE, MAKER, MAKES, MAKING)

Gen	1:26	Let Us **m** man in Our image,
Gen	2:18	I will **m** him a helper
Gen	9:12	of the covenant which I **m**
Gen	11: 4	let us **m** a name for
Gen	12: 2	I will **m** you a great nation;
Gen	12: 2	I will bless you And **m**
Gen	13:16	And I will **m** your descendants
Gen	17: 2	And I will **m** My covenant
Gen	17: 6	and I will **m** nations of you,
Ex	20: 4	You shall not **m** for yourself
Ex	20:23	You shall not **m** anything to
Ex	28: 2	And you shall **m** holy garments
Ex	29:36	cleanse the altar when you **m**
Ex	32: 1	**m** us gods that shall go
Ex	33:19	I will **m** all My goodness pass
Lev	4:35	So the priest shall **m**
Lev	22:22	nor **m** an offering by fire of
Lev	26: 1	You shall not **m** idols for
Lev	26: 6	and none will **m** you afraid;
Lev	26:22	and **m** you few in number; and
Num	5:21	the LORD **m** you a curse and
Num	5:22	and **m** your belly swell and
Num	5:24	And he shall **m** the woman
Num	6:25	The LORD **m** His face shine
Num	12: 6	**m** Myself known to him in a
Num	15:38	Tell them to **m** tassels on
Num	21: 8	**M** a fiery serpent, and set
Deut	4:25	and act corruptly and **m** a
Deut	12:11	LORD your God chooses to **m**
Deut	20:12	if the city will not **m**
Deut	22: 8	then you shall **m** a parapet

Deut	23:21	When you **m** a vow to the
Deut	32:39	I kill and I **m** alive; I
Josh	1: 8	For then you will **m** your way
Josh	9: 7	so how can we **m** a covenant
Judg	8:24	I would like to **m** a request
Judg	9:48	**m** haste and do as I have
Ruth	3: 3	but do not **m** yourself known
Ruth	4:11	The LORD **m** the woman who is
1Sa	1: 6	to **m** her miserable, because
1Sa	2:19	his mother used to **m** him a
1Sa	6: 7	**m** a new cart, take two milk
1Sa	8: 5	Now **m** us a king to judge us
1Sa	13:19	Lest the Hebrews **m** swords or
1Sa	20:38	**M** haste, hurry, do not
2Sa	7:11	tells you that He will **m**
2Sa	7:23	to **m** for Himself a name—and
1Ki	1:37	and **m** his throne greater
1Ki	8:33	and pray and **m** supplication
1Ki	12:10	but you **m** it lighter on
2Ki	4:10	let us **m** a small upper room
2Ki	8: 3	and she went to **m** an appeal
1Ch	16: 8	**M** known His deeds among the
Ps	39: 4	**m** me to know my end, And
Ps	100: 1	**M** a joyful shout to the
Ps	105: 1	**M** known His deeds among the
Ps	110: 1	Till I **m** Your enemies Your
Ps	115: 8	Those who **m** them are like
Ps	119:27	**M** me understand the way of
Ps	139: 8	If I **m** my bed in hell,
Prov	1:16	And they **m** haste to shed
Is	1:15	Even though you **m** many
Is	41:15	I will **m** you into a new
Is	53:10	When You **m** His soul an
Is	55: 3	And I will **m** an everlasting
Jer	31:31	when I will **m** a new covenant
Jer	46:27	No one shall **m** him afraid.
Ezek	24:17	**m** no mourning for the dead;
Ezek	30:12	I will **m** the rivers dry,
Ezek	30:12	I will **m** the land waste,
Ezek	34:25	I will **m** a covenant of peace
Ezek	35:11	and I will **m** Myself known
Ezek	37:19	and **m** them one stick, and
Ezek	37:22	and I will **m** them one nation
Ezek	37:26	Moreover I will **m** a covenant
Ezek	45:15	to **m** atonement for them,"
Dan	4:25	and they shall **m** you eat
Dan	5:15	read this writing and **m**
Dan	6: 7	a royal statute and to **m** a
Dan	9:24	To **m** an end of sins, To
Dan	9:24	To **m** reconciliation for
Dan	11:35	and **m** them white, until
Hos	2:18	To **m** them lie down safely.
Hos	11: 8	How can I **m** you like Admah?
Amos	8: 9	That I will **m** the sun go down
Mic	1:16	**M** yourself bald and cut off
Mic	4: 4	And no one shall **m** them
Hab	1:14	Why do You **m** men like fish
Hab	2: 2	Write the vision And **m** it
Hab	3: 2	In the midst of the years **m**
Hab	3:19	He will **m** my feet like
Hab	3:19	And He will **m** me walk on my
Zeph	3:13	And no one shall **m** them
Hag	2:23	and will **m** you like a signet
Mal	3:17	On the day that I **m** them My

Matt	1:19	and not wanting to **m** her a
Matt	3: 3	**M** His paths straight.'
Matt	4:19	and I will **m** you fishers of
Matt	5:36	because you cannot **m** one
Matt	8: 2	You can **m** me clean."
Matt	12:16	Yet He warned them not to **m**
Matt	12:33	Either **m** the tree good and
Matt	17: 4	let us **m** here three
Matt	22:44	Till I **m** Your enemies
Matt	23: 5	They **m** their phylacteries
Matt	23:14	and for a pretense **m** long
Matt	23:15	you **m** him twice as much a
Matt	24:47	I say to you that he will **m**
Matt	25:21	I will **m** you ruler over many
Matt	28:19	Go therefore and **m** disciples
Mark	14:15	there **m** ready for us."
Luke	1:17	to **m** ready a people prepared
Luke	9:14	**M** them sit down in groups of
Luke	11:39	Now you Pharisees **m** the
Luke	11:40	Ho who made the outside **m**
Luke	14:18	with one accord began to **m**
Luke	15:19	**M** me like one of your hired
Luke	15:29	that I might **m** merry with my
Luke	16: 9	**m** friends for yourselves by
Luke	19: 5	**m** haste and come down, for
Luke	19:42	the things that **m** for your
Luke	22:12	there **m** ready."
John	2:16	these things away! Do not **m**
John	6:15	and take Him by force to **m**
John	8:32	and the truth shall **m** you
John	8:53	Whom do You **m** Yourself out
John	10:33	**m** Yourself God."
John	14:23	We will come to him and **m**
Acts	2:28	You will **m** me full of
Rom	1: 9	that without ceasing I **m**
Rom	2.17	and **m** your boast in God,
Rom	3: 3	Will their unbelief **m** the
Rom	3:31	Do we then **m** void the law
Rom	9:21	from the same lump to **m** one
Rom	9:22	to show His wrath and to **m**
Rom	13:14	and **m** no provision for the
Rom	14: 4	for God is able to **m** him
Rom	14:19	pursue the things which **m**
1Co	8:13	lest I **m** my brother stumble.
1Co	10:13	the temptation will also **m**
1Co	14: 7	when they **m** a sound, unless
2Co	8: 1	we **m** known to you the grace
2Co	9: 8	And God is able to **m** all
Gal	3:17	that it should **m** the promise
Gal	6:12	As many as desire to **m** a good
Eph	3: 9	and to **m** all see what is the
Eph	6:19	open my mouth boldly to **m**
Col	4: 4	that I may **m** it manifest, as
1Th	3:12	And may the Lord **m** you
2Th	3: 9	but to **m** ourselves an
2Ti	3: 6	creep into households and **m**
2Ti	3:15	which are able to **m** you wise
Heb	1:13	Till I **m** Your enemies
Heb	2:17	to **m** propitiation for the
Heb	7:25	since He always lives to **m**
Heb	8: 8	when I will **m** a new
Heb	13:21	**m** you complete in every good
Jas	3:18	sown in peace by those who **m**
Jas	4:13	and **m** a profit";

M

2Pe	1:10	be even more diligent to **m**
1Jn	1:10	we **m** Him a liar, and His
Rev	11: 7	of the bottomless pit will **m**
Rev	13: 7	It was granted to him to **m**
Rev	21: 5	I **m** all things new." And He

MAKER (see MAKE)

Job	4:17	man be more pure than his M?
Ps	95: 6	kneel before the LORD our M.
Is	45: 9	him who strives with his M!
Is	51:13	you forget the LORD your M,
Is	54: 5	For your M is your husband,
Hos	8:14	Israel has forgotten his M,
Heb	11:10	whose builder and **m** is God.

MAKES (see MAKE, VOWS)

1Sa	2: 6	The LORD kills and **m** alive;
1Sa	2: 7	The LORD **m** poor and makes
Ps	18:33	He **m** my feet like the feet
Ps	23: 2	He **m** me to lie down in green
Ps	46: 9	He **m** wars cease to the end
Ps	104: 3	Who **m** the clouds His
Ps	104: 4	Who **m** His angels spirits,
Ps	104:15	And wine that **m** glad the
Prov	10: 1	A wise son **m** a glad father,
Prov	13:12	Hope deferred **m** the heart
Prov	16: 7	He **m** even his enemies to be
Is	44:15	Indeed he **m** a god and
Matt	5:45	for He **m** His sun rise on the
Mark	7:37	He **m** both the deaf to hear
John	8:36	Therefore if the Son **m** you
Rom	8:26	but the Spirit Himself **m**
1Co	4: 7	For who **m** you differ from
Heb	1: 7	Who **m** His angels spirits
Jas	4: 4	be a friend of the world **m**

MAKING (see MAKE)

1Ch	15:28	**m** music with stringed
Ps	19: 7	**m** wise the simple;
Eccl	12:12	Of **m** many books there is
Is	45: 9	forms it, 'What are you **m**?
Mark	7:13	**m** the word of God of no
John	5:18	**m** Himself equal with God.
Eph	1:16	**m** mention of you in my
Eph	5:19	singing and **m** melody in your
1Th	1: 2	**m** mention of you in our

MALE (see MALES)

Gen	1:27	**m** and female He created
Gen	17:10	Every **m** child among you
Deut	4:16	the likeness of **m** or female,
1Ki	11:15	after he had killed every **m**
Dan	8: 5	suddenly a **m** goat came from
Matt	2:16	and put to death all the **m**
Matt	19: 4	made them **m** and female,'
Luke	2:23	Every **m** who opens the
Gal	3:28	there is neither **m** nor
Rev	12: 5	She bore a **m** Child who was to

MALES (see MALE)

Ex	23:17	times in the year all your **m**

MALICE

1Co	5: 8	nor with the leaven of **m** and
Col	3: 8	all these: anger, wrath, **m**,

MAMMON

Matt	6:24	You cannot serve God and **m**.
Luke	16: 9	yourselves by unrighteous **m**,

MAN (see MAN'S, MANKIND, MEN, SON)

Gen	1:26	Let Us make **m** in Our image,
Gen	1:27	So God created **m** in His own
Gen	2: 7	And the LORD God formed **m**
Gen	2: 7	and **m** became a living being.
Gen	2:18	It is not good that **m**
Gen	9: 5	I will require the life of **m**.
Gen	9: 6	By **m** his blood shall be
Gen	9: 6	the image of God He made **m**.
Ex	15: 3	The LORD is a **m** of war;
Ex	33:11	as a **m** speaks to his friend.
Ex	33:20	for no **m** shall see Me, and
Num	23:19	"God is not a **m**,
Deut	8: 3	but **m** lives by every word
Deut	22:25	But if a **m** finds a betrothed
Deut	22:25	and the **m** forces her and
Deut	24: 5	When a **m** has taken a new
Deut	24: 7	If a **m** is found kidnapping
Deut	25: 5	the widow of the dead **m**
Deut	33: 1	with which Moses the **m** of
Josh	3:12	one **m** from every tribe.
Josh	5:13	a M stood opposite him with
Josh	8:17	There was not a **m** left in Ai
Josh	10:14	heeded the voice of a **m**;
Josh	23:10	One **m** of you shall chase a
Judg	3:17	(Now Eglon was a very fat **m**.
Judg	5:30	To every **m** a girl or two;
Judg	6:12	you mighty **m** of valor!"
Judg	11:39	he had vowed. She knew no **m**.
Judg	13: 6	A M of God came to me, and
Judg	16: 7	and be like any other **m**.
Judg	17: 5	The **m** Micah had a shrine, and
Judg	17:11	content to dwell with the **m**;
Judg	17:12	and the young **m** became his
Judg	18:15	house of the young Levite **m**—
Judg	19:22	Bring out the **m** who came to
Judg	19:25	So the **m** took his concubine
Judg	20: 1	gathered together as one **m**
Judg	21:11	woman who has known a **m**
Ruth	2: 1	a **m** of great wealth, of the
Ruth	2:20	This **m** is a relation of
Ruth	3:18	for the **m** will not rest
Ruth	4: 7	one **m** took off his sandal
1Sa	2:27	Then a **m** of God came to Eli
1Sa	9: 1	There was a **m** of Benjamin
1Sa	9: 6	there is in this city a **m**
1Sa	9: 9	when a **m** went to inquire of
1Sa	9:10	to the city where the **m** of
1Sa	10: 6	and be turned into another **m**.
1Sa	13:14	has sought for Himself a **m**
1Sa	14: 1	of Saul said to the young **m**
1Sa	14: 6	said to the young **m** who
1Sa	15:29	relent. For He is not a **m**,
1Sa	16: 7	LORD does not see as **m**
1Sa	16: 7	for **m** looks at the outward

1Sa	16:16	to seek out a **m** who is a
1Sa	16:18	a mighty **m** of valor, a man
1Sa	16:18	a **m** of war, prudent in
1Sa	17:26	shall be done for the **m** who
1Sa	17:58	son are you, young **m**?
1Sa	21:14	you see the **m** is insane. Why
1Sa	27: 9	he left neither **m** nor woman
1Sa	27:11	David would save neither **m**
1Sa	28:14	An old **m** is coming up, and he
2Sa	3:38	that a prince and a great **m**
2Sa	7:19	Is this the manner of **m**,
2Sa	12: 2	The rich **m** had exceedingly
2Sa	12: 3	But the poor **m** had nothing,
2Sa	12: 7	You are the **m**! Thus says the
2Sa	14:21	bring back the young **m**
2Sa	16: 7	Como out! You bloodthirsty **m**,
2Sa	18:12	anyone touch the young **m**
2Sa	19:22	Shall any **m** be put to death
2Sa	20: 1	Every **m** to his tents, O
2Sa	21:20	where there was a **m** of
2Sa	22:49	me from the violent **m**.
2Sa	24:14	me fall into the hand of **m**.
1Ki	1:42	for you are a prominent **m**,
1Ki	1:52	he proves himself a worthy **m**,
1Ki	4:25	each **m** under his vine and
1Ki	8:25	shall not fail to have a **m**
1Ki	13: 1	a **m** of God went from Judah
1Ki	13:29	took up the corpse of the **m**
1Ki	17:18	O **m** of God? Have you come to
2Ki	1: 9	**M** of God, the king has said,
2Ki	4: 9	know that this is a holy **m**
1Ch	12: 4	a mighty **m** among the thirty,
Neh	9:29	Which if a **m** does, he shall
Job	1: 1	There was a **m** in the land of
Job	1: 8	a blameless and upright **m**,
Job	2: 4	all that a **m** has he will
Job	5: 7	Yet **m** is born to trouble,
Job	7: 1	like the days of a hired **m**?
Job	7:17	"What is **m**, that You
Job	9:32	"For He is not a **m**,
Job	14: 1	**M** who is born of woman Is
Job	25: 6	a maggot, And a son of **m**,
Job	33:12	For God is greater than **m**.
Ps	1: 1	Blessed is the **m** Who walks
Ps	8: 4	What is **m** that You are
Ps	8: 4	And the son of **m** that You
Ps	19: 5	rejoices like a strong **m** to
Ps	22: 6	But I am a worm, and no **m**;
Ps	32: 2	Blessed is the **m** to whom
Ps	34: 6	This poor **m** cried out, and
Ps	56:11	What can **m** do to me?
Ps	84: 5	Blessed is the **m** whose
Ps	119: 9	How can a young **m** cleanse
Prov	9: 8	hate you; Rebuke a wise **m**,
Prov	14:12	that seems right to a **m**,
Prov	19: 6	And every **m** is a friend to
Prov	24:34	your need like an armed **m**.
Prov	29:22	An angry **m** stirs up strife,
Eccl	1: 3	What profit has a **m** from all
Eccl	2:22	For what has **m** for all his
Eccl	2:24	Nothing is better for a **m**
Eccl	11: 9	Rejoice, O young **m**,
Eccl	12: 5	For **m** goes to his eternal
Song	8: 7	If a **m** would give for love
Is	6: 5	undone! Because I am a **m**
Is	36: 6	on which if a **m** leans, it
Is	52:14	was marred more than any **m**,
Is	53: 3	A **M** of sorrows and
Is	55: 7	And the unrighteous **m** his
Jer	3: 1	If a **m** divorces his wife,
Jer	9:23	Let not the wise **m** glory in
Jer	9:23	Let not the mighty **m** glory
Jer	9:23	Nor let the rich **m** glory
Jer	10:23	I know the way of **m** is not
Jer	10:23	It is not in **m** who walks
Jer	15:10	A **m** of strife and a man of
Jer	22:30	Write this **m** down as
Jer	31:22	woman shall encompass a **m**.
Jer	31:34	No more shall every **m** teach
Jer	31:34	and every **m** his brother,
Jer	33:17	David shall never lack a **m** to
Lam	3: 1	I am the **m** who has seen
Ezek	1: 5	they had the likeness of a **m**.
Ezek	2: 1	Ho said to me, "Son of **m**,
Ezek	20:11	if a **m** does, he shall live
Dan	2:10	There is not a **m** on earth who
Dan	7:13	One like the Son of **M**,
Dan	8:17	me, "Understand, son of **m**,
Dan	9:21	the **m** Gabriel, whom I had
Hos	11: 9	For I am God, and not **m**,
Amos	2: 7	A **m** and his father go in to
Mic	6: 8	He has shown you, O **m**,
Zech	13: 7	Against the **M** who is My
Mal	3: 8	Will a **m** rob God? Yet you
Matt	1:19	her husband, being a just **m**,
Matt	4: 4	**M** shall not live by
Matt	7: 9	Or what **m** is there among you
Matt	7:24	I will liken him to a wise **m**
Matt	7:26	will be like a foolish **m** who
Matt	8: 9	For I also am a **m** under
Matt	8:20	but the Son of **M** has nowhere
Matt	9: 6	may know that the Son of **M**
Matt	11:19	The Son of **M** came eating and
Matt	12: 8	For the Son of **M** is Lord even
Matt	12:29	he first binds the strong **m**?
Matt	12:35	A good **m** out of the good
Matt	12:35	and an evil **m** out of the
Matt	12:40	so will the Son of **M** be
Matt	12:45	the last state of that **m**
Matt	13:31	which a **m** took and sowed in
Matt	15:11	into the mouth defiles a **m**;
Matt	16:13	men say that I, the Son of **M**,
Matt	18: 7	but woe to that **m** by whom
Matt	19: 6	let not **m** separate."
Matt	19:20	The young **m** said to Him,
Matt	19:24	a needle than for a rich **m**
Matt	20:18	and the Son of **M** will be
Matt	24:30	the sign of the Son of **M**
Matt	24:30	they will see the Son of **M**
Matt	24:37	the coming of the Son of **M**
Matt	25:14	of heaven is like a **m**
Matt	25:24	I knew you to be a hard **m**,
Matt	26:72	I do not know the **M**!"
Matt	27:57	there came a rich **m** from
Mark	2: 7	Why does this **M** speak
Mark	5: 2	met Him out of the tombs a **m**
Mark	8:22	and they brought a blind **m**
Mark	12: 1	A **m** planted a vineyard and

Mark	14:51	Now a certain young **m**	Rom	5: 7	scarcely for a righteous **m**
Mark	15:39	Truly this **M** was the Son of	Rom	5: 7	yet perhaps for a good **m**
Luke	1:18	know this? For I am an old **m,**	Rom	5:12	just as through one **m** sin
Luke	1:27	to a virgin betrothed to a **m**	Rom	5:15	by the grace of the one **M,**
Luke	1:34	be, since I do not know a **m?**	Rom	6: 6	that our old **m** was crucified
Luke	2:25	there was a **m** in Jerusalem	Rom	7:22	according to the inward **m.**
Luke	2:25	and this **m** was just and	Rom	9:10	also had conceived by one **m,**
Luke	5:12	a **m** who was full of leprosy	1Co	2: 9	into the heart of **m**
Luke	5:18	men brought on a bed a **m** who	1Co	2:11	For what **m** knows the things
Luke	6:48	He is like a **m** building a	1Co	2:14	But the natural **m** does not
Luke	7: 8	For I also am a **m** placed	1Co	7: 1	It is good for a **m** not to
Luke	7:12	a dead **m** was being carried	1Co	7:26	that it is good for a **m** to
Luke	7:14	And He said, "Young **m,**	1Co	9: 8	these things as a mere **m?**
Luke	8:33	the demons went out of the **m**	1Co	10:13	such as is common to **m;**
Luke	8:41	there came a **m** named Jairus,	1Co	11: 3	that the head of every **m** is
Luke	13: 6	A certain **m** had a fig tree	1Co	11: 3	the head of woman is **m,**
Luke	13:19	which a **m** took and put in	1Co	11: 7	but woman is the glory of **m.**
Luke	15: 2	This **M** receives sinners and	1Co	11: 8	For **m** is not from woman, but
Luke	15:11	A certain **m** had two sons.	1Co	11:28	But let a **m** examine himself,
Luke	16:22	The rich **m** also died and was	1Co	13:11	child; but when I became a **m,**
Luke	18: 2	not fear God nor regard **m.**	1Co	15:21	For since by **m** came death,
Luke	18:25	a needle than for a rich **m**	1Co	15:45	The first **m** Adam became
Luke	19: 2	there was a **m** named	1Co	15:47	the second **M** is the Lord
Luke	19:21	because you are an austere **m.**	2Co	4:16	Even though our outward **m** is
Luke	22:48	you betraying the Son of **M**	2Co	4:16	yet the inward **m** is being
Luke	22:58	them." But Peter said, "**M,**	2Co	12: 2	I know a **m** in Christ who
Luke	23: 4	"I find no fault in this **M.**	Gal	1: 1	(not from men nor through **m,**
Luke	23:18	saying, "Away with this **M,**	Eph	2:15	create in Himself one new **m**
Luke	23:41	but this **M** has done nothing	Eph	3:16	His Spirit in the inner **m,**
Luke	23:47	this was a righteous **M!"**	Eph	4:22	the old **m** which grows
John	1: 6	There was a **m** sent from God,	Eph	4:24	that you put on the new **m**
John	1: 7	This **m** came for a witness, to	Eph	5:31	For this reason a **m**
John	1: 9	which gives light to every **m**	Phil	2: 8	found in appearance as a **m,**
John	1:13	flesh, nor of the will of **m,**	Col	1:28	warning every **m** and teaching
John	1:30	After me comes a **M** who is	Col	1:28	that we may present every **m**
John	1:51	descending upon the Son of **M.**	Col	3: 9	you have put off the old **m**
John	2:10	Every **m** at the beginning sets	Col	3:10	and have put on the new **m**
John	2:25	for He knew what was in **m.**	2Th	2: 3	and the **m** of sin is
John	3: 2	This **m** came to Jesus by night	1Ti	2: 5	the **M** Christ Jesus,
John	3: 4	How can a **m** be born when he	1Ti	3: 1	If a **m** desires the position
John	3:14	even so must the Son of **M** be	1Ti	6:11	O **m** of God, flee these
John	4:29	see a **M** who told me all	1Ti	6:16	whom no **m** has seen or can
John	6:53	the flesh of the Son of **M**	2Ti	3:17	that the **m** of God may be
John	7:15	How does this **M** know letters,	Heb	2: 6	What is **m** that You are
John	7:46	No **m** ever spoke like this	Heb	2: 6	Or the son of **m** that
John	9: 2	this **m** or his parents, that	Heb	7: 4	consider how great this **m**
John	9:11	A **M** called Jesus made clay	Heb	11:12	Therefore from one **m,**
John	12:23	has come that the Son of **M**	Heb	13: 6	What can **m** do to
John	12:34	The Son of **M** must be lifted	Jas	1: 8	he is a double-minded **m,**
John	18:40	again, saying, "Not this **M,**	Jas	1:11	So the rich **m** also will fade
John	19: 5	Behold the **M!"**	Jas	1:23	he is like a **m** observing his
Acts	6: 5	a **m** full of faith and the	Jas	1:24	forgets what kind of **m** he
Acts	7:56	opened and the Son of **M**	Jas	3: 8	But no **m** can tame the tongue.
Acts	10:22	the centurion, a just **m,**	Jas	5:16	prayer of a righteous **m**
Acts	13:22	a **m** after My own	1Pe	1:24	all the glory of **m** as
Acts	16: 9	A **m** of Macedonia stood and	2Pe	1:21	never came by the will of **m,**
Acts	17:31	in righteousness by the **M**	Rev	1:13	One like the Son of **M,**
Acts	22:26	for this **m** is a Roman."	Rev	4: 7	creature had a face like a **m,**
Acts	23: 9	"We find no evil in this **m;**	Rev	13:18	for it is the number of a **m:**
Rom	1:23	made like corruptible **m—**	Rev	21:17	to the measure of a **m,**
Rom	2: 1	you are inexcusable, O **m**			
Rom	3: 4	let God be true but every **m**			**MAN'S** (*see* MAN)
Rom	3: 5	wrath? (I speak as a **m.**	Gen	8:21	curse the ground for **m** sake,
Rom	4: 6	the blessedness of the **m** to	Gen	8:21	the imagination of **m** heart

Gen	9: 6	Whoever sheds **m** blood, By
Prov	16: 7	When a **m** ways please the
Prov	20:24	A **m** steps are of the LORD;
Mic	7: 6	A **m** enemies are the men of
Matt	10:36	a **m** enemies will be
Rom	15:20	I should build on another **m**
1Co	2:13	not in words which **m** wisdom

MANASSEH
Gen	41:51	the name of the firstborn **M:**
Gen	48: 5	your two sons, Ephraim and **M,**
Deut	3:13	gave to half the tribe of **M.**
2Ki	21:11	Because **M** king of Judah has
2Ki	24: 3	because of the sins of **M,**
Matt	1:10	Hezekiah begot **M,**

MANDRAKES
Gen	30:14	me some of your son's **m.**
Song	7:13	The **m** give off a fragrance,

MANGER
Luke	2: 7	cloths, and laid Him in a **m,**
Luke	2:16	and the Babe lying in a **m.**

MANIFEST (see MANIFESTATION, MANIFESTED)
John	14:21	and I will love him and **m**
Rom	1:19	may be known of God is **m** in
Eph	5:13	that are exposed are made **m**
1Pe	1:20	but was **m** in these last
1Jn	3:10	children of the devil are **m:**

MANIFESTATION (see MANIFEST)
Luke	1:80	till the day of his **m** to
1Co	12: 7	But the **m** of the Spirit is

MANIFESTED (see MANIFEST)
John	2:11	and **m** His glory; and His
John	17: 6	I have **m** Your name to the
2Co	4:10	life of Jesus also may be **m**
1Ti	3:16	God was **m** in the flesh,
1Jn	1: 2	the life was **m,**
1Jn	4: 9	this the love of God was **m**

MANIFOLD
Ps	104:24	how **m** are Your works! In
1Pe	4:10	as good stewards of the **m**

MANKIND (see MAN)
Gen	5: 2	them and called them **M** in
Acts	15:17	So that the rest of **m**

MANNA
Ex	16:31	of Israel called its name **M.**
Ex	16:33	a pot and put an omer of **m**
Josh	5:12	Then the **m** ceased on the day
Ps	78:24	Had rained down **m** on them to
John	6:31	Our fathers ate the **m** in the
Heb	9: 4	golden pot that had the **m,**
Rev	2:17	give some of the hidden **m**

MANNER
Gen	31:35	for the **m** of women is with
2Sa	7:19	Is this the **m** of man, O

Acts	1:11	will so come in like **m** as
1Co	11:25	In the same **m** He also took
1Co	11:29	and drinks in an unworthy **m**
Gal	3:15	I speak in the **m** of men:
Heb	10:25	as is the **m** of some, but
1Pe	1:11	or what **m** of time, the
2Pe	3:11	what **m** of persons ought
1Jn	3: 1	Behold what **m** of love the

MANOAH
Judg	13: 9	but **M** her husband was not

MANSIONS†
John	14: 2	My Father's house are many **m;**

MANSLAYER
Num	35: 6	to which a **m** may flee. And

MANTLE
2Ki	2: 8	Now Elijah took his **m,**

MARCH
Josh	6: 3	You shall **m** around tne city,

MARK (see MARKS)
Gen	4:15	And the LORD set a **m** on
Ps	130: 3	should **m** iniquities, O
Ezek	9: 4	and put a **m** on the foreheads
Rev	13:16	to receive a **m** on their

MARK* (see JOHN)
Acts	12:12	of John whose surname was **M,**
2Ti	4:11	Get **M** and bring him with
1Pe	5:13	and so does **M** my son.

MARKS (see MARK)
Gal	6:17	for I bear in my body the **m**

MARRED
Is	52:14	So His visage was **m** more
Jer	18: 4	that he made of clay was **m**

MARRIAGE (see MARRY)
Matt	22:30	marry nor are given in **m,**
1Co	7:38	then he who gives her in **m**
Heb	13: 4	**M** is honorable among all,
Rev	19: 9	who are called to the **m**

MARRIED (see MARRY)
1Ki	3: 1	and **m** Pharaoh's daughter;
Is	62: 4	And your land shall be **m.**
Matt	22:25	first died after he had **m,**
Rom	7: 3	though she has **m** another
1Co	7:10	Now to the **m** I command, yet
1Co	7:33	But he who is **m** cares about

MARRIES (see MARRY)
Matt	5:32	and whoever **m** a woman who is
Luke	16:18	and whoever **m** her who is
Rom	7: 3	she **m** another man, she will
1Co	7:28	sinned; and if a virgin **m,**

MARROW
Heb	4:12	spirit, and of joints and **m,**

M

MARRY (see MARRIAGE, MARRIED, MARRIES, MARRYING, UNMARRIED)

Is	62: 5	So shall your sons **m** you;
Matt	19:10	wife, it is better not to **m**.
Matt	22:30	resurrection they neither **m**
Luke	20:34	The sons of this age **m** and
1Co	7: 9	For it is better to **m** than
1Co	7:36	He does not sin; let them **m**.
1Ti	4: 3	forbidding to **m**,

MARRYING (see MARRY)

Matt	24:38	**m** and giving in marriage,

MARTHA

Luke	10:40	But **M** was distracted with
John	11: 1	of Mary and her sister **M**.

MARTYRS (see MARTYR)

Rev	17: 6	and with the blood of the **m**

MARVEL (see MARVELED, MARVELOUS)

John	3: 7	Do not **m** that I said to you,

MARVELED (see MARVEL)

Matt	8:10	When Jesus heard it, He **m**,
Luke	20:26	And they **m** at His answer and
John	4:27	and they **m** that He talked
Acts	2: 7	they were all amazed and **m**,

MARVELOUS (see MARVEL)

Ps	9: 1	I will tell of all Your **m**
Ps	98: 1	new song! For He has done **m**
Ps	118:23	It is **m** in our eyes.
Ps	139:14	**M** are Your works, And
Joel	2:21	For the LORD has done **m**
Matt	21:42	And it is **m** in our
John	9:30	this is a **m** thing, that you
1Pe	2: 9	out of darkness into His **m**

MARY

Matt	1:16	Joseph the husband of **M**,
Matt	1:18	After His mother **M** was
Matt	27:56	whom were **M** Magdalene,
Matt	27:56	**M** the mother of James and
Mark	6: 3	the carpenter, the Son of **M**,
Mark	16: 9	He appeared first to **M**
Luke	1:27	The virgin's name was **M**.
Luke	2:19	But **M** kept all these things
John	11: 2	It was that **M** who anointed
John	11:19	women around Martha and **M**,
John	19:25	**M** the wife of Clopas, and
John	20:16	**M**!" She turned and said to
Acts	1:14	with the women and **M** the

MASONS

2Sa	5:11	trees, and carpenters and **m**.
2Ki	12:12	and to **m** and stonecutters,

MASTER (see MASTER'S, MASTERS)

Gen	24:12	O LORD God of my **m** Abraham,
Prov	8:30	I was beside Him as a **m**
Hos	2:16	And no longer call Me 'My **M**,
Mal	1: 6	My honor? And if I am a **M**,

Matt	10:24	nor a servant above his **m**.
Matt	24:45	whom his **m** made ruler over
Matt	24:46	is that servant whom his **m**,
Mark	14:14	say to the **m** of the house,
Luke	13:25	When once the **M** of the house
Luke	14:21	Then the **m** of the house,
Luke	16: 5	'How much do you owe my **m**?
Luke	16: 8	So the **m** commended the unjust
John	2: 8	and take it to the **m** of the
John	13:16	is not greater than his **m**;
1Co	3:10	as a wise **m** builder I have
Gal	4: 1	though he is **m** of all,
Eph	6: 9	knowing that your own **M** also
2Ti	2:21	and useful for the **M**,

MASTER'S (see MASTER)

2Sa	12: 8	I gave you your **m** house and
Is	1: 3	owner And the donkey its **m**

MASTERS (see MASTER, TASKMASTERS)

Matt	6:24	"No one can serve two **m**;
Acts	16:16	who brought her **m** much
Eph	6: 9	And you, **m**, do the same
Col	3:22	obey in all things your **m**
Col	4: 1	**M**, give your bondservants
1Ti	6: 2	those who have believing **m**,

MATTHEW (see LEVI)

Matt	9: 9	He saw a man named **M** sitting
Matt	10: 3	Thomas and **M** the tax
Mark	3:18	Philip, Bartholomew, **M**,

MATURE

1Co	2: 6	wisdom among those who are **m**,
1Co	14:20	but in understanding be **m**.

MEAL (see GRAIN)

Matt	13:33	hid in three measures of **m**

MEAN (see MEANS, MEANT)

Josh	4: 6	What do these stones **m** to

MEANS (see MEAN)

Matt	9:13	go and learn what this **m**:
Matt	12: 7	you had known what this **m**,
John	6:37	comes to Me I will by no **m**
1Co	9:22	that I might by all **m** save
2Th	2: 3	no one deceive you by any **m**;
1Pe	2: 6	on Him will by no **m**

MEANT (see MEAN)

Gen	50:20	you **m** evil against me; but
Gen	50:20	but God **m** it for good, in

MEASURE (see MEASURED, MEASURES, MEASURING)

Luke	6:38	will be given to you: good **m**,
John	3:34	not give the Spirit by **m**.
Rom	12: 3	has dealt to each one a **m**
Eph	4: 7	given according to the **m** of
Eph	4:13	to the **m** of the stature of

MEASURED (see MEASURE)

Is	40:12	Who has **m** the waters in the
Matt	7: 2	it will be **m** back to you.

MEASURES (see MEASURE)

Prov	20:10	weights and diverse **m**,
Matt	13:33	took and hid in three **m** of

MEASURING (see MEASURE)

Zech	2: 1	a man with a **m** line in his

MEAT

Ex	16: 8	when the LORD gives you **m**
Num	11:13	over me, saying, 'Give us **m**,
Num	11:18	and you shall eat **m**;
Ps	78:20	Can He provide **m** for His
Ps	78:27	He also rained **m** on them
Is	44:16	With this half he eats **m**;
Dan	10: 3	no **m** or wine came into my
Rom	14:21	is good neither to eat **m**
1Co	8:13	I will never again eat **m**,
1Co	10:25	whatever is sold in the **m**

MEDE† (see MEDES, MEDIA)

Dan	5:31	And Darius the M received the
Dan	11: 1	first year of Darius the M,

MEDES (see MEDE)

Esth	1:19	of the Persians and the M,
Is	13:17	I will stir up the M against
Dan	5:28	and given to the M and
Dan	6: 8	to the law of the M and
Acts	2: 9	Parthians and M and Elamites,

MEDIA (see MEDE)

Ezra	6: 2	is in the province of M,
Esth	1:14	princes of Persia and M,
Dan	8:20	they are the kings of M and

MEDIATOR†

Job	9:33	Nor is there any **m** between
Job	33:23	is a messenger for him, A **m**,
Gal	3:19	angels by the hand of a **m**.
Gal	3:20	Now a **m** does not mediate for
1Ti	2: 5	there is one God and one M
Heb	8: 6	inasmuch as He is also M of
Heb	9:15	for this reason He is the M
Heb	12:24	to Jesus the M of the new

MEDITATE (see MEDITATES, MEDITATION)

Gen	24:63	And Isaac went out to **m** in
Josh	1: 8	but you shall **m** in it day
Ps	119:15	I will **m** on Your precepts,
Ps	119:148	That I may **m** on Your word.
Phil	4: 8	**m** on these things.
1Ti	4:15	M on these things; give

MEDITATES (see MEDITATE)

Ps	1: 2	And in His law he **m** day and

MEDITATION (see MEDITATE)

Ps	19:14	words of my mouth and the **m**
Ps	119:97	love Your law! It is my **m**

MEDIUM

1Sa	28: 7	is a woman who is a **m** at

MEEK (see MEEKNESS)

Ps	37:11	But the **m** shall inherit the
Matt	5: 5	Blessed are the **m**,

MEEKNESS (see MEEK)

Col	3:12	kindness, humility, **m**,
1Pe	3:15	with **m** and fear;

MEET (see MEETING, MET)

Gen	18: 2	ran from the tent door to **m**
Ex	25:22	And there I will **m** with you,
Amos	4:12	Prepare to **m** your God, O
1Th	4:17	them in the clouds to **m** the

MEETING (see MEET)

Ex	27:21	"In the tabernacle of **m**,
Ex	39:40	for the tent of **m**;

MEGIDDO

Judg	5:19	Taanach, by the waters of M;
1Ki	9:15	wall of Jerusalem, Hazor, M,
2Ch	35:22	to fight in the Valley of M.

MELCHIZEDEK

Gen	14:18	Then M king of Salem brought
Ps	110: 4	According to the order of M.
Heb	5: 6	to the order of M";
Heb	7: 1	For this M, king of Salem,
Heb	7:15	if, in the likeness of M,

MELODY

Eph	5:19	singing and making **m** in your

MELT

Josh	14: 8	the heart of the people **m**,
Ps	97: 5	The mountains **m** like wax at
2Pe	3:10	and the elements will **m** with

MEMBER (see MEMBERS)

1Co	12:14	fact the body is not one **m**
1Co	12:26	And if one **m** suffers, all the
Jas	3: 5	so the tongue is a little **m**

MEMBERS (see MEMBER)

Matt	5:29	for you that one of your **m**
Rom	6:13	And do not present your **m** as
Rom	7: 5	law were at work in our **m**
Rom	7:23	law of sin which is in my **m**.
Rom	12: 4	For as we have many **m** in one
1Co	6:15	know that your bodies are **m**
1Co	12:12	body is one and has many **m**,
Eph	4:25	for we are **m** of one
Eph	5:30	For we are **m** of His body, of
Jas	4: 1	pleasure that war in your **m**?

MEMORIAL

Ex	12:14	this day shall be to you a **m**;
Ex	13: 9	you on your hand and as a **m**
Josh	4: 7	stones shall be for a **m** to
Matt	26:13	will also be told as a **m** to

M

MEN (*see* MAN, MEN-PLEASERS, MEN'S, PEOPLE)

Gen	4:26	Then **m** began to call on the
Gen	6: 1	when **m** began to multiply on
Gen	6: 2	God saw the daughters of **m**,
Gen	6: 4	Those were the mighty **m** who
Gen	6: 4	were of old, **m** of renown.
Gen	11: 5	tower which the sons of **m**
Gen	13:13	But the **m** of Sodom were
Gen	18: 2	three **m** were standing by
Gen	32:28	with God and with **m**,
Ex	7:11	also called the wise **m** and
Ex	18:25	And Moses chose able **m** out of
Deut	1:15	wise and knowledgeable **m**,
Deut	3:18	All you **m** of valor shall
Josh	1:14	all your mighty **m** of valor,
Judg	9: 9	which they honor God and **m**,
Judg	9:13	cheers both God and **m**,
Ruth	2: 9	I not commanded the young **m**
Ruth	2:21	stay close by my young **m**
1Sa	31: 4	lest these uncircumcised **m**
2Sa	7:14	him with the rod of **m** and
2Sa	7:14	the blows of the sons of **m**.
2Sa	10: 7	all the army of the mighty **m**.
2Sa	11:16	knew there were valiant **m**.
2Sa	23: 9	one of the three mighty **m**
1Ki	9:22	because they were **m** of war
1Ch	12:33	stouthearted **m** who could
1Ch	22:15	and all types of skillful **m**
1Ch	26:31	found among them capable **m**
2Ch	6:18	God indeed dwell with **m** on
Esth	1:13	the king said to the wise **m**
Job	4:13	When deep sleep falls on **m**,
Job	7:20	done to You, O watcher of **m**?
Job	12:12	Wisdom is with aged **m**,
Job	33:15	deep sleep falls upon **m**,
Ps	4: 2	How long, O you sons of **m**,
Ps	12: 1	from among the sons of **m**.
Ps	62: 9	Surely **m** of low degree are
Ps	62: 9	**M** of high degree are a
Ps	68:18	have received gifts among **m**,
Ps	107: 8	that **m** would give thanks to
Ps	107: 8	works to the children of **m**!
Ps	116:11	All **m** are liars."
Ps	148:12	Both young **m** and maidens;
Ps	148:12	Old **m** and children.
Prov	8:31	was with the sons of **m**.
Prov	17: 6	are the crown of old **m**,
Prov	20:29	The glory of young **m** is
Is	7:13	thing for you to weary **m**,
Is	9: 3	As **m** rejoice when they
Is	19:12	they? Where are your wise **m**?
Is	31: 3	Now the Egyptians are **m**,
Is	38:16	by these things **m** live;
Is	45:24	To Him **m** shall come, And
Is	52:14	form more than the sons of **m**;
Is	53: 3	despised and rejected by **m**,
Lam	1:15	me To crush my young **m**;
Lam	2:21	My virgins and my young **m**
Ezek	9: 4	on the foreheads of the **m**
Ezek	14:14	"Even if these three **m**,
Ezek	26:17	one inhabited by seafaring **m**,
Ezek	27: 8	your oarsmen; Your wise **m**,

Ezek	34:31	of My pasture; you are **m**,
Dan	1:15	flesh than all the young **m**
Dan	1:17	As for these four young **m**,
Dan	2:12	to destroy all the wise **m**
Dan	3:21	Then these **m** were bound in
Dan	3:23	And these three **m**,
Dan	3:25	I see four **m** loose, walking
Dan	4:17	rules in the kingdom of **m**,
Dan	4:33	he was driven from **m** and ate
Dan	5: 8	Now all the king's wise **m**
Hos	6: 7	But like **m** they transgressed
Hos	13: 2	Let the **m** who sacrifice kiss
Joel	2:28	Your old **m** shall dream
Joel	2:28	Your young **m** shall see
Amos	6: 9	that if ten **m** remain in one
Amos	8:13	virgins And strong young **m**
Jon	1:13	Nevertheless the **m** rowed hard
Jon	1:16	Then the **m** feared the LORD
Mic	5: 5	and eight princely **m**.
Zeph	1:17	they shall walk like blind **m**,
Matt	2: 1	wise **m** from the East came to
Matt	4:19	I will make you fishers of **m**.
Matt	5:13	and trampled underfoot by **m**.
Matt	5:16	your light so shine before **m**,
Matt	5:19	and teaches **m** so, shall be
Matt	6: 1	charitable deeds before **m**,
Matt	6: 2	they may have glory from **m**.
Matt	6: 5	that they may be seen by **m**.
Matt	6:14	For if you forgive **m** their
Matt	6:15	if you do not forgive **m**
Matt	6:16	that they may appear to **m**
Matt	7:12	whatever you want **m** to do to
Matt	7:16	Do **m** gather grapes from
Matt	8:28	Him two demon-possessed **m**,
Matt	9: 8	had given such power to **m**.
Matt	10:32	confesses Me before **m**,
Matt	12:31	blasphemy will be forgiven **m**,
Matt	12:31	will not be forgiven **m**.
Matt	12:36	that for every idle word **m**
Matt	12:41	The **m** of Nineveh will rise up
Matt	14:21	were about five thousand **m**,
Matt	15:38	who ate were four thousand **m**,
Matt	16:13	Who do **m** say that I, the Son
Matt	17:22	betrayed into the hands of **m**,
Matt	19:26	With **m** this is impossible,
Matt	21:25	from? From heaven or from **m**?
Matt	24:40	Then two **m** will be in the
Matt	28: 4	him, and became like dead **m**.
Mark	2: 3	who was carried by four **m**.
Mark	7: 7	the commandments of **m**.
Mark	7: 8	you hold the tradition of **m**—
Mark	7:21	out of the heart of **m**,
Luke	2:14	goodwill toward **m**!"
Luke	2:52	and in favor with God and **m**.
Luke	6:44	For **m** do not gather figs
Luke	11:46	lawyers! For you load **m** with
Luke	16:15	justify yourselves before **m**,
Luke	17:12	there met Him ten **m** who were
Luke	18: 1	that **m** always ought to pray
Luke	18:11	that I am not like other **m**—
John	1: 4	the life was the light of **m**.
John	2:24	them, because He knew all **m**,
John	3:19	and **m** loved darkness rather
John	5:41	do not receive honor from **m**.

Acts	1:10	two **m** stood by them in white
Acts	1:11	**M** of Galilee, why do you
Acts	1:16	**M** and brethren, this
Acts	2: 5	in Jerusalem Jews, devout **m**,
Acts	2:17	Your young **m** shall see
Acts	2:17	Your old **m** shall dream
Acts	2:22	**M** of Israel, hear these
Acts	4:12	under heaven given among **m**
Acts	4:13	uneducated and untrained **m**,
Acts	5: 4	You have not lied to **m** but
Acts	5:29	to obey God rather than **m**.
Acts	6: 3	out from among you seven **m**
Acts	11: 3	went in to uncircumcised **m**
Acts	13:50	women and the chief **m** of
Acts	14:15	We also are **m** with the same
Acts	17: 5	took some of the evil **m** from
Acts	17:12	prominent women as well as **m**.
Acts	17:22	**M** of Athens, I perceive that
Acts	17:26	one blood every nation of **m**
Acts	17:30	but now commands all **m**
Rom	1:18	and unrighteousness of **m**,
Rom	1:27	**m** with men committing what
Rom	2:29	whose praise is not from **m**
Rom	5:12	thus death spread to all **m**,
Rom	5:18	judgment came to all **m**,
Rom	5:18	free gift came to all **m**,
Rom	12:17	things in the sight of all **m**.
Rom	12:18	live peaceably with all **m**.
1Co	1:25	of God is wiser than **m**,
1Co	2: 5	not be in the wisdom of **m**
1Co	3: 3	and behaving like mere **m**?
1Co	7: 7	For I wish that all **m** were
1Co	9:19	though I am free from all **m**,
1Co	9:22	become all things to all **m**,
1Co	13: 1	speak with the tongues of **m**
1Co	14: 2	a tongue does not speak to **m**
1Co	14:21	With **m** of other tongues
1Co	15:19	we are of all **m** the most
1Co	15:39	is one kind of flesh of **m**,
2Co	3: 2	known and read by all **m**;
2Co	5:11	of the Lord, we persuade **m**;
Gal	1: 1	an apostle (not from **m** nor
Gal	1:10	For do I now persuade **m**,
Eph	4: 8	And gave gifts to **m**.
Eph	6: 7	as to the Lord, and not to **m**,
Phil	2: 7	coming in the likeness of **m**.
Phil	4: 5	gentleness be known to all **m**.
Col	3:23	as to the Lord and not to **m**,
1Th	1: 5	as you know what kind of **m**
1Th	2: 4	we speak, not as pleasing **m**,
1Th	2:13	it not as the word of **m**,
1Ti	2: 4	who desires all **m** to be saved
1Ti	2: 5	Mediator between God and **m**,
1Ti	2: 8	desire therefore that the **m**
1Ti	4:10	who is the Savior of all **m**,
1Ti	6: 9	harmful lusts which drown **m**
2Ti	2: 2	commit these to faithful **m**
2Ti	3:13	But evil **m** and impostors will
Tit	2: 2	that the older **m** be sober,
Tit	2:11	has appeared to all **m**,
Heb	9:27	as it is appointed for **m** to
Heb	12:23	to the spirits of just **m**
Jas	3: 9	and with it we curse **m**,
1Pe	2:15	the ignorance of foolish **m**—

2Pe	1:21	but holy **m** of God spoke as
2Pe	3: 7	and perdition of ungodly **m**.
1Jn	2:13	I write to you, young **m**,
Jude	4	For certain **m** have crept in
Rev	9: 7	were like the faces of **m**.
Rev	16:21	**M** blasphemed God because of
Rev	18:13	and bodies and souls of **m**.
Rev	21: 3	tabernacle of God is with **m**,

MEN-PLEASERS† (*see* MEN)

Eph	6: 6	not with eyeservice, as **m**,
Col	3:22	not with eyeservice, as **m**,

MEN'S (*see* MEN)

Matt	23:27	inside are full of dead **m**
Luke	21:26	**m** hearts failing them from
2Co	10:15	in other **m** labors, but

MENDING

Matt	4:21	**m** their nets. He called

MENE

Dan	5:25	that was written: MENE, **M**,

MENTION

Rom	1: 9	without ceasing I make **m** of
Eph	1:16	making **m** of you in my

MEPHIBOSHETH

2Sa	9: 6	Then David said, "**M**?
2Sa	19:24	Now **M** the son of Saul came

MERCHANDISE

John	2:16	Father's house a house of **m**!

M

MERCIES (*see* MERCY)

Gen	32:10	of the least of all the **m**
Neh	9:27	to Your abundant **m** You
Ps	25: 6	Your tender **m** and Your
Ps	51: 1	multitude of Your tender **m**,
Ps	89: 1	I will sing of the **m** of the
Is	55: 3	The sure **m** of David.
Lam	3:22	Through the LORD's **m** we
Dan	9:18	but because of Your great **m**.
Acts	13:34	give you the sure **m**
Rom	12: 1	by the **m** of God, that you
2Co	1: 3	the Father of **m** and God of

MERCIFUL (*see* MERCY, UNMERCIFUL)

Gen	19:16	the LORD being **m** to him,
Ex	34: 6	**m** and gracious,
Ps	18:25	With the **m** You will show
Ps	41: 4	be **m** to me; Heal my soul,
Ps	56: 1	Be **m** to me, O God, for man
Ps	67: 1	God be **m** to us and bless us,
Ps	103: 8	The LORD is **m** and
Joel	2:13	For He is gracious and **m**,
Jon	4: 2	You are a gracious and **m**
Matt	5: 7	Blessed are the **m**,
Luke	18:13	be **m** to me a sinner!'
Heb	2:17	that He might be a **m** and

MERCY (*see* MERCIES, MERCIFUL)

Ex	20: 6	but showing **m** to thousands,

Ex	25:17	You shall make a **m** seat of
Lev	16:15	and sprinkle it on the **m**
Num	14:18	and abundant in **m**,
Deut	5:10	but showing **m** to thousands,
Deut	7: 9	God who keeps covenant and **m**
1Ch	16:34	for He is good! For His **m**
Ps	4: 1	Have **m** on me, and hear my
Ps	18:50	And shows **m** to His
Ps	23: 6	Surely goodness and **m** shall
Ps	25: 7	According to Your **m**
Ps	31: 7	glad and rejoice in Your **m**,
Ps	32:10	**m** shall surround him.
Ps	33:18	On those who hope in His **m**,
Ps	51: 1	Have **m** upon me, O God,
Ps	59:16	I will sing aloud of Your **m**,
Ps	85:10	**M** and truth have met
Ps	90:14	satisfy us early with Your **m**,
Ps	98: 3	He has remembered His **m** and
Ps	100: 5	His **m** is everlasting, And
Ps	103: 8	to anger, and abounding in **m**.
Ps	103:11	So great is His **m** toward
Ps	103:17	But the **m** of the LORD is
Ps	106: 1	for He is good! For His **m**
Ps	119:64	O LORD, is full of Your **m**;
Ps	130: 7	with the LORD there is **m**,
Ps	136: 1	for He is good! For His **m**
Ps	145: 8	to anger and great in **m**.
Is	55: 7	And He will have **m** on him;
Hos	1: 6	I will no longer have **m** on
Hos	2:23	who had not obtained **m**;
Hos	4: 1	There is no truth or **m** Or
Hos	6: 6	For I desire **m** and not
Hos	14: 3	You the fatherless finds **m**.
Mic	6: 8	to do justly, To love **m**,
Mic	7:18	Because He delights in **m**.
Hab	3: 2	known; In wrath remember **m**.
Matt	5: 7	For they shall obtain **m**.
Matt	9:13	I desire **m** and not
Matt	9:27	have **m** on us!"
Matt	23:23	justice and **m** and faith.
Luke	1:50	And His **m** is on those who
Luke	1:78	Through the tender **m** of our
Rom	9:15	I will have **m** on
Rom	9:16	runs, but of God who shows **m**.
Rom	9:23	glory on the vessels of **m**,
Rom	11:30	yet have now obtained **m**
Gal	6:16	peace and **m** be upon them,
Eph	2: 4	But God, who is rich in **m**,
Phil	2: 1	if any affection and **m**,
1Ti	1:13	but I obtained **m** because I
Tit	3: 5	but according to His **m** He
Heb	4:16	that we may obtain **m** and
Heb	9: 5	of glory overshadowing the **m**
1Pe	1: 3	according to His abundant **m**
1Pe	2:10	who had not obtained **m** but

MERODACH-BALADAN†

Is	39: 1	At that time **M** the son of

MERRY

Eccl	8:15	than to eat, drink, and be **m**;
Luke	12:19	ease; eat, drink, and be **m**.

MESHA

2Ki	3: 4	Now **M** king of Moab was a

MESHACH (see MISHAEL)

Dan	1: 7	Shadrach; to Mishael, **M**;
Dan	3:12	of Babylon: Shadrach, **M**,

MESHECH

Ezek	32:26	There are **M** and Tubal and

MESOPOTAMIA (see ARAM)

Gen	24:10	And he arose and went to **M**,
Judg	3: 8	Cushan-Rishathaim king of **M**;
Acts	2: 9	those dwelling in **M**,
Acts	7: 2	Abraham when he was in **M**,

MESSAGE (see MESSENGER)

1Co	1:18	For the **m** of the cross is
1Co	1:21	the foolishness of the **m**
1Jn	1: 5	This is the **m** which we have

MESSENGER (see MESSAGE)

Job	1:14	and a **m** came to Job and said,
Is	42:19	Or deaf as My **m** whom I
Mal	2: 7	For he is the **m** of the
Mal	3: 1	"Behold, I send My **m**,
Mal	3: 1	Even the **M** of the covenant,
Matt	11:10	I send My **m** before
2Co	12: 7	a **m** of Satan to buffet me,

MESSIAH†

Dan	9:25	and build Jerusalem Until **M**
Dan	9:26	after the sixty-two weeks **M**
John	1:41	We have found the **M**" (which
John	4:25	I know that **M** is coming"

MET (see MEET)

Ps	85:10	Mercy and truth have **m**

METHUSELAH

Gen	5:27	So all the days of **M** were

MICAH

Judg	17: 1	Ephraim, whose name was **M**.
Jer	26:18	**M** of Moresheth prophesied in
Mic	1: 1	of the LORD that came to **M**

MICHAEL

Dan	10:21	except **M** your prince.
Jude	9	Yet **M** the archangel, in
Rev	12: 7	**M** and his angels fought with

MICHAL

2Sa	3:14	saying, "Give me my wife **M**,

MIDDLE

Ezek	1:16	a wheel in the **m** of a wheel.
Eph	2:14	and has broken down the **m**

MIDIAN (see MIDIANITE)

Ex	2:15	and dwelt in the land of **M**;
Ex	18: 1	And Jethro, the priest of **M**,
Judg	7: 8	Now the camp of **M** was below

MIDIANITE (see MIDIAN, MIDIANITES)

Gen	37:28	Then M traders passed by; so

MIDIANITES (see MIDIANITE)

Gen	37:36	Now the M had sold him in
Judg	6:14	from the hand of the M.

MIDNIGHT

Ex	12:29	And it came to pass at m

MIDWIVES

Ex	1:17	But the m feared God, and did

MIGHT (see MIGHTILY, MIGHTY, STRENGTH)

Eccl	9:10	to do, do it with your m;
Is	11: 2	The Spirit of counsel and m,
Jer	9:23	mighty man glory in his m,
Zech	4: 6	Not by m nor by power, but by
Eph	3:16	to be strengthened with m
Eph	6:10	and in the power of His m.

MIGHTIER (see MIGHT, MIGHTY)

Ex	1: 9	of Israel are more and m
Matt	3:11	who is coming after me is m

MIGHTILY (see MIGHT)

Judg	14: 6	Spirit of the LORD came m
Acts	19:20	the word of the Lord grew m
Col	1:29	working which works in me m.

MIGHTY (see MIGHT, MIGHTIER)

Gen	6: 4	Those were the m men who
Gen	10: 9	Like Nimrod the m hunter
Gen	49:24	By the hands of the M God
Ex	32:11	great power and with a m
Num	22: 6	for they are too m for me.
Deut	9:29	You brought out by Your m
Josh	1:14	all your m men of valor, and
2Sa	23: 9	one of the three m men with
Ps	24: 8	The LORD strong and m,
Ps	24: 8	The LORD m in battle.
Ps	29: 1	O you m ones, Give unto the
Ps	50: 1	The M One, God the LORD,
Ps	89: 8	Who is m like You, O
Ps	150: 1	Praise Him in His m
Is	1:24	the M One of Israel, "Ah,
Is	5:22	Woe to men m at drinking
Is	9: 6	M God, Everlasting Father,
Is	10:21	To the M God.
Is	43:16	And a path through the m
Is	49:26	the M One of Jacob."
Is	63: 1	righteousness, m to save."
Jer	9:23	Let not the m man glory in
Jer	32:18	the M God, whose name is
Jer	33: 3	and show you great and m
Jer	51:30	The m men of Babylon have
Dan	4:30	for a royal dwelling by my m
Dan	8:24	His power shall be m,
Dan	11: 3	Then a m king shall arise,
Amos	5:24	And righteousness like a m
Jon	1: 4	and there was a m tempest on
Zeph	3:17	The M One, will save; He
Matt	11:20	in which most of His m

Mark	6: 5	Now He could do no m work
Luke	1:49	For He who is m has done
Luke	1:52	He has put down the m from
Luke	24:19	who was a Prophet m in deed
Acts	2: 2	as of a rushing m wind, and
Acts	7:22	and was m in words and
Acts	18:24	an eloquent man and m in
1Co	1:26	to the flesh, not many m,
1Co	1:27	shame the things which are m;
2Co	10: 4	are not carnal but m in
2Co	13: 3	but m in you.
Eph	1:19	to the working of His m
2Th	1: 7	from heaven with His m
1Pe	5: 6	yourselves under the m hand
Rev	18:10	that m city! For in one hour

MILE†

Matt	5:41	compels you to go one m,

MILK

Ex	3: 8	to a land flowing with m and
Ex	23:19	young goat in its mother's m.
Judg	5:25	asked for water, she gave m;
Is	55: 1	buy wine and m Without
1Co	3: 2	I fed you with m and not with
Heb	5:12	and you have come to need m
1Pe	2: 2	desire the pure m of the

MILLSTONE

Judg	9:53	woman dropped an upper m on
Matt	18: 6	be better for him if a m

MINA

Luke	19:16	your m has earned ten

M

MIND (see MINDED, MINDFUL, MINDS)

Gen	37:11	kept the matter in m.
Neh	4: 6	for the people had a m to
Ps	26: 2	Try my m and my heart.
Ps	73:21	And I was vexed in my m.
Is	26: 3	Whose m is stayed on
Is	65:17	be remembered or come to m.
Jer	12: 2	mouth But far from their m.
Jer	17:10	the heart, I test the m,
Lam	3:21	This I recall to my m,
Matt	22:37	and with all your m.
Mark	5:15	clothed and in his right m.
Luke	12:29	drink, nor have an anxious m.
Rom	1:28	them over to a debased m,
Rom	7:23	against the law of my m,
Rom	8: 7	Because the carnal m is
Rom	11:34	who has known the m
Rom	12: 2	by the renewing of your m,
Rom	14: 5	fully convinced in his own m.
1Co	1:10	together in the same m and
1Co	2:16	who has known the m of
1Co	2:16	But we have the m of
2Co	8:12	there is first a willing m,
2Co	8:19	and to show your ready m,
Phil	1:27	with one m striving together
Phil	2: 3	but in lowliness of m let
Phil	2: 5	Let this m be in you which
Phil	4: 2	to be of the same m in the
Col	2:18	puffed up by his fleshly m,

Col	3: 2	Set your **m** on things above,
1Th	4:11	to **m** your own business, and
2Ti	1: 7	and of love and of a sound **m**.
Heb	8:10	put My laws in their **m**
1Pe	3: 8	all of you be of one **m**,

MINDED (see MIND)

Matt	1:19	was **m** to put her away
Rom	8: 6	For to be carnally **m** is

MINDFUL (see MIND)

Ps	8: 4	What is man that You are **m**
Heb	2: 6	is man that You are **m**

MINDS (see MIND)

Jer	31:33	I will put My law in their **m**,
Jer	34:11	they changed their **m** and
2Co	3:14	But their **m** were blinded. For
2Co	4: 4	whose **m** the god of this age
Phil	4: 7	will guard your hearts and **m**
1Ti	6: 5	of men of corrupt **m** and
Rev	2:23	I am He who searches the **m**

MINGLED

Matt	27:34	they gave Him sour wine **m**
Luke	13: 1	whose blood Pilate had **m**

MINISTER (see MINISTERED, MINISTERING, MINISTERS, MINISTRY)

Ex	28: 1	that he may **m** to Me as
Matt	25:44	and did not **m** to You?'
Rom	13: 4	For he is God's **m** to you for
1Co	9:13	not know that those who **m**
Eph	3: 7	of which I became a **m**
1Ti	4: 6	you will be a good **m** of
Heb	1:14	spirits sent forth to **m** for
Heb	8: 2	a **M** of the sanctuary and of

MINISTERED (see MINISTER)

Matt	4:11	angels came and **m** to Him.

MINISTERING (see MINISTER)

Rom	15:16	**m** the gospel of God, that
Heb	1:14	Are they not all **m** spirits
Heb	10:11	And every priest stands **m**

MINISTERS (see MINISTER)

Ex	28:35	be upon Aaron when he **m**,
Ps	103:21	You **m** of His, who do His
Ps	104: 4	His **m** a flame of fire.
Luke	1: 2	were eyewitnesses and **m** of
Rom	13: 6	for they are God's **m**
2Co	6: 4	we commend ourselves as **m**
2Co	11:23	Are they **m** of Christ?—I speak
Heb	1: 7	spirits And His **m** a
1Pe	4:11	oracles of God. If anyone **m**,

MINISTRIES† (see MINISTRY)

1Co	12: 5	There are differences of **m**,

MINISTRY (see MINISTER, MINISTRIES)

Luke	3:23	Jesus Himself began His **m**
Acts	6: 4	to prayer and to the **m** of
1Co	16:15	devoted themselves to the **m**

2Co	3: 8	how will the **m** of the Spirit
2Co	3: 9	For if the **m** of condemnation
Eph	4:12	the saints for the work of **m**,
1Ti	1:12	putting me into the **m**,
2Ti	4: 5	evangelist, fulfill your **m**.
2Ti	4:11	for he is useful to me for **m**.
Heb	8: 6	obtained a more excellent **m**,

MINT

Matt	23:23	For you pay tithe of **m** and

MIRACLE (see MIRACLES)

Ex	7: 9	Show a **m** for yourselves,'
Mark	9:39	for no one who works a **m** in
Luke	23: 8	and he hoped to see some **m**
Acts	4:22	years old on whom this **m** of

MIRACLES (see MIRACLE, SIGNS)

Acts	2:22	attested by God to you by **m**,
Acts	19:11	Now God worked unusual **m** by
1Co	12:10	to another the working of **m**,
1Co	12:28	third teachers, after that **m**,

MIRE (see MIRY)

Ps	69:14	Deliver me out of the **m**,
Is	57:20	Whose waters cast up **m** and
Jer	38: 6	So Jeremiah sank in the **m**.

MIRIAM

Ex	15:20	Then **M** the prophetess, the
Num	12:10	suddenly **M** became leprous,
Num	26:59	and Moses and their sister **M**.

MIRROR

1Co	13:12	For now we see in a **m**,
2Co	3:18	beholding as in a **m** the
Jas	1:23	his natural face in a **m**;

MIRTH

Ps	137: 3	plundered us requested **m**,

MIRY† (see MIRE)

Ps	40: 2	Out of the **m** clay, And set

MISERABLE

Job	16: 2	**M** comforters are you all!
Rev	3:17	that you are wretched, **m**,

MISHAEL (see MESHACH)

Dan	1: 6	were Daniel, Hananiah, **M**,

MIST

Gen	2: 6	but a **m** went up from the
Job	36:27	distill as rain from the **m**,

MISTRESS

Gen	16: 4	her **m** became despised in her

MITE† (see MITES)

Luke	12:59	have paid the very last **m**.

MITES (see MITE)

Mark	12:42	came and threw in two **m**,

MIXED
Ex	12:38	A m multitude went up with
Dan	2:41	just as you saw the iron m

MIZPAH
Gen	31:49	also M, because he said,
Jer	40: 8	they came to Gedaliah at M—

MOAB (see MOABITESS)
Gen	19:37	a son and called his name M;
Num	23: 7	Balak the king of M has
Num	25: 1	harlotry with the women of M.
Num	26:63	of Israel in the plains of M
Deut	34: 5	died there in the land of M,
Ruth	1: 1	to dwell in the country of M,
2Ki	1: 1	M rebelled against Israel

MOABITESS (see MOAB)
Ruth	1:22	and Ruth the M her

MOCK (see MOCKED, MOCKER)
Gen	39:14	in to us a Hebrew to m us.

MOCKED (see MOCK)
Judg	16:15	You have m me these three
1Ki	18:27	that Elijah m them and said,
Neh	4: 1	and m the Jews.
Job	12: 4	I am one m by his friends,
Lam	1: 7	adversaries saw her And m
Matt	27:29	the knee before Him and m
Luke	18:32	the Gentiles and will be m
Luke	22:63	the men who held Jesus m
Luke	23:36	The soldiers also m Him,
Acts	17:32	of the dead, some m,
Gal	6: 7	be deceived, God is not m;

MOCKER† (see MOCK, MOCKERS)
Prov	20: 1	Wine is a m,

MOCKERS (see MOCKER)
Jer	15:17	sit in the assembly of the m,
Jude	18	you that there would be m

MODESTY†
1Co	12:23	parts have greater m,

MOLDED
Ex	32: 4	and made a m calf. Then they
Ex	34:17	You shall make no m gods for
Num	33:52	destroy all their m images,
Judg	17: 3	make a carved image and a m
Judg	17: 4	into a carved image and a m
2Ch	28: 2	and made m images for the
Ps	106:19	And worshiped the m image.
Is	41:29	Their m images are wind
Jer	10:14	For his m image is

MOLECH
Lev	18:21	pass through the fire to M,
1Ki	11: 7	and for M the abomination of

MOMENT
Job	20: 5	hypocrite is but for a m?
Ps	30: 5	His anger is but for a m,
Luke	4: 5	of the world in a m of time.
1Co	15:52	in a m, in the twinkling of
2Co	4:17	which is but for a m,

MONEY (see MONEY CHANGERS)
Gen	17:23	who were bought with his m,
Ex	22:25	If you lend m to any of My
Ex	30:16	shall take the atonement m
Num	3:51	gave their redemption m to
Deut	21:14	shall not sell her for m;
2Ki	17: 3	and paid him tribute m.
Is	52: 3	shall be redeemed without m.
Is	55: 1	buy wine and milk Without m
Is	55: 2	Why do you spend m for what
Mic	3:11	her prophets divine for m.
Matt	17:27	you will find a piece of m;
Matt	22:19	"Show Me the tax m.
Matt	25:18	ground, and hid his lord's m.
Luke	16:14	who were lovers of m,
Luke	19:23	then did you not put my m
John	2:15	poured out the changers' m
John	13:29	because Judas had the m box,
Acts	8:20	Your m perish with you,
1Ti	3: 3	violent, not greedy for m,
1Ti	6:10	For the love of m is a root
2Ti	3: 2	of themselves, lovers of m,

MONEY CHANGERS† (see MONEY)
Matt	21:12	overturned the tables of the m
John	2:14	and the m doing business.

MONTH (see MONTHS)
Ex	12: 2	it shall be the first m of
Ex	12: 6	fourteenth day of the same m.
Ex	13: 4	in the m Abib.
Luke	1:26	Now in the sixth m the angel
Rev	22: 2	yielding its fruit every m.

MONTHS (see MONTH)
Ex	2: 2	child, she hid him three m.
Ex	12: 2	be your beginning of m;
John	4:35	There are still four m and

MONUMENT
2Sa	18:18	day it is called Absalom's M.

MOON (see MOONS)
Gen	37: 9	this time, the sun, the m,
Num	29: 6	grain offering for the New M,
Josh	10:12	still over Gibeon; And M,
Josh	10:13	And the m stopped, Till
2Ki	23: 5	Baal, to the sun, to the m,
Ps	8: 3	The m and the stars, which
Ps	72: 5	As long as the sun and m
Ps	72: 7	Until the m is no more.
Ps	121: 6	Nor the m by night.
Ps	136: 9	The m and stars to rule by
Ps	148: 3	Praise Him, sun and m;
Joel	2:10	The sun and m grow dark,
Joel	2:31	And the m into blood,
Joel	3:15	The sun and m will grow
Amos	8: 5	When will the New M be past,
Hab	3:11	The sun and m stood still in

M

Acts	2:20	And the **m** into blood,
1Co	15:41	sun, another glory of the **m**,
Rev	6:12	and the **m** became like blood.

MOONS (*see* MOON)

1Ch	23:31	Sabbaths and on the New **M**

MORDECAI

Esth	2: 5	Jew whose name was **M** the

MORIAH†

Gen	22: 2	and go to the land of **M**,
2Ch	3: 1	at Jerusalem on Mount **M**,

MORNING

Gen	1: 5	So the evening and the **m**
Gen	21:14	Abraham rose early in the **m**,
Gen	22: 3	Abraham rose early in the **m**
Ex	7:15	"Go to Pharaoh in the **m**,
Ex	12:10	none of it remain until **m**,
Ex	16:19	one leave any of it till **m**.
Ex	18:13	stood before Moses from **m**
1Ki	18:26	on the name of Baal from **m**
Neh	8: 3	of the Water Gate from **m**
Job	1: 5	he would rise early in the **m**
Job	24:17	For the **m** is the same to
Job	38: 7	When the **m** stars sang
Job	38:12	Have you commanded the **m**
Ps	30: 5	But joy comes in the **m**.
Ps	55:17	Evening and **m** and at noon I
Ps	59:16	aloud of Your mercy in the **m**;
Ps	88:13	And in the **m** my prayer
Ps	90: 5	In the **m** they are like
Ps	90: 6	In the **m** it flourishes and
Ps	92: 2	Your lovingkindness in the **m**,
Ps	110: 3	from the womb of the **m**,
Ps	130: 6	those who watch for the **m**—
Ps	139: 9	I take the wings of the **m**,
Prov	7:18	our fill of love until **m**;
Eccl	11: 6	In the **m** sow your seed, And
Is	5:11	who rise early in the **m**,
Is	14:12	son of the **m**! How you are
Is	58: 8	shall break forth like the **m**,
Jer	20:16	him hear the cry in the **m**
Lam	3:23	They are new every **m**;
Ezek	24:18	and the next **m** I did as I
Dan	6:19	arose very early in the **m**
Hos	6: 4	faithfulness is like a **m**
Amos	4: 4	your sacrifices every **m**,
Amos	4:13	And makes the **m** darkness,
Jon	4: 7	But as **m** dawned the next day
Matt	16: 3	"and in the **m**,
Matt	20: 1	who went out early in the **m**
Mark	13:35	of the rooster, or in the **m**—
Mark	16: 2	Very early in the **m**,
Acts	5:21	the temple early in the **m**
2Pe	1:19	the day dawns and the **m**
Rev	2:28	and I will give him the **m**
Rev	22:16	the Bright and **M** Star."

MORSEL

Prov	17: 1	Better is a dry **m** with
Heb	12:16	who for one **m** of food sold

MORTAL (*see* MORTALITY)

Job	4:17	Can a **m** be more righteous
Rom	6:12	not let sin reign in your **m**
Rom	8:11	also give life to your **m**
1Co	15:53	and this **m** must put on
2Co	4:11	may be manifested in our **m**

MORTALITY (*see* MORTAL)

2Co	5: 4	that **m** may be swallowed up

MORTAR

Gen	11: 3	and they had asphalt for **m**.
Ex	1:14	with hard bondage—in **m**,

MOSES (*see* MOSES')

Ex	2:10	So she called his name **M**,
Ex	5:20	they met **M** and Aaron who
Ex	14:31	the LORD and His servant **M**.
Num	12: 1	and Aaron spoke against **M**
Num	12: 3	(Now the man **M** was very
Num	12: 7	Not so with My servant **M**;
Deut	31: 9	So **M** wrote this law and
Deut	31:22	Therefore **M** wrote this song
Deut	31:24	when **M** had completed writing
Deut	33: 1	the blessing with which **M**
Deut	34: 7	**M** was one hundred and twenty
Deut	34:10	in Israel a prophet like **M**,
Josh	1: 1	After the death of **M** the
Josh	1: 2	**M** My servant is dead. Now
Josh	8:31	in the Book of the Law of **M**:
Josh	8:32	a copy of the law of **M**,
Josh	23: 6	in the Book of the Law of **M**,
1Ki	2: 3	is written in the Law of **M**,
1Ki	8: 9	two tablets of stone which **M**
2Ki	14: 6	in the Book of the Law of **M**,
2Ki	18: 4	the bronze serpent that **M**
2Ki	23:25	to all the Law of **M**;
1Ch	23:15	The sons of **M** were Gershon
2Ch	8:13	to the commandment of **M**,
2Ch	25: 4	in the Law in the Book of **M**,
2Ch	30:16	according to the Law of **M**
2Ch	33: 8	ordinances by the hand of **M**.
Ezra	7: 6	scribe in the Law of **M**,
Ps	77:20	a flock By the hand of **M**
Ps	99: 6	**M** and Aaron were among His
Ps	103: 7	He made known His ways to **M**,
Ps	106:23	Had not **M** His chosen one
Is	63:12	them by the right hand of **M**,
Jer	15: 1	Even if **M** and Samuel stood
Matt	8: 4	and offer the gift that **M**
Matt	17: 3	**M** and Elijah appeared to
Matt	17: 4	one for You, one for **M**,
Matt	19: 7	Why then did **M** command to
Matt	22:24	**M** said that if a man dies,
Mark	7:10	For **M** said, 'Honor your
Mark	10: 4	**M** permitted a man to write
Mark	12:19	**M** wrote to us that if a
Mark	12:26	not read in the book of **M**,
Luke	2:22	according to the law of **M**
Luke	16:31	If they do not hear **M** and the
Luke	24:27	And beginning at **M** and all
Luke	24:44	written in the Law of **M** and
John	1:17	the law was given through **M**,

John	1:45	have found Him of whom **M**
John	3:14	And as **M** lifted up the
John	5:45	is one who accuses you—**M**,
John	5:46	"For if you believed **M**,
John	6:32	**M** did not give you the bread
John	7:19	Did not **M** give you the law,
John	9:29	know that God spoke to **M**;
Acts	6:11	blasphemous words against **M**
Acts	7:22	And **M** was learned in all the
Acts	13:39	be justified by the law of **M**.
Acts	15: 1	according to the custom of **M**,
Acts	15:21	For **M** has had throughout many
Acts	21:21	the Gentiles to forsake **M**,
Acts	26:22	which the prophets and **M**
Acts	28:23	from both the Law of **M** and
Rom	5:14	death reigned from Adam to **M**,
Rom	9:15	For He says to **M**,
Rom	10: 5	For **M** writes about the
Rom	10:19	First **M** says: "I will
1Co	9: 9	is written in the law of **M**,
1Co	10: 2	all were baptized into **M** in
2Co	3:15	when **M** is read, a veil lies
2Ti	3: 8	and Jambres resisted **M**,
Heb	3: 2	as **M** also was faithful in
Heb	8: 5	as **M** was divinely instructed
Heb	11:23	By faith **M**, when he was
Jude	9	disputed about the body of **M**,
Rev	15: 3	They sing the song of **M**,

MOSES' (see MOSES)

Ex	34:35	that the skin of **M** face
Matt	23: 2	and the Pharisees sit in **M**

MOTH

Job	4:19	Who are crushed before a **m**?
Matt	6:20	where neither **m** nor rust

MOTHER (see GRANDMOTHER,
  MOTHER IN LAW, MOTHER'S, MOTHERS)

Gen	2:24	leave his father and **m** and
Gen	3:20	because she was the **m** of all
Gen	20:12	but not the daughter of my **m**;
Ex	20:12	your father and your **m**,
Ex	21:15	strikes his father or his **m**
Ex	21:17	curses his father or his **m**
Judg	5: 7	Arose a **m** in Israel.
Ruth	2:11	left your father and your **m**
1Sa	2:19	Moreover his **m** used to make
2Sa	20:19	to destroy a city and a **m**
1Ki	1:11	spoke to Bathsheba the **m** of
1Ki	2:19	throne set for the king's **m**;
1Ki	3:27	kill him; she is his **m**.
1Ki	15:13	from being queen **m**,
1Ki	17:23	house, and gave him to his **m**.
2Ki	4:30	And the **m** of the child said,
2Ki	9:22	as the harlotries of your **m**
Job	17:14	You are my **m** and my sister,'
Ps	35:14	one who mourns for his **m**.
Ps	51: 5	And in sin my **m** conceived
Ps	113: 9	Like a joyful **m** of
Ps	131: 2	a weaned child with his **m**;
Prov	1: 8	forsake the law of your **m**;
Prov	10: 1	son is the grief of his **m**.
Prov	15:20	a foolish man despises his **m**.
Prov	31: 1	the utterance which his **m**
Song	3: 4	him to the house of my **m**,
Song	6: 9	one, The only one of her **m**,
Is	8: 4	to cry 'My father' and 'My **m**,
Jer	15:10	Woe is me, my **m**,
Jer	20:14	not be blessed in which my **m**
Jer	20:17	That my **m** might have been
Ezek	16: 3	was an Amorite and your **m**
Ezek	16:44	proverb against you: 'Like **m**,
Hos	2: 5	For their **m** has played the
Hos	4: 5	And I will destroy your **m**.
Matt	2:13	the young Child and His **m**,
Matt	2:20	the young Child and His **m**,
Matt	8:14	He saw his wife's **m** lying
Matt	10:37	He who loves father or **m** more
Matt	12:47	Your **m** and Your brothers are
Matt	12:48	Who is My **m** and who are My
Matt	14: 8	been prompted by her **m**,
Matt	14:11	and she brought it to her **m**.
Matt	15: 4	your father and your **m**'
Matt	19: 5	leave his father and **m**
Matt	19:29	or sisters or father or **m**
Mark	1:30	But Simon's wife's **m** lay sick
Luke	1:43	that the **m** of my Lord should
Luke	2:51	but His **m** kept all these
Luke	12:53	**m** against daughter and
John	2: 1	and the **m** of Jesus was
John	19:25	by the cross of Jesus His **m**,
John	19:27	Behold your **m**!" And from
Acts	1:14	the women and Mary the **m** of
Gal	4:26	which is the **m** of us all.
Eph	5:31	leave his father and **m**
Eph	6: 2	your father and **m**,
1Th	2: 7	just as a nursing **m**
2Ti	1: 5	grandmother Lois and your **m**
Heb	7: 3	without father, without **m**,
Rev	17: 5	THE **M** OF HARLOTS AND OF

M

MOTHER-IN-LAW (see MOTHER)

Ruth	1:14	and Orpah kissed her **m**,
Ruth	3: 1	Then Naomi her **m** said to her,

MOTHER'S (see MOTHER)

Job	1:21	Naked I came from my **m** womb,
Ps	50:20	You slander your own **m** son.
John	3: 4	a second time into his **m**
Gal	1:15	who separated me from my **m**

MOTHERS (see MOTHER)

Mark	10:30	brothers and sisters and **m**

MOUNT (see MOUNTAIN)

Gen	22:14	In the **M** of The LORD it
Gen	36: 8	So Esau dwelt in **M** Seir. Esau
Ex	19:18	Now **M** Sinai was completely
Num	20:23	to Moses and Aaron in **M** Hor
Deut	11:29	shall put the blessing on **M**
Deut	11:29	Gerizim and the curse on **M**
Josh	19:26	it reached to **M** Carmel.
1Sa	31: 1	and fell slain on **M** Gilboa.
Ps	48: 2	Is **M** Zion on the sides of
Song	4: 1	Going down from **M** Gilead.
Is	40:31	They shall **m** up with wings
Zech	14: 4	feet will stand on the **M** of

Matt	24: 3	Now as He sat on the **M** of
Gal	4:25	for this Hagar is **M** Sinai in
Heb	12:22	But you have come to **M** Zion

MOUNTAIN (*see* MOUNT, MOUNTAINS)

Ex	3: 1	the **m** of God.
Ex	3:12	shall serve God on this **m**.
Ex	19:12	Whoever touches the **m** shall
Ex	19:16	and a thick cloud on the **m**;
Ex	19:18	and the whole **m** quaked
Ex	24:18	And Moses was on the **m** forty
Ex	25:40	which was shown you on the **m**.
Is	2: 2	latter days That the **m** of
Is	2: 3	and let us go up to the **m** of
Is	11: 9	nor destroy in all My holy **m**,
Is	40: 4	be exalted And every **m** and
Dan	2:35	the image became a great **m**
Dan	2:45	stone was cut out of the **m**
Mic	3:12	And the **m** of the temple
Mic	4: 1	latter days That the **m** of
Mic	4: 2	and let us go up to the **m** of
Matt	4: 8	up on an exceedingly high **m**,
Matt	5: 1	He went up on a **m**,
Matt	8: 1	He had come down from the **m**,
Matt	17: 1	led them up on a high **m** by
Matt	17:20	seed, you will say to this **m**,
Luke	19:29	at the **m** called Olivet,
John	4:20	fathers worshiped on this **m**,
Heb	8: 5	shown you on the **m**.
Heb	12:18	you have not come to the **m**
2Pe	1:18	were with Him on the holy **m**.

MOUNTAINS (*see* MOUNTAIN)

Gen	7:20	and the **m** were covered.
Gen	8: 4	on the **m** of Ararat.
Gen	8: 5	the tops of the **m** were seen.
Gen	19:17	the plain. Escape to the **m**,
Gen	22: 2	offering on one of the **m** of
2Sa	1:21	O **m** of Gilboa, Let there
Ps	46: 2	And though the **m** be carried
Ps	90: 2	Before the **m** were brought
Ps	104: 6	waters stood above the **m**.
Ps	114: 4	The **m** skipped like rams,
Ps	148: 9	**M** and all hills
Is	2: 2	on the top of the **m**,
Is	40:12	Weighed the **m** in scales
Is	52: 7	How beautiful upon the **m**
Is	55:12	The **m** and the hills Shall
Ezek	34:13	I will feed them on the **m** of
Ezek	34:14	in rich pasture on the **m** of
Nah	1:15	on the **m** The feet of him
Hab	3: 6	And the everlasting **m** were
Matt	24:16	are in Judea flee to the **m**.
1Co	13: 2	so that I could remove **m**,
Heb	11:38	wandered in deserts and **m**,
Rev	17: 9	The seven heads are seven **m**

MOURN (*see* MOURNED, MOURNERS, MOURNING)

Gen	23: 2	and Abraham came to **m** for
Job	2:11	together to come and **m** with
Eccl	3: 4	time to laugh; A time to **m**,
Is	61: 2	God; To comfort all who **m**,
Is	61: 3	To console those who **m** in

Lam	1: 4	The roads to Zion **m** Because
Ezek	24:16	yet you shall neither **m** nor
Ezek	24:23	you shall neither **m** nor
Hos	4: 3	Therefore the land will **m**;
Amos	1: 2	pastures of the shepherds **m**,
Zech	12:10	they will **m** for Him as one
Matt	5: 4	Blessed are those who **m**,
Matt	9:15	friends of the bridegroom **m**
Matt	24:30	tribes of the earth will **m**,
Luke	6:25	For you shall **m** and weep.
Rev	1: 7	tribes of the earth will **m**
Rev	18:11	of the earth will weep and **m**

MOURNED (*see* MOURN)

Gen	37:34	and **m** for his son many days.
Gen	50: 3	and the Egyptians **m** for him
1Sa	15:35	Nevertheless Samuel **m** for
2Sa	1:12	And they **m** and wept and
2Sa	11:26	she **m** for her husband.
2Sa	13:37	And David **m** for his son
Is	38:14	I **m** like a dove; My eyes
Luke	23:27	and women who also **m** and

MOURNERS (*see* MOURNER)

Eccl	12: 5	And the **m** go about the
Hos	9: 4	shall be like bread of **m**

MOURNING (*see* MOURN)

Gen	37:35	the grave to my son in **m**.
Gen	50:10	He observed seven days of **m**
Ps	38: 6	I go **m** all the day long.
Ps	42: 9	Why do I go **m** because of
Eccl	7: 2	to go to the house of **m**
Is	61: 3	ashes, The oil of joy for **m**,
Jer	16: 5	not enter the house of **m**,
Jer	31:13	For I will turn their **m** to
Jas	4: 9	laughter be turned to **m** and
Rev	18: 8	death and **m** and famine. And

MOUTH (*see* MOUTHS)

Gen	4:11	which has opened its **m** to
Gen	8:11	olive leaf was in her **m**;
Ex	4:11	him, "Who has made man's **m**?
Ex	4:12	and I will be with your **m**
Ex	4:15	and put the words in his **m**.
Ex	13: 9	LORD's law may be in your **m**;
Num	16:32	and the earth opened its **m**
Num	23: 5	put a word in Balaam's **m**,
Num	30: 2	that proceeds out of his **m**.
Deut	8: 3	that proceeds from the **m** of
Deut	18:18	will put My words in His **m**,
Deut	19:15	by the **m** of two or three
Deut	30:14	in your **m** and in your heart,
Josh	1: 8	shall not depart from your **m**,
Job	29:10	stuck to the roof of their **m**.
Ps	8: 2	Out of the **m** of babes and
Ps	10: 7	His **m** is full of cursing and
Ps	19:14	Let the words of my **m** and
Ps	22:21	Save Me from the lion's **m**
Ps	33: 6	them by the breath of His **m**.
Ps	34: 1	continually be in my **m**.
Ps	40: 3	has put a new song in my **m**—
Ps	51:15	And my **m** shall show forth
Ps	62: 4	They bless with their **m**,

Ps	89: 1	With my **m** will I make known
Ps	119:103	than honey to my **m**!
Ps	137: 6	cling to the roof of my **m**—
Prov	5: 3	And her **m** is smoother than
Prov	30:20	She eats and wipes her **m**,
Prov	31:26	She opens her **m** with wisdom,
Song	1: 2	me with the kisses of his **m**—
Is	1:20	For the **m** of the LORD has
Is	6: 7	And he touched my **m** with
Is	11: 4	earth with the rod of His **m**,
Is	45:23	word has gone out of My **m**
Is	53: 7	So He opened not His **m**.
Is	53: 9	was any deceit in His **m**.
Is	55:11	be that goes forth from My **m**;
Is	58:14	The **m** of the LORD has
Jer	1: 9	His hand and touched my **m**,
Jer	1: 9	have put My words in your **m**.
Jer	12: 2	You are near in their **m**
Dan	7: 5	and had three ribs in its **m**
Matt	4: 4	proceeds from the **m** of
Matt	5: 2	Then He opened His **m** and
Matt	12:34	of the heart the **m** speaks.
Matt	13:35	I will open My **m** in
Matt	15: 8	to Me with their **m**,
Matt	15:11	Not what goes into the **m**
Matt	18:16	by the **m** of two or
Matt	21:16	Out of the **m** of babes
Mark	9:18	him down; he foams at the **m**,
Mark	9:20	wallowed, foaming at the **m**.
Luke	1:64	Immediately his **m** was opened
Luke	1:70	As He spoke by the **m** of His
Luke	19:22	Out of your own **m** I will
Luke	22:71	it ourselves from His own **m**.
John	19:29	hyssop, and put it to His **m**.
Acts	4:25	who by the **m** of Your servant
Acts	8:32	He opened not His **m**.
Acts	23: 2	him to strike him on the **m**.
Rom	3:14	Whose **m** is full of
Rom	3:19	that every **m** may be stopped,
Rom	10: 8	in your **m** and in your
Rom	10: 9	if you confess with your **m**
Eph	6:19	that I may open my **m** boldly
Col	3: 8	language out of your **m**.
2Th	2: 8	with the breath of His **m**
2Ti	4:17	I was delivered out of the **m**
Jas	3:10	Out of the same **m** proceed
1Pe	2:22	deceit found in His **m**'
Rev	1:16	out of His **m** went a sharp
Rev	3:16	I will vomit you out of My **m**.

MOUTHS (*see* MOUTH)

Ps	17:10	With their **m** they speak
Ps	22:13	gape at Me with their **m**,
Ps	135:17	there any breath in their **m**.
Is	29:13	draw near with their **m** And
Is	52:15	Kings shall shut their **m** at
Dan	6:22	angel and shut the lions' **m**,
Heb	11:33	stopped the **m** of lions,

MOVE (*see* MOVED)

Gen	9: 2	on all that **m** on the earth,
Matt	17:20	to there,' and it will **m**;
Acts	17:28	for in Him we live and **m** and

MOVED (*see* MOVE)

Gen	12: 8	And he **m** from there to the
Gen	13:18	Then Abram **m** his tent, and
Deut	32:21	They have **m** Me to anger by
1Sa	1:13	her heart; only her lips **m**,
Ps	10: 6	heart, "I shall not be **m**;
Ps	62: 6	defense; I shall not be **m**.
Ps	66: 9	not allow our feet to be **m**.
Ps	125: 1	Zion, Which cannot be **m**,
Is	7: 2	heart of his people were **m**
Matt	9:36	He was **m** with compassion for
Heb	11: 7	**m** with godly fear, prepared
2Pe	1:21	God spoke as they were **m**
Rev	6:14	mountain and island was **m**

MULBERRY

2Sa	5:24	in the tops of the **m** trees,

MULTIPLIED (*see* MULTIPLY)

Ex	1: 7	**m** and grew exceedingly
Is	9: 3	You have **m** the nation And
Acts	6: 7	number of the disciples **m**
Acts	12:24	the word of God grew and **m**.
1Pe	1: 2	Grace to you and peace be **m**.

MULTIPLY (*see* MULTIPLIED, MULTIPLYING)

Gen	1:22	saying, "Be fruitful and **m**,
Gen	3:16	I will greatly **m** your sorrow
Gen	6: 1	when men began to **m** on the
Gen	9: 1	to them: "Be fruitful and **m**,
Gen	17: 2	and will **m** you
Deut	17:16	But he shall not **m** horses for

MULTIPLYING (*see* MULTIPLY)

Gen	22:17	and **m** I will multiply your
Heb	6:14	and **m** I will multiply

MULTITUDE (*see* MULTITUDES)

Gen	16:10	shall not be counted for **m**.
Gen	48:19	shall become a **m** of nations.
Ex	12:38	A mixed **m** went up with them
Deut	1:10	as the stars of heaven in **m**.
Judg	7:12	sand by the seashore in **m**.
1Ki	4:20	as the sand by the sea in **m**,
Ps	51: 1	According to the **m** of Your
Prov	11:14	But in the **m** of counselors
Matt	15:32	"I have compassion on the **m**,
Luke	2:13	was with the angel a **m** of
Heb	11:12	as the stars of the sky in **m**—
Jas	5:20	from death and cover a **m** of
1Pe	4: 8	love will cover a **m** of
Rev	7: 9	a great **m** which no one could

MULTITUDES (*see* MULTITUDE)

Joel	3:14	**m** in the valley of decision!
Matt	4:25	Great **m** followed Him—from

MURDER (*see* MURDERED, MURDERER, MURDERS)

Ex	20:13	"You shall not **m**.
Deut	5:17	'You shall not **m**.
Jer	7: 9	"Will you steal, **m**,
Matt	5:21	of old, 'You shall not **m**,

M

Luke	23:25	who for rebellion and **m** had
Acts	9: 1	breathing threats and **m**
Rom	1:29	full of envy, **m**,
Rom	13: 9	"You shall not **m**,

MURDERED (see MURDER)

Matt	23:31	you are sons of those who **m**
Acts	5:30	raised up Jesus whom you **m**

MURDERER (see MURDER, MURDERERS)

Num	35:16	the **m** shall surely be put to
2Ki	9:31	**m** of your master?"
John	8:44	He was a **m** from the
Acts	28: 4	"No doubt this man is a **m**,
1Pe	4:15	none of you suffer as a **m**,
1Jn	3:15	hates his brother is a **m**,

MURDERERS (see MURDERER)

1Ti	1: 9	murderers of fathers and **m**
Rev	21: 8	unbelieving, abominable, **m**,

MURDERS (see MURDER)

Matt	5:21	and whoever **m** will be in
Matt	15:19	proceed evil thoughts, **m**,
Mark	7:21	adulteries, fornications, **m**,
Gal	5:21	envy, **m**, drunkenness,

MUSIC (see MUSICAL, MUSICIAN)

1Sa	18:10	So David played **m** with his

MUSICAL (see MUSIC)

1Sa	18: 6	and with **m** instruments.
Amos	6: 5	invent for yourselves **m**

MUSICIAN (see MUSIC, MUSICIANS)

Hab	3:19	high hills. To the Chief **M.**

MUST

Luke	2:49	Did you not know that I **m** be
John	3: 7	You **m** be born again.'
John	3:14	even so **m** the Son of Man be
John	3:30	He **m** increase, but I must
John	9: 4	I **m** work the works of Him who
Acts	4:12	among men by which we **m** be
Acts	·16:30	what **m** I do to be saved?"

MUSTARD

Matt	13:31	of heaven is like a **m** seed,
Matt	17:20	if you have faith as a **m**

MUTE

Ex	4:11	mouth? Or who makes the **m**,
Ezek	24:27	speak and no longer be **m**.
Matt	9:33	the **m** spoke. And the
Matt	12:22	demon-possessed, blind and **m**;

MUZZLE

Deut	25: 4	You shall not **m** an ox while
1Co	9: 9	You shall not **m** an ox
1Ti	5:18	You shall not **m** an ox

MYRRH

Gen	37:25	bearing spices, balm, and **m**,
Song	1:13	A bundle of **m** is my beloved

Song	5:13	lilies, Dripping liquid **m**.
Matt	2:11	gold, frankincense, and **m**.
Mark	15:23	Him wine mingled with **m** to

MYRTLE

Zech	1: 8	and it stood among the **m**

MYSTERIES (see MYSTERY)

Matt	13:11	given to you to know the **m**
Luke	8:10	been given to know the **m** of
1Co	13: 2	and understand all **m** and all

MYSTERY (see MYSTERIES)

Mark	4:11	been given to know the **m** of
Rom	11:25	should be ignorant of this **m**,
Rom	16:25	to the revelation of the **m**
1Co	15:51	Behold, I tell you a **m:**
Eph	1: 9	made known to us the **m** of
Eph	3: 9	is the fellowship of the **m**,
Eph	5:32	This is a great **m**,
Col	1:26	the **m** which has been hidden
Col	2: 2	to the knowledge of the **m** of
2Th	2: 7	For the **m** of lawlessness is
1Ti	3: 9	holding the **m** of the faith
1Ti	3:16	controversy great is the **m**
Rev	17: 5	a name was written: **M**,

N

NAAMAN

2Ki	5:20	my master has spared **N** this
Luke	4:27	them was cleansed except **N**

NABAL

1Sa	25:25	**N** is his name, and folly

NABOTH

1Ki	21: 2	So Ahab spoke to **N**,
1Ki	21: 7	give you the vineyard of **N**

NADAB

Num	3: 4	**N** and Abihu had died before
1Ki	15:25	Now **N** the son of Jeroboam

NAHOR

Gen	11:27	Terah: Terah begot Abram, **N**,
Gen	24:10	to the city of **N**.

NAHSHON

Num	1: 7	**N** the son of Amminadab;
Matt	1: 4	Amminadab begot **N**,

NAHUM

Nah	1: 1	The book of the vision of **N**

NAILED† (see NAILS)

Col	2:14	having **n** it to the cross.

NAILS (see NAILED)

Eccl	12:11	are like well-driven **n**,
Dan	7:19	its teeth of iron and its **n**
John	20:25	His hands the print of the **n**,

NAIN†

Luke	7:11	He went into a city called **N**;

NAKED (*see* NAKEDNESS)

Gen	2:25	And they were both **n**,
Gen	3: 7	they knew that they were **n**;
1Sa	19:24	and lay down **n** all that day
Job	1:21	**N** I came from my mother's
Eccl	5:15	**n** shall he return, To go as
Matt	25:36	I was **n** and you clothed Me;
Mark	14:52	cloth and fled from them.
Heb	4:13	but all things are **n** and
Jas	2:15	If a brother or sister is **n**
Rev	3:17	poor, blind, and **n**—

NAKEDNESS (*see* NAKED)

Gen	9:23	backward and covered the **n**
Lev	18: 7	The **n** of your father or the
Rom	8:35	persecution, or famine, or **n**,
2Co	11:27	often, in cold and **n**—

NAME (*see* NAMED, NAME'S, NAMES)

Gen	4:26	men began to call on the **n**
Gen	11: 4	let us make a **n** for
Gen	12: 2	bless you And make your **n**
Gen	17: 5	but your **n** shall be Abraham;
Gen	35:10	but Israel shall be your **n**.
Ex	3:13	say to me, 'What is His **n**?
Ex	3:15	This is My **n** forever, and
Ex	6: 3	but by My **n** LORD I was not
Ex	20: 7	You shall not take the **n** of
Ex.	34: 5	and proclaimed the **n** of the
Ex	34:14	whose **n** is Jealous, is a
Lev	18:21	nor shall you profane the **n**
Lev	19:12	you shall not swear by My **n**
Lev	24:11	son blasphemed the **n** of
Deut	12:11	God chooses to make His **n**
Ruth	4: 5	to perpetuate the **n** of the
2Sa	7:13	shall build a house for My **n**,
2Sa	12:24	and he called his **n** Solomon.
2Sa	12:25	So he called his **n** Jedidiah,
1Ch	16:29	LORD the glory due His **n**;
2Ch	7:14	who are called by My **n** will
Job	1:21	Blessed be the **n** of the
Ps	8: 1	How excellent is Your **n** in
Ps	20: 5	And in the **n** of our God we
Ps	22:22	I will declare Your **n** to My
Ps	29: 2	LORD the glory due to His **n**;
Ps	34: 3	And let us exalt His **n**
Ps	68: 4	By His **n** YAH, And rejoice
Ps	99: 3	Your great and awesome **n**—
Ps	100: 4	to Him, and bless His **n**.
Ps	103: 1	bless His holy **n**!
Ps	113: 2	Blessed be the **n** of the
Ps	118:10	But in the **n** of the LORD
Ps	118:26	is he who comes in the **n**
Ps	138: 2	Your word above all Your **n**.
Ps	147: 4	He calls them all by **n**.
Prov	22: 1	A good **n** is to be chosen
Prov	30: 4	the earth? What is His **n**,
Prov	30: 4	and what is His Son's **n**,
Is	7:14	and shall call His **n**
Is	9: 6	And His **n** will be called

Is	57:15	whose **n** is Holy: "I dwell
Is	62: 2	shall be called by a new **n**,
Jer	7:10	which is called by My **n**,
Zech	14: 9	is one," And His **n** one.
Matt	1:21	and you shall call His **n**
Matt	6: 9	heaven, Hallowed be Your **n**.
Matt	7:22	we not prophesied in Your **n**,
Matt	10:42	cup of cold water in the **n**
Matt	18:20	gathered together in My **n**,
Matt	21: 9	He who comes in the **n**
Matt	28:19	baptizing them in the **n** of
Luke	1:13	and you shall call his **n**
Luke	1:27	The virgin's **n** was Mary.
Luke	1:49	for me, And holy is His **n**.
Luke	24:47	should be preached in His **n**
John	1: 6	whose **n** was John.
John	1:12	those who believe in His **n**:
John	3:18	he has not believed in the **n**
John	5:43	have come in My Father's **n**,
John	10: 3	he calls his own sheep by **n**
John	12:28	"Father, glorify Your **n**.
John	14:13	whatever you ask in My **n**,
John	17: 6	I have manifested Your **n** to
John	17:12	world, I kept them in Your **n**.
John	20:31	you may have life in His **n**.
Acts	2:21	whoever calls on the **n**
Acts	2:38	of you be baptized in the **n**
Acts	4: 7	By what power or by what **n**
Acts	4:12	for there is no other **n**
Acts	4:18	at all nor teach in the **n**
Acts	5:41	to suffer shame for His **n**.
Acts	9:15	vessel of Mine to bear My **n**
Acts	10:48	to be baptized in the **n** of
Acts	16:18	I command you in the **n** of
Rom	2:24	the **n** of God is blasphemed
Rom	10:13	whoever calls on the **n**
1Co	1:13	were you baptized in the **n**
Eph	1:21	and every **n** that is named,
Phil	2: 9	name which is above every **n**,
Phil	2:10	that at the **n** of Jesus every
Col	3:17	do all in the **n** of the Lord
Heb	1: 4	obtained a more excellent **n**
Heb	2:12	I will declare Your **n** to
Jas	5:14	him with oil in the **n** of
1Pe	4:14	are reproached for the **n** of
1Jn	5:13	to you who believe in the **n**
Rev	2:13	And you hold fast to My **n**,
Rev	2:17	and on the stone a new **n**
Rev	3: 5	I will not blot out his **n**
Rev	3:12	name of My God and the **n** of
Rev	6: 8	And the **n** of him who sat on
Rev	8:11	The **n** of the star is
Rev	13:17	who has the mark or the **n**
Rev	13:17	or the number of his **n**.
Rev	15: 4	O Lord, and glorify Your **n**?
Rev	16: 9	and they blasphemed the **n** of
Rev	17: 5	And on her forehead a **n** was
Rev	19:13	and His **n** is called The Word

NAMED (*see* NAME)

Rom	15:20	not where Christ was **n**,
Eph	1:21	and every name that is **n**,
Eph	3:15	in heaven and earth is **n**,
Eph	5: 3	let it not even be **n** among

NAME'S (see NAME)

Ps	23: 3	of righteousness For His n
Matt	24: 9	by all nations for My n
Acts	9:16	he must suffer for My n

NAMES (see NAME)

Gen	2:20	So Adam gave n to all cattle,
Luke	10:20	rejoice because your n are
Phil	4: 3	whose n are in the Book of
2Ti	2:19	Let everyone who n the name
Rev	3: 4	You have a few n even in
Rev	17: 8	whose n are not written in

NAOMI

Ruth	1: 2	the name of his wife was N,
Ruth	1:22	So N returned, and Ruth the
Ruth	3: 1	Then N her mother-in-law said

NAPHTALI

Gen	35:25	maidservant, were Dan and N;
2Ki	15:29	Galilee, all the land of N;
Is	9: 1	of Zebulun and the land of N,
Matt	4:15	and the land of N,

NARROW

Matt	7:14	Because n is the gate and

NATHAN

2Sa	7: 2	that the king said to N the
1Ki	1:11	So N spoke to Bathsheba the

NATHANAEL (see BARTHOLOMEW)

John	1:45	Philip found N and said to
John	21: 2	N of Cana in Galilee, the

NATION (see NATIONS)

Gen	12: 2	I will make you a great n;
Ex	19: 6	of priests and a holy n.
Deut	4: 7	For what great n is there
2Sa	7:23	the one n on the earth whom
Ps	33:12	Blessed is the n whose God
Prov	14:34	Righteousness exalts a n,
Is	1: 4	Alas, sinful n, A people
Is	2: 4	not lift up sword against n,
Is	9: 3	You have multiplied the n
Is	18: 2	to a n tall and smooth of
Is	26:15	You have increased the n,
Jer	18: 7	I speak concerning a n and
Jer	18: 8	if that n against whom I have
Mic	4: 3	not lift up sword against n,
Matt	24: 7	nation will rise against n,
Luke	7: 5	"for he loves our n,
Luke	23: 2	fellow perverting the n,
John	11:50	and not that the whole n
John	11:51	Jesus would die for the n,
John	11:52	and not for that n only, but
Acts	2: 5	from every n under heaven.
Acts	10:35	But in every n whoever fears
Acts	17:26	made from one blood every n
Rom	10:19	those who are not a n,
1Pe	2: 9	a royal priesthood, a holy n,
Rev	5: 9	and tongue and people and n,

Rev	13: 7	every tribe, tongue, and n.
Rev	14: 6	on the earth—to every n,

NATIONS (see NATION)

Gen	10: 5	their families, into their n.
Gen	10:31	lands, according to their n.
Gen	17: 4	shall be a father of many n.
Gen	17:16	shall be a mother of n;
Gen	18:18	and all the n of the earth
Gen	25:23	Two n are in your womb, Two
1Sa	8:20	also may be like all the n,
Ps	2: 1	Why do the n rage, And the
Ps	22:27	all the families of the n
Ps	22:28	And He rules over the n.
Ps	46:10	will be exalted among the n,
Ps	47: 3	And the n under our feet.
Ps	79:10	there be known among the n
Ps	96: 3	His glory among the n,
Ps	110: 6	He shall judge among the n,
Is	2: 2	And all n shall flow to it.
Is	2: 4	shall judge between the n,
Is	5:26	lift up a banner to the n
Is	40:15	the n are as a drop in a
Is	52:15	So shall He sprinkle many n.
Is	56: 7	a house of prayer for all n.
Jer	1: 5	you a prophet to the n.
Jer	1:10	this day set you over the n
Ezek	37:22	shall no longer be two n,
Dan	4: 1	the king, To all peoples, n,
Mic	4: 2	Many n shall come and say,
Mic	4: 3	And rebuke strong n afar
Hag	2: 7	'and I will shake all n,
Hag	2: 7	come to the Desire of All N,
Zech	9:10	shall speak peace to the n;
Matt	24: 9	you will be hated by all n
Matt	28:19	make disciples of all the n,
Mark	11:17	of prayer for all n'?
Mark	13:10	be preached to all the n.
Luke	12:30	For all these things the n of
Acts	4:25	Why did the n rage, And
Acts	13:19	He had destroyed seven n in
Gal	3: 8	In you all the n shall
Rev	7: 9	one could number, of all n,
Rev	12: 5	Child who was to rule all n
Rev	17:15	are peoples, multitudes, n,
Rev	18: 3	For all the n have drunk of

NATURAL (see NATURE)

Deut	34: 7	eyes were not dim nor his n
Rom	11:24	who are n branches, be
1Co	2:14	But the n man does not
1Co	15:44	It is sown a n body, it is

NATURE (see NATURAL)

Acts	17:29	to think that the Divine N
Rom	1:26	use for what is against n.
Eph	2: 3	and were by n children of
Jas	3: 6	sets on fire the course of n;
2Pe	1: 4	be partakers of the divine n,

NAZARENE† (see NAZARENES, NAZARETH)

Matt	2:23	"He shall be called a N.

NAZARENES† (*see* NAZARENE)

Acts 24: 5 of the sect of the N.

NAZARETH (*see* NAZARENE)

Matt 2:23 and dwelt in a city called N,
Matt 21:11 the prophet from N of
Matt 26:71 also was with Jesus of N.
John 1:46 anything good come out of N?
John 19:19 the writing was: JESUS OF N,

NAZIRITE (*see* NAZIRITES)

Num 6: 2 to take the vow of a N,
Num 6:18 Then the N shall shave his
Num 6:20 After that the N may drink
Judg 13: 5 for the child shall be a N

NAZIRITES (*see* NAZIRITE)

Amos 2:12 But you gave the N wine to

NEBO (*see* PISGAH)

Deut 34: 1 plains of Moab to Mount N,
Is 46: 1 N stoops; Their idols were

NEBUCHADNEZZAR

Dan 2: 1 N had dreams; and his spirit
Dan 5: 2 vessels which his father N

NECESSARY

Job 23:12 of His mouth More than my n

NECESSITY

1Co 9:16 for n is laid upon me; yes,
2Co 9: 7 not grudgingly or of n;

NECHO (*see* PHARAOH)

2Ki 23:29 And Pharaoh N killed him

NECK (*see* NECKS)

Gen 41:42 a gold chain around his n.
Gen 45:14 and Benjamin wept on his n.
Ex 13:13 then you shall break its n.
Deut 31:27 rebellion and your stiff n.
Ps 69: 1 waters have come up to my n.
Prov 3: 3 Bind them around your n,
Prov 3:22 soul And grace to your n.
Prov 29: 1 rebuked, and hardens his n,
Song 7: 4 Your n is like an ivory
Is 8: 8 He will reach up to the n;
Dan 5: 7 a chain of gold around his n;
Luke 15:20 and ran and fell on his n

NECKS (*see* NECK)

Josh 10:24 put their feet on their n.
2Ki 17:14 hear, but stiffened their n,
Neh 9:16 proudly, Hardened their n,
Is 3:16 walk with outstretched n

NEED (*see* NEEDED, NEEDFUL, NEEDS, NEEDY, WANT)

Prov 6:11 And your n like an armed
Matt 3:14 I n to be baptized by You,
Matt 6: 8 knows the things you have n
Matt 6:32 Father knows that you n all

Matt 9:12 who are well have no n of a
Matt 21: 3 The Lord has n of them,' and
Mark 2:25 David did when he was in n
Luke 15: 7 just persons who n no
Luke 22:71 further testimony do we n?
Acts 2:45 among all, as anyone had n.
1Co 12:21 I have no n of you."
Eph 4:28 to give him who has n.
Phil 2:25 one who ministered to my n;
Phil 4:12 to abound and to suffer n.
Phil 4:19 God shall supply all your n
1Th 1: 8 so that we do not n to say
2Ti 2:15 a worker who does not n to
Heb 4:16 grace to help in time of n.
Heb 5:12 you n someone to teach you
1Jn 3:17 and sees his brother in n,
Rev 3:17 and have n of nothing'—and
Rev 21:23 The city had no n of the sun
Rev 22: 5 They n no lamp nor light of

NEEDED (*see* NEED)

John 4: 4 But He n to go through
Acts 17:25 as though He n anything,

NEEDFUL† (*see* NEED)

Phil 1:24 in the flesh is more n for

NEEDLE

Matt 19:24 to go through the eye of a n

NEEDS (*see* NEED)

Rom 12:13 distributing to the n of the

NEEDY (*see* NEED)

Deut 15:11 to your poor and your n,
Ps 9:18 For the n shall not always
Ps 37:14 To cast down the poor and n,
Ps 40:17 But I am poor and n;
Ps 72:13 will save the souls of the n.
Is 10: 2 To rob the n of justice,
Ezek 18:12 has oppressed the poor and n,
Amos 4: 1 the poor, Who crush the n,
Amos 8: 4 you who swallow up the n,
Amos 8: 6 And the n for a pair of

NEGLECT (*see* NEGLECTED)

Col 2:23 and n of the body, but are
1Ti 4:14 Do not n the gift that is in
Heb 2: 3 how shall we escape if we n

NEGLECTED† (*see* NEGLECT)

Matt 23:23 and have n the weightier
Acts 6: 1 because their widows were n

NEHEMIAH

Ezra 2: 2 Zerubbabel were Jeshua, N,

NEIGHBOR (*see* NEIGHBOR'S)

Ex 3:22 woman shall ask of her n,
Ex 20:16 false witness against your n.
Ex 21:14 premeditation against his n,
Ex 22:14 borrows anything from his n,
Lev 19:13 'You shall not cheat your n,
Lev 19:18 but you shall love your n as

N

Deut	4:42	flee there, who kills his **n**
1Sa	15:28	and has given it to a **n** of
Ps	101: 5	secretly slanders his **n**,
Prov	14:20	is hated even by his own **n**,
Prov	24:28	be a witness against your **n**
Prov	27:10	Better is a **n** nearby than
Jer	31:34	shall every man teach his **n**,
Jer	34:15	proclaiming liberty to his **n**;
Zech	8:16	each man the truth to his **n**;
Matt	5:43	You shall love your **n** and
Luke	10:29	to Jesus, "And who is my **n**?
Rom	13: 9	You shall love your **n** as
Rom	13:10	Love does no harm to a **n**;
Eph	4:25	speak truth with his **n**,
Heb	8:11	them shall teach his **n**,

NEIGHBOR'S (*see* NEIGHBOR)

Ex	20:17	shall not covet your **n**

NEST (*see* NESTED, NESTS)

Matt	13:32	birds of the air come and **n**

NESTED† (*see* NEST)

Luke	13:19	and the birds of the air **n**

NESTS (*see* NEST)

Matt	8:20	and birds of the air have **n**,

NET (*see* NETS)

Ps	57: 6	They have prepared a **n** for
Matt	4:18	casting a **n** into the sea;
John	21: 6	Cast the **n** on the right side
John	21:11	the **n** was not broken.

NETS (*see* NET)

Ps	141:10	wicked fall into their own **n**,
Ezek	26:14	a place for spreading **n**,
Matt	4:20	immediately left their **n**

NEW (*see* NEWBORN, NEWNESS, NEWS)

Ex	1: 8	Now there arose a **n** king
Num	18:12	all the best of the **n** wine
Ps	33: 3	Sing to Him a **n** song; Play
Ps	40: 3	He has put a **n** song in my
Ps	96: 1	sing to the LORD a **n** song!
Eccl	1: 9	And there is nothing **n**
Is	1:13	The N Moons, the Sabbaths,
Is	42: 9	And **n** things I declare;
Is	42:10	Sing to the LORD a **n** song,
Is	43:19	I will do a **n** thing, Now it
Is	65:17	I create **n** heavens and a new
Lam	3:23	They are **n** every morning;
Ezek	11:19	and I will put a **n** spirit
Ezek	18:31	and get yourselves a **n** heart
Ezek	18:31	a new heart and a **n** spirit.
Amos	8: 5	When will the N Moon be past,
Matt	9:17	But they put new wine into **n**
Matt	26:28	this is My blood of the **n**
Mark	2:21	or else the **n** piece pulls
John	13:34	A **n** commandment I give to
John	19:41	and in the garden a **n** tomb
Acts	2:13	They are full of **n** wine."
Acts	17:21	to tell or to hear some **n**
1Co	5: 7	that you may be a **n** lump,

1Co	11:25	This cup is the **n** covenant in
2Co	3: 6	as ministers of the **n**
2Co	5:17	he is a **n** creation; old
Gal	6:15	anything, but a **n** creation.
Eph	2:15	to create in Himself one **n**
Eph	4:24	and that you put on the **n** man
Col	3:10	and have put on the **n** man
Heb	8: 8	when I will make a **n**
Heb	9:15	He is the Mediator of the **n**
Heb	10:20	by a **n** and living way which
2Pe	3:13	look for **n** heavens and a new
Rev	2:17	and on the stone a **n** name
Rev	3:12	the N Jerusalem, which comes
Rev	5: 9	And they sang a **n** song,
Rev	21: 1	I saw a new heaven and a **n**
Rev	21: 5	I make all things **n**.

NEWBORN† (*see* NEW)

1Pe	2: 2	as **n** babes, desire the pure

NEWNESS (*see* NEW)

Rom	6: 4	so we also should walk in **n**

NEWS (*see* NEW, TIDINGS)

2Sa	18:27	man, and comes with good **n**.
1Ki	14: 6	sent to you with bad **n**.
Prov	25:25	So is good **n** from a far
Is	52: 7	of him who brings good **n**,
Jer	20:15	be cursed Who brought **n**
1Th	3: 6	and brought us good **n** of

NICODEMUS

John	3: 1	man of the Pharisees named N,
John	7:50	N (he who came to Jesus by

NIGHT (*see* NIGHTS)

Gen	1: 5	and the darkness He called N.
Gen	1:14	to divide the day from the **n**;
Gen	1:16	lesser light to rule the **n**.
Josh	1: 8	meditate in it day and **n**,
Job	35:10	Who gives songs in the **n**,
Ps	1: 2	law he meditates day and **n**.
Ps	19: 2	And night unto **n** reveals
Ps	22: 2	And in the **n** season, and am
Ps	30: 5	Weeping may endure for a **n**,
Ps	90: 4	And like a watch in the **n**.
Ps	91: 5	be afraid of the terror by **n**,
Ps	121: 6	by day, Nor the moon by **n**.
Ps	136: 9	moon and stars to rule by **n**,
Is	21:11	"Watchman, what of the **n**?
Jer	9: 1	I might weep day and **n** For
Jon	4:10	which came up in a **n** and
Luke	2: 8	watch over their flock by **n**.
Luke	12:20	Fool! This **n** your soul will
John	3: 2	This man came to Jesus by **n**
John	9: 4	the **n** is coming when no one
John	13:30	immediately. And it was **n**.
Rom	13:12	The **n** is far spent, the day
1Co	11:23	Lord Jesus on the same **n**
1Th	5: 2	so comes as a thief in the **n**.
1Th	5: 5	We are not of the **n** nor of
2Pe	3:10	come as a thief in the **n**,
Rev	21:25	by day (there shall be no **n**

NIGHTS (see NIGHT)

Gen	7: 4	earth forty days and forty **n**,
1Ki	19: 8	food forty days and forty **n**
Jon	1:17	fish three days and three **n**.
Matt	4: 2	forty days and forty **n**,
Matt	12:40	was three days and three **n**

NIMROD

Gen	10: 9	Like N the mighty nunter

NINETY-NINE

Gen	17:24	Abraham was **n** years old when
Matt	18:12	does he not leave the **n** and
Luke	15: 7	who repents than over **n**

NINEVEH

Gen	10:11	went to Assyria and built N,
Jon	1: 2	"Arise, go to N,
Jon	3: 2	"Arise, go to N,
Jon	4:11	"And should I not pity N,
Nah	3: 7	N is laid waste! Who will
Luke	11:32	The men of N will rise up in

NINTH

Matt	20: 5	about the sixth and the **n**
Matt	27:46	And about the **n** hour Jesus
Acts	3: 1	of prayer, the **n** hour.

NISAN (see ABIB)

Esth	3: 7	which is the month of N,

NOAH

Gen	5:32	and N begot Shem, Ham, and
Gen	6: 8	But N found grace in the eyes
Gen	8: 1	Then God remembered N,
Gen	9: 1	So God blessed N and his
Is	54: 9	is like the waters of N to
Ezek	14:20	"even though N,
Luke	17:26	as it was in the days of N,
Heb	11: 7	By faith N, being divinely
1Pe	3:20	waited in the days of N,
2Pe	2: 5	ancient world, but saved N,

NOBLE (see NOBLEMAN)

1Co	1:26	not many mighty, not many **n**,
Phil	4: 8	true, whatever things are **n**,
Jas	2: 7	Do they not blaspheme that **n**

NOBLEMAN (see NOBLE)

Luke	19:12	A certain **n** went into a far
John	4:46	And there was a certain **n**

NOD†

Gen	4:16	and dwelt in the land of N

NOISE

Ex	32:17	There is a **n** of war in the
Ex	32:18	It is not the **n** of the
2Ki	7: 6	the **n** of a great army; so
Ps	42: 7	calls unto deep at the **n** of
Ps	93: 4	is mightier Than the **n** of
Is	29: 6	and earthquake and great **n**,
Is	66: 6	The sound of **n** from the

Jer	4:19	heart! My heart makes a **n**
Jer	49:21	The earth shakes at the **n** of
Ezek	1:24	I heard the **n** of their
Ezek	3:13	and the **n** of the wheels
Ezek	37: 7	I prophesied, there was a **n**,
Amos	5:23	Take away from Me the **n** of
Zeph	1:14	The **n** of the day of the
2Pe	3:10	pass away with a great **n**,

NOON (see NOONDAY)

Acts	22: 6	near Damascus at about **n**,

NOONDAY (see NOON)

Ps	91: 6	that lays waste at **n**.

NORTH

Job	26: 7	He stretches out the **n** over
Ps	48: 2	Zion on the sides of the **n**,
Ps	107: 3	From the **n** and from the
Is	14:13	the farthest sides of the **n**;
Jer	1:14	Out of the **n** calamity shall

NOSE

Gen	24:30	when he saw the **n** ring, and
2Ki	19:28	I will put My hook in your **n**
Song	7: 4	Your **n** is like the tower
Ezek	8:17	put the branch to their **n**.

NOSTRILS

Gen	2: 7	and breathed into his **n** the
Gen	7:22	All in whose **n** was the
Ex	15: 8	with the blast of Your **n**
Num	11:20	it comes out of your **n** and
2Sa	22: 9	Smoke went up from His **n**,
Ps	18:15	of the breath of Your **n**.
Lam	4:20	The breath of our **n**,

NOURISHED (see NOURISHES)

2Sa	12: 3	which he had bought and **n**;
Is	1: 2	I have **n** and brought up
Col	2:19	**n** and knit together by
1Ti	4: 6	**n** in the words of faith and

NOURISHES (see NOURISHED)

Eph	5:29	but **n** and cherishes it, just

NUMBER (see NUMBERED)

Gen	13:16	so that if a man could **n** the
Gen	15: 5	stars if you are able to **n**
Num	1: 3	You and Aaron shall **n** them
Deut	7: 7	because you were more in **n**
2Sa	24: 1	**n** Israel and Judah."
1Ch	21: 1	and moved David to **n** Israel.
Ps	90:12	So teach us to **n** our days,
Dan	9: 2	by the books the **n** of the
Acts	11:21	and a great **n** believed and
Acts	16: 5	and increased in **n** daily.
Rev	7: 9	which no one could **n**,
Rev	13:18	of a man: His **n** is 666.

NUMBERED (see NUMBER)

Gen	13:16	descendants also could be **n**.
Is	53:12	And He was **n** with the
Dan	5:26	God has **n** your kingdom, and

N

Matt	10:30	hairs of your head are all **n**.
Mark	15:28	And He was **n** with the

NUN

Ex	33:11	servant Joshua the son of **N**,
Num	13: 8	Ephraim, Hoshea the son of **N**;

NURSE (*see* NURSED, NURSING)

Ex	2: 7	that she may **n** the child for
Ruth	4:16	and became a **n** to him.

NURSED (*see* NURSE)

Ex	2: 9	woman took the child and **n**
Luke	11:27	and the breasts which **n**
Luke	23:29	and breasts which never **n**!'

NURSING (*see* NURSE)

Is	11: 8	The **n** child shall play by
Is	49:15	Can a woman forget her **n**

O

OATH (*see* OATHS)

Gen	21:31	the two of them swore an **o**
Deut	7: 8	because He would keep the **o**
Deut	29:14	this covenant and this **o**,
Josh	2:20	we will be free from your **o**
Ps	106:26	up His hand in an **o**
Eccl	9: 2	He who takes an **o** as he
Matt	26:63	I put you under **o** by the

OATHS (*see* OATH)

Matt	5:33	but shall perform your **o** to

OBADIAH

1Ki	18: 3	And Ahab had called **O**,
Obad	1	The vision of **O**.

OBED

Ruth	4:21	begot Boaz, and Boaz begot **O**;
Matt	1: 5	Boaz begot **O** by Ruth, Obed

OBEDIENCE (*see* OBEDIENT)

Gen	49:10	to Him shall be the **o** of
Rom	1: 5	grace and apostleship for **o**
Rom	5:19	so also by one Man's **o** many
Rom	6:16	or of **o** leading to
Rom	16:19	For your **o** has become known
Rom	16:26	for **o** to the faith—
2Co	10: 5	into captivity to the **o** of
Heb	5: 8	yet He learned **o** by the
1Pe	1: 2	for **o** and sprinkling of the

OBEDIENT (*see* OBEDIENCE, OBEY)

Ex	24: 7	said we will do, and be **o**.
Is	1:19	If you are willing and **o**,
Acts	6: 7	many of the priests were **o**
Rom	15:18	deed, to make the Gentiles **o**—
Eph	6: 5	be **o** to those who are your
Phil	2: 8	Himself and became **o** to
Tit	2: 5	**o** to their own husbands,

Tit	2: 9	bondservants to be **o** to
1Pe	1:14	as **o** children, not conforming

OBEY (*see* OBEDIENT, OBEYED, OBEYING)

Gen	27:43	**o** my voice: arise, flee to
Ex	5: 2	that I should **o** His voice to
Ex	19: 5	if you will indeed **o** My
Deut	4:30	to the LORD your God and **o**
Deut	11:13	be that if you earnestly **o**
Deut	15: 5	only if you carefully **o** the
Josh	24:24	and His voice we will **o**!"
1Sa	8:19	the people refused to **o** the
1Sa	12:14	LORD and serve Him and **o**
1Sa	15:22	to **o** is better than
1Sa	28:18	Because you did not **o** the
Jer	7:28	is a nation that does not **o**
Jer	11: 3	is the man who does not **o**
Jer	18:10	sight so that it does not **o**
Dan	7:27	dominions shall serve and **o**
Matt	8:27	the winds and the sea **o** Him?
Mark	1:27	and they **o** Him."
Acts	5:29	We ought to **o** God rather than
Acts	5:32	God has given to those who **o**
Acts	7:39	our fathers would not **o**,
Rom	2: 8	self-seeking and do not **o**
Rom	6:12	that you should **o** it in its
Rom	6:16	yourselves slaves to **o**,
Eph	6: 1	**o** your parents in the Lord,
Col	3:20	**o** your parents in all
Col	3:22	**o** in all things your masters
2Th	1: 8	and on those who do not **o**
2Th	3:14	And if anyone does not **o** our
Tit	3: 1	rulers and authorities, to **o**,
Heb	3:18	but to those who did not **o**?
Heb	5: 9	salvation to all who **o** Him,
Heb	13:17	**O** those who rule over you,
1Pe	3: 1	that even if some do not **o**
1Pe	4:17	end of those who do not **o**

OBEYED (*see* OBEY)

Gen	22:18	because you have **o** My
Gen	26: 5	because Abraham **o** My voice
Dan	9:10	We have not **o** the voice of
Dan	9:14	though we have not **o** His
Rom	6:17	yet you **o** from the heart
Rom	10:16	But they have not all **o** the
Heb	11: 8	By faith Abraham **o** when he
1Pe	3: 6	as Sarah **o** Abraham, calling

OBEYING (*see* OBEY)

Judg	2:17	in **o** the commandments of the
1Sa	15:22	As in **o** the voice of the
Gal	5: 7	Who hindered you from **o** the

OBSERVE (*see* OBSERVING)

Deut	4: 1	which I teach you to **o**,
Deut	5:12	**O** the Sabbath day, to keep
Matt	28:20	teaching them to **o** all things

OBSERVING (*see* OBSERVE)

Jas	1:23	he is like a man **o** his

OBSOLETE

Heb	8:13	He has made the first **o**.

OBTAIN (see OBTAINED, OBTAINS)

Gen	16: 2	perhaps I shall o children
Matt	5: 7	For they shall o mercy.
Rom	11:31	shown you they also may o
1Co	9:25	Now they do it to o a
1Th	5: 9	but to o salvation through
Heb	4:16	that we may o mercy and find
Heb	11:35	that they might o a better

OBTAINED (see OBTAIN)

Rom	11:30	yet have now o mercy through
Eph	1:11	In Him also we have o an
1Ti	1:16	for this reason I o mercy,
Heb	1: 4	as He has by inheritance o
Heb	8: 6	But now He has o a more
Heb	9:12	having o eternal redemption.
Heb	11: 2	For by it the elders o a
Heb	11: 4	through which he o witness
Heb	11:33	o promises, stopped the
Heb	11:39	having o a good testimony
1Pe	2:10	who had not o mercy but now

OBTAINS (see OBTAIN)

Prov	8:35	And o favor from the LORD;
Prov	12: 2	A good man o favor from the

OCCASION

Rom	7:11	taking o by the commandment,

OFFEND (see OFFENDED, OFFENSE)

Matt	13:41	kingdom all things that o,
Luke	17: 2	than that he should o one of

OFFENDED (see OFFEND)

Prov	18:19	A brother o is harder to
Matt	11: 6	blessed is he who is not o
Matt	13:57	So they were o at Him. But

OFFENSE (see OFFEND, OFFENSES)

Is	8:14	of stumbling and a rock of o
Matt	16:23	Satan! You are an o to Me,
Matt	18: 7	to that man by whom the o
Rom	5:15	For if by the one man's o
Rom	9:33	stone and rock of o,
1Co	10:32	Give no o, either to the
Gal	5:11	Then the o of the cross has
Phil	1:10	may be sincere and without o
1Pe	2: 8	And a rock of o.

OFFENSES (see OFFENSE)

Matt	18: 7	to the world because of o!

OFFER (see OFFERED, OFFERING)

Gen	22: 2	and o him there as a burnt
Ex	23:18	You shall not o the blood of
2Sa	24:12	I o you three things; choose
2Ki	17:36	and to Him you shall o
1Ch	29:17	who are present here to o
Job	1: 5	early in the morning and o
Job	42: 8	and o up for yourselves a
Ps	16: 4	of blood I will not o,
Ps	50:14	O to God thanksgiving, And
Ps	51:19	Then they shall o bulls on

Jer	11:12	to the gods to whom they o
Jer	33:18	lack a man to o burnt
Ezek	43:22	the second day you shall o
Ezek	44:27	he must o his sin offering
Hos	9: 4	They shall not o wine
Amos	4: 5	O a sacrifice of
Amos	5:22	Though you o Me burnt
Amos	5:25	Did you o Me sacrifices and
Hag	2:14	and what they o there is
Mal	1: 7	You o defiled food on My
Mal	1: 8	And when you o the blind as
Luke	6:29	o the other also. And from
Luke	11:12	will he o him a scorpion?
Heb	5: 3	to o sacrifices for sins.
Heb	7:27	to o up sacrifices, first
Heb	8: 3	One also have something to o.
Heb	9:25	not that He should o Himself
Heb	10: 1	which they o continually
Heb	13:15	by Him let us continually o
1Pe	2: 5	to o up spiritual sacrifices

OFFERED (see OFFER)

Gen	8:20	and o burnt offerings on the
Gen	22:13	and o it up for a burnt
Lev	10: 1	and o profane fire before
Mark	15:36	and o it to Him to drink,
Acts	7:41	o sacrifices to the idol,
Acts	15:29	you abstain from things o
Acts	21:25	themselves from things o
1Co	8: 4	the eating of things o to
1Co	10:19	or what is o to idols is
Heb	5: 7	when He had o up prayers and
Heb	7:27	did once for all when He o
Heb	9: 7	which he o for himself and
Heb	9:14	through the eternal Spirit o
Heb	9:28	so Christ was o once to bear
Heb	10:12	after He had o one sacrifice
Heb	11: 4	By faith Abel o to God a
Heb	11:17	o up Isaac, and he who had
Heb	11:17	had received the promises o
Jas	2:21	by works when he o Isaac

OFFERING (see OFFER, OFFERINGS)

Gen	4: 4	respected Abel and his o,
Gen	4: 5	not respect Cain and his o.
Gen	22: 2	him there as a burnt o on
Lev	4: 3	without blemish as a sin o.
Lev	4: 8	fat of the bull as the sin o.
Lev	4:25	of the altar of burnt o,
Lev	5:15	sanctuary, as a trespass o.
Lev	6:14	is the law of the grain o:
Lev	7:13	thanksgiving of his peace o.
Lev	7:16	is a vow or a voluntary o,
Lev	9:15	he brought the people's o,
Lev	10:14	The breast of the wave o and
Lev	10:15	The thigh of the heave o and
Lev	23:13	and its drink o shall be
Lev	27:28	'Nevertheless no devoted o
Num	7:88	This was the dedication o
Deut	23:18	your God for any vowed o,
Neh	10:34	for bringing the wood o
Ps	40: 6	Sacrifice and o You did not
Ps	40: 6	Burnt o and sin offering
Ps	51:16	do not delight in burnt o.

O

Ps	51:19	offering and whole burnt o;
Ps	96: 8	due His name; Bring an o,
Is	53:10	You make His soul an o for
Is	57: 6	you have poured a drink o,
Jer	11:17	to provoke Me to anger in o
Ezek	40:42	slaughtered the burnt o and
Ezek	45:19	of the blood of the sin o
Ezek	45:23	the goats daily for a sin o.
Dan	2:46	they should present an o
Dan	9:21	the time of the evening o.
Dan	9:27	an end to sacrifice and o.
Mal	1:10	Nor will I accept an o from
Mal	2:13	So He does not regard the o
Mal	3: 3	offer to the LORD An o in
Luke	5:14	and make an o for your
Luke	23:36	coming and to Him sour wine,
Rom	15:16	that the o of the Gentiles
Eph	5: 2	an o and a sacrifice to God
2Ti	4: 6	poured out as a drink o,
Heb	10: 5	Sacrifice and o You did
Heb	10: 8	saying, "Sacrifice and o,
Heb	10:10	sanctified through the o of
Heb	10:11	ministering daily and o
Heb	10:14	For by one o He has perfected
Heb	10:18	there is no longer an o

OFFERINGS (see OFFERING).

Gen	8:20	and offered burnt o on the
Ex	20:24	on it your burnt o and your
Lev	8:28	They were consecration o
1Sa	15:22	great delight in burnt o
2Sa	1:21	upon you, Nor fields of o.
2Ki	12:16	money from the trespass o
2Ch	1: 6	offered a thousand burnt o
2Ch	29:34	not skin all the burnt o;
2Ch	31: 3	the burnt o for the Sabbaths
2Ch	35: 6	slaughter the Passover o,
Ezra	3: 3	morning and evening burnt o.
Ezra	8:35	offered burnt o to the God
Neh	12:44	of the storehouse for the o,
Job	1: 5	morning and offer burnt o
Ps	16: 4	Their drink o of blood I
Ps	20: 3	May He remember all your o,
Ps	66:13	into Your house with burnt o;
Ps	119:108	the freewill o of my mouth,
Prov	7:14	I have peace o with me;
Is	1:11	have had enough of burnt o
Jer	7:18	and they pour out drink o
Jer	19: 5	sons with fire for burnt o
Jer	33:18	before Me, to kindle grain o,
Jer	41: 5	with o and incense in their
Ezek	20:28	and provoked Me with their o.
Ezek	42:13	shall eat the most holy o.
Ezek	45:17	and the peace o to make
Hos	6: 6	of God more than burnt o.
Amos	5:22	regard your fattened peace o.
Amos	5:25	offer Me sacrifices and o
Mic	6: 6	come before Him with burnt o,
Mal	3: 8	You?' In tithes and o.
Mark	12:33	than all the whole burnt o
1Co	9:13	the altar partake of the o
Heb	10: 6	In burnt o and sacrifices
Heb	10: 8	and o for sin You did

OFFICE (see OFFICER)

Gen	41:13	He restored me to my o,
1Ch	9:22	them to their trusted o.
Ps	109: 8	And let another take his o.
Matt	9: 9	Matthew sitting at the tax o.
Mark	2:14	sitting at the tax o.
Luke	5:27	Levi, sitting at the tax o.
Acts	1:20	another take his o.

OFFICER (see OFFICE)

Gen	37:36	an o of Pharaoh and captain
Matt	5:25	judge hand you over to the o,
Luke	12:58	and the o throw you into

OFFSPRING

Gen	15: 3	You have given me no o;
Deut	7:13	of your cattle and the o of
Judg	8:30	sons who were his own o,
Ruth	4:12	because of the o which the
Job	39: 3	young, They deliver their o.
Ps	21:10	Their o You shall destroy
Ps	22:23	all you o of Israel!
Is	44: 3	And My blessing on your o;
Is	48:19	And the o of your body like
Is	57: 4	O of falsehood,
Lam	2:20	the women eat their o,
Mal	2:15	why one? He seeks godly o.
Matt	22:24	his wife and raise up o for
Matt	22:25	had married, and having no o,
Mark	12:20	and dying, he left no o.
Acts	17:28	said, 'For we are also His o.
Acts	17:29	since we are the o of God,
Rev	22:16	I am the Root and the O of

OG

Num	21:33	So O king of Bashan went out
Ps	135:11	O king of Bashan, And all

OIL

Gen	28:18	and poured o on top of it.
Ex	25: 6	o for the light, and spices
Ex	25: 6	spices for the anointing o
Ex	29: 2	cakes mixed with o,
Ex	30:24	and a hin of olive o.
Ex	37:29	made the holy anointing o
Deut	7:13	and your new wine and your o,
Deut	32:13	And o from the flinty rock;
1Sa	10: 1	Samuel took a flask of o
1Sa	16: 1	Fill your horn with o,
1Ki	17:12	and a little o in a jar; and
2Ki	4: 6	So the o ceased.
Job	29: 6	rock poured out rivers of o
Ps	23: 5	You anoint my head with o;
Ps	45: 7	anointed You With the o of
Ps	104:15	O to make his face shine,
Ps	109:18	And like o into his bones.
Ps	133: 2	It is like the precious o
Prov	5: 3	mouth is smoother than o;
Eccl	9: 8	And let your head lack no o.
Is	61: 3	The o of joy for mourning,
Jer	31:12	wheat and new wine and o,
Ezek	32:14	make their rivers run like o,
Ezek	45:25	grain offering, and the o.

Hos	2: 5	My **o** and my drink.'
Mic	6: 7	Ten thousand rivers of **o**?
Zech	4:12	from which the golden **o**
Matt	25: 4	but the wise took **o** in their
Matt	26: 7	of very costly fragrant **o**,
Luke	10:34	pouring on **o** and wine; and
Heb	1: 9	You With the **o** of
Jas	5:14	anointing him with **o** in the

OINTMENT (see OINTMENTS)

Ex	30:25	an **o** compounded according to
Prov	27: 9	**O** and perfume delight the
Eccl	7: 1	is better than precious **o**,
Is	1: 6	bound up, Or soothed with **o**.

OINTMENTS (see OINTMENT)

Song	1: 3	the fragrance of your good **o**,
Amos	6: 6	yourselves with the best **o**,

OLD (see OLDER)

Gen	6: 4	mighty men who were of **o**,
Gen	15:15	shall be buried at a good **o**
Gen	17: 1	was ninety-nine years **o**,
Gen	18:11	Abraham and Sarah were **o**,
Gen	19:31	younger, "Our father is **o**,
Gen	21: 2	bore Abraham a son in his **o**
Gen	21: 4	when he was eight days **o**,
Gen	25: 8	last and died in a good **o**
Gen	25: 8	an **o** man and full of
Deut	32: 7	"Remember the days of **o**,
Deut	34: 7	hundred and twenty years **o**
Josh	9: 5	**o** and patched sandals on
1Sa	2:22	Now Eli's was very **o**;
2Ch	31:17	Levites from twenty years **o**
Job	22:15	Will you keep to the **o** way
Job	42:17	**o** and full of days.
Ps	25: 6	For they are from of **o**.
Ps	32: 3	my bones grew **o** Through my
Ps	37:25	been young, and now am **o**;
Ps	55:19	He who abides from of **o**.
Ps	74:12	God is my King from of **o**,
Ps	77: 5	considered the days of **o**,
Ps	77:11	remember Your wonders of **o**.
Ps	78: 2	will utter dark sayings of **o**,
Ps	92:14	shall still bear fruit in **o**
Ps	102:25	Of **o** You laid the foundation
Ps	102:26	they will all grow **o** like a
Ps	148:12	**O** men and children.
Prov	8:22	way, Before His works of **o**.
Is	43:18	consider the things of **o**.
Is	46: 4	Even to your **o** age, I am
Is	46: 9	the former things of **o**,
Is	50: 9	they will all grow **o** like a
Is	65:20	die one hundred years **o**,
Lam	5:21	Renew our days as of **o**,
Joel	2:28	Your **o** men shall dream
Mic	5: 2	goings forth are from of **o**,
Mic	6: 6	With calves a year **o**?
Mic	7:20	our fathers From days of **o**.
Matt	2:16	from two years **o** and under,
Matt	5:21	it was said to those of **o**,
Matt	9:16	of unshrunk cloth on an **o**
Matt	9:17	do they put new wine into **o**
Matt	13:52	treasure things new and **o**.

Luke	1:18	For I am an **o** man, and my
Luke	1:36	conceived a son in her **o**
Luke	2:42	when He was twelve years **o**,
Luke	9: 8	by others that one of the **o**
Luke	9:19	say that one of the **o**
John	3: 4	a man be born when he is **o**?
John	8:57	are not yet fifty years **o**,
John	21:18	wished; but when you are **o**,
Acts	2:17	Your **o** men shall dream
Rom	6: 6	that our **o** man was crucified
1Co	5: 7	Therefore purge out the **o**
2Co	3:14	in the reading of the **O**
2Co	5:17	**o** things have passed away;
Eph	4:22	the **o** man which grows
Col	3: 9	you have put off the **o** man
1Ti	4: 7	But reject profane and **o**
Heb	1:11	they will all grow **o**
Heb	8:13	obsolete and growing **o** is
2Pe	1: 9	he was cleansed from his **o**
1Jn	2: 7	but an **o** commandment which
Rev	12: 9	cast out, that serpent of **o**,
Rev	20: 2	dragon, that serpent of **o**,

OLDER (see OLD)

Gen	25:23	And the **o** shall serve the
Rom	9:12	The **o** shall serve the
1Ti	5: 1	Do not rebuke an **o** man, but
1Ti	5: 2	**o** women as mothers, younger
Tit	2: 2	that the **o** men be sober,

OLIVE (see OLIVES)

Gen	8:11	a freshly plucked **o** leaf
Ex	23:11	your vineyard and your **o**
Deut	6:11	vineyards and **o** trees which
Judg	9: 8	And they said to the **o**
Neh	8:15	and bring **o** branches,
Zech	4: 3	Two **o** trees are by it, one
Rom	11:17	being a wild **o** tree, were
Rom	11:24	be grafted into their own **o**
Rev	11: 4	These are the two **o** trees and

OLIVES (see OLIVE)

Ex	27:20	you pure oil of pressed **o**
2Sa	15:30	Ascent of the Mount of **O**,
Zech	14: 4	will stand on the Mount of **O**,
Matt	26:30	went out to the Mount of **O**.
Mark	13: 3	as He sat on the Mount of **O**

OLIVET

Luke	19:29	at the mountain called **O**,

OMEGA†

Rev	1: 8	"I am the Alpha and the **O**,
Rev	1:11	"I am the Alpha and the **O**,
Rev	21: 6	I am the Alpha and the **O**,
Rev	22:13	"I am the Alpha and the **O**,

OMNIPOTENT†

Rev	19: 6	For the Lord God **O** reigns!

OMRI

1Ki	16:23	**O** became king over Israel,
1Ki	16:25	**O** did evil in the eyes of the

1Ki	16:29	Ahab the son of O became
Mic	6:16	For the statutes of O are

ONCE (see ONE)

Gen	18:32	and I will speak but o more:
Lev	16:34	o a year." And he did as
Josh	6:14	marched around the city o
Judg	6:39	just o more with the fleece;
Job	40: 5	O I have spoken, but I will
Rom	6:10	He died to sin o for all;
1Co	15: 6	five hundred brethren at o,
Gal	1:23	the faith which he o tried
Eph	2: 2	in which you o walked
Eph	2:13	in Christ Jesus you who o
Eph	5: 8	For you were o darkness, but
Col	1:21	who o were alienated and
Col	3: 7	in which you yourselves o
Heb	6: 4	for those who were o
Heb	7:27	for this He did o for all
Heb	9: 7	high priest went alone o a
Heb	9:12	the Most Holy Place o for
Heb	9:27	appointed for men to die o,
Heb	9:28	so Christ was offered o to
Heb	12:26	Yet o more I shake not
1Pe	2:10	who o were not a people but
1Pe	3:18	For Christ also suffered o
Jude	3	for the faith which was o

ONE (see GOD, ONCE)

Gen	2:24	and they shall become o
Gen	31:49	and me when we are absent o
Num	7:89	he heard the voice of O
Deut	6: 4	our God, the LORD is o!
1Sa	13: 1	Saul reigned o year; and when
2Ki	19:22	Against the Holy O of
Ps	3: 3	My glory and the O who
Ps	14: 3	who does good, No, not o.
Ps	16:10	will You allow Your Holy O
Ps	19: 6	Its rising is from o end of
Ps	27: 4	O thing I have desired of
Ps	34:20	Not o of them is broken.
Ps	50: 1	The Mighty O, God the
Ps	53: 3	Every o of them has turned
Ps	53: 3	who does good, No, not o.
Ps	71:22	O Holy O of Israel.
Ps	83: 5	consulted together with o
Ps	105:13	When they went from o nation
Ps	132: 2	And vowed to the Mighty O
Ps	132: 5	place for the Mighty O of
Ps	137: 3	Sing us o of the songs of
Ps	142: 4	For there is no o who
Ps	144: 2	My shield and the O in
Prov	9:10	the knowledge of the Holy O
Prov	28: 1	The wicked flee when no o
Prov	30: 3	have knowledge of the Holy O.
Eccl	4: 9	Two are better than o,
Song	2:10	up, my love, my fair o,
Is	1: 4	to anger The Holy O of
Is	1:24	the Mighty O of Israel,
Is	6: 2	each o had six wings: with
Is	6: 6	Then o of the seraphim flew
Is	12: 6	For great is the Holy O of
Is	29:23	And hallow the Holy O of
Is	40: 3	The voice of o crying in

Is	42: 1	My Elect O in whom My
Is	53: 6	We have turned, every o,
Is	57:15	says the High and Lofty O
Is	63: 1	This O who is glorious
Jer	32:39	then I will give them o heart
Ezek	1:28	and I heard a voice of O
Dan	7:13	O like the Son of Man,
Dan	12: 1	Every o who is found
Hos	11: 9	The Holy O in your midst;
Mic	4: 4	And no o shall make them
Mic	5: 2	come forth to Me The O to
Zech	14: 9	is one," And His name o.
Matt	6:13	deliver us from the evil o.
Matt	6:24	No o can serve two masters;
Matt	8: 4	"See that you tell no o;
Matt	11: 3	Him, "Are You the Coming O,
Matt	19: 5	the two shall become o
Matt	19:17	No o is good but One, that
Matt	23: 8	for O is your Teacher, the
Matt	23: 9	for O is your Father, He who
Mark	10:21	O thing you lack: Go your
Mark	12:29	God, the LORD is o.
Luke	12:25	of you by worrying can add o
Luke	12:27	was not arrayed like o of
Luke	15: 4	and go after the o which is
Luke	15: 7	be more joy in heaven over o
Luke	15:19	Make me like o of your hired
Luke	16:13	either he will hate the o
Luke	16:31	they be persuaded though o
Luke	17: 2	that he should offend o of
Luke	18:22	You still lack o thing. Sell
1Co	11:21	and o is hungry and another
1Co	12: 3	and no o can say that Jesus
1Co	12:11	But o and the same Spirit
1Co	12:12	For as the body is o and has
1Co	12:13	For by o Spirit we were all
1Co	12:13	we were all baptized into o
1Co	12:26	And if o member suffers, all
1Co	15: 8	as by o born out of due
1Co	15:23	But each o in his own order:
2Co	2:16	To the o we are the aroma
2Co	3:16	Nevertheless when o turns to
2Co	5:14	that if O died for all, then
2Co	9: 7	So let each o give as he
2Co	11:24	forty stripes minus o.
Gal	3:11	But that no o is justified by
Gal	3:28	for you are all o in Christ
Gal	6: 1	spiritual restore such a o
Gal	6: 2	Bear o another's burdens, and
Eph	2:14	peace, who has made both o,
Eph	2:15	so as to create in Himself o
Eph	2:18	Him we both have access by o
Eph	4: 4	just as you were called in o
Eph	4: 5	o Lord, one faith, one
Eph	4: 6	o God and Father of all, who
Eph	4:32	And be kind to o another,
Eph	4:32	forgiving o another, just as
Eph	5:21	submitting to o another in
Eph	5:29	For no o ever hated his own
Eph	6:16	fiery darts of the wicked o.
Phil	2: 2	being of o accord, of one
Phil	3:13	but o thing I do,
Col	2:16	So let no o judge you in food
Col	3: 9	Do not lie to o another,

Col	3:13	bearing with o another, and
Col	3:13	and forgiving o another, if
Col	3:15	also you were called in o
Col	3:16	teaching and admonishing o
1Th	5:11	each other and edify o
1Th	5:15	See that no o renders evil
2Th	2: 8	And then the lawless o will
1Ti	2: 5	For there is o God and one
1Ti	3: 2	the husband of o wife,
1Ti	3: 4	o who rules his own house
1Ti	4:12	Let no o despise your youth,
Heb	6:13	He could swear by no o
Heb	10:14	For by o offering He has
Heb	10:25	but exhorting o another,
Heb	11:12	Therefore from o man, and him
Heb	12:14	without which no o will see
Jas	2:10	and yet stumble in o point,
1Pe	3: 8	all of you be of o mind,
2Pe	3: 8	and a thousand years as o
1Jn	1: 7	we have fellowship with o
1Jn	2:13	have overcome the wicked o.
1Jn	3:11	that we should love o
1Jn	4:12	No o has seen God at any
1Jn	5: 7	and these three are o.
1Jn	5: 8	and these three agree as o.
Rev	1:13	of the seven lampstands O
Rev	3: 7	and shuts and no o
Rev	7: 4	O hundred and forty-four
Rev	7: 9	a great multitude which no o
Rev	14:14	and on the cloud sat O like
Rev	16: 5	The O who is and who was
Rev	22:12	to give to every o according

ONESIMUS†

Col	4: 9	with O, a faithful and
Phm	1:10	I appeal to you for my son O,

ONESIPHORUS

2Ti	1:16	mercy to the household of O,

ONIONS†

Num	11: 5	the melons, the leeks, the o,

OPEN (see OPENED, OPENING, OPENLY, OPENS)

Ex	34:19	All that o the womb are
Ps	34:15	And His ears are o to
Ps	51:15	o my lips, And my mouth
Ps	118:19	O to me the gates of
Ps	119:18	O my eyes, that I may see
Is	22:22	shut, and no one shall o.
Is	42: 7	To o blind eyes, To bring
Dan	6:10	with his windows o toward
Amos	1:13	Because they ripped o the
Matt	25:11	'Lord, Lord, o to us!'
John	1:51	you shall see heaven o,
John	9:26	How did He o your eyes?"
Acts	16:27	seeing the prison doors o,
Rom	3:13	Their throat is an o
2Co	7: 2	O your hearts to us
Col	4: 3	that God would o to us a
Heb	4:13	all things are naked and o
Heb	6: 6	and put Him to an o shame.
1Pe	3:12	And His ears are o to

Rev	3: 8	I have set before you an o
Rev	5: 2	Who is worthy to o the scroll

OPENED (see OPEN)

Gen	3: 5	of it your eyes will be o,
Gen	7:11	the windows of heaven were o.
Gen	29:31	He o her womb; but Rachel
Num	16:32	and the earth o its mouth and
2Ki	4:35	and the child o his eyes.
Ps	40: 6	desire; My ears You have o.
Ps	106:17	The earth o up and swallowed
Is	35: 5	eyes of the blind shall be o,
Is	53: 7	Yet He o not His mouth; He
Ezek	1: 1	that the heavens were o and
Ezek	3: 2	So I o my mouth, and He
Ezek	37:13	when I have o your graves, O
Dan	7:10	And the books were o.
Matt	3:16	the heavens were o to Him,
Matt	5: 2	Then He o His mouth and
Matt	7: 7	and it will be o to you.
Matt	27:52	and the graves were o;
Mark	7:34	that is, "Be o.
Mark	7:35	Immediately his ears were o,
Luke	1:64	Immediately his mouth was o
Luke	4:17	and when He had o the book,
Luke	24:32	and while He o the
Luke	24:45	And He o their understanding,
John	9:14	Jesus made the clay and o
Acts	5:19	an angel of the Lord o the
Acts	7:56	Look! I see the heavens o and
Acts	8:32	So He o not His mouth.
Acts	8:35	Then Philip o his mouth, and
1Co	16: 9	and effective door has o to
Rev	6: 1	Now I saw when the Lamb o one
Rev	9: 2	And he o the bottomless pit,
Rev	19:11	Now I saw heaven o,
Rev	20:12	before God, and books were o.

OPENING (see OPEN)

Is	61: 1	And the o of the prison to

OPENLY (see OPEN)

Matt	6: 6	in secret will reward you o.

OPENS (see OPEN)

Ex	13: 2	whatever o the womb among
Num	16:30	and the earth o its mouth
Ps	146: 8	The LORD o the eyes of
Luke	2:23	Every male who o the
John	10: 3	"To him the doorkeeper o,
Rev	3: 7	shuts and no one o":
Rev	3:20	anyone hears My voice and o

OPHIR

1Ki	10:11	which brought gold from O,

OPINION (see OPINIONS)

Rom	11:25	should be wise in your own o,
Rom	12:16	Do not be wise in your own o.

OPINIONS† (see OPINION)

1Ki	18:21	you falter between two o?

O

OPPORTUNITY

Matt	26:16	from that time he sought **o**
Rom	7: 8	taking **o** by the commandment,
Gal	5:13	do not use liberty as an **o**
Gal	6:10	Therefore, as we have **o**,
Phil	4:10	did care, but you lacked **o**.
1Ti	5:14	give no **o** to the adversary

OPPRESS (see OPPRESSED, OPPRESSION, OPPRESSOR)

Ex	3: 9	with which the Egyptians **o**
Lev	25:14	you shall not **o** one another.
Ps	17: 9	From the wicked who **o** me,
Amos	4: 1	Who **o** the poor, Who crush
Zech	7:10	Do not **o** the widow or the
Acts	7: 6	them into bondage and **o**

OPPRESSED (see OPPRESS)

1Sa	12: 4	have not cheated us or **o** us,
Ps	9: 9	will be a refuge for the **o**,
Ps	10:18	to the fatherless and the **o**,
Ps	76: 9	To deliver all the **o** of the
Ps	103: 6	justice for all who are **o**.
Is	53: 7	He was **o** and He was
Is	58: 6	To let the **o** go free, And
Amos	3: 9	And the **o** within her.
Luke	4:18	liberty those who are **o**;
Acts	10:38	and healing all who were **o**

OPPRESSION (see OPPRESS)

Ex	3: 7	I have surely seen the **o** of
Ps	12: 5	For the **o** of the poor, for
Ps	42: 9	go mourning because of the **o**
Ps	55: 3	Because of the **o** of the
Ps	72:14	redeem their life from **o**
Is	5: 7	for justice, but behold, **o**;
Jer	6: 6	She is full of **o** in her
Acts	7:34	have surely seen the **o**

OPPRESSOR (see OPPRESS)

Ps	72: 4	will break in pieces the **o**.
Prov	3:31	Do not envy the **o**,
Is	1:17	Seek justice, Rebuke the **o**;
Is	9: 4	shoulder, The rod of his **o**,
Is	14: 4	How the **o** has ceased, The

ORACLE (see ORACLES)

Num	23: 7	And he took up his **o** and
Ps	36: 1	An **o** within my heart
Jer	23:33	What is the **o** of the LORD?'

ORACLES (see ORACLE)

Acts	7:38	who received the living **o**
Rom	3: 2	to them were committed the **o**
Heb	5:12	first principles of the **o**
1Pe	4:11	let him speak as the **o** of

ORDAIN† (see ORDAINED)

1Co	7:17	And so I **o** in all the

ORDAINED (see ORDAIN)

Ps	8: 3	the stars, which You have **o**,
Jer	1: 5	I **o** you a prophet to the

Acts	17:31	by the Man whom He has **o**.
1Co	2: 7	hidden wisdom which God **o**

ORDER (see ORDERED)

Gen	22: 9	and placed the wood in **o**;
2Ki	23: 4	the priests of the second **o**,
Ps	110: 4	forever According to the **o**
Is	9: 7	To **o** it and establish it
Luke	1: 1	taken in hand to set in **o** a
Luke	1: 8	priest before God in the **o**
1Co	14:40	be done decently and in **o**.
1Co	15:23	But each one in his own **o**:
Heb	5: 6	According to the **o** of

ORDERED (see ORDER)

Ps	37:23	steps of a good man are **o**

ORDINANCE (see ORDINANCES)

Ex	12:14	a feast by an everlasting **o**.

ORDINANCES (see ORDINANCE)

Luke	1: 6	all the commandments and **o**
Eph	2:15	commandments contained in **o**,

ORPAH

Ruth	1:14	and **O** kissed her

ORPHANS

John	14:18	"I will not leave you **o**;
Jas	1:27	to visit **o** and widows in

OTHNIEL

Judg	3: 9	**O** the son of Kenaz, Caleb's

OUTCRY

Gen	18:20	Because the **o** against Sodom

OUTRAN†

2Sa	18:23	and **o** the Cushite.
John	20: 4	and the other disciple **o**

OUTSTRETCHED

Ex	6: 6	I will redeem you with an **o**
Deut	5:15	by a mighty hand and by an **o**
Is	3:16	And walk with **o** necks And

OUTWARD (see OUTWARDLY)

1Sa	16: 7	for man looks at the **o**
2Co	4:16	Even though our **o** man is
2Co	10: 7	at things according to the **o**
1Pe	3: 3	your adornment be merely **o**—

OUTWARDLY (see OUTWARD)

Matt	23:27	indeed appear beautiful **o**,
Rom	2:28	is not a Jew who is one **o**,

OVEN

Gen	15:17	there appeared a smoking **o**
Hos	7: 4	Like an **o** heated by a
Mal	4: 1	coming, Burning like an **o**,
Matt	6:30	is thrown into the **o**,

OVERCAME† (see OVERCOME)

Rev	3:21	as I also o and sat down
Rev	12:11	And they o him by the blood

OVERCOME (see OVERCAME, OVERCOMES)

John	16:33	I have o the world."
Rom	3: 4	And may o when You
Rom	12:21	Do not be o by evil, but
1Jn	2:13	Because you have o the
1Jn	2:14	And you have o the wicked
1Jn	5: 4	is the victory that has o
Rev	17:14	and the Lamb will o them,

OVERCOMES (see OVERCOME)

1Jn	5: 4	whatever is born of God o
Rev	2: 7	To him who o I will give to

OVERLOOKED†

Acts	17:30	times of ignorance God o,

OVERLY

Eccl	7:16	Do not be o righteous, Nor

OVERSEER (see OVERSEERS)

1Pe	2:25	to the Shepherd and O of

OVERSEERS (see OVERSEER)

Acts	20:28	Holy Spirit has made you o,
1Pe	5: 2	is among you, serving as o,

OVERSHADOW†

Luke	1:35	power of the Highest will o

OVERTAKE (see OVERTAKEN)

Gen	19:19	lest some evil o me and I
Hos	2: 7	But not o them; Yes, she
Amos	9:13	When the plowman shall o the
Acts	8:29	Go near and o this chariot."
1Th	5: 4	so that this Day should o

OVERTAKEN (see OVERTAKE)

Ps	40:12	My iniquities have o me, so
1Co	10:13	No temptation has o you
Gal	6: 1	if a man is o in any

OVERTHREW (see OVERTHROW)

Gen	19:25	So He o those cities, all the
Ex	14:27	So the LORD o the Egyptians
Jer	50:40	As God o Sodom and Gomorrah

OVERTHROW (see OVERTHREW, OVERTHROWN)

Gen	19:29	out of the midst of the o,
Deut	29:23	like the o of Sodom and

OVERTHROWN (see OVERTHROW)

Jon	3: 4	and Nineveh shall be o!"

OVERTURNED

Matt	21:12	and o the tables of the
John	2:15	the changers' money and o

OVERWHELMED

Ps	142: 3	When my spirit was o within
Dan	10:16	vision my sorrows have o me,

OWE (see OWES)

Matt	18:28	Pay me what you o!'
Luke	16: 5	How much do you o my master?'
Rom	13: 8	O no one anything except to
Phm	1:19	to mention to you that you o

OWES† (see OWE)

Phm	1:18	if he has wronged you or o

OWN (see OWNER)

Gen	1:27	So God created man in His o
Gen	5: 3	and begot a son In his o
Gen	15: 4	who will come from your o
Josh	2:19	blood shall be on his o
Judg	7: 2	My o hand has saved me.'
Judg	17: 6	what was right in his o
Ruth	4: 6	lest I ruin my o
1Sa	13:14	Himself a man after His o
1Sa	18: 3	he loved him as his o soul.
2Sa	7:24	people Israel Your very o
Prov	3: 5	And lean not on your o
Prov	3: 7	Do not be wise in your o
Prov	5:15	running water from your o
Prov	12:15	of a fool is right in his o
Prov	26: 5	Lest he be wise in his o
Prov	31:31	And let her o works praise
Is	2: 8	That which their o fingers
Is	31: 7	which your o hands have made
Is	37:35	to save it For My o sake
Is	53: 6	to his o way; And the LORD
Is	59:16	Therefore His o arm brought
Is	66: 3	as they have chosen their o
Jer	1:16	the works of their o hands.
Jer	9:14	to the dictates of their o
Jer	31:30	one shall die for his o
Lam	4:10	women Have cooked their o
Ezek	13: 3	who follow their o spirit
Ezek	37:21	and bring them into their o
Dan	3:28	any god except their o God!
Dan	6:17	king sealed it with his o
Dan	9:19	act! Do not delay for Your o
Joel	3: 4	your retaliation upon your o
Jon	2: 8	idols Forsake their o
Matt	2:12	they departed for their o
Matt	6:34	for the day is its o
Matt	7: 3	the plank in your o eye?
Matt	8:22	let the dead bury their o
Matt	10:36	will be those of his o
Matt	16:26	and loses his o soul? Or
Matt	25:27	have received back my o
Matt	27:31	put His o clothes on Him,
Mark	6: 4	honor except in his o
Luke	2: 3	everyone to his o city.
Luke	2:35	will pierce through your o
Luke	6:44	every tree is known by its o
John	1:11	He came to His o,
John	1:41	He first found his o brother
John	4:44	has no honor in his o
John	5:30	because I do not seek My o

O

John	5:43	if another comes in his **o**
John	7:17	or whether I speak on My **o**
John	10: 3	and he calls his **o** sheep by
John	10:12	one who does not **o** the
John	11:51	this he did not say on his **o**
John	13: 1	having loved His **o** who were
John	19:27	disciple took her to his **o**
Acts	1: 7	the Father has put in His **o**
Acts	1:19	field is called in their **o**
Acts	1:25	that he might go to his **o**
Acts	2: 8	each in our **o** language in
Acts	5: 4	remained, was it not your **o**?
Acts	13:22	a man after My **o**
Acts	17:28	as also some of your **o** poets
Acts	20:28	He purchased with His **o**
Acts	28:30	two whole years in his **o**
Rom	4:19	he did not consider his **o**
Rom	5: 8	But God demonstrates His **o**
Rom	8: 3	God did by sending His **o**
Rom	8:32	He who did not spare His **o**
Rom	10: 3	seeking to establish their **o**
Rom	11:25	you should be wise in your **o**
Rom	16:18	but their **o** belly, and by
1Co	1:15	that I had baptized in my **o**
1Co	3: 8	reward according to his **o**
1Co	3:19	the wise in their **o**
1Co	4:12	working with our **o** hands.
1Co	6:18	sins against his **o** body.
1Co	6:19	God, and you are not your **o**?
1Co	7: 2	let each man have his **o**
1Co	7: 4	have authority over her **o**
1Co	10:33	not seeking my **o** profit, but
1Co	11:21	each one takes his **o** supper
1Co	13: 5	rudely, does not seek its **o**,
1Co	14:35	let them ask their **o**
1Co	15:23	But each one in his **o** order:
1Co	16:21	The salutation with my **o**
Gal	6: 4	let each one examine his **o**
Gal	6: 5	each one shall bear his **o**
Eph	5:22	submit to your **o** husbands,
Eph	5:28	ought to love their **o** wives
Eph	5:29	For no one ever hated his **o**
Phil	2: 4	look out not only for his **o**
Phil	2:12	work out your **o** salvation
1Th	4:11	to mind your **o** business, and
2Th	3:17	of Paul with my **o** hand,
1Ti	3: 5	not know how to rule his **o**
1Ti	5: 8	does not provide for his **o**,
Tit	2:14	purify for Himself His **o**
Heb	3: 6	Christ as a Son over His **o**
Heb	7:27	first for His **o** sins and
Heb	9:12	but with His **o** blood He
Jas	1:14	he is drawn away by his **o**
1Pe	2: 9	His **o** special people, that
1Pe	2:24	bore our sins in His **o** body
2Pe	2:22	dog returns to his **o**
2Pe	3:16	people twist to their **o**
Jude	6	but left their **o** abode, He
Rev	1: 5	us from our sins in His **o**

OWNER (see OWN)

Ex	21:28	but the **o** of the ox shall
Ex	22:12	make restitution to the **o**
Is	1: 3	The ox knows its **o** And the

Matt	13:27	So the servants of the **o** came
Matt	20: 8	the **o** of the vineyard said

OX (see OXEN)

Ex	20:17	female servant, nor his **o**,
Ex	21:28	If an **o** gores a man or a
Deut	25: 4	You shall not muzzle an **o**
Is	1: 3	The **o** knows its owner And
Is	11: 7	shall eat straw like the **o**.
Ezek	1:10	four had the face of an **o**
1Co	9: 9	shall not muzzle an **o**
1Ti	5:18	shall not muzzle an **o**

OXEN (see OX)

Gen	12:16	her sake. He had sheep, **o**,
1Sa	15:14	and the lowing of the **o**
2Sa	6: 6	for the **o** stumbled.
Ps	8: 7	All sheep and **o**—
Dan	4:25	make you eat grass like **o**.
Amos	6:12	one plow there with **o**?
John	2:14	the temple those who sold **o**

P

PAID (see PAY)

Matt	5:26	out of there till you have **p**
Heb	7: 9	**p** tithes through Abraham, so

PAIN (see PAINFUL, PAINS)

Gen	3:16	In **p** you shall bring forth
Jer	6:24	**P** as of a woman in labor.
Jer	15:18	Why is my **p** perpetual And
Rev	21: 4	There shall be no more **p**,

PAINFUL (see PAIN)

Job	2: 7	and struck Job with **p** boils
Heb	12:11	for the present, but **p**;

PAINS (see PAIN)

1Sa	4:19	for her labor **p** came upon
Ps	116: 3	The **p** of death surrounded
Acts	2:24	having loosed the **p** of

PAIR

Amos	2: 6	And the poor for a **p** of
Amos	8: 6	And the needy for a **p** of
Luke	2:24	A **p** of turtledoves or

PALACE (see PALACES)

Ps	45:13	all glorious within the **p**;
Dan	5: 5	of the wall of the king's **p**;

PALACES (see PALACE)

Ps	45: 8	cassia, Out of the ivory **p**,

PALM (see PALMS)

Ex	15:27	wells of water and seventy **p**
Deut	34: 3	the city of **p** trees, as far
Judg	4: 5	she would sit under the **p**
Neh	8:15	**p** branches, and branches of
Ps	92:12	shall flourish like a **p**
John	12:13	took branches of **p** trees and

| John | 18:22 | by struck Jesus with the **p** |
| Rev | 7: 9 | with **p** branches in their |

PALMS (see PALM)

Judg	1:16	went up from the City of **P**
Is	49:16	have inscribed you on the **p**
Matt	26:67	struck Him with the **p** of

PANELED

| Hag | 1: 4 | to dwell in your **p** houses, |

PANGS

Ps	18: 4	The **p** of death surrounded
Ps	116: 3	And the **p** of Sheol laid
Is	21: 3	like the **p** of a woman in
Jer	48:41	heart of a woman in birth **p**.
Mic	4: 9	For **p** have seized you like
Rom	8:22	and labors with birth **p**

PANTS

| Ps | 38:10 | My heart **p**, my strength |
| Ps | 42: 1 | As the deer **p** for the water |

PAPYRUS

| Is | 19: 7 | The **p** reeds by the River, by |

PARABLE (see PARABLES)

| Matt | 13:18 | Therefore hear the **p** of the |
| Mark | 4:13 | you not understand this **p**? |

PARABLES (see PARABLE)

Ezek	20:49	of me, 'Does he not speak **p**?
Matt	13:10	do You speak to them in **p**?
Mark	4: 2	taught them many things by **p**,
Luke	8:10	the rest it is given in **p**,

PARADISE†

Luke	23:43	you will be with Me in **P**.
2Co	12: 4	how he was caught up into **P**
Rev	2: 7	is in the midst of the **P** of

PARALYTIC (see PARALYZED)

| Matt | 9: 2 | they brought to Him a **p** |
| Mark | 2: 9 | is easier, to say to the **p**, |

PARALYZED (see PARALYTIC)

Matt	8: 6	servant is lying at home **p**,
John	5: 3	sick people, blind, lame, **p**,
Acts	8: 7	and many who were **p** and lame

PARCHMENTS†

| 2Ti | 4:13 | the books, especially the **p**. |

PARDON (see PARDONED, PARDONING)

Ex	34: 9	and **p** our iniquity and our
1Sa	15:25	please **p** my sin, and return
Neh	9:17	You are God, Ready to **p**,
Is	55: 7	For He will abundantly **p**.

PARDONED (see PARDON)

| Is | 40: 2 | That her iniquity is **p**; |

PARDONING† (see PARDON)

| Mic | 7:18 | **P** iniquity And passing |

PARENTS

Luke	2:41	His **p** went to Jerusalem
Luke	18:29	one who has left house or **p**
John	9: 2	sinned, this man or his **p**,
Rom	1:30	things, disobedient to **p**,
Eph	6: 1	obey your **p** in the Lord, for
2Ti	3: 2	disobedient to **p**,

PART (see PARTLY, PARTS, SHARE)

Ps	51: 6	And in the hidden **p** You
Luke	10:42	Mary has chosen that good **p**,
John	13: 8	you have no **p** with Me."
Acts	5: 3	Spirit and keep back **p** of
Rom	11:25	that blindness in **p** has
1Co	13: 9	in part and we prophesy in **p**.
1Co	13:10	then that which is in **p** will
1Co	13:12	to face. Now I know in **p**,
Eph	4:16	working by which every **p**
1Pe	4:14	On their **p** He is blasphemed,
Rev	22:19	God shall take away his **p**

PARTAKE (see PARTAKER)

| 1Co | 9:13 | who serve at the altar **p** of |
| 1Co | 10:17 | for we all **p** of that one |

PARTAKER (see PARTAKE, PARTAKERS)

| 1Pe | 5: 1 | and also a **p** of the glory |

PARTAKERS (see PARTAKER)

Eph	3: 6	and **p** of His promise in
Col	1:12	has qualified us to be **p** of
Heb	3: 1	**p** of the heavenly calling,
Heb	6: 4	and have become **p** of the
Heb	12:10	that we may be **p** of His
2Pe	1: 4	through these you may be **p**

PARTIALITY

Ex	23: 3	You shall not show **p** to a
Acts	10:34	perceive that God shows no **p**.
Rom	2:11	For there is no **p** with God.
1Ti	5:21	doing nothing with **p**.
Jas	2: 9	but if you show **p**,

PARTLY (see PART)

| Dan | 2:33 | feet partly of iron and **p** |
| Dan | 2:42 | shall be partly strong and **p** |

PARTS (see PART)

Ps	51: 6	desire truth in the inward **p**,
Ps	139: 9	dwell in the uttermost **p** of
Ps	139:13	For You formed my inward **p**;

PASS (see PASSED, PASSES)

Ex	12:13	I will **p** over you; and the
Ex	15:16	Till Your people **p** over, O
1Sa	16:10	made seven of his sons **p**
Ps	8: 8	the fish of the sea That **p**
Ps	37: 5	And He shall bring it to **p**.
Is	42: 9	former things have come to **p**,
Lam	1:12	all you who **p** by? Behold
Matt	5:18	till heaven and earth **p**
Matt	5:18	tittle will by no means **p**
Matt	26:39	let this cup **p** from Me;

P

Mark	14:35	the hour might **p** from Him.
Jas	1:10	of the field he will **p** away.
2Pe	3:10	in which the heavens will **p**

PASSED (see PASS)

Ex	12:27	who **p** over the houses of the
1Ki	19:11	the LORD **p** by, and a great
Ps	90: 9	For all our days have **p** away
Luke	10:31	he **p** by on the other side.
John	5:24	but has **p** from death into
2Co	5:17	old things have **p** away;
1Jn	3:14	We know that we have **p** from
Rev	21: 1	and the first earth had **p**
Rev	21: 4	for the former things have **p**

PASSES (see PASS)

Hos	13: 3	like the early dew that **p**
Eph	3:19	the love of Christ which **p**

PASSION (see PASSIONS)

1Co	7: 9	marry than to burn with **p**.

PASSIONS (see PASSION)

Rom	1:26	God gave them up to vile **p**.
Gal	5:24	the flesh with its **p** and

PASSOVER

Ex	12:11	haste. It is the LORD's **P**.
Ex	12:21	and kill the **P** lamb.
Ex	12:27	It is the **P** sacrifice of the
Ex	34:25	of the Feast of the **P** be
Josh	5:10	and kept the **P** on the
2Ki	23:22	Such a **P** surely had never
Matt	26:17	prepare for You to eat the **P**?
Mark	14:12	when they killed the **P**
Mark	14:14	in which I may eat the **P**
Luke	22:15	I have desired to eat this **P**
John	2:13	Now the **P** of the Jews was at
John	12: 1	Then, six days before the **P**,
John	19:14	the Preparation Day of the **P**,
1Co	5: 7	For indeed Christ, our **P**,
Heb	11:28	By faith he kept the **P** and

PAST

Job	9:10	He does great things **p**
Song	2:11	For lo, the winter is **p**,
Jer	8:20	"The harvest is **p**,
Amos	8: 5	will the New Moon be **p**,
Rom	11:33	His judgments and His ways **p**
1Co	7:36	if she is **p** the flower of
2Ti	2:18	resurrection is already **p**;
Heb	1: 1	ways spoke in time **p** to the
Heb	11:11	bore a child when she was **p**

PASTORS†

Eph	4:11	and some **p** and teachers,

PASTURE (see PASTURES)

Ps	95: 7	we are the people of His **p**,
Ps	100: 3	and the sheep of His **p**.
Jer	23: 1	scatter the sheep of My **p**!
Ezek	34:14	"I will feed them in good **p**,
John	10: 9	go in and out and find **p**.

PASTURES (see PASTURE)

Ps	23: 2	me to lie down in green **p**;

PATH (see PATHS)

Ps	1: 1	Nor stands in the **p** of
Ps	16:11	You will show me the **p** of
Ps	27:11	And lead me in a smooth **p**,
Ps	77:19	Your **p** in the great waters,
Ps	78:50	He made a **p** for His anger;
Ps	119:105	my feet And a light to my **p**.
Prov	2: 9	Equity and every good **p**.
Prov	4:18	But the **p** of the just is

PATHS (see PATH)

Ps	8: 8	That pass through the **p** of
Ps	23: 3	He leads me in the **p** of
Ps	25: 4	O LORD; Teach me Your **p**.
Prov	2: 8	He guards the **p** of justice,
Prov	2:18	And her **p** to the dead;
Prov	3: 6	And He shall direct your **p**.
Prov	3:17	And all her **p** are peace.
Is	2: 3	And we shall walk in His **p**.
Jer	6:16	see, And ask for the old **p**,
Matt	3: 3	Make His **p** straight.'
Heb	12:13	and make straight **p** for your

PATIENCE (see PATIENT)

Luke	21:19	By your **p** possess your souls.
Rom	15: 4	that we through the **p** and
Rom	15: 5	Now may the God of **p** and
2Co	6: 4	ministers of God: in much **p**,
Col	1:11	for all **p** and longsuffering
1Th	1: 3	and **p** of hope in our Lord
2Th	3: 5	love of God and into the **p**
1Ti	6:11	godliness, faith, love, **p**,
Heb	6:12	who through faith and **p**
Jas	1: 3	of your faith produces **p**.
Jas	1: 4	But let **p** have its perfect
Jas	5:10	example of suffering and **p**.
Rev	2: 2	works, your labor, your **p**,
Rev	14:12	Here is the **p** of the saints;

PATIENT (see PATIENCE, PATIENTLY)

Rom	2: 7	life to those who by **p**
Rom	12:12	**p** in tribulation, continuing
1Th	5:14	the weak, be **p** with all.
2Ti	2:24	to all, able to teach, **p**,
Jas	5: 7	Therefore be **p**, brethren,

PATIENTLY (see PATIENT)

Ps	37: 7	and wait **p** for Him; Do not
Ps	40: 1	I waited **p** for the LORD;
Heb	6:15	after he had **p** endured, he
Jas	5: 7	waiting **p** for it until it
1Pe	2:20	your faults, you take it **p**?

PATMOS†

Rev	1: 9	the island that is called **P**

PATRIARCH† (see PATRIARCHS)

Acts	2:29	speak freely to you of the **p**
Heb	7: 4	to whom even the **p** Abraham

PATRIARCHS (*see* PATRIARCH)

| Acts | 7: 8 | Jacob begot the twelve **p**. |

PATTERN

Ex	25: 9	the **p** of the tabernacle and
Ex	25:40	them according to the **p**
2Ti	1:13	Hold fast the **p** of sound
Heb	8: 5	according to the **p**

PAUL (*see* SAUL)

Acts	13: 9	Saul, who also is called **P**,
Acts	13:46	Then **P** and Barnabas grew bold
Acts	15:40	but **P** chose Silas and
Acts	19:15	and **P** I know; but who are
1Co	1:12	of you says, "I am of **P**,
1Co	1:13	Was **P** crucified for you? Or
1Co	1:13	baptized in the name of **P**?
1Co	3:22	whether **P** or Apollos or
2Pe	3:15	also our beloved brother **P**,

PAVEMENT

| John | 19:13 | place that is called The **P**, |

PAVILION

| Ps | 27: 5 | He shall hide me in His **p**; |

PAW

| 1Sa | 17:37 | who delivered me from the **p** |

PAY (*see* PAID)

Ex	22: 7	he shall **p** double.
Ps	22:25	I will **p** My vows before
Eccl	5: 4	**P** what you have vowed—
Jon	2: 9	I will **p** what I have vowed.
Matt	22:17	Is it lawful to **p** taxes to
Matt	23:23	hypocrites! For you **p** tithe

PEACE (*see* PEACEABLE, PEACEMAKERS)

Gen	15:15	go to your fathers in **p**;
Num	6:26	upon you, And give you **p**.
Num	25:12	give to him My covenant of **p**;
Judg	6:23	**P** be with you; do not fear,
Ps	4: 8	I will both lie down in **p**,
Ps	28: 3	Who speak **p** to their
Ps	29:11	will bless His people with **p**.
Ps	34:14	Seek **p** and pursue it.
Ps	85: 8	For He will speak **p** To His
Ps	85:10	Righteousness and **p** have
Ps	119:165	Great **p** have those who love
Ps	120: 7	I am for **p**; But when I
Ps	122: 6	Pray for the **p** of Jerusalem:
Ps	125: 5	**P** be upon Israel!
Prov	3:17	And all her paths are **p**.
Prov	16: 7	even his enemies to be at **p**
Eccl	3: 8	of war, And a time of **p**.
Is	9: 6	Father, Prince of **P**.
Is	9: 7	of His government and **p**
Is	26: 3	will keep him in perfect **p**,
Is	45: 7	I make **p** and create
Is	48:22	"There is no **p**," says the
Is	52: 7	good news, Who proclaims **p**,
Is	53: 5	The chastisement for our **p**
Is	54:10	Nor shall My covenant of **p**
Is	57:21	"There is no **p**," Says my
Is	59: 8	The way of **p** they have not
Jer	6:14	people slightly, Saying, '**P**,
Jer	6:14	**p**!' When there is no
Jer	29: 7	And seek the **p** of the city
Jer	29: 7	in its peace you will have **p**.
Ezek	34:25	will make a covenant of **p**
Nah	1:15	Who proclaims **p**! O Judah,
Matt	10:34	I did not come to bring **p**
Mark	4:39	and said to the sea, "**P**,
Luke	2:14	the highest, And on earth **p**,
Luke	19:38	name of the LORD!' **P**
Luke	19:42	that make for your **p**! But
John	14:27	**P** I leave with you, My peace
John	16:33	that in Me you may have **p**.
Acts	10:36	preaching **p** through Jesus
Rom	1: 7	Grace to you and **p** from God
Rom	3:17	And the way of **p** they
Rom	5: 1	we have **p** with God through
Rom	8: 6	minded is life and **p**.
Rom	10:15	preach the gospel of **p**,
Rom	14:19	things which make for **p**
Rom	15:33	Now the God of **p** be with you
Rom	16:20	And the God of **p** will crush
1Co	7:15	But God has called us to **p**.
1Co	14:33	of confusion but of **p**,
Gal	5:22	the Spirit is love, joy, **p**,
Gal	6:16	**p** and mercy be upon them,
Eph	2:14	For He Himself is our **p**,
Eph	2:15	the two, thus making **p**,
Eph	2:17	And He came and preached **p** to
Eph	4: 3	the Spirit in the bond of **p**.
Eph	6:15	of the gospel of **p**;
Phil	4: 7	and the **p** of God, which
Phil	4: 9	and the God of **p** will be
Col	1:20	having made **p** through the
Col	3:15	And let the **p** of God rule in
Heb	7: 2	Salem, meaning "king of **p**,
Heb	13:20	Now may the God of **p** who
Jas	2:16	says to them, "Depart in **p**,
1Pe	3:11	Let him seek **p** and
Rev	6: 4	one who sat on it to take **p**

PEACEABLE (*see* PEACE, PEACEABLY)

1Ti	2: 2	we may lead a quiet and **p**
Heb	12:11	afterward it yields the **p**
Jas	3:17	above is first pure, then **p**,

PEACEABLY (*see* PEACEABLE)

| Rom | 12:18 | live **p** with all men. |

PEACEMAKERS† (*see* PEACE)

| Matt | 5: 9 | Blessed are the **p**, |

PEARL† (*see* PEARLS)

| Matt | 13:46 | when he had found one **p** of |
| Rev | 21:21 | individual gate was of one **p**. |

PEARLS (*see* PEARL)

| Matt | 7: 6 | nor cast your **p** before |

PEDDLING†

| 2Co | 2:17 | **p** the word of God; but as of |

PEN

Ps	45: 1	My tongue is the **p** of a
Jer	8: 8	the false **p** of the scribe
3Jn	13	wish to write to you with **p**

PENIEL† (see PENUEL)

Gen	32:30	the name of the place **P**:

PENNY†

Matt	5:26	you have paid the last **p**.

PENTECOST†

Acts	2: 1	When the Day of **P** had fully
Acts	20:16	if possible, on the Day of **P**.
1Co	16: 8	tarry in Ephesus until **P**.

PENUEL (see PENIEL)

Gen	32:31	Just as he crossed over **P** the

PEOPLE (see MEN, PEOPLES)

Gen	11: 6	Indeed the **p** are one and
Gen	17:14	shall be cut off from his **p**;
Gen	25: 8	and was gathered to his **p**.
Gen	49:10	be the obedience of the **p**.
Ex	5: 1	Let My **p** go, that they may
Ex	15:24	And the **p** complained against
Ex	19: 5	treasure to Me above all **p**;
Ex	32: 9	it is a stiff-necked **p**!
Lev	26:12	God, and you shall be My **p**.
Deut	4:33	Did any **p** ever hear the
Deut	7: 6	For you are a holy **p** to the
Deut	7: 6	God has chosen you to be a **p**
Deut	7: 7	in number than any other **p**,
Judg	7: 4	The **p** are still too many;
Ruth	1: 6	the LORD had visited His **p**
Ruth	1:16	Your **p** shall be my
2Sa	3:18	I will save My **p** Israel from
2Sa	7: 8	sheep, to be ruler over My **p**,
2Sa	7:23	"And who is like Your **p**,
2Sa	7:23	to redeem for Himself as a **p**,
2Sa	7:24	Israel Your very own **p**
2Ch	7:14	if My **p** who are called by My
Neh	4: 6	for the **p** had a mind to
Neh	8: 5	all the **p** stood up.
Neh	8: 7	helped the **p** to understand
Neh	8: 9	For all the **p** wept, when
Job	12: 2	"No doubt you are the **p**,
Ps	2: 1	And the **p** plot a vain
Ps	9:11	His deeds among the **p**.
Ps	14: 4	Who eat up my **p** as they
Ps	14: 7	back the captivity of His **p**,
Ps	22: 6	men, and despised by the **p**.
Ps	29:11	will give strength to His **p**;
Ps	29:11	The LORD will bless His **p**
Ps	72: 2	He will judge Your **p** with
Ps	77:20	You led Your **p** like a flock
Ps	79:13	Your **p** and sheep of Your
Ps	85: 8	will speak peace To His **p**
Ps	95: 7	And we are the **p** of His
Ps	100: 3	We are His **p** and the
Ps	144:15	Happy are the **p** whose God
Prov	14:34	sin is a reproach to any **p**.
Prov	29:18	the **p** cast off restraint;

Prov	30:25	The ants are a **p** not
Is	1: 3	My **p** do not consider."
Is	1: 4	A **p** laden with iniquity, A
Is	6: 5	I dwell in the midst of a **p**
Is	6: 9	said, "Go, and tell this **p**:
Is	6:10	Make the heart of this **p**
Is	9: 2	The **p** who walked in darkness
Is	11:10	stand as a banner to the **p**;
Is	19:25	"Blessed is Egypt My **p**,
Is	40: 1	comfort My **p**!" Says your
Is	40: 7	Surely the **p** are grass.
Is	42: 6	You as a covenant to the **p**,
Is	49: 8	You As a covenant to the **p**,
Is	53: 8	the transgressions of My **p**
Is	55: 4	him as a witness to the **p**,
Is	55: 4	and commander for the **p**.
Is	62:10	Prepare the way for the **p**;
Is	65: 2	day long to a rebellious **p**,
Jer	7:16	do not pray for this **p**,
Jer	7:23	God, and you shall be My **p**.
Jer	31:33	God, and they shall be My **p**.
Jer	32:38	They shall be My **p**,
Jer	34: 8	a covenant with all the **p**
Jer	38: 4	seek the welfare of this **p**,
Lam	1: 1	city That was full of **p**!
Ezek	37:23	Then they shall be My **p**,
Hos	1: 9	For you are not My **p**,
Hos	2: 1	Say to your brethren, 'My **p**,
Hos	4: 6	My **p** are destroyed for lack
Hos	4: 9	And it shall be: like **p**,
Amos	7:15	prophesy to My **p** Israel.'
Matt	1:21	for He will save His **p** from
Matt	2: 6	Who will shepherd My **p**
Matt	4:16	The **p** who sat in
Matt	9:35	every disease among the **p**.
Matt	13:15	the hearts of this **p**
Matt	15: 8	These **p** draw near to Me
Mark	6:12	out and preached that **p**
Mark	7: 6	This **p** honors Me with
Mark	12:37	And the common **p** heard Him
Luke	1:17	to make ready a **p** prepared
Luke	1:25	away my reproach among **p**.
Luke	2:10	joy which will be to all **p**.
Luke	2:32	And the glory of Your **p**
Luke	3:21	When all the **p** were
Luke	9:13	and buy food for all these **p**.
Luke	23: 5	saying, "He stirs up the **p**,
Luke	23:35	And the **p** stood looking on.
John	7:31	And many of the **p** believed in
John	11:50	one man should die for the **p**,
John	12:29	Therefore the **p** who stood by
John	18:14	one man should die for the **p**.
Acts	2:47	having favor with all the **p**.
Acts	4:25	And the **p** plot vain
Acts	5:16	bringing sick **p** and those
Acts	5:26	for they feared the **p**,
Acts	5:37	and drew away many **p** after
Acts	6: 8	and signs among the **p**.
Acts	10: 2	alms generously to the **p**,
Acts	15:14	to take out of them a **p** for
Acts	18:10	for I have many **p** in this
Acts	21:39	permit me to speak to the **p**.
Acts	26:23	light to the Jewish **p** and
Acts	28:27	the hearts of this **p**

Rom	9:25	will call them My **p**,
Rom	10:21	and contrary **p**.
Rom	11: 1	has God cast away His **p**?
Rom	11: 2	God has not cast away His **p**
1Co	10: 7	The **p** sat down to eat
2Co	6:16	they shall be My **p**.
Tit	2:14	Himself His own special **p**,
Heb	2:17	for the sins of the **p**.
Heb	4: 9	therefore a rest for the **p**
Heb	8:10	and they shall be My **p**.
Heb	9:19	book itself and all the **p**,
Heb	10:30	LORD will judge His **p**.
Heb	11:25	affliction with the **p** of
Heb	13:12	that He might sanctify the **p**
1Pe	2: 9	nation, His own special **p**,
1Pe	2:10	a people but are now the **p**
2Pe	2: 5	Noah, one of eight **p**,
Rev	5: 9	tribe and tongue and **p** and
Rev	14: 6	nation, tribe, tongue, and **p**—

PEOPLES (*see* PEOPLE)

Gen	17:16	kings of **p** shall be from
Gen	25:23	Two **p** shall be separated
Deut	7: 6	treasure above all the **p** on
Deut	7: 7	you were the least of all **p**;
Deut	32: 8	set the boundaries of the **p**
1Ch	16: 8	known His deeds among the **p**!
Ps	7: 8	The LORD shall judge the **p**;
Ps	33:10	makes the plans of the **p** of
Ps	47: 1	all you **p**! Shout to God
Ps	49: 1	Hear this, all **p**;
Ps	65: 7	And the tumult of the **p**.
Ps	67: 3	Let the **p** praise You, O God;
Ps	67: 3	Let all the **p** praise You.
Ps	87: 6	When He registers the **p**:
Ps	96:13	And the **p** with His truth.
Ps	98: 9	And the **p** with equity.
Ps	99: 2	He is high above all the **p**.
Ps	105: 1	known His deeds among the **p**!
Is	12: 4	His deeds among the **p**,
Is	49:22	set up My standard for the **p**;
Is	51: 4	rest As a light of the **p**.
Is	62:10	Lift up a banner for the **p**!
Ezek	32:10	I will make many **p**
Dan	3: 4	you it is commanded, O **p**,
Dan	4: 1	the king, To all **p**,
Hos	7: 8	mixed himself among the **p**;
Mic	4: 1	And **p** shall flow to it.
Mic	4: 3	shall judge between many **p**,
Zeph	3: 9	I will restore to the **p** a
Zech	10: 9	will sow them among the **p**,
John	12:32	will draw all **p** to
Rev	7: 9	of all nations, tribes, **p**,
Rev	11: 9	Then those from the **p**,

PEOR

Num	23:28	took Balaam to the top of **P**,
Num	25: 3	was joined to Baal of **P**,

PERCEIVE (*see* PERCEIVED)

Deut	29: 4	not given you a heart to **p**
Prov	1: 2	To **p** the words of
Is	6: 9	on seeing, but do not **p**.
Matt	13:14	you will see and not **p**;

Luke	6:41	but do not **p** the plank in
John	4:19	I **p** that You are a prophet.
Acts	10:34	In truth I **p** that God shows
Acts	17:22	I **p** that in all things you

PERCEIVED (*see* PERCEIVE)

2Sa	12:19	David **p** that the child was
Luke	5:22	But when Jesus **p** their
Luke	8:46	for I **p** power going out from
Gal	2: 9	**p** the grace that had been

PERDITION

John	17:12	is lost except the son of **p**,
2Th	2: 3	is revealed, the son of **p**,
2Pe	3: 7	the day of judgment and **p**
Rev	17: 8	bottomless pit and go to **p**.

PERES† (*see* UPHARSIN)

Dan	5:28	"**P**: Your kingdom has

PEREZ

1Ch	4: 1	The sons of Judah were **P**,
Matt	1: 3	Judah begot **P** and Zerah by

PERFECT (*see* PERFECTED, PERFECTION)

Gen	6: 9	**p** in his generations. Noah
Deut	25:15	a **p** and just measure, that
Deut	32: 4	is the Rock, His work is **p**;
2Sa	22:33	And He makes my way **p**.
Ps	19: 7	The law of the LORD is **p**,
Ps	138: 8	The LORD will **p** that
Ps	139:22	I hate them with **p** hatred;
Prov	4:18	ever brighter unto the **p**
Is	26: 3	You will keep him in **p**
Ezek	27: 3	I am **p** in beauty.'
Ezek	28:12	Full of wisdom and **p** in
Matt	5:48	"Therefore you shall be **p**,
Matt	5:48	your Father in heaven is **p**.
Luke	1: 3	having had **p** understanding
John	17:23	that they may be made **p** in
Rom	12: 2	good and acceptable and **p**
1Co	13:10	But when that which is **p** has
2Co	12: 9	for My strength is made **p** in
Eph	4:13	to a **p** man, to the measure
Col	1:28	we may present every man **p**
Col	4:12	that you may stand **p** and
1Th	3:10	we may see your face and **p**
Heb	2:10	captain of their salvation **p**
Heb	7:19	for the law made nothing **p**;
Heb	12:23	spirits of just men made **p**,
Jas	1: 4	But let patience have its **p**
Jas	1:17	Every good gift and every **p**
Jas	1:25	But he who looks into the **p**
Jas	2:22	by works faith was made **p**?
Jas	3: 2	he is a **p** man, able also to
1Pe	5:10	you have suffered a while, **p**,
1Jn	4:18	but **p** love casts out fear,
Rev	3: 2	have not found your works **p**

PERFECTED (*see* PERFECT)

Matt	21:16	infants You have **p**
Luke	13:32	the third day I shall be **p**.
Phil	3:12	attained, or am already **p**;
Heb	7:28	the Son who has been **p**

Heb	10:14	For by one offering He has **p**
1Jn	2: 5	truly the love of God is **p**

PERFECTION (see PERFECT)

Col	3:14	love, which is the bond of **p**.
Heb	6: 1	of Christ, let us go on to **p**,
Heb	7:11	if **p** were through the

PERFORM

Deut	25: 5	and **p** the duty of a
Judg	16:25	that he may **p** for us." So
Is	9: 7	of the LORD of hosts will **p**
Rom	4:21	He was also able to **p**.

PERGAMOS

Rev	1:11	to Ephesus, to Smyrna, to **P**,

PERIL† (see PERILOUS)

Rom	8:35	famine, or nakedness, or **p**,

PERILOUS (see PERIL)

2Ti	3: 1	that in the last days **p**

PERISH (see PERISHABLE, PERISHED, PERISHES, PERISHING)

Gen	41:36	that the land may not **p**
Deut	4:26	that you will soon utterly **p**
Esth	4:16	against the law; and if I **p**,
Job	3: 3	May the day **p** on which I was
Job	3:11	Why did I not **p** when I
Job	4:20	They **p** forever, with no one
Job	34:15	All flesh would **p** together,
Ps	1: 6	way of the ungodly shall **p**.
Ps	2:12	And you **p** in the way,
Ps	37:20	But the wicked shall **p**;
Ps	41: 5	will he die, and his name **p**?
Ps	49:12	is like the beasts that **p**.
Ps	80:16	They **p** at the rebuke of
Ps	92: 9	behold, Your enemies shall **p**;
Ps	102:26	They will **p**, but You will
Is	31: 3	They all will **p** together.
Jer	18:18	for the law shall not **p** from
Ezek	7:26	But the law will **p** from the
Dan	2:18	his companions might not **p**
Jon	1: 6	us, so that we may not **p**.
Jon	1:14	please do not let us **p** for
Jon	3: 9	anger, so that we may not **p**?
Matt	5:29	that one of your members **p**,
Matt	18:14	these little ones should **p**.
Matt	26:52	who take the sword will **p**
Luke	13: 3	you will all likewise **p**.
Luke	15:17	and I **p** with hunger!
John	3:16	in Him should not **p** but
John	10:28	life, and they shall never **p**;
John	11:50	the whole nation should **p**.
Acts	8:20	Your money **p** with you,
Rom	2:12	without law will also **p**
1Co	8:11	shall the weak brother **p**,
Heb	1:11	They will **p**, but You

PERISHABLE† (see PERISH)

1Co	9:25	they do it to obtain a **p**

PERISHED (see PERISH)

Job	4: 7	who ever **p** being innocent?
Ps	9: 6	Even their memory has **p**.
Jer	49: 7	Has counsel **p** from the
Jon	4:10	came up in a night and **p** in
Mic	7: 2	The faithful man has **p** from
Luke	11:51	the blood of Zechariah who **p**
1Co	15:18	asleep in Christ have **p**.
2Pe	3: 6	world that then existed **p**,
Jude	11	and **p** in the rebellion of

PERISHES (see PERISH)

Is	57: 1	The righteous **p**,
John	6:27	labor for the food which **p**,
1Pe	1: 7	precious than gold that **p**,

PERISHING (see PERISH)

Prov	31: 6	strong drink to him who is **p**,
Matt	8:25	save us! We are **p**!"

PERMIT (see PERMITTED)

1Ti	2:12	And I do not **p** a woman to

PERMITTED (see PERMIT)

Deut	22:29	he shall not be **p** to divorce
Matt	19: 8	**p** you to divorce your wives,

PERPETUAL

Ex	30: 8	a **p** incense before the LORD
Jer	15:18	Why is my pain **p** And my

PERPLEXED

2Co	4: 8	yet not crushed; we are **p**,

PERSECUTE (see PERSECUTED, PERSECUTING, PERSECUTION)

Ps	31:15	And from those who **p** me.
Ps	119:86	They **p** me wrongfully; Help
Jer	17:18	Let them be ashamed who **p**
Dan	7:25	Shall **p** the saints of the
Matt	5:11	you when they revile and **p**
Matt	5:44	who spitefully use you and **p**
Matt	23:34	in your synagogues and **p**
Luke	11:49	of them they will kill and **p**,
John	15:20	they will also **p** you. If
Rom	12:14	Bless those who **p** you; bless

PERSECUTED (see PERSECUTE)

Ps	109:16	But **p** the poor and needy
Ps	143: 3	For the enemy has **p** my soul;
Matt	5:10	are those who are **p** for
Matt	5:12	for so they **p** the prophets
John	15:20	If they **p** Me, they will
Acts	22: 4	I **p** this Way to the death,
1Co	15: 9	because I **p** the church of
2Co	4: 9	**p**, but not forsaken;

PERSECUTING (see PERSECUTE)

Acts	9: 5	"I am Jesus, whom you are **p**.
Phil	3: 6	**p** the church; concerning the

PERSECUTION (see PERSECUTE,
  PERSECUTIONS)

Matt	13:21	For when tribulation or **p**
Acts	8: 1	At that time a great **p** arose
Acts	11:19	were scattered after the **p**
Rom	8:35	or distress, or **p**,
Gal	6:12	that they may not suffer **p**
2Ti	3:12	Christ Jesus will suffer **p**.

PERSECUTIONS (see PERSECUTION)

Mark	10:30	children and lands, with **p**—
2Ti	3:11	what **p** I endured. And out of

PERSEVERANCE

Rom	5: 3	that tribulation produces **p**;
2Co	12:12	among you with all **p**,
2Ti	3:10	longsuffering, love, **p**,
Jas	5:11	You have heard of the **p** of
2Pe	1: 6	to **p** godliness,

PERSIA (see ELAM, PERSIAN)

2Ch	36:22	year of Cyrus king of **P**,
Ezra	4: 7	to Artaxerxes king of **P**;
Ezra	4:24	reign of Darius king of **P**.
Esth	1: 3	the powers of **P** and Media,
Dan	10:13	prince of the kingdom of **P**
Dan	10:20	fight with the prince of **P**;

PERSIAN † (see ELAMITES, PERSIA, PERSIANS)

Neh	12:22	the reign of Darius the **P**,
Dan	6:28	in the reign of Cyrus the **P**.

PERSIANS (see PERSIAN)

Dan	5:28	and given to the Medes and **P**.
Dan	6: 8	the law of the Medes and **P**,

PERSISTENCE†

Luke	11: 8	yet because of his **p** he will

PERSON (see PERSONS)

Matt	27:24	of the blood of this just **P**.
Rom	14: 5	One **p** esteems one day above
Heb	1: 3	the express image of His **p**,
1Pe	3: 4	let it be the hidden **p**

PERSONS (see PERSON)

Luke	15: 7	over ninety-nine just **p** who
2Pe	3:11	what manner of **p** ought you

PERSUADE (see PERSUADED, PERSUASIVE)

Acts	26:28	You almost **p** me to become a
2Co	5:11	we **p** men; but we are well
Gal	1:10	For do I now **p** men, or God?

PERSUADED (see PERSUADE)

Luke	16:31	neither will they be **p**
Acts	18: 4	and **p** both Jews and Greeks.
Rom	8:38	For I am **p** that neither death
2Ti	1: 5	and I am **p** is in you also.
2Ti	1:12	I have believed and am **p**

PERSUASIVE (see PERSUADE)

1Co	2: 4	preaching were not with **p**

PERTAIN (see PERTAINING)

Rom	9: 4	to whom **p** the adoption, the
1Co	6: 3	things that **p** to this life?

PERTAINING (see PERTAIN)

Acts	1: 3	speaking of the things **p** to
1Co	6: 4	concerning things **p** to this
Heb	2:17	High Priest in things **p** to
Heb	5: 1	for men in things **p** to God,

PERVERSE (see PERVERT)

Deut	32: 5	A **p** and crooked generation.
1Sa	20:30	to him, "You son of a **p**,
Prov	4:24	And put **p** lips far from
Prov	10:31	But the **p** tongue will be
Prov	11:20	Those who are of a **p** heart
Is	19:14	The LORD has mingled a **p**
Matt	17:17	O faithless and **p** generation,
Phil	2:15	the midst of a crooked and **p**

PERVERT (see PERVERSE)

Ex	23: 2	turn aside after many to **p**
Job	8: 3	Or does the Almighty **p**
Amos	2: 7	And **p** the way of the
Gal	1: 7	trouble you and want to **p**

PESTILENCE (see PESTILENCES)

Ps	91: 3	And from the perilous **p**.
Ps	91: 6	Nor of the **p** that walks in
Jer	27: 8	sword, the famine, and the **p**,
Hab	3: 5	Before Him went **p**,

PESTILENCES (see PESTILENCE)

Matt	24: 7	And there will be famines, **p**,

PETER (see CEPHAS, SIMON)

Matt	4:18	two brothers, Simon called **P**,
Matt	26:69	Now **P** sat outside in the
Matt	26:75	And **P** remembered the word of
Mark	3:16	to whom He gave the name **P**;
Mark	8:33	His disciples, He rebuked **P**,
Mark	14:33	And He took **P**, James, and
Mark	14:67	And when she saw **P** warming
Mark	16: 7	go, tell His disciples—and **P**—
Luke	22:34	He said, "I tell you, **P**,
Luke	22:58	But **P** said, "Man, I am
Luke	22:61	Lord turned and looked at **P**.
Luke	22:62	So **P** went out and wept
John	1:44	the city of Andrew and **P**.
John	18:10	Then Simon **P**, having a
John	18:18	And **P** stood with them and
John	18:26	of him whose ear **P** cut
John	18:27	**P** then denied again; and
John	20: 4	the other disciple outran **P**
Acts	1:13	where they were staying: **P**,
Acts	1:15	And in those days **P** stood up
Acts	2:38	Then **P** said to them,
Acts	3: 1	Now **P** and John went up
Acts	3: 6	Then **P** said, "Silver and
Acts	4: 8	Then **P**, filled with the
Acts	4:13	they saw the boldness of **P**
Acts	5:29	But **P** and the other apostles
Acts	10: 5	for Simon whose surname is **P**.

P

Acts	10:13	voice came to him, "Rise, **P**;
Acts	10:14	But **P** said, "Not so, Lord!
Acts	10:25	As **P** was coming in, Cornelius
Acts	12: 6	that night **P** was sleeping,
Acts	12: 7	and he struck **P** on the side
Acts	12:13	And as **P** knocked at the door
Gal	1:18	up to Jerusalem to see **P**,
1Pe	1: 1	**P**, an apostle of Jesus
2Pe	1: 1	Simon **P**, a bondservant

PETITION (*see* PETITIONS)

1Sa	1:17	God of Israel grant your **p**
Esth	5: 7	My **p** and request is this:
Dan	6:13	but makes his **p** three times

PETITIONS (*see* PETITION)

Ps	20: 5	the LORD fulfill all your **p**.
Dan	6: 7	that whoever **p** any god or
1Jn	5:15	we know that we have the **p**

PHARAOH (*see* NECHO)

Gen	12:15	The princes of **P** also saw her
Gen	37:36	an officer of **P** and captain
Gen	41: 1	that **P** had a dream; and
Ex	1:11	And they built for **P** supply
Ex	6:11	tell **P** king of Egypt to let
Ex	7: 1	I have made you as God to **P**,
Ex	8:32	But **P** hardened his heart at
Ex	11: 5	from the firstborn of **P** who
Deut	6:21	We were slaves of **P** in Egypt,
Neh	9:10	signs and wonders against **P**,
Acts	7:10	wisdom in the presence of **P**,
Rom	9:17	For the Scripture says to **P**,

PHARISEE (*see* PHARISEES)

Matt	23:26	"Blind **P**, first cleanse the
Luke	11:37	a certain **P** asked Him to
Luke	18:10	one a **P** and the other a tax
Acts	5:34	a **P** named Gamaliel, a
Acts	23: 6	a Pharisee, the son of a **P**;
Acts	26: 5	of our religion I lived a **P**.
Phil	3: 5	concerning the law, a **P**;

PHARISEES (*see* PHARISEE)

Matt	5:20	of the scribes and **P**,
Matt	9:14	Why do we and the **P** fast
Matt	16: 1	Then the **P** and Sadducees
Matt	16: 6	of the leaven of the **P** and
Matt	16:12	but of the doctrine of the **P**
Matt	21:45	when the chief priests and **P**
Matt	22:15	Then the **P** went and plotted
Matt	23: 2	The scribes and the **P** sit in
Matt	23:14	"Woe to you, scribes and **P**,
Mark	2:18	of John and of the **P** fast,
Luke	5:30	And their scribes and the **P**
Luke	6: 7	So the scribes and **P** watched
Luke	7:30	But the **P** and lawyers
Luke	16:14	Now the **P**, who were
John	3: 1	There was a man of the **P**
John	7:45	to the chief priests and **P**
John	9:13	formerly was blind to the **P**.
John	11:47	the chief priests and the **P**
Acts	23: 7	arose between the **P** and the

PHILADELPHIA†

Rev	1:11	to Thyatira, to Sardis, to **P**,
Rev	3: 7	the angel of the church in **P**

PHILIP (*see* PHILIP'S)

Mark	3:18	Andrew, **P**, Bartholomew,
Luke	3: 1	his brother **P** tetrarch of
John	1:45	**P** found Nathanael and said to
John	12:22	**P** came and told Andrew, and
Acts	6: 5	and the Holy Spirit, and **P**,
Acts	8:26	angel of the Lord spoke to **P**,
Acts	8:29	Then the Spirit said to **P**,
Acts	21: 8	and entered the house of **P**

PHILIP'S (*see* PHILIP)

Matt	14: 3	his brother **P** wife.

PHILIPPI

Acts	16:12	and from there to **P**,
Phil	1: 1	in Christ Jesus who are in **P**,
1Th	2: 2	were spitefully treated at **P**,

PHILISTINE (*see* PHILISTINES)

1Sa	17:23	the **P** of Gath, Goliath by
1Sa	17:26	who is this uncircumcised **P**,

PHILISTINES (*see* PHILISTINE)

Gen	21:32	to the land of the **P**.
Gen	26: 1	to Abimelech king of the **P**,
Ex	13:17	by way of the land of the **P**,
Josh	13: 3	the five lords of the **P**—
Judg	16: 9	The **P** are upon you,
Judg	16:30	Let me die with the **P**!" And
1Sa	5: 1	Then the **P** took the ark of
1Sa	18:25	hundred foreskins of the **P**,
2Sa	8: 1	that David attacked the **P**

PHILOSOPHERS† (*see* PHILOSOPHY)

Acts	17:18	Epicurean and Stoic **p**

PHILOSOPHY† (*see* PHILOSOPHERS)

Col	2: 8	anyone cheat you through **p**

PHINEHAS

Josh	22:30	Now when **P** the priest and
1Sa	1: 3	sons of Eli, Hophni and **P**,

PHOEBE†

Rom	16: 1	I commend to you **P** our

PHYLACTERIES†

Matt	23: 5	They make their **p** broad and

PHYSICIAN (*see* PHYSICIANS)

Jer	8:22	Is there no **p** there? Why
Matt	9:12	are well have no need of a **p**,
Luke	4:23	say this proverb to Me, '**P**,
Col	4:14	Luke the beloved **p** and Demas

PHYSICIANS (*see* PHYSICIAN)

Gen	50: 2	his servants the **p** to
Job	13: 4	You are all worthless **p**.

Mark	5:26	many things from many **p**.
Luke	8:43	all her livelihood on **p** and

PIECE (*see* PIECES)

Matt	9:16	No one puts a **p** of unshrunk
Matt	17:27	you will find a **p** of money;
John	19:23	woven from the top in one **p**.

PIECES (*see* PIECE)

Gen	15:17	that passed between those **p**.
Gen	37:33	doubt Joseph is torn to **p**.
Ps	2: 9	You shall dash them to **p**
Dan	2:40	as iron breaks in **p** and
Dan	2:40	kingdom will break in **p**
Zech	11:12	out for my wages thirty **p**
Matt	26:15	counted out to him thirty **p**

PIERCE (*see* PIERCED, PIERCING)

Ex	21: 6	and his master shall **p** his
2Ki	18:21	will go into his hand and **p**
Job	41: 2	Or **p** his jaw with a hook?
Luke	2:35	a sword will **p** through your

PIERCED (*see* PIERCE)

Ps	22:16	They **p** My hands and My
Zech	12:10	will look on Me whom they **p**.
John	19:34	But one of the soldiers **p** His
John	19:37	on Him whom they **p**.
1Ti	6:10	and **p** themselves through
Rev	1: 7	even they who **p** Him. And all

PIERCING† (*see* PIERCE)

Heb	4:12	**p** even to the division of

PIGEON† (*see* PIGEONS)

Gen	15: 9	a turtledove, and a young **p**.
Lev	12: 6	and a young **p** or a

PIGEONS (*see* PIGEON)

Lev	5: 7	turtledoves or two young **p**,
Luke	2:24	or two young **p**.

PILATE

Matt	27: 2	delivered Him to Pontius **P**
Luke	3: 1	Pontius **P** being governor of
Luke	13: 1	the Galileans whose blood **P**
Luke	23:12	That very day **P** and Herod
John	18:33	Then **P** entered the Praetorium
1Ti	6:13	confession before Pontius **P**,

PILGRIMS

Heb	11:13	they were strangers and **p**

PILLAR (*see* PILLARS)

Gen	19:26	and she became a **p** of salt.
Gen	28:18	his head, set it up as a **p**,
Gen	31:52	and this **p** is a witness,
Ex	13:21	and by night in a **p** of fire
2Sa	18:18	had taken and set up a **p**
Jer	1:18	fortified city and an iron **p**,
1Ti	3:15	the **p** and ground of the

PILLARS (*see* PILLAR)

Ex	24: 4	and twelve **p** according to

Judg	16:26	Let me feel the **p** which
Job	26:11	The **p** of heaven tremble,
Prov	9: 1	has hewn out her seven **p**;
Joel	2:30	Blood and fire and **p** of
Gal	2: 9	and John, who seemed to be **p**,

PIM

1Sa	13:21	for a sharpening was a **p**

PINNACLE

Matt	4: 5	set Him on the **p** of the

PISGAH (*see* NEBO)

Deut	34: 1	Mount Nebo, to the top of P,

PIT

Gen	37:22	but cast him into this **p**
Ps	28: 1	those who go down to the **p**.
Ps	40: 2	me up out of a horrible **p**,
Ps	49: 9	And not see the P.
Ps	88: 6	have laid me in the lowest **p**,
Prov	23:27	For a harlot is a deep **p**,
Is	14:15	the lowest depths of the P.
Is	24:17	Fear and the **p** and the snare
Jer	48:43	Fear and the **p** and the snare
Ezek	28: 8	throw you down into the P,
Jon	2: 6	up my life from the **p**,
Matt	12:11	and if it falls into a **p** on
Rev	9:11	angel of the bottomless **p**,

PITCH

Gen	6:14	it inside and outside with **p**.
Ex	2: 3	daubed it with asphalt and **p**,

PITCHER (*see* PITCHERS)

Gen	24:15	came out with her **p** on her
Eccl	12: 6	Or the **p** shattered at the
Mark	14:13	will meet you carrying a **p**

PITCHERS (*see* PITCHER, VESSELS)

Judg	7:16	and torches inside the **p**.

PITIABLE† (*see* PITY)

1Co	15:19	we are of all men the most **p**.

PITIES (*see* PITY)

Ps	103:13	As a father **p** his children,

PITY (*see* PITIABLE, PITIES)

2Sa	12: 6	and because he had no **p**.
Jon	4:11	And should I not **p** Nineveh,
Matt	18:33	just as I had **p** on you?'

PLAGUE (*see* PLAGUES)

Ex	11: 1	will bring yet one more **p**
Lev	13:47	if a garment has a leprous **p**
Deut	28:61	every sickness and every **p**,
1Ch	21:14	So the LORD sent a **p** upon
Ps	91:10	Nor shall any **p** come near
Acts	24: 5	we have found this man a **p**,

PLAGUES (*see* PLAGUE)

Gen	12:17	and his house with great **p**
Hos	13:14	I will be your **p**! O Grave,

P

Rev	9:18	By these three **p** a third of
Rev	15: 1	having the seven last **p**,
Rev	22:18	God will add to him the **p**

PLAIN (see PLAINLY)

Gen	19:29	the cities of the **p**,
Ezek	8: 4	vision that I saw in the **p**.
Hab	2: 2	the vision And make it **p**

PLAINLY (see PLAIN)

Num	12: 8	him face to face, Even **p**,
Mark	7:35	was loosed, and he spoke **p**.
John	10:24	are the Christ, tell us **p**.

PLANS

Prov	6:18	heart that devises wicked **p**,
Prov	16: 9	A man's heart **p** his way,
Jer	18:18	Come and let us devise **p**

PLANT (see PLANTED)

Gen	2: 5	before any **p** of the field was
Eccl	3: 2	a time to die; A time to **p**,
Is	5: 7	of Judah are His pleasant **p**.
Is	53: 2	up before Him as a tender **p**,
Jer	1:10	down, To build and to **p**.
Jer	18: 9	to build and to **p** it,
Jon	4: 6	the LORD God prepared a **p**

PLANTED (see PLANT)

Gen	2: 8	The LORD God **p** a garden
Gen	9:20	and he **p** a vineyard.
Ps	1: 3	He shall be like a tree **P**
Ps	80:15	which Your right hand has **p**,
Ps	94: 9	He who **p** the ear, shall He
Eccl	3: 2	a time to pluck what is **p**;
Is	40:24	Scarcely shall they be **p**,
Jer	17: 8	he shall be like a tree **p**
1Co	3: 6	I **p**, Apollos watered, but

PLAY (see PLAYING)

Ex	32: 6	and drink, and rose up to **p**.
Ex	34:15	and they **p** the harlot with
1Sa	16:17	me now a man who can **p** well,
1Co	10: 7	and rose up to **p**.

PLAYING (see PLAY)

1Sa	16:18	who is skillful in **p**,

PLEAD

Ps	35: 1	**P** my cause, O LORD, with
Is	1:17	**P** for the widow.

PLEASANT (see PLEASANTNESS)

Gen	3: 6	that it was **p** to the eyes,
Ps	16: 6	lines have fallen to me in **p**
Ps	133: 1	how good and how **p** it is
Is	5: 7	the men of Judah are His **p**

PLEASANTNESS† (see PLEASANT)

Prov	3:17	Her ways are ways of **p**,

PLEASE (see PLEASED, PLEASES, PLEASING)

Prov	16: 7	When a man's ways **p** the
Is	55:11	it shall accomplish what I **p**,

Rom	8: 8	are in the flesh cannot **p**
Rom	15: 3	For even Christ did not **p**
1Co	7:32	how he may **p** the Lord.
1Co	7:33	how he may **p** his wife.
1Co	7:34	how she may **p** her husband.
Heb	11: 6	it is impossible to **p**

PLEASED (see PLEASE)

Is	53:10	Yet it **p** the LORD to
Mic	6: 7	Will the LORD be **p** with
Matt	3:17	Son, in whom I am well **p**.
1Co	1:21	it **p** God through the
Heb	11: 5	testimony, that he **p** God.
Heb	13:16	sacrifices God is well **p**.
2Pe	1:17	Son, in whom I am well **p**.

PLEASES (see PLEASE)

Ps	115: 3	He does whatever He **p**.
Ps	135: 6	Whatever the LORD **p** He
Song	2: 7	nor awaken love Until it **p**.

PLEASING (see PLEASE)

Acts	7:20	and was well **p** to God; and
Phil	4:18	sacrifice, well **p** to God.
Col	1:10	fully **p** Him, being fruitful
1Th	2: 4	not as **p** men, but God who
Heb	13:21	in you what is well **p** in

PLEASURE (see PLEASURES)

Ps	51:18	Do good in Your good **p** to
Ps	103:21	of His, who do His **p**.
Ps	147:11	The LORD takes **p** in those
Eccl	12: 1	I have no **p** in them":
Is	53:10	And the **p** of the LORD
Is	58:13	From doing your **p** on My
Luke	12:32	it is your Father's good **p**
2Co	12:10	Therefore I take **p** in
Eph	1: 5	according to the good **p** of
Phil	2:13	and to do for His good **p**.
1Ti	5: 6	But she who lives in **p** is
2Ti	3: 4	lovers of **p** rather than
Heb	10: 8	nor had **p** in them"
Heb	10:38	My soul has no **p** in
Jas	4: 1	from your desires for **p**

PLEASURES (see PLEASURE)

Ps	16:11	At Your right hand are **p**
Tit	3: 3	serving various lusts and **p**,
Heb	11:25	than to enjoy the passing **p**
Jas	4: 3	you may spend it on your **p**.

PLEDGE

Ex	22:26	neighbor's garment as a **p**,
Deut	24:17	a widow's garment as a **p**.
Prov	17:18	shakes hands in a **p**,
Amos	2: 8	altar on clothes taken in **p**,

PLENTIFUL (see PLENTY)

Gen	41:34	land of Egypt in the seven **p**
Matt	9:37	"The harvest truly is **p**,

PLENTY (see PLENTIFUL)

Gen	41:53	Then the seven years of **p**
Jer	44:17	For then we had **p** of food,

PLOT (*see* COUNSEL)
| Ps | 2: 1 | And the people **p** a vain |
| Acts | 4:25 | And the people **p** vain |

PLOW (*see* PLOWED, PLOWMAN, PLOWSHARES)
| Deut | 22:10 | You shall not **p** with an ox |
| Luke | 9:62 | having put his hand to the **p**, |

PLOWED (*see* PLOW)
Judg	14:18	If you had not **p** with my
Jer	26:18	Zion shall be **p** like a
Mic	3:12	of you Zion shall be **p**

PLOWMAN (*see* PLOW)
| Amos | 9:13 | When the **p** shall overtake the |

PLOWSHARES (*see* PLOW)
Is	2: 4	beat their swords into **p**,
Joel	3:10	Beat your **p** into swords And
Mic	4: 3	beat their swords into **p**,

PLUCK (*see* PLUCKED)
Deut	23:25	you may **p** the heads with
Eccl	3: 2	And a time to **p** what is
Jer	18: 7	to **p** up, to pull down, and
Matt	5:29	**p** it out and cast it from
Matt	12: 1	and began to **p** heads of

PLUCKED (*see* PLUCK)
| Gen | 8:11 | a freshly **p** olive leaf was |
| Luke | 6: 1 | And His disciples **p** the |

PLUMB
| Amos | 7: 7 | on a wall made with a **p** |
| Zech | 4:10 | seven rejoice to see The **p** |

PLUNDER (*see* PLUNDERED)
| Ex | 3:22 | So you shall **p** the |
| Matt | 12:29 | a strong man's house and **p** |

PLUNDERED (*see* PLUNDER)
| Ex | 12:36 | Thus they **p** the Egyptians. |

POETS†
| Acts | 17:28 | as also some of your own **p** |

POINT (*see* POINTS)
| Phil | 2: 8 | became obedient to the **p** |
| Jas | 2:10 | and yet stumble in one **p**, |

POINTS (*see* POINT)
| Prov | 6:13 | He **p** with his fingers; |
| Heb | 4:15 | but was in all **p** tempted as |

POISON
Ps	140: 3	The **p** of asps is under
Rom	3:13	The **p** of asps is under
Jas	3: 8	evil, full of deadly **p**.

POLLUTED
| Acts | 15:20 | to abstain from things **p** by |

POMEGRANATE (*see* POMEGRANATES)
| Ex | 28:34 | "a golden bell and a **p**, |

POMEGRANATES (*see* POMEGRANATE)
| Ex | 39:24 | on the hem of the robe **p** of |

PONDERED
| Luke | 2:19 | kept all these things and **p** |

POOL
2Ki	18:17	aqueduct from the upper **p**,
John	5: 7	no man to put me into the **p**
John	9: 7	wash in the **p** of Siloam"

POOR
Gen	41:19	**p** and very ugly and gaunt,
Deut	15: 4	when there may be no **p**
Deut	15:11	For the **p** will never cease
Ruth	3:10	whether **p** or rich.
2Sa	12: 4	but he took the **p** man's lamb
Job	5:16	So the **p** have hope, And
Job	24:10	They cause the **p** to go
Job	24:14	He kills the **p** and needy;
Job	29:16	I was a father to the **p**,
Job	34:28	caused the cry of the **p** to
Ps	34: 6	This **p** man cried out, and
Ps	40:17	But I am **p** and needy; Yet
Ps	82: 3	Defend the **p** and fatherless;
Ps	113: 7	He raises the **p** out of the
Ps	132:15	I will satisfy her **p** with
Prov	14:20	The **p** man is hated even by
Prov	14:31	He who oppresses the **p**
Prov	19:22	And a **p** man is better than
Prov	22: 9	gives of his bread to the **p**.
Prov	22:16	He who oppresses the **p** to
Prov	22:22	Do not rob the **p** because he
Prov	31:20	extends her hand to the **p**,
Is	3:15	grinding the faces of the **p**?
Is	41:17	The **p** and needy seek water,
Is	61: 1	preach good tidings to the **p**;
Amos	2: 6	And the **p** for a pair of
Amos	8: 6	That we may buy the **p** for
Matt	5: 3	Blessed are the **p** in spirit,
Matt	11: 5	are raised up and the **p**
Matt	19:21	you have and give to the **p**,
Matt	26:11	For you have the **p** with you
Mark	12:42	Then one **p** widow came and
Mark	14: 5	denarii and given to the **p**.
Luke	4:18	the gospel to the **p**;
Luke	6:20	"Blessed are you **p**,
Luke	14:13	give a feast, invite the **p**,
Luke	19: 8	half of my goods to the **p**;
Rom	15:26	contribution for the **p**
1Co	13: 3	all my goods to feed the **p**,
2Co	6:10	yet always rejoicing; as **p**,
2Co	8: 9	for your sakes He became **p**,
Jas	2: 2	should also come in a **p** man
Rev	3:17	are wretched, miserable, **p**,
Rev	13:16	small and great, rich and **p**,

PORCH (*see* PORCHES)
| John | 10:23 | the temple, in Solomon's **p**. |

PORCHES (*see* PORCH)

John	5: 2	Bethesda, having five **p.**

PORTION (*see* PORTIONS, SHARE)

Deut	21:17	by giving him a double **p** of
1Sa	1: 5	he would give a double **p,**
2Ki	2: 9	Please let a double **p** of your
Ps	16: 5	You are the **p** of my
Ps	119:57	You are my **p,** O LORD;
Is	53:12	I will divide Him a **p** with
Jer	10:16	The **P** of Jacob is not like
Luke	15:12	give me the **p** of goods that

PORTIONS (*see* PORTION)

Neh	8:10	and send **p** to those for whom

POSSESS (*see* POSSESSED, POSSESSES, POSSESSION, POSSESSOR)

Deut	4: 5	the land which you go to to **p.**
Josh	1:11	to go in to **p** the land which
Luke	18:12	give tithes of all that I **p.**

POSSESSED (*see* POSSESS)

Prov	8:22	The LORD **p** me at the
Acts	16:16	that a certain slave girl **p**

POSSESSES (*see* POSSESS)

Luke	12:15	abundance of the things he **p.**

POSSESSION (*see* POSSESS, POSSESSIONS)

Gen	17: 8	Canaan, as an everlasting **p;**
Gen	36:43	in the land of their **p.**
Ps	2: 8	of the earth for Your **p.**
Acts	7: 5	to give it to him for a **p,**
Eph	1:14	of the purchased **p,**

POSSESSIONS (*see* POSSESSION)

Gen	15:14	shall come out with great **p.**
Matt	19:22	for he had great **p.**
Luke	15:13	and there wasted his **p** with
Acts	2:45	and sold their **p** and goods,

POSSESSOR (*see* POSSESS)

Gen	14:19	**P** of heaven and earth;

POSSIBLE

Matt	19:26	with God all things are **p.**
Matt	24:24	and wonders to deceive, if **p,**
Matt	26:39	"O My Father, if it is **p,**
Mark	9:23	all things are **p** to him who
Luke	18:27	impossible with men are **p**
Rom	12:18	If it is **p,** as much as
Heb	10: 4	For it is not **p** that the

POT (*see* POTSHERD)

Ex	16:33	Take a **p** and put an omer of
Eccl	7: 6	of thorns under a **p,**
Jer	1:13	I said, "I see a boiling **p,**
Zech	14:21	every **p** in Jerusalem and
Heb	9: 4	in which were the golden **p**

POTENTATE†

1Ti	6:15	is the blessed and only **P,**

POTIPHAR

Gen	37:36	had sold him in Egypt to **P,**

POTSHERD (*see* POT)

Job	2: 8	And he took for himself a **p**

POTTER (*see* POTTER'S)

Is	29:16	turned around! Shall the **p**
Is	41:25	As the **p** treads clay.
Is	64: 8	are the clay, and You our **p;**
Jer	18: 4	marred in the hand of the **p;**
Zech	11:13	Throw it to the **p**"—that
Rom	9:21	Does not the **p** have power

POTTER'S (*see* POTTER)

Ps	2: 9	dash them to pieces like a **p**
Jer	18: 6	as the clay is in the **p**

POUR (*see* POURED)

Ex	29:12	and **p** all the blood beside
Lev	4:25	and **p** its blood at the base
Lev	17:13	he shall **p** out its blood and
Ps	42: 4	I **p** out my soul within me.
Ps	62: 8	**P** out your heart before
Is	44: 3	I will **p** My Spirit on your
Joel	2:28	afterward That I will **p**
Joel	2:29	My maidservants I will **p**
Mal	3:10	the windows of heaven And **p**

POURED (*see* POUR)

Gen	28:18	and **p** oil on top of it.
Lev	4:12	where the ashes are **p** out,
Lev	8:15	And he **p** the blood at the
Lev	21:10	the anointing oil was **p** and
1Sa	1:15	but have **p** out my soul
Ps	22:14	I am **p** out like water, And
Is	32:15	Until the Spirit is **p** upon
Is	53:12	Because He **p** out His soul
Jer	7:20	anger and My fury will be **p**
Matt	26: 7	and she **p** it on His head as
John	13: 5	He **p** water into a basin and
Phil	2:17	and if I am being **p** out as

POVERTY

Prov	6:11	So shall your **p** come on you
Prov	11:24	right, But it leads to **p.**
Prov	31: 7	him drink and forget his **p,**
Mark	12:44	but she out of her **p** put in
2Co	8: 2	their joy and their deep **p**
2Co	8: 9	that you through His **p** might
Rev	2: 9	and **p** (but you are rich);

POWDER

Ex	32:20	fire, and ground it to **p;**
Matt	21:44	it will grind him to **p.**

POWER (*see* POWERFUL, POWERS)

Ex	9:16	that I may show My **p** in
1Ch	29:11	The **p** and the glory, The
Ps	22:20	precious life from the **p**
Ps	49:15	redeem my soul from the **p**
Ps	65: 6	Being clothed with **p;**
Ps	90:11	Who knows the **p** of Your

Is	40:29	He gives **p** to the weak, And
Dan	2:37	has given you a kingdom, **p**,
Dan	4:30	dwelling by my mighty **p** and
Dan	6:27	delivered Daniel from the **p**
Nah	1: 3	slow to anger and great in **p**,
Zech	4: 6	'Not by might nor by **p**,
Matt	6:13	is the kingdom and the **p**
Matt	9: 6	that the Son of Man has **p**
Matt	9: 8	who had given such **p** to men.
Matt	24:30	the clouds of heaven with **p**
Matt	26:64	at the right hand of the **P**,
Luke	1:17	Him in the spirit and **p** of
Luke	1:35	and the **p** of the Highest
Luke	4:14	Jesus returned in the **p** of
Luke	6:19	for **p** went out from Him and
Luke	24:49	until you are endued with **p**
John	10:18	I have **p** to lay it down, and
John	19:11	You could have no **p** at all
Acts	1: 8	But you shall receive **p** when
Acts	4: 7	By what **p** or by what name
Acts	6: 8	Stephen, full of faith and **p**,
Acts	26:18	and from the **p** of Satan to
Rom	1: 4	be the Son of God with **p**
Rom	1:16	for it is the **p** of God to
Rom	1:20	even His eternal **p** and
Rom	9:22	His wrath and to make His **p**
1Co	1:18	are being saved it is the **p**
1Co	1:24	Christ the **p** of God and the
1Co	4:20	God is not in word but in **p**.
1Co	15:43	weakness, it is raised in **p**.
2Co	4: 7	the excellence of the **p** may
2Co	12: 9	that the **p** of Christ may
Eph	1:19	greatness of His **p** toward
Eph	1:19	the working of His mighty **p**
Eph	1:21	all principality and **p** and
Eph	2: 2	to the prince of the **p** of
Eph	3: 7	effective working of His **p**.
Phil	3:10	I may know Him and the **p** of
Col	1:11	according to His glorious **p**,
Col	2:10	of all principality and **p**.
1Th	1: 5	in word only, but also in **p**,
2Th	1: 9	and from the glory of His **p**,
2Ti	1: 7	but of **p** and of love and of
2Ti	3: 5	godliness but denying its **p**.
Heb	1: 3	things by the word of His **p**,
Heb	7:16	but according to the **p** of an
1Pe	1: 5	who are kept by the **p** of God
Jude	25	and majesty, Dominion and **p**,
Rev	4:11	glory and honor and **p**;
Rev	20: 6	the second death has no **p**,

POWERFUL (*see* POWER)

Ps	29: 4	voice of the LORD is **p**;
Heb	4:12	word of God is living and **p**,

POWERS (*see* POWER)

Rom	8:38	nor principalities nor **p**,
Eph	3:10	to the principalities and **p**
1Pe	3:22	angels and authorities and **p**

PRACTICE

Rom	1:32	that those who **p** such things

PRAISE (*see* PRAISED, PRAISES, PRAISING, THANK)

Ps	9: 1	I will **p** You, O LORD, with
Ps	33: 2	**P** the LORD with the harp
Ps	34: 1	His **p** shall continually
Ps	42: 5	for I shall yet **p** Him For
Ps	67: 3	Let the peoples **p** You, O
Ps	69:34	Let heaven and earth **p** Him,
Ps	100: 4	And into His courts with **p**.
Ps	104:33	I will sing **p** to my God
Ps	104:35	O my soul! **P** the LORD!
Ps	135: 1	**P** the LORD! Praise the
Ps	145: 4	One generation shall **p** Your
Ps	148: 1	**P** Him in the heights!
Ps	150: 1	Praise the LORD! **P** God in
Ps	150: 2	**P** Him for His mighty acts
Prov	31:31	And let her own works **p** her
Is	60:18	Salvation, And your gates **P**.
Matt	21:16	You have perfected **p**'?
John	12:43	for they loved the **p** of men
Rom	2:29	whose **p** is not from men but
Eph	1: 6	to the **p** of the glory of His
Phil	1:11	to the glory and **p** of God.
Heb	2:12	assembly I will sing **p**
Heb	13:15	offer the sacrifice of **p** to
1Pe	1: 7	by fire, may be found to **p**,
Rev	19: 5	**P** our God, all you His

PRAISED (*see* PRAISE)

1Ch	16:25	great and greatly to be **p**;
Ps	18: 3	who is worthy to be **p**;
Ps	48: 1	and greatly to be **p** In the
Prov	31:30	the LORD, she shall be **p**.
Dan	5: 4	and **p** the gods of gold and

PRAISES (*see* PRAISE)

Ps	9:11	Sing **p** to the LORD, who
Ps	22: 3	Enthroned in the **p** of
Ps	47: 6	Sing **p** to God, sing praises!

PRAISING (*see* PRAISE)

Luke	1:64	and he spoke, **p** God.
Luke	2:13	of the heavenly host **p** God
Luke	2:20	glorifying and **p** God for all

PRAY (*see* PRAYED, PRAYER, PRAYING)

Gen	20: 7	and he will **p** for you and
2Ch	7:14	and **p** and seek My face, and
Job	42: 8	and My servant Job shall **p**
Ps	55:17	and at noon I will **p**,
Ps	122: 6	**P** for the peace of Jerusalem
Jer	7:16	Therefore do not **p** for this
Matt	5:44	and **p** for those who
Matt	6: 5	For they love to **p** standing
Matt	6: 6	**p** to your Father who is in
Matt	6: 9	this manner, therefore, **p**:
Matt	9:38	Therefore **p** the Lord of the
Matt	14:23	the mountain by Himself to **p**.
Matt	26:41	"Watch and **p**, lest you
Luke	11: 1	Him, "Lord, teach us to **p**,
John	14:16	And I will **p** the Father, and
John	17: 9	I **p** for them. I do not pray
John	17:20	I do not **p** for these alone,

P

Rom	8:26	do not know what we should **p**
1Co	11:13	it proper for a woman to **p**
1Co	14:13	him who speaks in a tongue **p**
1Co	14:14	For if I **p** in a tongue, my
1Co	14:15	I will **p** with the spirit,
Col	1: 9	do not cease to **p** for you,
1Th	5:17	**p** without ceasing,
1Th	5:25	Brethren, **p** for us.
Jas	5:13	you suffering? Let him **p**.
Jas	5:14	and let them **p** over him,

PRAYED (*see* PRAY)

Gen	20:17	So Abraham **p** to God; and God
Mark	14:35	and **p** that if it were
Luke	22:41	and He knelt down and **p**,
Acts	4:31	And when they had **p**,
Jas	5:17	and he **p** earnestly that it
Jas	5:18	And he **p** again, and the

PRAYER (*see* PRAY, PRAYERS)

Ps	4: 1	mercy on me, and hear my **p**.
Ps	17: 1	Give ear to my **p** which is
Ps	39:12	"Hear my **p**, O LORD, And
Ps	42: 8	A **p** to the God of my life.
Is	56: 7	be called a house of **p** for
Dan	9:17	hear the **p** of Your servant,
Hab	3: 1	A **p** of Habakkuk the prophet,
Matt	17:21	does not go out except by **p**
Matt	21:13	be called a house of **p**,
Matt	21:22	whatever things you ask in **p**,
Acts	1:14	with one accord in **p** and
Acts	3: 1	the temple at the hour of **p**,
Rom	10: 1	my heart's desire and **p** to
Rom	12:12	continuing steadfastly in **p**;
1Co	7: 5	yourselves to fasting and **p**;
Eph	6:18	praying always with all **p** and
Phil	1: 4	always in every **p** of mine
Phil	4: 6	but in everything by **p** and
1Ti	4: 5	by the word of God and **p**.
Jas	5:15	And the **p** of faith will save
Jas	5:16	fervent **p** of a righteous man

PRAYERS (*see* PRAYER)

Ps	72:20	The **p** of David the son of
Matt	23:14	for a pretense make long **p**.
Luke	20:47	for a pretense make long **p**.
Acts	2:42	breaking of bread, and in **p**.
Acts	10: 4	Your **p** and your alms have
Rom	1: 9	of you always in my **p**,
2Ti	1: 3	I remember you in my **p**
Heb	5: 7	when He had offered up **p** and
1Pe	3: 7	that your **p** may not be
Rev	5: 8	which are the **p** of the

PRAYING (*see* PRAY)

Dan	6:11	and found Daniel **p** and
Mark	11:25	"And whenever you stand **p**,
Eph	6:18	**p** always with all prayer and
Col	1: 3	**p** always for you,
Jude	20	**p** in the Holy Spirit,

PREACH (*see* PREACHED, PREACHER,
  PREACHES, PREACHING, PROCLAIM)

Is	61: 1	LORD has anointed Me To **p**

Matt	4:17	that time Jesus began to **p**
Matt	10:27	**p** on the housetops.
Mark	3:14	He might send them out to **p**,
Mark	16:15	into all the world and **p**
Acts	15:21	generations those who **p** him
Rom	1:15	I am ready to **p** the gospel
Rom	10: 8	word of faith which we **p**):
Rom	10:15	And how shall they **p** unless
Rom	15:20	I have made it my aim to **p**
1Co	1:17	but to **p** the gospel, not
1Co	1:23	but we **p** Christ crucified, to
1Co	9:14	commanded that those who **p**
1Co	9:16	woe is me if I do not **p** the
2Co	4: 5	For we do not **p** ourselves,
Gal	1: 8	**p** any other gospel to you
Phil	1:15	Some indeed **p** Christ even
Col	1:28	Him we **p**, warning every
2Ti	4: 2	**P** the word! Be ready in

PREACHED (*see* PREACH)

Matt	11: 5	the poor have the gospel **p**
Matt	24:14	of the kingdom will be **p** in
Mark	13:10	the gospel must first be **p**
Mark	14: 9	wherever this gospel is **p** in
Acts	8:35	**p** Jesus to him.
Acts	10:37	the baptism which John **p**:
1Co	9:27	when I have **p** to others, I
1Co	15:12	Now if Christ is **p** that He
Gal	3: 8	**p** the gospel to Abraham
Eph	2:17	And He came and **p** peace to
Phil	1:18	or in truth, Christ is **p**;
Heb	4: 2	For indeed the gospel was **p**
1Pe	3:19	by whom also He went and **p** to

PREACHER (*see* PREACH)

Eccl	1: 2	of vanities," says the **P**;
Rom	10:14	shall they hear without a **p**?
1Ti	2: 7	which I was appointed a **p**
2Pe	2: 5	a **p** of righteousness,

PREACHES† (*see* PREACH)

2Co	11: 4	For if he who comes **p** another
Gal	1: 9	if anyone **p** any other gospel

PREACHING (*see* PREACH)

Matt	3: 1	John the Baptist came **p** in
Matt	4:23	**p** the gospel of the kingdom,
Matt	12:41	they repented at the **p** of
Luke	9: 6	**p** the gospel and healing
Acts	10:36	**p** peace through Jesus
Acts	11:20	**p** the Lord Jesus.
1Co	2: 4	And my speech and my **p** were
1Co	15:14	then our **p** is empty and

PRECEPT

Is	28:10	precept must be upon **p**,

PRECIOUS

Ps	22:20	My **p** life from the power
Ps	36: 7	How **p** is Your
Ps	116:15	**P** in the sight of the LORD
Ps	133: 2	It is like the **p** oil upon
Ps	139:17	How **p** also are Your thoughts
Prov	3:15	She is more **p** than rubies,

1Co	3:12	**p** stones, wood, hay, straw,
1Pe	1: 7	being much more **p** than gold
1Pe	1:19	but with the **p** blood of
1Pe	2: 6	cornerstone, elect, **p**,
1Pe	3: 4	which is very **p** in the sight
2Pe	1: 4	us exceedingly great and **p**

PREDESTINED

Rom	8:29	He also **p** to be conformed
Eph	1: 5	having **p** us to adoption as

PREEMINENCE

Col	1:18	all things He may have the **p**.

PREPARATION (*see* PREPARE)

Matt	27:62	which followed the Day of **P**,
Eph	6:15	shod your feet with the **p**

PREPARE (*see* PREPARATION, PREPARED)

Is	40: 3	**P** the way of the LORD; Make
Amos	4:12	**P** to meet your God, O
Mal	3: 1	And he will **p** the way
Matt	3: 3	**P** the way of the LORD;
Matt	26:17	Where do You want us to **p** for
John	14: 2	I go to **p** a place for you.

PREPARED (*see* PREPARE)

Neh	8:10	those for whom nothing is **p**;
Ps	31:19	Which You have **p** for those
Jon	1:17	Now the LORD had **p** a great
Jon	4: 6	And the LORD God **p** a plant
Jon	4: 7	dawned the next day God **p** a
Jon	4: 8	that God **p** a vehement east
Matt	25:34	inherit the kingdom **p** for
Matt	25:41	into the everlasting fire **p**
Matt	26:19	and they **p** the Passover.
Luke	1:17	to make ready a people **p** for
Rom	9:23	which He had **p** beforehand
1Co	2: 9	things which God has **p**
Eph	2:10	which God **p** beforehand that
2Ti	2:21	**p** for every good work.
Heb	10: 5	a body You have **p** for
Heb	11: 7	**p** an ark for the saving of
Rev	21: 2	**p** as a bride adorned for her

PRESENCE (*see* PRESENT)

Gen	3: 8	hid themselves from the **p**
Ex	33:14	My **P** will go with you, and
Ps	16:11	In Your **p** is fullness of
Ps	23: 5	a table before me in the **p**
Ps	51:11	not cast me away from Your **p**,
Ps	100: 2	Come before His **p** with
Ps	116:14	to the LORD Now in the **p**
Ps	139: 7	where can I flee from Your **p**?
Is	63: 9	And the Angel of His **P**
Phil	2:12	not as in my **p** only, but now
2Th	1: 9	destruction from the **p** of
1Ti	6:12	good confession in the **p** of
Heb	6:19	and which enters the **P**
Jude	24	faultless Before the **p** of

PRESENT (*see* PRESENCE)

Ps	46: 1	A very **p** help in trouble.
Luke	2:22	Him to Jerusalem to **p** Him

Rom	6:13	And do not **p** your members as
Rom	8:18	the sufferings of this **p**
Rom	8:38	nor things **p** nor things to
Rom	12: 1	that you **p** your bodies a
1Co	5: 3	as absent in body but **p** in
1Co	15: 6	greater part remain to the **p**,
2Co	5: 8	from the body and to be **p**
2Co	5: 9	whether **p** or absent, to be
Gal	1: 4	deliver us from this **p** evil
Eph	5:27	that He might **p** her to
Col	1:22	to **p** you holy, and
Col	1:28	that we may **p** every man
2Ti	4:10	having loved this **p** world,
Tit	2:12	and godly in the **p** age,
Heb	12:11	seems to be joyful for the **p**,
Jude	24	And to **p** you faultless

PRESERVE (*see* PRESERVED)

Ps	16: 1	**P** me, O God, for in You I
Ps	32: 7	You shall **p** me from
Ps	64: 1	**P** my life from fear of the
Ps	121: 7	He shall **p** your soul.
Ps	121: 8	The LORD shall **p** your going
Luke	17:33	loses his life will **p** it.

PRESERVED (*see* PRESERVE)

1Th	5:23	and body be **p** blameless at

PRESS (*see* PRESSED)

Phil	3:12	but I **p** on, that I may lay
Phil	3:14	I **p** toward the goal for the

PRESSED (*see* PRESS)

Mark	3:10	as many as had afflictions **p**
Luke	6:38	**p** down, shaken together, and
2Co	4: 8	We are hard **p** on every

PRESUMPTUOUS

Ps	19:13	Your servant also from **p**

PREVAIL (*see* PREVAILED)

Is	7: 1	but could not **p** against it.
Matt	16:18	gates of Hades shall not **p**

PREVAILED (*see* PREVAIL)

Gen	7:24	And the waters **p** on the earth
Gen	32:28	God and with men, and have **p**.
Hos	12: 4	with the Angel and **p**;

PRICE

Is	55: 1	Without money and without **p**.
Matt	13:46	found one pearl of great **p**,
Acts	5: 3	keep back part of the **p** of
1Co	6:20	For you were bought at a **p**;
1Co	7:23	You were bought at a **p**;

PRIDE (*see* PROUD)

Prov	16:18	**P** goes before destruction,
1Ti	3: 6	lest being puffed up with **p**
1Jn	2:16	and the **p** of life—is not of

PRIEST (*see* PRIESTHOOD, PRIESTS)

Gen	14:18	he was the **p** of God Most
Ex	18: 1	the **p** of Midian, Moses'

P

Ex	31:10	garments for Aaron the **p**
Num	5:17	The **p** shall take holy water
Num	35:28	the death of the high **p**.
Judg	17:13	since I have a Levite as **p**!
1Sa	2:35	up for Myself a faithful **p**
Ezra	7:11	Artaxerxes gave Ezra the **p**,
Ezra	10:10	Then Ezra the **p** stood up and
Neh	8: 2	So Ezra the **p** brought the Law
Neh	8: 9	Ezra the **p** and scribe, and
Ps	110: 4	You are a **p** forever
Jer	23:11	For both prophet and **p** are
Ezek	1: 3	expressly to Ezekiel the **p**,
Ezek	7:26	law will perish from the **p**,
Hos	4: 9	be: like people, like **p**.
Matt	8: 4	way, show yourself to the **p**,
Matt	26:51	the servant of the high **p**,
Matt	26:57	away to Caiaphas the high **p**,
Mark	2:26	days of Abiathar the high **p**,
Luke	1: 5	a certain **p** named Zacharias,
Luke	10:31	Now by chance a certain **p**
John	11:49	being high **p** that year, said
Acts	4: 6	as well as Annas the high **p**,
Acts	14:13	Then the **p** of Zeus, whose
Acts	23: 4	"Do you revile God's high **p**?
Heb	2:17	and faithful High **P** in
Heb	3: 1	the Apostle and High **P** of
Heb	4:14	that we have a great High **P**
Heb	5: 6	You are a **p** forever
Heb	7: 1	**p** of the Most High God, who
Heb	7: 3	remains a **p** continually.
Heb	7:20	as He was not made **p**
Heb	8: 1	We have such a High **P**,
Heb	9: 7	the second part the high **p**
Heb	9:11	But Christ came as High **P**
Heb	9:25	as the high **p** enters the

PRIESTHOOD (see PRIEST)

Num	25:13	covenant of an everlasting **p**,
Heb	7:12	For the **p** being changed, of
Heb	7:24	has an unchangeable **p**.
1Pe	2: 5	a spiritual house, a holy **p**,
1Pe	2: 9	chosen generation, a royal **p**,

PRIESTS (see PRIEST)

Ex	19: 6	be to Me a kingdom of **p** and
Is	61: 6	you shall be named the **p** of
Matt	16:21	from the elders and chief **p**
Matt	20:18	be betrayed to the chief **p**
Matt	26: 3	Then the chief **p**,
Matt	27: 3	of silver to the chief **p**
Mark	2:26	to eat, except for the **p**,
Mark	15: 3	And the chief **p** accused Him
Luke	6: 4	lawful for any but the **p** to
Luke	17:14	show yourselves to the **p**.
Luke	23: 4	Pilate said to the chief **p**
Acts	9:21	them bound to the chief **p**?
Acts	26:10	authority from the chief **p**;
Rev	1: 6	and has made us kings and **p**
Rev	5:10	have made us kings and **p** to

PRINCE (see PRINCES)

Gen	23: 6	You are a mighty **p** among
Ex	2:14	Who made you a **p** and a judge
Ezra	1: 8	out to Sheshbazzar the **p** of

Is	9: 6	Father, **P** of Peace.
Ezek	28: 2	say to the **p** of Tyre, 'Thus
Ezek	38: 2	the **p** of Rosh, Meshech, and
Dan	8:11	himself as high as the **P**
Dan	8:25	even rise against the **P** of
Dan	9:25	Until Messiah the **P**,
Dan	9:26	And the people of the **p** who
Dan	10:20	return to fight with the **p**
Dan	10:20	indeed the **p** of Greece will
Dan	10:21	these, except Michael your **p**.
Dan	11:22	and also the **p** of the
Hos	3: 4	many days without king or **p**,
Acts	3:15	and killed the **P** of life,
Acts	5:31	to His right hand to be **P**
Eph	2: 2	according to the **p** of the

PRINCES (see PRINCE)

Gen	12:15	The **p** of Pharaoh also saw her
Gen	17:20	He shall beget twelve **p**,
Judg	5: 3	O **p**! I, even I, will sing
1Sa	18:30	Then the **p** of the Philistines
Job	12:21	He pours contempt on **p**,
Ps	45:16	Whom You shall make **p** in
Ps	105:22	To bind his **p** at his
Ps	107:40	He pours contempt on **p**,
Ps	113: 8	He may seat him with **p**—
Ps	118: 9	Than to put confidence in **p**.
Ps	146: 3	Do not put your trust in **p**,
Ps	148:11	**P** and all judges of the
Prov	8:16	By me **p** rule, and nobles,
Is	1:23	Your **p** are rebellious, And
Jer	1:18	of Judah, Against its **p**,
Jer	48: 7	His priests and his **p**
Lam	5:12	**P** were hung up by their
Dan	8:25	rise against the Prince of **p**;
Dan	10:13	Michael, one of the chief **p**,
Hos	7: 3	And **p** with their lies.
Hos	8: 4	but not by Me; They made **p**,
Hos	9:15	All their **p** are
Zeph	3: 3	Her **p** in her midst are

PRINCIPALITIES (see PRINCIPALITY)

Rom	8:38	nor angels nor **p** nor powers,
Eph	6:12	and blood, but against **p**,
Col	2:15	Having disarmed **p** and powers,

PRINCIPALITY (see PRINCIPALITIES)

Eph	1:21	far above all **p** and power and

PRINCIPLES†

Col	2: 8	according to the basic **p** of
Col	2:20	Christ from the basic **p** of
Heb	5:12	teach you again the first **p**
Heb	6: 1	of the elementary **p** of

PRISCILLA

Acts	18: 2	from Italy with his wife **P**
Rom	16: 3	Greet **P** and Aquila, my

PRISON (see PRISONER)

Gen	39:20	him and put him into the **p**,
Judg	16:21	he became a grinder in the **p**.
Is	53: 8	He was taken from **p** and from
Is	61: 1	And the opening of the **p** to

Matt	4:12	that John had been put in **p**,
Matt	14:10	and had John beheaded in **p**.
Matt	25:36	I was in **p** and you came to
Luke	12:58	the officer throw you into **p**.
Acts	12: 5	was therefore kept in **p**,
Acts	16:27	And the keeper of the **p**,
1Pe	3:19	preached to the spirits in **p**,

PRISONER (see PRISON, PRISONERS)

2Ti	1: 8	of our Lord, nor of me His **p**,
Phm	1: 1	a **p** of Christ Jesus, and
Phm	1:23	my fellow **p** in Christ Jesus,

PRISONERS (see PRISONER)

Gen	39:20	a place where the king's **p**
Is	42: 7	To bring out **p** from the

PRIVATE (see PRIVATELY)

2Pe	1:20	of Scripture is of any **p**

PRIVATELY (see PRIVATE)

Matt	17:19	disciples came to Jesus **p**

PRIZE

1Co	9:24	run, but one receives the **p**?
Phil	3:14	toward the goal for the **p**

PROCEED (see PROCEEDED, PROCEEDS)

Is	51: 4	For law will **p** from Me,
Matt	15:19	For out of the heart **p** evil
Eph	4:29	Let no corrupt word **p** out of
Jas	3:10	Out of the same mouth **p**

PROCEEDED (see PROCEED)

John	8:42	for I **p** forth and came from
Rev	19:21	with the sword which **p** from

PROCEEDS (see PROCEED)

Deut	8: 3	lives by every word that **p**
Matt	4: 4	by every word that **p**
John	15:26	the Spirit of truth who **p**

PROCLAIM (see PREACH, PROCLAIMED, PROCLAIMS)

Ex	33:19	and I will **p** the name of the
Lev	25:10	and **p** liberty throughout
2Sa	1:20	**P** it not in the streets of
Ps	26: 7	That I may **p** with the voice
Ps	96: 2	**P** the good news of His
Is	61: 1	To **p** liberty to the
Is	61: 2	To **p** the acceptable year of
Mark	1:45	he went out and began to **p**
Luke	4:19	To **p** the acceptable
1Co	11:26	you **p** the Lord's death till
1Pe	2: 9	that you may **p** the praises

PROCLAIMED (see PROCLAIM)

Ex	34: 5	and **p** the name of the LORD.
Ps	68:11	the company of those who **p**
Jon	3: 5	**p** a fast, and put on
Mark	7:36	the more widely they **p** it.
Luke	12: 3	in inner rooms will be **p** on

PROCLAIMS (see PROCLAIM)

Is	52: 7	Who **p** peace, Who brings

Nah	1:15	Who **p** peace! O Judah, keep

PRODIGAL†

Luke	15:13	his possessions with **p**

PRODUCES

Rom	5: 3	knowing that tribulation **p**
2Co	7:10	For godly sorrow **p** repentance
Jas	1: 3	the testing of your faith **p**

PROFANE

Lev	10: 1	and offered **p** fire before
Lev	18:21	nor shall you **p** the name of
1Ti	4: 7	But reject **p** and old wives'
2Ti	2:16	But shun **p** and idle

PROFESSING

Rom	1:22	**P** to be wise, they became

PROFIT (see ADVANTAGE, PROFITABLE, PROFITS)

Prov	14:23	In all labor there is **p**,
Eccl	1: 3	What **p** has a man from all
Mark	8:36	For what will it **p** a man if
Acts	16:16	brought her masters much **p**
2Ti	2:14	strive about words to no **p**,
Jas	2:14	What does it **p**, my brethren,

PROFITABLE (see PROFIT, UNPROFITABLE)

Matt	5:29	for it is more **p** for you
1Ti	4: 8	but godliness is **p** for all
2Ti	3:16	and is **p** for doctrine, for
Tit	3: 8	These things are good and **p**
Phm	1:11	but now is **p** to you and to

PROFITS (see PROFIT)

John	6:63	the flesh **p** nothing. The
1Co	13: 3	it **p** me nothing.
1Ti	4: 8	For bodily exercise **p** a

PROLONG (see PROLONGED)

Deut	5:33	and that you may **p** your
Ps	85: 5	Will You **p** Your anger to
Is	53:10	He shall **p** His days, And

PROLONGED (see PROLONG)

Deut	6: 2	and that your days may be **p**.

PROMISE (see PROMISED, PROMISES)

1Ki	8:56	one word of all His good **p**,
Luke	24:49	I send the **P** of My Father
Acts	1: 4	but to wait for the **P** of the
Acts	2:39	For the **p** is to you and to
Acts	13:23	seed, according to the **p**,
Rom	4:14	is made void and the **p** made
Rom	4:20	He did not waver at the **p** of
Rom	9: 9	For this is the word of **p**:
Gal	3:14	that we might receive the **p**
Gal	3:18	law, it is no longer of **p**;
Gal	3:18	God gave it to Abraham by **p**.
Gal	3:19	should come to whom the **p**
Gal	3:29	and heirs according to the **p**.
Gal	4:23	of the freewoman through **p**,
Gal	4:28	was, are children of **p**.

P

Eph	1:13	with the Holy Spirit of **p**,
Eph	2:12	from the covenants of **p**,
Eph	3: 6	and partakers of His **p** in
Eph	6: 2	the first commandment with **p**:
1Ti	4: 8	having **p** of the life that
Heb	4: 1	since a **p** remains of
Heb	6:15	endured, he obtained the **p**.
Heb	6:17	to the heirs of **p** the
Heb	9:15	called may receive the **p** of
Heb	11: 9	heirs with him of the same **p**;
Heb	11:39	faith, did not receive the **p**,
2Pe	3: 4	Where is the **p** of His coming?
2Pe	3: 9	not slack concerning His **p**,
2Pe	3:13	we, according to His **p**,
1Jn	2:25	And this is the **p** that He has

PROMISED (see PROMISE)

Deut	9:28	them to the land which He **p**
Rom	1: 2	which He **p** before through His
Rom	4:21	that what He had **p** He was
Tit	1: 2	**p** before time began,
Heb	10:23	for He who **p** is faithful.
Heb	11:11	Him faithful who had **p**.
Jas	1:12	of life which the Lord has **p**

PROMISES (see PROMISE)

2Co	1:20	For all the **p** of God in Him
2Co	7: 1	Therefore, having these **p**,
Heb	6:12	and patience inherit the **p**.
Heb	7: 6	blessed him who had the **p**.
Heb	8: 6	was established on better **p**.
Heb	11:13	not having received the **p**,
Heb	11:17	he who had received the **p**
Heb	11:33	righteousness, obtained **p**,
2Pe	1: 4	great and precious **p**,

PROMOTED

Dan	2:48	Then the king **p** Daniel and
Dan	3:30	Then the king **p** Shadrach,

PROOFS†

Acts	1: 3	by many infallible **p**,

PROPER

Jude	6	who did not keep their **p**

PROPHECIES (see PROPHECY)

1Co	13: 8	But whether there are **p**,

PROPHECY (see PROPHECIES, PROPHESY, PROPHETIC)

Dan	9:24	To seal up vision and **p**,
Rom	12: 6	let us use them: if **p**,
1Co	13: 2	I have the gift of **p**,
1Ti	4:14	which was given to you by **p**
2Pe	1:20	that no **p** of Scripture is of
2Pe	1:21	for **p** never came by the will
Rev	1: 3	who hear the words of this **p**,
Rev	19:10	of Jesus is the spirit of **p**.
Rev	22: 7	keeps the words of the **p** of

PROPHESIED (see PROPHESY)

Num	11:25	upon them, that they **p**,
1Sa	10:10	and he **p** among them.

Jer	2: 8	The prophets **p** by Baal,
Jer	20: 1	heard that Jeremiah **p** these
Matt	7:22	have we not **p** in Your name,
Matt	11:13	the prophets and the law **p**
Luke	1:67	with the Holy Spirit, and **p**,
John	11:51	high priest that year he **p**
Acts	19: 6	spoke with tongues and **p**.
1Pe	1:10	who **p** of the grace that
Jude	14	**p** about these men also,

PROPHESIES (see PROPHESY)

Jer	28: 9	As for the prophet who **p** of
1Co	11: 5	every woman who prays or **p**
1Co	14: 4	but he who **p** edifies the

PROPHESY (see PROPHECY, PROPHESIED, PROPHESIES, PROPHET, PROPHETESS)

Jer	5:31	The prophets **p** falsely, And
Ezek	21:14	therefore, son of man, **p**,
Ezek	37: 4	**P** to these bones, and say to
Ezek	37: 9	**P** to the breath, prophesy,
Joel	2:28	and your daughters shall **p**,
Amos	3: 8	has spoken! Who can but **p**?
Amos	7:12	eat bread, And there **p**.
Amos	7:13	But never again **p** at Bethel,
Matt	15: 7	Well did Isaiah **p** about you,
Matt	26:68	**P** to us, Christ! Who is the
Luke	22:64	**P**! Who is the one who struck
Acts	2:17	your daughters shall **p**,
Rom	12: 6	let us **p** in proportion to
1Co	13: 9	we know in part and we **p** in
1Co	14: 1	especially that you may **p**.
1Co	14:39	desire earnestly to **p**,

PROPHET (see PROPHESY, PROPHETS)

Gen	20: 7	man's wife; for he is a **p**,
Ex	7: 1	your brother shall be your **p**.
Num	12: 6	If there is a **p** among you,
Deut	13: 1	there arises among you a **p**
Deut	18:15	will raise up for you a **P**
Deut	18:20	But the **p** who presumes to
Deut	18:20	other gods, that **p** shall die.'
Deut	34:10	has not arisen in Israel a **p**
1Sa	9: 9	he who is now called a **p**
1Ki	18:22	I alone am left a **p** of the
Is	9:15	The **p** who teaches lies, he
Jer	1: 5	I ordained you a **p** to the
Jer	18:18	nor the word from the **p**.
Jer	23:11	For both **p** and priest are
Jer	23:28	The **p** who has a dream, let
Dan	9: 2	LORD through Jeremiah the **p**,
Amos	7:14	Nor was I a son of a **p**,
Hag	1: 3	LORD came by Haggai the **p**,
Mal	4: 5	I will send you Elijah the **p**
Matt	1:22	by the Lord through the **p**,
Matt	2: 5	thus it is written by the **p**:
Matt	2:17	was spoken by Jeremiah the **p**,
Matt	3: 3	who was spoken of by the **p**
Matt	10:41	He who receives a **p** in the
Matt	11: 9	did you go out to see? A **p**?
Matt	11: 9	to you, and more than a **p**.
Matt	12:39	it except the sign of the **p**
Matt	13:57	A **p** is not without honor
Matt	21:11	the **p** from Nazareth of

Matt	21:26	for all count John as a **p**.
Matt	24:15	spoken of by Daniel the **p**,
Mark	6:15	others said, "It is the **P**,
Luke	4:17	was handed the book of the **p**
Luke	4:24	no **p** is accepted in his own
Luke	24:19	who was a **P** mighty in deed
John	6:14	This is truly the **P** who is to
Acts	2:16	is what was spoken by the **p**
Acts	3:22	raise up for you a **P**
Acts	7:37	raise up for you a **P**
Acts	8:28	he was reading Isaiah the **p**.
Acts	13: 6	certain sorcerer, a false **p**,
Acts	13:20	years, until Samuel the **p**.
Rev	20:10	the beast and the false **p**

PROPHETESS (see PROPHESY)

Ex	15:20	Then Miriam the **p**,
Judg	4: 4	Now Deborah, a **p**,
2Ki	22:14	Asaiah went to Huldah the **p**,
Luke	2:36	there was one, Anna, a **p**,

PROPHETIC† (see PROPHECY)

Rom	16:26	and by the **p** Scriptures has
2Pe	1:19	And so we have the **p** word

PROPHETS (see PROPHET)

Num	11:29	the LORD's people were **p**
1Sa	10: 5	you will meet a group of **p**
1Sa	10:12	"Is Saul also among the **p**?
2Ki	2: 3	Now the sons of the **p** who
2Ki	17:13	to you by My servants the **p**.
1Ch	16:22	And do My **p** no harm."
Neh	9:30	by Your Spirit in Your **p**.
Ps	105:15	And do My **p** no harm."
Jer	23:21	"I have not sent these **p**,
Dan	9: 6	heeded Your servants the **p**,
Dan	9:10	us by His servants the **p**.
Amos	3: 7	secret to His servants the **p**.
Zech	7:12	Spirit through the former **p**.
Matt	2:23	which was spoken by the **p**,
Matt	5:17	to destroy the Law or the **P**.
Matt	7:15	"Beware of false **p**,
Matt	11:13	For all the **p** and the law
Matt	16:14	Jeremiah or one of the **p**.
Matt	23:30	them in the blood of the **p**.
Mark	6:15	or like one of the **p**.
Luke	1:70	by the mouth of His holy **p**,
Luke	16:16	The law and the **p** were until
Luke	16:29	'They have Moses and the **p**;
Luke	24:44	the Law of Moses and the **P**
Acts	3:25	"You are sons of the **p**,
Acts	10:43	To Him all the **p** witness
Acts	15:15	with this the words of the **p**
Rom	1: 2	before through His **p** in the
Rom	11: 3	have killed Your **p** and
1Co	12:28	first apostles, second **p**,
1Co	12:29	all apostles? Are all **p**?
1Co	14:29	Let two or three **p** speak, and
1Co	14:32	And the spirits of the **p** are
1Co	14:32	are subject to the **p**.
Eph	2:20	of the apostles and **p**,
Eph	4:11	to be apostles, some **p**,
Heb	1: 1	past to the fathers by the **p**,
Heb	11:32	David and Samuel and the **p**:

1Pe	1:10	Of this salvation the **p** have
2Pe	2: 1	But there were also false **p**
1Jn	4: 1	because many false **p** have
Rev	10: 7	to His servants the **p**.

PROPITIATION

Rom	3:25	whom God set forth as a **p** by
Heb	2:17	to make **p** for the sins of
1Jn	4:10	sent His Son to be the **p**

PROPORTION

Rom	12: 6	let us prophesy in **p** to

PROSELYTE†

Matt	23:15	land and sea to win one **p**,
Acts	6: 5	a **p** from Antioch,

PROSPER (see PROSPEROUS)

Gen	24:40	His angel with you and **p**
Josh	1: 7	that you may **p** wherever you
Ps	1: 3	whatever he does shall **p**.
Ps	122: 6	May they **p** who love you.
Is	53:10	of the LORD shall **p** in His

PROSPEROUS (see PROSPER)

Gen	24:21	had made his journey **p** or
Josh	1: 8	you will make your way **p**,

PROUD (see PRIDE)

Prov	6:17	A **p** look, A lying tongue,
Jas	4: 6	"God resists the **p**,
1Pe	5: 5	"God resists the **p**,

PROVE (see TEST, TRY)

Ps	26: 2	and **p** me; Try my mind and
Rom	12: 2	that you may **p** what is that

PROVERB (see PROVERBS)

Prov	1: 6	To understand a **p** and an

PROVERBS (see PROVERB)

1Ki	4:32	He spoke three thousand **p**,
Prov	1: 1	The **p** of Solomon the son of
Prov	10: 1	The **P** of Solomon: A wise son
Prov	25: 1	These also are **p** of Solomon
Eccl	12: 9	out and set in order many **p**.

PROVIDE (see PROVIDED, PROVISION)

Gen	22: 8	God will **p** for Himself the
1Ti	5: 8	But if anyone does not **p** for

PROVIDED (see PROVIDE)

Gen	22:14	of The LORD it shall be **p**.
Heb	11:40	God having **p** something better

PROVISION (see PROVIDE)

Rom	13:14	and make no **p** for the flesh,

PROVOKE (see PROVOKED, PROVOKING)

Ex	23:21	do not **p** Him, for He will
Deut	4:25	of the LORD your God to **p**
Rom	10:19	I will **p** you to jealousy
1Co	10:22	Or do we **p** the Lord to
Eph	6: 4	do not **p** your children to

P

PROVOKED (see PROVOKE)

Deut	32:16	They **p** Him to jealousy with
1Sa	1: 6	And her rival also **p** her
Is	1: 4	They have **p** to anger The
Acts	17:16	his spirit was **p** within him
1Co	13: 5	not seek its own, is not **p**,

PROVOKING (see PROVOKE)

| Gal | 5:26 | **p** one another, envying one |

PRUDENCE (see PRUDENT)

| Prov | 1: 4 | To give **p** to the simple, To |
| Eph | 1: 8 | us in all wisdom and **p**, |

PRUDENT (see PRUDENCE, PRUDENTLY)

1Sa	16:18	**p** in speech, and a handsome
Prov	14: 8	The wisdom of the **p** is to
Matt	11:25	things from the wise and **p**

PRUDENTLY (see PRUDENT)

| Is | 52:13 | My Servant shall deal **p**; |

PRUNES† (see PRUNING)

| John | 15: 2 | that bears fruit He **p**, |

PRUNING (see PRUNES)

Is	2: 4	And their spears into **p**
Joel	3:10	into swords And your **p**
Mic	4: 3	And their spears into **p**

PSALM (see PSALMIST, PSALMS)

1Ch	16: 7	first delivered this **p**
Ps	98: 5	harp and the sound of a **p**,
Acts	13:33	also written in the second **P**:
1Co	14:26	each of you has a **p**,

PSALMIST† (see PSALM)

| 2Sa | 23: 1 | And the sweet **p** of Israel: |

PSALMS (see PSALM)

Luke	20:42	said in the Book of **P**:
Luke	24:44	and the Prophets and the **P**
Acts	1:20	is written in the book of **P**:
Eph	5:19	to one another in **p** and
Col	3:16	one another in **p** and hymns
Jas	5:13	cheerful? Let him sing **p**.

PUBLIC†

| Matt | 1:19 | not wanting to make her a **p** |
| Col | 2:15 | He made a **p** spectacle of |

PUFFED (see PUFFS)

1Co	4: 6	that none of you may be **p** up
1Co	13: 4	is not **p** up;
1Ti	3: 6	lest being **p** up with pride

PUFFS† (see PUFFED)

| 1Co | 8: 1 | Knowledge **p** up, but love |

PUNISHMENT

Gen	4:13	My **p** is greater than I can
Is	10: 3	will you do in the day of **p**,
Jer	8:12	In the time of their **p**

Jer	11:23	even the year of their **p**.
Hos	9: 7	The days of **p** have come;
Amos	1: 3	I will not turn away its **p**,
Matt	25:46	go away into everlasting **p**,
Heb	10:29	Of how much worse **p**,

PURCHASED

| Acts | 20:28 | the church of God which He **p** |
| Eph | 1:14 | the redemption of the **p** |

PURE (see PURER, PURIFY, PURITY)

Ex	25:17	make a mercy seat of **p** gold;
Ps	12: 6	words of the LORD are **p**
Ps	18:26	With the **p** You will show
Ps	19: 8	of the LORD is **p**,
Ps	24: 4	who has clean hands and a **p**
Ps	73: 1	To such as are **p** in heart.
Prov	30: 5	Every word of God is **p**;
Dan	7: 9	hair of His head was like **p**
Matt	5: 8	Blessed are the **p** in heart,
Phil	4: 8	just, whatever things are **p**,
1Ti	1: 5	is love from a **p** heart,
1Ti	3: 9	of the faith with a **p**
1Ti	5:22	sins; keep yourself **p**.
Heb	10:22	and our bodies washed with **p**
Jas	1:27	**P** and undefiled religion
Jas	3:17	is from above is first **p**,
1Pe	2: 2	desire the **p** milk of the
1Jn	3: 3	himself, just as He is **p**.
Rev	15: 6	clothed in **p** bright linen,
Rev	21:21	street of the city was **p**

PURER† (see PURE)

| Hab | 1:13 | You are of **p** eyes than to |

PURGE (see PURGED)

| Ps | 51: 7 | **P** me with hyssop, and I |
| 1Co | 5: 7 | Therefore **p** out the old |

PURGED (see PURGE, PURIFIED)

| Is | 6: 7 | taken away, And your sin **p**. |
| Heb | 1: 3 | when He had by Himself **p** our |

PURIFICATION (see PURIFY)

| Lev | 12: 4 | until the days of her **p** are |
| Luke | 2:22 | Now when the days of her **p** |

PURIFIED (see PURGED, PURIFY)

| Heb | 9:22 | law almost all things are **p** |
| 1Pe | 1:22 | Since you have **p** your souls |

PURIFIES† (see PURIFY)

| 1Jn | 3: 3 | who has this hope in Him **p** |

PURIFY (see PURE, PURIFICATION, PURIFIED, PURIFIES, PURIFYING)

| Gen | 35: 2 | **p** yourselves, and change |
| Jas | 4: 8 | and **p** your hearts, you |

PURIFYING (see PURIFY)

| Acts | 15: 9 | **p** their hearts by faith. |
| Heb | 9:13 | sanctifies for the **p** of the |

PURIM
Esth   9:26   So they called these days **P**,

PURITY (see PURE)
1Ti   4:12   in spirit, in faith, in **p**.

PURPLE
Dan   5:29   they clothed Daniel with **p**
John   19: 5   crown of thorns and the **p**
Acts   16:14   She was a seller of **p** from
Rev   17: 4   The woman was arrayed in **p**

PURPOSE (see COUNSEL, PURPOSES)
Eccl   3: 1   A time for every **p** under
Luke   4:43   because for this **p** I have
John   12:27   But for this **p** I came to
Acts   2:23   by the determined **p** and
Rom   8:28   called according to His **p**.
Rom   9:17   For this very **p** I have
Gal   3:19   What **p** then does the law
Eph   1:11   according to the **p** of Him
Eph   3:11   according to the eternal **p**
1Jn   3: 8   For this **p** the Son of God

PURPOSES (see PURPOSE)
2Co   9: 7   let each one give as he **p**

PURSUE (see PURSUES)
Ex   14: 4   so that he will **p** them; and
Ps   34:14   Seek peace and **p** it.
Hos   6: 3   Let us **p** the knowledge of
1Th   5:15   but always **p** what is good
1Pe   3:11   him seek peace and **p**

PURSUES (see PURSUE)
Lev   26:17   you shall flee when no one **p**
Prov   28: 1   wicked flee when no one **p**,
Hos   12: 1   And **p** the east wind; He

Q

QUAIL (see QUAILS)
Num   11:32   and gathered the **q** (he who

QUAILS† (see QUAIL)
Ex   16:13   So it was that **q** came up at

QUAKED
Ex   19:18   and the whole mountain **q**
Matt   27:51   to bottom; and the earth **q**,

QUALIFIED
Col   1:12   to the Father who has **q** us

QUEEN
1Ki   10: 1   Now when the **q** of Sheba heard
Matt   12:42   The **q** of the South will rise
Rev   18: 7   in her heart, 'I sit as **q**,

QUENCH (see QUENCHED, UNQUENCHABLE)
Song   8: 7   Many waters cannot **q** love,

Is   42: 3   smoking flax He will not **q**;
Matt   12:20   flax He will not **q**,
1Th   5:19   Do not **q** the Spirit.

QUENCHED (see QUENCH)
Mark   9:43   fire that shall never be **q**—
Heb   11:34   **q** the violence of fire,

QUESTION (see QUESTIONED, QUESTIONS)
Job   38: 3   I will **q** you, and you shall
Matt   22:35   a lawyer, asked Him a **q**,
Matt   22:46   day on did anyone dare **q**

QUESTIONED (see QUESTION)
Luke   23: 9   Then he **q** Him with many

QUESTIONS (see QUESTION)
1Ki   10: 3   Solomon answered all her **q**;
Luke   2:46   to them and asking them **q**.

QUICKLY (see HASTILY)
Deut   11:17   and you perish **q** from the
John   13:27   to him, "What you do, do **q**.
2Ti   4: 9   Be diligent to come to me **q**;
Rev   3:11   I am coming **q**! Hold fast
Rev   22:20   says, "Surely I am coming **q**.

QUIET (see QUIETNESS)
Is   7: 4   to him: 'Take heed, and be **q**;
Jer   47: 6   How long until you are **q**?
Mark   1:25   rebuked him, saying, "Be **q**,
1Th   4:11   you also aspire to lead a **q**
1Pe   3: 4   beauty of a gentle and **q**

QUIETNESS (see QUIET)
Is   30:15   In **q** and confidence shall

QUIRINIUS†
Luke   2: 2   first took place while **Q**

QUIVER
Ps   127: 5   is the man who has his **q**
Is   49: 2   In His **q** He has hidden

QUOTA
Ex   5: 8   you shall lay on them the **q**

R

RAAMSES† (see RAMESES,
Ex   1:11   supply cities, Pithom and **R**.

RABBI (see RABBONI)
Matt   23: 7   and to be called by men, '**R**,
Matt   26:25   Him, answered and said, "**R**,
Mark   9: 5   and said to Jesus, "**R**,
John   1:49   and said to Him, "**R**,

RABBONI (see RABBI)
John   20:16   **R**!" (which is to say,

R

RACA†
Matt 5:22 R!' shall be in danger of the

RACE
Ps 19: 5 a strong man to run its r
Eccl 9:11 The r is not to the swift,
Zech 9: 6 A mixed r shall settle in
1Co 9:24 that those who run in a r
2Ti 4: 7 fight, I have finished the r,
Heb 12: 1 us run with endurance the r

RACHEL
Gen 29:11 Then Jacob kissed R,
Gen 35:19 So R died and was buried on
Ruth 4:11 coming to your house like R
Jer 31:15 R weeping for her children,
Matt 2:18 R weeping for her

RAGE (see RAGING)
Ps 2: 1 Why do the nations r,
Acts 4:25 did the nations r,

RAGING (see RAGE)
Ps 22:13 Like a r and roaring lion.
Jon 1:15 the sea ceased from its r

RAGS
Is 64: 6 are like filthy r;
Jer 38:12 put these old clothes and r

RAHAB
Josh 2: 1 house of a harlot named R,
Ps 89:10 You have broken R in pieces,
Matt 1: 5 Salmon begot Boaz by R,
Heb 11:31 By faith the harlot R did not
Jas 2:25 was not R the harlot also

RAIN (see RAINED, RAINS)
Gen 2: 5 God had not caused it to r
Gen 7: 4 days I will cause it to r
Ex 16: 4 I will r bread from heaven
Deut 11:14 the early r and the latter
2Sa 1:21 there be no dew nor r
1Ki 17: 1 there shall not be dew nor r
1Ki 18:41 the sound of abundance of r
Eccl 11: 3 If the clouds are full of r,
Eccl 12: 2 do not return after the r;
Song 2:11 The r is over and gone.
Is 55:10 For as the r comes down, and
Hos 6: 3 will come to us like the r,
Matt 5:45 and sends r on the just and
Matt 7:25 and the r descended, the
Jas 5:17 and it did not r on the land
Jas 5:18 again, and the heaven gave r,

RAINBOW
Gen 9:13 I set My r in the cloud, and

RAINED (see RAIN)
Gen 19:24 Then the LORD r brimstone
Ex 9:23 And the LORD r hail on the
Ps 78:24 Had r down manna on them to

Ps 78:27 He also r meat on them like
Luke 17:29 Lot went out of Sodom it r

RAINS (see RAIN)
2Sa 21:10 of harvest until the late r
Hos 10:12 Till He comes and r

RAISE (see LIFT, RAISED)
Deut 18:18 I will r up for them a
Hos 6: 2 On the third day He will r
Matt 10: 8 r the dead, cast out demons.
John 2:19 and in three days I will r
John 6:40 and I will r him up at the
Acts 2:30 He would r up the Christ to
1Co 15:15 whom He did not r up—if in
2Co 4:14 the Lord Jesus will also r
Heb 11:19 that God was able to r
Jas 5:15 and the Lord will r him up.

RAISED (see LIFTED, RAISE)
Judg 2:16 the LORD r up judges who
Judg 3: 9 the LORD r up a deliverer
Matt 11: 5 the dead are r up and the
Matt 16:21 and be r the third day.
Matt 26:32 "But after I have been r,
Matt 27:52 who had fallen asleep were r;
John 12: 1 whom He had r from the dead.
Acts 2:32 This Jesus God has r up, of
Acts 3:26 having r up His Servant
Acts 4:10 whom God r from the dead, by
Rom 4:24 us who believe in Him who r
Rom 4:25 and was r because of our
Rom 6: 4 that just as Christ was r
Rom 8:11 if the Spirit of Him who r
Rom 9:17 very purpose I have r
Rom 10: 9 in your heart that God has r
1Co 6:14 And God both r up the Lord
1Co 15:12 preached that He has been r
1Co 15:42 it is r in incorruption.
2Co 4:14 knowing that He who r up the
Eph 2: 6 and r us up together, and
Col 2:12 in which you also were r
Heb 11:35 Women received their dead r

RAM (see RAM'S, RAMS)
Gen 15: 9 goat, a three-year-old r,
Gen 22:13 Abraham went and took the r,
Ruth 4:19 Hezron begot R,
Dan 8: 3 was a r which had two horns,
Matt 1: 4 R begot Amminadab, Amminadab

RAM'S (see RAM)
Josh 6: 5 a long blast with the r

RAMAH
Jer 31:15 "A voice was heard in R,
Matt 2:18 voice was heard in R,

RAMESES (see RAAMSES)
Gen 47:11 the land, in the land of R,
Ex 12:37 of Israel journeyed from R

RAMS (*see* RAM)

Ex	29: 1	one young bull and two **r**
1Sa	15:22	to heed than the fat of **r**.
Ps	114: 4	mountains skipped like **r**,
Mic	6: 7	pleased with thousands of **r**,

RAN (*see* RUN)

Gen	18: 2	he **r** from the tent door to
Gen	33: 4	But Esau **r** to meet him, and
1Sa	3: 5	So he **r** to Eli and said,
1Sa	17:51	Therefore David **r** and stood
1Ki	18:35	So the water **r** all around the
Jer	23:21	these prophets, yet they **r**
Matt	8:32	the whole herd of swine **r**
Matt	28: 8	and **r** to bring His disciples
Luke	24:12	But Peter arose and **r** to the
John	2: 3	And when they **r** out of wine,
Acts	27:41	they **r** the ship aground; and
Gal	5: 7	You **r** well. Who hindered you

RANSOM (*see* RANSOMED)

Num	35:31	you shall take no **r** for the
Ps	49: 7	Nor give to God a **r** for
Prov	13: 8	The **r** of a man's life is
Hos	13:14	I will **r** them from the power
Matt	20:28	and to give His life a **r** for
Mark	10:45	and to give His life a **r** for
1Ti	2: 6	who gave Himself a **r** for all,

RANSOMED (*see* RANSOM)

Is	35:10	And the **r** of the LORD shall
Jer	31:11	And **r** him from the hand of

RARE

1Sa	3: 1	the word of the LORD was **r**

RAVEN (*see* RAVENS)

Gen	8: 7	Then he sent out a **r**,
Song	5:11	wavy, And black as a **r**

RAVENOUS

Matt	7:15	but inwardly they are **r**

RAVENS (*see* RAVEN)

1Ki	17: 6	The **r** brought him bread and
Luke	12:24	"Consider the **r**,

RAZOR

Num	6: 5	vow of his separation no **r**
Judg	13: 5	And no **r** shall come upon his
1Sa	1:11	and no **r** shall come upon his

READ (*see* READER, READING, READS)

Deut	17:19	and he shall **r** it all the
Neh	8: 3	Then he **r** from it in the open
Neh	8: 8	So they **r** distinctly from the
Dan	5: 8	but they could not **r** the
Matt	12: 5	Or have you not **r** in the law
Luke	4:16	day, and stood up to **r**.
John	19:20	Then many of the Jews **r** this
Acts	8:32	in the Scripture which he **r**
Acts	13:27	of the Prophets which are **r**
2Co	3: 2	known and **r** by all men;

2Co	3:15	to this day, when Moses is **r**,
Col	4:16	Now when this epistle is **r**

READER† (*see* READ)

Mark	13:14	it ought not" (let the **r**

READINESS† (*see* READY)

Acts	17:11	received the word with all **r**,

READING (*see* READ)

Neh	8: 8	them to understand the **r**.
Acts	8:28	he was **r** Isaiah the prophet.
Acts	8:30	understand what you are **r**?
1Ti	4:13	I come, give attention to **r**,

READS† (*see* READ)

Dan	5: 7	Whoever **r** this writing, and
Hab	2: 2	That he may run who **r** it.
Matt	24:15	the holy place" (whoever **r**,
Rev	1: 3	Blessed is he who **r** and

READY (*see* READINESS)

Ex	19:15	Be **r** for the third day; do
Luke	1:17	to make **r** a people prepared
Rom	1:15	I am **r** to preach the
2Co	12:14	for the third time I am **r**
1Pe	1: 5	faith for salvation **r** to be
1Pe	3:15	and always be **r** to give a
1Pe	4: 5	an account to Him who is **r**

REAP (*see* REAPER, REAPING, REAPS)

Ps	126: 5	who sow in tears Shall **r**
Prov	22: 8	He who sows iniquity will **r**
Hos	8: 7	And **r** the whirlwind. The
Matt	6:26	for they neither sow nor **r**
Matt	25:26	you knew that I **r** where I
2Co	9: 6	sows sparingly will also **r**
Gal	6: 7	sows, that he will also **r**
Gal	6: 8	flesh will of the flesh **r**

REAPER (*see* REAP, REAPERS)

Amos	9:13	plowman shall overtake the **r**,

REAPERS (*see* REAPER)

Ruth	2: 3	in the field after the **r**
Matt	13:39	and the **r** are the angels.

REAPING (*see* REAP)

Matt	25:24	**r** where you have not sown,

REAPS (*see* REAP)

John	4:36	he who sows and he who **r**

REASON (*see* REASONABLE, REASONING)

Ps	90:10	And if by **r** of strength
Is	1:18	and let us **r** together,"
Matt	16: 8	why do you **r** among
Luke	23:22	I have found no **r** for death
Eph	5:31	For this **r** a man shall
1Pe	3:15	to everyone who asks you a **r**

REASONABLE† (*see* REASON)

Rom	12: 1	which is your **r** service.

R

REASONING (see REASON)

Luke	5:22	Why are you r in your hearts?

REBECCA† (see REBEKAH)

Rom	9:10	but when R also had

REBEKAH (see REBECCA)

Gen	25:28	but R loved Jacob.

REBELLED (see REBELLION, REBELLIOUS)

Is	1: 2	And they have r against Me;

REBELLION (see REBELLED, REBELLIOUS)

1Sa	15:23	For r is as the sin of
Ps	95: 8	your hearts, as in the r,
Heb	3: 8	hearts as in the r,
Jude	11	and perished in the r of

REBELLIOUS (see REBELLED, REBELLION)

Deut	21:20	of ours is stubborn and r;
Ps	78: 8	A stubborn and r
Prov	7:11	She was loud and r,
Is	30: 1	Woe to the r children," says
Is	65: 2	My hands all day long to a r
Jer	5:23	people has a defiant and r
Ezek	2: 5	for they are a r house—yet
Hos	9:15	All their princes are r

REBUILD (see REBUILDING, REBUILT)

Is	61: 4	And they shall r the old

REBUILDING (see REBUILD)

Ezra	5:11	and we are r the temple that
Neh	6: 6	you are r the wall, that you

REBUILT (see REBUILD)

Ezra	5:15	let the house of God be r

REBUKE (see REBUKED, REPROOF)

Ruth	2:16	and do not r her."
Ps	6: 1	do not r me in Your anger,
Prov	9: 8	R a wise man, and he will
Prov	30: 6	Lest He r you, and you be
Is	1:17	R the oppressor; Defend
Jer	15:15	Your sake I have suffered r
Mic	4: 3	And r strong nations afar
Zech	3: 2	The LORD r you, Satan! The
1Ti	5: 1	Do not r an older man, but
2Ti	4: 2	out of season. Convince, r,
Tit	2:15	and r with all authority.

REBUKED (see REBUKE)

Gen	37:10	and his father r him and
Ps	9: 5	You have r the nations, You
Ps	105:14	He r kings for their sakes,
Prov	29: 1	He who is often r,
Matt	17:18	And Jesus r the demon, and it
Mark	8:33	He r Peter, saying, "Get
Heb	12: 5	when you are r by Him;

RECALL

Lam	3:21	This I r to my mind,
Heb	10:32	But r the former days in

RECEDED

Gen	8: 3	And the waters r continually
Rev	6:14	Then the sky r as a scroll

RECEIVE (see RECEIVED, RECEIVES, RECEIVING)

Ps	24: 5	He shall r blessing from the
Ps	49:15	For He shall r me. Selah
Ps	73:24	And afterward r me to
Mal	3:10	not be room enough to r
Matt	10:14	And whoever will not r you
Matt	10:41	name of a prophet shall r a
Matt	11:14	if you are willing to r
Luke	18:30	who shall not r many times
Luke	23:41	for we r the due reward of
John	1:11	and His own did not r Him.
John	12:48	and does not r My words, has
John	14: 3	I will come again and r you
John	14:17	whom the world cannot r,
John	16:24	My name. Ask, and you will r,
John	20:22	R the Holy Spirit.
Acts	1: 8	But you shall r power when
Acts	2:38	and you shall r the gift of
Acts	3:21	whom heaven must r until the
Acts	7:59	Lord Jesus, r my spirit."
Acts	20:35	blessed to give than to r
1Co	2:14	the natural man does not r
1Co	4: 7	you have that you did not r?
Gal	3: 2	Did you r the Spirit by the
Gal	4: 5	that we might r the adoption
Heb	11:39	did not r the promise,
Jas	1:12	he will r the crown of life
Jas	4: 3	You ask and do not r,
1Pe	5: 4	you will r the crown of
1Jn	3:22	And whatever we ask we r from
Rev	4:11	To r glory and honor and
Rev	13:16	to r a mark on their right

RECEIVED (see RECEIVE)

Is	40: 2	For she has r from the
Matt	10: 8	demons. Freely you have r,
Mark	16:19	He was r up into heaven, and
Luke	9:51	had come for Him to be r up,
John	1:12	But as many as r Him, to them
John	1:16	His fullness we have all r,
Acts	1: 9	and a cloud r Him out of
Acts	8:17	and they r the Holy Spirit.
Acts	15: 4	they were r by the church
Rom	1: 5	Through Him we have r grace
Rom	5:11	through whom we have now r
Rom	8:15	but you r the Spirit of
1Co	4: 7	boast as if you had not r
1Co	11:23	For I r from the Lord that
1Co	15: 3	of all that which I also r:
1Ti	3:16	R up in glory.
Heb	10:26	willfully after we have r
Heb	11:13	not having r the promises,
1Pe	4:10	As each one has r a gift,

RECEIVES (see RECEIVE)

Prov	15: 5	But he who r correction is
Matt	7: 8	"For everyone who asks r,
Matt	10:40	He who r you receives Me,

Matt	10:41	He who r a prophet in the
Matt	18: 5	Whoever r one little child
1Co	9:24	but one r the prize? Run in
Heb	6: 7	r blessing from God;
Heb	12: 6	every son whom He r

RECEIVING (see RECEIVE)

Rom	1:27	and r in themselves the
Heb	12:28	since we are r a kingdom
1Pe	1: 9	r the end of your faith—the

RECOGNIZE (see RECOGNIZED)

Job	2:12	and did not r him, they

RECOGNIZED (see RECOGNIZE)

Gen	42: 8	So Joseph r his brothers, but

RECOMPENSE

Deut	32:35	Vengeance is Mine, and r;

RECONCILE (see RECONCILED,
RECONCILIATION, RECONCILING)

Eph	2:16	and that He might r them both
Col	1:20	and by Him to r all things to

RECONCILED (see RECONCILE)

Matt	5:24	First be r to your brother,
Rom	5:10	we were enemies we were r
2Co	5:20	be r to God.

RECONCILIATION (see RECONCILE)

Rom	5:11	we have now received the r
2Co	5:18	given us the ministry of r,
2Co	5:19	to us the word of r

RECONCILING (see RECONCILE)

2Co	5:19	that God was in Christ r the

RECOVERY

Luke	4:18	to the captives And r

RED (see REDNESS)

Gen	25:25	And the first came out r
Gen	25:30	feed me with that same r
Ex	10:19	and blew them into the R
Prov	23:31	on the wine when it is r,
Is	1:18	Though they are r like
Is	63: 2	Why is Your apparel r,
Zech	1: 8	a man riding on a r horse,
Matt	16: 2	weather, for the sky is r';
Heb	11:29	they passed through the R
Rev	6: 4	Another horse, fiery r,

REDEEM (see REDEEMED, REDEEMER,
REDEEMING, REDEEMS, REDEMPTION)

Ex	6: 6	and I will r you with an
Ex	13:13	of a donkey you shall r
Ex	13:15	the firstborn of my sons I r
Lev	25:25	relative comes to r it,
Lev	27:20	if he does not want to r
Ruth	4: 4	If you will r it, redeem
Ps	49:15	But God will r my soul from
Mic	4:10	There the LORD will r you

Luke	24:21	it was He who was going to r
Gal	4: 5	to r those who were under the

REDEEMED (see REDEEM)

2Sa	4: 9	who has r my life from all
Ps	55:18	He has r my soul in peace
Ps	77:15	You have with Your arm r
Ps	107: 2	Let the r of the LORD say
Is	62:12	The R of the LORD; And
Gal	3:13	Christ has r us from the
1Pe	1:18	knowing that you were not r
Rev	5: 9	And have r us to God by

REDEEMER (see REDEEM)

Job	19:25	For I know that my R lives,
Ps	19:14	LORD, my strength and my R.
Is	41:14	says the LORD And your R,
Is	49: 7	The R of Israel, their Holy
Is	49:26	am your Savior, And your R,
Is	63:16	Our R from Everlasting is

REDEEMING (see REDEEM)

Eph	5:16	r the time, because the days

REDEEMS (see REDEEM)

Ps	103: 4	Who r your life from

REDEMPTION (see REDEEM)

Ps	130: 7	And with Him is abundant r
Luke	2:38	all those who looked for r
Luke	21:28	because your r draws near."
Rom	3:24	by His grace through the r
Rom	8:23	the r of our body.
1Co	1:30	and sanctification and r—
Eph	1: 7	In Him we have r through His
Eph	4:30	were sealed for the day of r
Col	1:14	in whom we have r through His
Heb	9:12	having obtained eternal r

REDNESS† (see RED)

Prov	23:29	Who has r of eyes?

REED (see REEDS)

Is	42: 3	A bruised r He will not
Matt	11: 7	A r shaken by the wind?
Matt	12:20	A bruised r He will

REEDS (see REED)

Ex	2: 5	she saw the ark among the r,

REFORMATION†

Heb	9:10	imposed until the time of r

REFRAIN

Eccl	3: 5	And a time to r from

REFRESHING

Acts	3:19	so that times of r may come

REFUGE

Num	35: 6	appoint six cities of r,
Deut	33:27	The eternal God is your r,
Ruth	2:12	wings you have come for r
Ps	9: 9	A r in times of trouble.

R

Ps	46: 1	God is our **r** and strength,
Ps	46: 7	The God of Jacob is our **r**
Heb	6:18	who have fled for **r** to lay

REFUSE (see REFUSED, REFUSING)

Is	7:15	that He may know to **r** the
Heb	12:25	See that you do not **r** Him

REFUSED (see REFUSE)

Gen	37:35	but he **r** to be comforted,
1Sa	16: 7	because I have **r** him. For
Ps	77: 2	My soul **r** to be comforted.
Is	8: 6	Inasmuch as these people **r**
Heb	11:24	**r** to be called the son of

REFUSING (see REFUSE)

Jer	31:15	**R** to be comforted for her
Matt	2:18	**R** to be comforted,

REGARD (see REGARDED)

Ps	66:18	If I **r** iniquity in my heart,
Luke	18: 2	who did not fear God nor **r**
2Co	5:16	we **r** no one according to the

REGARDED (see REGARD)

Luke	1:48	For He has **r** the lowly state

REGENERATION

Tit	3: 5	through the washing of **r** and

REGIONS

2Co	10:16	preach the gospel in the **r**

REGISTERED

Luke	2: 1	all the world should be **r**
Luke	2: 5	to be **r** with Mary, his
Heb	12:23	of the firstborn who are **r**

REHOBOAM

1Ki	12:21	restore the kingdom to **R**
Matt	1: 7	Solomon begot **R**,

REIGN (see REIGNED, REIGNS)

Gen	37: 8	Shall you indeed **r** over us?
Ex	15:18	The LORD shall **r** forever and
Judg	9: 8	**R** over us!'
1Sa	8:11	of the king who will **r** over
Prov	8:15	By me kings **r**,
Luke	1:33	And He will **r** over the house
Luke	3: 1	the fifteenth year of the **r**
Rom	5:17	of righteousness will **r** in
Rom	5:21	even so grace might **r**
Rom	6:12	Therefore do not let sin **r** in
1Co	15:25	For He must **r** till He has put
Rev	11:15	and He shall **r** forever and
Rev	20: 6	and shall **r** with Him a
Rev	22: 5	And they shall **r** forever and

REIGNED (see REIGN)

Gen	36:31	of Edom before any king **r**
1Sa	13: 1	Saul **r** one year; and when he
Rom	5:14	Nevertheless death **r** from
Rom	5:21	so that as sin **r** in death,
Rev	20: 4	And they lived and **r** with

REIGNS (see REIGN)

Ps	96:10	the nations, "The LORD **r**;
Rev	19: 6	the Lord God Omnipotent **r**!

REJECTED (see CAST, REJECTS)

1Sa	8: 7	for they have not **r** you, but
1Sa	15:23	Because you have **r** the word
Ps	118:22	stone which the builders **r**
Is	5:24	Because they have **r** the law
Is	53: 3	He is despised and **r** by men,
Matt	21:42	which the builders **r**
Acts	4:11	stone which was **r** by you
Heb	12:17	the blessing, he was **r**,
1Pe	2: 7	which the builders **r**

REJECTS (see REJECTED)

Luke	10:16	he who **r** you rejects Me, and

REJOICE (see REJOICED, REJOICES, REJOICING)

1Sa	2: 1	Because I **r** in Your
Ps	2:11	And **r** with trembling.
Ps	9: 2	I will be glad and **r** in You;
Ps	9:14	I will **r** in Your salvation.
Ps	14: 7	Let Jacob **r** and Israel be
Ps	33: 1	**R** in the LORD, O you
Ps	51: 8	bones You have broken may **r**
Ps	63: 7	of Your wings I will **r**
Ps	85: 6	That Your people may **r** in
Ps	90:14	That we may **r** and be glad
Ps	97: 1	reigns; Let the earth **r**;
Ps	107:42	The righteous see it and **r**,
Ps	118:24	We will **r** and be glad in
Ps	119:162	I **r** at Your word As one who
Prov	5:18	And **r** with the wife of your
Eccl	3:22	than that a man should **r** in
Eccl	11: 9	**R**, O young man,
Is	9: 3	As men **r** when they divide
Is	25: 9	We will be glad and **r** in
Is	35: 1	And the desert shall **r** and
Is	65:13	Behold, My servants shall **r**,
Jer	15:17	of the mockers, Nor did I **r**;
Hab	3:18	Yet I will **r** in the LORD,
Zech	9: 9	**R** greatly, O daughter of
Matt	5:12	**R** and be exceedingly glad,
Luke	1:14	and many will **r** at his
Luke	1:28	the angel said to her, "**R**,
Luke	6:23	**R** in that day and leap for
Luke	10:20	but rather **r** because your
Luke	15: 6	**R** with me, for I have found
John	4:36	sows and he who reaps may **r**
Rom	5: 2	and **r** in hope of the glory
Rom	5:11	but we also **r** in God through
Rom	12:15	**R** with those who rejoice, and
1Co	13: 6	does not **r** in iniquity, but
Gal	4:27	For it is written: "**R**,
Phil	1:18	is preached; and in this I **r**,
Phil	4: 4	**R** in the Lord always. Again I
Col	1:24	I now **r** in my sufferings for
1Th	5:16	**R** always,
1Pe	1: 6	In this you greatly **r**,
1Pe	1: 8	you **r** with joy inexpressible
1Pe	4:13	but **r** to the extent that you
Rev	19: 7	Let us be glad and **r** and give

REJOICED (see REJOICE)

Matt	2:10	they **r** with exceedingly
Luke	1:47	And my spirit has **r** in God
John	8:56	Your father Abraham **r** to see
Phil	4:10	But I **r** in the Lord greatly

REJOICES (see REJOICE)

1Sa	2: 1	My heart **r** in the LORD; My
Ps	19: 5	And **r** like a strong man to
Matt	18:13	he **r** more over that sheep
1Co	13: 6	but **r** in the truth;

REJOICING (see REJOICE)

Ps	19: 8	**r** the heart; The
Ps	107:22	declare His works with **r**
Ps	119:111	For they are the **r** of my
Ps	126: 6	doubtless come again with **r**,
Jer	15:16	was to me the joy and **r** of
Acts	5:41	**r** that they were counted
Acts	8:39	and he went on his way **r**
Rom	12:12	**r** in hope, patient in
2Co	6:10	as sorrowful, yet always **r**;
1Th	2:19	hope, or joy, or crown of **r**?

RELEASE (see LOOSE, RELEASED)

Lev	16:22	and he shall **r** the goat in
Deut	15: 9	seventh year, the year of **r**,
Matt	27:17	Whom do you want me to **r** to

RELEASED (see RELEASE)

Lev	16:26	And he who **r** the goat as the
Matt	27:26	Then he **r** Barabbas to them;

RELENT (see RELENTED, RELENTS)

1Sa	15:29	not a man, that He should **r**
Ps	110: 4	has sworn And will not **r**,
Jer	18: 8	I will **r** of the disaster
Heb	7:21	sworn And will not **r**,

RELENTED (see RELENT)

Jon	3:10	and God **r** from the disaster

RELENTS† (see RELENT)

Joel	2:13	And He **r** from doing harm.
Jon	4: 2	One who **r** from doing harm.

RELIGION (see RELIGIOUS)

Jas	1:27	Pure and undefiled **r** before

RELIGIOUS† (see RELIGION)

Acts	17:22	in all things you are very **r**;
Jas	1:26	among you thinks he is **r**,

REMAIN (see REMAINS, REMNANT)

Ex	12:10	You shall let none of it **r**
John	15:11	that My joy may **r** in you,
John	15:16	that your fruit should **r**,
1Co	7:11	let her **r** unmarried or be
1Co	7:26	it is good for a man to **r**
1Th	4:15	that we who are alive and **r**
Heb	1:11	will perish, but You **r**;
Heb	12:27	which cannot be shaken may **r**

REMAINS (see REMAIN)

Gen	8:22	"While the earth **r**,
John	9:41	see.' Therefore your sin **r**
John	12:24	it **r** alone; but if it dies,
1Co	7:40	But she is happier if she **r**
2Ti	2:13	He **r** faithful; He cannot
Heb	4: 9	There **r** therefore a rest for
Heb	7: 3	**r** a priest continually.
1Jn	3: 9	for His seed **r** in him; and

REMEDY

Prov	6:15	he shall be broken without **r**
Prov	29: 1	and that without **r**.

REMEMBER (see REMEMBERED, REMEMBERING, REMEMBERS, REMEMBRANCE)

Gen	9:15	and I will **r** My covenant
Gen	40:23	the chief butler did not **r**
Ex	20: 8	**R** the Sabbath day, to keep
Deut	9: 7	"**R**! Do not forget how
Neh	13:31	**R** me, O my God, for good!
Ps	25: 7	Do not **r** the sins of my
Ps	25: 7	According to Your mercy **r**
Ps	42: 4	When I **r** these things, I
Ps	42: 6	Therefore I will **r** You from
Ps	63: 6	When I **r** You on my bed, I
Ps	77:10	But I will **r** the years
Ps	79: 8	do not **r** former iniquities
Ps	105: 5	**R** His marvelous works which
Ps	137: 6	If I do not **r** you, Let my
Eccl	12: 1	**R** now your Creator in the
Is	43:18	Do not **r** the former things,
Is	46: 9	**R** the former things of old,
Jer	31:34	and their sin I will **r** no
Lam	3:19	**R** my affliction and
Hab	3: 2	In wrath **r** mercy.
Luke	17:32	**R** Lot's wife.
Luke	23:42	**r** me when You come into Your
Col	4:18	**R** my chains. Grace be with
2Ti	1: 3	as without ceasing I **r** you
Rev	2: 5	**R** therefore from where you

REMEMBERED (see REMEMBER, REMEMBERS)

Gen	8: 1	Then God **r** Noah, and every
Gen	19:29	that God **r** Abraham, and sent
Gen	42: 9	Then Joseph **r** the dreams
Ex	6: 5	and I have **r** My covenant.
Ps	98: 3	He has **r** His mercy and His
Ps	105:42	For He **r** His holy promise,
Ps	111: 4	His wonderful works to be **r**;
Ps	136:23	Who **r** us in our lowly state,
Ps	137: 1	we wept When we **r** Zion.
Is	65:17	the former shall not be **r**
Hos	2:17	And they shall be **r** by
Jon	2: 7	I **r** the LORD; And my
Matt	26:75	And Peter **r** the word of Jesus
Luke	24: 8	And they **r** His words.
Rev	18: 5	and God has **r** her

REMEMBERING (see REMEMBER)

Mark	11:21	And Peter, **r**, said to Him,
1Th	1: 3	**r** without ceasing your work

R

REMEMBERS (see REMEMBER)

Ps	103:14	He r that we are dust.
Ps	103:16	And its place r it no more.
Ps	105: 8	He r His covenant forever,

REMEMBRANCE (see REMEMBER)

Ex	17:14	will utterly blot out the r
Deut	25:19	you will blot out the r of
Ps	6: 5	in death there is no r of
Ps	112: 6	will be in everlasting r
Eccl	1:11	There is no r of former
Mal	3:16	So a book of r was written
Luke	1:54	In r of His mercy,
Luke	22:19	do this in r of Me."
1Co	11:24	do this in r of Me."
1Co	11:25	drink it, in r of Me."
Phil	1: 3	I thank my God upon every r
2Ti	1: 5	when I call to r the genuine

REMISSION

Matt	26:28	is shed for many for the r
Luke	1:77	to His people By the r of
Luke	24:47	and that repentance and r of
Acts	10:43	in Him will receive r of
Heb	9:22	of blood there is no r
Heb	10:18	Now where there is r of

REMNANT (see REMAIN)

Is	1: 9	left to us a very small r,
Is	10:21	The r will return, the
Is	10:21	the r of Jacob, To the
Ezek	6: 8	"Yet I will leave a r,
Amos	5:15	Will be gracious to the r
Mic	2:12	I will surely gather the r
Mic	5: 7	Then the r of Jacob Shall
Rom	9:27	The r will be saved.
Rom	11: 5	present time there is a r

REMOVE (see REMOVED, TAKE)

Prov	22:28	Do not r the ancient
1Co	13: 2	so that I could r mountains,

REMOVED (see REMOVE)

Ps	103:12	So far has He r our

REND†

Is	64: 1	that You would r the
Joel	2:13	So r your heart, and not

RENDER

Ps	38:20	Those also who r evil for
Ps	116:12	What shall I r to the LORD
Matt	22:21	R therefore to Caesar the
Rom	2: 6	will r to each one
Rom	13: 7	R therefore to all their due:
1Co	7: 3	Let the husband r to his wife

RENEW (see RENEWED, RENEWING)

Ps	51:10	And r a steadfast spirit
Ps	104:30	And You r the face of the
Is	40:31	wait on the LORD Shall r
Heb	6: 6	to r them again to

RENEWED (see RENEW)

Ps	103: 5	So that your youth is r
2Co	4:16	the inward man is being r
Eph	4:23	and be r in the spirit of
Col	3:10	on the new man who is r in

RENEWING† (see RENEW)

Rom	12: 2	but be transformed by the r
Tit	3: 5	of regeneration and r of

RENOWN

Gen	6: 4	who were of old, men of r

REPAY

Ruth	2:12	The LORD r your work, and a
1Sa	26:23	May the LORD r every man
Ps	54: 5	He will r my enemies for
Is	59:18	deeds, accordingly He will r,
Luke	10:35	I will r you.'
Rom	12:17	R no one evil for evil. Have
Rom	12:19	is Mine, I will r,
2Ti	4:14	May the Lord r him according
Phm	1:19	with my own hand. I will r—
Heb	10:30	is Mine, I will r,

REPENT (see REPENTANCE, REPENTED, REPENTS)

Num	23:19	son of man, that He should r
Job	42: 6	And r in dust and ashes."
Jer	25: 5	R now everyone of his evil
Ezek	14: 6	says the Lord GOD: "R,
Hos	11: 5	Because they refused to r
Matt	3: 2	and saying, "R,
Matt	4:17	to preach and to say, "R,
Mark	1:15	kingdom of God is at hand. R,
Luke	13: 3	but unless you r you will
Acts	3:19	R therefore and be converted,
Acts	17:30	all men everywhere to r,
Acts	26:20	Gentiles, that they should r,
Rev	2: 5	r and do the first works, or
Rev	3: 3	and heard; hold fast and r
Rev	9:20	did not r of the works of

REPENTANCE (see REPENT)

Matt	3: 8	bear fruits worthy of r,
Matt	3:11	you with water unto r,
Matt	9:13	righteous, but sinners, to r
Mark	1: 4	and preaching a baptism of r
Luke	3: 8	bear fruits worthy of r,
Luke	15: 7	just persons who need no r
Luke	24:47	and that r and remission of
Acts	11:18	granted to the Gentiles r
Acts	13:24	the baptism of r to all the
Acts	20:21	r toward God and faith
Acts	26:20	and do works befitting r
Rom	2: 4	of God leads you to r?
2Co	7: 9	that your sorrow led to r.
2Co	7:10	For godly sorrow produces r
Heb	6: 1	again the foundation of r
Heb	6: 6	to renew them again to r,
Heb	12:17	for he found no place for r,
2Pe	3: 9	that all should come to r.

REPENTED (see REPENT)

Matt	11:21	they would have r long ago
Luke	11:32	for they r at the preaching
2Co	12:21	before and have not r of

REPENTS (see REPENT)

Luke	15:10	of God over one sinner who r

REPETITIONS†

Matt	6: 7	do not use vain r as the

REPORT

Gen	37: 2	and Joseph brought a bad r
Is	53: 1	Who has believed our r?
John	12:38	who has believed our r?
Rom	10:16	who has believed our r?
Phil	4: 8	things are of good r,

REPROACH (see REPROACHED, REPROACHES)

Gen	30:23	"God has taken away my r
Ps	22: 6	A r of men, and despised by
Ps	69: 7	for Your sake I have borne r;
Prov	14:34	But sin is a r to any
Luke	1:25	to take away my r among
Col	1:22	and above r in His sight—
1Ti	4:10	we both labor and suffer r,
Heb	11:26	esteeming the r of Christ
Heb	13:13	the camp, bearing His r.
Jas	1: 5	all liberally and without r,

REPROACHED (see REPROACH)

Rom	15: 3	of those who r You
1Pe	4:14	If you are r for the name of

REPROACHES (see REPROACH)

Ps	69: 9	And the r of those who
Rom	15: 3	The r of those who

REPROOF (see REBUKE)

2Ti	3:16	for doctrine, for r,

REPUTATION

Acts	6: 3	you seven men of good r,
Phil	2: 7	but made Himself of no r,

REQUEST (see REQUESTS)

1Co	1:22	For Jews r a sign, and Greeks
Phil	1: 4	prayer of mine making r for

REQUESTS (see REQUEST)

Phil	4: 6	let your r be made known to

REQUIRE (see REQUIRED, REQUIREMENT)

Gen	9: 5	of every beast I will r it,
Gen	9: 5	man's brother I will r the
Ps	40: 6	sin offering You did not r
Ezek	3:18	but his blood I will r at
Mic	6: 8	And what does the LORD r

REQUIRED (see REQUIRE)

Luke	12:20	night your soul will be r
Luke	12:48	from him much will be r;
1Co	4: 2	Moreover it is r in stewards

REQUIREMENT† (see REQUIRE, REQUIREMENTS)

Rom	8: 4	that the righteous r of the

REQUIREMENTS (see REQUIREMENT)

Rom	2:26	man keeps the righteous r

RESCUE

Ex	6: 6	I will r you from their
Ps	22: 8	let Him r Him; Let Him

RESERVED

1Ki	19:18	Yet I have r seven thousand
Job	21:30	For the wicked are r for the
1Pe	1: 4	r in heaven for you,
2Pe	2: 4	to be r for judgment;
2Pe	2:17	for whom is r the blackness
2Pe	3: 7	are r for fire until the day
Jude	6	He has r in everlasting

RESIST (see RESISTED, RESISTS)

Jas	4: 7	R the devil and he will flee
1Pe	5: 9	R him, steadfast in the

RESISTED (see RESIST)

Rom	9:19	For who has r His will?"
Heb	12: 4	You have not yet r to

RESISTS (see RESIST)

Jas	4: 6	God r the proud, But
1Pe	5: 5	God r the proud, But

RESPECT

Gen	4: 5	but He did not r Cain and his
Ps	40: 4	And does not r the proud,
Ps	74:20	Have r to the covenant; For
Is	22:11	Nor did you have r for Him
Matt	21:37	They will r my son.'
Acts	5:34	of the law held in r by all
Heb	12: 9	us, and we paid them r.

REST (see RESTED, RESTING, RESTS)

Ex	16:23	'Tomorrow is a Sabbath r,
Ex	23:11	year you shall let it r
Ex	23:12	the seventh day you shall r,
Ex	33:14	you, and I will give you r
Deut	12: 9	you have not come to the r
Deut	31:16	you will r with your
Judg	3:11	So the land had r for forty
2Sa	7: 1	the LORD had given him r
1Ki	11:41	Now the r of the acts of
1Ch	28: 2	heart to build a house of r
Ezra	3: 8	and the r of their brethren
Ezra	4: 3	and Jeshua and the r of the
Ezra	4: 7	and the r of their
Neh	6:14	Noadiah and the r of the
Esth	9:22	days on which the Jews had r
Job	3:17	there the weary are at r
Ps	16: 9	My flesh also will r in
Ps	37: 7	R in the LORD, and wait
Ps	55: 6	would fly away and be at r
Ps	95:11	'They shall not enter My r
Ps	116: 7	Return to your r,

R

Prov	24:33	folding of the hands to r;
Is	11: 2	Spirit of the LORD shall r
Is	14: 7	The whole earth is at r and
Is	18: 4	to me, "I will take My r,
Is	28:12	may cause the weary to r,
Is	34:14	the night creature shall r
Is	57:20	sea, When it cannot r,
Jer	6:16	Then you will find r for
Jer	47: 6	R and be still!
Matt	11:28	laden, and I will give you r
Matt	11:29	and you will find r for your
1Co	7:12	But to the r I, not the Lord,
2Co	12: 9	the power of Christ may r
2Th	1: 7	you who are troubled r with
Heb	3:11	shall not enter My r
Heb	4: 9	There remains therefore a r
1Pe	1:13	and r your hope fully upon
Rev	4: 8	And they do not r day or

RESTED (see REST)

Gen	2: 2	and He r on the seventh day
Ex	20:11	and r the seventh day.
Num	11:25	when the Spirit r upon them,
1Ki	2:10	So David r with his fathers,
Heb	4: 4	And God r on the seventh

RESTING (see REST)

Gen	8: 9	But the dove found no r place
Ps	132:14	This is My r place forever;

RESTITUTION

Ex	22: 3	He should make full r;

RESTORATION† (see RESTORE)

Acts	3:21	until the times of r of all

RESTORE (see RESTORATION, RESTORED, RESTORES)

Gen	20: 7	r the man's wife; for he is
2Sa	12: 6	And he shall r fourfold for
Ps	51:12	R to me the joy of Your
Ps	60: 1	Oh, r us again!
Dan	9:25	forth of the command To r
Joel	2:25	So I will r to you the years
Matt	17:11	is coming first and will r
Luke	19: 8	I r fourfold."
Acts	1: 6	will You at this time r the
Gal	6: 1	you who are spiritual r

RESTORED (see RESTORE)

Ex	4: 7	it was r like his other
2Ki	5:10	and your flesh shall be r to
Dan	4:36	I was r to my kingdom, and
Mark	3: 5	and his hand was r as whole

RESTORES (see RESTORE)

Ps	23: 3	He r my soul; He leads me
Mark	9:12	is coming first and r all

RESTRAINS (see RESTRAINT)

2Th	2: 7	only He who now r will do

RESTRAINT (see RESTRAINS)

Prov	29:18	the people cast off r;

RESTS (see REST)

2Ki	2:15	The spirit of Elijah r on
1Pe	4:14	of glory and of God r upon

RESURRECTION

Matt	22:23	who say there is no r,
Matt	27:53	of the graves after His r,
John	5:29	to the r of life, and those
John	5:29	to the r of condemnation.
John	11:24	he will rise again in the r
John	11:25	I am the r and the life. He
Acts	1:22	a witness with us of His r
Acts	17:18	to them Jesus and the r
Acts	17:32	when they heard of the r of
Acts	23: 6	concerning the hope and r of
Acts	23: 8	say that there is no r—
Rom	1: 4	by the r from the dead.
Rom	6: 5	in the likeness of His r,
1Co	15:13	But if there is no r of the
1Co	15:42	So also is the r of the
Phil	3:10	Him and the power of His r,
Phil	3:11	I may attain to the r from
2Ti	2:18	saying that the r is already
Heb	11:35	they might obtain a better r
1Pe	1: 3	a living hope through the r
1Pe	3:21	through the r of Jesus
Rev	20: 6	who has part in the first r

RETAIN (see RETAINED)

John	20:23	if you r the sins of any,
Rom	1:28	as they did not like to r

RETAINED (see RETAIN)

John	20:23	the sins of any, they are r

RETURN (see RETURNED, RETURNING, RETURNS)

Gen	3:19	And to dust you shall r
Ex	13:17	and r to Egypt."
Deut	17:16	You shall not r that way
Ruth	1: 8	r each to her mother's
1Sa	7: 3	If you r to the LORD with
2Sa	12:23	but he shall not r to me."
Neh	7: 5	had come up in the first r,
Job	1:21	And naked shall I r there.
Job	10:21	from which I shall not r,
Job	16:22	I shall go the way of no r
Job	34:15	And man would r to dust.
Ps	59: 6	At evening they r,
Ps	116: 7	R to your rest, O my soul,
Prov	2:19	None who go to her r,
Eccl	1: 7	There they r again.
Eccl	3:20	and all r to dust.
Eccl	5:15	womb, naked shall he r,
Eccl	12: 2	And the clouds do not r
Eccl	12: 7	Then the dust will r to the
Eccl	12: 7	And the spirit will r to
Is	6:10	And r and be healed."
Is	10:21	The remnant shall r,
Is	55: 7	Let him r to the LORD,
Is	55:11	It shall not r to Me void,
Hos	2: 7	I will go and r to my first
Hos	6: 1	and let us r to the LORD;

Mal	3: 7	'In what way shall we **r**?
Matt	10:13	let your peace **r** to you.
1Pe	2:23	reviled, did not revile in **r**;

RETURNED (see RETURN)

Ezra	2: 1	and who **r** to Jerusalem and
Neh	7: 6	and who **r** to Jerusalem and
Is	38: 8	So the sun **r** ten degrees
Dan	4:34	and my understanding **r** to
Amos	4: 6	Yet you have not **r** to Me,"
Luke	2:20	Then the shepherds **r**,
Luke	10:17	Then the seventy **r** with joy,
Luke	24: 9	Then they **r** from the tomb and
Luke	24:52	and **r** to Jerusalem with
Acts	1:12	Then they **r** to Jerusalem
1Pe	2:25	but have now **r** to the

RETURNING (see RETURN)

Is	30:15	In **r** and rest you shall be
1Pe	3: 9	not **r** evil for evil or

RETURNS (see RETURN)

Prov	26:11	As a dog **r** to his own vomit,
2Pe	2:22	A dog **r** to his own

REUBEN

Gen	35:23	the sons of Leah were **R**,
Gen	46: 8	**R** was Jacob's firstborn.
Num	13: 4	names: from the tribe of **R**,

REUEL (see JETHRO)

Ex	2:18	When they came to **R** their

REVEAL (see REVEALED, REVEALS, REVELATION)

Esth	2:10	had charged her not to **r**
Dan	2:47	since you could **r** this
Matt	11:27	to whom the Son wills to **r**
1Co	4: 5	things of darkness and **r**
Gal	1:16	to **r** His Son in me, that I
Phil	3:15	God will **r** even this to you.

REVEALED (see REVEAL)

1Sa	3: 7	the word of the LORD yet **r**
Is	40: 5	of the LORD shall be **r**,
Is	53: 1	the arm of the LORD been **r**?
Dan	2:19	Then the secret was **r** to
Matt	10:26	covered that will not be **r**,
Matt	11:25	wise and prudent and have **r**
Matt	16:17	flesh and blood has not **r**
Luke	2:26	And it had been **r** to him by
Luke	2:35	of many hearts may be **r**
Luke	17:30	day when the Son of Man is **r**
John	1:31	but that He should be **r** to
John	9: 3	works of God should be **r** in
John	12:38	of the LORD been **r**?
Acts	23:22	no one that you have **r**
Rom	1:17	righteousness of God is **r**
Rom	1:18	For the wrath of God is **r**
Rom	3:21	God apart from the law is **r**,
Rom	8:18	the glory which shall be **r**
1Co	2:10	But God has **r** them to us
1Co	3:13	because it will be **r** by
1Co	14:25	secrets of his heart are **r**;

Gal	3:23	which would afterward be **r**
Col	1:26	but now has been **r** to His
2Th	1: 7	us when the Lord Jesus is **r**
2Th	2: 3	and the man of sin is **r**,
2Th	2: 8	the lawless one will be **r**,
2Ti	1:10	but has now been **r** by the
1Pe	1: 5	for salvation ready to be **r**
1Pe	1:12	To them it was **r** that, not to
1Pe	4:13	that when His glory is **r**,
1Pe	5: 1	of the glory that will be **r**:
1Jn	3: 2	and it has not yet been **r**
1Jn	3: 2	we know that when He is **r**,

REVEALS (see REVEAL)

Ps	19: 2	And night unto night **r**
Dan	2:28	is a God in heaven who **r**
Amos	3: 7	Unless He **r** His secret to

REVELATION (see REVEAL)

1Sa	3: 1	there was no widespread **r**
Prov	29:18	Where there is no **r**,
Luke	2:32	A light to bring **r** to the
1Co	14: 6	I speak to you either by **r**,
1Co	14:26	has a tongue, has a **r**,
Gal	1:12	but it came through the **r**
Gal	2: 2	And I went up by **r**,
Eph	1:17	the spirit of wisdom and **r**
Eph	3: 3	how that by **r** He made known
1Pe	1: 7	and glory at the **r** of Jesus
1Pe	1:13	be brought to you at the **r**
Rev	1: 1	The **R** of Jesus Christ, which

REVERENCE (see REVERENT)

1Ti	2: 2	life in all godliness and **r**
1Ti	3: 4	in submission with all **r**

REVERENT (see REVERENCE)

1Ti	3: 8	deacons must be **r**,
1Ti	3:11	their wives must be **r**,
Tit	2: 2	the older men be sober, **r**,

REVILE (see REVILED)

Matt	5:11	are you when they **r**
1Pe	2:23	did not **r** in return; when He

REVILED (see REVILE)

Mark	15:32	were crucified with Him **r**
1Pe	2:23	who, when He was **r**,

REVIVE (see REVIVED)

Ps	71:20	Shall **r** me again, And
Ps	85: 6	Will You not **r** us again,
Is	57:15	To **r** the spirit of the
Is	57:15	And to **r** the heart of the
Hab	3: 2	**r** Your work in the midst of

REVIVED (see REVIVE)

2Ki	13:21	he **r** and stood on his feet.
Rom	7: 9	sin **r** and I died.

REWARD (see REWARDER)

Gen	15: 1	your exceedingly great **r**
Ps	19:11	them there is great **r**
Ps	127: 3	fruit of the womb is a **r**

R

Prov	25:22	And the LORD will r you.
Matt	5:12	for great is your r in
Matt	5:46	what r have you? Do not even
Matt	6: 1	Otherwise you have no r from
Matt	6: 4	in secret will Himself r
Matt	10:41	shall receive a prophet's r
Matt	10:42	shall by no means lose his r
Matt	16:27	and then He will r each
Luke	23:41	for we receive the due r of
Heb	2: 2	received a just r,
Heb	10:35	which has great r
Heb	11:26	for he looked to the r

REWARDER† (see REWARD)

Heb	11: 6	and that He is a r of those

RHODA†

Acts	12:13	a girl named R came to

RIB

Gen	2:22	Then the r which the LORD

RICH (see RICHES, RICHLY)

Gen	13: 2	Abram was very r in
Gen	14:23	say, 'I have made Abram r'—
Is	53: 9	But with the r at His death,
Jer	9:23	Nor let the r man glory in
Matt	19:23	you that it is hard for a r
Matt	19:24	eye of a needle than for a r
Matt	27:57	there came a r man from
Luke	1:53	And the r He has sent away
Luke	12:21	and is not r toward God."
Luke	16:21	which fell from the r man's
Rom	10:12	the same Lord over all is r
1Co	4: 8	full! You are already r!
2Co	6:10	as poor, yet making many r;
2Co	8: 9	Christ, that though He was r,
2Co	8: 9	His poverty might become r
Eph	2: 4	who is r in mercy, because
Jas	1:11	So the r man also will fade
Rev	2: 9	and poverty (but you are r);
Rev	3:17	"Because you say, 'I am r,

RICHES (see RICH)

1Ki	3:11	nor have asked r for
Prov	8:18	R and honor are with me,
Prov	11:28	He who trusts in his r will
Prov	19:14	Houses and r are an
Prov	22: 1	chosen rather than great r,
Prov	27:24	For r are not forever, Nor
Jer	9:23	the rich man glory in his r;
Matt	13:22	and the deceitfulness of r
Mark	10:24	is for those who trust in r
Rom	2: 4	Or do you despise the r of
Rom	9:23	He might make known the r
Rom	11:33	the depth of the r both of
Eph	1:18	what are the r of the glory
Eph	2: 7	might show the exceeding r
Eph	3: 8	Gentiles the unsearchable r
Phil	4:19	need according to His r in
Col	1:27	to make known what are the r
1Ti	6:17	nor to trust in uncertain r
Heb	11:26	of Christ greater r than

RICHLY† (see RICH)

Col	3:16	of Christ dwell in you r in
1Ti	6:17	who gives us r all things to

RIDDLE

Judg	14:12	Let me pose a r to you. If

RIDE (see RIDER, RIDING)

Ps	45: 4	And in Your majesty r

RIDER (see RIDE)

Ex	15: 1	The horse and its r He

RIDING (see RIDE)

Zech	9: 9	Lowly and r on a donkey, A

RIGHT (see RIGHTLY)

Gen	18:25	Judge of all the earth do r?
Gen	48:13	Ephraim with his r hand
Deut	12:28	you do what is good and r
Deut	21:17	the r of the firstborn is
Judg	17: 6	everyone did what was r in
Ruth	4: 6	You redeem my r of
1Ki	11:33	in My ways to do what is r
1Ki	15:11	Asa did what was r in the
2Ki	14: 3	And he did what was r in
2Ki	16: 2	he did not do what was r
2Ch	3:17	the name of the one on the r
Job	33:27	and perverted what was r,
Job	35: 2	"Do you think this is r?
Job	40:14	to you That your own r
Job	42: 7	not spoken of Me what is r,
Ps	9: 4	You have maintained my r
Ps	16: 8	Because He is at my r
Ps	16:11	At Your r hand are
Ps	19: 8	statutes of the LORD are r,
Ps	20: 6	the saving strength of His r
Ps	33: 4	the word of the LORD is r,
Ps	44: 3	But it was Your r hand,
Ps	63: 8	Your r hand upholds me.
Ps	73:23	You hold me by my r hand.
Ps	78:54	This mountain which His r
Ps	80:17	be upon the man of Your r
Ps	91: 7	And ten thousand at your r
Ps	98: 1	His r hand and His holy arm
Ps	107: 7	He led them forth by the r
Ps	110: 1	Sit at My r hand, Till I
Ps	110: 5	The Lord is at Your r hand;
Ps	121: 5	is your shade at your r
Ps	137: 5	Let my r hand forget its
Ps	138: 7	And Your r hand will save
Ps	139:10	And Your r hand shall hold
Prov	14:12	is a way that seems r to
Prov	21: 2	Every way of a man is r in
Is	41:10	you with My righteous r
Is	45: 1	whose r hand I have held—To
Is	62: 8	LORD has sworn by His r
Jer	32: 7	for the r of redemption is
Jer	32: 8	for the r of inheritance is
Ezek	21:27	Until He comes whose r it
Jon	4: 9	Is it r for you to be angry
Jon	4:11	discern between their r
Matt	5:29	If your r eye causes you to

Matt	20:21	one on Your r hand and the
Matt	22:44	Sit at My r hand, Till
Matt	25:33	will set the sheep on His r
Matt	26:64	Son of Man sitting at the r
Mark	5:15	and clothed and in his r
Mark	16:19	and sat down at the r hand
John	1:12	to them He gave the r to
John	21: 6	Cast the net on the r side of
Acts	2:25	For He is at my r
Acts	7:55	and Jesus standing at the r
Rom	8:34	who is even at the r hand of
Eph	1:20	and seated Him at His r
Eph	6: 1	in the Lord, for this is r
Heb	1: 3	sat down at the r hand of
Heb	1:13	Sit at My r hand, Till

RIGHTEOUS (see RIGHTEOUSLY,
     RIGHTEOUSNESS, UNRIGHTEOUS)

Gen	7: 1	I have seen that you are r
Gen	18:23	You also destroy the r with
Gen	18:24	Suppose there were fifty r
Gen	38:26	She has been more r than I,
Job	22:19	The r see it and are glad,
Job	34: 5	"For Job has said, 'I am r,
Ps	1: 5	in the congregation of the r
Ps	1: 6	LORD knows the way of the r,
Ps	7: 9	For the r God tests the
Ps	14: 5	with the generation of the r
Ps	19: 9	the LORD are true and r
Ps	37:16	A little that a r man has
Ps	37:17	But the LORD upholds the r
Ps	37:25	Yet I have not seen the r
Ps	37:29	The r shall inherit the
Ps	92:12	The r shall flourish like a
Ps	143: 2	sight, no one living is r
Ps	145:17	The LORD is r in all His
Prov	10: 7	The memory of the r is
Prov	11:10	it goes well with the r,
Prov	11:28	But the r will flourish
Prov	11:30	The fruit of the r is a
Prov	13:22	is stored up for the r
Prov	15:29	He hears the prayer of the r
Prov	18:10	The r run to it and are
Eccl	7:16	Do not be overly r,
Is	41:10	I will uphold you with My r
Is	53:11	By His knowledge My r
Is	57: 1	The r perishes, And no man
Ezek	3:21	if you warn the r man that
Amos	2: 6	Because they sell the r for
Matt	9:13	I did not come to call the r,
Matt	10:41	And he who receives a r man
Matt	13:43	Then the r will shine forth
Matt	23:28	you also outwardly appear r
Luke	23:47	Certainly this was a r Man!"
John	5:30	judge; and My judgment is r,
John	17:25	O r Father! The world has not
Rom	1:32	knowing the r judgment of
Rom	3:10	"There is none r,
Rom	5: 7	For scarcely for a r man will
Rom	5:19	many will be made r
Rom	8: 4	that the r requirement of the
2Ti	4: 8	the r Judge, will give to me
Jas	5:16	fervent prayer of a r man
1Pe	4:18	If the r one is scarcely

2Pe	2: 7	and delivered r Lot, who
1Jn	2: 1	Father, Jesus Christ the r
Rev	16: 7	true and r are Your

RIGHTEOUSLY (see RIGHTEOUS)

Tit	2:12	we should live soberly, r,

RIGHTEOUSNESS (see RIGHTEOUS,
     RIGHTEOUSNESS', RIGHTEOUSNESSES)

Gen	15: 6	He accounted it to him for r
Ps	4: 1	O God of my r! You have
Ps	7: 8	O LORD, according to my r,
Ps	7:17	the LORD according to His r,
Ps	9: 8	shall judge the world in r,
Ps	23: 3	leads me in the paths of r
Ps	24: 5	And r from the God of his
Ps	35:28	shall speak of Your r And
Ps	40: 9	the good news of r In the
Ps	45: 6	A scepter of r is the
Ps	45: 7	You love r and hate
Ps	85:10	R and peace have kissed.
Ps	96:13	shall judge the world with r,
Ps	103:17	And His r to children's
Ps	106:31	was accounted to him for r
Ps	111: 3	And His r endures forever.
Prov	2:20	And keep to the paths of r
Prov	10: 2	But r delivers from death.
Prov	11:19	As r leads to life, So he
Prov	14:34	R exalts a nation, But sin
Prov	16: 8	Better is a little with r,
Prov	16:12	a throne is established by r
Is	5: 7	behold, oppression; For r,
Is	11: 4	But with r He shall judge
Is	11: 5	R shall be the belt of His
Is	28:17	And r the plummet; The
Is	45:23	gone out of My mouth in r,
Is	61:10	me with the robe of r,
Jer	23: 5	raise to David a Branch of r;
Jer	23: 6	be called: THE LORD OUR R.
Ezek	14:14	only themselves by their r,
Ezek	33:13	but he trusts in his own r
Dan	9:24	To bring in everlasting r,
Dan	12: 3	those who turn many to r
Hos	2:19	betroth you to Me In r and
Hos	10:12	Till He comes and rains r
Amos	5:24	And r like a mighty stream.
Mal	4: 2	fear My name The Sun of R
Matt	3:15	for us to fulfill all r
Matt	5: 6	who hunger and thirst for r,
Matt	5:20	that unless your r exceeds
Matt	6:33	the kingdom of God and His r,
John	16: 8	the world of sin, and of r,
Acts	17:31	He will judge the world in r
Acts	24:25	Now as he reasoned about r,
Rom	1:17	For in it the r of God is
Rom	4: 3	accounted to him for r
Rom	4: 5	his faith is accounted for r,
Rom	4: 6	man to whom God imputes r
Rom	4:11	a seal of the r of the faith
Rom	6:13	as instruments of r to God.
Rom	6:18	sin, you became slaves of r
Rom	8:10	Spirit is life because of r
Rom	9:31	pursuing the law of r,
Rom	10: 3	being ignorant of God's r,

R

Rom	10: 3	to establish their own r,
Rom	10: 4	the end of the law for r to
Rom	10:10	heart one believes unto r,
Rom	14:17	but r and peace and joy in
2Co	5:21	that we might become the r
2Co	6: 7	by the armor of r on the
2Co	11:15	into ministers of r,
Gal	2:21	for if r comes through the
Gal	3: 6	accounted to him for r.
Eph	6:14	put on the breastplate of r,
Phil	3: 9	in Him, not having my own r,
1Ti	6:11	these things and pursue r,
2Ti	2:22	youthful lusts; but pursue r,
2Ti	3:16	for instruction in r,
2Ti	4: 8	up for me the crown of r,
Tit	3: 5	not by works of r which we
Heb	1: 8	A scepter of r is the
Heb	1: 9	You have loved r and
Heb	7: 2	being translated "king of r,
Jas	2:23	accounted to him for r.
1Pe	2:24	to sins, might live for r—
2Pe	2: 5	people, a preacher of r,
2Pe	3:13	and a new earth in which r

RIGHTEOUSNESS' (*see* RIGHTEOUSNESS)

Matt	5:10	who are persecuted for r

RIGHTEOUSNESSES† (*see* RIGHTEOUSNESS)

Is	64: 6	And all our r are like

RIGHTLY (*see* RIGHT)

Gen	27:36	Is he not r named Jacob? For
2Ti	2:15	r dividing the word of

RING

Prov	11:22	As a r of gold in a swine's
Luke	15:22	and put a r on his hand and

RIPE

Jer	24: 2	the figs that are first r;

RISE (*see* AWAKE, RISEN, RISES, RISING, ROSE)

Num	24:17	A Scepter shall r out of
Deut	6: 7	and when you r up.
Neh	2:18	Let us r up and build." Then
Job	14:12	man lies down and does not r.
Ps	27: 3	Though war should r against
Prov	31:28	Her children r up and call
Song	2:10	R up, my love, my fair one,
Matt	5:45	for He makes His sun r on
Matt	12:41	The men of Nineveh will r up
Matt	20:19	And the third day He will r
Matt	24: 7	For nation will r against
Matt	24:11	many false prophets will r
Matt	27:63	'After three days I will r
Luke	5:23	R up and walk'?
Luke	22:46	R and pray, lest you enter
John	11:23	Your brother will r again."
Acts	3: 6	r up and walk."
1Co	15:15	in fact the dead do not r
1Th	4:16	the dead in Christ will r

RISEN (*see* RISE)

Matt	17: 9	until the Son of Man is r

Matt	28: 6	is not here; for He is r,
Mark	6:14	John the Baptist is r from
Mark	16:14	had seen Him after He had r
Luke	24: 6	but is r! Remember how He
Luke	24:34	The Lord is r indeed, and has
1Co	15:13	dead, then Christ is not r

RISES (*see* RISE)

Eccl	1: 5	The sun also r,
Eccl	12: 4	When one r up at the sound
2Pe	1:19	and the morning star r in

RISING (*see* RISE)

Ps	19: 6	Its r is from one end of
Ps	139: 2	my sitting down and my r up;
Luke	2:34	destined for the fall and r

RIVER (*see* RIVERS)

Gen	2:10	Now a r went out of Eden to
Gen	15:18	from the r of Egypt to the
Gen	15:18	of Egypt to the great r,
Ps	46: 4	There is a r whose streams
Mark	1: 5	by him in the Jordan R,

RIVERS (*see* RIVER)

Ps	1: 3	a tree Planted by the r of
Ps	78:44	Turned their r into blood,
Ps	137: 1	By the r of Babylon, There
Mic	6: 7	Ten thousand r of oil?
John	7:38	of his heart will flow r of

ROAD

Acts	26:13	along the r I saw a light

ROAR (*see* ROARED, ROARING, ROARS)

Ps	96:11	be glad; Let the sea r,

ROARED (*see* ROAR)

Amos	3: 8	A lion has r! Who will not

ROARING (*see* ROAR)

Ps	22:13	Like a raging and r lion.
1Pe	5: 8	devil walks about like a r

ROARS (*see* ROAR)

Amos	1: 2	The LORD r from Zion, And

ROB (*see* ROBBER, ROBBERY)

Mal	3: 8	Will a man r God? Yet you

ROBBER (*see* ROB, ROBBERS)

John	10: 1	the same is a thief and a r

ROBBERS (*see* ROBBER)

Matt	27:38	Then two r were crucified
John	10: 8	before Me are thieves and r,

ROBBERY (*see* ROB)

Phil	2: 6	did not consider it r to be

ROBE (*see* ROBES)

Ex	28: 4	a breastplate, an ephod, a r,
Ex	29: 5	and the r of the ephod, the
1Sa	2:19	used to make him a little r,

1Sa	15:27	seized the edge of his **r**
1Sa	24: 4	cut off a corner of Saul's **r**
2Sa	13:18	Now she had on a **r** of many
2Sa	15:32	to meet him with his **r** torn
Esth	6: 8	let a royal **r** be brought
Job	1:20	Then Job arose, tore his **r**
Job	2:12	and each one tore his **r** and
Song	5: 3	I have taken off my **r**;
Is	6: 1	and the train of His **r**
Is	61:10	has covered me with the **r**
Matt	27:28	Him and put a scarlet **r** on
Luke	15:22	Bring out the best **r** and put
John	19: 2	they put on Him a purple **r**
Rev	6:11	Then a white **r** was given to
Rev	19:13	He was clothed with a **r**

ROBES (*see* ROBE)

Ps	45:14	be brought to the King in **r**
Is	63: 3	And I have stained all My **r**
Mark	12:38	to go around in long **r**
Rev	7: 9	Lamb, clothed with white **r**
Rev	7:14	and washed their **r** and made

ROCK (*see* ROCKS)

Ex	17: 6	and you shall strike the **r**
Ex	33:22	you in the cleft of the **r**
Num	20: 8	water for them out of the **r**
Num	20:11	his hand and struck the **r**
Deut	32: 4	He is the **R**,
Deut	32:13	him draw honey from the **r**
1Sa	2: 2	Nor is there any **r** like
2Sa	22: 2	The LORD is my **r** and my
Job	19:24	they were engraved on a **r**
Ps	18: 2	The LORD is my **r** and my
Ps	27: 5	shall set me high upon a **r**
Ps	28: 1	You I will cry, O LORD my **R**:
Ps	31: 3	For You are my **r** and my
Ps	40: 2	And set my feet upon a **r**
Ps	61: 2	Lead me to the **r** that is
Ps	78:16	brought streams out of the **r**
Ps	81:16	And with honey from the **r**
Ps	94:22	And my God the **r** of my
Ps	137: 9	little ones against the **r**!
Prov	30:19	The way of a serpent on a **r**
Is	8:14	a stone of stumbling and a **r**
Is	32: 2	As the shadow of a great **r**
Is	51: 1	Look to the **r** from which
Jer	23:29	a hammer that breaks the **r**
Matt	7:24	who built his house on the **r**:
Matt	7:25	for it was founded on the **r**
Matt	16:18	and on this **r** I will build
Matt	27:60	he had hewn out of the **r**;
Luke	8: 6	"Some fell on **r**;
Rom	9:33	a stumbling stone and **r**
1Co	10: 4	drank of that spiritual **R**
1Co	10: 4	and that **R** was Christ.
1Pe	2: 8	of stumbling And a **r**

ROCKS (*see* ROCK)

1Sa	13: 6	in caves, in thickets, in **r**
1Ki	19:11	mountains and broke the **r**
Amos	6:12	Do horses run on **r**?
Matt	27:51	and the **r** were split,
Acts	27:29	should run aground on the **r**

ROD (*see* RODS)

Ex	4: 4	and it became a **r** in his
Ex	4:20	And Moses took the **r** of God
Ex	7:12	But Aaron's **r** swallowed up
Ex	8:16	Aaron, 'Stretch out your **r**
Num	20:11	the rock twice with his **r**;
2Sa	7:14	will chasten him with the **r**
Ps	2: 9	shall break them with a **r**
Ps	23: 4	Your **r** and Your staff, they
Prov	13:24	He who spares his **r** hates
Prov	22:15	The **r** of correction will
Prov	23:13	if you beat him with a **r**
Is	9: 4	The **r** of his oppressor, As
Is	10: 5	the **r** of My anger And the
Is	11: 1	There shall come forth a **R**
Heb	9: 4	Aaron's **r** that budded, and
Rev	2:27	rule them with a **r** of

RODS (*see* ROD)

2Co	11:25	times I was beaten with **r**;

ROLL (*see* ROLLED)

Mark	16: 3	Who will **r** away the stone

ROLLED (*see* ROLL)

Gen	29:10	that Jacob went near and **r**
Is	9: 5	And garments **r** in blood,
Is	34: 4	And the heavens shall be **r**
Matt	27:60	and he **r** a large stone
Rev	6:14	as a scroll when it is **r** up,

ROMAN (*see* ROME)

Acts	22:26	you do, for this man is a **R**.

ROME (*see* ROMAN)

Acts	23:11	must also bear witness at **R**.
2Ti	1:17	but when he arrived in **R**,

ROOF

Gen	19: 8	under the shadow of my **r**
2Sa	11: 2	his bed and walked on the **r**
Ps	137: 6	my tongue cling to the **r** of
Matt	8: 8	You should come under my **r**
Mark	2: 4	they uncovered the **r** where

ROOM

Mal	3:10	there will not be **r**
Matt	6: 6	you pray, go into your **r**
Luke	2: 7	because there was no **r** for
Luke	14:22	and still there is **r**
Acts	1:13	went up into the upper **r**

ROOSTER

Matt	26:34	before the **r** crows, you will
Mark	14:30	before the **r** crows twice,

ROOT (*see* ROOTED, ROOTS)

Deut	29:18	may not be among you a **r**
Job	19:28	Since the **r** of the matter
Is	11:10	that day there shall be a **R**
Is	53: 2	And as a **r** out of dry
Matt	3:10	now the ax is laid to the **r**
Matt	13: 6	and because they had no **r**

R

Rom	11:16	and if the r is holy, so
1Ti	6:10	the love of money is a r of
Heb	12:15	lest any r of bitterness
Rev	5: 5	the R of David, has
Rev	22:16	I am the R and the Offspring

ROOTED (see ROOT)

Eph	3:17	being r and grounded in

ROOTS (see ROOT)

Amos	2: 9	his fruit above And his r

ROPES

Judg	15:13	bound him with two new r
Jer	38: 6	let Jeremiah down with r

ROSE (see RISE)

Gen	4: 8	that Cain r up against Abel
Gen	22: 3	So Abraham r early in the
Ex	32: 6	and r up to play.
Josh	6:15	the seventh day that they r
Ruth	2:15	And when she r up to glean,
1Sa	25:42	So Abigail r in haste and
2Ch	13: 6	r up and rebelled against
Ps	18:39	under me those who r up
Ps	124: 2	When men r up against us,
Song	2: 1	I am the r of Sharon, And
Is	35: 1	rejoice and blossom as the r;
John	11:31	when they saw that Mary r up
John	13: 4	r from supper and laid aside
Acts	5:36	some time ago Theudas r
Acts	18:12	the Jews with one accord r
Rom	14: 9	this end Christ died and r
1Co	10: 7	and r up to play."
1Co	15: 4	and that He r again the
2Co	5:15	Him who died for them and r
1Th	4:14	that Jesus died and r again,

ROSH

Ezek	38: 3	you, O Gog, the prince of R,

ROTTENNESS

Prov	14:30	But envy is r to the

ROUGH

Is	40: 4	be made straight And the r
Luke	3: 5	straight And the r

ROYAL

Jas	2: 8	If you really fulfill the r
1Pe	2: 9	a r priesthood, a holy

RUBBISH

Phil	3: 8	things, and count them as r,

RUBIES

Job	28:18	price of wisdom is above r
Prov	3:15	is more precious than r,
Prov	8:11	wisdom is better than r,
Prov	31:10	her worth is far above r.

RUDDER

Jas	3: 4	are turned by a very small r

RUDDY

1Sa	16:12	him in. Now he was r,
Song	5:10	My beloved is white and r,

RUIN (see RUINED, RUINS)

Luke	6:49	And the r of that house was
2Ti	2:14	to the r of the hearers.

RUINED (see RUIN)

Matt	9:17	and the wineskins are r

RUINS (see RUIN)

Is	61: 4	they shall rebuild the old r,
Jer	9:11	make Jerusalem a heap of r,
Jer	26:18	shall become heaps of r,
Amos	9:11	I will raise up its r,
Mic	3:12	shall become heaps of r,
Hag	1: 4	this temple to lie in r?
Acts	15:16	I will rebuild its r,

RULE (see RULER, RULES)

Gen	1:16	the greater light to r the
Gen	3:16	And he shall r over you."
Gen	4: 7	but you should r over it."
Judg	8:23	the LORD shall r over
Ps	110: 2	R in the midst of Your
Ps	136: 8	The sun to r by day, For
Prov	8:16	By me princes r,
Is	3: 4	And babes shall r over
Is	3:12	And women r over them. O
Is	40:10	And His arm shall r for
1Co	15:24	He puts an end to all r and
Gal	6:16	as walk according to this r,
Phil	3:16	let us walk by the same r,
Col	3:15	And let the peace of God r in
1Ti	3: 5	a man does not know how to r
1Ti	5:17	Let the elders who r well be
Heb	13:17	Obey those who r over you,
Rev	2:27	He shall r them with a

RULER (see RULE, RULERS)

2Sa	5: 2	and be r over Israel.'"
2Sa	7: 8	to be r over My people, over
Dan	2:38	and has made you r over them
Dan	5: 7	and he shall be the third r
Mic	5: 2	to Me The One to be R in
Matt	2: 6	of you shall come a R
Matt	25:21	I will make you r over many
John	3: 1	a r of the Jews.
John	12:31	now the r of this world will
Acts	7:27	Who made you a r and a

RULERS (see RULER)

Ex	18:21	r of hundreds, rulers of
Ps	2: 2	And the r take counsel
Matt	2: 6	the least among the r
Acts	3:17	as did also your r
Rom	13: 3	For r are not a terror to
1Co	2: 6	nor of the r of this age,
Eph	6:12	against the r of the

RULES (see RULE)

Ps	59:13	let them know that God r in

Ps	103:19	And His kingdom r over all.
Prov	16:32	And he who r his spirit
Dan	4:17	know That the Most High r
Dan	4:26	come to know that Heaven r
1Ti	3: 4	one who r his own house well,
2Ti	2: 5	competes according to the r

RUMORS

Matt	24: 6	you will hear of wars and r

RUN (*see* RAN, RUNNING, RUNS)

2Ch	16: 9	the eyes of the LORD r
Ps	18:29	For by You I can r against a
Ps	19: 5	like a strong man to r its
Prov	18:10	The righteous r to it and
Is	40:31	They shall r and not be
Jer	12: 5	If you have r with the
Dan	12: 4	many shall r to and fro, and
Amos	5:24	But let justice r down like
Hab	2: 2	That he may r who reads it.
1Co	9:24	not know that those who r
Gal	2: 2	lest by any means I might r,
2Th	3: 1	the word of the Lord may r
Heb	12: 1	and let us r with endurance
1Pe	4: 4	it strange that you do not r
Jude	11	have r greedily in the error

RUNNING (*see* RUN)

Ps	133: 2	R down on the beard, The

RUNS (*see* RUN)

Ps	23: 5	My cup r over.
Rom	9:16	who wills, nor of him who r,

RUSHING

Acts	2: 2	as of a r mighty wind, and

RUST

Matt	6:19	where moth and r destroy and

S

SABACHTHANI†

Matt	27:46	saying, "Eli, Eli, lama s?
Mark	15:34	saying, "Eloi, Eloi, lama s?

SABAOTH†

Rom	9:29	Unless the Lord of S
Jas	5: 4	the ears of the Lord of S.

SABBATH (*see* SABBATHS)

Ex	16:23	Tomorrow is a S rest, a holy
Ex	20: 8	Remember the S day, to keep
Ex	20:11	the LORD blessed the S day
Ex	31:15	does any work on the S day,
Num	15:32	gathering sticks on the S
Matt	12: 2	is not lawful to do on the S!
Matt	12: 8	of Man is Lord even of the S.
Mark	2:27	man, and not man for the S.
Acts	1:12	a S day's journey.

SABBATHS (*see* SABBATH)

Lev	23:15	seven S shall be completed.

SACK

Gen	42:25	every man's money to his s,
Gen	44:12	was found in Benjamin's s.

SACKCLOTH

Jon	3: 5	a fast, and put on s,
Matt	11:21	have repented long ago in s

SACRIFICE (*see* SACRIFICED, SACRIFICES)

Ex	3:18	that we may s to the LORD
Ex	12:27	It is the Passover s of the
1Sa	1:21	to the LORD the yearly s
1Sa	15:22	to obey is better than s,
2Ch	7:12	for Myself as a house of s.
Ps	40: 6	S and offering You did not
Ps	50: 5	made a covenant with Me by s.
Ps	51:16	For You do not desire s,
Dan	9:27	He shall bring an end to s
Dan	12:11	the time that the daily s
Hos	6: 6	I desire mercy and not s,
Matt	9:13	desire mercy and not s.
Matt	12: 7	desire mercy and not s,
Rom	12: 1	your bodies a living s,
Eph	5: 2	an offering and a s to God
Phil	4:18	aroma, an acceptable s,
Heb	10: 5	S and offering You did
Heb	10:12	after He had offered one s
Heb	10:26	there no longer remains a s
Heb	11: 4	to God a more excellent s

SACRIFICED (*see* SACRIFICE)

1Co	5: 7	our Passover, was s for us.
Rev	2:14	to eat things s to idols,

SACRIFICES (*see* SACRIFICE)

Ps	4: 5	Offer the s of
Ps	51:17	The s of God are a broken
Ps	106:28	And ate s made to the dead
Ps	107:22	Let them sacrifice the s of
Is	1:11	is the multitude of your s
Is	1:13	Bring no more futile s;
Is	43:23	you honored Me with your s.
Dan	8:11	and by him the daily s were
Hos	14: 2	For we will offer the s of
Amos	4: 4	Bring your s every morning,
Amos	5:25	Did you offer Me s and
Mal	1:14	But s to the Lord what is
Luke	13: 1	had mingled with their s.
Acts	7:41	offered s to the idol, and
1Co	10:18	not those who eat of the s
Heb	5: 1	may offer both gifts and s
Heb	5: 3	to offer s for sins.
Heb	7:27	high priests, to offer up s,
Heb	9:23	themselves with better s
Heb	10: 6	burnt offerings and s
Heb	10:11	repeatedly the same s,
Heb	13:16	for with such s God is well
1Pe	2: 5	to offer up spiritual s

S

SAD

| 1Sa | 1:18 | her face was no longer s. |
| Neh | 2: 2 | to me, "Why is your face s, |

SADDUCEES

| Matt | 3: 7 | many of the Pharisees and S |
| Acts | 23: 8 | For S say that there is no |

SAFE (see SAFELY, SAFETY)

| Prov | 18:10 | run to it and are s. |

SAFELY (see SAFE)

| 1Ki | 4:25 | And Judah and Israel dwelt s, |

SAFETY (see SAFE)

Prov	11:14	of counselors there is s.
Is	14:30	the needy will lie down in s;
1Th	5: 3	Peace and s!" then sudden

SAINTS

1Sa	2: 9	will guard the feet of His s,
Ps	30: 4	You s of His, And give
Ps	34: 9	you His s! There is no
Ps	89: 5	in the assembly of the s.
Ps	97:10	preserves the souls of His s;
Ps	116:15	Is the death of His s.
Dan	7:18	But the s of the Most High
Dan	7:21	was making war against the s,
Matt	27:52	and many bodies of the s who
Rom	1: 7	of God, called to be s:
Rom	8:27	makes intercession for the s
Rom	12:13	to the needs of the s,
Rom	15:25	to minister to the s.
Rom	16: 2	in a manner worthy of the s,
1Co	1: 2	Jesus, called to be s,
1Co	6: 2	Do you not know that the s
1Co	14:33	in all the churches of the s.
1Co	16: 1	the collection for the s,
1Co	16:15	to the ministry of the s—
2Co	1: 1	with all the s who are in
Eph	1:15	and your love for all the s,
Eph	1:18	of His inheritance in the s,
Eph	2:19	fellow citizens with the s
Eph	3: 8	than the least of all the s,
Eph	3:18	to comprehend with all the s
Eph	4:12	for the equipping of the s
Eph	6:18	supplication for all the s—
Col	1:12	of the inheritance of the s
1Th	3:13	Jesus Christ with all His s.
2Th	1:10	to be glorified in His s and
Jude	3	for all delivered to the s.
Jude	14	with ten thousands of His s,
Rev	5: 8	are the prayers of the s.
Rev	13: 7	him to make war with the s
Rev	15: 3	O King of the s!
Rev	17: 6	with the blood of the s and

SAKE

Ps	23: 3	For His name's s.
Phil	1:29	but also to suffer for His s,
Col	1:24	for the s of His body, which
1Jn	2:12	you for His name's s.

SALEM (see JERUSALEM)

Gen	14:18	Then Melchizedek king of S
Ps	76: 2	In S also is His tabernacle,
Heb	7: 1	this Melchizedek, king of S,

SALOME

| Mark | 16: 1 | and S bought spices, that |

SALT

Gen	14: 3	(that is, the S Sea).
Gen	19:26	and she became a pillar of s.
Num	18:19	it is a covenant of s
Judg	9:45	the city and sowed it with s.
Matt	5:13	You are the s of the earth;
Col	4: 6	with grace, seasoned with s,

SALVATION (see SAVE)

Ex	14:13	and see the s of the LORD,
Ex	15: 2	And He has become my s;
Deut	32:15	esteemed the Rock of his s.
1Sa	2: 1	Because I rejoice in Your s.
2Sa	22: 3	shield and the horn of my s,
Ps	3: 8	S belongs to the LORD
Ps	9:14	I will rejoice in Your s.
Ps	27: 1	LORD is my light and my s;
Ps	51:12	to me the joy of Your s,
Ps	51:14	O God, The God of my s,
Ps	89:26	God, and the rock of my s.
Ps	95: 1	to the Rock of our s.
Ps	96: 2	the good news of His s from
Ps	98: 2	LORD has made known His s;
Ps	98: 3	of the earth have seen the s
Ps	116:13	I will take up the cup of s,
Ps	118:14	And He has become my s.
Is	45:17	LORD With an everlasting s;
Is	52: 7	things, Who proclaims s,
Is	52:10	the earth shall see The s
Is	59:16	His own arm brought s for
Is	59:17	And a helmet of s on His
Jon	2: 9	S is of the LORD."
Zech	9: 9	He is just and having s,
Luke	1:69	has raised up a horn of s
Luke	2:30	my eyes have seen Your s
Luke	3: 6	flesh shall see the s
Luke	19: 9	Today s has come to this
John	4:22	for s is of the Jews.
Acts	4:12	Nor is there s in any other,
Acts	16:17	proclaim to us the way of s.
Rom	1:16	it is the power of God to s
Rom	10:10	confession is made unto s.
Rom	13:11	for now our s is nearer
2Co	6: 2	behold, now is the day of s.
Eph	1:13	truth, the gospel of your s;
Eph	6:17	And take the helmet of s,
Phil	2:12	work out your own s with
1Th	5: 8	as a helmet the hope of s.
1Th	5: 9	but to obtain s through our
2Ti	3:15	able to make you wise for s
Heb	1:14	for those who will inherit s?
Heb	2: 3	if we neglect so great a s,
Heb	2:10	make the captain of their s
Heb	5: 9	the author of eternal s to
1Pe	1: 9	the s of your souls.

1Pe	1:10	Of this s the prophets have

SALVE†

Rev	3:18	anoint your eyes with eye s,

SAMARIA (see SAMARITAN)

1Ki	16:24	And he bought the hill of **S**
1Ki	16:24	the city which he built, **S**,
John	4: 4	He needed to go through **S**.
John	4: 7	A woman of **S** came to draw
Acts	1: 8	and in all Judea and **S**,

SAMARITAN† (see SAMARIA, SAMARITANS)

Luke	10:33	"But a certain **S**,
Luke	17:16	Him thanks. And he was a **S**.
John	4: 9	a **S** woman?" For Jews have
John	8:48	say rightly that You are a **S**

SAMARITANS (see SAMARITAN)

John	4: 9	Jews have no dealings with **S**.

SAMSON

Judg	16: 6	So Delilah said to **S**,
Judg	16:29	And **S** took hold of the two
Heb	11:32	of Gideon and Barak and **S**

SAMUEL

1Sa	1:20	a son, and called his name **S**,
1Sa	3:10	**S**! Samuel!" And Samuel
1Sa	7:15	And **S** judged Israel all the
1Sa	16:13	Then **S** took the horn of oil
1Sa	25: 1	Then **S** died; and the
1Sa	28:11	Bring up **S** for me."
1Sa	28:12	When the woman saw **S**,
Acts	3:24	from **S** and those who follow,
Acts	13:20	until **S** the prophet.
Heb	11:32	also of David and **S** and the

SANBALLAT

Neh	6:14	God, remember Tobiah and **S**,

SANCTIFICATION (see SANCTIFY)

1Co	1:30	and righteousness and s and
1Th	4: 3	is the will of God, your s:
1Th	4: 4	possess his own vessel in s
2Th	2:13	you for salvation through s

SANCTIFIED (see SANCTIFY)

Gen	2: 3	the seventh day and s it,
Jer	1: 5	Before you were born I s
John	10:36	say of Him whom the Father s
John	17:19	that they also may be s by
Acts	20:32	among all those who are s.
Acts	26:18	among those who are s by
Rom	15:16	s by the Holy Spirit.
1Co	1: 2	to those who are s in Christ
1Co	6:11	were washed, but you were s,
1Co	7:14	unbelieving husband is s by
2Ti	2:21	s and useful for the Master,
Jude	1	s by God the Father, and

SANCTIFIES (see SANCTIFY)

Heb	2:11	For both He who s and those
Heb	9:13	s for the purifying of the

SANCTIFY (see SANCTIFICATION, SANCTIFIED, SANCTIFIES)

Num	6:11	and he shall s his head that
Neh	13:22	to s the Sabbath day.
Ezek	36:23	And I will s My great name,
Ezek	38:23	I will magnify Myself and s
John	17:17	**S** them by Your truth. Your
John	17:19	And for their sakes I s
Eph	5:26	that He might s and cleanse
1Th	5:23	the God of peace Himself s
Heb	13:12	that He might s the people
1Pe	3:15	But s the Lord God in your

SANCTUARY

Ex	25: 8	"And let them make Me a s,
Ex	30:13	to the shekel of the s (a
Lev	16:33	atonement for the Holy **S**,
Ps	96: 6	and beauty are in His s.
Ps	150: 1	LORD! Praise God in His s;
Dan	9.26	destroy the city and the s.
Heb	9: 1	service and the earthly s.
Heb	13:11	blood is brought into the s

SAND

Gen	22:17	of the heaven and as the s
Gen	32:12	your descendants as the s
Matt	7:26	who built his house on the s:
Rom	9:27	of Israel be as the s

SANDAL (see SANDALS)

Mark	1: 7	whose s strap I am not

SANDALS (see SANDAL)

Ex	3: 5	Take your s off your feet,
Deut	29: 5	and your s have not worn out
Amos	2: 6	the poor for a pair of s.
Matt	3:11	whose s I am not worthy to

SANG (see SING)

Job	38: 7	When the morning stars s
Rev	5: 9	And they s a new song,

SANK (see SINK)

Judg	5:27	At her feet he s,
1Sa	17:49	so that the stone s into his
Jer	38: 6	So Jeremiah s in the mire.

SAPPHIRA†

Acts	5: 1	with **S** his wife, sold a

SARAH (see SARAI)

Gen	17:19	**S** your wife shall bear you a
Gen	18:12	Therefore **S** laughed within
Gen	21: 1	And the LORD visited **S** as He
Is	51: 2	And to **S** who bore you;
Heb	11:11	By faith **S** herself also

SARAI (see SARAH)

Gen	11:29	name of Abram's wife was **S**,

SARGON†

Is	20: 1	when **S** the king of Assyria

S

SAT (see SIT)

Ex	32: 6	and the people s down to eat
Ps	137: 1	There we s down, yea, we
Jer	15:17	I s alone because of Your
Mark	11: 2	tied, on which no one has s.
Mark	16:19	and s down at the right hand
Luke	10:39	who also s at Jesus' feet
1Co	10: 7	The people s down to eat
Heb	1: 3	s down at the right hand of
Rev	4: 2	and One s on the throne.
Rev	14:14	and on the cloud s One like
Rev	19:19	make war against Him who s

SATAN

1Ch	21: 1	Now S stood up against
Job	1: 6	and S also came among them.
Zech	3: 1	and S standing at his right
Matt	4:10	S! For it is written, 'You
Matt	12:26	If S casts out Satan, he is
Matt	16:23	S! You are an offense to Me,
Mark	1:13	forty days, tempted by S,
Luke	10:18	I saw S fall like lightning
Luke	11:18	If S also is divided against
Luke	22: 3	Then S entered Judas,
Rom	16:20	God of peace will crush S
1Co	5: 5	deliver such a one to S for
2Co	12: 7	a messenger of S to buffet
1Th	2:18	but S hindered us.
1Ti	1:20	whom I delivered to S that
Rev	2: 9	but are a synagogue of S.
Rev	2:24	not known the depths of S,
Rev	12: 9	old, called the Devil and S,
Rev	20: 7	S will be released from his

SATISFIED (see SATISFY)

Ps	63: 5	My soul shall be s as with
Prov	27:20	the eyes of man are never s.
Eccl	1: 8	The eye is not s with
Is	53:11	labor of His soul, and be s.
Hab	2: 5	like death, and cannot be s,

SATISFIES (see SATISFY)

Ps	103: 5	Who s your mouth with good

SATISFY (see SATISFIED, SATISFIES)

Ps	91:16	With long life I will s him,

SAUL (see PAUL)

1Sa	9: 3	And Kish said to his son S,
1Sa	9:17	And when Samuel saw S,
1Sa	11:15	and there they made S king
1Sa	14: 1	that Jonathan the son of S
1Sa	18: 7	S has slain his thousands,
2Sa	1:17	this lamentation over S and
Acts	7:58	feet of a young man named S.
Acts	9: 4	a voice saying to him, "S,
Acts	13:21	so God gave them S the son

SAVE (see SALVATION, SAVED, SAVING, SAVIOR)

Ps	3: 7	S me, O my God! For You
Ps	6: 4	s me for Your mercies' sake!
Ps	22:21	S Me from the lion's mouth
Ps	44: 3	Nor did their own arm s
Ps	57: 3	send from heaven and s me;
Ps	59: 2	And s me from bloodthirsty
Ps	69: 1	S me, O God! For the waters
Ps	72:13	And will s the souls of the
Ps	86:16	And s the son of Your
Ps	138: 7	And Your right hand will s
Is	45:20	pray to a god that cannot s.
Is	49:25	And I will s your children.
Is	59: 1	shortened, That it cannot s;
Is	63: 1	righteousness, mighty to s.
Jer	15:20	For I am with you to s you
Jer	17:14	S me, and I shall be saved,
Jer	46:27	I will s you from afar, And
Ezek	3:18	to s his life, that same
Ezek	13:22	from his wicked way to s
Ezek	34:22	therefore I will s My flock,
Hos	1: 7	Will s them by the LORD
Zeph	3:19	I will s the lame, And
Matt	1:21	for He will s His people
Matt	8:25	s us! We are perishing!"
Matt	16:25	For whoever desires to s his
Matt	18:11	the Son of Man has come to s
Matt	27:40	s Yourself! If You are the
Matt	27:42	others; Himself He cannot s.
Matt	27:49	see if Elijah will come to s
Mark	3: 4	to s life or to kill?" But
Mark	8:35	and the gospel's will s it.
Mark	15:30	s Yourself, and come down
Luke	23:37	of the Jews, s Yourself."
John	12:27	s Me from this hour'? But
1Co	9:22	that I might by all means s
1Ti	1:15	came into the world to s
1Ti	4:16	for in doing this you will s
Heb	5: 7	to Him who was able to s
Heb	7:25	He is also able to s to the
Jas	1:21	which is able to s your
Jas	2:14	Can faith s him?
Jas	5:15	the prayer of faith will s

SAVED (see SAVE)

Ps	18: 3	So shall I be s from my
Ps	34: 6	And s him out of all his
Ps	80: 3	And we shall be s!
Is	30:15	and rest you shall be s;
Is	45:22	"Look to Me, and be s,
Is	63: 9	the Angel of His Presence s
Jer	8:20	And we are not s!"
Jer	17:14	Save me, and I shall be s,
Joel	2:32	of the LORD Shall be s.
Matt	10:22	endures to the end will be s.
Matt	19:25	saying, "Who then can be s?
Matt	27:42	He s others; Himself He
Mark	16:16	and is baptized will be s;
Luke	7:50	Your faith has s you. Go in
John	3:17	world through Him might be s.
John	10: 9	enters by Me, he will be s,
Acts	2:21	the LORD Shall be s.
Acts	2:47	daily those who were being s.
Acts	4:12	men by which we must be s.
Acts	16:30	what must I do to be s?
Acts	16:31	Christ, and you will be s.
Rom	5: 9	we shall be s from wrath
Rom	5:10	we shall be s by His life.
Rom	10: 1	Israel is that they may be s.

Rom   10: 9 from the dead, you will be **s**.
Rom   10:13 the LORD shall be **s**.
Rom   11:26 And so all Israel will be **s**,
1Co   1:18 but to us who are being **s** it
1Co   5: 5 that his spirit may be **s** in
2Co   2:15 among those who are being **s**
Eph   2: 8 For by grace you have been **s**
1Ti   2: 4 who desires all men to be **s**
1Ti   2:15 Nevertheless she will be **s** in
Tit   3: 5 according to His mercy He **s**
1Pe   3:20 were **s** through water.
1Pe   4:18 one is scarcely **s**,

SAVING (*see* SAVE)

Heb   10:39 those who believe to the **s**
Heb   11: 7 prepared an ark for the **s** of

SAVIOR

Ps   106:21 They forgot God their **S**,
Is   19:20 and He will send them a **S**
Is   43: 3 Holy One of Israel, your **S**;
Is   43:11 besides Me there is no **s**.
Is   45:21 Me, A just God and a **S**,
Luke   1:47 has rejoiced in God my **S**.
Luke   2:11 day in the city of David a **S**,
John   4:42 the **S** of the world."
Eph   5:23 and He is the **S** of the body.
Phil   3:20 also eagerly wait for the **S**,
1Ti   1: 1 the commandment of God our **S**
1Ti   4:10 who is the **S** of all men,
Tit   2:13 of our great God and **S**
2Pe   1: 1 of our God and **S** Jesus
2Pe   1:11 kingdom of our Lord and **S**
1Jn   4:14 has sent the Son as **S** of

SCAPEGOAT

Lev   16:10 and to let it go as the **s**

SCARCELY

Rom   5: 7 For **s** for a righteous man
1Pe   4:18 the righteous one is **s**

SCARLET

Gen   38:28 and the midwife took a **s**
Josh   2:18 you bind this line of **s** cord
Prov   31:21 household is clothed with **s**.
Is   1:18 your sins are like **s**,
Matt   27:28 stripped Him and put a **s**
Heb   9:19 **s** wool, and hyssop, and
Rev   17: 3 I saw a woman sitting on a **s**

SCATTERED (*see* SCATTERS)

Gen   11: 8 So the LORD **s** them abroad
Ezek   34: 6 My flock was **s** over the
Zech   13: 7 And the sheep will be **s**;
Mark   14:27 the sheep will be **s**.

SCATTERS (*see* SCATTERED)

Matt   12:30 does not gather with Me **s**
John   10:12 wolf catches the sheep and **s**

SCEPTER

Gen   49:10 The **s** shall not depart from
Num   24:17 A **S** shall rise out of

Ps   45: 6 A **s** of righteousness is
Heb   1: 8 A **s** of righteousness

SCORNFUL

Ps   1: 1 sits in the seat of the **s**;

SCORPION

Luke   11:12 egg, will he offer him a **s**?

SCOURGE (*see* SCOURGED, SCOURGES)

Mark   10:34 and **s** Him, and spit on Him,

SCOURGED (*see* SCOURGE)

John   19: 1 then Pilate took Jesus and **s**

SCOURGES (*see* SCOURGE)

Heb   12: 6 And **s** every son whom

SCRIBE (*see* SCRIBES)

Ezra   7:11 gave Ezra the priest, the **s**,
Ezra   7:12 a **s** of the Law of the God of
Is   33:18 terror: "Where is the **s**?
Jer   36:32 and gave it to Baruch the **s**,
Matt   8:19 Then a certain **s** came and
1Co   1:20 the wise? Where is the **s**?

SCRIBES (*see* SCRIBE)

Matt   2: 4 all the chief priests and **s**
Matt   5:20 righteousness of the **s** and
Matt   7:29 authority, and not as the **s**.
Matt   23:14 **s** and Pharisees, hypocrites!

SCRIPTURE (*see* SCRIPTURES)

Dan   10:21 you what is noted in the **S**
Mark   15:28 So the **S** was fulfilled which
Luke   4:21 Today this **S** is fulfilled in
John   2:22 and they believed the **S** and
John   7:38 as the **S** has said, out of
John   10:35 word of God came (and the **S**
Acts   8:35 and beginning at this **S**,
Rom   4: 3 For what does the **S** say?
2Ti   3:16 All **S** is given by
Jas   2: 8 royal law according to the **S**,
Jas   4: 5 Or do you think that the **S**
1Pe   2: 6 is also contained in the **S**,
2Pe   1:20 that no prophecy of **S** is of

SCRIPTURES (*see* SCRIPTURE)

Matt   21:42 you never read in the **S**:
Matt   22:29 not knowing the **S** nor the
Matt   26:54 How then could the **S** be
Luke   24:27 to them in all the **S** the
Luke   24:32 and while He opened the **S** to
Luke   24:45 they might comprehend the **S**.
John   5:39 "You search the **S**,
Acts   17: 2 with them from the **S**,
Acts   17:11 and searched the **S** daily to
Acts   18:24 man and mighty in the **S**,
Acts   18:28 showing from the **S** that
Rom   1: 2 His prophets in the Holy **S**,
Rom   16:26 and by the prophetic **S** has
1Co   15: 3 our sins according to the **S**,
2Ti   3:15 you have known the Holy **S**,
2Pe   3:16 do also the rest of the **S**.

S

SCROLL

Ps	40: 7	In the s of the book it
Is	34: 4	shall be rolled up like a s;
Jer	36: 4	and Baruch wrote on a s of a
Jer	36:27	the king had burned the s
Ezek	3: 1	what you find; eat this s,
Zech	5: 1	and saw there a flying s.
Rev	5: 2	is worthy to open the s
Rev	6:14	Then the sky receded as a s

SEA (see SEAS, SEASHORE)

Gen	1:21	So God created great s
Gen	1:26	over the fish of the s,
Gen	14: 3	Siddim (that is, the Salt S).
Gen	32:12	as the sand of the s,
Ex	10:19	and blew them into the Red S.
Ex	20:11	heavens and the earth, the s,
Num	34: 6	you shall have the Great S
Ps	8: 8	And the fish of the s That
Ps	72: 8	have dominion also from s
Ps	95: 5	The s is His, for He made
Ps	96:11	Let the s roar, and all its
Ps	107:23	Those who go down to the s
Ps	114: 3	The s saw it and fled;
Ps	114: 5	What ails you, O s,
Ps	139: 9	the uttermost parts of the s,
Eccl	1: 7	Yet the s is not full;
Is	9: 1	her, By the way of the s,
Is	11: 9	As the waters cover the s.
Is	43:16	who makes a way in the s
Is	57:20	are like the troubled s,
Dan	7: 3	beasts came up from the s,
Hos	1:10	be as the sand of the s,
Hab	2:14	As the waters cover the s.
Matt	4:15	By the way of the s,
Matt	4:18	walking by the S of Galilee,
Matt	8:27	even the winds and the s
Matt	8:32	the steep place into the s,
Matt	14:26	saw Him walking on the s,
1Co	10: 1	all passed through the s,
1Co	10: 2	in the cloud and in the s,
2Co	11:26	in perils in the s,
Heb	11:29	passed through the Red S as
Jas	1: 6	is like a wave of the s
Rev	13: 1	beast rising up out of the s,
Rev	20:13	The s gave up the dead who
Rev	21: 1	Also there was no more s.

SEAL (see SEALED)

Job	38:14	on form like clay under a s,
Song	8: 6	Set me as a s upon your
Is	8:16	S the law among my
Dan	8:26	Therefore s up the vision,
Dan	12: 4	and s the book until the
John	6:27	the Father has set His s on
2Ti	2:19	of God stands, having this s:
Rev	6: 3	When He opened the second s,
Rev	10: 4	S up the things which the
Rev	22:10	Do not s the words of the

SEALED (see SEAL)

Jer	32:10	I signed the deed and s
Dan	12: 9	words are closed up and s

2Co	1:22	who also has s us and given
Eph	1:13	you were s with the Holy
Eph	4:30	by whom you were s for the

SEARCH (see SEARCHED, SEARCHES, SEARCHING)

Job	3:21	And s for it more than
Job	11: 7	Can you s out the deep things
Ps	139:23	S me, O God, and know my
Prov	2: 4	And s for her as for
Jer	17:10	s the heart, I test the
Jer	29:13	when you s for Me with all
Ezek	34:11	Indeed I Myself will s for My
Matt	2: 8	Go and s carefully for the
John	5:39	You s the Scriptures, for in

SEARCHED (see SEARCH)

Gen	31:34	And Laban s all about the
Ps	139: 1	You have s me and known me.
Eccl	2: 3	I s in my heart how to
Acts	12:19	But when Herod had s for him
Acts	17:11	and s the Scriptures daily
1Pe	1:10	prophets have inquired and s

SEARCHES (see SEARCH)

1Ch	28: 9	for the LORD s all hearts
Rom	8:27	Now He who s the hearts knows
1Co	2:10	For the Spirit s all things,
Rev	2:23	know that I am He who s the

SEARCHING (see SEARCH)

1Pe	1:11	s what, or what manner of

SEARED

1Ti	4: 2	their own conscience s with

SEAS (see SEA)

Gen	1:10	of the waters He called S.
Ps	8: 8	through the paths of the s.
Ps	24: 2	He has founded it upon the s,

SEASHORE (see SEA)

Gen	22:17	the sand which is on the s;
Ex	14:30	the Egyptians dead on the s.
1Ki	4:29	heart like the sand on the s.
Heb	11:12	the sand which is by the s.

SEASON (see SEASONED, SEASONS)

Ps	1: 3	forth its fruit in its s,
Ps	22: 2	hear; And in the night s,
Ps	104:27	them their food in due s.
Prov	15:23	And a word spoken in due s,
Eccl	3: 1	everything there is a s,
Matt	24:45	to give them food in due s?
Mark	11:13	for it was not the s for
Gal	6: 9	for in due s we shall reap
2Ti	4: 2	the word! Be ready in s

SEASONED (see SEASON)

Matt	5:13	flavor, how shall it be s?
Mark	9:49	every sacrifice will be s
Col	4: 6	s with salt, that you may

SEASONS (see SEASON)

Gen	1:14	let them be for signs and s,
Ps	16: 7	instructs me in the night s.
Dan	2:21	changes the times and the s;
Matt	21:41	to him the fruits in their s.
Acts	1: 7	for you to know times or s
1Th	5: 1	the times and the s,

SEAT (see SEATED)

Ex	25:22	you from above the mercy s,
Lev	16:15	sprinkle it on the mercy s
Ps	1: 1	Nor sits in the s of the
Ezek	28: 2	I sit in the s of gods,
Matt	23: 2	Pharisees sit in Moses' s.
Matt	27:19	sitting on the judgment s,
Rom	14:10	stand before the judgment s
2Co	5:10	before the judgment s of
Heb	9: 5	overshadowing the mercy s.

SEATED (see SEAT)

Eph	1:20	Him from the dead and s
Heb	8: 1	who is s at the right hand

SECOND

Rev	20:14	This is the s death.

SECRET (see SECRETLY, SECRETS)

Deut	29:29	The s things belong to the
Judg	16: 9	So the s of his strength was
Ps	19:12	Cleanse me from s faults.
Ps	27: 5	In the s place of His
Ps	90: 8	Our s sins in the light of
Ps	91: 1	He who dwells in the s place
Ps	139:15	You, When I was made in s,
Eccl	12:14	Including every s thing,
Dan	2:19	Then the s was revealed to
Amos	3: 7	Unless He reveals His s to
Matt	6: 4	your Father who sees in s
Luke	8:17	For nothing is s that will
Rom	16:25	of the mystery kept s since

SECRETLY (see SECRET)

Matt	1:19	was minded to put her away s.

SECRETS (see SECRET)

Dan	2:28	God in heaven who reveals s,
Rom	2:16	when God will judge the s
1Co	14:25	And thus the s of his heart

SEED (see SEEDS, SEEDTIME)

Gen	1:11	the herb that yields s,
Gen	3:15	And between your s and her
Gen	21:12	for in Isaac your s shall be
Gen	22:18	In your s all the nations of
Ps	126: 6	Bearing s for sowing,
Is	6:13	So the holy s shall be
Is	53:10	sin, He shall see His s,
Is	55:10	That it may give s to the
Matt	13: 4	some s fell by the wayside;
Matt	13:24	like a man who sowed good s
Matt	13:31	heaven is like a mustard s,
Matt	17:20	have faith as a mustard s,
Luke	1:55	To Abraham and to his s

Luke	8:11	The s is the word of God.
Acts	3:25	And in your s all the
Acts	13:23	"From this man's s,
Rom	1: 3	who was born of the s of
Rom	9: 7	In Isaac your s shall be
Rom	9: 8	promise are counted as the s.
Rom	11: 1	of the s of Abraham, of the
2Co	9:10	Now may He who supplies s to
Gal	3:16	of one, "And to your S,
Gal	3:29	then you are Abraham's s,
Heb	11:18	In Isaac your s shall be
1Pe	1:23	not of corruptible s but
1Jn	3: 9	for His s remains in him;

SEEDS (see SEED)

Matt	13:32	is the least of all the s;
Gal	3:16	He does not say, "And to s,

SEEDTIME† (see SEED)

Gen	8:22	S and harvest, Cold and

SEEK (see SEEKING, SEEKS, SOUGHT)

Deut	4:29	you will find Him if you s
2Ch	7:14	and pray and s My face, and
Ps	14: 2	understand, who s God.
Ps	24: 6	generation of those who s
Ps	27: 4	of the LORD, That will I s:
Ps	34:14	S peace and pursue it.
Ps	53: 2	understand, who s God.
Ps	63: 1	Early will I s You; My
Prov	2: 4	If you s her as silver, And
Eccl	1:13	And I set my heart to s and
Is	1:17	S justice, Rebuke the
Is	41:12	You shall s them and not
Is	55: 6	S the LORD while He may be
Jer	29: 7	And s the peace of the city
Jer	29:13	And you will s Me and find
Jer	45: 5	And do you s great things for
Ezek	34:16	I will s what was lost and
Amos	5: 4	S Me and live;
Amos	5: 6	S the LORD and live, Lest
Amos	5:14	S good and not evil, That
Mal	3: 1	And the Lord, whom you s,
Matt	2:13	for Herod will s the young
Matt	6:32	these things the Gentiles s.
Matt	6:33	But s first the kingdom of
Matt	7: 7	it will be given to you; s,
Matt	28: 5	for I know that you s Jesus
Mark	8:12	Why does this generation s a
Mark	16: 6	You s Jesus of Nazareth, who
Luke	12:29	And do not s what you should
Luke	12:30	the nations of the world s
Luke	13:24	will s to enter and will not
Luke	19:10	the Son of Man has come to s
Luke	24: 5	Why do you s the living among
John	1:38	to them, "What do you s?
John	4:27	no one said, "What do You s?
John	5:30	because I do not s My own
John	7:34	You will s Me and not find
John	8:50	And I do not s My own glory;
Acts	6: 3	s out from among you seven
Acts	10:21	"Yes, I am he whom you s.
Acts	15:17	rest of mankind may s
Acts	17:27	so that they should s the

S

Rom	10:20	by those who did not s
Rom	11: 3	and they s my life"?
1Co	1:22	and Greeks s after wisdom;
1Co	7:27	Do not s a wife.
1Co	13: 5	does not s its own, is not
Gal	1:10	Or do I s to please men? For
Phil	2:21	For all s their own, not the
Phil	4:17	Not that I s the gift, but I
1Th	2: 6	Nor did we s glory from men,
Heb	11: 6	of those who diligently s
Heb	11:14	declare plainly that they s
Heb	13:14	but we s the one to come.
1Pe	3:11	Let him s peace and

SEEKING (see SEEK)

John	4:23	for the Father is s such to
John	18: 4	to them, "Whom are you s?
John	20:15	you weeping? Whom are you s?
Rom	10: 3	and s to establish their own
1Pe	5: 8	s whom he may devour.

SEEKS (see SEEK)

Matt	7: 8	and he who s finds, and to
Matt	12:39	and adulterous generation s
Rom	3:11	There is none who s

SEEN

Ex	19: 4	You have s what I did to the
Judg	6:22	O Lord GOD! For I have s
Judg	13:22	because we have s God!"
Ps	37:25	Yet I have not s the
Is	6: 5	For my eyes have s the
Is	9: 2	walked in darkness Have s
John	1:18	No one has s God at any time.
John	3:11	and testify what We have s,
John	3:32	And what He has s and heard,
John	9:37	You have both s Him and it is
John	14: 7	on you know Him and have s
John	14: 9	He who has s Me has seen the
John	20:18	the disciples that she had s
John	20:25	We have s the Lord." So he
John	20:29	because you have s Me, you
John	20:29	are those who have not s
Acts	13:31	He was s for many days by
Rom	8:24	but hope that is s is not
1Co	2: 9	"Eye has not s,
1Co	9: 1	Have I not s Jesus Christ
1Co	15: 5	and that He was s by Cephas,
2Co	4:18	at the things which are s,
1Ti	3:16	S by angels, Preached
1Ti	6:16	whom no man has s or can
Heb	11: 1	the evidence of things not s.
Heb	11: 3	that the things which are s
Heb	11: 7	warned of things not yet s,
Heb	11:13	but having s them afar off
1Pe	1: 8	whom having not s you love.
1Jn	1: 1	which we have s with our
1Jn	4:12	No one has s God at any
1Jn	4:20	his brother whom he has s,
Rev	1:19	the things which you have s,

SEER

1Sa	9: 9	was formerly called a s.
Amos	7:12	you s! Flee to the land of

SELF-CONTROL

Acts	24:25	about righteousness, s,
1Co	7: 5	because of your lack of s.
Gal	5:23	gentleness, s. Against such
2Pe	1: 6	to knowledge s,

SELL (see SOLD)

Gen	25:31	S me your birthright as of
Gen	37:27	Come and let us s him to the

SEND (see SENDS, SENT)

Gen	24: 7	He will s His angel before
Gen	38:17	I will s a young goat from
Ex	3:10	and I will s you to Pharaoh
Ex	8:21	I will s swarms of flies
Ex	23:20	I s an Angel before you to
Neh	2: 5	I ask that you s me to
Neh	2: 6	So it pleased the king to s
Neh	8:10	and s portions to those for
Ps	20: 2	May He s you help from the
Ps	43: 3	s out Your light and Your
Ps	57: 3	He shall s from heaven and
Ps	104:30	You s forth Your Spirit,
Is	6: 8	saying: "Whom shall I s,
Is	6: 8	Here am I! S me."
Is	42:19	as My messenger whom I s?
Jer	1: 7	shall go to all to whom I s
Jer	14:15	in My name, whom I did not s,
Ezek	7: 3	And I will s My anger
Ezek	39: 6	And I will s fire on Magog
Amos	1: 7	But I will s a fire upon the
Mal	3: 1	I s My messenger, And he
Mal	4: 5	I will s you Elijah the
Matt	9:38	the Lord of the harvest to s
Matt	10:16	I s you out as sheep in the
Matt	11:10	I s My messenger before
Matt	14:15	S the multitudes away, that
Matt	24:31	And He will s His angels with
Mark	5:12	S us to the swine, that we
Mark	6: 7	and began to s them out two
Luke	12:49	I came to s fire on the
Luke	24:49	I s the Promise of My Father
John	3:17	For God did not s His Son
John	16: 7	I will s Him to you.
John	20:21	I also s you."
Acts	11:29	determined to s relief to
1Co	1:17	For Christ did not s me to
Phil	2:19	trust in the Lord Jesus to s
2Th	2:11	for this reason God will s
Rev	1:11	write in a book and s it to

SENDS (see SEND)

Ps	68:33	He s out His voice, a mighty
Matt	5:45	and s rain on the just and

SENNACHERIB

2Ki	18:13	S king of Assyria came up
2Ch	32: 2	And when Hezekiah saw that S

SENSE†

Neh	8: 8	of God; and they gave the s,
Hos	7:11	like a silly dove, without s—
Heb	11:19	him in a figurative s.

SENT (see SEND)

Ex	3:12	a sign to you that I have s
Ex	3:14	I AM has s me to you.'"
Num	21: 6	So the LORD s fiery serpents
Is	55:11	the thing for which I s
Is	61: 1	He has s Me to heal the
Jer	26:12	The LORD s me to prophesy
Jer	28:15	the LORD has not s you, but
Ezek	39:28	who s them into captivity
Matt	10: 5	These twelve Jesus s out and
Matt	10:40	Me receives Him who s Me.
Matt	15:24	I was not s except to the
Mark	9:37	not Me but Him who s Me.
Luke	4:18	He has s Me to heal
Luke	10: 1	and s them two by two before
Luke	10:16	Me rejects Him who s Me.
John	1: 6	There was a man s from God,
John	1: 8	but was s to bear witness
John	4:34	to do the will of Him who s
John	5:24	and believes in Him who s
John	5:37	who s Me, has testified of
John	6:39	will of the Father who s Me,
John	8:16	I am with the Father who s
John	9: 4	work the works of Him who s
John	9: 7	(which is translated, S).
John	13:16	sent greater than he who s
John	13:20	Me receives Him who s Me.
John	17: 3	Jesus Christ whom You have s.
John	20:21	to you! As the Father has s
Rom	10:15	preach unless they are s?
Gal	4: 4	God s forth His Son, born of
Heb	1:14	all ministering spirits s
1Pe	1:12	to you by the Holy Spirit s
1Jn	4: 9	that God has s His only
1Jn	4.10	but that He loved us and s
1Jn	4:14	that the Father has s the
Rev	1: 1	And He s and signified it

SEPARATE (see SEPARATED)

Matt	19: 6	together, let not man s.
Acts	13: 2	Now s to Me Barnabas and Saul
Rom	8:35	Who shall s us from the love
Rom	8:39	shall be able to s us from
2Co	6:17	among them And be s,
Heb	7:26	s from sinners, and has

SEPARATED (see DIVIDED, SEPARATE)

Is	59: 2	But your iniquities have s
Rom	1: 1	s to the gospel of God
Gal	1:15	who s me from my mother's

SERAPHIM†

Is	6: 2	Above it stood s;
Is	6: 6	Then one of the s flew to

SERPENT (see SERPENTS)

Gen	3: 1	Now the s was more cunning
Ex	7:15	rod which was turned to a s
Num	21: 8	to Moses, "Make a fiery s,
Num	21: 9	So Moses made a bronze s,
2Ki	18: 4	in pieces the bronze s that
Job	26:13	hand pierced the fleeing s.
Prov	23:32	the last it bites like a s,
Is	27: 1	Leviathan the fleeing s,
Mic	7:17	shall lick the dust like a s;
Matt	7:10	a fish, will he give him a s?
John	3:14	as Moses lifted up the s in
2Co	11: 3	as the s deceived Eve by his
Rev	12: 9	that s of old, called the
Rev	20: 2	that s of old, who is the

SERPENTS (see SERPENT)

Matt	10:16	Therefore be wise as s and
Mark	16:18	"they will take up s;
Luke	10:19	authority to trample on s

SERVANT (see MAIDSERVANT, SERVANTS, SERVE)

Gen	9:25	A s of servants He shall
Gen	9:26	And may Canaan be his s.
Gen	18: 3	do not pass on by Your s.
Gen	24:34	he said, "I am Abraham's s.
Gen	26:24	your descendants for My s
Gen	39:17	Hebrew s whom you brought
Ex	14:31	the LORD and His s Moses.
Ex	21: 2	"If you buy a Hebrew s,
Num	12: 7	Not so with My s Moses; He
Deut	34: 5	So Moses the s of the LORD
Josh	1: 2	Moses My s is dead. Now
1Sa	3: 9	for Your s hears.'" So
2Sa	3:18	By the hand of My s David, I
Job	1: 8	Have you considered My s Job,
Job	42: 8	and My s Job shall pray for
Ps	19:11	Moreover by them Your s is
Ps	19:13	Keep back Your s also from
Ps	27: 9	Do not turn Your s away in
Ps	31:16	Your face shine upon Your s;
Ps	69:17	hide Your face from Your s,
Ps	86:16	Your strength to Your s,
Ps	89: 3	I have sworn to My s David:
Ps	116:16	O LORD, truly I am Your s;
Ps	119:17	bountifully with Your s,
Ps	119:135	Your face shine upon Your s,
Ps	136:22	A heritage to Israel His s,
Prov	17: 2	A wise s will rule over a
Is	20: 3	Just as My s Isaiah has
Is	41: 8	you, Israel, are My s,
Is	41: 9	said to you, 'You are My s,
Is	42: 1	Behold! My S whom I uphold,
Is	42:19	Who is blind but My s,
Is	43:10	And My s whom I have chosen,
Is	44:21	formed you, you are My s;
Is	49: 3	said to me, 'You are My s,
Is	50:10	obeys the voice of His S?
Is	52:13	My S shall deal prudently;
Is	53:11	His knowledge My righteous S
Dan	6:20	s of the living God, has
Dan	9:17	hear the prayer of Your s,
Zech	3: 8	I am bringing forth My S the
Matt	8: 6	my s is lying at home
Matt	8: 8	and my s will be healed.
Matt	10:24	nor a s above his master.
Matt	12:18	Behold! My S whom I
Matt	24:45	is a faithful and wise s,
Matt	25:21	done, good and faithful s;
Matt	25:30	'And cast the unprofitable s
Matt	26:51	struck the s of the high

Luke	1:54	He has helped His s Israel,
Luke	2:29	now You are letting Your s
Luke	7: 2	And a certain centurion's s,
Luke	12:43	Blessed is that s whom his
Luke	16:13	No s can serve two masters;
John	12:26	there My s will be also. If
John	13:16	a s is not greater than his
Acts	3:13	glorified His S Jesus, whom
Acts	3:26	having raised up His S
Acts	4:30	the name of Your holy S
Rom	14: 4	are you to judge another's s?
Rom	15: 8	Jesus Christ has become a s
1Co	9:19	I have made myself a s to
Col	4: 7	and fellow s in the Lord,
Heb	3: 5	in all His house as a s,
Rev	1: 1	it by His angel to His s

SERVANTS (see SERVANT)

Job	1:15	they have killed the s with
Ps	34:22	redeems the soul of His s,
Ps	90:13	have compassion on Your s.
Ps	113: 1	O s of the LORD, Praise
Ps	135:14	have compassion on His s.
Eccl	2: 7	I acquired male and female s,
Dan	3:26	s of the Most High God, come
Amos	3: 7	reveals His secret to His s
Matt	18:23	settle accounts with his s.
Matt	21:36	"Again he sent other s,
Mark	1:20	in the boat with the hired s,
Luke	15:17	many of my father's hired s
Luke	15:19	me like one of your hired s.
Luke	17:10	say, 'We are unprofitable s.
Luke	19:13	"So he called ten of his s,
John	15:15	"No longer do I call you s,
John	18:36	My s would fight, so that I
1Co	4: 1	as s of Christ and stewards
1Pe	2:18	S, be submissive to your
Rev	1: 1	God gave Him to show His s—
Rev	19: 5	all you His s and those who
Rev	22: 3	and His s shall serve Him.

SERVE (see SERVANT, SERVED, SERVICE
    SERVING)

Gen	25:23	And the older shall s the
Ex	3:12	you shall s God on this
Ex	4:23	let My son go that he may s
Ex	20: 5	not bow down to them nor s
Ex	21: 2	he shall s six years; and in
Ex	21: 6	and he shall s him forever.
Ex	23:33	For if you s their gods, it
Deut	7: 4	to s other gods; so the
Josh	24:15	this day whom you will s,
Josh	24:15	we will s the LORD."
Josh	24:21	but we will s the LORD!"
Ps	2:11	S the LORD with fear, And
Ps	72:11	All nations shall s Him.
Ps	100: 2	S the LORD with gladness
Jer	27: 7	So all nations shall s him
Dan	1: 5	of that time they might s
Dan	3:17	our God whom we s is able to
Dan	3:18	that we do not s your gods,
Dan	6:16	whom you s continually, He
Matt	4:10	Him only you shall s.
Matt	6:24	No one can s two masters;

Matt	6:24	You cannot s God and mammon.
Matt	20:28	come to be served, but to s,
Mark	10:45	come to be served, but to s,
Luke	1:74	Might s Him without fear,
Acts	6: 2	leave the word of God and s
Rom	1: 9	whom I s with my spirit in
Rom	7:25	with the mind I myself s the
Rom	9:12	The older shall s the
Rom	16:18	those who are such do not s
1Co	9:13	and those who s at the altar
Gal	3:19	then does the law s?
Gal	5:13	but through love s one
Col	3:24	for you s the Lord Christ.
1Th	1: 9	to God from idols to s the
1Ti	3:10	then let them s as deacons,
2Ti	1: 3	whom I s with a pure
Heb	9:14	from dead works to s the
Heb	13:10	from which those who s the
Rev	7:15	and s Him day and night in
Rev	22: 3	and His servants shall s

SERVED (see SERVE)

Matt	8:15	And she arose and s them.
Matt	20:28	of Man did not come to be s,
Mark	10:45	of Man did not come to be s,
John	12: 2	Him a supper; and Martha s,
Rom	1:25	and worshiped and s the
Gal	4: 8	you s those which by nature
Phil	2:22	a son with his father he s

SERVICE (see SERVE)

Ex	1:14	and in all manner of s in
Ex	27:19	the tabernacle for all its s,
John	16: 2	think that he offers God s.
Rom	12: 1	which is your reasonable s.
Heb	9: 1	had ordinances of divine s

SERVING (see SERVE)

Luke	10:40	was distracted with much s,
Rom	12:11	in spirit, s the Lord;
Jude	12	s only themselves. They

SETH

Gen	4:25	bore a son and named him S,
1Ch	1: 1	Adam, S, Enosh,
Luke	3:38	son of Enos, the son of S,

SETTLE (see SETTLED)

1Pe	5:10	strengthen, and s you.

SETTLED (see SETTLE)

Ps	119:89	Your word is s in heaven.

SEVEN (see SEVENTH)

Gen	7: 2	You shall take with you s
Gen	8:10	And he waited yet another s
Gen	29:20	So Jacob served s years for
Gen	33: 3	himself to the ground s
Gen	41: 2	came up out of the river s
Gen	41: 5	and suddenly s heads of
Gen	41:53	Then the s years of plenty
Gen	41:54	and the s years of famine
Ex	12:19	For s days no leaven shall be
Ex	23:15	eat unleavened bread s days,

Ex	25:37	You shall make s lamps for
Lev	4:17	the blood and sprinkle it s
Lev	23:15	s Sabbaths shall be
Lev	23:42	shall dwell in booths for s
Num	12:14	be shut out of the camp s
Deut	15: 1	At the end of every s years
Deut	16:13	the Feast of Tabernacles s
Josh	6: 4	march around the city s
1Sa	16:10	Thus Jesse made s of his sons
2Ki	5:14	So he went down and dipped s
Prov	9: 1	She has hewn out her s
Dan	4:16	And let s times pass over
Dan	9:25	There shall be s weeks
Matt	12:45	he goes and takes with him s
Matt	15:36	And He took the s loaves and
Matt	15:37	and they took up s large
Matt	18:21	Up to s times?"
Matt	18:22	but up to seventy times s.
Matt	22:28	whose wife of the s will she
Luke	2:36	had lived with a husband s
Luke	8: 2	out of whom had come s
Luke	11:26	goes and takes with him s
Luke	24:13	which was s miles from
Acts	6: 3	seek out from among you s
Rom	11: 4	reserved for Myself s
Heb	11:30	they were encircled for s
Rev	1: 4	to the s churches which are
Rev	1: 4	and from the s Spirits who
Rev	1:12	And having turned I saw s
Rev	1:16	He had in His right hand s
Rev	5: 1	sealed with s seals.
Rev	8: 2	and to them were given s
Rev	10: 3	s thunders uttered their
Rev	12: 3	fiery red dragon having s
Rev	15: 7	gave to the seven angels s
Rev	15: 8	the seven plagues of the s
Rev	17:10	There are also s kings. Five
Rev	17:11	the eighth, and is of the s,
Rev	21: 9	bowls filled with the s

SEVENFOLD
Gen	4:24	If Cain shall be avenged s,

SEVENTEEN
Gen	37: 2	being s years old, was

SEVENTH (see SEVEN)
Gen	2: 2	and He rested on the s day
Gen	2: 3	Then God blessed the s day
Ex	12:15	the first day until the s
Ex	20:10	but the s day is the Sabbath
Ex	20:11	and rested the s day.
Ex	23:11	but the s year you shall let
Heb	4: 4	God rested on the s
Jude	14	the s from Adam, prophesied

SEVENTY
Ex	1: 5	descendants of Jacob were s
Ex	24: 1	and s of the elders of
Ps	90:10	days of our lives are s
Jer	25:11	serve the king of Babylon s
Dan	9: 2	that He would accomplish s
Dan	9:24	S weeks are determined For
Zech	1:12	which You were angry these s

Matt	18:22	but up to s times seven.
Luke	10: 1	things the Lord appointed s

SEVENTY-SEVENFOLD†
Gen	4:24	sevenfold, Then Lamech s.

SEVERITY
Rom	11:22	consider the goodness and s

SEXUAL
Matt	5:32	wife for any reason except s
Matt	19: 9	except for s immorality, and
Acts	15:29	and from s immorality. If
Acts	21:25	and from s immorality."
Rom	1:29	s immorality, wickedness,
1Co	5: 1	reported that there is s
1Co	6:13	Now the body is not for s
1Co	6:18	Flee s immorality. Every sin
1Co	7: 2	because of s immorality, let
1Th	4: 3	you should abstain from s
Jude	7	given themselves over to s
Rev	2:14	and to commit s immorality.
Rev	9:21	their sorceries or their s

SHACKLES
Mark	5: 4	had often been bound with s
Luke	8:29	bound with chains and s;

SHADE
Ps	121: 5	The LORD is your s at
Dan	4:12	beasts of the field found s
Jon	4: 5	and sat under it in the s,
Mark	4:32	the air may nest under its s.

SHADOW
Gen	19: 8	they have come under the s
2Ki	20: 9	shall the s go forward ten
Job	8: 9	our days on earth are a s.
Ps	17: 8	Hide me under the s of Your
Ps	23: 4	through the valley of the s
Ps	91: 1	Shall abide under the s of
Is	9: 2	dwelt in the land of the s
Is	32: 2	As the s of a great rock in
Is	49: 2	In the s of His hand He has
Matt	4:16	in the region and s
Luke	1:79	sit in darkness and the s
Col	2:17	which are a s of things to
Heb	8: 5	who serve the copy and s of
Jas	1:17	there is no variation or s

SHADRACH (see HANANIAH)
Dan	3:28	"Blessed be the God of S,

SHAKE (see SHAKEN)
Job	4:14	Which made all my bones s.
Ps	46: 3	Though the mountains s
Ps	109:25	they s their heads.
Is	2:19	When He arises to s the
Hag	2: 6	is a little while) I will s
Hag	2:21	I will s heaven and earth.
Matt	10:14	s off the dust from your
Heb	12:26	Yet once more I s not

S

SHAKEN (see SHAKE)

Ps	112: 6	Surely he will never be s;
Matt	11: 7	A reed s by the wind?
Matt	24:29	of the heavens will be s.
Luke	6:38	s together, and running over
Acts	4:31	assembled together was s;
Acts	16:26	of the prison were s;
2Th	2: 2	not to be soon s in mind or
Heb	12:27	things that are being s,
Heb	12:28	a kingdom which cannot be s,

SHAME (see SHAMEFUL)

2Sa	13:13	I, where could I take my s?
Ps	4: 2	you turn my glory to s?
Ps	35: 4	Let those be put to s and
Ps	69: 7	S has covered my face.
Ps	69:19	You know my reproach, my s,
Ps	71: 1	Let me never be put to s.
Ps	71:24	For they are brought to s
Ps	119:31	do not put me to s!
Ps	129: 5	who hate Zion Be put to s
Prov	10: 5	is a son who causes s.
Prov	19:26	Is a son who causes s and
Is	20: 4	to the s of Egypt.
Jer	17:18	do not let me be put to s;
Dan	9: 8	to us belongs s of face, to
Dan	12: 2	Some to s and everlasting
Joel	2:26	shall never be put to s.
Nah	3: 5	And the kingdoms your s.
Acts	5:41	counted worthy to suffer s
Rom	9:33	will not be put to s.
Rom	10:11	will not be put to s.
1Co	1:27	of the world to put to s
1Co	6: 5	I say this to your s.
Heb	6: 6	and put Him to an open s.
Heb	12: 2	the cross, despising the s,
1Pe	2: 6	no means be put to s.

SHAMEFUL (see SHAME)

Jer	11:13	set up altars to that s
Rom	1:27	men committing what is s,
1Co	11: 6	But if it is s for a woman
1Co	14:35	for it is s for women to
Eph	5:12	For it is s even to speak of

SHARE (see PART, PORTION)

2Sa	20: 1	We have no s in David, Nor
1Ki	12:16	What s have we in David? We
Gal	6: 6	who is taught the word s in
Eph	4:16	which every part does its s,
1Ti	6:18	ready to give, willing to s,
2Ti	1: 8	but s with me in the
Heb	13:16	forget to do good and to s,

SHARON

1Ch	27:29	over the herds that fed in S,
Song	2: 1	I am the rose of S,

SHARP (see SHARPER)

Prov	5: 4	S as a two-edged sword.

SHARPENS

Prov	27:17	As iron s iron, So a man

SHARPER (see SHARP)

Heb	4:12	and s than any two-edged

SHATTERED

Eccl	12: 6	Or the pitcher s at the

SHAVE (see SHAVED)

Lev	21: 5	nor shall they s the edges
Num	6:18	Then the Nazirite shall s his
Judg	16:19	for a man and had him s off

SHAVED (see SHAVE)

Num	6:19	the Nazirite after he has s
1Co	11: 6	for a woman to be shorn or s,

SHEAF (see SHEAVES)

Gen	37: 7	and bowed down to my s.

SHEAR-JASHUB†

Is	7: 3	you and S your son, at the

SHEARER† (see SHEARERS, SHORN)

Acts	8:32	as a lamb before its s

SHEARERS (see SHEARER)

Is	53: 7	as a sheep before its s is

SHEATH

John	18:11	"Put your sword into the s.

SHEAVES (see SHEAF)

Gen	37: 7	and indeed your s stood all
Ps	126: 6	Bringing his s with him.

SHEBA

1Ki	10: 4	And when the queen of S had

SHECHEM (see SYCHAR)

Gen	33:18	came safely to the city of S,
Gen	37:12	their father's flock in S.
Judg	9:23	Abimelech and the men of S;
1Ki	12: 1	And Rehoboam went to S,

SHED (see SHEDDING, SHEDS)

Gen	9: 6	By man his blood shall be s;
Prov	6:17	Hands that s innocent
Matt	23:35	all the righteous blood s
Matt	26:28	which is s for many for the
Luke	11:50	all the prophets which was s
Luke	22:20	which is s for you.
Acts	22:20	of Your martyr Stephen was s,
Rom	3:15	feet are swift to s

SHEDDING (see SHED)

Heb	9:22	and without s of blood there

SHEDS (see SHED)

Gen	9: 6	Whoever s man's blood, By

SHEEP (see SHEEPFOLD, SHEEPSKINS)

Gen	4: 2	Now Abel was a keeper of s,
Gen	29: 6	Rachel is coming with the s.
Gen	30:32	the speckled and spotted s,

Ps	95: 7	And the **s** of His hand.
Ps	100: 3	are His people and the **s**
Ps	119:176	gone astray like a lost **s**;
Is	53: 6	All we like **s** have gone
Is	53: 7	And as a **s** before its
Ezek	34:11	Myself will search for My **s**
Zech	13: 7	And the **s** will be
Matt	9:36	like **s** having no shepherd.
Matt	10: 6	go rather to the lost **s**
Matt	10:16	I send you out as **s** in the
Matt	12:11	among you who has one **s**,
Matt	18:12	If a man has a hundred **s**,
Mark	14:27	And the **s** will be
Luke	15: 6	for I have found my **s** which
John	10: 2	is the shepherd of the **s**.
John	10: 3	and the **s** hear his voice;
John	10: 7	you, I am the door of the **s**.
John	10:11	gives His life for the **s**.
John	10:16	And other **s** I have which are
John	21:16	He said to him, "Tend My **s**.
John	21:17	said to him, "Feed My **s**.
Acts	8:32	He was led as a **s** to
Rom	8:36	We are accounted as **s**
Heb	13:20	that great Shepherd of the **s**,
1Pe	2:25	For you were like **s** going

SHEEPFOLD (see SHEEP)

2Sa	7: 8	"I took you from the **s**,
John	10: 1	he who does not enter the **s**

SHEEPSKINS† (see SHEEP)

Heb	11:37	They wandered about in **s** and

SHEET

Acts	10:11	and an object like a great **s**

SHEKEL (see SHEKELS)

Amos	8: 5	the ephah small and the **s**

SHEKELS (see SHEKEL)

Gen	23:15	is worth four hundred **s**
Ex	21:32	to their master thirty **s** of
Lev	27: 4	valuation shall be thirty **s**;

SHELTER

Ps	61: 4	I will trust in the **s** of
Is	4: 6	and for a **s** from storm and
Jon	4: 5	There he made himself a **s**

SHEM

Gen	6:10	And Noah begot three sons: **S**,

SHEOL

2Sa	22: 6	The sorrows of **S** surrounded
Job	11: 8	can you do? Deeper than **S**—
Job	17:16	go down to the gates of **S**?
Ps	16:10	will not leave my soul in **S**,
Ps	116: 3	And the pangs of **S** laid
Is	14:15	shall be brought down to **S**,
Jon	2: 2	Out of the belly of **S** I

SHEPHERD (see SHEPHERDS)

Gen	49:24	Jacob (From there is the **S**,
Num	27:17	like sheep which have no **s**.

2Sa	7: 7	whom I commanded to **s** My
Ps	23: 1	The LORD is my **s**;
Ps	80: 1	O **S** of Israel, You who lead
Eccl	12:11	nails, given by one **S**.
Is	40:11	will feed His flock like a **s**;
Is	44:28	says of Cyrus, 'He is My **s**,
Ezek	34:12	As a **s** seeks out his flock on
Ezek	37:24	they shall all have one **s**;
Zech	13: 7	of hosts. "Strike the **S**,
Matt	2: 6	a Ruler Who will **s**
Matt	9:36	like sheep having no **s**.
Matt	26:31	'I will strike the **S**,
John	10: 2	enters by the door is the **s**
John	10:11	"I am the good **s**.
John	10:16	will be one flock and one **s**.
Acts	20:28	to **s** the church of God which
Heb	13:20	that great **S** of the sheep,
1Pe	2:25	have now returned to the **S**
1Pe	5: 2	**S** the flock of God which is
1Pe	5: 4	and when the Chief **S** appears,

SHEPHERDS (see SHEPHERD)

Ex	2:17	Then the **s** came and drove
Jer	23: 1	Woe to the **s** who destroy and
Ezek	34: 2	Woe to the **s** of Israel who
Ezek	34:10	I am against the **s**,
Amos	1: 2	The pastures of the **s**
Luke	2: 8	were in the same country **s**

SHIBBOLETH†

Judg	12: 6	**S**'!" And he would say,

SHIELD

Gen	15: 1	afraid, Abram. I am your **s**,
Ps	18: 2	My **s** and the horn of my
Ps	18:30	He is a **s** to all who trust
Ps	28: 7	is my strength and my **s**;
Ps	33:20	He is our help and our **s**.
Ps	84:11	LORD God is a sun and **s**;
Eph	6:16	taking the **s** of faith with

SHILOAH† (see SILOAM)

Is	8: 6	refused The waters of **S**

SHILOH

Gen	49:10	Until **S** comes; And to Him
Josh	18: 9	to Joshua at the camp in **S**.
Judg	18:31	the house of God was in **S**.
Jer	26: 6	will make this house like **S**,

SHINAR

Gen	11: 2	a plain in the land of **S**,
Gen	14: 1	days of Amraphel king of **S**,

SHINE (see SHINED, SHINES, SHINING, SHONE)

Num	6:25	The LORD make His face **s**
Ps	31:16	Make Your face **s** upon Your
Ps	80: 3	O God; Cause Your face to **s**,
Ps	104:15	Oil to make his face **s**,
Is	60: 1	Arise, **s**; For your light
Dan	12: 3	Those who are wise shall **s**
Matt	5:16	Let your light so **s** before
2Co	4: 6	God who commanded light to **s**
Phil	2:15	among whom you **s** as lights

S

Rev   21:23   the sun or of the moon to **s**

SHINED† (*see* SHINE)
Is   9: 2   Upon them a light has **s**.

SHINES (*see* SHINE)
Prov   4:18   That **s** ever brighter unto
John   1: 5   And the light **s** in the
2Pe   1:19   to heed as a light that **s**

SHINING (*see* SHINE)
Mark   9: 3   His clothes became **s**,
Luke   24: 4   two men stood by them in **s**
John   5:35   He was the burning and **s**
1Jn   2: 8   the true light is already **s**.
Rev   1:16   was like the sun **s** in its

SHIP (*see* SHIPS, SHIPWRECK)
Jon   1: 3   and found a **s** going to

SHIPS (*see* SHIP)
Ps   107:23   who go down to the sea in **s**,
Is   23: 1   you **s** of Tarshish! For it
Ezek   27: 9   All the **s** of the sea And

SHIPWRECK† (*see* SHIP, SHIPWRECKED)
1Ti   1:19   the faith have suffered **s**,

SHIPWRECKED† (*see* SHIPWRECK)
2Co   11:25   stoned; three times I was **s**;

SHOD†
Eph   6:15   and having **s** your feet with

SHONE (*see* SHINE)
Ex   34:35   the skin of Moses' face **s**,
Matt   17: 2   His face **s** like the sun, and
Luke   2: 9   and the glory of the Lord **s**
Acts   9: 3   and suddenly a light **s**
2Co   4: 6   who has **s** in our hearts to

SHORN (*see* SHEARER)
1Co   11: 6   for a woman to be **s** or

SHORT (*see* SHORTENED)
Job   20: 5   of the wicked is **s**,
Rom   3:23   all have sinned and fall **s**
1Co   7:29   brethren, the time is **s**,
Heb   12:15   lest anyone fall **s** of the

SHORTENED (*see* SHORT)
Matt   24:22   unless those days were **s**,

SHOULDER (*see* SHOULDERS)
Gen   24:15   with her pitcher on her **s**.
Is   9: 6   will be upon His **s**.

SHOULDERS (*see* SHOULDER)
Gen   9:23   laid it on both their **s**,
1Sa   9: 2   From his **s** upward he was
Is   49:22   shall be carried on their **s**;
Matt   23: 4   and lay them on men's **s**;
Luke   15: 5   it, he lays it on his **s**,

SHOUT (*see* SHOUTED)
Ps   32:11   And **s** for joy, all you
Ps   35:27   Let them **s** for joy and be
Ps   47: 1   all you peoples! **S** to God
Ps   47: 5   God has gone up with a **s**,
Ps   66: 1   Make a joyful **s** to God, all
Ps   98: 4   **S** joyfully to the LORD, all
Ps   100: 1   Make a joyful **s** to the
Zech   9: 9   O daughter of Zion! **S**,
Gal   4:27   Break forth and **s**,
1Th   4:16   descend from heaven with a **s**,

SHOUTED (*see* SHOUT)
Job   38: 7   And all the sons of God **s**

SHOW (*see* SHOWED, SHOWING, SHOWN, SHOWS)
Gen   12: 1   To a land that I will **s**
Ex   33:18   **s** me Your glory."
Ps   16:11   You will **s** me the path of
Ps   18:25   the merciful You will **s**
Ps   25: 4   **S** me Your ways, O LORD
Ps   51:15   And my mouth shall **s** forth
Matt   8: 4   **s** yourself to the priest,
John   14: 9   **S** us the Father'?
Acts   7: 3   a land that I will **s**
1Co   12:31   And yet I **s** you a more
Eph   2: 7   the ages to come He might **s**
Jas   2:18   **S** me your faith without
Rev   4: 1   and I will **s** you things

SHOWBREAD
Num   4: 7   On the table of **s** they shall
1Ch   9:32   in charge of preparing the **s**
Matt   12: 4   house of God and ate the **s**
Heb   9: 2   the table, and the **s**,

SHOWED (*see* SHOW)
Matt   4: 8   and **s** Him all the kingdoms
Luke   10:37   He who **s** mercy on him." Then
Luke   24:40   He **s** them His hands and His

SHOWERS
Ps   72: 6   Like **s** that water the
Ezek   34:26   there shall be **s** of
Zech   10: 1   He will give them **s** of

SHOWING (*see* SHOW)
Ex   20: 6   but **s** mercy to thousands, to
Acts   18:28   **s** from the Scriptures that
Tit   3: 2   **s** all humility to all men.

SHOWN (*see* SHOW)
Ex   25:40   to the pattern which was **s**
Ps   78:11   His wonders that He had **s**
Mic   6: 8   He has **s** you, O man, what
John   10:32   Many good works I have **s** you
Acts   10:28   But God has **s** me that I
Rom   1:19   for God has **s** it to them.
Heb   8: 5   to the pattern **s** you
Jas   2: 4   have you not **s** partiality

SHOWS (see SHOW)

Deut	10:17	who s no partiality nor
2Sa	22:51	And s mercy to His
Ps	19: 1	And the firmament s His
Ps	37:21	But the righteous s mercy
Mark	14:70	and your speech s it."
Acts	10:34	truth I perceive that God s
Rom	9:16	but of God who s mercy.
Rom	12: 8	he who s mercy, with

SHULAMITE

Song	6:13	Return, return, O S;

SHUN† (see SHUNNED)

2Ti	2:16	But s profane and idle

SHUNNED

Job	1: 1	and one who feared God and s

SHUT (see SHUTS)

Gen	7:16	and the LORD s him in.
Gen	19: 6	s the door behind him,
Num	12:15	So Miriam was s out of the
Josh	6: 1	Now Jericho was securely s up
1Ki	8:35	When the heavens are s up
Neh	13:19	commanded the gates to be s,
Ps	69:15	And let not the pit s its
Ps	88: 8	I am s up, and I cannot
Eccl	12: 4	When the doors are s in the
Is	6:10	And s their eyes; Lest
Is	22:22	open, and no one shall s;
Is	44:18	For He has s their eyes, so
Is	52:15	Kings shall s their mouths
Jer	20: 9	like a burning fire S up
Jer	32: 2	Jeremiah the prophet was s
Ezek	44: 2	me, "This gate shall be s;
Dan	6:22	God sent His angel and s
Dan	12: 4	s up the words, and seal the
Matt	6: 6	and when you have s your
Matt	25:10	wedding; and the door was s.
Luke	3:20	that he s John up in prison.
Luke	4:25	when the heaven was s up
John	20:26	came, the doors being s,
Acts	20:10	and many of the saints I s
Rev	3: 8	and no one can s it; for you
Rev	21:25	Its gates shall not be s at

SHUTS (see SHUT)

Rev	3: 7	who opens and no one s,

SICK (see SICKNESS)

2Ki	20: 1	In those days Hezekiah was s
Neh	2: 2	sad, since you are not s?
Prov	13:12	deferred makes the heart s,
Is	1: 5	more. The whole head is s,
Dan	8:27	fainted and was s for days;
Mal	1: 8	you offer the lame and s,
Matt	4:24	they brought to Him all s
Matt	8:14	his wife's mother lying s
Matt	8:16	and healed all who were s,
Matt	9:12	but those who are s.
Matt	10: 8	"Heal the s, cleanse
Matt	25:36	I was s and you visited Me;

Mark	6:13	with oil many who were s,
Mark	16:18	they will lay hands on the s,
John	11: 2	whose brother Lazarus was s.
1Co	11:30	reason many are weak and s
Phil	2:27	For indeed he was s almost
Jas	5:14	Is anyone among you s?
Jas	5:15	of faith will save the s,

SICKLE

Deut	16: 9	you begin to put the s to
Joel	3:13	Put in the s, for the harvest
Mark	4:29	immediately he puts in the s,
Rev	14:14	and in His hand a sharp s.

SICKNESS (see SICK, SICKNESSES)

Deut	28:61	Also every s and every
Is	38: 9	and had recovered from his s:
Matt	4:23	and healing all kinds of s
John	11: 4	This s is not unto death, but

SICKNESSES (see SICKNESS)

Matt	8:17	And bore our s.

SIDE (see SIDES)

Ex	32:26	is on the LORD's s—
Ps	91: 7	thousand may fall at your s,
Ps	118: 6	The LORD is on my s;
Ps	124: 1	the LORD who was on our s,
Mark	16: 5	robe sitting on the right s;
Luke	1:11	standing on the right s of
Luke	10:31	he passed by on the other s.
John	19:18	with Him, one on either s,
John	19:34	the soldiers pierced His s
John	20:20	them His hands and His s.
John	20:25	and put my hand into His s,
2Co	4: 8	are hard pressed on every s,
2Co	7: 5	we were troubled on every s.

SIDES (see SIDE)

Ps	48: 2	Is Mount Zion on the s of

SIDON

Josh	11: 8	and chased them to Greater S,
Judg	10: 6	gods of Syria, the gods of S,
Matt	15:21	to the region of Tyre and S.

SIFT

Luke	22:31	that he may s you as wheat.

SIGH (see SIGHING)

Ps	90: 9	finish our years like a s.

SIGHING (see SIGH)

Is	35:10	And sorrow and s shall flee

SIGHT

Gen	2: 9	that is pleasant to the s
Ex	3: 3	aside and see this great s,
Num	13:33	grasshoppers in our own s,
Judg	2:11	of Israel did evil in the s
Ruth	2:13	me find favor in your s,
1Sa	1:18	find favor in your s.
2Sa	7:19	was a small thing in Your s,
2Sa	12:11	with your wives in the s of

S

2Sa	16:22	concubines in the s of all
1Ki	11: 6	Solomon did evil in the s of
1Ki	14:22	Now Judah did evil in the s
1Ki	15:26	And he did evil in the s of
2Ki	1:13	yours be precious in your s.
2Ki	14: 3	what was right in the s
2Ki	17:18	and removed them from His s;
Neh	1:11	grant him mercy in the s of
Esth	5: 2	she found favor in his s,
Job	15:15	are not pure in His s,
Job	25: 5	stars are not pure in His s,
Ps	18:24	of my hands in His s.
Ps	19:14	Be acceptable in Your s,
Ps	51: 4	done this evil in Your s—
Ps	90: 4	a thousand years in Your s
Ps	116:15	Precious in the s of the
Prov	4: 3	and the only one in the s
Eccl	6: 9	Better is the s of the eyes
Is	43: 4	you were precious in My s,
Hos	6: 2	That we may live in His s.
Luke	4:18	And recovery of s to
Luke	15:21	against heaven and in your s,
Luke	24:31	and He vanished from their s.
John	9:11	and washed, and I received s.
Acts	1: 9	received Him out of their s.
Acts	9: 9	he was three days without s,
Acts	22:13	Saul, receive your s.
2Co	5: 7	we walk by faith, not by s.
Heb	13:21	is well pleasing in His s,
Jas	4:10	Humble yourselves in the s of
1Pe	3: 4	is very precious in the s
1Jn	3:22	that are pleasing in His s.

SIGN (see SIGNED, SIGNS)

Gen	9:12	This is the s of the
Gen	17:11	and it shall be a s of the
Ex	3:12	And this shall be a s to
Ex	12:13	Now the blood shall be a s
Ex	31:17	It is a s between Me and the
Deut	6: 8	You shall bind them as a s on
Is	7:11	Ask a s for yourself from the
Is	7:14	Himself will give you a s:
Is	20: 3	three years for a s and a
Matt	12:39	generation seeks after a s,
Matt	12:39	be given to it except the s
Luke	2:12	And this will be the s to
John	4:54	This again is the second s
1Co	1:22	For Jews request a s,
1Co	14:22	tongues are for a s,

SIGNED (see SIGN)

| Dan | 6:10 | knew that the writing was s, |

SIGNIFYING

| John | 12:33 | s by what death He would |

SIGNS (see MIRACLES, SIGN)

Gen	1:14	and let them be for s and
Ex	4: 9	not believe even these two s,
Ex	7: 3	and multiply My s and My
Deut	34:11	in all the s and wonders
Is	8:18	given me! We are for s
Dan	6:27	And He works s and wonders
Matt	16: 3	you cannot discern the s

Mark	16:20	through the accompanying s.
Luke	21:25	And there will be s in the
John	2:11	This beginning of s Jesus did
John	3: 2	for no one can do these s
John	4:48	Unless you people see s and
John	6:26	not because you saw the s,
John	7:31	will He do more s than these
John	9:16	who is a sinner do such s?
Acts	2:22	and s which God did through
Acts	5:12	of the apostles many s and
Acts	6: 8	did great wonders and s
Acts	8:13	seeing the miracles and s
Rom	15:19	in mighty s and wonders, by
2Co	12:12	Truly the s of an apostle
2Th	2: 9	of Satan, with all power, s,
Heb	2: 4	bearing witness both with s
Rev	13:13	He performs great s,

SILAS (see SILVANUS)

| Acts | 15:40 | but Paul chose S and |

SILENCE (see SILENT)

Ps	8: 2	That You may s the enemy
Ps	115:17	Nor any who go down into s.
Eccl	3: 7	to sew; A time to keep s,
Is	41: 1	Keep s before Me, O
Hab	2:20	Let all the earth keep s
1Ti	2:11	Let a woman learn in s with
Rev	8: 1	there was s in heaven for

SILENT (see SILENCE)

2Ki	2: 3	"Yes I know; keep s!"
Esth	4:14	if you remain completely s
Job	13: 5	Oh, that you would be s,
Ps	22: 2	night season, and am not s.
Ps	32: 3	When I kept s,
Ps	83: 1	Do not keep s,
Is	53: 7	before its shearers is s,
Matt	26:63	But Jesus kept s.
Mark	3: 4	to kill?" But they kept s.
Acts	8:32	before its shearer is s,
1Co	14:28	let him keep s in church,
1Co	14:34	Let your women keep s in the

SILOAM (see SHILOAH)

| Luke | 13: 4 | on whom the tower in S fell |
| John | 9: 7 | wash in the pool of S" |

SILVANUS (see SILAS)

| 1Th | 1: 1 | Paul, S, and Timothy, |

SILVER (see SILVERSMITH)

Gen	23:15	four hundred shekels of s.
Gen	37:28	for twenty shekels of s.
Gen	44: 2	the s cup, in the mouth of
Ex	20:23	gods of s or gods of gold you
Ex	21:32	master thirty shekels of s,
Num	10: 2	Make two s trumpets for
Deut	17:17	shall he greatly multiply s
Ps	66:10	You have refined us as s is
Ps	115: 4	Their idols are s and gold,
Prov	2: 4	If you seek her as s,
Prov	25:11	of gold In settings of s.
Dan	2:32	its chest and arms of s,

Dan	5: 4	the gods of gold and s,
Amos	2: 6	sell the righteous for s,
Amos	8: 6	we may buy the poor for s,
Hag	2: 8	The s is Mine, and the gold
Zech	11:12	my wages thirty pieces of s.
Mal	3: 3	refiner and a purifier of s;
Matt	26:15	to him thirty pieces of s.
Luke	15: 8	having ten s coins, if she
Acts	3: 6	S and gold I do not have, but
Acts	17:29	Nature is like gold or s or
1Co	3:12	foundation with gold, s,
1Pe	1:18	like s or gold, from your

SILVERSMITH (*see* SILVER)

Acts	19:24	man named Demetrius, a s,

SIMEON

Gen	34:25	S and Levi, Dinah's
Num	2:12	shall be the tribe of S,
Acts	13: 1	S who was called Niger,

SIMON (*see* BAR-JONAH, CEPHAS, PETER)

Matt	4:18	S called Peter, and Andrew
Matt	10: 4	S the Canaanite, and Judas
Matt	13:55	His brothers James, Joses, S,
Matt	16:17	S Bar-Jonah, for flesh and
Mark	15:21	S a Cyrenian, the father of
Luke	6:15	and S called the Zealot;
John	6:71	Iscariot, the son of S,
John	18:10	Then S Peter, having a sword,

SIMPLE

Ps	19: 7	is sure, making wise the s;
Ps	116: 6	The LORD preserves the s;
Ps	119:130	gives understanding to the s.
Prov	1: 4	To give prudence to the s,
Prov	9: 4	"Whoever is s, let him turn
Rom	16:18	deceive the hearts of the s.
Rom	10:19	and s concerning evil.

SIN (*see* SINFUL, SINNED, SINNER, SINNING, SINS)

Gen	4: 7	s lies at the door. And its
Gen	18:20	and because their s is very
Gen	39: 9	and s against God?"
Ex	10:17	please forgive my s only
Ex	20:20	you, so that you may not s.
Ex	29:36	a bull every day as a s
Ex	32:30	have committed a great s.
Ex	32:30	make atonement for your s.
Ex	34: 7	and transgression and s,
Ex	34: 7	our iniquity and our s,
Lev	4: 3	bull without blemish as a s
Lev	4:29	hand on the head of the s
Lev	5: 9	some of the blood of the s
Lev	5:10	on his behalf for his s
Lev	6:25	This is the law of the s
Lev	12: 6	or a turtledove as a s
Lev	16: 5	two kids of the goats as a s
Lev	19:22	And the s which he has
Lev	20:20	They shall bear their s;
Num	9:13	that man shall bear his s.
Num	12:11	Please do not lay this s
Num	15:22	If you s unintentionally,

Num	19:17	for purification from s,
Num	27: 3	but he died in his own s;
Num	32:23	and be sure your s will find
Num	33:11	in the Wilderness of S.
Deut	15: 9	and it become s among you.
Deut	21:22	a man has committed a s
Deut	23:21	and it would be s to you.
Deut	24:16	put to death for his own s.
1Sa	15:23	rebellion is as the s of
1Sa	15:25	please pardon my s,
1Ki	8:46	is no one who does not s),
1Ki	14:16	sinned and who made Israel s.
1Ki	22:52	Nebat, who had made Israel s;
Job	1:22	In all this Job did not s
Ps	32: 1	Whose s is covered.
Ps	32: 5	I acknowledged my s to You,
Ps	32: 5	forgave the iniquity of my s.
Ps	40: 6	Burnt offering and s
Ps	51: 2	And cleanse me from my s.
Ps	51: 3	And my s is always before
Ps	51: 5	And in s my mother
Ps	119:11	That I might not s against
Prov	14:34	But s is a reproach to
Prov	20: 9	I am pure from my s"?
Eccl	7:20	does good And does not s.
Is	6: 7	And your s purged."
Is	30: 1	That they may add s to sin;
Is	53:10	His soul an offering for s,
Is	53:12	And He bore the s of many,
Jer	31:34	and their s I will remember
Ezek	3:20	he shall die in his s,
Mic	6: 7	fruit of my body for the s
Matt	5:29	right eye causes you to s,
Matt	18:21	how often shall my brother s
John	1:29	of God who takes away the s
John	5:14	S no more, lest a worse
John	8: 7	He who is without s among
John	8:11	go and s no more."
John	8:34	whoever commits s is a slave
John	8:46	of you convicts Me of s?
John	9:41	blind, you would have no s;
John	9:41	Therefore your s remains.
John	16: 8	will convict the world of s,
John	19:11	Me to you has the greater s.
Rom	3: 9	that they are all under s.
Rom	4: 8	shall not impute s.
Rom	5:12	just as through one man s
Rom	5:12	world, and death through s,
Rom	5:20	But where s abounded, grace
Rom	5:21	so that as s reigned in
Rom	6: 1	Shall we continue in s that
Rom	6: 6	no longer be slaves of s.
Rom	6: 7	died has been freed from s.
Rom	6:10	He died to s once for all;
Rom	6:14	For s shall not have dominion
Rom	6:17	though you were slaves of s,
Rom	6:23	For the wages of s is death,
Rom	7: 7	I would not have known s
Rom	7: 9	s revived and I died.
Rom	7:14	I am carnal, sold under s.
Rom	7:17	but s that dwells in me.
Rom	8: 2	me free from the law of s
Rom	8: 3	He condemned s in the flesh,
Rom	14:23	is not from faith is s.

S

1Co	15:56	The sting of death is **s**,
1Co	15:56	and the strength of **s** is
2Co	5:21	He made Him who knew no **s**
2Th	2: 3	and the man of **s** is
Heb	4:15	as we are, yet without **s**.
Heb	9:26	has appeared to put away **s**
Heb	10: 8	and offerings for **s** You
Heb	10:26	For if we **s** willfully after
Heb	11:25	the passing pleasures of **s**,
Heb	12: 1	and the **s** which so easily
Jas	1:15	it gives birth to **s**;
Jas	4:17	not do it, to him it is **s**.
1Pe	2:22	"Who committed no **s**,
1Jn	1: 7	Son cleanses us from all **s**.
1Jn	1: 8	If we say that we have no **s**,
1Jn	3: 4	and **s** is lawlessness.
1Jn	3: 6	abides in Him does not **s**.
1Jn	3: 9	been born of God does not **s**,
1Jn	3: 9	in him; and he cannot **s**,
1Jn	5:16	There is **s** leading to
1Jn	5:17	All unrighteousness is **s**,

SINAI (see HOREB)

Ex	19: 1	came to the Wilderness of **S**.
Ex	19:20	LORD came down upon Mount **S**,
Gal	4:25	for this Hagar is Mount **S** in

SINCERE (see SINCERITY)

1Ti	1: 5	and from **s** faith

SINCERITY (see SINCERE)

Josh	24:14	serve Him in **s** and in truth,
1Co	5: 8	the unleavened bread of **s**
Eph	6: 5	in **s** of heart, as to Christ;
Col	3:22	but in **s** of heart, fearing

SINFUL (see SIN)

Luke	5: 8	for I am a **s** man, O Lord!"
Luke	24: 7	into the hands of **s** men,
Rom	8: 3	own Son in the likeness of **s**

SING (see SANG, SINGING, SONG, SUNG)

Ex	15: 1	I will **s** to the LORD, For
Ps	33: 3	**S** to Him a new song
Ps	47: 6	**S** praises to God, sing
Ps	89: 1	I will **s** of the mercies of
Ps	95: 1	let us **s** to the LORD! Let
Ps	96: 1	**s** to the LORD a new song!
Ps	137: 4	How shall we **s** the LORD's
Is	5: 1	Now let me **s** to my
Is	12: 5	**S** to the LORD, For He has
Is	42:10	**S** to the LORD a new song,
1Co	14:15	I will **s** with the spirit,

SINGED†

Dan	3:27	of their head was not **s** nor

SINGING (see SING)

Ps	100: 2	before His presence with **s**.
Song	2:12	The time of **s** has come,
Is	14: 7	They break forth into **s**.
Acts	16:25	and Silas were praying and **s**
Eph	5:19	**s** and making melody in your
Col	3:16	**s** with grace in your hearts

SINK (see SANK)

Matt	14:30	and beginning to **s** he cried

SINNED (see SIN)

1Sa	15:24	said to Samuel, "I have **s**,
2Sa	12:13	I have **s** against the LORD."
2Sa	24:10	I have **s** greatly in what I
Ps	51: 4	You, You only, have I **s**,
Is	43:27	Your first father **s**,
Hos	4: 7	The more they **s** against Me;
Luke	15:18	I have **s** against heaven and
John	9: 2	Him, saying, "Rabbi, who **s**,
John	9: 3	this man nor his parents **s**,
Rom	3:23	for all have **s** and fall short
Rom	5:12	to all men, because all **s**—
2Pe	2: 4	not spare the angels who **s**,
1Jn	1:10	If we say that we have not **s**,
1Jn	3: 8	for the devil has **s** from the

SINNER (see SIN, SINNERS)

Prov	11:31	more the ungodly and the **s**.
Luke	15: 7	joy in heaven over one **s**
Luke	18:13	be merciful to me a **s**!'
John	9:24	We know that this Man is a **s**.
1Pe	4:18	the ungodly and the **s**

SINNERS (see SINNER)

Ps	1: 1	Nor stands in the path of **s**,
Ps	1: 5	Nor **s** in the congregation
Ps	51:13	And **s** shall be converted to
Matt	9:10	many tax collectors and **s**
Matt	9:13	to call the righteous, but **s**,
Matt	26:45	betrayed into the hands of **s**.
John	9:31	that God does not hear **s**;
Rom	5: 8	that while we were still **s**,
1Ti	1:15	into the world to save **s**,

SINNING (see SIN)

Gen	20: 6	I also withheld you from **s**
1Jn	5:16	anyone sees his brother **s** a

SINS (see SIN)

Ps	19:13	also from presumptuous **s**;
Ps	25:18	pain, And forgive all my **s**.
Ps	51: 9	Hide Your face from my **s**,
Ps	90: 8	Our secret **s** in the light
Ps	103:10	with us according to our **s**,
Prov	10:12	But love covers all **s**.
Is	1:18	Though your **s** are like
Is	38:17	For You have cast all my **s**
Is	40: 2	hand Double for all her **s**.
Is	43:25	I will not remember your **s**.
Ezek	18: 4	The soul who **s** shall die.
Dan	9:24	To make an end of **s**,
Mic	7:19	You will cast all our **s**
Matt	1:21	save His people from their **s**.
Matt	9: 2	your **s** are forgiven you."
Matt	9: 6	power on earth to forgive **s**'
Matt	18:15	if your brother **s**
Matt	26:28	many for the remission of **s**.
Luke	11: 4	And forgive us our **s**,
John	8:24	that you will die in your **s**;
John	20:23	If you forgive the **s** of any,

Acts	2:38	for the remission of **s**;
Acts	3:19	that your **s** may be blotted
1Co	15: 3	that Christ died for our **s**
1Co	15:17	you are still in your **s**!
Gal	1: 4	who gave Himself for our **s**,
Eph	1: 7	blood, the forgiveness of **s**,
Eph	2: 1	dead in trespasses and **s**,
Heb	1: 3	had by Himself purged our **s**,
Heb	2:17	make propitiation for the **s**
Heb	5: 3	to offer sacrifices for **s**.
Heb	7:27	first for His own **s** and then
Heb	9:28	offered once to bear the **s**
Heb	10: 4	and goats could take away **s**.
Heb	10:12	offered one sacrifice for **s**
Jas	5:20	and cover a multitude of **s**.
1Pe	2:24	who Himself bore our **s** in His
1Pe	2:24	that we, having died to **s**,
1Pe	3:18	also suffered once for **s**,
1Pe	4: 8	cover a multitude of **s**.
1Jn	1: 9	If we confess our **s**,
1Jn	2: 1	may not sin. And if anyone **s**,
1Jn	2: 2	the propitiation for our **s**,
1Jn	3: 8	He who **s** is of the devil, for
Rev	1: 5	us and washed us from our **s**

SIR

John	4:15	The woman said to Him, "**S**,
John	20:15	gardener, said to Him, "**S**,

SISTER (*see* SISTERS)

Gen	12:13	"Please say you are my **s**,
Gen	20:12	indeed she is truly my **s**.
Gen	26: 7	She is my **s**"; for he was
Gen	34:13	he had defiled Dinah their **s**.
Ex	2: 7	Then his **s** said to Pharaoh's
Ex	15:20	the **s** of Aaron, took the
Song	4: 9	ravished my heart, My **s**,
Matt	12:50	heaven is My brother and **s**
Jas	2:15	If a brother or **s** is naked

SISTERS (*see* SISTER)

Matt	19:29	houses or brothers or **s** or

SIT (*see* SAT, SITS, SITTING)

Deut	6: 7	talk of them when you **s** in
Ps	110: 1	**S** at My right hand, Till I
Mic	4: 4	But everyone shall **s** under
Matt	8:11	and **s** down with Abraham,
Matt	22:44	**S** at My right hand,
Acts	2:34	**S** at My right hand,
Eph	2: 6	and made us **s** together in
Heb	1:13	**S** at My right hand,

SITS (*see* SIT)

Ps	1: 1	Nor **s** in the seat of the
Ps	2: 4	He who **s** in the heavens

SITTING (*see* SIT)

Ps	139: 2	You know my **s** down and my
Is	6: 1	I saw the Lord **s** on a
Matt	21: 5	and **s** on a donkey, A
Col	3: 1	**s** at the right hand of God.

SIX (*see* SIXTH)

Ex	20: 9	**S** days you shall labor and do
Ex	20:11	For in **s** days the LORD made
Ex	21: 2	he shall serve **s** years; and
Is	6: 2	each one had **s** wings: with
Rev	4: 8	each having **s** wings, were

SIXTH (*see* SIX)

Gen	1:31	and the morning were the **s**
Matt	27:45	Now from the **s** hour until

SKILL (*see* SKILLED, SKILLFUL)

Ex	35:35	He has filled them with **s** to
1Ki	5: 6	is none among us who has **s**
Ps	137: 5	right hand forget its **s**!
Dan	1:17	gave them knowledge and **s**
Dan	9:22	come forth to give you **s** to

SKILLED (*see* SKILL)

2Ch	2:14	**s** to work in gold and
Ezra	7: 6	and he was a **s** scribe in

SKILLFUL (*see* SKILL, SKILLFULLY)

Gen	25:27	And Esau was a **s** hunter, a
1Sa	16:16	seek out a man who is a **s**

SKILLFULLY (*see* SKILLFUL)

Ps	139:15	And **s** wrought in the

SKIN

Gen	3:21	LORD God made tunics of **s**,
Ex	34:35	that the **s** of Moses' face
Job	2: 4	Skin for **s**! Yes, all that a
Job	7: 5	My **s** is cracked and breaks
Job	19:20	My bone clings to my **s** and
Job	19:20	I have escaped by the **s** of
Job	19:26	And after my **s** is destroyed,
Job	30:30	My **s** grows black and falls
Ps	102: 5	My bones cling to my **s**.
Jer	13:23	the Ethiopian change his **s**

SKIPPED

Ps	114: 4	The mountains **s** like rams,

SKULL

Judg	9:53	head and crushed his **s**.
Matt	27:33	that is to say, Place of a **S**,

SKY

Ps	89:37	faithful witness in the **s**.
Matt	16: 2	for the **s** is red';
Matt	16: 3	to discern the face of the **s**,
Heb	11:12	many as the stars of the **s**

SLACK (*see* SLACKNESS)

2Pe	3: 9	The Lord is not **s** concerning

SLACKNESS† (*see* SLACK)

2Pe	3: 9	promise, as some count **s**,

SLAIN (*see* SLAY)

1Sa	18: 7	Saul has **s** his thousands,
Hos	6: 5	I have **s** them by the words

S

Rev	5: 6	Lamb as though it had been s,
Rev	5: 9	its seals; For You were s,
Rev	6: 9	of those who had been s for
Rev	13: 8	Book of Life of the Lamb s

SLAUGHTER

Ps	44:22	accounted as sheep for the s.
Prov	24:11	those stumbling to the s.
Is	53: 7	was led as a lamb to the s,
Jer	7:32	Hinnom, but the Valley of S;
Acts	8:32	as a sheep to the s;
Rom	8:36	as sheep for the s.
Jas	5: 5	your hearts as in a day of s.

SLAVE (see SLAVES)

Deut	5:15	remember that you were a s
Ps	105:17	was sold as a s.
Jer	2:14	Is he a homeborn s?
Jer	34: 9	free his male and female s—
Matt	20:27	among you, let him be your s—
Mark	10:44	to be first shall be s of
John	8:34	whoever commits sin is a s
Acts	16:16	that a certain s girl
1Co	7:22	in the Lord while a s is
1Co	7:22	while free is Christ's s.
Gal	3:28	there is neither s nor free,
Gal	4: 7	you are no longer a s but a
Eph	6: 8	whether he is a s or free.
Col	3:11	s nor free, but Christ is
Phm	1:16	no longer as a s but more

SLAVES (see SLAVE)

Lev	25:42	they shall not be sold as s.
Lev	25:44	may buy male and female s.
Lev	25:46	shall be your permanent s.
Deut	6:21	We were s of Pharaoh in
Esth	7: 4	sold as male and female s,
Jer	34:10	free his male and female s,
Rom	6: 6	we should no longer be s of
Rom	6:16	you present yourselves s to
Rom	6:17	that though you were s of
Rom	6:18	you became s of
Rom	6:19	your members as s of
Rom	6:22	and having become s of God,
1Co	7:23	do not become s of men.
1Co	12:13	whether s or free—and have

SLAY (see SLAIN)

Gen	18:25	to s the righteous with the
Gen	22:10	and took the knife to s his
Job	13:15	Though He s me, yet will I
Ps	37:14	To s those who are of
Ps	94: 6	They s the widow and the
Ps	139:19	that You would s the wicked,

SLEEP (see SLEEPING, SLEPT)

Gen	2:21	LORD God caused a deep s
Gen	15:12	a deep s fell upon Abram;
Job	4:13	When deep s falls on men,
Ps	13: 3	Lest I s the sleep of
Ps	44:23	Awake! Why do You s,
Ps	121: 4	Shall neither slumber nor s.
Ps	127: 2	so He gives His beloved s.
Prov	6:10	A little s, a little

Prov	6:10	folding of the hands to s—
Dan	12: 2	And many of those who s in
Luke	22:46	said to them, "Why do you s?
Rom	13:11	high time to awake out of s;
1Co	11:30	sick among you, and many s.
1Co	15:51	mystery: We shall not all s,
Eph	5:14	says: "Awake, you who s,
1Th	4:14	bring with Him those who s
1Th	5: 6	Therefore let us not s,
1Th	5:10	that whether we wake or s,

SLEEPING (see SLEEP)

1Ki	18:27	or perhaps he is s and must
Matt	9:24	the girl is not dead, but s.

SLEPT (see SLEEP)

Gen	2:21	to fall on Adam, and he s;
2Sa	11: 9	But Uriah s at the door of
Matt	25: 5	they all slumbered and s.
Matt	28:13	stole Him away while we s.

SLING

Judg	20:16	every one could s a stone at
1Sa	17:40	and his s was in his hand.

SLIP (see SLIPS)

Ps	17: 5	my footsteps may not s.
Ps	18:36	me, So my feet did not s.

SLIPS (see SLIP)

Ps	38:16	me, Lest, when my foot s,

SLOW

Ex	4:10	but I am s of speech and
Neh	9:17	S to anger, Abundant in
Ps	103: 8	S to anger, and abounding
Ps	145: 8	S to anger and great in
Joel	2:13	S to anger, and of great
Jon	4: 2	s to anger and abundant in
Nah	1: 3	The LORD is s to anger and
Luke	24:25	and s of heart to believe in
Jas	1:19	s to speak, slow to wrath;

SLUGGARD (see LAZY)

Prov	6: 6	you s! Consider her ways

SLUMBER

Ps	121: 3	He who keeps you will not s.
Ps	121: 4	Israel Shall neither s nor
Ps	132: 4	sleep to my eyes Or s to
Prov	6:10	A little sleep, a little s,

SMALL (see SMALLER)

1Ki	18:44	as s as a man's hand, rising
1Ki	19:12	and after the fire a still s
Ps	104:25	Living things both s and
Zech	4:10	has despised the day of s
Rev	20:12	s and great, standing before

SMALLER (see SMALL)

Mark	4:31	is s than all the seeds on

SMELL

Gen	27:27	the s of my son Is like

Dan   3:27   and the **s** of fire was not on

SMITTEN†
Is   53: 4   **S** by God, and afflicted.

SMOKE (see SMOKING)
Gen   19:28   the **s** of the land which went
Ex   19:18   Sinai was completely in **s**,
Is   6: 4   the house was filled with **s**.
Joel   2:30   and fire and pillars of **s**.
Acts   2:19   fire and vapor of **s**.

SMOKING† (see SMOKE)
Gen   15:17   there appeared a **s** oven and
Ex   20:18   trumpet, and the mountain **s**;
Is   7: 4   for these two stubs of **s**
Is   42: 3   And **s** flax He will not
Matt   12:20   And **s** flax He will

SMOOTH
Gen   27:16   on his hands and on the **s**
1Sa   17:40   he chose for himself five **s**
Is   40: 4   And the rough places **s**;
Luke   3: 5   And the rough ways **s**;
Rom   16:18   and by **s** words and

SNARE (see SNARES)
Ps   91: 3   deliver you from the **s** of
Ps   119:110   The wicked have laid a **s** for
Eccl   9:12   Like birds caught in a **s**,
Is   24:17   Fear and the pit and the **s**
Jer   48:43   Fear and the pit and the **s**

SNARES (see SNARE)
Ps   18: 5   The **s** of death confronted

SNATCH
John   10:28   neither shall anyone **s** them

SNEEZED†
2Ki   4:35   then the child **s** seven

SNOUT†
Prov   11:22   ring of gold in a swine's **s**,

SNOW
Ex   4: 6   hand was leprous, like **s**.
Num   12:10   leprous, as white as **s**.
Ps   51: 7   and I shall be whiter than **s**.
Prov   31:21   She is not afraid of **s** for
Is   1:18   They shall be as white as **s**;
Is   55:10   and the **s** from heaven, And
Dan   7: 9   His garment was white as **s**,
Matt   28: 3   his clothing as white as **s**.
Rev   1:14   like wool, as white as **s**,

SOBER (see SOBERLY)
1Th   5: 6   but let us watch and be **s**.
1Th   5: 8   us who are of the day be **s**,
Tit   2: 2   that the older men be **s**,
1Pe   1:13   the loins of your mind, be **s**,
1Pe   5: 8   Be **s**, be vigilant;

SOBERLY (see SOBER)
Rom   12: 3   to think, but to think **s**,

SOCKET
Gen   32:25   He touched the **s** of his hip;

SODOM
Gen   13:10   the LORD destroyed **S** and
Gen   18:26   If I find in **S** fifty
Gen   19:24   brimstone and fire on **S** and
Deut   29:23   like the overthrow of **S** and
Is   1: 9   We would have become like **S**,
Is   1:10   the LORD, You rulers of **S**;
Lam   4: 6   punishment of the sin of **S**,
Ezek   16:48   neither your sister **S** nor her
Matt   10:15   tolerable for the land of **S**
Matt   11:23   in you had been done in **S**,
Rom   9:29   have become like **S**,
Jude   7   as **S** and Gomorrah, and the
Rev   11: 8   spiritually is called **S** and

SOFT
Prov   15: 1   A **s** answer turns away wrath,

SOLD (see SELL)
Gen   25:33   and **s** his birthright to
Gen   37:28   and **s** him to the Ishmaelites
Matt   13:46   went and **s** all that he had
Matt   21:12   all those who bought and **s**
Matt   26: 9   oil might have been **s** for
Luke   17:28   drank, they bought, they **s**,
John   2:14   in the temple those who **s**
Acts   2:45   and **s** their possessions and
Acts   4:34   of lands or houses **s** them,
Acts   5: 4   your own? And after it was **s**,
Acts   7: 9   **s** Joseph into Egypt. But God
Rom   7:14   I am carnal, **s** under sin.
1Co   10:25   Eat whatever is **s** in the meat
Heb   12:16   who for one morsel of food **s**

SOLDIER (see SOLDIERS)
Acts   10: 7   servants and a devout **s**
Phil   2:25   fellow worker, and fellow **s**,
2Ti   2: 3   endure hardship as a good **s**

SOLDIERS (see SOLDIER)
Matt   8: 9   having **s** under me. And I say
Matt   28:12   large sum of money to the **s**,
Mark   15:16   Then the **s** led Him away into
John   19:34   But one of the **s** pierced His
Acts   12: 6   two chains between two **s**;

SOLE
Gen   8: 9   no resting place for the **s**
Deut   28:35   and from the **s** of your foot
Job   2: 7   painful boils from the **s** of
Is   1: 6   From the **s** of the foot even

SOLID
1Co   3: 2   you with milk and not with **s**
Heb   5:12   come to need milk and not **s**

SOLOMON (see SOLOMON'S)
1Ki   1:11   to Bathsheba the mother of **S**,

S

1Ki	3: 5	the LORD appeared to S in
1Ki	4:29	And God gave S wisdom and
1Ki	6:14	So S built the temple and
1Ki	11: 1	But King S loved many foreign
2Ch	9: 1	Sheba heard of the fame of S,
2Ch	9: 1	came to Jerusalem to test S
Prov	1: 1	The proverbs of S the son of
Prov	10: 1	The Proverbs of S:
Prov	25: 1	also are proverbs of S
Song	3:11	And see King S with the
Matt	1: 6	David the king begot S by
Matt	6:29	I say to you that even S in
Matt	12:42	to hear the wisdom of S;
Matt	12:42	and indeed a greater than S
Acts	7:47	But S built Him a house.

SOLOMON'S (see SOLOMON)

1Ki	4:30	Thus S wisdom excelled the
Song	1: 1	song of songs, which is S.
Song	3: 7	it is S couch, With sixty
John	10:23	in the temple, in S porch.

SON (see GRANDSON, MAN, SON'S, SONS)

Gen	22: 2	He said, "Take now your s,
Gen	22:16	and have not withheld your s,
Gen	22:16	your son, your only s—
Ex	4:22	the LORD: "Israel is My s,
Ex	4:23	let My s go that he may
Ex	13:14	when your s asks you in time
Ex	33:11	his servant Joshua the s of
Num	1:20	of Reuben, Israel's oldest s,
Num	4:28	authority of Ithamar the s
Num	13:16	Moses called Hoshea the s
Num	14: 6	But Joshua the s of Nun and
Num	20:25	Aaron and Eleazar his s,
Num	23:19	Nor a s of man, that He
Num	27: 1	families of Manasseh the s
Num	27: 8	'If a man dies and has no s,
Deut	7: 3	your daughter to their s,
Deut	18:10	you anyone who makes his s
Deut	21:16	firstborn status on the s
Deut	21:16	wife in preference to the s
Deut	21:20	This s of ours is stubborn
Josh	18:16	before the Valley of the S
Josh	22:32	And Phinehas the s of
Judg	1:13	And Othniel the s of Kenaz,
Judg	3:15	Ehud the s of Gera, the
Judg	3:31	him was Shamgar the s of
Judg	5: 1	Deborah and Barak the s of
Judg	6:29	Gideon the s of Joash has
Judg	8:23	nor shall my s rule over
Judg	8:29	Then Jerubbaal the s of
Judg	9: 1	Then Abimelech the s of
Judg	13: 3	shall conceive and bear a s.
Ruth	4:13	conception, and she bore a s.
Ruth	4:17	There is a s born to Naomi."
1Sa	1:20	conceived and bore a s,
1Sa	9: 2	had a choice and handsome s
1Sa	10:21	And Saul the s of Kish was
1Sa	13:16	Saul, Jonathan his s,
1Sa	14: 3	the s of Eli, the LORD's
1Sa	17:17	Then Jesse said to his s
1Sa	17:58	Whose s are you, young
1Sa	20:30	You s of a perverse,

1Sa	26: 5	and Abner the s of Ner, the
2Sa	1: 5	Saul and Jonathan his s are
2Sa	2: 8	took Ishbosheth the s of
2Sa	2:13	And Joab the s of Zeruiah,
2Sa	13: 1	After this Absalom the s of
2Sa	18:33	"O my son Absalom—my s,
1Ch	17:13	Father, and he shall be My s;
Ps	2: 7	said to Me, 'You are My S,
Ps	2:12	Kiss the S, lest He be
Ps	8: 4	And the s of man that You
Ps	72: 1	to the king's S.
Ps	72:20	The prayers of David the s
Ps	116:16	the s of Your maidservant;
Ps	144: 3	Or the s of man, that You
Prov	1: 1	proverbs of Solomon the s
Prov	1: 8	My s, hear the instruction
Prov	10: 1	A wise s makes a glad
Prov	10: 1	But a foolish s is the
Prov	13:24	spares his rod hates his s,
Prov	19:18	Chasten your s while there
Eccl	1: 1	the s of David, king in
Is	1: 1	The vision of Isaiah the s
Is	7:14	shall conceive and bear a S,
Is	9: 6	Unto us a S is given; And
Is	14:12	s of the morning! How you
Ezek	2: 1	S of man, stand on your feet,
Ezek	21: 3	S of man, I am sending you to
Ezek	18:20	bear the guilt of the s.
Ezek	37: 3	S of man, can these bones
Dan	3:25	of the fourth is like the S
Dan	7:13	One like the S of Man,
Dan	8:17	s of man, that the vision
Hos	11: 1	out of Egypt I called My s.
Amos	7:14	Nor was I a s of a
Matt	1: 1	the S of David, the Son of
Matt	1:20	s of David, do not be afraid
Matt	1:21	she will bring forth a S,
Matt	2:15	of Egypt I called My S.
Matt	3:17	"This is My beloved S,
Matt	4: 3	If You are the S of God,
Matt	4:21	James the s of Zebedee,
Matt	7: 9	if his s asks for bread,
Matt	8:20	but the S of Man has nowhere
Matt	9: 6	you may know that the S of
Matt	9:27	S of David, have mercy on
Matt	11:19	The S of Man came eating and
Matt	11:27	and no one knows the S
Matt	12: 8	For the S of Man is Lord even
Matt	12:32	speaks a word against the S
Matt	13:37	sows the good seed is the S
Matt	13:55	this not the carpenter's s?
Matt	16:13	the S of Man, am?"
Matt	16:16	the S of the living God."
Matt	20:18	and the S of Man will be
Matt	20:30	O Lord, S of David!"
Matt	21: 9	Hosanna to the S of David!
Matt	22:42	Whose S is He?" They said
Matt	24:27	will the coming of the S of
Matt	24:30	Then the sign of the S of Man
Matt	26:63	the S of God!"
Matt	27:54	Truly this was the S of
Matt	28:19	of the Father and of the S
Mark	1: 1	Jesus Christ, the S of God.
Mark	2: 5	said to the paralytic, "S,

Mark	3:11	You are the S of God."
Mark	5: 7	S of the Most High God? I
Mark	6: 3	the S of Mary, and brother
Mark	14:61	the S of the Blessed?"
Mark	15:39	Truly this Man was the S of
Luke	1:13	Elizabeth will bear you a s,
Luke	1:31	womb and bring forth a S,
Luke	1:32	and will be called the S of
Luke	1:35	be born will be called the S
Luke	2: 7	forth her firstborn S,
Luke	2:48	His mother said to Him, "S,
Luke	3:23	(as was supposed) the s of
Luke	3:38	son of Adam, the s of God.
Luke	6:16	Judas the s of James, and
Luke	10: 6	And if a s of peace is there,
Luke	12:53	will be divided against s
Luke	12:53	be divided against son and s
Luke	15:13	the younger s gathered all
Luke	15:19	worthy to be called your s.
Luke	15:25	Now his older s was in the
Luke	17:30	it be in the day when the S
Luke	18: 8	when the S of Man comes,
Luke	18:38	S of David, have mercy on
Luke	20:44	how is He then his S?
Luke	22:48	are you betraying the S of
John	1:18	time. The only begotten S,
John	1:42	You are Simon the s of Jonah.
John	1:49	You are the S of God! You
John	1:51	and descending upon the S
John	3:14	even so must the S of Man be
John	3:16	He gave His only begotten S,
John	3:17	For God did not send His S
John	3:35	"The Father loves the S,
John	3:36	He who believes in the S has
John	3:36	who does not believe the S
John	6:53	you eat the flesh of the S
John	8:36	Therefore if the S makes you
John	10:36	I am the S of God'?
John	12:23	hour has come that the S of
John	12:34	The S of Man must be lifted
John	19:26	behold your s!"
John	21:15	s of Jonah, do you love Me
Acts	8:37	that Jesus Christ is the S
Acts	13:33	Psalm: 'You are My S,
Rom	1: 4	and declared to be the S
Rom	1: 9	in the gospel of His S,
Rom	5:10	through the death of His S,
Rom	8: 3	did by sending His own S
Rom	8:29	to the image of His S,
Rom	8:32	who did not spare His own S,
Gal	1:16	to reveal His S in me, that I
Gal	2:20	I live by faith in the S of
Gal	4: 4	come, God sent forth His S,
Gal	4: 6	forth the Spirit of His S
Gal	4: 7	no longer a slave but a s,
Col	1:13	into the kingdom of the S
1Th	1:10	and to wait for His S from
2Th	2: 3	the s of perdition,
1Ti	1: 2	a true s in the faith:
2Ti	1: 2	To Timothy, a beloved s:
Heb	1: 2	days spoken to us by His S,
Heb	1: 5	say: "You are My S,
Heb	1: 5	shall be to Me a S"?
Heb	1: 8	But to the S He says:

Heb	2: 6	Or the s of man that
Heb	5: 5	to Him: "You are My S,
Heb	5: 8	though He was a S,
Heb	7: 3	but made like the S of God,
Heb	10:29	who has trampled the S of
Heb	11:17	up his only begotten s,
Heb	11:24	refused to be called the s
Heb	12: 6	And scourges every s
2Pe	1:17	"This is My beloved S,
1Jn	1: 3	the Father and with His S
1Jn	1: 7	blood of Jesus Christ His S
1Jn	4: 9	has sent His only begotten S
1Jn	4:14	the Father has sent the S
1Jn	4:15	that Jesus is the S of God,
1Jn	5:10	He who believes in the S of
1Jn	5:11	and this life is in His S.
1Jn	5:12	He who has the S has life; he
Rev	1:13	lampstands One like the S
Rev	21: 7	his God and he shall be My s.

SON'S (see SON)

Prov	30: 4	and what is His S name, If

SONG (see SING, SONGS)

Ex	15: 1	of Israel sang this s to
Ex	15: 2	LORD is my strength and s,
Judg	5:12	sing a s! Arise, Barak, and
Ps	33: 3	Sing to Him a new s;
Ps	40: 3	He has put a new s in my
Ps	96: 1	sing to the LORD a new s!
Ps	118:14	LORD is my strength and s,
Ps	137: 3	away captive asked of us a s,
Ps	137: 4	shall we sing the LORD's s
Song	1: 1	The s of songs, which is
Is	5: 1	to my Well-beloved A s of
Is	12: 2	LORD, is my strength and s;
Is	42:10	Sing to the LORD a new s,
Rev	5: 9	And they sang a new s,
Rev	15: 3	They sing the s of Moses, the
Rev	15: 3	and the s of the Lamb,

SONGS (see SONG)

Job	35:10	Who gives s in the night,
Ps	137: 3	Sing us one of the s of
Song	1: 1	The song of s,
Eph	5:19	and hymns and spiritual s,
Col	3:16	and hymns and spiritual s,

SONS (see SON)

Gen	6: 2	that the s of God saw the
Ruth	4:15	better to you than seven s,
1Sa	1: 8	not better to you than ten s?
Job	1: 6	there was a day when the s
Job	38: 7	And all the s of God
Jer	19: 5	to burn their s with fire
Jer	19: 9	to eat the flesh of their s
Hos	1:10	You are s of the living
Joel	2:28	Your s and your daughters
Matt	5: 9	For they shall be called s
Matt	5:45	that you may be s of your
Matt	8:12	But the s of the kingdom will
Matt	13:38	but the tares are the s of
Matt	20:21	Grant that these two s of
Matt	26:37	Him Peter and the two s of

S

Mark	3:17	**S** of Thunder";
Mark	3:28	sins will be forgiven the **s**
Luke	6:35	and you will be **s** of the
Luke	11:19	by whom do your **s** cast them
Luke	16: 8	For the **s** of this world are
Luke	16: 8	their generation than the **s**
Luke	20:34	The **s** of this age marry and
Luke	20:36	being **s** of the resurrection.
John	12:36	that you may become **s** of
Rom	8:14	these are **s** of God.
Rom	9:26	they shall be called **s**
Gal	3: 7	who are of faith are **s** of
Gal	3:26	For you are all **s** of God
Gal	4: 5	receive the adoption as **s**.
Gal	4:22	that Abraham had two **s**:
Eph	1: 5	us to adoption as **s** by
Eph	2: 2	who now works in the **s** of
Eph	5: 6	of God comes upon the **s** of
Col	3: 6	of God is coming upon the **s**
1Th	5: 5	You are all **s** of light and
Heb	2:10	in bringing many **s** to glory,
Heb	12: 8	are illegitimate and not **s**.

SORCERER (see SORCERERS, SORCERY)

Deut	18:10	who interprets omens, or a **s**,
Acts	13: 8	But Elymas the **s** (for so his

SORCERERS (see SORCERER)

Ex	7:11	the wise men and the **s**;
Dan	2: 2	the astrologers, the **s**,

SORCERY (see SORCERER)

Acts	8: 9	who previously practiced **s**
Gal	5:20	idolatry, **s**, hatred,

SORES

Ex	9: 9	boils that break out in **s**
Is	1: 6	and bruises and putrefying **s**;
Luke	16:20	named Lazarus, full of **s**,

SORROW (see SORROWFUL, SORROWS)

Gen	3:16	greatly multiply your **s** and
Gen	42:38	down my gray hair with **s** to
Ps	13: 2	Having **s** in my heart
Ps	35:12	To the **s** of my soul.
Ps	90:10	boast is only labor and **s**;
Ps	116: 3	me; I found trouble and **s**.
Prov	10:22	And He adds no **s** with it.
Prov	22: 8	sows iniquity will reap **s**,
Prov	23:29	Who has woe? Who has **s**?
Eccl	1:18	knowledge increases **s**.
Is	35:10	And **s** and sighing shall
Is	51:11	**S** and sighing shall flee
Jer	30:15	Your **s** is incurable.
Luke	22:45	found them sleeping from **s**.
John	16: 6	**s** has filled your heart.
Rom	9: 2	that I have great **s** and
2Co	7:10	For godly **s** produces
1Th	4:13	lest you **s** as others who
Rev	21: 4	be no more death, nor **s**,

SORROWFUL (see SORROW)

Matt	19:22	that saying, he went away **s**,
Matt	26:38	"My soul is exceedingly **s**,

SORROWS (see SORROW)

Ex	3: 7	for I know their **s**.
Ps	127: 2	late, To eat the bread of **s**;
Is	53: 3	A Man of **s** and acquainted
Is	53: 4	griefs And carried our **s**;
Matt	24: 8	are the beginning of **s**.
1Ti	6:10	through with many **s**.

SORRY

Gen	6: 6	And the LORD was **s** that He
Mark	6:26	the king was exceedingly **s**;

SOUGHT (see SEEK)

2Ch	14: 7	because we have **s** the LORD
Ps	34: 4	I **s** the LORD, and He heard
Ps	119:10	my whole heart I have **s** You;
Ps	119:94	For I have **s** Your precepts.
Song	3: 1	I **s** him, but I did not find
Luke	2:48	Your father and I have **s** You

SOUL (see SOULS)

Lev	17:11	makes atonement for the **s**.
Deut	4:29	heart and with all your **s**.
Deut	6: 5	your heart, with all your **s**,
1Sa	1:26	O my lord! As your **s** lives,
1Sa	18: 1	loved him as his own **s**.
Ps	16:10	You will not leave my **s** in
Ps	19: 7	perfect, converting the **s**;
Ps	23: 3	He restores my **s**;
Ps	24: 4	has not lifted up his **s** to
Ps	25: 1	You, O LORD, I lift up my **s**.
Ps	30: 3	You brought my **s** up from the
Ps	33:19	To deliver their **s** from
Ps	33:20	Our **s** waits for the LORD;
Ps	34: 2	My **s** shall make its boast in
Ps	34:22	The LORD redeems the **s** of
Ps	42: 1	So pants my **s** for You, O
Ps	42: 2	My **s** thirsts for God, for
Ps	42: 4	I pour out my **s** within me.
Ps	42: 5	are you cast down, O my **s**?
Ps	49:15	But God will redeem my **s**
Ps	56:13	For You have delivered my **s**
Ps	63: 1	My **s** thirsts for You; My
Ps	84: 2	My **s** longs, yes, even faints
Ps	86: 4	You, O Lord, I lift up my **s**.
Ps	103: 1	Bless the LORD, O my **s**;
Ps	106:15	sent leanness into their **s**.
Ps	107: 9	He satisfies the longing **s**,
Ps	107: 9	And fills the hungry **s** with
Ps	116: 7	Return to your rest, O my **s**,
Ps	116: 8	For You have delivered my **s**
Ps	121: 7	He shall preserve your **s**.
Ps	123: 4	Our **s** is exceedingly filled
Ps	130: 6	My **s** waits for the Lord
Ps	139:14	And that my **s** knows very
Ps	141: 8	Do not leave my **s**
Ps	142: 4	me; No one cares for my **s**.
Prov	3:22	they will be life to your **s**
Prov	16:24	Sweetness to the **s** and
Prov	25:25	As cold water to a weary **s**,
Eccl	6: 3	but his **s** is not satisfied
Is	38:15	In the bitterness of my **s**.
Is	42: 1	My Elect One in whom My **s**

Is	53:10	When You make His **s** an
Is	53:11	shall see the labor of His **s**,
Is	53:12	He poured out His **s** unto
Is	55: 2	And let your **s** delight
Is	55: 3	and your **s** shall live; And
Jer	32:41	My heart and with all My **s**.
Ezek	18: 4	The **s** of the father As
Ezek	18: 4	The **s** who sins shall die.
Ezek	24:21	eyes, the delight of your **s**;
Mic	6: 7	my body for the sin of my **s**?
Matt	10:28	body but cannot kill the **s**.
Matt	10:28	is able to destroy both **s**
Matt	12:18	Beloved in whom My **s**
Matt	16:26	world, and loses his own **s**?
Matt	16:26	give in exchange for his **s**?
Matt	22:37	heart, with all your **s**,
Matt	26:38	My **s** is exceedingly
Luke	1:46	My **s** magnifies the Lord,
Luke	2:35	pierce through your own **s**
Luke	12:19	I will say to my soul, "**S**,
Luke	12:20	Fool! This night your **s** will
John	12:27	Now My **s** is troubled, and
Acts	2:43	Then fear came upon every **s**,
Acts	4:32	were of one heart and one **s**;
Rom	13: 1	Let every **s** be subject to the
2Co	1:23	God as witness against my **s**,
1Th	5:23	and may your whole spirit, **s**,
Heb	4:12	even to the division of **s**
Heb	6:19	have as an anchor of the **s**,
Heb	10:38	My **s** has no pleasure
Heb	10:39	to the saving of the **s**.
Jas	5:20	of his way will save a **s**
1Pe	2:11	which war against the **s**,

SOULS (see SOUL)

Lev	17:11	to make atonement for your **s**;
Num	16:38	sinned against their own **s**,
Ps	72:13	And will save the **s** of the
Ps	97:10	evil! He preserves the **s**
Prov	11:30	And he who wins **s** is wise.
Prov	14:25	A true witness delivers **s**,
Jer	6:16	will find rest for your **s**.
Ezek	18: 4	all **s** are Mine; The soul of
Matt	11:29	will find rest for your **s**.
Luke	21:19	your patience possess your **s**.
Acts	2:41	day about three thousand **s**
Jas	1:21	which is able to save your **s**.
1Pe	1: 9	salvation of your **s**.
1Pe	2:25	and Overseer of your **s**.
1Pe	3:20	a few, that is, eight **s**,
2Pe	2:14	sin, enticing unstable **s**.
Rev	6: 9	I saw under the altar the **s**

SOUND (see SOUNDED, SOUNDING, VOICE)

Gen	3: 8	And they heard the **s** of the
Ps	89:15	who know the joyful **s**!
Ps	150: 3	Praise Him with the **s** of the
Eccl	12: 4	When one rises up at the **s**
Acts	2: 2	And suddenly there came a **s**
1Co	14: 8	trumpet makes an uncertain **s**,
1Co	15:52	For the trumpet will **s**,
2Co	5:13	or if we are of a **s** mind, it
2Ti	1: 7	and of love and of a **s** mind.
2Ti	1:13	Hold fast the pattern of **s**

2Ti	4: 3	when they will not endure **s**
Rev	19: 6	as the **s** of many waters and

SOUNDED (see SOUND)

1Th	1: 8	the word of the Lord has **s**

SOUNDING (see SOUND)

1Co	13: 1	I have become **s** brass or a

SOUR

Jer	31:29	The fathers have eaten **s**
Ezek	18: 2	The fathers have eaten **s**
Matt	27:34	they gave Him **s** wine mingled

SOUTH

Matt	12:42	The queen of the **S** will rise

SOW (see SOWED, SOWER, SOWN, SOWS)

Ex	23:10	Six years you shall **s** your
Ps	126: 5	Those who **s** in tears Shall
Hos	8: 7	They **s** the wind, And reap
Matt	6:26	for they neither **s** nor reap
Matt	13: 3	a sower went out to **s**.
Luke	19:21	and reap what you did not **s**.

SOWED (see SOW)

Matt	13: 4	"And as he **s**, some seed fell

SOWER (see SOW)

Is	55:10	it may give seed to the **s**
Matt	13: 3	a **s** went out to sow.
Matt	13:18	hear the parable of the **s**:
2Co	9:10	who supplies seed to the **s**,

SOWN (see SOW)

Is	40:24	Scarcely shall they be **s**,
Jer	2: 2	wilderness, In a land not **s**.
Matt	25:24	reaping where you have not **s**,
Mark	4:15	wayside where the word is **s**.
1Co	9:11	If we have **s** spiritual things
1Co	15:42	The body is **s** in

SOWS (see SOW)

Prov	22: 8	He who **s** iniquity will reap
Matt	13:37	He who **s** the good seed is the
Mark	4:14	The sower **s** the word.
John	4:37	One **s** and another reaps.'
2Co	9: 6	He who **s** sparingly will also
Gal	6: 7	mocked; for whatever a man **s**,

SPAIN

Rom	15:24	whenever I journey to **S**,

SPARE (see SPARES, SPARINGLY)

Gen	18:24	destroy the place and not **s**
Job	2: 6	but **s** his life."
Ezek	5:11	you; My eye will not **s**,
Luke	15:17	have bread enough and to **s**,
Rom	8:32	He who did not **s** His own Son,
Rom	11:21	For if God did not **s** the
2Pe	2: 4	For if God did not **s** the

SPARES (see SPARE)

Prov	13:24	He who **s** his rod hates his

S

SPARINGLY† (*see* SPARE)

2Co	9: 6	He who sows s will also reap

SPARKS

Job	5: 7	As the s fly upward.

SPARROWS

Matt	10:29	Are not two s sold for a
Matt	10:31	of more value than many s.

SPAT (*see* SPIT)

Matt	26:67	Then they s in His face and
John	9: 6	He s on the ground and made

SPEAK (*see* SPEAKING, SPEAKS, SPEECH, SPOKE, SPOKEN)

Ex	4:14	I know that he can s well.
Num	12: 6	I s to him in a dream.
Num	12: 8	I s with him face to face,
Deut	18:18	and He shall s to them all
Deut	18:20	prophet who presumes to s a
Deut	18:20	have not commanded him to s,
1Sa	3:10	And Samuel answered, "S,
Job	11: 5	But oh, that God would s,
Ps	17:10	With their mouths they s
Ps	51: 4	may be found just when You s,
Ps	85: 8	For He will s peace To His
Ps	115: 5	mouths, but they do not s;
Ps	119:172	My tongue shall s of Your
Eccl	3: 7	silence, And a time to s;
Is	8:10	S the word, but it will not
Is	19:18	in the land of Egypt will s
Is	30:10	S to us smooth things,
Is	40: 2	S comfort to Jerusalem, and
Is	41: 1	come near, then let them s;
Is	45:19	s righteousness, I declare
Is	50: 4	I should know how to s A
Jer	1: 6	GOD! Behold, I cannot s,
Jer	1: 7	I command you, you shall s.
Jer	1:17	And s to them all that I
Jer	8: 6	But they do not s aright.
Jer	9: 5	taught their tongue to s
Jer	12: 6	Even though they s smooth
Jer	18: 7	The instant I s concerning a
Jer	20: 9	Nor s anymore in His
Jer	23:16	They s a vision of their
Jer	34: 2	Go and s to Zedekiah king of
Jer	43: 2	You s falsely! The LORD our
Ezek	2: 7	You shall s My words to them,
Ezek	3:18	nor s to warn the wicked
Ezek	17: 2	and s a parable to the house
Ezek	20: 3	s to the elders of Israel,
Ezek	24:27	you shall s and no longer be
Dan	7:25	He shall s pompous words
Dan	11:36	shall s blasphemies against
Hos	1: 2	When the LORD began to s
Zech	9:10	He shall s peace to the
Matt	8: 8	But only s a word, and my
Matt	10:19	how or what you should s.
Matt	10:20	"for it is not you who s,
Matt	12:36	every idle word men may s,
Matt	13:34	a parable He did not s to
Mark	7:37	to hear and the mute to s.

Mark	9:39	My name can soon afterward s
Mark	16:17	they will s with new
Luke	1:20	be mute and not able to s
Luke	6:26	Woe to you when all men s
Luke	7:15	dead sat up and began to s.
John	3:11	We s what We know and
John	4:26	I who s to you am He."
John	6:63	The words that I s to you
John	7:17	is from God or whether I s
John	9:21	He will s for himself."
Acts	2: 4	Holy Spirit and began to s
Acts	2: 6	everyone heard them s in
Acts	4:20	For we cannot but s the
Acts	5:40	that they should not s in
Acts	10:46	For they heard them s with
Acts	21:37	Can you s Greek?
Acts	26: 1	You are permitted to s for
Rom	3: 5	(I s as a man.)
Rom	6:19	I s in human terms because
1Co	1:10	that you all s the same
1Co	2: 6	we s wisdom among those who
1Co	12:30	Do all s with tongues? Do
1Co	13: 1	Though I s with the tongues
1Co	14:19	the church I would rather s
1Co	14:35	is shameful for women to s
Eph	6:20	boldly, as I ought to s.
Tit	3: 2	to s evil of no one, to be
Heb	9: 5	things we cannot now s in
Jas	1:19	be swift to hear, slow to s,
Jas	4:11	Do not s evil of one
1Pe	4:11	let him s as the oracles
2Jn	12	I hope to come to you and s

SPEAKING (*see* SPEAK)

Acts	2:11	we hear them s in our own
Acts	26:14	I heard a voice s to me and
1Co	14: 6	if I come to you s with
1Co	14: 9	For you will be s into the
Eph	4:15	s the truth in love, may
Eph	5:19	s to one another in psalms
1Ti	2: 7	I am s the truth in Christ
1Pe	3:10	And his lips from s

SPEAKS (*see* SPEAK)

Ex	33:11	as a man s to his friend.
Deut	18:20	or who s in the name of
Deut	18:22	when a prophet s in the name
Ps	15: 2	And s the truth in his
Matt	12:34	of the heart the mouth s.
1Co	14: 2	For he who s in a tongue does
1Co	14:27	If anyone s in a tongue, let
Heb	11: 4	it he being dead still s.
Heb	12:24	blood of sprinkling that s
Heb	12:25	you do not refuse Him who s
Jas	4:11	He who s evil of a brother
1Pe	4:11	If anyone s, let him speak

SPEAR (*see* SPEARS)

1Sa	19:10	and he drove the s into the
John	19:34	pierced His side with a s,

SPEARS (*see* SPEAR)

1Sa	13:19	the Hebrews make swords or s.
Is	2: 4	And their s into pruning

Joel	3:10	your pruning hooks into s;
Mic	4: 3	And their s into pruning

SPECIAL

Ex	19: 5	then you shall be a s
Deut	7: 6	a s treasure above all the
Deut	26:18	proclaimed you to be His s
Tit	2:14	for Himself His own s
1Pe	2: 9	His own s people, that you

SPECK

Matt	7: 3	why do you look at the s in

SPECKLED

Gen	30:32	and the spotted and s among

SPECTACLE

1Co	4: 9	for we have been made a s to
Col	2:15	He made a public s of them,

SPEECH (see SPEAK)

Gen	11: 1	had one language and one s.
Gen	11: 7	understand one another's s.
Ex	4:10	but I am slow of s and slow
1Sa	16:18	a man of war, prudent in s,
Ps	19: 2	Day unto day utters s,
Ps	19: 3	There is no s nor language
Matt	26:73	for your s betrays you."
Mark	7:32	had an impediment in his s,
Col	4: 6	Let your s always be with

SPEND (see SPENT)

Gen	19: 2	your servant's house and s
Judg	19: 9	please s the night. See, the
Is	55: 2	Why do you s money for what
1Co	16: 6	or even s the winter with

SPENT (see SPEND)

Rom	13:12	The night is far s,
2Co	12:15	very gladly spend and be s

SPICES

Gen	37:25	with their camels, bearing s,
Mark	16: 1	James, and Salome bought s,

SPIED (see SPY)

Num	13:21	So they went up and s out
Josh	7: 2	So the men went up and s

SPIES (see SPY)

Gen	42:31	honest men; we are not s.

SPIN

Matt	6:28	they neither toil nor s;

SPIRIT (see HOLY, SPIRITS)

Gen	1: 2	And the S of God was
Gen	6: 3	My S shall not strive with
Gen	41:38	a man in whom is the S of
Ex	28: 3	I have filled with the s of
Ex	31: 3	I have filled him with the S
Num	11:29	the LORD would put His S
Num	27:18	you, a man in whom is the S,
Judg	3:10	The S of the LORD came upon

1Sa	10:10	then the S of God came upon
1Sa	16:14	and a distressing s from the
1Sa	28:13	I saw a s ascending out of
2Sa	23: 2	The S of the LORD spoke by
2Ki	2: 9	a double portion of your s
2Ki	2:15	The s of Elijah rests on
Job	33: 4	The S of God has made me,
Ps	31: 5	Your hand I commit my s;
Ps	32: 2	And in whose s there is
Ps	34:18	such as have a contrite s.
Ps	51:10	And renew a steadfast s
Ps	51:11	And do not take Your Holy S
Ps	51:12	me by Your generous S.
Ps	51:17	of God are a broken s,
Ps	106:33	they rebelled against His S,
Ps	139: 7	Where can I go from Your S?
Ps	146: 4	His s departs, he returns to
Prov	16:18	And a haughty s before a
Prov	16:32	And he who rules his s than
Prov	18:14	But who can bear a broken s?
Eccl	12: 7	And the s will return to
Is	4: 4	by the s of judgment and by
Is	11: 2	The S of the LORD shall
Is	11: 2	The S of wisdom and
Is	30: 1	plans, but not of My S,
Is	31: 3	horses are flesh, and not s.
Is	32:15	Until the S is poured upon
Is	40:13	Who has directed the S of
Is	42: 1	delights! I have put My S
Is	44: 3	I will pour My S on your
Is	57:15	has a contrite and humble s,
Is	57:15	To revive the s of the
Is	61: 1	The S of the Lord GOD is
Is	63:10	and grieved His Holy S;
Is	63:11	is He who put His Holy S
Ezek	2: 2	Then the S entered me when He
Ezek	11:19	and I will put a new s
Ezek	18:31	a new heart and a new s.
Ezek	36:27	I will put My S within you
Ezek	37: 1	and brought me out in the S
Ezek	37:14	I will put My S in you, and
Dan	4: 8	in him is the S of the Holy
Dan	4:18	for the S of the Holy God
Joel	2:28	That I will pour out My S
Joel	2:29	I will pour out My S in
Zech	4: 6	nor by power, but by My S,
Zech	6: 8	have given rest to My S in
Matt	1:18	with child of the Holy S.
Matt	3:11	baptize you with the Holy S
Matt	3:16	and He saw the S of God
Matt	4: 1	Jesus was led up by the S
Matt	5: 3	are the poor in s,
Matt	12:28	I cast out demons by the S
Matt	12:31	the blasphemy against the S
Matt	12:32	speaks against the Holy S,
Matt	26:41	The s indeed is willing,
Matt	27:50	voice, and yielded up His s.
Matt	28:19	of the Son and of the Holy S,
Mark	1:10	heavens parting and the S
Luke	1:15	be filled with the Holy S,
Luke	1:35	The Holy S will come upon
Luke	1:41	was filled with the Holy S.
Luke	2:26	to him by the Holy S that
Luke	11:13	Father give the Holy S to

S

Luke	12:10	against the Holy S,
Luke	23:46	hands I commit My s.
Luke	24:39	for a s does not have flesh
John	1:32	I saw the S descending from
John	3: 5	is born of water and the S,
John	4:23	worship the Father in s and
John	4:24	"God is S, and those who
John	6:63	It is the S who gives life;
John	6:63	that I speak to you are s,
John	7:39	for the Holy S was not yet
John	14:17	the S of truth, whom the
John	14:26	"But the Helper, the Holy S,
John	19:30	His head, He gave up His s.
John	20:22	them, "Receive the Holy S.
Acts	1: 5	be baptized with the Holy S
Acts	1: 8	power when the Holy S has
Acts	1:16	which the Holy S spoke
Acts	2: 4	all filled with the Holy S
Acts	2:17	will pour out of My S
Acts	2:33	the promise of the Holy S,
Acts	2:38	the gift of the Holy S.
Acts	5: 3	heart to lie to the Holy S
Acts	7:51	You always resist the Holy S;
Acts	7:59	"Lord Jesus, receive my s.
Acts	15:28	it seemed good to the Holy S,
Acts	19: 2	Did you receive the Holy S
Acts	19: 2	whether there is a Holy S.
Rom	7: 6	in the newness of the S and
Rom	8: 2	For the law of the S of life
Rom	8: 9	anyone does not have the S
Rom	8:10	but the S is life because
Rom	8:11	But if the S of Him who
Rom	8:16	The S Himself bears witness
Rom	8:23	the firstfruits of the S,
Rom	8:27	what the mind of the S is,
Rom	12:11	in diligence, fervent in s,
Rom	14:17	peace and joy in the Holy S.
1Co	2: 4	in demonstration of the S
1Co	2:10	For the S searches all
1Co	5: 3	in body but present in s,
1Co	5: 5	that his s may be saved in
1Co	6:19	is the temple of the Holy S
1Co	6:20	in your body and in your s,
1Co	7:40	I think I also have the S
1Co	12: 3	no one speaking by the S of
1Co	12: 4	of gifts, but the same S.
1Co	12: 7	the manifestation of the S
1Co	12: 8	word of wisdom through the S,
2Co	3: 3	not with ink but by the S
2Co	3: 6	of the letter but of the S;
2Co	3: 6	but the S gives life.
2Co	3:17	and where the S of the Lord
2Co	11: 4	you receive a different s
2Co	13:14	the communion of the Holy S
Gal	3: 2	Did you receive the S by the
Gal	3: 3	Having begun in the S,
Gal	4:29	born according to the S,
Gal	5:16	I say then: Walk in the S,
Gal	5:17	flesh lusts against the S,
Gal	5:18	But if you are led by the S,
Gal	5:22	But the fruit of the S is
Gal	6: 8	but he who sows to the S
Eph	1:13	were sealed with the Holy S
Eph	2:18	we both have access by one S

Eph	4: 3	to keep the unity of the S
Eph	4: 4	is one body and one S,
Eph	4:30	do not grieve the Holy S of
Eph	5:18	but be filled with the S,
Eph	6:17	and the sword of the S,
Phil	2: 1	if any fellowship of the S,
1Th	1: 6	with joy of the Holy S,
1Th	5:19	Do not quench the S.
1Ti	3:16	flesh, Justified in the S,
1Ti	4: 1	Now the S expressly says that
Tit	3: 5	and renewing of the Holy S,
Heb	2: 4	and gifts of the Holy S,
Heb	3: 7	as the Holy S says:
Heb	4:12	the division of soul and s,
Heb	6: 4	partakers of the Holy S,
Heb	10:29	and insulted the S of grace?
Jas	2:26	as the body without the s
Jas	4: 5	The S who dwells in us yearns
1Pe	1: 2	in sanctification of the S,
1Pe	3:18	but made alive by the S,
2Pe	1:21	were moved by the Holy S.
1Jn	5: 6	And it is the S who bears
1Jn	5: 7	the Word, and the Holy S;
Rev	1:10	I was in the S on the Lord's
Rev	2: 7	let him hear what the S says
Rev	22:17	And the S and the bride say,

SPIRITISTS

1Sa	28: 3	put the mediums and the s

SPIRITS (see SPIRIT)

Lev	19:31	to mediums and familiar s;
Num	16:22	the God of the s of all
Ps	104: 4	Who makes His angels s,
Zech	6: 5	These are four s of heaven,
Matt	8:16	And He cast out the s with a
Luke	8: 2	had been healed of evil s
1Co	12:10	to another discerning of s,
1Co	14:32	And the s of the prophets are
Heb	1: 7	Who makes His angels s
Heb	1:14	they not all ministering s
Heb	12:23	to the s of just men made
1Pe	3:19	went and preached to the s
Rev	1: 4	and from the seven S who are

SPIRITUAL (see SPIRITUALLY)

Rom	7:14	we know that the law is s,
1Co	2:13	comparing s things with
1Co	3: 1	not speak to you as to s
1Co	10: 3	all ate the same s food,
1Co	12: 1	Now concerning s gifts,
1Co	14: 1	and desire s gifts, but
1Co	15:44	it is raised a s body. There
Gal	6: 1	you who are s restore such
Eph	1: 3	has blessed us with every s
Eph	5:19	in psalms and hymns and s
Eph	6:12	against s hosts of
1Pe	2: 5	are being built up a s

SPIRITUALLY (see SPIRITUAL)

Rom	8: 6	but to be s minded is life
1Co	2:14	because they are s

SPIT (*see* SPAT)

| Mark | 8:23 | And when He had **s** on his |

SPITEFULLY

| Matt | 5:44 | and pray for those who **s** use |

SPOIL

| Song | 2:15 | The little foxes that **s** the |
| Is | 53:12 | And He shall divide the **s** |

SPOKE (*see* SPEAK, SPOKEN)

Ps	33: 9	For He **s**, and it was done;
John	7:46	No man ever **s** like this
Acts	1:16	which the Holy Spirit **s**
Acts	19: 6	and they **s** with tongues and
1Co	13:11	I **s** as a child, I understood
Heb	1: 1	times and in various ways **s**
2Pe	1:21	but holy men of God **s** as

SPOKEN (*see* SPEAK, SPOKE)

Ex	19: 8	All that the LORD has **s** we
Ps	87: 3	Glorious things are **s** of
Prov	15:23	And a word **s** in due
Prov	25:11	A word fitly **s** is like
Matt	1:22	be fulfilled which was **s** by
Matt	24:15	**s** of by Daniel the prophet,
Mark	12:32	You have **s** the truth, for
Luke	2:34	for a sign which will be **s**
Luke	12: 3	whatever you have **s** in the
Luke	20:39	You have **s** well."
Luke	24:25	that the prophets have **s**!
John	12:29	An angel has **s** to Him."
John	12:49	For I have not **s** on My own
John	14:25	These things I have **s** to you
Acts	1: 9	Now when He had **s** these
Acts	2:16	But this is what was **s** by the
Acts	16: 2	He was well **s** of by the
Rom	1: 8	that your faith is **s** of
Heb	1: 2	has in these last days **s** to
Heb	2: 2	For if the word **s** through
Heb	3: 5	things which would be **s**
Heb	4: 4	For He has **s** in a certain
Heb	13: 7	who have **s** the word of God

SPOKESMAN

| Ex | 4:16 | So he shall be your **s** to the |

SPONGE

| Mark | 15:36 | someone ran and filled a **s** |

SPOT (*see* UNSPOTTED)

Lev	13: 2	a scab, or a bright **s**,
Song	4: 7	And there is no **s** in you.
Eph	5:27	not having **s** or wrinkle or
Heb	9:14	offered Himself without **s**
1Pe	1:19	blemish and without **s**.
2Pe	3:14	without **s** and blameless;

SPREAD

Ex	40:19	And he **s** out the tent over
Lev	13: 5	and the sore has not **s** on
Ps	140: 5	They have **s** a net by the
Prov	7:16	I have **s** my bed with

Is	1:15	When you **s** out your hands,
Is	37:14	and **s** it before the LORD.
Is	42: 5	Who **s** forth the earth and
Matt	9:31	they **s** the news about Him in
Matt	21: 8	from the trees and **s** them
Mark	11: 8	And many **s** their clothes on
Acts	6: 7	Then the word of God **s**,
Acts	13:49	word of the Lord was being **s**
Rom	5:12	and thus death **s** to all men,
2Co	4:15	having **s** through the many,
2Ti	2:17	And their message will **s** like

SPRING (*see* SPRINGING, WELLSPRING)

2Sa	11: 1	It happened in the **s** of the
Ps	84: 6	of Baca, They make it a **s**;
Ps	92: 7	When the wicked **s** up like
Prov	4:23	For out of it **s** the issues
Prov	25:26	wicked Is like a murky **s**
Song	4:12	A **s** shut up, A fountain
Is	42: 9	Before they **s** forth I tell
Is	58: 8	Your healing shall **s** forth
Jas	3:11	Does a **s** send forth fresh

SPRINGING (*see* SPRING)

| John | 4:14 | in him a fountain of water **s** |
| Heb | 12:15 | any root of bitterness **s** up |

SPRINKLE (*see* SPRINKLED, SPRINKLING)

Ex	29:16	shall take its blood and **s**
Ex	29:21	and **s** it on Aaron and on
Lev	1: 5	shall bring the blood and **s**
Lev	14:16	and shall **s** some of the oil
Lev	16:14	the blood of the bull and **s**
Lev	16:14	the mercy seat he shall **s**
Num	8: 7	**S** water of purification on
Is	52:15	So shall He **s** many nations.
Ezek	36:25	Then I will **s** clean water on

SPRINKLED (*see* SPRINKLE)

Ex	24: 6	and half the blood he **s** on
Ex	24: 8	**s** it on the people, and
2Ki	16:13	his drink offering and **s**
Job	2:12	each one tore his robe and **s**
Heb	9:19	and **s** both the book itself
Heb	10:22	having our hearts **s** from an

SPRINKLING (*see* SPRINKLE)

| Heb | 12:24 | and to the blood of **s** that |
| 1Pe | 1: 2 | for obedience and **s** of the |

SPY (*see* SPIED, SPIES)

Josh	6:25	whom Joshua sent to **s** out
Judg	18: 2	to **s** out the land and search
Gal	2: 4	came in by stealth to **s** out

SQUARE

Gen	19: 2	the night in the open **s**.
Ex	27: 1	wide—the altar shall be **s**—
Judg	19:15	he sat down in the open **s** of
Job	29: 7	I took my seat in the open **s**,
Rev	21:16	The city is laid out as a **s**;

STAFF (*see* STAFFS)

| Gen | 38:25 | signet and cord, and **s**. |

S

Ex	12:11	and your s in your hand. So
Ps	23: 4	me; Your rod and Your s,
Is	9: 4	of his burden And the s of
Mark	6: 8	for the journey except a s—
Heb	11:21	leaning on the top of his s.

STAFFS† (*see* STAFF)

Zech	11: 7	I took for myself two s:
Matt	10:10	tunics, nor sandals, nor s;
Luke	9: 3	neither s nor bag nor bread

STAKES

Is	54: 2	And strengthen your s.

STALL†

Amos	6: 4	from the midst of the s;
Luke	13:15	his ox or donkey from the s,

STAND (*see* STANDS, STOOD)

Ex	3: 5	for the place where you s
Ex	9:11	the magicians could not s
Ex	14:13	S still, and see the
Josh	10:12	s still over Gibeon; And
Job	19:25	And He shall s at last on
Ps	1: 5	the ungodly shall not s in
Ps	24: 3	Or who may s in His holy
Ps	76: 7	And who may s in Your
Ps	130: 3	O Lord, who could s?
Is	7: 7	GOD: "It shall not s,
Is	14:24	purposed, so it shall s:
Is	46:10	Saying, 'My counsel shall s,
Jer	15:19	You shall s before Me; If
Ezek	2: 1	s on your feet, and I will
Ezek	22:30	and s in the gap before Me
Dan	2:44	and it shall s forever.
Dan	7: 4	the earth and made to s on
Dan	12: 1	that time Michael shall s
Amos	7: 2	pray! Oh, that Jacob may s,
Zech	4: 2	and on the s seven lamps
Zech	14: 4	in that day His feet will s
Mal	3: 2	And who can s when He
Matt	12:25	against itself will not s.
Matt	12:26	How then will his kingdom s?
Mark	11:25	And whenever you s praying,
John	8:44	and does not s in the
Acts	1:11	why do you s gazing up into
Acts	4:26	the earth took their s,
Acts	25:10	I s at Caesar's judgment
Rom	5: 2	this grace in which we s,
Rom	9:11	to election might s,
Rom	11:20	and you s by faith. Do not
Rom	14:10	For we shall all s before
1Co	15: 1	received and in which you s,
1Co	15:30	And why do we s in jeopardy
1Co	16:13	s fast in the faith, be
Gal	5: 1	S fast therefore in the
Eph	6:11	that you may be able to s
Eph	6:13	and having done all, to s.
Eph	6:14	S therefore, having girded
Phil	4: 1	so s fast in the Lord,
Col	4:12	that you may s perfect and
1Th	3: 8	if you s fast in the Lord.
Jas	2: 3	You s there," or, "Sit here

1Pe	5:12	grace of God in which you s.
Rev	3:20	I s at the door and knock.

STANDS (*see* STAND)

Ps	1: 1	Nor s in the path of
Is	40: 8	But the word of our God s
1Co	10:12	let him who thinks he s

STAR (*see* STARS)

Matt	2: 2	For we have seen His s in
1Co	15:41	for one s differs from
2Pe	1:19	day dawns and the morning s
Rev	2:28	will give him the morning s.
Rev	22:16	the Bright and Morning S.

STARS (*see* STAR)

Gen	1:16	He made the s also.
Gen	15: 5	and count the s if you are
Gen	22:17	your descendants as the s
Gen	37: 9	and the eleven s bowed down
Judg	5:20	The s from their courses
Job	38: 7	When the morning s sang
Ps	8: 3	fingers, The moon and the s,
Ps	136: 9	The moon and s to rule by
Ps	148: 3	all you s of light!
Is	14:13	exalt my throne above the s
Dan	12: 3	to righteousness Like the s
Matt	24:29	the s will fall from heaven,
Rev	1:16	in His right hand seven s,
Rev	6:13	And the s of heaven fell to

STATE

Ps	136:23	remembered us in our lowly s,
Matt	12:45	and the last s of that man
Luke	1:48	He has regarded the lowly s
Phil	4:11	I have learned in whatever s

STATURE

Num	13:32	in it are men of great s.
1Sa	2:26	the child Samuel grew in s,
Matt	6:27	can add one cubit to his s?
Luke	2:52	increased in wisdom and s,
Eph	4:13	to the measure of the s of

STATUTE (*see* STATUTES)

Dan	6:15	that no decree or s which

STATUTES (*see* STATUTE)

Lev	26: 3	If you walk in My s and keep
Deut	11:32	to observe all the s and
Deut	30:10	His commandments and His s
1Ki	11:11	kept My covenant and My s,
2Ch	33: 8	to the whole law and the s
Ezra	7:10	and to teach s and
Neh	9:13	Good s and commandments.
Ps	18:22	I did not put away His s
Ps	19: 8	The s of the LORD are
Ps	119:12	O LORD! Teach me Your s!
Ps	119:71	That I may learn Your s.
Ps	119:118	those who stray from Your s,
Ezek	5: 6	they have not walked in My s.
Mic	6:16	For the s of Omri are kept;

STEADFAST (see STEADFASTLY)

Ps	51:10	And renew a s spirit within
Ps	57: 7	My heart is s,
Ps	78:37	For their heart was not s
1Co	15:58	my beloved brethren, be s,
Col	1:23	in the faith, grounded and s,
Heb	3:14	of our confidence s to the
Heb	6:19	of the soul, both sure and s,
1Pe	5: 9	s in the faith, knowing that

STEADFASTLY (see STEADFAST)

Luke	9:51	that He s set His face to go
Acts	1:10	And while they looked s
Acts	2:42	And they continued s in the
Rom	12:12	continuing s in prayer;

STEAL (see STOLE)

Gen	31:30	but why did you s my
Ex	20:15	"You shall not s.
Deut	5:19	"You shall not s.
Matt	6:19	where thieves break in and s;
Matt	19:18	'You shall not s,
John	10:10	does not come except to s,
Eph	4:28	Let him who stole s no

STEPHEN

Acts	6: 5	multitude. And they chose S,
Acts	7:59	And they stoned S as he was

STEPS

Ps	37:23	The s of a good man are
Prov	16: 9	But the LORD directs his s.
Prov	20:24	A man's s are of the LORD;
1Pe	2:21	that you should follow His s:

STEW

Gen	25:34	Jacob gave Esau bread and s

STEWARD (see STEWARDS, STEWARDSHIP)

Gen	44: 4	off, Joseph said to his s,
Matt	20: 8	the vineyard said to his s,
Luke	12:42	is that faithful and wise s,
Luke	16: 8	commended the unjust s
Tit	1: 7	as a s of God, not

STEWARDS (see STEWARD)

1Co	4: 2	it is required in s that
1Pe	4:10	as good s of the manifold

STEWARDSHIP (see STEWARD)

Luke	16: 2	Give an account of your s,
1Co	9:17	have been entrusted with a s.

STICK (see STICKS)

Job	33:21	And his bones s out which
Ezek	37:19	Judah, and make them one s,

STICKS (see STICK)

Num	15:32	found a man gathering s on
Prov	18:24	there is a friend who s

STIFF-NECKED

Ex	32: 9	and indeed it is a s
Deut	10:16	and be s no longer.

STILL

Josh	10:12	stand s over Gibeon; And
1Ki	19:12	and after the fire a s small
Job	1:16	While he was s speaking,
Ps	23: 2	He leads me beside the s
Ps	46:10	Be s, and know that I am
Is	5:25	His hand is stretched out s.
Jer	47: 6	Rest and be s!
Hab	3:11	The sun and moon stood s in
Mark	4:39	be s!" And the wind ceased
Rom	5: 6	For when we were s without
Rom	5: 8	in that while we were s
1Co	15:17	you are s in your sins!
Heb	11: 4	through it he being dead s

STILLBORN

Job	3:16	was I not hidden like a s

STING

1Co	15:55	Death, where is your s?

STIR (see STIRRED, STIRS)

Song	2: 7	Do not s up nor awaken love
Is	13:17	I will s up the Medes

STIRRED (see STIR)

Ex	35:21	came whose heart was s,
John	5: 4	time into the pool and s up

STIRS (see STIR)

Prov	10:12	Hatred s up strife, But
Prov	15: 1	But a harsh word s up
Prov	15:18	A wrathful man s up strife,
Luke	23: 5	He s up the people, teaching

STOLE (see STEAL, STOLEN)

Matt	28:13	came at night and s Him
Eph	4:28	Let him who s steal no

STOLEN (see STOLE)

Gen	31:19	and Rachel had s the
Prov	9:17	S water is sweet, And bread

STOMACH (see STOMACH'S)

Num	5:22	the curse go into your s,
Matt	15:17	the mouth goes into the s
Mark	7:19	enter his heart but his s,
1Co	6:13	Foods for the s and the

STOMACH'S† (see STOMACH)

1Ti	5:23	use a little wine for your s

STONE (see STONED, STONES, STONY)

Gen	49:24	the S of Israel),
Ex	34: 1	Cut two tablets of s like the
Num	14:10	the congregation said to s
Deut	17: 5	and shall s to death that
Deut	28:36	serve other gods—wood and s.
Josh	24:27	this s shall be a witness to

S

Judg	20:16	every one could sling a s at
1Sa	17:50	with a sling and a s,
1Sa	25:37	him, and he became like a s.
Job	38:30	The waters harden like s,
Job	41:24	His heart is as hard as s,
Ps	91:12	dash your foot against a s.
Ps	118:22	The s which the builders
Prov	27: 3	A s is heavy and sand is
Is	8:14	But a s of stumbling and a
Is	28:16	I lay in Zion a s for a
Jer	2:27	are my father,' And to a s,
Ezek	1:26	appearance like a sapphire s;
Ezek	36:26	I will take the heart of s
Dan	2:34	You watched while a s was cut
Dan	2:35	And the s that struck the
Dan	6:17	Then a s was brought and laid
Amos	5:11	have built houses of hewn s,
Zech	3: 9	Upon the s are seven eyes.
Matt	4: 6	your foot against a s.
Matt	7: 9	for bread, will give him a s?
Matt	21:42	The s which the builders
Matt	21:44	whoever falls on this s
Matt	24: 2	not one s shall be left
Matt	27:60	and he rolled a large s
John	2: 6	set there six waterpots of s,
John	8: 7	let him throw a s at her
John	10:31	took up stones again to s
John	11:39	said, "Take away the s.
Acts	4:11	s which was rejected by
Acts	17:29	is like gold or silver or s,
Rom	9:33	in Zion a stumbling s
2Co	3: 3	not on tablets of s but on
1Pe	2: 4	to Him as to a living s,
1Pe	2: 7	The s which the builders
1Pe	2: 8	A s of stumbling And a
Rev	2:17	I will give him a white s,
Rev	2:17	and on the s a new name

STONED (see STONE)

Ex	19:13	but he shall surely be s or
Josh	7:25	So all Israel s him with
1Ki	21:14	Naboth has been s and is
Matt	21:35	killed one, and s another.
John	8: 5	us that such should be s.
Acts	7:59	And they s Stephen as he was
Acts	14:19	they s Paul and dragged
2Co	11:25	with rods; once I was s;
Heb	11:37	They were s, they were sawn

STONES (see STONE)

Josh	4: 3	for yourselves twelve s
Josh	4: 6	What do these s mean to
1Sa	17:40	for himself five smooth s
Eccl	3: 5	And a time to gather s;
Is	5: 2	it up and cleared out its s,
Matt	3: 9	to Abraham from these s.
Matt	4: 3	command that these s become
Luke	13:34	who kills the prophets and s
Luke	19:40	the s would immediately cry
John	8:59	Then they took up s to throw
John	10:31	Then the Jews took up s
1Co	3:12	gold, silver, precious s,
1Pe	2: 5	you also, as living s,

STONY (see STONE)

Ezek	11:19	and take the s heart out of
Matt	13: 5	Some fell on s places, where

STOOD (see STAND)

Ps	33: 9	commanded, and it s fast.
Hab	3:11	The sun and moon s still in
Matt	2: 9	till it came and s over
Luke	4:16	and s up to read.
Luke	17:12	who s afar off.
Luke	24: 4	two men s by them in shining
Luke	24:36	Jesus Himself s in the midst
John	20:19	Jesus came and s in the
Acts	1:10	two men s by them in white
Acts	3: 8	s and walked and entered the
Acts	16: 9	A man of Macedonia s and
Acts	21:40	Paul s on the stairs and
2Ti	4:16	At my first defense no one s
2Ti	4:17	But the Lord s with me and

STOOP (see STOOPED)

Mark	1: 7	strap I am not worthy to s

STOOPED (see STOOP)

John	8: 6	But Jesus s down and wrote

STOPPED

Rom	3:19	that every mouth may be s,
Heb	11:33	s the mouths of lions,

STORE (see STOREHOUSE)

Gen	41:35	and s up grain under the
Prov	10:14	Wise people s up knowledge,
Luke	12:17	since I have no room to s my

STOREHOUSE (see STORE)

Mal	3:10	all the tithes into the s,

STORM

Nah	1: 3	the whirlwind and in the s,

STRAIGHT

Ps	5: 8	Make Your way s before my
Prov	9:15	Who go s on their way:
Eccl	1:15	is crooked cannot be made s,
Is	40: 3	Make s in the desert A
Is	40: 4	places shall be made s And
Is	45: 2	make the crooked places s;
Matt	3: 3	Make His paths s.
John	1:23	Make s the way of the
Acts	9:11	go to the street called S,
Heb	12:13	and make s paths for your

STRAIN†

Matt	23:24	who s out a gnat and swallow

STRANGE (see STRANGER)

Prov	23:33	Your eyes will see s things,
Heb	13: 9	about with various and s
Jude	7	immorality and gone after s

STRANGER (*see* FOREIGNER, STRANGE, STRANGERS)

Gen	17: 8	land in which you are a **s**,
Ex	12:48	And when a **s** dwells with you
Ex	22:21	shall neither mistreat a **s**
Ps	119:19	I am a **s** in the earth; Do
Matt	25:35	I was a **s** and you took Me

STRANGERS (*see* STRANGER)

Gen	15:13	your descendants will be **s**
Ps	105:12	very few, and **s** in it.
Eph	2:12	of Israel and **s** from the
Heb	13: 2	Do not forget to entertain **s**,

STRANGLED

Acts	15:20	immorality, from things **s**,
Acts	15:29	from blood, from things **s**,

STRAP

Gen	14:23	from a thread to a sandal **s**,
Mark	1: 7	whose sandal **s** I am not

STRAW

Ex	5: 7	no longer give the people **s**
Ex	5:12	gather stubble instead of **s**.
Is	11: 7	And the lion shall eat **s**
1Co	3:12	stones, wood, hay, **s**,

STREAM (*see* STREAMS)

Jer	15:18	to me like an unreliable **s**,
Amos	5:24	like a mighty **s**.

STREAMS (*see* STREAM)

Ps	46: 4	There is a river whose **s**
Is	35: 6	And **s** in the desert.

STREET (*see* STREETS)

Is	42: 2	voice to be heard in the **s**.
Acts	9:11	Arise and go to the **s** called
Rev	21:21	And the **s** of the city was

STREETS (*see* STREET)

Eccl	12: 4	the doors are shut in the **s**,
Eccl	12: 5	the mourners go about the **s**.
Matt	12:19	His voice in the **s**.

STRENGTH (*see* MIGHT, STRENGTHEN)

Gen	4:12	shall no longer yield its **s**
Ex	15: 2	The LORD is my **s** and song,
Deut	6: 5	soul, and with all your **s**.
Deut	33:25	so shall your **s** be.
Judg	8:21	as a man is, so is his **s**.
Judg	16: 9	So the secret of his **s** was
Judg	16:19	and his **s** left him.
1Sa	2: 9	For by **s** no man shall
1Sa	2:10	He will give **s** to His king,
1Sa	15:29	And also the **S** of Israel will
1Ki	19: 8	and he went in the **s** of that
1Ch	16:11	Seek the LORD and His **s**;
2Ch	6:41	You and the ark of Your **s**.
Neh	8:10	joy of the LORD is your **s**.
Job	9:19	If it is a matter of **s**,
Job	12:13	Him are wisdom and **s**,

Ps	8: 2	infants You have ordained **s**,
Ps	18: 1	will love You, O LORD, my **s**.
Ps	18: 2	my deliverer; My God, my **s**,
Ps	18:32	is God who arms me with **s**,
Ps	18:39	You have armed me with **s**
Ps	19:14	my **s** and my Redeemer.
Ps	20: 6	heaven With the saving **s**
Ps	21: 1	shall have joy in Your **s**,
Ps	22:15	My **s** is dried up like a
Ps	22:19	not be far from Me; O My **S**,
Ps	27: 1	The LORD is the **s** of my
Ps	28: 7	The LORD is my **s** and my
Ps	29: 1	unto the LORD glory and **s**.
Ps	29:11	The LORD will give **s** to His
Ps	31:10	My **s** fails because of my
Ps	33:16	is not delivered by great **s**.
Ps	38:10	my **s** fails me; As for the
Ps	43: 2	You are the God of my **s**;
Ps	46: 1	God is our refuge and **s**,
Ps	68:34	Ascribe **s** to God; His
Ps	71:16	I will go in the **s** of the
Ps	81: 1	Sing aloud to God our **s**;
Ps	84: 7	They go from **s** to strength;
Ps	86:16	mercy on me! Give Your **s**
Ps	90:10	And if by reason of **s** they
Ps	93: 1	has girded Himself with **s**.
Ps	96: 6	**S** and beauty are in His
Ps	96: 7	to the LORD glory and **s**.
Ps	110: 2	send the rod of Your **s** out
Ps	118:14	The LORD is my **s** and song,
Ps	132: 8	You and the ark of Your **s**.
Prov	20:29	of young men is their **s**,
Prov	31: 3	Do not give your **s** to women,
Prov	31:17	She girds herself with **s**,
Prov	31:25	**S** and honor are her
Is	12: 2	is my **s** and song; He also
Is	26: 4	the LORD, is everlasting **s**.
Is	40:31	LORD Shall renew their **s**;
Jer	17: 5	man And makes flesh his **s**,
Dan	2:37	you a kingdom, power, **s**,
Dan	2:41	yet the **s** of the iron shall
Dan	10: 8	and no **s** remained in me; for
Hos	7: 9	Aliens have devoured his **s**,
Hos	12: 3	And in his **s** he struggled
Mark	12:30	and with all your **s**.
Rom	5: 6	when we were still without **s**,
1Co	15:56	and the **s** of sin is the
2Co	12: 9	for My **s** is made perfect in
Rev	3: 8	it; for you have a little **s**,

STRENGTHEN (*see* STRENGTH, STRENGTHENED, STRENGTHENS)

Is	35: 3	**S** the weak hands, And make
Is	54: 2	And **s** your stakes.
Luke	22:32	**s** your brethren."
Heb	12:12	Therefore **s** the hands which
1Pe	5:10	while, perfect, establish, **s**,

STRENGTHENED (*see* STRENGTHEN)

Eph	3:16	to be **s** with might through
Col	1:11	**s** with all might, according

STRENGTHENS (*see* STRENGTHEN)

Phil	4:13	things through Christ who **s**

S

STRETCH (*see* STRETCHED, STRETCHES)

Ex	7: 5	when I s out My hand on
Ex	7:19	Take your rod and s out your
Ps	68:31	Ethiopia will quickly s out
Ps	104: 2	Who s out the heavens like
Matt	12:13	**S** out your hand." And he
John	21:18	you will s out your hands,

STRETCHED (*see* STRETCH)

Ex	9:15	Now if I had s out My hand
Ex	9:23	And Moses s out his rod
Is	5:25	But His hand is s out

STRETCHES (*see* STRETCH)

Job	26: 7	He s out the north over
Is	40:22	Who s out the heavens like

STRICKEN

Is	53: 4	Yet we esteemed Him s,
Is	53: 8	of My people He was s.

STRIFE

Gen	13: 7	And there was s between the
Prov	10:12	Hatred stirs up s,
Jer	15:10	A man of s and a man of
Rom	13:13	not in s and envy.

STRIKE (*see* STRIKES, STRUCK)

Ex	3:20	stretch out My hand and s
Ex	7:17	I will s the waters which
Ex	17: 6	and you shall s the rock,
Ps	121: 6	The sun shall not s you by
Zech	13: 7	S the Shepherd, And the
Matt	26:31	I will s the Shepherd,
Acts	23: 3	God will s you, you

STRIKES (*see* STRIKE)

Ex	21:15	And he who s his father or

STRINGED

2Sa	6: 5	on s instruments, on
Ps	150: 4	Praise Him with s

STRIPE† (*see* STRIPES)

Ex	21:25	for wound, s for stripe.

STRIPES (*see* STRIPE)

Is	53: 5	And by His s we are healed.
Luke	12:47	shall be beaten with many s.
2Co	11:24	times I received forty s
1Pe	2:24	by whose s you were healed.

STRIPPED (*see* STRIPS)

Gen	37:23	that they s Joseph of his
Matt	27:28	And they s Him and put a

STRIPS (*see* STRIPPED)

Gen	30:37	peeled white s in them, and
John	19:40	and bound it in s of linen

STRIVE (*see* STRIVING)

Gen	6: 3	My Spirit shall not s with
Ps	103: 9	He will not always s with

STRIVING (*see* STRIVE)

Heb	12: 4	s against sin.

STRONG (*see* STRONGER)

Ex	6: 1	and with a s hand he will
Deut	31: 7	Be s and of good courage, for
Josh	1: 6	Be s and of good courage, for
Ps	19: 5	And rejoices like a s man
Ps	22:12	S bulls of Bashan have
Ps	24: 8	The LORD s and mighty,
Ps	136:12	With a s hand, and with an
Eccl	9:11	Nor the battle to the s,
Eccl	12: 3	And the s men bow down;
Song	8: 6	For love is as s as
Ezek	34:16	destroy the fat and the s,
Matt	12:29	unless he first binds the s
Rom	15: 1	We then who are s ought to
1Co	4:10	but you are s! You are
2Co	12:10	when I am weak, then I am s.
Eph	6:10	be s in the Lord and in the
2Ti	2: 1	be s in the grace that is in
Heb	11:34	out of weakness were made s,

STRONGER (*see* STRONG)

1Co	1:25	and the weakness of God is s

STRONGHOLD (*see* STRONGHOLDS)

2Sa	5: 7	David took the s of Zion
Ps	18: 2	horn of my salvation, my s.

STRONGHOLDS (*see* STRONGHOLD)

2Co	10: 4	in God for pulling down s,

STRUCK (*see* STRIKE)

Ex	7:20	he lifted up the rod and s
Ex	8:17	his hand with his rod and s
Ex	12:29	at midnight that the LORD s
Ps	78:20	He s the rock, So that the
Dan	2:35	And the stone that s the
Matt	26:51	s the servant of the high
Matt	26:67	and others s Him with the

STRUGGLED

Gen	32:28	for you have s with God and
Hos	12: 3	And in his strength he s
Hos	12: 4	he s with the Angel and

STUBBLE

Ex	5:12	land of Egypt to gather s

STUDY†

Eccl	12:12	and much s is wearisome to

STUMBLE (*see* STUMBLED, STUMBLES, STUMBLING)

Prov	3:23	And your foot will not s.
Is	28: 7	they s in judgment.
1Co	8:13	if food makes my brother s,
Jas	2:10	and yet s in one point, he

STUMBLED (*see* STUMBLE)

2Sa	6: 6	hold of it, for the oxen s.
Ps	73: 2	for me, my feet had almost s;

STUMBLES (see STUMBLE)

Rom 14:21 by which your brother s or

STUMBLING (see STUMBLE)

Prov 24:11 And hold back those s to
Is 8:14 But a stone of s and a rock
Is 57:14 Take the s block out of the
Rom 9:33 I lay in Zion a s
Rom 14:13 not to put a s block or a
1Co 1:23 to the Jews a s block and to
1Co 8: 9 liberty of yours become a s
1Pe 2: 8 A stone of s And a
1Jn 2:10 and there is no cause for s
Jude 24 is able to keep you from s,

STUMP

Job 14: 8 And its s may die in the
Is 6:13 holy seed shall be its s.

SUBDUE (see SUBDUED)

Gen 1:28 fill the earth and s it;

SUBDUED (see SUBDUE)

Heb 11:33 who through faith s kingdoms,

SUBJECT (see SUBJECTED, SUBJECTION)

Luke 2:51 and was s to them, but His
Luke 10:20 that the spirits are s to
1Co 14:32 of the prophets are s to
1Co 15:28 when all things are made s
Eph 5:24 just as the church is s to

SUBJECTED (see SUBJECT)

Rom 8:20 For the creation was s to

SUBJECTION (see SUBJECT)

1Co 9:27 my body and bring it into s,
Heb 2: 8 put all things in s

SUBMISSION (see SUBMIT)

1Ti 2:11 learn in silence with all s.

SUBMIT (see SUBMISSION)

Eph 5:22 s to your own husbands, as
Jas 4: 7 Therefore s to God. Resist

SUBSIDED

Gen 8: 1 the earth, and the waters s.

SUBSTANCE

Ps 139:16 Your eyes saw my s,
Heb 11: 1 Now faith is the s of things

SUCCESS

Gen 24:12 please give me s this day,
Josh 1: 8 then you will have good s.

SUDDENLY

Prov 29: 1 Will s be destroyed, and
Luke 2:13 And s there was with the

SUFFER (see SUFFERED, SUFFERING, SUFFERS)

Luke 24:46 for the Christ to s and to
Acts 17: 3 that the Christ had to s
Rom 8:17 if indeed we s with Him,
1Co 3:15 he will s loss; but he
Phil 1:29 but also to s for His sake,
Phil 4:12 both to abound and to s
Heb 11:25 choosing rather to s
1Pe 4:15 But let none of you s as a

SUFFERED (see SUFFER)

Luke 24:26 not the Christ to have s
Phil 3: 8 for whom I have s the loss
Heb 2:18 For in that He Himself has s,
Heb 13:12 s outside the gate.
1Pe 2:21 because Christ also s for
1Pe 5:10 after you have s a while,

SUFFERING (see SUFFER, SUFFERINGS)

Heb 2: 9 for the s of death crowned
Jas 5:13 Is anyone among you s?
1Pe 2:19 grief, s wrongfully.

SUFFERINGS (see SUFFERING)

Rom 8:18 For I consider that the s of
2Co 1: 5 For as the s of Christ abound
2Co 1: 7 you are partakers of the s,
Phil 3:10 and the fellowship of His s,
Col 1:24 I now rejoice in my s for
2Ti 1: 8 but share with me in the s
Heb 2:10 salvation perfect through s.
1Pe 1:11 testified beforehand the s
1Pe 4:13 you partake of Christ's s,
1Pe 5: 9 knowing that the same s are

SUFFERS (see SUFFER)

1Co 12:26 And if one member s,
1Co 13: 4 Love s long and is kind;
1Pe 4:16 Yet if anyone s as a

SUFFICIENCY (see SUFFICIENT)

2Co 3: 5 but our s is from God,

SUFFICIENT (see SUFFICIENCY)

Matt 6:34 S for the day is its own
John 14: 8 and it is s for us."
2Co 2:16 And who is s for these
2Co 12: 9 My grace is s for you, for My

SUMMER

Gen 8:22 and heat, Winter and s,
Jer 8:20 The s is ended, And we are
Amos 8: 1 a basket of s fruit.
Matt 24:32 you know that s is near.

SUMPTUOUSLY†

Luke 16:19 and fine linen and fared s

SUN (see SUNDIAL)

Josh 10:12 the sight of Israel: "S,
Ps 19: 4 set a tabernacle for the s,
Ps 84:11 For the LORD God is a s

S

Ps	121: 6	The s shall not strike you
Eccl	1: 3	which he toils under the s?
Eccl	1: 5	The s also rises, and the
Eccl	1: 9	is nothing new under the s.
Joel	3:15	The s and moon will grow
Mal	4: 2	you who fear My name The S
Matt	5:45	for He makes His s rise on
Matt	17: 2	His face shone like the s,
Acts	2:20	The s shall be turned
Eph	4:26	do not let the s go down on
Rev	21:23	city had no need of the s
Rev	22: 5	no lamp nor light of the s,

SUNDIAL (see SUN)

2Ki	20:11	it had gone down on the s

SUNG (see SING)

Matt	26:30	And when they had s a hymn,

SUPPER

Luke	22:20	also took the cup after s,
1Co	11:20	is not to eat the Lord's S.
1Co	11:25	also took the cup after s,
Rev	19: 9	called to the marriage s of

SUPPLICATION (see SUPPLICATIONS)

Ps	6: 9	The LORD has heard my s;
Ps	55: 1	not hide Yourself from my s.
Zech	12:10	the Spirit of grace and s;
Acts	1:14	one accord in prayer and s,
Eph	6:18	with all prayer and s in
Eph	6:18	with all perseverance and s
Phil	4: 6	everything by prayer and s

SUPPLICATIONS (see SUPPLICATION)

Ps	28: 6	has heard the voice of my s!
Ps	86: 6	attend to the voice of my s.
Dan	9: 3	make request by prayer and s,
1Ti	2: 1	I exhort first of all that s,
Heb	5: 7	had offered up prayers and s,

SUPPLIES (see SUPPLY)

Eph	4:16	by what every joint s,
1Pe	4:11	with the ability which God s,

SUPPLY (see SUPPLIES)

Ex	1:11	And they built for Pharaoh s
Phil	2:30	to s what was lacking in
Phil	4:19	And my God shall s all your

SUPPRESS†

Rom	1:18	who s the truth in

SUPREME†

1Pe	2:13	whether to the king as s,

SURE (see SURETY)

Num	32:23	and be s your sin will find
Ps	19: 7	testimony of the LORD is s,
Is	55: 3	The s mercies of David.
Acts	13:34	I will give you the s
2Pe	1:10	your call and election s,

SURETY (see SURE)

Heb	7:22	more Jesus has become a s

SURPASSES† (see SURPASSING)

Phil	4: 7	which s all understanding,

SURPASSING† (see SURPASSES)

2Sa	1:26	S the love of women.

SURROUNDED

Judg	19:22	s the house and beat on the
Ps	18: 4	The pangs of death s me,
Ps	22:12	Many bulls have s Me;
Jon	2: 3	And the floods s me; All
Luke	21:20	when you see Jerusalem s by
Heb	12: 1	since we are s by so great a

SWADDLING

Ezek	16: 4	with salt nor wrapped in s
Luke	2: 7	and wrapped Him in s cloths,

SWALLOW (see SWALLOWED)

Num	16:34	Lest the earth s us up
Is	25: 8	He will s up death forever,
Jon	1:17	prepared a great fish to s
Matt	23:24	who strain out a gnat and s

SWALLOWED (see SWALLOW)

Ex	7:12	But Aaron's rod s up their
Ex	15:12	The earth s them.
1Co	15:54	Death is s up in

SWEAR (see SWEARS, SWORE, SWORN)

Matt	5:34	do not s at all: neither by
Heb	6:13	because He could s by no one
Heb	6:16	For men indeed s by the

SWEARS (see SWEAR)

Num	30: 2	or s an oath to bind himself
Ps	15: 4	He who s to his own hurt
Prov	29:24	He s to tell the truth, but
Matt	23:16	Whoever s by the temple, it

SWEAT

Gen	3:19	In the s of your face you
Luke	22:44	Then His s became like great

SWEET (see SWEET-SMELLING, SWEETER, SWEETNESS)

Ex	15:25	the waters were made s.
Lev	1: 9	a s aroma to the LORD.
Judg	14:14	the strong came something s.
2Sa	23: 1	And the s psalmist of
Neh	8:10	eat the fat, drink the s,
Ps	119:103	How s are Your words to my
Prov	3:24	and your sleep will be s.
Prov	9:17	"Stolen water is s,
Song	5:16	His mouth is most s,
Is	5:20	Who put bitter for s,
Jer	31:26	and my sleep was s to me.

SWEET-SMELLING (*see* SWEET)

| Eph | 5: 2 | a sacrifice to God for a **s** |
| Phil | 4:18 | a **s** aroma, an acceptable |

SWEETER (*see* SWEET)

| Judg | 14:18 | What is **s** than honey? And |
| Ps | 19:10 | **S** also than honey and the |

SWEETNESS (*see* SWEET)

Judg	9:11	Should I cease my **s** and my
Prov	16:24	**S** to the soul and health to
Ezek	3: 3	in my mouth like honey in **s**.

SWIFT

Prov	6:18	Feet that are **s** in running
Eccl	9:11	race is not to the **s**,
Rom	3:15	Their feet are **s** to shed

SWINE (*see* SWINE'S)

Deut	14: 8	Also the **s** is unclean for
Matt	7: 6	cast your pearls before **s**,
Matt	8:32	the whole herd of **s** ran

SWINE'S (*see* SWINE)

| Prov | 11:22 | As a ring of gold in a **s** |
| Is | 65: 4 | Who eat **s** flesh, And the |

SWORD (*see* SWORDS)

Gen	3:24	and a flaming **s** which turned
Gen	34:26	son with the edge of the **s**,
Judg	7:18	The **s** of the LORD and of
2Sa	2:26	Shall the **s** devour forever?
Ps	22:20	Deliver Me from the **s**,
Ps	57: 4	And their tongue a sharp **s**.
Prov	5: 4	Sharp as a two-edged **s**.
Is	2: 4	Nation shall not lift up **s**
Jer	47: 6	O you **s** of the LORD, How
Amos	7:11	shall die by the **s**,
Mic	4: 3	Nation shall not lift up **s**
Matt	10:34	come to bring peace but a **s**.
Matt	26:51	out his hand and drew his **s**,
Matt	26:52	Put your **s** in its place, for
Matt	26:52	sword will perish by the **s**.
Luke	2:35	a **s** will pierce through your
Rom	8:35	or nakedness, or peril, or **s**?
Rom	13: 4	for he does not bear the **s**
Eph	6:17	and the **s** of the Spirit,
Heb	4:12	sharper than any two-edged **s**,
Rev	1:16	went a sharp two-edged **s**,
Rev	19:15	of His mouth goes a sharp **s**,

SWORDS (*see* SWORD)

Is	2: 4	They shall beat their **s**
Joel	3:10	your plowshares into **s** And
Mic	4: 3	They shall beat their **s**
Luke	22:38	look, here are two **s**.

SWORE (*see* SWEAR)

1Ki	1:17	you **s** by the LORD your God
Ps	95:11	So I **s** in My wrath, 'They
Dan	12: 7	and **s** by Him who lives
Heb	3:11	So I **s** in My wrath,

| Heb | 6:13 | He **s** by Himself, |
| Rev | 10: 6 | and **s** by Him who lives |

SWORN (*see* SWEAR)

Gen	22:16	said: "By Myself I have **s**,
Ps	24: 4	Nor **s** deceitfully.
Ps	110: 4	The LORD has **s** And will
Is	62: 8	The LORD has **s** by His right
Heb	7:21	The LORD has **s** And

SYCAMORE

| Amos | 7:14 | And a tender of **s** fruit. |
| Luke | 19: 4 | and climbed up into a **s** |

SYCHAR† (*see* SHECHEM)

| John | 4: 5 | of Samaria which is called **S**, |

SYMPATHIZE†

| Heb | 4:15 | a High Priest who cannot **s** |

SYNAGOGUE (*see* SYNAGOGUES)

Matt	13:54	He taught them in their **s**,
Mark	1:21	the Sabbath He entered the **s**
Rev	2: 9	but are a **s** of Satan.

SYNAGOGUES (*see* SYNAGOGUE)

Matt	23: 6	the best seats in the **s**,
Mark	1:39	He was preaching in their **s**
John	16: 2	will put you out of the **s**;

SYRIA (*see* ARAM, SYRIAN)

1Ki	19:15	Hazael as king over **S**.
1Ki	20:20	and Ben-Hadad the king of **S**
Luke	2: 2	Quirinius was governing **S**.

SYRIAN (*see* SYRIA, SYRIANS,
SYRO-PHOENICIAN)

| 2Ki | 5:20 | has spared Naaman this **S**, |
| Luke | 4:27 | cleansed except Naaman the **S**. |

SYRIANS (*see* SYRIAN)

| 2Sa | 8: 5 | When the **S** of Damascus came |

SYRO-PHOENICIAN† (*see* SYRIAN)

| Mark | 7:26 | a **S** by birth, and she kept |

T

TABERNACLE (*see* TABERNACLES)

Ex	25: 9	the pattern of the **t** and the
Ex	26: 7	to be a tent over the **t**.
Ex	27:21	In the **t** of meeting, outside
Ex	38:21	the **t** of the Testimony,
Ps	15: 1	who may abide in Your **t**?
Ps	19: 4	In them He has set a **t** for
Ps	27: 5	the secret place of His **t**
Ps	43: 3	holy hill And to Your **t**.
Ps	46: 4	The holy place of the **t** of
Ps	76: 2	In Salem also is His **t**,
Ps	78:60	So that He forsook the **t** of
Ps	84: 1	How lovely is Your **t**,
Amos	9:11	day I will raise up The **t**

Acts	15:16	will rebuild the t of
Heb	8: 2	sanctuary and of the true t
Heb	9: 8	manifest while the first t
Heb	9:11	greater and more perfect t
Rev	21: 3	the t of God is with men,

TABERNACLES (*see* TABERNACLE)

Deut	16:13	shall observe the Feast of T
John	7: 2	Now the Jews' Feast of T was

TABITHA (*see* DORCAS)

Acts	9:40	to the body he said, "T,

TABLE (*see* TABLES)

Num	4: 7	On the t of showbread they
2Sa	9: 7	you shall eat bread at my t
Ps	23: 5	You prepare a t before me in
Ps	78:19	Can God prepare a t in the
Matt	15:27	fall from their masters' t.
Matt	26: 7	head as He sat at the t.
Luke	16:21	fell from the rich man's t.
Luke	22:30	may eat and drink at My t
1Co	10:21	partake of the Lord's t and

TABLES (*see* TABLE)

Matt	21:12	and overturned the t of the
John	2:15	money and overturned the t.
Acts	6: 2	the word of God and serve t.

TABLET (*see* TABLETS)

Prov	3: 3	Write them on the t of your
Ezek	4: 1	take a clay t and lay it
Luke	1:63	And he asked for a writing t,

TABLETS (*see* TABLET)

Ex	31:18	He gave Moses two t of the
Ex	34: 1	Cut two t of stone like the
Deut	9: 9	the t of the covenant which
Deut	10: 5	and put the t in the ark
Hab	2: 2	And make it plain on t,
2Co	3: 3	on tablets of stone but on t
Heb	9: 4	and the t of the covenant;

TAIL

Ex	4: 4	hand and take it by the t'
Deut	28:13	you the head and not the t;
Judg	15: 4	turned the foxes t to

TAKE (*see* REMOVE, TAKEN, TAKES, TAKING, TOOK)

Gen	22: 2	T now your son, your only
Gen	24: 4	and t a wife for my son
Ex	19:12	T heed to yourselves that
Ex	20: 7	You shall not t the name of
Job	23:10	He knows the way that I t;
Ps	51:11	And do not t Your Holy
Matt	2:13	t the young Child and His
Matt	9: 6	t up your bed, and go to
Matt	10:38	And he who does not t his
Matt	11:12	and the violent t it by
Matt	11:29	T My yoke upon you and learn
Matt	16:24	and t up his cross, and
Matt	24:34	away till all these things t
Matt	25:38	we see You a stranger and t

Matt	26:26	the disciples and said, "T,
Matt	26:52	for all who t the sword will
Mark	14: 1	sought how they might t Him
Mark	14:36	T this cup away from Me;
Mark	16:18	they will t up serpents; and
Luke	9: 3	T nothing for the journey,
Luke	9:23	and t up his cross daily,
Luke	12:19	t your ease; eat, drink,
Luke	21:32	pass away till all things t
Luke	22:42	t this cup away from Me;
John	6:15	were about to come and t
John	10:17	down My life that I may t
John	16:14	for He will t of what is
Acts	1:20	Let another t his
Rom	11:27	When I t away their
1Co	10:12	him who thinks he stands t
1Co	11:24	He broke it and said, "T,
Eph	6:13	Therefore t up the whole
Eph	6:17	And t the helmet of
Heb	2: 6	son of man that You t
Heb	10: 4	of bulls and goats could t
1Pe	2:20	if you t it patiently, this
Rev	1: 1	which must shortly t
Rev	22:17	let him t the water of life
Rev	22:19	God shall t away his part

TAKEN (*see* TAKE, TRANSLATED)

Gen	2:23	Because she was t out of
Gen	3:23	ground from which he was t.
2Ki	2: 9	before I am t away from
Job	1:21	and the LORD has t away;
Is	6: 6	a live coal which he had t
Is	6: 7	Your iniquity is t away,
Is	53: 8	He was t from prison and
Matt	24:40	one will be t and the other
Matt	25:29	even what he has will be t
John	20:13	Because they have t away my
Acts	1: 2	the day in which He was t
Acts	1:11	who was t up from you into
2Co	3:14	because the veil is t away
Heb	11: 5	By faith Enoch was t away so

TAKES (*see* TAKE)

Ex	20: 7	hold him guiltless who t
John	1:29	The Lamb of God who t away
John	10:18	No one t it from Me, but I

TAKING (*see* TAKE)

Ps	119: 9	By t heed according to Your
Phil	2: 7	t the form of a bondservant,

TALENTS

Matt	18:24	who owed him ten thousand t.
Matt	25:15	"And to one he gave five t,

TAMAR

Gen	38:11	Then Judah said to T his
Ruth	4:12	whom T bore to Judah,
2Sa	13:10	Then Amnon said to T,
Matt	1: 3	begot Perez and Zerah by T,

TAME

Jas	3: 8	But no man can t the tongue.

TANNER

Acts   9:43   in Joppa with Simon, a **t**.

TARES

Matt   13:25   his enemy came and sowed **t**

TARSHISH

Ps   48: 7   You break the ships of **T**
Jon   1: 3   But Jonah arose to flee to **T**

TARSUS

Acts   9:11   for one called Saul of **T**,

TASKMASTERS (see MASTERS)

Ex   1:11   Therefore they set **t** over

TASTE (see TASTED)

Ps   34: 8   **t** and see that the LORD is
Ps   119:103   sweet are Your words to my **t**,
Matt   16:28   here who shall not **t** death
Col   2:21   "Do not touch, do not **t**,
Heb   2: 9   might **t** death for everyone.

TASTED (see TASTE)

Heb   6: 4   and have **t** the heavenly

TAUGHT (see TEACH)

Matt   7:29   for He **t** them as one having
Mark   9:31   For He **t** His disciples and
John   8:28   but as My Father **t** Me, I
Gal   1:12   nor was I **t** it, but it

TAX (see TAXES)

Matt   5:46   Do not even the **t** collectors
Matt   10: 3   Thomas and Matthew the **t**
Matt   17:24   who received the temple **t**

TAXES (see TAX)

Matt   22:17   Is it lawful to pay **t** to
Rom   13: 7   taxes to whom **t** are due,

TEACH (see TAUGHT, TEACHER, TEACHES, TEACHING)

Ex   4:12   be with your mouth and **t**
Ex   18:20   And you shall **t** them the
Deut   6: 7   You shall **t** them diligently
Deut   11:19   You shall **t** them to your
Job   21:22   Can anyone **t** God knowledge,
Job   32: 7   multitude of years should **t**
Ps   25: 4   O LORD; **T** me Your paths.
Ps   27:11   **T** me Your way, O LORD, And
Ps   51:13   Then I will **t** transgressors
Ps   90:12   So **t** us to number our days,
Is   2: 3   He will **t** us His ways, And
Jer   31:34   No more shall every man **t** his
Dan   1: 4   and whom they might **t** the
Matt   22:16   and **t** the way of God in
Luke   11: 1   **t** us to pray, as John also
John   14:26   He will **t** you all things,
Acts   1: 1   Jesus began both to do and **t**,
1Co   4:17   as I **t** everywhere in every
1Co   14:19   that I may **t** others also,
1Ti   1: 3   may charge some that they **t**

1Ti   2:12   I do not permit a woman to **t**
1Ti   3: 2   hospitable, able to **t**;
2Ti   2: 2   men who will be able to **t**
2Ti   2:24   be gentle to all, able to **t**,

TEACHER (see TEACH, TEACHERS)

Matt   8:19   came and said to Him, "**T**,
Matt   9:11   Why does your **T** eat with tax
Matt   10:24   disciple is not above his **t**,
Matt   23: 8   'Rabbi'; for One is your **T**,
Mark   10:17   Him, and asked Him, "Good **T**,
John   3: 2   we know that You are a **t**
John   3:10   Are you the **t** of Israel, and

TEACHERS (see TEACHER)

Ps   119:99   understanding than all my **t**,
Luke   2:46   in the midst of the **t**,
1Co   12:28   second prophets, third **t**,
Eph   4:11   and some pastors and **t**,
2Ti   4: 3   heap up for themselves **t**;
Jas   3: 1   let not many of you become **t**,
2Pe   2: 1   as there will be false **t**

TEACHES (see TEACH)

Ps   25: 8   Therefore He **t** sinners in
Ps   94:10   He who **t** man knowledge?
Rom   12: 7   our ministering; he who **t**,

TEACHING (see TEACH)

Matt   7:28   were astonished at His **t**,
Matt   28:20   **t** them to observe all things
Rom   12: 7   he who teaches, in **t**;
Col   3:16   **t** and admonishing one

TEAR (see TEARS, TORE, TORN)

Eccl   3: 7   A time to **t**, and a time
Matt   9:16   and the **t** is made worse.
Rev   21: 4   God will wipe away every **t**

TEARS (see TEAR)

Ps   56: 8   Put my **t** into Your bottle;
Ps   126: 5   Those who sow in **t** Shall
Is   25: 8   Lord GOD will wipe away **t**
Jer   9: 1   And my eyes a fountain of **t**,
Luke   7:38   to wash His feet with her **t**,

TEETH (see TOOTH)

Num   11:33   was still between their **t**,
Job   19:20   escaped by the skin of my **t**.
Jer   31:29   And the children's **t** are
Ezek   18: 2   And the children's **t** are
Dan   7: 7   strong. It had huge iron **t**;
Amos   4: 6   I gave you cleanness of **t**
Matt   8:12   be weeping and gnashing of **t**.
Matt   13:42   be wailing and gnashing of **t**.

TEKEL

Dan   5:25   was written: MENE, MENE, **T**,

TEKOA

Amos   1: 1   among the sheepbreeders of **T**,

T

TEMPEST

Jon	1: 4	and there was a mighty **t** on
Matt	8:24	And suddenly a great **t** arose

TEMPLE (see TEMPLES, THRESHOLD)

Judg	4:21	and drove the peg into his **t**,
Judg	16:26	pillars which support the **t**,
Judg	16:30	and the **t** fell on the lords
2Ki	10:21	So they came into the **t** of
Ezra	3:12	men who had seen the first **t**,
Ezra	5:11	and we are rebuilding the **t**
Ps	11: 4	The LORD is in His holy **t**,
Ps	18: 6	heard my voice from His **t**,
Ps	27: 4	And to inquire in His **t**.
Is	6: 1	of His robe filled the **t**.
Jer	7: 4	the **t** of the LORD are
Dan	5: 3	had been taken from the **t**
Mic	3:12	And the mountain of the **t**
Hab	2:20	the LORD is in His holy **t**.
Hag	2: 3	among you who saw this **t** in
Mal	3: 1	Will suddenly come to His **t**,
Matt	4: 5	Him on the pinnacle of the **t**,
Matt	27:51	the veil of the **t** was torn
Luke	11:51	between the altar and the **t**.
John	2:15	drove them all out of the **t**,
John	2:19	to them, "Destroy this **t**,
Acts	3: 1	went up together to the **t**
1Co	3:16	not know that you are the **t**
1Co	6:19	that your body is the **t** of
Eph	2:21	grows into a holy **t** in the
Rev	15: 8	The **t** was filled with smoke
Rev	21:22	and the Lamb are its **t**.

TEMPLES (see TEMPLE)

Acts	17:24	does not dwell in **t** made

TEMPT (see TEMPTATION, TEMPTED, TEMPTER)

Deut	6:16	You shall not **t** the LORD
Matt	4: 7	You shall not **t** the
1Co	7: 5	so that Satan does not **t**
Jas	1:13	nor does He Himself **t**

TEMPTATION (see TEMPT)

Matt	6:13	And do not lead us into **t**,
1Co	10:13	No **t** has overtaken you except

TEMPTED (see TEMPT)

Matt	4: 1	into the wilderness to be **t**
Gal	6: 1	yourself lest you also be **t**.
Heb	2:18	has suffered, being **t**,
Jas	1:13	I am **t** by God"; for God

TEMPTER (see TEMPT)

Matt	4: 3	Now when the **t** came to Him,

TEN (see TENTH)

Gen	18:32	Suppose **t** should be found
Gen	31: 7	me and changed my wages **t**
Ex	34:28	the **T** Commandments.
Ps	91: 7	And **t** thousand at your
Mic	6: 7	**T** thousand rivers of oil?

TEND (see TENDER)

Gen	2:15	in the garden of Eden to **t**
John	21:16	to him, "**T** My sheep."

TENDER (see TEND, TENDERHEARTED)

Ps	51: 1	to the multitude of Your **t**
Is	53: 2	grow up before Him as a **t**

TENDERHEARTED (see TENDER)

Eph	4:32	be kind to one another, **t**,

TENT (see TENTMAKERS, TENTS)

Gen	9:21	became uncovered in his **t**.
Num	9:15	the **t** of the Testimony; from
Josh	7:22	it was, hidden in his **t**,
Judg	4:21	took a **t** peg and took a
2Co	5: 1	our earthly house, this **t**,
2Pe	1:14	shortly I must put off my **t**,

TENTH (see TEN)

Gen	28:22	me I will surely give a **t**
Num	18:26	the LORD, a **t** of the tithe.
Deut	23: 2	even to the **t** generation
Is	6:13	But yet a **t** will be in it,
Heb	7: 2	whom also Abraham gave a **t**

TENTMAKERS† (see TENT)

Acts	18: 3	by occupation they were **t**.

TENTS (see TENT)

Ps	84:10	my God Than dwell in the **t**
Heb	11: 9	dwelling in **t** with Isaac and

TERAH

Gen	11:32	and **T** died in Haran.
Luke	3:34	of Abraham, the son of **T**,

TERAPHIM†

Hos	3: 4	pillar, without ephod or **t**.

TERRESTRIAL

1Co	15:40	also celestial bodies and **t**

TERRIBLE (see TERROR)

Deut	1:19	through all that great and **t**
Dan	7: 7	fourth beast, dreadful and **t**,

TERROR (see TERRIBLE, TERRORS)

Ps	91: 5	not be afraid of the **t** by
Prov	3:25	not be afraid of sudden **t**,
Is	2:10	From the **t** of the LORD
Rom	13: 3	For rulers are not a **t** to

TERRORS (see TERROR)

Job	18:14	him before the king of **t**.
Eccl	12: 5	And of **t** in the way; When

TEST (see PROVE, TESTED, TESTING, TESTS)

Ex	20:20	for God has come to **t** you,
Num	14:22	and have put Me to the **t** now
Deut	8: 2	to humble you and **t** you, to
Deut	8:16	you and that He might **t** you,
Judg	2:22	that through them I may **t**

Judg	6:39	just once more: Let me t,
1Ki	10: 1	she came to t him with hard
1Ch	29:17	that You t the heart and
Ps	11: 4	His eyelids t the sons of
Is	7:12	nor will I t the LORD!"
Dan	1:12	Please t your servants for
Matt	22:18	Why do you t Me, you
John	6: 6	But this He said to t him,
Acts	5: 9	have agreed together to t
Acts	15:10	why do you t God by putting
1Co	3:13	and the fire will t each
2Co	2: 9	I might put you to the t,
2Co	13: 5	T yourselves. Do you not
1Th	5:21	T all things; hold fast what
1Jn	4: 1	but t the spirits, whether
Rev	3:10	to t those who dwell on the

TESTAMENT (see COVENANT, TESTATOR)

2Co	3:14	in the reading of the Old T,

TESTATOR (see TESTAMENT)

Heb	9:16	be the death of the t.

TESTED (see TEST)

Gen	22: 1	these things that God t
Ps	17: 3	You have t my heart; You
Ps	66:10	have t us; You have refined
Heb	11:17	faith Abraham, when he was t,
1Pe	1: 7	though it is t by fire, may

TESTIFIED (see TESTIFY)

John	1:34	And I have seen and t that
John	5:37	has t of Me. You have
John	19:35	And he who has seen has t,
Heb	2: 6	But one t in a certain place,
1Pe	1:11	was indicating when He t

TESTIFIES (see TESTIFY)

John	3:32	seen and heard, that He t;
John	21:24	This is the disciple who t of
Acts	20:23	that the Holy Spirit t in
Rev	22:20	He who t to these things

TESTIFY (see TESTIFIED, TESTIFIES)

John	5:39	and these are they which t
John	15:26	the Father, He will t of Me.

TESTIMONIES (see TESTIMONY)

Deut	4:45	These are the t, the statutes,
Mark	14:56	but their t did not agree.

TESTIMONY (see TESTIMONIES)

Ex	16:34	laid it up before the T,
Ex	25:22	are on the ark of the T,
Ex	31:18	Moses two tablets of the T,
Num	1:50	over the tabernacle of the T,
Num	35:30	be put to death on the t of
Ps	19: 7	The t of the LORD is
Is	8:16	Bind up the t, Seal the
Is	8:20	To the law and to the t! If
Matt	8: 4	commanded, as a t to them."
Luke	22:71	What further t do we need?
John	1:19	Now this is the t of John,
John	3:33	He who has received His t has

John	21:24	and we know that his t is
1Ti	3: 7	he must have a good t among
Heb	11: 2	elders obtained a good t.
1Jn	5:10	he has not believed the t
Rev	1: 9	word of God and for the t

TESTING (see TEST)

Matt	19: 3	t Him, and saying to Him,
Jas	1: 3	knowing that the t of your

TESTS (see TEST)

Prov	17: 3	But the LORD t the hearts.
1Th	2: 4	but God who t our hearts.

TETRARCH

Luke	3: 1	Herod being t of Galilee,

THADDAEUS (see JUDAS)

Mark	3:18	the son of Alphaeus, T,

THANK (see PRAISE, THANKFUL, THANKS)

Dan	2:23	I t You and praise You, O
Matt	11:25	I t You, Father, Lord of
Luke	18:11	I t You that I am not like
Rom	1: 8	I t my God through Jesus
1Co	1:14	I t God that I baptized none
Phil	1: 3	I t my God upon every
Phm	1: 4	I t my God, making mention

THANKFUL† (see THANK, UNTHANKFUL)

Ps	100: 4	Be t to Him, and bless His
Rom	1:21	Him as God, nor were t,
Col	3:15	called in one body; and be t.

THANKS (see THANK, THANKSGIVING)

Ps	18.49	Therefore I will give t to
Ps	92: 1	It is good to give t to
Ps	105: 1	give t to the LORD! Call
Ps	107: 1	give t to the LORD, for He
Ps	107: 8	that men would give t to
Ps	136: 2	give t to the God of gods!
Matt	26:27	He took the cup, and gave t,
Rom	14: 6	not eat, and gives God t.
1Co	11:24	and when He had given t,
1Co	15:57	But t be to God, who gives
2Co	9:15	T be to God for His
Eph	1:16	do not cease to give t for
Eph	5:20	giving t always for all
1Th	3: 9	For what t can we render to
1Th	5:18	in everything give t;

THANKSGIVING (see THANKS)

Lev	7:12	with the sacrifice of t,
Ps	95: 2	before His presence with t;
Ps	100: 4	Enter into His gates with t,
Phil	4: 6	and supplication, with t,
1Ti	4: 4	if it is received with t;
Rev	7:12	T and honor and power and

THE-LORD-IS-MY-BANNER† (see LORD)

Ex	17:15	altar and called its name, T;

THE-LORD-WILL-PROVIDE† (see LORD)

Gen	22:14	the name of the place, T;

T

THEOPHILUS†
Luke	1: 3	account, most excellent T,
Acts	1: 1	former account I made, O T,

THESSALONICA
Acts	17: 1	Apollonia, they came to T,

THICK
Ex	8:24	T swarms of flies came
Ex	10:22	and there was t darkness in
Ex	19: 9	I come to you in the t
Zeph	1:15	A day of clouds and t

THICKET
Gen	22:13	was a ram caught in a t by

THIEF (see THIEVES)
Ex	22: 2	If the t is found breaking
Matt	24:43	had known what hour the t
John	10: 1	the same is a t and a
1Th	5: 2	of the Lord so comes as a t
2Pe	3:10	of the Lord will come as a t
Rev	3: 3	I will come upon you as a t,

THIEVES (see THIEF)
Jer	7:11	become a den of t in your
Matt	6:19	and rust destroy and where t
Matt	21:13	have made it a 'den of t.
Luke	10:30	to Jericho, and fell among t,
John	10: 8	ever came before Me are t

THIGH (see THIGHS)
Gen	24: 2	put your hand under my t,

THIGHS (see THIGH)
Dan	2:32	its belly and t of bronze,

THINK (see THINKS, THOUGHT)
John	5:39	for in them you t you have
Rom	12: 3	not to t of himself more
Eph	3:20	above all that we ask or t,

THINKS (see THINK)
Prov	23: 7	For as he t in his heart, so
1Co	10:12	Therefore let him who t he
1Co	13: 5	not provoked, t no evil;

THIRD (see THREE)
Ex	20: 5	on the children to the t
Hos	6: 2	On the t day He will raise
Matt	16:21	and be raised the t day.
Luke	24:46	to rise from the dead the t
1Co	15: 4	and that He rose again the t
2Co	12: 2	a one was caught up to the t

THIRST (see THIRSTS, THIRSTY)
Ps	69:21	And for my t they gave me
Matt	5: 6	are those who hunger and t
John	4:13	drinks of this water will t
John	6:35	believes in Me shall never t.
John	19:28	fulfilled, said, I t!"

THIRSTS (see THIRST, THIRSTY)
Ps	42: 2	My soul t for God, for the
Is	55: 1	"Ho! Everyone who t,
John	7:37	out, saying, "If anyone t,
Rev	21: 6	of life freely to him who t.
Rev	22:17	Come!" And let him who t

THIRSTY (see THIRST)
Ps	63: 1	for You In a dry and t
Matt	25:35	I was t and you gave Me
Rom	12:20	feed him; If he is t,

THIRTY
2Sa	23:24	of Joab was one of the t;
Zech	11:12	weighed out for my wages t
Matt	26:15	they counted out to him t
Luke	3:23	His ministry at about t

THISTLES
Gen	3:18	Both thorns and t it shall
Matt	7:16	thornbushes or figs from t?

THOMAS
Mark	3:18	Bartholomew, Matthew, T,
John	20:27	Then He said to T,

THORN (see THORNS)
2Co	12: 7	a t in the flesh was given

THORNS (see THORN)
Gen	3:18	Both t and thistles it shall
Hos	2: 6	hedge up your way with t,
Matt	13: 7	"And some fell among t,
Matt	27:29	had twisted a crown of t,
Luke	6:44	do not gather figs from t,
John	19: 5	wearing the crown of t and

THOUGHT (see THINK, THOUGHTS)
1Co	13:11	I t as a child; but when I
2Co	10: 5	bringing every t into

THOUGHTS (see THOUGHT)
Gen	6: 5	that every intent of the t
Job	4:13	In disquieting t from the
Job	20: 2	Therefore my anxious t make
Ps	92: 5	are Your works! Your t are
Ps	94:11	The LORD knows the t of
Ps	139:17	precious also are Your t to
Prov	12: 5	The t of the righteous are
Prov	15:26	The t of the wicked are an
Is	55: 7	the unrighteous man his t;
Is	55: 8	For My t are not your
Dan	4:19	and his t troubled him. So
Matt	9: 4	But Jesus, knowing their t,
Matt	15:19	of the heart proceed evil t,
Rom	1:21	but became futile in their t,
Heb	4:12	and is a discerner of the t

THOUSAND (see THOUSANDS)
Ps	84:10	courts is better than a t.
Ps	90: 4	For a t years in Your sight
Ps	91: 7	A t may fall at your side,
Is	30:17	One t shall flee at the

Mic	6: 7	Ten **t** rivers of oil? Shall
Matt	14:21	had eaten were about five **t**
Matt	15:38	those who ate were four **t**
Acts	2:41	and that day about three **t**
Acts	4: 4	men came to be about five **t**.
1Co	14:19	than ten **t** words in a
2Pe	3: 8	the Lord one day is as a **t**
Rev	20: 2	and bound him for a **t** years;
Rev	20: 6	and shall reign with Him a **t**

THOUSANDS (see THOUSAND)

Ex	20: 6	but showing mercy to **t**,
Ex	34: 7	"keeping mercy for **t**,
1Sa	18: 7	"Saul has slain his **t**,
Mic	5: 2	you are little among the **t**
Mic	6: 7	the LORD be pleased with **t**

THREATENING (see THREATS)

Matt	16: 3	for the sky is red and **t**.

THREATS (see THREATENING)

Acts	9: 1	still breathing **t** and murder

THREE (see THIRD)

Gen	18: 2	**t** men were standing by him;
Ex	23:17	**T** times in the year all your
Deut	17: 6	on the testimony of two or **t**
Deut	19:15	by the mouth of two or **t**
Job	2:11	Now when Job's **t** friends
Amos	1: 3	For **t** transgressions of
Jon	1:17	of the fish three days and **t**
Matt	12:40	For as Jonah was **t** days and
Matt	18:16	the mouth of two or **t**
Matt	18:20	For where two or **t** are
Matt	26:34	you will deny Me **t** times."
Matt	27:63	After **t** days I will rise.'
John	2:19	and in **t** days I will raise
1Co	13:13	faith, hope, love, these **t**;
1Jn	5: 7	For there are **t** that bear
1Jn	5: 7	and these **t** are one.

THRESHED (see THRESHING)

Judg	6:11	while his son Gideon **t** wheat
Amos	1: 3	Because they have **t** Gilead

THRESHING (see THRESHED)

Ruth	3: 6	So she went down to the **t**
2Sa	24:24	So David bought the **t**
1Ch	21:18	altar to the LORD on the **t**
Matt	3:12	thoroughly clean out His **t**

THRESHOLD (see TEMPLE)

1Sa	5: 4	were broken off on the **t**;
1Sa	5: 5	house tread on the **t** of
Zeph	1: 9	those who leap over the **t**,

THROAT

Ps	5: 9	Their **t** is an open tomb;
Matt	18:28	him and took him by the **t**,
Rom	3:13	Their **t** is an open tomb;

THRONE (see THRONES)

Gen	41:40	only in regard to the **t** will
Ex	11: 5	of Pharaoh who sits on his **t**,
Deut	17:18	when he sits on the **t** of his
2Sa	3:10	and set up the **t** of David
2Sa	7:16	Your **t** shall be established
1Ki	2: 4	not lack a man on the **t** of
1Ki	22:19	the LORD sitting on His **t**,
Ps	11: 4	The LORD's **t** is in
Ps	45: 6	Your **t**, O God, is
Ps	89:14	the foundation of Your **t**;
Ps	103:19	LORD has established His **t**
Is	6: 1	saw the Lord sitting on a **t**,
Is	9: 7	Upon the **t** of David and
Is	14:13	I will exalt my **t** above the
Is	66: 1	LORD: "Heaven is My **t**,
Zech	6:13	shall be a priest on His **t**,
Matt	5:34	by heaven, for it is God's **t**;
Matt	19:28	Son of Man sits on the **t** of
Luke	1:32	God will give Him the **t** of
Acts	2:30	the Christ to sit on his **t**,
Acts	7:49	'Heaven is My **t**, And earth
Heb	1: 8	Son He says: "Your **t**,
Heb	4:16	come boldly to the **t** of
Heb	8: 1	at the right hand of the **t**
Rev	1: 4	Spirits who are before His **t**,
Rev	2:13	where Satan's **t** is. And you
Rev	3:21	down with My Father on His **t**.
Rev	4: 3	was a rainbow around the **t**,
Rev	4: 9	to Him who sits on the **t**,
Rev	20:11	Then I saw a great white **t**
Rev	22: 1	proceeding from the **t** of God

THRONES (see THRONE)

Matt	19:28	Me will also sit on twelve **t**,
Col	1:16	whether **t** or dominions or
Rev	4: 4	throne were twenty-four **t**,

THROW (see THROWN)

Eccl	3: 6	And a time to **t** away;
Jer	1:10	To destroy and to **t** down,
Matt	4: 6	**t** Yourself down. For it is
Luke	22:41	from them about a stone's **t**,
John	8:59	they took up stones to **t** at

THROWN (see THROW)

Ex	15: 1	and its rider He has **t**
Matt	3:10	good fruit is cut down and **t**
Matt	5:13	for nothing but to be **t** out
Matt	5:25	and you be **t** into prison.
Matt	6:30	and tomorrow is **t** into the
John	3:24	For John had not yet been **t**

THUMMIM (see URIM)

Ezra	2:63	consult with the Urim and **T**.

THUNDER

Mark	3:17	that is, "Sons of **T**";

THYATIRA

Acts	16:14	of purple from the city of **T**,
Rev	2:18	the angel of the church in **T**

TIBERIAS

John	6: 1	which is the Sea of **T**.

T

TIBERIUS† (see CAESAR)
Luke   3: 1   year of the reign of **T**

TIDINGS (see NEWS)
Ps   112: 7   will not be afraid of evil **t**;
Is   40: 9   Zion, You who bring good **t**,
Is   52: 7   Who brings glad **t** of good
Is   61: 1   Me To preach good **t** to the
Nah   1:15   of him who brings good **t**,
Luke   2:10   I bring you good **t** of great
Rom   10:15   Who bring glad **t** of

TIGLATH-PILESER
2Ki   15:29   **T** king of Assyria came and

TIMBREL (see TIMBRELS)
Ps   150: 4   Praise Him with the **t** and

TIMBRELS (see TIMBREL)
Ex   15:20   went out after her with **t**
Judg   11:34   out to meet him with **t** and

TIME (see TIMES)
Gen   24:11   the **t** when women go out to
2Sa   11: 1   at the **t** when kings go out
Esth   4:14   to the kingdom for such a **t**
Ps   27: 5   For in the **t** of trouble He
Ps   37:19   not be ashamed in the evil **t**,
Ps   69:13   LORD, in the acceptable **t**;
Ps   113: 2   of the LORD From this **t**
Eccl   3: 1   A **t** for every purpose under
Eccl   3: 2   A **t** to be born, And a time
Eccl   3:11   everything beautiful in its **t**.
Eccl   9:11   But **t** and chance happen to
Song   2:12   The **t** of singing has come,
Is   49: 8   In an acceptable **t** I have
Jer   46:21   The **t** of their punishment.
Dan   7:25   time and times and half a **t**.
Dan   8:19   happen in the latter **t** of
Dan   11:35   until the **t** of the end;
Dan   12: 9   up and sealed till the **t** of
Amos   5:13   time, For it is an evil **t**.
Matt   8:29   to torment us before the **t**?
Matt   26:18   My **t** is at hand; I will keep
Mark   1:15   The **t** is fulfilled, and the
Luke   1:57   Now Elizabeth's full **t** came
Luke   12:56   you do not discern this **t**?
John   1:18   No one has seen God at any **t**.
John   3: 4   Can he enter a second **t** into
John   7: 6   My **t** has not yet come, but
John   21:17   He said to him the third **t**,
Acts   1: 6   will You at this **t** restore
Acts   17:21   were there spent their **t** in
Rom   5: 6   in due **t** Christ died for the
Rom   13:11   that now it is high **t** to
1Co   4: 5   judge nothing before the **t**,
1Co   7:29   the **t** is short, so that
1Co   15: 8   as by one born out of due **t**.
2Co   6: 2   In an acceptable **t** I
2Co   6: 2   now is the accepted **t**;
Gal   4: 4   when the fullness of the **t**
Eph   2:12   that at that **t** you were
Eph   5:16   redeeming the **t**, because

1Ti   2: 6   to be testified in due **t**,
2Ti   1: 9   us in Christ Jesus before **t**
2Ti   4: 6   and the **t** of my departure is
Heb   1: 1   in various ways spoke in **t**
Heb   4:16   and find grace to help in **t**
Heb   9:10   imposed until the **t** of
Heb   9:28   He will appear a second **t**,
Heb   11:32   For the **t** would fail me to
Jas   4:14   that appears for a little **t**
1Pe   1: 5   to be revealed in the last **t**.
1Pe   1:11   what, or what manner of **t**,
1Pe   5: 6   He may exalt you in due **t**,
1Jn   4:12   one has seen God at any **t**.
Rev   1: 3   in it; for the **t** is near.
Rev   12:14   time and times and half a **t**,
Rev   22:10   for the **t** is at hand.

TIMES (see TIME)
Gen   31: 7   and changed my wages ten **t**,
Gen   33: 3   to the ground seven **t**,
Ex   23:17   Three **t** in the year all your
Josh   6: 4   around the city seven **t**,
Ps   9: 9   A refuge in **t** of trouble.
Ps   31:15   My **t** are in Your hand;
Ps   34: 1   bless the LORD at all **t**;
Ps   77: 5   old, The years of ancient **t**.
Ps   119:164   Seven **t** a day I praise You,
Prov   17:17   A friend loves at all **t**,
Is   41:26   we may know? And former **t**,
Is   46:10   And from ancient **t** things
Dan   4:16   And let seven **t** pass over
Dan   7:25   his hand For a time and **t**
Matt   16: 3   discern the signs of the **t**.
Matt   26:34   you will deny Me three **t**.
Acts   1: 7   is not for you to know **t**
Acts   3:19   so that **t** of refreshing may
Acts   17:30   these **t** of ignorance God
Eph   1:10   of the fullness of the **t** He
1Ti   4: 1   says that in latter **t** some
2Ti   3: 1   in the last days perilous **t**
Heb   1: 1   who at various **t** and in
1Pe   1:20   was manifest in these last **t**

TIMOTHY
Acts   16: 1   disciple was there, named **T**,
Acts   17:14   but both Silas and **T**
2Co   1:19   by us—by me, Silvanus, and **T**—
Phil   1: 1   Paul and **T**, bondservants
Heb   13:23   Know that our brother **T** has

TINGLE†
1Sa   3:11   everyone who hears it will **t**.
2Ki   21:12   of it, both his ears will **t**.
Jer   19: 3   hears of it, his ears will **t**.

TITHE (see TITHES)
Gen   14:20   And he gave him a **t** of all.
Num   18:26   the LORD, a tenth of the **t**.
Matt   23:23   hypocrites! For you pay **t** of

TITHES (see TITHE)
Mal   3: 8   In **t** and offerings.
Mal   3:10   Bring all the **t** into the
Luke   18:12   I give **t** of all that I

Heb	7: 6	from them received t from
Heb	7: 9	paid t through Abraham, so

TITTLE

| Matt | 5:18 | one jot or one t will by no |

TITUS

| 2Co | 2:13 | because I did not find T my |
| Gal | 2: 1 | and also took T with me. |

TODAY

Deut	30:15	I have set before you t life
Ps	2: 7	T I have begotten You.
Ps	95: 7	the sheep of His hand. T,
Matt	6:30	which t is, and tomorrow is
Acts	13:33	T I have begotten
Heb	1: 5	T I have begotten
Heb	3: 7	the Holy Spirit says: "T,
Heb	3:13	while it is called "T,
Heb	5: 5	T I have begotten
Heb	13: 8	is the same yesterday, t,

TOES

| Judg | 1: 6 | cut off his thumbs and big t. |
| Dan | 2:41 | you saw the feet and t, |

TOIL

| Gen | 3:17 | In t you shall eat of it |
| Matt | 6:28 | they neither t nor spin; |

TOMB (see TOMBS)

Ps	5: 9	Their throat is an open t;
Matt	27:60	and laid it in his new t
Luke	24: 2	stone rolled away from the t.
John	12:17	called Lazarus out of his t
Acts	2:29	and his t is with us to this
Rom	3:13	throat is an open t;

TOMBS (see TOMB)

| Matt | 8:28 | men, coming out of the t, |
| Matt | 23:27 | you are like whitewashed t |

TOMORROW

Prov	27: 1	Do not boast about t,
Is	22:13	and drink, for t we die!"
Matt	6:34	do not worry about t,
1Co	15:32	and drink, for t we die!"

TONGS

| Is | 6: 6 | he had taken with the t |

TONGUE (see TONGUES)

Ex	4:10	slow of speech and slow of t.
Ps	22:15	And My t clings to My jaws;
Ps	34:13	Keep your t from evil, And
Ps	39: 1	ways, Lest I sin with my t;
Ps	57: 4	And their t a sharp sword.
Ps	137: 6	Let my t cling to the roof
Prov	6:17	A proud look, A lying t,
Prov	25:15	And a gentle t breaks a
Luke	16:24	in water and cool my t;
Rom	14:11	And every t shall
1Co	14: 2	He who speaks in a t edifies
1Co	14:19	ten thousand words in a t.

Phil	2:11	and that every t should
Jas	1:26	and does not bridle his t
Jas	3: 6	And the t is a fire, a world
Jas	3: 8	But no man can tame the t.
Rev	5: 9	Out of every tribe and t

TONGUES (see TONGUE)

Ps	140: 3	They sharpen their t like a
Mark	16:17	they will speak with new t;
Acts	2: 3	appeared to them divided t,
Acts	2: 4	began to speak with other t,
Acts	2:11	them speaking in our own t
1Co	12:10	the interpretation of t.
1Co	13: 1	Though I speak with the t of
1Co	13: 8	fail; whether there are t,
1Co	14: 5	I wish you all spoke with t,
1Co	14:39	not forbid to speak with t.
Rev	7: 9	tribes, peoples, and t,

TOOK (see CAUGHT, MADE, TAKE)

Gen	5:24	he was not, for God t him.
Matt	8:17	He Himself t our
Matt	25:35	I was a stranger and you t

TOOTH (see TEETH)

| Ex | 21:24 | "eye for eye, tooth for t, |
| Matt | 5:38 | for an eye and a t |

TOP

Gen	11: 4	and a tower whose t is in
Gen	28:12	and its t reached to heaven;
Ex	25:21	put the mercy seat on t of
Matt	27:51	was torn in two from t to

TORCH (see TORCHES)

| Gen | 15:17 | oven and a burning t that |
| Judg | 15: 4 | and put a t between each |

TORCHES (see TORCH)

| Judg | 7:16 | and t inside the pitchers. |

TORE (see TEAR)

Gen	37:34	Then Jacob t his clothes, put
1Ki	11:30	and t it into twelve
1Ki	14: 8	and t the kingdom away from
Amos	1:11	His anger t perpetually,
Matt	26:65	Then the high priest t his

TORMENT (see TORMENTED)

Judg	16:19	Then she began to t him, and
Matt	8:29	Have You come here to t us
Luke	16:28	also come to this place of t.

TORMENTED (see TORMENT)

| Heb | 11:37 | destitute, afflicted, t— |
| 2Pe | 2: 8 | t his righteous soul from |

TORN (see TEAR)

Gen	37:33	Without doubt Joseph is t to
1Sa	15:28	The LORD has t the kingdom
1Ki	19:10	t down Your altars, and
Matt	27:51	veil of the temple was t in

T

TOSSED
Matt	14:24	t by the waves, for the wind
Eph	4:14	t to and fro and carried
Jas	1: 6	of the sea driven and t by

TOUCH (see TOUCHED, TOUCHES, TOUCHING)
Gen	3: 3	nor shall you t it, lest you
Ruth	2: 9	the young men not to t you?
Job	1:11	stretch out Your hand and t
Job	2: 5	and t his bone and his
Ps	105:15	Do not t My anointed ones,
Ps	144: 5	T the mountains, and they
Is	52:11	T no unclean thing; Go
Matt	14:36	Him that they might only t
Mark	3:10	pressed about Him to t Him.
1Co	7: 1	is good for a man not to t
Col	2:21	"Do not t, do not taste,

TOUCHED (see TOUCH)
Gen	32:25	He t the socket of his hip;
1Sa	10:26	him, whose hearts God had t.
2Ki	13:21	the man was let down and t
Is	6: 7	And he t my mouth with it,
Is	6: 7	this has t your lips; Your
Jer	1: 9	put forth His hand and t my
Matt	8:15	So He t her hand, and the
Matt	20:34	Jesus had compassion and t
Mark	5:30	Who t My clothes?"
Luke	22:51	And He t his ear and
Heb	12:18	the mountain that may be t

TOUCHES (see TOUCH)
Zech	2: 8	for he who touches you t the

TOUCHING (see TOUCH)
Luke	7:39	of woman this is who is t

TOWEL
John	13: 4	took a t and girded Himself.

TOWER
Gen	11: 4	and a t whose top is in the
Ps	144: 2	My high t and my deliverer,
Prov	18:10	of the LORD is a strong t;
Song	4: 4	Your neck is like the t of
Mic	4: 8	O t of the flock, The

TRADITION (see TRADITIONS)
Matt	15: 6	God of no effect by your t.
Mark	7: 8	you hold the t of men—the
1Pe	1:18	conduct received by t from

TRADITIONS (see TRADITION)
1Co	11: 2	in all things and keep the t
2Th	2:15	stand fast and hold the t

TRAIN† (see TRAINED)
Prov	22: 6	T up a child in the way he
Is	6: 1	and the t of His robe

TRAINED (see TRAIN)
Heb	12:11	to those who have been t by
2Pe	2:14	They have a heart t in

TRAITOR†
Luke	6:16	Iscariot who also became a t.

TRAMPLE (see TRAMPLED)
Is	1:12	your hand, To t My courts?

TRAMPLED (see TRAMPLE)
Matt	5:13	but to be thrown out and t
Heb	10:29	be thought worthy who has t

TRANCE
Acts	10:10	made ready, he fell into a t

TRANSFIGURED
Matt	17: 2	and He was t before them. His

TRANSFORM (see TRANSFORMED, TRANSFORMS)
Phil	3:21	who will t our lowly body

TRANSFORMED† (see TRANSFORM)
Rom	12: 2	but be t by the renewing of
2Co	3:18	are being t into the same

TRANSFORMS† (see TRANSFORM)
2Co	11:14	wonder! For Satan himself t

TRANSGRESS (see TRANSGRESSION, TRANSGRESSOR)
Matt	15: 2	Why do Your disciples t the

TRANSGRESSION (see TRANSGRESS, TRANSGRESSIONS)
Ex	34: 7	forgiving iniquity and t and
Ps	19:13	shall be innocent of great t.
Ps	32: 1	Blessed is he whose t is
Prov	17: 9	He who covers a t seeks
Dan	9:24	holy city, To finish the t,
Mic	3: 8	To declare to Jacob his t
Mic	6: 7	give my firstborn for my t,
Rom	4:15	is no law there is no t.
Rom	5:14	to the likeness of the t of

TRANSGRESSIONS (see TRANSGRESSION)
Ps	32: 5	I will confess my t to the
Ps	51: 1	mercies, Blot out my t.
Ps	51: 3	For I acknowledge my t,
Ps	103:12	far has He removed our t
Is	44:22	like a thick cloud, your t,
Is	53: 5	He was wounded for our t,
Is	53: 8	For the t of My people He
Amos	1: 3	For three t of Damascus, and

TRANSGRESSOR (see TRANSGRESS, TRANSGRESSORS)
Rom	2:27	are a t of the law?
Jas	2:11	you have become a t of the

TRANSGRESSORS (see TRANSGRESSOR)
Ps	51:13	Then I will teach t Your
Is	53:12	He was numbered with the t,
Is	53:12	made intercession for the t.

Hos	14: 9	But t stumble in them.
Mark	15:28	was numbered with the t.

TRANSLATED (see TAKEN)

Ezra	4: 7	and t into the Aramaic
Matt	1:23	Immanuel," which is t,

TREAD (see TREADS)

Ps	91:13	You shall t upon the lion
Amos	5:11	because you t down the poor

TREADS (see TREAD)

Deut	11:24	the sole of your foot t
Deut	25: 4	not muzzle an ox while it t
1Co	9: 9	an ox while it t out
1Ti	5:18	an ox while it t out
Rev	19:15	He Himself t the winepress

TREASON

2Ki	11:14	T! Treason!"

TREASURE (see TREASURES)

Ex	19: 5	you shall be a special t to
Ps	119:162	As one who finds great t.
Matt	6:21	For where your t is, there
Matt	12:35	good man out of the good t
Matt	13:44	kingdom of heaven is like t
Matt	13:52	who brings out of his t
Matt	19:21	and you will have t in
Luke	6:45	evil man out of the evil t
Luke	12:21	So is he who lays up t for
2Co	4: 7	But we have this t in
Jas	5: 3	You have heaped up t in the

TREASURES (see TREASURE)

Job	3:21	for it more than hidden t;
Prov	2. 4	for her as for hidden t,
Matt	6:19	not lay up for yourselves t
Col	2: 3	in whom are hidden all the t
Heb	11:26	greater riches than the t

TREATED

Gen	12:16	He t Abram well for her sake.
1Th	2: 2	and were spitefully t at

TREE (see TREES)

Gen	1:11	and the fruit t that
Gen	2: 9	The t of life was also in
Gen	2: 9	and the t of the knowledge
Gen	40:19	from you and hang you on a t;
Deut	12: 2	and under every green t.
Job	14: 7	"For there is hope for a t,
Ps	1: 3	He shall be like a t
Prov	3:18	She is a t of life to those
Prov	11:30	of the righteous is a t
Song	8: 5	you under the apple t.
Jer	17: 8	For he shall be like a t
Mic	4: 4	his vine and under his fig t,
Matt	7:17	every good t bears good
Matt	12:33	for a t is known by its
Matt	21:19	Immediately the fig t
Matt	24:32	this parable from the fig t:
Acts	10:39	killed by hanging on a t.
Rom	11:17	you, being a wild olive t,

Gal	3:13	who hangs on a t"),
1Pe	2:24	in His own body on the t,
Rev	2: 7	will give to eat from the t
Rev	22: 2	The leaves of the t were
Rev	22:14	may have the right to the t

TREES (see TREE)

Deut	34: 3	Jericho, the city of palm t,
Ps	104:16	The t of the LORD are full
Zech	1:11	who stood among the myrtle t,
Matt	3:10	is laid to the root of the t.
Matt	21: 8	cut down branches from the t
Mark	8:24	and said, "I see men like t,
John	12:13	took branches of palm t and
Rev	11: 4	These are the two olive t and

TREMBLE (see TREMBLED, TREMBLING)

Ps	60: 2	You have made the earth t;
Ps	96: 9	the beauty of holiness! T
Ps	99: 1	Let the peoples t! He
Eccl	12: 3	the keepers of the house t,
Dan	6:26	of my kingdom men must t
Jas	2:19	demons believe—and t!

TREMBLED (see TREMBLE)

Gen	27:33	Then Isaac t exceedingly, and
Ex	19:16	who were in the camp t.
Ex	20:18	they t and stood afar off.
Ps	18: 7	Then the earth shook and t;
Mark	16: 8	for they t and were amazed.

TREMBLING (see TREMBLE)

Is	51:22	of your hand The cup of t,
1Co	2: 3	in fear, and in much t.
Phil	2:12	salvation with fear and t;

TRESPASS (see TRESPASSES)

Gen	50:17	forgive the t of the
Lev	14:14	some of the blood of the t
Gal	6: 1	a man is overtaken in any t,

TRESPASSES (see TRESPASS)

Matt	6:14	if you forgive men their t,
2Co	5:19	not imputing their t to
Eph	2: 1	who were dead in t and sins,
Col	2:13	being dead in your t and the

TRIAL (see TRIALS)

1Pe	4:12	concerning the fiery t
Rev	3:10	keep you from the hour of t

TRIALS (see TRIAL)

Jas	1: 2	when you fall into various t,
1Pe	1: 6	been grieved by various t,

TRIBE (see TRIBES)

Ex	31: 2	of Hur, of the t of Judah.
Rev	5: 5	the Lion of the t of Judah,
Rev	14: 6	the earth—to every nation, t,

TRIBES (see TRIBE)

Gen	49:28	these are the twelve t of
1Ki	11:35	and give it to you—ten t.
Is	49: 6	Servant To raise up the t

T

Matt	19:28	judging the twelve t of
Matt	24:30	and then all the t of the
Jas	1: 1	To the twelve t which are
Rev	7: 9	number, of all nations, t,

TRIBULATION (*see* TRIBULATIONS)

Matt	13:21	For when t or persecution
Matt	24: 9	will deliver you up to t
Matt	24:21	then there will be great t,
Matt	24:29	Immediately after the t of
John	16:33	In the world you will have t;
Rom	5: 3	knowing that t produces
Rom	8:35	the love of Christ? Shall t,
Rom	12:12	in hope, patient in t,
2Co	1: 4	who comforts us in all our t,
Rev	2:22	with her into great t,
Rev	7:14	who come out of the great t,

TRIBULATIONS (*see* TRIBULATION)

Acts	14:22	We must through many t enter
Acts	20:23	saying that chains and t
Rom	5: 3	but we also glory in t,

TRIUMPH

Ps	25: 2	Let not my enemies t over
Ps	47: 1	to God with the voice of t!
Ps	94: 3	How long will the wicked t?
2Co	2:14	who always leads us in t in

TRODDEN

Is	63: 3	I have t the winepress

TROUBLE (*see* TROUBLED, TROUBLER, TROUBLES)

Josh	7:25	The LORD will t you this
2Ki	19: 3	'This day is a day of t,
Neh	9:27	And in the time of their t,
Job	4: 8	who plow iniquity And sow t
Job	5: 7	Yet man is born to t,
Job	14: 1	of few days and full of t.
Ps	9: 9	A refuge in times of t.
Ps	20: 1	answer you in the day of t;
Ps	27: 5	For in the time of t He
Ps	46: 1	A very present help in t.
Ps	50:15	upon Me in the day of t;
Ps	54: 7	delivered me out of all t;
Ps	116: 3	I found t and sorrow.
Jer	30: 7	it is the time of Jacob's t,
Dan	12: 1	there shall be a time of t,
2Ti	2: 9	for which I suffer t as an

TROUBLED (*see* TROUBLE)

Ps	6: 3	My soul also is greatly t;
Is	57:20	the wicked are like the t
Matt	2: 3	king heard this, he was t,
Luke	1:29	she was t at his saying, and
Luke	24:38	to them, "Why are you t?
John	12:27	"Now My soul is t,
John	14: 1	"Let not your heart be t;
2Co	7: 5	but we were t on every side.

TROUBLER (*see* TROUBLE)

1Ki	18:17	that you, O t of Israel?"

TROUBLES (*see* TROUBLE)

Ps	34: 6	saved him out of all his t.
Mark	13: 8	there will be famines and t.
Acts	7:10	him out of all his t,

TRUE (*see* TRUTH)

Ps	19: 9	of the LORD are t and
Jer	10:10	But the LORD is the t God;
John	1: 9	That was the t Light which
John	4:23	when the t worshipers will
John	8:17	testimony of two men is t.
John	15: 1	I am the t vine, and My
John	17: 3	the only t God, and Jesus
John	21:24	know that his testimony is t.
Rom	3: 4	let God be t but every man a
2Co	6: 8	as deceivers, and yet t;
Eph	4:24	in t righteousness and
Phil	4: 8	whatever things are t,
1Th	1: 9	to serve the living and t
1Ti	1: 2	a t son in the faith:
Heb	10:22	let us draw near with a t
1Jn	2: 8	and the t light is already
1Jn	5:20	This is the t God and
Rev	3:14	the Faithful and T Witness,
Rev	6:10	long, O Lord, holy and t,
Rev	19:11	was called Faithful and T,
Rev	22: 6	words are faithful and t.

TRUMPET (*see* TRUMPETS)

Judg	7:16	and he put a t into every
Ps	150: 3	Him with the sound of the t;
1Co	14: 8	For if the t makes an
1Co	15:52	of an eye, at the last t.
1Co	15:52	For the t will sound, and
1Th	4:16	and with the t of God. And

TRUMPETS (*see* TRUMPET)

Num	10: 2	Make two silver t for

TRUST (*see* TRUSTED, TRUSTS)

Job	13:15	yet will I t Him. Even so,
Ps	2:12	all those who put their t
Ps	7: 1	my God, in You I put my t;
Ps	18: 2	strength, in whom I will t;
Ps	31: 1	In You, O LORD, I put my t;
Ps	37: 3	T in the LORD, and do good
Ps	37: 5	T also in Him, And He
Ps	91: 2	My God, in Him I will t.
Ps	118: 8	It is better to t in the
Prov	3: 5	T in the LORD with all your
Matt	12:21	name Gentiles will t.
John	5:45	you—Moses, in whom you t.
1Ti	1:11	which was committed to my t.
1Ti	6:17	nor to t in uncertain riches
1Ti	6:20	what was committed to your t,

TRUSTED (*see* TRUST)

Ps	13: 5	But I have t in Your mercy;
Ps	22: 4	Our fathers t in You; They
Ps	22: 8	He t in the LORD, let Him
Matt	27:43	He t in God; let Him deliver
Eph	1:12	that we who first t in Christ

TRUSTS (*see* TRUST)

Ps	57: 1	to me! For my soul t in
Prov	31:11	of her husband safely t her;
Is	26: 3	Because he t in You.

TRUTH (*see* TRUE)

Ex	34: 6	abounding in goodness and t,
Deut	32: 4	A God of t and without
Ps	15: 2	And speaks the t in his
Ps	25: 5	Lead me in Your t and teach
Ps	43: 3	out Your light and Your t!
Ps	51: 6	You desire t in the inward
Ps	85:10	Mercy and t have met
Ps	96:13	And the peoples with His t.
Ps	100: 5	And His t endures to all
Ps	145:18	all who call upon Him in t.
Prov	29:24	He swears to tell the t,
Dan	10:21	noted in the Scripture of T.
Matt	22:16	teach the way of God in t;
John	1:14	Father, full of grace and t.
John	1:17	but grace and t came
John	3:21	But he who does the t comes
John	4:23	the Father in spirit and t;
John	4:24	must worship in spirit and t.
John	8:32	"And you shall know the t,
John	8:32	and the t shall make you
John	8:44	does not stand in the t,
John	14: 6	him, "I am the way, the t,
John	16:13	when He, the Spirit of t,
John	16:13	He will guide you into all t;
John	17:17	"Sanctify them by Your t.
John	17:17	Your truth. Your word is t.
John	18:37	Everyone who is of the t
John	18:38	said to Him, "What is t?
Rom	1:18	who suppress the t in
Rom	1:25	who exchanged the t of God
Rom	9: 1	I tell the t in Christ, I am
1Co	5: 8	bread of sincerity and t.
1Co	13: 6	but rejoices in the t;
Gal	2: 5	that the t of the gospel
Eph	1:13	you heard the word of t,
Eph	4:15	speaking the t in love, may
Eph	4:21	as the t is in Jesus.
Eph	5: 9	righteousness, and t),
Eph	6:14	girded your waist with t,
Phil	1:18	whether in pretense or in t,
1Th	2:13	of men, but as it is in t,
1Ti	2: 4	to the knowledge of the t.
1Ti	2: 7	I am speaking the t in Christ
1Ti	3:15	pillar and ground of the t.
2Ti	2:15	dividing the word of t.
2Ti	2:18	strayed concerning the t,
Heb	10:26	the knowledge of the t,
Jas	5:19	among you wanders from the t,
2Pe	2: 2	of whom the way of t will
1Jn	1: 6	and do not practice the t.
1Jn	1: 8	and the t is not in us.
1Jn	2: 4	and the t is not in him.
1Jn	3:18	tongue, but in deed and in t.
1Jn	5: 6	because the Spirit is t.
2Jn	1	children, whom I love in t,
2Jn	4	your children walking in t,

TRY (*see* PROVE)

Ps	26: 2	T my mind and my heart.
Ps	139:23	T me, and know my
Mal	3:10	And t Me now in this,"
1Pe	4:12	fiery trial which is to t

TUBAL

Ezek	38: 2	of Rosh, Meshech, and T,

TURN (*see* TURNED, TURNING, TURNS)

Ex	3: 3	I will now t aside and see
2Ch	7:14	and t from their wicked
Ps	40: 4	nor such as t aside to lies.
Prov	4:27	Do not t to the right or the
Prov	29: 8	But wise men t away wrath.
Ezek	33: 9	if you warn the wicked to t
Dan	12: 3	And those who t many to
Mal	4: 6	And he will t The hearts of
Acts	13:46	we t to the Gentiles.
Phil	1:19	I know that this will t out
Jude	4	who t the grace of our God

TURNED (*see* TURN)

Gen	3:24	and a flaming sword which t
1Ki	2:15	the kingdom has been t over,
Ps	14: 3	They have all t aside, They
Is	5:25	all this His anger is not t
Is	53: 6	have gone astray; We have t,
Joel	2:31	The sun shall be t into
Jon	3:10	that they t from their evil
Mal	2: 6	And t many away from
Matt	16:23	But He t and said to Peter,
John	16:20	but your sorrow will be t
John	20:14	she t around and saw Jesus
Acts	2:20	The sun shall be t
Acts	7:42	Then God t and gave them up
Acts	11:21	great number believed and t
Acts	17: 6	These who have t the world
1Th	1: 9	and how you t to God from
1Ti	5:15	For some have already t aside
Jas	4: 9	Let your laughter be t to

TURNING (*see* TURN)

John	21:20	t around, saw the disciple
Acts	3:26	in t away every one of you
Acts	15:19	the Gentiles who are t to
Jas	1:17	no variation or shadow of t.

TURNS (*see* TURN)

Deut	29:18	whose heart t away today
Prov	15: 1	A soft answer t away wrath,
Prov	26:14	As a door t on its hinges,
Ezek	3:20	when a righteous man t from
Ezek	18:21	But if a wicked man t from
2Co	3:16	Nevertheless when one t to

TURTLEDOVE (*see* TURTLEDOVES)

Gen	15: 9	a three-year-old ram, a t,
Lev	12: 6	and a young pigeon or a t as
Song	2:12	And the voice of the t Is

TURTLEDOVES (*see* TURTLEDOVE)

Lev	5: 7	two t or two young pigeons:

T

Lev	12: 8	then she may bring two **t** or
Luke	2:24	A pair of **t** or two

TUTOR

Gal	3:24	Therefore the law was our **t**

TWELVE

Gen	35:22	the sons of Jacob were **t**:
Gen	49:28	All these are the **t** tribes
Ex	24: 4	and **t** pillars according to
Ex	39:14	There were **t** stones
Josh	4: 9	Then Joshua set up **t** stones
Judg	19:29	and divided her into **t**
1Ki	7:44	and **t** oxen under the Sea;
1Ki	10:20	**T** lions stood there, one on
1Ki	11:30	and tore it into **t** pieces.
1Ki	18:31	And Elijah took **t** stones,
Matt	10: 1	And when He had called His **t**
Matt	10: 2	Now the names of the **t**
Matt	19:28	Me will also sit on **t**
Matt	19:28	judging the **t** tribes of
Matt	26:53	provide Me with more than **t**
Luke	2:42	And when He was **t** years old,
Acts	7: 8	and Jacob begot the **t**
1Co	15: 5	by Cephas, then by the **t**.
Jas	1: 1	To the **t** tribes which are
Rev	7: 5	of the tribe of Reuben **t**
Rev	21:12	a great and high wall with **t**
Rev	22: 2	which bore **t** fruits, each

TWENTY

Lev	27: 3	is of a male from **t** years

TWENTY-FOUR

1Ch	27: 1	each division having **t**
Rev	4:10	the **t** elders fall down before

TWICE

Ex	16:22	that they gathered **t** as
Num	20:11	hand and struck the rock **t**
Job	42:10	Indeed the LORD gave Job **t**
Mark	14:30	before the rooster crows **t**,

TWILIGHT

Ex	12: 6	of Israel shall kill it at **t**.
Ex	29:39	lamb you shall offer at **t**.
Deut	16: 6	sacrifice the Passover at **t**,
Job	24:15	adulterer waits for the **t**,

TWINKLING†

1Co	15:52	in the **t** of an eye, at the

TWIN (see TWINS)

John	11:16	Thomas, who is called the **t**

TWINS (see TWIN)

Gen	25:24	indeed there were **t** in her
Gen	38:27	**t** were in her womb.

TWIST (see TWISTED)

2Pe	3:16	and unstable people **t** to

TWISTED (see TWIST)

Is	27: 1	Leviathan that **t** serpent;
Mark	15:17	and they **t** a crown of

TWO (see TWO-EDGED)

Gen	7:15	the ark to Noah, two by **t**,
Ex	31:18	He gave Moses **t** tablets of
Deut	21:15	If a man has **t** wives, one
1Ki	3:25	the living child in **t**,
Amos	3: 3	Can **t** walk together, unless
Matt	18:20	For where **t** or three are
Mark	6: 7	to send them out two by **t**,
2Co	13: 1	By the mouth of **t** or

TWO-EDGED (see TWO)

Prov	5: 4	Sharp as a **t** sword.
Heb	4:12	and sharper than any **t**
Rev	1:16	of His mouth went a sharp **t**

TYPE† (see ANTITYPE)

Rom	5:14	who is a **t** of Him who was to

TYRE

Josh	19:29	to the fortified city of **T**;
2Sa	5:11	Then Hiram king of **T** sent
Matt	11:22	be more tolerable for **T** and
Mark	3: 8	and those from **T** and Sidon,

U

UNAPPROACHABLE†

1Ti	6:16	dwelling in **u** light, whom no

UNAWARE

Rom	1:13	I do not want you to be **u**,
1Co	10: 1	I do not want you to be **u**

UNBELIEF (see BELIEF, UNBELIEVING)

Matt	13:58	there because of their **u**.
Mark	9:24	I believe; help my **u**!"
Rom	4:20	the promise of God through **u**,
Rom	11:23	if they do not continue in **u**,
1Ti	1:13	I did it ignorantly in **u**.
Heb	3:12	of you an evil heart of **u**
Heb	3:19	not enter in because of **u**.

UNBELIEVER (see BELIEVER, UNBELIEVERS)

1Co	7:15	But if the **u** departs, let him
2Co	6:15	has a believer with an **u**?
1Ti	5: 8	faith and is worse than an **u**.

UNBELIEVERS (see UNBELIEVER)

2Co	6:14	yoked together with **u**.

UNBELIEVING (see UNBELIEF)

John	20:27	into My side. Do not be **u**,
1Co	7:14	For the **u** husband is
Rev	21: 8	"But the cowardly, **u**,

UNCERTAIN (see CERTAIN)

1Co	14: 8	if the trumpet makes an **u**

1Ti 6:17 nor to trust in **u** riches but

UNCHANGEABLE† (see CHANGE)
Heb 7:24 has an **u** priesthood.

UNCIRCUMCISED (see CIRCUMCISE, UNCIRCUMCISION)
Ex 6:12 for I am of **u** lips?"
Lev 26:41 if their **u** hearts are
Jer 6:10 Indeed their ear is **u**,
Ezek 44: 7 **u** in heart and uncircumcised
Rom 2:27 will not the physically **u**,
Rom 4:12 Abraham had while still **u**.
Col 3:11 nor Jew, circumcised nor **u**,

UNCIRCUMCISION (see UNCIRCUMCISED)
1Co 7:19 is nothing and **u** is nothing,
Eph 2:11 who are called **U** by what is

UNCLEAN (see CLEAN, UNCLEANNESS)
Gen 7: 2 each of animals that are **u**,
Lev 5: 2 if a person touches any **u**
Lev 10:10 and between **u** and clean,
Lev 12: 2 then she shall be **u** seven
Lev 13:45 and cry, 'U! Unclean!'
Is 6: 5 Because I am a man of **u**
Is 52:11 Touch no **u** thing; Go out
Is 64: 6 But we are all like an **u**
Luke 4:33 man who had a spirit of an **u**
Acts 10:14 eaten anything common or **u**.
Acts 10:28 not call any man common or **u**.
1Co 7:14 your children would be **u**,
Heb 9:13 a heifer, sprinkling the **u**,
Rev 16:13 And I saw three **u** spirits

UNCLEANNESS (see UNCLEAN)
Deut 24: 1 because he has found some **u**
Matt 23:27 dead men's bones and all **u**.
Rom 1:24 God also gave them up to **u**,
Rom 6:19 your members as slaves of **u**,
1Th 4: 7 For God did not call us to **u**,

UNCOVERED
Gen 9:21 and became **u** in his tent.
1Co 11: 5 prophesies with her head **u**
1Co 11:13 pray to God with her head **u**?

UNDEFILED (see DEFILE)
Heb 7:26 who is holy, harmless, **u**,
Heb 13: 4 among all, and the bed **u**;
Jas 1:27 Pure and **u** religion before
1Pe 1: 4 incorruptible and **u** and

UNDERFOOT
Heb 10:29 trampled the Son of God **u**,

UNDERSTAND (see UNDERSTANDING, UNDERSTANDS, UNDERSTOOD)
Neh 8: 7 helped the people to **u** the
Job 42: 3 uttered what I did not **u**,
Ps 14: 2 see if there are any who **u**,
Ps 19:12 Who can **u** his errors?
Ps 82: 5 do not know, nor do they **u**;
Ps 139: 2 You **u** my thought afar off;

Prov 2: 5 Then you will **u** the fear of
Is 6: 9 on hearing, but do not **u**;
Is 6:10 And **u** with their heart,
Is 43:10 And **u** that I am He.
Dan 12: 8 I heard, I did not **u**.
Dan 12:10 but the wise shall **u**.
Matt 13:15 Lest they should **u**
Matt 24:15 (whoever reads, let him **u**),
John 6:60 saying; who can **u** it?"
John 13: 7 I am doing you do not **u** now,
Acts 8:30 Do you **u** what you are
1Co 13: 2 and **u** all mysteries and all
Eph 5:17 but **u** what the will of the
Heb 11: 3 By faith we **u** that the worlds
2Pe 3:16 are some things hard to **u**,

UNDERSTANDING (see UNDERSTAND)
1Ki 3: 9 give to Your servant an **u**
Job 28:28 to depart from evil is **u**.
Ps 111:10 A good **u** have all those who
Ps 119:99 I have more **u** than all my
Ps 119:130 It gives **u** to the simple.
Ps 147: 5 in power; His **u** is infinite.
Prov 2: 2 And apply your heart to **u**;
Prov 3: 5 And lean not on your own **u**;
Prov 3:19 By **u** He established the
Prov 9:10 of the Holy One is **u**.
Prov 16:22 **U** is a wellspring of life
Is 11: 2 The Spirit of wisdom and **u**,
Is 40:28 His **u** is unsearchable.
Luke 2:47 Him were astonished at His **u**
1Co 14:15 I will also pray with the **u**.
1Co 14:19 speak five words with my **u**,
1Co 14:20 but in **u** be mature.
Eph 1:18 the eyes of your **u** being
Eph 4:18 having their **u** darkened,
Phil 4: 7 God, which surpasses all **u**,
Col 1: 9 all wisdom and spiritual **u**;

UNDERSTANDS (see UNDERSTAND)
Jer 9:24 That he **u** and knows Me,
Rom 3:11 There is none who **u**;
1Co 14: 2 for no one **u** him; however,

UNDERSTOOD (see UNDERSTAND)
Neh 8:12 because they **u** the words
Is 40:21 Have you not **u** from the
Dan 9: 2 **u** by the books the number of
Rom 1:20 being **u** by the things that
1Co 13:11 I **u** as a child, I thought as

UNDIGNIFIED†
2Sa 6:22 And I will be even more **u**

UNDONE
Is 6: 5 for I am **u**! Because I am a
Matt 23:23 without leaving the others **u**.

UNEQUALLY† (see EQUAL)
2Co 6:14 Do not be **u** yoked together

UNEXPECTEDLY (see EXPECT)
Ps 35: 8 destruction come upon him **u**,
Luke 21:34 and that Day come on you **u**.

U

UNFORGIVING† (see FORGIVE)
Rom	1:31	untrustworthy, unloving, **u**,
2Ti	3: 3	unloving, **u**, slanderers,

UNFORMED† (see FORM)
Ps	139:16	my substance, being yet **u**.

UNFRUITFUL (see FRUITFUL)
Matt	13:22	the word, and he becomes **u**.
Eph	5:11	no fellowship with the **u**
2Pe	1: 8	be neither barren nor **u** in

UNGODLINESS (see UNGODLY)
Is	32: 6	iniquity: To practice **u**,
Rom	1:18	from heaven against all **u**
Tit	2:12	denying **u** and worldly lusts,

UNGODLY (see GODLY, UNGODLINESS)
Ps	1: 1	not in the counsel of the **u**,
Ps	1: 6	But the way of the **u** shall
Rom	4: 5	on Him who justifies the **u**,
Rom	5: 6	time Christ died for the **u**.
1Pe	4:18	Where will the **u** and
2Pe	3: 7	judgment and perdition of **u**
Jude	4	**u** men, who turn the grace of

UNHOLY (see HOLY)
Lev	10:10	between holy and **u**,
1Ti	1: 9	for the **u** and profane, for
2Ti	3: 2	to parents, unthankful, **u**,

UNITED (see UNITY)
Rom	6: 5	For if we have been **u**

UNITY (see UNITED)
Ps	133: 1	to dwell together in **u**!
Eph	4: 3	endeavoring to keep the **u** of
Eph	4:13	till we all come to the **u** of

UNJUST (see JUST)
Matt	5:45	on the just and on the **u**.
Luke	16: 8	the master commended the **u**
Luke	18: 6	Hear what the **u** judge said.
1Pe	3:18	for sins, the just for the **u**,
2Pe	2: 9	and to reserve the **u** under
Rev	22:11	"He who is **u**, let him be

UNKNOWN (see KNOW)
Acts	17:23	TO THE U GOD. Therefore, the

UNLEAVENED (see LEAVEN)
Ex	12: 8	with **u** bread and with
Ex	12:17	observe the Feast of U
Matt	26:17	day of the Feast of the U
Acts	12: 3	it was during the Days of U
1Co	5: 7	lump, since you truly are **u**.

UNLOVED (see LOVE, UNLOVING)
Gen	29:31	LORD saw that Leah was **u**,
Deut	21:15	one loved and the other **u**,

UNLOVING (see UNLOVED)
Rom	1:31	untrustworthy, **u**,

UNMARRIED (see MARRY)
1Co	7: 8	But I say to the **u** and to the
1Co	7:32	He who is **u** cares for the

UNMERCIFUL† (see MERCIFUL)
Rom	1:31	unloving, unforgiving, **u**;

UNPROFITABLE (see PROFITABLE)
Matt	25:30	And cast the **u** servant into
Luke	17:10	We are **u** servants. We have
Rom	3:12	have together become **u**;
Phm	1:11	who once was **u** to you, but

UNQUENCHABLE (see QUENCH)
Matt	3:12	burn up the chaff with **u**

UNRIGHTEOUS (see RIGHTEOUS, UNRIGHTEOUSNESS)
Is	55: 7	And the **u** man his thoughts;
Luke	16: 9	friends for yourselves by **u**
1Co	6: 9	Do you not know that the **u**

UNRIGHTEOUSNESS (see UNRIGHTEOUS)
Ps	92:15	and there is no **u** in Him.
John	7:18	and no **u** is in Him.
Rom	1:18	who suppress the truth in **u**,
Rom	6:13	as instruments of **u** to sin,
Rom	9:14	Is there **u** with God?
2Th	2:12	truth but had pleasure in **u**.
2Pe	2:13	will receive the wages of **u**,
1Jn	1: 9	and to cleanse us from all **u**.

UNSEARCHABLE
Ps	145: 3	And His greatness is **u**.
Rom	11:33	and knowledge of God! How **u**
Eph	3: 8	among the Gentiles the **u**

UNSPOTTED† (see SPOT)
Jas	1:27	and to keep oneself **u** from

UNSTABLE
Jas	1: 8	man, **u** in all his ways.
2Pe	2:14	enticing **u** souls. They

UNTHANKFUL (see THANKFUL)
2Ti	3: 2	disobedient to parents, **u**,

UNVEILED† (see VEIL)
2Co	3:18	with **u** face, beholding as in

UNWASHED (see WASH)
Matt	15:20	but to eat with **u** hands does

UNWISE (see WISE)
Rom	1:14	both to wise and to **u**.
Eph	5:17	Therefore do not be **u**,

UNWORTHY (see WORTHY)
1Co	11:27	cup of the Lord in an **u**

UPHARSIN† (see PERES)
Dan	5:25	MENE, MENE, TEKEL, U

UPHOLD (*see* UPHOLDING)

Ps	51:12	And **u** me by Your generous
Ps	119:116	U me according to Your word,
Is	42: 1	My Servant whom I **u**,

UPHOLDING† (*see* UPHOLD)

Heb	1: 3	and **u** all things by the word

UPPER

2Ki	4:10	let us make a small **u** room
Dan	6:10	And in his **u** room, with his
Mark	14:15	he will show you a large **u**
Acts	1:13	they went up into the **u** room

UPRIGHT (*see* UPRIGHTLY)

Gen	37: 7	sheaf arose and also stood **u**;
Job	1: 1	that man was blameless and **u**,
Ps	25: 8	Good and **u** is the LORD;
Ps	111: 1	In the assembly of the **u**
Prov	2: 7	up sound wisdom for the **u**;
Prov	15:19	But the way of the **u** is a
Eccl	7:29	found: That God made man **u**,
Hab	2: 4	His soul is not **u** in him;

UPRIGHTLY (*see* UPRIGHT)

Ps	84:11	From those who walk **u**.
Prov	2: 7	a shield to those who walk **u**;

UPSIDE

Acts	17: 6	who have turned the world **u**

UPWARD

Job	5: 7	As the sparks fly **u**.
Phil	3:14	goal for the prize of the **u**

UR

Gen	11:28	in U of the Chaldeans.
Neh	9: 7	And brought him out of U of

URIAH

2Sa	11: 3	the wife of U the Hittite?"
2Sa	11:17	and U the Hittite died also.
Matt	1: 6	had been the wife of U.

URIM (*see* THUMMIM)

Ex	28:30	of judgment the U and the
1Sa	28: 6	either by dreams or by U or

USURY

Lev	25:36	Take no **u** or interest from
Neh	5: 7	Each of you is exacting **u**

UTTER (*see* UTTERANCE, UTTERED, UTTERS)

Ps	119:171	My lips shall **u** praise, For

UTTERANCE (*see* UTTER)

Acts	2: 4	as the Spirit gave them **u**.
Eph	6:19	that **u** may be given to me,

UTTERED (*see* UTTER)

Rom	8:26	groanings which cannot be **u**.

UTTERMOST

Ps	139: 9	And dwell in the **u** parts
Heb	7:25	also able to save to the **u**

UTTERS (*see* UTTER)

Ps	19: 2	Day unto day **u** speech, And

UZ

Job	1: 1	was a man in the land of U,

UZZAH

2Sa	6: 6	U put out his hand to the

UZZIAH (*see* AZARIAH)

2Ch	26:21	King U was a leper until the
Is	6: 1	In the year that King U died,
Hos	1: 1	of Beeri, in the days of U,
Amos	1: 1	Israel in the days of U
Zech	14: 5	In the days of U king of
Matt	1: 8	Joram, and Joram begot U.

V

VAGABOND

Gen	4:12	A fugitive and a **v** you shall

VAIN (*see* EMPTY)

Ex	20: 7	who takes His name in **v**.
Ps	2: 1	And the people plot a **v**
Ps	127: 1	They labor in **v** who build
Ps	139:20	take Your name in **v**.
Eccl	6:12	all the days of his **v** life
Jn	15:19	Who did not create it in **v**,
Matt	6: 7	do not use **v** repetitions as
Acts	4:25	And the people plot **v**
Rom	13: 4	does not bear the sword in **v**;
1Co	15: 2	you—unless you believed in **v**.
1Co	15:58	that your labor is not in **v**
Gal	2:21	law, then Christ died in **v**.
Gal	3: 4	vain—if indeed it was in **v**?
Phil	2:16	run in vain or labored in **v**.

VALLEY (*see* VALLEYS)

Josh	10:12	in the V of Aijalon."
Ps	23: 4	though I walk through the **v**
Is	40: 4	Every **v** shall be exalted
Joel	3:14	the LORD is near in the **v**
Luke	3: 5	Every **v** shall be filled

VALLEYS (*see* VALLEY)

Deut	11:11	is a land of hills and **v**,
Song	2: 1	And the lily of the **v**.

VALUE (*see* FULL)

Matt	6:26	Are you not of more **v** than
Matt	27: 9	the **v** of Him who was

VANISH (*see* VANISHED)

Is	51: 6	For the heavens will **v** away
1Co	13: 8	knowledge, it will **v** away.
Heb	8:13	growing old is ready to **v**

VANISHED (see VANISH)
Luke   24:31   and He **v** from their sight.

VANITIES† (see VANITY)
Eccl   1: 2   "Vanity of **v**," says the
Eccl   12: 8   "Vanity of **v**," says the

VANITY (see VANITIES)
Eccl   2: 1   but surely, this also was **v**.
Hos   12:11   idols—Surely they are **v**—

VAPOR
Ps   39:11   Surely every man is **v**.
Acts   2:19   Blood and fire and **v**
Jas   4:14   It is even a **v** that appears

VARIATION† (see VARIETIES)
Jas   1:17   with whom there is no **v** or

VARIETIES† (see VARIATION, VARIOUS)
1Co   12:28   **v** of tongues.

VARIOUS (see DIFFERENT, VARIETIES)
Heb   1: 1   who at **v** times and in

VASHTI
Esth   1:12   But Queen **V** refused to come

VEHEMENT
Song   8: 6   of fire, A most **v** flame.
Heb   5: 7   with **v** cries and tears to

VEIL (see UNVEILED)
Ex   26:33   The **v** shall be a divider for
Ex   34:33   he put a **v** on his face.
Lev   16:15   bring its blood inside the **v**,
Matt   27:51   the **v** of the temple was torn
2Co   3:13   who put a **v** over his face
2Co   3:15   a **v** lies on their heart.
Heb   6:19   the Presence behind the **v**,
Heb   10:20   for us, through the **v**,

VENGEANCE
Gen   4:15   **v** shall be taken on him
Deut   32:35   **V** is Mine, and recompense
Ps   94: 1   to whom **v** belongs—O God, to
Is   61: 2   And the day of **v** of our
Jer   46:10   GOD of hosts, A day of **v**,
Mic   5:15   And I will execute **v** in
Nah   1: 2   The LORD will take **v** on
Luke   21:22   these are the days of **v**,
Rom   12:19   **V** is Mine, I will repay,"
2Th   1: 8   in flaming fire taking **v** on
Heb   10:30   **V** is Mine, I will repay,"
Jude   7   suffering the **v** of eternal

VESSEL (see VESSELS)
Ps   2: 9   to pieces like a potter's **v**.
Jer   18: 4   made it again into another **v**,
Jer   19:11   as one breaks a potter's **v**,
Acts   9:15   for he is a chosen **v** of Mine
Rom   9:21   the same lump to make one **v**
1Th   4: 4   how to possess his own **v** in

2Ti   2:21   he will be a **v** for honor,
1Pe   3: 7   the wife, as to the weaker **v**,

VESSELS (see PITCHERS, VESSEL)
Dan   5: 2   bring the gold and silver **v**
Rom   9:23   of His glory on the **v** of
2Co   4: 7   this treasure in earthen **v**,

VICTORY
Ps   98: 1   arm have gained Him the **v**.
Matt   12:20   sends forth justice to **v**;
1Co   15:54   is swallowed up in **v**.
1Co   15:57   who gives us the **v** through
1Jn   5: 4   And this is the **v** that has

VIGILANT
1Pe   5: 8   Be sober, be **v**; because your

VIGOR
Deut   34: 7   not dim nor his natural **v**

VILE
Judg   19:24   this man do not do such a **v**
Rom   1:26   reason God gave them up to **v**

VINE (see GRAPEVINE, VINEDRESSER, VINES, VINEYARD)
Judg   9:12   the trees said to the **v**,
1Ki   4:25   each man under his **v** and his
Ps   128: 3   be like a fruitful **v** In
Is   5: 2   it with the choicest **v**.
Mic   4: 4   shall sit under his **v** and
Mark   14:25   drink of the fruit of the **v**
John   15: 1   "I am the true **v**,

VINEDRESSER† (see VINE)
John   15: 1   vine, and My Father is the **v**.

VINEGAR
Num   6: 3   he shall drink neither **v**
Ps   69:21   my thirst they gave me **v** to

VINES (see VINE)
Song   2:15   foxes that spoil the **v**,

VINEYARD (see VINE)
Gen   9:20   a farmer, and he planted a **v**.
1Ki   21:16   to take possession of the **v**
Is   5: 1   my Beloved regarding His **v**:
Is   5: 7   For the **v** of the LORD of
Matt   20: 1   to hire laborers for his **v**.
Matt   21:28   'Son, go, work today in my **v**.

VIOLENCE (see VIOLENT)
Gen   6:11   the earth was filled with **v**.
Job   16:17   Although no **v** is in my
Ps   27:12   And such as breathe out **v**.
Is   53: 9   Because He had done no **v**,
Hab   1: 2   **V**!" And You will not save.
Matt   11:12   kingdom of heaven suffers **v**,

VIOLENT (see VIOLENCE)
Matt   11:12   and the **v** take it by force.

1Ti	3: 3	not given to wine, not **v**,
Tit	1: 7	not given to wine, not **v**,

VIPERS

Matt	12:34	Brood of **v**! How can you,

VIRGIN (see VIRGINS)

Gen	24:16	beautiful to behold, a **v**;
Is	7:14	the **v** shall conceive and
Is	47: 1	O **v** daughter of Babylon;
Jer	31: 4	O **v** of Israel! You shall
Matt	1:23	the **v** shall be with
Luke	1:27	to a **v** betrothed to a man

VIRGINS (see VIRGIN)

Matt	25: 1	shall be likened to ten **v**
1Co	7:25	Now concerning **v**:

VIRTUE (see VIRTUOUS)

Phil	4: 8	if there is any **v** and if
2Pe	1: 5	add to your faith **v**,

VIRTUOUS † (see VIRTUE)

Ruth	3:11	town know that you are a **v**
Prov	31:10	Who can find a **v** wife? For

VISAGE † (see VISION)

Is	52:14	So His **v** was marred more

VISIBLE (see VISION)

Heb	11: 3	made of things which are **v**.

VISION (see VISAGE, VISIBLE, VISIONS)

Gen	15: 1	LORD came to Abram in a **v**,
Num	12: 6	Myself known to him in a **v**;
Is	1: 1	The **v** of Isaiah the son of
Dan	2:19	to Daniel in a night **v**.
Dan	8: 1	reign of King Belshazzar a **v**
Dan	8:26	Therefore seal up the **v**,
Dan	10:14	for the **v** refers to many
Hab	2: 2	Write the **v** And make it
Acts	9:10	to him the Lord said in a **v**,
Acts	11: 5	and in a trance I saw a **v**,
Acts	26:19	to the heavenly **v**,

VISIONS (see VISION)

Ezek	1: 1	were opened and I saw **v** of
Dan	7: 7	this I saw in the night **v**,
Joel	2:28	Your young men shall see **v**.
Acts	2:17	young men shall see **v**,

VISIT (see VISITATION, VISITED, VISITING)

Ps	8: 4	the son of man that You **v**
Matt	25:43	in prison and you did not **v**
Jas	1:27	to **v** orphans and widows in

VISITATION † (see VISIT)

Luke	19:44	not know the time of your **v**.
1Pe	2:12	glorify God in the day of **v**.

VISITED (see VISIT)

Gen	21: 1	And the LORD **v** Sarah as He
Matt	25:36	I was sick and you **v** Me; I
Luke	1:78	from on high has **v** us;

VISITING † (see VISIT)

Ex	20: 5	**v** the iniquity of the
Ex	34: 7	**v** the iniquity of the
Num	14:18	**v** the iniquity of the
Deut	5: 9	**v** the iniquity of the

VOICE (see SOUND)

Gen	3:10	I heard Your **v** in the garden,
Gen	4:10	The **v** of your brother's
Gen	22:18	because you have obeyed My **v**.
Gen	27:22	The **v** is Jacob's voice, but
Ex	19: 5	if you will indeed obey My **v**
Deut	4:12	form; you only heard a **v**.
1Sa	15:22	As in obeying the **v** of the
1Ki	19:12	the fire a still small **v**.
Ps	19: 3	language Where their **v** is
Ps	29: 4	The **v** of the LORD is
Ps	86: 6	And attend to the **v** of my
Ps	95: 7	if you will hear His **v**:
Song	2:12	And the **v** of the turtledove
Is	6: 4	door were shaken by the **v**
Is	6: 8	Also I heard the **v** of the
Is	40: 3	The **v** of one crying in the
Is	42: 2	Nor cause His **v** to be heard
Is	65:19	The **v** of weeping shall no
Jer	7:34	streets of Jerusalem the **v**
Jer	31:15	A **v** was heard in Ramah,
Matt	2:18	A **v** was heard in Ramah,
Matt	3: 3	The **v** of one crying in
John	10: 4	him, for they know his **v**.
John	10:27	"My sheep hear My **v**,
John	18:37	is of the truth hears My **v**.
Acts	9: 7	hearing a **v** but seeing no
Acts	22: 7	to the ground and heard a **v**
1Th	4:10	with the **v** of an archangel,
Heb	3: 7	if you will hear His **v**,
Rev	1:15	and His **v** as the sound of
Rev	3:20	If anyone hears My **v** and
Rev	14: 2	like the **v** of many waters,
Rev	18:23	and the **v** of bridegroom and

VOID

Gen	1: 2	was without form, and **v**;
Is	55:11	It shall not return to Me **v**,
Jer	4:23	it was without form, and **v**;

VOLUME

Heb	10: 7	In the **v** of the book

VOMIT (see VOMITED)

Lev	18:28	lest the land **v** you out also
Prov	26:11	a dog returns to his own **v**,
2Pe	2:22	returns to his own **v**,
Rev	3:16	I will **v** you out of My

VOMITED (see VOMIT)

Jon	2:10	and it **v** Jonah onto dry

VOW (see VOWED, VOWS)

Gen	28:20	Then Jacob made a **v**,
Num	6: 2	an offering to take the **v**
Judg	11:30	And Jephthah made a **v** to the

V

| Judg | 11:39 | and he carried out his **v** |
| Eccl | 5: 4 | When you make a **v** to God, |

VOWED (see VOW)

| Eccl | 5: 4 | fools. Pay what you have **v**— |
| Jon | 2: 9 | I will pay what I have **v**. |

VOWS (see MAKES, VOW)

| Prov | 31: 2 | womb? And what, son of my **v**? |

W

WAGES

Gen	31: 7	me and changed my **w** ten
Is	55: 2	And your **w** for what does
Hag	1: 6	Earns **w** to put into a bag
Luke	10: 7	laborer is worthy of his **w**.
Rom	6:23	For the **w** of sin is death,
1Ti	5:18	laborer is worthy of his **w**.

WAILING

| Matt | 13:42 | There will be **w** and gnashing |

WAIT (see WAITED, WAITING, WAITS)

Ps	25: 5	On You I **w** all the day.
Ps	27:14	**W** on the LORD; Be of
Ps	37: 7	and **w** patiently for Him; Do
Ps	37: 9	But those who **w** on the
Ps	62: 5	**w** silently for God alone,
Prov	1:11	Let us lie in **w** to shed
Is	40:31	But those who **w** on the LORD
Is	42: 4	And the coastlands shall **w**
Hab	2: 3	**w** for it; Because it will
Acts	1: 4	but to **w** for the Promise of
Phil	3:20	which we also eagerly **w** for
1Th	1:10	and to **w** for His Son from

WAITED (see WAIT)

| Ps | 40: 1 | I **w** patiently for the LORD; |

WAITING (see WAIT)

Luke	2:25	**w** for the Consolation of
John	5: 3	**w** for the moving of the
Rom	8:23	eagerly **w** for the adoption,
1Co	1: 7	eagerly **w** for the revelation
Jas	5: 7	**w** patiently for it until it

WAITS (see WAIT)

Ps	33:20	Our soul **w** for the LORD;
Ps	130: 5	for the LORD, my soul **w**,
Dan	12:12	"Blessed is he who **w**,
Rom	8:19	of the creation eagerly **w**

WAKE

| 1Th | 5:10 | that whether we **w** or sleep, |

WALK (see WALKED, WALKING, WALKS)

Gen	17: 1	**w** before Me and be
Deut	6: 7	when you **w** by the way, when
Ps	23: 4	though I **w** through the
Ps	84:11	withhold From those who **w**
Is	30:21	**w** in it," Whenever you

Is	40:31	They shall **w** and not faint.
Amos	3: 3	Can two **w** together, unless
Mic	6: 8	And to **w** humbly with your
Matt	9: 5	or to say, 'Arise and **w**'?
Matt	11: 5	blind see and the lame **w**;
John	8:12	who follows Me shall not **w**
Rom	6: 4	even so we also should **w** in
Rom	8: 1	who do not **w** according to
2Co	5: 7	For we **w** by faith, not by
Eph	2:10	beforehand that we should **w**
Eph	5: 2	And **w** in love, as Christ also
Eph	5: 8	**W** as children of light
Col	1:10	that you may **w** worthy of the
Col	2: 6	the Lord, so **w** in Him,
Col	4: 5	**W** in wisdom toward those who
1Th	4: 1	from us how you ought to **w**
1Jn	1: 7	But if we **w** in the light as
Rev	3: 4	and they shall **w** with Me in

WALKED (see FOLLOWED, WALK)

Gen	5:24	And Enoch **w** with God; and he
Gen	6: 9	Noah **w** with God.
Is	9: 2	The people who **w** in darkness
Matt	14:29	he **w** on the water to go to
John	5: 9	well, took up his bed, and **w**.
Eph	2: 2	in which you once **w** according
Col	3: 7	which you yourselves once **w**
1Jn	2: 6	also to walk just as He **w**.

WALKING (see WALK)

Gen	3: 8	sound of the LORD God **w** in
Matt	14:25	to them, **w** on the sea.
Mark	8:24	"I see men like trees, **w**.

WALKS (see WALK)

Ps	1: 1	Blessed is the man Who **w**
Ps	91: 6	of the pestilence that **w**
Ps	104: 3	Who **w** on the wings of the
1Pe	5: 8	your adversary the devil **w**
1Jn	2:11	is in darkness and **w** in

WALL (see WALLS)

Ex	14:22	and the waters were a **w** to
Josh	2:15	her house was on the city **w**;
Josh	6:20	that the **w** fell down flat.
Neh	2:17	Come and let us build the **w**
Dan	5: 5	on the plaster of the **w** of
Acts	23: 3	you whitewashed **w**! For you
Eph	2:14	broken down the middle **w** of

WALLOWING†

| 2Pe | 2:22 | to her **w** in the mire." |

WALLS (see WALL)

Ps	51:18	Build the **w** of Jerusalem.
Ps	122: 7	Peace be within your **w**,
Jer	1:18	And bronze **w** against the
Heb	11:30	By faith the **w** of Jericho

WANDERED

| Heb | 11:37 | They **w** about in sheepskins |

WANT (see NEED, WANTING)

| Ps | 23: 1 | my shepherd; I shall not **w**. |

WANTING (*see* WANT)

Dan	5:27	in the balances, and found **w**;

WAR (*see* WARFARE, WARRING, WARS)

Ex	15: 3	The LORD is a man of **w**;
Ex	32:17	There is a noise of **w** in
Num	31:21	priest said to the men of **w**
Josh	11:23	Then the land rested from **w**.
Ps	27: 3	Though **w** should rise
Ps	120: 7	I speak, they are for **w**.
Eccl	3: 8	a time to hate; A time of **w**,
Is	2: 4	Neither shall they learn **w**
Mic	4: 3	Neither shall they learn **w**

WARFARE† (*see* WAR)

Is	40: 2	That her **w** is ended, That
2Co	10: 4	For the weapons of our **w** are
1Ti	1:18	them you may wage the good **w**,
2Ti	2: 4	No one engaged in **w** entangles

WARMED

John	18:25	Now Simon Peter stood and **w**
Jas	2:16	be **w** and filled," but you

WARN (*see* WARNED, WARNING)

Ezek	3:19	if you **w** the wicked, and he
Ezek	33: 9	Nevertheless if you **w** the
Acts	20:31	years I did not cease to **w**

WARNED (*see* WARN)

Gen	43: 3	The man solemnly **w** us,
Ps	19:11	by them Your servant is **w**,
Matt	2:12	being divinely **w** in a dream
Matt	2:22	And being **w** by God in a
Matt	3: 7	Brood of vipers! Who **w** you to
Heb	11: 7	being divinely **w** of things

WARNING (*see* WARN)

Ezek	3:18	die,' and you give him no **w**,
Col	1:28	**w** every man and teaching

WARRING (*see* WAR)

Rom	7:23	**w** against the law of my

WARS (*see* WAR)

Num	21:14	is said in the Book of the **W**
Ps	46: 9	He makes **w** cease to the end
Matt	24: 6	hear of wars and rumors of **w**.
Jas	4: 1	Where do **w** and fights come

WASH (*see* UNWASHED, WASHED, WASHING)

Gen	18: 4	and **w** your feet, and rest
Gen	19: 2	and **w** your feet; then you
Ex	29:17	**w** its entrails and its legs,
Lev	16:26	as the scapegoat shall **w**
Ruth	3: 3	Therefore **w** yourself and
1Sa	25:41	a servant to **w** the feet of
2Ki	5:10	Go and **w** in the Jordan seven
Ps	51: 2	**W** me thoroughly from my
Ps	51: 7	**W** me, and I shall be whiter
Is	1:16	**W** yourselves, make yourselves
Matt	15: 2	For they do not **w** their
Luke	7:38	and she began to **w** His feet

WASH (*see* WASH)

John	9: 7	**w** in the pool of Siloam"
John	13: 5	into a basin and began to **w**
John	13: 8	You shall never **w** my feet!"
John	13:14	you also ought to **w** one
Acts	22:16	and **w** away your sins,

WASHED (*see* WASH)

Gen	43:24	and they **w** their feet; and
Gen	43:31	Then he **w** his face and came
Ex	19:14	and they **w** their clothes.
Ps	73:13	And **w** my hands in
Song	5:12	**W** with milk, And fitly
Is	4: 4	When the Lord has **w** away the
Matt	27:24	he took water and **w** his
Luke	7:44	but she has **w** My feet with
Luke	11:38	that He had not first **w**
John	9: 7	Sent). So he went and **w**,
John	9:15	put clay on my eyes, and I **w**,
John	13:12	So when He had **w** their feet,
1Co	6:11	some of you. But you were **w**,
Heb	10:22	conscience and our bodies **w**
Rev	1: 5	To Him who loved us and **w** us
Rev	7:14	and **w** their robes and made

WASHING (*see* WASH)

Mark	7: 4	like the **w** of cups, pitchers
Luke	5: 2	gone from them and were **w**
John	13: 6	are You **w** my feet?"
Eph	5:26	and cleanse her with the **w**
Tit	3: 5	**w** of regeneration

WASTE (*see* WASTED)

Ps	31:10	And my bones **w** away.
Ps	91: 6	destruction that lays **w** at
Matt	26: 8	saying, "Why this **w**?

WASTED (*see* WASTE)

Mark	14: 4	was this fragrant oil **w**?
Luke	15:13	and there **w** his possessions

WATCH (*see* WATCHER, WATCHES, WATCHING, WATCHMAN)

Gen	31:49	May the LORD **w** between you
Ps	90: 4	And like a **w** in the night.
Ps	130: 6	Lord More than those who **w**
Hab	2: 1	I will stand my **w** And set
Matt	24:42	**W** therefore, for you do not
Matt	26:40	Could you not **w** with Me one
Matt	26:41	**W** and pray, lest you enter
Luke	2: 8	keeping **w** over their flock

WATCHER (*see* WATCH, WATCHERS)

Job	7:20	O **w** of men? Why have You

WATCHERS (*see* WATCHER)

Dan	4:17	is by the decree of the **w**,

WATCHES (*see* WATCH)

Ps	63: 6	on You in the night **w**.
Rev	16:15	thief. Blessed is he who **w**,

WATCHING (*see* WATCH)

Luke	12:37	when he comes, will find **w**.

WATCHMAN (*see* WATCH, WATCHMEN)

Ps	127: 1	The **w** stays awake in vain.
Ezek	3:17	I have made you a **w** for the
Ezek	33: 7	I have made you a **w** for the

WATCHMEN (*see* WATCHMAN)

| Song | 3: 3 | The **w** who go about the city |

WATER (*see* WATERED, WATERFALLS, WATERS)

Gen	24:11	when women go out to draw **w**.
Ex	2:10	I drew him out of the **w**.
Ex	20: 4	or that is in the **w** under
Num	5:17	priest shall take holy **w** in
Num	5:18	in his hand the bitter **w**
Job	15:16	Who drinks iniquity like **w**!
Ps	1: 3	Planted by the rivers of **w**,
Ps	22:14	I am poured out like **w**,
Ps	42: 1	As the deer pants for the **w**
Ps	63: 1	land Where there is no **w**.
Ps	72: 6	Like showers that **w** the
Ps	105:41	and **w** gushed out; It ran in
Ps	107:35	a wilderness into pools of **w**,
Prov	5:15	Drink **w** from your own
Prov	5:15	And running **w** from your own
Prov	9:17	Stolen **w** is sweet, And bread
Prov	20: 5	of man is like deep **w**,
Prov	25:21	give him **w** to drink;
Prov	25:25	As cold **w** to a weary soul,
Is	55:10	But **w** the earth, And make
Jer	2:13	cisterns that can hold no **w**.
Jer	9:18	And our eyelids gush with **w**.
Jer	13: 1	but do not put it in **w**.
Lam	1:16	eye, my eye overflows with **w**;
Lam	5: 4	We pay for the **w** we drink,
Ezek	47: 1	the **w** was flowing from under
Ezek	47: 4	the **w** came up to my
Ezek	47: 5	**w** in which one must swim, a
Dan	1:12	us vegetables to eat and **w**
Amos	5:24	let justice run down like **w**,
Amos	8:11	bread, Nor a thirst for **w**,
Matt	3:11	indeed baptize you with **w**
Matt	10:42	ones only a cup of cold **w**
Matt	14:28	me to come to You on the **w**.
Matt	17:15	fire and often into the **w**.
Mark	1: 8	indeed baptized you with **w**,
Mark	9:22	the fire and into the **w** to
Mark	14:13	you carrying a pitcher of **w**;
Luke	8:25	even the winds and **w**,
Luke	16:24	the tip of his finger in **w**
John	1:26	saying, "I baptize with **w**,
John	2: 7	"Fill the waterpots with **w**.
John	2: 9	the feast had tasted the **w**
John	3: 5	unless one is born of **w** and
John	4: 7	of Samaria came to draw **w**.
John	4:10	have given you living **w**.
John	5: 3	for the moving of the **w**.
John	7:38	will flow rivers of living **w**.
John	13: 5	He poured **w** into a basin and
John	19:34	and immediately blood and **w**
Acts	1: 5	John truly baptized with **w**,
Acts	8:38	eunuch went down into the **w**,
Acts	10:47	"Can anyone forbid **w**,
Acts	11:16	'John indeed baptized with **w**,

Eph	5:26	her with the washing of **w**
1Ti	5:23	No longer drink only **w**,
Heb	10:22	bodies washed with pure **w**.
Jas	3:11	a spring send forth fresh **w**
1Pe	3:20	souls, were saved through **w**.
2Pe	3: 5	the earth standing out of **w**
1Jn	5: 6	This is He who came by **w** and
1Jn	5: 8	on earth: the Spirit, the **w**,
Rev	22: 1	showed me a pure river of **w**
Rev	22:17	let him take the **w** of life

WATERED (*see* WATER)

| Gen | 2: 6 | up from the earth and **w** the |
| 1Co | 3: 6 | I planted, Apollos **w**, |

WATERFALLS† (*see* WATER)

| Ps | 42: 7 | deep at the noise of Your **w**; |

WATERS (*see* FLOODWATERS, WATER)

Gen	1: 2	over the face of the **w**.
Gen	1: 6	divide the waters from the **w**.
Ex	14:21	and the **w** were divided.
Ex	15:25	the **w** were made sweet. There
Ps	23: 2	leads me beside the still **w**.
Ps	24: 2	established it upon the **w**.
Ps	29: 3	of the LORD is over the **w**;
Ps	69: 1	O God! For the **w** have come
Ps	69: 2	I have come into deep **w**,
Ps	77:19	Your path in the great **w**,
Ps	107:23	Who do business on great **w**,
Eccl	11: 1	Cast your bread upon the **w**,
Song	8: 7	Many **w** cannot quench love,
Is	40:12	Who has measured the **w** in
Is	43: 2	When you pass through the **w**,
Is	43:16	a path through the mighty **w**,
Is	55: 1	who thirsts, Come to the **w**;
Is	57:20	Whose **w** cast up mire and
Jer	2:13	Me, the fountain of living **w**,
Jer	9: 1	Oh, that my head were **w**,
Jer	15:18	stream, As **w** that fail?
Jer	17:13	The fountain of living **w**.
Hab	2:14	As the **w** cover the sea.
Rev	1:15	voice as the sound of many **w**;
Rev	7:17	to living fountains of **w**.

WAVE (*see* WAVED, WAVES)

| Jas | 1: 6 | he who doubts is like a **w** |

WAVED (*see* WAVE)

| Ex | 29:27 | the wave offering which is **w**, |

WAVER†

| Rom | 4:20 | He did not **w** at the promise |

WAVES (*see* WAVE)

| Ps | 42: 7 | All Your **w** and billows have |
| Jon | 2: 3 | All Your billows and Your **w** |

WAX

| Ps | 22:14 | joint; My heart is like **w**; |
| Ps | 97: 5 | The mountains melt like **w** at |

WAY (*see* WAYS, WAYSIDE)

| Gen | 3:24 | sword which turned every **w**, |

Ex	2:12	looked this way and that **w**,
Deut	1:33	to show you the **w** you should
Deut	6: 7	when you walk by the **w**,
Deut	11:28	but turn aside from the **w**
Josh	1: 8	then you will make your **w**
Neh	8:10	he said to them, "Go your **w**,
Ps	1: 6	For the LORD knows the **w** of
Ps	1: 6	But the **w** of the ungodly
Ps	2:12	And you perish in the **w**,
Ps	18:30	His **w** is perfect; The word
Ps	25: 9	the humble He teaches His **w**.
Ps	27:11	Teach me Your **w**, O LORD,
Ps	37: 5	Commit your **w** to the LORD,
Ps	37: 7	of him who prospers in his **w**,
Ps	119: 9	a young man cleanse his **w**?
Ps	119:104	I hate every false **w**.
Ps	139:24	if there is any wicked **w**
Ps	139:24	And lead me in the **w**
Prov	2:12	To deliver you from the **w** of
Prov	2:20	So you may walk in the **w** of
Prov	7:27	Her house is the **w** to hell,
Prov	8:22	me at the beginning of His **w**,
Prov	14:12	There is a **w** that seems
Prov	14:12	But its end is the **w** of
Prov	22: 6	Train up a child in the **w** he
Prov	30:19	And the **w** of a man with a
Is	9: 1	By the **w** of the sea,
Is	30:21	saying, "This is the **w**,
Is	40: 3	Prepare the **w** of the LORD;
Is	40:27	My **w** is hidden from the
Is	53: 6	every one, to his own **w**;
Is	55: 7	the wicked forsake his **w**,
Jer	10:23	I know the **w** of man is not
Jer	21: 8	the way of life and the **w**
Ezek	3:18	the wicked from his wicked **w**,
Ezek	18:25	is it not My **w** which is
Ezek	33: 8	warn the wicked from his **w**,
Hos	2: 6	I will hedge up your **w** with
Jon	3:10	turned from their evil **w**;
Matt	2:12	their own country another **w**.
Matt	3: 3	Prepare the **w** of the
Matt	4:15	By the **w** of the sea,
Matt	7:13	the gate and broad is the **w**
Luke	20:21	but teach the **w** of God in
John	14: 6	said to him, "I am the **w**,
Acts	9: 2	found any who were of the **W**,
Acts	16:17	who proclaim to us the **w** of
Acts	18:26	and explained to him the **w**
Acts	19:23	great commotion about the **W**.
Acts	24:22	accurate knowledge of the **W**,
1Co	12:31	show you a more excellent **w**.
Heb	9: 8	that the **w** into the Holiest
Heb	10:20	by a new and living **w** which
Jude	11	For they have gone in the **w**

WAYS (*see* WAY)

Deut	10:12	to walk in all His **w** and to
2Ch	7:14	and turn from their wicked **w**,
Job	40:19	He is the first of the **w** of
Ps	25: 4	Show me Your **w**, O LORD;
Ps	51:13	teach transgressors Your **w**,
Ps	91:11	To keep you in all your **w**.
Ps	145:17	is righteous in all His **w**,
Prov	3: 6	In all your **w** acknowledge

Prov	16: 7	When a man's **w** please the
Is	2: 3	He will teach us His **w**,
Is	55: 8	Nor are your **w** My ways,"
Is	55: 9	My ways higher than your **w**,
Jer	7: 3	Amend your **w** and your doings,
Ezek	33:11	turn from your evil **w**! For
Mic	4: 2	He will teach us His **w**,
Hag	1: 5	of hosts: "Consider your **w**!
Zech	1: 4	Turn now from your evil **w** and
Luke	3: 5	And the rough **w** smooth;
Acts	2:28	known to me the **w** of
Rom	11:33	are His judgments and His **w**
Heb	1: 1	times and in various **w**
Jas	1: 8	man, unstable in all his **w**.
Rev	15: 3	Just and true are Your **w**,

WAYSIDE (*see* WAY)

Matt	13: 4	some seed fell by the **w**;

WEAK (*see* WEAKER, WEAKNESS)

Is	35: 3	Strengthen the **w** hands,
Is	40:29	He gives power to the **w**,
Matt	26:41	willing, but the flesh is **w**.
Rom	4:19	And not being **w** in faith, he
Rom	8: 3	not do in that it was **w**
1Co	1:27	and God has chosen the **w**
1Co	8: 7	their conscience, being **w**,
1Co	9:22	to the weak I became as **w**,
1Co	11:30	For this reason many are **w**

WEAKER (*see* WEAK)

1Pe	3: 7	as to the **w** vessel, and as

WEAKNESS (*see* WEAK, WEAKNESSES)

1Co	1:25	and the **w** of God is stronger
1Co	15:43	in glory. It is sown in **w**,
2Co	12: 9	is made perfect in **w**.
Heb	11:34	out of **w** were made strong,

WEAKNESSES† (*see* WEAKNESS)

Rom	8:26	Spirit also helps in our **w**.
Heb	4:15	cannot sympathize with our **w**,

WEALTH

Ps	112: 3	**W** and riches will be in
Prov	19: 4	**W** makes many friends, But
Eccl	5:19	God has given riches and **w**,

WEAPONS

2Sa	1:27	And the **w** of war perished!"
2Co	10: 4	For the **w** of our warfare are

WEAR (*see* WORN)

Matt	6:31	drink?' or 'What shall we **w**?
Matt	11: 8	those who **w** soft clothing

WEARIED (*see* WEARY)

Jer	12: 5	and they have **w** you, Then
John	4: 6	being **w** from His journey,

WEARISOME (*see* WEARY)

Eccl	12:12	and much study is **w** to the

WEARY (*see* WEARIED, WEARISOME)

Gen	19:11	so that they became **w**
Job	3:17	And there the **w** are at
Ps	6: 6	I am **w** with my groaning;
Ps	69: 3	I am **w** with my crying; My
Is	7:13	a small thing for you to **w**
Is	32: 2	of a great rock in a **w** land.
Is	40:30	youths shall faint and be **w**,
Is	40:31	They shall run and not be **w**,
Jer	6:11	I am **w** of holding it in.
Gal	6: 9	And let us not grow **w** while
2Th	3:13	do not grow **w** in doing

WEATHER

Matt	16: 2	say, 'It will be fair **w**,

WEAVE

Judg	16:13	If you **w** the seven locks of

WEDDING

Matt	22: 3	who were invited to the **w**;
John	2: 1	the third day there was a **w**

WEEK (*see* WEEKS)

Gen	29:27	"Fulfill her **w**, and we will
Dan	9:27	covenant with many for one **w**;
Mark	16: 2	on the first day of the **w**,
Acts	20: 7	on the first day of the **w**,
1Co	16: 2	On the first day of the **w**

WEEKS (*see* WEEK)

Ex	34:22	shall observe the Feast of **W**,
Dan	9:24	Seventy **w** are determined

WEEP (*see* WEEPING, WEPT)

Eccl	3: 4	A time to **w**, And a time
Jer	9: 1	That I might **w** day and
Jer	13:17	My eyes will **w** bitterly
Luke	6:21	Blessed are you who **w**
Luke	23:28	do not **w** for Me, but weep
John	11:31	is going to the tomb to **w**
Rom	12:15	and **w** with those who weep.
1Co	7:30	those who **w** as though they
1Co	7:30	as though they did not **w**,
Jas	5: 1	**w** and howl for your miseries

WEEPING (*see* WEEP)

Esth	4: 3	the Jews, with fasting, **w**,
Ps	6: 8	has heard the voice of my **w**.
Ps	30: 5	**W** may endure for a night,
Ps	126: 6	who continually goes forth **w**,
Jer	31:15	Rachel **w** for her children,
Ezek	8:14	women were sitting there **w**
Matt	2:18	Rachel **w** for her children,
Matt	8:12	There will be **w** and gnashing
John	11:33	when Jesus saw her **w**,
John	20:11	stood outside by the tomb **w**,
John	20:13	her, "Woman, why are you **w**?

WEIGHED (*see* WEIGHS)

1Sa	2: 3	And by Him actions are **w**.
Is	40:12	**W** the mountains in scales

Dan	5:27	You have been **w** in the
Zech	11:12	So they **w** out for my wages

WEIGHS (*see* WEIGHED, WEIGHT)

Prov	21: 2	But the LORD **w** the hearts.

WEIGHT (*see* WEIGHS, WEIGHTIER, WEIGHTS)

2Co	4:17	exceeding and eternal **w** of
Heb	12: 1	let us lay aside every **w**,

WEIGHTIER† (*see* WEIGHT)

Matt	23:23	and have neglected the **w**

WEIGHTS (*see* WEIGHT)

Lev	19:36	have honest scales, honest **w**,
Mic	6:11	with the bag of deceitful **w**?

WELL (*see* WELLSPRING)

Gen	21:19	and she saw a **w** of water.
Ex	2:15	and he sat down by a **w**.
Prov	5:15	water from your own **w**.
John	4: 6	Now Jacob's **w** was there.

WELLSPRING (*see* SPRING, WELL)

Prov	16:22	Understanding is a **w** of

WEPT (*see* WEEP)

Gen	37:35	Thus his father **w** for him.
Gen	45:14	Benjamin's neck and **w**,
2Sa	12:22	was alive, I fasted and **w**;
2Ki	20: 3	And Hezekiah **w** bitterly.
Neh	1: 4	words, that I sat down and **w**,
Neh	8: 9	weep." For all the people **w**,
Job	2:12	lifted their voices and **w**;
Ps	137: 1	we **w** When we remembered
Hos	12: 4	Angel and prevailed; He **w**,
Luke	19:41	He saw the city and **w** over
Luke	22:62	So Peter went out and **w**
John	11:35	Jesus **w**.

WEST

Ps	103:12	as the east is from the **w**,
Matt	8:11	will come from east and **w**,

WHEAT

Ps	81:16	also with the finest of **w**;
Jer	23:28	What is the chaff to the **w**?
Amos	8: 5	That we may trade **w**?
Matt	3:12	and gather His **w** into the
Matt	13:25	and sowed tares among the **w**
Luke	22:31	that he may sift you as **w**.
John	12:24	unless a grain of **w** falls

WHEEL (*see* WHEELS)

Eccl	12: 6	Or the **w** broken at the
Ezek	1:16	a wheel in the middle of a **w**.

WHEELS (*see* WHEEL)

Ezek	1:19	the **w** were lifted up.

WHIP (*see* WHIPS)

Prov	26: 3	A **w** for the horse, A bridle
John	2:15	When He had made a **w** of

WHIPS (*see* WHIP)

1Ki	12:11	father chastised you with **w**,

WHIRLWIND

2Ki	2: 1	up Elijah into heaven by a **w**,
Job	38: 1	answered Job out of the **w**,
Prov	1:27	destruction comes like a **w**,
Hos	8: 7	the wind, And reap the **w**.

WHISPER

Job	4:12	And my ear received a **w** of
Job	26:14	And how small a **w** we hear
Is	8:19	who **w** and mutter," should

WHITE (*see* WHITER, WHITEWASHED)

Num	12:10	as **w** as snow. Then Aaron
Eccl	9: 8	your garments always be **w**,
Is	1:18	They shall be as **w** as snow;
Dan	7: 9	His garment was **w** as snow,
Matt	28: 3	and his clothing as **w** as
Luke	9:29	and His robe became **w** and
John	4:35	for they are already **w** for
Rev	1:14	His head and hair were **w**
Rev	2:17	And I will give him a **w**
Rev	3: 4	they shall walk with Me in **w**,
Rev	19:11	a **w** horse. And He who sat on
Rev	20:11	Then I saw a great **w** throne

WHITER (*see* WHITE)

Ps	51: 7	and I shall be **w** than snow.

WHITEWASHED† (*see* WHITE)

Matt	23:27	For you are like **w** tombs
Acts	23: 3	you **w** wall! For you sit to

WHOLE (*see* WHOLLY)

Gen	11: 1	Now the **w** earth had one
Gen	13: 9	Is not the **w** land before
Ps	9: 1	with my **w** heart; I will
Ps	48: 2	The joy of the **w** earth,
Ps	51:19	With burnt offering and **w**
Eccl	12:13	hear the conclusion of the **w**
Is	6: 3	The **w** earth is full of His
Matt	12:13	and it was restored as **w** as
Matt	16:26	to a man if he gains the **w**
Acts	2: 2	and it filled the **w** house
Acts	4:10	man stands here before you **w**.
Acts	20:27	to declare to you the **w**
1Co	5: 6	little leaven leavens the **w**
Eph	6:11	Put on the **w** armor of God,
Jas	2:10	For whoever shall keep the **w**

WHOLLY (*see* WHOLE)

Josh	14: 8	but I **w** followed the LORD

WICKED (*see* EVIL, WICKEDLY, WICKEDNESS)

Gen	13:13	of Sodom were exceedingly **w**
Gen	18:25	the righteous with the **w**,
2Ch	7:14	and turn from their **w** ways,
Job	3:17	There the **w** cease from
Ps	10:15	Break the arm of the **w** and
Ps	22:16	The congregation of the **w**
Ps	36: 1	the transgression of the **w**:

Ps	37:17	For the arms of the **w** shall
Ps	37:20	But the **w** shall perish; And
Ps	91: 8	And see the reward of the **w**.
Ps	92: 7	When the **w** spring up like
Ps	92:11	hear my desire on the **w**
Ps	112:10	The **w** will see it and be
Ps	139:19	that You would slay the **w**,
Ps	139:24	see if there is any **w**
Prov	4:14	not enter the path of the **w**,
Prov	6:18	A heart that devises **w**
Prov	11: 7	When a **w** man dies, his
Prov	13: 9	But the lamp of the **w** will
Prov	15:26	The thoughts of the **w** are
Prov	16: 4	even the **w** for the day of
Prov	18: 5	to show partiality to the **w**,
Prov	24:20	The lamp of the **w** will be
Prov	26:23	Fervent lips with a **w** heart
Prov	28: 1	The **w** flee when no one
Eccl	7:17	Do not be overly **w**,
Is	5:23	Who justify the **w** for a
Is	11: 4	His lips He shall slay the **w**.
Is	48:22	says the LORD, "for the **w**.
Is	53: 9	made His grave with the **w**—
Is	55: 7	Let the **w** forsake his way,
Is	57:20	But the **w** are like the
Is	57:21	Says my God, "for the **w**.
Jer	17: 9	things, And desperately **w**;
Ezek	3:18	nor speak to warn the **w** from
Ezek	3:18	warn the wicked from his **w**
Ezek	3:18	that same **w** man shall die
Ezek	3:19	"Yet, if you warn the **w**,
Ezek	33: 8	do not speak to warn the **w**
Ezek	33: 8	that **w** man shall die in his
Ezek	33:11	in the death of the **w**,
Matt	12:45	seven other spirits more **w**
Matt	12:45	shall it also be with this **w**
Matt	13:38	tares are the sons of the **w**
Matt	16: 4	A **w** and adulterous generation
Matt	18:32	You **w** servant! I forgave you
Eph	6:16	all the fiery darts of the **w**
2Pe	2: 7	the filthy conduct of the **w**
1Jn	2:13	you have overcome the **w** one.

WICKEDLY (*see* WICKED)

Gen	19: 7	brethren, do not do so **w**!
Judg	19:23	do not act so **w**! Seeing
Dan	9:15	sinned, we have done **w**!

WICKEDNESS (*see* WICKED)

Gen	6: 5	the LORD saw that the **w** of
Ps	45: 7	righteousness and hate **w**;
Ps	84:10	dwell in the tents of **w**.
Is	58: 6	To loose the bonds of **w**,
Ezek	3:19	he does not turn from his **w**,
Ezek	18:27	man turns away from the **w**
Ezek	33:19	the wicked turns from his **w**
Eph	6:12	spiritual hosts of **w** in

WIDE (*see* BROAD)

Matt	7:13	for **w** is the gate and broad

WIDOW (*see* WIDOWS)

Lev	21:14	A **w** or a divorced woman or a
Deut	10:18	for the fatherless and the **w**,

W

Deut	25: 5	the **w** of the dead man shall
Is	1:17	fatherless, Plead for the **w**.
Luke	2:37	and this woman was a **w** of
1Ti	5: 4	But if any **w** has children or

WIDOWS (see WIDOW)

Ps	68: 5	fatherless, a defender of **w**,
1Ti	5: 3	Honor **w** who are really
Jas	1:27	to visit orphans and **w** in

WIFE (see WIFE'S, WIVES)

Gen	2:24	and be joined to his **w**,
Gen	4: 1	Now Adam knew Eve his **w**,
Ex	20:17	not covet your neighbor's **w**,
Deut	21:17	the son of the unloved **w**
Prov	18:22	He who finds a **w** finds a
Prov	31:10	Who can find a virtuous **w**?
Eccl	9: 9	Live joyfully with the **w**
Jer	16: 2	"You shall not take a **w**,
Ezek	24:18	and at evening my **w** died;
Hos	1: 2	take yourself a **w** of
Hos	2: 2	For she is not My **w**,
Matt	5:31	'Whoever divorces his **w**,
Matt	19:29	or father or mother or **w** or
Matt	22:24	brother shall marry his **w**
Matt	22:28	whose **w** of the seven will
Luke	17:32	"Remember Lot's **w**.
1Co	5: 1	a man has his father's **w**!
1Co	7: 2	let each man have his own **w**,
1Co	7: 4	The **w** does not have authority
1Co	7:11	is not to divorce his **w**.
1Co	7:14	and the unbelieving **w** is
1Co	7:27	Are you bound to a **w**?
1Co	7:33	he may please his **w**.
Eph	5:23	the husband is head of the **w**,
Eph	5:31	and be joined to his **w**,
1Ti	3: 2	the husband of one **w**,
Tit	1: 6	the husband of one **w**,
1Pe	3: 7	giving honor to the **w**,
Rev	21: 9	you the bride, the Lamb's **w**.

WIFE'S (see WIFE)

Mark	1:30	But Simon's **w** mother lay sick

WILD

Gen	37:20	Some **w** beast has devoured
Is	5: 2	But it brought forth **w**
Matt	3: 4	his food was locusts and **w**
Acts	10:12	**w** beasts, creeping things,
Rom	11:17	being a **w** olive tree, were

WILDERNESS (see DESERT)

Ex	5: 1	hold a feast to Me in the **w**.
Ex	19: 2	had come to the **W** of Sinai,
Lev	16:10	as the scapegoat into the **w**.
Num	14: 2	only we had died in this **w**!
Deut	1:19	that great and terrible **w**
Deut	8: 2	these forty years in the **w**,
Is	40: 3	voice of one crying in the **w**:
Matt	3: 1	came preaching in the **w** of
Matt	3: 3	of one crying in the **w**:
Matt	4: 1	up by the Spirit into the **w**
John	3:14	up the serpent in the **w**,
John	6:49	ate the manna in the **w**,

2Co	11:26	city, in perils in the **w**,

WILES†

Eph	6:11	able to stand against the **w**

WILL (see COUNSEL, WILLFULLY, WILLING)

Lev	19: 5	offer it of your own free **w**.
Ps	40: 8	I delight to do Your **w**,
Ps	143:10	Teach me to do Your **w**,
Matt	6:10	Your **w** be done On earth as
Matt	7:21	but he who does the **w** of My
Matt	26:42	drink it, Your **w** be done."
Luke	22:42	"Father, if it is Your **w**,
John	1:13	nor of the **w** of the flesh,
John	4:34	My food is to do the **w** of Him
John	5:30	I do not seek My own **w** but
John	7:17	anyone wants to do His **w**,
Rom	9:19	For who has resisted His **w**?
Rom	12: 2	acceptable and perfect **w** of
1Co	1: 1	Jesus Christ through the **w**
Eph	1: 5	the good pleasure of His **w**,
Eph	1: 9	to us the mystery of His **w**,
Eph	1:11	to the counsel of His **w**,
Eph	5:17	but understand what the **w** of
1Th	4: 3	For this is the **w** of God,
Heb	10: 7	of Me—To do Your **w**,
Heb	13:21	every good work to do His **w**,
1Pe	2:15	For this is the **w** of God,
2Pe	1:21	never came by the **w** of man,
1Jn	2:17	but he who does the **w** of God
1Jn	5:14	anything according to His **w**,

WILLFULLY (see WILL)

Heb	10:26	For if we sin **w** after we

WILLING (see WILL, WILLINGLY)

Ex	35:21	everyone whose spirit was **w**,
Matt	8: 2	saying, "Lord, if You are **w**,
Matt	11:14	And if you are **w** to receive
Matt	26:41	The spirit indeed is **w**,
Acts	18:21	return again to you, God **w**.
1Co	7:12	and she is **w** to live with
2Co	8:12	For if there is first a **w**
2Pe	3: 9	not **w** that any should perish

WILLINGLY (see WILLING)

1Co	9:17	For if I do this **w**, I have
1Pe	5: 2	not by compulsion but **w**,

WILLOWS

Ps	137: 2	hung our harps Upon the **w**

WIN (see WINS)

Matt	23:15	you travel land and sea to **w**
1Co	9:19	that I might **w** the more;
1Co	9:20	that I might **w** Jews; to

WIND (see WINDS)

1Ki	19:11	the LORD was not in the **w**;
Ps	1: 4	like the chaff which the **w**
Ps	18:10	flew upon the wings of the **w**.
Prov	11:29	own house will inherit the **w**,
Hos	8: 7	"They sow the **w**, And reap
Matt	11: 7	see? A reed shaken by the **w**?

Matt	14:32	the boat, the **w** ceased.
Mark	4:39	He arose and rebuked the **w,**
Mark	4:41	that even the **w** and the sea
John	3: 8	The **w** blows where it wishes,
Acts	2: 2	as of a rushing mighty **w,**
Eph	4:14	carried about with every **w**
Jas	1: 6	driven and tossed by the **w.**

WINDOW (see WINDOWS)

Gen	8: 6	that Noah opened the **w** of
Josh	2:21	the scarlet cord in the **w.**
1Sa	19:12	let David down through a **w.**
Acts	20: 9	And in a **w** sat a certain
2Co	11:33	in a basket through a **w** in

WINDOWS (see WINDOW)

Gen	7:11	and the **w** of heaven were
Dan	6:10	with his **w** open toward
Mal	3:10	will not open for you the **w**

WINDS (see WIND)

Matt	7:25	and the **w** blew and beat on
Matt	8:27	that even the **w** and the sea
Matt	24:31	His elect from the four **w,**

WINE (see WINEBIBBER, WINEPRESS, WINESKINS)

Gen	9:24	So Noah awoke from his **w,**
Gen	14:18	brought out bread and **w;**
Gen	19:32	us make our father drink **w,**
Num	6: 3	separate himself from **w** and
Num	6:20	the Nazirite may drink **w.**
Deut	28:51	leave you grain or new **w** or
Judg	13: 7	Now drink no **w** or similar
Neh	2: 1	that I took the **w** and gave
Prov	20: 1	**W** is a mocker, Strong
Prov	23:30	who linger long at the **w,**
Prov	23:31	Do not look on the **w** when it
Prov	31: 4	is not for kings to drink **w,**
Song	1: 2	your love is better than **w.**
Is	55: 1	buy **w** and milk Without
Jer	35: 6	said, "We will drink no **w,**
Hos	2: 8	I gave her grain, new **w,**
Amos	2:12	you gave the Nazirites **w** to
Amos	4: 1	to your husbands, "Bring **w,**
Amos	6: 6	Who drink **w** from bowls, And
Matt	9:17	Nor do they put new **w** into
Matt	27:34	they gave Him sour **w** mingled
Luke	1:15	and shall drink neither **w**
Luke	10:34	wounds, pouring on oil and **w;**
John	2: 9	the water that was made **w,**
John	2:10	You have kept the good **w**
Acts	2:13	"They are full of new **w.**
Eph	5:18	And do not be drunk with **w,**
1Ti	3: 3	not given to **w,** not violent,
1Ti	5:23	but use a little **w** for your
Rev	14:10	shall also drink of the **w**

WINEBIBBER (see WINE)

| Matt | 11:19 | 'Look, a glutton and a **w,** |

WINEPRESS (see WINE)

| Is | 63: 3 | I have trodden the **w** alone, |

WINESKINS (see WINE)

| Josh | 9: 4 | old **w** torn and mended, |
| Matt | 9:17 | they put new wine into old **w,** |

WING (see WINGED, WINGS)

| Ruth | 3: 9 | maidservant under your **w,** |
| Dan | 9:27 | And on the **w** of abominations |

WINGED (see WING)

| Gen | 1:21 | and every **w** bird according |

WINGS (see WING)

Ex	19: 4	I bore you on eagles' **w** and
Ruth	2:12	under whose **w** you have come
Ps	17: 8	under the shadow of Your **w,**
Ps	18:10	He flew upon the **w** of the
Ps	55: 6	that I had **w** like a dove!
Ps	57: 1	in the shadow of Your **w** I
Ps	61: 4	in the shelter of Your **w.**
Ps	91: 4	And under His **w** you shall
Ps	104: 3	Who walks on the **w** of the
Ps	139: 9	If I take the **w** of the
Is	6: 2	seraphim; each one had six **w:**
Is	40:31	They shall mount up with **w**
Mal	4: 2	arise With healing in His **w;**
Matt	23:37	her chicks under her **w,**
Rev	4: 8	creatures, each having six **w,**

WINNOWING†

| Ruth | 3: 2 | he is **w** barley tonight at |
| Matt | 3:12 | His **w** fan is in His hand, |

WINS† (see WIN)

| Prov | 11:30 | And he who **w** souls is |

WINTER

Gen	8:22	**W** and summer, And day and
Song	2:11	the **w** is past, The rain is
Jer	36:22	king was sitting in the **w**
Matt	24:20	your flight may not be in **w**
John	10:22	in Jerusalem, and it was **w.**
2Ti	4:21	your utmost to come before **w.**

WIPE (see WIPED)

Is	25: 8	And the Lord GOD will **w**
John	13: 5	and to **w** them with the
Rev	21: 4	And God will **w** away every

WIPED (see WIPE)

| John | 11: 2 | with fragrant oil and **w** His |
| Col | 2:14 | having **w** out the handwriting |

WISDOM (see WISE)

Ex	28: 3	filled with the spirit of **w,**
Ex	31: 3	with the Spirit of God, in **w,**
1Ki	4:29	And God gave Solomon **w** and
Job	12: 2	And **w** will die with you!
Job	28:18	For the price of **w** is
Job	28:28	fear of the Lord, that is **w,**
Ps	51: 6	You will make me to know **w.**
Ps	90:12	we may gain a heart of **w.**
Ps	111:10	LORD is the beginning of **w;**
Ps	136: 5	To Him who by **w** made the

Prov	1: 2	To know **w** and instruction,
Prov	1: 7	But fools despise **w** and
Prov	1:20	**W** calls aloud outside; She
Prov	3:19	The LORD by **w** founded the
Prov	4: 5	Get **w**! Get understanding!
Prov	4: 7	**W** is the principal thing
Prov	9: 1	**W** has built her house, She
Prov	9:10	LORD is the beginning of **w**,
Eccl	1:16	and have gained more **w** than
Eccl	1:17	And I set my heart to know **w**
Eccl	9:10	or device or knowledge or **w**
Is	11: 2	The Spirit of **w** and
Jer	9:23	the wise man glory in his **w**,
Dan	1: 4	gifted in all **w**, possessing
Luke	2:40	in spirit, filled with **w**;
Luke	2:52	And Jesus increased in **w** and
Luke	11:49	Therefore the **w** of God also
Acts	6: 3	of the Holy Spirit and **w**,
Rom	11:33	of the riches both of the **w**
1Co	1:17	not with **w** of words, lest
1Co	1:19	I will destroy the **w** of
1Co	1:20	not God made foolish the **w**
1Co	1:22	and Greeks seek after **w**;
1Co	1:24	the power of God and the **w**
1Co	2: 4	persuasive words of human **w**,
1Co	2: 6	yet not the **w** of this age,
1Co	2: 7	the hidden **w** which God
1Co	3:19	For the **w** of this world is
2Co	1:12	not with fleshly **w** but by
Eph	1:17	give to you the spirit of **w**
Col	2: 3	all the treasures of **w** and
Col	3:16	dwell in you richly in all **w**,
Col	4: 5	Walk in **w** toward those who
Jas	1: 5	If any of you lacks **w**,
Jas	3:17	But the **w** that is from above
Rev	5:12	power and riches and **w**,
Rev	13:18	Here is **w**. Let him who

WISE (see UNWISE, WISDOM, WISER)

Gen	3: 6	desirable to make one **w**,
1Ki	3:12	I have given you a **w** and
Ps	19: 7	making **w** the simple;
Prov	3: 7	Do not be **w** in your own
Prov	6: 6	Consider her ways and be **w**,
Prov	9: 8	Rebuke a **w** man, and he
Prov	10: 1	A **w** son makes a glad
Prov	11:30	And he who wins souls is **w**.
Prov	14: 1	The **w** woman builds her
Prov	26: 5	Lest he be **w** in his own
Prov	30:24	But they are exceedingly **w**:
Eccl	7:16	righteous, Nor be overly **w**:
Jer	9:23	Let not the **w** man glory in
Jer	18:18	nor counsel from the **w**,
Dan	12: 3	Those who are **w** shall shine
Matt	2: 1	**w** men from the East came to
Matt	10:16	Therefore be **w** as serpents
Matt	25: 2	"Now five of them were **w**,
Rom	1:14	both to **w** and to unwise.
Rom	1:22	Professing to be **w**,
Rom	11:25	lest you should be **w** in your
1Co	1:19	the wisdom of the **w**,
1Co	1:26	that not many **w** according to
Eph	5:15	not as fools but as **w**,
1Ti	1:17	to God who alone is **w**,

2Ti	3:15	are able to make you **w** for
Jude	25	our Savior, Who alone is **w**,

WISER (see WISE)

1Ki	4:31	For he was **w** than all
1Co	1:25	the foolishness of God is **w**

WISH

John	12:21	we **w** to see Jesus."

WITHER (see WITHERED, WITHERS)

Ps	1: 3	Whose leaf also shall not **w**;
Ps	37: 2	And **w** as the green herb.
Is	40:24	on them, And they will **w**,
Matt	21:20	How did the fig tree **w** away

WITHERED (see WITHER)

Matt	12:10	there was a man who had a **w**
Matt	21:19	Immediately the fig tree **w**
John	15: 6	out as a branch and is **w**;

WITHERS (see WITHER)

Ps	90: 6	evening it is cut down and **w**.
Is	40: 7	The grass **w**, the flower
1Pe	1:24	the grass. The grass **w**,

WITHHELD (see WITHHOLD)

Gen	22:12	since you have not **w** your

WITHHOLD (see WITHHELD)

Ps	84:11	No good thing will He **w**

WITHSTOOD

Gal	2:11	I **w** him to his face, because

WITNESS (see EYEWITNESSES, WITNESSES)

Gen	31:50	God is **w** between you and
Ex	20:16	shall not bear false **w**
Num	17: 7	LORD in the tabernacle of **w**.
Deut	4:26	call heaven and earth to **w**
Job	16:19	Surely even now my **w** is in
Is	55: 4	I have given him as a **w** to
Matt	19:18	shall not bear false **w**,
Matt	24:14	in all the world as a **w** to
John	1: 7	This man came for a **w**,
John	1:15	John bore **w** of Him and cried
Acts	14:17	not leave Himself without **w**,
Rom	1: 9	For God is my **w**, whom
Rom	2:15	conscience also bearing **w**,
Rom	8:16	The Spirit Himself bears **w**
Rom	10: 2	For I bear them **w** that they
Phil	1: 8	For God is my **w**, how greatly
1Jn	1: 2	and we have seen, and bear **w**,
1Jn	5: 6	it is the Spirit who bears **w**,
1Jn	5: 7	there are three that bear **w**
Rev	1: 5	Jesus Christ, the faithful **w**,
Rev	3:14	the Faithful and True **W**,
Rev	20: 4	been beheaded for their **w**

WITNESSES (see WITNESS)

Deut	17: 6	testimony of two or three **w**;
Matt	18:16	of two or three **w**
Matt	26:60	Even though many false **w**
Acts	1: 8	and you shall be **w** to Me in

Acts	7:58	And the **w** laid down their
2Co	13: 1	of two or three **w**
2Ti	2: 2	heard from me among many **w,**
Heb	10:15	But the Holy Spirit also **w** to
Heb	10:28	testimony of two or three **w.**
Heb	12: 1	by so great a cloud of **w,**
Rev	11: 3	will give power to my two **w,**

WITS'†

Ps	107:27	And are at their **w** end.

WIVES (see WIFE, WIVES')

Gen	4:19	took for himself two **w:**
Deut	17:17	shall he multiply **w**
Deut	21:15	"If a man has two **w,**
1Ki	11: 3	And he had seven hundred **w,**
Ezra	10:17	men who had taken pagan **w.**
Matt	19: 8	you to divorce your **w,**
Eph	5:22	**W,** submit to your own
Eph	5:25	Husbands, love your **w,**
Col	3:18	**W,** submit to your own
1Pe	3: 1	**W,** likewise, be submissive

WIVES'† (see WIVES)

1Ti	4: 7	profane and old **w** fables,

WOE

Prov	23:29	Who has **w**? Who has sorrow?
Is	5: 8	**W** to those who join house
Is	6: 5	**W** is me, for I am undone!
Amos	5:18	**W** to you who desire the day
Amos	6: 1	**W** to you who are at ease
Matt	11:21	**W** to you, Chorazin! Woe to
Matt	23:14	**W** to you, scribes and
Matt	23:16	**W** to you, blind guides, who
1Co	9:16	**w** is me if I do not preach
Rev	8:13	with a loud voice, "Woe, **w,**

WOLF (see WOLVES)

Is	11: 6	The **w** also shall dwell with
Is	65:25	The **w** and the lamb shall
John	10:12	sees the **w** coming and leaves

WOLVES (see WOLF)

Matt	10:16	as sheep in the midst of **w.**

WOMAN (see WOMEN)

Gen	2:23	She shall be called **W,**
Gen	3:15	Between you and the **w,**
2Sa	14: 2	brought from there a wise **w,**
2Sa	20:16	Then a wise **w** cried out from
Job	14: 1	Man who is born of **w** Is of
Prov	2:16	you from the immoral **w,**
Prov	6:24	To keep you from the evil **w,**
Prov	14: 1	The wise **w** builds her house,
Prov	21: 9	shared with a contentious **w.**
Prov	31:30	But a **w** who fears the
Matt	5:28	that whoever looks at a **w**
John	2: 4	Jesus said to her, "**W,**
John	4:21	Jesus said to her, "**W,**
John	19:26	He said to His mother, "**W,**
John	20:15	Jesus said to her, "**W,**
1Co	7: 1	for a man not to touch a **w.**
1Co	7:34	The unmarried **w** cares about

1Co	11: 3	the head of **w** is man, and
1Co	11: 7	but **w** is the glory of man.
1Co	11: 8	For man is not from **w,**
1Co	11:15	But if a **w** has long hair, it
Gal	4: 4	forth His Son, born of a **w,**
1Ti	2:11	Let a **w** learn in silence with
1Ti	2:12	And I do not permit a **w** to
1Ti	2:14	but the **w** being deceived,

WOMB

Gen	38:27	behold, twins were in her **w.**
Deut	7:13	bless the fruit of your **w**
Judg	13: 5	a Nazirite to God from the **w;**
1Sa	1: 5	the LORD had closed her **w.**
Job	1:21	I came from my mother's **w,**
Ps	22: 9	He who took Me out of the **w;**
Ps	110: 3	from the **w** of the morning,
Ps	127: 3	The fruit of the **w** is a
Prov	31: 2	son? And what, son of my **w?**
Is	44: 2	And formed you from the **w,**
Jer	1: 5	I formed you in the **w** I
Jer	20:17	did not kill me from the **w,**
Hos	12: 3	brother by the heel in the **w,**
Luke	1:41	the babe leaped in her **w;**
Luke	11:27	Blessed is the **w** that bore
John	3: 4	time into his mother's **w**
Rom	4:19	the deadness of Sarah's **w.**
Gal	1:15	me from my mother's **w** and

WOMEN (see WOMAN)

Gen	24:11	the time when **w** go out to
Gen	31:35	for the manner of **w** is with
2Sa	1:26	Surpassing the love of **w.**
1Ki	11: 1	Solomon loved many foreign **w,**
Job	2:10	as one of the foolish **w**
Amos	1:13	they ripped open the **w** with
Matt	11:11	among those born of **w** there
Luke	1:28	blessed are you among **w!**"
Luke	1:42	"Blessed are you among **w,**
Rom	1:26	For even their **w** exchanged
1Co	14:34	Let your **w** keep silent in the
2Ti	3: 6	make captives of gullible **w**
Heb	11:35	**W** received their dead raised

WONDER (see WONDERFUL, WONDERS, WONDROUS)

Deut	13: 1	he gives you a sign or a **w,**
Acts	3:10	and they were filled with **w**
2Co	11:14	And no **w!** For Satan himself

WONDERFUL (see WONDER, WONDERFULLY)

Judg	13:18	ask My name, seeing it is **w?**
2Sa	1:26	me; Your love to me was **w,**
Job	42: 3	Things too **w** for me, which
Ps	107: 8	And for His **w** works to the
Ps	139: 6	Such knowledge is too **w**
Prov	30:18	things which are too **w**
Is	9: 6	His name will be called **W,**
Is	28:29	Who is **w** in counsel and
Acts	2:11	in our own tongues the **w**

WONDERFULLY† (see WONDERFUL)

Ps	139:14	for I am fearfully and **w**

WONDERS (see WONDER)

Ex	3:20	strike Egypt with all My **w**
Deut	4:34	by trials, by signs, by **w**,
Ps	77:14	You are the God who does **w**;
Ps	105:27	And **w** in the land of Ham.
Ps	136: 4	Him who alone does great **w**,
Dan	4: 3	And how mighty His **w**! His
Dan	6:27	And He works signs and **w**
Matt	7:22	and done many **w** in Your
Mark	13:22	rise and show signs and **w**
John	4:48	you people see signs and **w**,
Rom	15:19	in mighty signs and **w**,
2Th	2: 9	power, signs, and lying **w**,
Heb	2: 4	both with signs and **w**,

WONDROUS (see WONDER)

1Ch	16: 9	Talk of all His **w** works!
Ps	26: 7	And tell of all Your **w**
Ps	72:18	Who only does **w** things!
Ps	119:18	that I may see **W** things

WOOD (see WOODEN)

Gen	22: 6	So Abraham took the **w** of the
Ex	25:10	make an ark of acacia **w**;
Lev	14: 4	and clean birds, cedar **w**,
Is	44:19	down before a block of **w**?
Dan	5: 4	and iron, **w** and stone.
Hab	2:19	Woe to him who says to **w**,
Luke	23:31	these things in the green **w**,
1Co	3:12	silver, precious stones, **w**,

WOODEN (see WOOD)

Ex	34:13	and cut down their **w** images

WOOL

Prov	31:13	She seeks **w** and flax, And
Is	1:18	crimson, They shall be as **w**.
Dan	7: 9	of His head was like pure **w**.
Hos	2: 5	My **w** and my linen, My oil
Rev	1:14	and hair were white like **w**,

WORD (see WORDS)

Gen	15: 4	the **w** of the LORD came to
Ex	8:10	it be according to your **w**,
Deut	8: 3	but man lives by every **w**
Deut	30:14	But the **w** is very near you,
1Ki	6:12	then I will perform My **w**
1Ki	8:56	There has not failed one **w**
2Ki	18:36	and answered him not a **w**;
Job	2:13	and no one spoke a **w** to him,
Ps	33: 4	For the **w** of the LORD is
Ps	33: 6	By the **w** of the LORD the
Ps	68:11	The Lord gave the **w**;
Ps	119: 9	heed according to Your **w**.
Ps	119:11	Your **w** I have hidden in my
Ps	119:16	I will not forget Your **w**.
Ps	119:89	Your **w** is settled in
Ps	119:105	Your **w** is a lamp to my
Ps	119:114	my shield; I hope in Your **w**.
Ps	119:162	I rejoice at Your **w** As one
Ps	138: 2	You have magnified Your **w**
Ps	139: 4	For there is not a **w** on my

Prov	15: 1	But a harsh **w** stirs up
Prov	25:11	A **w** fitly spoken is like
Prov	30: 5	Every **w** of God is pure;
Is	40: 8	But the **w** of our God stands
Is	45:23	The **w** has gone out of My
Is	55:11	So shall My **w** be that goes
Jer	23:29	Is not My **w** like a fire?"
Zech	9: 1	The burden of the **w** of the
Zech	12: 1	The burden of the **w** of the
Mal	1: 1	The burden of the **w** of the
Matt	4: 4	but by every **w** that
Matt	8: 8	my roof. But only speak a **w**,
Matt	13:22	of riches choke the **w**,
Luke	1: 2	and ministers of the **w**
Luke	7: 7	come to You. But say the **w**,
Luke	8:11	The seed is the **w** of God.
Luke	24:19	mighty in deed and **w** before
John	1: 1	In the beginning was the **W**,
John	1: 1	and the **W** was with God, and
John	1: 1	and the **W** was God.
John	1:14	And the **W** became flesh and
John	8:31	Him, "If you abide in My **w**,
John	17:17	Your **w** is truth.
Acts	6: 4	and to the ministry of the **w**.
Acts	6: 7	Then the **w** of God spread, and
Rom	10: 8	The **w** is near you, in
Rom	10:17	and hearing by the **w** of God.
1Co	4:20	kingdom of God is not in **w**
2Co	2:17	peddling the **w** of God; but
Phil	2:16	holding fast the **w** of life,
Col	3:16	Let the **w** of Christ dwell in
Col	3:17	And whatever you do in **w** or
1Th	1: 5	did not come to you in **w**
1Th	2:13	welcomed it not as the **w**
2Th	2: 2	either by spirit or by **w** or
2Th	2:15	whether by **w** or our epistle.
1Ti	4: 5	it is sanctified by the **w**
1Ti	4:12	to the believers in **w**,
1Ti	5:17	those who labor in the **w**
2Ti	2: 9	but the **w** of God is not
2Ti	2:15	rightly dividing the **w** of
2Ti	4: 2	Preach the **w**! Be ready in
Heb	1: 3	all things by the **w** of His
Heb	2: 2	For if the **w** spoken through
Heb	4:12	For the **w** of God is living
Heb	5:13	milk is unskilled in the **w**
Heb	6: 5	and have tasted the good **w** of
Heb	11: 3	worlds were framed by the **w**
Jas	1:21	meekness the implanted **w**,
Jas	1:22	But be doers of the **w**,
Jas	3: 2	anyone does not stumble in **w**,
1Pe	1:25	But the **w** of the LORD
1Pe	2: 2	the pure milk of the **w**,
2Pe	1:19	so we have the prophetic **w**
2Pe	3: 5	that by the **w** of God the
2Pe	3: 7	now preserved by the same **w**,
1Jn	1: 1	concerning the **W** of life—
1Jn	1:10	and His **w** is not in us.
1Jn	2: 5	But whoever keeps His **w**,
1Jn	2:14	and the **w** of God abides in
1Jn	3:18	let us not love in **w** or in
1Jn	5: 7	in heaven: the Father, the **W**,
Rev	1: 2	who bore witness to the **w** of

Rev	1: 9	is called Patmos for the **w**
Rev	12:11	of the Lamb and by the **w** of
Rev	19:13	His name is called The **W** of
Rev	20: 4	to Jesus and for the **w** of

WORDS (see WORD)

Ex	20: 1	And God spoke all these **w,**
Ex	34: 1	on these tablets the **w**
Deut	18:18	and will put My **w** in His
Deut	18:19	whoever will not hear My **w,**
Josh	24:26	Then Joshua wrote these **w** in
Job	38: 2	who darkens counsel By **w**
Ps	12: 6	The **w** of the LORD are pure
Ps	19: 4	And their **w** to the end of
Ps	19:14	Let the **w** of my mouth and
Ps	22: 1	And from the **w** of My
Ps	119:103	How sweet are Your **w** to my
Ps	119:130	The entrance of Your **w** gives
Prov	1: 6	The **w** of the wise and their
Prov	2: 1	My son, if you receive my **w,**
Eccl	1. 1	The **w** of the Preacher, the
Eccl	9:17	**W** of the wise, spoken
Eccl	12:11	The **w** of the wise are like
Is	59: 4	They trust in empty **w** and
Jer	1: 9	I have put My **w** in your
Jer	7: 4	not trust in these lying **w,**
Jer	11: 2	Hear the **w** of this covenant,
Jer	15:16	Your **w** were found, and I ate
Jer	36:32	added to them many similar **w.**
Amos	7:10	not able to bear all his **w.**
Mal	2:17	the LORD with your **w;**
Matt	6: 7	be heard for their many **w.**
Mark	10:24	were astonished at His **w.**
Mark	12:13	to catch Him in His **w.**
Luke	1:20	you did not believe my **w**
John	3:34	God has sent speaks the **w**
John	5:47	how will you believe My **w?**
John	6:68	You have the **w** of eternal
John	12:47	And if anyone hears My **w** and
John	14:10	The **w** that I speak to you I
John	14:24	love Me does not keep My **w;**
John	15: 7	and My **w** abide in you, you
Acts	2:22	of Israel, hear these **w:**
Acts	6:11	him speak blasphemous **w**
Acts	7:22	and was mighty in **w** and
Rom	10:18	And their **w** to the
Rom	16:18	and by smooth **w** and
1Co	1:17	gospel, not with wisdom of **w,**
1Co	14: 9	you utter by the tongue **w**
1Co	14:19	I would rather speak five **w**
1Co	14:19	than ten thousand **w** in a
1Ti	6: 4	and arguments over **w,**
Heb	13:22	have written to you in few **w.**
Rev	1: 3	and those who hear the **w**
Rev	22: 6	These **w** are faithful and
Rev	22: 9	and of those who keep the **w**
Rev	22:18	to everyone who hears the **w**
Rev	22:19	takes away from the **w** of

WORK (see WORKER, WORKING,
　　WORKMANSHIP, WORKS)

Gen	2: 2	seventh day God ended His **w**

Ex	14:31	Thus Israel saw the great **w**
Ex	20: 9	labor and do all your **w,**
Ex	20:10	In it you shall do no **w:**
Ex	23:12	days you shall do your **w,**
Ex	31:15	**W** shall be done for six days,
Ex	34:21	"Six days you shall **w,**
Neh	4: 6	the people had a mind to **w.**
Neh	6: 3	"I am doing a great **w,**
Job	1:10	You have blessed the **w** of
Job	10: 3	You should despise the **w** of
Job	24: 5	They go out to their **w,**
Job	34:11	man according to his **w,**
Ps	8: 3	the **w** of Your fingers, The
Ps	62:12	each one according to his **w.**
Ps	74: 6	they break down its carved **w,**
Ps	77:12	also meditate on all Your **w,**
Ps	90:17	And establish the **w** of our
Ps	104:23	Man goes out to his **w** And
Ps	115: 4	The **w** of men's hands.
Prov	24:29	the man according to his **w.**
Eccl	9:10	for there is no **w** or
Eccl	12:14	For God will bring every **w**
Is	2: 8	They worship the **w** of their
Is	28:21	do His work, His awesome **w,**
Is	64: 8	And all we are the **w** of
Hab	1: 5	For I will work a **w** in
Hab	3: 2	revive Your **w** in the midst
Mark	6: 5	Now He could do no mighty **w**
John	4:34	sent Me, and to finish His **w.**
John	6:28	that we may **w** the works of
John	6:29	This is the **w** of God, that
John	9: 4	I must **w** the works of Him who
John	9: 4	is coming when no one can **w.**
John	17: 4	I have finished the **w** which
Rom	4: 5	But to him who does not **w**
Rom	7: 5	by the law were at **w** in our
Rom	8:28	we know that all things **w**
1Co	3:13	fire will test each one's **w,**
1Co	9: 1	Are you not my **w** in the
1Co	15:58	always abounding in the **w** of
2Co	9: 8	abundance for every good **w.**
Gal	6: 4	each one examine his own **w,**
Eph	4:12	of the saints for the **w** of
Phil	1: 6	He who has begun a good **w**
Phil	2:12	**w** out your own salvation
Col	1:10	fruitful in every good **w**
1Th	4:11	and to **w** with your own
2Th	2:17	you in every good word and **w.**
2Th	3:10	this: If anyone will not **w,**
1Ti	3: 1	bishop, he desires a good **w.**
2Ti	3:17	equipped for every good **w.**
2Ti	4: 5	do the **w** of an evangelist,
Tit	3: 1	to be ready for every good **w,**
Heb	1:10	the heavens are the **w**
Heb	13:21	complete in every good **w** to
Jas	1: 4	patience have its perfect **w,**
1Pe	1:17	according to each one's **w,**
Rev	22:12	every one according to his **w.**

W

WORKER (see WORK, WORKERS)

Eccl	3: 9	What profit has the **w** from

Matt	10:10	for a **w** is worthy of his
Rom	16: 9	our fellow **w** in Christ, and
Rom	16:21	Timothy, my fellow **w**,
2Ti	2:15	a **w** who does not need to be

WORKERS (see WORKER)

1Co	3: 9	For we are God's fellow **w**;
1Co	12:29	Are all **w** of miracles?
2Co	6: 1	as **w** together with Him
Phil	4: 3	and the rest of my fellow **w**,
Col	4:11	are my only fellow **w** for

WORKING (see WORK)

John	5:17	My Father has been **w** until
1Co	4:12	**w** with our own hands. Being
1Co	12:10	to another the **w** of miracles,
Gal	5: 6	but faith **w** through love.
Eph	1:19	according to the **w** of His
Eph	4:16	to the effective **w** by which
Eph	4:28	**w** with his hands what is
Heb	13:21	**w** in you what is well
Jas	2:22	Do you see that faith was **w**

WORKMANSHIP (see WORK)

Eph	2:10	For we are His **w**,

WORKS (see WORK)

Ps	8: 6	to have dominion over the **w**
Ps	66: 3	How awesome are Your **w**!
Ps	66: 5	Come and see the **w** of God;
Ps	103:22	Bless the LORD, all His **w**,
Ps	104:24	how manifold are Your **w**! In
Ps	105: 2	Talk of all His wondrous **w**!
Ps	139:14	made; Marvelous are Your **w**,
Ps	145:10	All Your **w** shall praise You,
Prov	8:22	Before His **w** of old.
Prov	31:31	And let her own **w** praise
Matt	5:16	they may see your good **w**
Matt	11:21	For if the mighty **w** which
John	5:20	He will show Him greater **w**
John	6:28	that we may work the **w** of
John	9: 3	but that the **w** of God should
John	9: 4	I must work the **w** of Him who
John	14:12	and greater **w** than these he
Acts	26:20	to God, and do **w** befitting
Rom	4: 2	Abraham was justified by **w**,
Rom	4: 4	Now to him who **w**,
Rom	4: 6	righteousness apart from **w**:
Rom	9:11	not of **w** but of Him who
Rom	11: 6	then it is no longer of **w**;
Rom	13:12	let us cast off the **w** of
1Co	12: 6	but it is the same God who **w**
1Co	12:11	one and the same Spirit **w**
Gal	2:16	in Christ and not by the **w**
Gal	5:19	Now the **w** of the flesh are
Eph	2: 2	the spirit who now **w** in the
Eph	2: 9	not of **w**, lest anyone
Eph	2:10	in Christ Jesus for good **w**,
Eph	3:20	to the power that **w** in us,
Phil	2:13	for it is God who **w** in you
2Ti	4:14	repay him according to his **w**.
Tit	2:14	people, zealous for good **w**.

Tit	3: 5	not by **w** of righteousness
Tit	3: 8	careful to maintain good **w**.
Heb	2: 7	set him over the **w** of
Heb	6: 1	of repentance from dead **w**
Heb	10:24	to stir up love and good **w**,
Jas	2:14	faith but does not have **w**?
Jas	2:18	me your faith without your **w**,
Jas	2:20	that faith without **w** is
1Jn	3: 8	that He might destroy the **w**
Rev	2: 2	"I know your **w**, your labor,
Rev	20:13	each one according to his **w**.

WORLD (see FOREVER, WORLDS)

Ps	19: 4	words to the end of the **w**.
Ps	22:27	All the ends of the **w** Shall
Ps	24: 1	The **w** and those who dwell
Ps	90: 2	formed the earth and the **w**,
Ps	96:13	He shall judge the **w** with
Ps	98: 7	The **w** and those who dwell
Is	23:17	all the kingdoms of the **w**
Matt	4: 8	all the kingdoms of the **w**
Matt	5:14	"You are the light of the **w**.
Matt	13:22	and the cares of this **w** and
Matt	13:35	the foundation of the **w**.
Matt	13:38	"The field is the **w**,
Matt	16:26	man if he gains the whole **w**,
Mark	16:15	Go into all the **w** and preach
John	1: 9	every man coming into the **w**.
John	1:10	and the **w** was made through
John	1:29	takes away the sin of the **w**!
John	3:16	For God so loved the **w** that
John	3:17	the world to condemn the **w**,
John	3:19	light has come into the **w**,
John	8:12	"I am the light of the **w**.
John	9: 5	"As long as I am in the **w**,
John	13: 1	His own who were in the **w**,
John	14:17	whom the **w** cannot receive,
John	14:27	not as the **w** gives do I give
John	14:30	for the ruler of this **w** is
John	15:19	therefore the **w** hates you.
John	16: 8	He will convict the **w** of
John	16:28	I leave the **w** and go to the
John	16:33	cheer, I have overcome the **w**.
John	17: 5	I had with You before the **w**
John	17:21	that the **w** may believe that
John	18:36	kingdom is not of this **w**.
John	21:25	I suppose that even the **w**
Acts	17: 6	who have turned the **w**
Acts	17:31	on which He will judge the **w**
Rom	1:20	since the creation of the **w**,
Rom	5:12	one man sin entered the **w**,
Rom	10:18	to the ends of the **w**.
Rom	12: 2	not be conformed to this **w**,
1Co	1:20	foolish the wisdom of this **w**?
1Co	1:27	the weak things of the **w** to
1Co	6: 2	the saints will judge the **w**?
1Co	7:31	For the form of this **w** is
1Co	7:33	about the things of the **w**—
2Co	5:19	in Christ reconciling the **w**
Gal	6:14	to me, and I to the **w**.
Eph	2:12	and without God in the **w**.
Phil	2:15	you shine as lights in the **w**,
Col	2: 8	basic principles of the **w**,

1Ti	1:15	Jesus came into the **w** to
1Ti	3:16	Believed on in the **w**,
1Ti	6: 7	brought nothing into this **w**,
2Ti	4:10	having loved this present **w**,
Heb	1: 6	the firstborn into the **w**,
Heb	11: 7	by which he condemned the **w**
Heb	11:38	of whom the **w** was not worthy.
Jas	2: 5	chosen the poor of this **w**
Jas	4: 4	to be a friend of the **w**
2Pe	2: 5	did not spare the ancient **w**,
1Jn	2: 2	but also for the whole **w**.
1Jn	2:15	Do not love the **w** or the
1Jn	2:17	And the **w** is passing away,
1Jn	4: 9	only begotten Son into the **w**,
1Jn	4:14	the Son as Savior of the **w**.
1Jn	5: 4	born of God overcomes the **w**.
Rev	11:15	The kingdoms of this **w** have

WORLDS† (see WORLD)

Heb	1: 2	whom also He made the **w**;
Heb	11: 3	we understand that the **w**

WORM

Ps	22: 6	But I am a **w**, and no
Is	41:14	you **w** Jacob, You men of
Is	66:24	For their **w** does not die,
Jon	4: 7	next day God prepared a **w**,
Mark	9:44	Their **w** does not die,

WORMWOOD

Prov	5: 4	the end she is bitter as **w**,
Amos	5: 7	You who turn justice to **w**,
Rev	8:11	The name of the star is **W**.

WORN (see WEAR)

Deut	29: 5	Your clothes have not **w** out

WORRY

Matt	6:25	do not **w** about your life,
Matt	6:34	for tomorrow will **w** about

WORSHIP (see WORSHIPED)

Gen	22: 5	and I will go yonder and **w**,
Ex	34:14	(for you shall **w** no other
Ps	29: 2	**W** the LORD in the beauty
Ps	95: 6	let us **w** and bow down; Let
Ps	96: 9	**w** the LORD in the beauty of
Ps	97: 7	**W** Him, all you gods.
Matt	4: 9	if You will fall down and **w**
Matt	4:10	You shall **w** the LORD
John	4:20	place where one ought to **w**.
John	4:24	who worship Him must **w** in
Heb	1: 6	the angels of God **w**
Rev	14:11	who **w** the beast and his
Rev	22: 9	of this book. **W** God."

WORSHIPED (see WORSHIP)

Matt	8: 2	a leper came and **w** Him,
Matt	9:18	a ruler came and **w** Him,
John	4:20	Our fathers **w** on this

Acts	17:25	Nor is He **w** with men's hands,
Rev	13: 4	and they **w** the beast,

WORTHY (see UNWORTHY)

Ps	18: 3	who is **w** to be praised;
Matt	3:11	whose sandals I am not **w** to
Luke	10: 7	for the laborer is **w** of his
Luke	15:19	and I am no longer **w** to be
Eph	4: 1	beseech you to walk **w** of the
Col	1:10	that you may walk **w** of the
1Ti	1:15	is a faithful saying and **w**
1Ti	5:18	The laborer is **w** of his
Heb	11:38	of whom the world was not **w**.
Rev	3: 4	Me in white, for they are **w**.
Rev	4:11	"You are **w**, O Lord, To
Rev	5:12	**W** is the Lamb who was slain

WOUNDED

Is	53: 5	But He was **w** for our

WRAPPED

Matt	27:59	he **w** it in a clean linen
Luke	2: 7	and **w** Him in swaddling

WRATH

Deut	9: 8	you provoked the LORD to **w**,
Ps	2: 5	shall speak to them in His **w**,
Ps	2:12	When His **w** is kindled but a
Ps	38: 1	do not rebuke me in Your **w**,
Ps	95:11	So I swore in My **w**,
Prov	14:29	He who is slow to **w** has
Prov	15: 1	A soft answer turns away **w**,
Hab	3: 2	In **w** remember mercy.
Zeph	1:15	That day is a day of **w**,
John	3:36	but the **w** of God abides on
Rom	1:18	For the **w** of God is revealed
Rom	2: 5	wrath in the day of **w** and
Rom	9:22	the vessels of **w** prepared
Rom	12:19	but rather give place to **w**;
Eph	2: 3	were by nature children of **w**,
Eph	4:26	the sun go down on your **w**,
Eph	6: 4	provoke your children to **w**,
1Th	1:10	who delivers us from the **w**
1Th	5: 9	God did not appoint us to **w**,
Heb	3:11	So I swore in My **w**,
Rev	6:17	For the great day of His **w**

WRESTLE† (see WRESTLED)

Eph	6:12	For we do not **w** against flesh

WRESTLED (see WRESTLE)

Gen	32:25	hip was out of joint as He **w**

WRETCHED†

Rom	7:24	O **w** man that I am! Who will
Rev	3:17	do not know that you are **w**,

WRINKLE

Eph	5:27	not having spot or **w** or any

WRITE (see WRITING, WRITTEN, WROTE)

Ex	17:14	**W** this for a memorial in the
Deut	6: 9	You shall **w** them on the

Deut	17:18	that he shall **w** for himself
Prov	3: 3	W them on the tablet of
Jer	31:33	and **w** it on their hearts;
Hab	2: 2	W the vision And make it
1Jn	1: 4	And these things we **w** to you
2Jn	12	Having many things to **w** to
3Jn	13	but I do not wish to **w** to
Rev	1:11	**w** in a book and send it to

WRITING (see WRITE)

2Ch	36:22	and also put it in **w**,
Ezra	1: 1	and also put it in **w**,
Dan	5: 8	they could not read the **w**,
Dan	6:10	when Daniel knew that the **w**
Phm	1:19	am **w** with my own hand. I

WRITTEN (see WRITE)

Ex	31:18	**w** with the finger of God.
Ex	32:15	The tablets were **w** on both
Job	19:23	that my words were **w**! Oh,
Ps	40: 7	of the book it is **w** of me.
Dan	12: 1	Every one who is found **w** in
Matt	4: 4	answered and said, "It is **w**,
Luke	10:20	because your names are **w** in
John	19:22	answered, "What I have **w**,
John	20:31	but these are **w** that you may
John	21:25	the books that would be **w**.
Rom	1:17	faith to faith; as it is **w**,
Rom	2:27	even with your **w** code and
Rom	4:23	Now it was not **w** for his sake
Rom	15: 4	For whatever things were **w**
Rom	15:15	I have **w** more boldly to you
1Co	10:11	and they were **w** for our
2Co	3: 2	You are our epistle **w** in our
2Co	3: 3	**w** not with ink but by the
Gal	6:11	what large letters I have **w**
Heb	10: 7	of the book it is **w**
Heb	13:22	for I have **w** to you in few
1Jn	2:14	I have **w** to you, fathers,
1Jn	2:14	I have **w** to you, young men,
1Jn	2:26	These things I have **w** to you
Rev	1: 3	those things which are **w** in
Rev	2:17	on the stone a new name **w**
Rev	5: 1	sat on the throne a scroll **w**
Rev	14: 1	having His Father's name **w**
Rev	20:12	by the things which were **w**
Rev	20:15	And anyone not found **w** in the
Rev	22:18	him the plagues that are **w**

WRONG

Job	1:22	sin nor charge God with **w**.
Dan	6:22	I have done no **w** before
Luke	23:41	this Man has done nothing **w**.
1Co	6: 7	do you not rather accept **w**?

WROTE (see WRITE)

Ex	24: 4	And Moses **w** all the words of
Deut	4:13	and He **w** them on two tablets
Deut	31: 9	So Moses **w** this law and
Deut	31:22	Therefore Moses **w** this song

Jer	36: 4	and Baruch **w** on a scroll of
Dan	5: 5	the part of the hand that **w**.
John	5:46	for he **w** about Me.
John	8: 6	Jesus stooped down and **w** on

Y

YAH (see LORD)

Ps	68: 4	the clouds, By His name **Y**,
Is	12: 2	and not be afraid; 'For **Y**,

YEAR (see YEARS)

Ex	12: 2	the first month of the **y** to
Ex	12: 5	a male of the first **y**.
Ex	23:17	Three times in the **y** all your
Lev	25: 5	for it is a **y** of rest for
Lev	25:10	consecrate the fiftieth **y**,
Lev	25:13	In this **Y** of Jubilee, each
Deut	15: 9	the **y** of release, is at
Ps	65:11	You crown the **y** with Your
Is	61: 2	proclaim the acceptable **y**
Mic	6: 6	With calves a **y** old?
Luke	4:19	the acceptable **y** of
Heb	9: 7	priest went alone once a **y**,

YEARNS

Job	19:27	How my heart **y** within me!

YEARS (see YEAR)

Gen	1:14	seasons, and for days and **y**;
Gen	29:20	So Jacob served seven **y** for
Gen	37: 2	being seventeen **y** old, was
Gen	41:26	seven good cows are seven **y**,
Ex	30:14	from twenty **y** old and above,
Lev	25: 8	seven times seven **y**;
Lev	25: 8	of the seven sabbaths of **y**
Num	14:33	in the wilderness forty **y**,
Ps	90: 4	For a thousand **y** in Your
Ps	90: 9	We finish our **y** like a
Ps	90:10	of our lives are seventy **y**;
Ps	90:10	strength they are eighty **y**,
Eccl	12: 1	And the **y** draw near when
Jer	25:11	king of Babylon seventy **y**.
Luke	2:42	And when He was twelve **y** old
Luke	3:23	at about thirty **y** of age,
John	8:57	You are not yet fifty **y** old,
Rev	20: 6	reign with Him a thousand **y**.

YESTERDAY

Ps	90: 4	in Your sight Are like **y**
Heb	13: 8	Jesus Christ is the same **y**,

YIELDED

Matt	27:50	and **y** up His spirit.

YOKE (see YOKED)

1Ki	12: 4	Your father made our **y** heavy;
1Ki	12:11	on you, I will add to your **y**;
Jer	28:14	I have put a **y** of iron on the
Matt	11:29	Take My **y** upon you and learn
Matt	11:30	For My **y** is easy and My
Gal	5: 1	be entangled again with a **y**

YOKED† (*see* YOKE)

1Sa	6: 7	cows which have never been **y**,
2Co	6:14	Do not be unequally **y**

YOU-ARE-THE-GOD-WHO-SEES† (*see* GOD)

Gen	16:13	LORD who spoke to her, **Y**;

YOUNG (*see* YOUNGER, YOUTH)

Gen	4:23	Even a **y** man for hurting
Ps	37:25	I have been **y**, and now am
Ps	119: 9	How can a **y** man cleanse his
Ps	148:12	Both **y** men and maidens; Old
Is	11: 6	shall lie down with the **y**
Is	40:11	lead those who are with **y**.
Is	40:30	And the **y** men shall utterly
Dan	1: 4	**y** men in whom there was no
Joel	2:28	Your **y** men shall see
Acts	2:17	Your **y** men shall see
Acts	20: 9	in a window sat a certain **y**

YOUNGER (*see* YOUNG)

Gen	9:24	and knew what his **y** son had
Gen	25:23	the older shall serve the **y**.
Gen	29:26	to give the **y** before the
Rom	9:12	older shall serve the **y**.

YOUTH (*see* YOUNG, YOUTHFUL, YOUTHS)

Gen	8:21	heart is evil from his **y**;
Ps	103: 5	So that your **y** is renewed
Ps	110: 3	You have the dew of Your **y**.
Prov	2:17	the companion of her **y**,
Prov	5:18	with the wife of your **y**.
Eccl	12: 1	in the days of your **y**,
Jer	1: 6	cannot speak, for I am a **y**.
Jer	1: 7	"Do not say, 'I am a **y**,
Matt	19:20	things I have kept from my **y**.
1Ti	4:12	Let no one despise your **y**,

YOUTHFUL (*see* YOUTH)

2Ti	2:22	Flee also **y** lusts; but pursue

YOUTHS (*see* YOUTH)

2Ki	2:24	mauled forty-two of the **y**.
Is	40:30	Even the **y** shall faint and

Z

ZACCHAEUS

Luke	19: 5	him, and said to him, "**Z**,

ZACHARIAS (*see* ZECHARIAH)

Luke	1: 5	a certain priest named **Z**,
Luke	3: 2	came to John the son of **Z**

ZAREPHATH

1Ki	17: 9	"Arise, go to **Z**, which
Luke	4:26	was Elijah sent except to **Z**, which

ZEAL (*see* ZEALOT, ZEALOUS)

Ps	69: 9	Because **z** for Your house has

John	2:17	**Z** for Your house has
Rom	10: 2	witness that they have a **z**
Phil	3: 6	concerning **z**, persecuting
Col	4:13	that he has a great **z** for

ZEALOT (*see* ZEAL)

Acts	1:13	of Alphaeus and Simon the **Z**;

ZEALOUS (*see* ZEAL)

1Ki	19:10	I have been very **z** for the
Tit	2:14	people, **z** for good works.

ZEBEDEE

Matt	4:21	James the son of **Z**,
Mark	10:35	and John, the sons of **Z**,

ZEBULUN

Gen	35:23	Levi, Judah, Issachar, and **Z**;
Is	9: 1	esteemed The land of **Z** and
Matt	4:15	The land of **Z** and the

ZECHARIAH (*see* ZACHARIAS)

Ezra	5: 1	the prophet Haggai and **Z**
Luke	11:51	of Abel to the blood of **Z**

ZEDEKIAH

2Ki	25: 7	eyes, put out the eyes of **Z**,
Jer	37:18	Jeremiah said to King **Z**,

ZERAH

1Ch	2: 4	bore him Perez and **Z**.
Matt	1: 3	Judah begot Perez and **Z** by

ZERUBBABEL

Ezra	3: 2	and **Z** the son of Shealtiel
Hag	2: 4	'Yet now be strong, **Z**,
Hag	2:23	**Z** My servant, the son of
Zech	4:10	plumb line in the hand of **Z**.
Matt	1:12	and Shealtiel begot **Z**.

ZEUS

Acts	14:12	And Barnabas they called **Z**,

ZION

1Ki	8: 1	City of David, which is **Z**.
2Ki	19:21	virgin, the daughter of **Z**,
Ps	2: 6	King On My holy hill of **Z**.
Ps	48: 2	Is Mount **Z** on the sides
Ps	50: 2	Out of **Z**, the perfection
Ps	76: 2	And His dwelling place in **Z**.
Ps	97: 8	**Z** hears and is glad, And
Ps	99: 2	The LORD is great in **Z**,
Ps	125: 1	the LORD Are like Mount **Z**,
Song	3:11	Go forth, O daughters of **Z**,
Is	1: 8	So the daughter of **Z** is left
Is	2: 3	For out of **Z** shall go
Is	28:16	I lay in **Z** a stone for a
Is	37:22	virgin, the daughter of **Z**,
Is	51: 3	the LORD will comfort **Z**,
Is	51:11	And come to **Z** with singing,
Is	59:20	Redeemer will come to **Z**,
Is	61: 3	console those who mourn in **Z**,
Jer	26:18	**Z** shall be plowed like a
Jer	51:10	and let us declare in **Z** the

Z

Joel	2: 1	Blow the trumpet in **Z**,
Joel	3:16	LORD also will roar from **Z**,
Amos	1: 2	"The LORD roars from **Z**,
Amos	6: 1	you who are at ease in **Z**,
Mic	3:12	because of you **Z** shall be
Mic	4: 2	For out of **Z** the law
Zech	1:17	LORD will again comfort **Z**,
Zech	9: 9	O daughter of **Z**! Shout, O
Matt	21: 5	the daughter of **Z**,
Rom	9:33	I lay in **Z** a stumbling
Rom	11:26	will come out of **Z**,
Heb	12:22	But you have come to Mount **Z**
1Pe	2: 6	I lay in **Z** A chief

ZIPPORAH

Ex	4:25	Then **Z** took a sharp stone and
Ex	18: 2	Moses' father-in-law, took **Z**,

ZOPHAR

Job	2:11	and **Z** the Naamathite. For

Nelson's Quick-Reference™ Series

Nelson's Quick-Reference™ Bible Dictionary

More like a "mini-encyclopedia" than a standard dictionary, this compact reference offers an A-Z way to discover fascinating details about the Bible—its characters, history, setting, and doctrines.

784 pages / 0-8407-6906-7 / available now

Nelson's Quick-Reference™ Bible Handbook

Helps you read each of the Bible's 66 books, plus those of the Apocrypha. Offers book introductions, brief summaries, historical and faith-and-life highlights, at-a-glance charts, and detailed teaching outlines. Suggests individual reading plans and schedules for group study.

416 pages / 0-8407-6904-0 / available now

Nelson's Quick-Reference™ Bible Questions and Answers

Learning is fun, lively, and exciting with the over 6,000 questions and answers covering the whole Bible. Variety keeps interest high—short answer, true/false, multiple choice, fill in the blank, and sentence completion.

384 pages / 0-8407-6905-9 / available now

Nelson's Quick-Reference™ Introduction to the Bible

Introduces the Bible as a whole and describes all its parts from an historical and evangelical theological perspective. Explore the fascinating variety in Scripture—story and song, poetry and prophecy, and more. Discover its divinely revealed answers to the most important questions of life.

approx 400 pages / 0-8407-3206-6 / August, 1993

Nelson's Quick-Reference™ Bible People and Places

From Aaron to Zurishaddain, and from Dan to Beersheba, quickly identify each person and place in the Bible—and many key events. One list, arranged from A to Z, gives brief descriptions and Scripture references, and tells what the names mean,

how to say them, and which refer to the same person or place. Variant spellings make this guide useful with any translation.
approx 400 pages / 0-8407-6912-1 / August, 1993

Nelson's Quick-Reference™ Bible Maps and Charts

Make any Bible a study Bible with this unique collection of maps, book charts, and other visuals that present clear information about Bible people, events, and teachings in ways that heighten your interest, retention, and understanding in Bible study. Seeing it helps you believe it!
approx 300 pages / 0-8407-6908-3 / April, 1994